American Government

Clayton State University Edition

Dautrich | Yalof | Fleischmann | Pierannunzi

CENGAGE
Learning·

Australia • Brazil • Japan • Korea • Mexico • Singapore • Spain • United Kingdom • United States

American Government

The Enduring Democracy, 3rd Edition
Kenneth Dautrich | David Yalof

© 2014 Cengage Learning. All rights reserved.

Senior Project Development Manager:
Linda deStefano

Market Development Manager:
Heather Kramer

Senior Production/Manufacturing Manager:
Donna M. Brown

Production Editorial Manager:
Kim Fry

Sr. Rights Acquisition Account Manager:
Todd Osborne

For product information and technology assistance, contact us at
Cengage Learning Customer & Sales Support, 1-800-354-9706

For permission to use material from this text or product,
submit all requests online at **cengage.com/permissions**
Further permissions questions can be emailed to
permissionrequest@cengage.com

This book contains select works from existing Cengage Learning resources and was produced by Cengage Learning Custom Solutions for collegiate use. As such, those adopting and/or contributing to this work are responsible for editorial content accuracy, continuity and completeness.

Compilation © 2013 Cengage Learning
ISBN-13: 978-1-285-56116-5

ISBN-10: 1-285-56116-3

Cengage Learning
5191 Natorp Boulevard
Mason, Ohio 45040
USA
Cengage Learning is a leading provider of customized learning solutions with office locations around the globe, including Singapore, the United Kingdom, Australia, Mexico, Brazil, and Japan. Locate your local office at:
international.cengage.com/region.

Cengage Learning products are represented in Canada by Nelson Education, Ltd.
For your lifelong learning solutions, visit **www.cengage.com/custom.**
Visit our corporate website at **www.cengage.com.**

Printed in the United States of America

Brief Contents

Model Course Syllabus: American National Government POLS 1101 1

Model Course Syllabus: American National Government POLS 1101
(Online Course Syllabus) 5

Political Science Degree Program Outcomes and Assessments
(Bachelor of Science Degree) 7

Clayton State University Political Science Program Mission Statement 11

The Importance of Civil Engagement 13

Excerpted from:
The Enduring Democracy, 3rd Edition, includes Aplia Printed Access Card.
Kenneth Dautrich | David Yalof

Preface xxiv

PART I   FOUNDATIONS

Chapter 1   The More Things Change, the More They Stay the Same 3

Chapter 2   The Founding and the Constitution 23

              Annotated Constitution of the United States of American C-1

Chapter 3   Federalism 51

Chapter 4   Civil Liberties 73

Chapter 5   Civil Rights, Equality and Social Movements 105

PART II   INSTITUTIONS

Chapter 6   Congress 139

Chapter 7   The Presidency 171

Chapter 8   The Federal Bureaucracy 201

Chapter 9   The Judiciary 229

PART III   POLITICAL BEHAVIOR

Chapter 10   Public Opinion 263

Chapter 11   Interest Groups 291

Chapter 12   The Media and American Politics...317
Chapter 13   Political Parties and Voting 345
Chapter 14   Campaigns and Elections..387

PART IV   PUBLIC POLICY
Chapter 15   American Domestic Policy 421
Chapter 16   American Foreign Policy 451

              Appendix..477
              Answers to the Test-Yourself Multiple-Choice Questions.............491
              Glossary 495
              Notes 511
              Index 525
              Maps: Electoral College
              Maps: Results from 1984 to 2012

Excerpted from:
Georgia's Constitution and Government, 6th Edition
Arnold Fleischman | Carol Pierannunzi

Introduction 1
Section 1   The U.S. Constituion and Federalism 2
Section 2   State Constitutions 4
Section 3   Constitutional Development in Georgia 8
Section 4   Georgia's Governmental Institutions.......................................20
Section 5   Elections...36
Section 6   Rights and Liberties 39
Section 7   The Continuing Significance of Georgia's Constitution 50
Notes 51

Model Course Syllabus

AMERICAN NATIONAL GOVERNMENT POLS 1101

(Classroom Course Syllabus)

Course Description: (3-0-3) American National Government in an International Context is an introductory level survey of the American political system, emphasizing a cross-cultural approach to the study of the structure and processes of policy decision-making. The course incorporates a comparison of the American political system and other types of political systems. The course also includes the study of world geography, emphasizing a knowledge of the global configuration of nation-states. This course satisfies the Georgia legislative requirement for the study of the United States and Georgia Constitutions.

Format: Class will meet each regularly scheduled calendar day unless announced otherwise. All dates of assignments, tests and exams are listed later in this syllabus. Scheduled regular class sessions generally will follow a lecture/discussion format. You are expected to have read each assignment by the date set for its consideration in class.

NOTE: The instructor and students will treat each other with the proper respect at all times.

Course Computer Usage: Students will not be requested to bring a computer to class on a daily basis. Students will make regular remote site use of their computers to access course related email, course websites, complete assignments and communicate with the instructor.

Attendance: All students are expected to attend class each day we meet. If you are unable to attend, obtain information on what has been missed from a fellow student, and then see the instructor with any further questions. Roll will be taken daily.

Classroom Conduct: students are expected to conduct themselves in a manner that evidences respect for students, the instructor and the learning environment.

Students must abide by policies in the CSU Catalog & Student Handbook.

Disruption of the Learning Environment: Behavior which disrupts the teaching–learning process during class activities will not tolerated. This includes belligerent, abusive, profane, and/or threatening behavior. A student who fails to respond to reasonable faculty direction regarding classroom behavior and/or behavior while participating in classroom activities may be dismissed from class. A student who is dismissed is entitled to due process and will be afforded such rights as soon as possible following dismissal. If found in violation, a student may be administratively withdrawn and may receive a grade of WF.

http://a-s.clayton.edu/DisruptiveClassroomBehavior.htm

Click on this link to read the Clayton State University
Basic Undergraduate Student Responsibilities Statement.

The instructor and students will treat each other with the proper respect at all times.

***Children are NOT permitted in any CSU classroom under any circumstances,
nor may they be left unattended anywhere on the campus.***

Please turn your cell phone to "vibrate" or turn it off during class.

***Cheating will not be tolerated and will be dealt with in keeping
with in keeping with the CSU Conduct Code.***

CSU Conduct Code and Judicial Procedure

Civic Engagement:

Civic Engagement at Clayton State University is defined as an intentional learning experience
that contributes to a student's understanding *of social and civic responsibility, community
leadership, and service* to a diverse, democratic *society*. Civic Engagement outcomes are located
at the Political Science Program website:

http://a-s.clayton.edu/politicalscience/default.htm

For information on earning a political science degree at CSU:

http://a-s.clayton.edu/politicalscience/default.htm

Political Science Degree Program Outcomes and Assessments:

Outcomes: *Graduating political science majors should*

- Apply concepts related to the structures and principles of the U.S.
  Constitution to historical and current politics.

- Explain and criticize U.S. political institutions and processes.

- Define and distinguish how aspects of the Georgia Constitution and
  government differ from the U.S. Constitution and government.

- Assess and compare how other national political systems and   international
  political organizations differ from the U.S. political system and recognize the
  importance of political geography.

- Research and compose a project report in a subfield of political science.

- Successfully complete a political science related internship.

Assessments:

- POLS 1101 pre and post assessment surveys & geography tests

- POLS 4490/POLS 4491 Internship/Practicum Site Supervisor Evaluation

- POLS 3000 and 4000 level course research papers

- POLS 4500 Senior Seminar research paper

- POLS 4500 Senior Political Science Program Exit Survey

- ACAT Area Concentration Achievement Test taken by graduating seniors

Midterm Grades: A course midterm grade will be posted on the DUCK by midterm each semester. The midterm grade will only reflect graded work completed to the middle of the semester. Typically more than half of the scored work in this course is completed after the midterm date. If you have questions, please contact your instructor.

Withdrawals and Incompletes: Students may wish to review college policy regarding course withdrawals and incompletes in the CSU catalog. Do not hesitate to speak with your instructor or your advisor if you need information relating to deadlines for course withdrawals or incompletes.

Disabilities: For information about Disability Services or to obtain this document in an alternative format, contact Disability Services in the Student Center building: Student Center 255, 678-466-5445: disabilityservices@mail.clayton.edu .

Required Textbook: (Available in the CSU Bookstore)
Note: All POLS 1101 classroom and online classes use the same identical course textbook. Be sure to purchase the new 2013 edition of the custom textbook for this course.

Dautrich and Yalof, American Government POLS 1101 American Government Clayton State University Edition, Cengage, 2013.

Keep Informed: Current events will often be discussed in class. Read a major daily newspaper such as *The Atlanta Journal Constitution, The Wall Street Journal* or *The New York Times*, or a news magazine such as *Newsweek, Time* or *U.S. News and World Report, or The Economist*. Watch a daily national network news program on a network such as ABC, CBS, FOX, NBC, PBS, CNN or MSNBC, and/or listen to National Public Radio (6:00 - 9:00 a.m. and 4:00 - 6:30 p.m.) on WABE FM 90.1.

<u>Course Expectations</u>:
1. Attend all class lectures and discussions;
2. Complete all course assignments;
3. Take all geography tests and major examinations;
4. Earn a passing course grade.

This syllabus is subject to revision where necessary to achieve course goals.

Model Course Syllabus

AMERICAN NATIONAL GOVERNMENT POLS 1101

(Online Course Syllabus)

Course Description: (3-0-3) American National Government in an International Context is an introductory level survey of the American political system, emphasizing a cross-cultural approach to the study of the structure and processes of policy decision-making. The course incorporates a comparison of the American political system and other types of political systems. The course also includes the study of world geography, emphasizing a knowledge of the global configuration of nation-states. This course satisfies the Georgia legislative requirement for the study of the United States and Georgia Constitutions.

Attendance: This class will meet on the CSU campus only 4 times. Therefore, it is essential that ALL students attend the course on-campus orientation and the three on-campus examinations. Please make an effort to be on time - once an examination begins you will have only the allotted time to complete your examination.

Format: Class will meet each regularly scheduled calendar day unless announced otherwise. All dates of assignments, tests and exams are listed later in this syllabus. You are expected to have read all assigned material included in each examination.

In selecting an online course approach to learning the course material, you have decided that an independent study approach to this course will work well for you. Because you will be learning outside of a traditional college classroom environment, truly extraordinary discipline must be exercised. The instructor is available to advise and assist you, but you must study ALL assigned textbook chapters and other required course materials in order to succeed. This approach gives you a lot of freedom to study when you choose. However, keep in mind that typically, a student must devote approximately 5 hours a week to an online course reading assignments in the course textbook, and studying for examinations to earn a C grade or better. Less time devoted to this course may result in an unsuccessful experience and a lower course grade than desired.

Course Computer Usage: Students will not be requested to bring a computer to class on a daily basis. Students will make regular remote site use of their computers to access course related email, course websites, complete assignments and communicate with the instructor.

Attendance: All students are expected to attend class each day we meet. If you are unable to attend, obtain information on what has been missed from a fellow student, and then see the instructor with any further questions. Roll will be taken daily.

Classroom Conduct: students are expected to conduct themselves in a manner that evidences respect for students, the instructor and the learning environment.

Students must abide by policies in the CSU Catalog & Student Handbook.

Disruption of the Learning Environment:

Behavior which disrupts the teaching–learning process during class activities will not tolerated. This includes belligerent, abusive, profane, and/or threatening behavior. A student who fails to respond to reasonable faculty direction regarding classroom behavior and/or behavior while participating in classroom activities may be dismissed from class. A student who is dismissed is entitled to due process and will be afforded such rights as soon as possible following dismissal. If found in violation, a student may be administratively withdrawn and may receive a grade of WF.

http://a-s.clayton.edu/DisruptiveClassroomBehavior.htm

**Click on this link to read the Clayton State University
Basic Undergraduate Student Responsibilities Statement.**

The instructor and students will treat each other with the proper respect at all times.

*Children are NOT permitted in any CSU classroom under any circumstances,
nor may they be left unattended anywhere on the campus.*

Please turn your cell phone to "vibrate" or turn it off during class.

*Cheating will not be tolerated and will be dealt with in keeping
with in keeping with the CSU Conduct Code.*

CSU Conduct Code and Judicial Procedure

Civic Engagement:

Civic Engagement at Clayton State University is defined as an intentional learning experience that contributes to a student's understanding *of social and civic responsibility, community leadership, and service* to a diverse, democratic *society.* Civic Engagement outcomes are located at the Political Science Program website:

http://a-s.clayton.edu/politicalscience/default.htm

For information on earning a political science degree at CSU:

http://a-s.clayton.edu/politicalscience/default.htm

Political Science Degree Program Outcomes and Assessments:

Outcomes: *Graduating political science majors should*

- Apply concepts related to the structures and principles of the U.S. Constitution to historical and current politics.

- Explain and criticize U.S. political institutions and processes.

- Define and distinguish how aspects of the Georgia Constitution and government differ from the U.S. Constitution and government.

- Assess and compare how other national political systems and international political organizations differ from the U.S. political system and recognize the importance of political geography.

- Research and compose a project report in a subfield of political science.

- Successfully complete a political science related internship.

Assessments:

- POLS 1101 pre and post assessment surveys & geography tests

- POLS 4490/POLS 4491 Internship/Practicum Site Supervisor Evaluation

- POLS 3000 and 4000 level course research papers

- POLS 4500 Senior Seminar research paper

- POLS 4500 Senior Political Science Program Exit Survey

- ACAT Area Concentration Achievement Test taken by graduating seniors

Midterm Grades: A course midterm grade will be posted on the DUCK by midterm each semester. The midterm grade will only reflect graded work completed to the middle of the semester. Typically more than half of the scored work in this course is completed after the midterm date. If you have questions, please contact your instructor.

Withdrawals and Incompletes: Students may wish to review college policy regarding course withdrawals and incompletes in the CSU catalog. Do not hesitate to speak with your instructor or your advisor if you need information relating to deadlines for course withdrawals or incompletes.

Disabilities: For information about Disability Services or to obtain this document in an alternative format, contact Disability Services in the Student Center building:Student Center 255, 678-466-5445: disabilityservices@mail.clayton.edu .

Required Textbook Materials: (Available in the CSU Bookstore)
Note: All POLS 1101 classroom and online classes use the same identical course textbook. Be sure to purchase the 2013 edition of the custom textbook for this course.

Dautrich and Yalof, American Government, POLS 1101 American Government Clayton State University, Cengage, 2013.

Keep Informed: Current events will often be discussed in class. Read a major daily newspaper such as *The Atlanta Journal Constitution, The Wall Street Journal* or *The New York Times*, or a news magazine such as *Newsweek, Time* or *U.S. Newsand World Report, or The Economist.* Watch a daily national network news program on a network such as ABC, CBS, FOX, NBC, PBS, CNN or MSNBC, and/or listen to National Public Radio (6:00 - 9:00 a.m. and 4:00 - 6:30 p.m.) on WABE FM 90.1.

Course Expectations:
1. Attend the course orientation;
2. Complete all reading course assignments;
3. Take course major examinations;
4. Earn a passing course grade.

This syllabus is subject to revision where necessary to achieve course goals.

Political Science

Social Sciences

Program Description

This political science program places special emphasis on preparing students for community service, public service, law school, and graduate school to meet the expanding needs of South Metropolitan Atlanta.

What is Political Science?

Political science is the study of governments and the governing procedures in individual countries and in international bodies such as the United Nations. Irrespective of the unit of government political science deals with, it is primarily concerned with "the authoritative allocation of values" - namely, how individuals and groups go about obtaining the most of what they cherish and value.

Political scientists study how governments are structured, how governments make decisions, as well as the content of those decisions, and how governments solve societal conflicts, and what conditions are most conducive to the orderly process of government. Specifically, political scientists study such phenomena as political parties and voting behavior, public opinion, interest groups, bureaucracies and administrative procedures, national security and international organization, executive politics and legislative behavior, courts and the administration of justice, intergovernmental relations, political personality, mass movements, revolution, ideologies, political philosophy, community organization and urban politics, and the expanding field of policy studies.

Political Science Program Outcomes

1. Understand the structure and perspective of Political Science.

2. Understand the research processes of Political Science.

3. Understand the institutions of government and politics at the local, state, national and international levels.

4. Understand alternative political systems.

5. Understand the importance of civic engagement in American society.

6. Demonstrate effective written communication skills.

7. Demonstrate the ability to analyze data and textual materials, and to think critically.

Political Science Home

Political Sciences at Clayton State University

Program Outcomes & Assessments

Political Science Advisor Assignments

Curriculum Worksheet

Core Curriculum

Previous Catalog POLS Degree Requirements

Political Science Three-Year Program

Political Science Minor

Course Descriptions

Course Offerings 2012-2017

Internships

Change of Major Forms

Graduation Application, Fall 2011 -

Graduation Application, 2006-2011 Catalogs

Graduation Application, 2005 Catalog

Thinking About Law School

Social Sciences Home

College of Arts & Sciences Home

What you can do with a Political Science degrees
Careers in Political Science

Websites for the Political Science Major
Internet Resources

Department Chair
A. Rafik Mohamed

Political Science Advisors
Joe Trachtenberg
Augustine Ayuk
Joseph Corrado
Sean Mattie

LOCATIONS

Main Campus, 2000 Clayton State Boulevard, Morrow, GA 30260, (678) 466-4000
Clayton State East, 5823 Trammell Road, Morrow, GA 30260
Fayette, 100 World Drive, Suite 100, Peachtree City, GA 30269, (678) 466-5000
Henry, 401 Tomlinson St., McDonough, GA 30253

FOLLOW US

Political Science Program Mission Statement

The Political Science Program at Clayton State University immerses undergraduate major students in the study of government and public policy and of the political behavior of individuals and groups. Students are expected to develop the facility to apply both normative and behavioral perspectives and skills in their studies. Political analysis will involve the study of political systems and processes in the State of Georgia, the United States, the comparative study of other nations' political systems and international relations. Students will demonstrate a knowledge of world political geography. Political science majors should understand the dynamics of a constantly changing domestic and international political world and the implications of political change for domestic and international politics. Students should develop an understanding of how politics works, motivating factors behind public policy, and the use of political power. The political science major is designed to expose students to the philosophical and practical problems of political organization, action, and governance and to encourage critical thinking about the nature of citizenship, rights, and duties in contemporary society. Majors will experience politics first-hand through a required internship learning experience. In the process of their studies students also will acquire the analytic and writing skills necessary to communicate effectively in a challenging socio-political world and their chosen career.

The Importance of Civic Engagement

Tom Ehrlich, a senior scholar for the Carnegie Foundation for the Advancement of Teaching, gave this definition of the characteristics of a civically engaged individual:

"Civic engagement means working to make a difference in the civic life of our communities and developing the combination of knowledge, skills, values and motivation to make that difference. It means promoting the quality of life in a community, through both political and nonpolitical processes. A morally and civically responsible individual recognizes himself and herself as a member of a larger social fabric and therefore considers social problems to be at least partly his or her own; such an individual is willing to see the moral and civic dimensions of issues, to make and justify informed moral and civic judgments and to take action when appropriate."[1]

Unfortunately, Americans are often less knowledgeable and active than citizens in other democracies. In a 33 question test on civic knowledge, compiled by the Intercollegiate Studies Institute, the average American scored 49%.[2] While the 2008 election was closely followed by more Americans than other recent elections, only 14% felt very confident that they would attempt to change local policies in schools, neighborhoods, or the workplace. Less than 20% of Americans were sure they would talk about the issues raised during the presidential campaign.[3] In your POLS 1101 courses you will gain some knowledge about the Constitution, U.S. political institutions, and the political behavior of interest groups, political parties, and citizens. To be a good citizen it is your responsibility to use this knowledge to improve your social and political world.

You can start by getting involved in activities on campus. Clayton State University is an active member of the American Democracy Project (ADP). The ADP is a multi-campus initiative focused on higher education's role in preparing the next generation of informed, engaged citizens for our democracy. Each year, CSU celebrates Constitution Day (September 17th) with a week full of events including the reading of the Constitution and a speaker covering some Constitutional issue. CSU holds New York Times talks. These are discussions about current events facilitated by a faculty member over a free lunch of pizza and soda held on about 5 Tuesdays during the spring and fall semesters. Recently, an undergraduate research conference on the 2008 election was initiated.

Clayton State University is only one place to be more involved. Do you know who represents you in Congress? Have you ever attended a school board meeting or a city council meeting? There are endless reasons why you should consider becoming active in your communities, university, and in politics. Here are two: 1) Approximately 1 in 3 people aged 18-34 are without health insurance. 2) The cost of higher education is increasing. Tamara Draught notes that, "Over 25 percent of college graduates in 2003 had student loan debt higher than $25,000 up from 7 percent in 1992-1993."[4]

1 Thomas Ehrlich (Ed.) Civic Responsibility and Higher Education. Phoenix: Oryx Press, 2000.

2 http://www.ncoc.net/

3 2008 Civic Health Index: Beyond the Vote (Executive Summary) http://www.ncoc.net/

4 http://www.strappedthebook.com/facts.php

Here are some websites that you can use to become more civically engaged:

 To find out who represents you in Congress:

www.congress.org

For non-partisan election information and a link to a voter registration form: www.lwv.org

The American Democracy Project:

http://americandemocracyproject.pbwiki.com and http://www.aascu.org/programs/adp/

To learn more about student debt:

http://www.projectonstudentdebt.org

These sites encourage young people to participate regardless of their political affiliation:

http://www.rockthevote.com and http://www.mobilize.org

The Clayton County Board of Education: http://www.clayton.k12.ga.us/administration/boardofeducation/

Clayton County's government:

http://www.co.clayton.ga.us/

Georgia's Government:

www.georgia.gov

This book is dedicated to the next generation of responsible citizens who will inherit the American government, in particular, our students and our own children:

ALLISON, BENJAMIN, JANE, KENNY, AND RACHEL

BRIEF CONTENTS

PART I FOUNDATIONS
Chapters 1 through 5

President Obama: Jewel Samad/AFP/Getty Images President Truman: George Skadding/Time Life Pictures/Getty Images

CHAPTER 1
The More Things Change . . . The More They Stay the Same 2

© Michael Ventura/Alamy

CHAPTER 2
The Founding and the Constitution. 22

Dennie Cody/Getty Images

CHAPTER 3
Federalism 56

Douglas Graham/Roll Call/Getty Images

CHAPTER 4
Civil Liberties 72

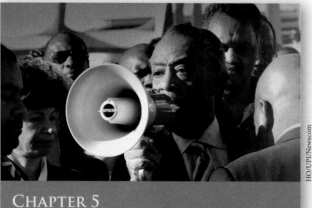

HO/UPI/Newscom

CHAPTER 5
Civil Rights, Equality and Social Movements 104

PART II INSTITUTIONS
Chapters 6 through 9

© iStockphoto.com/oversnap

CHAPTER 6
Congress 138

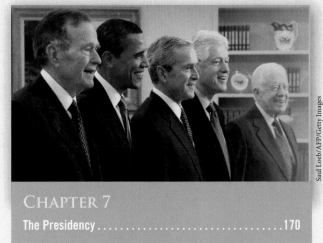

Saul Loeb/AFP/Getty Images

CHAPTER 7
The Presidency 170

© iStockphoto.com/Skyhobo

CHAPTER 8
The Federal Bureaucracy 200

AP Photo/Charles Dharapak

CHAPTER 9
The Judiciary 228

Part III Political Behavior
Chapters 10 through 14

© iStockphoto.com/P_We

Chapter 10
Public Opinion.....................................262

William Thomas Cain/Getty Images

Chapter 11
Interest Groups.....................................290

AP Photo/Brad Barket

Chapter 12
The Media and American Politics.....................316

Political buttons: © Lynne Fernandes/The Image Works
Background: Joe Raedle/Newsmakers/Getty Images

Chapter 13
Political Parties and Voting 344

Daniel Acker/Bloomberg via Getty Images

Chapter 14
Campaigns and Elections 386

PART IV PUBLIC POLICY
Chapters 15 and 16

Chip Somodevilla/Getty Images

CHAPTER 15

American Domestic Policy 420

REUTERS/White House/Pete Souza/LANDOV

CHAPTER 16

American Foreign Policy 450

CONTENTS

PART I

FOUNDATIONS

CHAPTER 1 THE MORE THINGS CHANGE . . . THE MORE THEY STAY THE SAME

CHECK the List: Incumbent Presidents Who Enjoy Reelection Success 4

History Repeats Itself 4

   A New Communications Medium Paves the Way to Electoral Victory 4

   A Bruising, Negative Primary Fight Sets the Stage for a Difficult General Election Against an Incumbent 5

Forms and Functions of Government. 7

American Government and Politics. 8

Jewel Samad/AFP/Getty Images

American Political Culture. 10

The More Things Change, The More They Stay the Same: Constitutional Amendments That Have Extended Voting Rights in the United States 11

Is American Democracy in Decline? 15

   The Case for Decline. 15

   But Do These Problems Really Signify a Decline? 17

From Your Perspective: Courting the Youth Vote. 19

Summary: Putting It All Together. 20

CHAPTER 2 THE FOUNDING AND THE CONSTITUTION

The Beginnings of a New Nation 26

   British Actions. 26

   Colonial Responses. 26

CHECK the List: Top 10 Most Important Founders? 28

   The Decision for Independence 29

   The First National Government: The Articles of Confederation. 30

The Constitutional Convention 32

   Plans and Compromises 32

   The Slavery Issue 34

The New Constitution 35

© Michael Ventura/Alamy

The Ratification Battle 37

Federalists versus Anti-Federalists 37

The Federalist Papers 38

The More Things Change, The More They Stay the Same: The Continuing
Call to the Federalist Papers 40

A Bill of Rights 41

Changing the Constitution 42

The Formal Amendment Process 42

Informal Processes of Change 45

From Your Perspective: One Student's Term Paper Proves That the
Constitution Is Indeed a "Living Document" 46

ANNOTATED CONSTITUTION OF THE UNITED STATES OF AMERICA C-1

Summary: Putting It All Together 47

CHAPTER 3 FEDERALISM

Dennie Cody/Getty Images

What Is Federalism? 54

Comparing Federalism to Other Systems of Government 54

Government Powers in a Federal System 56

The Supremacy Clause 57

Relations Between the States 57

The History of American Federalism 58

CHECK the List: Dramatic Variations in State-Level Approaches
to Health Care 59

State-Centered Federalism, 1789–1819 60

National Supremacy Period, 1819–1837 60

Cooperative Federalism, 1937–1990 62

The "New Federalism," 1990–Present 64

The More Things Change, The More They Stay the Same: When Must the Federal
Government Put State Governments in Their Place? 65

Why Federalism? Advantages and Disadvantages 67

Advantages of Federalism 67

Disadvantages of Federalism 67

From Your Perspective: The Real-Life Benefits of Attending College
Close to Home 68

Summary: Putting It All Together 69

CHAPTER 4 CIVIL LIBERTIES

Douglas Graham/Roll Call/Getty Images

The Bill of Rights: Origins and Evolution 76

Freedom of Religion and the Establishment Clause 78

   The Free Exercise of Religion *78*

   The Establishment Clause *80*

Free Expression Rights 83

   Free Speech During the Early Twentieth Century: The Clear
   and Present Danger Test *84*

   The Warren Court and the Rise of the "Preferred Freedoms" Doctrine *84*

   The Freedom of the Press, Libel Laws, and Prior Restraints *85*

   Obscenity and Pornography *86*

   Symbolic Speech and the Flag-Burning Controversy *87*

   Hate Speech Codes *88*

   Regulating the Internet *88*

The Second Amendment Right to Bear Arms 89

The Rights of the Criminally Accused 90

   Fourth Amendment Rights *91*

The More Things Change, The More They Stay the Same: Balancing
Police Surveillance Techniques With the Need for Individual Privacy 93

   Fifth Amendment Rights *94*

   Sixth Amendment Rights *96*

   Eighth Amendment Rights *97*

The Modern Right to Privacy 97

CHECK the List: Nearly All Western Democracies Have Abolished
the Death Penalty 98

From Your Perspective: Shedding Fourth Amendment
Rights at the Schoolhouse Door 100

Summary: Putting It All Together 101

CHAPTER 5 CIVIL RIGHTS, EQUALITY AND SOCIAL MOVEMENTS

Types of Equality 108

The Struggle for Equality: Approaches and Tactics 108

The African American Struggle for Equality and Civil Rights 110

   Racial Discrimination: From Slavery to Reconstruction *110*

CHECK the List: The 11 Largest Political Demonstrations
Held in Washington, D.C. 112

HO/UPI/Newscom

Racial Segregation and Barriers to Equality. 112

The Beginnings of the Civil Rights Movement 115

Birmingham 1963: The Turning Point of the Civil Rights Movement 116

Continuing Struggles over Racial Equality. 119

The More Things Change, The More They Stay the Same:
Tolerance Can Be Hard to Come by . . . Even in Congress 120

The Women's Movement and Gender Equality 124

Judicial Scrutiny of Gender Discrimination and the Equal
Rights Amendment. 125

Legal Challenges to Gender Discrimination 125

Other Struggles for Equality. 127

Native Americans. 127

Asian Americans 128

Muslim Americans 129

Hispanic Americans 129

Older Americans. 130

Individuals with Disabilities. 131

Gays and Lesbians 131

From Your Perspective: Title IX Brings Gender Equality—and
Controversy—to a Campus Near You 133

Summary: Putting It All Together. 134

PART II

INSTITUTIONS

CHAPTER 6 CONGRESS

Article I and the Creation of Congress. 142

The Structure and Organization of Congress 143

The House of Representatives: The "People's House" 144

The Senate: A Stabilizing Factor 145

Leadership in Congress. 146

Leadership in the House of Representatives 147

Leadership in the Senate 148

CHECK the List: The Top 10 Largest Partisan Gains in House
Elections Since 1914 149

© iStockphoto.com/oversnap

The Committee System 150

    Types of Committees in Congress *151*

    Leadership of Congressional Committees *153*

    Partisan Nature of the Committee System *153*

    Congressional Staffing *153*

The More Things Change, The More They Stay the Same:
The Power of Congressional Caucuses within the Major Parties 155

How a Bill Becomes a Law 156

    Step 1: A Bill Is Introduced *156*

    Step 2: The Bill Is Sent to a Standing Committee for Action *157*

    *Step 3: The Bill Goes to the Full House and Senate
for Consideration* *158*

    Step 4: Conference Committee Action *159*

    Step 5: Presidential Action *160*

Oversight and Personnel Functions of Congress 160

    Congressional Oversight *161*

    Confirmation of Presidential Nominations and Approval of Treaties *162*

    Impeachment and Removal of Federal Judges and High Executives *163*

Constituent Service: Helping People Back Home 163

From Your Perspective: An Internship as a Steppingstone 165

Summary: Putting It All Together 166

CHAPTER 7 THE PRESIDENCY

Where Do Presidents Come From? Presidential Comings and Goings 174

The Evolution of the American Presidency 175

    The President as "Chief Clerk" of the United States, 1789–1836 . . . . *176*

    The Weakened Presidency in the Wilderness Years, 1837–1900 . . . . *177*

    *The Birth of the Modern Presidency and Its Rise to Dominance,
1901–1945* *178*

CHECK the List: The 10 Greatest Presidents of All Time 180

    The Imperial Presidency Comes Under Attack, 1945–1980 . . . . *180*

    Redefining the Presidency in an Era of Divisiveness, 1981–2012 . . . . *181*

Express Powers and Responsibilities of the President 182

    Head of State *182*

Saul Loeb/AFP/Getty Images

Chief Executive and Head of Government *183*

The More Things Change, The More They Stay the Same: Foreign Policy
Successes That Defined a Young Presidency 185

    Chief Diplomat *186*

    Chief Legislator *186*

    Commander in Chief *188*

Implied Powers and Responsibilities of the President 189

    Crisis Manager *189*

    Party Leader *189*

    Executive Orders and Agreements *190*

Presidential Resources 190

    The Vice President *191*

    The Cabinet *191*

    The Executive Office of the President and the White House Staff *192*

    The First Lady *192*

Important Presidential Relationships 193

    The President and the Public *193*

    The President and Congress *194*

    The President and the Media *195*

From Your Perspective: Another "Tweet" from the Commander in Chief:
The Interactive Presidency of Barack Obama 197

Summary: Putting It All Together 197

CHAPTER 8 THE FEDERAL BUREAUCRACY

What Is Bureaucracy? 204

What Does the Federal Bureaucracy Do? 206

    Policy Implementation *206*

    Bureaucratic Legislation *206*

CHECK the List: Senator Proxmire's Top 10 Golden Fleece Awards 208

    Bureaucratic Adjudication *209*

The Development of the Federal Bureaucracy 209

Getting Control of the Growing Bureaucracy 211

The Organization of the Federal Bureaucracy 212

    Cabinet Departments *212*

    The Department of Homeland Security *216*

© iStockphoto.com/Skyhobo

The More Things Change, The More They Stay the Same:
Conflicts Within the President's Cabinet 217

    Independent Agencies 218

    Regulatory Agencies 218

    Government Corporations 219

    The Executive Office of the President 220

The Federal Workforce 220

    Political Appointees and Career Professionals 220

    The Civil Service 221

From Your Perspective: You, Your Parents, and the
Dreaded FAFSA Form 223

Summary: Putting It All Together 224

CHAPTER 9 THE JUDICIARY

Types of Law 232

The Structure of the U.S. Legal System 233

    State Legal Systems and State Courts 233

    Development of the Federal Court System 234

The Adversarial System of Justice 236

    Elements of Civil Litigation 236

    The Criminal Justice System at Work 237

Judicial Review and its Implications 238

CHECK the List: Five Justices Who Received No Legal Education
at a College or University 240

Limitations on Courts 241

Electing and Appointing Judges 244

    The Nomination Process 244

    The Confirmation Process 247

How a Case Proceeds within the U.S. Supreme Court 249

Why the Justices Vote the Way They Do 252

The More Things Change, The More They Stay the Same:
"Swing Justices" Who Kept a Nation on Edge 253

Current Debates over the Exercise of Judicial Power 255

From Your Perspective: Is Law School the Right Choice for You,
and If So, When Should You Apply? 256

Summary: Putting It All Together 258

AP Photo/Charles Dharapak

PART III

POLITICAL BEHAVIOR

© iStockphoto.com/P_We

CHAPTER 10 PUBLIC OPINION

Public Opinion in American Politics 266

How Is Public Opinion Expressed? 267

The Levels of Public Opinion 268

    Values and Beliefs 268

    Political Orientations 269

    Political Preferences 270

How Informed Is Public Opinion? 271

How Does Public Opinion Form? 272

    Family 273

    Friends and Peer Groups 273

    The Schools 274

    The Media 275

    Religion 275

How Is Public Opinion Measured? 275

    The History of Political Polling 276

The More Things Change, The More They Stay the Same:
Polling Problems in Presidential Elections 277

    Scientific Sampling 278

    Unscientific Polls 278

    Pseudo-Polls 281

    Sample Size 281

    Asking Questions on Polls 282

CHECK the List: Items That Should be Disclosed About Any
Publicly Released Poll 283

Interpreting Public Opinion Data 284

From Your Perspective: College Students Making
Their Voices Heard in Occupy Wall Street 286

Summary: Putting It All Together 286

CHAPTER 11 INTEREST GROUPS

Pluralism and the Interest-Group System 294

What Is an Interest Group? 294

The Pros and Cons of Interest Groups 295

Interest Groups versus Political Parties 296

Interest Groups and Social Movements 297

Interest Groups in Action 298

The Growth of Interest Groups 298

Iron Triangles, Issue Networks, and the Influence of Groups 299

Membership in Groups 300

What Makes Some Groups More Powerful Than Others? 301

CHECK the List: The Top 10 Most Influential Interest Groups 302

Types of Interest Groups 303

Economic Groups 303

Noneconomic Groups 306

How Interest Groups Achieve Their Goals 308

Lobbying 308

The More Things Change, The More They Stay the Same:
High-Powered Lobbyists in American History 309

Supporting Candidates and Parties in Elections 310

Litigation 311

Persuasion Campaigns 311

From Your Perspective: "Before the Lecture Begins,
Students from PIRG Have an Announcement . . ." 312

Summary: Putting It All Together 313

William Thomas Cain/Getty Images

CHAPTER 12 THE MEDIA AND AMERICAN POLITICS

The Media in American Politics 320

Government Regulation of the Media 320

Functions of the Media in American Politics 321

CHECK the List: Top 10 Political Blogs, as of April 2012 322

Historical Development of the Media 324

The Era of the Partisan Press 324

The Emergence of Electronic Media 325

AP Photo/Brad Barket

The Mass Media Today 328

The More Things Change, The More They Stay the Same:
Political Satire Throughout the Years 329

The Print Media 330

The Electronic Media 332

Ownership of the Media 334

The Effects of the Media 336

Criticisms of the News Media 337

From Your Perspective: Are You a Blogger? 339

Summary: Putting It All Together 340

CHAPTER 13 POLITICAL PARTIES AND VOTING

Political buttons: © Lynne Fernandes/The
Image Works Background: Joe Raedle/
Newsmakers/Getty Images

The Development of Political Parties in the United States 348

The First Parties in America 349

A Second Party System Emerges 351

The Modern Party System in America: Democrats versus Republicans 352

The Functions of Political Parties 354

Contesting Elections 354

Recruiting and Nominating Candidates 355

Providing a Framework for Voters to Make Vote Choices 355

Providing Organization for the Operations of Government 358

Why a Two-Party System? 359

Reasons for the Two-Party System in the United States 360

Minor and Third Parties 361

Party Organizations 362

Are Parties in Decline? 364

Voting 365

The Legal Structure for Voting in the United States 366

Toward Universal Suffrage 366

Voter Registration Laws 368

The More Things Change, The More They Stay the Same:
Breaking Down Traditional Barriers to Winning the White House 369

Exercising the Franchise 370

Who Turns Out to Vote? 371

How Do They Vote? Methods of Casting a Ballot 371

Why Don't More People Vote? *373*

Voting in the United States Compared with Other Democracies *374*

Is Nonvoting a Problem? *377*

CHECK the List: The Top 10 and Bottom 10 Popular Vote Winners
in Presidential Elections *377*

Participation Beyond Voting *378*

From Your Perspective: How Might Television Shape Your Own
Views of What Is Politically Possible? *380*

Summary: Putting It All Together *381*

CHAPTER 14 CAMPAIGNS AND ELECTIONS

Daniel Acker/Bloomberg via Getty Images

American Presidential Elections in Historical Perspective *390*

The Nomination Phase *390*

The General Election Phase *391*

The Prenomination Campaign *393*

The More Things Change, The More They Stay the Same: New Romances
and Old Horses in the Race for the Presidential Nomination *394*

The Nomination Campaign *395*

Primaries and Caucuses *395*

*The Traditional Importance of the Iowa and New Hampshire
Contests* *396*

The Nominating Conventions *398*

The General Election Campaign *399*

Incumbent Race versus Open Election *399*

The Choice of a Vice Presidential Candidate *400*

Gathering a Winning Coalition of States *401*

CHECK the List: Top Battleground States in 2012 . . . . *402*

The Presidential Debates *403*

The Advertising *404*

The Electoral College Vote *404*

Making a Vote Choice *407*

Candidate Familiarity *407*

Party Identification *407*

Issue Voting *408*

Retrospective Voting *408*

Candidate Image Voting *409*

Campaign Funding 409

  Sources of Funding *409*

  Regulating Campaign Financing *412*

Congressional Campaigns and Elections 413

From Your Perspective: Getting Involved in Political Campaigns 416

Summary: Putting It All Together 417

PART IV

PUBLIC POLICY

Chip Somodevilla/Getty Images

CHAPTER 15 AMERICAN DOMESTIC POLICY

An Overview of the Policymaking Process 424

Theory and Practice in Fiscal Policy 426

  Assessing the Economy's Performance *427*

  The Federal Budget-Making Process *429*

  Taxation Policy *431*

  Spending Policies—Dividing the Pie *434*

Theories and Practice in Monetary Policy 435

CHECK the List: The G-7 Nations, Ranked According to Income
Tax Rates Imposed on Their Citizens 437

The Nature and Practice of Crime Policy 438

The Welfare State and Programs for the Poor 439

The Social Security System 441

The More Things Change, The More Things Stay the Same:
States as "Laboratories of Democracy" That Point the Way for National
Domestic Policy 442

Health Care Policy 444

From Your Perspective: Realistic Options for National Service 445

Summary: Putting It All Together 446

CHAPTER 16 AMERICAN FOREIGN POLICY

The Constitutional Framework of American Foreign Policy 454

The Roots of American Foreign Policy 454

  The Isolationist Tradition and the Monroe Doctrine *455*

  Expansionism and the Birth of a Superpower *456*

REUTERS/White House/Pete Souza/
LANDOV

New World Order and New World Disorder. *459*

The U.S. Government Confronts the Middle East *460*

The More Things Change, The More Things Stay the Same:
Assassinating Foreign Leaders 461

Navigating the New World Order After the September 11 Attacks *462*

The Structure of American Foreign Policymaking 463

Other Foreign Policy Actors and Interests *466*

American Foreign Policy and Public Opinion *467*

Foreign Policy Dilemmas for the Twenty-first Century 468

Is the "Preemption Doctrine" Justifiable? *469*

Cultivating Relations with the New Russian Federation *469*

What Role Does Foreign Aid Play in the New International Order? *470*

Does the United Nations Still Serve an Important Function? *470*

CHECK the List: Who Is in the "Nuclear Club"? 471

From Your Perspective: Is the American Military Draft
a Thing of the Past? 473

Summary: Putting It All Together 473

SPECIAL FEATURES

CHECK THE LIST

Incumbent Presidents Who Enjoy Reelection Success 4

Top 10 Most Important Founders? 28

Dramatic Variations in State-Level Approaches to Health Care 59

Nearly All Western Democracies Have Abolished the Death Penalty 98

The 11 Largest Political Demonstrations Held in Washington, D.C. 112

The Top 10 Largest Partisan Gains in House Elections Since 1914 149

The 10 Greatest Presidents of All Time 180

Senator Proxmire's Top 10 Golden Fleece Awards 208

Five Justices Who Received No Legal Education at a College or University 240

Items That Should Be Disclosed about Any Publicly Released Poll 283

The Top 10 Most Influential Interest Groups 302

Top 10 Political Blogs, as of April 2012 322

The Top 10 and Bottom 10 Popular Vote Winners in Presidential Elections 377

Top Battleground States in 2012 402

The G-7 Nations, Ranked According to Income Tax Rates Imposed on Their Citizens 437

Who Is in the "Nuclear Club"? 471

THE MORE THINGS CHANGE . . .

Constitutional Amendments That Have Extended Voting Rights in the United States 11

The Continuing Call to the Federalist Papers 40

When Must the Federal Government Put State Governments in Their Place? 65

Balancing Police Surveillance Techniques with the Need for Individual Privacy 93

Tolerance Can Be Hard to Come by . . . Even in Congress 120

The Power of Congressional Caucuses within the Major Parties 155

Foreign Policy Successes That Defined a Young Presidency 185

Conflicts Within the President's Cabinet 217

"Swing Justices" Who Kept a Nation on Edge 253

Polling Problems in Presidential Elections 277

High-Powered Lobbyists in American History 309

Political Satire Throughout the Years 329

Breaking Down Traditional Barriers to Winning the White House 369

New Romances and Old Horses in the Race for the Presidential Nomination 394

States as "Laboratories of Democracy" That Point the Way for National Domestic Policy 442

Assassinating Foreign Leaders 461

FROM YOUR PERSPECTIVE

Courting the Youth Vote 19

One Student's Term Paper Proves That the Constitution Is Indeed a "Living Document" .46

The Real-Life Benefits of Attending College Close to Home 68

Shedding Fourth Amendment Rights at the Schoolhouse Door 100

Title IX Brings Gender Equality—and Controversy—to a Campus Near You 133

An Internship as a Steppingstone 165

Another "Tweet" from the Commander in Chief: The Interactive Presidency of Barack Obama 197

You, Your Parents, and the Dreaded FAFSA Form 223

Is Law School the Right Choice for You, and If So, When Should You Apply? 256

College Students Making Their Voices Heard in Occupy Wall Street 286

"Before the Lecture Begins, Students from PIRG Have an Announcement . . ." 312

Are You a Blogger? 339

How Might Television Shape Your Own Views of What Is Politically Possible? 380

Getting Involved in Political Campaigns 416

Realistic Options for National Service. 445

Is the American Military Draft a Thing of the Past? 473

PREFACE

AN INTRODUCTION TO AMERICAN GOVERNMENT

This is a textbook about the American government, the success of which depends upon a responsible citizenry willing to ask tough questions of its leaders and demand reasonable answers in return. This book encourages student-readers to hone their critical thinking skills, ask the tough questions, and become responsible citizens.

We encourage students to engage by demonstrating how the problems and controversies characterizing American government today have been successfully tackled in America's past. Indeed, history tends to repeat itself, and we certainly can learn from the lessons of history to better address the problems we face today and will face tomorrow. Despite all the changes that have occurred over the course of the nation's history, the past is replete with examples from which we can learn. The challenge facing instructors of American government today is how to take adequate account of all these changes while never losing sight of the issues and events from the nation's past and their significance today.

We offer in this third edition of *The Enduring Democracy* all the nuts and bolts of the U.S. government and how it works; but as with our previous editions, we do not settle for mere surface descriptions and analysis of American government and politics. We also seek to educate students about American politics in ways that go beyond the essentials of government by placing current political issues and debates in historical perspective. By examining the current state of American politics through the lens of American history, we hope to encourage students to think critically about the significance of certain persons, places, and events in American politics and consider all the different ways in which they might be viewed and interpreted. We are particularly interested in a historical perspective, as college students in recent years have been witness to seismic shifts in American politics: Barack Obama's two presidential campaigns and the emergence of a more energetic and younger voting contingent as a force in recent elections; the unified resistance of moderate and conservative Republicans to most aspects of the Obama administration's agenda; the rise of the Tea Party and Occupy Wall Street movements; the passage of landmark health care legislation and the political fallout of the Obama administration's legislative agenda on the outcome of the 2010 congressional elections; and, of course, the hallmark 2012 presidential and congressional election outcomes. All of these events offer unprecedented opportunities for testing political theories and concepts against modern-day realities.

As educators, we never want to let students accept at face value these and other essential aspects of American politics—we thus offer tools to help students think more critically about American government and politics. For example, we don't want students to assume that all victories in the American political system are equally important; we want them to realize that prevailing political circumstances exert a powerful influence on how different entities may define "victory." For example, some observers criticized Barack Obama and the Democrats for passing comprehensive health care legislation in early 2010 on the strength of an exceedingly slim partisan majority; and yet when Lyndon Johnson, at the height of his party's political power in early 1965, was informed by one top aide that the White House had just won passage of desired legislation by a wide margin, the president purportedly remarked: "How much more could we have gotten had we been willing to win by just one vote?" In similar fashion, some defeats may still advance the given cause, such as when losses generate attention or publicity for a previously unrecognized issue. The newly formed Republican Party's defeat in the 1856 presidential election set the stage for Abraham Lincoln's election as the first Republican president in 1860, and the eloquent dissents written by Supreme Court Justice Oliver Wendell Holmes early in the twentieth century pointed the way to the more liberal free speech doctrines embraced by a majority of Supreme Court justices in the 1960s.

Throughout *The Enduring Democracy*, we offer students of American government and politics the means by which to think critically about those topics. Blinded by what is in front of us now, we often ignore lessons from the past. American government and politics have changed dramatically in the more than two centuries of the nation's existence, yet certain issues persist. In this textbook we investigate America's political institutions and processes from a number of different viewpoints in an effort to take the full measure of American politics.

We offer in these pages no polemic or theoretical argument about what American politics should look like or stand for, either now or in the years ahead. To the degree it's possible, we attempt to avoid normative judgments about American political institutions or individuals based on a particular ideological point of view—whether conservative or liberal, radical or moderate. Instead, we aim to provide a more measured view of government institutions and processes. We complement the text presentation of the essentials of American government with a focus on placing current issues and controversies into historical perspective, allowing students to view current issues and problems through the lens of history. This perspective allows students to see how what might seem to be "new" challenges and issues have been effectively resolved in the past. We also frame contemporary problems from the perspective of what they mean to college students, thus highlighting the relevance of American government to their lives.

The idea that "history repeats itself" or that "the more things change, the more they stay the same" is not merely a piece of conventional wisdom. Looking back provides important lessons applicable to today's challenges. In examining the past we find that some of our new and "unprecedented" political controversies are neither new nor unprecedented. The faces may have changed and the policies may have been transformed, but the challenges the nation faces today are often newer versions of past dilemmas and problems.

Viewing American politics through the prism of history allows students to gain a greater appreciation for American government—both its flaws and its successes. Furthermore, placing American government in historical perspective facilitates an understanding of how the modern political system works. For example, the smoke-filled rooms of the nineteenth century in which political party bosses often selected political candidates threatened democracy and undermined accountability to the majority. Those smoke-filled rooms no longer exist today, as progressive reforms introduced in the early part of the twentieth century forced major political parties to use slightly more democratic means to choose candidates. Still, party bosses continue to exert considerable influence by determining where the party will allocate its resources. A thorough examination of past problems, issues, and conflicts does not negate the uniqueness of the current American condition, but it does offer a better understanding of contemporary issues. In some cases, studying the past assures us that the political process does work in a positive way; in other cases, it reminds us that we are not the first to face certain difficulties, and it suggests that we may want to seek more direction from the past about what works and what does not.

Although the historical framework is the primary analytic tool we use to present contemporary political issues, students of American history also recognize that each of them views American politics through his or her own narrow prism. American military interventions abroad are one thing, but when the U.S. government actually drafts college-age students into the army—as occurred most recently during the Vietnam War—students may come to see the intervention with an entirely different eye. By the same token, the passage of landmark health care legislation means something entirely different for those students who can now remain longer on their family health care policies and thus put off worrying about obtaining their own health care insurance until much farther into the future. *The Enduring Democracy* thus offers students a window into American politics that looks specifically at their own vantage points—with the understanding, of course, that students come from a wide range of backgrounds and experiences.

ORGANIZATION OF THE TEXT

PART I—FOUNDATIONS

Part I ("Foundations," Chapters 1 through 5) of the textbook begins with a discussion of how the roadmap of history provides a guide to the future, how the use of a historical perspective on American politics can add to and help shape our understanding of contemporary problems and the creation and evolution of its institutions and processes. In Chapter 1, after reviewing the forms and functions of government in general and highlighting fundamental aspects of American political culture, we pose a hypothetical question: Is American democracy on the decline? We then consider evidence that has been offered in recent years to support and contradict that controversial proposition, using an examination of historical perspectives in order to place contentions such as these in their proper contexts. Chapters 2 through 5 begin the textbook's consideration of the American political system with a discussion of the origins of the American government and the Constitution (Chapter 2), the federal system and the rights and liberties that derive from the Constitution (Chapter 3), and the Bill of Rights and subsequent amendments that guarantee equality (Chapters 4 and 5).

PART II—INSTITUTIONS

Part II ("Institutions," Chapters 6 through 9) considers the major institutions of government formed under the Constitution. Congress (Chapter 6), the executive branch (Chapter 7), and the judiciary (Chapter 9) were all established by the first three articles of the Constitution, although their appearance and functions today might surprise many of the founders who designed them. The bureaucracy (Chapter 8) is not specifically mentioned in the Constitution but it is an inevitable product of a government expected to tackle the problems of a nation that is home to a diverse population of over 300 million people.

PART III—POLITICAL BEHAVIOR

In Part III ("Political Behavior," Chapters 10 through 14), we consider political behavior and its evolution. Interest groups (Chapter 11) and political parties (Chapter 13) are not modern phenomena; they were outgrowths of the American political system from the beginning and have always had an important influence in American governance. Public opinion (Chapter 10) and the media (Chapter 12), although they look very different today than in the past, continue to alter the political landscape significantly. Voting and elections (Chapter 14) in America are just as contentious and competitive today as ever.

PART IV—PUBLIC POLICY

In Part IV ("Public Policy," Chapters 15 and 16), we discuss the so-called "outputs" of government. Following a discussion of the nature of public policymaking in general, we consider domestic policymaking (Chapter 15) and foreign policymaking (Chapter 16) in American government.

NEW AND UPDATED FEATURES OF THE THIRD EDITION

This revised third edition of *The Enduring Democracy* offers new features, updated coverage, and updated features that will assist students as they grapple with the constantly shifting realities of American politics.

- Each chapter begins with a **Then and Now** feature, which highlights how contemporary political events and controversies compare with related historical precedents. In Chapter 2, for example, we show how contemporary challenges to the constitutionality of provisions of the 2010 health care reform legislation are in fact remarkably similar to the challenges lodged against many provisions of the New Deal laws in the 1930s. In other chapters, we depict the striking similarities of both the Occupy Wall Street and Tea Party movements to other movements in America's political past. Moreover, we show how the current era of divisiveness in politics is nothing new, nor are the challenges faced by groups, such as gays and lesbians, fighting for their equal rights.

- In the initial pages of each chapter, we include a set of **Fact or Fiction** statements to engage students in the chapter topic. These statements are intended to provoke student curiosity by highlighting surprising material, calling attention to lesser known but important details of the political system.

- In each chapter, we include succinctly written **learning objectives**, and we conclude each chapter with a review of those objectives, supported by **review test questions** that students can use to gauge their own mastery of the chapter's material. Additionally, within each chapter **key terms** are highlighted in boldface type and defined in the margins of the pages. These key terms are also listed at the end of the chapter, and the terms and definitions are repeated in a glossary at the end of the book.

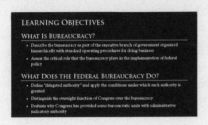 

- **Critical thinking questions** are provided at the end of the thematic boxes, which encourage students in turn to think about the material in new and interesting ways, and that may be used to spark discussion of the material in class;

- Late-night television host David Letterman is not the only one to offer "Top 10" lists—such lists have become part of American culture, whether they feature the top 10 movies of the year, the top 10 political cartoons of the month, or the top 40 songs of week. In each chapter of the text, the **Check the List** feature presents a list (sometimes, but not always, a ranked list) of people, places, events, issues, and so on that addresses some aspect of American politics.

- Each chapter features a box entitled **The More Things Change, the More They Stay the Same.** Here, the premise that American political history has a habit of repeating itself receives ample attention—it is thus no wonder that "those who cannot remember the past are condemned to repeat it." Certainly the specific names and details change, but most contemporary problems and controversies have been identified, tackled, and in some cases outright resolved over and over at different points in the past:

- Finally, each chapter also includes a **From Your Perspective** feature, which considers contemporary political issues from the unique perspective of college students, tapping into the experiences they bring to bear when studying American government.

UPDATED COVERAGE IN THE THIRD EDITIONS

In recent years we have witnessed a significant transformation of the American political landscape. The collapse of the economy in 2007–2008 was followed by Barack Obama's historic victory in the November 2008 presidential election. Despite having united party government under the Democrats, the Obama administration's first two years in office proved contentious, as President Obama and his party allies in Congress pushed through their legislative agenda against strong resistance from Republicans and newly formed outside groups such as the Tea Party. The bitterly contested 2010 congressional midterm elections were a product of growing unrest; they led to divided government, with the GOP making historic gains in the House. The result? Washington, D.C., was home to a legislative logjam throughout much of 2011 and 2012. The historic 2012 presidential election campaign was filled with just as much contention, negativity, and conflict as might have been predicted given the years leading up to that election.

This third edition of *The Enduring Democracy* features fresh new chapter content to bring our discussion of American government fully up to date. Not only is the text fully updated, but the boxes, tables, and figures have been updated to bring the book up to speed with all the new political realities facing government in 2013 and beyond.

Many other textbooks subtly (and, in some cases, not so subtly) offer the authors' own "take" on American politics. Although some instructors may appreciate that more polemical approach, we aim to provide something different. Recognizing that students come to the introductory American government course from a variety of different backgrounds and with varying levels of understanding about American politics, we present all the nuts and bolts they need to understand the system in as straightforward and clear a manner as possible. But then we go a step further: To complement that foundation of basic information, we offer materials that highlight the important events and clues in American history that guide an understanding of contemporary political events and controversies.

The historical perspective—as well as the materials that address American politics from students' own perspectives—do not interfere with the description of essential foundations. If anything, they should spark students' interest in revisiting what they learned in high school, from the media, and elsewhere about American politics with a more discerning and critical eye. Perhaps many students will take this critical approach beyond the course itself and become actual participants in the process. If they do so with a more critical and skeptical eye, our democratic system can only benefit.

SUPPLEMENTS FOR THE INSTRUCTORS

POWERLECTURE DVD WITH EXAMVIEW® AND JOININ® FOR DAUTRICH & YALOF'S *THE ENDURING DEMOCRACY*, 3E

ISBN: 9781285060880

An all-in-one multimedia resource for class preparation, presentation, and testing, this DVD includes Microsoft® PowerPoint® slides, a test bank in both Microsoft® Word and ExamView® formats, online polling and JoinIn™ clicker questions, an Instructor Manual, and a Resource Integration Guide.

The book-specific **PowerPoint® slides** of lecture outlines, as well as photos, figures, and tables from the text, make it easy for you to assemble lectures for your course, and the **media-enhanced PowerPoint® slides** help bring your lecture to life with audio and video clips; animated learning modules illustrating key concepts; and tables, statistical charts, graphs, and photos from the book as well as outside sources.

The **test bank**, offered in Microsoft Word® and ExamView® formats, includes 60+ multiple-choice questions with answers and page references along with 10 essay questions for each chapter. ExamView® features a user-friendly testing environment that allows you to not only publish traditional paper and computer-based tests, but also Web-deliverable exams. **JoinIn**™ offers "clicker" questions covering key concepts, enabling instructors to incorporate student-response systems into their classroom lectures.

The **Instructor's Manual** includes learning objectives, chapter outlines, summaries, discussion questions, class activities and projects suggestions, tips on integrating media into your class, and suggested readings and Web resources. A **Resource Integration Guide** provides a chapter-by-chapter outline of all available resources to supplement and optimize learning. Contact your Cengage representative to receive a copy upon adoption.

THE WADSWORTH NEWS DVD FOR AMERICAN GOVERNMENT 2014

ISBN: 9781285053455

This collection of two- to five-minute video clips on relevant political issues serves as a great lecture or discussion launcher.

ONLINE RESOURCES

POLITICAL SCIENCE COURSEMATE FOR DAUTRICH & YALOF'S *THE ENDURING DEMOCRACY*, 3E

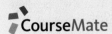

ISBN: 9781285060842 PAC (Printed Access Card)
ISBN: 9781285061467 IAC (Instant Access Code)
To order the text with a Printed Access Card for CourseMate, please use ISBN: 9781285485621

Cengage Learning's Political Science CourseMate brings course concepts to life with interactive learning, study tools, and exam-preparation tools that support the printed textbook. Use **Engagement Tracker** to assess student preparation and engagement in the course, and watch student comprehension soar as your class works with the textbook-specific website. An **interactive eBook** allows students to take notes, highlight, search, and interact with embedded media. Other resources include video activities, animated learning modules, simulations, case studies, interactive quizzes, and timelines.

The American Government NewsWatch is a real-time news and information resource, updated daily, that includes interactive maps, videos, podcasts, and hundreds of articles from leading journals, magazines, and newspapers from the United States and around the world. Also included is the **KnowNow! American Government Blog**, which highlights three current events stories per week and consists of a succinct analysis of the story, multimedia, and discussion-starter questions. Access your course via www.cengage.com/login.

New to this edition is "**The Connections App**," an interactive web app that helps students better understand the relationship between historical and current events and their connection with basic concepts. The App is available through CourseMate. It is also available for free for students at www.cengage.com/login.

FREE COMPANION WEBSITE FOR DAUTRICH & YALOF'S THE ENDURING DEMOCRACY, 3E

ISBN: 9781285060224

This password-protected website for instructors features all of the free student assets plus an Instructor's Manual, book-specific PowerPoint® presentations, JoinIn™ "clicker" questions, a Resource Integration Guide, and a test bank. Access your resources by logging into your account at www.cengage.com/login.

COURSEREADER: AMERICAN GOVERNMENT 0–30 SELECTIONS

ISBN: 9781111479954 PAC (Printed Access Card)
ISBN: 9781111479978 IAC (Instant Access Code)

CourseReader: American Government allows you to create your reader, your way, in just minutes. This affordable, fully customizable online reader provides access to thousands of permissions-cleared readings, articles, primary sources, and audio and video selections from the regularly updated Gale research library database. This easy-to-use solution allows you to search for and select just the material you want for your courses.

Each selection opens with a descriptive introduction to provide context, and concludes with critical thinking and multiple-choice questions to reinforce key points. CourseReader is loaded with convenient tools such as highlighting, printing, note-taking, and downloadable MP3 audio files for each reading.

CourseReader is the perfect complement to any political science course. It can be bundled with your current textbook, sold alone, or integrated into your learning management system. CourseReader 0–30 allows access to up to 30 selections in the reader.

Please contact your Cengage sales representative for details, or please visit us at **www.cengage .com/login.** Click on "New Faculty User" and fill out the registration page. Once you are in your new SSO account, search for "CourseReader" from your dashboard and select "CourseReader: American Government." Then click "CourseReader 0–30: American Government Instant Access Code" and click "Add to my bookshelf." To access the live CourseReader, click on "CourseReader 0–30: American Government" under "Additional resources" on the right side of your dashboard.

APLIA FOR DAUTRICH & YALOF'S *THE ENDURING DEMOCRACY,* 3E

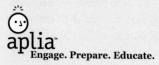

ISBN: 9781133952947 PAC (Printed Access Card)
ISBN: 9781133952978 IAC (Instant Access Code)

Easy to use, affordable, and effective, Aplia helps students learn and saves you time. It's like a virtual teaching assistant! Aplia helps you have more productive classes by providing assignments that get students thinking critically, reading assigned material, and reinforcing basic concepts—all before coming to class. The interactive questions also help students better understand the relevance of what they're learning and how to apply those concepts to the world around them.

Visually engaging videos, graphs, and political cartoons help capture students' attention and imagination, and an automatically included eBook provides convenient access. Aplia is instantly accessible via CengageBrain or through the bookstore via printed access card.

Please contact your local Cengage sales representative for more information, and go to www.aplia.com/politicalscience to view a demo.

ELECTION 2012: AN AMERICAN GOVERNMENT SUPPLEMENT

ISBN: 9781285090931 PAC (Printed Access Card)
ISBN: 9781285420080 IAC (Instant Access Code)

Written by John Clark and Brian Schaffner, this booklet addresses the 2012 congressional and presidential races, with real-time analysis and references. Access your course via www.cengage.com/login.

CUSTOM ENRICHMENT MODULE: LATINO-AMERICAN POLITICS SUPPLEMENT

ISBN: 9781285184296

This revised and updated 32-page supplement uses real examples to detail politics related to Latino Americans and can be added to your text via our custom publishing solutions.

FOR STUDENTS, WHEN REQUESTED BY YOUR INSTRUCTORS

POLITICAL SCIENCE COURSEMATE FOR DAUTRICH & YALOF'S *THE ENDURING DEMOCRACY*, 3E

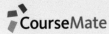

Cengage Learning's Political Science CourseMate brings course concepts to life with interactive learning, study tools, and exam-preparation tools that support the printed textbook. The more you study, the better the results. Make the most of your study time by accessing everything you need to succeed in one place. Read your textbook, take notes, watch videos, read case studies, take practice quizzes, and more—online with CourseMate. CourseMate also gives you access to the American Government **NewsWatch website**, a real-time news and information resource updated daily, and **KnowNow!**, the go-to blog about current events in American government. Additionally, CourseMate for *The Enduring Democracy* includes "**The Connections App**," an interactive web app that helps you better understand the relationship between historical and current events and their connection with basic concepts.

Purchase instant access via CengageBrain or via a printed access card in your bookstore. Visit www.cengagebrain.com for more information. CourseMate should be purchased only when assigned by your instructor as part of your course.

APLIA FOR DAUTRICH & YALOF'S *THE ENDURING DEMOCRACY*, 3E

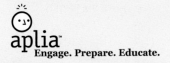

Easy to use, affordable, and convenient, Aplia helps you learn more and improve your grade in the course. Through interactive assignments, including videos, graphs, and political cartoons, you can better understand the essential concepts of American government and how they apply to real life.

Aplia helps prepare you to be more involved in class by strengthening your critical thinking skills, reinforcing what you need to know, and helping you understand why it all matters. For your studying convenience, Aplia includes an eBook, accessible right next to your assignments. Get instant access via CengageBrain or via a printed access card in your bookstore. Visit www.cengagebrain.com for more information. Aplia should be purchased only when assigned by your instructor as part of your course.

ABOUT THE AUTHORS

KENNETH J. DAUTRICH (Ph.D., Rutgers, 1995) is an associate professor of public policy at the University of Connecticut in Storrs. He is also the founder and former director of the Center for Survey Research & Analysis at the University of Connecticut. Previously, Dr. Dautrich was a Research Fellow at the Media Studies Center in New York and has served as a senior faculty fellow at the Heldrich Center at Rutgers. His first book, *How the News Media Fail American Voters* (Columbia University Press, 1997), received scholarly praise in numerous political science circles. He also co-authored *The First Amendment and the Media in the Court of Public Opinion* (Cambridge University Press, 2002) and *The Future of the First Amendment* (Rowman & Littlefield, 2008). Dr. Dautrich's research and teaching focus on public opinion and American elections. For the past four years he has directed a set of national surveys on civic literacy in the American public and the role of higher education in advancing knowledge about American government. He is currently writing a book on findings from this project.

DAVID A. YALOF (Ph.D., Johns Hopkins University, 1997; J.D., University of Virginia, 1991) is a professor of political science and director of undergraduate studies at the University of Connecticut. His first book, *Pursuit of Justices: Presidential Politics and the Selection of Supreme Court Nominees* (University of Chicago Press, 1999), was awarded the American Political Science Association's Richard E. Neustadt Award as the best book published on presidential studies in 1999. His most recent book is *Prosecution Among Friends: Presidents, Attorneys General and Executive Branch Wrongdoing* (Texas A & M University Press, 2012). He is also the co-author of *The First Amendment and the Media in the Court of Public Opinion* (Cambridge University Press, 2002), *The Future of the First Amendment* (Rowman & Littlefield, 2008), and another textbook, *Constitutional Law: Civil Liberty and Individual Rights* (Foundation Press, 2007). Dr. Yalof has written extensively on issues in constitutional law and Supreme Court appointment politics—his work has been published in *Political Research Quarterly, Judicature, Constitutional Commentary*, and various other journals.

ACKNOWLEDGMENTS

The third edition of *The Enduring Democracy* (formerly under the title, *American Government: Historical, Popular, and Global Perspectives*) is a product of the hard work of many, many people. First and foremost among them is our executive editor, Carolyn Merrill. At Cengage she has been the prime mover of this project, just as she was for our earlier editions. It is impossible to imagine pulling off a project like this without the management skills, temperament, and good humor that Carolyn provides. As the textbook industry has undergone especially significant changes over the past few years, she has been on top of every last development. Much of the credit for this book's continued success belongs to her.

Tops among all of the great decisions Carolyn made was the hiring of Kate Scheinman as our development editor. Kate has been a no-nonsense editor, and her suggestions have been invaluable. Norine Strang has been an effective senior project manager, guiding this book through the production process. We are also indebted to Alexa Orr for her photo research, and Allison Eigel Zade for keeping the production machinery running smoothly. Senior managers at Cengage also played a hands-on role in the development of this second edition, including Sean Wakely, P. J. Boardman, our publisher Suzanne Jeans, and Dan Silverburg. Their guidance and commitment to our book is, as always, greatly appreciated. We also extend our gratitude to the many other members of the Cengage staff we have come to depend upon in writing and producing this book and its supplemental materials: our awesome "brand manager" Lydia LeStar, as well as, Laura Hildebrand, Josh Allen, Scott Greenan, and Suzanne St. Clair.

The many sales representatives at Cengage not only do a great job in getting the word out on our book, but they also have collected feedback from instructors and relayed it back to us. In many instances, our reps have provided their own guidance and feedback as well. Thankfully, all their efforts have helped improve the content of the book, and make it more responsive to the perspective of instructors who use it. Our hats are off to this terrific sales force. We are grateful for your many efforts.

Appreciation also goes to our colleagues at the University of Connecticut, especially those in the Department of Political Science and the Department of Public Policy, of which there are too many to list by name. Their patience, support, and advice in our writing of this third edition have not gone unnoticed; nor has the input we have received from our graduate students and undergraduate users of the text. Special thanks to Rebecca Barry for compiling data for the many new graphs and tables in the book.

The many professionals, colleagues, and students who provide support and advice are not the only ones who influence the writing of a textbook. Our families must live with us through the writing and production cycles. Not only do they tolerate the fact that we often bring our work home, but they also give us strong motivation to get the job done. We cannot thank our better halves, Andrea and Mary Beth, enough. Our children, to whom this book is dedicated, are not shy about offering their ideas either. The book benefits from their youthful perspectives and advice.

Finally, there are many members of our profession and many practitioners in American politics who put in countless hours and intellectual energy aiding in the writing of this manuscript. Some participated in focus groups; others in informal conversations with us; and still others who spent much time marking up chapters. We are indebted to all those who have generously given time to this effort. A list of these contributors is found below. Please note, however, that any errors that remain are entirely our own.

Reviewers of the Third Edition

Kara Lindaman *Winona State University*

Christi Dayley *Weatherford College*

Joseph Engle *Blinn College, Bryan Campus*

Augustine Ayuk *Clayton State University*

Nicholas D'Arecca *Temple University*

Donna Hooper *North Central Texas College*

Joseph Jozwiak *Texas A&M Corpus Christi*

Bernard Fitzpatrick *Naugatuck Valley Community College*

Tracy Cook *Central Texas College*

Michael Lenaghan *Miami Dade College*

J. Wesley Leckrone *Widener University*

Chief Justice Richard Barajas (Ret.) *Cathedral High School / El Paso Community College*

Richard Kiefer *Waubonsee Community College*

Chris Newman *Elgin Community College*

Steven Collins *Oklahoma State University-Oklahoma City*

Reviewers of the Second Edition

Mary Balchunis *LaSalle University*

Murray Bessette *Morehead State University*

Holly Brasher *University of Alabama at Birmingham*

Robert Bromber *University of Maryland—University College*

Steven Collins *Oklahoma State University—Oklahoma City*

Thom Costa *Florida State College at Jacksonville*

Lance Denning *Metropolitan State College of Denver*

Sheng Ding *Bloomsburg University*

Donald Gawronski *Maricopa Campus Community College—Mesa*

Lauren Hall *Rochester Institute of Technology*

M. Ahad *Hayaud-Din Brookhaven College*

David Head *John Tyler Community College*

Timothy Hoye *Texas Woman's University*

Melody Huckaby *Cameron University*

Terri Jett *Butler University*

Gina Keel *SUNY Oneonta*

Patricia Knol *Triton College*

Christopher Latimer *SUNY Cortland*

Randolph Lightfoot *Saint Petersburg College—Tarpon Springs*

Gary Malecha *University of Portland*

Roger Marietta *Darton College*

Scott Meinke *Bucknell College*

Jason Mycoff *University of Delaware*

Chris Newman *Elgin Community College*

Richard Pacelle *Georgia Southern University*

Greg Rabb *Jamestown Community College*

Cherry Rain *Redlands Community College*

Mitzi Ramos *University of Illinois at Champaign*

Susan Roomberg *University of Texas at San Antonio*

David Ross *Stark State College of Technology*

Sandy Self *Hardin-Simmons University*

Patrick Shade *Edison Community College*

Dari Sylvester *University of the Pacific*

Roy Tate *Redlands Community College*

1

THE MORE THINGS CHANGE ... THE MORE THEY STAY THE SAME

LEARNING OBJECTIVES

HISTORY REPEATS ITSELF

- Analyze current problems and issues in American government by applying historical perspective

FORMS AND FUNCTIONS OF GOVERNMENT

- Explain the philosophical underpinnings of the American political system through the exploration of important theories such as the "social contract" theory and the concept of the "natural law"
- Compare and contrast democracy with other forms of government

AMERICAN GOVERNMENT AND POLITICS

- Assess the importance of the value of popular sovereignty, and how that value is realized through "representative democracy" in the United States

AMERICAN POLITICAL CULTURE

- Define *political culture* and describe the unique combination of political beliefs and values that forms the American political culture, including majority rule, liberty, limited government, diversity, individualism, and equality of economic opportunity

IS AMERICAN DEMOCRACY IN DECLINE?

- Assess the health of American democracy and evaluate whether the American system is in decline by applying an historical perspective on contemporary politics
- Evaluate contemporary problems by placing them in historical context

Perhaps the most salient lesson to be learned from the 2012 presidential election concerns the power of incumbency. President Barack Obama's first term was plagued by soaring unemployment, stagnated wages, and a skyrocketing national debt. Still, the incumbent managed to secure a decisive electoral college victory. Many were skeptical that Obama would win again during such fiscally distressed times. What could possibly allow Obama to win reelection under such conditions?

A broader view of American history, however, places this incumbent president's victory into context. Just eight years earlier in 2004, President George W. Bush ran for reelection on a record that featured the decision to launch a controversial war in Iraq, one that was producing mounting numbers of casualties. And yet Bush was reelected. Similarly, Harry S Truman, thrust into the White House three years earlier upon the death of FDR, surprised pundits by winning the 1948 election. Earlier in the 20th century, Woodrow Wilson defied expectations by winning reelection in 1916 amid a difficult fiscal environment and the looming threat of war from Europe.

The lesson of the 2012 election is one that has played out many times before in American history. Voters may express frustration with incumbents, but when the sitting president seeks reelection, he may well receive the benefit of the doubt. Thus President Obama's success in 2012 should have surprised no one. Once elected, Americans tend to stand behind their leader—through good times and bad times as well. To be sure, some incumbents have fallen permanently out of the public's favor. Yet that happened a mere three times in the past century compared to the 11 successful incumbent reelections. Historical context helps us understand not only presidential elections, but many other aspects of American politics. This book explores the current American political system, and uses history as a guide to the future.

Jewel Samad/AFP/Getty Images

✓ CHECK THE LIST

Incumbent Presidents Who Enjoy Reelection Success

Those who make it to the presidency have been quite successful in getting reelected. During the past 100 years, 17 different men have served as president. Two died in their first terms (Harding and Kennedy). Three assumed office and ran for reelection (Coolidge, Truman and Ford). Among the incumbents (either elected or appointed), 11 have won reelection, and only 3 have lost. Below are the incumbents since 1916 who have successfully sought reelection:

1916	Woodrow Wilson	1972	Richard Nixon
1924	Calvin Coolidge	1984	Ronald Reagan
1936, 1940 and 1944	Franklin Roosevelt	1996	Bill Clinton
1948	Harry Truman	2004	George W. Bush
1956	Dwight Eisenhower	2012	Barack Obama
1964	Lyndon Johnson		

- To craft his "Declaration of Independence" from Great Britain, Thomas Jefferson was inspired primarily by British philosophers.

- The U.S. government continued with its open immigration policy until World War II, when the free flow of immigrants became overwhelming.

- America's political culture rejects the "Horatio Alger" myth in favor of a more "caring society" in which government offers individuals the means to get started on the road to eventual success.

HISTORY REPEATS ITSELF

The patterns of history provide a powerful tool for understanding American government today. Let's consider a few important dynamics of the political system today and the historical patterns that shed light on those dynamics.

A New Communications Medium Paves the Way to Electoral Victory

The Internet and social media have revolutionized American politics. In 2008, presidential candidate Barack Obama used Facebook to build extensive volunteer networks and campaign donations to the tune of a half-billion dollars. Obama captured the attention of young people and those affected by the Great Recession of 2008, offering a message of hope and change. His campaign actively encouraged social networking to mobilize voters to his cause. The result: voter turnout and interest spiked, and helped to pave the way to victory. Other politicians have tried to duplicate Obama's model; by 2012, social media began to dominate the campaign process. Voters of all political persuasions use social media to connect with their favorite campaigns. Consider the possibilities: in 2011 Facebook subscribed 150 million voting-age users, each with an average of 130 friends. Not only is this a massive audience, but it is an active audience, as social networks allow users to trade and share information and opinions with their friends and families. In the past, political strategists were forced to rely on the paid TV spot as the primary way to communicate with voters. Today, however, there is a noticeable shift toward using social media to send messages, raise money, and mobilize voters. Why? A message from a friend is considered much more personal, powerful, and effective than an impersonal TV spot.

Of course social network sites like Facebook are not the only type of breakthrough technology to revolutionize political campaigns. Although Barack Obama was the first candidate to win the presidency by making extensive use of social media, John F. Kennedy pioneered the use of television to win the White House over a half-century ago. When he ran for the presidency in 1960, TV was dramatically changing American society, just as social media are changing it today. As a relatively new medium with a mass audience in Kennedy's time, TV provided prospective voters with what no communications platform had offered ever before—the chance to see the candidates campaign on a daily basis. Television audiences could tune in to watch TV spots, and they could see the candidates actually debate each other live in their own living rooms; voters saw the candidates in action. Kennedy's youth and enthusiasm made effective use of television commercials touting his candidacy. His ability to "out-charisma" Richard Nixon in the 1960 debates led to a surge in turnout, and helped to pave the way for a Kennedy victory. Kennedy's use of this new medium provided a model for how presidents would interact with voters over the next four decades. By 1964, candidates had mastered the art of the 30-second spot, as evidenced by Lyndon Johnson and his now-famous "Daisy Girl" commercial.

"Daisy Girl," featured in the 1964 political commercial of the Lyndon Johnson campaign, is shown above. The ad cut to a mushroom cloud explosion of an atomic bomb as the girl pulled off the last petal of the daisy.

Although revolutionary, TV was not the first communications medium to transform political campaigns. Radio, which by 1932 had reached most U.S. households, enabled voters to listen to the candidates' voices, instead of just reading their speeches or statements. Franklin Delano Roosevelt (FDR) and President Herbert Hoover both used radio addresses and advertising extensively during the 1932 campaign. However, whereas Roosevelt's voice on the radio inspired confidence and enthusiasm for tackling the ills of the Great Depression, Hoover's logical and monotone monologue was far less effective. From that point forward candidates could not just focus on the words that they used; they also had to excel in articulating those words with passion. FDR's use of radio eventually mobilized voters, particularly those who were most negatively affected by the economic doldrums of the Great Depression. After winning the 1932 election, FDR continued to use radio to personally connect with voters and inspire them through his "fireside chats," which he broadcast for the next 12 years.

One hundred years earlier, yet another communications revolution occurred that had a lasting impact on political campaigns. By the 1830s, newspapers were changing in a number of ways. The invention of the "rotary press" in 1815 facilitated the mass production of affordable newspapers, and eventually gave way to the so-called "penny press." A decade later, the invention of the telegraph enabled penny-press papers to quickly produce stories on breaking news events. Further, the laying of railroads to all parts of the country to accommodate rapid westward expansion paved the way for mass distribution of newspapers. Americans gobbled up this new source of information, and Andrew Jackson used this medium to engage voters, bypass the political elite, and communicate his message of rugged individualism and "the rise of the common man" to help him capture the White House in 1832. The newspaper, which became a common person's medium, enabled Jackson to distribute his message widely to an audience that was willing and eager to read what he had to say. Jackson's use of the newspaper was critical to his success, just as Obama's use of social media was critical to his own success. Never again would presidential political campaigns be targeted exclusively at political elites, thanks to Jackson's use of the penny press to effectively appeal to the masses.

A Bruising, Negative Primary Fight Sets the Stage for a Difficult General Election Against an Incumbent

President Barack Obama began 2012 as an extremely vulnerable incumbent, and Republicans smelled blood in the water. For six months the three leading Republican hopefuls waged a bitter war against each other for the Republican nomination. The frontrunner in the group, former Massachusetts Governor Mitt Romney, began the year with a campaign war chest that exceeded that of all the other candidates combined, and he used it to run mostly negative attack ads against his competitors (according to one study, two-thirds of Romney's ads were primarily negative). The one-time Pennsylvania Senator Rick Santorum aggressively mocked Romney's conservative credentials and accused the frontrunner of rank dishonesty for distancing himself from his moderate credentials. Former Speaker of the House Newt Gingrich doubted whether either of those two men could stand up to Obama in a debate, but he struggled to win outside of his home region in the South. Libertarian Congressman Ron Paul also stuck around for much of the spring, providing many barbs of his own. While other candidates such as Rep. Michelle Bachmann, pizza industry magnate Herman Cain, and Texas Governor Rick Perry saw their campaigns initially soar before fizzling out, Romney, Santorum, and Gingrich stuck around for the longer haul.

As these final contenders pummeled each other throughout the spring of 2012, party regulars began to fear that they were destroying the Republicans' chances of beating Obama in November. The new rules governing campaign donations only exacerbated the nastiness: A political action campaign (PAC), dubbed a super-PAC, supporting Gingrich accused Romney of being a "corporate raider" and of taking "blood money" from a corporation. One Romney ad accused Gingrich of supporting China's "one-child policy," leading Gingrich to consider a slander lawsuit. According to polls in early March 2012, Romney's onslaught of negative advertising all but destroyed the favorable impression he once enjoyed among independents. And despite Santorum's initial promise to stay positive, his campaign aired ads accusing Romney of hiding from his "big-government Romneycare" and of supporting "job-killing cap-and-trade" policies. The combination of unrestricted super-PACs, a 24-hour news cycle, and three determined candidates meant that Ronald Reagan's Eleventh Commandment, "thou shalt not speak poorly of a fellow Republican," would be ignored. Of course nobody could have been happier about this development than President Obama himself; without any primary challenges of his own, the incumbent could lay in wait for what he hoped would be a bloodied opponent in the fall.

Shown below are Barry Goldwater (top picture, at right) and Rick Santorum (bottom), the GOP candidates in 1964 and 2012 who ran aggressive conservative campaigns in their quest for the nomination.

The 2012 Republican primaries were highly negative in tone, but such incivility is nothing new in the rough-and-tumble world of American politics. One of the most negative campaigns ever fought was between two revered founders of the nation, then-Vice President Thomas Jefferson and the sitting President John Adams, as they battled for the White House in 1800. During that nasty campaign, Jefferson used partisan newspapers to launch negative attacks on Adams, though Jefferson himself stayed behind the scenes. Some of the nastiest fights have occurred within a party's race for the presidential nomination. Consider the Republicans' drawn-out battle during the spring of 1964 to take on incumbent President Lyndon Johnson later that fall. The Grand Old Party (GOP) was badly divided between its more conservative faction led by Senator Barry Goldwater and its moderate-liberal factions. After Goldwater voted against the Civil Rights Act, Pennsylvania Governor William Scranton immediately jumped into the race because he was so offended by Goldwater's action. New York Governor Nelson Rockefeller, the self-identified leader of the liberal faction of the GOP, launched an anti-Goldwater campaign all the way to the convention in San Francisco, where he was booed off the platform for declaring that the Republican Party was killing itself. Meanwhile, moderate Michigan Governor George Romney (Mitt Romney's father) took another route by storming out of

Bettmann/CORBIS

© Planetpix / Alamy

the convention in protest of its "political extremism." President Johnson—facing no significant challenge in his own party—took much delight in the GOP candidates bloodying each other. Thus while the 2012 Republican race will not be remembered as a "lovefest" among like-minded individuals, it hardly marks a new and unprecedented negative phase of presidential election politics.

In this book we examine the major topics and concepts in American government and politics. We attempt to answer sweeping questions about how American government works: How does public policy get made? Who are the major players and institutions that make laws? How do these major players achieve their position? How do disputes get settled? What is the role of the American people in governing? In this discussion, we draw on lessons learned from nearly 250 years of nationhood, and apply those lessons to better understand contemporary issues and controversies in politics. Contemporary American government is a product of American history.

FORMS AND FUNCTIONS OF GOVERNMENT

Government is the collection of public institutions in a nation that establish and enforce the rules by which the members of that nation must live. Even the most primitive of societies have found government to be necessary. Without government, society would be in a state of **anarchy**, a situation characterized by lawlessness and discord in the political system. Thomas Hobbes, a seventeenth-century British political philosopher, wrote that without government, life would be "solitary, poor, nasty, brutish and short."[1] Government is necessary to make the rules by which citizens must abide, promoting order, stability, and protection for the society. It exists in part to resolve conflicts that naturally arise when people live in communities. Elaborating on the role of government, Jean-Jacques Rousseau, an eighteenth-century French philosopher, posited that in fact a "social contract" exists.[2] A **social contract** is an agreement people make with one another to form a government and abide by its rules and laws. In return, the government promises to protect the people's rights and welfare and to promote their best interests.

A government's **authority** over its citizens refers to the ability of public institutions and the officials within them to make laws, independent of the power to execute them. People obey authority out of respect, whereas they obey power out of fear. Numerous different forms of government with governing authority can be found around the nations of the world. One such form—the form that will receive extended attention throughout this book—is **democracy**, defined as a government in which the people, either directly or through elected representatives, hold power and authority. The word *democracy* is derived from the Greek *demos kratos*, meaning "rule by the people."

By contrast, an **oligarchy** is a form of government in which a small exclusive class, which may or may not attempt to rule on behalf of the people as a whole, holds supreme power. In a **theocracy**, a particular religion or faith plays a dominant role in the government; Iran is just one example of a theocratic nation in the world today. A **monarchy** is a form of government in which one person, usually a member of a royal family or a royal designate, exercises supreme authority. The monarch may be a king or queen, such as Queen Elizabeth II of Great Britain. In the past monarchies were quite common; today they are rarely practiced in the absolute sense. Although the United Kingdom continues to pay homage to its royalty, true political power rests in the Parliament, the members of which are elected by the people.

Many of the nations in the world today have an **authoritarian** form of government in which one political party, group, or person maintains such complete control over the nation that it may refuse to recognize, and may even choose to suppress, all other political parties and interests. The nation of Iraq, before the American military intervention in 2003, was considered by most to be an authoritarian government under the dictatorial rule of Saddam Hussein. North Korea under Kim Jong-Il is an authoritarian government in existence today.

An important characteristic of any government, whether democratic or not, is its power to exercise authority over people. **Power** is the capacity to get individuals to do something that

government: The collection of public institutions in a nation that establish and enforce the rules by which the members of that nation must live.

anarchy: A state of lawlessness and discord in the political system caused by lack of government.

social contract: From the philosophy of Jean-Jacques Rousseau, an agreement people make with one another to form a government and abide by its rules and laws, and in return, the government promises to protect the people's rights and welfare and promote their best interests.

authority: The ability of public institutions and the officials within them to make laws, independent of the power to execute them.

democracy: Form of government in which the people, either directly or through elected representatives, hold power and authority. The word *democracy* is derived from the Greek *demos kratos*, meaning "rule by the people."

oligarchy: A form of government in which a small exclusive class, which may or may not attempt to rule on behalf of the people as a whole, holds supreme power.

theocracy: A form of government in which a particular religion or faith plays a dominant role in the government.

monarchy: A form of government in which one person, usually a member of a royal family or a royal designate, exercises supreme authority.

authoritarianism: A form of government in which one political party, group, or person maintains such complete control over the nation that it may refuse to recognize and may even suppress all other political parties and interests.

power: The ability to get individuals to do something that they may not otherwise do, such as pay taxes, stop for red lights, or submit to a search before boarding an airplane.

legitimacy: The extent to which the people afford the government the authority and right to exercise power.

politics: The way in which the institutions of government are organized to make laws, rules, and policies, and how those institutions are influenced.

they may not otherwise do, such as pay taxes, stop for red lights, or submit to a search before boarding an airplane. Without power, it would be very difficult for a government to enforce rules. The sustained power of any government largely rests on its legitimacy. **Legitimacy** is the extent to which the people (or the "governed") afford the government the authority and right to exercise power. The more that people subscribe to the goals of a government, and the greater the degree to which that government guarantees the people's welfare (for example, by supporting a strong economy or providing protection from foreign enemies), the higher will be the government's level of legitimacy. When the governed grant a high level of legitimacy to their government, the government wields its power to make and enforce rules more successfully.

AMERICAN GOVERNMENT AND POLITICS

Politics is defined as the way in which the institutions of government are organized to make laws, rules, and policies, and how those institutions are influenced. More than 70 years ago, political scientist Harold Lasswell proposed a brief but very useful definition of politics as "who gets what, when and how." In American politics, the "who" includes actors within and outside the formal government, such as citizens, elected officials, interest groups, and state and local governments. The "what" are the decisions the government makes and take the form of what government funds, the way it raises revenue, and the policies it produces and enforces. The "when" relates to setting priorities about what government does. The concerns and issues that government addresses differ in importance, and issues of greater importance tend to be addressed more quickly. Finally, the "how" refers to the way in which the government goes about its work, based on the political institutions that exist and the formal and informal procedures and rules that define the governing process. In describing American politics, this book provides answers to Lasswell's "who gets what, when and how?"[3]

Government in the United States is especially complex. It is organized into multiple layers (national, state, and local) and contains many governing units, as shown in Table 1.1. It encompasses a number of political institutions that share power—the executive (the president), the legislature (Congress), and the judiciary (the courts); and it provides countless methods for individuals and groups to influence the decisions made by those institutions. In this book, we will examine this complex organization of American government, describe the political institutions that exercise power, and explore the varied ways that people and groups exert influence. As we sort through this complexity of American government, we will seek to explain how and why the American political system has been able to endure the conflicts, both internal and external, that it has faced and currently faces. We will attempt to show how the American government is uniquely designed to stand up to its many challenges.

The strength and stability of the U.S. government are grounded in the high level of legitimacy it maintains with the American public. Americans may disagree vehemently with public officials, but rarely do they question their claim to authority. The Framers of the U.S. Constitution were keenly aware of the importance of the legitimacy of the system. They knew that if the

Portrait of George Washington and the Constitution's drafters at the Constitutional Convention in 1787.

Bettmann/CORBIS

TABLE 1.1 Governments in the United States

The government of the United States might be more correctly described as a system of governments. In addition to the federal government, there are 50 state governments and thousands of local governments. The 2007 edition of the *Statistical Abstract of the United States* listed these totals for the number of governments operating throughout the nation.

Government	Number
Federal	1
State	50
County	3,033
Municipal	19,492
School district	13,051
Township/town	16,519
Special district	37,381
Total	89,476

government was to withstand the test of time, it must serve the people well. These ideas about legitimacy drew largely on the theories of seventeenth-century British political philosopher John Locke (1632–1704).[4] Locke proposed that people are born with certain *natural rights*, which derive from **natural law**, the rules of conduct inherent in the relationship among human beings and thus more fundamental than any law that a governing authority might make. Government cannot violate these natural rights, which include life, liberty, and property. Therefore, government, or human law, must be based on the "consent of the governed." That is, citizens are responsible for choosing their government and its leaders. This theory loomed large in the mind of Thomas Jefferson as he drafted the Declaration of Independence to justify the American colonies' split with the British government: "All men . . . are endowed by their creator with certain unalienable rights . . . [and] whenever any form of government becomes destructive of these ends, it is the right of the people to alter or abolish it." A government maintains legitimacy as long as the governed are served well and as long as government respects the natural rights of individuals.

Drawing on this philosophy, the Framers drafted a Constitution that created a political system able to manage the inevitable conflicts that occur in any society. Mindful of Thomas Hobbes's notion that the essence of government is to manage naturally occurring conflicts, the Framers designed a government that encourages conflict and competition rather than attempting to repress it. As we shall see in the chapters that follow, the U.S. Constitution includes a number of mechanisms that allow naturally occurring conflict to play out in as productive a manner as possible. Mechanisms are also in place to resolve conflicts and arrive at consensus on issues. Those who disagree and come up on the short side of political battles are guaranteed rights and liberties nonetheless. Further, the rules by which conflicts are settled are predicated on fairness and proper procedures.

The significance of what the Framers of the Constitution accomplished cannot be overstated. They not only addressed the short-term problems challenging the new nation, they also drafted a blueprint for how government should go about dealing with problems and conflicts into the future. The U.S. Constitution has served as the cornerstone of an American political system that routinely attempts to tackle some of the thorniest problems imaginable. In Chapter 2 of this book, we examine the enduring principles and processes outlined in the Constitution.

The Constitution provides a way for the American government to navigate through the many problems and conflicts that have faced the nation, including severe economic depressions, two world wars, nuclear confrontations with the former Soviet Union, and persisting questions of equality. Through all these difficulties, the American government has endured. The foresight of the Framers to create a Constitution that possesses the flexibility to adapt to

natural law: According to John Locke, the most fundamental type of law, which supersedes any law that is made by government. Citizens are born with certain natural rights (including life, liberty, and property) that derive from this law and that government cannot take away.

To craft his "Declaration of Independence" from Great Britain, Thomas Jefferson was inspired primarily by British philosophers.

Fact.

When Thomas Jefferson drafted the Declaration of Independence in 1776, he drew heavily on the philosophy of British theorist John Locke, who had articulated principles of natural law and the "consent of the governed," as well as British philosopher Thomas Hobbes, who argued that the essence of government is to manage naturally occurring conflicts.

ARPL/HIP/The Image Works

"I agree to this Constitution, with all of its faults, if they are such: because I think a general government necessary for us, and there is no form of government but what may be a blessing to the people if well administered. I doubt too whether any convention we can obtain may be able to make a better constitution. For when you assemble a number of men to have the advantage of their joint wisdom, you inevitably assemble with those men all their prejudices, their passions, their errors of opinion, their local interests, and their selfish views. From such an assembly can a perfect production be expected? It therefore astonishes me . . . to find this system approaching so near to perfection."

—Benjamin Franklin (1788)

---

popular sovereignty: The idea that the ultimate source of power in the nation is held by the people.

---

representative democracy: A form of government designed by the U.S. Constitution whereby free, open, and regular elections are held to allow voters to choose those who govern on their behalf; it is also referred to as *indirect democracy* or a *republican* form of government.

changing times has served as a basis for the enduring democracy of the United States.

The preamble to the U.S. Constitution perhaps best summarizes the broad goals of American government:

> We the People of the United States, in Order to form a more perfect Union, establish Justice, insure domestic Tranquility, provide for the common defense, promote the general Welfare, and secure the Blessings of Liberty to ourselves and our Posterity, do ordain and establish this Constitution for the United States of America.

It is no accident that the first three words of the Constitution are "We the People." With this phrase the Framers acknowledged that the ultimate source of power rests with the people, a concept known as **popular sovereignty**. The U.S. Constitution provided for a form of **representative democracy**, under which regular elections are held to allow voters to choose those who govern on their behalf. In this sense, individual citizens do not directly make policies, rules, and other governing decisions (that system of government is known as a **direct democracy**). Rather, representative democracy, also referred to as *indirect democracy* or a *republican* form of government, rests on the notion that consent of the governed is achieved through free, open, and regular elections of those who are given the responsibility of governing. An important source of the legitimacy of the U.S. government is the nation's commitment to representative democracy, which features the notion of majority rule. Majorities (more than 50 percent of the voters) and pluralities (the leading vote getters, whether or not they constitute absolute majorities) choose the winners of election contests, and so officeholders take their positions on the basis of whom most voters prefer. If officeholders fall from public favor, they may be removed in subsequent elections.

Legitimacy is also enhanced by broad public support for the specific purposes of government stated in the preamble to the Constitution: to "insure domestic tranquility" (produce laws that maintain a peaceful and organized approach to living in the nation), to "provide for the common defense" (establish and maintain a military force to protect the nation from outside threats), to "promote the general welfare" (develop domestic policy programs to promote the welfare of the people), and to "secure the blessings of liberty" (guarantee basic freedoms, such as the rights of free expression and the ownership of property, even to those in the minority). Though people may have different opinions on how to achieve these broad goals, few in the United States would disagree with the ideals as stated in the abstract, or with the broad outlines of our republican form of government. Problems arise when public officials stray so far from these goals that their actions are deemed illegitimate by a near, if not absolute, majority. Yet the political system as a whole has been able to maintain its legitimacy, even under such trying circumstances, because it has been flexible enough to eventually rid itself of those ineffective actors, whether through elections, impeachment, or some other means. The relatively high degree of legitimacy that is maintained in the United States has helped the American government persist under the U.S. Constitution through good times and bad since 1789.

AMERICAN POLITICAL CULTURE

Political culture refers to the core values about the role of government and its operations and institutions that are widely held among citizens in a society. Political culture defines the essence of how a society thinks politically. It is transmitted from one generation to the next, and thus has

THE MORE THINGS CHANGE, THE MORE THEY STAY THE SAME

Constitutional Amendments That Have Extended Voting Rights in the United States

In several states, approval of the new U.S. Constitution drafted in 1789 hinged on adding a bill of rights. Supporters of the Constitution agreed, and the first 10 amendments, which compose the formal Bill of Rights, were added to the Constitution in 1791. Since then, the Constitution has been amended 17 times. Six of these 17 amendments extend Americans' voting rights, and no amendment has ever in any way restricted voting rights. Over the years, changes to the original Constitution have led to greater empowerment of the American people in determining the direction that government takes.

In 1870, the Fifteenth Amendment provided that the right to vote may not be denied on the basis of race.

In 1913, the Seventeenth Amendment changed the method of selection of U.S. senators from having state legislatures choose senators to having senators directly elected by the voters of a state.

In 1920, the Nineteenth Amendment provided voting rights to women by not allowing states to deny women the right to vote.

In 1961, the Twenty-third Amendment provided residents of the District of Columbia with electoral votes in presidential elections.

In 1962, the Twenty-fourth Amendment prevented states from levying a tax on people in order for them to vote in federal elections. Some states used a poll tax to discourage poor people and African Americans from voting.

In 1971, the Twenty-sixth Amendment provided voting rights to those who are 18 years of age by not allowing states to deny the franchise to those who have obtained this age.

For Critical Thinking and Discussion

1. What are the values in American political culture that have produced constitutional changes promoting the extension of the franchise?

2. Can you think of any other possible amendments that might further promote voting rights?

---

an enduring influence on the politics of a nation. Every nation has a political culture, and the United States is no exception.

Whereas common ancestry characterizes the core of the political culture of many other nations, the United States has no common ancestry. Most other nations around the world, such as France, Britain, China, and Japan, are bound by a common birth lineage that serves to define the cultural uniqueness of the nation. For example, the Russian people share common political values and beliefs as part of their ancestors' historical experiences with czars, and then later with the communist regime. Britain, despite being a democracy, retains a monarchy as a symbolic gesture toward its historical antecedents. In many nations rich with such common ethnic traditions, these routines often serve to underscore the political culture of the nation.

The United States has no such common ancestry to help define its political culture. Its land was first occupied by many different Native American tribes, and then settled by people from many different parts of the world. Most of the immigrants who settled the colonies were seeking a better life from the political or religious persecution they experienced in their native countries, or they were seeking improved economic opportunities for themselves and their families. As America continued to grow through the centuries, it attracted immigrants from around the world, anxious to find a better life. These circumstances had a profound influence on the core values that have become engrained in the American political culture. The ideas generated by democratic political philosophers such as Thomas Hobbes and John Locke also significantly contributed

direct democracy: A system of government in which all citizens participate in making policy, rules, and governing decisions.

political culture: The values and beliefs about government, its purpose, and its operations and institutions that are widely held among citizens in a society; it defines the essence of how a society thinks politically and is transmitted from one generation to the next.

President Barack Obama speaks to a gathering of the National Association for the Advancement of Colored Peoples (NAACP) at the group's 100th anniversary celebration in July 2009.

to American political culture. These ideas were used by the Founders to justify the Declaration of Independence and the U.S. Constitution, and they continue to underlie American political culture today.

The circumstances surrounding America's first and current immigrants, as well as the great ideas generated by Enlightenment philosophers, form the core set of values that define the American political culture. One of these core values is **majority rule**. From its earliest times, the American nation has been committed to the notion that the "will of the people" ought to guide public policy, thus underscoring the importance of popular sovereignty in the thinking of the Founders. Majority rule is the way in which popular sovereignty is actually exercised. Rarely will all of the people agree all of the time; and so it is what the majority of people prefer that generally guides decision making. Early local governments, such as town governments in some of the New England colonies, relied on town meetings, where all citizens were invited to attend, discuss, and vote, to make governmental decisions. Elections for most local and state offices, and elections for the U.S. Congress, are all based on the idea that those who make and enforce laws are duly elected by majorities. A more recent aspect of U.S. commitment to majority rule is its heavy reliance on public opinion polling as a gauge for assessing the performance of elected leaders, and to ensure that leaders respect public preferences for certain policy positions.

majority rule: The notion that the will of the majority should guide decisions made by American government.

Although the preferences of the majority rule the day, another core value in the American political culture is minority rights. Those in the minority enjoy certain rights and liberties that cannot be taken away by government. The idea of the natural law (e.g., that people are "endowed by their creator with certain unalienable rights" that government cannot deny) is an important corollary to majority rule. The rights to speak freely, to choose a religion, or to decide not to practice religion at all are among the many liberties that are protected by the U.S. Bill of Rights, and are widely endorsed by the American public.

These rights are intended to inspire debate on issues, to guarantee religious freedoms, and to afford due-process rights to those accused of crimes. The American political culture places a high value on individual liberty. The fact that many immigrants came to this country for the promise of greater freedom adds further credence to this proposition. Certainly there are some terrible black marks in American history that belie this claim. Among them are the perpetuation of slavery in the country up until the Civil War, the internment of Japanese Americans during World War II, and the treatment of early 1960s civil rights protesters in the South. Still, many Americans today view their nation as the world's "garden" of freedom and liberty, even if it has come to this status only slowly and sometimes with reluctance during its more than two centuries of existence.

limited government: The value that promotes the idea that government power should be as restricted as possible.

Another core value in American political culture is the idea of **limited government**. Americans have generally supported the idea expressed by Thomas Jefferson that "the government that governs least governs best." From the days of the American Revolution, the colonists believed that the corruptive power of King George III and the British Parliament led to unfair treatment of the colonies. Suspicion of the government and those with power is firmly rooted in the psyche of American political culture. The "watchdog" function of the press, the separation of powers and the system of checks and balances among political institutions, and the rather negative connotation of the word "politics" all reflect an appreciation for limits and checks on those with authority. Corresponding to the value of limited government is the notion that communities and the private sector should take a role in helping fellow citizens. Problems that may be solved without government should be solved that way. The French journalist Alexis de Tocqueville observed this tradition when he visited the United States in the early 1800s and credited the success of the American political system in part to citizens' strong interest in community and helping one another apart from government.[5]

TABLE 1.2 Daniel Elazar's Typology of American Political Culture

Many observers of American politics have used different approaches and typologies to describe American political culture. The late political scientist Daniel Elazar described three competing political subcultures, which he believed differentiated American political culture from that found in any other country in the world:*

Subculture	Description
Individualistic subculture	Is skeptical of authority, keeps government's role limited, and celebrates the United States' general reliance on the marketplace
Moralistic subculture	Has faith in the American government's capacity to advance the public interest and encourages citizens to participate in the noble cause of politics
Traditionalistic subculture	Maintains a more ambivalent attitude toward both government and the marketplace, believing that politicians must come from society's elite, whereas ordinary citizens are free to stand on the sidelines

According to Elazar, different subcultures can be found in different geographic areas, and sometimes within a single area itself. For example, he described the political subculture in Texas as part traditionalistic (as manifested in the long history of one-party dominance in state politics) and part individualistic (as seen in the state government's commitment to support for private business and its opposition to big government).

*See Daniel J. Elazar, *American Federalism: A View from the States* (New York: Thomas Y. Crowell, 1966).

Because the United States has no common ancestral or cultural bloodline, American political culture recognizes the value and strength derived from the diversity of its population—another important core value. At the base of the Statue of Liberty in New York Harbor is inscribed a poem by Emma Lazarus beginning with the phrase "Bring me your huddled masses, yearning to be free." Until the U.S. government adopted a restrictive immigration policy in the early 1920s, those huddled masses arrived in waves from different parts of the world, as the United States became the chosen destination for those seeking a better life. Joining freed African American slaves who were originally brought here against their will were legions of Italians, Irish, Germans, and other immigrants from Europe and elsewhere. The United States today is one of the most racially and ethnically diverse nations in the world. Integrating these many people into a united nation has not come easy; in fact, resistance to the notion of a "melting pot" has been common. The nation has been wracked at times with racial and ethnic strife to a degree that more homogeneous countries can more easily avoid. Government officials occasionally exacerbate these tensions by promoting policies that discriminate against various groups, including Native Americans, African Americans, Asian Americans, and Hispanic Americans. No stranger to ethnic and racial tensions himself, German dictator Adolph Hitler calculated that the diversity of the United States would eventually hamper its resistance against Germany's totalitarian aggression; in fact, American soldiers of different backgrounds, ethnicities, and religions fought in World War II. Much to Hitler's chagrin, U.S. diversity proved to be a source of strength, rather than weakness. Indeed, many Americans today believe that the heterogeneity of our society enhances the quality of our culture and helps guarantee the fairness of the government.

Americans also generally subscribe to the notion that individuals are primarily responsible for their lot in life—a value referred to as **individualism**. The seeds of this value were sown hundreds of years ago with the Puritans and their commitment to a strong work ethic that stressed that "what one sows determines what one reaps." In other words, hard work and intelligence should be rewarded. Although the U.S. government has assumed some responsibility to provide a safety net for citizens who suffer economically, the American political culture, through its primary reliance on a capitalist economic system, free markets, and individual effort, is one that promotes individual initiative and responsibility. Figure 1.1 depicts the heightened importance of the value of individualism in the American political culture, compared to other European democracies.

Fact or **Fiction?**

The U.S. government continued with its open immigration policy until World War II, when the free flow of immigrants became overwhelming.

Fiction.

The U.S. government adopted a restrictive immigration policy beginning in the early 1920s.

individualism: The value that individuals are primarily responsible for their own lot in life and that promotes and rewards individual initiative and responsibility. This value underlies America's reliance on a capitalist economy and free market system.

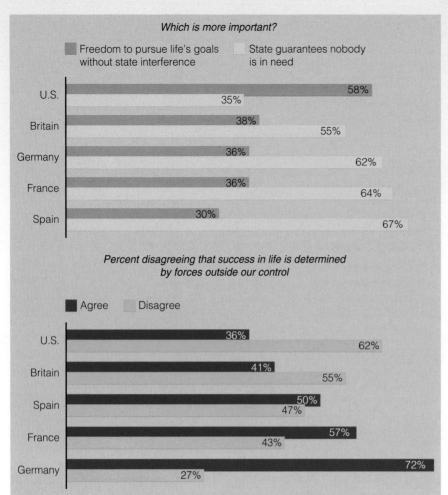

Which is more important?

■ Freedom to pursue life's goals without state interference   □ State guarantees nobody is in need

U.S.	58%	
	35%	
Britain	38%	
	55%	
Germany	36%	
	62%	
France	36%	
	64%	
Spain	30%	
	67%	

Percent disagreeing that success in life is determined by forces outside our control

■ Agree   □ Disagree

U.S.	36%	
	62%	
Britain	41%	
	55%	
Spain	50%	
	47%	
France	57%	
	43%	
Germany	72%	
	27%	

FIGURE 1.1 Individualism as a Value in the United States Compared to Other Democracies

The Pew Global Survey in 2011 shows that Americas are more likely than their European counterparts to believe that "it is more important to pursue life's goals without government interference" and to disagree with the statement "success in life is determined by forces outside our control."

The value of individualism promotes another core value—equality of opportunity, or the idea that the role of government is to set the stage for individuals to achieve on their own, and that everyone should be given the same opportunity to achieve success. Indeed, America has been an attractive place for highly motivated individuals from around the world to immigrate so that they might have a fair chance of achieving personal success. Many immigrants today, particularly from Asia and Latin America, are attracted to the United States for the opportunities to achieve individual success.

The United States has long set itself apart from those nations whose histories include traditions of a rigid class system of privileged aristocracies and oligarchies and peasants with few or no rights or freedoms. In the United States there is no formal recognition of a class system; nor is there a tradition of royalty, nobility, or monarchy. Indeed, Article I of the Constitution specifically prohibits both the federal government and the state governments from granting any title of nobility upon its citizens. Instead, American political culture values the so-called Horatio Alger myth. Alger was a popular writer in the late 1800s whose characters came from impoverished backgrounds but through pluck, determination, and hard work achieved huge success. Although this idealistic rags-to-riches notion often ignores the many harsh economic disparities that exist in the United States, it remains central to the American political culture. The stories of Benjamin Franklin and Abraham Lincoln exemplified this road to success, as do the more recent examples of Presidents Bill Clinton and Ronald Reagan, both of whom came from less-than-privileged circumstances to win the nation's highest political office and become leaders of the free world. Perhaps it is because of these success stories that so many Americans believe that they have boundless opportunities to better their lot on the basis of diligence and hard work.

These core values provide a window into American political culture. To be sure, there is plenty of room for disagreement as to how these values might be applied to specific situations, which we address in Chapter 10. In addition, these values are often in conflict. At the heart

Fact or Fiction?

America's political culture rejects the "Horatio Alger" myth in favor of a more "caring society" in which government offers individuals the means to get started on the road to eventual success.

Fiction.

American political culture has always embraced the idealistic "rags-to-riches" notion whereby individuals rise solely on the basis of their own hard work and determination.

of the debate over affirmative action, for example, lies the value conflict pitting individualism against equality of opportunity. Those who oppose affirmative action in hiring claim that individuals should be evaluated exclusively based on who they are and what they can do rather than on their gender, race, or other demographic characteristic. Those supporting affirmative action claim that historical discrimination has led to a current job market that provides unequal opportunities for certain groups, such as racial minorities and women. Although these values do not always solve problems and policy debates, they do lay the groundwork for how American politics goes about settling problems and debating issues.

IS AMERICAN DEMOCRACY IN DECLINE?

The old saying that "those who ignore the problems of the past are destined to repeat them" holds as true in American politics as it does in any other context. Certainly new issues and problems may arise, requiring innovative new thinking to address them. But many other difficulties the United States faces can be effectively addressed by casting an eye on the distant or not-so-distant past. A historical view can help place modern dilemmas in proper perspective.

The Case for Decline

Some recent observers of American politics have suggested that the American political system is in decline. Are we currently witnessing a deterioration of democracy in the United States? Is the American political system in jeopardy? Are the problems that the American system of government faces today beyond repair? To try to answer these questions, let's first look at the factors some cite as contemporary indicators of the decline of American democracy.

1. **The Decline of the United States as an Economic Superpower?** The growth of the national economy from the Industrial Revolution through the post–World War II era established the United States as the preeminent fiscal power in the world for much of the twentieth century. This fiscal strength enabled the United States to establish the dollar as the benchmark unit of currency for the world, to defeat the Soviet Union in the Cold War, to build a military capability vastly superior to that of other nations, and to provide the leadership that brought democracy to many other nations. However, the significant growth of the Chinese economy over the past decade, coupled with the exploding U.S. national debt (and the willingness of China to underwrite much of that debt) has raised serious questions about the future of U.S. dominance over the world's economy. Concerns over the economic rise of China and decline of the United States are summarized in a recent study by the Congressional Research Service: ". . . the emergence of China as a major economic superpower has raised concern among many U.S. policymakers. . . . that China will overtake the United States as the world's largest trade economy in a few years and the world's largest economy within the next two decades. In this context, China's rise is viewed as America's relative decline."[6] This report offers evidence of a decline in economic power citing projections of U.S. and Chinese Gross Domestic Product, depicted in Table 1.3.

TABLE 1.3 Projections of U.S. and Chinese Gross Domestic Product (GDP), in Billions (from Global Insight)

	China	U.S.
2005	9,838	13,244
2010	13,882	16,041
2015	22,210	20,169
2020	35,734	27,584
2025	57,145	35,963

2. **The Death of Capitalism?** The collapse of many of the largest financial institutions in the United States in 2008, and the subsequent "Great Recession," has raised questions about the viability of the free market system in contemporary society. In large part, the financial industry's drive in the 1990s and 2000s to capitalize on rising real estate markets drove financial institutions to rely on increasingly risky lending practices. Risky loans were bundled and sold off to investors in the form of real estate securities. Multibillion-dollar financial institutions, such as Citibank, Morgan Stanley, Lehman Brothers, Countrywide Mortgage, and AIG, among many others, found themselves in the red at the exact same time that the real estate market collapsed, thus freezing credit in the United States. The stock market tumbled, and the U.S. government needed to bail out many of the largest financial institutions just to keep the nation's financial system from collapse. The frantic drive for profits among the largest of these companies was identified as the source of economic ills not only in the United States, but around the world. Greed, inspired by capitalism, seemed to be the culprit of the world's economic woes, thus leading to questions about the viability of the free market system in the modern age.

3. **Policy paralysis caused by partisan gridlock?** Relations between the two major parties tend to ebb and flow with changing political moods and circumstances. Still, cross-party relations between Republicans and Democrats seemed to have reached such a low by 2011 that policymaking ceased to function. In recent years, whichever party has carried the White House has been forced to brace for a Senate opposition that uses the filibuster freely and without any limitation to impose a supermajority requirement of 60 senators for all legislative enactments. Many other bills can never even get out of committee. Meanwhile, in the House of Representatives, the president's opposition has ruled with an iron hand, rendering matters that had in the past proven perfunctory (such as the routine raising of the nation's debt ceiling) into a knockdown, drag-out fight between the two parties in Congress. The prospect of a government shutdown has loomed over every budget fight. Even more significant, party-line votes on most major legislative initiatives indicate a lack of any common ground whatsoever. The recent retirements of such moderates as Sen. Olympia Snowe (R.–Maine) and Sen. Ben Nelson (D.–Nebraska) all but ensures that the two parties will continue to grow farther apart in the years to come.

4. **Weak candidates for high office?** The relentless media hoards, 24-hour news cycles, and other impositions on the privacy of public figures has scared off nearly all of the most qualified public servants from seeking high public office. Whereas the prospect of a reduced income was once the primary disincentive to individuals taking on the burdens of public service, today a prospective politician must live a perfect life or risk being raked over the coals by his or her political rivals, media figures, and others. With so many experienced public servants reluctant to run, it is no wonder that a movie star (Arnold Schwarzenegger) and a WWF wrestler (Jesse Ventura) could rise to power in two of the most populated states in the union. Those Democrats who were looking for an alternative to Barack Obama in 2012 had to accept the reality that Obama had scared off all potential party challengers. Republican constituents who expressed frustration with their choice of candidates in the Republican primaries of 2012 were left to wonder why such popular Republican figures as New Jersey Governor Chris Christie and Indiana Governor Daniels never even joined the 2012 race. Democrats saw numerous party luminaries such as New Mexico Governor William Richardson and former Senate Majority Leader Thomas Daschle banished from the Obama administration for transgressions that might have been ignored in years past. Americans used to celebrate the proposition that in this country "anyone can grow up to be president"—today perhaps what's wrong with

During the 2012 race for the GOP nomination, many Republicans were critical of the strength of the leading contenders, including Mitt Romney and Newt Gingrich, pictured below.

Charles Dharapak/AFP/Getty Images

America is that "anyone can grow up to be president." Among the most qualified individuals, few do.

5. **Has money ruined American politics?** "Big money" now dominates American elections, in the form of contributions from those who seek to influence future officials, personal expenditures from candidates themselves, and general expenditures by political parties. The Supreme Court's landmark decision in *Citizens United v. FEC* (2010) seemed to cement the role that big money plays in determining election outcomes, paving the way for independent-expenditure political action committees (often called "super-PACs") to accept unlimited contributions from individuals, unions, and corporations for the purpose of making so-called "independent expenditures" on behalf of candidates; it thus enabled wealthy individuals to dominate the process. In 2011, just 22 donors provided the money for half of the $67 million funded by super-PACs! In some instances, anonymous outside groups poured millions of dollars into the process. Others were willing to stand up and be counted: consider that billionaire Sheldon Adelson singlehandedly kept Newt Gingrich's struggling presidential campaign afloat in 2012 with his donation of $10 million to a pro-Gingrich super-PAC. With a handful of individuals responsible for a large percentage of the donations in these campaigns, the corruptive influence of money appears to have reached new, dangerous heights.

But Do These Problems Really Signify a Decline?

If we reexamine some of the criticisms of contemporary American politics with the benefit of historical perspective, we may reach far different conclusions about whether American democracy is now in a state of decline.

1. **The U.S. will remain an economic superpower.** Challenges to U.S. fiscal dominance, such as the current challenge of China, are nothing new. Forty years ago, for example, many policymakers expressed similar concerns about the imminent decline of U.S. economic power. In this era the concern was focused not on China, but on Japan. The Japanese economy flourished in the decades after World War II. A latecomer to modernization, Japan was able to avoid the pitfalls of industrialization experienced by the United States and other advanced democracies prior to World War II. Once converted to a free market system after the war, Japan's economy took off quickly. By the 1970s, Japan had the world's second largest economy and appeared to be closing in on the United States. Gross domestic product (GDP) in Japan grew from $8 billion in 1955, to $32 billion in 1965, to $148 billion in 1975, to $323 billion in 1985. By 1990 Japan's per capita GDP exceeded per capita GDP in the United States. The sharp upward trajectory alarmed many U.S. policymakers, who felt that Japan's rise would ultimately derail the U.S. dominance of world fiscal policy. Yet today Japan offers no significant threat to the economic power of the United States. The rapid rise of Japan's economy left it unable to effectively deal with a recessionary period of any length. Consequently, the dire predictions of the U.S. economic fall to Japan were never realized. Furthermore, in 2012 China's economy is already showing signs of slower growth, leading economists to recognize the likely continued dominance of the United States into the 21st Century.[6]

2. **Capitalism is not dead.** The Great Recession of 2008 and the events that led up to it certainly do not mark the first time that speculation in free markets led to economic catastrophe. A panic in 1837 led to stymied economic growth for more than three years, a severe recession in 1873 retracted growth for six years, and an economic panic in 1893 set off a series of bank failures. A stock market crash in 1929 produced a decade-long "Great Depression." These and many other economic downturns in U.S. history, aggravated by speculation and overly exuberant investors, have led to extremely tough economic times. But the ills of the free market have never limited the ability of capitalism to provide the medicine for recovery, and then some. Panics, recessions, and depressions have always been corrected by bull markets, opportunities, and resurgences. Capitalism has been declared dead many times in U.S. history. The approach of each economic downturn was accompanied by claims that the U.S.

Trading on the floor of the New York Stock Exchange remains an important symbol of American capitalism.

experiment with a free market system had finally failed. In fact, the free markets operate in natural cycles of growth and retraction. Just as the free market system was declared dead at earlier times in American history, so too were many claiming that the Great Recession of 2008 was the last nail in the coffin of American capitalism. However, just as the cyclical nature of free market growth calmed the fears of the skeptics before, so too has the recent growth of the U.S. economy quieted the naysayers once again.

3. **The polarization of the two major political parties has not paralyzed the lawmaking process.** The political parties' recent polarization is hardly unprecedented: at various times in history (e.g., during the Civil War, the New Deal) the parties have stood in stark contrast on nearly all the major issues of the time. Some democratic theorists argue that a marked differentiation between the two parties may actually contribute to democracy under a "responsive theory of democracy": the two parties disagree on the issues and then allow the public to express its opinion through elections. For all the talk of polarization, the 111th Congress passed 43 major pieces of legislation in 2009–2010, including the Obama administration's centerpiece, health care reform. Even after the 2010 midterm elections, emboldened Republicans and deflated Democrats managed to approve over 60 bills and resolutions through March 2012. They also averted a threatened government showdown. The parties may be growing more distinct, but that has not translated into true gridlock by any real definition.

4. **The pool of candidates who run for high office is strong.** The dream of exercising political power continues to attract many of the most qualified individuals to run for president and other powerful positions in government. In recent years the Senate has been described as an institution of 100 men and women, "all of whom want to be president," and many have tossed their hats in the ring only to be rejected by voters. Meanwhile, those who are successful can hardly be deemed unqualified for the position: Of the last five men to hold the presidency, four sported degrees from Harvard or Yale; two of those chief executives (Reagan and George W. Bush) sported experience running two of the largest states in the nation (California and Texas, respectively). That elite group also included among them a Rhodes Scholar (Clinton) and a two-term vice president (George H.W. Bush). Americans frustrated with the choice of candidates must face up to the reality that stars of the two political parties tend to lose their luster the moment they run for high office. Consider

that public opinion polls showed Bill Bradley as a popular candidate for the presidency throughout the 1990s; yet when Bradley finally joined the fray in 2000, Democratic primary voters quickly soured on his candidacy. Perhaps the grass always seems greener somewhere else . . . in truth, candidates for the presidency today are as qualified as ever.

5. **The influence of money does not spell the end of American politics.** American elections have always been dominated by individuals with immense power and influence. For much of this nation's history, political machines all but controlled the nomination process and wielded heavy influence on politicians who benefitted from their respective handouts and other forms of largesse. Whether it was Boss Tweed and Tammany Hall in New York City, the Thomas Prendergast political machine in Missouri, or the Daley machine in Chicago, power has always been wielded by a relatively few, elite individuals. The recent dominance of money in politics has shifted the source of power from those machines to the extremely wealthy, but that may actually represent a positive development of sorts, as both parties have enjoyed their share of big donors and fundraising prowess in recent years. Those who think money corrupts politics might want to consider the far less attractive alternative that used to mark the elections process.

FROM YOUR PERSPECTIVE

Courting the Youth Vote

Candidates and political parties often try to increase turnout as a means of enhancing their prospects in an election. However, numerous nonpartisan organizations also engage in special efforts to encourage the so-called youth vote in particular. These organizations may target young voters primarily for two reasons: (1) young voters represent the future of American democracy, and (2) youth turnout has tended to be lower than turnout among older Americans. Even in 2008 and 2012—when the youth vote increased substantially as compared to past presidential elections—barely more than half of eligible voters aged 18 to 29 voted, leaving that group well behind turnout rates of the electorate as a whole (more than 60 percent or more of eligible Americans voted in 2008 and 2012).

Among the many organizations that run programs to encourage young voters to exercise their voting rights are the following:

- Rock the Vote, which claims to have registered more than 2 million new voters in 2008 alone (see rockthevote.com);
- CIRCLE (Center for Information and Research on Civic Learning and Engagement), which conducts research on the dynamics of young people's voting behavior (see www.civicyouth.org); and
- YouthVote.org, a Web site that provides a plethora of information for young people to learn how to register to vote and why it is important to do so.

Courtesy of Rock the Vote

Pictured above are college students participating in the "Rock the Vote" campaign.

For Critical Thinking and Discussion

1. Which of the presidential candidates do you think won the vote among college students in 2012? Why did this candidate appeal more to students?

2. Why do you think college-age students turn out in relatively lower numbers, as compared to older voters?

3. How much did the candidates in 2012 address issues that were important to college students?

History does not literally repeat itself. The specific people, circumstances, and events certainly change. But history can help us identify patterns, recurring problems, and trends in how the American political system functions and resolves conflicts. The preceding discussion of some of the contemporary arguments for why American democracy may be in a state of decline helps us frame current conditions. In doing so, we may gain a greater understanding of the challenges facing the nation today. Certainly, many contemporary challenges are no less daunting than problems the nation has encountered over the past two centuries. Throughout this book, a historical perspective on contemporary problems offers a sense of how the past might help us understand politics today.

SUMMARY: PUTTING IT ALL TOGETHER

FORMS AND FUNCTIONS OF GOVERNMENT

- The development of the American political system is grounded in the philosophy of John Locke and Jean-Jacques Rousseau, who argued that government is necessary and that it exists for the purpose of protecting the people that it serves. The "social contract" theory states that natural law gives people certain unalienable rights that government cannot take away, and that the people give government authority to rule, but the people can withdraw that authority if government does not serve the people's interests.

Test Yourself on This Section

1. The "social contract" theory between the governing and the governed was first developed by
   a. Thomas Jefferson.
   b. Socrates.
   c. Thomas Hobbes.
   d. Jean Jacques Rousseau.

2. A form of government in which one political party, one group, or one person maintains control and suppresses the views of outsiders is
   a. a theocracy.
   b. an oligarchy.
   c. authoritarian.
   d. in anarchy.

3. Distinguish between the political concepts of "power" and "legitimacy."

AMERICAN GOVERNMENT AND POLITICS

- Democracy includes at its core the idea of popular sovereignty. The United States practices a form of democracy known as "representative democracy," where the people indirectly rule by electing leaders who are responsible for making and carrying out policies and laws.

Test Yourself on This Section

1. The form of government that best describes that in the United States is
   a. direct democracy.
   b. representative democracy.
   c. oligarchy.
   d. monarchy.

2. Which of the following documents establishes the principle of popular sovereignty?
   a. the preamble to the Constitution
   b. the Bill of Rights
   c. the Declaration of Independence
   d. Article I of the Constitution

3. What did John Locke mean by the term *natural law*, and how is that concept reflected in the Declaration of Independence?

AMERICAN POLITICAL CULTURE

- The political culture in America is reflected in the Constitution and the way in which the political system deals with and decides political debates. Among the core values guiding the American political culture are majority rule, liberty, limited government, diversity, individualism, and equality of economic opportunity.

Test Yourself on This Section

1. Which of the following of Elazar's "subcultures" in the United States is characterized by a skeptical view of authority and a desire to limit the role of government?
   a. individualistic
   b. moralistic → advance public interest
   c. traditionalistic → Attitude toward both Gov'nt & market place
   d. rationalistic

2. The notion of popular sovereignty is best supported by which of the following values?
   a. minority rights
   b. diversity
   c. individualism
   d. majority rule

3. Individualism and equality are two values that underlie the American political culture. Define each and describe how these values may come into conflict on a specific policy issue.

IS AMERICAN DEMOCRACY IN DECLINE?

- Although the current American government has been in place for more than 200 years, questions have been raised about whether this political system is in a state of decline. Lower voter turnout, confusing election outcomes, negativity in politics, and the influence of money in policy outcomes have been offered as evidence of a decline. However, a review of historical patterns in American politics suggests that these seemingly contemporary problems are chronic, and the American political system has effectively dealt with these and many other problems in the past.

- Viewing American government from a historical perspective may enrich our understanding of how the political system works. History can help us identify patterns, recurring problems, and trends in how the American political system functions and resolves conflicts. Many contemporary challenges are no more significant than problems the nation has encountered over the past two centuries.

Test Yourself on This Section

1. Today many policymakers are concerned that China will soon overtake the role of the world's leading economic power. In the 1970s and 1980s, which nation was the subject of similar fears?
   a. Germany
   b. Brazil
   c. Japan
   d. Pakistan

2. The U.S. Supreme Court ruling in 2010 that paved the way for the so-called "super-PACS" was
   a. *Citizen's United v. F.E.C.*
   b. *Miller v. California*
   c. *Miranda v. Arizona*
   d. *U.S. v. Davis*

3. What are the key arguments in support of and in opposition to the notion that partisan gridlock has paralyzed policymaking over the past few years? Which side of the argument do you support? Why?

KEY TERMS

anarchy (p. 7)
authoritarianism (p. 8)
authority (p. 7)
democracy (p. 7)
direct democracy (p. 11)
government (p. 7)
individualism (p. 13)

legitimacy (p. 8)
limited government (p. 12)
majority rule (p. 12)
monarchy (p. 7)
natural law (p. 9)
oligarchy (p. 7)
political culture (p. 11)

politics (p. 8)
popular sovereignty (p. 10)
power (p. 8)
representative democracy (p. 10)
social contract (p. 7)
theocracy (p. 7)

2

THE FOUNDING AND THE CONSTITUTION

LEARNING OBJECTIVES

THE BEGINNINGS OF A NEW NATION

- Discuss the origins and causes of the American Revolution
- Describe the first national government under the Articles of Confederation, including its strengths, weaknesses, and struggles

THE CONSTITUTIONAL CONVENTION

- Compare and contrast the various plans for the new constitution and the obstacles to agreement among the different colonies

THE NEW CONSTITUTION

- Explain the principles incorporated in the new constitution, including popular sovereignty, the separation of powers, federalism, and limited government

THE RATIFICATION BATTLE

- Evaluate the advantages enjoyed by those seeking to ratify the new constitution
- Assess the role that the Federalist Papers played in ratification
- Explain the origins of the Bill of Rights and its role in securing ratification

CHANGING THE CONSTITUTION

- Describe the process of amending the Constitution
- Outline the informal types of constitutional change, including different forms of constitutional interpretation

The U.S. Constitution has governed the affairs of the United States continuously since 1789; it is the longest-lasting governing document in the world today. Thus the enduring capacity of the U.S. Constitution to govern for better than two centuries represents something of a miracle: by one estimate, the average lifespan of national constitutions over this same period was just 17 years. Foreign constitutions have been especially vulnerable during crises; by contrast, the U.S. Constitution has survived many such crises, including the Civil War of the 1860s, the Great Depression of the 1930s, two world wars, the Cold War against the Soviet Union, and the 9/11 terrorist attacks. How has the American constitutional experiment succeeded where so many others have failed? The secret lies in its capacity to serve two functions at the same time: it provides stability (just 17 amendments passed during the last two centuries) while at the same time offering the flexibility to adapt to changes in America's political culture. Woodrow Wilson addressed this when he wrote: "the Constitution of the United States is not a mere lawyers' document: it is a vehicle of life, and its spirit is always the spirit of the age."

1910   1920   1930   1940   1950

Then

1933

Franklin Delano Roosevelt, signing into law emergency economic relief legislation in May 1933, during the first 100 days of his administration.

Source: Bettmann/CORBIS

The Constitution's capacity to evolve with changing times is hardly a given: when change does occur it takes place slowly, and often with numerous starts and stops along the way. As the United States sunk further into the Great Depression during the early 1930s, certain principles of government relations remained essentially unchanged from the early days of the republic. That included the "non-delegation doctrine," which prohibited Congress from passing its constitutionally prescribed lawmaking powers to other branches. Beginning in 1933, a forceful new chief executive, Franklin Roosevelt (FDR), offered new and innovative solutions to the nation's economic woes. Rejecting the laissez-faire approach to government's role in the economy, FDR encouraged the promulgation of new rules for industries that had never been regulated before, as the unwieldy size of Congress left that branch largely powerless to effectively hold those businesses accountable with detailed regulations. FDR had already pressed Congress to pass broad economic regulations under an expanded definition of the interstate commerce clause. Next, he planned to stretch the Constitution further than ever before. Specifically, on June 16, 1933, he signed into law the National Industrial Recovery Act (NIRA), by which Congress authorized the chief executive to approve codes generated by trade associations regarding maximum hours of labor, minimum rates of pay, and working conditions in different lines of business. The Roosevelt administration approved over 700 industry codes in all before the Supreme Court invalidated portions of the NIRA in *Schechter Poultry Corp v. U.S.* (1935). Still, even that legal setback could not stop the growth of the welfare state under Roosevelt and his successors: Between 1935 and 1980 the federal government grew exponentially on the backs of executive agencies issuing rules and regulations that clearly amounted to lawmaking. The constitutional system today would grind to a halt if Congress had to issue all those regulations. The Constitution's capacity to stretch eventually afforded the federal government more flexibility to offer innovative solutions for an increasingly complex society.

2010

Now

President Barack Obama, addressing the "Families USA Health Action Conference" on January 28, 2011.

Source: AP Photo/J. Scott Applewhite

A decade into the twenty-first century, the promise of universal health care remained unfulfilled despite the efforts of several earlier presidents to shepherd such legislation through Congress. The election of President Barack Obama gave new hope to universal care advocates that their day might finally arrive. In 2010 the Democratic Congress abided by the President's wishes when it narrowly passed health care reform that approached a universal care standard by requiring all individuals to purchase some form of health insurance by January 1, 2014, or be subject to financial penalties. The so-called "individual mandate" had enjoyed the support of conservatives two decades earlier; but now it was opposed vehemently by Republicans in Congress, conservative interest groups, and, perhaps most notably, many constitutional traditionalists. Obama's critics claimed that the mandate was a symbol of "social totalitarianism"; meanwhile, defenders of the law argued that fairness dictated such a requirement, given that any individual may find him- or herself in need of expensive emergency care at some point. Lower courts divided on the issue: while a handful of appellate courts upheld the law, the U.S. Court of Appeals for the 11th Circuit ruled that the mandate represents "a wholly novel and potentially unbounded assertion of congressional authority: the ability to compel Americans to purchase an expensive health insurance product they have elected not to buy. . . ." In short, President Obama was trying to stretch the Constitution in new and unprecedented ways. On June 28, 2012, the Supreme Court accepted President Obama's argument that the individual mandate was constitutional on the ground that it was a valid exercise of Congress's taxing power. Clearly federal government's efforts to offer innovative solutions to modern problems will continue to push traditional constitutional principles in new directions. In that sense, the battle over policy initiatives such as health care reform remains inextricably bound to a larger battle over the nature of the Constitution itself, and its capacity to adapt to changing times.

THE BEGINNINGS OF A NEW NATION

Throughout the seventeenth and early eighteenth centuries, thousands of people, many of them British subjects, migrated to North America. Many came in search of greater economic opportunities; others fled to escape religious persecution and sought freedom to worship as they pleased. Slowly, a culture dedicated to the protection of social and civil rights began to take shape in the colonies.

The political structures that governed the colonies up through the early 1760s roughly paralleled those of England during the same period: (1) royal governors served as substitutes for the king in each individual colony; (2) a governor's council in each colony served as a mini House of Lords, with the most influential men in the colony serving effectively as a high court; and (3) the general assembly in each colony was elected directly by the qualified voters in each colony and served essentially as a House of Commons, passing ordinances and regulations that would govern the colony. Up until the middle of the eighteenth century, the colonies' diverse histories and economies had provided little incentive for them to join together to meet shared goals. In fact, Great Britain feared other European powers attempting to encroach on their American holdings far more than they feared any form of uprising on the part of the colonists.

The French and Indian War that was waged in the colonies from 1754 through 1763 was a significant turning point in British–colonial relations.[1] For nearly a decade, the French, from their base in Canada, fought the British in the colonies for control of the North American empire. Both nations were interested in rights to the territory that extended west of the colonial settlements along the Atlantic seaboard and over the Appalachian Mountains into the Ohio Valley. Britain defeated France, and under the terms of the Treaty of Paris (1763), which settled the war, all territory from the Arctic Ocean to the Gulf of Mexico between the Atlantic Ocean and the Mississippi River (except for New Orleans, which was ceded to Spain, an ally of Britain during the war) was awarded to Britain. But along with the acquisition of all this new territory came a staggering debt of approximately 130 million pounds. Administering its huge new North American empire would be a costly undertaking for Britain.

British Actions

Following the war, Britain imposed upon its colonies a series of regulatory measures intended to make the colonists help pay the war debts and share the costs of governing the empire. To prevent colonists from ruining the prosperous British fur trade, the Proclamation of 1763 restricted them to the eastern side of the Appalachian chain, angering those interested in settling, cultivating, and trading in this new region. The Sugar Act (1764) was the first law passed by Parliament for the specific purpose of raising money in the colonies for the Crown. (Other regulatory acts passed earlier had been enacted for the purpose of controlling trade.) The Sugar Act (1) increased the duties on sugar; (2) placed new import duties on textiles, coffee, indigo, wines, and other goods; and (3) doubled the duties on foreign goods shipped from England to the colonies. The Stamp Act (1765) required the payment of a tax on the purchase of all newspapers, pamphlets, almanacs, and commercial and legal documents in the colonies. Both acts drew outrage from colonists, who argued that Parliament could not tax those who were not formally represented in its chambers. Throughout late 1765 and early 1766, angry colonists protested the Stamp Act by attacking stamp agents who attempted to collect the tax, destroying the stamps, and boycotting British goods. When English merchants complained bitterly about the loss of revenue they were suffering as a result of these colonial protests, Parliament repealed the Stamp Act in March 1766.[2]

Colonial Responses

As a result of the Stamp Act fiasco, positions on the state of British rule were articulated both in the colonies and in Parliament. Following the lead of the Virginia assembly, which sponsored the Virginia Resolves that had declared the principle of "no taxation without representation," an intercolonial Stamp Act Congress met in New York City in 1765. This first congressional body in America issued a Declaration of Rights and Grievances that acknowledged allegiance to the Crown, but reiterated the right to not be taxed without consent. Meanwhile, the British

Parliament—on the same day that it repealed the Stamp Act—passed into law the Declaratory Act, asserting that the king and Parliament had "full power and authority" to enact laws binding on the colonies "in all cases whatsoever."

Despite the colonists' protests, Parliament continued to pass legislation designed to raise revenue from the colonies. The Townshend Acts, passed in 1767, imposed duties on various items, including tea, imported into the colonies and created a Board of Customs Commissioners to enforce the acts and collect the duties. When the colonists protested by boycotting British goods, in 1770 Parliament repealed all the duties except that on tea. The Tea Act, enacted in 1773, was passed to help the financially troubled British East India Company by relaxing export duties and allowing the company to sell its tea directly in the colonies. These advantages allowed the company to undersell colonial merchants. Angry colonists saw the act as a trick to lure Americans into buying the cheaper tea and thus ruining American tea sellers. On December 16, 1773, colonists disguised as Mohawk Indians boarded ships in Boston Harbor, and threw overboard their cargoes of tea. Outraged by this defiant Boston Tea Party, Parliament in 1774 passed the Intolerable Acts (known in the colonies as the Coercive Acts), designed to punish the rebellious colonists. The acts closed the port of Boston, revised the Massachusetts colonial government, and required the colonists to provide food and housing for British troops stationed in the colonies.

The colonists had had enough. In September 1774, 56 leaders from 12 colonies (there were no delegates from Georgia) met in Philadelphia to plan a united response to Parliament's actions. This First Continental Congress denounced British policy and organized a boycott of British goods. Although the Congress did not advocate outright independence from England, it did encourage the colonial militias to arm themselves and began to collect and store weapons in an arsenal in Concord, Massachusetts. The British governor general of Massachusetts ordered British troops to seize and destroy the weapons. On their way to Concord, the troops

Patrick Henry, a leading revolutionary who coined the phrase "Give me liberty or give me death," speaking before the Virginia House of Burgesses in 1775.

CHECK **THE LIST**

Top 10 Most Important Founders?

Jim Allison, an independent researcher from Virginia Beach, Virginia, recently tried to identify those Founders who most influenced the early republic. Rejecting traditional forms of subjective or impressionistic analysis, Allison invented his own ranking system, which allotted to each Founder a specific number of points for participation in selected activities. For example, he awarded two points for signing the Declaration of Independence, two points for attending the Constitutional Convention, one point for authoring documents that had an impact on state government, and so on. The ranking system can be found at http://members.tripod.com/~candst/tnppage/quote1.htm. Allison's system has its flaws; most notably, it awards to each person the same number of points for participating in an activity, even though some obviously had more influence on the outcome of these activities than others. Thus the appearance of James Madison at the top of the list seems reasonable, whereas Thomas Jefferson's low ranking (19th) may be explained in part by his absence from America (he was in France) during both the Constitutional Convention and subsequent congressional debates over the Bill of Rights. Perhaps what is most surprising about Allison's list is the absence of such well-known figures as George Washington, Benjamin Franklin, and John Adams.

Who would you list as the 10 most important Founding Fathers? The list of Allison's top 10 is as follows:

Founder	Points	State
1. James Madison, key drafter of Constitution, author of some Federalist Papers, congressional sponsor of Bill of Rights, fourth president of the United States	364	VA
2. Roger Sherman, author of the Great Compromise that saved the Constitutional Convention	295	CT
3. James Wilson, played a leading role at the Constitutional Convention, one of the first Supreme Court justices	276	PA
4. Rufus King, delegate to Constitutional Convention, early-eighteenth-century candidate for president, vice president	272	MA
5. Elbridge Gerry, delegate to Constitutional Convention, American commissioner to Paris, vice president	214	MA
6. Edmund Randolph, proposed Virginia Plan at the Constitutional Convention, first U.S. attorney general, second secretary of state	154	VA
7. George Mason, key revolutionary statesman, opposed the Great Compromise, fought for federal Bill of Rights	131	VA
8. Alexander Hamilton, author of Federalist Papers, Secretary of the Treasury, inspired creation of national bank	125	NY
9. Gouverneur Morris, led floor debates at Constitutional Convention, prepared final draft of Constitution	119	PA
10. John Rutledge, member of Continental Congress, delegate to the Constitutional Convention, associate justice of the Supreme Court, nominee for Supreme Court chief justice	112	SC

▶ **POINT TO PONDER:** Can a list of influential Founders that excludes George Washington be taken seriously? Or should this list lead us to revisit our traditional measures of historical influence?

met a small force of colonial militiamen at Lexington. Shots were exchanged, but the militiamen were soon routed and the British troops marched on to Concord. There they encountered a much larger group of colonial militia. Shots again were fired, and this time the British retreated. The American Revolution had begun.

After the skirmishes at Lexington and Concord in early 1775, a Second Continental Congress met in May of that year, this time with all 13 colonies represented. This Congress established a continental army and appointed George Washington as its commander-in-chief, initiating the process that resulted in independence for the colonies and the formation of a new nation, the United States of America.[3]

The Decision for Independence

Despite the events of the early 1770s, many leading colonists continued to hold out hope that some settlement could be reached between the colonies and Britain. The tide turned irrevocably in early 1776, when one of the most influential publications of this period, *Common Sense*, first appeared. In it, Thomas Paine attacked King George III as responsible for the provocations against the colonies, and converted many wavering Americans to the cause of independence.[4]

On June 7, 1776, Richard Henry Lee, a delegate to the Second Continental Congress from Virginia, proposed a resolution stating that "these United Colonies are, and of right ought to be, free and independent States." Of course the Congress needed a formal document both to state the colonies' list of grievances and to articulate their new intention to seek independence. The Congress thus appointed a committee to draft a document that would meet those objectives.

The committee, consisting of Thomas Jefferson, John Adams, Roger Sherman, Robert Livingston, and Benjamin Franklin, appointed Jefferson to compose the document. At first, Jefferson may have seemed an unlikely choice to produce such a declaration. The 33-year-old lawyer and delegate to the Continental Congresses of 1775 and 1776 had played a relatively minor role in those bodies' deliberations. But according to historian David McCullough, Adams initially believed that the document was really just a symbolic "side show," and quickly justified the choice of Jefferson over himself as follows: "Reason first: you are a Virginian and a Virginian ought to appear at the head of this business. Reason second: I am obnoxious, suspected and unpopular. You are very much otherwise. Reason third: You can write ten times better than I can." Later, Adams fumed for decades over the larger-than-life reputation Jefferson gained on the basis of authoring the nation's first great political document.[5]

The committee submitted its draft to Congress on July 2, 1776; after making some changes, Congress formally adopted the document on July 4. The **Declaration of Independence** restated John Locke's theory of natural rights and the social contract between government and the governed.[6] Locke had argued that although citizens sacrifice certain rights when they consent to be governed as part of a social contract, they retain other inalienable rights. In the Declaration, Jefferson reiterated this argument with the riveting sentence: "We hold these truths to be self-evident, that all men are created equal, that they are endowed by their Creator with certain inalienable rights, that among these are life, liberty and the pursuit of happiness." Jefferson went on to state that whenever government fails in its duty to secure such rights, the people have the right to "alter" or "abolish" it and institute a new one. Through the centuries, America's political leaders have consistently invoked the Declaration of Independence as perhaps the truest written embodiment of the American Revolution. Before independence could become a reality, however, the colonists had to fight and win a war with Great Britain.

Declaration of Independence: Formal document listing colonists' grievances and articulating the colonists' intention to seek independence; formally adopted by the Second Continental Congress on July 4, 1776.

Jeffrey Sylvester/Taxi/Getty Images

The Declaration of Independence.

The First National Government: The Articles of Confederation

Articles of Confederation: The document creating a "league of friendship" governing the 13 states during and immediately after the war for independence; hampered by the limited power the document vested in the legislature to collect revenue or regulate commerce, the Articles eventually proved unworkable for the new nation.

The colonies also needed some sort of plan of government to direct the war effort. The Second Continental Congress drew up the **Articles of Confederation**, a written statement of rules and principles to guide the first continent-wide government in the colonies during the war and beyond. Although the document was initially adopted by Congress in 1777, it was not formally ratified by all 13 states until 1781. The Articles of Confederation created a "league of friendship" among the states, but the states remained sovereign and independent, with the power and authority to rule the colonists' daily lives. The sole body of the new national government was the Congress, in which each state had one vote. As shown in Table 2.1, the Congress enjoyed only limited authority to govern the colonies: it could wage war and make peace, coin money, make treaties and alliances with other nations, operate a postal service, and manage relations with the Native Americans.[7] But Congress had no power to raise troops, regulate commerce, or levy taxes, which left it dependent on state legislatures to raise and support armies or provide other services. Congress's inability to raise funds significantly hampered the efforts of George Washington and the Continental Army during the war against Britain. Although Congress employed a "requisition system" in the 1780s, which essentially asked that states voluntarily meet contribution quotas to the federal government, the system proved ineffective. New Jersey, for example, consistently refused to pay such requisitions. Reflecting the colonists' distrust of a strong centralized government, the Articles made no provision for a chief executive who could enforce Congress's laws.

TABLE 2.1 The Articles of Confederation and the U.S. Constitution: Key Features

Articles of Confederation Provisions	Problems Generated	1787 Federal Constitution
Unicameral (one-house) Congress with each state having one vote, regardless of population	Gave smaller, less populated states disproportionate power in lawmaking	Bicameral (two-house) legislature with one house apportioned by population (House of Representatives) and second house (Senate) apportioned equally among states (two senators from each state)
Approval by 9 of 13 states required for most legislative matters	Restricted lawmaking by simple majorities, halting the legislative process in most cases	Approval of simple majority (one-half plus one) of both houses required for most legislation
No separate executive or judiciary	Legislative abuses went unchecked	Three separate branches of government: legislative, executive, and judicial
Congress did not have the power to regulate foreign or interstate commerce	States negotiated separately among themselves and with foreign powers on commercial matters, to the detriment of the overall economy	Congress given power to regulate interstate and foreign commerce
Congress did not have the power to levy or collect taxes	Suffering from the economic depression and saddled with their own war debts, states furnished only a small portion of the money sought by Congress	Congress given power to levy and collect taxes
Congress did not have power to raise an army	Once the war with Britain had ended, states were reluctant to provide any support for an army	Congress given power to raise and support armies
Amendments to Articles required unanimous approval of state legislatures	Articles were practically immune from modification, and thus inflexible to meet changing demands of a new nation	Amendments to Constitution require two-thirds vote of both houses of Congress, ratification by three-fourths of states

The limited powers of the central government posed many problems, but changing the Articles of Confederation to meet the needs of the new nation was no easy task. The Articles could be amended only by the assent of all 13 state legislatures, a provision that made change of any kind nearly impossible. Wealthy property owners and colonial merchants were frustrated with the Articles for various reasons. Because Congress lacked the power to regulate interstate and foreign commerce, it was exceedingly difficult to obtain commercial concessions from other nations. Quarrels among states disrupted interstate commerce and travel. Finally, a few state governments (most notably, Pennsylvania) had come to be dominated by radical movements that further threatened the property rights of many wealthy, landowning colonists.

These difficulties did not disappear when the war ended with the Americans' victory in 1783. Instead, an economic depression, partially caused by the loss of trade with Great Britain and the West Indies, aggravated the problems facing the new nation. In January 1785, an alarmed Congress appointed a committee to consider amendments to the Articles. Although the committee called for expanded congressional powers to enter commercial treaties with other nations, no action was taken. Further proposals to revise the Articles by creating federal courts and strengthening the system of soliciting contributions from states were never even submitted to the states for approval; congressional leaders apparently despaired of ever winning the unanimous approval of the state legislatures needed to create such changes.

Then in September 1786, nine states accepted invitations to attend a convention in Annapolis, Maryland, to discuss interstate commerce. Yet when the Annapolis Convention opened on September 11, delegates from only five states (New York, New Jersey, Delaware,

North Wind/North Wind Picture Archives

Daniel Shays leads a rebellion of farmers to a Massachusetts courthouse in 1786 to protest the state legislature's inaction.

Pennsylvania, and Virginia) attended. A committee led by Alexander Hamilton, a leading force at the Annapolis meeting, issued a report calling upon all 13 states to attend a convention in Philadelphia the following May to discuss all matters necessary "to render the constitution of the federal government adequate to the exigencies of the Union." At the time, few knew whether this proposal would attract more interest than had previous calls for a new government.

Events in Massachusetts in 1786–1787 proved a turning point in the creation of momentum for a new form of government. A Revolutionary War veteran, Daniel Shays, was also one of many debt-ridden farmers in Massachusetts, where creditors controlled the state government. Shays and his men rebelled against the state courts' foreclosing on the farmers' mortgages for failure to pay debts and state taxes.[8] When the state legislature failed to resolve the farmers' grievances, Shays's rebels stormed two courthouses and a federal arsenal.[9] Eventually the state militia put down the insurrection, known as **Shays's Rebellion**, but the message was clear: a weak and unresponsive government carried with it the danger of disorder and violence. In February 1787, Congress endorsed the call for a convention to serve the purpose of drafting amendments to the Articles of Confederation, and by May 11 states had acted to name delegates to the convention to be held in Philadelphia.

THE CONSTITUTIONAL CONVENTION

Portrait of George Washington, circa 1775. Washington was elected president of the Constitutional Convention in Philadelphia.

Time Life Pictures/Getty Images

Shays's Rebellion: Armed uprising by debt-ridden Massachusetts farmers frustrated with the state government.

Constitutional Convention: Meeting of delegates from 12 states in Philadelphia during the summer of 1787, at which was drafted an entirely new system to govern the United States.

The **Constitutional Convention** convened on May 25, 1787, with 29 delegates from 9 states in attendance. Over the next four months, 55 delegates from 12 states would participate. Fiercely resistant to any centralized power, Rhode Island sent no delegates. Some heroes of the American Revolution like Patrick Henry refused appointments due to their opposition to the feelings of nationalism that had spurred the convention to be held in the first place. Meanwhile, lending authority to the proceedings were such well-known American figures as George Washington, Alexander Hamilton, and Benjamin Franklin. (The 36-year-old James Madison of Virginia was only beginning to establish a reputation for himself when he arrived in Philadelphia; meanwhile, John Adams and Thomas Jefferson were both on diplomatic assignment in Europe.)

The delegates, who unanimously selected Washington to preside over the convention, were united by at least four common concerns: (1) the United States was being treated with contempt by other nations, and foreign trade had suffered as a consequence; (2) the economic radicalism of Shays's Rebellion might spread in the absence of a stronger central government; (3) the Native Americans had responded to encroachment on their lands by threatening frontiersmen and land speculators, and the national government had been ill-equipped to provide citizens with protection; and (4) the postwar economic depression had worsened, and the national government was powerless to take any action to address it.[10] Of course, on many other matters the delegates differed. Those from bigger, more heavily populated states such as Virginia and Pennsylvania wanted a central government that reflected their larger population bases, whereas those from smaller states like Georgia and Delaware hoped to maintain the one-state, one-vote principle of the Articles.

Plans and Compromises

It quickly became evident that a convention originally called to discuss amendments to the Articles of Confederation would be undertaking a more drastic overhaul of the American system of government. Members of the Virginia delegation got the ball rolling when they introduced the **Virginia Plan**, also known as the "large states plan," which proposed a national government consisting of three branches—a legislature, an executive, and a judiciary. The legislature would consist of two houses, with membership in each house proportional to each state's population. The people would elect members of one house, and the members of that house would then choose members of the second house. The legislature would have the power to choose a chief executive and members of the judiciary, as well as the authority to legislate in "all cases to which the states are incompetent" or when the "harmony of the United States" demands it. Finally, the legislature would have power to veto any state law. Under the plan, the only real check on the legislature would be a Council of Revision, consisting of the executive and several members of the judiciary, which could veto the legislature's acts.

To counter the Virginia Plan, delegates from less populous states proposed the **New Jersey Plan**, which called for a one-house legislature in which each state, regardless of size, would have equal representation. The New Jersey Plan also provided for a national judiciary and an executive committee chosen by the legislature; expanded the powers of Congress to include the power to levy taxes and regulate foreign and interstate commerce; and asserted that the new constitution and national laws would become the "supreme law of the United States." Both the Virginia and New Jersey plans rejected a model of government in which the executive would be given extensive authority.

By July 2, 1787, disagreements over the design of the legislature and the issue of representation had brought the convention to a near dead end. The delegates then agreed to submit the matter to a smaller committee in the hope that it might craft some form of compromise.

The product of that committee's deliberations was a set of compromises, termed the **Great Compromise** by historians. (Formally proposed by delegate Roger Sherman of Connecticut, the agreement is also known as the Connecticut Compromise.) As shown in Table 2.2, its critical features included (1) a bicameral (two-house) legislature with an upper house or "Senate" in which the states would have equal power with two representatives from each state, and a lower House of Representatives in which membership would be apportioned on the basis of population; and (2) the guarantee that all revenue bills would originate in the lower house. The convention delegates settled as well on granting Congress the authority to regulate interstate and foreign commerce by a simple majority vote, but required that treaties be approved by a two-thirds vote of the upper house. The Great Compromise was eventually approved by a narrow 5–4 margin of the state delegations. Connecticut, New Jersey, Delaware, Maryland, and

Virginia Plan: A proposal known also as the "large states plan" that empowered three separate branches of government, including a legislature with membership proportional to population.

New Jersey Plan: A proposal known also as the "small states plan" that would have retained the Articles of Confederation's principle of a legislature where states enjoyed equal representation.

Great Compromise: A proposal also known as the "Connecticut Compromise" that provided for a bicameral legislature featuring an upper house based on equal representation among the states and a lower house whose membership was based on each state's population; approved by a 5–4 vote of the state delegations.

TABLE 2.2 The Virginia Plan, the New Jersey Plan, and the Great Compromise

The Virginia Plan	The New Jersey Plan	The Great Compromise
Introduced on May 29, 1787, by Edmund Randolph of Virginia; favored initially by delegates from Virginia, Pennsylvania, and Massachusetts	Introduced on June 15, 1787, by William Paterson of New Jersey; favored initially by delegates from New Jersey, New York, Connecticut, Maryland, and Delaware	Introduced by Roger Sherman of Connecticut; approved at the convention by a narrow 5–4 vote on July 16, 1787
Bicameral legislature with one house elected by the people and second house chosen by the first	Unicameral legislature elected by the people	Bicameral legislature with one house elected by the people and second house chosen by state legislatures
All representatives and senators apportioned by population	Equal representation among states	Members of one house (representatives) apportioned by population (five slaves counted as three free men); members of second house (senators) apportioned equally among states
Singular executive chosen by the legislature	Plural executive chosen by the legislature	Singular executive chosen by the "electoral college" (electors appointed by state legislatures choose president; if no one receives majority, House chooses president)
Congress can legislate wherever "states are incompetent" or to preserve the "harmony of the United States"	Congress has power to tax and regulate commerce	Congress has power to tax only in proportion to representation in the lower House; all appropriation bills must originate in lower House

North Carolina approved; Pennsylvania, Virginia, South Carolina, and Georgia opposed; New York and New Hampshire were absent, and the Massachusetts delegation was deadlocked. Thus a vote margin of just one state paved the way for the creation of a new federal government.

Compromise also resolved disagreement over the nature of the executive. Although rejecting the New Jersey Plan's call for a plural executive—in which officials would have exercised executive power through a multi-person council—the delegates split on whether the executive should be elected by members of Congress or directly by the people. The agreement reached called for the president (and vice president) to be elected by an electoral college. Because the number of electors equaled that of the number of representatives and senators from each state, this system gave disproportionately greater influence to smaller states. As chief executive, the president would have the power to veto acts of Congress, make treaties and appointments with the consent of the Senate, and serve as commander-in-chief of the nation's armed forces.

The Slavery Issue

The issue of representation collided with another thorny issue looming over the convention proceedings: the issue of slavery. Four Southern states—Maryland, Virginia, North Carolina, and South Carolina—had slave populations of more than a hundred thousand each.

FIGURE 2.1 Concentration of Slavery (by County), Circa 1790

Source: "GIS for History" project at the University of Illinois at Chicago, http://gis.uchicago.edu/data.htm

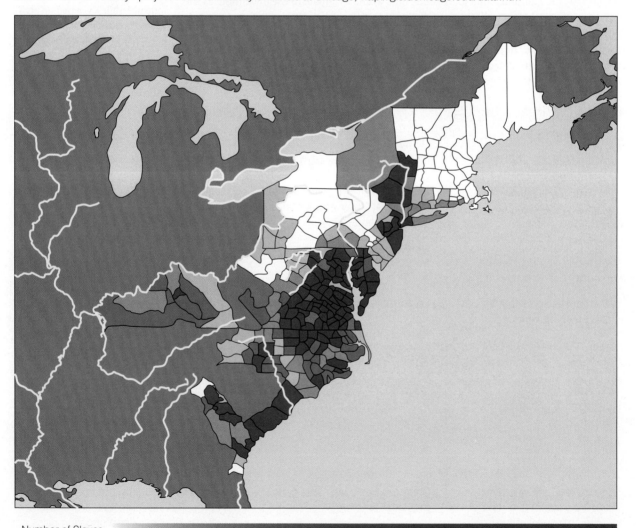

Number of Slaves

0   25.317   50.634

Meanwhile, as shown in Figure 2.1, two New England states, Maine and Massachusetts, had already banned slavery and another four Northern states—Vermont, New Hampshire, Rhode Island, and Connecticut—maintained extremely low concentrations of slavery within their borders. The steady march of abolition in the North was matched by a Southern slave population that had been doubling every two decades. The convention delegates who advocated a new form of government were wary of the role slavery would play in this new nation, but they were even more wary of offending Southern sentiments to the point that consensus at the convention would be endangered.

Some delegates from the Northern states who had already voted in favor of banning slavery sought a similar emancipation of slaves in all the colonies by constitutional edict. Southerners hoping to protect their plantation economy, which depended on slave labor, wanted to prevent future Congresses from interfering with the institution of slavery and the importation of slaves. Moreover, even among Northerners there was disagreement on how emancipation should proceed: some favored outright freedom, whereas others argued for some form of colonization of the slaves, which would in effect ship them back to Africa. Many delegates feared that any extended discussion of slavery at the convention would become so divisive that it might bring the entire gathering to a standstill.

Southern delegates also wanted slaves to be counted equally with free people in determining the apportionment of representatives; Northerners opposed such a scheme for representation because it would give the Southern states more power, but the North did want slaves counted equally for purposes of apportioning taxes among the states. In an effort to forestall the convention's collapse, the delegates crafted a series of compromises that amounted to misdirection, and in some instances outright silence on the issue of slavery.[11] By the agreement known as the **Three-Fifths Compromise**, five slaves would be counted as the equivalent of three "free persons" for purposes of taxes *and* representation. Delegates from Southern states also feared that a Congress dominated by representatives from more populous Northern states might take action against the slave trade. Most Northerners continued to favor gradual emancipation. Once again, neither side got exactly what it wanted. The new constitution said nothing about either preserving or outlawing slavery. Indeed, the only specific provision about slavery was a time limit on legislation banning slave importation: Congress was forbidden from doing so for at least 20 years. In 1807, however, with the slave population steadily outgrowing demand, many Southerners allied with opponents of the slave trade to ban the importation of slaves. Not until the Civil War decades later would the conflict over slavery be finally resolved.

On September 17, 1787, after four months of compromises and negotiations, the 12 state delegations present approved the final draft of the new constitution. By the terms of Article VII of the document, the new constitution was to become operative once ratified by 9 of the 13 states.

Three-Fifths Compromise: A compromise proposal in which five slaves would be counted as the equivalent of three free people for purposes of taxes and representation.

THE NEW CONSTITUTION

As a consequence of the many compromises in the draft constitution, few of the delegates were pleased with every aspect of the new document. Even James Madison, later heralded as the "Father of the Constitution" for his many contributions as a spokesman at the convention, had furiously opposed the Great Compromise; he hinted at one point that a majority of the states might be willing to form a union outside the convention if the compromise were ever approved, and he convinced the Virginia delegation to vote "no" when it came up for a formal vote.

Nonetheless, the central desire of most of the delegates to craft a new government framework did lead them to consensus on a set of guiding principles that are evident throughout the document. The following principles continue to guide politicians, lawyers, and scholars today as they study the many ambiguous provisions of the U.S. Constitution:

- Recognizing that calls for fairer representation of colonists' interests lay at the heart of the Declaration of Independence, popular sovereignty was a guiding principle behind the new constitution. The document's preamble beginning with "We the People" signified the coming together of people, not states, for the purposes of creating a new government. Under the proposed constitution, no law could be passed without the approval of the House of Representatives, a "people's house" composed of members apportioned by population and subject to reelection every two years. Of even greater significance, the delegates agreed that all revenue measures must originate in the House, an explicit affirmation of the principle that there would be "no taxation without representation."

separation of powers: The principle that each branch of government enjoys separate and independent powers and areas of responsibility.

- The delegates recognized the need for a **separation of powers**. The Founders drew upon the ideas of the French political philosopher Baron de Montesquieu, who had argued that when legislative, executive, and judicial power are not exercised by the same institution, power cannot be so easily abused. Mindful of the British model in which Parliament combined legislative and executive authority, the drafters of the new constitution assigned specific responsibilities and powers to each branch of the government— Congress (the legislative power), the president (the executive power), and the Supreme Court (the judicial power). In the new government, individuals were generally prohibited from serving in more than one branch of government at the same time. The vice president's role as president of the Senate was a notable exception to this rule.

checks and balances: A system of limits imposed by the Constitution that gives each branch of government the limited right to change or cancel the acts of other branches.

- While establishing separate institutions, the drafters of the new constitution also created a system of **checks and balances** to require that the branches of government would have to work together to formulate policy (see Figure 2.2). This system of "separate institutions sharing power" helped ensure that no one interest or faction could easily dominate the government. Through the exercise of presidential vetoes, Senate advice and consent, and judicial interpretations and other tools, each institution would have an opportunity to contend for influence.

FIGURE 2.2 Checks and Balances in the U.S. Constitution

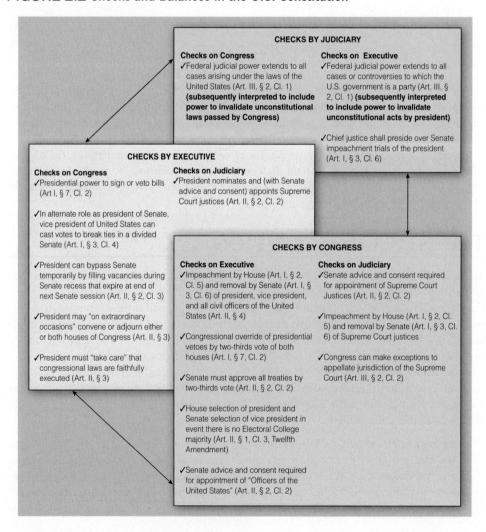

- Dividing sovereign powers between the states and the federal government—a system later termed *federalism*—is also a defining characteristic of the government framework established by the new constitution. Rather than entrusting all powers to a centralized government and essentially reducing the states to mere geographical subdivisions of the nation, the convention delegates divided powers between two levels of government: the states and the federal government. The distinction drawn between local concerns— controlled by state governments—and national concerns—controlled by the federal government—was as confusing then as it is today. But the delegates determined that such a division was necessary if they hoped to achieve any consensus. It would be politically impossible to convince the states to become mere geographic subdivisions of a larger political whole.

- Although united by the belief that the national government needed to be strengthened, the framers of the new constitution were products of a revolutionary generation that had seen governmental power abused. Thus, they were committed to a government of limited or **enumerated powers**. The new constitution spelled out the powers of the new federal government in detail, and it was assumed that the government's authority did not extend beyond those powers. By rejecting a government of unlimited discretionary power, James Madison argued, individual rights, including those "inalienable rights" cited in the Declaration of Independence, would be protected from the arbitrary exercise of authority.

  enumerated powers: Express powers explicitly granted by the Constitution, such as the taxing power specifically granted to Congress.

- Finally, some delegates believed that the new constitution should be a "living" document; that is, it should have some measure of flexibility in order to meet the changing demands placed on it over time. Perhaps the most frustrating aspect of the Articles of Confederation was the near impossibility of any sort of modification: because any change to the Articles required the unanimous consent of the states, even the most popular reform proposals stood little chance of being implemented. Thus, the Framers decided that the new constitution would go into effect when it had been ratified by 9 of the 13 states. Furthermore, once ratified, the constitution could be amended by a two-thirds vote of each house of Congress (subject to subsequent ratification by three-fourths of the state legislatures).

THE RATIFICATION BATTLE

Federalists versus Anti-Federalists

Once Congress submitted the new constitution to the states for approval, battle lines were formed between the **Federalists**, who supported ratification of the new document, and the **Anti-Federalists**, who opposed it. From the outset, the Federalists enjoyed a number of structural and tactical advantages in this conflict:

Federalists: Those who supported ratification of the proposed constitution of the United States between 1787 and 1789.

- **Nonunanimous consent.** The rules of ratification for the new constitution, requiring approval of just 9 of the 13 states, were meant to ease the process of adopting the new document. The delegates understood that once the constitution had been approved, it would be difficult for even the most stubborn of state holdouts to exist as an independent nation surrounded by this formidable new national entity, the United States of America.

Anti-Federalists: Those who opposed ratification of the proposed constitution of the United States between 1787 and 1789.

- **Special "ratifying conventions."** The delegates realized that whatever form the new constitution might take, state legislatures would have the most to lose from an abandonment of the Articles. Thus they decided that the constitution would be sent for ratification not to state legislatures, but instead to special state ratifying conventions that would be more likely to approve it.

- **The rule of secrecy.** The Constitutional Convention's agreed-upon rule of secrecy, which forbade publication or discussion of the day-to-day proceedings of the convention, followed the precedent established in colonial assemblies and the First Continental Congress, where it was thought that members might speak more freely and openly if their remarks were not subject to daily scrutiny by the public at large. In the fall of 1787, the

Portrait of James Madison, the "Father of the Constitution."

Roger-Violle /The Image Works

rule of secrecy also gave the Federalists on the inside a distinct advantage over outside opponents, who had little knowledge of the new document's provisions until publicized. Because the number of convention delegates who supported the new constitution far exceeded the number of delegates opposed, the rule of secrecy gave the Federalists a distinct advantage. As it turned out, five state ratifying conventions approved the new constitution within four months of the convention's formal conclusion, just as Anti-Federalist forces were collecting their strength for the battle ahead.

• **Conventions held in the winter limited rural participation.** Winter was approaching just as the fight over the new constitution was being launched. This timing gave the Federalists another advantage, especially in the critical ratification battlegrounds of Massachusetts, New Hampshire, and New York. It would be difficult for rural dwellers—mostly poor farmers resistant to a strong central government and thus opposed to the new constitution—to attend the ratification conventions if they were held in the dead of winter. Supporters of the new constitution successfully pressed for the ratifying conventions to be held as soon as possible. And of the six states that held such conventions over the winter, all voted to ratify by substantial margins.

The Federalist Papers

Between the fall of 1787 and the summer of 1788, the Federalists launched an aggressive media campaign that was unusually well organized for its time. James Madison, Alexander Hamilton, and John Jay wrote 77 essays explaining and defending the new constitution and urging its ratification. Signed under the name "Publius," the essays were printed in New York newspapers and magazines. These essays—along with eight others by the same men—were then collected, printed, and published in book form under the title *The Federalist*.[12] The essays allayed fears and extolled the benefits of the new constitution by emphasizing the inadequacy of the Articles of Confederation and the need for a strong government. Today these essays are considered classic works of political philosophy. The following are among the most frequently cited Federalist Papers:

Federalist Papers: A series of articles authored by Alexander Hamilton, James Madison, and John Jay, which argued in favor of ratifying the proposed constitution of the United States; the Federalist Papers outlined the philosophy and motivation of the document.

• **Federalist No. 10.** In Madison's first offering in the **Federalist Papers**, he analyzes the nature, causes, and effects of *factions*, by which he meant groups of people motivated by a common economic and/or political interest. Noting that such factions are both the product and price of liberty, Madison argued that by extending the sphere in which they can act, "you make it less probable that a majority of the whole will have a common motive to invade the rights of other citizens." Political theorists often cite Federalist No. 10 as justification for pluralist theory—the idea that competition among groups for power produces the best approximation of overall public good.

• **Federalist No. 15.** Hamilton launched his attack on the Articles of Confederation in this essay. Specifically, he pointed to the practical impossibility of engaging in concerted action when each of the 13 states retained virtual power to govern.

• **Federalist No. 46.** In this essay, Madison defended the system of federalism set up by the new constitution. He contended that the system allowed the states sufficient capacity to resist the "ambitious encroachments of the federal government."

• **Federalist No. 51.** In perhaps the most influential of the essays, Madison described how the new constitution would prevent the government from abusing its citizens. His argument is that the "multiplicity of interests" that influences so many different parts of the government would guarantee the security of individual rights. Because the federal system of government divides the government into so many parts (federal versus state; legislative versus executive versus judicial branches; and so on), "the rights of the individual, or of the minority, will be in little danger from interested combinations of the majority."

- **Federalist No. 69.** Hamilton in this essay defined the "real character of the executive," which, unlike the king of Great Britain, is accountable to the other branches of government and to the people.

- **Federalist No. 70.** In this essay, Hamilton presented his views on executive power, which had tempered considerably since the convention, when he advocated an executive for life. Still, Hamilton argued for a unitary, one-person executive to play a critical role as a check on the legislative process (that is, by exercising vetoes), as well as in the process of negotiating treaties and conducting war. According to Hamilton, "energy in the executive is a leading character in the definition of good government"; by contrast, "the species of security" sought for by those who advocate a plural executive is "unattainable."

- **Federalist No. 78.** In this essay—often cited in U.S. Supreme Court opinions—Hamilton argues that the judiciary would be the weakest of the three branches because it has "neither FORCE nor WILL, but merely judgment." Because the Court depends on the other branches to uphold that judgment, Hamilton called it "the least dangerous branch."

In late 1787 and early 1788, Anti-Federalists countered the Federalist Papers with a media campaign of their own.[13] In letters written under the pseudonyms "Brutus" and "The Federal Farmer" and published by newspapers throughout the colonies, the Anti-Federalists claimed that they were invoking a cause more consistent with that of the revolution—the cause of freedom from government tyranny. For them, the new national government's power to impose internal taxes on the states amounted to a revival of the British system of internal taxation. Perhaps the Anti-Federalists' most effective criticism was that the new constitution lacked a bill of rights that explicitly protected citizens' individual rights. They rejected Madison's contention in Federalist No. 51 that limitations on the central government provided those protections.

Ratification ultimately succeeded, but by a somewhat narrow margin (see Table 2.3). Of the first five states to ratify, four (Delaware, New Jersey, Georgia, and Connecticut) did so with little or no opposition, whereas Pennsylvania did so only after a bitter conflict at its ratifying

Fact or Fiction?

Alexander Hamilton originally proposed that the new constitution should feature a chief executive who would serve for life.

Fact.

Hamilton proposed a unitary, one-person executive to serve for life, but later tempered that position when it gained so little support at the convention.

TABLE 2.3 Ratifying the Constitution

State	Vote	Date of Ratification
Delaware	30–0	December 7, 1787
Pennsylvania	43–23	December 12, 1787
New Jersey	38–0	December 18, 1787
Georgia	25–0	January 2, 1788
Connecticut	128–40	January 9, 1788
Massachusetts	187–168	February 16, 1788
Maryland	63–11	April 26, 1788
South Carolina	149–73	May 23, 1788
New Hampshire	57–46	June 21, 1788
Virginia	89–79	June 25, 1788
New York	30–27	June 26, 1788
North Carolina*	194–77	November 21, 1789
Rhode Island	34–32	May 29, 1790

*Despite strong Federalist sentiment at the convention, North Carolina withheld its vote in 1788 until a draft bill of rights was formally introduced. The submission by Congress of 12 proposed amendments to the states on September 25, 1789, led North Carolina to hold a second ratifying convention the following November.

Source: © Cengage Learning

THE MORE THINGS CHANGE, THE MORE THEY STAY THE SAME

The Continuing Call to the Federalist Papers

The Federalist Papers had a significant impact on the birth of the new nation. The essays argued persuasively that the Articles of Confederation were inadequate. Many scholars today attribute the narrow margin in favor of ratification of the new constitution at New York's ratification convention to the sophisticated media campaign waged by the Federalists, especially through the Federalist Papers.

In 1905, the Supreme Court's controversial decision in *Lochner v. New York*, which invalidated a New York State health regulation restricting the hours that bakers could be exposed to flour dust, set off a furious political debate about the role government should play in a newly industrialized society. Advocates on both sides of the debate repeatedly cited the Federalist Papers to bolster their arguments. Those who supported government regulation argued that it was not the job of courts to disagree with the decisions of legislatures on such public-interest issues; even if factions and interest groups had produced such legislation, they cited Federalist No. 10 to claim that the corrupting spirit of "factions" distinguished democracy from true republics. Opponents of government regulations countered that Madison's preference for more factions was simply his way of reaching toward an ideal politics in which all these factions would cancel themselves out—by contrast, they argued that factions remained heavily influential in state legislatures. In support of the Court's ruling, they cited Federalist No. 78, in which Hamilton argued that "the independence of the judges may be an essential safeguard against the effects of occasional ill humors in the society." Only a sudden switch by the Supreme Court to stop interfering with industrial regulations in 1937 saved the nation from a constitutional crisis fueled in part by dramatically contrasting readings of the Federalist Papers.

By 2012, same-sex marriage had become a reality in an increasing number of states. As of March 1, 2012, eight states had passed laws recognizing same-sex marriage; meanwhile, a handful of states actively considered joining that list, including New Jersey, whose legislature passed a same-sex marriage recognition law in mid-February. The Republican New Jersey Governor Chris Christie had previously indicated he would veto that bill if given the chance. Christie followed through on that promise on February 17, 2012, but the debate over Christie's actions raged on as the governor defended his action on talk shows and before the public as a whole. Knowing that a direct vote of the population on same-sex marriage was likely to support his view, Christie called for voters to petition for a constitutional amendment that would change the definition of marriage. Critics charged that by asking for a popular vote and ignoring the vote of the people's representatives, Christie ran up against the purpose of the U.S. Constitution as outlined by **Federalist No. 51**, in which Madison described the ideals of republican government over a democratic one as the most crucial "political safeguard against tyrannical majorities . . . if a majority be united by a common interest, the rights of the minority will be insecure." Christie's call for a popular vote clearly placed him on the side of democracy; the Federalist Papers offered Christie and others a reminder that many of the Constitution's founders never intended it to promote the interests of a majority over the minority.

For Critical Thinking and Discussion:

1. Are calls to the Federalist Papers still persuasive in the modern age?

2. Given that the Constitution has been amended 27 times since it was ratified, should excerpts from the Federalist Papers (written to defend the new constitution prior to those amendments being ratified) still carry the same degree of authority?

convention. Massachusetts became the sixth state to ratify when proponents of the new constitution swung the convention narrowly in their favor only by promising to push for a bill of rights after ratification. By June, three more states (Maryland, South Carolina, and New Hampshire) had voted to ratify, providing the critical threshold of nine states required under the new constitution. Still, the Federalists worried that without ratification by the major states of New York and Virginia, the new union would not succeed.

Opposition in Virginia was formidable, with Patrick Henry leading the Anti-Federalist forces against James Madison and the Federalists.[14] Eventually Madison gained the upper hand with an assist from George Washington, whose eminent stature helped capture numerous votes for the Federalists. Madison also promised to support adding a bill of rights to the new constitution. Then, Alexander Hamilton and John Jay capitalized on the positive news from Virginia to secure victory at the New York ratifying convention. With more than the required nine states—including the crucial states of New York and Virginia—the Congress did not wait for the votes from North Carolina or Rhode Island; on July 2, 1788, it appointed a committee to prepare for the new government.

A Bill of Rights

Seven of the state constitutions created during the Revolutionary War featured a statement of individual rights in some form. The Virginia Declaration of Rights of 1776, for example, had borrowed (from John Locke) its grounding of individual rights in a conception of natural law and social contract: "All men are by nature equally free and independent, and have certain inherent rights, of which, when they enter into a state of society, they cannot, by any compact, deprive or divest their posterity." Later, during the battle over ratification, five state ratifying conventions had stressed the need for amendments to the proposed constitution in the form of a bill of rights, which would expressly protect fundamental rights against encroachment by the national government.[15]

Still, not all Federalists saw the need for a federal bill of rights. Madison, for one, believed a bill of rights was unnecessary because the central government held only those powers enumerated in the Constitution. He explained: "The rights in question are reserved by the manner in which the federal powers are granted . . . the limited powers of the federal government and the jealousy of the subordinate governments afford a security which has not existed in the case of the state governments, and exists in no other." Madison was also concerned about the dangers of trying to enumerate all important rights: "There is great reason to fear that a positive declaration of some of the most essential rights could not be obtained," leaving some essential rights omitted for the future. Hamilton underscored this sentiment in Federalist No. 84, arguing that such a list of rights might invite governmental attempts to exercise power over those rights not included in the list.

Among the most ardent supporters of adding a bill of rights to the Constitution was Thomas Jefferson, who warned about the dangers of abuses of power.[16] From his distant vantage point in France, where he continued to serve as an American minister, Jefferson was in the dark about the new constitution until November 1787. Then, in a December 20, 1787, letter to his friend and political protégé from Virginia, James Madison, Jefferson wrote: "A bill of rights is what the people are entitled to against every government on earth, general or particular, and what no just government should refuse, or rest on inference." Although recognizing Madison's fears of omissions as legitimate, Jefferson continued to argue the point. In a subsequent letter dated March 15, 1789, Jefferson argued that "half a loaf is better than no bread. If we cannot secure all our rights, let us secure what we can."

In the end Jefferson's arguments prevailed, and Madison (by this time a congressman from Virginia) became a principal sponsor of a bill of rights in the first Congress. Introducing the bill in the House of Representatives, he declared: "They will be an impenetrable bulwark against every assumption of power in the legislative or executive." On September 9, 1789, the House of Representatives voted to submit a list of 12 **amendments** to the states; 10 of these were ratified by the required nine states by December 15, 1791, and compose today's **Bill of Rights**.

Among the rights protected by the Bill of Rights are the rights of free religious exercise, free speech, free press, and assembly (First Amendment); rights against search and seizure without a warrant stating "probable cause" (Fourth Amendment); and rights of due process and no self-incrimination (Fifth Amendment). The two amendments not ratified in 1791 did not relate to individual rights at all. They were (1) a prohibition on salary increases for legislators taking effect prior to the next congressional election (in 1992—more than two hundred years later—this became the Twenty-seventh Amendment); and (2) a provision defining the rules for determining the number of members of the House of Representatives.

amendments: Modifications or additions to the U.S. Constitution passed in accordance with the amendment procedures laid out in Article V.

Bill of Rights: The first 10 amendments to the U.S. Constitution, which protect various rights of the people against the new federal government.

CHANGING THE CONSTITUTION

The Formal Amendment Process

Though political circumstances dictated that the Bill of Rights be passed in a relatively speedy fashion, future proposed amendments would not have it so easy. In crafting the rules for amending the new constitution, the Framers sought to balance two competing interests: (1) the need to protect the Constitution from short-lived or temporary passions by making amendments exceedingly difficult to pass; and (2) sufficient flexibility to allow for amendments to be added when the needs of the nation demanded change. Their determination to strike such a balance was shaped by their experience in dealing with the Articles of Confederation, whose "unanimous consent of states" rule had left the document immune from even the most necessary of reforms.

As shown in Figure 2.3, Article V of the Constitution specifies two ways in which amendments can be proposed and two methods of ratification. Congress may propose an amendment by a two-thirds vote of both houses; alternatively, two-thirds of the state legislatures may apply to Congress to call a special national convention for proposing amendments. Amendments take effect when ratified either by a vote of three-fourths of the state legislatures or by special ratifying conventions held in three-fourths of the states. To date, all 27 amendments (including the Bill of Rights) have been proposed by Congress, and all but one (the Twenty-first Amendment) have been ratified by the state legislatures.

No national convention has ever been called for the purpose of proposing amendments. Indeed, the closest the states have ever come to applying to Congress for such an event occurred in 1967, when 33 states (just one short of the required number) petitioned Congress to call a convention that would propose an amendment reversing the 1964 Supreme Court ruling requiring that both houses of each state legislature be apportioned according to population. Given the ambiguity of Article V, numerous questions have been raised about the form such a convention would take. How would delegates be chosen? When Congress proposed the Twenty-first Amendment, it left it to each state to determine the manner in which delegates to the ratifying conventions would be chosen. How would the convention be run? Could a convention go beyond the limitations placed on it by Congress? What would happen if a convention went far afield and proposed an entirely new constitution, just as the convention in 1787 did? Congress has to date refused to pass laws dictating the terms of future conventions, in part because it has not wanted to encourage such an event.[17]

FIGURE 2.3 How an Amendment Gets Proposed and Ratified

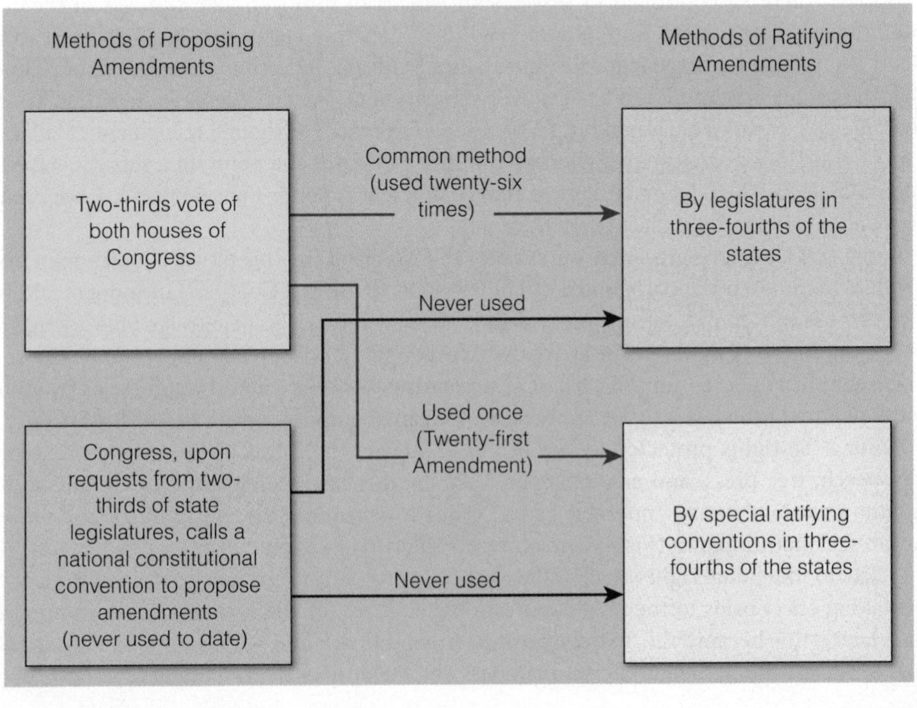

Critics of the amendment process charge that it is undemocratic, as today just 13 of the 50 states can block amendments desired by a large majority. Additionally, amendments, especially those ratified by special conventions, may be adopted even if they lack widespread popular support.

Although 27 amendments have been ratified since 1789, only 17 of those were ratified after 1791 (see Table 2.4 on next page). More than 5,000 amendments have been introduced in Congress since that time, but only 33 have been formally proposed by Congress. Today, as shown in Figure 2.4, different amendments garner varying levels of support. Among the proposed amendments that failed in the ratification process are the following:

- An amendment that would withdraw citizenship from any person who has accepted a title of nobility or who has received (without the consent of Congress) an office or salary from a foreign power (proposed in 1810)

- An amendment proposed on the eve of the Civil War in 1861 that would have prohibited further interference by the federal government with slavery in any state

- An amendment that would have prohibited labor by young children (proposed in 1924)

The Equal Rights Amendment (ERA) proposed by Congress in 1972 also came up short during the ratification process, after years of effort to secure its passage. Although the courts have consistently held that ratification of an amendment must take place within a "reasonable time," it has been left up to Congress to determine what constitutes a reasonable time. When drafting the proposed Eighteenth Amendment in 1917, Congress placed into the text of

FIGURE 2.4 Popular Support for Constitutional Amendments Today
Source: Aspen Ideas poll, based on 1,000 online interviews conducted June 18–20, 2010.

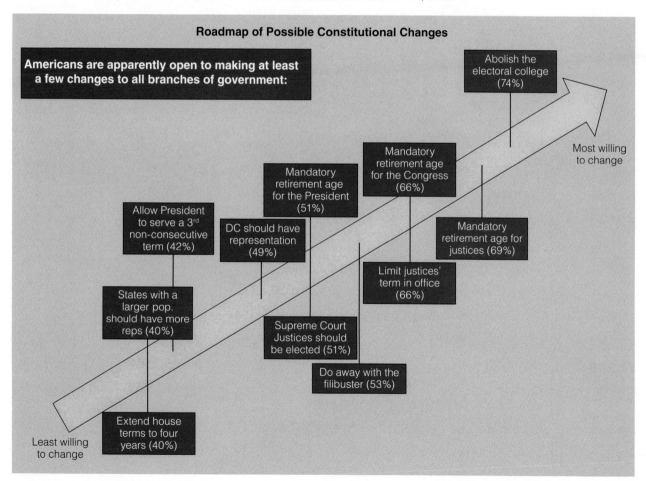

TABLE 2.4 Amendments, Date of Ratification, and Length of Ratification Process

Amendment	Subject of Amendment	Date Proposed	Date Ratified	Length
Bill of Rights				
First	Free speech, press, religion, assembly	Sept. 25, 1789	Dec. 15, 1791	2+ years
Second	Right to bear arms			
Third	No quartering of troops in homes			
Fourth	No unreasonable searches/seizures			
Fifth	Right to due process, grand jury, no double jeopardy, self-incrimination			
Sixth	Right to speedy and public trial, counsel			
Seventh	Right to trial by jury in civil cases			
Eighth	No excessive bail, fines, cruel/unusual punishment			
Ninth	Rights not enumerated retained by people			
Tenth	Powers not delegated to Congress or prohibited to states belong to states or people			
Subsequent Amendments				
Eleventh	No federal cases between state, citizen of other state	March 5, 1794	Jan. 8, 1798	3+ years
Twelfth	Modification of electoral college rules	Dec. 12, 1803	July 16, 1787	9+ months
Thirteenth	Ban on slavery	Feb. 1, 1865	Dec. 18, 1865	10+ months
Fourteenth	States can't deprive right to due process, equal protection, privileges and immunities	June 16, 1866	July 28, 1868	2+ years
Fifteenth	Right to vote can't be denied by race	Feb. 27, 1869	March 30, 1870	1+ years
Sixteenth	Congress can levy individual income taxes	July 12, 1909	Feb. 25, 1913	3+ years
Seventeenth	Direct election of senators	May 16, 1912	May 31, 1913	1+ years
Eighteenth	Prohibition of liquors	Dec. 18, 1917	Jan. 29, 1919	1+ years
Nineteenth	Women's right to vote	June 4, 1919	Aug. 26, 1920	1+ years
Twentieth	Dates for inauguration, Congress's session	March 2, 1932	Feb. 6, 1933	1+ months
Twenty-first	Repeal of prohibition	Feb. 20, 1933	Dec. 5, 1933	9+ months
Twenty-second	Presidential term limits	March 24, 1947	Feb. 26, 1951	3+ years
Twenty-third	D.C. residents' vote for president	June 16, 1960	March 29, 1961	9+ months
Twenty-fourth	Ban on poll taxes	Aug. 27, 1962	Jan. 23, 1964	1+ years
Twenty-fifth	Appointment of new vice president, presidential incompetence	July 6, 1965	Feb. 10, 1967	1+ years
Twenty-sixth	Eighteen-year-olds' right to vote	March 23, 1971	July 1, 1971	3+ months
Twenty-seventh	Congressional pay raises effective only after election	Sept. 25, 1789	May 7, 1992	202+ years

the amendment a seven-year limit on ratification and continued to do so with subsequent amendments it proposed up until 1960. That year, when Congress proposed the Twenty-third Amendment giving residents of the District of Columbia the right to vote in presidential elections, it began the practice of setting time limits in the resolution accompanying submission of the amendment to Congress, rather than in the formal part of the amendment. As a consequence, when it appeared that the ERA would not be ratified, proponents of the amendment managed to get the ratification period extended to June 30, 1982 (an additional three years and three months beyond the original deadline), by a majority vote of both houses. Despite the extension, however, the proposed amendment died when it failed to win the approval of more than 35 state legislatures, 3 short of the 38 necessary for passage.

Demonstrators (including Rep. Carolyn Maloney [D-NY], at the podium) urging reintroduction of the ERA as an amendment to the Constitution.

The "reasonable time" requirement for ratification of an amendment reached an extreme with the Twenty-seventh Amendment (forbidding congressional pay raises from taking effect until an intervening election in the House of Representatives has occurred). Originally proposed in 1789 as part of the Bill of Rights, it was finally ratified in 1992, just over 202 years later. (See the "From Your Perspective" box for more detailed discussion of what occurred.)

Informal Processes of Change

After the Constitution and Bill of Rights were ratified, there remained the difficult task of interpreting those documents for use by the different branches of government. Among the Framers, Alexander Hamilton was perhaps most attuned to the danger that Anti-Federalists and other opponents of the Constitution might attempt to overturn the convention's carefully crafted compromises so many years later by judicial fiat. Certainly most of the Constitution's provisions were vague enough that they allowed discretion for maneuvering by the generation that interprets them—but how much discretion was justified in the process of constitutional interpretation?

As it turned out, the Supreme Court under Chief Justice John Marshall was the first to put its own lasting imprint on the Constitution. Marshall, who hailed from Virginia, served as the chief justice of the United States[18] from 1801 until his death in 1835. Marshall believed in a **loose construction** (or interpretation) of the Constitution, meaning that under his leadership, many of the Constitution's provisions enjoyed broad and quite open-ended meanings. Thus, for example, Article I, Section 8, Clause 18 empowered Congress "to make all laws which shall be necessary and proper for carrying into execution" any of the powers specifically listed in the Constitution. Marshall's loose construction of that provision gave the federal government considerable implied powers (those not explicitly stated) to regulate the economy. For example, in the 1819 case of *McCulloch v. Maryland*,[19] the Marshall Court ruled that Congress had the power to create a national bank, even though the Constitution said nothing explicitly about such a power. The Court determined that a national bank was "necessary and proper" to assist in regulating commerce or raising armies. This philosophy of loose constitutional interpretation underlies the concept of a "living Constitution," one that is adaptable to changing times and conditions.

Thomas Jefferson, James Madison, and many others viewed the powers of the central government more narrowly. They favored a **strict construction**, arguing that the government possessed only those powers explicitly stated in the Constitution. Thus, although Article I, Section 8, Clause 3 gave Congress the power to regulate interstate commerce, it could not do so by creating a national bank or utilizing any other means not specifically mentioned in the Constitution. They supported a "fixed Constitution," one that could be changed only by the formal amendment process, not by congressional action or judicial ruling.

Fact (or) **Fiction?**

More than two centuries passed between formal proposal and the ratification of the Twenty-seventh Amendment to the U.S. Constitution.

Fact.

The Twenty-seventh Amendment—delaying congressional pay raises until after an intervening election—was proposed as part of the original Bill of Rights in 1789, but not ratified until 1992.

loose construction: Constitutional interpretation that gives constitutional provisions broad and open-ended meanings.

strict construction: Constitutional interpretation that limits the government to only those powers explicitly stated in the Constitution.

FROM YOUR PERSPECTIVE

One Student's Term Paper Proves That the Constitution Is Indeed a "Living Document"?

College students may be forgiven for assuming that classroom assignments that invite them to propose constitutional amendments are strictly theoretical exercises. Yet in the case of one University of Texas student, such an assignment on constitutional change became much more than theoretical. Gregory Watson chose as the topic for his research a long-forgotten amendment to forbid congressional pay raises from taking effect until an intervening election in the House of Representatives had occurred. Originally proposed in 1789 as part of the Bill of Rights, the amendment was finally ratified 203 years later, thanks largely to Watson. The sophomore had discovered the amendment while doing research for a paper on American government. Watson's final paper—in which he argued that the amendment was still viable for ratification—garnered a mere "C" from his professor. But Watson continued his quest to secure ratification of the amendment. Tapping into the resentment of citizens over various instances in which members of Congress had quietly passed pay raises for themselves without calling attention to their actions, Watson joined forces with several state lawmakers to get the required number of states to ratify the provision. Their efforts succeeded, and the Twenty-seventh Amendment was eventually ratified in May 1992. Although Watson's grade from a decade earlier remained unchanged, he at least had the satisfaction of knowing that he had made history—literally.

Zigy Kaluzny. All Rights Reserved.

Greg Watson, whose efforts helped to ratify the Twenty-seventh Amendment in 1992.

For Critical Thinking and Discussion

1. What amendments to the Constitution would you like to see implemented?
2. Would you be willing to sacrifice your own time, energy, and resources to organize interest-group activities on an amendment's behalf?

The tension between advocates of strict and loose constructions of the Constitution continues to this day. Robert Bork, a former Yale law professor and failed Supreme Court nominee, argues that overly loose interpretations of the Constitution are outside the Court's proper task. In particular, Bork says, the Supreme Court has "simply abandoned" the Constitution by refusing to enforce limits on the subjects that come within congressional reach.[20] Another strict constructionist, Justice Antonin Scalia, rejects the notion of constitutional standards evolving over time; in 2008 Scalia told one reporter that while change in a society can be reflected in legislation, "society doesn't change through a Constitution."[21] In accordance with this philosophy, the more conservative Supreme Court of the late 1990s (which included Scalia) struck down federal statutes regulating guns in the schools and domestic violence, on the theory that such regulations were not grounded in any specifically enumerated power of Congress, such as the power to regulate interstate commerce.

This strict-construction approach contrasts markedly with the approach advocated by Professors Lawrence Tribe[22] and John Hart Ely,[23] as well as Supreme Court Justice William Brennan, who argued for a loose or more flexible interpretation of the Constitution. Advocates of a loose construction view the document as evolving with the times. In the 1960s and 1970s, the Supreme Court utilized a loose-construction approach to interpret congressional power more broadly to include the power to create civil rights legislation and federal criminal laws.

With so few amendments proposed and ratified during the nation's history, students of American politics may wonder how a Constitution written in 1787 has developed to meet the needs of a changing nation. In truth, an informal constitutional convention occurs on a frequent basis in the American political system. Congress, the president, and the courts engage in constitutional interpretation every day through their respective activities, both official and unofficial. Thus the Constitution has not been a straitjacket at all—rather, its elegant vagueness has opened it up to a variety of interpretations.

Much of the rise in presidential power during the twentieth century occurred in the absence of any formal amendments conferring new powers on the chief executive; the president of the United States reacted to circumstances facing the executive office by assuming greater authority over foreign and domestic policymaking, and the other branches of government have allowed the president considerable latitude to do so. With its ruling in *Marbury v. Madison* (1803),[24] the Supreme Court asserted its right of judicial review, that is, its authority to review acts of Congress for their constitutionality and void those that the Court determines are contrary to the Constitution. As part of its decision in *McCulloch v. Maryland* (1819), the Court ruled that when state and federal powers collide, federal powers take precedence. With some notable exceptions, the other branches of the federal government and state courts have more or less acquiesced to such exercises of power.

When the states in 1791 ratified the Bill of Rights, citizens must have marveled at the flexibility of the new U.S. Constitution. After all, it had been amended 10 times in just two years! And yet the Constitution has proven remarkably resistant to change since then, incorporating only 17 additional amendments over the next 220 years. How has the federal Constitution survived so long, and in nearly the same form as the original document? The demands of modern government, which manages an advanced welfare state that serves the needs of hundreds of millions of Americans, press the Constitution into service even when traditional rules of constitutional interpretation would seem to offer an insurmountable obstacle. Advocates of the New Deal were undaunted by the strictures of the "non-delegation doctrine," and they stretched the Constitution's language to advance the modern welfare state; supporters of President Obama's individual health care mandate similarly pressed ahead, confident that more traditional constitutional principles would not stand in the way if the measures proved popular. The calculus is straight forward: The so-called "higher law" found in the Constitution must ultimately defer to the same public that vests it with that supreme authority in the first place.

SUMMARY: PUTTING IT ALL TOGETHER

THE BEGINNINGS OF A NEW NATION

- Britain's victory in the French and Indian War put the British Empire into significant debt. Following the war, Britain imposed numerous regulatory measures on the colonies that were intended to raise money; those measures generated outrage, protests, and eventually outright resistance from the colonists.

- After a series of military skirmishes, the Second Continental Congress in 1776 authorized the drafting of a Declaration of Independence listing the colonists' grievances and justifying its call for independence based on John Locke's theory of natural rights and the social contract.

- The Articles of Confederation created a "league of friendship" among the 13 states by vesting them with equal authority in the central government during and immediately after America's successful war for independence. Under the Articles, the central government also possessed only limited powers to raise revenue and regulate commerce.

- Congress's inability to raise funds hampered the U.S. government's war effort and its economic relations with foreign nations.

Test Yourself on This Section

1. The first law passed by Parliament for the purpose of raising money from the colonies for the British Crown was the
   a. The Sugar Act
   b. The Stamp Act
   c. The Townsend Acts
   d. The Tea Act

2. Which of the following political philosophers helped inspire ideas found in the Declaration of Independence?
   a. Voltaire
   b. Hobbes
   c. Descartes
   d. Locke

3. Thomas Paine's *Common Sense* most directly impacted which of the following?
   a. the Boston Tea Party
   b. the Declaration of Independence
   c. the Articles of Confederation
   d. Shays's Rebellion

4. What were the main weaknesses of the Articles of Confederation?

THE CONSTITUTIONAL CONVENTION

- A Constitutional Convention consisting of delegates from 12 states convened in the summer of 1787 in an attempt to revise the Articles. The delegates immediately began to consider the "Virginia Plan," which proposed to overhaul the Articles by empowering a new government with three separate branches and the power to raise revenue.

- The Virginia Plan favored large and more populous states by allotting membership in its proposed legislature based on each state's population; delegates from less populous states countered with the "New Jersey Plan," based on the principle of equal representation of the states. The Constitutional Convention eventually resolved the conflict by accepting the so-called Great Compromise, which proposed a bicameral legislature with a House of Representatives apportioned by population, and a Senate that allots equal power to each of the states.

- With the issue of slavery dividing Northern and Southern states, the convention sidestepped the issue by settling on the "Three-Fifths Compromise" (counting five slaves as three people for purposes of taxes and representation) and by deferring a ban on slave importation for at least 20 years.

Test Yourself on This Section

1. The compromise plan at the Constitutional Convention that featured a Senate with states equally represented, and a House whose members would be apportioned by popular vote, was called which of the following?
   a. the New Jersey Plan
   b. the Connecticut Plan
   c. the Virginia Plan
   d. the Georgia Plan

2. Who was selected to be the presiding officer at the Constitutional Convention?
   a. George Washington
   b. Thomas Jefferson
   c. John Adams
   d. Alexander Hamilton

3. What was the "Three-Fifths Compromise," and why was it adopted at the Constitutional Convention?

THE NEW CONSTITUTION

- The new constitution combined features of popular sovereignty, separation of powers, and checks and balances with a commitment to a system of "federalism," which divides sovereignty between state and federal governments.

Test Yourself on This Section

1. The powers that are expressly granted to Congress in the Constitution are referred to as
   a. implied powers.
   b. enumerated powers.
   c. reserved powers.
   d. shared powers.

2. The sharing of powers between the national government and the state governments is based on a principle known as
   a. checks and balances.
   b. separation of powers.
   c. federalism.
   d. distributed authority.

3. Identify three "checks" that Congress has on the power of the president.

THE RATIFICATION BATTLE

- The battle over ratification was waged between Federalists (who supported the new constitution) and Anti-Federalists (who opposed it).
- The Federalists' carefully crafted media campaign, which included publication of the Federalist Papers justifying various provisions of the new constitution, helped ensure its ratification.
- Several state ratifying conventions insisted that the new government add a bill of rights to the Constitution; James Madison, the "father of the Constitution," was initially reluctant to propose such a bill for fear that it might omit important rights, but eventually sponsored a new Bill of Rights in the first Congress.

Test Yourself on This Section

1. The fact that the proposed constitution would be debated by the states during the winter months gave an advantage to
   - **a.** the Federalists.
   - **b.** the Anti-Federalists.
   - **c.** smaller states.
   - **d.** none of the above.

2. In order for the proposed constitution to be adopted, how many of the 13 states had to ratify it?
   - **a.** 7
   - **b.** 9
   - **c.** 11
   - **d.** all 13

3. In order to guarantee that the proposed constitution would be adopted, Federalists promised that which of the following would be incorporated into the new constitution by the first Congress?
   - **a.** the Declaration of Independence
   - **b.** Federalist No. 10
   - **c.** *Common Sense*
   - **d.** a bill of rights

4. Why did the Anti-Federalists oppose the adoption of the new constitution?

CHANGING THE CONSTITUTION

- Article V of the Constitution makes it exceedingly difficult to amend the Constitution. Since the Bill of Rights was ratified in 1791, only 17 additional amendments have been ratified.
- The Supreme Court under Chief Justice John Marshall favored a loose construction of several constitutional provisions, giving the federal government considerable implied powers; Thomas Jefferson and Jeffersonian Republicans favored a stricter construction of the Constitution's provisions.

Test Yourself on This Section

1. Which of the following is NOT required for passage of a constitutional amendment?
   - **a.** two-thirds vote in both houses of Congress
   - **b.** approval by three-quarters of the state legislatures or ratifying conventions
   - **c.** presidential approval
   - **d.** All of the above are required.

2. Would those who are concerned about limiting the power of the federal government favor a "loose" or "strict" construction of the Constitution? Why?

KEY TERMS

amendments (p. 41)
Anti-Federalists (p. 37)
Articles of Confederation (p. 30)
Bill of Rights (p. 41)
checks and balances (p. 36)
Constitutional Convention (p. 32)

Declaration of Independence (p. 29)
enumerated powers (p. 37)
Federalist Papers (p. 38)
Federalists (p. 37)
Great Compromise (p. 33)
loose construction (p. 45)

New Jersey Plan (p. 33)
separation of powers (p. 36)
Shays's Rebellion (p. 32)
strict construction (p. 45)
Three-Fifths Compromise (p. 35)
Virginia Plan (p. 33)

Annotated Constitution
of the United States
# of America

The Constitution of the United States of America

We the people of the United States, in order to form a more perfect union, establish justice, insure domestic tranquility, provide for the common defense, promote the general welfare, and secure the blessings of liberty to ourselves and our posterity, do ordain and establish this Constitution for the United States of America.

As a statement containing the essential reasons for drafting the Constitution and the purposes of the new central government, the Preamble theoretically does not confer any actual power on government. Nevertheless, on numerous occasions the Supreme Court has cited the preamble to illustrate the origin, scope, and purposes of the Constitution, as well as to help discern the meaning of certain constitutional provisions that follow it. Most notably in McCulloch v. Maryland (1819), Chief Justice John Marshall quoted from the Preamble at length to confirm that the Constitution comes directly from the people, and not from the states.

Article I

Section 1. All legislative powers herein granted shall be vested in a Congress of the United States, which shall consist of a Senate and House of Representatives.

The placement of provisions for congressional power in Article I confirms what the Founders undoubtedly assumed to be true: that Congress would be the preeminent branch of the new central government. Section 1 established two important principles. First, by specifying "powers herein granted" it declared that the national government is one of enumerated powers. Despite the broadening of powers implied by the necessary and proper clause of Section 8, this statement of Section 1 still means that Congress theoretically cannot do whatever it wants to do. Rather, it must ground its exercise of power (whether explicitly stated or implied) in a specific provision of Article I. Second, Section 1 established the principle of bicameralism—the presence of two separate but equally powerful legislative bodies as a further safeguard against government tyranny.

Section 2. The House of Representatives shall be composed of members chosen every second year by the people of the several states, and the electors in each state shall have the qualifications requisite for electors of the most numerous branch of the state legislature.

No person shall be a Representative who shall not have attained to the age of twenty five years, and been seven years a citizen of the United States, and who shall not, when elected, be an inhabitant of that state in which he shall be chosen.

Representatives and direct taxes shall be apportioned among the several states which may be included within this union, according to their respective numbers, which shall be determined by adding to the whole number of free persons, including those bound to service for a term of years, and excluding Indians not taxed, three fifths of all other Persons. The actual Enumeration shall be made within three years after the first meeting of the Congress of the United States, and within every subsequent term of ten years, in such manner as they shall by law direct. The number of Representatives shall not exceed one for every thirty thousand, but each state shall have at least one Representative; and until such enumeration shall be made, the state of New Hampshire shall be entitled to chuse three, Massachusetts eight, Rhode Island and Providence Plantations one, Connecticut five, New York six, New Jersey four, Pennsylvania eight, Delaware one, Maryland six, Virginia ten, North Carolina five, South Carolina five, and Georgia three.

When vacancies happen in the Representation from any state, the executive authority thereof shall issue writs of election to fill such vacancies.

The House of Representatives shall choose their speaker and other officers; and shall have the sole power of impeachment.

> *Section 2 of Article I establishes a House of Representatives as the lower House of the Congress. The membership of the U.S. House of Representatives is apportioned according to each state's population; the so-called Three-Fifths Compromise (only three fifths of the population of slaves would be counted for enumeration purposes) helped resolve an impasse at the Convention between Southern states, who wanted slaves to count as more, and Northern states, who wanted them to count as less. Although the number of House members has grown with the population, since 1911 it has been fixed by statute at 435. As constituted, the House is as powerful as the U.S. Senate, and in one respect is even more powerful: the House has the sole power to originate revenue bills. Section 2 also lays out the two-year term rule and qualifications for each House member, as well as providing procedures for apportionment and filling vacancies. Finally, it authorizes the House to choose top officials, including the Speaker.*

Section 3. The Senate of the United States shall be composed of two Senators from each state, chosen by the legislature thereof, for six years; and each Senator shall have one vote.

Immediately after they shall be assembled in consequence of the first election, they shall be divided as equally as may be into three classes. The seats of the Senators of the first class shall be vacated at the expiration of the second year, of the second class at the expiration of the fourth year, and the third class at the expiration of the sixth year, so that one third may be chosen every second year; and if vacancies happen by resignation, or otherwise, during the recess of the legislature of any state, the executive thereof may make temporary appointments until the next meeting of the legislature, which shall then fill such vacancies.

No person shall be a Senator who shall not have attained to the age of thirty years, and been nine years a citizen of the United States and who shall not, when elected, be an inhabitant of that state for which he shall be chosen.

The Vice President of the United States shall be President of the Senate, but shall have no vote, unless they be equally divided.

The Senate shall choose their other officers, and also a President pro tempore, in the absence of the Vice President, or when he shall exercise the office of President of the United States.

The Senate shall have the sole power to try all impeachments. When sitting for that purpose, they shall be on oath or affirmation. When the President of the United States is tried, the Chief Justice shall preside: And no person shall be convicted without the concurrence of two thirds of the members present.

Judgment in cases of impeachment shall not extend further than to removal from office, and disqualification to hold and enjoy any office of honor, trust or profit under the United States: but the party convicted shall nevertheless be liable and subject to indictment, trial, judgment and punishment, according to law.

> *Just as Section 2 does for the House of Representative, Section 3 establishes various powers and procedures for the U.S. Senate. Individual senators may be more powerful than their counterparts in the House because of the longer length of their terms (six years) and because there are far fewer members in the body; however, there is no constitutional basis for the claim that the Senate is a superior chamber. Although the vice president theoretically presides over the Senate as its president, and the president pro tempore serves in the vice president's absence, in actual practice the president pro tempore usually deputizes a more junior senator to preside over most Senate business. The provisions of Clause 1 and Clause 2 that state legislatures choose senators have been overturned by the Seventeenth Amendment, which now provides that senators are chosen by popular election.*

Section 4. The times, places and manner of holding elections for Senators and Representatives, shall be prescribed in each state by the legislature thereof; but the Congress may at any time by law make or alter such regulations, except as to the places of choosing Senators.

The Congress shall assemble at least once in every year, and such meeting shall be on the first Monday in December, unless they shall by law appoint a different day.

> *According to Article I, Section 4, states can regulate the time, place, and manner of all federal elections, but Congress can still establish a single uniform date for elections (and it has done so on the first Tuesday following the first Monday in November).*

Section 5. Each House shall be the judge of the elections, returns and qualifications of its own members, and a majority of each shall constitute a quorum to do business; but a smaller number may adjourn from day to day, and may be authorized to compel the attendance of absent members, in such manner, and under such penalties as each House may provide.

Each House may determine the rules of its proceedings, punish its members for disorderly behavior, and, with the concurrence of two thirds, expel a member.

Each House shall keep a journal of its proceedings, and from time to time publish the same, excepting such parts as may in their judgment require secrecy; and the yeas and nays of the members of either House on any question shall, at the desire of one fifth of those present, be entered on the journal.

Neither House, during the session of Congress, shall, without the consent of the other, adjourn for more than three days, nor to any other place than that in which the two Houses shall be sitting.

Section 6. The Senators and Representatives shall receive a compensation for their services, to be ascertained by law, and paid out of the treasury of the United States. They shall in all cases, except treason, felony and breach of the peace, be privileged from arrest during their attendance at the session of their respective Houses, and in going to and returning from the same; and for any speech or debate in either House, they shall not be questioned in any other place.

No Senator or Representative shall, during the time for which he was elected, be appointed to any civil office under the authority of the United States, which shall have been created, or the emoluments whereof shall have been increased during such time: and no person holding any office under the United States, shall be a member of either House during his continuance in office.

> *Article I, Section 6 extends to members of Congress various immu-nities. The speech and debate clause of Section 6 prevents House members or senators from being sued for slander during congres-sional debates, committee hearings, or most other official con-gressional business. In deference to the principle of separation of powers, Clause 2 ensures that members of Congress cannot hold another civil office while retaining their legislative seats.*

Section 7. All bills for raising revenue shall originate in the House of Representatives; but the Senate may propose or concur with amendments as on other Bills.

Every bill which shall have passed the House of Representatives and the Senate, shall, before it become a law, be presented to the President of the United States; if he approve he shall sign it, but if not he shall return it, with his objections to that House in which it shall have originated, who shall enter the objections at large on their journal, and proceed to reconsider it. If after such reconsideration two thirds of that House shall agree to pass the bill, it shall be sent, together with the objections, to the other House, by which it shall likewise be reconsidered, and if approved by two thirds of that House, it shall become a law. But in all such cases the votes of both Houses shall be determined by yeas and nays, and the names of the persons voting for and against the bill shall be entered on the journal of each House respectively. If any bill shall not be returned by the President within ten days (Sundays excepted) after it shall have been presented to him, the same shall be a law, in like manner as if he had signed it, unless the Congress by their adjournment prevent its return, in which case it shall not be a law.

Every order, resolution, or vote to which the concurrence of the Senate and House of Representatives may be necessary (except on a question of adjournment) shall be presented to the President of the United States; and before the same shall take effect, shall be approved by him, or being disapproved by him, shall be repassed by two thirds of the Senate and House of Representatives, according to the rules and limita-tions prescribed in the case of a bill.

> *Article I, Section 7 is often referred to as the presentment clause. It estab-lishes the procedures by which Congress presents bills to the president for approval; it also lays out the process by which the president may veto legislation, either by refusing to sign it and sending it back, or by keeping the bill for a period of ten days without signing it while Con-gress has adjourned in the interim (referred to as a pocket veto). In 1996, Congress passed the Line Item Veto Act, which allowed the president to veto specific expenditures at the time of signing; the Supreme Court declared the Line Item Veto Act unconstitutional in* Clinton v. City of New York *(1998) because it gave the president the power to repeal parts of duly enacted statutes in a manner different from the "finely wrought and exhaustively considered procedure" described in this section.*

Section 8. The Congress shall have power to lay and collect taxes, duties, imposts and excises, to pay the debts and provide for the common defense and general welfare of the United States; but all duties, imposts and excises shall be uniform throughout the United States;

To borrow money on the credit of the United States;

To regulate commerce with foreign nations, and among the several states, and with the Indian tribes;

To establish a uniform rule of naturalization, and uniform laws on the subject of bankruptcies throughout the United States;

To coin money, regulate the value thereof, and of foreign coin, and fix the standard of weights and measures;

To provide for the punishment of counterfeiting the securities and current coin of the United States;

To establish post offices and post roads;

To promote the progress of science and useful arts, by securing for limited times to authors and inventors the exclusive right to their respective writings and discoveries;

To constitute tribunals inferior to the Supreme Court;

To define and punish piracies and felonies committed on the high seas, and offenses against the law of nations;

To declare war, grant letters of marque and reprisal, and make rules concerning captures on land and water;

To raise and support armies, but no appropriation of money to that use shall be for a longer term than two years;

To provide and maintain a navy;

To make rules for the government and regulation of the land and naval forces;

To provide for calling forth the militia to execute the laws of the union, suppress insurrections and repel invasions;

To provide for organizing, arming, and disciplining, the militia, and for governing such part of them as may be employed in the service of the United States, reserving to the states respectively, the appointment of the officers, and the authority of training the militia according to the discipline prescribed by Congress;

To exercise exclusive legislation in all cases whatsoever, over such District (not exceeding ten miles square) as may, by cession of particular states, and the acceptance of Congress, become the seat of the government of the United States, and to exercise like authority over all places purchased by the consent of the legislature of the state in which the same shall be, for the erection of forts, magazines, arsenals, dockyards, and other needful buildings;—And

To make all laws which shall be necessary and proper for carrying into execution the foregoing powers, and all other powers vested by this Constitution in the government of the United States, or in any department or officer thereof.

Article I, Section 8 may be the most heavily cited clause in the original Constitution, as it lays out all the enumerated powers of Congress. The 18th clause listed, the necessary and proper clause, was the source of significant controversy in the early republic. In McCulloch v. Maryland (1819), Chief Justice John Marshall interpreted the clause as essentially aiding Congress in carrying out its expressed powers. Combining the powers granted by the 18th clause with other powers allows Congress to exercise implied powers not explicitly listed in the Constitution, so long as those powers offer a theoretical means of achieving the enumerated powers. Thus Congress successfully incorporated a bank of the United States because it was deemed necessary and proper to achieve the power to coin money and regulate its value (Clause 5), as well as other powers. No wonder the necessary and proper clause has also been called the elastic clause: it gives Congress the power to enact laws on almost any subject it desires. The power to regulate interstate commerce under Clause 3 has been especially useful in this regard. Citing the commerce clause, Congress since 1937 has regulated minimum wages of state employees, outlawed loan sharking, and passed numerous civil rights laws, among other legislation. The modern limits to that practice were outlined by

the Supreme Court in United States v. Lopez *(1995)*, United States
v. Morrison *(2000), and* NFIB v. Sebelius *(2012)—the law in question must regulate affirmative activities that are at least directly
economic in nature. By comparison, the Supreme Court recently held
that Congress may regulate even inactivity (e.g. a refusal to purchase health insurance) under its power to collect taxes in clause 1.*

Section 9. The migration or importation of such persons as any of the states now existing shall think proper to admit, shall not be prohibited by the Congress prior to the
year one thousand eight hundred and eight, but a tax or duty may be imposed on such
importation, not exceeding ten dollars for each person.

The privilege of the writ of habeas corpus shall not be suspended, unless when in
cases of rebellion or invasion the public safety may require it.

No bill of attainder or ex post facto Law shall be passed.

No capitation, or other direct, tax shall be laid, unless in proportion to the census
or enumeration herein before directed to be taken.

No tax or duty shall be laid on articles exported from any state.

No preference shall be given by any regulation of commerce or revenue to the
ports of one state over those of another: nor shall vessels bound to, or from, one state,
be obliged to enter, clear or pay duties in another.

No money shall be drawn from the treasury, but in consequence of appropriations
made by law; and a regular statement and account of receipts and expenditures of all
public money shall be published from time to time.

No title of nobility shall be granted by the United States: and no person holding
any office of profit or trust under them, shall, without the consent of the Congress,
accept of any present, emolument, office, or title, of any kind whatever, from any
king, prince, or foreign state.

> *Section 9 places some explicit limits on congressional power, includ-
> ing restrictions on the power to ban the import of slaves (at least
> through 1808), the power to bestow titles of nobility, and the
> power to lay direct taxes not apportioned to the states' popula-
> tions. This last restriction was effectively removed by ratification of
> the Sixteenth Amendment in 1913. It also prohibits Congress from
> issuing bills of attainder (legislative acts that inflict punishment
> without a judicial trial) or from passing ex post facto laws (crimi-
> nal laws that apply retroactively to acts committed in the past).*

Section 10. No state shall enter into any treaty, alliance, or confederation; grant letters
of marque and reprisal; coin money; emit bills of credit; make anything but gold and
silver coin a tender in payment of debts; pass any bill of attainder, ex post facto law, or
law impairing the obligation of contracts, or grant any title of nobility.

No state shall, without the consent of the Congress, lay any imposts or duties on
imports or exports, except what may be absolutely necessary for executing its inspec-
tion laws: and the net produce of all duties and imposts, laid by any state on imports
or exports, shall be for the use of the treasury of the United States; and all such laws
shall be subject to the revision and control of the Congress.

No state shall, without the consent of Congress, lay any duty of tonnage, keep
troops, or ships of war in time of peace, enter into any agreement or compact with
another state, or with a foreign power, or engage in war, unless actually invaded, or
in such imminent danger as will not admit of delay.

> *The final section of Article I limits states from exercising powers
> reserved exclusively to the federal government. Most controversial of
> these clauses was the contracts clause, which prohibits states from*

impairing the obligation of contracts. Added to the Constitution largely to prevent state laws that undermined the collection of valid debts, it was later used to protect certain franchises or special privileges that corporations had received from state legislatures. Thus the Supreme Court held in Trustees of Dartmouth College v. Woodward *(1819) that the charter given to Dartmouth by a colonial legislature in 1769 could not be changed without Dartmouth's consent. State legislatures complained that the contracts clause unduly restricted their ability to legislate; thus, the Supreme Court over the course of two centuries has narrowed the meaning of the clause to allow states greater freedom to operate, relying on the theory that such contracts are by implication the laws of the state and thus may be modified by the state. The Court has also upheld state bankruptcy laws when the laws are applied to debts incurred after passage of the law.*

Article II

Section 1. The executive power shall be vested in a President of the United States of America. He shall hold his office during the term of four years, and, together with the Vice President, chosen for the same term, be elected, as follows:

Each state shall appoint, in such manner as the Legislature thereof may direct, a number of electors, equal to the whole number of Senators and Representatives to which the State may be entitled in the Congress: but no Senator or Representative, or person holding an office of trust or profit under the United States, shall be appointed an elector.

The electors shall meet in their respective states, and vote by ballot for two persons, of whom one at least shall not be an inhabitant of the same state with themselves. And they shall make a list of all the persons voted for, and of the number of votes for each; which list they shall sign and certify, and transmit sealed to the seat of the government of the United States, directed to the President of the Senate. The President of the Senate shall, in the presence of the Senate and House of Representatives, open all the certificates, and the votes shall then be counted. The person having the greatest number of votes shall be the President, if such number be a majority of the whole number of electors appointed; and if there be more than one who have such majority, and have an equal number of votes, then the House of Representatives shall immediately choose by ballot one of them for President; and if no person have a majority, then from the five highest on the list the said House shall in like manner choose the President. But in choosing the President, the votes shall be taken by States, the representation from each state having one vote; A quorum for this purpose shall consist of a member or members from two thirds of the states, and a majority of all the states shall be necessary to a choice. In every case, after the choice of the President, the person having the greatest number of votes of the electors shall be the Vice President. But if there should remain two or more who have equal votes, the Senate shall choose from them by ballot the Vice President.

The Congress may determine the time of choosing the electors, and the day on which they shall give their votes; which day shall be the same throughout the United States.

No person except a natural born citizen, or a citizen of the United States, at the time of the adoption of this Constitution, shall be eligible to the office of President; neither shall any person be eligible to that office who shall not have attained to the age of thirty five years, and been fourteen Years a resident within the United States.

In case of the removal of the President from office, or of his death, resignation, or inability to discharge the powers and duties of the said office, the same shall devolve on the Vice President, and the Congress may by law provide for the case of removal, death, resignation or inability, both of the President and Vice President, declaring what officer shall then act as President, and such officer shall act accordingly, until the disability be removed, or a President shall be elected.

The President shall, at stated times, receive for his services, a compensation, which shall neither be increased nor diminished during the period for which he shall have been elected, and he shall not receive within that period any other emolument from the United States, or any of them.

Before he enter on the execution of his office, he shall take the following oath or affirmation:—'I do solemnly swear (or affirm) that I will faithfully execute the office of President of the United States, and will to the best of my ability, preserve, protect and defend the Constitution of the United States.'

Article II, Section 1 lays out the manner by which the president and vice president are selected, the qualifications for those two offices, and the means for removal and succession. (Clause 2 on presidential elections has been replaced by the Twelfth Amendment.) Section 1 begins with the vague declaration that the "executive power shall be vested in a president of the United States of America." Does this clause serve as a source of independent power for the chief executive? Beginning in the twentieth century, the Supreme Court has held that the president possesses broad "inherent powers" to exercise certain powers not specifically enumerated in the Constitution. These vast executive powers included, for example, Franklin Roosevelt's various executive agreements extending the scope of the federal government during the 1930s. On the other hand, the Supreme Court ruled in Youngstown Sheet and Tune Co. v. Sawyer *(1951) that a president's inherent powers did not include President Truman's attempt to seize the steel mills to avert a strike without congressional approval; similarly, in* United States v. Nixon *(1974) the Court held that the chief executive's inherent powers did not encompass President Richard Nixon's refusal to turn over important documents in a criminal matter.*

Section 2. The President shall be commander in chief of the Army and Navy of the United States, and of the militia of the several states, when called into the actual service of the United States; he may require the opinion, in writing, of the principal officer in each of the executive departments, upon any subject relating to the duties of their respective offices, and he shall have power to grant reprieves and pardons for offenses against the United States, except in cases of impeachment.

He shall have power, by and with the advice and consent of the Senate, to make treaties, provided two thirds of the Senators present concur; and he shall nominate, and by and with the advice and consent of the Senate, shall appoint ambassadors, other public ministers and consuls, judges of the Supreme Court, and all other officers of the United States, whose appointments are not herein otherwise provided for, and which shall be established by law: but the Congress may by law vest the appointment of such inferior officers, as they think proper, in the President alone, in the courts of law, or in the heads of departments.

The President shall have power to fill up all vacancies that may happen during the recess of the Senate, by granting commissions which shall expire at the end of their next session.

Article II, Section 2 is striking for how few express powers are granted to the president, as compared to the long list of powers granted to Congress in Article I, Section 8. In the twentieth century the powers granted to the president expanded to create a far more powerful presidency than the Founders envisioned. Thus, invoking their power as commander-in-chief, modern presidents have deployed troops around the world in military battles even without a formal declaration of war by Congress. Recent presidents have occasionally terminated treaties without the consent of the Senate. Presidents have also asserted the power to terminate officers of the United States without cause. The combined Supreme Court precedents of Myers v. United States *(1926) and* Humphrey's Executor v. United States *(1935) authorize them to do so in the case of purely executive officers, but not in the case of independent agency heads.*

Section 3. He shall from time to time give to the Congress information of the state of the union, and recommend to their consideration such measures as he shall judge necessary and expedient; he may, on extraordinary occasions, convene both Houses, or either of them, and in case of disagreement between them, with respect to the time of adjournment, he may adjourn them to such time as he shall think proper; he shall receive ambassadors and other public ministers; he shall take care that the laws be faithfully executed, and shall commission all the officers of the United States.

Article II, Section 3 lists numerous presidential responsibilities, including the obligation to give a report on the "state of the union" to Congress (today this occurs in the form of a yearly address), and the duty to "take care that laws be faithfully executed." Citing this latter phrase, presidents have asserted the power to impound money appropriated by Congress, and to suspend the writ of habeas corpus. Though reluctant to afford the chief executive such unbridled authority the Supreme Court has upheld nearly all efforts by the president to call upon the military to assist in faithfully executing the law. President Eisenhower, for example, exercised this power when he used federal troops to enforce desegregation decrees in Arkansas and Mississippi in the late 1950s.

Section 4. The President, Vice President and all civil officers of the United States, shall be removed from office on impeachment for, and conviction of, treason, bribery, or other high crimes and misdemeanors.

Article II, Section 4 lays out the process of impeachment and conviction of civil officers, but the phrase "high crimes and misdemeanors" is vague and subject to conflicting interpretations. Regardless, the House of Representatives has asserted its authority to decide on its own how to define the term. Only two chief executives have ever been formally impeached under this section: Andrew Johnson in 1868, and Bill Clinton in 1998. However, in both cases, the U.S. Senate failed to provide the required two-thirds vote necessary for conviction.

Article III

Section 1. The judicial power of the United States, shall be vested in one Supreme Court, and in such inferior courts as the Congress may from time to time ordain and establish. The judges, both of the supreme and inferior courts, shall hold their offices during good behaviour, and shall, at stated times, receive for their services, a compensation, which shall not be diminished during their continuance in office.

Section 2. The judicial power shall extend to all cases, in law and equity, arising under this Constitution, the laws of the United States, and treaties made, or which shall be made, under their authority;—to all cases affecting ambassadors, other public ministers and consuls;—to all cases of admiralty and maritime jurisdiction;—to controversies to which the United States shall be a party;—to controversies between two or more states;—between a state and citizens of another state;—between citizens of different states;—between citizens of the same state claiming lands under grants of different states, and between a state, or the citizens thereof, and foreign states, citizens or subjects.

In all cases affecting ambassadors, other public ministers and consuls, and those in which a state shall be party, the Supreme Court shall have original jurisdiction. In all the other cases before mentioned, the Supreme Court shall have appellate jurisdiction, both as to law and fact, with such exceptions, and under such regulations as the Congress shall make.

The trial of all crimes, except in cases of impeachment, shall be by jury; and such trial shall be held in the state where the said crimes shall have been committed; but when not committed within any state, the trial shall be at such place or places as the Congress may by law have directed.

Section 3. Treason against the United States, shall consist only in levying war against them, or in adhering to their enemies, giving them aid and comfort. No person shall be convicted of treason unless on the testimony of two witnesses to the same overt act, or on confession in open court.

The Congress shall have power to declare the punishment of treason, but no attainder of treason shall work corruption of blood, or forfeiture except during the life of the person attainted.

> *Article III establishes a U.S. Supreme Court, spells out the terms of office of its members, and lists the various cases to which its judicial power extends. Just as important, it provides the basis for a more elaborate judicial system featuring numerous levels of courts, which Congress may establish at its discretion. Note how vague and general this Article is compared to Articles I and II: only one court (the Supreme Court) is specifically mentioned, and there are no provisions that specify the size or composition of the court. Congress subsequently established that federal judges on the courts of appeals and the district courts, like justices of the Supreme Court, are appointed by the president and confirmed by the Senate. They too serve for indefinite terms on good behavior, which provides the equivalent of life tenure to federal judges on those three levels of courts. Article III does not specifically grant the Supreme Court the power of judicial review, that is, the power to review the actions of other branches for their constitutionality. The Supreme Court seized that power for itself in* Marbury v. Madison *(1803), and it remains a fundamental precept of the federal judicial system today.*

Article IV

Section 1. Full faith and credit shall be given in each state to the public acts, records, and judicial proceedings of every other state. And the Congress may by general laws prescribe the manner in which such acts, records, and proceedings shall be proved, and the effect thereof.

Section 2. The citizens of each state shall be entitled to all privileges and immunities of citizens in the several states.

A person charged in any state with treason, felony, or other crime, who shall flee from justice, and be found in another state, shall on demand of the executive authority of the state from which he fled, be delivered up, to be removed to the state having jurisdiction of the crime.

No person held to service or labor in one state, under the laws thereof, escaping into another, shall, in consequence of any law or regulation therein, be discharged from such service or labor, but shall be delivered up on claim of the party to whom such service or labor may be due.

Section 3. New states may be admitted by the Congress into this union; but no new states shall be formed or erected within the jurisdiction of any other state; nor any state be formed by the junction of two or more states, or parts of states, without the consent of the legislatures of the states concerned as well as of the Congress.

The Congress shall have power to dispose of and make all needful rules and regulations respecting the territory or other property belonging to the United States; and nothing in this Constitution shall be so construed as to prejudice any claims of the United States, or of any particular state.

Section 4. The United States shall guarantee to every state in this union a republican form of government, and shall protect each of them against invasion; and on application of the legislature, or of the executive (when the legislature cannot be convened) against domestic violence.

Article IV describes the responsibilities states have to one another under the Constitution, and the obligations of the federal government to the states. It also provides the procedures for admitting new states to the union (no state has been admitted since the entry of Alaska and Hawaii in 1959). In recent years, the most controversial aspect of Article IV has been the full faith and credit clause of Section 1, which theoretically binds states to respect the public acts and proceedings of other states, including the granting of drivers' licenses and child custody rulings. Does the full faith and credit clause apply as well to the institution of same-sex marriage? The federal government and various states have sought to evade the recognition of gay marriages sanctioned elsewhere through legislation, including the Defense of Marriage Act of 1996. (At the time of this writing, six states have sanctioned the practice by a vote of their respective legislatures; two others recognize same-sex marriage under certain conditions, but do not actually grant same-sex marriage licenses.)

The ambiguous privileges and immunities clause of Article IV, Section 2 requires that states not discriminate against citizens of other states in favor of its own citizens, although the Supreme Court has allowed states to establish more favorable terms for in-state residents when distributing certain recreational rights such as amateur fishing licenses or permits to use state parks; taxes on commuters, by contrast, may be unconstitutional if they penalize out-of-state residents who work or do business in the state. The requirement in Section 4 that the United States guarantee to every state a republican form of government was invoked in the 1840s when President John Tyler threatened the use of federal troops after a rebellion occurred in Rhode Island. Today that provision is obscure and little-used.

Article V

The Congress, whenever two thirds of both houses shall deem it necessary, shall propose amendments to this Constitution, or, on the application of the legislatures of two thirds of the several states, shall call a convention for proposing amendments, which, in either case, shall be valid to all intents and purposes, as part of this Constitution, when ratified by the legislatures of three fourths of the several states, or by conventions in three fourths thereof, as the one or the other mode of ratification may be proposed by the Congress; provided that no amendment which may be made prior to the year one thousand eight hundred and eight shall in any manner affect the first and fourth clauses in the ninth section of the first article; and that no state, without its consent, shall be deprived of its equal suffrage in the Senate.

Article V spells out the process for amending the Constitution. By far the most common form of constitutional amendment has been by congressional proposal, with state legislatures ratifying the proposal. Twenty-six of the twenty-seven amendments have been adopted in this way. The sole exception was the Twenty-first Amendment, which was ratified by specially chosen state ratifying conventions to assure that farmer-dominated state legislatures would not undermine the effort to repeal Prohibition. The procedure by which the requisite number of state legislatures (two thirds) apply to Congress to call a convention for proposing amendments has never been used. Article V does not provide a deadline for considering proposed amendments, although Congress has the power to set such deadlines in the language of the proposed amendment. Congress did not do so in the case of the Twenty-seventh Amendment, which received the approval of the required three fourths of states necessary for ratification in 1992—fully 203 years after the amendment was first proposed.

Article VI

All debts contracted and engagements entered into, before the adoption of this Constitution, shall be as valid against the United States under this Constitution, as under the Confederation.

This Constitution, and the laws of the United States which shall be made in pursuance thereof; and all treaties made, or which shall be made, under the authority of the United States, shall be the supreme law of the land; and the judges in every state shall be bound thereby, anything in the Constitution or laws of any State to the contrary notwithstanding.

The Senators and Representatives before mentioned, and the members of the several state legislatures, and all executive and judicial officers, both of the United States and of the several states, shall be bound by oath or affirmation, to support this Constitution; but no religious test shall ever be required as a qualification to any office or public trust under the United States.

Article VI establishes that the Constitution, laws, and treaties are to be the supreme law of the land. In interpreting this supremacy clause, the U.S. Supreme Court has countenanced little resistance. Thus the Supreme Court has consistently struck down attempts by states to control federal institutions, and it has reminded state governments that even state constitutions are subordinate to federal statutes. Even more important, in Cooper v. Aaron *(1957) the U.S. Supreme Court stated in no uncertain terms that its own rulings are to be treated as if they are the words of the Constitution itself, heading off attempts by some state governments to resist Supreme Court rulings on desegregation by offering their own interpretations of the federal Constitution as authority.*

The ratification of the conventions of nine states, shall be sufficient for the establishment of this Constitution between the states so ratifying the same. Done in convention by the unanimous consent of the states present the seventeenth day of September in the year of our Lord one thousand seven hundred and eighty seven and of the independence of the United States of America the twelfth. In witness whereof We have hereunto subscribed our Names,

G. Washington—Presidt. and deputy from Virginia

New Hampshire
John Langdon
Nicholas Gilman
Massachusetts
Nathaniel Gorham
Rufus King

Connecticut
Wm. Saml. Johnson
Roger Sherman

New York
Alexander Hamilton

New Jersey
Wil. Livingston
David Brearly
Wm. Paterson
Jona. Dayton

Pennsylvania
B. Franklin
Thomas Mifflin

Robt. Morris
Geo. Clymer
Thos. FitzSimons
Jared Ingersoll
James Wilson
Gouv Morris

Delaware
Geo. Read
Gunning Bedford jun
John Dickinson
Richard Bassett
Jaco. Broom

Maryland
James McHenry
Dan of St Thos. Jenifer
Danl Carroll

Virginia
John Blair—
James Madison Jr.

North Carolina
Wm. Blount
Richd. Dobbs Spaight
Hu Williamson

South Carolina
J. Rutledge
Charles Cotesworth
  Pinckney
Charles Pinckney
Pierce Butler

Georgia
William Few
Abr Baldwin

Amendments to the Constitution of the United States

The Bill of Rights, ratified in 1791, consists of the first ten amendments to the Constitution. Since that time, seventeen additional amendments have been ratified by the states. Originally the Bill of Rights applied only to the federal government and not to the state governments; however, through a process known as incorporation, the Supreme Court has ruled that the Fourteenth Amendment (adopted in 1868) made most of the provisions found in the Bill of Rights applicable to the states as well. Subsequent amendments have extended the franchise, established (and repealed) Prohibition, and clarified important procedures that the federal government must follow.

Amendment I (1791)

Congress shall make no law respecting an establishment of religion, or prohibiting the free exercise thereof; or abridging the freedom of speech, or of the press; or the right of the people peaceably to assemble, and to petition the government for a redress of grievances.

Although many provisions of the original Bill of Rights are based on aspects of English law, the extensive guarantees found in the First Amendment have no true English equivalent. The First Amendment offered one of the first written guarantees of religious freedom, and it formed the basis for extensive free speech and free press protection as well. Yet its unqualified language notwithstanding, the First Amendment has never conveyed absolute freedom to Americans. Whether it was the Alien and Sedition Acts of 1798, the aggressive application of the Espionage Act during World War I, or the "red scare" of the late 1940s, government has often found ways to evade the First Amendment, especially during times of crisis. The Supreme Court has also specifically exempted obscenity, libel, fighting words, and incitement from free speech protections. Nor has the separate and independent provision for the freedom of the press been interpreted to give members of the press any more protection than is afforded to ordinary citizens. Finally, as noted above, although the first word of the amendment implies that its protections apply only against actions of the federal government, today the First Amendment offers protection against the state governments as well.

Amendment II (1791)

A well regulated militia, being necessary to the security of a free state, the right of the people to keep and bear arms, shall not be infringed.

The Second Amendment originated as a compromise in the debate between those who feared mob rule by the people, and those committed to give the people everything they need to fight governmental tyranny. In 2008, the U.S. Supreme Court ruled for the first time that certain gun control laws may violate an individual's Second Amendment right to "bear arms." Two years later it went a step further, applying those protections against all 50 states governments and their subdivisions. See District of Columbia v. Heller, *554 U.S. 570 (2008);* McDonald v. Chicago, *561 U.S. ___ (2010).*

Amendment III (1791)

No soldier shall, in time of peace be quartered in any house, without the consent of the owner, nor in time of war, but in a manner to be prescribed by law.

> *The Third Amendment has been all but lost to history. The Quartering Act, which required the American colonists to provide shelter and supplies for British troops, was one of the grievances that provoked the Declaration of Independence and ultimately the Revolution. Many colonists resented having to house British soldiers in private homes. The Third Amendment aimed to protect private citizens from such intrusions.*

Amendment IV (1791)

The right of the people to be secure in their persons, houses, papers, and effects, against unreasonable searches and seizures, shall not be violated, and no warrants shall issue, but upon probable cause, supported by oath or affirmation, and particularly describing the place to be searched, and the persons or things to be seized.

> *Like the First Amendment, the Fourth Amendment is a uniquely American right. It arose out of colonists' anger over the warrantless searches and so-called General Warrants by which British authorities would conduct raids of colonists' homes virtually at their own discretion. The Fourth Amendment guarantees that with certain carefully specified exceptions (consent of the owner, urgent circumstances, etc.), government authorities can conduct searches only when they possess a reasonably specific warrant demonstrating probable cause. Enforcement of the Fourth Amendment occurs primarily through application of the controversial exclusionary rule, which excludes from trial all evidence seized in violation of a defendant's constitutional rights.*

Amendment V (1791)

No person shall be held to answer for a capital, or otherwise infamous crime, unless on a presentment or indictment of a grand jury, except in cases arising in the land or naval forces, or in the militia, when in actual service in time of war or public danger; nor shall any person be subject for the same offense to be twice put in jeopardy of life or limb; nor shall be compelled in any criminal case to be a witness against himself, nor be deprived of life, liberty, or property, without due process of law; nor shall private property be taken for public use, without just compensation.

> *The Fifth Amendment is a collection of various rights, most of which are important primarily to those accused of a crime. Those who "take the Fifth" under oath are normally invoking the privilege against self-incrimination; under current precedents they can invoke that privilege in other contexts as well, such as whenever they are being questioned by police or other authorities. The grand jury requirement has never been incorporated to apply against state governments. The requirement against double jeopardy prevents defendants who have been acquitted from being retried for the same offense by the same government. The due process clause of the Fifth Amendment was later duplicated in the Fourteenth Amendment and applied to states as well. Finally, the takings clause limits the traditional power of eminent domain by requiring that the government must pay compensation whenever it takes private property for public use.*

Amendment VI (1791)

In all criminal prosecutions, the accused shall enjoy the right to a speedy and public trial, by an impartial jury of the state and district wherein the crime shall have been committed, which district shall have been previously ascertained by law, and to be informed of the nature and cause of the accusation; to be confronted with the witnesses against him; to have compulsory process for obtaining witnesses in his favor, and to have the assistance of counsel for his defense.

The Sixth Amendment offers the accused numerous constitutional protections. The need for a speedy and public trial dates back to concerns raised by imprisoned enemies of the British crown who were detained indefinitely and without notice. The right to a jury trial—considered a sacred aspect of the American political culture—is not all-encompassing either: it applies only to nonpetty offenses (punishable by more than six months of prison).

Amendment VII (1791)

In suits at common law, where the value in controversy shall exceed twenty dollars, the right of trial by jury shall be preserved, and no fact tried by a jury, shall be otherwise reexamined in any court of the United States, than according to the rules of the common law.

The Seventh Amendment is the only amendment in the Bill of Rights that focuses on elements of civil trials exclusively. It preserves the distinction the English system draws between courts of common law (in which juries grant monetary relief) and courts of equity (in which a judge grants nonmonetary relief, such as an injunction).

Amendment VIII (1791)

Excessive bail shall not be required, nor excessive fines imposed, nor cruel and unusual punishments inflicted.

The Eighth Amendment offers protections that come directly from the English Bill of Rights. The prohibition against excessive bail was established to prevent judges from keeping the accused indefinitely imprisoned while waiting for trials on minor offenses; it has subsequently been interpreted to allow judges to deny bail in instances where the charges are sufficiently serious, or where preventative detention is warranted for the safety of the community. The prohibition against cruel and unusual punishment forbids some punishments entirely (drawing and quartering, burning alive, and other forms of torture), while forbidding other punishments only when they are excessive compared to the crime. Aside from the four-year period from 1972 through 1976, the Supreme Court has consistently held that with proper safeguards, capital punishment is not cruel and unusual punishment. However, consistent with this clause it may not be imposed for rape or crimes lesser than murder, and it may not be imposed against the mentally retarded or against juvenile offenders.

Amendment IX (1791)

The enumeration in the Constitution, of certain rights, shall not be construed to deny or disparage others retained by the people.

The Ninth Amendment has been nicknamed the Madison Amendment in deference to James Madison's general concerns about the Bill of Rights. During debates over ratification of the Constitution, Anti-Federalists called for a bill of rights to protect the people against a potentially abusive new central government. In correspondence with Thomas Jefferson, Madison expressed the fear that by listing exceptions to congressional powers, such a bill of rights would effectively deny the existence of rights that did not happen to appear on the list. Eventually, as a member of the House of Representatives in the First Congress, Madison sponsored passage of the Bill of Rights, but he included this amendment as a way to ensure that the listing of certain rights did not mean that other rights were denied. As interpreted, the Ninth Amendment has not had much impact on the constitutional landscape. Likened by some to an "inkblot," it has been most commonly viewed not as a source of rights, but rather as a loose guideline on how to interpret the Constitution.

Amendment X (1791)

The powers not delegated to the United States by the Constitution, nor prohibited by it to the states, are reserved to the states respectively, or to the people.

The Tenth Amendment lays out in explicit terms that the federal government is limited only to the powers granted to it in the Constitution. For most of the twentieth century, the Supreme Court regarded this amendment largely as a redundant truism, adding little to the Constitution as it was originally ratified. Yet since the early 1990s the Supreme Court has began to put teeth into the amendment, interpreting it as a prohibition on attempts by Congress to force states to participate in federal programs.

Amendment XI (1798)

The judicial power of the United States shall not be construed to extend to any suit in law or equity, commenced or prosecuted against one of the United States by citizens of another state, or by citizens or subjects of any foreign state.

The Eleventh Amendment was ratified to modify the Supreme Court's controversial decision in Chisholm v. Georgia *(1793), which upheld the authority of federal courts to hear lawsuits brought by citizens of one state against another state. The Supreme Court has ruled that the Eleventh Amendment provide states with some form of sovereign immunity, which means that it generally protects states from civil or criminal prosecution. The Supreme Court has also determined that under the Eleventh Amendment, a state cannot be sued by one of its own citizens.*

Amendment XII (1804)

The electors shall meet in their respective states and vote by ballot for President and Vice-President, one of whom, at least, shall not be an inhabitant of the same state with themselves; they shall name in their ballots the person voted for as President, and in distinct ballots the person voted for as Vice-President, and they shall make distinct lists of all persons voted for as President, and of all persons voted for as Vice-President, and of the number of votes for each, which lists they shall sign and certify, and transmit sealed to the seat of the government of the United States, directed to the President of the Senate;—The President of the Senate shall, in the presence of the Senate and House of Representatives, open all the certificates and the votes shall then be counted;—the person having the greatest number of votes for President, shall be the President, if such number be a majority of the whole number of electors appointed; and if no person have such majority, then from the persons having the highest numbers not exceeding three on the list of those voted for as President, the House of Representatives shall choose immediately, by ballot, the President. But in choosing the President, the votes shall be taken by states, the representation from each state having one vote; a quorum for this purpose shall consist of a member or members from two-thirds of the states, and a majority of all the states shall be necessary to a choice. And if the House of Representatives shall not choose a President whenever the right of choice shall devolve upon them, before the fourth day of March next following, then the Vice-President shall act as President, as in the case of the death or other constitutional disability of the President. The person having the greatest number of votes as Vice-President, shall be the Vice-President, if such number be a majority of the whole number of electors appointed, and if no person have a majority, then from the two highest numbers on the list, the Senate shall choose the Vice-President; a quorum for the purpose shall consist of two-thirds of the whole number of Senators, and a majority of the whole number shall be necessary to a choice. But no person constitutionally ineligible to the office of President shall be eligible to that of Vice-President of the United States.

The Twelfth Amendment altered the Constitution's original procedures for holding presidential elections. Under Article II, the winner of a majority of Electoral College votes would become president, and the runner-up would become vice president. The election of 1800 exposed the peculiarity that if every member of the Electoral College voted for both members of a party ticket, each member of the most popular ticket would receive the same number of votes, resulting in a deadlock. The Twelfth Amendment cured that flaw by requiring electors to cast separate votes for president and vice president, and by ensuring that if a deadlock occurred anyway and the House of Representatives failed to choose a president, then the candidate who received the highest number of votes on the vice presidential ballot would act as president (thus all vice presidents must be constitutionally eligible to serve as president).

Amendment XIII (1865)

Section 1. Neither slavery nor involuntary servitude, except as a punishment for crime whereof the party shall have been duly convicted, shall exist within the United States, or any place subject to their jurisdiction.
Section 2. Congress shall have power to enforce this article by appropriate legislation.

The Thirteenth Amendment was the first of the three Civil War Amendments. It officially prohibited slavery in all states, and with certain exceptions (such as in the case of convicts) involuntary servitude. Immediately prior to its ratification in December 1865, slavery remained legal in only two states, Kentucky and Delaware. (Slavery in the former confederate states had been outlawed by the Emancipation Proclamation of 1863.)

Amendment XIV (1868)

Section 1. All persons born or naturalized in the United States, and subject to the jurisdiction thereof, are citizens of the United States and of the state wherein they reside.

No state shall make or enforce any law which shall abridge the privileges or immunities of citizens of the United States; nor shall any state deprive any person of life, liberty, or property, without due process of law; nor deny to any person within its jurisdiction the equal protection of the laws.

Section 2. Representatives shall be apportioned among the several states according to their respective numbers, counting the whole number of persons in each state, excluding Indians not taxed. But when the right to vote at any election for the choice of electors for President and Vice President of the United States, Representatives in Congress, the executive and judicial officers of a state, or the members of the legislature thereof, is denied to any of the male inhabitants of such state, being twenty-one years of age, and citizens of the United States, or in any way abridged, except for participation in rebellion, or other crime, the basis of representation therein shall be reduced in the proportion which the number of such male citizens shall bear to the whole number of male citizens twenty-one years of age in such state.

Section 3. No person shall be a Senator or Representative in Congress, or elector of President and Vice President, or hold any office, civil or military, under the United States, or under any state, who, having previously taken an oath, as a member of Congress, or as an officer of the United States, or as a member of any state legislature, or as an executive or judicial officer of any state, to support the Constitution of the United States, shall have engaged in insurrection or rebellion against the same, or given aid or comfort to the enemies thereof. But Congress may by a vote of two-thirds of each House, remove such disability.

Section 4. The validity of the public debt of the United States, authorized by law, including debts incurred for payment of pensions and bounties for services in suppressing insurrection or rebellion, shall not be questioned. But neither the United States nor any state shall assume or pay any debt or obligation incurred in aid of insurrection or rebellion against the United States, or any claim for the loss or emancipation of any slave; but all such debts, obligations and claims shall be held illegal and void.

Section 5. The Congress shall have power to enforce, by appropriate legislation, the provisions of this article.

The Fourteenth Amendment was ratified in an attempt to secure rights for freed slaves by broadening the definition of national citizenship and offering all persons equal protection of the law as well as due process of law from state governments. In the Slaughterhouse Cases (1873), the Supreme Court held that the privileges and immunities of national citizenship are actually quite limited: they include visiting the seat of government, petitioning Congress, using the nation's navigable waters, and other narrow privileges. By contrast, the equal protection clause provided the basis during the twentieth century for dismantling legally enforced segregation in Brown v. Board of Education (1954) and other cases. It also has been used to extend equal protection to groups other than African Americans, including women and other ethnic minorities. Of equal significance, the Supreme Court has also interpreted the equal protection clause to require states to apportion their congressional districts and state legislative seats on a "one-person, one-vote" basis.

The due process clause has been interpreted to provide procedural safeguards before the government deprives a person of life, liberty, or property. More controversially, in the early part of the twentieth century the Supreme Court in Lochner v. New York (1905) interpreted the clause as providing substantive protection to private contracts and other economic agreements. In later rulings the clause sparked considerable controversy when the Court used

it as the basis for protecting substantive privacy rights not explic-
itly spelled out in the Constitution, such as that of a woman's right
to an abortion (in the Court's 1973 Roe v. Wade decision), and of
homosexual sodomy (in its 2003 ruling in Lawrence v. Texas).

Amendment XV (1870)

Section 1. The right of citizens of the United States to vote shall not be denied or abridged by the United States or by any state on account of race, color, or previous condition of servitude.

Section 2. The Congress shall have power to enforce this article by appropriate legislation.

> *The Fifteenth Amendment was ratified in order to enfranchise all*
> *the former male slaves. (As was the case with all women, former*
> *female slaves would have to wait for passage of the Nineteenth*
> *Amendment to gain the franchise.) Unfortunately, the promise of*
> *the franchise was subsequently undermined in many states by the*
> *proliferation of rigorous voter qualification laws, including literacy*
> *tests and poll taxes. Not until passage of the Voting Rights Act of*
> *1965 and the elimination of poll taxes did the franchise become a*
> *reality for African American voters in many parts of the South.*

Amendment XVI (1913)

The Congress shall have power to lay and collect taxes on incomes, from whatever source derived, without apportionment among the several states, and without regard to any census of enumeration.

> *The Sixteenth Amendment was ratified in response to the Supreme*
> *Court's controversial decision in Pollack v. Farmer's Loan & Trust Co.*
> *(1895), which held that a tax on incomes derived from property was a*
> *"direct tax." Prior to the Pollack case, income taxes had been considered*
> *"indirect" taxes, and thus well within the powers given to Congress by the*
> *Constitution. "Direct taxes," by contrast, could be imposed only if they*
> *were apportioned among the states according to each state's population*
> *(Article I, Section 9). The effect of the Pollack decision was to make an*
> *income tax all but impractical; the Sixteenth Amendment remedied the*
> *situation by placing income taxes back in the category of "indirect taxes."*

Amendment XVII (1913)

The Senate of the United States shall be composed of two Senators from each state, elected by the people thereof, for six years; and each Senator shall have one vote. The electors in each state shall have the qualifications requisite for electors of the most numerous branch of the state legislatures.

When vacancies happen in the representation of any state in the Senate, the executive authority of such state shall issue writs of election to fill such vacancies: Provided, that the legislature of any state may empower the executive thereof to make temporary appointments until the people fill the vacancies by election as the legislature may direct.

This amendment shall not be so construed as to affect the election or term of any Senator chosen before it becomes valid as part of the Constitution.

> *The Seventeenth Amendment changed the method by which U.S. sena-*
> *tors were elected, overturning the provisions in Article I, Section 3. The*

amendment was the culmination of an extended effort of Progressive Era reformers at the beginning of the twentieth century, who frequently targeted institutions marked by economic privilege and corrupt politics. Eventually they demanded that U.S. senators should be more responsive to the public will—the best way to accomplish that goal was to require that senators should be chosen by popular election, rather than by state legislatures. Prior to the amendment's ratification, many states had already amended their primary laws to allow a popular vote for party nominees, and a handful of states had bound their respective legislatures to select the candidate who received the highest number of popular votes in the general election. The Seventeenth Amendment soon followed, receiving the approval of the required number of states (three fourths) less than a year after it was first introduced.

Amendment XVIII (1919)

Section 1. After one year from the ratification of this article the manufacture, sale, or transportation of intoxicating liquors within, the importation thereof into, or the exportation thereof from the United States and all territory subject to the jurisdiction thereof for beverage purposes is hereby prohibited.

Section 2. The Congress and the several states shall have concurrent power to enforce this article by appropriate legislation.

Section 3. This article shall be inoperative unless it shall have been ratified as an amendment to the Constitution by the legislatures of the several states, as provided in the Constitution, within seven years from the date of the submission hereof to the states by the Congress.

> *The Eighteenth Amendment slipped into the Constitution on the strength of efforts by the Anti-Saloon League and other groups who believed that intoxicating liquors were harmful and sinful. The amendment was proposed immediately after the end of World War I, and the Prohibition era began a year after its formal ratification on January 16, 1919.*

Amendment XIX (1920)

The right of citizens of the United States to vote shall not be denied or abridged by the United States or by any state on account of sex.

Congress shall have power to enforce this article by appropriate legislation.

> *The Nineteenth Amendment was a reform spurred by the Progressive movement. Although women had been fighting for their right to vote since before the Civil War, the drive for woman suffrage started achieving success only with the entry of Western states such as Wyoming, which extended the right to vote to women upon its admission to the Union in 1890. (Five other Western states followed suit in subsequent decades.) By concentrating their efforts on a federal constitutional amendment guaranteeing women the right to vote, woman suffrage activists brought immediate pressure to bear on Congress and the president to support the movement. With momentum clearly on its side, the Nineteenth Amendment was ratified less than fifteen months after it was first proposed.*

Amendment XX (1933)

Section 1. The terms of the President and Vice President shall end at noon on the 20th day of January, and the terms of Senators and Representatives at noon on the 3d day of

January, of the years in which such terms would have ended if this article had not been ratified; and the terms of their successors shall then begin.

Section 2. The Congress shall assemble at least once in every year, and such meeting shall begin at noon on the 3d day of January, unless they shall by law appoint a different day.

Section 3. If, at the time fixed for the beginning of the term of the President, the President elect shall have died, the Vice President elect shall become President. If a President shall not have been chosen before the time fixed for the beginning of his term, or if the President elect shall have failed to qualify, then the Vice President elect shall act as President until a President shall have qualified; and the Congress may by law provide for the case wherein neither a President elect nor a Vice President elect shall have qualified, declaring who shall then act as President, or the manner in which one who is to act shall be selected, and such person shall act accordingly until a President or Vice President shall have qualified.

Section 4. The Congress may by law provide for the case of the death of any of the persons from whom the House of Representatives may choose a President whenever the right of choice shall have devolved upon them, and for the case of the death of any of the persons from whom the Senate may choose a Vice President whenever the right of choice shall have devolved upon them.

Section 5. Sections 1 and 2 shall take effect on the 15th day of October following the ratification of this article.

Section 6. This article shall be inoperative unless it shall have been ratified as an amendment to the Constitution by the legislatures of three-fourths of the several states within seven years from the date of its submission.

The Twentieth Amendment brought an end to the excessively long period of time between the November election and the March inauguration of a new president. Given advances in transportation and communications systems over the previous century, such a delay in the president taking office—with the outgoing president reluctant to act even during times of crisis—could no longer be justified. The amendment also limited Congress's lame duck sessions that followed the November elections: newly elected members of Congress could now begin their service to constituents in early January, rather than waiting thirteen months until the following December. Finally, the amendment authorized Congress to provide for a line of succession in the event that neither a president-elect nor a vice president–elect qualified to serve by the January 20th date.

Amendment XXI (1933)

Section 1. The eighteenth article of amendment to the Constitution of the United States is hereby repealed.

Section 2. The transportation or importation into any state, territory, or possession of the United States for delivery or use therein of intoxicating liquors, in violation of the laws thereof, is hereby prohibited.

Section 3. This article shall be inoperative unless it shall have been ratified as an amendment to the Constitution by conventions in the several states, as provided in the Constitution, within seven years from the date of the submission hereof to the states by the Congress.

The Twenty-first Amendment repealed Prohibition. The enforcement of the Eighteenth Amendment had proven too difficult and expensive, as thousands of illegal sources arose to meet the continuing public demand for alcohol. Crime gangs involved in the illegal liquor trade spread violence and bloodshed throughout the nation, which pressured politicians to end Prohibition. Finally, when both political parties came out in favor of repeal during the 1932 election, Prohibition's days were clearly numbered. After the Twenty-first Amendment was ratified on December 5, 1933, states would thereafter have the exclusive power to prevent the import and use of liquor in their respective jurisdictions.

Amendment XXII (1951)

Section 1. No person shall be elected to the office of the President more than twice, and no person who has held the office of President, or acted as President, for more than two years of a term to which some other person was elected President shall be elected to the office of the President more than once. But this article shall not apply to any person holding the office of President when this article was proposed by the Congress, and shall not prevent any person who may be holding the office of President, or acting as President, during the term within which this article becomes operative from holding the office of President or acting as President during the remainder of such term.

Section 2. This article shall be inoperative unless it shall have been ratified as an amendment to the Constitution by the legislatures of three-fourths of the several states within seven years from the date of its submission to the states by the Congress.

Franklin Roosevelt's election to a record fourth term as president in 1944 sent politicians clamoring for a means of restoring the unwritten two-term tradition originally established by George Washington. Within two years of FDR's death, Congress proposed the Twenty-second Amendment, and it was adopted soon thereafter. In addition to setting a limit on the number of terms (two) to which a president may be elected, the amendment also sets a maximum of ten years less one day for a president to serve in the event he or she also succeeds to a part of another president's term. The amendment was worded so as not to apply to the then-sitting president, Harry S Truman, but it has applied to Dwight Eisenhower and all other presidents since.

Amendment XXIII (1961)

Section 1. The District constituting the seat of government of the United States shall appoint in such manner as the Congress may direct:

A number of electors of President and Vice President equal to the whole number of Senators and Representatives in Congress to which the District would be entitled if it were a state, but in no event more than the least populous state; they shall be in addition to those appointed by the states, but they shall be considered, for the purposes of the election of President and Vice President, to be electors appointed by a state; and they shall meet in the District and perform such duties as provided by the twelfth article of amendment.

Section 2. The Congress shall have power to enforce this article by appropriate legislation.

The Twenty-third Amendment cured the anomaly of U.S. citizens being denied the right to vote for federal officials (including president of the United States) so long as they remained permanent residents of the District of Columbia. Since ratification of the amendment in 1961, DC residents have been entitled to vote for presidential and vice-presidential candidates, but the amendment did not authorize residents of DC to elect members to either branch of Congress. Nor did it provide DC residents with home rule or the power to run their own local government. Since 1973 Congress has authorized the DC government to be run primarily by locally elected officials, subject to the oversight and supervision of Congress.

Amendment XXIV (1964)

Section 1. The right of citizens of the United States to vote in any primary or other election for President or Vice President, for electors for President or Vice President, or for Senator or Representative in Congress, shall not be denied or abridged by the United States or any state by reason of failure to pay any poll tax or other tax.

Section 2. The Congress shall have power to enforce this article by appropriate legislation.

The Twenty-fourth Amendment eliminated yet another vestige of legally enforced racism in the South and elsewhere. Many states had already eliminated the requirement that voters pay a tax before voting, a restriction that created an undue hardship on lower economic classes, including disproportionate numbers of racial minorities. Still, as late as 1964, five states (Alabama, Arkansas, Mississippi, Texas, and Virginia) continued to tie a poll tax to the voting privilege. In 1966 the Supreme Court ruled in Harper v. Board of Education *that poll taxes also violated the equal protection clause of the Fourteenth Amendment.*

Amendment XXV (1967)

Section 1. In case of the removal of the President from office or of his death or resignation, the Vice President shall become President.

Section 2. Whenever there is a vacancy in the office of the Vice President, the President shall nominate a Vice President who shall take office upon confirmation by a majority vote of both Houses of Congress.

Section 3. Whenever the President transmits to the President pro tempore of the Senate and the Speaker of the House of Representatives his written declaration that he is unable to discharge the powers and duties of his office, and until he transmits to them a written declaration to the contrary, such powers and duties shall be discharged by the Vice President as Acting President.

Section 4. Whenever the Vice President and a majority of either the principal officers of the executive departments or of such other body as Congress may by law provide, transmit to the President pro tempore of the Senate and the Speaker of the House of Representatives their written declaration that the President is unable to discharge the powers and duties of his office, the Vice President shall immediately assume the powers and duties of the office as Acting President.

Thereafter, when the President transmits to the President pro tempore of the Senate and the Speaker of the House of Representatives his written declaration that no inability exists, he shall resume the powers and duties of his office unless the Vice President and a majority of either the principal officers of the executive department or of such other body as Congress may by law provide, transmit within four days to the President pro tempore of the Senate and the Speaker of the House of Representatives their written declaration that the President is unable to discharge the powers and duties of his office. Thereupon Congress shall decide the issue, assembling within forty-eight hours for that purpose if not in session. If the Congress, within twenty-one days after receipt of the latter written declaration, or, if Congress is not in session, within twenty-one days after Congress is required to assemble, determines by two-thirds vote of both Houses that the President is unable to discharge the powers and duties of his office, the Vice President shall continue to discharge the same as Acting President; otherwise, the President shall resume the powers and duties of his office.

The Twenty-fifth Amendment clarified several ambiguous aspects of presidential succession. At the outset, it formalized an unwritten precedent first established by John Tyler, who succeeded to the presidency upon the death of William Henry Harrison in 1841: If the office of president becomes vacant because of the president's death or resignation, the vice president becomes president and assumes all powers and duties of the office. If the vice presidency is vacant, the amendment establishes new procedures for filling the position between elections: the president nominates a successor, to be confirmed by a majority vote of both houses of Congress. Since its adoption in 1967, two vice presidents have been selected in this manner: Gerald Ford in 1973, and Nelson Rockefeller in 1974. When Gerald Ford succeeded to the presidency upon the resignation of Richard Nixon in 1974, he became the first—and to date, the only—president in American history to hold that office without being formally elected to either the presidency or the vice presidency.

The amendment also addresses the vexing problem of presidential disabilities. In the early twentieth century, Woodrow Wilson was an invalid for more than a year of his presidency; in the 1950s, Dwight Eisenhower suffered a stroke once during each of his two terms in office. The Twenty-fifth Amendment addresses the problem of presidential disability by providing procedures for the president to temporarily discharge the duties and powers of the office to the officer next in line (normally the vice president), who then becomes "acting president." This has happened only twice: in 1985, when Vice President George H. W. Bush received a transmission of power temporarily while President Ronald Reagan underwent a minor medical procedure; and in 2002, when President George W. Bush temporarily transferred his powers to Vice President Dick Cheney while he underwent a colonoscopy. The amendment further authorizes the vice president and certain members of the executive branch to declare the president disabled or incapacitated, subject (within twenty-seven days) to Congress upholding the finding of incapacity. This final provision has never been invoked.

Amendment XXVI (1971)

Section 1. The right of citizens of the United States, who are 18 years of age or older, to vote, shall not be denied or abridged by the United States or any state on account of age.

Section 2. The Congress shall have the power to enforce this article by appropriate legislation.

The Twenty-sixth Amendment extended suffrage to those age eighteen and older. At the time of its passage, soldiers under the age of twenty-one were fighting in Vietnam, creating intense pressure on Congress and state legislatures to extend the vote to all those who were old enough to fight. The amendment does not apply to the denial of rights other than voting to those who are between eighteen and twenty-one years of age. Thus the National Minimum Drinking Age

*Act of 1984 obliges states to establish a twenty-one-year-old drinking
age or risk the loss of federal highway funds. Additionally, Utah and
Alaska have established nineteen as the minimum age for tobacco use.*

Amendment XXVII (1992)

No law, varying the compensation for the services of the Senators and Representatives,
shall take effect, until an election of Representatives shall have intervened.

*The Twenty-seventh Amendment was intended to serve as a
restraint on the power of Congress to raise its own pay—it may
only do so if the raise takes effect after a subsequent general election. Although the Supreme Court has never ruled on the issue,
lower courts have held that this amendment does not prevent Congress from receiving cost of living adjustments immediately.*

FEDERALISM

The national cemetery at Gettysburg, where states' rights were contested most violently in 1863.

LEARNING OBJECTIVES

WHAT IS FEDERALISM?

- Define *federalism* and compare it to other forms of government, including confederations and unitary systems of government

- Explain how the Constitution differentiates between federal government powers, state government powers, and concurrent powers

- Describe the powers accorded to Congress under Article I

- Explain the significance of the supremacy clause, the preemption doctrine, and the full faith and credit clause of Article IV in distributing sovereignty

THE HISTORY OF AMERICAN FEDERALISM

- Define the five eras of American federalism and assess the role played by the Supreme Court in articulating state–federal relations during each era

- Evaluate different forms of federalism (layer-cake federalism versus marble-cake federalism) in the modern era

WHY FEDERALISM? ADVANTAGES AND DISADVANTAGES

- Identify the advantages and disadvantages of federalism in terms of fairness and accountability

The term *federal* comes from the Latin *foedus*, which means a covenant, or an agreement linking different entities. A federal (or federated) system of government is one in which power is divided between a central authority and constituent political subunits. Both types of government are linked in order to provide for the pursuit of common ends; at the same time, each government maintains its own integrity. Federalism, the doctrine underlying such a system, generally requires the existence of a central government tier and at least one major subnational tier of governments (usually referred to as "states" or "provinces"). Each tier is then assigned its own significant government powers. What may sound simple in the abstract has proven quite difficult to implement and practice. How exactly does a political system divide sovereignty between two thriving branches of government without creating animosities among the competing branches that may threaten to undermine the system in the first place?

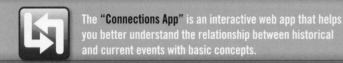

The "Connections App" is an interactive web app that helps you better understand the relationship between historical and current events with basic concepts.

1830 1840 1850 1860 1870

1850

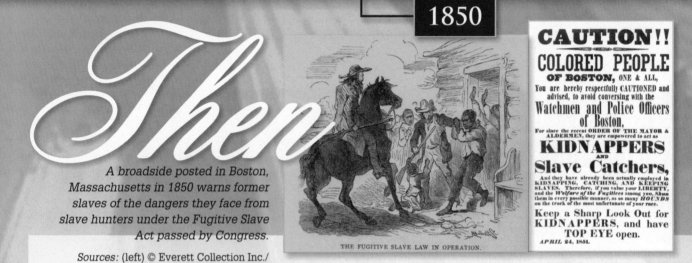

Then

A broadside posted in Boston, Massachusetts in 1850 warns former slaves of the dangers they face from slave hunters under the Fugitive Slave Act passed by Congress.

THE FUGITIVE SLAVE LAW IN OPERATION.

CAUTION!!
COLORED PEOPLE
OF BOSTON, ONE & ALL,
You are hereby respectfully CAUTIONED and advised, to avoid conversing with the
Watchmen and Police Officers of Boston,
For since the recent ORDER OF THE MAYOR & ALDERMEN, they are empowered to act as
KIDNAPPERS
AND
Slave Catchers,
And they have already been actually employed in KIDNAPPING, CATCHING, AND KEEPING SLAVES. Therefore, if you value your LIBERTY, and the *Welfare of the Fugitives* among you, *Shun* them in every possible manner, as so many *HOUNDS* on the track of the most unfortunate of your race.
Keep a Sharp Look Out for
KIDNAPPERS, and have
TOP EYE open.
APRIL 24, 1851.

Sources: (left) © Everett Collection Inc./ Alamy, (right) Picture History/Newscom

Though Congress often injects itself into the most hotly debated issues of the times, state governments and their own agendas are never far from the battle. Indeed, in a system of federalism such as ours, some state interests are often responsible for spurring federal legislation forward, while competing state interests are busy offering resistance at every turn. Consider that by 1850, slave states had grown tired of Congress's half-hearted efforts at stopping fugitive slaves from escaping their southern masters; though the federal legislature had passed a series of fugitive slave laws during the late eighteenth and early- to mid-nineteenth centuries, none were effective at overcoming Northern resistance. Certainly none of them proved as far reaching or as tough as Congress's final effort in this regard: the Fugitive Slave Act of 1850. Southern officials had insisted on federal legislation that protected their states' interests through heightened judicial enforcement; accordingly, the 1850 act—passed as part of the overall Compromise of 1850—offered slave states unprecedented protection from Northern resistors. The provisions of the law included: (1) harsh penalties imposed on marshals who refused to enforce the law; (2) the virtual elimination of jury trials that favored the fugitive; and (3) the establishment of so-called "special commissioners" with jurisdiction to enforce the law, with or without the assistance of courts. Of course with Southern interests now emboldened, frustrated officials from Northern states continued to fight back. Eight Northern state legislatures passed so-called "Personal Liberty Laws" between 1850 and 1854—all directed at undermining the Fugitive Slave Act by forbidding the use of state jails and requiring that bounty hunters provide more elaborate proof. Clearly state governments from different regions were at loggerheads, but that didn't stop the two sides from increasingly exerting their respective wills on Congress. With room for compromise slowly dwindling, this battle over states' rights and the implications of federalism would rage on for another decade until a Civil War would resolve the issue of slavery once and for all.

2010

Now

Protesters rally against Arizona's immigration bill in front of the U.S. Supreme Court on April 25, 2012.

Source: Kevin Dietsch/UPI/Landov

Immigration has become ground zero in the latest wars over federalism, with states lining up for—or in many cases against—the compromises that have been crafted in Washington, D.C. Federal immigration law during the first part of the twenty-first century established rules specifying the treatment of aliens in the United States: all residents over the age of 14 who were born in or belong to another country, and who had not acquired U.S. citizenship, were required to register with the federal government if they remained in the United States for more than two weeks. Although federal law also requires that aliens maintain registration documents in their possession, the systematic enforcement of those provisions remains a thorny question, as border states in particular seek more stringent measures to discourage illegal immigration. In 2010, Arizona took an especially bold step in this direction when its legislature passed the Support Our Law Enforcement and Safe Neighborhoods Act, better known as SB 1070. The Arizona act made it a crime for an alien to be without registration documents at all times, and it authorized the police to arrest individuals if there was a "suspicion" that the persons were illegal immigrants. Viewing the law as a form of racial profiling, protests against the law were widespread. Many critics complained that the law was directed at those who merely "looked" like they were from foreign

countries, undermining federal immigration laws in the process. President Barack Obama declared that the law "undermined basic notions of fairness . . . as well as the trust between police and our communities . . ." and the Department of Justice eventually challenged the Arizona law in the U.S. Supreme Court. On June 25, 2012, the Court struck down most provisions of the Arizona law including (1) the requirement that all immigrants carry registration documents; and (2) the power of police to arrest a person on the mere suspicion that he or she is an illegal immigrant. At the same time, the Court gave a nod to states' interests by allowing Arizona police to investigate the status of legitimately stopped or detained individuals if there was also a "reasonable suspicion" that he or she was an illegal immigrant. Even as the Arizona law was being challenged in federal court, bills similar to SB 1070 were introduced in Pennsylvania, Rhode Island, Michigan, Minnesota, and South Carolina. The continued popularity of Arizona's controversial law in so many circles (and the various attempts to duplicate it elsewhere) thus revealed significant fissures on the question of immigration law more generally. Is there a role for states to play on that subject in a system that divides sovereignty between the state governments and the federal government?

As already noted, **federalism** is the doctrine underlying a political system in which power is divided between a central authority and constituent political subunits. For a system of federalism to maintain itself, it must sustain this division of powers by whatever means possible, including—but not limited to—a resort to the courts to define the proper bounds of authority. Perhaps the greatest challenge facing any federalist system is the task of determining **sovereignty**, defined as the supreme political power of a government to regulate its affairs without outside interference. In a system based on federalism, sovereignty resides not just in the central government, but also within each of the subunits, which in the case of the United States are the individual 50 states. Yet how can there be two separate sovereign governments sharing power over the exact same territory? The distribution of national and local responsibilities to more than one sovereign power depends on how the terms *national* and *local* are defined. These definitions are important, for a government based on federalism must both achieve national unity for certain overarching purposes and also preserve local governments' autonomy so they can respond to diverse subsets of citizens.

Related to these issues are complex questions concerning the nature of national citizenship. American federalism rests on the principle that two separate sovereigns—the state government and the federal government—both exert authority over the individual. But can an individual citizen really be subject to two separate sovereign governments at the same time? U.S. citizens have official status as citizens both of the state where they reside and of the nation as a whole. Many take pride in *both* associations. What remain unclear are the obligations and duties that dual citizenship requires. Is national citizenship every citizen's primary form of identification? To which sovereign government is the citizen obligated when the nation and individual states are in conflict? Although these conceptual difficulties tend to be unique to a federal system, there are other forms of government that involve multiple governments or tiers of government, and these alternative forms have significant problems of their own.

Comparing Federalism to Other Systems of Government

A federal system of government can be thought of as existing on a continuum of different forms of government. At one end of the continuum is a **confederation** (or "confederacy"), defined as a league of two or more independent states that unite to achieve certain specified common aims. Those aims may be quite limited, as is often the case with offensive or defensive military alliances. For example, the Articles of Confederation, which prescribed the rules of government for the newly independent colonies until 1788, featured 13 states entering into "a firm league of friendship with each other, for their common defense, the security of their liberties, and their mutual and general welfare." Recently the European Community, a collection of European nations united in a commercial alliance, has acquired its own status as a type of confederation.[1] Similarly, the United Nations is a league of countries from around the world that work together to enforce various provisions of international law. Although a confederation may be a useful arrangement to achieve some aims, it can result in political chaos, as when separate member countries bound only by limited rules strike out on their own at critical times, often to the detriment of the larger confederation.

At the other end of the continuum is a **unitary system of government**, which subordinates the independent aims of constituent states (if any even exist) to the goals of the central whole. Although individual states within such a government may enjoy some form of representation in the central legislature (such as through the election of state senators) and may even assert their own systems of municipal law, sovereignty rests in the central government alone, with states exerting authority over citizens only through the larger government entity. Of the Western industrialized nations, Great Britain and France perhaps come closest to this unitary government ideal, with their provinces and subunits having little or no power independent of the national government. Problems with a unitary system of government often arise from the tendency toward *hypercentralism*, that is, the more or less complete reliance on the central government and the extinguishing of individual state differences. Such a system often hampers local officials from responding to the particular needs of their varying constituencies.

---

federalism: The doctrine underlying a system of government in which power is divided between a central government and constituent political subunits.

---

sovereignty: The supreme political power of a government to regulate its affairs without outside interference.

---

confederation: A system of government (or "league") in which two or more independent states unite to achieve certain specified common aims.

---

unitary system of government: A system of government in which the constituent states are strictly subordinated to the goals of the central government as a whole.

As Figure 3.1 shows, a federal system of government sits in the middle of this continuum, granting its member states significant power but still subordinating them to the national government in critical instances. James Madison believed this federal system was the preferred "middle ground" of government types. At least 20 countries today, including Canada, Germany, Australia, and Switzerland, may be characterized as federal systems. It is the

FIGURE 3.1 Comparing Systems of Government

These three figures illustrate the most common configurations for (1) federal systems of government, (2) unitary systems of government, and (3) confederate systems of government. The directions of the arrows indicate the relationship that exists between the different forms of government. Note the two-way arrows found in the federal system.

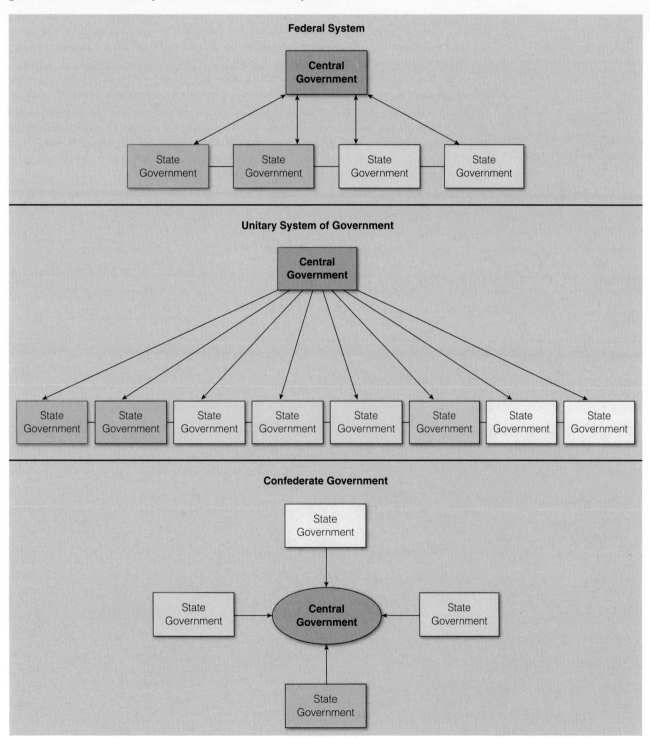

United States' brand of federalism, however—first established with the ratification of the Constitution in 1788—that represents the most significant breakthrough in the evolution of this government type among modern nation-states.

Government Powers in a Federal System

Under the U.S. Constitution, the national government of the United States was formed to serve a community of 13 states, and each state delegated to the new central government significant powers while retaining full powers within its own constitutionally designated sphere of authority. The Framers of this new government relied on no overarching philosophy or political theory in designing this federalist form of government; federalism was simply a political compromise calculated to build consensus among them. The powers delegated to Congress under Article I of the Constitution are called enumerated powers. The powers retained by the states are **reserved powers**. And the powers shared by the federal and state governments are generally referred to as **concurrent powers** (see Table 3.1).

Article I, Section 8 enumerates the specific powers held by the national legislature. Among these are economic powers such as the authority to levy and collect taxes, borrow money, coin money, and regulate interstate commerce and bankruptcies; military powers such as the authority to provide for the common defense, declare war, raise and support armies and navies, and regulate the militia; and legislative powers such as the authority to establish regulations governing immigration and naturalization. Congress also enjoys the prerogative to make laws that are "necessary and proper" to carry out these foregoing powers.[2]

reserved powers: Those powers expressly retained by the state governments under the Constitution.

concurrent powers: Those powers shared by the federal and state governments under the Constitution.

TABLE 3.1   The Powers of the Federal and State Governments Under the Constitution

Federal Government Powers (Enumerated Powers)	State Government Powers (Reserved Powers)	Concurrent Powers (Shared Powers)
Borrow money on U.S. credit	Regulate intrastate commerce	Spend money for general welfare
Regulate foreign commerce	Regulate state militias	Regulate interstate commerce
Regulate commerce with Indian nations	Conduct elections/qualify voters	Establish bankruptcy laws
Conduct foreign affairs	Regulate safety/health/morals	Lay and collect taxes
Coin money/punish counterfeiting	Ratify amendments	Charter/regulate banks
Establish courts inferior to Supreme Court		Establish courts
Establish post offices		Establish highways
Establish patent/copyright laws		Take private property for public purposes (with compensation)
Define/punish high-seas offenses		
Declare war		
Raise and support armies, navies		
Call forth militias		
Govern District of Columbia matters		
Admit new states to the Union		
Establish rules of naturalization		

Source: © Cengage Learning

On its face, the Constitution appears to draw clear and explicit lines between the powers afforded the state and national governments. In brief, the national government is to assume responsibility for great matters of national importance, including the protection of national economic interests, relations with other countries, and the military security of the United States. All local and/or internal matters—including the health, safety, and welfare of citizens—were to be to the province of state governments. Indeed, in a delayed victory for states' rights advocates who had opposed the proposed constitution before its ratification, the Tenth Amendment restates this fundamental division of powers: that any specific power not assigned to the federal government by the Constitution may be exercised by the states, unless the Constitution prohibits the states from exercising that power.

The Framers of the Constitution believed that Congress should legislate only within its enumerated powers under Article I; in their view the **necessary and proper clause** (later referred to as the elastic clause) was *not* to be used as an instrument to expand federal legislative authority unnecessarily. Yet within a few years, competing views of the necessary and proper clause would arise, giving the national government far more discretion in determining how to carry out its enumerated powers.

The Supremacy Clause

Overlaying this explicit system of enumerated powers for Congress and reserved powers for the states is the **supremacy clause** of Article VI, which provides that the Constitution and the laws passed by Congress shall be "the supreme law of the land," overriding any conflicting provisions in state constitutions or state laws. The supremacy clause gives special weight to the federal Constitution by ensuring that it cannot be interpreted differently from state to state. In the landmark case of *Martin v. Hunter's Lessee* (1816),[3] the U.S. Supreme Court rejected the Virginia Supreme Court's attempt to interpret the federal Constitution in a way that conflicted with the U.S. Supreme Court's own rulings. Accordingly, each state legislature and state judiciary not only must abide by the terms of the federal Constitution, it must also abide by the interpretation of those terms laid out by the U.S. Supreme Court.

The language of the supremacy clause also gives rise to the doctrine of preemption. When Congress exercises power granted to it under Article I, the federal law it creates may supersede state laws, in effect "preempting" state authority. In practice, when a federal law clearly bars state action, the doctrine of **preemption** is relatively uncontroversial. For example, when the federal government acted to regulate the commercial advertising of tobacco products, it essentially "occupied the field," and all state rules governing tobacco advertising immediately gave way to the new federal standard. But when Congress enacts a law that does not clearly articulate its intentions with regard to state laws, a court may have to decide whether the doctrine of preemption applies, subject to later court review. In addition, Congress's lack of action within its enumerated powers opens the door to limited state regulations. For example, a state government can enact transportation regulations affecting truck drivers in the state so long as Congress has not passed any similar laws and the state law does not burden interstate commerce.

Relations Between the States

A federalist system must not only manage relations between the state governments and the federal government, it must also arbitrate disagreements among member states. A feature of American federalism in this regard is the requirement that individual states must respect the civil laws of all other states, as guaranteed by the **full faith and credit clause** of Article IV, Section 1 of the Constitution. This clause provides that each state must abide by the decisions of other state and local governments, including their judicial proceedings. This clause acts to assure stability in commercial and personal relations that extend beyond one state's borders. For example, contracts duly entered into in California under the laws of that state cannot simply be ignored or invalidated by the courts in Arizona or any other state. Similarly, when an unhappy married couple meets the legal requirements of divorce in one state and ends their marriage, they are not required to meet new divorce requirements in other states,

necessary and proper clause: The clause in Article I, Section 8 of the Constitution that affords Congress the power to make laws that serve as a means to achieving its expressly delegated powers.

supremacy clause: The provision in Article VI, Clause 2 of the Constitution that provides that the Constitution and federal laws override any conflicting provisions in state constitutions or state laws.

Martin v. Hunter's Lessee (1816): The Supreme Court case that established that state governments and state courts must abide by the U.S. Supreme Court's interpretation of the federal Constitution.

preemption: The constitutional doctrine that holds that when Congress acts affirmatively in the exercise of its own granted power, federal laws supersede all state laws on the matter.

Under the Constitution, a legal marriage performed and executed by the state of Nevada must be honored fully by the state of Texas.

Fact.

The full faith and credit clause of Article IV requires that every state in the United States respect the public proceedings of every other state. Though the Defense of Marriage Act of 1996 aimed to create an exception to this principle in the case of same-sex marriages, the Obama administration indicated that it would refuse to defend the law's constitutionality in court.

Gay marriage ceremony in Massachusetts.

Ellis Island.

On a Florida highway, Florida state police may target out-of-state vehicles for speeding tickets as a way of discouraging out-of-state businesspersons from stealing business from in-state entities.

Fiction.

The privileges and immunities clause of Article IV prevents states from treating citizens of other states in a discriminatory manner when they pursue a profession or trade in that state.

as the divorce decree of one state must be recognized as valid by every other state.

Even though the full faith and credit clause has traditionally required states to respect the public proceedings of every other state, many state legislatures have attempted to prevent same-sex couples from asserting their newfound status as married couples. At least 31 states have at some point passed laws denying recognition to same-sex marriages. In denying this recognition, these states enjoy the theoretical support of Congress, which in 1996 passed the Defense of Marriage Act, authorizing any state to deny a "marriage-like" relationship between persons of the same sex, even when such unions are recognized by another state.

These states have not received the energetic and full-hearted support of all recent presidents, however: the Obama administration announced in 2011 that while it would continue to enforce the law, it would no longer defend it as constitutional in court. Ultimately, the U.S. Supreme Court may have to once and for all resolve whether the Defense of Marriage Act and similar laws passed at the state level unconstitutionally evade the full faith and credit clause of the Constitution.

Another clause that provides for the equal treatment of out-of-state citizens is the privileges and immunities clause of Article IV. Through this clause, which guarantees that the citizens of each state are "entitled to all Privileges and Immunities of Citizens in the several States," the Constitution protects the rights of every citizen to travel through other states, to reside in any state, and to participate in trade, agriculture, and professional pursuits in any state.[4] Some states have tried to limit memberships to in-state residents, or to impose hefty commuter taxes on out-of-staters who cross state lines each day for work. Such legislative efforts potentially conflict with the privileges and immunities clause. Article IV also provides that the criminal laws of individual states must be respected across state lines. When a criminal in one state escapes to another state, he or she is normally "extradited" or handed over to the original state either to stand trial or to complete a previously imposed sentence.

Article III, Section 2 of the Constitution gives the U.S. Supreme Court the authority to decide disputes between states. Although such jurisdiction is rarely exercised, the Court has taken its responsibility to arbitrate state conflicts seriously on those occasions when it has been asked to do so. For example, when officials in New York and New Jersey were battling in the late 1990s over which of those two states could claim sovereign authority over Ellis Island, the site where millions of immigrants to the United States were initially processed, the Supreme Court authorized a fact-finding investigation on the issue. Presented with the evidence of that investigation, the Court ruled that Ellis Island was within the state boundaries of New Jersey—news no doubt to the millions of immigrants who thought they had disembarked in New York.[5] The Framers of the Constitution believed it was critically important that the highest federal court enjoy the power to arbitrate disputes between state governments, a key component of American federalism.

THE HISTORY OF AMERICAN FEDERALISM

In the more than two centuries that have passed since the ratification of the Constitution, different conceptions of federalism have prevailed during different eras. Some of these shifting patterns in state–federal relations were inevitable given the changing state of the nation and the increasingly important role it would play in world politics. The dominance of a

CHECK THE LIST

Dramatic Variations in State-Level Approaches to Health Care

Federalism affords state governments considerable discretion in choosing what social services to provide to their citizens; accordingly, states services differ dramatically. Indeed, the recent controversy over the Obama administration's health care reform legislation may have obscured a more fundamental point about health care in America: that there remains tremendous variation among individual states in the nature of health care insurance and access to care. Consider some telling examples: whereas the percentage of insured adults in Massachusetts (where coverage is now mandatory) is 93 percent, it is just 69 percent in Texas. And while only 33 percent of diabetics in Mississippi receive recommended care, in Minnesota, that figure doubles to nearly 67 percent.

In 2009 *Forbes* magazine publicized a study from the New York–based Commonwealth Fund that measured "the best states for health care" according to five measures: (1) access to health care, (2) prevention and treatment, (3) potentially avoidable hospital use and costs, (4) health care differences among ethnic and income groups, and (5) "healthy lives." According to the study, the top 10 states were as follows:

1. Vermont
2. Hawaii
3. Iowa (tie)
4. Minnesota
5. Maine

6. New Hampshire (tie)
7. Massachusetts
8. Connecticut
9. North Dakota
10. Wisconsin

▶ **POINT TO PONDER:** While midwestern and New England states dominate the top of this list, Great Plains states, Pacific coast states (excluding Hawaii), and the southern states are nowhere to be found. Are attitudes toward health care based in part on region? Why would states in New England and the Midwest be more concerned about access to health care?

Source: Brian Wingfield and Aleksandra Kulczuga, "The Best States for Health Care," Forbes.com. October 9, 2009 (see http://www.forbes.com/2009/10/09/best-states-healthcare-business-washington-reform.html).

---

global economy in the late twentieth and early-twenty-first centuries, changing patterns in population growth, and technological developments in communication and transportation all spurred wholesale reexamination of the nature of federal and state governmental functions. Various government figures—presidents, Supreme Court justices, and members of Congress—have also played a role in shaping the nature of federalism. The flexibility of the federalist system has allowed it to adapt to changing circumstances.

Although a clear delineation of periods may oversimplify history, scholars have identified at least five eras of American federalism:

1. state-centered federalism, 1789–1819;
2. national supremacy period, 1819–1837;
3. dual federalism, 1837–1937;
4. cooperative federalism, 1937–1990; and
5. the "new federalism," 1990–present.

Each of these periods is defined by some shift in the power relationship between the national and state governments.

full faith and credit clause: The provision in Article IV, Section 1 of the Constitution that forces states to abide by the official acts and proceedings of all other states.

State-Centered Federalism, 1789–1819

The Framers' vision of federalism was relatively clear at the time the Constitution was ratified: other than in those policy areas clearly identified in Article I as subject to the national government's control (the military, foreign affairs, creation of currency, and so on), state governments would have full sovereignty over all other matters. Indeed, it is tough to imagine the Constitution being ratified by the requisite number of states had it called for any further subordination of traditional state authority. And with some notable exceptions, the national government's reach was exceedingly limited during the first 30 years of the Constitution's history.[6] At the urging of Treasury Secretary Alexander Hamilton, the Washington administration cautiously undertook some first steps in nationwide economic planning when it chartered the first National Bank of the United States and the federal government assumed all the debts of the state governments. Nevertheless, during this earliest period of federalism states remained the principal authority for American citizens. For the most part, each state managed its own affairs, often with little interference from the federal government.

National Supremacy Period, 1819–1837

Just before leaving office in 1801, President John Adams installed as chief justice of the Supreme Court a fellow nationalist, John Marshall of Virginia. That appointment may have been the most significant act of Adams's presidency; although the Federalists would never again occupy the White House or control Congress, the national-government-oriented party would influence American politics through Chief Justice Marshall for the next three decades.

national supremacy doctrine: Chief Justice John Marshall's interpretation of federalism as holding that states have extremely limited sovereign authority, whereas Congress is supreme within its own sphere of constitutional authority.

Marshall's **national supremacy doctrine** of federalism is most evident in the Supreme Court decision in ***McCulloch v. Maryland*** **(1819)**,[7] which concerned the National Bank of the United States. As Secretary of the Treasury during the Washington administration, Alexander Hamilton successfully pushed for Congress to charter the first bank of the United States in 1792, arguing that such an institution would help provide for a sound national currency and a national system of credit. Thomas Jefferson, then Secretary of State, and James Madison opposed the bank, believing that the Constitution gave Congress no authority to charter such a bank. Consequently, when the bank's 20-year charter expired, the Jeffersonian Republican–controlled Congress declined to recharter it. Recognizing that the lack of a national bank had hindered American efforts to obtain needed financial resources throughout the War of 1812, many in the Democratic-Republican Party, including Madison, who was now president, swallowed their pride and supported the chartering of a second national bank in 1816.

McCulloch v. Maryland (1819): The Supreme Court case that established that Congress enjoys broad and extensive authority to make all laws that are "necessary and proper" to carry out its constitutionally delegated powers.

Marshall's Court also refuted the power of state courts to interpret and apply the Constitution in ways that conflicted with the Supreme Court's own interpretations. Thus the Constitution assumed its status as the uniform governing law of all the states. To Marshall, the Court's duty was not to preserve state sovereignty, but rather "to protect national power against state encroachments." Consistent with this view, the Marshall Court routinely interpreted Congress's legislative authority quite broadly. In *Gibbons v. Ogden* (1824),[8] for example, the Court invalidated a monopoly granted by the New York legislature covering the operation of steamboats in New York waters, because the New York monopoly was in conflict with a federal license.

Gibbons v. Ogden (1824): The Supreme Court case that held that under the Constitution, a federal license to operate steamboats overrides a state-granted monopoly of New York water rights.

The national supremacy doctrine articulated by Marshall was not without its critics. State politicians accused the Court of ignoring the sovereign power of the states. Some national politicians were no less sympathetic. As president, Andrew Jackson opposed the National Bank and all internal improvements (such as the building of roads or canals) ordered by Congress as unconstitutional. He even vetoed a rechartering of the bank in 1832. Yet, at the same time, he also applied Marshall's national supremacy doctrine in defending the Tariff of 1828. After Congress passed a highly protectionist tariff over the objections of Southern free-trade adherents, the South Carolina legislature adopted a series of resolutions negating the tariff on the theory that state sovereignty allowed each state to nullify any law passed by Congress that the state deemed unconstitutional. (New Englanders had used that same argument during the War of 1812 when a convention of the region's states met in Hartford, Connecticut, in early 1815 and endorsed the right of states to interpose themselves against "dangerous infractions" of the Constitution by the federal government.) In response to the action by South Carolina, President Jackson declared that such a nullification was an "impractical absurdity" and rejected the right of individual states to refuse to obey federal laws. A call by South Carolina Senator John Calhoun and others for a "general convention of the states" to reconsider state–federal relations, including possible secession from the Union, elicited enthusiasm from numerous Southern states, but eventually the nullification crisis passed when Congress approved a compromise tariff that progressively lowered rates until they reached the same level they had been at in 1816.[9]

Although slavery was a crucial component of the fight between the Union and the Confederacy, the Civil War was at its core a struggle about the relationship between the states and the federal government. The Union's victory undermined dual federalism's "compact of states" premise by rejecting the authority of states to leave the compact. Then, in a series of cases handed down after the Civil War, a newly constituted Supreme Court acknowledged national power and congressional authority to set the terms for readmitting former Confederate states into the Union. This power was considered an outgrowth of Congress's exclusive and unquestioned authority not only to regulate the territories of the United States, but also to oversee the admission of new states to the Union. With 24 of the 50 states joining the Union between 1836 and 1912 (see Figure 3.2), admission to statehood was an important function of the federal government during this period.

Under **dual federalism**, however, the states did retain considerable authority to regulate economic affairs that were not directly within the "stream of commerce" between two or more states, including matters

Portrait of John Calhoun, circa 1830.

concerning the manufacturing of products and the health and safety of factory workers. Ignoring *McCulloch v. Maryland*, the Supreme Court refused to give Congress the discretionary authority it enjoyed during the era of the national supremacy doctrine. Regulatory legislation passed by Congress, such as child labor laws and many minimum wage laws, were set aside as unconstitutional. Once again the Court had greatly diminished the scope of the necessary and proper clause. Despite the onset of the Industrial Revolution, Congress was eventually rendered helpless to regulate the abuses of some businesses. Later, in the 1930s, the Court struck down a series of New Deal laws implementing pension and retirement systems for workers and regulating industrial relations.[10] In this way, dual federalism prevented Congress from addressing the hardships brought on by the Great Depression.

dual federalism: The doctrine of federalism that holds that state authority acts as a significant limit on congressional power under the Constitution.

FIGURE 3.2 Admission of States to the Union

Source: © Cengage Learning

Cooperative Federalism, 1937–1990

Faced with judicial opposition to New Deal policies regulating the workplace, retirement policies, and other subjects traditionally ceded to the states, President Franklin D. Roosevelt (FDR) and his supporters grew increasingly frustrated. To them, the economic hardships of the Great Depression demanded an activist federal government, and a conservative Supreme Court now stood in the way. FDR and his allies in Congress proposed slowly expanding the size of the Supreme Court from 9 to what would eventually become 15, which would allow Roosevelt to "pack" the Supreme Court with advocates of a broader vision of federal legislative power.[11] The proposed "court-packing plan" became unnecessary, however. As public frustration with the Court was mounting, one member of the Court in 1937 (Justice Owen Roberts) suddenly did an about-face, abandoning dual federalist principles in favor of a more expansive view of congressional authority. A shift in just one vote had a significant impact; a shift in two votes on the Supreme Court meant that nearly all federal legislation would now survive High Court scrutiny. Once Roosevelt was able to add his own judicial appointees to the mix, the Court as a whole was ready to support unprecedented exercises of congressional power.

Social scientists speak of the post–New Deal period as marking a shift from **layer-cake federalism**, in which the authority of state and federal governments is distinct and more easily delineated, to a system of **marble-cake federalism**, in which state and federal authority are intertwined in an inseparable mixture. This new era, later labeled as the period of **cooperative federalism**, in some ways harkened back to the national supremacy doctrine articulated by John Marshall. Congress once again became the judge of its own powers, including those powers implied under the necessary and proper clause. Congress could, for example, restrict the activities of labor unions, criminalize loan sharking, or enact any policy under the theory that it may be "necessary and proper" to exercise enumerated powers such as the power to regulate interstate commerce. The limits on congressional power under so-called cooperative federalism were thus quite small: so long as some link to commerce could be offered, for example, no matter how tenuous such a link might be, Congress remained free to exert its authority over the states. When Congress passed civil rights laws in 1964 under the premise that racial discrimination in restaurants and hotels "burdened" interstate commerce, the Supreme Court barely batted an eye at what was in fact an extremely broad reading of congressional authority.[12]

Cooperative federalism, however, can be distinguished from Marshall's doctrine of national superiority. Whenever concurrent legislative power is exercised, Congress can act in one of three ways:

1. Preempt the states altogether and assert exclusive control over the subject matter.

2. Leave the states to act on their own.

3. Provide that the operation of its own law depends on or is qualified by existing state laws.

This last category provides an opening in state–federal relationships that even Marshall could not have anticipated: the possibility that the federal government might actually enlist state officials and other state actors to implement federal policies.

The positive aspects of cooperative federalism are obvious. The expansion of the central government beginning in the 1930s into the $6.3-trillion-per-year behemoth that it is today means that federal officials now have huge sums of money at their disposal, as shown in Figure 3.3. Individual states can benefit from this pool of funds whenever the federal government passes on some of its revenues directly to the states to initiate and administer programs. **Grants-in-aid** from the federal government to the states have been used to fund state educational initiatives, build roads, and provide unemployment relief, among other programs that fulfill purposes expressly approved by Congress and/or its federal regulatory agencies. Federal grants also help balance the economic inequities that arise because states have vastly different tax bases. Occasionally the federal government has transformed grants-in-aid, which are allocated only for specific programs or policies, into **block grants**, which a state or local government may use at its discretion for more generalized programs.

---

layer-cake federalism: Description of federalism as maintaining that the authority of state and federal governments exists in distinct and separate spheres.

---

marble-cake federalism: Description of federalism as intertwining state and federal authority in an inseparable mixture.

---

cooperative federalism: The doctrine of federalism that affords Congress nearly unlimited authority to exercise its powers through means that often coerce states into administering and/or enforcing federal policies.

---

grants-in-aid: Grants from the federal government to states that allow state governments to pursue specific federal policies, such as highway construction.

---

block grants: Grants from the federal government to the states that may be used at the discretion of states to pursue more generalized aims.

FIGURE 3.3 Comparing Federal Expenditures to State Expenditures

The system of federalism dictates that the federal government, not the states, must provide national defense. By contrast, state expenditures focus on educational expenses, criminal justice, and social services in particular. Although different systems of categorization make budget comparisons among governments difficult, a glimpse of the budgets of the federal government and two state governments provides some interesting insights as to where your tax dollars are going . . . or not going.

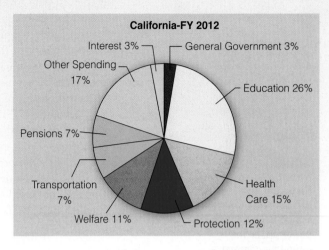

California-FY 2012

Source: State of California Legislative Analyst's Office

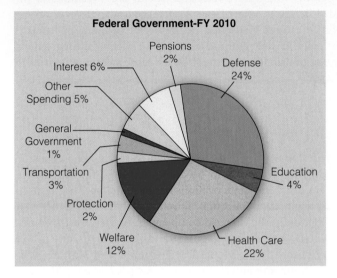

Federal Government-FY 2010

Source: Office of Management and Budget

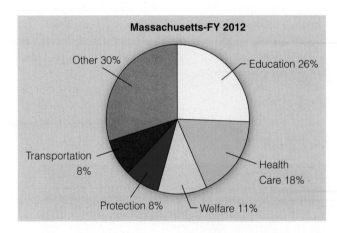

Massachusetts-FY 2012

Source: Massachusetts Budget and Policy Center (www.massbudget.org)

The collaboration between state governments and the federal government in the era of co-operative federalism also carried some negative implications for state sovereignty. Federal government officials increasingly insisted that federal appropriations to the states be accompanied by various conditions. Often these consisted of "protective conditions," designed to ensure that the state would administer its program consistent with the objectives of Congress. For example, Congress required that states receiving educational assistance meet federal requirements for educating handicapped children, including the creation of individualized education programs for students with special needs. On occasion, however, Congress has imposed coercive burdens on states that increasingly rely on such federal assistance. In 1984, for example, Congress passed the National Minimum Drinking Age Amendment, which withheld 5 percent of federal highway funds from any state "in which the purchase or public possession of any alcoholic beverage by a person who is less than 21 years of age" is lawful. The purpose of the law was to decrease the number of serious automobile accidents among those aged 18 to 20—statistics showed that this group was responsible for a high percentage of accidents on the nation's highways.

Although the conditions imposed by the National Minimum Drinking Age Amendment essentially coerced state governments to pass laws at the behest of the federal government, the Supreme Court generally approved of such tactics in *South Dakota v. Dole* (1987).[13] Yet when Ronald Reagan was elected president in 1980, he openly trumpeted federal initiatives to return policymaking authority to the states. In his first State of the Union Address in early 1981, Reagan proposed to terminate the federal role in welfare and return to the states 43 other major federal grant programs.

The voluntary transfer of power by the central government to state or local governments is known as "devolution."[14] If Reagan's proposals had been fully implemented, such a large-scale devolution of federal programs would have returned federal–state relations to the version of federalism that existed before the New Deal. As it turned out, however, strong resistance from the Democratic-controlled House led to the defeat of many of Reagan's devolution initiatives. Nonetheless, Reagan administration rhetoric emphasizing federal deregulation and increased state responsibilities set the stage for more sweeping reforms to be implemented in the years ahead.

The "New Federalism," 1990–Present

Scholars assessing the state of federalism since 1990 have failed to reach a consensus on the proper label for characterizing what appears to be a counterthrust favoring states' rights in certain areas. This new era of federal–state relations has been marked by a resuscitation of state authority, helped by a Supreme Court that, since the early 1990s, has been far more attentive to protecting states' rights. The changed composition of the Court accounts for this shift. Between 1991 and 2005, four Reagan appointees to the Court (Chief Justice Rehnquist and Associate Justices Antonin Scalia, Sandra Day O'Connor, and Anthony Kennedy) and one of George H. W. Bush's appointees (Associate Justice Clarence Thomas) generally favored states' rights in federalism disputes.[15] (Subsequent appointments to the Supreme Court have done little to reverse this trend.) The modern Court's decisions on federalism fit into a number of different categories.

Second, since the mid-1990s, Congress's virtually unlimited authority to regulate interstate commerce has been scaled back somewhat. In *United States v. Lopez* (1995), the Supreme Court declared that Congress could not ban guns in school zones.[16] Whereas during the cooperative federalism era Congress regulated all manner of criminal and social activities, the present-day Supreme Court has more strenuously insisted that Congress must show a clear connection with commerce when exercising its power to regulate interstate commerce, for example. Then, in 1997, Congress ran into more obstacles when it enacted a law entitling sexual assault victims to sue their perpetrators in federal court. Once again, the Supreme Court stood firm for state sovereignty, ruling in *United States v. Morrison* (2000) that the law was unconstitutional, on the grounds that domestic abuse had only a slight connection to commerce.[17]

This radioactive waste plant in New Mexico was built by the state with strong monetary incentives from the federal government.

Joe Raedle/Getty Images

Meanwhile a Supreme Court increasingly intent on protecting states' rights has given new teeth to the Eleventh Amendment, which bars citizens of one state from bringing suit against another state in federal court. As a result of Court decisions, many plaintiffs are now restricted from bringing lawsuits in federal court against public employers; instead, plaintiffs must bring suit in state courts.[18]

Of course Supreme Court decisions are not solely responsible for the resurrection of state sovereignty that has occurred over the past decade and a half. Political developments have also altered the character of American federalism in important ways. Many of President Reagan's federalism initiatives met with limited success in a Democratic-controlled House of

---

South Dakota v. Dole (1987): The Supreme Court Case that allowed Congress to coerce state governments to pass state laws by conditioning grants to those states, so long as the requirements are related to the overall spending in question.

THE MORE THINGS CHANGE,
THE MORE THEY STAY THE SAME

When Must the Federal Government Put State Governments in Their Place?

Citizens of the United States are also citizens of one of the 50 states. Policies in the states are by no means uniform. Notwithstanding some of the uniform testing requirements imposed by federal No Child Left Behind legislation, educational policy differs widely from state to state. So too will an individual accused of a crime find one state's criminal justice system far more onerous and difficult than another. The federal government (which includes federal courts) has occasionally stepped in to smooth out those differences, much to the chagrin of states that prefer to maintain their own unique identity on specific issues. Sometimes uniformity is favored as a matter of good policy; at other times it may be mandated by the Constitution itself. This delicate balancing act between state interests and the need to maintain states' unique political and cultural identities has never been easy to maintain.

In 1850, Congress debated a legislative compromise at a time when Northern and Southern senators were growing increasingly anxious about the future course of slavery in the United States. Though Southern legislators recognized the right of Northern states to forbid slavery, they rejected all efforts to undermine Southern laws that allowed the practice. In passing the Compromise of 1850, Congress defused the confrontation and put off the threat of secession for the time being by ensuring that new territories like New Mexico and Utah could decide on their own whether to be slave states; it also strengthened the enforcement of fugitive slave acts. Thus while Congress did not mandate uniform laws on slavery, it did manage to bring Northern states into line with the clear expectations of Southern states. In this instance uniformity was not possible, and the only feasible compromise would have to accept that reality for the time being.

In 1963, uniformity in the treatment of criminal defendants was squarely at issue before the U.S. Supreme Court. By late 1962, close to half of the states were automatically providing indigent defendants a right to free counsel whenever jail time was a possibility. In fact, just prior to the landmark Supreme Court case of *Gideon v. Wainwright* (1963),[19] 22 of those states urged the Court to adopt this right as a federal standard. By contrast, many states (including Florida) provided such counsel only on a case-by-case basis—if an indigent defendant seemed competent enough to try his or her own case, judges usually insisted that he or she do so. Could such a patchwork of protections stand under the Sixth Amendment? "No," said the Supreme Court, which in *Gideon* effectively nationalized the requirement that counsel be provided to indigent defendants. Following the landmark decision, the second half of the 1960s witnessed the creation of public defender programs across the country.

In 2010, the U.S. Supreme Court once again inserted itself into a social and cultural debate where individual feelings tend to run high. This time the issue was gun control. In 2007 the Court ruled that the Second Amendment protects an individual's right to possess a firearm for public use. Its ruling was limited, however, to federal restrictions on firearms (in that case it was a D.C. law); the Supreme Court did not address whether the Second Amendment applied to state laws as well under the process known as *incorporation*. (Incorporation is discussed in detail in Chapter 4). Certainly the possession of firearms has different implications for residents of the South Bronx than it does for residents of rural farmland in Wyoming. Does the Fourteenth Amendment hold all governments accountable to the protections afforded by the Second Amendment? The Supreme Court's answer was "yes." On June 28, 2010, the Court held in *McDonald v. Chicago* that the Second Amendment right to bear arms applies to all 50 states as well as the District of Columbia.

For Critical Thinking and Discussion

1. If the Bill of Rights was intended to provide certain fundamental rights for all citizens, shouldn't those rights be uniform from state to state?

2. Can you justify, for example, giving criminal defendants in one state less constitutional protection than defendants in another state? On what basis?

Like this Texan, many citizens take pride in their home states.

Representatives. For example, his own Republican Party's platform in the 1980s called for the abolition of the Department of Education; yet that controversial proposal proved a nonstarter in the Congress. Still, his administration managed to push through deregulation initiatives in a number of partially preempted programs, and it relaxed federal oversight of state performance to a considerable degree. In addition, six years after Reagan left office, Republicans took control of both the House and the Senate for the first time since the early 1950s. In 1994, Newt Gingrich (R-GA), then House Minority Whip, and 366 other Republican candidates for Congress rallied around the "Contract with America," a series of initiatives they promised to introduce in the first one hundred days of the 104th Congress. (Republicans would maintain control of at least one and usually both houses of Congress for more than a decade, up until the Democratic sweep of both houses in 2006.)

In the end, that Congress passed few revolutionary new laws. A standoff between President Bill Clinton, who refused to sign the budget resolutions, and Congress, which threatened to close down the government unless the president gave way, led to government shutdowns in November 1995 and January 1996; eventually, on April 26, 1996, Clinton signed a budget bill that cut federal domestic discretionary spending for the first time in three decades. Yet the bill did not achieve anything close to the revolution that the leaders of the 104th Congress had hoped for. Devolution of programs to the states has instead evolved far more gradually, through legislation like the Personal Responsibility and Work Opportunity Reconciliation Act of 1996, which capped federal block grants to states for welfare aid. States have been encouraged by the law to create their own, cost-efficient welfare benefits programs. But the states' rights movement stopped significantly short of the vaunted "devolution revolution" promised by Republican House leaders when they first took control in 1995.

In the wake of the terrorist attacks that occurred on September 11, 2001, Americans rallied around the flag, offering their support for a strong and emboldened federal government, as seen in Figure 3.4. But in the decade since then, support for the federal government has dropped sharply, falling even below pre 9/11 levels. For better or worse, public frustration with the immense size and power of the federal government is a modern reality, and politicians in Washington, D.C., must account for this sentiment when they introduce new programs.

FIGURE 3.4 Has the Federal Government Gotten Too Big?

Source: Gallup poll, January 19, 2012. (http://www.gallup.com/poll/152096/Americans-Anti-Big-Business-Big-Gov.aspx)

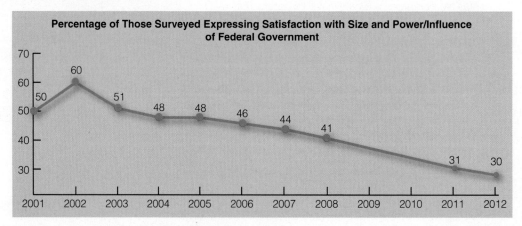

WHY FEDERALISM? ADVANTAGES AND DISADVANTAGES

Supporters of federalism point to several advantages offered by this form of government, and opponents of federalism counter with arguments of their own concerning the disadvantages of this form of government.

Advantages of Federalism

Supporters of federalism cite among the specific advantages of this form of government that it is more likely to accommodate the needs of a diverse citizenry, to strengthen liberty by dividing powers between levels of government, to encourage experimentation, and to respond to change.

Accommodation of diversity. If a unitary system of government threatens to treat citizens of different states as interchangeable parts for purposes of quick and easy administration, federalism acts as an important counterbalance to this trend. A citizen of the United States can also take pride in being a citizen of Texas or some other state with a clearly defined culture or character. State and local politicians can perhaps respond to the specific demands or needs of their citizens better than a central government can. The culture of a state may be reflected in that state's handgun control laws, its rules on the distribution of alcohol, or its laws concerning abortion, prostitution, the use of land, and many other issues that tend to receive differing levels of support across America.

Strengthening of liberty through the division of powers. In Federalist No. 51, James Madison argued that "in the compound republic of America" the power surrendered by the people is divided between two distinct governments. This division provides security against a concentration of power in a single, unitary government. Madison also considered the division of such power "essential to the preservation of liberty," because it becomes harder for a corrupt agreement between these two separate governments to last for long—in the unlikely event that one entire government turns corrupt, the other government would still be available to check that government's abuses. Thus the existence of two distinct levels of government, combined with the separation of executive, legislative, and judicial powers within each of those governments, offers individuals considerable protection. Accordingly, Madison argued that "a double security arises to the rights of the people."

Encouragement of laboratories of democracy. In 1932, Supreme Court Justice Louis Brandeis made famous a metaphor for creative federalism when he wrote that "a single courageous state may, if its citizens choose, serve as a laboratory, and try social and economic experiments without risk to the rest of the country."[20] This notion of states serving as "laboratories of democracy" is encouraged by a federalist system that gives the states authority to craft policies at the outset, while at the same time affording the central government authority to implement policies that prove successful throughout the nation. During the 1930s, FDR borrowed from the experience of various states in crafting many New Deal policies. In 1993, the Brady Bill passed by Congress drew heavily on successful state gun-control provisions that established waiting periods for handgun purchases. The flip side of such successes is also significant: state policies that proved to be failures discourage broad-based applications by the federal government. For example, given that California's deregulation of utilities helped bring about an energy crisis in that state in early 2001, it seems unlikely that other states or the federal government will seek similar forms of deregulation anytime soon.

Disadvantages of Federalism

Opponents of federalism present arguments of their own concerning the disadvantages of this form of government. Chief among their objections to a federalist system are the unfairness caused by economic disparities among the states, questions about government accountability for many public programs that are inherent with competing sovereigns, and the system's heavy reliance on the courts to define the nature of federalism.

FROM YOUR PERSPECTIVE

The Real-Life Benefits of Attending College Close to Home

Many high school seniors dream of attending colleges or universities in distant and exotic locations, far from the watchful eyes of parents or guardians who may be footing the bill. Did you ever dream of attending the University of Hawaii, or perhaps the Florida Keys Community College?

UCLA students walking to class on the school's Westwood campus. In recent years, state universities such as UCLA have increased the number of admissions offers extended to non-residents as a means of generating more revenue.

While admission standards to such schools may or may not pose an obstacle, the bigger issue may be financial. State legislatures try to attract in-state students by offering lower-cost in-state tuition: They know that those students will often stay in the state after graduation and secure good jobs, contributing to the state's economy. For example, if you live in Wisconsin and you want to go to the University of Rhode Island, your college tuition in 2011 would have cost you $25,912. But if you were from Rhode Island, it would only cost you $9,824. UCLA offers perhaps the biggest home-state discount in the country: $35,564 in tuition per year for out-of-staters, as compared to just $12,686 for California residents.

For Critical Thinking and Discussion

1. Did you consider attending (or are you currently attending) a school far from your own home state?

2. As a high school senior, were you aware of the significant disparities in tuition charged by some public universities to students from other states?

3. Should states be allowed to financially discriminate against out-of-state applicants? Why or why not?

Fiscal disparities among the states. States differ markedly in the wealth of their citizens, and thus in the taxable resources available to them for programs. According to the U.S. Department of Commerce's Bureau of Economic Analysis, Connecticut's citizens in 2007 boasted a per capita personal income of $54,117, nearly twice that of citizens in Mississippi ($28,845).[21] Because of these fiscal differences, the amount that states have available to spend on governmental programs varies widely. Furthermore, when the central government defers to state entities in the governing process, such as when it requires states to fund their own welfare programs, wide fiscal inequalities among states (and localities) may mean disparate—and inequitable—programs for citizens in different states. Advocates of social equity and justice routinely complain about this consequence of federalism. Although federal financing of state developmental projects or other state programs relieves some of these inequities, the current trend toward reducing state dependency on the federal government promises more, not less, equity in the distribution of government benefits across states.

Lack of accountability. Numerous government programs fall under the exclusive authority of neither the state nor the federal governments; both may act, either may act, or, in some cases, neither may act. At least in the abstract, federalism creates the prospect of multiple levels of government vying for the opportunity to address economic or social problems. In practice, however, the federal and state governments often play a game of "chicken," each hoping the other will

Kevork Djansezian/Getty Images

act first and assume greater economic responsibility, and perhaps accountability for failures. In an era when public frustration with rising taxes discourages government spending, this "blame game" may go on for years, with both sides accusing the other of shirking its responsibilities to the public. During the 1990s, for example, many state governments eliminated benefits for the needy and imposed stricter requirements on those seeking welfare. State legislatures facing growing budget deficits hoped to "push" the poverty problem onto other states by passing laws that encouraged poor people to move to states with more liberal benefits programs. During this same period Congress passed welfare legislation in 1996 that transferred welfare responsibilities back to states. Critics charge that this arrangement of shared accountability quickly transforms into a lack of accountability, with neither government accepting responsibility for dealing with problems.

Frank Cezus/Getty Images

An interstate highway beset with construction. Many states must rely heavily on federal construction funds to help them maintain roads and highways.

Contentious issues often begin as debates over the substance of legislation: Should fugitive slaves who escape to freedom be returned to their masters? Should immigration enforcement extend to local police officers stopping individuals and demanding that they produce evidence of citizenship? Yet when significant questions about resources and enforcement inevitably arise, those issues quickly transform into even larger questions of jurisdiction and sovereignty: Can the federal government order law enforcement officials in free states to return escaped slaves to their masters? Do Arizona officials have the power to impose additional obligations on aliens that go beyond established federal rules and standards? States tend to line up for or against the federal government's exercise of power based on where they stand; apparently one state's defense of another state's sovereignty extends only so far as the former state believes that sovereignty is being exercised in the interests of its own citizens as well. Sometimes uniformity makes sense to avoid confusion and prevent abuse; at other times, variations among the states allows for valuable policy experimentation as well as the protection of local concerns and interests. Dividing sovereignty is never easy: In the case of fugitive slave acts and the recent battle over immigration policy, it has been especially controversial. No one ever said federalism was a simple doctrine. As long as federal and state governments keep the public interest in mind, the debate over applications of federalism should continue to serve as a mostly healthy (if a bit uncomfortable) form of political dialogue.

SUMMARY: PUTTING IT ALL TOGETHER

WHAT IS FEDERALISM?

- The American system of federalism links the central government to all 50 state governments. Sovereignty (the power of a government to regulate its affairs) resides concurrently in both the central government and state governments.
- Federal systems of government can be distinguished from confederations (simple alliances of independent states) or unitary systems of government (in which subunits are subordinate to the central government).

- The Framers of the Constitution assigned to the national government matters of great national importance (including foreign and military affairs) and assigned to the states all local and internal matters, including those relating to the health, safety, and welfare of citizens.
- The supremacy clause of Article VI provides that the Constitution and all federal laws override conflicting provisions in state constitutions or state laws.
- The full faith and credit clause of Article IV requires that states respect each other's acts and official proceedings.

Test Yourself on This Section

1. The provision of the Constitution declaring that state constitutions and state laws my not conflict with the Constitution is known as the
   a. elastic clause.
   b. supremacy clause.
   c. necessary and proper clause.
   d. dominance clause.

2. The requirement that all states recognize and abide by the official acts of other states is known as
   ✓a. full faith and credit.
   b. preemption.
   c. privileges and immunities.
   d. extradition.

3. The specific powers delegated to Congress, such as the power to coin money, are referred to as
   a. reserved powers.
   b. concurrent powers.
   c. shared powers.
   d. enumerated powers.

4. What clause in the U.S. Constitution makes it quite easy for a citizen to change his or her official state of residence? In what other ways do Americans benefit from this clause?

THE HISTORY OF AMERICAN FEDERALISM

- Beginning in 1819, the Supreme Court under Chief Justice John Marshall substituted the Framers' vision of federalism (state-centered federalism) with its own national supremacy doctrine, which held that Congress was supreme within the sphere of its own constitutional powers.
- In *McCulloch v. Maryland* (1819), Chief Justice Marshall applied the national supremacy doctrine to uphold the authority of Congress to create a national bank under a broader interpretation of the necessary and proper clause in Article I.
- Beginning in 1837, a system of "dual federalism," in which state authority under the Constitution served as a limit on congressional power, reigned for nearly a century.
- The economic hardships of the Great Depression led to an activist federal government; facing these realities, the Supreme Court eventually adopted a more expansive view of congressional authority.
- The era of "cooperative federalism" (1937–1990) barely limited Congress in the exercise of its powers. Through grants-in-aid and block grants, the federal government has placed huge sums of money at the disposal of states.
- Critics of cooperative federalism note that by attaching conditions to these funds, the federal government often coerces states and state officials to administer federal laws.
- The rhetoric of the Reagan administration emphasized increased state responsibilities; Reagan's Supreme Court appointees helped usher in a period of "new federalism" (1990–present) in which state sovereignty has once again been resuscitated to resist certain forms of congressional coercion.

Test Yourself on This Section

1. Which of the following Supreme Court cases did NOT favor broad federal government power to regulate?
   a. *McCulloch v. Maryland*
   b. *Gibbons v. Ogden*
   c. *South Dakota v. Dole*
   d. *Lopez v. United States*

2. The doctrine of federalism that gives Congress nearly unlimited authority to exercise its powers to coerce states into enforcing federal policies is
   a. dual federalism.
   b. layer-cake federalism.
   c. marble-cake federalism.
   ✓d. cooperative federalism.

3. Funds provided by the federal government to the states that may be used at the discretion of the states for more generalized policy goals are called

a. grants-in-aid.

✓**b.** block grants.

c. federal matching funds.

d. continuing appropriations.

4. In this period of "new federalism," the Supreme Court has issued a number of decisions that have resuscitated state authority. What are some of these decisions and how did they empower state authority?

WHY FEDERALISM? ADVANTAGES AND DISADVANTAGES

- Supporters of federalism argue that it accommodates diversity, strengthens liberty, and encourages states to serve as "laboratories of democracy" where they may try social and economic policy experiments without risk to the entire country.

- Opponents of federalism object to the unfairness caused by economic disparities among the states. They also complain about the lack of government accountability for programs managed by competing sovereign powers, as well as the system's heavy reliance on the judiciary to define the nature of federalism and enforce its perimeters.

Test Yourself on This Section

1. Which of the following individuals made famous the metaphor that states might serve as "laboratories of democracy"?

a. Thomas Jefferson

b. James Madison

✓**c.** Louis Brandeis

d. Ronald Reagan

2. Differences in per capita income among states

a. lead states to spend different amounts of money on government programs.

b. do not matter, thanks to federal financing initiatives.

c. decrease state dependency on the federal government.

d. are relatively insignificant.

3. What are the main arguments that have been advanced in favor of the system of federalism in the United States?

4. What are the main arguments against the system of federalism in the United States?

KEY TERMS

block grants (p. 62)
concurrent powers (p. 56)
confederation (p. 54)
cooperative federalism (p. 62)
dual federalism (p. 61)
federalism (p. 54)
full faith and credit clause (p. 59)

Gibbons v. Ogden (1824) (p. 60)
grants-in-aid (p. 62)
layer-cake federalism (p. 62)
marble-cake federalism (p. 62)
Martin v. Hunter's Lessee (1816) (p. 57)
McCulloch v. Maryland (1819) (p. 60)
national supremacy doctrine (p. 60)

necessary and proper clause (p. 57)
preemption (p. 57)
reserved powers (p. 56)
South Dakota v. Dole (1987) (p. 64)
sovereignty (p. 54)
supremacy clause (p. 57)
unitary system of government (p. 54)

4 CIVIL LIBERTIES

LEARNING OBJECTIVES

THE BILL OF RIGHTS: ORIGINS AND EVOLUTION

- Compare civil rights to civil liberties; discuss the origins of the Bill of Rights and the process of incorporation

FREEDOM OF RELIGION AND THE ESTABLISHMENT CLAUSE

- Describe the free exercise clause and the rules for granting exemptions
- Identify the rules governing the separation of church and state; explain the tests for upholding government accommodations of religion

FREE EXPRESSION RIGHTS

- Outline the theories that justify giving heightened protection to expression rights
- Assess the scope of free speech rights, free press rights, and symbolic speech; summarize the rules for exempting from protection lesser-value speech, including libel and obscenity

THE SECOND AMENDMENT RIGHT TO BEAR ARMS

- Identify the scope of the right to bear arms and the constitutional limits on gun control laws

THE RIGHTS OF THE CRIMINALLY ACCUSED

- Assess the scope of Fourth Amendment rights and the privacy issues raised by technology
- Identify the rules against double jeopardy and the privilege against self-incrimination
- Summarize the rights granted under the Sixth and Eighth Amendments

THE MODERN RIGHT TO PRIVACY

- Define the modern privacy rights that apply to government restrictions on abortion, sodomy, and euthanasia.

T he concept of **civil liberties**—those specific individual rights that cannot be denied by government—dates all the way back to the original English legal charter, the Magna Carta of 1215. Yet civil liberties remain just as significant and hotly contested today. In the United States, most discussions of civil liberties begin with the Bill of Rights, which was amended to the Constitution in 1791. The Bill of Rights affords to individuals numerous protections, including the freedom of speech and the right of protection against self-incrimination. All these individual rights are subject to formal interpretation from the courts, and to informal interpretation by those charged with their enforcement. Civil liberties may be distinguished from civil rights (sometimes called *equal rights*), which refer to rights that members of various groups (racial, ethnic, sexual, and so on) have to equal treatment by government under the law and equal access to society's opportunities. Chapter 4 deals with civil liberties, whereas Chapter 5 deals with civil rights.

civil liberties: Those specific individual rights that are guaranteed by the Constitution and cannot be denied to citizens by government. Most of these rights are in the first 10 amendments to the Constitution, known as the Bill of Rights.

The "Connections App" is an interactive web app that helps you better understand the relationship between historical and current events with basic concepts.

1780   1790   1800   1810   1820

1798

Then

An alien suspected of having "treasonable leanings" is arrested in accordance with the Alien Act of 1798.

Source: MultiEducator, Inc.

When a democratic nation like the United States faces a crisis of epic proportions—whether foreign or domestic—a frightened population may be willing to compromise its civil liberties to achieve greater safety and security. But to what end and for how long? Consider the dilemma facing President John Adams in 1798, when his administration was gearing up for hostilities against the French dictator Napoleon Bonaparte. Napoleon's forces had already captured Rome and invaded Switzerland and Egypt earlier that year, and now Napoleon's aides intimated to American diplomats that a war against the young American republic might just be next. Congress passed 20 acts to help consolidate the national defense against France and prepare for the possibility of invasion. The most controversial of these acts were the Alien Act, which authorized the president to deport from the United States all aliens suspected of "trea-sonable or secret" inclinations; the Alien Enemies Act, which allowed the president during wartime to arrest aliens subject to an enemy power; and the Sedition Act, which criminalized the publication of materials that brought the U.S. government into "disrepute." Fearful of being viewed as weak on foreign policy, Adams approved of all three laws. Though Adams did not issue any deportation orders during his presidency, several Republican editors were jailed for violating the Sedition Act. War fever captured the nation's imagination for a while, but when the actual war against France did not materialize, the public struck back, helping throw Adams and the Federalist Party out of office two years later. Still, none of those controversial laws was ever declared unconstitutional, allowing for their possible return when future presidents deemed them as once again necessary.

1980   1990   2000   2010   2020

2009

Now

Despite President Obama's efforts in early 2009 to close the Guantanamo Bay detention camp (right), the controversial prison was still operating four years later.

Source: Kyodo /Landov (left); Brennan Linsley/AFP/Getty Images (right)

Presidents George W. Bush and Barack Obama were the first two chief executives to direct the U.S. government's post-9/11 antiterrorism policies. The Bush administration launched wars in Afghanistan and Iraq in the years immediately following the September 11, 2001, terrorist attacks. Spurred on by a scared populace, Congress enacted the USA Patriot Act, authorizing President Bush to take numerous steps to prosecute the war, including giving the federal government broad new powers to detain suspects without hearings at the Guantanamo Military Base ("Gitmo") in Cuba and elsewhere. The law targeted aliens in particular, allowing authorities to hold noncitizens suspected of terrorism for seven days without

charging them, and utilized a system of military tribunals with limited due process protections. In 2008 Barack Obama campaigned for the White House among a citizenry that had soured on many aspects of the war on terrorism, including the use of torture to interrogate prisoners. As president, Obama did halt the use of torture; however, he refused to roll back the Bush administration's other antiterrorism measures, including the practice of indefinitely detaining prisoners deemed "unlawful combatants," denying them habeas corpus rights. More than a decade after 9/11, the foundation of civil liberties in the United States had been shaken to its core, even with a new president in office and a new set of challenges facing him.

THE BILL OF RIGHTS: ORIGINS AND EVOLUTION

What are rights? Strictly speaking, they are powers or privileges to which individuals are entitled. The central question is: where do rights come from, and are they absolute? *Natural rights*, which are based on the natural laws of human society, exist even in the absence of a formal government. Because natural rights theoretically transcend government entities, no authority can legitimately take them away. As Thomas Jefferson so eloquently stated in the Declaration of Independence, human beings are endowed with certain rights that are "inalienable," which means they cannot be denied by government.

Positive rights, by comparison, are granted by government authority and can usually be shaped and modified by that authority according to certain rules. An indigent person's right to a lawyer paid by the state in felony cases, for example, is a positive right. The term *liberty* refers to a right received from a higher authority, such as a government. As they articulated the basis for a new government, many of the Framers grappled with these and other terms in the nation's founding documents.

It is sometimes easy to forget that, as U.S. Supreme Court Justice Antonin Scalia once stated, individual rights are only "the fruits, rather than the roots, of the Constitutional tree."[1] The Constitution of the United States was intended to provide individuals with protection by guaranteeing a framework of limited government based on a theory of enumerated powers—the central government was allowed to exercise only those powers delegated to it by the Constitution. As James Madison wrote in Federalist No. 14, "the general government is not to be charged with the whole power of making and administering laws . . . its jurisdiction is limited to *certain enumerated objects*."[2] Thus by Madison's logic, separate provisions for the protection of individual rights were unnecessary; protection for those rights was inherent in the nature of limited government with enumerated powers. Because the government possessed no explicit power to infringe on those rights in the first place, they should never be in danger.

Yet Madison's logic ran up against an early American tradition that called for the explicit delineation of individual rights. The Declaration of Independence not only formally recognized that certain "unalienable rights" exist, it also stated that when a government created by "the consent of the governed" fails to protect those rights, the people have the right to "alter or abolish such government." At the time of the founding, individual rights were considered an important element of America's political culture, because they embodied the principles that justified the American Revolution. Many of the former colonists wanted those rights clearly spelled out, lest there be any doubt of their significance to the new nation.

When the U.S. Constitution was created in 1787, most state governments already maintained a bill of rights to protect citizens against government encroachment. As the final draft of the proposed constitution was being debated at ratification conventions in the states, it became evident to the new constitution's supporters that its approval was going to require the inclusion of a more formal bill of rights to protect citizens against the federal government. George Mason and Patrick Henry of Virginia cast votes against ratification, in part because the proposed constitution lacked a formal statement of rights. Thomas Jefferson was also an early proponent of a bill of rights. To Madison's fears that such a declaration of rights could never be comprehensive, and thus might leave out something important, Jefferson replied: "Half a loaf is better than no bread."[3]

Eventually it was Madison who framed the list of rights that the first Congress proposed in 1789—10 amendments to the Constitution in all were ratified by the required three-fourths of state legislatures. These are normally regarded as the Bill of Rights. Whereas the first eight amendments guarantee specific rights, the Ninth and Tenth Amendments offer more general statements describing divisions of power between the federal and state governments under the Constitution.

The provisions listed in the Bill of Rights enjoyed little influence in late-eighteenth-and early-nineteenth-century America, because they were understood to be restrictions on the federal government only. The Supreme Court confirmed as much in the case of *Barron v. Baltimore* (1833),[4] which pitted a wharf owner against the city of Baltimore. City officials had lowered the water level around the wharves, causing him a significant economic loss. The wharf owner thus sued the city under the Fifth Amendment's "taking clause," which stated that no private property could be taken from an individual for public use without just compensation. But the Supreme Court dismissed the suit because at that time only the federal government could be held up to the standards of the Bill of Rights. In light of the dominant role state governments played in regulating individuals' daily lives during most of this period, the *Barron v. Baltimore* decision essentially reduced the Bill of Rights to paper guarantees that only occasionally provided protection for ordinary citizens.

That all changed in the twentieth century, as the Supreme Court grew increasingly willing to protect individuals against intrusive state actions. Its instrument for doing so was the Fourteenth Amendment (ratified in 1868), which provided that no *state* could "deprive any person of life, liberty or property without due process of law." The Fourteenth Amendment had been passed immediately after the Civil War to protect freed slaves from discriminatory state laws. Yet at the beginning of the twentieth century and increasingly throughout the century, the Supreme Court, by a process known as **incorporation** (or "nationalization"), demonstrated a new willingness to hold state governments accountable to the Bill of Rights by utilizing the Fourteenth Amendment's vague requirement that states respect "due process." Specifically, the Court carefully considered individual clauses from the Bill of Rights, and if the right was deemed fundamental enough, the Court held that no state could legitimately ignore the right without depriving an individual of the right to "life, liberty and property, without due process of law." By this incorporation process, states were required to live up to the dictates of the First Amendment free speech clause beginning in 1925, the Fourth Amendment right against unreasonable searches and seizures beginning in 1949, and the Sixth Amendment right to a speedy trial beginning in 1967. (See Table 4.1.)

incorporation: The process by which the U.S. Supreme Court used the due process clause of the Fourteenth Amendment to make most of the individual rights guaranteed by the Bill of Rights also applicable to the states. Incorporation provided that state and local governments, as well as the federal government, could not deny these rights to citizens.

TABLE 4.1 Incorporating the Bill of Rights to Apply to the States

Provision (Amendment)	Year	Case
Protection from government taking property without just compensation (Fifth)	1897	*Chicago, Burl. & Quincy Rwy. v. Chicago*
Freedom of speech (First)	1925	*Gitlow v. New York*
Freedom of the press (First)	1931	*Near v. Minnesota*
Right to assistance of counsel in capital cases (Sixth)	1932	*Powell v. Alabama*
Freedom of assembly (First)	1937	*Delaware v. Van Arsdall*
Free exercise of religion (First)	1940	*Cantwell v. Connecticut*
Protection from establishment of religion (First)	1947	*Everson v. Board of Education*
Right to public trial (Sixth)	1948	*In re Oliver*
Right against unreasonable search and seizure (Fourth)	1949	*Wolf v. Colorado*
Exclusionary rule (Fourth and Fifth)	1961	*Mapp v. Ohio*
Protection against cruel and unusual punishment (Eighth)	1962	*Robinson v. California*
Right to paid counsel for indigents in felony cases (Sixth)	1963	*Gideon v. Wainwright*
Right against self-incrimination (Fifth)	1964	*Malloy v. Hogan*
Right to confront witnesses (Sixth)	1965	*Pointer v. Texas*
Right to an impartial jury (Sixth)	1966	*Parker v. Gladden*
Right to compulsory process to obtain witnesses (Sixth)	1967	*Washington v. Texas*
Right to speedy trial (Sixth)	1967	*Klopfer v. North Carolina*
Right to jury in nonpetty criminal cases (Sixth)	1968	*Duncan v. Louisiana*
Right against double jeopardy (Fifth)	1969	*Benton v. Maryland*
Right to keep and bear arms (Second)	2010	*McDonald v. Chicago*

Source: © Cengage Learning

Slowly but surely the provisions of the Bill of Rights were incorporated by the Fourteenth Amendment to apply to state governments as well as to the federal government.

At present there remain a handful of provisions of the Bill of Rights that theoretically provide protection against the federal government only:

- The Third Amendment safeguard against the involuntary quartering of troops
- The Fifth Amendment requirement that defendants be indicted by a grand jury
- The Seventh Amendment guarantee of a trial by jury in civil cases
- The Eighth Amendment prohibition against excessive bail and fines

Virtually all other provisions contained within the first eight amendments of the Constitution are considered applicable to all state governments and to all local governments within the states in exactly the same manner as they are applicable to the federal government.

FREEDOM OF RELIGION AND THE ESTABLISHMENT CLAUSE

THE FIRST AMENDMENT: *Congress shall make no law respecting an establishment of religion, or prohibiting the free exercise thereof. . . .*

Although the first words of the Bill of Rights speak to the freedom of religion, the actual rights guaranteeing religious freedom did not become widespread until the latter half of the twentieth century. In early America, Protestantism played a highly influential role in public life, and the First Amendment was intended to provide a limited barrier against its influence. In 1802, Thomas Jefferson described the First Amendment as erecting a "wall of separation" between church and state,[5] but that metaphor captured his hopes more than the reality of the time. Although there existed no official church of the United States, government aid to religion—in particular to certain Protestant sects—stood little chance of being overturned by a court on constitutional grounds. And for much of American history, minority religious groups such as Mormons, Jehovah's Witnesses, and the Amish were forced to change or abandon some of their religious practices whenever public policy conflicted with them. By the 1940s, however, American public life had grown increasingly secular, and application of the First Amendment's guarantees of freedom of religion was transformed. Even today the interest in accommodating religion continues to run up against the desire to create a "wall of separation" emphasizing government neutrality.

The Free Exercise of Religion

The **free exercise clause** of the First Amendment bans government laws that prohibit the free exercise of religion. Debate over the clause has largely focused on whether government laws can force adherents of a certain religion to engage in activities that are prohibited by their religious beliefs or prevent them from performing acts that are compelled by their religious beliefs. During the heart of World War II, the Supreme Court in *West Virginia v. Barnette* (1943)[6] ordered school officials to reinstate the children of Jehovah's Witnesses who had been suspended for refusing to salute the American flag in their public school classrooms. Yet although those children could claim legitimate religious objections to the law (the Jehovah's Witnesses' creed forbids them from saluting any "graven image"), they also could claim more generally the right of free expression—those who disagreed with the U.S. government were free to withhold displays of public support for the nation's symbol. It remained for the Court in subsequent years to sort out what rights of religious freedom might exist under the free exercise clause.

Seventh-Day Adventists and the Refusal to Work. In the landmark case of *Sherbert v. Verner* (1963),[7] the Supreme Court ordered the state of South Carolina to pay unemployment benefits to a Seventh-Day Adventist who refused to work on Saturdays. Even though the state's unemployment laws required that she make herself available for work on Saturday, the Court refused

free exercise clause: The religious freedom clause in the First Amendment that denies government the ability to prohibit the free exercise of religion. Debate over the clause has largely focused on whether government laws can force adherents of a certain religion to engage in activities that are prohibited by their religious beliefs or prevent them from performing acts that are compelled by their religious beliefs.

The Amish at work moving haystacks. In 1972 the Supreme Court ruled that Amish children could not be forced to attend school after the eighth grade, as it would undermine the religion's emphasis on "community welfare" and "learning by doing."

to apply that law to this worker because Saturday is the Seventh-Day Adventists' sabbath. Although the state could provide legitimate reasons for refusing to pay her benefits (guarding the unemployment insurance fund against running low, for example), the Supreme Court declared that only a *compelling state interest* could justify denying her such an exception on the basis of religion. What interest counts as "compelling"? Although no precise definition is available, the Court has held that administrative convenience is not compelling; rather, the Court must be convinced that the government program (whether the draft, Social Security, unemployment benefits, and so on) would be significantly undermined by religious exemptions in order to say that the government's interest is compelling.

The Amish and Mandatory School Attendance. Continuing to accept exemptions for religious reasons, the Supreme Court in *Wisconsin v. Yoder* (1972)[8] held that members of the Amish religion were not required to send their children to school after the eighth grade. Even though Wisconsin law compelled high school attendance, the Court ruled that the enforcement of that law would undermine Amish religious principles, which include the value of "learning through doing" and support for "community welfare" over all other interests.

The Mormons and Polygamy Laws. Up until the late nineteenth century, a central tenet of the Mormon Church, also called the Church of Jesus Christ of Latter-Day Saints, required some of its adherents to practice polygamy—the act of having multiple spouses "when circumstances would permit." During the 1870s, many Mormons were prosecuted under a federal antibigamy statute that applied to federal territories, including the new Utah territory where many Mormons had settled. George Reynolds, secretary of one of the founders of the Mormon Church in America as well as the founder of Brigham Young University, brought suit in 1878, challenging the law as destructive to the Mormon Church, and thus a violation of the free exercise clause of the First Amendment.

The Supreme Court, in a unanimous decision, rejected Reynolds's argument that the First Amendment protects plural marriage. According to the Court, religious practices that impair the "public interest" do not receive constitutional protection; such practices were to be distinguished from religious "beliefs," which the government had no power to regulate. *Reynolds v. United States*[9] remains the law today, and polygamy is now banned in all 50 states. Additionally, since 1890 the Mormon Church has formally renounced the practice of polygamy by its members.

Illegal Drug Use and the *Smith* Case. In 1990, the Supreme Court adopted a new approach to the free exercise of religion, one that dramatically diminished the likelihood that future religious exemptions might be granted. Two Native Americans were dismissed from their jobs as drug rehabilitation counselors when it was discovered that they had ingested the illegal drug peyote as part of their tribe's religious rituals. Because their drug use violated the Oregon criminal code, the two men were subsequently denied unemployment compensation. The Supreme Court ruled in *Employment Division v. Smith* (1990)[10] that the state's legitimate interest in maintaining its unemployment insurance fund at a high level outweighed the Native Americans' religious rights and thus that it could deny the two men unemployment benefits. State governments may choose to accommodate otherwise illegal acts done in pursuit of religious beliefs, but they are not *required* to do so.[11]

Today *Smith* remains the rule for judicial interpretation of free exercise cases: instead of being forced to show a *compelling* government interest (which is extremely hard to do), a government interested in applying its neutral laws over religious objections may do so based on any *legitimate state interest* it might claim. What is a legitimate state interest? The bar here is quite low; only an arbitrary or irrational objective by government will fail the test of legitimacy. The Religious Freedom Restoration Act passed by Congress in 1993 attempted to reverse the Court's holding in *Smith* and revert to the more liberal rules established in the *Sherbert* and *Yoder* decisions. However, the Supreme Court invalidated the religious freedom law in 1997 (*Yoder* and *Sherbert* remain as valid exceptions to the Smith doctrine). The Supreme Court—and not the Congress—holds the lever of power in the debate over religious exemptions. And, at least for the time being, that means the courts generally will not grant such exemptions.

The Establishment Clause

establishment clause: The clause in the First Amendment that prohibits government from enacting any law "respecting an establishment of religion." Separationist interpretations of this clause affirm that government should not support any religious activity. Accommodationists say that support for a religion is legal provided that all religions are equally supported.

Even more controversial than the debate over religious exemptions from public policies has been the battle over what role religion may play in American public life under the **establishment clause**, which prohibits the government from enacting laws "respecting an establishment of religion." Most Americans take it for granted that during the holiday season they will see Christmas decorations prominently displayed in government buildings, in front of the town hall, and in public squares. But what about nativity scenes? Menorahs? The Ten Commandments? What types of religious activities and symbols are considered acceptable in public places, and which ones run afoul of the First Amendment, whose prohibition of government "respecting an establishment of religion" has been interpreted to mean creating a "wall of separation" between church and state?

Modern debates over the proper role religion may play under the establishment clause generally divide advocates into two camps. Those who advocate a strict dividing line between church and state support a principle of "separation," which holds that government should have no involvement whatsoever with religious practices, although religion remains free to flourish privately on its own, with its own resources.[12] Opponents of strict separation argue instead for the principle of "accommodation," which holds that government neutrality toward religion requires only that it treat all religions equally. Government should be free to aid and subsidize religious activities as long as it does so fairly across different religions, and aids comparable nonreligious activities as well. In recent decades, the Supreme Court has moved from a position of especially strict separation to one that shifts back and forth between principles of separation and accommodation.

Historically Accepted Practices. Certain religious practices have been a part of political and public life for generations, and the Supreme Court has generally allowed such activities to continue. Congress opens each legislative session with a prayer from a clergy member, chaplains serve in religious capacities with the U.S. armed forces, and U.S. currency proclaims "In God We Trust." Even the Supreme Court opens every court session to a marshal's bellowing pronouncement: "God save this honorable court!" All of these are considered acceptable practices, products of the American historical tradition. But not all religious displays on public property will be automatically deemed as "historically accepted practices." On occasion, the Court has ordered the removal of nativity scenes and other religious displays during Christmastime.

In Kentucky, versions of the Ten Commandments were posted on the walls of several county courthouses. In Texas, a six-foot-high monolith inscribed with the Ten Commandments sits among numerous other monuments and historical markers outside the state capitol building commemorating the "people, ideals, and events that compose Texan identity." Do these public displays of the Ten Commandments, which feature such statements as "Thou shalt have no other gods before me" and "Thou shalt not take the name of the Lord thy God in vain," violate the establishment clause of the First Amendment?

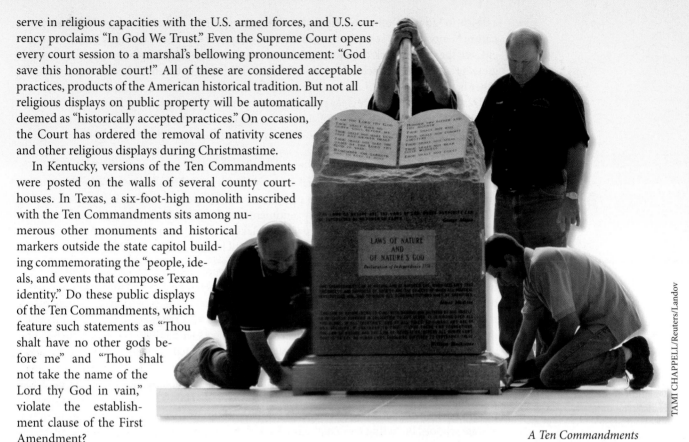

A Ten Commandments monument is moved outside the Alabama Judicial Building in Montgomery, 2003.

TAMI CHAPPELL/Reuters/Landov

In a set of cases handed down in 2005, the Supreme Court ordered the Kentucky courthouses to remove their displays, but allowed the Texas display to remain standing. In explaining its different approach to these cases, the Court ruled that even though the Ten Commandments are inherently religious, their placement in a monument outside the state capitol is an essentially "passive" act, whereas their placement within the courthouse had been motivated by a desire on the part of legislators to advance religion. Of course the members of the U.S. Supreme Court need not be reminded that a frieze in their own courtroom depicts Moses holding tablets exhibiting a portion of the secularly phrased Commandments in the company of 17 other lawgivers. Perhaps the Court believes that there is little risk that such a depiction of Moses would strike an observer as evidence of the federal government violating religious neutrality.

Religious Prayers in Public School Classrooms. The public school classroom has always been viewed as a unique context in which to assess claims that the government has violated the establishment clause. Judges and politicians alike assume that students—particularly elementary school students—have not yet formed firm beliefs about religion and thus may be susceptible to even subtle forms of religious coercion. Public officials interested in promoting religion in society as a whole have focused on the school as a place to encourage religious practices; as a consequence, school policies touching on the subject of religion have undergone serious scrutiny in the courts.

In 1962, the Supreme Court in *Engel v. Vitale*[13] invalidated the New York public schools' policy of having each class recite a specified nondenominational religious prayer each day. That prayer, which proclaimed in nondenominational terms, "Almighty God, we acknowledge our dependence upon thee," was held to be a violation of the First Amendment's prohibition against the establishment of religion. In *Abington School District v. Schempp* (1963),[14] the Court refused to allow spiritual Bible readings in public school classrooms, and in *Wallace v. Jaffree* (1985)[15] it outlawed "moments of silence" authorized by government officials to encourage religious prayer during those moments. The Court held that in neither of those instances was the government acting with a "secular purpose"—one not grounded in a desire to "advance religion." These decisions are especially difficult to enforce, as the closed nature of most public school classrooms allows prayer to escape the notice of those seeking to enforce these landmark decisions. And it remains unclear whether the general ban on religious prayer in public schools extends to the teaching of the Ten Commandments, among other issues.

Despite these seemingly clear rulings against school prayer, some teachers continue to lead students in prayer in public school classrooms across the country. Defiance has become widespread in some instances, forcing one court in Alabama to forbid prayer in schools throughout the state fully 35 years after *Engel v. Vitale* invalidated the practice. Anecdotal evidence of violations continue to mount as well: in one highly publicized case, officials in DeKalb County, Georgia, helped lead a religious revival at a public high school in admitted disobedience of the Supreme Court. Defiance persists in part because public schools are so rarely challenged in court for their violations. Community sentiment has also played an influential role in squelching potential litigation, as dissenting parents quickly realize that only continued and expensive litigation over many years will bring a defiant school into line.

Financial Aid and the *Lemon* Test. During the last several decades, government officials seeking to promote religion as part of the educational process have expanded the variety and scope of their efforts. Many initiatives have occurred in public schools—provisions for school prayer recitations, released-time programs (allowing students to visit religious schools for instruction during normal school hours), and the teaching of subjects with religious content, such as creationism. Efforts to provide religious private schools that teach students full-time with public funds have met with some recent success. In 2000, the Supreme Court approved of a program to provide government-funded computers and other teaching aids to certain parochial schools. Two years later, the Court in *Zelman v. Simmons-Harris* (2002)[16] upheld a system of private school vouchers, whereby parents are given coupons that can be used to pay tuition at private schools, including parochial schools. Such programs continue to be a source of heated policy debate between proponents of separation and accommodation.

Since 1971, issues involving the separation of church and state have often been governed by the *Lemon* test articulated by the Supreme Court in the landmark decision of *Lemon v. Kurtzman* (1971).[17] Under the test, government aid to public or private schools is considered unconstitutional if it fails to meet three separate criteria: "First, the statute must have a secular [that is, not religious] purpose; second, its principal or primary effect must be one that neither advances nor inhibits religion; finally, the statute must not foster 'an excessive government entanglement with religion.'" The test has been criticized by many, including a number of the Supreme Court justices, who assert that its requirements are so stringent that literally all deliberate government accommodation of religion is presumptively invalid. The Court has never renounced the test, and it continues to play a role in the consideration of various types of financial aid.

Prayers at Graduation Ceremonies and Football Games. In recent years, some school officials have attempted to facilitate student prayers in school contexts outside of the classroom. Those efforts have met with little success.

***Lemon* test:** The legal test that determines if a government statute aiding public or private schools is an unconstitutional violation of the establishment clause. The statute is unconstitutional if the statute has no secular purpose, if its principal or primary effect advances or inhibits religion, or if it fosters "an excessive government entanglement with religion."

Group prayer before a high school football game in Austin, Texas.

Bob Daemmrich/The Image Works

In *Lee v. Weisman* (1992),[18] the Supreme Court ordered a Providence, Rhode Island, middle school to stop its practice of permitting prayers to be read at the school's graduation ceremony, even though attendance was voluntary. Eight years later, in *Santa Fe v. Doe* (2000),[19] the Court ruled that a student-led prayer before a football game at a Texas public high school violated the separation of church and state. The Court believed that both practices forced all of those present to participate in an act of religious worship. In addition, these practices could have been interpreted as state endorsements of prayer, which is unconstitutional.

The debate over the role religion should play in American public life remains a highly charged topic. Public schools especially will continue to be a focus of intense interest, as the proponents of a greater role for religion seek ever more creative ways to combine the educational process with efforts to encourage spirituality and religious participation.

FREE EXPRESSION RIGHTS

THE FIRST AMENDMENT: *Congress shall make no law . . . abridging the freedom of speech, or of the press.*

Among the many civil liberties guaranteed by the Bill of Rights, the First Amendment rights of free speech and press enjoy especially revered status. That wasn't always the case. The Sedition Act of the late 1790s egregiously restricted speech that negatively reflected on the Federalists who were in power; during the Civil War, the Lincoln administration took harsh action against those who sought to undermine the Union's cause. Today, nearly all politicians openly celebrate rights of free expression, at least in the abstract. For many, these rights of free expression serve as a cornerstone for all other individual rights, facilitating the more effective realization of such freedoms as the right to vote and participate in the democratic process.

What accounts for the lofty status of free expression rights in the American political system? Several theories have been offered to justify this high level of respect:

- **"The marketplace of ideas,"** a phrase coined by Supreme Court Justice Oliver Wendell Holmes in 1919, is a metaphor for the premise that the best test of truth is the free trade of ideas; only through such free exchange and presentation of all arguments, valid and invalid, can the truth prevail. To ensure a robust "marketplace of ideas," government restrictions on speech must be kept to a minimum.

- **Self-governance** is another frequently cited justification for protecting free expression. Speech is considered essential to representative government, because it provides the mechanism by which citizens deliberate on important issues of public policy. Free speech also serves as a means for ordinary citizens to check the abuse of power by public officials.

- **Self-fulfillment.** Some philosophers have emphasized the importance of free speech and expression as a means of achieving individual self-fulfillment. The human capacity to create ideas and express oneself is thus considered central to human existence; government restrictions on free speech invariably threaten that human capacity. Such a justification of free speech rights extends as well to the protection of music, pictures, and other forms of artistic expression.

- **A "safety valve."** Free speech also serves a critical role in encouraging adaptability and flexibility according to the changing circumstances in society. If the suppression of free speech forces citizens to adopt more extreme means of enacting change, such as violence, the promotion of free speech provides an essential mechanism for balancing the need for order with cries for reform.

Each of these justifications for free speech protection may be subject to legitimate criticisms as well. But for better or worse, the First Amendment's protection of free expression today enjoys a special status in our constitutional system, even though that was not always the case.

Free Speech During the Early Twentieth Century: The Clear and Present Danger Test

The modern status of free expression rights is a far cry from the low level of protection the First Amendment afforded to free speech nearly a century ago. Many of the early cases pitting dissenting speakers against the government came before the Court when tensions were great—first during wartime, then at the height of the Cold War when fears of communist infiltration in American society gripped many ordinary Americans. In neither instance did free speech fare well.

The Supreme Court gave birth to the "clear and present danger" test in *Schenck v. United States* (1919).[20] In 1917, with the United States readying for active participation in World War I, Charles Schenck, a general secretary for the American Socialist Party, was tried and convicted for distributing leaflets arguing that the military draft was immoral. Although the pamphlet posed little danger of interfering with the draft, the Supreme Court refused to release Schenck from jail. Writing the majority opinion for a unanimous court, Justice Oliver Wendell Holmes stated that there was in fact "a clear and present danger" that the pamphlet could bring about the damage being claimed by the government.

In practice, the clear and present danger test soon became a hammer on speakers' rights rather than a shield against government suppression. Under the doctrine, members of the Socialist and Communist parties were tried and punished for participating in organizational meetings or declaring allegiance to their party's principles. Justice Holmes was clearly alarmed by the legacy his *Schenck* decision had wrought; in subsequent decisions he modified his earlier view by insisting that the present danger must relate to an "immediate evil" and a specific action. But Holmes was now in the minority, and there was little he could do to stop the momentum. During the late 1940s and early 1950s, when the fear of communism in the United States was reaching a fever pitch, members of the Communist Party were convicted for their advocacy of sedition. In *Dennis v. United States* (1951),[21] the Supreme Court gave a measure of credibility to this red scare when it upheld the convictions of numerous communist defendants for "teaching and advocating the overthrow and destruction of the Government of the United States."

The Warren Court and the Rise of the "Preferred Freedoms" Doctrine

By the late 1950s, fears of subversion and communist infiltration in the United States were beginning to subside. However, it was the ascension of former California Governor Earl Warren to the position of chief justice of the United States in 1953 that eventually changed the Court's free speech doctrine from one that offered little protection to dissenting speakers into one that protected even the most unpopular speakers against suppression by the majority. The Warren Court brought about this change by embracing a doctrine first articulated by Justice Harlan Fiske Stone in 1938. In a footnote to the otherwise forgettable case of *United States v. Carolene Products* (1938),[22] Justice Stone declared that various civil liberties guaranteed in the Bill of Rights, including the right of free expression, enjoyed a "preferred position" in constitutional law. Stone's explicit support for this preferred freedoms doctrine did not take immediate hold. Yet in the 1960s, when new social tensions such as the battle over civil rights and resistance to the Vietnam War threatened to wreak havoc on civil liberties, the Warren Court issued several key decisions that shattered any possibility that the government might be able to suppress the exercise of free speech rights under the Constitution, as it had in the earlier part of the century.

In 1969, the Supreme Court in *Brandenburg v. Ohio* (1969)[23] abandoned the clear and present danger test and replaced it with a test that was much more protective of free speech. A Ku Klux Klan rally in Cincinnati, Ohio, featured numerous figures in white hoods uttering phrases that demeaned African Americans and Jews. The principal speaker had argued that some form of vengeance be taken against both groups. The group's leader was convicted under a law criminalizing the advocacy of violence. The Supreme Court overturned his conviction.

In the process, it declared a new "imminent danger" test for such speech: first, is the speech "directed to inciting or producing imminent lawless action," and second, is the advocacy *likely* to produce such action? Few of the speakers jailed in the previous half century for seditious speech could have been convicted under this new standard.[24]

The preferred freedoms doctrine also offered protection to those exercising their rights of free expression in other contexts—to writers and publishers, filmmakers and protesters, for example. Indeed, it provided a foundation for the protection of such modern activities as the dissemination of information on the Internet. Even speakers and publishers of certain categories of speech that have not traditionally enjoyed First Amendment protection—obscenity and libel, for example—soon discovered that the preferred freedoms doctrine provided protection for their activities.

The Freedom of the Press, Libel Laws, and Prior Restraints

Freedom of the press enjoys a long and storied tradition in the United States. Well before the American Revolution or the drafting of the Constitution, the trial of newspaper publisher John Peter Zenger in 1734 on charges of libel laid the foundation for robust press freedoms. **Libel** is the crime of printing or disseminating false statements that harm someone. Zenger was accused of attacking the corrupt administration of New York's colonial governor in his weekly newspaper. When he was acquitted on the basis of his lawyer's argument that he had printed true facts, Zenger's case helped to establish the legal principle that truth would serve as a defense to any libel action. In the late 1790s, after many Republican editors and publishers had been jailed under the highly controversial Sedition Act, public distaste for the act helped to catapult Thomas Jefferson and his Republican Party into power in the election of 1800.

libel: Printing or disseminating false statements that harm someone.

Despite the general recognition of the importance of the press, newspapers traditionally enjoyed few special privileges under the law. Specifically, individuals whose reputations were harmed were free to bring libel suits against newspapers and other publications without any implications for the First Amendment. That all changed in 1964 with the landmark decision of *New York Times v. Sullivan*.[25] A Montgomery, Alabama, police commissioner sued the *New York Times* in March 1960 for an advertisement the newspaper had published. The ad—charging the existence of "an unprecedented wave of terror" against blacks in Montgomery—had been signed by several black clergymen. In its description of events that had transpired, the ad also contained some minor inaccuracies. Although the police commissioner was unable to prove that he had suffered any actual economic harm, he still sought a $500,000 judgment against the *Times*. But the Supreme Court refused to allow the official to claim damages, and in the process articulated a much more stringent test to be met by public officials suing for libel: they must prove that the newspapers had published false facts with malice (bad intentions) or reckless disregard for the truth (they ignored clear evidence of contrary facts).[26]

In subsequent years, the *New York Times v. Sullivan* decision has applied to public figures as well as public officials; today a libel lawsuit brought by any famous person—whether it's the president of the United States, Tiger Woods, or Julia Roberts—must prove that the newspaper or magazine in question not only printed false facts, but did so either with "malicious intent" or in "reckless disregard" for the truth. Of course, an important question remains: Who is a public figure? This was the question raised in the case of Richard Jewell, a security guard suspected of setting off a bomb in Centennial Park in Atlanta, Georgia, during the 1996 Summer Olympics. Two people died in the explosion. Jewell was initially portrayed as a hero for his role in discovering the bomb, alerting authorities, and evacuating bystanders from the immediate vicinity. But when Jewell's status changed from hero to suspect, the resulting media coverage of the criminal investigation caused Jewell and his family considerable anguish. Although the investigation ultimately cleared Jewell of any involvement in the bombing, his reputation had been harmed enough that he decided to sue the *Atlanta Journal-Constitution*, which had rushed to judgment against him.

Jewell's entire lawsuit rested on the premise that he was (and continued to be) a private figure. Unlike public figures who had to prove the libeling newspaper had demonstrated a "reckless disregard for the truth," private figures seeking monetary damages need only show that the newspaper was "negligent." Immediately following the bomb explosion, but before he became a suspect, Jewell granted one photo shoot and 10 interviews to the media, including *Larry King Live* and the *Today* show. During the course of these interviews, Jewell repeatedly stated that he had spotted a suspicious bag after a group of rowdy, college-age men had left the park, and announced that he had matched one of the men to a composite sketch. These interviews proved Jewell's undoing, as both a trial judge and the Georgia Court of Appeals ruled that his media activities meant he had "voluntarily assumed a position of influence in the controversy," and thus was a public figure for purposes of his lawsuit. Jewell never received any monetary relief from the *Atlanta Journal-Constitution*.

prior restraint: The government's requirement that material be approved by government before it can be published.

Whereas libel laws punish publications after the fact, a **prior restraint** imposes a limit on publication *before* the material has actually been published. Securing a prior restraint is very difficult for government to accomplish. In the *Pentagon Papers Case* (1971),[27] the Supreme Court refused the U.S. government's request to stop the *Washington Post* and the *New York Times* from publishing a classified study of U.S. decision making about the Vietnam War. The courts have made it very difficult for government to implement a prior restraint of expression. In only the rarest of cases, such as the publication of information about troop movements during wartime, has government been able to block the publication of a story.

Obscenity and Pornography

Despite the exalted status free expression rights enjoy under the Constitution, obscenity has long been recognized as an exception to the rule. Even through the so-called sexual revolution of the 1960s and 1970s, the Supreme Court continued to adhere to the premise that truly obscene speech—words or publications that tend to violate accepted standards of decency by their very lewdness—may under certain circumstances be regulated. When asked how he would define obscene pornography, Justice Potter Stewart in 1964 uttered his now celebrated phrase: "I can't define it, but I know it when I see it." Stewart's statement captures the often confusing state of obscenity law in the United States. The First Amendment does not allow governments simply to ban all sexually explicit materials. But what types of materials can be banned? Is all pornography to be considered "obscene"?

Poster advertising Lady Chatterley's Lover. *The film was based on a book that was the target of a New York State ban during the 1950s.*

In *Miller v. California* (1973),[28] the Supreme Court created the modern legal test for determining what sexually explicit materials may be legitimately subject to regulation under the Constitution. According to the Court, a work is obscene if *all* of these three conditions are met:

1. The average person applying contemporary community standards would think that the work (taken as a whole) appeals to the "prurient" (that is, lustful) interest.

2. The work depicts sexual conduct in a patently offensive way.

3. The work taken as a whole lacks "serious literary, artistic, political or scientific value."

This third condition has come to be known as the **SLAPS test** (derived from taking the first letter of each word in the quoted phrase). In theory, adherence to the SLAPS test allows a jury to apply its own conception of "contemporary community standards" and thus ban relatively innocent sexual materials. In practice, however, courts have found very few materials able to survive the SLAPS test (after all, who is to say what possesses "artistic value"?). None of the above rules apply to child pornography, which enjoys no First Amendment protection whatsoever under the Constitution.

The rise of the Internet as a medium of communication in recent years has caused even more confusion as to what types of obscenity and/or pornography can be regulated. In *Reno v. ACLU* (1997),[29] the Supreme Court invalidated a federal law passed to protect minors from "indecent" and "patently offensive" communications on the Internet. The Court feared that in denying minors access to potentially harmful speech, the law had suppressed a large amount of speech that adults have a constitutional right to receive. Still, the question of how to restrict sexually explicit speech on the Internet will remain an issue for years to come.

SLAPS test: A standard that courts established to determine if material is obscene based in part on whether the material has serious literary, artistic, political, or scientific value. If it does, then the material is not obscene.

Symbolic Speech and the Flag-Burning Controversy

When school officials in Des Moines, Iowa, suspended two students for wearing black armbands in protest of the Vietnam War in the 1960s, they claimed they were not restricting free speech rights at all—rather, the students were engaging in conduct that could be regulated by authorities.[30] The Supreme Court in 1969 disagreed and the students were vindicated;[31] but the line between speech and conduct remains difficult to draw. Protesters often engage in disruptive activities that make powerful statements about important issues of public policy. They may camp out in public parks overnight to bring attention to the plight of the homeless, or burn their draft cards as a statement of opposition to a war. Are such forms of **symbolic speech** protected by the First Amendment?

symbolic speech: Nonspoken forms of speech that might be protected by the First Amendment, such as flag burning, wearing armbands at school to protest a war, or camping out in public parks to protest the plight of the homeless.

In 1968, the Supreme Court in *United States v. O'Brien*[32] refused to allow a Vietnam War protester to burn his draft card in violation of federal law. That case introduced three criteria for determining whether the regulation of symbolic speech may be justified:

1. The government interest must be valid and important.

2. The interest must be unrelated to the suppression of free speech.

3. The restriction should be no greater than is essential to the furtherance of that interest.

In *United States v. O'Brien*, the key was motive: the Court believed the government actions were motivated by the need to operate a military registration system during wartime, rather than simply to suppress the ideas and message of this particular protester. Similarly, protesters do not have the right to violate federal park service rules and sleep

Antiwar demonstrators burn their draft cards on the steps of the Pentagon during the Vietnam War.

Hulton Archive/Getty Images

in parks after closing—those rules were established for one reason: to prevent damage to public property. By contrast, students were granted the constitutional right to wear black armbands in school to protest the Vietnam War—their "conduct" was considered the equivalent of "pure speech," and school officials' arguments about the maintenance of order and discipline were given little credibility.

The constitutionality of flag burning has been a source of considerable debate in recent years. To many the American flag is a symbol of nationhood and national unity, and thus must be preserved at all costs. For that very reason, protesters seeking to attract publicity for their ideas have burned or desecrated the flag in public places. The Supreme Court ended the legal debate over flag burning with its decision in *Texas v. Johnson* (1989).[33] In 1984, Gregory Lee Johnson was arrested and convicted for "desecrating a venerated object" at a political demonstration in Dallas, the site of the Republican National Convention. Johnson had been leading a protest against the Reagan administration; he eventually set an American flag on fire, after which he and the other protesters chanted: "America, the red, white and blue, we spit on you." But the Supreme Court threw out Johnson's conviction because the "government may not prohibit the expression of an idea simply because society finds the idea itself offensive or disagreeable."[34]

Despite the Supreme Court's apparent resolution of the matter, heated feelings on both sides of the flag-burning issue have kept it alive. After an initial attempt by Congress to pass flag-burning legislation failed to withstand judicial scrutiny in 1990, some members of Congress proposed passage of an amendment to the Constitution that would make flag burning unconstitutional. Although that proposed amendment has on several occasions achieved the necessary level of support in the House of Representatives, the U.S. Senate has so far failed to approve it, thus preventing it from being promulgated to state legislatures for ratification.

Hate Speech Codes

Since the 1970s, communities have sought to prevent speakers who preach hatred for certain groups—whether racial, religious, or some other classification—from exercising their rights of free speech in certain specified neighborhoods or other places where the perceived harms may be great. Such efforts have not always passed constitutional muster. In one instance during the late 1970s, the courts refused to deny neo-Nazis the right to march in a parade in Skokie, Illinois, home to a large number of Holocaust victims.[35] By contrast, efforts to ban cross burning and other controversial forms of expression have sometimes been upheld. In *Virginia v. Black* (2003),[36] the U.S. Supreme Court ruled that the state of Virginia could prohibit cross burning with the "intent to intimidate any person or group," because the law applied only to intimidation and not to cross burning in general. The law also applied to all groups, not just racial or ethnic groups.

It is a considerable challenge for school officials to restrict hate speech by students at public colleges and universities, even when that speech proves disruptive to the school's mission of providing a constructive environment for learning.[37] In 1988, the University of Michigan passed a regulation subjecting individuals to discipline for "behavior, verbal or physical" that stigmatized or victimized an individual on the basis of race, ethnicity, religion, sex, or a host of other criteria. Stanford University similarly attempted to prohibit "discriminatory harassment," which was defined to include speech intended to stigmatize or insult on the basis of sex, race, and so on. Lower courts invalidated both of these "hate speech codes" on grounds that they violated the First Amendment.

Regulating the Internet

Meanwhile, high school principals and superintendents face their own set of twenty-first-century challenges, thanks to the Internet and popular social networking sites like Facebook and Twitter. Recently, some public school students found themselves the target of "cyberbullying" from classmates who posted nasty comments about them on social media sites. If the

Courts are still sorting out whether students — many of whom spend time at home on social network sites such as Facebook — may still be subject to discipline by school officials for harassing fellow students in cyberspace.

harassing posts originated from a school or library computer, the school would obviously have the authority to punish the cyberbullies. But what if a student posted the harassing comment from his or her own computer or a mobile device while at home? What if the student posted the offending comments on a discussion thread open only to his or her closest friends? Does school authority extend to students' behaviors in their own private spheres? Lower courts are still sorting out such issues as they await eventual judgment from the U.S. Supreme Court.

What about congressional attempts to curb the online theft of music, movies, and other popular content? The 112th Congress considered two new bills—the Stop On-Line Piracy Act (SOPA) and the Protect Intellectual Property Act—that would have made the unauthorized streaming of protected content a criminal offense. Fearful that law enforcement might use the laws to block access to entire Internet domains, some Internet companies argued that the bills would harm the "free, secure and open Internet" and encourage censorship. As a means of protest, Wikipedia and over 7,000 other websites led a self-imposed blackout of their own content for a 12-hour period on January 18, 2012. The show of force proved effective, as members of Congress postponed plans to move forward with SOPA until it could create a wider consensus on a solution. In the years to come, Congress is expected to keep searching for a solution that strikes a balance between deterring piracy on one hand and encouraging the open exchange of information on the other hand.

THE SECOND AMENDMENT RIGHT TO BEAR ARMS

THE SECOND AMENDMENT: *A well regulated militia, being necessary to the security of a free State, the right of the people to keep and bear Arms, shall not be infringed.*

The Second Amendment "right to keep and bear arms" remains something of a puzzle for Americans. On one hand, the second part of the amendment appears to trumpet the "people's" right to own firearms at their discretion, and has taken its place as a central tenet in the platforms of interest groups such as the National Rifle Association (NRA), which opposes nearly all government attempts to restrict gun ownership. On the other hand, the first part of the amendment speaks directly of a "well-regulated militia," and implies that some relationship

Gabriel Bouys/AFP/Getty Images

A man buying a handgun at a gun shop in California. The 2008 Supreme Court decision in District of Columbia v. Heller *held that the Second Amendment protects a person's right to own a handgun.*

must exist between the private gun owner's rights and more formal state activities. The U.S. Supreme Court finally weighed in on the subject in 2008. In *District of Columbia v. Heller* (2008),[38] the Supreme Court by a 5–4 vote held that the Second Amendment forbids the government from banning all forms of handgun possession in the home for purposes of immediate self-defense.

In *McDonald v. Chicago* (2010),[39] the Supreme Court went a step further, ruling that the right to bear arms is incorporated by the due process clause of the Fourteenth Amendment, and thus applies to all 50 states as well. However, this Second Amendment right is not absolute: the Court in *Heller* noted that government can still regulate the commercial sale of handguns; it can also prohibit their possession by felons and the mentally ill, or in sensitive places such as school buildings.

Second Amendment considerations aside, Congress has been reluctant to regulate gun ownership—only rarely are the sponsors of gun control able to overcome fierce lobbying efforts by the NRA and others in opposition. Advocates of gun control scored some success following the attempted assassination of President Ronald Reagan in 1981. Reagan was wounded in the attempt, as was James Brady, his press secretary. Although the president fully recovered from his injuries in a matter of weeks, Brady sustained serious head injuries because a bullet tore into his temple and lodged in the base of his brain. He ultimately experienced a partial recovery, though he permanently lost the use of his left arm and left leg and suffers from slurred speech.

In 1985 Brady and his wife, Sarah, became spokespersons for gun control measures. Their efforts resulted in the Brady Handgun Violence Prevention Act, signed by President Clinton in 1993. The "Brady Law" required a five-day waiting period and a background check on handgun purchases from licensed firearms dealers to ensure that felons, drug users, fugitives, and other specified categories of individuals are not permitted to purchase guns. The NRA avoided any direct court challenges to the law on Second Amendment grounds, hammering instead at more peripheral aspects of the law, such as the requirement that local sheriffs conduct these checks as part of a federal regulatory scheme. In 1997, the Supreme Court struck down this aspect of the Brady Law as a violation of federalism, although leaving the substance of the law in place. Congress has also attempted to restrict the carrying of firearms near schools, even though some of these efforts have been invalidated by the Supreme Court on the grounds that the federal government cannot commandeer the states to enforce federal legislation.

THE RIGHTS OF THE CRIMINALLY ACCUSED

A few rights for the accused may be found in the language of the original Constitution. Article I prohibits Congress from passing a **bill of attainder**, which is an act of a legislature declaring a person (or group) guilty of some crime and then carrying out punishment without a trial. It also prohibits **ex post facto laws**, which are new criminal laws retroactively applied to those who engaged in activities when they were not yet illegal. But the vast majority of constitutional rights for those accused of crimes are contained in the Fourth, Fifth, Sixth, and Eighth Amendments to the Constitution. Despite the seemingly explicit protections found in those four amendments, accused individuals enjoyed only limited substantive protection from arbitrary violations of criminal due process for better than a century and a half of this nation's history, as they protected defendants primarily only against intrusions by the federal government.

bill of attainder: An act of a legislature declaring a person (or group) guilty of some crime, and then carrying out punishment without a trial. The Constitution denies Congress the ability to issue a bill of attainder.

ex post facto law: A law that punishes someone for an act that took place in the past, at a time when the act was not illegal. The Constitution denies government the ability to write laws ex post facto.

Much of that changed in the 1960s with a number of decisions handed down by the Warren Court. During that period the Supreme Court applied many of the provisions of the Bill of Rights against state governments by incorporating most of the protections given accused persons in the federal judicial system. In addition, the Warren Court gave increased substance to these rights, holding government officials accountable under the Bill of Rights for their actions at highway road stops, during the interrogation of witnesses at the police station, and elsewhere.[40] Even the right to counsel was broadened to extend to far more of those accused of committing crimes. During the late 1980s and 1990s under Chief Justice William Rehnquist, the Court scaled back some of these protections. Nevertheless, defendants forced to weave their way through the criminal justice system today still enjoy numerous rights protections that were not guaranteed before the Warren Court era.

Fourth Amendment Rights

THE FOURTH AMENDMENT: *The right of the people to be secure in their persons, houses, papers and effects, against unreasonable searches and seizures, shall not be violated, and no Warrants shall issue, but upon probable cause. . . .*

The right of citizens to be free from unreasonable searches and seizures has a long history in America. Before the American Revolution, colonists loudly protested English abuses of the power to inspect merchants' goods through the use of an unlimited "general warrant." Although the Fourth Amendment had been in place for nearly two centuries, the Warren Court modernized the rules governing police searches with its decision in *Katz v. United States* (1967).[41] The Court's ruling created the *Katz* **test**, which requires that the government attain a warrant demonstrating "probable cause" for any investigative activity that violates a person's reasonable expectation of privacy, whether or not the person is at home. A **warrant** is a document issued by a judge or magistrate that allows law enforcement to search or seize items at a home, business, or anywhere else that might be specified.

Perhaps the most controversial aspect of the Fourth Amendment is the mechanism by which it is enforced. Although no specific provision for enforcing civil liberties is provided in the amendment, since its 1961 decision in *Mapp v. Ohio,*[42] the Supreme Court has demanded that the states adhere to the **exclusionary rule**, by which all evidence obtained by police in violation of the Bill of Rights must be "excluded" from admission in a court of law, where it might have assisted in convicting those who have been accused of committing crimes. Complaints about the exclusionary rule focus on its most likely beneficiaries: those who are guilty of committing some wrongdoing. They are the ones with the most potential evidence against them and thus have the most to gain from such exclusion. Detractors also complain about the "injustice" of the rule—whenever evidence is thrown out because of a warrantless search by police, "the criminal is to go free because the constable has blundered." Defenders of the rule counter that without a means of excluding such evidence, the government could violate the rights of guilty and innocent individuals alike by conducting the equivalent of fishing expeditions.

Since the 1960s, the Court has modified application of the exclusionary rule somewhat, although it has refused to back down from its central requirements. The most significant of these modifications is the **good faith exception** to the rule, which was first instituted in 1984: if a search warrant is invalid through no fault of the police (for example, the judge puts the wrong date on the warrant), evidence obtained under that warrant may still be admitted into court. Police may also under certain circumstances conduct warrantless searches of a defendant's premises. The allowable circumstances for a warrantless search include (1) the search is incidental to a lawful arrest; (2) the defendant has given consent to be searched; (3) the police are in "hot pursuit" of the defendant; and (4) the evidence is in "plain view" of police standing in a place where they have the legal right to be. Police may also briefly stop individuals driving in their cars, or conduct a "pat down" of suspicious individuals for weapons—in neither case is a warrant required. Nevertheless, police should conduct such warrantless searches with caution, as the good faith exception may be relied on only when conducting searches under the authority of a warrant.

Katz **test:** The legal standard that requires the government to attain a warrant demonstrating "probable cause" for any "search" that violates a person's actual and reasonable expectation of privacy.

warrant: A document issued by a judge or magistrate that allows law enforcement to search or seize items at a home, business, or anywhere else that might be specified.

exclusionary rule: The legal rule requiring that all evidence illegally obtained by police in violation of the Bill of Rights must be "excluded" from admission in a court of law, where it might have assisted in convicting those accused of committing crimes.

good faith exception: An exception to the exclusionary rule stating that if a search warrant is invalid through no fault of the police, evidence obtained under that warrant may still be admitted into court.

Fact or Fiction?

When the police stop your car for speeding, they can require you to open your trunk to find additional evidence of wrongdoing.

Fiction.

If the police stop a driver for speeding or some other driving offense, they must have a warrant issued upon probable cause to search a suspect's trunk.

Advances in technology and new innovations in police work have invited new types of Fourth Amendment civil liberties claims, and a potential reinterpretation of those rights by the U.S. Supreme Court. The testing of defendants for drug or alcohol use through breathalyzer tests and the taking of blood samples may require the police to jump through a series of procedural hoops imposed on them by the state, but no warrant is generally required in either instance when the defendant is in the legitimate custody of the police. Similarly, the DNA testing of defendants has provided a significant breakthrough in the prosecution of difficult cases that lack eyewitnesses or other "hard" evidence of the crime. The use of thermal imaging scans, which expand police investigative tactics from afar, has also been tested in the courts. A thermal imaging scan detects infrared radiation, which then converts radiation into images based on relative warmth, operating somewhat like a video camera showing heat images. In the mid-1990s, police forces began to employ the device to detect the presence of indoor halide lights used to grow marijuana plants inside large buildings; police are able to conduct these scans from vehicles parked across the street from the buildings in question. Do such scans violate a person's reasonable expectation of privacy? "Yes," said the Supreme Court, in a narrow 5–4 decision handed down in 2001:[43] "Where the Government uses a device that is not in general public use, to explore details of the home that would previously have been unknowable without physical intrusion, the surveillance is a 'search' and is presumptively unreasonable without a warrant."

Recently, some communities have posted cameras at stoplights that produce photographic evidence of traffic violations. Other communities have installed cameras on street corners in busy areas. When used in conjunction with computer databanks of convicted criminals, these cameras can provide surveillance capable of instantly detecting the presence of such figures on the street. Officials in Tampa, Florida, have recently turned to closed-circuit television systems to assist police departments in performing surveillance. Specifically, face-recognition software programmed to identify certain wanted individuals has been employed on the streets of Tampa as well as in certain airports; an extensive network of cameras deployed throughout those areas can theoretically identify the faces of wanted individuals, and alert authorities quickly and efficiently of their presence.

A thermal imaging instrument used by police to detect intense heat emissions. The Supreme Court banned its use without a warrant in 2001.

AP Photo/Gary Tramontina

THE MORE THINGS CHANGE, THE MORE THEY STAY THE SAME

Balancing Police Surveillance Techniques With the Need for Individual Privacy

Americans have long accepted that even in a free society they must accept some degree of police surveillance of their activities. When an individual takes a walk in a public park or drives a car along a public thoroughfare, he or she can expect those activities will be observed by complete strangers, including members of law enforcement. Under Fourth Amendment precedents, the government must have a warrant to search someone—even in a public place—if the person maintains a "reasonable expectation of privacy" in his or her actions. Of course law enforcement officers' increasing use of technology for surveillance purposes complicates this area of the law, forcing the Court to weigh the interests of society against those of the individual in this context.

In 1967, the Supreme Court for the first time ruled that nonphysical government intrusion may require a warrant. In *Katz v. United States*, the court considered the case of Charles Katz, who made illegal gambling wagers by using a public pay phone booth—the Federal Bureau of Investigation (FBI) had secretly attached an electronic bugging device (without a warrant or probable cause) to the outside of the booth to record all conversations. The government defended its actions by asserting that the phone booth was in the public, and the bugging device was on the outside of the booth, where others could legally go. The Supreme Court rejected this argument: By a 7–1 vote, it held that the recording of Katz's conversation violated the privacy "upon which he justifiably relied." *Katz* established

that the Fourth Amendment protects not just "things," but the reasonable expectations of people as well.

In 1986, the Court ruled that this new Fourth Amendment doctrine was not unlimited. In *California v. Ciraolo*, Dante Ciraolo was charged with growing marijuana in his backyard. Ciraolo put up two large fences to keep the activity private; meanwhile, the Santa Clara police photographed the marijuana plants from a private airplane 400 feet above the ground. This time, by a 5–4 vote, the Supreme Court held that so long as the plants were visible to the "naked eye" from above, the government did not require a search warrant, and Ciraolo's reasonable expectation of privacy was not violated.

In 2012, the police learned that they could not overrely on technology to conduct surveillance. In *U.S. v. Jones*, the Supreme Court ruled that the police decision to attach a GPS device to a vehicle without a warrant, thus allowing them to monitor its movements on a nearly continuous basis, was unconstitutional. The Court held that because the police had physically intruded onto the defendant's private property to attach the device, the information discovered from the device could not be admitted in court. Unfortunately, the government left many significant questions unanswered: Could the government monitor movements from a distance if no physical intrusion was necessary? What about the acquisition of text messages and e-mails retained by the individuals' cell phone providers? As technology grows more sophisticated, the police will enjoy a significant advantage over targets, so long as privacy expectations do not raise even more red flags in the Court.

In 2012 the Supreme Court ruled that the police cannot attach GPS tracking devices such as this one to cars without a warrant.

For Critical Thinking and Discussion

1. Have advances in modern technology expanded or contracted citizens' conceptions of what privacy they actually enjoy? Is it still reasonable to assume that conversations on cell phones remain private? What about e-mail messages and texts? Is anything that you do or write on a social networking site such as Facebook actually private?

2. What steps must an individual take to keep his or her activities private from government?

Reviews of this technology have so far been mixed: Critics complain that the system often makes false matches in the same way that humans so often are mistaken. Civil libertarians further complain that the use of surveillance cameras in general violates many citizens' privacy rights, which they believe extend beyond the privacy of their own homes. Tampa abandoned the face-recognition system in April 2001, but other cities continue to rely on closed-circuit cameras in general as a means of detecting crime—or, if possible, preventing it from taking place.

To date, none of these modern police tactics has been successfully challenged on Fourth Amendment grounds. But as the use of these techniques is broadened—perhaps to facilitate racial profiling or other controversial forms of police investigation—it is certain that legal challenges will be waged.

Fifth Amendment Rights

THE FIFTH AMENDMENT: *No person shall be held to answer for a capital, or otherwise infamous crime, unless on a presentment or indictment of a grand jury . . . nor shall any person be subject for the same offense to be twice put in jeopardy of life or limb; nor shall be compelled in any criminal case to be a witness against himself.*

Under the Fifth Amendment, the accused enjoy an assortment of rights that may prove crucial to their defense. The requirement that a grand jury, a jury that meets to decide whether the evidence is sufficient to justify a prosecutor's request that a case go to trial, be convened for serious crimes is theoretically significant; it forces prosecutors to convince an initial jury that a defendant should rightfully be forced to go to trial. (Grand juries do not decide on a defendant's guilt or innocence.) In practice, however, the grand jury requirement is rarely much of an obstacle to a skilled prosecutor, who can selectively present evidence to the jury members outside the view of the defendant or the defendant's lawyer. Moreover, because the grand jury requirement was never incorporated, it applies only to federal prosecutors in federal court.[44] The **double jeopardy clause** is a source of much greater protection for defendants: it provides that no defendant may be tried twice for the same crime. Prosecutors must weigh carefully their probability of success at trial and bring forth all the relevant resources at their disposal. If the jury acquits the defendant, the prosecutor cannot try the defendant again. Still, the double jeopardy clause does not stop an altogether different government from retrying the defendant for violating that government's own laws. This occurred in the high-profile case of several white Los Angeles police officers who were accused in 1991 of beating Rodney King, an African American motorist whom they had stopped for a traffic violation. The acquittal of the police set off a series of race riots in Los Angeles. Later, federal charges were brought against the police for violating King's civil rights. At the federal trial, the officers were convicted.

Another provision of the Fifth Amendment is the so-called self-incrimination clause, which prevents individuals from being compelled to testify against themselves. Although originally interpreted to provide protection for defendants only in the courtroom, the self-incrimination clause today offers substantial protection to defendants being questioned by police at the station house or elsewhere. Certainly the clause protects defendants from being coerced or tortured into confessing to crimes. (That form of protection is valuable enough: as shown in Figure 4.1, the right against self-incrimination ranks high in public support, above the right to health care and the right not to be tortured.) But the Warren Court truly changed this area of the law in the now famous case of *Miranda v. Arizona* (1966).[45] In that ruling, the Supreme Court announced the requirement that *Miranda* warnings be read to all defendants in custody before they are questioned by police.

Ernesto Miranda was convicted of the March 1963 kidnapping and rape of an 18-year-old girl in Phoenix, Arizona. Soon after the crime, the police picked up Miranda, who fit the description of the girl's attacker. Officers immediately took him into an interrogation room and told him (falsely) that he had been positively identified by his victim. After two hours of questioning, Miranda confessed. At trial, the defense counsel prodded one of the detectives into admitting that Miranda had never been given the opportunity to seek advice from an attorney prior to his interrogation. Miranda was nevertheless convicted and sentenced to

double jeopardy clause: The constitutional protection that those accused of a crime cannot be tried twice for the same crime.

Miranda **warning:** The U.S. Supreme Court's requirement that an individual who is arrested must be read a statement that explains the person's right to remain silent and the right to an attorney.

David R. Frazier / The Image Works

"You have the right to remain silent. Anything you say will be used against you in a court of law. You have the right to an attorney during interrogation; if you cannot afford an attorney, one will be appointed to you."

—*Miranda* warning,
  Miranda v. Arizona

40 to 60 years in prison. On appeal, the U.S. Supreme Court in 1966 set aside Miranda's conviction. Chief Justice Warren wrote: "Prior to any questioning, the person must be warned that he has a right to remain silent, that any statement he does make may be used as evidence against him, and that he has a right to the presence of an attorney, either retained or appointed. . . ."

Miranda was retried, this time without his confession being introduced into evidence at the trial, and again convicted. Although his original confession could not be used, a former girlfriend testified that Miranda had told her about the kidnapping and rape. After Miranda was paroled in 1972, he spent time in and out of prison before being stabbed fatally in a bar at the age of 34. Thanks to police drama shows and movies, the *Miranda* warnings are better

FIGURE 4.1 Americans' Attitudes on Rights That Should Be Guaranteed

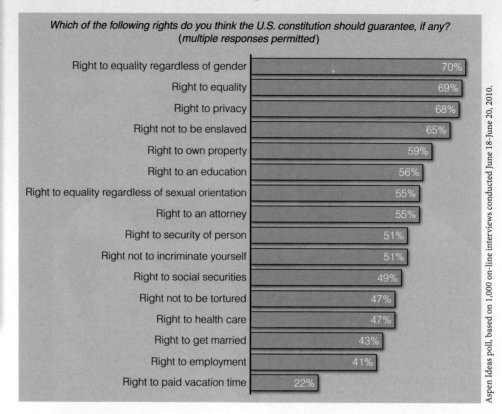

known to citizens today than are any other constitutional protections: police must routinely tell suspects being questioned that they have the right to remain silent and the right to a court-appointed attorney, and confirm that the suspects understand these rights. Perhaps that's why a more conservative Supreme Court conceded in the case of *United States v. Dickerson* (2000) that *Miranda* has become so "embedded in routine police practice" that the warnings have become "part of our national culture." Thus a failure to read the list of *Miranda* rights to witnesses may still result in any subsequent confession to the police being thrown out of court by virtue of the exclusionary rule.[46]

Sixth Amendment Rights

THE SIXTH AMENDMENT: *In all criminal prosecutions, the accused shall ... have the Assistance of Counsel for his defense.*

Images of beleaguered and confused defendants trying desperately to defend themselves against experienced and well-seasoned prosecutors are now mostly a thing of the past. In 1963, the Supreme Court in *Gideon v. Wainwright*[47] ordered a new trial for an indigent defendant who had been ordered by the state of Florida to defend himself in a criminal trial, even though he possessed no legal training. Under prevailing Sixth Amendment standards today, no indigent criminal defendant can be sentenced to jail unless the defendant has been provided with a lawyer at no cost. This constitutional right to the assistance of counsel even extends beyond the trial: a court-appointed lawyer must assist the defendant in preparing the case and in all other hearings and meetings before trial. Some critics of the criminal justice system cite the disparity that often exists between the quality of court-appointed counsel and of paid counsel for well-off defendants. Nevertheless, public defenders' offices have been established all over the country in response to the requirement that indigent defendants be provided with lawyers.

Eighth Amendment Rights

THE EIGHTH AMENDMENT: *Excessive bail shall not be required, nor excessive fines imposed, nor cruel and unusual punishments inflicted.*

The Eighth Amendment deals in a limited way with defendants being held for trial: according to its language, **bail**, which is an amount of money paid to the court as security against a defendant's illegal flight before trial, may not be excessive. In practice, that provision applies only when bail is proper in the first place; many high-risk defendants are held either to prevent flight or to ensure that they do not cause more harm while on release. In those instances, bail may be denied altogether without any violation of the Constitution.

bail: An amount of money determined by a judge that the accused must pay to a court as security against his or her freedom before trial.

Far more significant are the concluding words of the Eighth Amendment with respect to "cruel and unusual punishment." No government may impose a cruel and unusual punishment on an individual, but there remains heated debate over what is "cruel and unusual." Traditionally, the clause prohibited only those punishments that even the drafters of the Bill of Rights would have disapproved of—drawing and quartering, beheading, and other forms of extreme torture. In recent times, the Court has added to the mix the requirement of "proportionality," in which serious punishments may not be imposed for relatively minor offenses. Thus, for instance, the Court struck down imprisonment for the controversial offense of "being addicted to the use of narcotics" on the ground that the state was punishing someone for an illness.

The Supreme Court has never held the death penalty to be inherently cruel and unusual. Most modern lawsuits by prisoners on "death row" focus on the manner by which the death sentence has been imposed. Any judge or jury that imposes capital punishment must have the opportunity to consider mitigating circumstances that might generate some sympathy for the accused. Nor can a jury impose a death sentence at the same time that it finds the defendant guilty; the defendant's lawyers must be given a chance to argue against imposition of the death penalty without also having to prove the defendant is innocent. Finally, certain defendants may not receive the death penalty. In 2002, the Court in *Atkins v. Virginia* ruled executions impermissible in the case of mentally retarded defendants.[48] Then in 2005, the Court also ruled executions impermissible for defendants who committed their crimes while under the age of 18.

Critics of the system claim that so many death penalty cases are held up on appeal that bad luck and misfortune are inevitable in the process.[49] Furthermore, advances in DNA testing technology have revealed that some prisoners on death row were innocent of the crime for which they had been sentenced to death. Even in the face of unrelenting popular support for the death penalty, governors in Illinois and Maryland recently announced a "moratorium" on executions in their respective states, to be continued as long as the process by which death sentences are determined remains so riddled with errors.

THE MODERN RIGHT TO PRIVACY

Perhaps no single constitutional right garnered more controversial attention during the second half of the twentieth century than the right to have an abortion. Unlike all the other rights mentioned so far in this chapter, however, neither the specific right to abortion nor the more general right to privacy is explicitly referred to in the Constitution or in the amendments to the Constitution. The right to privacy is thus often referred to as an unwritten or "unenumerated" right. The Ninth Amendment counsels against dismissing such rights offhand. It reads: "The enumeration in the Constitution of certain rights, shall not be construed to deny or disparage others retained by the people." In other words, the fact that other rights such as freedom of speech are written down in the Bill of Rights does not mean that the Constitution doesn't also recognize certain unwritten rights.

The recognition of unstated rights in the Constitution raises difficult questions, such as how to justify recognizing certain unenumerated rights but not others. In 1965, the Supreme Court stepped into this controversy with its decision in *Griswold v. Connecticut*,[50] when it invalidated an 1879 Connecticut law prohibiting the dissemination of information about and the sale of contraceptives. Seven of the nine justices ruled that although the right to birth control is not

CHECK THE LIST

Nearly All Western Democracies Have Abolished the Death Penalty

Americans' support for the death penalty (recent polls show that about two-thirds of Americans support capital punishment under some circumstances) defies worldwide trends, as 95 countries have taken steps to abolish capital punishment. That includes all but one European country (Belarus is the exception), many Pacific-area states (including Australia and New Zealand), and Canada. In 2009, just 18 countries still carried out executions worldwide. Following is a list of the 12 original NATO member states (all are Western-style republics or democracies), and the year each of those countries formally abolished the death penalty:

1. Iceland	1928	7. France	1981
2. Canada	1976	8. Italy	1994
3. Portugal	1976	9. Belgium	1996
4. Denmark	1978	10. United Kingdom	1998
5. Luxembourg	1979	11. Netherlands	2010
6. Norway	1979	12. United States	Not abolished

▶ **POINT TO PONDER:** Why do you think the United States remains a holdout on capital punishment?

explicitly mentioned in the Constitution, several provisions of the Bill of Rights (the First, Third, Fourth, and Fifth) and the Fourteenth Amendment, taken together, suggest that these provisions create a "zone of privacy" that includes within it the right to decide whether or not to bear a child. Although the Supreme Court's methods were considered highly speculative, widespread acceptance of birth control devices allowed the Supreme Court to avoid controversy in the years following the decision.[51]

No such sidestepping of heated controversy was possible in 1973, when the Supreme Court formally recognized the constitutional right to abortion in *Roe v. Wade*.[52] By the early 1970s, nearly 15 states had passed liberal abortion laws, but lawyers for Norma McCorvey (she used the pseudonym of "Jane Roe" for purposes of her lawsuit) argued that the decision to end a pregnancy was a constitutional right that *all 50 states* must adhere to. McCorvey herself had been unable to secure a legal abortion in Texas and so eventually gave birth and put her baby up for adoption. The Supreme Court agreed to take her case and rule on the general constitutionality of abortion restrictions.

In ruling in McCorvey's favor, the Supreme Court affirmed that the Constitution recognizes a right to privacy in general—and thus a right to abortion more specifically—even though neither of those rights is ever spelled out explicitly. Such a right is not absolute throughout the term of the pregnancy, however. The author of the opinion, Justice Harry Blackmun, divided the pregnancy into three stages as part of a highly controversial *trimester framework*. During the first trimester, a woman's right to end her pregnancy is absolute. During the second trimester, the right is nearly absolute, although the government has the right to restrict abortions that might pose threats to a woman's health. Finally, in the third trimester (when the fetus is potentially viable), the state government is allowed to impose any abortion restrictions on the mother, so long as they do not limit efforts to protect the life or health of the mother.[53]

The number of legal abortions that occurred in the United States rose dramatically in the years immediately following *Roe v. Wade*. The decision also unleashed a fury of controversy from antiabortion interest groups and conservative lawmakers. The election of Ronald Reagan to the presidency in 1980 and his reelection in 1984 set the stage for *Roe v. Wade*'s weakening; as a candidate for high office, Reagan had specifically targeted *Roe v. Wade* as a case of illegitimate judicial activism and had promised to nominate Supreme Court justices who would overturn the controversial decision. Reagan's more conservative Supreme Court appointments began to make their presence known during the late 1980s, when increasingly severe restrictions on abortion were upheld by the Court.

In 1992, the Supreme Court overhauled *Roe v. Wade*'s controversial trimester framework in *Planned Parenthood v. Casey*.[54] Although the Court did not specifically overturn *Roe*, the justices replaced the trimester framework with a less stringent *undue burden test*: does the restriction at issue—regardless of what trimester it affects—*unduly burden* a woman's right to privacy under the Constitution? One example of this new constitutional test at work can be found in the Court's approach to state-mandated 24-hour waiting periods for abortions. Under *Roe v. Wade*, the requirement that a woman wait for an abortion in either of the first two trimesters would have been unconstitutional. Yet in *Casey*, the Court held that such a waiting period does not unduly burden the woman's right to privacy. Other regulations that have been upheld under the *Casey* framework include the requirement that minors seek permission from a parent or a court before having an abortion, and the requirement that women seeking abortions be provided information about the specific medical effects an abortion will have on the fetus.

Not all abortion restrictions are allowed under this new framework. In *Casey*, the Supreme Court invalidated a requirement that women notify their spouses of their intention to have abortions. Yet many more provisions restricting abortion have been upheld since 1992 under the less restrictive *Casey* doctrine. In *Gonzales v. Carhart* (2007),[55] the Supreme Court upheld the Partial Birth Abortion Act of 2003, which effectively banned the use of the "intact dilation and extraction" abortion procedure, most often performed during the second trimester of pregnancy.

Once the unwritten right to privacy became a reality in constitutional law, it seemed inevitable that citizens might try to claim other unwritten rights implicating privacy in the same fashion. Although most efforts to expand the right to privacy beyond abortion and birth control have met with limited success, the Court has not always shut the door on these claims. In 1986, the Court held that a Georgia law that criminalized acts of sodomy by homosexuals was constitutional. Seventeen years later in the case of *Lawrence v. Texas*,[56] the Court reversed itself, holding that a Texas law making it a crime for two people of the same sex to engage in certain types of intimate sexual conduct did in fact violate the individual's right to due process.

The highly visible prosecutions of Dr. Jack Kevorkian for helping terminally ill patients end their lives has brought added attention to the issue of physician-assisted suicide in recent years. On April 13, 1999, Kevorkian, a retired pathologist, was sentenced to jail in Michigan for helping a terminally ill man die by direct injection, a form of voluntary euthanasia. Kevorkian, labeled by many of his opponents as "Dr. Death," had already acknowledged publicly that he had helped at least 90 other people to die by assisted suicide in Michigan between 1990 and 1997. Indeed, when enforcement authorities in Michigan initially refused to charge Kevorkian with killing his most recent patient, he took a tape of the incident to CBS television and aired it on the widely watched news program *60 Minutes*. On the program, Kevorkian challenged the state to act: three days later he got his wish.

Questions remain about Kevorkian's tactics—do terminally ill patients have the right to end their lives, and if so, can a licensed physician assist them in doing so? Although the Court has been willing to recognize a right of terminally ill patients to end their medical treatment, it has steadfastly refused to extend that privilege to the active termination of one's life. In 1997, the Supreme Court held that no such constitutional right exists, although the justices were significantly divided as to the specific reasons why that is so. But the Court also indicated that states are free to legalize physician-assisted suicide. Since then, only one state (Oregon) has enacted an assisted-suicide law. As for Kevorkian, after serving eight years of his prison sentence for second-degree murder, he was granted parole on June 1, 2007, and died four years later at the age of 83.

Shedding Fourth Amendment Rights at the Schoolhouse Door

Justice Abe Fortas once wrote that "students do not . . . shed their constitutional rights when they enter the schoolhouse door." His comment held true in *Tinker v. Des Moines* (1967), when the Court upheld the rights of students to wear black armbands in protest of the Vietnam War. Yet the Court has not been so kind to students in subsequent civil liberties cases. This has been especially true within the schoolhouse itself, where Fourth Amendment rights may be implicated. When the state's power to search and seize conflicts with student claims of privacy, all the advantages lie with the state.

The leading Supreme Court case addressing students' Fourth Amendment rights is *New Jersey v. TLO* (1985), involving the search of a high school student for contraband after she was caught smoking. The assistant vice principal's subsequent search of her purse without a warrant revealed drug paraphernalia and marijuana. The U.S. Supreme Court held that the search was constitutional so long as it was "deemed reasonable given the circumstances." Because the student was caught and taken directly to the office, it was considered "reasonable" to assume the purse contained some evidence of wrongdoing.

For Critical Thinking and Discussion

1. Do you think the rights of college students on your campus should be equivalent to the rights adults enjoy in the workplace, or should they be equivalent to the more limited rights of high school students?

2. Is the location of the search relevant?

3. Should college students enjoy the same rights against unreasonable searches and seizures in their dorm rooms as they enjoy elsewhere on campus?

4. Should private colleges and universities have greater power to search students than public colleges or universities? Why or why not?

© Mikael Karlsson Alamy

A trained police dog checking bags and lockers at a Nebraska high school.

Passionate debates over constitutional rights are hardly a new phenomenon. With a tradition of robust press protections in America dating back to John Peter Zenger's acquittal in the early eighteenth century, the Sedition Act of 1798 stood little chance of long-term success; America's policy of openness to immigrants from abroad similarly doomed the Alien Act passed that same year. (Both acts were repealed just three years after their passage.) As a candidate, Barack Obama attacked the George W. Bush administration for violating the rights of the accused in prosecuting the war on terror; yet once he became president, he left many of his predecessor's more controversial measures in place, and he failed to effectively modify a handful of others. Where necessary, Obama vigorously defended those initiatives as necessary for national security. Ultimately, President Obama must strike a balance between the interests of national security and the integrity of these constitutional rights. Certainly not all presidents are able to strike that balance with the same degree of political success: John Adams suffered at the polls in 1800; George W. Bush served two terms, but left office with record-low approval ratings. President Obama treaded on similar ground when he assumed the presidency in 2009—how will history judge his presidency on this issue?

Summary: Putting It All Together

The Bill of Rights: Origins and Evolution

- Civil liberties are those specific individual rights guaranteed by the Constitution that government cannot deny to citizens. Most of these rights are found in the Bill of Rights.
- The original Constitution did not include a bill of rights, and the way the Framers guaranteed ratification of the proposed constitution was to promise that the first Congress would take up as its first task the passage of these amendments.
- Civil liberties are subject to formal interpretation by the courts and informal interpretation by those charged with their enforcement. The courts' interpretation of these rights has evolved greatly over the past two centuries. Originally, these rights were protected from intrusion by the federal government, not necessarily by state or local governments.
- Beginning in the mid-twentieth century, the U.S. Supreme Court, through a process known as incorporation, used the Fourteenth Amendment's due process clause to require state and local governments to uphold most of these protections as well.

Test Yourself on This Section

1. Who framed the original Bill of Rights in the First Congress, prior to its formal ratification in 1791?
   a. Alexander Hamilton
   b. John Jay
   c. Thomas Jefferson
   d. James Madison

2. What provision of the Constitution was used by the Supreme Court to "incorporate" most of the Bill of Rights against the states as well as the federal government?
   a. the Fourteenth Amendment's "due process" clause
   b. Article I's "elastic" clause
   c. Article I's "enumerated powers"
   d. the Fourteenth Amendment's "equal protection" clause

3. The "inalienable rights" that Jefferson talked about in the Declaration of Independence constitute what kind of rights?
   a. positive rights
   b. equal rights
   c. natural rights
   d. fundamental rights

4. Distinguish between "civil liberties" and "civil rights." Give an example of each.

Freedom of Religion and the Establishment Clause

- The free exercise clause bans government laws that prohibit the free exercise of religion. Debate over the clause has largely focused on whether government can force adherents of a certain religion to engage in activities that are prohibited by their religious beliefs or prevent them from performing acts that are compelled by their religious beliefs.
- The establishment clause prohibits the government from enacting any law "respecting an establishment of religion." In recent decades, the Supreme Court has moved from a position of especially strict separation to one that shifts back and forth between principles of separation and accommodation.

Test Yourself on This Section

1. Which of the following practices by government have been upheld as constitutional by the Supreme Court?
   a. providing private school vouchers to parents
   b. offering a religious prayer for students during the school day
   c. reading of a religious prayer at a high school graduation ceremony
   d. having a religious prayer read at the start of a high school football game

2. Which Supreme Court decision articulated a controversial three-part test to determine if a law or practice violates the establishment clause?
   a. *Barron v. Baltimore*
   b. *Lemon v. Kurtzman*
   c. *Engel v. Vitale*
   d. *Lee v. Weisman*

3. What are the different schools of thought when it comes to interpreting the "establishment" clause?

FREE EXPRESSION RIGHTS

- The First Amendment rights of free speech and press enjoy especially revered status in the United States because free expression promotes the marketplace of ideas, acts as a watchdog on government, and advances the capacity for individuals to create ideas and improve society.

- The press is afforded a great deal of latitude because the courts have made libel suits very difficult to prosecute, and only under very few conditions may government issue a prior restraint on the publication of a story. Speech is not just the spoken word—it also includes such things as flag burning, referred to as symbolic speech, which also enjoys a high level of protection from the courts.

Test Yourself on this Section

1. Which Supreme Court ruling effectively ended the legal debate over flag burning by declaring it a form of constitutionally protected speech?
   a. *Miller v. California*
   b. *Texas v. Johnson* ✓
   c. *Tinker v. Des Moines*
   d. *United States v. O'Brien*

2. The "SLAPS" test was articulated by the Supreme Court in *Miller v. California* to provide a framework for determining
   a. speech that is libelous.
   b. speech that is slanderous.
   c. speech that promotes riotous behavior.
   d. speech that is obscene. ✓

3. The current test that is used to determine whether political speech that advocates unlawful action is protected is the
   a. clear and present danger test.
   b. imminent danger test. ✓
   c. compelling state interest test.
   d. legitimate state interest test.

4. What is "symbolic" speech? What forms of symbolic speech has the Supreme Court ruled are protected by the Constitution? *burning*

THE SECOND AMENDMENT RIGHT TO BEAR ARMS

- The Constitution protects the right of individuals to possess a firearm; still, the government retains the power to enact a broad range of firearms laws, including reasonable restrictions on possession by felons, or in sensitive places such as schools or government buildings.

Test Yourself on This Section

1. What was the Supreme Court case that ruled that the Second Amendment forbids the government from banning all forms of handgun possession in the home for the immediate purpose of self-defense?
   a. *McDonald v. Chicago*
   b. *Virginia v. Black*
   c. *Reno v. ACLU*
   d. *District of Columbia v. Heller* ✓

2. What is it about the language of the Second Amendment that has caused differences in interpretations about the right to own a gun? *NRA*

THE RIGHTS OF THE CRIMINALLY ACCUSED

- The right of citizens to be free from unreasonable searches and seizures has a long history in America, and is the subject of the Fourth Amendment. Although there are some exceptions to the exclusion of evidence based on a warrantless search, the basic notion that probable cause is a requirement for a warrant and that a warrant is necessary for a search holds true.

- Modern technologies have given the police and investigators new methods of search and surveillance. Some of these modern police tactics have been successfully challenged on Fourth Amendment grounds. But as the use of these techniques is broadened—perhaps to facilitate racial profiling or other controversial forms of police investigation—it is certain that legal challenges will be waged.

- Additional rights of the accused are articulated in the Fifth Amendment, including the double jeopardy clause, the grand jury requirement, and the self-incrimination clause. The U.S. Supreme Court has ruled that police must read the "*Miranda* warnings" to anyone who is arrested, which indicates not only the right to remain silent, but also the right to an attorney—a right protected by the Sixth Amendment. Failure to read the *Miranda* rights may lead to a confession being excluded as evidence at trial.

Test Yourself on This Section

1. An act of a legislature that declares a person to be guilty of a crime without a trial is called a(n)
   a. ex post facto law.
   c. bill of attainder.
   b. habeas corpus law.
   d. letter of marquee.

2. Which of the following is NOT a valid exception to the Fourth Amendment requirement that the police obtain a proper warrant?
   a. At a traffic stop, a police officer seizes a gun that he sees on the back seat of a car.
   b. A police officer searches an apartment for a weapon based on a reliable tip from an informant.
   c. A police officer searches a suspect running from the scene of a crime.
   d. A warrant unintentionally lists the wrong address to be searched and the search (conducted in good faith) produces valuable evidence.

3. The legal standard that a judge uses to determine whether or not a warrant should be issued is
   a. reasonable cause.
   c. clear and present danger.
   b. imminent danger.
   d. probable cause.

4. How did the Supreme Court's decision in *Gideon v. Wainwright* alter the Sixth Amendment's mandate for a "right to an attorney"?   MIRANDA   RIGHT

THE MODERN RIGHT TO PRIVACY

- The Ninth Amendment indicates that just because an individual right is not explicitly spelled out does not mean that the right is not protected. Two such high-profile rights are the subject of much national debate: the right to privacy and the right to die. The former served as the basis for *Roe v. Wade*—the case that first established abortion rights under the Constitution.

- A more recent conservative Supreme Court (since the decision in *Planned Parenthood v. Casey*) has allowed the states to place more restrictions on current abortion rights.

- Although the Court has been willing to recognize the right of terminally ill patients to end their medical treatment, it has steadfastly refused to extend that privilege to the active termination of one's life. The Supreme Court has also recognized the rights of gays and lesbians to sexual privacy.

Test Yourself on This Section

1. Which was the first Supreme Court case that recognized a right that was not explicitly mentioned in the Constitution?
   a. *Roe v. Wade*
   c. *Griswold v. Connecticut*
   b. *Planned Parenthood v. Casey*
   d. *Lawrence v. Texas*

2. *Roe v. Wade* guaranteed a women's right to an abortion
   a. unconditionally during the first three months of a pregnancy.
   b. only when the mother's life is in danger.
   c. only in cases of rape or incest.
   d. with consent of the fetus' father.

KEY TERMS

bail (p. 97)
bill of attainder (p. 90)
civil liberties (p. 73)
double jeopardy clause (p. 94)
establishment clause (p. 80)
ex post facto laws (p. 90)

exclusionary rule (p. 91)
free exercise clause (p. 78)
good faith exception (p. 91)
incorporation (p. 77)
Katz test (p. 91)
Lemon test (p. 82)

libel (p. 85)
Miranda warning (p. 94)
prior restraint (p. 86)
SLAPS test (p. 87)
symbolic speech (p. 87)
warrant (p. 91)

5 CIVIL RIGHTS, EQUALITY AND SOCIAL MOVEMENTS

Civil rights activists led by the Rev. Al Sharpton (center, holding megaphone), demonstrate in front of the Edmund Pettus Bridge in Selma, Alabama on March 4, 2012. Thousands joined them to commemorate the historic 1965 voting rights march from Selma to Montgomery.

LEARNING OBJECTIVES

TYPES OF EQUALITY

- Define civil rights and the three types of equality: political, social, and economic

THE STRUGGLE FOR EQUALITY: APPROACHES AND TACTICS

- List the means groups employ to pursue equality within and outside the system

THE AFRICAN AMERICAN STRUGGLE FOR EQUALITY AND CIVIL RIGHTS

- Assess the history of racial discrimination against African Americans, including the role courts played in initially denying African Americans full equality
- Describe the Court-created framework of equality and the challenges it presented
- Evaluate voting rights laws and the more recent battles waged over affirmative action and racial profiling

THE WOMEN'S MOVEMENT AND GENDER EQUALITY

- Summarize the history of women's rights, including the role of the courts in recognizing such rights, from women's suffrage up through the present
- Explain Title IX's effect on women's rights

OTHER STRUGGLES FOR EQUALITY

- Trace the struggles for equality waged by other racial, religious, and ethnic groups, including Native Americans, Asian Americans, Muslims, and Hispanic Americans
- Discuss the struggles of older Americans, Americans with disabilities, and gays and lesbians

I n the abstract, the word *equality* sits alongside terms such as *liberty*, *freedom*, and *justice* as lofty values that underlie American political culture. Unfortunately, when it comes to settling on a formal definition of equality, no consensus exists. "All men are created equal," Thomas Jefferson wrote in the Declaration of Independence of 1776. But Jefferson never intended that document to extend to African American slaves, at least not in the short run. When Abraham Lincoln warned in 1859 that "those who deny freedom to others, deserve it not for themselves," the future president of the United States did not consider the lot of women in American society, who at that time were not yet guaranteed the freedom to vote or own property, among other rights. As with any other abstract ideal, we must fully define *equality* and appreciate its implications in order to understand all that it encompasses.

HO/UPI/Newscom

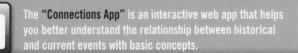

1900   1910   1920   1930   1940

1919

Then

Suffragettes marching for the right to vote in May 1912

Source: © Bettmann/CORBIS

In the quest for equal treatment, rarely is progress linear: small breakthroughs are often followed by intermittent setbacks, until the larger public offers more general acceptance, reluctant as it may be, of the general principle. Beginning in the 1860s and continuing through World War I, demands for women's suffrage stood front and center in the battle lines of equality. Activists at the outset were mostly older women of English or German descent; frustrated that Congress had placed the African American male's right to vote as a higher priority, several women's groups began working to achieve the right to vote, including the New England Woman Suffrage Association and the American Woman Suffrage Association. By the 1890s, these voices had merged into a movement, led at first by Susan B. Anthony. Opposition was widespread: upper-class women worried that their behind-the-scenes influence would be diluted once all women could vote; southern white males feared that African American women would vote, and liquor interests worried that women voters would favor prohibition. Pro-suffrage groups managed some limited victories, particularly in the newly settled western states of Utah, Colorado, Idaho, and Wyoming, which all granted women suffrage before the turn of the century. Still, they experienced continued setbacks at the federal level during the first decade of the new century. The tide may have finally turned with President Woodrow Wilson's call for American entry into World War I. When Wilson termed the battle ahead as a "war for democracy," his point rang hollow among disenfranchised women. Reluctantly, Wilson shifted his position in favor of women suffrage. Finally, in 1919, the Nineteenth Amendment passed, guaranteeing women the right vote nationwide.

2011

NOW

At left, Washington Governor Christine Gregoire raises her arms as legislators and supporters cheer immediately after she signed a state law legalizing same-sex marriage on February 13, 2012; at right, A protestor holding up a rainbow flag in support of same-sex marriage in Marysville, California.

Source: (Left) http://www.theblaze.com/stories/its-official-washington-state-governor-signs-gay-marriage-into-law/ (Right) AP Photo/Elaine Thompson.

By the 1970s, gay and lesbian advocacy groups had begun organizing to achieve equality on a number of fronts. In 1973, just three years after Jack Baker and Michael McConnell applied unsuccessfully for a marriage license in Minnesota, Maryland became the first state to statutorily ban same-sex marriage. In the following three decades, 44 more states followed Maryland's lead, as gay advocacy groups struggled to realize the goal of equal access to marriage. The Democratic Party strategically embraced gay rights as a general matter, but its platform refused support for same-sex marriage specifically. Then in 1996 President Bill Clinton signed into law the Defense of Marriage Act (DOMA), which banned federal recognition of same-sex unions. By 2000, gay and lesbian groups had

achieved limited success in Vermont, which established a law providing for same-sex civil unions, and several other states followed Vermont's lead. Yet gay advocacy groups continued to push for equal marital rights. Once the movement enjoyed its first real breakthrough in 2004, there would be no turning back. That year Massachusetts became the first state to authorize same-sex marriages. Nine states (including, most recently, Washington, Maine and Maryland) soon followed suit. In 2011, a Gallup poll found for the first time that a majority of Americans (53 percent) favored legal gay marriage. That same year gay advocacy groups achieved their first victory on the federal level when President Barack Obama announced that the Department of Justice would no longer defend DOMA in court.

political equality: A condition in which members of different groups possess substantially the same rights to participate actively in the political system. In the United States, these rights include voting, running for office, petitioning the government for redress of grievances, free speech, free press, and the access to an education.

social equality: Equality and fair treatment of all groups within the various institutions in society, both public and private, that serve the public at large, including in stores, theaters, restaurants, hotels, and public transportation facilities, among many other operations open to the public.

economic equality: May be defined as providing all groups the equality of opportunity for economic success, or as the equality of results. In the United States, the latter has been the more common understanding of economic equality.

TYPES OF EQUALITY

References to different types of equality tend to appear again and again in discussions of American politics; political equality, social equality, and economic equality are among those most often referred to.

Political equality generally refers to a condition in which members of different groups possess substantially the same rights to participate actively in the political system. These rights include voting, running for office, and formally petitioning the government for redress of grievances. In a democracy, the rights to free speech, to free press, and to a quality education may also be considered necessary elements of political quality, as those who are denied such rights often are less able to exercise influence over the political process in any meaningful way. In the years immediately following the Civil War, some moderates in Congress argued that if freed slaves were simply given formal political equality, other benefits and privileges would inevitably follow. Reality quickly proved otherwise, as even African Americans in the North who were able to exercise their right to vote were generally unable to influence the political process.

Social equality extends beyond the granting of political rights; it refers additionally to equality and fair treatment within the various institutions in society, both public and private, that serve the public at large. Social equality calls for a sameness of treatment in stores, theaters, restaurants, hotels, and public transportation facilities, among many other operations open to the public. Jim Crow laws passed in the South during the late nineteenth century segregated many of these institutions, thus denying social equality to African Americans.

Economic equality remains the most controversial form of equality—indeed, its very mention often touches off heated debate among political officials. To some, society's responsibility to promote economic equality requires only that it provide equality of economic "opportunity," by which different groups enjoy substantially the same rights to enter contracts, marry, purchase and sell property, and otherwise compete for resources in society. To others, economic equality extends beyond equality of economic opportunity to something approaching an "equality of results." Whichever meaning one gives to the term, economic equality has been exceedingly difficult to achieve. Although the government has introduced a graduated income tax and other resource-leveling measures during the past century to improve economic opportunities for the poor, large variances in the quality of education afforded to different groups continue to render economic equality an elusive ideal.

The term **civil rights** has traditionally referred to those positive rights, whether political, social, or economic, conferred by the government on individuals or groups that had previously been denied them. What type of equality does the guarantee of civil rights promote? Immediately after the Civil War, civil rights legislation that would have provided for extensive social equality (equal accommodations in hotels, restaurants, trains, and other public facilities) was struck down as unconstitutional by the U.S. Supreme Court. As a result, the package of civil rights granted to freed slaves included only limited political rights, including the right to vote. In the late 1950s and 1960s, renewed efforts to guarantee equality in all areas of American life led to the civil rights movement.[1]

Many civil rights battles in American history have been waged by African Americans, but other ethnic groups, women, the physically disabled, the aged, and homosexuals have also sought the political, social, and economic equality denied them. The Constitution of the United States and the amendments to it have provided a framework for these groups to use to win equality. As a result, the meaning of civil rights has been significantly expanded both in the scope of its protection and in the variety of groups who seek its guarantees.

THE STRUGGLE FOR EQUALITY: APPROACHES AND TACTICS

The methods and tactics various groups use to achieve equality have evolved since the end of the Civil War. Initially, the battle over what constituted the most effective means of fostering change—at least in the context of challenging racial discrimination against African Americans—pitted two competing philosophies against each other. Booker T. Washington,

Paul J. Richards/AFP/Getty Images

Members of the Congressional Black Caucus at the August 2008 Democratic National Convention in Denver, Colorado.

who founded Tuskegee Normal and Industrial Institute (today Tuskegee University) in Alabama in 1881, advocated a philosophy of *accommodation*, which promoted vocational education for African Americans and opposed confrontation with the mostly white power structure in place in post–Civil War America. Washington urged his fellow African Americans to accept existing conditions, even to the point of tolerating racial segregation and all but surrendering the newly won right to vote. According to his philosophy, only by engaging in law-abiding practices and standing by their former white oppressors would African Americans become prepared for the exercise of the franchise. Washington's philosophy of accommodation fit comfortably within the dominant conservative political and economic structure of his time. Although some critics charged him with accepting second-class citizenship for his race, Washington was perhaps the most powerful and influential figure in African American affairs until his death in 1915.[1]

Washington's passive approach contrasted with the philosophy of *agitation*, which challenged racial discrimination and injustice through various forms of political activity. Among Washington's contemporaries, the most widely recognized proponent of this alternative approach was W. E. B. Du Bois. At the beginning of the twentieth century, Du Bois and his associates proposed a specific platform of legal, political, and social reforms to achieve social, economic, and political equality for African Americans.[2] Their demands included the unfettered right to vote and an immediate end to all segregation. Agitation eventually replaced accommodation as the dominant mode by which African Americans and other groups sought equality in twentieth-century America. New debates emerged, however, over what would be the most effective means and methods for achieving these reforms. Tactics that various groups have used to seek their civil rights are discussed next.

Working Within the Political System. Some groups have used the political process to implement reforms to end discrimination. In recent decades, for example, African Americans have used their substantial power as a voting bloc to influence the outcome of some elections. Various groups have expanded their influence more directly over public policies and programs by lobbying and petitioning government officials; in some cases members of these groups have been elected to high public office, giving them a place at the table of political power.

Litigation. When the political arena fails to provide adequate remedies to discrimination, a lawsuit brought before a court may afford a better opportunity for success. Founded in 1909 for the purpose of ensuring the political, educational, social, and economic equality of rights of all Americans, the National Association for the Advancement of Colored People (NAACP) focused its efforts on legal challenges to discrimination and segregation because the political arena had offered inadequate remedies. Civil rights legislation in particular had proven

civil rights: Those positive rights, whether political, social, or economic, conferred by the government on individuals or groups.

Women could not vote in any state until 1919, when the Nineteenth Amendment was finally ratified.

Fiction.

By 1900, at least four states (Idaho, Colorado, Utah, and Wyoming) had already enfranchised women; several other states followed suit even before the Nineteenth Amendment was ratified in 1919.

ineffective, with Southern state legislatures either ignoring or circumventing the laws. The NAACP won a string of legal battles that gradually broke down racial barriers in education and elsewhere. These efforts culminated with the U.S. Supreme Court's decision in *Brown v. Board of Education* (1954),[3] which ordered desegregation of public schools. In subsequent years women's groups, disabled people, and other victims of discrimination have similarly turned to the courts for remedies to discriminatory practices.

Legal Boycott. The organized refusal to buy, sell, or use certain goods or to perform certain services has long been a tool in economic battles waged between employers and unions. Adopting this tactic for use in the war on racial discrimination, African American citizens of Montgomery, Alabama, refused to ride the city's buses for more than a year in the mid-1950s; their efforts drained the city's public transportation budget and ultimately forced city officials to desegregate the bus system. In 2003, women's rights organizations discouraged some companies from sponsoring the Masters Golf Tournament held at the all-male Augusta National Golf Club in Augusta, Georgia.

Civil Disobedience. Sometimes citizens resort to passive resistance to what they see as an unjust government policy or law by openly refusing to obey it. Such a tactic may result in arrests, fines, or even jail time for those who practice it. Still, civil disobedience may also call attention to a group's plight in an especially effective way. The Reverend Martin Luther King Jr., who had studied the methods used by Mohandas Gandhi of India and other nonviolent protestors, applied these methods to the civil rights movement in the American South.

THE AFRICAN AMERICAN STRUGGLE FOR EQUALITY AND CIVIL RIGHTS

Colonists who supported the American Revolution trumpeted the notion of equality as a means of justifying their war with England. Yet when the U.S. Constitution was drafted in 1787, the document said nothing about such a call to equality, nor did the Bill of Rights (ratified in 1791) guarantee to all citizens "equal protection of the law." The period following the Revolution offered equality primarily to property-owning white men. Nowhere did Jefferson's call for equality, as stated in the Declaration of Independence, seem more hollow than in the area of racial discrimination. Throughout the North, African Americans were denied the right to vote and numerous other economic and social privileges enjoyed by white citizens. And in the South, the institution of slavery thrived for more than a half century after the Constitution was ratified.

Racial Discrimination: From Slavery to Reconstruction

The organized antislavery movement in the United States began in the late eighteenth century as an effort to eradicate slavery through progressive elimination. Advocates of gradual emancipation believed that by preventing the extension of slavery to new areas and relocating emancipated slaves to areas outside the United States, slavery would eventually die out. Opposed to gradual emancipation were the abolitionists, who sought the immediate emancipation of all slaves. A leader of the abolitionist movement was William Lloyd Garrison, who founded the antislavery periodical *The Liberator* in 1831. It is noteworthy, however, that even extreme abolitionists such as Garrison believed that the "fatal characteristic" of slavery was that it denied African Americans the basic legal rights to own property, enter into contracts, and testify in court. Many abolitionists at the time did *not* believe that emancipation automatically entitled freed slaves to the right to vote or serve on juries. Even among some of the most ardent advocates of equality before the Civil War, a sharp distinction was often drawn between economic rights—which they felt African Americans were entitled to—and basic political rights including suffrage, which were somehow not viewed as natural entitlements.

Neither conception of civil rights for slaves gained much favor in the South, where the economy of the plantation system depended on slave labor. The southerners' approach to racial equality was perhaps best summed up by Chief Justice Roger Taney of Maryland, who in the landmark Supreme Court case of *Dred Scott v. Sandford* (1857)[4] wrote that blacks were "so far

Brown v. Board of Education (1954): The 1954 U.S. Supreme Court decision that declared school segregation to be unconstitutional.

inferior that they had no rights which the white man was bound to respect." The initial rhetoric surrounding the outbreak of the Civil War in 1861 focused on issues such as states' rights and territorial expansion in addition to slavery. The Emancipation Proclamation issued by President Lincoln in 1863 declared the freedom of all slaves in states fighting the Union and allowed blacks to enlist in the Union Army. By the end of the struggle in 1865, the war was essentially transformed into a battle over the end of the institution of slavery.

With the Union victory in the Civil War, the complete emancipation of African Americans after the war was a foregone conclusion. Former slaves were able to legally marry, worship as they wished, and migrate to different parts of the country. But the years following the Civil War—normally referred to as the Reconstruction era (1865–1877) in American history—proved a mixed blessing for the newly freed slaves.[5] The **Civil War Amendments** to the Constitution did grant African Americans the rights of citizenship. The Thirteenth Amendment (ratified in 1865) banished slavery from all states and U.S. territories. The Fourteenth Amendment (ratified in 1868) granted full U.S. and state citizenship to all people born or naturalized in the United States and guaranteed to each person "the equal protection of the laws." Finally, the Fifteenth Amendment (1870) forbade the denial or abridgement of the right to vote by any government on account of race. The Republican-controlled Congress hoped that these three amendments would institutionalize freedom for the former slaves and protect their rights from being undermined by future generations.

During the Reconstruction era, many freed slaves were successful in getting on ballots in the former Confederate states—in all, 22 African Americans were elected to the House and 1 (Hiram Revels of Mississippi) was elected to the Senate during the latter part of the nineteenth century. African American participation in Congress trailed off at the beginning of the twentieth century, however, because restrictions on the franchise curtailed the political viability of most black candidates. No African American served in either house of Congress for most of the first three decades of the twentieth century, and just four served in the House up to 1954. After George Henry White (R-NC) left Congress in 1901, no African American was elected from a Southern state again until 1973, when Barbara Jordan (D-TX) and Andrew Young (D-GA) were elected to serve in the 93rd Congress.

Although African Americans achieved some gains during Reconstruction, the Reconstruction-era generation posed the greatest threat to those civil rights victories. The Fourteenth Amendment had been proposed in part to negate the infamous *Black Codes* passed by the southern states, which denied African Americans numerous economic and social rights. However, in *The Slaughterhouse Cases* (1873),[6] a conservative U.S. Supreme Court narrowly defined the scope of rights protected by the Fourteenth Amendment, holding that the great body of civil rights still lay under the protection of state governments, not the U.S. Constitution. The Civil Rights Act of 1875 attempted to ensure the social and political rights of freed slaves by, among other provisions, prohibiting discrimination in public accommodations. The Supreme Court invalidated the act in *The Civil Rights Cases* (1883),[7] ruling that whereas the Constitution prohibits the states from discriminating by race against certain civil rights, it does not protect the invasion of such civil rights by private individuals unaided by state authority. Therefore, privately owned restaurants and hotels could freely discriminate on the basis of race without violating the Constitution.

This judicial gutting of federal civil rights guarantees opened the way for numerous abuses of freed slaves once the federal government's military occupation of the South ended in 1877. Although the Fifteenth Amendment had given African American men the right to vote, the southern states imposed new barriers to disenfranchise the former slaves. They levied *poll taxes*, which a voter had to pay before being allowed to vote; they required potential voters to pass *literacy tests*; they demanded some form of property-owning and residency documentation; they issued a grandfather clause requirement, which stated that to be eligible to vote one's grandfather had to have voted; and they restricted blacks from participating in crucial party primaries. Discrimination against African Americans in all areas of public life soon became the norm. Terrorist groups like the Ku Klux Klan intimidated or threatened African Americans to keep them under control, sometimes backing up their threats with beatings, arson, or murder. White vigilante groups resorted to lynching in an effort to restore white supremacy and deny blacks their rights. Post–Civil War blacks might no longer be slaves, but they could hardly be considered fully equal citizens under the law.

Civil War Amendments: The Thirteenth Amendment (ratified in 1865) banished slavery from all states and U.S. territories. The Fourteenth Amendment (ratified in 1868) granted full U.S. and state citizenship to all people born or naturalized in the United States and guaranteed to each person "the equal protection of the laws." The Fifteenth Amendment (1870) forbade the denial or abridgement of the right to vote by any government on account of race.

CHECK **THE LIST**

The 11 Largest Political Demonstrations Held in Washington, D.C.

Demonstration	Date	Number of People
1. March for Women's Lives (favoring abortion and reproductive rights)	April 24, 2004	1,150,000
2. Vietnam Moratorium Rally	November 15, 1969	600,000
3. Vietnam "Out Now" rally	April 24, 1971	500,000
4. National Organization for Women March for Women's Lives	April 5, 1992	500,000
5. Million Man March	October 16, 1995	400,000
6. March on Washington II	August 20, 1983	300,000
7. Pro-Choice Rally	April 9, 1989	300,000
8. Lesbian and Gay Rights Rally	April 25, 1993	300,000
9. Solidarity Day Labor Rally	September 19, 1981	260,000
10. Solidarity Day for Labor	August 31, 1991	250,000
11. March on Washington	August 28, 1963	250,000

▶ **POINT TO PONDER:** All but one of the D.C. rallies listed above occurred at least one or more generations ago. Why do you think large rallies in D.C. have waned in recent years? Have protestors found another means of expressing dissatisfaction with the political process?

List does not include routine events such as presidential inaugurations or Fourth of July festivities.
Source: Gathered by authors from various sources.

Racial Segregation and Barriers to Equality

In the period immediately following the Civil War, some African Americans were able to use public accommodations as long as they could afford to pay for them. By the turn of the twentieth century, however, growing racial tensions, exacerbated by urbanization and industrialization, led to racial segregation throughout America. The southern states enacted **Jim Crow laws**, which required segregation of blacks and whites in public schools, railroads, buses, restaurants, hotels, theaters, and other public facilities. The laws excluded blacks from militias and denied them certain education and welfare services. When Homer Plessy (described in court filings as being "seven-eights Caucasian and one-eight African blood") was arrested on a Louisiana train for refusing to leave a seat in a coach section designated for whites, he challenged the Louisiana law requiring segregated railroad cars, arguing that the law violated the

Jim Crow laws: Laws used by some southern states that required segregation of blacks and whites in public schools, railroads, buses, restaurants, hotels, theaters, and other public facilities. The laws excluded blacks from militias and denied them certain education and welfare services.

equal protection clause of the Fourteenth Amendment. In *Plessy v. Ferguson* (1896),[8] the Supreme Court upheld the Louisiana law on the theory that as long as the accommodations between the racially segregated cars were equal, the equal protection clause was not violated. The Court's ruling established the constitutionality of racial segregation according to the *separate but equal* doctrine. To the argument that such an enforced separation of the two races stamps the colored race with a "badge of inferiority," the Supreme Court replied matter-of-factly: "If this be so, it is not by reason of anything found in the act, but solely because the colored race *chooses* to put that construction upon it."

African American leaders responded to the spread of segregation in different ways. Initially, Booker T. Washington's accommodationist philosophy prevailed. W. E. B. Du Bois, by contrast, advocated direct and militant challenges to segregation. Perhaps the greatest breakthrough against segregation occurred through the legal arm of the organization that Du Bois helped found: the NAACP. Beginning in the late 1930s, NAACP lawyers Charles Houston and Thurgood Marshall began attacking the legal basis for segregation in the courts.[9] As detailed in Table 5.1, they won their first battles against state-mandated segregation in institutions of higher education, as the Supreme Court in 1950 recognized that separate accommodations in law schools and colleges had failed to meet the essential requirements of equality mandated by the Fourteenth Amendment.

The NAACP's incremental approach to eliminating segregation in education reached its climax in 1954, with the Supreme Court's landmark decision in *Brown v. Board of Education*. Chief Justice Earl Warren, writing for a unanimous Court, held that racial segregation in any facet of public education constituted a denial of equal protection by the laws. Recognizing the psychological harms of segregation on African American children, the Court declared that segregated schools were "inherently unequal."

Plessy v. Ferguson (1896): The Supreme Court case that upheld a Louisiana segregation law on the theory that as long as the accommodations between the racially segregated facilities were equal, the equal protection clause was not violated. The Court's ruling effectively established the constitutionality of racial segregation and the notion of "separate but equal."

TABLE 5.1 Tracking the NAACP's Legal Assault on Racially Segregated Education

U.S. Supreme Court Case	Description
Missouri ex. rel. Gaines v. Canada (1938)	Invalidated the exclusion of black students from the University of Missouri's School of Law absent some other provision for their legal training.
Sipuel v. Bd. of Regents of Univ. of Okla. (1948)	Rejected Oklahoma's attempt to create a separate law school for blacks by roping off a section of the state capitol for black law students and assigning three law teachers to them; such a form of separation failed to comply with the constitutional requirement of "equality."
Sweatt v. Painter (1950)	Invalidated Texas's attempt to create an alternative to the University of Texas law school for blacks, because any such alternative would be inherently different in the reputation of its faculty, the experience of its administration, the position and influence of its alumni, its standing in the community, and so on.
McLaurin v. Okla. State Regents (1950)	Rejected as "unequal" Oklahoma's attempt to provide graduate education to a black student by making him sit in a classroom surrounded by a railing marked "reserved for colored," assigning him a segregated desk in the library, and requiring him to sit separately from whites in the cafeteria.
Brown v. Board of Education (1954)	Rejected the "separate but equal" doctrine altogether, declaring that in the field of public education, "separate educational facilities are inherently unequal."
Cooper v. Aaron (1958)	Condemned the attempts of the Little Rock, Arkansas, school board to postpone desegregation efforts, ruling that no scheme of racial discrimination against black schoolchildren can stand if "there is state participation through any arrangement, management, funds, or property."

Source: © Cengage Learning

The *Brown* decision also confirmed that in all future cases related to racial (and ethnic) discrimination, the Court would apply a standard of **strict scrutiny**, a level of judicial review that requires the government to prove that the racial classification of the law or practice in question is "narrowly tailored" to meet a "compelling state interest." What precisely does this mean? At a minimum, there should be no less-restrictive alternative means available for achieving the government's objectives, and those objectives should stand among the most necessary that may be pursued by any government. Many legal scholars and judges say the strict scrutiny standard tends to invalidate nearly all government laws and programs. In the years following *Brown*, the courts would apply the standard of strict scrutiny in decisions on segregated public swimming pools, police forces, and laws banning interracial marriages.

A year after handing down the *Brown* decision, the Supreme Court declared that its implementation should proceed "with all deliberate speed." Despite that decree, many local school boards resisted desegregation. The school board of Little Rock, Arkansas, adopted a plan for "phased integration" over a 10-year period, spurring more lawsuits to speed up the process. Undeterred, Arkansas Governor Orval Faubus declared that no "*Brown* decisions" enjoyed "the force of law" in his state. In one famous instance, he placed soldiers of the Arkansas National Guard at Little Rock's Central High School to stop African American students from entering the school. Governor Ross Barnett of Mississippi refused to comply with court desegregation orders on so many occasions that a federal court held him in contempt and committed him "to the custody of the Attorney General of the United States." Alabama Governor George Wallace blocked a University of Alabama doorway, refusing to allow black students to pass through, in 1963. One hundred members of Congress signed a "Southern Manifesto" declaring their intention to use "all lawful means" to reverse the *Brown* decision. On several occasions, the Supreme Court was forced to reassert its authority over state governments. In *Cooper v. Aaron* (1958),[10] for example, the Court held that the rights of African American students could "neither be nullified openly and directly by state legislatures or state executive officials . . . by evasive schemes for segregation."

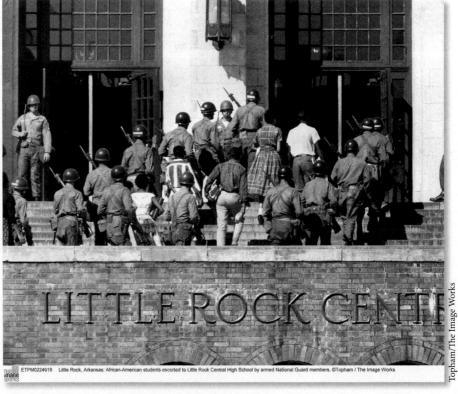

African American students are escorted through the doors of Little Rock's Central High School by the U.S. National Guard on September 25, 1957.

Despite the Supreme Court's increasingly clear edicts against segregation, many school districts in the South and North continued to drag their feet.[11] Significant and widespread change would not occur until after passage of civil rights legislation in the mid-1960s, which gave the executive branch of the government increased power to enforce school desegregation in local districts. Additionally, a sudden influx of federal money into local schools gave extra bite to court desegregation decrees. As scholar Gerald Rosenberg remarked: "Put simply, courts could hold up federal funds." Many school districts in the Deep South where less than half of all blacks were being educated alongside whites as late as 1967 were almost fully integrated by 1971.

In urban areas where whites and blacks lived largely apart, strict adherence to a neighborhood school system meant indefinitely perpetuating a racially unmixed setting; thus massive court-ordered "busing" in the late 1960s and 1970s became a controversial feature of efforts to integrate these schools. Many such court orders were issued in both Northern and Southern cities, as the Supreme Court required communities to cease both *de jure discrimination* (segregation sanctioned by the law), which was found mostly in the South, and *de facto discrimination* (segregation in reality, such as that which occurs when different racial groups voluntarily choose to live in different neighborhoods or attend different schools), which was found in both the North and the South. Yet busing was a remedy limited to a single metropolitan area, and comprehensive efforts to integrate schools were further hindered by white flight to suburbia, which left inner-city school districts in many large northern cities predominantly black and Hispanic. Today, fully 70 percent of the nation's African American students attend schools that are predominantly black. Thus more than 50 years after the *Brown* decision, de facto discrimination in public education remains a reality in many parts of America.

The Beginnings of the Civil Rights Movement

Although *Brown* signaled the end of state-sponsored segregation, the Supreme Court took pains to note that its holding applied only to discriminatory acts by the government. The extension of civil rights protections to all public accommodations did not occur until the civil rights movement began to gather momentum in the late 1950s and early 1960s. In December 1955, Rosa Parks, an African American seamstress in Montgomery, Alabama, was arrested for refusing to give up her seat at the front of a city bus. Her arrest sparked a racial boycott of the city's bus system. Leading the boycott was Martin Luther King Jr., pastor of the Dexter Avenue Baptist Church. King's eloquent speeches and his methods of nonviolent civil disobedience brought national attention to the boycott. King had been introduced to these tactics of nonviolent protest when he was a student at Crozer Theological

Michael Evans/Hulton Archive/Contributor/Getty Images

A 19-year-old student named Martin Luther King Jr. was first introduced to the pacifist philosophy of Mohandas Gandhi. By seeking a nonviolent confrontation with the segregation laws, King's followers practiced Gandhi's philosophy in a way that sent shock waves throughout the South and eventually the entire nation. King would continue to preach Gandhi's call for nonviolent protest up until his assassination in 1968.

Seminary in Chester, Pennsylvania, and studied the pacifist philosophy of Mohandas Gandhi of India, whose unshakable belief in nonviolent protest and religious tolerance helped secure independence for his country from Great Britain.

In 1957, King and other African American ministers in the South formed the Southern Christian Leadership Conference (SCLC), which encouraged Ghandian practices of nonviolent civil disobedience as a way to gain equal rights for blacks and spur white politicians into action. African American and white college students in numerous cities across the South eventually became the engine for pressing such change. One early tactic the students used was the sit-in. On February 1, 1960, four freshmen from the black North Carolina A&T College in Greensboro sat down at a whites-only lunch counter and refused to move after being denied service. The next day more students—black and white—joined them. Angry mobs harassed the students verbally and physically. Committed to nonviolence, the students endured the abuse. The episode brought considerable publicity to the civil rights movement. In 1961, interracial groups of students sponsored "Freedom Rides," traveling together from Washington, D.C., to the South to test court decisions prohibiting segregation on interstate buses and in bus terminals; many within the groups of interstate travelers of mixed races were beaten when their buses arrived in Alabama. Eventually President John F. Kennedy was forced to nationalize the Alabama police to help assure the freedom riders safe passage.

Birmingham 1963: The Turning Point of the Civil Rights Movement

The civil rights movement's strategy of nonviolent civil disobedience reached a climax between 1963 and 1965.[12] The year 1963 will long be remembered as the "Year of Birmingham." Tension was growing between King's SCLC and new civil rights groups that favored more radical and militant action, including the use of violence. Looking for a site where nonviolent demonstrations might succeed and draw national attention to the civil rights movement, King and his followers settled on Birmingham, Alabama. Birmingham was an obvious

Bettmann/Corbis

In 1963, firefighters in Birmingham, Alabama, sprayed civil rights demonstrators with fire hoses.

Barack Obama takes the oath of office as president of the United States on January 20, 2009.

target, for several reasons. First, as an industrial city (unlike most southern cities), it had a sizable concentration of workers. Also, during the 1930s and 1940s, the labor movement had introduced to the city a tradition of organized protest unusual throughout most of the South. And finally, the city was a stronghold of segregation; city leaders included the notoriously racist Public Safety Commissioner Eugene "Bull" Connor, who ruthlessly enforced segregation laws throughout the city.

In Birmingham, King led other demonstrators in a nonviolent march downtown, where he was arrested and placed in solitary confinement. While confined, he wrote his famous "Letter from Birmingham City Jail," addressed to the white Alabama clergymen who had criticized King's campaign. In the letter, King explained his philosophy and defended his strategy of nonviolent protest. Despite King's arrest, the demonstration in Birmingham continued. The marchers, including more than a thousand black schoolchildren, were met by attack dogs, cattle prods, and fire hoses. Pictures of children being attacked flashed across the nation's television sets and the violence was covered by newspapers and magazines across the world. The nation would be forever aroused by these events; the civil rights movement had finally been transformed into a truly national cause.

Birmingham businessmen, fearing damage to their downtown stores, hastened negotiations with King and his fellow civil rights leaders. An accord was eventually reached on May 10, 1963, with merchants agreeing to desegregate lunch counters and hire more black workers for clerical and sales positions. Yet the agreement did not bring peace to Birmingham: On the night of May 11, a Ku Klux Klan rally outside the city was followed by the explosion of bombs at the motel where King was staying. Riots erupted and some stores were set ablaze. This time, however, the federal government got involved; President Kennedy dispatched soldiers to Fort McClellan, 30 miles outside of Birmingham.

Civil Rights Act of 1964: The federal law that banned racial discrimination in all public accommodations, including those that were privately owned; prohibited discrimination by employers and created the Equal Employment Opportunity Commission to investigate complaints of discrimination; and denied public funds to schools that continued to discriminate on the basis of race.

Voting Rights Act of 1965: The federal law that invalidated literacy tests and property requirements and required select states and cities to apply for permission to the Justice Department to change their voting laws. As a consequence, millions of African Americans were effectively reenfranchised in the South.

Civil Rights Act of 1968: The federal law that banned race discrimination in housing and made interference with a citizen's civil rights a federal crime.

Nevertheless, in September a bombing at the city's Sixteenth Street Baptist Church killed four African American schoolgirls.

The events in Birmingham were neither the last of the civil rights demonstrations nor did they mark the end of violence in response to those activities. In August 1963, more than 250,000 people participated in the March on Washington, where King delivered his memorable "I Have a Dream" speech from the steps of the Lincoln Memorial. In 1964, the murder of three civil rights workers and a local NAACP leader in Mississippi revealed the depth of continuing opposition to racial equality. In 1965, King and other civil rights leaders organized a march from Selma, Alabama, to the state capital in Montgomery to bring attention to harsh political realities in the South, where African Americans had been denied the right to vote by illegitimate tests and in some instances outright intimidation.

President Lyndon Johnson and the U.S. Congress were eventually prodded into action. Johnson signed into law the **Civil Rights Act of 1964**, which banned racial discrimination in all public accommodations, including those that were privately owned; it also prohibited discrimination by employers and created the Equal Employment Opportunity Commission to investigate complaints of discrimination; and it denied public funds to schools that continued to discriminate on the basis of race.[13] The **Voting Rights Act of 1965**, enacted the following year, invalidated literacy tests and property requirements and required that certain states and cities with a history of voting discrimination obtain pre-approval from the Justice Department for all future changes to their voting laws. As shown in Table 5.2, the Act proved largely successful, as millions of African Americans were effectively reenfranchised in the South in subsequent decades.

The **Civil Rights Act of 1968** banned race discrimination in housing and made interference with a citizen's civil rights a federal crime. Even the state legislatures played a role in this civil rights transformation by ratifying the **Twenty-fourth Amendment** in 1964, which banned poll taxes in federal elections.

The focus of the civil rights movement began to shift in the mid- to late 1960s with the rise of "black nationalism," which was grounded in the belief that African Americans could not effectively work within the confines of a racist political system to produce effective change. Malcolm X, a leading advocate of black nationalism, sought to turn the characteristic of being black-skinned into a source of strength, and he urged African Americans to shun white culture

TABLE 5.2   The Effect of the Voting Rights Act on Registration Rates in the South

The following table compares black voter registration rates with white voter registration rates in seven southern states in 1965 and 1988. All numbers are percentage rates.

State	March 1965			November 1988		
	Black	White	Gap	Black	White	Gap
Alabama	19.3	69.2	49.9	68.4	75.0	6.6
Georgia	27.4	62.6	35.2	56.8	63.9	7.1
Louisiana	31.6	80.5	48.9	77.1	75.1	−2.0
Mississippi	6.7	69.9	63.2	74.2	80.5	6.3
North Carolina	46.8	96.8	50.0	58.2	65.6	7.4
South Carolina	37.3	75.7	38.4	56.7	61.8	5.1
Virginia	38.3	61.1	22.8	63.8	68.5	4.7

Source: The U.S. Commission on Civil Rights; Chandler Davidson and Bernard Grofman, *Quiet Revolution in the South* (Princeton, NJ: Princeton University Press, 1994).

and the values promoted by white society. He and other black nationalists criticized the civil rights leaders who advocated integration into white society rather than building separate black institutions. Following the assassination of Martin Luther King Jr. in 1968, the influence of black nationalism in the civil rights movement reached its peak during the late 1960s and early 1970s. Epitomizing a revolutionary vision of society that replaced the strategy of nonviolence with confrontational tactics, the Black Panther Party became a controversial militant presence in some cities.

Although the Black Panther Party had all but faded as a significant entity by 1972, black separatist organizations continue to maintain a strong presence. For example, the Nation of Islam (Black Muslims), led by Louis Farrakhan, preaches class consciousness and the concept of black self-rule. In 1995, Farrakhan's Nation of Islam led the Million Man March in Washington, D.C., which far outdrew the 1963 March on Washington. This Million Man March garnered international attention for Farrakhan's movement. Four years later, African American women held their own million women march.

Barack Obama's historic election as the first African American president in U.S. history may have fundamentally changed how many African Americans perceive their national government. Still, African Americans as a whole face immense challenges in making their voices heard in other institutions on the national political scene. Obama left a Senate chamber in November 2008 in which he had been the only African American then serving, and where he was just the third popularly elected African American senator to serve since Reconstruction. (His replacement as junior senator from Illinois, Roland Burris, also an African American, was appointed to the position, but was not reelected in 2010.) African Americans enjoyed a bit more success in the other house of Congress, as 42 African Americans (9.5 percent) served in the House of Representatives during the 111th Congress. Finally, African Americans have been mostly absent from the highest levels of state government: In 2006, Deval Patrick of Massachusetts became only the second popularly elected African American governor in history.

Continuing Struggles over Racial Equality

Two contemporary and hotly debated topics related to racial equality are affirmative action and racial profiling.

Affirmative Action. Some observers have called the civil rights movement a "Second Reconstruction," because it eliminated most of the vestiges of racial discrimination and segregation from the books. But would this successful legal revolution translate into real change? Various civil rights leaders in the 1970s and 1980s shifted their focus to affirmative action as a means of promoting African American gains in education and the workplace. **Affirmative action** programs are generally laws or practices designed to remedy past discriminatory hiring practices, government contracting, and school admissions. The women's movement too has benefited from affirmative action programs in the workplace and elsewhere. Although "quotas" (specifically defined numerical goals for hiring or admitting members of certain groups) have been used in the past, more often such programs involve giving some form of preferential treatment, whether by adding points to a mathematical score due to a person's status as a member of a particular racial group, or by creating economic or other incentives for administrative bodies to increase the diversity of their incoming workforce and/or educational institutions.

Proponents of affirmative action argue that past discriminatory practices have deprived certain racial groups and women of opportunities to get the skills or experiences they need to compete for jobs or college admissions on an equal footing with those who have not experienced such discrimination. The issue of affirmative action reached the U.S. Supreme Court in the case of *Regents of the University of California v. Bakke* (1978).[14] In 1973, Alan Bakke, one of 2,664 applicants for 100 seats at the University of California–Davis Medical School, interviewed with one of the school's officials, Dr. Theodore West. At that time, West told Bakke that he was a "very desirable applicant to the medical school." Thus Bakke was quite surprised when he was denied admission. Bakke in fact was rejected not once but twice for admission: in 1973 and again in 1974. In both instances, 16 applicants with lower grade point averages

Twenty-fourth Amendment: A 1964 constitutional amendment that banned poll taxes in federal elections.

affirmative action: Programs, laws, or practices designed to remedy past discriminatory hiring practices, government contracting, and school admissions.

Colleges can establish quotas determining the number of women, African Americans, and Hispanics to accept into a first-year class as a way of promoting racial diversity.

Fiction.

In 1978 the Court ruled in *Regents of the University of California v. Bakke* that hard quotas cannot be used as a means of promoting racial diversity in colleges and universities. Since then, the Supreme Court's rulings have, if anything, become even more restrictive concerning the use of affirmative action in higher education.

THE MORE THINGS CHANGE, THE MORE THEY STAY THE SAME

Tolerance Can Be Hard to Come by . . . Even in Congress

In **1917**, Montana's Jeanette Rankin, a Republican, arrived in Washington, D.C., as the first female to serve in the House of Representatives. Embracing her historic victory, she wrote a weekly newspaper column aimed at women suffragists and actively pressed for passage of child protection laws and other measures important to women. Still, many of her initial admirers were dismayed when in 1917 she cast the only vote in the House against U.S. entry into World War I, as they feared that her vote would handicap the cause of women's rights at a crucial time. The following year the Republican Party machine denied her the party's nomination and she lost her House seat. Rankin won her seat back again two decades later. Yet once again Rankin found her stay in Congress short-lived: On December 8, 1942, she became the only member of Congress to hold the distinction of voting against American involvement in *both* world wars. Of course by then Rankin was no longer a lone wolf, as eight other female House members served in the 77th Congress (along with the first female senator, Hattie Caraway of Arkansas).

In 1945 Adam Clayton Powell Jr. became the first African American from New York to hold a seat in Congress. When the Democratic congressman first took his seat, African Americans from northern states were frustrated that liberal white House members and Senators had thus far refused to challenge segregationists on the floor of Congress. Powell relished the opportunity to take on that challenge, even if it eventually rendered him an outcast in the House. On bill after bill Powell offered amendments and riders (all unsuccessful) denying funds to jurisdictions that maintained segregation. House members from his own party became increasingly frustrated with him; to make matters worse, Powell often broke from the Democratic Party ranks in high-profile ways, such as in 1956 when the party's weak civil rights plank led him to support Republican Dwight D. Eisenhower's presidential bid. By the mid-1960s, Powell came under attack for mismanaging the budget of the Education and Labor Committee he chaired; he was even accused of taking vacations at public expense. Democratic Party leaders eventually stripped him of his committee chairmanship and refused to seat him pending further investigation of the allegations. Luckily for Powell, he was rescued by another branch: In *Powell v. McCormack* (1969), the Supreme Court ruled that the

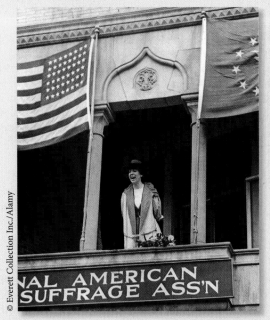

At left, Rep. Jeannette Rankin of Montana, speaking from the balcony of the National American Woman Suffrage Association; at right, Congressman-elect Keith Ellison, being sworn in to the House of Representatives in January 2007.

THE MORE THINGS CHANGE, THE MORE THEY STAY THE SAME

Tolerance Can Be Hard to Come by ... Even in Congress (continued)

House had acted unconstitutionally when it excluded Powell from his duly elected seat in Congress.

In 2006, Keith Maurice Ellison, a Democrat and member of the Farmer-Labor Party in Minnesota, became the first Muslim elected to the House of Representatives, and only the fourth elected Muslim official in American history. Ellison's landmark election occurred while the federal government's war on terrorism was continuing to spark unsupported allegations within the general public about the loyalty of Muslim Americans in general. Resistance even emerged from some of Ellison's own colleagues: when he announced plans to use the Koran for his unofficial swearing-in ceremony, Congressman Virgil Goode (R-Va) sent a letter to his own constituents warning that "if American citizens don't wake up and adopt the Virgil Goode position on immigration, there will likely be many more Muslims elected to office and demanding the use of the Koran." Undaunted, Ellison became a thorn in the side of the George W. Bush administration, opposing the troop surge in Iraq and advocating for Islamic causes.

For Critical Thinking and Discussion

1. What disadvantages do modern-day pioneers in battles over equality face? Is the fame they gain for being first worth the price they must pay from their opponents?

2. Why do you think Congress—and the House of Representatives in particular—is so slow to respond to the forces of demographic change?

---

and MCAT (Medical College Admission Test) scores than Bakke's were admitted to the school under a special minority admissions program. Bakke challenged the program as a violation of the Fourteenth Amendment's equal protection clause. In previous years, the courts had dismissed most lawsuits because they were quickly rendered "moot," a legal term that indicates that circumstances have removed the practical significance of deciding the case. (By attending some other school, those unsuccessful applicants had essentially prevented their cases from ever being decided.) But Bakke was determined to go to University of California–Davis Medical School and thus his case eventually reached the U.S. Supreme Court.

In deciding the case, the Supreme Court ruled that a university could take into account race and ethnicity when making decisions about the admission of students, as long as it did not utilize specifically assigned numerical goals. To the Court, no constitutional infirmity exists where "race or ethnic background is simply one element—to be weighed fairly against other elements—in the selection process." In his majority opinion, Justice Lewis Powell also heralded the benefits of a diverse student body, noting that students with particular racial backgrounds may bring to a school "experiences, outlooks and ideas that enrich the training of its student body."[15]

Five years after he was first denied admission, Bakke got what he wanted: on June 28, 1978, the U.S. Supreme Court directed that he be admitted to the university's medical school. Opponents of affirmative action thought they had received the victory they were looking for; after all, the Court held that the university could not use fixed racial quotas in this instance. But schools and universities took refuge in the Court's statements favoring the consideration of racial criteria more generally, and in the quarter century that followed, countless schools of higher education utilized race-conscious admissions programs. Thus although Alan Bakke won his personal battle for admission, the war over affirmative action would continue to be waged in the years that followed.

Opponents of affirmative action complain that such programs punish white applicants who played no role at all in the original discriminatory practices. They also claim that a racial divide that currently exists in this country may be exacerbated by affirmative action, because members of racial groups who benefit from such programs may be stigmatized by the perception that they are not fully deserving. Finally, affirmative action programs are explicit racial classifications, and thus may be thought to violate the principle of a "color-blind Constitution" that was celebrated by the Supreme Court's decision in *Brown v. Board of Education*.

A string of Supreme Court decisions in the late 1980s and 1990s has effectively brought an end to explicit affirmative action programs in public employment and contracting. The final nail in the coffin for affirmative action in contracting may have been the Court's decision in *Adarand v. Peña* (1995),[16] which held that any racial classification may be considered unconstitutional unless it meets the test of strict scrutiny: that it must be "narrowly tailored" to further a "compelling governmental interest," a standard that has proved nearly impossible for the government to meet. In fact, no affirmative action employment plan has been upheld as constitutional since the early 1990s.

By contrast, affirmative action in education remains steeped in controversy; the confusion over what is legal in this context was only partially resolved by two University of Michigan cases in 2003 that essentially reaffirmed *Bakke*'s finding that diversity constitutes a "compelling state interest" under certain circumstances. In *Grutter v. Bollinger* (2003),[17] the Court upheld the university's law school admission program because it only considered race as a positive factor in a review process where all individual applications were carefully reviewed and analyzed on their own merits. Yet that same day in *Gratz v. Bollinger* (2003),[18] the Supreme Court struck down the same university's undergraduate admissions program because instead of providing such careful, individualized review, it automatically awarded 20 points to all students from underrepresented groups, greatly enhancing their chances of being admitted. The Court declared that such a blanket award of benefits was not "narrowly tailored" enough to promote diversity.

In an attempt to balance the interests of having a diverse student body with frequently heard criticisms of affirmative action, state governments in Texas, Florida, and California have enacted alternative programs that would guarantee a place at the state's top universities for every student who finishes in the upper tier (normally the top 5 or 10 percent) of his or her high school class. Given that racial minorities tend to predominate at high schools both in the inner city and in especially poor rural neighborhoods in the South, these percentage plans tend to guarantee seats at major state universities to minority students who would

Students at the University of Michigan rally in support of affirmative action. In 2003 the U.S. Supreme Court upheld the use of affirmative action by the University of Michigan's Law School but struck down the affirmative action program utilized in undergraduate admissions.

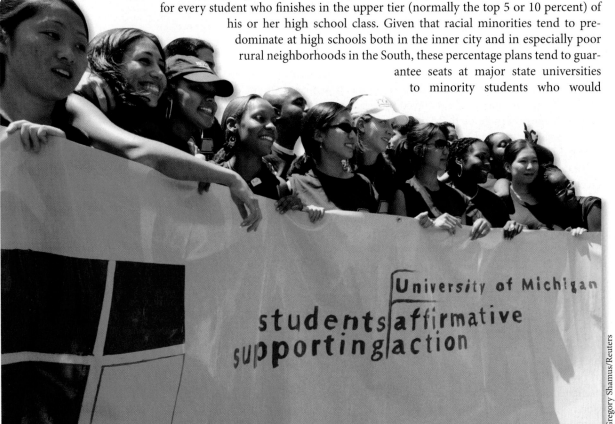

Gregory Shamus/Reuters

otherwise have been denied admission. Critics of the plans charge that they capitalize on patterns of segregation in housing and geography. Meanwhile the University of Texas program—which accepted 81 percent of incoming students through the "top 10 percent plan" and the rest through a review of various factors, including race—was under review by the Supreme Court at the time this edition went to press.

Racial inequality remains a fact of life in twenty-first-century America. According to a 2010 U.S. Census Bureau report, the mean and median income of African American households was just 65 percent that of all racial households combined.[19] Moreover, the *Journal of Blacks in Higher Education* recently reported that almost 37 percent of non-Hispanic white Americans age 30 to 34 hold at least a bachelor's degree, as compared to just 21 percent of all African Americans in that same age group.[20]

Racial Profiling. Statistics pertaining to the criminal justice system also testify to continuing racial inequality and racial tensions. For instance, although African American youth at the end of the twentieth century represented just 15 percent of the nation's total youth population, they made up 26 percent of the youth arrested, 31 percent of the youth referred to juvenile court, and 44 percent of the youth detained by the police.[21] African American males in particular compose a disproportionate number of those imprisoned. Critics of the system charge that it is racially biased, especially in how it metes out capital punishment. A study conducted by social scientist David Baldus in the early 1990s concluded that the victim's race was a significant factor in predicting which convicted murderers receive the death penalty. Specifically, killers of whites were 4.3 times more likely to be sentenced to death than killers of African Americans.

Racial discrimination may also characterize the initial phases of gathering information about a crime. For example, some law enforcement officials admit to using **racial profiling**—the practice of taking race into account when investigating crimes. African Americans may be stopped, questioned, and even held in custody not because there is specific evidence that links them to a particular crime, but because they fit a "profile" of the perpetrator that includes the characteristic of race.

Even in the wake of the civil rights revolution of the 1960s, little objection was raised against the practice, provided that it was done for purposes of "bona fide law enforcement" and not racial harassment, and so long as race was one of several factors that police officers considered when investigating crimes. But racial profiling became a source of considerable controversy in the 1990s.

racial profiling: The law enforcement practice of taking race into account when identifying possible suspects of crimes.

Scott Olson/Getty Images

A policeman interviews several teenagers on a street corner in Tucson, Arizona. The state's controversial new immigration law would allow officers to check any person's immigration status while in the process of enforcing other laws.

During the spring of 1999, victims of the New Jersey State Police force's allegedly overaggressive racial profiling testified at hearings held by the Black and Latino caucus of the state's legislature. President Bill Clinton publicly condemned racial profiling as a "morally indefensible, deeply corrosive practice." Finally, in March 2003, New Jersey became the first state in the nation to enact an antiprofiling law, which made any profiling by police punishable by five years in prison and a $15,000 fine. Yet by the end of that decade a majority of states still had not banned racial profiling as a law enforcement practice. In June 2003, President George W. Bush issued a directive that banned racial profiling by federal law enforcement agencies, though critics complained about both the law's exception for the use of racial profiling in "national security" investigations and the lack of enforcement mechanisms provided. Accordingly, claims of profiling in the past decade have focused on Naturalization, Customs, and Border Patrol agents accused of improperly restricting Muslims' entry or reentry into the United States.

Are criticisms of racial profiling exaggerated? Statistics overwhelmingly confirm that African American young men commit a disproportionate share of street crime in the United States. Thus not all racial profiling may be driven by prejudice against African Americans—civil rights leader Jesse Jackson admitted in 1993 that he was less fearful of white strangers than black strangers on dark streets, if only because, statistically speaking, he stands a greater risk of being robbed by a black person than a white person. At the same time, defenders of racial profiling (as one of many factors in the investigative process) tend to minimize the extent to which the practice adds to the sense of resentment of law enforcement felt by rich and poor blacks alike. No court has ever banned the practice outright. Moreover, even if a court did take such a bold action, it would be difficult to disprove an officer's claim that nonracial factors were in fact the primary consideration in his or her decision-making process.

The controversy over racial profiling entered the national conversation once again in 2012 with the fatal shooting of an unarmed 17-year-old African-American, Trayvon Martin, by a multi-racial neighborhood watch coordinator in a Sanford, Florida gated community. Though there was no indication that Martin was involved in any criminal activity, the coordinator, George Zimmerman, initially reported Martin to the police, and then shot him in an altercation that took place before the police arrived. The local police chose not to charge Zimmerman; nearly six weeks passed before Zimmerman was charged by a specially appointed prosecutor with second-degree murder. In the mean time, allegations of racist motivations both by the shooter and the police dominated media coverage of the incident. Critics also charged that laws like Florida's "Stand Your Ground Law"—which allows the use of force in self-defense without a duty to retreat—encourages racial profiling by citizens.

Controversies surrounding affirmative action and racial profiling highlight a vexing challenge in modern society. Even if all vestiges of formal racial classifications under the law are eliminated, calculations of racial differences inevitably enter into the subjective judgments of those in positions of authority. Thus for all the successful challenges launched against the racist legal and political structures that prevailed in American society during much of the twentieth century, the greater challenge of winning over the "hearts and minds" of individuals still remains.

The fatal shooting of Trayvon Martin, 17, led to charges of racism both against the shooter, and against the Sanford, Florida police department for its controversial handling of the matter.

THE WOMEN'S MOVEMENT AND GENDER EQUALITY

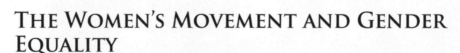

The process by which women achieved their own degree of equality during the course of the twentieth century took a circuitous route. In the early part of the twentieth century, women's rights leaders linked their calls for equality to other social movements of the same period, including those calling for child labor laws and increased literacy for immigrants. Initially, the women's rights movement pressed for protective laws, arguing that such legislation was necessary because of women's otherwise inferior legal status. For example, in *Muller v. Oregon* (1908),[22] the Supreme Court upheld an Oregon law that prohibited women laundry workers from being required to work more than 10 hours a day; similar laws applied to male workers had been invalidated as beyond the government's authority. Yet the reason for the holding could hardly have cheered advocates of women's equality: according to the Court, "a woman's physical structure and the performance of maternal functions place her at a disadvantage in the struggle for subsistence."

Judicial Scrutiny of Gender Discrimination and the Equal Rights Amendment

After ratification of the Nineteenth Amendment in 1920 guaranteed women the right to vote, women's rights groups began to alter their strategy for pursuing gender equality through the courts. In attempting to expand women's legal rights, these groups now argued that men and women should be treated equally. Their efforts met with only limited success at first. Although the NAACP achieved a string of successful challenges to racial discrimination in the 1940s and 1950s, the Supreme Court refused to view gender discrimination as similarly deserving of suspect scrutiny. In *Goesaert v. Cleary* (1948),[23] the Court upheld a Michigan law that banned women from tending bar unless they were the daughter or wife of the bar owner. Thirteen years later, the Court accepted as legitimate a Florida law that gave only women the right to excuse themselves from jury duty. In both cases, the Court continued to accept sex-role stereotypes of women as weak, and as dedicated above all else to taking care of the children at home. As the Court pointed out in *Hoyt v. Florida* (1961), "despite the enlightened emancipation of women from the restrictions and protections of bygone years . . . woman is still regarded as the center of home and family life."[24]

The women's rights movement did not achieve any significant breakthroughs in this regard until the early 1970s. Although the National Women's Party had first proposed an equal rights amendment to the Constitution in 1923 and in nearly every session of Congress since then, the amendment never got very far. In 1966, the newly formed National Organization for Women (NOW) became a new and forceful advocate for the Equal Rights Amendment (ERA) and other equal rights in education, employment, and political opportunities for women. NOW and other women's groups vigorously pressed for passage of the ERA, which stated simply that "equality of rights under the law shall not be denied or abridged by the United States or any state on account of sex." In 1972, Congress passed the amendment and sent it to the state legislatures for ratification. Even after the deadline for ratification was extended to June 1982, the amendment failed to achieve the approval of the three-fourths of state legislatures necessary for passage, falling just three states shy.

Although the ERA failed, women have recently achieved some noteworthy victories in politics. For example, women made political history in 2003, when Democrat Nancy Pelosi of California was elected minority leader in the House, the first woman ever to hold that high of a position in either branch of Congress. When Democrats won control of Congress after the 2006 midterm elections, Pelosi was elected Speaker of the House, again the first woman to hold that exalted position. (In 2011–2012, she served as House minority leader in the Republican-controlled Congress.) Pelosi's ascension to such high congressional leadership positions contrasts with the way women in Congress were often relegated to lesser committees and noninfluential positions in the past. When the 112th Congress began in 2011, there were 74 women serving in the U.S. House of Representatives (including 3 delegates) and 17 in the U.S. Senate.

Legal Challenges to Gender Discrimination

Ironically, some attributed the failure of the Equal Rights Amendment to other legal developments that may have rendered it unnecessary. The American Civil Liberties Union (ACLU), an organization traditionally dedicated to protecting the First Amendment rights of political dissidents and labor unions, turned its attention to women's rights in the late 1960s. Led in court by board member Ruth Bader Ginsburg (who was later appointed by President Clinton to the U.S. Supreme Court), the ACLU brought suit on behalf of women who charged that they had been victims of gender discrimination. Although the Court refused to accord gender discrimination the strict scrutiny normally reserved for racial discrimination, the ACLU achieved several victories in cases brought before the Supreme Court. In *Reed v. Reed* (1971),[25] the Court invalidated an Idaho law that gave males preference over females as administrators of estates. In *Frontiero v. Richardson* (1973),[26] the Court struck down a federal law requiring only female members of the armed forces to show proof that they contributed more than 50 percent to the income of their household in order to receive certain fringe benefits. And in the landmark case of *Craig v. Boren* (1976),[27] the Court invalidated an Oklahoma law that prohibited the sale of 3.2 percent beer to males under the age of 21 and to women under the age of 18.

Since *Craig*, the Supreme Court has applied *intermediate scrutiny* in all gender discrimination cases, a standard requiring the government to show that the gender classification is "substantially related to an important state interest." This level of scrutiny is less than that of strict scrutiny, which tends to invalidate all racial classifications. But under intermediate scrutiny, *nearly* all laws that discriminate against women will be invalidated. That fact alone distinguishes intermediate scrutiny from *rational basis* (or *minimum*) *scrutiny*, which asks only whether the law is "rationally related to a legitimate state interest"—a question to which courts can readily answer "yes" in nearly every instance.

In fact, in the modern era the Court has upheld only a handful of gender classifications as constitutional. For example, in 1981 the Court upheld a challenge to federal laws that required selective military service registration for males, but not for females. That same year the Court upheld a statutory rape law in California that punished men for having sex with underage females, although not vice versa. In each of those two instances, perceptions of real and relevant differences between men and women persuaded the Court to allow the discrimination to stand.

The highest-profile lawsuits charging gender discrimination targeted two all-male southern military academies, The Citadel in Charleston, South Carolina, and the Virginia Military Institute (VMI) in Lexington, Virginia. Both were classified as state institutions because they accepted significant funds from their respective states' budgets; thus each was hard-pressed to continue excluding women in violation of the Fourteenth Amendment's equal protection clause. Shannon Faulkner's frustrating experience as the first female cadet at The Citadel paved the way for future women to apply and be accepted to the institution in subsequent years. In an attempt to fend off gender integration of its own student body, VMI contracted with nearby Mary Baldwin College to create a parallel military program for women called the Virginia Women's Institute for Leadership (VWIL). But in 1996, the Supreme Court ruled that VWIL did not approximate VMI in terms of student body, faculty, course offerings, facilities, or opportunities for its alumni and ordered VMI to accept women. The issue of "separate but equal" that was resolved by the Supreme Court for racial classifications in 1954 was still being litigated for gender classifications well into the 1990s.

As with race discrimination, discrimination against women has been mostly eliminated in the formal sense. **Title IX** of the Federal Educational Amendments of 1972 prohibited the exclusion of women from an educational program or activity receiving financial assistance from the federal government. Courts have interpreted those provisions to force colleges and universities to provide as many athletic teams for women as they do for men. Title VII of the Civil Rights Act of 1964 extended to women's protection against discrimination in private and public businesses alike. Armed with equal rights to education and to entry in the workforce, women have made considerable occupational gains during the twentieth century.

Women have also benefited from affirmative action programs, especially in the workplace and in admission to professional and trade schools. To rectify long traditions of excluding women from certain occupations, scores of businesses and firms have aggressively recruited women. The period of most striking change occurred over the two decades between 1970 and 1990, when the proportion of women physicians doubled from 7.6 percent to 16.9 percent, and the percentage of women lawyers and judges nearly quadrupled from 5.8 percent to 22.7 percent. The percentage of women who are engineers rose over that same period from 1.3 percent to 8.6 percent. Still, complaints remain that in some occupations women continue to be clustered in low-paying positions. Thus women still compose only 3 percent of the nation's firefighters, 8 percent of state and local police officers, 1.9 percent of construction workers, 11.8 percent of college presidents, and 3 to 5 percent of senior-level positions in major companies. Some observers contend that a "glass ceiling" exists in many businesses, whereby women are prevented from receiving raises and promotions due them because of the subjective biases of their male bosses.

The securing of formal equality under the law and the proliferation of affirmative action programs have not always translated into actual equal opportunities to succeed. Women today continue to earn less than men in comparable positions—calls for "equal pay for equal work" have not always generated substantive changes in the pay structures of private companies or even the government. When women's salaries are compared with those of equally qualified men, the differences remain dramatic. Although Congress passed the Equal Pay Act in 1963

Title IX: The section of the Federal Educational Amendments Law of 1972 that prohibits the exclusion of women from an educational program or activity receiving financial assistance from the federal government. Courts have interpreted those provisions to force colleges and universities to provide as many athletic teams for women as they do for men.

to ensure that women would be paid the same as men for work that is "substantially equal" (that is, almost identical unless the pay difference is based on seniority, experience, or other legitimate factors), in the year 2008 a woman on average still earned only 77 cents for every dollar a man received.

A recent study conducted by the AFL-CIO revealed the salary discrepancies by gender for several different occupations:

- Female lawyers' median weekly earnings are nearly $500 less than those of male attorneys.

- Female clericals receive about $100 a week less than male clericals.

- Female doctors' median earnings are nearly $500 less each week than those of male doctors.

- Although 95 percent of nurses are women, they earn $100 less each week on average than the 5 percent of nurses who are men.

- Women elementary school teachers receive $70 less a week than men.

- Waitresses' weekly earnings are about $50 less than waiters' earnings.

Sexual harassment, normally in the form of unwelcome sexual advances by superiors, continues to pose a threat to working women in America. Since the mid-1980s the Supreme Court has considered such harassment—which includes any and all actions that create a hostile working environment, such as putting up provocative posters, making lewd comments, and so forth—to be a form of sexual discrimination actionable under Title VII of the 1964 Civil Rights Act. Still, many such sexual advances in the workplace continue despite the law, either because women remain unclear about the bounds of permissible conduct or because they fear reprisals for reporting the legal violations of superiors. Indeed, more than 4 in 10 women employed in federal agencies say they have experienced some form of harassment.[28] For all the legal equality that is now afforded to women, discrimination continues on a level that falls under the radar screen of the legal and judicial process.

OTHER STRUGGLES FOR EQUALITY

The political and legal systems in the United States directed increased attention during the late nineteenth and twentieth centuries to the plights of African Americans and women. The hardships suffered by these two groups inspired the passage of five constitutional amendments in all (the three Civil War Amendments, the Nineteenth Amendment granting women the right to vote, and the Twenty-fourth Amendment banning poll taxes) as well as many federal and state antidiscrimination laws. But both these groups' continuous quests for equal privileges under the law compose only part of the equal rights landscape. American history is replete with accounts of discrimination against other underrepresented groups as well. In recent years, these additional groups have begun to see their own claims to fairness and equal treatment recognized and vindicated within the American political system.

Native Americans

One of the nation's most unfortunate tales of mistreatment concerns Native Americans. For much of the eighteenth and nineteenth centuries, vast numbers of white Americans migrated west, pursuing what they viewed as their manifest destiny to settle across the continent. Consequently, millions of Native Americans were herded onto reservations according to a removal policy backed by the federal government. By a federal law passed in 1871, the government no longer agreed to recognize Native American tribes or nations as independent powers capable of entering treaties with the United States—all future tribal affairs were to be managed by the federal government without tribal consent. With passage of the Dawes Severalty Act in 1887, the U.S. government divided tribal lands still in existence among individual Indians who renounced their tribal holdings, further undermining tribal cultures and structures.

Although certain Native American tribes received piecemeal U.S. citizenship beginning in the 1850s and the Dawes Act granted citizenship to those who ceded their tribal holdings,

Native Americans protest federal policies by temporarily occupying Alcatraz Island in San Francisco Bay.

the class of Native Americans as a whole was not admitted to full citizenship until 1924, nearly 60 years after freed slaves had been afforded that same privilege. The federal government's attempt to undo the tribal structure did not produce widespread assimilation of Indians into American society as proponents of the Dawes Act intended; many chose to remain on reservations in an attempt to protect their culture from outside influences. Beginning in the middle of the twentieth century, some Native Americans turned to activism to protest their mistreatment by government authorities. From November 1969 until June 1971, 78 members of one tribe occupied Alcatraz Island in San Francisco Bay, demanding that it be made available as a cultural center to the tribes. Members of the American Indian Movement (AIM), an organization founded in 1968 to promote civil rights for Native Americans, occupied the Washington, D.C., offices of the Bureau of Indian Affairs in 1972, demanding that they receive the rights and privileges that had been promised them under the original treaties entered into by the federal government. This activism drew public attention to Native American causes and spurred action by Congress, which formally terminated its policy of assimilation and began to recognize the autonomy of Native American tribes to administer federal programs on their own lands. In the past quarter century, the U.S. government has settled millions of dollars in legal claims pressed by Native American tribes and has returned nearly half a million acres of land to the Navajo and Hopi tribes alone.

Asian Americans

Immigrants from East Asia—especially Japan and China—supplied much of the labor for building U.S. railroads in the nineteenth century. Even so, many were excluded from labor unions and denied other civil rights. Historically, the government has enacted several immigration acts specifically designed to limit or prevent Asian immigration. For example, the Chinese Exclusion Act passed in 1882 prohibited Chinese laborers from immigrating and denied U.S. citizenship to Chinese living in the United States. The 1907 Gentleman's Agreement with Japan prohibited the immigration of Japanese laborers. The National Origins Act of 1924 banned all Asians from further immigration to the United States.

Discrimination was especially rampant on the West Coast, where many Asian American populations were concentrated. Asian children were segregated into separate public schools in San Francisco, and the state of California restricted Japanese immigrants' rights to own farmland. Perhaps the most notorious incident of discrimination against Asian Americans occurred in 1942, when the U.S. government in response to the Japanese bombing of Pearl Harbor forcibly relocated 110,000 Japanese Americans to inland internment camps and seized their property. The Supreme Court upheld the internment policy in 1944, perpetuating an especially egregious brand of racial discrimination committed against legal residents of the country, including more than 60,000 legal U.S. citizens. National security concerns used to justify the policy at that time have been exposed in later decades as baseless claims.

In the post–World War II period, Asian Americans enjoyed increased economic prosperity and made significant civil rights gains as well. The ban on Asian immigration was officially lifted in 1952, and provisions of federal law encouraging the immigration of professionals helped attract to the United States large numbers of educated and highly skilled Asian professionals. The end of the Vietnam War in 1975 brought a great influx of immigrants from Vietnam, Laos, and Cambodia to the United States. With increasing numbers of immigrants from South Korea and the Philippines, the Asian American population today stands at approximately 4 percent of the American population as a whole.

Muslim Americans

The events of September 11, 2001, had a profound impact on America's foreign policy priorities and its approach to international terrorism. Those events have also taken a toll on citizens' perceptions of Muslim Americans, a group already set apart by its members' distinct religious practices and forms of dress. When plans for an Islamic community center and mosque to be built near the site of "Ground Zero" were revealed in early 2010, anger directed at Muslim Americans suddenly found a new cause. Polls showed a clear majority of Americans opposed to the project, even though most of those surveyed also recognized that the Muslim group had a legal right to build there. Politicians of all stripes, including Sarah Palin and Senate Majority Leader Harry Reid (D-NV), were quick to oppose the proposal, knowing that such opposition would offer them immediate political benefits.

The stereotype that associates the Islamic religion with terrorism is hardly applicable to the vast majority who practice the faith, but post–September 11 initiatives sanctioned by Congress under the USA Patriot Act targeted many Muslim Americans for questioning, and in some cases temporary detention. Of course African Americans have long suffered from racial profiling in criminal law enforcement, but the level and degree to which Muslim Americans have been singled out has created a special source of worry for civil rights groups.

Hispanic Americans

Hispanic Americans are defined as those of Spanish-speaking descent. A majority descended from Mexicans who were living in the Southwest when it became part of the United States in the 1840s. Even after immigration laws were tightened in the 1890s, hundreds of thousands of Mexicans continued to enter the United States illegally, drawn by opportunities in farming, mining, and other industries. Segregation of Mexican students from white students began in California in 1885 and continued through the 1950s; beginning in the 1960s, many Mexican Americans moved from rural areas to cities. Public schools in California, Texas, and elsewhere were forced to assimilate this growing population, including the children of illegal aliens, into overcrowded school districts.

Today, with more than 1,400 miles of border in common between the two nations, the United States and Mexico continue to be at odds over some important issues, including immigration. Meanwhile, more than 35 million people of Hispanic descent currently live in the United States, forming the nation's largest language minority. Cubans, Puerto Ricans, and numerous immigrants and refugees from other Central American countries contribute to the ranks of Hispanic Americans today. Some of the Cubans who left their native land hailed from privileged socioeconomic conditions; fleeing Castro's communistic agenda, their move to the United States was at least in part an effort to save their standard of living. Still, most immigrants from Hispanic countries such as Mexico and Cuba come from adverse economic circumstances in those nations. The crime linked to Mexican immigration in particular may be directly related to the impoverished conditions many of them live under in the United States.

Of course discrimination against Hispanics also contributes to the overall disproportionate levels of poverty and unemployment in this group. Unlike African Americans, Hispanics were never legally barred from the polls, and in New Mexico and California they have been a large and influential minority for several decades. And yet despite the large number of Hispanic Americans, the group's political power has yet to have its due influence on public policy, perhaps because many Hispanics are not yet citizens, and thus do not have the right to vote. Still, the appointment of Judge Sonia Sotomayor as the first Hispanic to the U.S. Supreme Court in 2009 was a source of pride among American Hispanic community.

As governor of Texas in the late 1990s before becoming president, George W. Bush regarded the Hispanic community as a potential source of growth within the more conservative Republican Party. Yet in the 2006 midterm elections, exit polls showed Hispanics voting in favor of the Democrats by a wide margin, helping them defeat many Republican incumbents. And in the 2008 presidential election, Hispanics voted for the Democratic ticket by a margin of more than two to one.

As Latin America (including Mexico) continues to dominate American immigration, Hispanic Americans have become by far the fastest growing ethnic minority in the country. As shown in Table 5.3, Mexico was the source for 29 percent of the overall growth in foreign-born persons living in the United States. Meanwhile, Latin America as whole accounted for 58 percent of the growth in the immigrant population from 2000 to 2010. It is no wonder, then, that both parties vied for the support of this crucial demographic in the lead-up to the 2012 president election. Hispanic Americans should see their political clout increase even more in the years to come.

Older Americans

Today approximately 13 percent of Americans are over the age of 65, compared with just 4 percent of Americans who were at that age at the beginning of the twentieth century. With their increased numbers has come increased political power; older Americans are among the most politically active of all citizens, and groups such as AARP (formerly the American Association of Retired Persons), with more than 40 million members on its rolls, have become especially

TABLE 5.3 Countries Sending the Most Immigrants to the United States, 1990, 2000, and 2010

Country	2010	2000	1990
1 Mexico	11,711,103	9,177,487	4,298,014
2 China, Hk, and Taiwan	2,166,526	1,518,652	921,070
3 India	1,780,322	1,022,552	450,406
4 Philippines	1,777,588	1,369,070	912,674
5 Vietnam	1,240,542	988,174	543,262
6 El Salvador	1,214,049	817,336	465,433
7 Cuba	1,104,679	872,716	736,971
8 Korea	1,100,422	864,125	568,397
9 Dominican Republic	879,187	687,677	347,858
10 Guatemala	830,824	480,665	225,739
11 Canada	798,649	820,771	744,830
12 United Kingdom	669,794	677,751	640,145
13 Jamaica	659,771	553,827	334,140
14 Colombia	636,555	509,872	286,124
15 Germany	604,616	706,704	711,929
16 Haiti	587,149	419,317	225,393
17 Honduras	522,581	282,852	108,923
18 Poland	475,503	466,742	388,328
19 Ecuador	443,173	298,626	143,314
20 Peru	428,547	278,186	144,199
All of Latin America	**21,224,087**	**16,086,974**	**8,407,837**
All Immigrants	39,955,854	31,107,889	19,767,316

Source: Center for Immigration Studies, http://www.cis.org/articles/2011/record-setting-decade.pdf

influential players on the political scene. This increased influence has been used to counteract incidents of age discrimination in the workplace and elsewhere. The Age Discrimination in Employment Act, passed in 1967 and broadened in 1986, makes it unlawful to hire or fire a person on the basis of age. Older Americans have also been at the forefront of lobbying efforts to protect Social Security trust funds and to ensure the continuation of cost-of-living adjustments to their payments. Ironically, older Americans' success at wielding influence within the political system has given credence to the suggestion that age classifications do not require suspect scrutiny by courts; at least in this instance, the political system appears to protect the civil rights of this particular subset of Americans.

Individuals with Disabilities

As with age classifications, discrimination against Americans with physical and mental disabilities has never received heightened scrutiny from the courts. Misperceptions about the nature of certain disabilities have on occasion led to discriminatory treatment of individuals with disabilities. In the 1920s, some states passed laws authorizing the sterilization of institutionalized "mental defectives"—Justice Oliver Wendell Holmes callously dismissed all legal challenges to such laws with the statement that "three generations of imbeciles are enough." Today, thanks to significant technological and medical advances, a more enlightened social understanding, and a more sophisticated approach to educating citizens about the nature of these limitations, millions of Americans with disabilities have been mainstreamed into society, attending school, going to work, and living otherwise normal lives. The Americans with Disabilities Act of 1990 established a national commitment to such mainstreaming efforts and extended to those with disabilities protection from discrimination in employment and public accommodations comparable to that afforded women and racial minorities under the 1964 Civil Rights Act.

Gays and Lesbians

Of all the groups that have claimed to be discriminated against in the United States, homosexuals stand among the least successful in having their claims to equal treatment vindicated under the law. Gays and lesbians have traditionally suffered discrimination in society, whether from those whose religions frown on homosexuality in general or from those who are simply uncomfortable with this lifestyle. In the period immediately following World War II, a movement for gay rights emerged with generally integrationist goals, encouraging homosexuals to conform to most existing social standards. Gays and lesbians assumed a more activist quest

Activists for the rights of individuals with disabilities at a rally advocating broader enforcement of the Americans with Disabilities Act of 1990.

On May 9, 2012, President Barack Obama announced in a television interview that he had personally reached the conclusion that "same sex couples should be able to get married."

for equality beginning in the late 1960s, marching for "gay power," urging reluctant gays to "out" themselves by openly admitting their sexual orientation, and interrupting government meetings to draw attention to their cause of equal treatment and nondiscrimination.

Although homosexual activists made advances, no significant antidiscrimination legislation followed. Some communities reacted by passing laws that prohibited the granting of "any special rights or privileges" to homosexuals. The Supreme Court in *Romer v. Evans* (1996)[28] struck down such a provision of the Colorado Constitution in 1996. Perhaps the biggest court victory of all for gays and lesbians occurred in 2003, when the Supreme Court in *Lawrence v. Texas[i]* struck down a Texas law that forbade same-sex partners from engaging in certain types of intimate relations. Despite these victories, the Supreme Court has still never recognized homosexuals as a protected class on a par with women or African Americans. Battles over the right to same-sex marriage—formally approved by at least nine states and D.C. as of December 1, 2012—remain a high priority on the gay rights agenda, promising to engage other state legislatures in debate for years to come.

The issue of homosexuals in the military first drew intense national attention when U.S. Army Colonel Margarethe Cammermeyer was discharged from the armed forces in June 1992 when, during a routine security clearance interview, she acknowledged that she was a lesbian. Cammermeyer hinged her hopes for restatement on a promise made to her by candidate Bill Clinton during his successful presidential campaign that fall. Yet soon after taking office, President Clinton began to backtrack on his promise: at his first televised news conference two weeks into his presidency, he indicated he might go along with a supposed compromise that would segregate gays within the military. The ultimate compromise reached was a "don't ask, don't tell" policy that would allow gays still in the closet to stay in the military, so long as they never publicized their status.

In his 2010 State of the Union Address, President Barack Obama indicated that he planned to work with Congress and the military to repeal the "don't ask, don't tell" rule. Eighteen months later he made good on this promise. After a federal court ruled in July 2011 that a ban on openly gay troops was unconstitutional, President Obama and the Chairman of the Joint Chiefs of Staff certified to Congress that ending the policy would not harm the nation's "military readiness." With the support of Congress, the federal government then formally ended the policy on September 20, 2011. Meanwhile, antigay violence continues. The 1998 murder of college student Matthew Shepard brought new calls for hate crime legislation directed at such criminal activity. Despite suffering countless setbacks, gays and lesbians continue to enjoy a significant presence in the political system, forging alliances with more liberal administrations and even electing some openly gay politicians. The attention paid to the Log Cabin Republicans—members of that party who actively promote gay and lesbian rights—provides some indication that homosexuals represent a political force in America today that can no longer be ignored.

Fact or Fiction?

As of December 1, 2012, same-sex marriage was still legal in less than one in five American states.

Fact.

By December 1, 2012, just nine states (Connecticut, Iowa, Maine, Maryland, Massachusetts, New Hampshire, New York, Washington and Vermont) and the District of Columbia were granting marriage licenses to same-sex couples.

Title IX Brings Gender Equality—and Controversy—to a Campus Near You

Every March on college campuses all across the country, many students get caught up in March Madness—the National Collegiate Athletic Association (NCAA) men's basketball tournament that crowns the sport's annual champion. In April, another event occurs that has become a serious business at many schools as well: the NCAA women's basketball tournament. Women have been crowned as NCAA champions since 1982; before that, between 1972 and 1982, women's college basketball championships were held by the Association for Intercollegiate Athletics for Women. Women who have won the NCAA championship may not realize that they owe some form of debt not just to the parents who supported them and the coaches who coached them, but also to the late Rep. Patsy Mink (D-HI), the first Asian American woman elected to Congress. In 1972 Representative Mink authored the Title IX Amendment to the Higher Education Act, which banned gender discrimination in any "education program or activity" receiving federal assistance. Though Mink's law made no explicit mention of intercollegiate athletics, that is where the law has had its most prominent impact to date.

The implications of Title IX are profound: courts have interpreted the statute to require gender equality in roster sizes for men's and women's athletic teams in general, as well as to require comparable budgets for recruiting, scholarships, coaches' salaries, and other expenses. The law has not been without controversy: some schools have eliminated successful men's athletic teams to bring the percentage of women's athletic scholarships up to par. Critics complain that men's football and basketball teams are normally the only sports teams that bring in revenue, and so they should be judged independently of all the other sports. Regardless, colleges and universities have fallen into line in the past 30 years; so much so, in fact, that in 2006 the Western Kentucky University Board of Regents ordered the upgrading of its football team (from Division 1-AA to 1-A), ostensibly because its share of female scholarship athletes had become disproportionately large.

For Critical Thinking and Discussion

1. Football and men's basketball generate more revenue for colleges and universities than all the other sports combined. Should the revenue generated by individual sports help determine whether those programs should be maintained?

2. Do you participate in other aspects of college life such as school-sponsored clubs or the school band where gender inequality exists in some form? Does the intense focus of Title IX enforcement on sports teams in particular tend to obscure gender discrimination where it exists elsewhere on campus?

AP Photo/Julie A. Jacobson

Notre Dame Head Women's Basketball Coach Muffet McGraw at a practice in 2012.

The civil rights movement continues to be waged in modern-day courts and legislatures. Despite all the gains of the past, battles are still being taken up by racial, ethnic, and religious groups, as well as by other traditionally disadvantaged groups, to attain equal rights under the law. Just as pioneers of the suffragette movement fought a slow and painful battle to achieve the right to vote for women, so too do gay rights activists continue to walk a difficult path to achieve support for same-sex marriage. Today other groups, such as Native Americans and Muslim Americans, walk this path as well, seeking recognition of rights traditionally denied to them by authorities acting on behalf of "the political majority." For every one or two steps they take forward, they are just as likely to take one other step backward. The hearts and minds of the majority are not so easily transformed. Fortunately, the openness of the American political system provides many mechanisms for groups to pursue and achieve equality over the long run.

SUMMARY: PUTTING IT ALL TOGETHER

TYPES OF EQUALITY

- References to equality in discussions of American politics often refer to one of three types: political equality, economic equality, and social equality.
- Civil rights are those political, social, or economic rights conferred by the government to individuals in groups that had previously been denied those rights. The battle for civil rights in American history has focused primarily on African Americans and other ethnic groups (Hispanics, Asian Americans, Native Americans, Muslim Americans), women, older Americans, individuals with physical disabilities, and gays and lesbians.

Test Yourself on This Section

1. The Civil Rights Act of 1968 was aimed primarily at advancing
   a. political equality.
   b. social equality. ✓
   c. economic equality.
   d. cultural equality.

2. The notion of "equality" as a value defining American political culture was articulated specifically in which of the following documents?
   a. Declaration of Independence
   b. Bill of Rights
   c. Articles of Confederation
   d. Article I of the Constitution

3. Distinguish between political and social equality. Give an example of each.

THE STRUGGLE FOR EQUALITY: APPROACHES AND TACTICS

- The tactics used by groups seeking to achieve civil rights include working within the existing rules and political process, litigation, boycotts, and civil disobedience.

Test Yourself on This Section

1. Which of the following Supreme Court decisions declared that racial segregation in public schools was unconstitutional?
   a. *Scott v. Sanford*
   b. *Plessy v. Ferguson*
   c. *Marbury v. Madison*
   d. *Brown v. Board of Education*

2. The civil rights leader who first advocated pursuing equality for African Americans using "agitation" techniques rather than accommodation was
   a. Booker T. Washington.
   b. W. E. B. DuBois.
   c. Al Sharpton.
   d. Martin Luther King Jr.

3. What is "civil disobedience," and how does its use advance the goals of the civil rights movement?

THE AFRICAN AMERICAN STRUGGLE FOR EQUALITY AND CIVIL RIGHTS

- The long and hard-fought African American struggle for equality included heated debate as early as the Constitutional Convention. The Civil War and the amendments that passed in its aftermath (Thirteenth, Fourteenth, and Fifteenth) ended slavery, granted citizenship to former slaves, guaranteed all Americans "equal protection under the laws," and denied states the ability to prevent voting rights on the basis of race.

- Despite these amendments, states have used many means to prevent African Americans from obtaining political, social, and economic equality, including Black Codes, literacy tests, poll taxes, and Jim Crow laws. A number of U.S. Supreme Court decisions, along with congressional legislation and constitutional amendments, have served to bring America closer to the goal of equality for African Americans.

- The *Brown v. Board of Education* decision of 1954 eliminated the "separate but equal" doctrine. The movement toward civil rights for minority groups in all public accommodations began in the later 1950s and emerged as a major force under the leadership of Martin Luther King Jr. and his use of nonviolent civil disobedience tactics.

- Two contemporary issues relating to civil rights are affirmative action and racial profiling. The courts have struck down many affirmative action programs, but many states continue to try to find ways for government to level the playing field in hiring and college admissions.

- King's legacy was memorialized through sweeping civil rights legislation, including the Civil Rights Act of 1964 (which banned racial discrimination in all public places), the Voting Rights Act of 1965 (which effectively reenfranchised millions of African Americans by eliminating the literacy test and property requirements for voting), and the Civil Rights Act of 1968 (which prohibited discrimination in housing and made it a federal crime to deny individuals their civil rights).

Test Yourself on This Section

1. Which of the following most directly played a role in bringing about the Civil War?
   a. *Plessy v. Ferguson*
   b. the *Dred Scott* decision
   c. the Kansas-Nebraska Act
   d. *Brown v. Board of Education*

2. Which of the following banished slavery from all states and U.S. territories?
   a. Thirteenth Amendment
   b. Fourteenth Amendment
   c. Fifteenth Amendment
   d. Sixteenth Amendment

3. The legal standard advanced in *Brown v. Board of Education* and other cases that tends to invalidate most state laws that discriminate on the basis of race is
   a. reasonable intent.
   b. probable cause.
   c. eminent domain.
   d. strict scrutiny.

4. In the *Bakke* decision, the Supreme Court ruled that
   a. the use of racial quotas violates the equal protection clause.
   b. quotas may be used to achieve equality.
   c. affirmative action of any kind is unconstitutional.
   d. quotas may be used in medical school admissions but not in law school admissions.

5. What is "affirmative action," and how has the court squared its application with the constitutional promise of "equal protection under law"?

THE WOMEN'S MOVEMENT AND GENDER EQUALITY

- The seeds were sown for the movement for gender equality in the early twentieth century with the ratification of the Nineteenth Amendment, guaranteeing women the right to vote.
- Not until the formation of the National Organization for Women (NOW) and its emergence as a significant political force did women's equality capture national attention.

Test Yourself on This Section

1. Which U.S. Supreme Court justice led the ACLU in its legal fight during the 1960s and 1970's to achieve protection against gender discrimination?
   - **a.** Sandra Day O'Connor
   - **b.** Ruth Bader Ginsburg
   - **c.** Elana Kagan
   - **d.** Sonia Sotomayor

2. Which of the following statements is true?
   - **a.** Women have achieved parity with men in salaries.
   - **b.** The Equal Rights Amendment was passed in 1972.
   - **c.** Title IX substantially increased women's opportunities to participate in college sports.
   - **d.** About half of all college presidents are now women.

3. What is meant by the legal standard of "intermediate scrutiny," and how does this concept apply to gender discrimination?

OTHER STRUGGLES FOR EQUALITY

- Some of the most heated contemporary debates over equality relate to discrimination against Muslim Americans (and how to protect their civil rights in the post-9/11 era), Hispanic Americans and immigration policy, and the rights of gays and lesbians, particularly as they relate to marriage.

Test Yourself on This Section

1. The law passed by Congress in 1887 that attempted to divide tribal lands and undermine Native American cultures was the
   - **a.** Indian Limitation Act.
   - **b.** Jim Crow Act.
   - **c.** Dawes Act.
   - **d.** Native American Assimilation Act.

2. The fastest growing minority group in the United States is
   - **a.** African Americans.
   - **b.** Asian Americans.
   - **c.** Native Americans.
   - **d.** Hispanic Americans.

3. The first state to pass a law formally authorizing the granting of licenses for same-sex marriages was
   - **a.** Vermont.
   - **b.** California.
   - **c.** Massachusetts.
   - **d.** Florida.

4. Why is the U.S. Patriot Act the subject of controversy among those who are concerned about equal rights for Muslim Americans?

KEY TERMS

affirmative action (p. 119)

Brown v. Board of Education (1954) (p. 110)

civil rights (p. 109)

Civil Rights Act of 1964 (p. 118)

Civil Rights Act of 1968 (p. 118)

Civil War Amendments (p. 111)

economic equality (p. 108)

Jim Crow laws (p. 112)

Plessy v. Ferguson (1896) (p. 113)

political equality (p. 108)

racial profiling (p. 123)

social equality (p. 108)

strict scrutiny (p. 114)

Title IX (p. 126)

Twenty-fourth Amendment (p. 119)

Voting Rights Act of 1965 (p. 118)

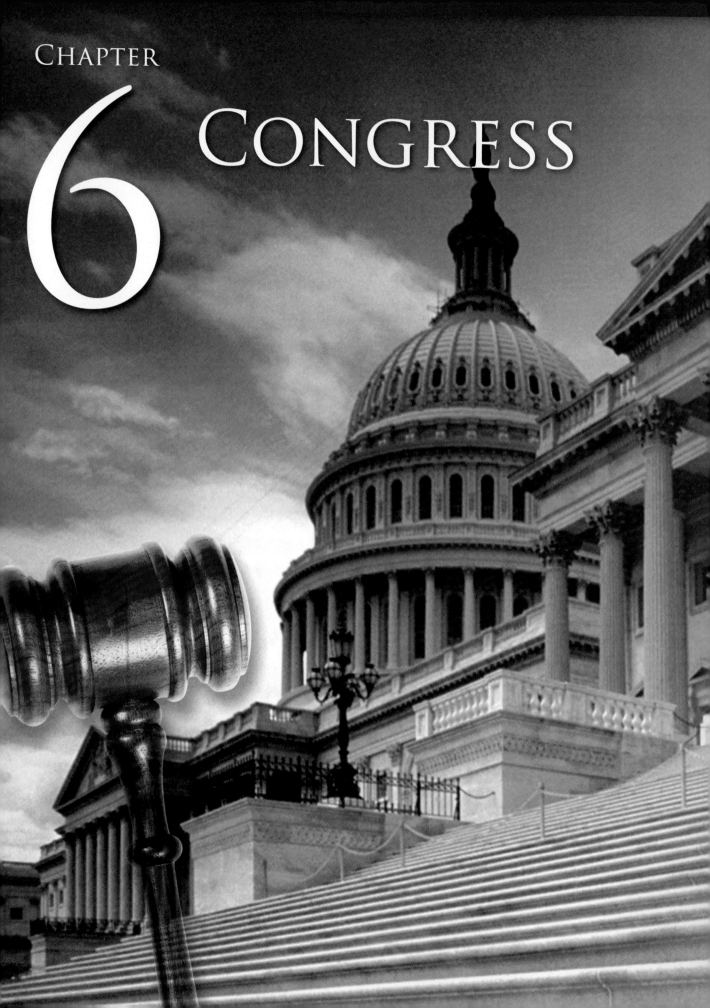

Learning Objectives

Article I and the Creation of Congress

- Define the role the U.S. Congress plays as the legislative branch of government, and how that role has evolved over time

The Structure and Organization of Congress

- Identify the structure and powers of Congress, explain bicameralism, and distinguish between the roles of the House and Senate
- Assess the role that political parties play in the leadership of Congress
- Identify key leadership positions and their functions in Congress
- Explain reapportionment and redistricting

The Committee System

- Compare and contrast the different types of committees found in Congress

How a Bill Becomes a Law

- Describe the various steps necessary for a bill to become a law

Oversight and Personnel Functions of Congress

- Explain why Congress often delegates its lawmaking authority to regulatory agencies
- Describe the role of the Senate in confirming presidential appointments, and the congressional procedures for impeachment and removal of executive and judicial officers

Constituent Service: Helping People Back Home

- Assess the "casework" functions of members of Congress in assisting constituents, educating them on policy issues, and performing other services on their behalf

C ongress is a large and complex institution. It is the branch of government that is primarily responsible for creating new laws, but it largely takes its cues from the White House. Although the Constitution makes no mention of the role that political parties might play in making laws, partisanship has become the primary factor that organizes Congress and its daily operations. Nonetheless, the nuances of the legislative process provide ample opportunities for the minority party, or even a small set of members, to thwart new laws from passage. Among the three branches of government, intense partisan divisiveness is most likely found in the halls of Congress. In this chapter, we explore the organization of the Congress and its leadership structure. We trace the steps of the tedious lawmaking process, the checks that Congress has on the other branches of government, and the important role the members of Congress play back in their home districts.

1840   1850   1860   1870   1880

1854

Then

Senator Preston Brooks shown clubbing Senator Charles Sumner on the floor of the U.S. Senate during an antislavery debate in 1856.

Source: © North Wind Picture Archives/Alamy

Partisan divisiveness often overtakes the halls of Congress, but during certain periods of our nation's history, the level of partisan nastiness and incivility has reached heights that all but paralyze the legislative branch. Consider the era of the 1850s, just before the Civil War. Historians often cite this period as representing the low point in relations between the parties in Congress, sometimes even characterized by physical violence. Most notably, House member Preston Brooks of South Carolina actually walked over to the Senate floor and clubbed Senator Charles Sumner of Massachusetts nearly to death because of their disagreements over slavery. Indeed, Congress was bitterly divided in all its feeble attempts at passing legislation. The issues that divided the parties were not limited to slavery, though the Kansas-Nebraska Act of 1854 proved so controversial that it actually gave birth to the Republican Party in opposition to it. The party divisions also reflected a commercial-versus-agricultural conflict. The term *filibuster*—from a Dutch word meaning "pirate"—first became popular during the 1850s, when it was applied to efforts by the Senate minority to hold the Senate floor in order to prevent a vote on a bill. The heightened divisiveness of the 1850s became dysfunction, driven by congressional party-based factions that could not work together to solve America's problems.

2011

Now

Rep. Joe Wilson shouts to President Obama "You lie!," during a 2009 Obama address to Congress during the health care reform debate.

Source: Chip Somodevilla/Getty Images

By 2012, congressional approval ratings had fallen to all-time lows, according to polls. Certainly, these ratings were a product of the vitriol and partisanship that began in 2009 with the 111th Congress. The Senate witnessed a record number of filibusters, as not one simple majority vote on a substantive bill prevailed throughout this period. The legislative battle over health care reform epitomized this bitter partisan reality, as Senate Republicans voted over and over along party lines to reject any and all bills proposed by the Democrats. Consider this telling statistic: for the first time ever, in the 111th Congress, the *National Journal*'s vote ratings showed that the most conservative Democratic senator was now to the left of the most liberal Republican, ensuring that there

was no longer any overlap ideologically between the parties. In the House there were contentious, drawn-out partisan battles as well. In a speech that President Obama delivered at the Capitol to promote health care reform, Representative Joe Wilson (R-SC) shouted "You lie!" in response to an Obama claim about coverage of illegal immigrants under the proposal. In 2011, a squabble over the normally perfunctory matter of raising the statutory debt ceiling ensued, jeopardizing a first-ever default. Moreover, Congress could not even manage a full-fledged substantive debate over such issues as climate change, jobs, or the continuing mortgage crisis. Indeed, the extreme partisan divisiveness in Congress beginning in 2009 had led to congressional dysfunction.

- Approximately half of the bills introduced into Congress end up being passed into law.

- In writing the Constitution, the Founders decided that all members of Congress would be directly elected by the people.

- The 2010 House elections produced a 63-seat shift to the GOP, the largest House gain by any party in the past century.

ARTICLE I AND THE CREATION OF CONGRESS

Article I of the U.S. Constitution created Congress; and the fact that it came first was no accident. James Madison, the Father of the Constitution, referred to Congress as the "first branch of government," and as a graduate student, Woodrow Wilson (later the 28th president of the United States) wrote in his book *Congressional Government* (1885) that "anyone who is unfamiliar with what Congress actually does and how it does it . . . is very far from a knowledge of the constitutional system under which we live."[1] As the legislative branch of the federal government, Congress has ultimate authority for enacting new laws. Because this authority is central to any system of government, the Founders engaged in considerable debate and took great care in building this first branch.

There was little question that a congress of some type would be the central institution in the new political system—a congress had been a central feature in all attempts to organize the states up through and including the Constitutional Convention of 1787. The Albany Congress of 1754 was the first attempt to unite the colonies—at the time for common defense against the French in the pending French and Indian War. The Albany Plan of Union called for the colonies to organize through the vehicle of a "congress." In addition, colonial efforts to deal with emerging conflicts with the British led to the formation of two congresses: the First Continental Congress in 1774, and then the Second Continental Congress in 1775. After the revolutionary war was won, the first official government of the United States, created under the Articles of Confederation, again used a congress as its organizing principle. It is not

Joseph Rainey of South Carolina was the first African American elected to Congress. He took office in 1870 and was reelected four times.

surprising, then, that Article I, Section 1 of the U.S. Constitution states: "All legislative powers herein granted shall be vested in a Congress of the United States."

The Founders engaged in plenty of debate, negotiation, and compromise in defining the powers, functions, and structure of the U.S. Congress. The complexity of this institution continues today. Congress is filled with paradoxes. On one hand, it is a highly democratic institution in which senators and representatives are selected in free and open elections; on the other hand, Congress often is responsive to an exceedingly narrow set of specialized interests. Citizens and journalists frequently criticize the institution as being too slow to act responsively; yet voters return more than 9 in 10 of their elected members to office. At times, such as in the weeks following the terrorist attacks of September 11, 2001, Congress can show enthusiasm for tackling large issues expeditiously: within days of the attacks it passed the USA Patriot Act, which featured numerous antiterrorism measures. At other times, it seems to avoid taking positions on important issues, such as campaign finance reform and abortion rights. Many of these factors have led to very low confidence ratings in Congress from the American public. Figure 6.1 shows the results of the Gallup Poll's 2011 survey on confidence levels in a variety of institutions. As the chart shows, confidence in Congress ranks the lowest.

Most significantly, Congress is the branch of the U.S. government that ensures representation of the people through the direct election of members of the House and, in more recent times, of members of the Senate as well. Through its 535 members, Congress provides representation of many groups throughout the country, such as women, African Americans, Native Americans, and Hispanics.

FIGURE 6.1 Confidence in Congress

Source: © Cengage Learning

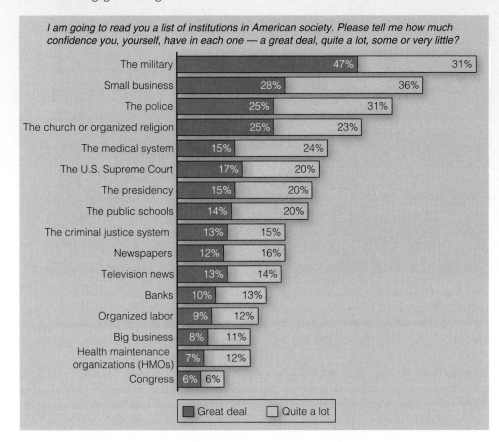

I am going to read you a list of institutions in American society. Please tell me how much confidence you, yourself, have in each one — a great deal, quite a lot, some or very little?

Institution	Great deal	Quite a lot
The military	47%	31%
Small business	28%	36%
The police	25%	31%
The church or organized religion	25%	23%
The medical system	15%	24%
The U.S. Supreme Court	17%	20%
The presidency	15%	20%
The public schools	14%	20%
The criminal justice system	13%	15%
Newspapers	12%	16%
Television news	13%	14%
Banks	10%	13%
Organized labor	9%	12%
Big business	8%	11%
Health maintenance organizations (HMOs)	7%	12%
Congress	6%	6%

THE STRUCTURE AND ORGANIZATION OF CONGRESS

A fundamental characteristic of Congress is that it is organized into two separate chambers, the Senate and the House of Representatives, and is thus termed a **bicameral legislature.** At the time the U.S. Constitution was written, 10 of the 13 states featured this type of legislature. Creating a bicameral legislature enabled the Founders to reach a compromise between two factions at the Constitutional Convention—those who represented large states and wanted congressional representation according to population, and those from small states who favored the model of the Articles of Confederation: that each state, regardless of population, would be equally represented in Congress. The "Great Compromise" reached by the convention delegates allowed for equal state representation in the Senate, and representation based on population in the House. These two chambers have shared lawmaking responsibilities since 1789.[2]

This nearly equal sharing of legislative power between the two chambers is significant. Many other nations in the world have bicameral legislatures, but the two legislative houses are rarely equal in power and usually do not share power. In the British Parliament, for example, the House of Lords has little power and serves a mostly symbolic function in that nation's politics, whereas the House of Commons wields the most authoritative power. Legislatures in other nations, such as Canada, France, Germany, Israel, and Japan, are also heavily dominated by one house. By contrast, in the U.S. Congress, the Senate and House are coequal chambers, with each enjoying about as much power as the other. Similar to the United States, the national legislatures in Italy and Mexico include two houses with nearly equal power. Many nations have *unicameral* legislatures that consist of only one body, such as the 275-member legislature elected to govern in Iraq in 2005.

bicameral legislature: A legislature composed of two separate chambers.

In 1916, Jeannette Rankin, a Republican from Montana, became the first woman elected to Congress. After one term in the House, she ran for the Senate and lost. She was reelected to the House in 1940. An ardent pacifist, she was the only member to vote against American entry into both World War I and World War II.

Bicameralism has important implications for the legislative process in American politics—passing new laws is difficult because the two chambers, constructed so differently, must come to absolute agreement before a new law is enacted. The slowness that so often characterizes lawmaking in Congress is, in part, a product of this reality. The sharing of power and the "checks" that each chamber has on the other are no mistake. Indeed, the Founders intentionally built a Congress that would move slowly and carefully in the adoption of new laws, a process that, although often characterized as gridlock, ensures that change is well contemplated before it is adopted.

The House of Representatives: The "People's House"

The Founders intended the House of Representatives to be the "people's house," or the institution through which ordinary people would be represented in government. At the time the Constitution was adopted, the only federal officials directly elected by the people were members of the House of Representatives. Senators were chosen by state legislatures; the president and vice president were selected by electors in the electoral college; and judges, ambassadors, and high-ranking officials in the executive branch were nominated by the president and approved by the Senate. In Federalist No. 51, James Madison admonished, "As it is essential to liberty that the government in general should have a common interest with the people, so it is particularly essential that the branch of it under consideration [the House] should have an immediate dependence on, and an intimate sympathy with, the people."[3] The House of Representatives thus directly connects voter sentiment with popular representation.

To ensure that members of the House would be accountable to voters, Article I, Section 2 sets the term of a House member at two years, keeping members constantly attentive to the currents of public opinion. Indeed, because of their relatively brief term of office, members of the House are typically consumed with concerns about winning reelection. This preoccupation has been well documented by scholars such as Thomas Mann, who argues that incumbent House members are in campaign mode most of the time, feeling "unsafe at any margin" of victory.[4]

Article I also ensures that the House of Representatives reflects the popular will by requiring that the number of representatives from each state be proportional to each state's population. States are not equally represented in the House of Representatives; rather, the population of each state is proportionately represented, at least to a large degree. This means that a more populous state has greater representation than a less populous one. The state of California, for example, now has 53 seats in the House of Representatives, compared to Wyoming, which has only 1.

The first Congress in 1789 included 65 members, consistent with the Article I requirement that the number of House members should not exceed one for every 30,000 people in a state. As the nation grew in both the number of states and number of people, the number of members of the House of Representatives also grew. If the ratio of 30,000 people to one representative persisted to today, there would be about 10,000 members of the House of Representatives! By the mid-1800s, Congress began enlarging the population size of a congressional district to keep the membership of the House from getting too large. Public Law 62-5, passed in 1911 to take effect in 1913, capped the total number of House seats at 435.[5]

Today there are still 435 **congressional districts**, each represented by one House member. The number of people who are represented in a congressional district is tied to a number that changes after every census. Since fixing the number of seats at 435, Congress has struggled to find an equitable way to allocate House seats to the states—a process known as **reapportionment**.

Several U.S. Supreme Court decisions in the early 1960s[6] established the basic principle that guides the process of reapportionment after every census—the "one person, one vote" principle. According to this principle, the population size of congressional districts must be as equal as possible. Currently, that amounts to roughly 650,000 people per district. The requirement that each state maintain at least one House district causes some variance among the population sizes of each district. The single congressional district for Wyoming, for example, has a population of about 570,000 because that is the number of people who live in that state. Consequently, Wyoming's population is proportionately "overrepresented," compared to most other congressional districts. Because congressional districts cannot cross state boundaries, the population size of congressional districts across states also varies. Yet once congressional districts are officially allocated to states based on the U.S. census, the size of each district within a state must be as close to equal as possible.

The Constitution requires that a new census of the population be taken every 10 years, which is used to reapportion seats in the House of Representatives to each state. The states are then responsible for **redistricting** congressional boundary lines to achieve equal representation in each of the congressional districts; that is, redrawing congressional district lines to achieve the "one person, one vote" principle within the borders of the state.

In addition to equalizing the size of congressional districts, parties in each state try to optimize the partisan characteristics of each district to their advantage. This drawing of district boundaries to favor one party over the other is referred to as **gerrymandering**, a term named for Elbridge Gerry, who was a signer of the Declaration of Independence, a Massachusetts delegate to the Constitutional Convention, a U.S. congressman, governor of Massachusetts, and vice president under James Madison. While governor, he endorsed legislation that redrew districts in Massachusetts, resulting in huge advantages for his political party, the Democratic-Republicans. The map of one of the new districts took on an odd shape, that of a salamander. Gerry's political opponents, the Federalists, dubbed the plan the "gerrymander plan." The political fallout for Gerry was significant—he lost his next bid for governor. But the legacy of gerrymandering continues. Every decade or so, parties in states with more than one House member must ultimately negotiate a redistricting plan based on gerrymandered district boundaries that each party hopes will optimize its electoral successes.

Article I requires that all members of the House of Representatives be at least 25 years of age, have been a U.S. citizen for a minimum of seven years, and live in the state (though not necessarily the congressional district) from which they are elected. These requirements are somewhat less restrictive than those for the Senate—another indication of the Founders' intention to give the people a greater role in deciding on who members of the House should be.

The Senate: A Stabilizing Factor

Whereas the Founders wanted to make the House of Representatives highly responsive to the people, their idea for the Senate was quite different. The Senate was to represent the states—with each state having two senators, thus being equally represented. As adopted, the Constitution specified that senators were to be elected not by the people of the state, but by the state legislatures, another way to recognize states' importance. Not until passage of the Seventeenth

congressional district: A geographic region (either a state itself or a region located entirely within one state) whose residents select one member to represent it in the House of Representatives.

reapportionment: The allocation of a fixed number of House seats to the states.

redistricting: The act of redrawing congressional boundaries to achieve equal representation in each of the congressional districts.

gerrymandering: The drawing of House district boundaries to the benefit of one political party over another. The term is named for Elbridge Gerry, a Massachusetts delegate to the Constitutional Convention, who (as governor) redrew districts in this fashion to favor the Democratic-Republicans.

Fact or Fiction?

In writing the Constitution, the Founders decided that all members of Congress would be directly elected by the people.

Fiction.

It wasn't until 1913, with the passage of the Seventeenth Amendment, that U.S. Senators were directly elected by the people. The Founders decided that senators would be selected by state legislatures.

Amendment to the Constitution in 1913 were senators elected directly by the people of the state they represented.

The Founders were also concerned that the "people's house" might be too prone to radical changes in membership resulting from swift changes in popular opinion. James Madison in particular regarded the U.S. Senate as "a necessary fence against this danger,"[7] able to resist fast changes in federal legislation because it was less accessible to the people. In fact, during the first five years of our constitutional government, the U.S. Senate met in closed session. By sharing legislative power with the House of Representatives, the Senate, a slower, more deliberative body, would be the mechanism for protecting against the potential tyranny of the masses. Thus the creation of new laws would be forced to proceed at a more thoughtful pace.

The Constitution sets the term of a U.S. senator at six years, three times the length of that for a House member. The Founders staggered the terms of senators. Every two years, only one-third of the seats in the Senate are up for reelection, as compared to all of the seats in the House. So although in theory all of the seats in the House can change every other year, the Senate may change only by a maximum of 34 seats every two years and is thus less prone to drastic changes in membership.

The qualifications for becoming a U.S. senator are also tighter. The minimum age is 30, five years older than in the House, with the idea being that older people are less likely to endorse radical change. Also, a U.S. senator must have been a citizen for at least nine years (rather than seven for the House) and be a resident of the state that he or she represents.

Article I requires that there be two senators from each state. The total number of senators grew from 26 in 1789 to 100 in 1959, the year Alaska and Hawaii became the 49th and 50th states, respectively, to join the Union. Although the size of the Senate has grown, it still remains small, at least relative to the size of the House of Representatives. The smaller size of the Senate is often cited as the primary reason why debate in the Senate tends to be more civil and camaraderie between individuals more important.

Leadership in Congress

Unlike the executive branch of American government, which is headed by the president, no one person or office leads Congress as a whole. Leadership is distinct in the Senate and the House of Representatives. Though both chambers must work together to pass new laws, each chamber maintains its own leadership structure to work on bills, pass laws, and conduct its other business. Cooperation between the House and Senate is necessary to accomplish legislation.

Rep. John Boehner (R-OH) making a tearful address on election night in November 2010, after he learned that the GOP would control the House, and that he would likely become the next Speaker.

The principal factor driving leadership in each chamber is the political party system, which, interestingly, is not mentioned in the U.S. Constitution.[8] The two-party system in America generates a majority of members from one of the two major parties, in both the Senate and House of Representatives. Since 1851, the majority party in each house has been either the Democratic Party or the Republican Party. Members of the party that has the majority of seats constitute the **majority caucus**, whereas those who are members of the party with a minority of seats constitute the **minority caucus**. The majority caucus in the House and the majority caucus in the Senate use their respective majorities to elect leaders and maintain control of their chamber. The larger the party's majority, and the more discipline and unity among party members, the stronger the power of the majority party's leadership ability.

majority caucus: The members of the party that has the majority of seats in a particular chamber.

minority caucus: The members of the party that has a minority of seats in a particular chamber.

Over the past 30 years, party control of the Senate has changed hands quite a few times. The 1980 elections gave Republicans control of the Senate for the first time since 1954, and they held at least a narrow margin of control up until the 1986 elections, when Democrats won back a majority. The 1994 elections swept the Republicans once again back into the majority, and they maintained control over that body until 2001, when the senate was equally divided. The Republicans regained control after the 2002 midterm elections, but then forfeited it once again in 2007, when 51 senators caucused with the Democrats and placed them back in control. As a result of the 2008 elections, the Democratic majority widened its margin to a 60–40 majority.

In the midterm elections of 2010, however, the GOP scored a number of victories in the Senate. While the Democrats retained control of the upper chamber (by a margin of 53–47), their margin of control was slashed significantly.

The Democrats then expanded upon that majority somewhat in the 2012 elections, ensuring that a friendly Senate would remain in place for Barack Obama at the outset of his second term as President.

By contrast, the House of Representatives has enjoyed a bit more stability, undergoing fewer changes in party control of the majority caucus since 1954. Up through 1994, the Democratic Party had maintained a seemingly iron grip of control over the House. Finally after 40 years, the 1994 elections transformed a Democratic majority to a Republican majority. The Republicans continued to dominate the House until the 2006 midterm elections, at which point the Democrats regained leadership of the people's chamber. Democratic control of the House, however, proved short lived. In 2010, the GOP won back more than 60 House seats from the Democrats and reestablished a Republican majority, which it then retained in the 2012 elections.

Leadership in the House of Representatives

The only guidance the Constitution offers regarding House leadership is contained in Article I, Section 2: "The House of Representatives shall choose their Speaker and other officers." The **Speaker of the House** is the title given to the leader of this chamber. Every two years, when a new Congress takes office, the full House of Representatives votes to determine who the Speaker will be from among its 435 members. In practice, the selection of Speaker is made by the political party in the House that holds the majority of seats. Members in the majority caucus meet prior to the vote for Speaker and agree on their leader, who receives virtually all the votes from the majority party members, thus guaranteeing that the majority party will occupy the Speaker of the House post.

Speaker of the House: The leader of the House of Representatives, responsible for assigning new bills to committees, recognizing members to speak in the House chamber, and assigning chairs of committees.

As presiding officer, the Speaker of the House is the most powerful member of the House of Representatives, although that was not always so. Throughout the first century of the American political system, the Speaker acted mostly as procedural leader, or presiding officer, of the House. However, with the accession of Joe Cannon to Speaker in 1903, this post became much more powerful. Cannon, a Republican from Illinois, served in the House for more than 50 years and was Speaker from 1903 to 1911. As Speaker, Cannon used the House Rules Committee to amass a tremendous amount of power.[9] Known as "Uncle Joe," he arbitrarily recognized who could speak in the House chamber and required that any measure passing the Rules Committee would have to be personally approved by him. Cannon also made a practice of

The 2010 House elections produced a 63-seat shift to the GOP, the largest House gain by any party in the past century.

Fiction.

The large GOP shift in seats in 2010 is tied for sixth place among partisan seat shifts over the past century. The single biggest shift in this era occurred in 1932, when Franklin D. Roosevelt helped the Democrats shift the margin in the House by 97.

filling important committee posts with those who were loyal to him. A coalition of Democrats and insurgent Republicans eventually unseated Cannon, but Uncle Joe permanently changed the visibility and power of the Speaker position.

The Speaker remains powerful today for a variety of reasons. First, as the person responsible for assigning new bills to committees, the Speaker can delay the assignment of a bill or assign it to a committee that is either friendly or hostile to its contents, a power that gives the Speaker control over much of the House agenda. Second, the Speaker has the ability to recognize members to speak in the House chamber. Because an important part of the legislative process involves members debating bills on the House floor, the Speaker's authority over this process is significant.

Third, the Speaker is the ultimate arbiter and interpreter of House rules. The ability to cast final judgment on a rule of order can make or break a piece of legislation. Fourth, the Speaker appoints members to serve on special committees, including conference committees, which iron out differences between similar bills passed in the House and Senate. The Speaker's influence is thus felt in the final changes made to a bill before Congress completes work on it. Fifth, the Speaker plays an influential role in assigning members to particular permanent committees. Some committees, as we will see later in this chapter, are more important than others. Being on the Speaker's "good side" can help in getting a good committee assignment. In addition, the Speaker hand-picks the nine members of the all-important Rules Committee. Finally, the Speaker has ultimate authority to schedule votes in the full House on a bill, an authority that allows the Speaker to speed the process or delay it, using timing to either improve or subvert a bill's chances of being passed.

Partisan control of the House is the key factor regarding how that body is organized to do its work. Because the party that holds a majority of seats selects the Speaker, the majority party controls the legislative agenda through members serving in other leadership posts, including chairs of committees.

To promote partisan leadership, the majority caucus in the House votes for a House **majority leader**, and the minority caucus for a House **minority leader**. These leaders oversee the development of their party platforms and are responsible for achieving party coherence in voting. Other important party leadership positions in the House are the House minority and majority **whips**. Whips report to their respective party leaders in the House and are primarily responsible for counting up the partisan votes on bills—that is, they contact members of their party caucus and try to convince them to vote the way their party leadership wants them to vote. The whips spend much of their time on the floor of the House, on the phone, or in the offices of their party colleagues, counting votes and urging their members to vote the party line on bills.

Leadership in the Senate

The Constitution prescribes that the presiding officer of the Senate is the vice president of the United States. In this capacity, the vice president also holds the title of president of the Senate. Unlike the Speaker of the House, who is necessarily a member of the House of Representatives, the president of the Senate is not a member of the Senate. The president of the Senate cannot engage in debate on the floor of the Senate and has no legislative duties in the Senate, with one notable exception: to cast a vote in the Senate in the event of a tie. John Adams, the first vice president of the United States, was the most frequent tiebreaker in U.S. history, casting a vote 21 times in the Senate.

In practice, the vice president rarely shows up on the Senate floor to preside over its session. The presiding officer, in the absence of the vice president, is the **president pro tempore** (*pro tempore* is Latin, meaning "for the time being"). By custom, the official president pro tempore is the senator in the majority caucus who has served the longest number of consecutive years in the Senate. Again, however, in practice the president pro tempore rarely exercises the authority to preside over the Senate. With fewer rules and a greater culture of respect to fellow members than in the House, the presiding officer of the Senate serves what is largely a ceremonial role.

CHECK THE LIST

The Top 10 Largest Partisan Gains in House Elections Since 1914*

The 2010 congressional elections produced historic gains by the Republican Party. In the modern era of congressional elections however, the GOP gains, while impressive, are by no means unprecedented. The 2010 GOP gains in the House are only the sixth highest total dating back to 1914.

Following are the top 10 partisan seat gains in House elections since 1914.

Partisan Gains in the House

✓	1932	Democrats	+ 97
✓	1938	Republicans	+ 80
✓	1922	Democrats	+ 75
✓	1948	Democrats	+ 75
✓	1914	Republicans	+ 66
✓	1920	Republicans	+ 63
✓	2010	Republicans	+ 63
✓	1946	Republicans	+ 56
✓	1994	Republicans	+ 54
✓	1930	Democrats	+ 53

▶ **POINT TO PONDER:** Over the past century, only two of the top 10 seat shifts in the House occurred in the past 50 years. Eight of the 10 occurred in the earlier part of the twentieth century. Why do you think larger shifts in House seats were more likely to happen before 1950?

*1914 is selected as the starting point for this list because that was the first congressional election after House membership was capped at 435 and the first congressional election after the Constitution was amended to require the direct election of U.S. Senators by a state's population of voters.

Leadership in the Senate is principally a function of partisanship, with the majority and minority caucuses organizing through leadership posts similar to those of the House of Representatives. As in the House, the majority party exercises tremendous power by controlling the agenda and mobilizing majority votes on important issues for the party. The majority caucus elects a Senate majority leader, and the minority caucus a Senate minority leader. These leaders are the main party spokespersons in the Senate, lead their party caucuses in proposing new laws, and are the chief architects of their party's platform. As leader of the majority, the Senate majority leader enjoys special power in making assignments to leadership of committees.

As in the House, the Senate majority and minority leaders are supported by whips, majority and minority. The whips in the Senate serve the same function as those in the House—they keep track of how caucus members are planning to vote on upcoming bills, and they communicate the positions of party leaders on upcoming legislative votes.

Leaders in the Senate generally have far less power than their counterparts in the House. The smaller number of senators requires less discipline in membership, and the culture of the Senate includes a greater amount of deference from one senator to another. Because there are fewer rules and formal procedures in the Senate, leaders and rule-making members have less power to control debate in that body.

Pictured here is the leadership of the Senate, beginning in the 110th Congress, which started its work in January 2007. Pictured with their Senate colleagues are Minority Leader Mitch McConnell (R-KY), left, and Majority Leader Harry Reid (D-NV).

THE COMMITTEE SYSTEM

The work of a member of Congress can be classified into four categories: (1) running for re-election, (2) serving constituents, (3) working on legislation, and (4) providing oversight of federal agencies. Working on legislation involves two activities—working on bills in committees and voting on proposed bills.[10] The bulk of work on legislation consists of what members do in committees, which includes generating ideas for new laws, debating the merits of those ideas, holding hearings, conducting investigations, listening to the testimony of experts, offering modifications and additions to proposed bills, and giving important advice to all House and Senate members regarding how they should vote on a new bill. Committee work also is the means through which members fulfill their role of oversight of federal agencies. Voting, on the other hand, is a rather simple and straightforward process. Members show up on the House or Senate floor and cast a vote of either "aye," "nay," or "present," indicating their support for, opposition to, or abstention from voting on a proposed piece of legislation.

bill: A proposed law presented for consideration to a legislative body.

Every year about ten thousand bills are introduced into Congress. A **bill** is a formally proposed piece of legislation, and many bills are long, complex documents with much legal and technical information. It is not practical to assume that each senator and House member reads and digests every bill that is introduced. As a way to manage the workload, both chambers of Congress rely heavily on a committee system. In both the House and Senate, each member is assigned to a few committees and becomes an expert in the subject area of the committee. Most of members' legislative work revolves around the committees to which they are assigned.

Congressional committees also include subcommittees, providing for even more specialization and division of labor. Currently there are more than one hundred subcommittees in the

House alone. Each of the subcommittees is also assigned a chair, so many members in the majority party of the House are chairs of either a committee or subcommittee. In the Senate, with fewer members, all members of the majority are usually the chair of at least one committee or subcommittee. A House member sits on an average of five different committees, whereas a senator sits on an average of seven committees.

What makes the committee system so powerful a force in legislation? It is the deference that most members give to the work of their colleagues in committees. Recognizing specialized knowledge, respecting the need for division of labor, and protecting one's own authority in the committees in which one serves all lead senators and House members to vote on the basis of a committee's recommendation on a bill.

Types of Committees in Congress

There are four general types of congressional committees: standing committees, select committees, conference committees, and joint committees.

In the summer of 2012, the White House and House Republicans sparred over the issue of college loan rates. Pictured above are college students enthused by President Obama's arguments for keeping rates low.

Standing committees are permanent committees that exist in both the House and Senate. Most standing committees focus on a particular substantive area of public policy, such as transportation, labor, foreign affairs, and the federal budget. A few focus on procedural matters of the House and Senate, such as the House Rules Committee and the Senate Rules and Administration Committee. The most significant power of the standing committee is that of **reporting legislation**—which means that the full House or Senate cannot vote on a bill unless the committee votes to approve it first. No other type of congressional committee has the power to report legislation. Table 6.1 lists the standing committees of the House and Senate.

Standing committees have been the heart and soul of congressional organization since the very early 1800s. Just like today, standing committees then were divided into substantive policy areas and had plenty of authority to determine the future of a bill within their jurisdiction. For example, in 1802 the House of Representatives established the Ways and Means Committee to set policies for America's federal tax system. Any bill dealing with changes in the tax system had to pass through this committee, as it still does today. The House Ways and Means Committee remains the primary author of tax bills, including the tax cuts approved by Congress and signed into law by President Bush in 2001 and 2003.

Though most standing committees focus on a substantive area of public policy, such areas of focus are often broad and complex. In order to further divide labor and provide for even greater levels of specialization, most standing committees include subcommittees. For example, the House Transportation and Infrastructure Committee includes the following subcommittees: Aviation; Coast Guard and Marine Transportation; Economic Development, Public Buildings, Hazardous Materials, and Pipeline Transportation; Ground Transportation; Oversight, Investigations, and Emergency Management; and Water Resources and Environment.

Before the House of Representatives or the Senate can vote on any bill, it must first be approved by a majority of members on the committee. A number of factors can affect a committee's consideration of a bill, which can seriously slow down the process of a bill becoming law and create a sense of "legislative gridlock." When a committee gets a new bill, the chair usually directs the bill to a subcommittee. The subcommittee discusses the bill, holds hearings, and makes changes, additions, or deletions to the bill. Usually, after a successful subcommittee vote, the bill moves back to the full committee, where additional debate and hearings might occur. Only after a successful committee vote is the bill ready to be considered by the full House and/or Senate. This process occurs in both the House and the Senate. There are, therefore, many opportunities for standing committees to slow the policymaking process, or bring it to a grinding halt.

standing committee: A permanent committee that exists in both the House and Senate; most standing committees focus on a particular substantive area of public policy, such as transportation, labor, foreign affairs, and the federal budget.

reporting legislation: The exclusive power of standing committees to forward legislation to the full House or Senate. Neither chamber can vote on a bill unless the committee votes to approve it first.

TABLE 6.1 The Standing Committees in Congress

Committees in the House	Committees in the Senate
Agriculture	Agriculture, Nutrition, and Forestry
Appropriations	Appropriations
Armed Services	Armed Services
Budgets	Banking, Housing, and Urban Affairs
Education and Labor	Budget
Energy and Commerce	Commerce, Science, and Transportation
Financial Services	Energy and Natural Resources
Homeland Security	Environment and Public Works
House Administration	Homeland Security and Governmental Affairs
Intelligence*	Finance
Judiciary	Foreign Relations
Natural Resources	Health, Education, Labor, and Pensions
Oversight and Government Reform	Judiciary
Rules	Rules and Administration
Science and Technology	Small Business and Entrepreneurship
Small Business	Veterans Affairs
Standards of Official Conduct	
Transportation and Infrastructure	
Veterans Affairs	
Ways and Means	

*Technically a "permanent select committee."

Source: © Cengage Learning

select committee: A committee established by a resolution in either the House or the Senate for a specific purpose and, usually, for a limited time.

A second general type of committee in Congress is the **select committee**, a special committee established to examine a particular issue of concern. Select committees do not have the power to report legislation, and they are not permanent. Once their work on a particular issue of the day is complete, the select committee is dissolved. Select committees are often formed to deal with a particularly serious national problem—a problem for which legislation may not be considered but rather a recommendation might be made. Recently, for example, select committees have been established to investigate the problem of illegal immigration and the national drug problem. House or Senate leaders may choose a select committee to deal with an issue for political reasons as well. If leaders suspect that a standing committee might have trouble reporting a bill to the full chamber, they might appoint a select committee, which does not have reporting power.

conference committee: A joint committee of Congress appointed by the House of Representatives and the Senate to resolve differences on a particular bill.

A third type of committee found in Congress is the **conference committee**. As described earlier in this chapter, the House and Senate are equal players in the legislative process. This means that both chambers debate, hold hearings on, comment on, and vote on individual pieces of legislation. A bill, then, is considered, modified, and voted on by both the House and the Senate. Assuming that a bill survives both chambers and passes, it is likely that the changes made to the bill during the standing committee process will differ between the House and Senate. Conference committees consist of both House members and senators, who work together to iron out differences in the House and Senate versions of a bill.

A fourth type of committee is the **joint committee**, which consists of members from both chambers. Joint committees do not propose legislation and have no reporting power, but rather are investigative in nature, focusing on issues of general concern, such as oversight of programs that are administered by the executive branch of the federal government. Unlike select committees, which are temporary and focus on a narrower topic, joint committees are typically permanent and focus on broader policy areas. An example is Congress's Joint Economic Committee. This committee keeps tabs on the performance of the nation's economy and provides oversight to the Federal Reserve Board, the unit that, among other things, has authority to adjust the federal prime interest rate.

joint committee: A committee composed of members of both the House and the Senate that is investigative in nature.

Leadership of Congressional Committees

Although there are a handful of broad leadership positions such as "presiding officers" and "party leaders" in the House and Senate, the vast majority of leaders are the chairs of the many committees and subcommittees in the two chambers. The power of the majority caucus is fully felt in the committee and subcommittee chairs, as all chairs are members of the majority caucus. Committees are where Congress gets most of its work done, and the chairs of committees have a great deal of power in determining what gets done and when it gets done.[11]

For example, the chairs decide how much time, if any, to spend on a new bill; they choose the people who will testify before the committee; and they allot the time to be spent on testimony and committee discussion. House and Senate leaders choose committee chairs from members of the majority caucus, a selection generally based on seniority and party allegiance. For each committee, the majority party's ranking, or senior, member is typically the person who becomes the committee chair, although the Speaker of the House ultimately determines the chairs for House committees and the Senate majority leader does the same for Senate committees.[12] Though seniority remains important, congressional reforms in 1974 and 1994 have somewhat reduced the power of seniority in the determination of committee chairs. More recently, the selection of chairs and the chairs' adherence to party leadership has provided a strong basis for party influence in congressional leadership.

Partisan Nature of the Committee System

The large number of standing committees and subcommittees, along with the significant power of the committee given its expertise in the policy area, disperses legislative power. It is in the interest of the majority party, however, to control what bills are given priority, how bills are written, and what bills get passed. Thus, the primary organizational characteristic of most committees in Congress is partisanship. To control the committee agenda and the committee votes, the majority caucus ensures that all committees have a majority of members of their party.[13] Furthermore, the chair of each committee is from the majority caucus. In addition, the majority caucus typically reserves a "supermajority" of seats on the most powerful committees, such as the Rules and Appropriations Committees.

Congressional Staffing

The 435 House members and 100 senators are supported by a large professional staff, many of whom are young, recent college graduates. Staffers perform a variety of support functions related to the roles of members of Congress. They conduct background research on bills, help generate new ideas for bills, provide services to constituents, and aid in the oversight of executive agencies. There are three categories of congressional staff.

First is the member's **congressional personal staff**. Members of Congress are given a budget to support a group of staffers to assist them. They typically have a staff in their Washington, D.C., office and one in their home district office. The personal staffers serve a number of legislative support functions, including tracking bills that the member has introduced and conducting research on ideas for new bills. They also work with the local media in the member's home district, answering journalists' questions and providing information on the member's legislative activities. Perhaps the personal staffers' most important responsibility is responding to constituents in

congressional personal staff: A group of workers who assist an individual member of Congress in performing his or her responsibilities.

The Library of Congress, Washington, D.C.

the district. House and Senate members receive many kinds of communications from constituents, ranging from requests for information about bills and explanations of why they voted a particular way, to letters expressing opinions on various issues and requests for speaking engagements. The personal staffers are responsible for dealing with these myriad constituent inquiries.

A second type of staffing resource at Congress's disposal is the **congressional committee staff**. Each standing committee of Congress employs a professional staff, many of whom are policy or legal experts in the policy area of the committee.

The third form of support for members of Congress is **congressional agencies**. The volume of legislative work has grown substantially over the years, as has the complexity of the federal budget and the policy issues that Congress deals with. One way that Congress has dealt with problems of growth and complexity has been to delegate authority to executive agencies of government, a consequence of which was that Congress began to lose control of the ability to keep tabs on what those agencies were doing. The explosion of budget deficits in the 1970s and suspicions about the administration that were inspired by the Watergate scandal also left Congress feeling that it lacked necessary information for effective monitoring of executive agencies under presidential control. Through the 1970s, Congress relied on budget data from the Office of Management and Budget (OMB), which reports to the president. Congress suspected that the budget figures produced by the OMB were compiled with an eye toward supporting the president's point of view. In response, in 1974 Congress created a new congressional agency, the Congressional Budget Office (CBO), to monitor the nation's economic situation and provide objective projections of the national budget. It reports directly to Congress. With the CBO, Congress no longer needs to depend exclusively on the executive branch to gather economic data and produce information to help Congress oversee the budget process.

At the same time, Congress also substantially expanded the size and funding of the Government Accountability Office (GAO; formerly called the General Accounting Office) and the Congressional Research Service (CRS). Congress uses the GAO to monitor executive agency expenditures. Essentially, the GAO audits the spending of federal organizations to find and remove any abuses. The CRS is Congress's information and statistical data archive. It provides members with information they might need in preparation for writing a bill, conducting a hearing or investigation, or making a speech. Other important agencies of Congress include the Library of Congress, which acts both as the de facto national library of the United States as well as a research arm for congressional members; and the Government Printing Office, which prints and provides access to documents produced by and for all three branches of the federal government.

congressional committee staff:
A group of workers assigned to congressional committees to support each committee's legislative work.

congressional agencies:
Government bodies formed by and relied on by Congress to support members of Congress in performing their functions.

The Power of Congressional Caucuses within the Major Parties

The two-party system in the United States features the Democratic and Republican parties, each of which has very broad bases of support. The diversity of views within parties is quite evident in the party caucuses in both the House and Senate. When a smaller group of members holds strong and passionate views on a particular topic, and those views are not as passionately held by (or even opposed by) other members in their party's caucus, that group will often form a special interest caucus to demonstrate their allegiance to the topic and to provide a framework for collective action.

By 1969, the number of African Americans elected to the House of Representatives had grown substantially. These members, such as Shirley Chisholm (D-NY), felt that the Nixon administration was particularly unresponsive to their concerns, and so formed the Democratic Select Committee as a way to organizationally advance their agenda. At the suggestion of Rep. Charles Rangel (D-NY), who still serves in the House, the group was renamed the Congressional Black Caucus (CBC) in 1971, and operated as a senate select committee to effectively promote the African American agenda. In 1995 the newly elected GOP majority abolished the 28 existing special select committees in the House, and so the CBC lost its public funding. The CBC reconstituted as a Congressional Member Organization, and continues to operate from private donations. Each year the CBC requests, and has been granted, a meeting with the president at the White House to ensure that its views are known.

In 2010, Rep. Michelle Bachmann (R-MN) launched the Tea Party Caucus. In his successful run for a senate

Pictured here are several members of the Tea Party caucus surrounding the caucus chair, Rep. Michelle Bachmann (R.-Minn).

AP Photo/Gerald Herbert

seat in 2010, Tea Party–endorsed candidate Rand Paul (R-KY) suggested that Bachmann form the caucus, and upon his victory Paul quickly signed up for the caucus. A number of other Tea Party–backed candidates won their election bids in 2010. The Caucus is particularly committed to advancing the goals of the Tea Party movement, which includes fiscal discipline in the form of cutting government spending, limited government, and a strict interpretation of the Constitution. In the 2011–2012 term of the 112th Congress, the Tea Party Caucus has been the primary force within the larger House GOP caucus responsible for rejecting Senate Democrat and President Obama's attempts to increase federal regulations. The Tea Party Caucus has also been the biggest advocate of decreasing federal spending and eliminating federal programs.

AP Photo/Carolyn Kaster

Members of the Congressional Black Caucus surround their chairman, Representative Emanuel Cleaver.

For Critical Thinking and Discussion

1. Do specialized caucuses within Congress, such as the Tea Party and CBC, provide advantages or disadvantages to the political party to which the caucus belongs?

2. Has the Tea Party Caucus helped or hurt the GOP?

3. Has the CBC helped or hurt the Democratic Party in the House?

HOW A BILL BECOMES A LAW

It is not easy for a bill to become a law. Though most work on bills occurs in committees, there are numerous other points at which a bill might be "killed." The Speaker of the House, the Senate majority leader, and the president all have means at their disposal to kill a bill. There are other points, as well, when bills might be stopped dead in their tracks. Not surprisingly, of the 10,000 or so bills introduced annually in Congress, only about 500 to 1,000 end up becoming law. And rarely does a bill, as originally introduced, become law without significant revision in the process. An important book on the process of a bill becoming law by is *The Dance of Legislation*, by Eric Redman.[14] As the title suggests, the lawmaking process involves many people and much politicking; the process is difficult and often follows no regular or consistent path. The steps to a bill becoming law (highlighted in Figure 6.2) are also highly influenced by partisan politics, lobbyists and special interests, public opinion, and powerful voices in and out of government. Even though the actual dance of legislation typically follows no neat pattern or order, we describe here the general way in which a bill becomes a law.

Step 1: A Bill Is Introduced

With the exception of tax or revenue proposals, which must originate in the House of Representatives, a bill can be first introduced into either the Senate or the House. The revenue exception, as stipulated in the Constitution, is a product of the American colonial experience with England, and the famous cry "no taxation without representation." Because the House provides popular representation, and representation is the philosophical basis undergirding taxation, the Founders gave the House sole authority to originate tax and revenue bills.

Whereas the Constitution requires that only a House member or a senator can introduce a bill, the ideas for new bills come from a variety of sources. Many come from the president of the United States or someone in the president's office or executive branch of government.

FIGURE 6.2 The Steps in a Bill Becoming a Law

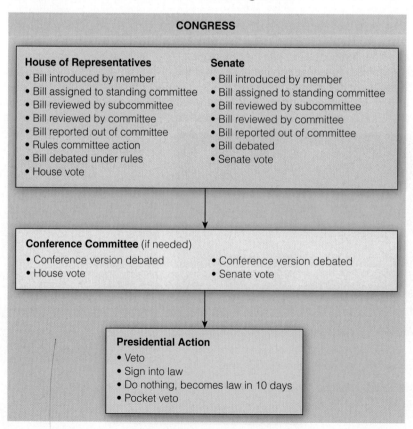

Others come from lobbyists. Because House members and senators depend on lobbyists for information, and lobbyists represent groups who support candidates for congressional office, those with access to members are an important source of ideas for new legislation. Business leaders, educators, journalists, and regular constituents may also generate ideas for new bills. The next step for those with a suggestion for a new law is to find a sponsor in the House or Senate to introduce the idea in the form of a bill.

Whether the idea for a law comes directly from a member of Congress or from some other source, the first official step in the process is for the sponsoring member to submit the bill to the House or Senate clerk, who issues a unique number to the bill. The clerk in the House sends the bill to the Speaker of the House; the Senate clerk forwards the bill to the Senate majority leader.

Step 2: The Bill Is Sent to a Standing Committee for Action

The next step in the process requires the bill to be assigned to the standing committee that has policy jurisdiction over the topic the bill addresses. A bill introduced in the Senate to raise the minimum wage, for example, would likely be sent to the Senate Labor and Human Resources Committee; a bill proposing increased criminal penalties for mail fraud introduced into the House might be assigned to the House Judiciary Committee.

Most bills die during their initial consideration by the committee. In some cases, the committee chair simply sits on the bill and ignores it. In other cases the full committee, without deliberation, votes to kill the bill. If the committee decides to give the bill serious consideration, the committee chair usually assigns it to a subcommittee. The subcommittee may hold hearings, conduct investigations, and deliberate on the merits of the bill. Often the subcommittee will make amendments to the bill before sending it back to the full committee.

When a bill is back in full committee, the recommendations of the subcommittee may be accepted, rejected, or further revised. The full committee may conduct additional hearings, call more witnesses and experts to testify, and debate the bill. At the end of this process, a "markup," or final version of the bill, is prepared. The markup is the proposed legislation on which the full committee will vote. If a majority of committee members vote against the bill, the bill goes no further, so here is another point in the process where a bill might be stopped. If a majority of committee members vote in favor of the bill, it moves forward in the process.

Federal Deposit Insurance Corporation (FDIC) Chair Sheila Blair, Assistant Treasury Secretary Neel Kashlari, and Assistant Housing and Urban Development (HUD) Secretary Brian Montgomery attend an October 2008 hearing of the Senate Banking Committee, which was meeting to address the U.S. financial crisis.

Step 3: The Bill Goes to the Full House and Senate for Consideration

At this next stage, the full House or Senate debates the bill and proposes amendments. The start of this process differs between the House and Senate. In the House, a bill that makes it through the committee is immediately assigned to the House **Rules Committee**. The Rules Committee decides when the bill will be debated, the amount of time that will be allotted for debate, and the extent to which amendments may be added from the floor of the House. The ability to control the timing and amount of time for debate is significant, thus making this committee one of the most important ones in the House. The ability to control the amendment process is even more powerful. If the Rules Committee issues a **closed rule**, House members are severely limited in their ability to amend the bill. An **open rule** order, on the other hand, permits amendments to the bill.

In the Senate, there are no rules set up ahead of time for debate. The Senate majority leader decides when to bring a bill to the floor. But, in theory, there are no limits on the amount of time the bill will be debated, and all senators are given the courtesy of speaking on any bill, if they so wish. The fact that the Senate includes far fewer members than the House allows for less structured debate. With no rules about how long a senator might speak, there is a possibility that a minority of senators—or even one senator—might try to block a bill from passage by refusing to end discussion, a process known as a **filibuster**.[15]

In 1917, a group of senators successfully filibustered to thwart a bill that would have armed American ships in anticipation of the nation's entry into World War I. In response to this event, the Senate adopted a **cloture** rule, which permitted the Senate to end debate and force a vote on a bill by approval of a two-thirds vote. The Senate left a loophole in place, however: if any senator, once properly recognized, refuses to concede the floor, he or she can exercise the equivalent of a one-person filibuster for as long as his or her voice will hold out. Accordingly, in 1957 South Carolina Senator Strom Thurmond spoke for more than 24 hours in an attempt to block the Senate from passing civil rights legislation. For many years, Senate filibusters successfully blocked legislation supported by a majority of senators. Then in 1975, the Senate modified the cloture requirement, so that currently a less stringent three-fifths vote of the Senate (60 out of 100 senators) is required to end debate.

In the 111th Congress, Senate Republicans increasingly resorted to the use of a filibuster in their attempts to block the Democratic majority from passing legislation endorsed by the Obama administration. At the end of 2009, the House and Senate each passed a version of the Obama administration's health care reform legislation. Yet final passage was initially thwarted by a threatened filibuster in the Senate after the election of Senator Scott Brown (R-MA) in February 2010 gave the Republicans the necessary 41 votes to defeat cloture on a party-line vote. (Ultimately the Obama administration pressed successfully for House passage of the original Senate version, which did not require a revote by the Senate in 2010.) In all, Senate Republicans made use of the filibuster more than a hundred times during the 111th Congress.

At the end of the debate and amendment process, the House and Senate take a vote on the proposed bill. Passage of a bill must achieve a majority of votes (half of all present for voting, plus one) from members on the floor. A majority of votes must be achieved in both the Senate and House for the bill to survive to the next step in the legislative process.

How any one member of the House or Senate makes the decision to vote "aye" or "nay" on a given proposed bill differs from one bill to another, and from one member to another. But there are six common explanations, which vary in importance, depending on the situation:

1. **Personal opinion and judgment.** Many members of Congress have strong personal opinions and convictions on issues, and cast their votes on bills on the basis of those opinions. Rep. Henry Waxman (D-CA), for example, is an ardent environmentalist and consistently votes this position on environmental bills. Similarly, Rep. Chris Smith's (R-NJ) pro-life stance on abortion leads him to vote that position on bills.

When member use their own personal judgment, they are said to be exercising their role as a "trustee."

2. **Constituent opinion.** Members of Congress want to be liked by their constituents, and most want to be reelected. In voting on particular bills, members often use results of polls, editorial commentary in local media, and letters written to them by their constituents to help them make up their minds in voting on a particular bill. When members use constituent opinion as a cue to casting a vote, they are said to be exercising their role as a "delegate" of the people they represent.

3. **Interest groups and lobbying.** As a way of achieving their goals, interest groups exert influence on congressional voting in a number of ways, including making contributions to congressional campaigns and hiring lobbyists to provide arguments to members regarding why they should vote a particular way on a bill. So members use both information provided by lobbyists to aid in their voting and the campaign support from interest groups to prompt how they will vote.

4. **Political parties.** The party of a member often conveys quite a bit about his or her political positions and ideology, with Democrats tending to be more liberal on social and economic issues, and Republicans tending to be more conservative on these issues. So party membership is an important cue. In addition, the leadership of each party is organized to influence party members to vote the "party line" on bills. Members voting with their party tend to be rewarded with better committee assignments and greater campaign funding, thus making party a very important factor in voting on legislation.

5. **The president.** Presidents are the focus of national attention and have, as President Teddy Roosevelt once said, a "bully pulpit" to make their case and influence others, including members of Congress. Presidents are quite influential in directing congressional members of their own party how to vote, but often exert influence on members of the opposition party as well. Particularly in times of international crisis, presidents can effectively make appeals to put partisanship aside and convince members to vote in the interests of the country.

6. **Logrolling.** Members often enter into an agreement with other members to vote a certain way on one bill in exchange for a favorable vote on another bill. This process is known as **logrolling**. Members vote on thousands of bills every term. Giving up a vote on less important bills in exchange for favorable votes on more important bills is a common practice, and one that often guides congressional voting behavior.

logrolling: The trading of influence or votes among legislators to achieve passage of projects that are of interest to one another.

Many Americans have expressed frustration over how Congress makes decisions on important bills before it. During the highly charged debate over the health care reform legislation in 2009 and 2010, for example, most Americans felt that Congress paid too little attention to the public and people who would be affected by the changes to heath care, and too much attention to the media and interest groups, as shown in Figure 6.3.

Step 4: Conference Committee Action

Often the version of a bill that passes the Senate differs from that passed by the House. To iron out any differences between Senate and House bills, Congress has two options. The first and most common route is to work out the differences informally. Of course the ability to do this depends on the extent of differences in the two versions of the bill and the closeness of the votes in committee and in the full chambers. When the versions are not far apart in content and when the margins of approval are large, informal discussions between House and Senate leaders and committee chairs are usually sufficient to strike a deal. When the prospects for informal agreement are less likely, then House and Senate leaders select a conference committee to work out the kinks. The conference committee consists of House and Senate members—usually drawn from the standing committees that worked on the bills.

FIGURE 6.3 Who Does Congress Listen To?

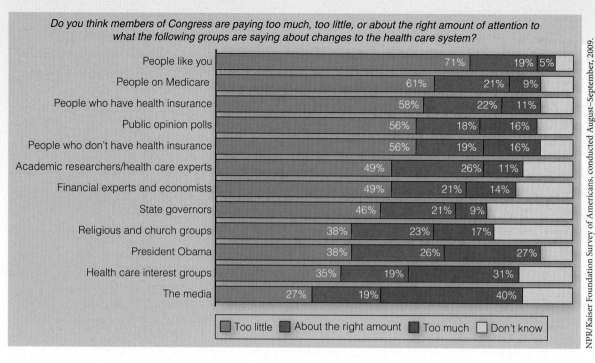

Do you think members of Congress are paying too much, too little, or about the right amount of attention to what the following groups are saying about changes to the health care system?

	Too little	About the right amount	Too much	Don't know
People like you	71%	19%	5%	
People on Medicare	61%	21%	9%	
People who have health insurance	58%	22%	11%	
Public opinion polls	56%	18%	16%	
People who don't have health insurance	56%	19%	16%	
Academic researchers/health care experts	49%	26%	11%	
Financial experts and economists	49%	21%	14%	
State governors	46%	21%	9%	
Religious and church groups	38%	23%	17%	
President Obama	38%	26%	27%	
Health care interest groups	35%	19%	31%	
The media	27%	19%	40%	

NPR/Kaiser Foundation Survey of Americans, conducted August–September, 2009.

Step 5: Presidential Action

The president plays both an informal and a formal role in the passage of new laws. The president's informal role is to develop new ideas for laws and urge members of Congress to introduce them. The president also lobbies Congress, attempting to persuade members to support or oppose certain bills. The president's strong presence in the American political system, along with attention from the national media, offers the president a unique platform from which to lobby on behalf of or against certain legislation.

The formal constitutional role that the president plays in legislation is the fifth step in the process by which a bill becomes law. Once both chambers of Congress have agreed to a bill, the bill is sent to the president for action. The president has three options for dealing with the congressionally approved bill. First, the president can sign the bill, which officially makes it new law. Second, the president can **veto** (or refuse assent to) the bill, which stops the bill from becoming law. If the bill is vetoed, Congress has one more opportunity to pass the bill, by **overriding** the presidential veto. This requires a two-thirds vote in favor of passage in both the Senate and the House, a margin substantially more difficult to achieve than the simple majority vote required prior to a presidential veto. Third, the president can decide not to act on a bill (that is, neither sign it nor veto it), in which case the bill automatically becomes law after it has sat on the president's desk for 10 days. If Congress passes a bill and sends it to the president within 10 days of the end of a congressional session and the president does not act on the bill, then the bill does not become law, a process known as a **pocket veto**.

veto: The constitutional procedure by which the president refuses to approve a bill or joint resolution and thus prevents its enactment into law.

overriding (a veto): The power of the Congress to enact legislation despite a president's veto of that legislation; requires a two-thirds vote of both houses of Congress.

pocket veto: The indirect veto of a bill received by the president within 10 days of the adjournment of Congress, effected by the president's retaining the bill unsigned until Congress adjourns.

OVERSIGHT AND PERSONNEL FUNCTIONS OF CONGRESS

In addition to creating new laws, Congress performs four other important constitutional functions: oversight of federal agencies, confirmation of top federal executives and judges, approval of treaties, and impeachment of top federal executives and judges.

President Obama signs the health care reform bill into law at the White House in March 2010.

Congressional Oversight

Congress's principal responsibility is to enact new laws to deal with national problems and concerns. But given the complexity of many issues (nuclear and toxic waste disposal, creating new sources of energy, promoting the role of high technology, and enhancing the performance of a multitrillion-dollar economy that has become highly integrated in the global economy, to name just a few), Congress often lacks the scientific and technological expertise needed to enact laws. In addition, for political reasons, sometimes Congress prefers not to deal with issues on its own, but rather to "pass the buck" to a bureaucratic agency. Defining the limits of genetic cloning is one such political hot potato. Whether the reason is technical capability or politics, Congress often delegates more specific legislative authority to the executive branch, which has the resources and expertise to make more highly technical policy decisions. The delegation of congressional power to the executive branch has become more frequent as our society has become more complex.

This delegation of authority, however, is not carried out blindly or without accountability. When Congress delegates its authority, it generally monitors the activities of agencies and administrators who are given this power through congressional oversight. One agency to which Congress has delegated considerable authority is the Federal Reserve Board (known as "the Fed"). Established by the Federal Reserve Act of 1913, the Fed has authority over credit rates and lending activities of the nation's banks. Congress created the agency because it recognized that specialized monitoring of the economy and the technical expertise of economists were necessary to make decisions about credit rates and lending activities in order to maintain a viable economy. The act gave the Fed the authority to adjust the supply of money to banks and to shift money from where there is too much to where there is too little. The Fed also has the power to take means to ensure that banks do not overextend themselves in lending so that a sudden economic scare will not cause a sudden run on banks for money. For nearly one hundred years, Congress has given this agency the power to set important monetary policy for the nation. But Congress retains its authority to exercise oversight of the Fed. The Joint Economic Committee in Congress carefully monitors the Fed's performance and regularly holds hearings to inquire about its policies and decisions. In addition, newly appointed members of the Federal Reserve Board must be approved by Congress.

In his book on Congress titled *Congress: The Keystone of the Washington Establishment*,[16] political scientist Morris Fiorina notes other important reasons for congressional delegation of power to executive agencies, including garnering political rewards while shifting blame to the executive branch, enabling Congress to blame federal agencies for failing to fulfill legislative intent, and taking credit for problem solving by holding oversight and investigative hearings.

Confirmation of Presidential Nominations and Approval of Treaties

The U.S. Senate plays a pivotal role in the selection of cabinet officers, other agency and executive branch heads, federal judges, and foreign ambassadors. The president nominates individuals for these posts, but the Senate must consent to the nomination with a majority vote in favor of the candidate. This function is one performed solely by the U.S. Senate, and not the House of Representatives.

At the beginning of a new presidential administration, the U.S. Senate is typically quite busy reviewing the president's nominations for high executive office positions.[17] Although the Senate usually endorses most nominees, there have been a number of high-profile instances when the Senate has been unwilling to confirm the nominee, typically occurring during eras of divided government when the political party of the president is different from the majority party in the Senate.

When there is a vacancy on the U.S. Supreme Court, a situation that often draws considerable interest from both the press and the public, the president nominates a new justice, whom the Senate also must confirm with a majority vote. Conflict between the Senate and the president over Supreme Court nominees goes all the way back to the first U.S. president, George Washington, and his choice of John Rutledge for chief justice of the United States. Although Rutledge appeared eminently qualified for the post (he was associate justice on the Supreme Court from 1789 to 1791 and chief justice of the South Carolina Court of Common Pleas from 1791 to 1795), he had openly criticized the highly controversial Jay Treaty with Britain (backed by Washington and the Federalists), which reneged on the terms of America's 1778 treaty with France. Rutledge's criticism was directed as much at its chief negotiator, John Jay, as at the treaty itself, which reassured Britain of American neutrality. Apparently, Rutledge still harbored a grudge against Jay, who had edged him out to become the nation's first chief justice in 1789. Although Washington stood behind his nominee and gave him a temporary recess appointment as chief justice, Federalist senators argued that confirmation of Rutledge would be an extreme embarrassment to their party and denounced him publicly. One called him a character "not very far above mediocrity." On December 15, 1795, the Senate rejected Rutledge's nomination by a 14–10 vote.

A more recent example of Senate opposition to a Supreme Court nominee occurred in the case of Clarence Thomas, nominated for the Court by President George H. W. Bush in 1991. The Democrat-controlled Senate opposed Thomas, an African American who held conservative views on numerous issues. Thomas's problems mounted further when one of his former employees at the Equal Employment Opportunity Commission, Anita Hill, testified that he had sexually harassed her while he was her boss. Thomas ultimately won confirmation by a close 52–48 vote and currently sits on the Supreme Court.

Under certain circumstances, Congress may also become involved in the selection of president and vice president of the United States. When no candidate receives a majority of electoral votes, the House of Representatives chooses the president and the Senate chooses the vice president. This has happened three times in the history of the nation—in 1801 when the House chose Thomas Jefferson as president, in 1825 when the House chose John Quincy Adams, and in 1877 when the House appointed a commission to resolve the controversial 1876 election (it chose Rutherford B. Hayes).

In the event of a vacancy in the vice presidency, the Twenty-fifth Amendment to the Constitution stipulates that the president's nomination of an individual to fill that position is subject to the approval of both the House and Senate by majority vote. This has happened twice since adoption of that amendment: in 1973 when Vice President Spiro Agnew resigned and Nixon's nomination of Gerald Ford was quickly approved, and in 1974 when Ford became president due to Nixon's resignation and Congress approved Ford's nomination of Nelson Rockefeller as vice president.

Finally, the Senate has the power to approve treaties that the president negotiates with foreign countries. The Constitution stipulates that approval of a treaty requires the consent of two-thirds of the Senate. Even though the standard for treaty approval is much higher than a simple majority, most treaties do obtain the necessary two-thirds approval. Perhaps the most important rejection concerned the Treaty of Versailles following World War I. The relatively low number of rejected treaties may be due to presidents' reluctance to negotiate treaties that they are not reasonably certain will pass. President Woodrow Wilson's failure to consult with the Senate and consider its objections to the Treaty of Versailles led to the treaty's twice being rejected by the Senate, once in 1919 and again in 1920. More recently, the House has also played an important role in approving treaties because most of them involve financial issues that require the approval of that chamber.

Impeachment and Removal of Federal Judges and High Executives

Congress also has the authority to impeach and remove federal judges, cabinet officers, the president, the vice president, and other civil officers. The removal process requires an impeachment action from the House and a trial in the Senate. Only two presidents (Andrew Johnson in 1867 and Bill Clinton in 1998) have been impeached, and neither was actually removed from office.

Impeachment is the formal process by which the House brings charges against federal officials. A judge, president, or executive official who is "impeached" by the House is not removed; he or she is charged with an offense. In this sense, the House acts as an initial forum that makes the decision about whether a trial is warranted. An impeachment occurs by a majority vote in the House of Representatives. An official may be impeached by the House on more than one charge, each of which is referred to as an article of impeachment.

Assuming the House passes at least one article of impeachment, the official must then stand trial in the Senate. The prosecutors in the trial are members of the House of Representatives and are referred to as House "managers." Selected by the House leadership, the House managers present the case for removal to the full Senate. If the defendant is the president, the chief justice of the U.S. Supreme Court presides over the trial; otherwise the vice president of the United States (who is president of the Senate) or the president pro tempore of the Senate presides. Other than in the impeachment of a president or vice president, the Senate in recent times has usually designated a committee to receive evidence and question the witnesses. The impeached official provides lawyers in his or her own defense. A two-thirds vote of the full Senate is required for removal of an official.

CONSTITUENT SERVICE: HELPING PEOPLE BACK HOME

Much of what has been discussed thus far in this chapter pertains to what members of Congress do in Washington. As the people's representatives, members are sent to Washington to develop new laws and deliberate on important issues. They are expected to safeguard the nation's security, act as watchdogs against fraud, and ensure that judges and high-ranking executive officers are qualified for office. An integral part of the way members serve their constituents is by reflecting the opinions and input of those whom they represent while carrying out these legislative functions.

Doug Murray/Reuters/Landov

Representative Allan West (R.-Fl.) talks to a constituent back in his congressional district in Boca Raton, FL.

However, the service of members of Congress does not stop with the work they do in Washington. Often constituents will call upon a House member or senator to provide information about federal programs, to render assistance in getting benefits from federal programs, or to prepare a talk or visit with a community group to educate its members about the political system or on a specific legislative or policy topic. Members are often asked by officials in state or local government to facilitate federal help for a local or state issue. The direct assistance that a member provides to a constituent, community group, or a local or state official, is referred to as **casework**. A now classic book by Richard F. Fenno Jr., titled *Home Style: House Members in Their Districts*, provides a rich description of this role played by members of Congress.[18]

Casework is important for a number of reasons. First is its electoral importance to members of Congress. Casework raises the visibility of members in their home state or district, which reflects positively on how well the member is regarded and gives members an advantage over their opponents in elections. More than 9 in 10 House and Senate members who run for re-election are returned to office, and effectively managing casework is an important reason for this high return rate.

It has also become an implicit responsibility of members to help their constituents navigate the complex federal bureaucracy. Federal programs are varied and complex, and constituents are often overwhelmed in their efforts to obtain the benefits for which they are eligible. For example, under the Workforce Development Act, the federal government has programs that provide assistance to "displaced workers," defined as those who have lost their jobs due to technological or broad trends in the workplace. Many workers in the manufacturing industry in the United States have lost their jobs over the past decade as the national economy has shifted away from manufacturing and toward technology and information services. Various programs are available for these displaced workers to help them obtain training in new skills necessary to adapt to the new workforce. Finding these programs is often difficult, and members provide information to connect constituents with available programs.

Third, casework provides a direct connection between members and their constituents. Casework requires members to keep in touch with those whom they represent. Giving a speech to a local Rotary club or League of Women Voters meeting, showing up to "cut the ribbon" at

An Internship as a Steppingstone

Many college students interested in politics and public policy seek internships with Congress during the summer. Such an experience allows them to see firsthand how Congress works, gain valuable experience, and prepare for a possible job with the federal government. In early 2010, the job search Web site Monster.com estimated that job opportunities in the federal government would grow from 2.1 million to 2.5 million by end of 2012. Building one's resume with an internship in Congress can help to jump-start a successful career in public service.

The dozens of committees in Congress all have spots for college interns, as do large congressional agencies such as the General Accounting Office, the Congressional Budget Office, and the Library of Congress. In addition, all 535 members of Congress maintain offices in Washington, D.C., as well as in their home state or district. Interns are commonly found helping with casework in many of these offices. Moreover, the partisan leadership offices, such as the majority and minority leaders and whips, frequently staff college interns to help them do their work, as do the Democratic and GOP House and Senate campaign committees. Many senators and representatives first got introduced to Congress through an internship that they themselves had. At a minimum, an internship with Congress provides a great resume item when applying for a full-time position in some part of the federal government.

If you are interested in a congressional internship, there are a number of ways to get one. You can contact the office of a member of the House or Senate directly and inquire about future openings. You can visit the internship coordinator at your college or in your university's political science department and ask what might be available and how to apply. Or you can visit the following Web sites for information about ongoing internship opportunities:

- http://dc.about.com/od/jobs/a/Internships.htm
- www.twc.edu
- www.cbo.gov/employment/intern.cfm

Congressional Hispanic Caucus Institute

A recent group of interns who work with the Congressional Hispanic Caucus.

For Critical Thinking and Discussion

An internship in Congress provides a wonderful experience for interested students to learn firsthand how our government works. However, there are only a handful of these internships, and so getting them is not easy. Should students who are interested in spending a semester in Washington have more opportunities to do so?

an opening of a new local school building or park, and coming to speak to a group of students or employees all provide face time between the members and their constituents. The experiences that members have and the type of work they do in Washington can shelter them from the real-life concerns of their constituents back home. Casework provides a constant reminder of the needs and interests of those whom members represent.

Another aspect of constituent service involves what is known as "pork-barrel" politics. The federal budget includes a great deal of money for local projects, such as parks, dams, and road improvements. Members secure federal funds to support these projects in their states and districts through what is often referred to as **pork-barrel legislation**. The pork-barrel reference is based on the idea that members are "bringing home the bacon." Members use their influence on congressional committees and leadership positions to add amendments to bills that authorize pork-barrel spending on projects back home. Though many observers of the political system decry the unfairness of pork-barrel legislation, it has been an important aspect of constituent service since the beginning of our political system and promises to remain so in the future.

pork-barrel legislation: A government project or appropriation that yields jobs or other benefits to a specific locale and patronage opportunities to its political representative.

When Congress is dealing with major problems or issues of the day, the process of creating new laws, approving new treaties, and approving presidential appointments can be very slow indeed—many observers use the word "gridlock" to describe congressional inaction. Congress's actions are slow and deliberate; there are many points at which the process may be halted, and many actors with the capacity to hinder progress. Further, the compromises necessary to achieve success in Congress rarely prove entirely satisfactory to everyone involved. The slow and grinding legislative process can even lead to bad behavior on the part of members of Congress, such as with Senator Preston Brooks' clubbing of Senator Charles Sumner in a debate on slavery in 1856, and Representative Joe Wilson's "You lie!" shout at President Obama in 2009 during the President's health care address. The power and significance of individual actors in the legislative process is also significant to understanding how Congress works. Strong individuals such as Senate Majority Leader Harry Reid and Speaker John Boehner dominated the debate in recent years. Congress is not simply two houses of 535 individuals who vote, with a majority obtaining victory. Those in leadership positions can exert a disproportionate influence on the process. Those with special communication skills enjoy more power, as do those who are highly informed on a particular issue.

SUMMARY: PUTTING IT ALL TOGETHER

ARTICLE I AND THE CREATION OF CONGRESS

- Congress, the legislative branch of the government, was the central institution in America's new political system at the beginning of the republic. Congress consists of two houses, a "people's house" apportioned by population (the House of Representatives), and a Senate in which the states, regardless of population, have equal representation.

- To ensure the principle of "one person, one vote" in the House, the population of congressional districts must be made as equal as possible based on the results of a federal census conducted every 10 years. Parties try to maximize their advantage in the House of Representatives by "gerrymandering," which means that they draw district boundaries in order to favor their party on Election Day.

Test Yourself on This Section

1. The first attempt to unite the colonies under a single "congress" was the
   a. Seneca Falls congress.
   c. Albany Congress.
   b. First Continental Congress.
   d. Congress of the States.

2. The primary power given to Congress by Article I of the constitution is to
   a. create laws.
   c. adjudicate disputes.
   b. implement laws.
   d. execute laws

3. Which of the following presidents was a congressional scholar and author of "Congressional Government?"
   a. Thomas Jefferson
   c. Woodrow Wilson
   b. Theodore Roosevelt
   d. Harry Truman

THE STRUCTURE AND ORGANIZATION OF CONGRESS

- The relative strength of political party membership determines leadership in each legislative chamber. The Constitution designates that the leader of the House carry the title Speaker of the House. The Speaker is responsible for assigning new bills to committees and recognizing members to speak in the House chamber. The Constitution also prescribes that the vice president is to be the presiding officer of the Senate. Unlike the Speaker, the president of the Senate can vote only to break ties. When the vice president is absent from the Senate chamber as is quite often the case), the presiding officer is the president pro tempore "for the time being").

Test Yourself on This Section

1. To qualify for membership in the House of Representatives, an individual must
   a. be 30 years old.
   c. be a natural-born citizen.
   b. reside in the congressional district he or she represents.
   d. have resided in the United States for at least 7 years.

2. Under the Constitution as it was adopted, which of the following was directly elected by voters?
   a. House members
   c. Speaker of the House
   b. Senate members
   d. Senate majority leader

3. The power structure in congress is primarily organized around
   a. seniority.
   c. the most powerful committees.
   b. partisan control.
   d. strong personalities.

4. What makes the position of Speaker of the House such a powerful one?

THE COMMITTEE SYSTEM

- There are four types of congressional committees: standing committees (permanent), select committees (established to look at a particular issue for a limited time), conference committees (reconcile differences between House and Senate versions of a bill), and joint committees (includes members from both houses, investigative in nature). Most members defer to committee recommendations on a bill.

Test Yourself on This Section

1. The type of committee that irons out differences between House and Senate versions of a bill is a
   a. standing committee.
   c. conference committee.
   b. joint committee.
   d. select committee.

2. The congressional office that provides objective analyses of the budget, separate from the White House analyses, is the
   a. CBO.
   c. GAO.
   b. OMB.
   d. CRS.

3. A committee appointed by both the Senate and the House of Representatives to iron out differences in the language of a bill is referred to as a

a. standing committee

b. conference committee

c. select committee

d. joint committee

4. What is the significance of a standing committee's power of "reporting legislation"?

HOW A BILL BECOMES A LAW

- The lawmaking process is often slow, and bills that survive frequently receive significant revisions along the way. After a bill is introduced by a member of Congress, it is usually sent to a committee for consideration (often in the form of hearings) and possible action. If the bill is endorsed by a majority of the committee, it then goes to the full House and Senate for consideration. Finally, if it is endorsed by a majority of each chamber, a conference committee reconciles differences in versions between the chambers, and then after a vote on the bill's final version, it goes to the president for signature.

- If the president vetoes the final bill, Congress can override the presidential veto by a two-thirds vote of both houses of Congress.

Test Yourself on This Section

1. What type of bill may NOT be introduced first into the Senate?

a. appropriations of money

b. defense bills

c. revenue bills

d. proposed constitutional amendments

2. Which of the following would NOT be found in the House of Representatives?

a. a Rules Committee

b. a filibuster

c. a majority leader

d. a minority caucus

3. The trading of influence or votes among legislators is known as

a. lobbying.

b. pocket vetoing.

c. reporting legislation.

d. logrolling.

4. What options does the president have when a bill passed by Congress arrives on his desk?

OVERSIGHT AND PERSONNEL FUNCTIONS OF CONGRESS

- Congress delegates considerable legislative authority to the executive branch, whether because it lacks the expertise of bureaucrats or because it wishes to shift blame for policies to the executive branch. Still, Congress may exercise oversight to ensure that the implementation of laws and regulations is consistent with national problems and concerns.

- The U.S. Senate plays an important role in consenting to the president's selection of cabinet officers, other executive branch officials, and judges. Senate confirmation
of Supreme Court nominees in particular has been the subject of considerable controversy.

- If a majority in the House of Representative impeaches a president, federal judge, or other executive official, the official must stand trial in the Senate. A two-thirds vote of the full Senate is required for the removal of an official from office.

Test Yourself on This Section

1. Which of the following is responsible for confirming presidential appointments?

a. the Senate

b. the House

c. both the Senate and House

d. the Senate Judiciary Committee

2. When no presidential candidate receives a majority of electoral votes, which of the following selects the president?

a. the Senate

b. the House

c. both the Senate and the House

d. the Supreme Court

3. Under what circumstances is Congress likely to delegate its authority to a bureaucratic agency?

CONSTITUENT SERVICE: HELPING PEOPLE BACK HOME

- Members of Congress play an important role doing
  casework for local constituents, whether by assisting them in getting federal benefits, educating them on policy issues, or performing some other service on their behalf. Casework provides a direct connection between members and their constituents.

Test Yourself on This Section

1. A government project that yields jobs or other benefits to a specific locale and patronage opportunities to its political representative is known as

   a. casework.

   b. pork-barrel legislation.

   c. a sausage-casing law.

   d. a continuing resolution.

2. What is meant by congressional "casework," and why is casework an important role of a member of congress?

KEY TERMS

bicameral legislature (p. 143)

bill (p. 150)

casework (p. 164)

closed rule (p. 158)

cloture (p. 158)

conference committee (p. 152)

congressional committee staff (p. 154)

congressional agencies (p. 154)

congressional district (p. 145)

congressional personal staff (p. 153)

filibuster (p. 158)

gerrymandering (p. 145)

joint committee (p. 153)

logrolling (p. 159)

majority caucus (p. 147)

majority leader (p. 148)

minority caucus (p. 147)

minority leader (p. 148)

open rule (p. 158)

overriding a veto (p. 160)

pocket veto (p. 160)

pork-barrel legislation (p. 166)

president pro tempore (p. 148)

reapportionment (p. 145)

redistricting (p. 145)

reporting legislation (p. 151)

Rules Committee (p. 158)

select committee (p. 152)

Speaker of the House (p. 147)

standing committee (p. 151)

veto (p. 160)

whip (majority and minority) (p. 148)

Chapter

7 The Presidency

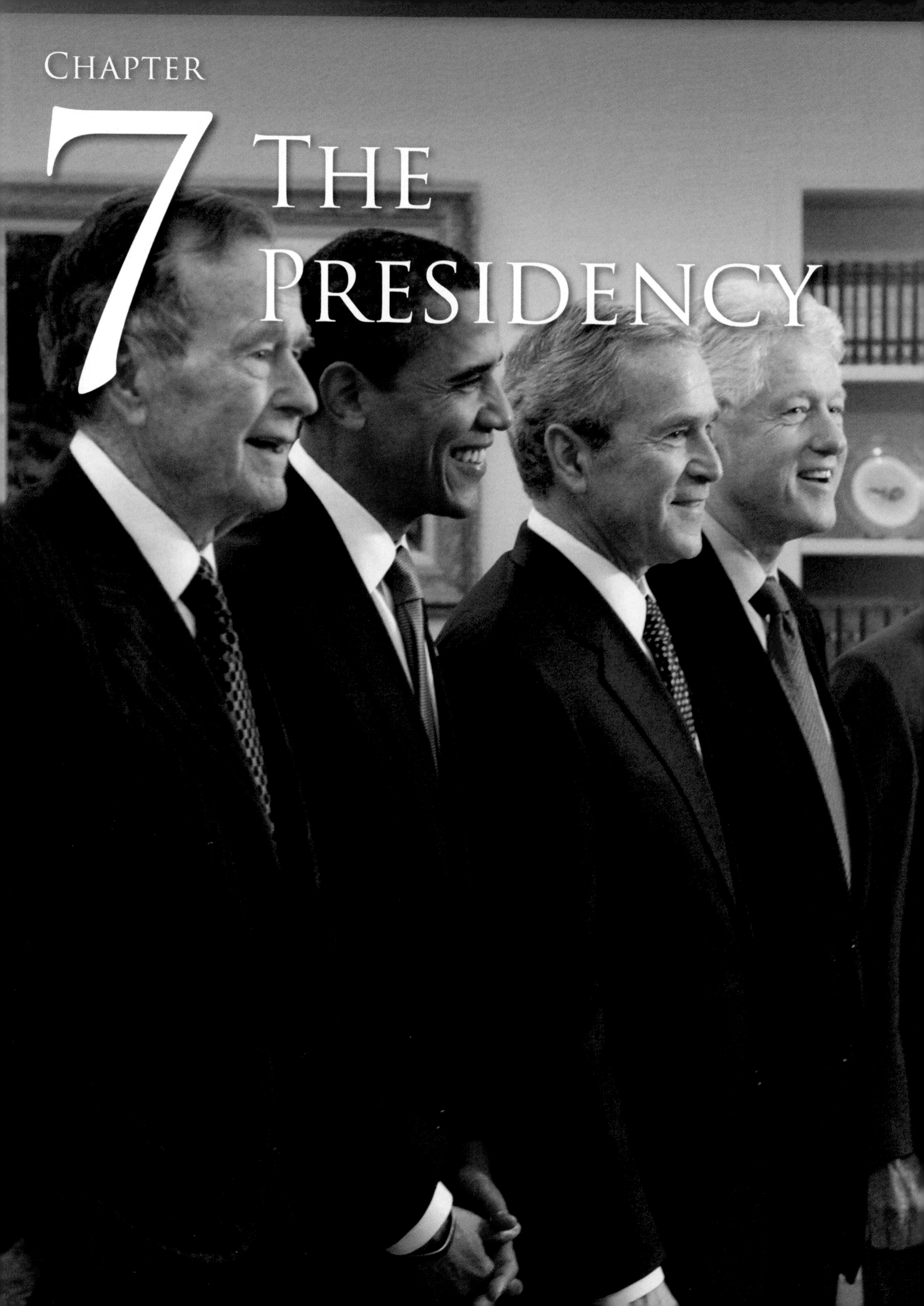

LEARNING OBJECTIVES

WHERE DO PRESIDENTS COME FROM? PRESIDENTIAL COMINGS AND GOINGS

- Identify the past traits of presidents; assess the requirements for holding the position
- Describe the process by which presidents may be impeached and removed from office; know the order of presidential succession

THE EVOLUTION OF THE AMERICAN PRESIDENCY

- Trace the evolution of the presidency from "chief clerk" in the late eighteenth and nineteenth centuries to eventual political dominance
- Explain how the modern presidency has persevered in the recent era of divisiveness

EXPRESS POWERS AND RESPONSIBILITIES OF THE PRESIDENT

- Define the formal powers vested in the president under Article II of the Constitution
- Explain how presidents use the veto, appointment and removal, and the pardon
- Define the powers and limits of the president as commander in chief

IMPLIED POWERS AND RESPONSIBILITIES OF THE PRESIDENT

- Discuss the implied powers of the presidency not spelled out in the Constitution, including executive orders and agreements

PRESIDENTIAL RESOURCES

- Describe the other individuals and offices in the executive branch that contribute to the modern presidency

IMPORTANT PRESIDENTIAL RELATIONSHIPS

- Assess how the power of the presidency is enhanced by communications with the public, the Congress, and the media

The world's oldest continuous republican chief executive office remains the U.S. presidency. Whereas most other countries divide political and symbolic functions among different officials, the Constitution combines both sets of functions into just one office: the president of the United States is both chief of state and head of the federal government. Unfortunately, the Constitution is deliberately vague on the meaning of the chief executive's primary responsibility under Article II: To "take care that the laws be faithfully executed." For more than a century it was the U.S. Congress—disciplined by the two major political parties—that served as the dominant institution of government. It was not until the twentieth century that the presidency became the central institution of American political life, with its executive powers expanded to include vast legislative, judicial, economic, administrative, and foreign policy responsibilities. Of course with that immense power comes an unprecedented level of accountability as well, especially in the modern era when the public watches the president's every move in real time thanks to wall-to-wall television coverage and the power of the Internet. Is presidential government in the early twenty-first century compatible with the Constitution and traditional notions of representative government? This much we know: the individual who occupies the White House will stand at the apex of international attention and power for as long as he or she remains president.

Saul Loeb/AFP/Getty Images

171

The "Connections App" is an interactive web app that helps you better understand the relationship between historical and current events with basic concepts.

1970   1975   1980   1985   1990

1981

Then

President Ronald Reagan addresses the nation in July 1981 on his proposed tax legislation and its impact on personal tax rates.

Source: Everett Collection

When the nation's economy runs out of gas, a Congress of 535 members is not well equipped to lead. In such a challenging environment, it is left to the president to step to the forefront and use his formidable powers as chief legislator and crisis manager to command the nation's attention, direct its spirits, and act decisively Consider the challenge facing Ronald Reagan in the summer of 1981. The severe economic recession that helped vault him into the White House was worsening: unemployment (then at 7.5 percent) was going up, inflation was in the double digits, and bank failures were on the rise. With his presidency at stake, Reagan offered an economic answer to the recession: so-called "Reaganomics."

Reagan's theory borrowed heavily from supply-side economics, which posited that economic growth would be stimulated by lowering income and corporate taxes so that consumers and businesses could more easily purchase and produce goods and services. Reagan pushed his plan through a reluctant Congress controlled in part by the Democratic opposition. Most notably, Reagan's policies cut the top marginal tax rate from 70.1 to 28.4 percent. And while U.S. debt levels exploded, Reagan's policies arguably helped produce the second longest peacetime economic expansion in U.S. history. On one point Reagan's critics and supporters both agreed: he had stuck to his economic principles, and Congress had followed suit.

2009

Now

President Obama and the Chairperson of his Economic Recovery Advisory Board, Paul Volcker, meeting with the press in 2009.

Source: Kevin Lamarque/Reuters/Landov

The "Great Recession" began to take its toll on the American economy in 2007–2008; thus by the time Barack Obama took office in January of 2009, he was ready to lead the battle to pass new legislation designed to jumpstart the fledgling economy. After huddling with his top economic advisors, Obama threw his administration's weight behind a quintessentially "Keynesian" solution. John Maynard Keynes was the late British economist who favored massive government spending as a way to promote economic growth. Accordingly, Obama pressed for passage of the American Recovery and Reinvestment Act (ARRA) of 2009, which provided a $787 billion fiscal stimulus. The new act expanded unemployment benefits; increased government spending in education, health care, and energy; and invested over $100 billion in transportation and other infrastructure. A year later, several independent macroeconomic firms, including Moody's and IHS Global Insight, estimated that the stimulus had saved or created 1.6 to 1.8 million jobs. On the other hand, the Congressional Budget Office conceded that the ARRA had increased the deficit by $200 billion for 2009 alone. Congress may be the branch entrusted to pass laws, but those laws have the president's stamp all over them, for better or worse.

WHERE DO PRESIDENTS COME FROM? PRESIDENTIAL COMINGS AND GOINGS

What career experiences have provided the most effective launching pads for the 43 individuals who have attained the presidency? Many vice presidents have gone on to immediate election as president, including most recently George H. W. Bush, vice president under Ronald Reagan, who in 1988 won the White House in his own right. Yet that form of promotion is actually quite rare. Although 5 of the last 13 vice presidents have become president, only Bush won election as a sitting vice president. In fact, in the 132-year-period between Vice President Martin Van Buren's presidential victory in 1836 and former Vice President Richard Nixon's election in 1968, every vice president who rose to the presidency did so (at least initially) only as a consequence of the president's untimely death in office.

Although the U.S. Senate has been aptly described as a body of one hundred individuals who all think they should be president, only 16 senators have eventually gone on to the White House, including Barack Obama, who won election as president in 2008. (And only three of those men—Warren Harding, John F. Kennedy, and Obama—moved *directly* from the Senate to the presidency.) By comparison, 19 governors and 19 members of the House of Representatives eventually served as president. Three presidents—William Henry Harrison, John Tyler, and Andrew Johnson—actually served in all three of those jobs. Another nine presidents formerly served in another president's cabinet, although none have held that distinction since Herbert Hoover, who was commerce secretary before he was elected president in 1928. The military has also been something of a breeding ground for presidents: 29 had some military experience, and 12 served as generals. Fully 27 of the 43 chief executives have been lawyers, but the cohort of presidents also includes among its ranks a mining engineer (Hoover), a peanut farmer (Carter), a baseball team executive (George W. Bush), and even a hat salesman (Truman).

As a formal matter, the adage that "anyone can grow up to be president" is not literally true. Article II of the Constitution imposes three prerequisites on those who aspire to the Oval Office. Every president must be (1) a "natural-born" citizen, (2) 35 years of age or older, and (3) a resident within the United States for at least 14 years. Although the Constitution poses no other formal obstacles to the presidency, as a practical matter the first 43 individual holders of the office have tended to fall into several clearly identifiable categories. All but one of these chief executives have been white males (Barack Obama is the lone African American president) between the ages of 42 and 77. All were born Christians, and nearly all identified themselves as Protestants at one point or another in their lifetimes. (John Kennedy was Catholic; Lyndon Johnson was mostly nonobservant in his adulthood.) Twenty-four were firstborn males in their families, and all but nine attended college (since 1897, every president except Harry Truman received some type of higher education degree). Some states have served as birthplaces for a disproportionate share of presidents, including Virginia (eight), Ohio (seven), Massachusetts (four), and New York (four). Although presidents are not royalty and none are entitled to serve for life, on several occasions birthright has played a role in helping an

Changing images of Franklin Delano Roosevelt (FDR), seen here in 1932, 1936, 1940, and 1944.

individual reach the Oval Office. Twenty-six presidents have been related to other presidents; these relationships encompass two father–son combinations (John and John Quincy Adams; George H. W. and George W. Bush), a grandfather–grandson combination (William Henry Harrison and Benjamin Harrison), and cousins (James Madison and Zachary Taylor were second cousins; Theodore Roosevelt and Franklin Roosevelt were fifth cousins).

When George Washington, after serving two terms as the nation's first president, declined to run again, he established an unwritten two-term precedent. No president challenged that precedent until Franklin Delano Roosevelt (FDR) sought a third term in 1940. FDR's successful election to four consecutive terms (he won in 1932, 1936, 1940, and then again in 1944) led to passage of the **Twenty-second Amendment** in 1951, which restricts any one person from being elected to the presidency "more than twice," or from acting as president for longer than two and a half terms. Four chief executives were assassinated while in office, and four others died of natural causes while still serving as president, including FDR, who died in 1945, only a few months into his unprecedented fourth term.

The constitutional means of removing a president from office is by **impeachment** and subsequent conviction. Article II, Section 4 of the U.S. Constitution provides that the president may be removed from office upon impeachment by a majority vote of the House and conviction by two-thirds of the Senate of "Treason, Bribery, or other high Crimes and Misdemeanors." Just what type of offense qualifies as a "high crime and misdemeanor"? It's difficult to say. Just two presidents, Andrew Johnson and Bill Clinton, have ever been impeached under these provisions, and both were impeached for primarily political reasons: Johnson was charged with illegally firing a cabinet member, pardoning traitors, and impeding ratification of the Fourteenth Amendment; Clinton was accused of lying to a grand jury about his sexual relationship with an intern and for obstructing justice. Both men were acquitted on all charges by the U.S. Senate and served out their respective terms.

The only president to resign was Richard Nixon, who was accused of obstructing justice in the now infamous Watergate scandal. Nixon left office less than halfway through his second term in 1974 under the looming threat of impeachment. In practice, unpopular presidents are usually turned out of office not by removal, but by a failed reelection. In recent times, three sitting presidents (Gerald Ford, Jimmy Carter, and George H. W. Bush) lost reelection bids; Lyndon Johnson chose not to run for reelection in 1968 when frustration with his unpopular Vietnam War policy undermined his prospects for victory in the November election.

When President John Adams was defeated for reelection in 1800 and turned over the White House to arch-rival Thomas Jefferson, he helped establish a precedent of peaceful transition between chief executives that has held firm to this day, despite the hostile feelings that sometimes exist between successive presidents. In the case of the president's removal by death, resignation, or inability to serve, the Constitution requires that the powers and duties of the president "devolve" on the vice president. When William Henry Harrison died barely a month after becoming president in 1841, Vice President John Tyler took over all the powers, duties, and responsibilities of the presidency, rejecting any notion that he was simply there to serve as a more limited "acting president" until the next election. Since Tyler, seven vice presidents have become chief executive in this manner, including most recently Lyndon Johnson, who assumed office after John F. Kennedy was assassinated in November 1963. Of the last six vice presidents thrust unexpectedly into office, four—Theodore Roosevelt, Calvin Coolidge, Harry Truman, and Lyndon Johnson—eventually secured election as presidents in their own right.

THE EVOLUTION OF THE AMERICAN PRESIDENCY

The U.S. Constitution places as many limitations on the office of the presidency as it grants the president specific powers and duties. Wary of the excessive authority wielded by the king of England, most of the Founders rejected Alexander Hamilton's radical suggestion that the president should be elected for life; instead, the Founders designed a chief executive who would be

Richard Nixon is the only president in American history to resign from office prior to the end of his elected term.

Fact.

The only president to resign was Richard Nixon, who left office as a result of the infamous Watergate scandal less than halfway through his second term in 1974. Had he not resigned, Nixon likely would have been impeached and removed from office.

North Wind Pictures

Military hero William Henry Harrison won election to the presidency in 1840. Yet for all of his strengths as a war hero, he was ultimately a victim of his own stubbornness. Inauguration Day, March 4, 1841, was one of the coldest and most blustery days of the year in Washington, D.C. Harrison refused to wear a hat and coat, and his nearly two-hour inaugural address was one of the longest in history. One month later Harrison died of pneumonia, probably contracted during his inaugural speech. He was the first president to die in office, but perhaps the last not to bundle up warmly for his inauguration day celebration.

powerful enough to respond quickly when necessary, but also would be limited by lack of lawmaking power and the need to gain congressional approval for most long-term commitments, whether foreign or domestic.

The presidency has evolved over the past two centuries not so much because of any constitutional expansion of the chief executive's powers, but rather through practice, tradition, and the personal energy of some presidents. The changing dynamics of policymaking in the United States from a mostly local focus to a national phenomenon has given presidents the opportunity to exert unprecedented influence over the process, and many have done exactly that. In many ways, the growth of the power of the presidency has paralleled the growth of the United States.

The President as "Chief Clerk" of the United States, 1789–1836

The earliest presidents established the office as a forceful power in the national government. Still, even the most popular presidents of the period were careful to avoid interfering with the clear legislative prerogatives of Congress. Several played a major role in helping steer America away from or toward war, despite the inclinations of Congress. But the truly dominant chief executive would not emerge until many years later.

When George Washington, the immensely popular former general of the Continental Army, agreed to be nominated as the nation's first president, widespread public confidence in his abilities helped secure immediate respect for this new office. Serving as the first chief executive from 1789 to 1797, Washington established various precedents that helped preserve a republican form of government in the nation's infancy. Washington rejected entrapments of royalty such as being referred to as "Your Majesty," preferring instead to be called "Mr. President." As a practical matter, Washington consulted constantly with the other branches—at one point he even asked the Supreme Court for an advisory opinion about his own interpretations of a foreign treaty. (The Court declined his invitation for comment.) Washington also established the executive's influential role in crafting public policy, siding with his Secretary of Treasury Alexander Hamilton's plans for industrialization and the creation of a national bank, and striving to maintain an isolationist foreign policy. Often serving as a mediator between differing positions in his administration, Washington rejected the less interventionist, farmer-friendly policies favored by his secretary of state, Thomas Jefferson.[1] For better or worse, most subsequent presidents would be forced to work within the framework of a divided party system that originated as an intramural fight within the Washington administration.

During the four decades after Washington's retirement, most presidents served more as chief "clerks" than as chief "executives," doing Congress's bidding and performing mostly administrative duties on behalf of the federal government. Upon winning the presidency in 1800, Thomas Jefferson (1801–1809)[2] put into practice his own theory of "that government is best which governs least." Accordingly, the Jefferson administration abolished many judgeships, trimmed government economic planning efforts, and scaled back the armed forces. The one crucial exception to such downsizing occurred in the area of land acquisition: Jefferson arranged for the purchase of the vast Louisiana territory from France, more than doubling the physical size of the country.

A presidency characterized by limited executive powers soon confronted unexpected challenges. When tensions between Great Britain and the United States erupted into the War of 1812, President James Madison (1809–1817) found himself hampered both by the small size of the federal army and by the lack of a powerful national bank capable of funding the government's prosecution of the war. This war with Britain revealed the limited powers of the president to influence national matters without strong institutional resources at his disposal. Madison's successor, James Monroe (1817–1825), exercised most of his influence in foreign affairs. Monroe's Secretary of State John Quincy Adams, who himself was president from 1825 to 1829, helped craft the "Monroe Doctrine," which declared that the United States would thereafter regard as an "unfriendly act" any attempt by a European nation to increase its possession or otherwise intervene on the American continent. Meanwhile, Congress led the way in domestic matters, crafting key compromises over slavery and paying off much of the public debt incurred during the War of 1812.

Andrew Jackson, who served as president from 1829 to 1837, remade the presidency into an office of tremendous political power. The military hero of the Battle of New Orleans in 1815, Jackson came to the White House as a political outsider but with overwhelming popular support. Capitalizing on this resource, Jackson wielded presidential power in a way that few of his predecessors had, dismissing hundreds of officeholders, forcing out cabinet members who angered him, using his constitutionally authorized power to veto Congress's bill to recharter the Second National Bank of the United States, and introducing the so-called spoils system of doling out federal offices to individuals as rewards for political service.[3]

Portrait of General Andrew Jackson, later the seventh president of the United States.

The Weakened Presidency in the Wilderness Years, 1837–1900

Andrew Jackson raised the profile and authority of the presidency to unprecedented heights, but its ascendancy was largely a product of his own popularity and energetic personality. The pre–Civil War presidents who followed Jackson also proved to be much weaker. The model of president as chief clerk seemed once again alive and well.

Perhaps the only effective president during this antebellum period was James K. Polk (1845–1849), who presided over a period of incredible westward expansion. Polk exercised his powers as commander in chief to instigate a successful war with Mexico over the Texas territory; his foreign relations successes included the acquisitions of the California and Arizona territories after the Mexican-American War, and the Oregon territory (including the current-day states of Oregon and Washington) from the British.[4] More typical were Presidents Franklin Pierce and James Buchanan during the 1850s; the failures of both to address growing sectional tensions over slavery left pro-slavery and abolitionist interests alike bitterly frustrated.

The presidency of Abraham Lincoln (1861–1865) thrived due to a rare combination of factors. Frequently underestimated as a great political mind, Lincoln was confronted with the single greatest threat in the history of the republic—the secession of 11 Southern states and the great battle between North and South to restore the Union. Although Lincoln proceeded carefully in his prosecution of the war against the South for fear of alienating crucial border states, those acts he did undertake were bold and unprecedented. At the outset of the war in April 1861, with Congress not even in session, Lincoln proclaimed a blockade of Southern ports and called on the Northern states to provide 75,000 soldiers for battle. He (at least in one court's opinion[5]) unconstitutionally suspended the writ of habeas corpus, by which anyone arrested is to be brought before a judge or court to determine if there is sufficient reason to hold the person for trial. Suspending the writ allowed Lincoln to hold some criminal defendants indefinitely. The president also spent freely from the U.S. Treasury without congressional approval. Although Congress ultimately ratified all his actions after the fact, Lincoln's bold exercise of authority essentially reinterpreted Article II into a source of executive authority during emergencies.

Following Lincoln's assassination in April 1865, Congress, dominated at that time by radical Republicans determined to punish the former Confederate states, quickly reasserted its control over the nation's agenda. For the remainder of the century, Congress would determine domestic policy. Indeed, after the former Civil War hero Ulysses Grant left office in 1877, no sitting president won election to a second term until William McKinley accomplished the feat in 1900.

President Abraham Lincoln delivering the Gettysburg Address in 1863.

LIBRARY OF CONGRESS/Getty Images

The Birth of the Modern Presidency and Its Rise to Dominance, 1901–1945

The beginning of the twentieth century marked the onset of a new era for the American presidency. In an increasingly global and interconnected world, the power of the presidency grew disproportionately. By the time two world wars had concluded, the presidency had emerged as the premier institution in American politics.

In the fall of 1901, William McKinley was assassinated during the first year of his second term, thrusting into office his young and ebullient vice president, 42-year-old Theodore Roosevelt. Roosevelt's presidency (1901–1909) ushered in a new era of presidential authority. He injected a forceful energy and enthusiasm into the office, using his position as "a bully pulpit" (Roosevelt's own words). As one observer noted, "He wanted to be the bride at every wedding; the corpse at every funeral." Unlike many of his predecessors, Roosevelt was willing to gamble political capital on bold assertions of presidential power: his efforts to break up corporate monopolies were narrowly upheld by the Supreme Court and forced Congress to enact new antitrust legislation. Roosevelt, through the creative use of executive orders, increased the acreage of national parks fivefold. When Roosevelt became president, foreign affairs were assuming an ever more significant place in the nation's list of priorities. In less than two full terms in office, Roosevelt encouraged a Panamanian revolution, initiated the building of the Panama Canal, won a Nobel Peace Prize for mediating war settlements between Japan and Russia, and sent the nation's naval fleet around the world as a demonstration of American military authority.[6] The first president to travel to foreign lands, Roosevelt expanded the Monroe Doctrine by advancing the "Roosevelt Corollary," which declared that the United States would serve as a police power to maintain stability in the Western Hemisphere by opposing any European interference in the affairs of Latin American nations. In foreign affairs, where force of personality is so important, Congress proved little match for this charismatic president.

Parade on the Rue Royale in front of Maxim's during the visit of President Woodrow Wilson to Paris in 1919.

Bridgeman Art Library

As president from 1913 to 1921, Woodrow Wilson achieved some significant successes and suffered some great failures: his aggressive industrial reform agenda marked a successful first term in office; during his second term he eventually led the United States into World War I and received accolades at the Paris Peace Conference following the war. But Wilson's hopes for a stable international order based on a system of collective security ultimately confronted political reality, as Senate leaders whom Wilson had excluded from the peace talks rejected U.S. membership in the League of Nations. Still, Wilson's presidency illustrated just how much more powerful the presidency had become since the mid-nineteenth century. In the early part of the twentieth century, the president began to dominate the political landscape.

The onset of the Great Depression during Herbert Hoover's presidency (1929–1933) and the looming threat of a second world war in the late 1930s called for a new and innovative approach to the office. Franklin Delano Roosevelt placed his own indelible stamp on the nation by transforming the presidency into an institution marked by permanent bureaucracies and well-established repositories of power. FDR tackled the Great Depression with **New Deal** policies that tied the economic fate of millions of Americans to the fate of the American government: a Social Security program of old-age insurance and unemployment insurance would provide income for the elderly and the jobless; the government would guarantee deposit accounts in commercial banks through the Federal Deposit Insurance Corporation (FDIC); and the government would provide federal jobs to the unemployed to perform various public works. Roosevelt communicated extensively with the American people through the media—millions listened to his "fireside chats" on the radio. By restoring public confidence with his energetic support for New Deal programs, FDR redefined the presidency as a source of national leadership. Future presidents would enjoy significant resources of power simply by taking the helms of the formidable institution FDR established.

Like Theodore Roosevelt and Woodrow Wilson, FDR felt especially at home in foreign affairs. Although adhering to popular sentiment that the United States should maintain strict neutrality in foreign wars, in the early days of World War II, Roosevelt met with British royalty and the British prime minister as a show of support, initiated a "lend-lease" policy by which Britain could purchase war supplies from the United States as long as it paid cash and transported the supplies in its own ships, and traded Britain 50 destroyers in exchange for rights to build military bases on British possessions in the Western Hemisphere—all without the consent of Congress. When America did enter the war in 1941 after the attack on Pearl Harbor, presidential power was put on full display. FDR met personally with British and Soviet leaders to craft military plans; then, near the end of the war, the Allied leaders carved Europe and the Middle East into "spheres of influence" that would establish an American presence across the Atlantic Ocean for decades. With the president playing a dominant role in both national and world affairs, the imperial presidency that took root at the beginning of the twentieth century came to fruition by the close of World War II.

New Deal: A set of aggressive federal domestic policies proposed by President Franklin Roosevelt in the 1930s and passed by Congress as a response to the Great Depression; it ultimately transformed the presidency into an institution marked by permanent bureaucracies and well-established repositories of power.

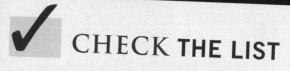

✓ CHECK THE LIST

The 10 Greatest Presidents of All Time

More than half a century ago, historian Arthur M. Schlesinger Jr. began the process of polling historians to rank the presidents of the United States. Recent surveys continue to borrow heavily from Schlesinger's original methodology. In 2009, the C-SPAN Survey of Presidential Leadership ranked the opinions of presidential historians and "professional observers of the presidency." Another poll of presidential scholars was conducted by the *Wall Street Journal* in 2005, with support from the Federalist Society. Interestingly, the results vary. Among the most significant differences: Ronald Reagan was ranked at No. 6 in the *Wall Street Journal* poll but barely broke the top 10 in the C-SPAN poll; Woodrow Wilson and John Kennedy landed in the top 10 of the C-SPAN poll but were ranked 11th and 15th, respectively, in the *Wall Street Journal* poll. While Washington, Lincoln, and Franklin D. Roosevelt usually top most lists, presidential scholars substantially disagree on how to complete the list of greatest presidents.

C-SPAN Survey—2009 Top 10	*Wall Street Journal* Poll—2005 Top 10
1. Lincoln	1. Washington
2. Washington	2. Lincoln
3. Roosevelt, F.	3. Roosevelt, F.
4. Roosevelt, T.	4. Jefferson
5. Truman	5. Roosevelt, T.
6. Kennedy	6. Reagan
7. Jefferson	7. Truman
8. Eisenhower	8. Eisenhower
9. Wilson	9. Polk
10. Reagan	10. Jackson

▶ **POINT TO PONDER:** Why do you think there is so much disagreement among experts about the relative places that Presidents Reagan, Wilson, and Kennedy sit in these rankings? Can ideological preferences truly be ignored when historians and/or journalists make such judgments? Why or why not?

Sources: "Presidential Leadership; The Rankings," *Wall Street Journal Online*, September 12, 2005.
http://legacy.c-span.org/PresidentialSurvey/presidential-leadership-survey.aspx

The Imperial Presidency Comes Under Attack, 1945–1980

By the end of World War II, the presidency had emerged as a very powerful office. FDR's fireside chats on the radio linked average Americans to the occupier of the White House in a fashion that was unimagined by the Founders. In the late 1940s, television became a central influence in American life, and presidents honed their skills with this new medium to further nurture their relationship with the public.

Now recognized as powerful chief executives, those who followed in the footsteps of FDR confronted a new and unprecedented threat to American national security: the presence of a second world military superpower—the Soviet Union. With presidential authority greatest in the area of national security, waging the Cold War that began in the late 1940s consumed much of these presidents' energies. Harry Truman, FDR's immediate successor, proclaimed the "Truman Doctrine" in foreign policy, by which the United States pledged military and economic aid to any nation threatened by communism or the Soviet Union. Like Truman, Presidents Eisenhower and Kennedy also focused their administrations' energies on containing the Soviet communist threat. As long as the Soviet Union challenged American interests, the presidency would remain the focus of attention in the American political system.

Not until the presidency of Lyndon Johnson (1963–1969) was a president able to enact a sweeping domestic agenda similar to FDR's New Deal. Johnson's **Great Society** program featured more than 60 reform measures, including increases in federal aid to education, the enactment of Medicare and Medicaid, and a voting rights act for African Americans. But Johnson's domestic policy success was offset by his failures in foreign policy. Exercising his authority as commander in chief, Johnson sent more than half a million troops to Vietnam to fight an increasingly unpopular war. The failure to stop the communists from taking over South Vietnam was laid squarely at the feet of Johnson, just as earlier foreign policy successes had been credited to his predecessors.

The presidents who followed Johnson came under increasing attack in the 1970s. Richard Nixon achieved foreign policy success by improving America's relationship with the Soviet Union and China, but in 1974 he became the first president in history to resign from office before the end of his term when the Watergate scandal enveloped his presidency. Jimmy Carter's presidency (1977–1981) was beset with hardships, as the nation's economy faltered in the 1970s. Carter's failure to resolve an Iranian revolution that included the taking of 50 American hostages further cemented his image as an inept commander in chief. Carter thus became the first elected president since 1932 to lose a reelection bid. By the end of the 1970s, the modern presidency created by Theodore Roosevelt and brought to new heights by Franklin Delano Roosevelt found itself increasingly under attack from an emboldened Congress and a frustrated public.

President Lyndon Baines Johnson.

Great Society: A set of aggressive federal domestic policies proposed by President Lyndon Johnson and passed by Congress in the 1960s that further enhanced the role of the presidency.

Redefining the Presidency in an Era of Divisiveness, 1981–2012

The election of Ronald Reagan to the White House in 1980 marked the return of the chief executive as an unmatched force over American politics. No president in the twentieth century (save perhaps FDR) could match Reagan's prowess as a "great communicator"; by speaking directly to the American people in terms they could understand, Reagan bypassed Congress and enjoyed early victories with passage of an economic program marked by tax cuts, decreased social spending, and a marked increase in defense spending. Reagan's legislative success was all the more remarkable given that he was working with a divided-party government. The Democrats controlled the House of Representatives in every year of Reagan's presidency; his legislative success thus contrasted favorably with that of previous presidents who had struggled to get legislation passed by a Congress controlled by the opposite party. In foreign policy, Reagan's aggressive program of military buildup combined with his own hard-line position against the Soviet Union is credited with helping bring about the fall of communist regimes in Eastern Europe, the breakup of the USSR, and thus victory in the Cold War. In addition, Reagan's immense popularity allowed him to weather numerous crises and scandals in a way that few of his predecessors had.

Reagan's successors also faced the reality of divided-party government at different points in their respective presidencies. George H. W. Bush took the lead in foreign policy, overseeing the dismantling of the Soviet Union and forging international alliances prior to mounting a successful war against Iraqi aggression in Kuwait. However, by compromising with the opposition Democrats on tax legislation, he frustrated some of his more conservative constituencies and undermined his efforts at reelection. Bill Clinton became the first Democratic president in a half century to serve two full terms. Clinton appealed to moderates largely by in effect borrowing central elements of the opposition party's domestic program—His three main legislative successes (free-trade agreements, budget cutting, and welfare reform) were all programs that had been more closely associated with Republicans than Democrats at the time Clinton took office in the early 1990s.

In the aftermath of the terrorist attacks of September 11, 2001, President George W. Bush moved quickly to position his administration as the eminent world leader in an emerging "war on terrorism." His early efforts to fight terrorism at home and abroad enjoyed congressional support from both parties: his aggressive military intervention against the Taliban-controlled government in Afghanistan in late 2001 proved extremely popular and helped cement his administration's image of toughness and resolve. Yet when the Bush administration expanded the war on terrorism to include military intervention in Iraq, justified on the basis of inaccurate reports that Iraq possessed weapons of mass destruction, these same policies became much more divisive. Though victorious in his 2004 reelection bid, George W. Bush's second term proved even more difficult than the first, with more Americans questioning the war in Iraq as U.S. casualties mounted. By the end of his second term, Bush's ratings had dropped to below 30 percent—in part the consequence of significant problems in the economy, exacerbated further by the Wall Street crisis of September 2008.

Barack Obama's presidency began—as most presidential terms do—buoyed by feelings of goodwill coming from both sides of the political aisle. A clear majority of the public hoped he would successfully tackle the economic crisis that befell the nation in 2008. They also hoped the young president was serious about his promises to bring "change" to Washington.

Obama's "honeymoon period" ended quickly, however, as the details of his administration's proposals for reform were laid bare for debate. President Obama benefitted from strong Democratic majorities in Congress; he muscled through his legislative agenda almost entirely on the strength of those majorities, and with little support from Republicans. The $787 billion fiscal stimulus bill (the American Recovery and Reinvestment Act of 2009) passed with the help of just three Republican Senators and no Republican House members; the landmark health care reform bill of 2010 was even more partisan, garnering not a single Republican vote from either branch of Congress. Facing an emboldened Republican majority following the 2010 midterm elections, Obama soon found himself at loggerheads with the GOP House leadership. The Republicans' refusal to approve increases in the federal debt ceiling—an approval that had previously been routine even in the most contentious of political times—cured the Democratic president of any notion that he might be able to shepherd through more initiatives before the 2012 presidential election. Obama thus learned an important political lesson: the rhetoric of bipartisanship does not easily translate into bipartisan votes.

EXPRESS POWERS AND RESPONSIBILITIES OF THE PRESIDENT

Article II of the Constitution provides that the president of the United States holds executive power, but it is not very detailed about what constitutes executive power. In fact, the Constitution lists only four specific powers of the president: (1) commander in chief of the armed forces, (2) power to grant reprieves or pardons, (3) power to "make" treaties (subject to Senate approval), and (4) power to make certain appointments, including those of ambassadors and justices of the Supreme Court (again subject to Senate approval). Despite this limited number of constitutionally expressed powers, presidents today serve many important functions in the American political system. Noting these varied roles, political scientist Clinton Rossiter referred to the many different "hats" that the president must wear during the course of a week, or even during just one day.[7] Some of these are specified in the Constitution and laws of the United States, which conceive of a limited executive, but one who possesses the authority to react quickly and energetically to unexpected crises.

Head of State

The office of the presidency combines the political and symbolic functions that are often divided in other countries. As the nation's head of state, the president fulfills numerous formal duties and obligations on behalf of the country. Most visiting foreign heads of state meet directly with the president; sometimes those visits include an official "state dinner" at the White House hosted by the president and attended by key political leaders from throughout Washington. Article II of the Constitution also carves out a more formal role for the president in foreign affairs; the president's role in receiving ambassadors and other public ministers has often been interpreted as granting the president the discretion to give or deny official recognition to foreign governments. Although such a power may seem mostly honorary, it can have a real political impact in some circumstances. President Woodrow Wilson's refusal to recognize the new

President Barack Obama greets Russian President Vladimir Putin at the G20 Summit in Los Cabos, Mexico in June 2012.

government of Mexico in 1913 caused considerable consternation among American supporters of the Mexican revolution, and led to growing tensions between the two neighbors. More recently, American presidents during the 1970s and 1980s refused to recognize the Palestine Liberation Organization as the legitimate representative of the Palestinian people, buttressing Israel's own hard-line stance against that organization.

Chief Executive and Head of Government

In his *Second Treatise of Government*, the political theorist John Locke argued that executive power was so fundamental that it predated civil society.[8] According to Locke, legislatures were ill-equipped to enforce their own laws because they need "perpetual execution," and legislatures sit only infrequently. Moreover, if the same entity both made and enforced the laws, it might be tempted to "suit the law to their own particular advantage," regardless of the law's language. Another political theorist, Baron de Montesquieu, also advocated the separation of legislative and executive powers—specifically, he decried the tendency of legislatures to exert too much influence over the executive, increasing the opportunity for abuse.[9]

Influenced in part by these arguments, the Framers of the Constitution vested all executive power in the president alone. Unfortunately, they failed to define that power with any specificity. At a minimum, the Constitution grants presidents alone the responsibility to execute the laws of the United States, which encompasses the implementation and enforcement of measures passed by Congress—in other words, to see that Americans actually abide by those laws in practice. A president's failure to "take care that the laws be faithfully executed"—whether intentionally or due to negligent administration of his subordinates—can have obvious implications for the effectiveness of such laws. Actual levels of execution sometimes lie squarely within the discretion of the chief executive. Presidents Reagan and Clinton, for example, defined antitrust laws in markedly different ways simply by offering contrasting approaches to the execution of those laws. During the 1980s, Reagan's lack of enthusiasm for government intervention in the marketplace translated into the prosecution of far fewer antitrust actions than had been brought by previous administrations. By contrast, under President Clinton the Justice Department applied the antitrust laws enthusiastically, such as when it brought suit against the Microsoft Corporation in 1997 for monopolistic practices that stifled competition in the software industry. More recently, Republican President George W. Bush and the Democrats in Congress sparred not just over the written terms of the USA Patriot Act, but also over the Bush administration's aggressive enforcement of those provisions against some individuals, which gave the laws far more teeth than was originally anticipated.

The president's power to see that laws are faithfully executed also implies some power to hire and fire those charged with administrative authority to help execute federal laws. The **power of appointment** thus stands among the president's most important executive powers.[10] The Constitution specifically authorizes the president to appoint ambassadors and other public ministers, judges of the Supreme Court, and all other federal officers under his charge. Additionally, the president appoints all federal judges. Most of these appointments require the consent of the Senate. In recent years, senators have subjected the president's nominees to intense scrutiny, occasionally even rejecting the president's choices. President George W. Bush withdrew his second choice for the Supreme Court, White House Counsel Harriet Miers, before she had even received a formal Senate vote in October 2005.

Although Supreme Court nominees often receive the most intense investigation, the Senate may occasionally question other executive appointments. In 1989, the U.S. Senate rejected President George H. W. Bush's choice for defense secretary, John Tower, due to allegations that Tower had a drinking problem. Barack Obama's first choice as secretary of health and human services, the former Senate Majority Leader Tom Daschle, withdrew his name from consideration in February 2009 amid a growing controversy over his failure to accurately report and pay income taxes.

The president's removal power has been a source of controversy as well. The Supreme Court's decision in *Myers v. United States* (1926) established that chief executives have the power to remove "purely executive officers" without congressional consent. Although independent agency heads can be removed only by congressional action, cabinet heads and military officials can be terminated by the president alone. In one famous instance during the Korean War, President Truman decided in 1951 to fire the extremely popular General Douglas MacArthur, commander of the United Nations forces in Korea.

Not only is the president responsible for the enforcement of all federal laws, he is also authorized by the Constitution to grant reprieves and pardons to individuals who violate those laws. The Founders vested this power in the chief executive because they believed that the prerogative of mercy, on which the pardon power is based, is most efficiently and equitably exercised by a single individual, as opposed to a body of legislators or judges. A **reprieve** reduces the severity of a punishment without removing the guilt; a full **pardon** relieves an individual of both the punishment and the guilt. A president's decision to exercise the pardon power can invite considerable negative comment and political backlash. Not surprisingly, then, most presidents wait until the end of their presidential terms to grant pardons. Less than two months after being denied his bid for reelection in 1992, President George H. W. Bush pardoned six officials for their involvement in the Iran-Contra scandal from 1987, including former Defense Secretary Casper Weinberger. President Clinton issued 140 pardons on his last day in office in 2001, including one to Marc Rich, who had previously fled the country for tax evasion and whose wife was a major contributor to Clinton's political campaigns. No president received more criticism for granting a pardon than Gerald Ford, who as vice president succeeded to the presidency when Richard Nixon resigned in 1974. Ford's pardon of his former boss for involvement in the Watergate scandal helped undermine his prospects for election to the White House in his own right two years later.

power of appointment: The president's constitutional power to hire and fire those charged with administrative authority to help execute federal laws, such as ambassadors; federal judges, including those on the Supreme Court; and all other federal officers under the president's charge. Most of these appointments require the consent of the Senate.

reprieve: The president's constitutional authority to reduce the severity of a punishment without removing the guilt for those who have violated the law.

pardon: The president's constitutional authority to relieve an individual of both the punishment and the guilt of violating the law.

Hulton Archive/Getty Images

President Richard Nixon and Vice President Gerald Ford conferring on August 9, 1974, the day Nixon resigned from office.

THE MORE THINGS CHANGE,
THE MORE THEY STAY THE SAME

Foreign Policy Successes That Boosted Young Presidents

Chief executives who campaign for office by promising domestic reforms often find themselves occupied by military or foreign policy crises. The dangers of foreign policy crises are obvious: these events may be difficult to control, and if they go bad, a president's entire domestic agenda may be overshadowed or ignored. On the other hand, foreign policy crises offer young presidents in particular the opportunity to establish their presence as a strong foreign policy commander and chief diplomat around the world.

In 1905, the 46-year-old President Theodore Roosevelt, fresh off his first national election victory (he succeeded to the presidency in 1901 upon the death of William McKinley), looked abroad for opportunities to make history. Roosevelt found what he was looking for in the summer of 1905, when he persuaded officials from Russia and Japan—countries locked in a Russo-Japanese War being waged on the other side of the world—to meet him at a peace conference in Portsmouth, New Hampshire. The imperial ambitions of those nations had led to the war; but Roosevelt's persistent and effective mediation led to the signing of the Treaty of Portsmouth on September 5, 1905. For his efforts, Roosevelt was awarded the Nobel Peace Prize, the first U.S. president to receive such an honor.

In 1962, the 45-year-old President John F. Kennedy faced a foreign policy crisis that placed the world on the brink of nuclear war. On October 14, 1962, U-2 reconnaissance flights produced evidence of a medium-range nuclear weapons buildup in Cuba—the Soviet Union had been supplying materials for the weapons, which would have the range to strike most of the continental United States. For 13 days President Kennedy and his national security team wrestled with options, including the possibility of an all-out military bombing assault on Cuba. Instead, he eventually settled on (1) a blockade of all incoming Russian ships and (2) active diplomacy using backchannels to achieve the Russian withdrawal of weapons from Cuba. Kennedy's strategy proved successful, and nuclear war was averted. Years later historians would learn just how close the United States came to trading nuclear blows with the Soviet Union.

In 2011, the 49-year-old President Barack Obama had his own opportunity to make a name for his administration in foreign policy and the war on terrorism. U.S. intelligence sources identified the man they believed to be Osama Bin Laden—mastermind of the 9/11 terrorist attacks—at a domestic compound in Pakistan. President Obama eventually chose to send in Navy seals by air to capture or kill Bin Laden early in the morning of May 1, 2011. The decision did not come free of significant risks; Obama ultimately chose the operation against the advice of Secretary of Defense Bob Gates as well as Vice President Joseph Biden. But President Obama's decision proved successful, as the U.S. military identified and killed Bin Laden during the operation he had personally approved.

Left: President John F. Kennedy, meeting with his national security team during the Cuban Missile Crisis in 1962;
Right: President Barack Obama, meeting with Vice President Biden and his national security team in the Situation Room of the White House on March 3, 2011.

(*Continued*)

Foreign Policy Successes That Boosted Young Presidents (continued)

AKHTAR SOOMRO/Reuters /Landov

A young boy plays in front of Osama bin Laden's former compound in Abbottabad, Pakistan, on May 5, 2011. Just a few days earlier, U.S. military operatives killed bin Laden in a secret raid at this location.

For Critical Thinking and Discussion

1. Why do presidents so often rely on foreign policy successes to provide a popular boost to their administrations?

2. Does the president's general dominance over the field of foreign policy render him nearly unaccountable in that arena? What are the dangers of the president enjoying such exclusive control over foreign policy?

Chief Diplomat

As chief diplomat of the United States, the president has the power to negotiate treaties and appoint diplomatic representatives to other countries, including ambassadors, ministers, and consuls. The president's power over treaties is limited to negotiation and execution—enactment of any treaties requires approval by two-thirds of the Senate. Still, the power to negotiate and execute the terms of treaties affords the president immense authority in the field of foreign affairs. John F. Kennedy used this power to negotiate an end to the Cuban missile crisis in 1962;[11] Jimmy Carter personally presided over the negotiation of the Panama Canal Treaty of 1977–1978, which relinquished U.S. control over the canal by the year 2000. Every president during the latter stages of the Cold War conducted arms control negotiations with the Soviet Union, working to check the spread of nuclear weapons to other nations. Bill Clinton surprised many in his own party when he completed negotiations on the North American Free Trade Agreement, an economic treaty with Canada and Mexico that was favored primarily by Republican presidents who came before him.

Chief Legislator

Although Congress is the branch of government authorized to make laws, modern presidents are involved in nearly every stage of federal lawmaking.[12] The Constitution's express provision that the president recommend for the consideration of Congress "such measures as he shall judge necessary and expedient" barely hints at the president's real role in this context: major legislation is often the product of a give-and-take process between the president and congressional leaders. Indeed, the president plays a critically important role in helping to set the lawmaking agenda for Congress, especially when the president's party is also in control of the legislative branch of government. While campaigning for the White House, the future president will lay out a policy agenda; once elected, he will claim a legislative mandate to follow through on those campaign proposals. In the **State of the Union address**, an annual speech made to Congress laying out the status of the nation, the president typically proposes suggestions for legislation. The legislative programs of FDR's New Deal and Lyndon Johnson's Great Society were both influenced heavily by the executive branch. Similarly, Congress's reorganization of various executive branch agencies into a unified Department of Homeland Security in 2002 was based on a plan drafted by officials within the Bush administration. According to social scientist Paul Light, recent presidents have tended to offer fewer legislative proposals than presidents of the mid-twentieth century, consistent with the modern administrations' increased emphasis on reducing the size of the federal government.[13] Still, when a national crisis demands legislative solutions, Congress often looks to the president for leadership. House and Senate leaders made few significant modifications to their respective health care bills in 2009 without first huddling with President Obama and his top White House aides; and it was the president's willingness to meet frequently with moderate Democratic members of Congress that kept many in the fold for the final passage of health care reform in 2010.

The **White House Office of Legislative Affairs** serves as a liaison between the president and Congress and helps develop the strategy used to promote passage of the president's legislative agenda. Administration officials often testify before congressional subcommittees on behalf of legislation, and presidents meet with congressional leaders frequently throughout the lawmaking process to negotiate details and discuss strategy. Many bills have the president's imprint squarely upon them, even though the power of lawmaking rests formally with Congress. The president's legislative authority also includes the constitutional power to veto, or reject, legislation that he opposes. Although Congress can technically override a veto by a two-thirds vote of both houses, barely 4 percent of presidential vetoes have been overridden in history.

During the twentieth century, vetoes became a routine form of political exercise for presidents, especially those confronting Congresses controlled by the opposite political party (see Table 7.1 on following page). That power includes so-called "pocket vetoes," by which presidents may refuse to sign a bill within 10 days of the adjournment of Congress, thus rendering it void. For Richard Nixon, Gerald Ford, and George H. W. Bush, the only three presidents during this span who never enjoyed unified party rule, the veto became something of an art form. Nixon and Bush vetoed 43 and 44 bills, respectively. (Only eight of those vetoes were overridden.) Gerald Ford vetoed 66 bills in just two and a half years, but more than one in five were overridden, a clear sign of the limited power Ford held during his brief term as president. With Republicans controlling the House during George W. Bush's first six years in office, he did not need to veto any bill until July 19, 2006, when he vetoed the Stem Cell Research Enhancement Bill, legislation that would have eased restrictions on federal funding for embryonic stem cell research. However, after the Democrats' takeover of Congress in 2007, Bush vetoed 11 more bills sent to him by the Democratic Congress. During President Obama's first two years in office he vetoed two bills: (1) a continuing appropriations bill; and (2) legislation that would have made it easier for banks to foreclose on homes by allowing foreclosure documents to be accepted among multiple states.

In recent times presidents have resorted to other means to undermine laws that stop short of an actual veto. For example, the president's distaste for a law may be so strong that even while signing the bill into law (perhaps for political reasons), the president will still express his intent to thereafter ignore the law in the form of a "signing statement." As shown in Figure 7.1, the past 30 years have seen a notable surge in such signing statements. President George W. Bush in particular heavily relied on such signing statements (over 800 times during his eight years in office); thus for example, in signing the Detainee Treatment Act of 2005, which prohibited cruel, inhumane, and degrading treatment of detainees in U.S. custody, Bush warned that the executive branch would construe the act in a manner consistent with his own views on a president's constitutional authority. To mark a shift in this practice, on March 9, 2009, President Barack Obama announced that he only planned to use signing statements when given legislation by Congress that contained unconstitutional provisions. Straying a bit from that self-imposed limit, President Obama issued 19 signing statements during his first three years in office.

State of the Union address: An annual speech that the president delivers to Congress laying out the status of the nation and offering suggestions for new legislation.

White House Office of Legislative Affairs: A presidential office that serves as a liaison between the president and Congress. This office helps the president develop the strategy used to promote passage of the president's legislative agenda.

TABLE 7.1 Vetoes Issued by Modern Presidents (Through September 1, 2012)

President	Congresses	Regular Vetoes	Pocket Vetoes	Total Vetoes	Vetoes Overridden
Theodore Roosevelt	57th–60th	42	40	82	1
William Taft	61st–62nd	30	9	39	1
Woodrow Wilson	63rd–66th	33	11	44	6
Warren Harding	67th	5	1	6	0
Calvin Coolidge	68th–70th	20	30	50	4
Herbert Hoover	71st–72nd	21	16	37	3
Franklin D. Roosevelt	73rd–79th	372	263	635	9
Harry Truman	79th–82nd	180	70	250	12
Dwight Eisenhower	83rd–86th	73	108	181	2
John F. Kennedy	87th–88th	12	9	21	0
Lyndon B. Johnson	88th–90th	16	14	30	0
Richard M. Nixon	91st–93rd	26	17	43	7
Gerald Ford	93rd–94th	48	18	66	12
Jimmy Carter	95th–96th	13	18	31	2
Ronald Reagan	97th–100th	39	39	78	9
George H. W. Bush	101st–102nd	29	15	44	1
William Clinton	103rd–106th	37	1	38	2
George W. Bush	107th–110th	11	1	12	4
Barack Obama	111th-112th	2	0	2	0

Source: U.S. Senate Reference Webpage on Vetoes, http://www.senate.gov/reference/Legislation/Vetoes/vetoCounts.htm

Commander in Chief

One of the defining features of the American political system is its commitment to civil control of the military, embodied in the president's status as head of the nation's armed forces. As commander in chief, the president is the nation's principal military leader, responsible for formulating and directing all military strategy and policy. Although the Constitution awards to Congress the formal power to "declare war," the balance of war-making power has shifted overwhelmingly from Congress to the president during the past century, as modern executives have assumed the nearly unlimited power to send troops into combat.[14] Terming it a "police action," President Harry Truman sent troops to Korea in June 1950 without even asking Congress for a formal declaration of war. In 1973, over President Nixon's veto, Congress passed the War Power Resolution, which theoretically limits the power of the president to unilaterally commit troops to battle. Ignoring its provisions, Presidents Reagan, George H. W. Bush, and Clinton have deployed U.S. troops to invade Grenada (1983), Panama (1989), and Haiti (1994), respectively. Similarly, in February 2009 President Obama announced his plans to bolster the U.S. military presence in Afghanistan by committing over 17,000 new troops to the region. Of course presidents are not entirely immune from public pressures in this context. In the two most recent Gulf War conflicts, the weight of popular opinion led both President Bushes to seek congressional authorization for the invasions of Iraq in 1991 and 2003.

FIGURE 7.1 Signing Statements Past and Present

Source: The Center for Media and Democracy's "PR Watch," http://www.prwatch.org/node/5156; The American Presidency Project, http://www.presidency.ucsb.edu/signingstatements .php#axzz1uoWd02o6

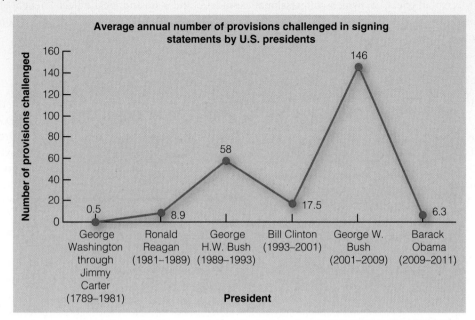

IMPLIED POWERS AND RESPONSIBILITIES OF THE PRESIDENT

Article II of the Constitution does not specifically spell out all the powers that a president may exercise; during the past two centuries presidents have assumed the right to exercise some "implied" or "inherent" powers not listed in the Constitution, and the Supreme Court has for the most part acceded in their right do so. These implied powers allow the president to act quickly in crisis situations, to serve as leader of his political party, and to issue executive orders and make executive agreements that do not require congressional approval.

Crisis Manager

More than any other official in government, the president is in a unique position to respond quickly and effectively to unexpected crises. Consequently, Americans look immediately to the president under such circumstances to provide assurances, comfort, and, where appropriate, a plan to address the difficulties. When a natural disaster strikes, the president will often visit the scene, meet with family members, and in many cases provide aid from the Federal Emergency Management Agency (FEMA). In the days following the September 11 attacks, George W. Bush redefined his presidency as a fight against terrorism—his visits to "Ground Zero," the site of the attacks on the World Trade Center, and his address to a joint session of Congress created indelible images in the media and won him widespread public support. President Obama continually expressed his personal resolve to tackle the nation's economic crisis up to and after his inauguration as president in 2009: within weeks he pressed forward with a proactive economic stimulus plan in hopes that it might reassure the public that his administration was not taking a passive approach to the problem.

Party Leader

Once elected, the president of the United States assumes the position of de facto leader of his own political party. Not surprisingly, presidents are normally well attuned to how their political decisions will reflect on the party as a whole. A popular president is often expected to campaign for the party's congressional candidates, and if possible, help secure control of Congress for the party. Any assistance the president provides to congressional candidates seeking election may have an important side effect: the president may now have the leverage to demand support from those members of Congress for his own legislative programs. Similarly, the "coattail effect," by which congressional candidates and state and local officials benefit at the polls from the votes of the president's supporters, may strengthen the president's position with party members during the upcoming term.

Executive Orders and Agreements

executive orders: Rules or regulations issued by the chief executive that have the force of law and do not require the consent of Congress.

On their own, presidents can issue **executive orders**, which are rules or regulations issued by the chief executive that have the force of law. Once thought to be an unconstitutional exercise of Congress's lawmaking power, executive orders have now become a routine feature of American government.[15] Since the beginning of the twentieth century, presidents have issued more than 13,000 executive orders regulating all manner of topics, including affirmative action, civil service, federal holidays, the classification of government documents, public land designations, and federal disaster relief. President George W. Bush issued more than 150 executive orders during his first term in office alone. On his first full day in office, Obama issued an executive order mandating that the interrogation of terrorism suspects not include torture.

Presidents may be reluctant to issue executive orders on especially controversial topics that may elicit a negative response from Congress, as any executive order can be partially or fully revoked by an act of Congress. FDR strategically issued executive orders to create agencies that Congress refused to establish; eventually, however, he was frustrated by the legislature's refusal to fund those agencies near the end of his presidency. Similarly, Richard Nixon's efforts to dismantle by executive order certain agencies created by his Democratic predecessors, such as the Office of Economic Opportunity, were often stymied, because the courts refused to allow the elimination of an agency established with the approval of Congress.

executive agreement: A pact reached between the president and a foreign government that does not require the consent of Congress.

An **executive agreement** is a pact, written or oral, reached between the president and a foreign government. As with executive orders, these agreements do not require the consent of Congress, although Congress does have the power to revoke them. Executive agreements have become important tools by which presidents conduct foreign affairs. FDR agreed to trade U.S. destroyers for British military bases in 1940, more than a year before the United States formally declared war on Germany, thus implicitly supporting the British military cause against Germany. In recent years, the U.S. government's military alliances with Great Britain and other countries in response to Iraqi aggression have not been spelled out in any treaties that required the advice and consent of the Senate; rather, those alliances came in the form of executive agreements between President Bush and the British government.

PRESIDENTIAL RESOURCES

Nearly a half century ago, Professor Richard Neustadt defined the central problem that all presidents face from the moment they are sworn into office: how do presidents mobilize the powers of the office to work for them? The federal bureaucracy has grown so vast that presidents cannot simply "command" the bureaucracy to do their will. So what exactly can presidents do to make their will felt within the executive branch, and to carry out their choices through that "maze of personalities and institutions called the government of the United States"?

In his landmark book *Presidential Power: The Politics of Leadership*, Neustadt argued that the president's most fundamental power is the "power to persuade."[16] Presidents use this power most effectively by keeping themselves informed, employing a system of information that allows them to be at the center of the decision-making apparatus, and carefully cultivating the image of a powerful president. Modern presidents have tended to emphasize certain individuals and offices under their control that play critical roles in the success of their administrations.

The Vice President

After Vice President Martin Van Buren's successful election to the White House in 1836, few vice presidents rose to the presidency by running and winning on their own accord. In fact, after Van Buren, no sitting vice president even emerged as a serious contender for the presidency until the Republicans nominated Richard Nixon in 1960. And the next sitting vice president after Van Buren to be elected president was George H. W. Bush in 1988.

Next in line for succession and thus "only a heartbeat away" from the presidency, vice presidents have often been relegated to the very fringes of presidential power.[17] FDR barely communicated with John Nance Garner, who was vice president during FDR's first two terms in office. Of course, Garner did not have a very high opinion of the vice presidency either, referring to the position (in a sanitized version of his remarks) as not

Vice President Joe Biden shakes hands with an Amtrak officer. Biden was a patron and supporter of Amtrak; when he was still a U.S. Senator he commuted 250 miles a day by train from his home in Wilmington, Delaware, when the Senate was in session.

worth "a bucket of warm spit." When asked toward the end of his presidency what ideas Vice President Richard Nixon had offered within his own administration, President Dwight D. Eisenhower quipped: "If you give me a week, I might think of one." In fact, up through the 1950s, vice presidents maintained their principal offices on Capitol Hill near the Senate Chamber, where they occasionally performed their one clearly defined constitutional responsibility: to preside over the Senate and to cast a vote in the event of a tie.

The vice presidency, however, has undergone a transformation in recent decades. Modern-day vice presidents have assumed roles as key advisers and executive branch officials working on behalf of the president. Walter Mondale developed U.S. policy on South Africa and was one of President Jimmy Carter's most trusted advisers. Al Gore headed the National Performance Review for the Clinton administration, leading to reforms to increase the federal government's efficiency and reduce its costs. Perhaps no federal official was more influential with President George W. Bush than Vice President Dick Cheney, the driving force behind Bush's controversial decision to invade Iraq in March 2003.[18] The current vice president, Joe Biden, has become famous for his salty language and verbal gaffes; notably, Biden's declaration on one news show that he was absolutely "comfortable" with granting same-sex couples full marital rights may have been the final factor that forced President Obama to declare his own support for same-sex marriage a few days later. Biden is also credited with helping to press the administration's legislative agenda forward by personally lobbying his former Senate colleagues for votes.

Constitutionally, the vice president is first in line to succeed the president in the event of death or incapacitation. By statute, if the vice president is not available to serve, succession falls in turn to the Speaker of the House, the president pro tempore of the Senate, and then to cabinet-level officials.

The Cabinet

The Constitution specifically affords presidents the power to solicit the advice of the principal officers in each of the executive departments. Thus in addition to running their own executive departments within the large federal bureaucracy, principal officers also serve as key advisers. Together, they form the president's **cabinet**. Today's cabinet consists of 15 heads of departments and 6 other important officials considered of "cabinet rank." In reality, such a large body of individuals with different areas of expertise can serve only limited functions for a president, and recent chief executives have convened their full cabinets to serve more as a sounding board and a communications device than as a significant instrument of policymaking. Nevertheless,

cabinet: The collection of the principal officers in each of the executive departments of the federal government who serve as key advisers to the president.

in individual meetings cabinet-level officials may still provide critical input to the president on issues related to their own departments.

The Executive Office of the President and the White House Staff

Created in 1939 to bring executive branch activities under tighter control, the Executive Office of the President (EOP) and its two thousand federal employees consists of numerous agencies that assist with the management and administration of executive branch departments. Some of these agencies, such as the Office of Management and Budget, the President's Council of Economic Advisors, the National Security Council, and the Office of the U.S. Trade Representatives, have near permanent status. Other EOP agencies come and go, depending on the policy priorities of the current administration. Thus during the height of the Cold War, the EOP included agencies that focused on preparedness and civil defense in the event of a nuclear attack.

The EOP also includes an expanded White House staff. Until 1939, this staff consisted mostly of assistant secretaries and clerks who helped the president with correspondence; the White House staff today consists of nearly six hundred employees and runs on an annual budget of almost $730 million. In charge of this bureaucracy is the **White House chief of staff**, who manages and organizes the staff to serve the president. Some modern presidents, including Ronald Reagan and George H. W. Bush, have adopted management styles that rely heavily on the chief of staff to control access to the president. Others, such as President Clinton, have utilized a "spokes-of-a-wheel" arrangement in which five or six different advisers have direct access to the president.[19] Regardless of the arrangement chosen, the White House chief of staff will have a significant hand in the success of the modern presidency. The principal duties of the White House staff include, but are not limited to, speechwriting, advance work for presidential appearances, scheduling, congressional relations, public relations, and communications.

White House chief of staff: The manager of the White House staff, which serves the president's organizational needs, including speechwriting, advance work for presidential appearances, scheduling, congressional relations, public relations, and communications.

The First Lady

All but one president (James Buchanan) have been married at some point in their lifetimes, and the spouses of sitting presidents, now referred to as first ladies, have come to assume an important role in the affairs of the nation. Until recently, presidents mainly relied on their spouses to help them perform social obligations, such as hosting state dinners. Woodrow Wilson's two wives broke somewhat with this mold: his first wife, Ellen, took public positions on bills being considered for Congress, and his second wife, Edith, served as an intermediary between the president and other government leaders while Wilson was recovering from a massive stroke in the fall of 1919. Eleanor Roosevelt, wife to Franklin Delano Roosevelt, charted a course for first ladies as aggressive public advocates. Mrs. Roosevelt launched one of the earliest civil rights organizations, the Southern Conference on Human Welfare; she actively supported the building of model communities; and she lobbied for refugees fleeing Nazi persecution. Occasionally, Mrs. Roosevelt even disagreed publicly with some of FDR's policies in foreign affairs.

Although no first lady after Eleanor Roosevelt was willing to so boldly challenge her husband's policies in the media, many did stake out policy areas where they could contribute, and some became active members of their husbands' administrations.[20] They have been assisted in this regard by a formal Office of the First Lady, now staffed by more than 20 aides. Rosalynn Carter lobbied Congress for mental health initiatives; Nancy Reagan became the public voice of the "Just Say No" to drugs campaign; and Barbara Bush (wife of George H. W. Bush) campaigned

First Lady Michelle Obama speaking at an event related to her "Let's Move" campaign against childhood obesity.

Saul Loeb/AFP/Getty Images

widely against the problem of illiteracy. A distinguished lawyer, Hillary Rodham Clinton led a task force in 1994 charged with reforming the nation's health care system; Mrs. Clinton's complex plan ultimately proved too ambitious, and it was rebuffed by Congress. In another series of unprecedented moves, Hillary Clinton ran for and won a seat in the U.S. Senate in 2000 and was reelected to the Senate in 2006; she was the front-running Democratic candidate for president (until she was defeated by Barack Obama in the Iowa caucuses), and became Secretary of State in 2009. Though an accomplished lawyer herself, Michelle Obama returned the Office of the First Lady to its more common role as lobbyist for a cause, expounding on the dangers of childhood obesity. Regardless of what roles first ladies may assume, modern presidents have increasingly come to rely on their spouses as advisers on a range of issues.

Although no woman has ever been nominated as a major party's candidate for the presidency, the day when that happens may be rapidly approaching. In 1984, Geraldine Ferraro, a member of Congress from New York, was the Democratic Party's candidate for vice president, a historic breakthrough to be sure. More recently, in 2008 the Republicans nominated Alaska governor Sarah Palin as the party's vice presidential candidate. Senator Hillary Clinton (D-NY) fell just short of capturing the Democratic presidential nomination, though she had been the early front-runner for the nomination from the time she first threw her hat into the race in early 2007. When a woman not only captures her party's nomination but goes on to win the presidency, a dilemma will be raised for the new chief executive in the event she is married: what role, if any, should be played by her spouse, who will be the first "first gentleman" in American history?

IMPORTANT PRESIDENTIAL RELATIONSHIPS

The power of the president is influenced by the relations that a president develops and cultivates with three important constituencies: the public, Congress, and the news media.

The President and the Public

Catering to the needs and demands of the public mattered little to presidents prior to 1824, when presidential nominees were chosen by congressional leaders in secret caucuses. By contrast, the presidency today is a truly public institution that depends heavily on its public popularity for political effectiveness. Modern presidential nominations and elections are won on an arduous campaign trail in which aspiring chief executives must reach out, communicate with, and ultimately gain acceptance from large segments of the public. Once in office, presidents must remain constantly attentive to the sentiments of the public at large. FDR was the first president to rely on public opinion polls, and his administration utilized them to monitor support for his New Deal policies. Through his fireside chats, he reached into the living rooms of millions of Americans, winning their support for and confidence in his domestic and foreign policies.

Most modern presidents continuously engage the public to support administration policies, whether through the annual State of the Union address to Congress and other special televised messages, staged events, or interviews and press conferences with the media where they attempt to promote the benefits of their programs. Presidents Richard Nixon and Ronald Reagan preferred the "set piece" speech presented from the Oval Office during prime time; Presidents Jimmy Carter and Bill Clinton occasionally held "town meetings" to discuss issues in open forums with concerned citizens. In bypassing legislators and appealing directly to their constituents, modern presidents have perfected the art of what social scientist Samuel Kernell calls "going public."[21]

Some recent presidents have come under criticism for being too dependent on public opinion polls. President Clinton's critics charged that he too quickly withdrew support for some of his more controversial appointments when public opinion swung against them. Notably, President Obama's decision in May 2012 to declare his own personal support for same-sex marriage coincided with recent polls showing a bare majority's support for that right for the first time in American history. On the other hand, presidents may find themselves in even greater political trouble when they refuse to heed public opinion. President Johnson's escalation of troops in Vietnam during the late 1960s ignored growing public opposition against that war and undermined his hopes for reelection. Just as the Watergate scandal began to engulf Richard Nixon's

Fact or Fiction?

Bill Clinton was the first president to rely heavily on public opinion polls to monitor the popularity of his policies and react accordingly.

Fiction.

Presidents dating back to FDR have relied on public opinion polls; FDR utilized them to monitor support for his New Deal policies.

presidency, his decision to hold press conferences less frequently only fed the impression that he was hiding from the public and fueled even more calls for his resignation. Whereas high levels of public support increase a president's chances to get legislation passed, precipitous drops in public support may stop a president's program in its tracks.

The President and Congress

The history of the American political system is marked by the ebb and flow of power between the president and Congress. For much of the nineteenth century, a form of "congressional government" prevailed, with most presidents acting as dutiful administrators of the laws passed by Congress. Buoyed by advances in communications technology that placed modern presidents at the center of American politics, presidents today play far more influential roles in the legislative process, at times even prodding Congress forward to meet their administrations' goals. Since the 1970s, the frequency of divided-party government, with the executive and the legislature controlled by opposing political parties, has placed the two branches in a near continuous battle over the nation's domestic policy agenda. Because credit for a program's success is rarely spread evenly among the two branches, tensions are inevitable and compromises often difficult to come by. President Reagan managed to get the Democrat-controlled House of Representatives to pass his program of tax decreases and spending cuts in 1981; when the economy rebounded a few years later, Reagan and the Republican Party benefited politically far more than did the Democrats. President Clinton's willingness to sign a welfare reform bill in 1996 aided him in that year's election, when he claimed to have lived up to his earlier promise to "end welfare as we know it." The Republican Congress that actually drafted and passed the welfare bill received far less credit for its accomplishments. In foreign policy, presidents continue to act nearly independent of Congress.

Presidents have many tools at their disposal to influence Congress. As party leader, the president can campaign for congressional candidates, and then leverage that assistance into support. Personal contacts by the president with members of Congress can be effective as well. The White House Office of Congressional Relations (OCR) serves as a liaison to Congress, rounding up support and monitoring events on Capitol Hill. Still, the most effective lobbying

Left: President Ronald Reagan giving a "set speech" from the Oval Office in 1986. Right: President Bill Clinton interacting with the public at a "town meeting" in 1993.

for a president's policies comes from members of Congress friendly to the administration, who persuade other members of Congress to vote in favor of the policies. The rewards for such service often come in the form of future appointments, pork-barrel projects for home districts or states, or financial support from the political party for future election bids. FDR rewarded Hugo Black, a key Senate supporter of the president's controversial 1937 plan to increase the size of the Supreme Court, with an appointment to the Court; Bill Clinton was prepared to reward Senate Majority Leader George Mitchell with the same prize in 1994, but held back because he needed Mitchell's support in Congress for a pending health care bill. (Despite Mitchell's efforts, Clinton's health care bill went down to defeat.)[22]

The President and the Media

The relationship between presidents and the media that cover their administrations is important. The media provide perhaps the most effective channel through which presidents can communicate information about their policies to the public. At the same time, the media's desire for interesting headlines to attract greater numbers of readers, listeners, viewers, and online observers leaves them to rely heavily on the executive branch for information. Effective media management has been a hallmark of the most successful modern presidents. Much of the responsibility rests with the **White House press secretary**, who plays an especially important role in briefing the press, organizing news conferences, and briefing the president on questions he may be forced to address.

The administration that ignores media management does so at its own peril. Social scientists Kathleen Hall Jamieson and Paul Waldman revealed how the mainstream media today does not so much report the news about presidents as create it, transforming "the raw stuff of experience into presumed fact" and "arranging facts into coherent stories" that can prove crucial to presidential success.[23] The media's focus on President George W. Bush talking with recovery workers at Ground Zero and issuing warnings to terrorists through a megaphone emphasized his toughness and compassion in dealing with the terrorist attacks of September 11, 2001. Yet nearly four years later that same press corps emphasized perceptions of President George W. Bush's aloofness aboard Air Force One after Hurricane Katrina killed thousands in and around New Orleans, Louisiana.

Today the president also relies on the White House director of communications to articulate a consistent and effective message to the public.[24] But even before that office came into being, chief executives felt the need to craft a message and hone their public images. Though known best for his fireside chats and effective public speeches, Franklin Roosevelt worked hard to cultivate good relations with the media, allowing his administration to set the news agenda and influence the content of the news. Many of his press conferences included off-the-record commentary that fed the media's appetite for information, yet allowed the president to change his position as circumstances changed. John F. Kennedy perfected the modern press conference in the East Room of the White House; his colorful banter with reporters played well as sound bites on the evening television news. Ronald Reagan's reputation as the "great communicator" was enhanced by positive media coverage. His administration perfected the use of "staged" or "pseudo" events, which presented the president in a positive light—perhaps visiting flag factories

White House press secretary: The person on the White House staff who plays an especially important role in briefing the press, organizing news conferences, and even briefing the president on questions that may be asked.

President John Kennedy in June 1963, taking questions at one of his many press conferences.

National Archives/Getty Images

or reading Shakespeare to children at elementary schools—all packaged in time for the evening newscasts. Even when scandals rocked Reagan's second term in office, his mostly friendly relations with the press paid off when they painted him as the unwitting victim of his own administration's follies.

Borrowing from Reagan's playbook, Presidents George W. Bush and Barack Obama have avoided live press conferences wherever possible, preferring controlled situations that could be molded to fit their respective messages. The Bush administration attempted to cultivate the image of a president working hard for the American people—even while vacationing at his ranch in Crawford, Texas, the president was often pictured clearing brush and performing various chores, rather than simply relaxing. President Obama in particular relished hitting the road to drum up support for his policies at large pep rallies. Thus his aides urged him to travel widely while key legislation was being debated to capitalize on those particular strengths.

Although presidents and their staffs take great care to present a positive public image through the media, the glare of the spotlight can sometimes catch off-the-cuff commentary or statements from chief executives that would have best been left unsaid. Some of the more notable gaffes spoken by recent presidents include these remarks:

- "I am not worried about the deficit. It is big enough to take care of itself."
  —President Ronald Reagan

- "At breakfast, she was complaining that it is impossible to get a decent bagel in Washington."
  —President Bill Clinton, on wife Hillary's run for a U.S. Senate seat from New York

- "We see nothing but increasingly brighter clouds every month," referring to an improving economy.
  —President Gerald Ford, speaking to a group of businesspeople

- "I don't see what's wrong with giving Bobby a little experience [as attorney general] before he starts to practice law."
  —President John Kennedy, reacting to critics who argued that his brother Robert was too young to be attorney general

- "When I need a little free advice about Saddam Hussein, I turn to country music."
  —President George H. W. Bush, at a country music awards ceremony

- "I would have made a good pope."
  —President Richard Nixon[25]

When unexpected crises confront the nation—military, economic, or otherwise—leadership must come from the president of the United States. As the nation's chief crisis manager, he must act boldly and decisively to reassure the nation that he has a plan to address whatever difficulties it may be facing. In the cases of Ronald Reagan and Barack Obama, supply-side economics and Keynesian economics offered bases, respectfully, for each administration's different approaches to dealing with financial crises facing the nation. Other presidents have chosen different approaches to leading the nation through economic difficulties. Regardless of the approach adopted, modern presidents are expected to act decisively in times of crisis.

Unfortunately, the Constitution does not spell out all of the roles and responsibilities that have become central to the modern presidency. The office has evolved over the course of the nation's history, and much of that evolution has occurred in response to crisis situations, economic or otherwise. Unlike the Congress, the president is just one person and so can act quickly and decisively. Additionally, the president and the vice president are the only two officials elected by the entire nation—thus, the president alone can claim a mandate to act on behalf of the American people as a whole, rather than on behalf of a state, a district, or one political party. In times of crisis, citizens look to presidents for strength because they alone are in a position to provide it. For that reason more than any other, presidents only rarely have to demonstrate their continued relevance in the modern political system.

FROM YOUR PERSPECTIVE

Another "Tweet" from the Commander in Chief: The Interactive Presidency of Barack Obama

Twitter, an online social networking service, allows every college student to follow friends, experts, celebrities, and breaking news in posts of up to 140 characters, known as "tweets." Enter the president of the United States into this modern world of communication by tweeting. The George W. Bush administration's White House Web site featured extensive videos and links to speeches and addresses by the 43rd president. By contrast, the Obama administration and its brand-new, state-of-the-art Web site at www.whitehouse.gov offers visitors the chance to stay connected to presidential events by Facebook, Flickr, and of course, Twitter. As of May 15, 2012, the president's daily (and sometimes hourly) "tweets" were followed by more than 15 million people around the world. In fact, that same day twitaholic.com's statistical algorithm ranked President Obama as the seventh most popular Twitter user in the United States, trailing only behind entertainers such as Lady Gaga, Justin Bieber, Katy Perry, Rihanna, Britney Spears, and Shakira.

Kevin Dietsch/UPI/Newscom

On July 6, 2011, President Obama responded live to "tweets" on health care, the economy and other issues at the White House's first ever "Twitter Townhall."

For Critical Thinking and Discussion

1. What advantages does a modern president have in his ability to communicate with a younger generation of citizens through Twitter?

2. Do the political views of a Twitter user affect his or her willingness to visit the White House Web site? Why or why not?

SUMMARY: PUTTING IT ALL TOGETHER

WHERE DO PRESIDENTS COME FROM? PRESIDENTIAL COMINGS AND GOINGS

- Although theoretically any American who is at least 35 years old, a "natural-born" citizen, and has lived in the United States for 14 years is eligible to be president, the 43 individuals who have held the office have been mostly older, well-educated, Caucasian Protestant men who have had prior political experience.

- Only two presidents in history have ever been impeached by the House, and none was removed by the Senate. When a president does leave office, succession falls to the vice president.

Test Yourself on This Section

1. How many U.S. presidents came to the White House directly after serving in the U.S. Senate?
   a. 2
   b. 3
   c. 6
   d. 13

2. The unwritten "two-term precedent" established by George Washington was first violated by

  a. Thomas Jefferson.

  b. Theodore Roosevelt.

  c. Franklin Roosevelt.

  d. Lyndon Johnson.

3. What are the constitutional requirements that must be met to serve as president?

THE EVOLUTION OF THE AMERICAN PRESIDENCY

- The office of the president has evolved over the nation's history. Over time, it has accumulated more power. For the century after George Washington's term, Congress dominated the federal government, with only a few exceptions—namely, during the presidencies of Andrew Jackson and Abraham Lincoln.

- The birth of the modern presidency occurred with the ascension of Theodore Roosevelt to office in 1901. His strong personality forced itself on the office. Taking strong pro-American positions in foreign policy and aggressive antimonopoly positions during the industrialization period, Roosevelt promoted power in the executive office.

- FDR's New Deal policies, in response to the failing economy of the 1930s, cemented a large role for the president in the American constitutional system. The growth of the federal bureaucracy under FDR significantly changed the role that the president would play and the power that office would yield.

- The emergence of the United States as a superpower after World War II cemented the role of the U.S. president as a dominant player in world and national politics. Contemporary presidents find themselves as the focal points of American politics, setting the political and legislative agenda and leading American foreign and domestic policy.

Test Yourself on This Section

1. Prior to the twentieth century, most American presidents functioned as

  a. strong national leaders.

  b. agents of the federal judiciary.

  c. "chief clerks" who serve Congress.

  d. military leaders.

2. Which of the following factors most influenced the development of presidential powers in the twentieth century?

  a. the increased importance of foreign policy

  b. the Twenty-second Amendment

  c. the war powers resolutions

  d. the emergence of Congress as a major power in the federal system

3. What factors helped produce the recent "era of divisiveness" between the president and Congress?

EXPRESS POWERS AND RESPONSIBILITIES OF THE PRESIDENT

- The powers of the president, as expressly stated in the Constitution, are (1) to be commander in chief of the armed forces, (2) to grant reprieves or pardons, (3) to "make" treaties (subject to Senate approval), and (4) to make certain appointments, including those of ambassadors and justices of the Supreme Court (again subject to Senate approval).

Test Yourself on This Section

1. The president's constitutional responsibilities regarding the military reflect the principle of

  a. the chain of command.

  b. civilian control of the military.

  c. the imperial presidency.

  d. congressional subordination to the president.

2. Which of the following presidents vetoed the most bills?

  a. Franklin Roosevelt

  b. Harry Truman

  c. Richard Nixon

  d. George W. Bush

3. Discuss the nature of the relationship between the chief executive and Congress under the Constitution.

IMPLIED POWERS AND RESPONSIBILITIES OF THE PRESIDENT

- Beyond the express powers granted to the president in the Constitution, presidents today also play a key role in setting the legislative agenda, managing national and international crises, and serving as leader of their political party.

- The singularity of leadership in the executive branch affords the president a unique position in the American political system, giving him the power to command the attention of the nation's people, Congress, and the media—thus enhancing the president's ability to persuade others concerning what to do.

Test Yourself on This Section

1. The president's party is an important resource to him because the party's members in Congress are needed to
   a. work on the president's campaign.
   b. fund the president's reelection effort.
   c. help him to pressure the judiciary.
   d. support the president's legislative agenda.

2. Which of the following presidents is NOT credited with skillfully exercising executive leadership during a time of crisis?
   a. George W. Bush
   b. Lyndon Johnson
   c. John Tyler
   d. Abraham Lincoln

3. Discuss the informal powers that modern presidents currently exercise.

PRESIDENTIAL RESOURCES

- The cabinet, the Executive Office of the President, and the White House staff provide large organizational support for the president to administer federal programs and agencies and lead the national government.

Test Yourself on This Section

1. Which of the following presidents most enhanced the role of the vice president?
   a. Franklin Roosevelt
   b. John F. Kennedy
   c. Gerald Ford
   d. Jimmy Carter

2. Historically speaking, the first lady who originally charted the course for presidential spouses to serve as aggressive public advocates was
   a. Hillary Clinton.
   b. Jacqueline Kennedy.
   c. Eleanor Roosevelt.
   d. Michelle Obama.

3. How has the Executive Office of the President served the White House in modern times?

IMPORTANT PRESIDENTIAL RELATIONSHIPS

- The president enhances his power by continually communicating with the public, maintaining a strong working relationship with congressional leaders from both parties, and cultivating a good relationship with the media through strategic management of the White House's activities.

Test Yourself on This Section

1. Which of the following is NOT a formal source of presidential power?
   a. patronage
   b. the cabinet
   c. the media
   d. the White House staff

2. Which of the following sets of two presidents preferred the "set piece" speech as a means of communicating to the public?
   a. Carter and Clinton
   b. Roosevelt and Truman
   c. Bush and Obama
   d. Nixon and Reagan

3. Have modern president become too dependent on public opinion polls? Explain.

KEY TERMS

cabinet (p. 191)
executive agreement (p. 190)
executive orders (p. 190)
Great Society (p. 181)
impeachment (p. 175)

New Deal (p. 179)
pardon (p. 184)
power of appointment (p. 184)
reprieve (p. 184)
State of the Union address (p. 187)

Twenty-second Amendment (p. 175)
White House chief of staff (p. 192)
White House Office of Legislative Affairs (p. 187)
White House press secretary (p. 195)

THE FEDERAL BUREAUCRACY

UNITED STATES
ENVIRONMENTA
PROTECTION AGEN

LEARNING OBJECTIVES

WHAT IS BUREAUCRACY?

- Describe the bureaucracy as part of the executive branch of government organized hierarchically with standard operating procedures for doing business
- Assess the critical role that the bureaucracy plays in the implementation of federal policy

WHAT DOES THE FEDERAL BUREAUCRACY DO?

- Define "delegated authority" and apply the conditions under which such authority is granted
- Distinguish the oversight function of Congress over the bureaucracy
- Evaluate why Congress has provided some bureaucratic units with administrative judicatory authority

THE DEVELOPMENT OF THE FEDERAL BUREAUCRACY

- Describe how the federal bureaucracy has evolved over time, including substantial growth spurts as a result of the New Deal and Great Society programs and the Cold War

GETTING CONTROL OF THE GROWING BUREAUCRACY

- Explain methods for attempting to control or reduce the size and scope of the federal bureaucracy through privatization, devolution, deregulation, and accountability

THE ORGANIZATION OF THE FEDERAL BUREAUCRACY

- Distinguish between the different types of agencies in the federal bureaucracy

THE FEDERAL WORKFORCE

- Describe the large scope of the federal workforce and the civil service rules governing federal employment

Bureaucracy is a term that usually conjures up negative images. It often refers to overgrown government, excessive rules and paperwork, or a burdensome process for getting something done. Political candidates often extol the vices of "the unresponsive, fat bureaucracy" to strike a sympathetic chord with voters.[1] Despite the negative connotations of the term, bureaucracy is necessary for any government to function. Laws must be enforced, programs must be administered, and regulations must be implemented. Without a federal bureaucracy, the government could not function. To be sure, there are many problems with bureaucracy. It is often hard to get things done in an efficient manner, or to fire workers who do not perform well, or to reward deserving workers. The buck often passes from one desk to another, and silly or irrelevant rules often dictate the actions of the bureaucrats. Despite its problems and the "bad rep" that the term often conjures up, bureaucracy is absolutely essential for any government to implement and carry out its laws and public policies.[2] New presidents quickly learn that to accomplish their policy goals, they must rely on the federal bureaucracy. They frequently are elected to office and claim a "mandate to get things done." Getting things done not only requires the passage of laws, but it also needs a bureaucracy to carry out those new laws.

The "Connections App" is an interactive web app that helps you better understand the relationship between historical and current events with basic concepts.

1920   1930   1940   1950   1960

1934

Then

Joseph P. Kennedy, the first chairman of the Securities Exchange Commission.

Source: AP Photo

Though public skepticism of big government is an ongoing reality, officials charged with tackling big problems invariably turn to new bureaucracies for answers. Consider the economic crisis that emerged at the end of the "roaring 1920s." American industry flourished in the six years prior to the 1929 stock market crash. The Dow Jones Industrial index grew by a factor of five over that period, luring Americans to the stock market with unprecedented returns on their investments. And invest they did. Few considered what they were actually risking in buying shares in companies that could just as easily fail as succeed. All this blind risk taking came to a halt on October 24, 1929, when the six-year-old stock bubble burst. On that day alone, the Dow Jones Industrial index suffered an 11 percent decline; through July 1932 the market suffered an 89 percent slide, gutting the savings of hundreds of thousands of Americans. Although a handful of elite investors avoided that fate by capitalizing on "insider information," many thousands of less fortunate investors were left to wonder what happened to their money. A new Democratic president entered office in March of 1933 with a mandate to redirect government toward the protection of ordinary consumers. Accordingly, Congress passed the Securities Act of 1933 and empowered it a year later when it established the Securities and Exchange Commission (SEC). Movie mogul and steel industry executive Joseph P. Kennedy was one of few Americans who escaped the stock market crash unscathed thanks to insider information and friends in high places. Who better than him to prevent other "insiders" like himself from manipulating the future market? Under the leadership of Kennedy, future father of the 35th president, the SEC promulgated new rules governing the disclosure of information affecting the sale and trade of stocks. Thereafter, issuers of securities would be forced to fully disclose all the information that a potential shareholder might need to help make up his or her mind about the investment, thus protecting consumers from deceptive corporate practices. A new bureaucratic agency, the SEC, now stood front and center in implementing this new way of life on Wall Street.

2010

Now

Richard Cordray, the first chairman of the Consumer Financial Protection Board.

Source: © ZUMA Press, Inc./Alamy

As the dark cloud of recession cast a shadow over the American economy in 2007 and 2008, millions of homeowners suddenly found themselves unable to afford their mortgage payments. The housing market had experienced high growth in the decade leading up to this recession as low interest rates, high levels of employment, and federal policies supporting the issuance of subprime loans lured Americans eager to take part in the American dream of homeownership. With the high demand for housing, property values skyrocketed and homeowners took pride in their suddenly lucrative investments. Financial institutions also cashed in on the booming real estate market by closing on new loans and selling those loans off in the form of market-based securities. Unfortunately, the race for profits led some financial institutions to engage in lending practices that caused unwitting consumers to sign up for risky loans they could not afford over the long run. These so-called "predatory lending practices" included foregoing proper background checks on loan applicants and "qualifying" homebuyers at artificially low initial interest rates, which over time ballooned to much higher rates. When the economy slowed, millions of new homeowners found themselves out of work and holding mortgage payments far higher than what they initially paid. By 2010, a record 2.87 million homes in the United States were in foreclosure. In response, Congress passed the Dodd-Frank Financial Reform Act, which, among other measures, created the Bureau of Consumer Financial Protection (BCFP). Harvard professor Elizabeth Warren helped to shape and build this new agency, which was charged with establishing new rules for loan-making practices and enforcing those rules to ensure that consumers didn't fall prey to predatory lending practices. Eighty years after the stock market crash kicked off the Great Depression, a new administration had once again re-tooled the federal bureaucracy to safeguard consumers. For better or worse, new ideas and programs often demand new bureaucracies to put those laws into practice.

bureaucracy: An organization set up in a logical and rational manner for the purpose of accomplishing specific functions.

WHAT IS BUREAUCRACY?

A **bureaucracy** is an organization set up in a logical and rational manner for the purpose of accomplishing specific functions. Sociologist Max Weber (pronounced VAY-ber), an early student of bureaucratic organizations, identified six characteristics of effective bureaucracies:[3]

1. **Bureaucracies are organized on the basis of specialization, expertise, and division of labor.** The organization is divided into subunits based on function, and subunits are staffed by employees who are qualified to administer those tasks.

2. **They are organized in a hierarchical manner with an identifiable "chain of command" from top to bottom.**

3. **A common set of rules for carrying out functions characterizes the operation.** These rules are often referred to as standard operating procedures (SOPs). Employees are trained to know and use these SOPs so that functions are performed smoothly and consistently.

4. **Bureaucracies maintain good records, or a "paper trail," of actions taken and decisions made.** Good record maintenance enables periodic review, efficiency of operation, and proof of action.

5. **Bureaucracies are characterized by an air of professionalism on the part of employees.**

6. **The hiring and promotion process within effective bureaucracies is characterized by merit-based criteria and is insulated from "politics."**

Bureaucracies are created within many types of organizations. Organizations typically exist to carry out a function, or set of functions. Bureaucracies are what actually carry out these functions. Large private companies typically have bureaucracies that divide labor functions into categories or departments such as sales, accounting, human resources (HR), management information systems (MISs), and other divisions. Colleges and universities have bureaucracies that usually include an admissions department, a registrar's office, an academic counseling center, an athletics department, and so on. Even small organizations such as physicians' offices feature a bureaucracy that includes medical support staff (e.g., nurses), a front-office staff (receptionist and secretary), and business offices (accountant and medical insurance specialist).

Governments maintain bureaucracies to carry out specific functions, and the federal government is no exception. As with political parties, there is no reference to the bureaucracy in the U.S. Constitution. But like parties, the federal bureaucracy is arguably one of the most important features of the American political system, because Americans have come to depend on it for many important things, such as the defense of U.S. interests around the world, protection against terrorist attacks, cleaning up the destruction caused by natural disasters, a financial safety net for those who are unemployed or retired, the maintenance and expansion of the nation's roads and airways, and research for cures to such health problems as heart disease, cancer, and AIDS. In American government, the federal bureaucracy has traditionally come under the authority and jurisdiction of the president and the executive branch. As we will see, however, the modern federal bureaucracy is a complex set of agencies and organizations, parts of which are accountable to the legislative and judicial branches as well.

Citizens are more likely to come into direct contact with the bureaucracy than any other part of government, and so for many Americans the bureaucracy comes to symbolize what government is. A visit to an unemployment office to register for unemployment benefits, a check in the mail from the Social Security Administration, a trip to the Department of Motor Vehicles to renew a driver's license, or a visit to the Web site of the Consumer Protection Agency to inquire about the safety of a child's car seat—these are just a few of the many ways citizens interact with the bureaucracy.

The federal bureaucracy, in fact, is a huge set of organizations that is expected to serve many different functions. As shown in Figure 8.1, it includes numerous departments, offices, agencies, bureaus, councils, foundations, commissions, boards, services, and authorities. Each of these units, as Weber's analysis of bureaucracies suggests, specializes in an area of public policy, is hierarchically organized to carry out its particular duties, conducts its operation on the basis

FIGURE 8.1 The Organization of the Federal Bureaucracy

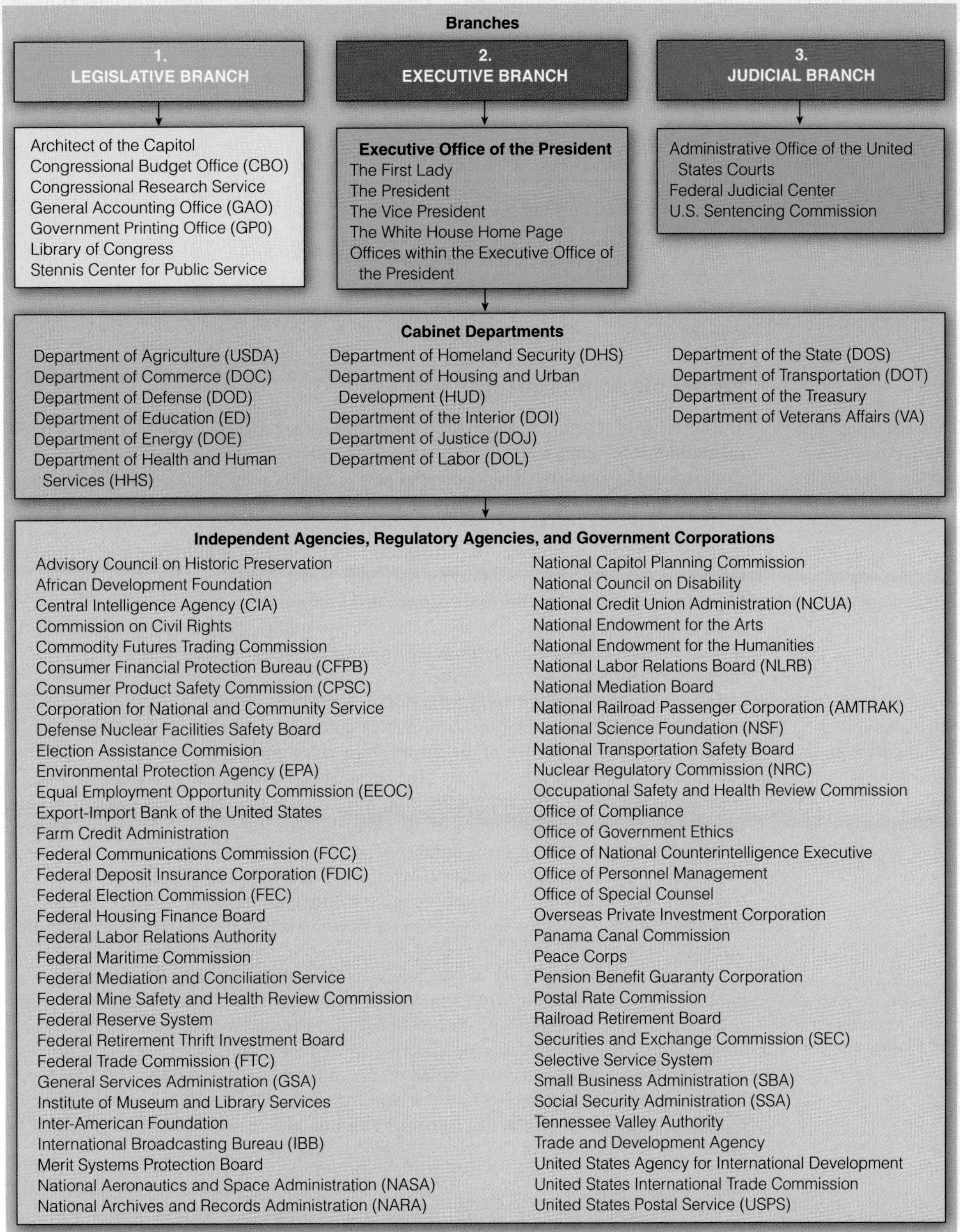

Branches

1. LEGISLATIVE BRANCH	2. EXECUTIVE BRANCH	3. JUDICIAL BRANCH

Architect of the Capitol Congressional Budget Office (CBO) Congressional Research Service General Accounting Office (GAO) Government Printing Office (GPO) Library of Congress Stennis Center for Public Service	**Executive Office of the President** The First Lady The President The Vice President The White House Home Page Offices within the Executive Office of the President	Administrative Office of the United States Courts Federal Judicial Center U.S. Sentencing Commission

Cabinet Departments

Department of Agriculture (USDA) Department of Commerce (DOC) Department of Defense (DOD) Department of Education (ED) Department of Energy (DOE) Department of Health and Human Services (HHS)	Department of Homeland Security (DHS) Department of Housing and Urban Development (HUD) Department of the Interior (DOI) Department of Justice (DOJ) Department of Labor (DOL)	Department of the State (DOS) Department of Transportation (DOT) Department of the Treasury Department of Veterans Affairs (VA)

Independent Agencies, Regulatory Agencies, and Government Corporations

Advisory Council on Historic Preservation	National Capitol Planning Commission
African Development Foundation	National Council on Disability
Central Intelligence Agency (CIA)	National Credit Union Administration (NCUA)
Commission on Civil Rights	National Endowment for the Arts
Commodity Futures Trading Commission	National Endowment for the Humanities
Consumer Financial Protection Bureau (CFPB)	National Labor Relations Board (NLRB)
Consumer Product Safety Commission (CPSC)	National Mediation Board
Corporation for National and Community Service	National Railroad Passenger Corporation (AMTRAK)
Defense Nuclear Facilities Safety Board	National Science Foundation (NSF)
Election Assistance Commision	National Transportation Safety Board
Environmental Protection Agency (EPA)	Nuclear Regulatory Commission (NRC)
Equal Employment Opportunity Commission (EEOC)	Occupational Safety and Health Review Commission
Export-Import Bank of the United States	Office of Compliance
Farm Credit Administration	Office of Government Ethics
Federal Communications Commission (FCC)	Office of National Counterintelligence Executive
Federal Deposit Insurance Corporation (FDIC)	Office of Personnel Management
Federal Election Commission (FEC)	Office of Special Counsel
Federal Housing Finance Board	Overseas Private Investment Corporation
Federal Labor Relations Authority	Panama Canal Commission
Federal Maritime Commission	Peace Corps
Federal Mediation and Conciliation Service	Pension Benefit Guaranty Corporation
Federal Mine Safety and Health Review Commission	Postal Rate Commission
Federal Reserve System	Railroad Retirement Board
Federal Retirement Thrift Investment Board	Securities and Exchange Commission (SEC)
Federal Trade Commission (FTC)	Selective Service System
General Services Administration (GSA)	Small Business Administration (SBA)
Institute of Museum and Library Services	Social Security Administration (SSA)
Inter-American Foundation	Tennessee Valley Authority
International Broadcasting Bureau (IBB)	Trade and Development Agency
Merit Systems Protection Board	United States Agency for International Development
National Aeronautics and Space Administration (NASA)	United States International Trade Commission
National Archives and Records Administration (NARA)	United States Postal Service (USPS)

Source: From http://www.firstgov.gov.

of a set of standard operating procedures, maintains records of its actions and decisions, is trained to carry out functions in a professional manner, and engages in hiring practices that are based on merit. The vast size and level of responsibility that these units have make the federal bureaucracy a complex and often confusing system to study.

WHAT DOES THE FEDERAL BUREAUCRACY DO?

Most of the federal bureaucracy is contained within the executive branch of government, and ultimately reports to the president of the United States.[4] Article II of the Constitution states that "the executive power shall be vested in a President of the United States of America." The executive power, or the power to carry out, administer, and enforce specific laws, then, falls mainly under the purview of presidential responsibility. The president uses the federal bureaucracy to exercise executive authority.

Policy Implementation

policy implementation: The process of carrying out laws, and the specific programs or services outlined in those laws.

The full range of activities in which the federal bureaucracy engages is known as **policy implementation**. Policy implementation is the process of carrying out a law. Laws that are passed by Congress often include the development of new or modification of existing federal programs or services. In order to carry out the specific programs or services outlined in a law, the federal bureaucracy is assigned the task of implementation. For example, in 1935 Congress passed the Social Security Act to provide older Americans with a stable source of income during their retirement years and to offer support for the children of deceased workers. The act created the Social Security Administration as the agency in the federal government that had the authority to carry out the provisions of the act. Today, the Social Security Administration remains the unit in the federal bureaucracy responsible for maintaining records and authorizing benefits to those eligible for Social Security payments.

regulations: Rules or other directives issued by government agencies.

Implementation of a law requires translating the congressional legislation into action. Bureaucratic units begin the process of implementation by developing **regulations,** or sets of rules that guide employees of the agency in carrying out its programs or services. These rules are supported by the force of law. The Social Security Administration, for example, has written a detailed set of regulations defining who is and who is not eligible for Social Security retirement benefits. The rules include a schedule for the amount of monthly payment benefit based on a person's age, the number of years he or she contributed to the Social Security system while working, and other criteria. Regulations are useful not only because they translate laws into actions, but, because they are written down and are usually very specific, they also provide a basis for employees in the bureaucracy to consistently apply them from one case to the next.

Federal Register: The journal that publishes regulations that implement a federal program.

Once an agency drafts a set of regulations to implement a program, the regulations are published in the *Federal Register*. This federal government publication is widely accessible to elected leaders, interest groups, corporations, the media, and regular citizens. The agencies authoring the regulations have an open period where they accept comments on the proposed rules and decide whether to redraft based on the commentary they receive. If the agency refuses to redraft based on an objection, the objector can ask Congress to require the agency to modify the regulations; or the objector might take the matter to court on the basis that the agency was acting outside of Congress's intentions in the law.

Bureaucratic Legislation

administrative discretion: The freedom of agencies to decide how to implement a vague or ambiguous law passed by Congress.

The types of laws passed by Congress are many and varied, and thus policy implementation encompasses many different bureaucratic activities. Some laws are very vague and offer agencies very little guidance about implementation. Other laws can be very specific in directing the agency on how to implement them. When laws are vague, agencies are said to have **administrative discretion**, which gives them considerable freedom in deciding how to implement the laws. Vague laws require an agency to spend more time and effort in developing regulations.

Two policy areas where congressional legislation tends to be vague and where agencies have much latitude in making rules and regulations are environmental quality and workplace safety. Important pieces of legislation, such as the Clean Air Act and the Occupational Safety and Health Act, have given agencies such as the Environmental Protection Agency (EPA) and Occupational Safety and Health Administration (OSHA) much discretion in setting specific standards for car emissions, pollution, and workplace safety standards. This discretion usually is the product of at least one of two conditions. First, Congress often does not have the technical expertise to define how to achieve clean air or workplace safety, and so it gives agencies that have such technical capabilities the discretion to set standards. Second, Congress sometimes chooses not to deal with politically difficult issues such as how to clean up toxic-waste dumps, and so it shifts the responsibility to the bureaucracy, forcing an agency to resolve the problem. When an agency makes an unpopular decision as a result of Congress's "passing the buck," the agency's action contributes further to the negative image of bureaucracies.

When Congress writes vague legislation and thus transfers legislative authority to an agency, it gives that agency the effective power to make laws, a constitutional power that is supposed to rest with the Congress alone. When Congress does this, it is said to have **delegated congressional power**. Laws that relate to the authority of administrative agencies and the rules promulgated by those agencies are referred to as **administrative law**. Congress has delegated considerable legislative authority to the EPA and OSHA to craft both environmental and workplace safety laws. Similarly, Congress has delegated a substantial amount of authority to the Federal Reserve to manage the nation's economy. The "Fed" has the power to adjust the prime interest rate in response to economic conditions to encourage investments and ward off inflation.

Delegation of power from Congress to bureaucratic agencies is not, however, typically open-ended. Congress may cede lawmaking authority to the bureaucracy, but it does not relinquish all power. **Congressional oversight** is the term used to describe Congress's regular monitoring of bureaucratic agency performance for the purpose of achieving accountability. Although the vast bulk of bureaucratic agencies ultimately report to the president as chief executive, Congress, through its oversight function, commands a significant amount of accountability from executive agencies.[5]

If Congress is not satisfied with an agency's performance, it has a variety of means to coerce change: it can reduce or eliminate an agency's budget; it can refuse to confirm presidential appointments to that agency; it can eliminate the agency; it can conduct investigations into the activities and performance of the agency; or it can establish a new agency and shift resources and powers to it. This strong system of checks often renders the federal bureaucracy just as (if not more) responsive to Congress as to the president.

Specific congressional oversight functions may be carried out in a number of ways. Particular committees (or subcommittees) in Congress hold hearings, on either a regularly scheduled or an ad hoc basis, to review agency performance. For example, the House Armed Services Committee meets with the secretary of defense and Joint Chiefs of Staff to review Pentagon programs. The Senate Environment and Public Works Committee holds regular meetings with the administrator of the EPA to review that agency's activities. The House Science and Technology Committee reviews the activities of the National Aeronautics and Space Administration (NASA). In addition, the House Appropriations Committee is divided into a number of subcommittees, each of which regularly reviews pending authorizations for funding individual agencies. These subcommittees often scrutinize agency spending.

Two bureaucratic agencies under the direct control of Congress (rather than the president) that support the oversight function of congressional committees are the Congressional Budget Office (CBO) and the Government Accountability Office (GAO). These offices compile data on federal programs and are staffed with program review and accounting professionals who comply with members' and committees' requests for information on agency performance and cost. Congress uses the GAO to investigate the actions or inactions of an agency, and it uses the CBO to conduct research, such as program effectiveness studies.

delegation of congressional power: Congress's transferring of its lawmaking authority to the executive branch of government.

administrative law: A law that relates to the authority of administrative agencies and the rules promulgated by those agencies.

congressional oversight: Congress's exercise of its authority to monitor the activities of agencies and administrators.

The Environmental Protection Agency once spent $1 million to preserve a Trenton, New Jersey, sewer as a historic monument.

Fact.

The EPA's million-dollar appropriation for the sewer monument made the all-time top 10 list for Senator Proxmire's Golden Fleece Awards.

CHECK **THE LIST**

Senator Proxmire's Top 10 Golden Fleece Awards

Stories of waste in bureaucratic spending always become fodder for calls to cut federal spending and eliminate unnecessary federal programs. Much of this "wasteful" spending is rooted in congressional pork-barrel spending, that is, spending on projects that benefit individual members' home districts. Perhaps no one took better aim at wasteful pork-barrel spending in the federal bureaucracy than U.S. Senator William Proxmire (D-WI). In 1975, Proxmire began what he called the "Golden Fleece Awards" to target bureaucratic agencies that spent money on wasteful programs. Proxmire announced 150 awards in all. Asked to identify the top 10 most egregious spending wastes, Proxmire provided the following list:

- ❑ **Tequila fish.** The National Institute on Alcohol Abuse and Alcoholism for spending millions of dollars to find out if drunken fish are more aggressive than sober fish, if young rats are more likely than old rats to consume alcohol in order to reduce anxiety, and if rats can be turned into alcoholics.
- ❑ **The Great Wall of Bedford.** The U.S. Department of Commerce for spending $20,000 to build an eight-hundred-foot limestone replica of the Great Wall of China in Bedford, Indiana.
- ❑ **Buying Worcestershire sauce.** The Department of the Army for spending $6,000 to prepare a 17-page document that told the federal government how to buy a bottle of Worcestershire sauce.
- ❑ **The New Jersey Sewer Museum.** The Environmental Protection Agency for spending $1 million to preserve a Trenton, New Jersey, sewer as a historical monument.
- ❑ **Lessons in watching TV.** The Office of Education for spending $220,000 to develop a curriculum to teach college students how to watch television.
- ❑ **Tennis cheating.** The National Endowment for the Humanities for a $25,000 grant to study why people cheat and act rudely on tennis courts in Virginia.
- ❑ **Tailhook.** The Department of the Navy for using 64 planes to fly 1,334 officers to the Hilton Hotel in Las Vegas for a reunion of the Tailhook Association.
- ❑ **$2 million patrol car.** The Law Enforcement Assistance Administration for spending $2 million on a prototype police car that was never completed.
- ❑ **Basketball therapy.** The Health Care Financing Administration for Medicaid payments to psychiatrists for unscheduled meetings with patients who were attending basketball games, which cost the federal government between $40 million and $80 million.
- ❑ **Surfing subsidy.** The Department of Commerce for giving the Honolulu city government $28,000 to study how to spend $250,000 for a good surfing beach.

▶ **POINT TO PONDER:** Can you reasonably justify any of the bureaucratic expenditures that made Proxmire's Golden Fleece Awards list? Go on your hometown's Web site. Can you find any examples of projects in your hometown that would similarly be classified as wasteful government spending?

Source: Taxpayers for Common Sense Web site, http://www.taxpayer.net

Bureaucratic Adjudication

Just as policy implementation sometimes includes the writing of legislation, it also may involve **bureaucratic adjudicating**, or determining the rights and duties of particular parties within the scope of an agency's rules or regulations. Such adjudication might include ruling on whether an individual is eligible to receive Social Security payments, or whether a company has violated an air pollution rule. Most adjudication takes place in the court system. However Congress, which has the authority to create federal adjudicating agencies, has placed judicial power in some bureaucratic agencies as well. For example, the Equal Employment Opportunity Commission (EEOC) has the authority to adjudicate cases where an individual or group of individuals charges that a company has violated federal laws preventing discrimination in hiring or promotion practices in the workplace. The EEOC can try a case against a company, and if the finding is that the company violated federal law, the EEOC is authorized to prescribe a punishment or corrective action.

bureaucratic adjudicating: Determining the rights and duties of particular parties within the scope of an agency's rules or regulations.

The EEOC and other agencies such as the EPA, the National Labor Relations Board, and the Federal Communications Commission (FCC) employ the personnel, procedures, and case law more typically seen in the judicial branch. Bureaucratic judicial personnel and powers include "administrative judges," appellate courts within the agency, and administrative hearings that resemble a trial. Ultimately, any administrative court decision may be appealed to the federal court system, because the power of adjudication ultimately rests in the hands of the judicial branch. In reality, however, federal courts routinely uphold cases appealed from administrative courts.

THE DEVELOPMENT OF THE FEDERAL BUREAUCRACY

The executive branch of government during the first four years of George Washington's presidency was very limited. Congress created just three departments to aid the first president in executing the law: the Department of State to oversee foreign affairs, the Department of Treasury to oversee fiscal affairs, and the Department of War to oversee military affairs. Washington selected and the Senate confirmed Thomas Jefferson, Alexander Hamilton, and Henry Knox to lead these departments, respectively. Shortly after these departments were created, the president was authorized to hire an attorney general and a postmaster general. During the first year of the Washington administration, the federal bureaucracy employed only about 50 individuals.

As the role of government expanded, and as the United States added new territories, there was a need to expand the size of the federal bureaucracy. Military operations, such as those conducted during the War of 1812, required increased support services and agencies to support military operations. Westward expansion brought with it the need for federal services to settle the new areas. A centralized national bank required federal agencies to centralize the economic and monetary system. By the mid-1800s, Congress saw the need to create a new cabinet department, the Department of the Interior, to manage federally owned lands and to aid in the westward expansion of the nation. The important role of farming in the nation's growth and development led to the establishment of the Department of Agriculture in 1862 to support and promote farming and farm-product commercialization. The Department of Justice was established in 1870 to aid the attorney general in the post–Civil War era in prosecuting violators of federal law and representing the federal government in the courts.

In 1884, a Bureau of Labor was created to address the concerns of the labor force that arose with the growth of the industrial economy. Large-scale industrialization and economic development led to the development of a Commerce Agency in 1888 to help regulate interstate and foreign trade. These agencies were elevated to cabinet status in the early 1900s to reflect the growing role they played in the federal government. The Great Depression set the stage for the election of Franklin Delano Roosevelt (FDR) in 1932. The FDR administration advocated an activist role for the federal government in responding to the economic crisis. Consequently, FDR's New Deal created a myriad of new federal agencies to deal with the nation's fiscal woes,

Many of the federal bureaucracy's "alphabet soup" agencies were created as New Deal programs during the administration of President Franklin Delano Roosevelt. Pictured above are workers at one such agency, the Tennessee Valley Authority, seen here assembling a new power generator at the Cherokee Dam on the Holston River in east Tennessee.

including the Social Security Administration, the Securities and Exchange Commission, the Civilian Conservation Corps, and a host of public works programs to provide jobs for the large number of unemployed. In 1936, Roosevelt established the Brownlow Committee (named for its chair Louis Brownlow) to investigate how to make the growing bureaucracy more efficient and more responsive to the president.[6] The committee unanimously agreed that the president's power should be enhanced to give the president greater authority as manager of the bureaucracy. The Brownlow Committee's recommendations led to the consolidation of presidential authority over the bureaucracy.

By 1940, the federal government accounted for 10 percent of the nation's gross domestic product (GDP), with $9.5 billion spent on federal programs, including the employment of about 700,000 Americans in the federal bureaucracy. The increased role of government led to greater demands for federal services, which in turn necessitated growth in the federal bureaucracy. Between 1940 and 1975, the federal bureaucracy experienced an unprecedented growth spurt. During this period, the number of federal employees more than tripled to 2.2 million, the federal budget increased to $332 billion, and the federal budget as a percentage of GDP reached 22 percent.[7]

Two factors accounted for this massive growth in the bureaucracy. First was President Lyndon B. Johnson's Great Society program of the 1960s. The Great Society encompassed numerous new laws aimed at social and economic improvements to American society through a highly activist role of the federal government. The post–World War II prosperity of the American economy allowed Johnson to convince a Democratic Congress that programs promoting social justice, a safety net for the impoverished, improvements to urban life, health care for the elderly, and greater access to educational opportunities should be guaranteed to all Americans and funded by the great wealth of the American economy. These programs had a large influence on growth of the bureaucracy through the 1970s.

A second factor contributing to the massive growth in the bureaucracy was the Cold War. World War II resulted in two superpowers, the United States and the Soviet Union, vying against each other for global influence. From 1945 to 1991, these superpowers developed expensive nuclear and other war technologies in search of military superiority. The federal budget for defense programs grew dramatically, as did the programs to support intelligence operations and aid to foreign nations for diplomatic purposes.

GETTING CONTROL OF THE GROWING BUREAUCRACY

During the mid- to late 1970s, the American economy began to slump. Whereas the prosperity of the 1960s facilitated the creation of a larger-size government to accomplish a number of policy goals, the sluggish economy of the late 1970s was unable to support the by now very large federal bureaucracy. Federal budget deficits began to accumulate, and the United States could no longer afford the huge federal bureaucracy that it had created. Ronald Reagan was elected president in 1980 with an agenda to scale back the federal bureaucracy. The Reagan administration targeted domestic programs to achieve the reduction in government. Since the 1980s, various administrations have attempted to reduce the size of the federal bureaucracy. The methods they have used include the following:

Privatization. **Privatization** means replacing government-provided services with services provided by the private sector. The theory of privatization is that if private companies compete to provide services, the cost of those services will be less than if government provides those services directly. Additionally, some contend that private corporations can more flexibly adapt to changing circumstances because they are not weighed down by civil service restrictions and government red tape. Accordingly, a number of federal programs were privatized during the 1980s. For example, the U.S. Department of Labor frequently provided job-training services to the unemployed during the 1960s and 1970s. Federal laws passed in the 1980s eliminated much of the federal management of job training and contracted out these services to private companies. More recently, the federal government has used a number of private contractors, including Halliburton (the company once run by former Vice President Dick Cheney) to help rebuild Iraq after the second Persian Gulf War, under the idea that the costs would be even greater if the federal government played a more direct role.

> **privatization:** The process of replacing government-provided services with services provided by the private sector.

Deregulation. The development of rules and regulations to achieve a policy goal requires units in the bureaucracy to ensure that such rules and regulations are followed. **Deregulation**, that is, eliminating government oversight and regulation of certain activities, results in less government to do the regulating. Prior to the mid-1970s, the trucking and railroad industries, long-distance telephone service, prices for air flights, and the activities of savings and loan institutions were regulated by the federal government. Deregulation of these and other activities resulted in the abolition of a number of federal agencies, including the Civil Aeronautics Board and eventually the Interstate Commerce Commission.

> **deregulation:** The elimination of government oversight and government regulation of certain activities.

Devolution. A central question in our federal system of government is which level of government—national or state—should have the authority to provide programs and services to citizens. The New Deal and Great Society programs gave the national government increased responsibility and authority for such services. In response to extensive growth of the national government, the 1980s witnessed a **devolution** of power and responsibility back to the states, mainly to shrink the size of the national government. For example, welfare reform in the mid-1990s shifted much responsibility for welfare from the federal to the state governments.

> **devolution:** The transfer of power and responsibilities for certain regulatory programs from the federal government back to the states.

"Reinventing government." When Bill Clinton was elected president in 1992, he promised to "reinvent government." This promise translated into an eight-year effort to promote bureaucratic accountability. The Clinton administration instituted mechanisms such as customer satisfaction research with those who received federal services and freedom-of-information policies that gave the public and the news media access to government documents to help promote accountability. In addition, the Government Performance and Results Act, passed in 1997, required that agencies establish goals and set out a plan for achieving those goals. In the book *Reinventing Government*, David Osborne and Ted Gaebler describe how bureaucracy and other aspects of the public sector in the United States have undergone a transformation.[8] They contend that the "entrepreneurial spirit" brought to bear on government performance, which includes market-driven and business-oriented planning, has improved the effectiveness and efficiency of bureaucracy at all levels of government.

In addition to implementing these strategies for reducing the size of the federal bureaucracy, the Cold War, which concluded in 1991 with the collapse of the Soviet Union, put an end to escalating defense budgets to support the arms race with the Soviets.

The end of the Cold War and the implementation of strategies that contain, if not reduce, the size of the federal bureaucracy do appear to have reversed the decades-long trend toward increasing the size of government. Between 1990 and 2000, the number of civilian employees in the federal government declined by about 500,000,[9] and the percentage of the GDP accounted for by federal spending dropped from 21.9 percent to 18.2 percent. Despite these efforts, however, federal spending on the bureaucracy continues to increase annually at a pace that exceeds inflation. In particular, defense spending to fight the war on terrorism and the war in Iraq in recent years have increased federal spending. Also, the Department of Homeland Security, created in response to the terrorist attacks of September 11, 2001, required increased federal dollars to protect the nation within its own borders.

More recently, the election of President Barack Obama and increased majorities of Democrats to Congress in 2008 during an economic recession ushered in a new growth spurt for the federal bureaucracy. A $787 billion federal spending plan to provide an economic stimulus along with a health care reform package and increased regulations of the financial services industry all significantly increased the scope and size of the bureaucracy. Most notably, the Obama administration championed the creation of a new Consumer Financial Protection Bureau designed to provide stricter regulations on the mortgage financing industry in particular.

The Organization of the Federal Bureaucracy

The federal bureaucracy is made up of a variety of different types of agencies that are empowered to carry out laws and federal programs. Some of these organizations have broad authority over a public policy area, whereas others have a narrow focus; some are empowered to implement laws and programs established by Congress, whereas others have the added responsibility of creating rules and policies, and adjudicating. Some report directly to the president, whereas others answer to both the president and Congress. Also, though most organizations in the federal bureaucracy are part of the executive branch, some are part of the legislative and judicial branches. Units of the federal bureaucracy include cabinet departments, independent agencies, regulatory agencies, government corporations, and the Executive Office of the President.

Cabinet Departments

Amid the complex web of bureaucratic units is a select set of 15 organizations called **cabinet departments**, which are the major administrative organizations of the executive branch. These departments described in Table 8.1, vary in terms of both size and importance. The Department of Defense, for example, employs nearly 1 million civilian workers and another 1.5 million military personnel. By contrast, the Department of Education has only about 5,000 employees.

At the head of each cabinet department is a secretary (with the exception of the Justice Department, which is headed by the attorney general) who reports directly to the president.

Along with a few other high-level presidential advisers and the vice president, these secretaries compose the president's cabinet, a set of high-level administrators who report directly to the president. Cabinet heads and their deputies are nominated by the president and must be confirmed by the Senate. Typically, a secretary shares the same views as the president on policy matters and often is a loyal political supporter (if not close friend) of the chief executive. The "inner cabinet" is a term used to describe the secretaries of the most important departments in the cabinet—State, Defense, Treasury, and Justice. Whereas the cabinet once served as the president's primary advisory panel, the growth in the Executive Office of the President, discussed later in this chapter, has shifted primary advisory responsibilities to that office.

Cabinet departments (sometimes referred to as executive departments) generally have a broad scope of authority over a particular policy area, such as the nation's military

cabinet departments: Those federal agencies that qualify as the major administrative organizations of the executive branch.

All of the leaders of the cabinet departments hold the official title of "Secretary."

Fiction.

All of the heads of cabinet departments hold the title of "Secretary" except the head of the U.S. Department of Justice, who holds the title "U.S. Attorney General."

Chip Somodevilla/Getty Images

President Obama meets with his cabinet in the Cabinet Room at the White House.

(the Department of Defense), federal law enforcement (the Department of Justice), the federal road and highway system (the Department of Transportation), and protecting the nation from terrorism and responding to emergency situations (Department of Homeland Security). The scope of activities in any one department tends to be so broad that most departments are best viewed as a collection of many different agencies and subagencies, each with a narrower policy focus.

The U.S. Department of Labor, for example, is charged with promoting the American labor force and the interests of labor. It is organized into a large array of agencies and offices, each of which focuses on a particular aspect of labor issues. The Occupational Safety and Health Administration (OSHA) develops standards to promote safe workplace environments, and implements regulations to ensure that employers live up to these standards. The Bureau of Labor Statistics is responsible for compiling data on the labor force on a regular basis. The Office of Labor-Management Standards sets policies for the conduct of negotiations between employers and employees.

Likewise, the U.S. Department of Defense manages the armed forces, and is organized into a number of subunits, including the U.S. Army, Navy, Air Force, and National Guard. The hierarchical organization of departments facilitates the bureaucratic goals of area specialization, division of labor, and chain of command.

Although the head of a cabinet department advises and reports directly to the president, only Congress has the authority to create a new department or eliminate an existing one. The power to define the scope, authority, and indeed the very existence of a specific major department in the federal bureaucracy is an important "check" that Congress exercises over the president.

TABLE 8.1 The Cabinet Departments

Department of State

The Department of State has been the leading U.S. foreign affairs agency since 1789, and the Secretary of State is the president's principal foreign policy adviser. The State Department engages in the following activities: it leads in the coordination and development of U.S. foreign policy; it manages the foreign affairs budget and other foreign affairs resources; it represents the United States abroad, conveying U.S. foreign policy to foreign governments and international organizations through U.S. embassies and consulates in foreign countries and diplomatic missions to international organizations; and it negotiates agreements and treaties on issues ranging from trade to nuclear weapons.

Department of Treasury

The Treasury Department, also established in 1789, is entrusted with a broad range of duties and functions. It is responsible for paying all the bills of the federal government, collecting federal taxes, borrowing money for the federal government, printing money, and overseeing the operations of national banks. In addition to these monetary functions, the Department of the Treasury also oversees critical functions in enforcement and economic policy development. The Internal Revenue Service and the U.S. Mint are part of the Treasury Department.

Department of Defense

Called the Department of War when it was established in 1789, the Department of Defense currently employs nearly 1 million civilians, far more than any other agency in the federal bureaucracy. Most of these employees work at military bases around the United States. In 1947, the separate Departments of the Army, Navy, Air Force, Marines, and Coast Guard were reorganized into the new Department of Defense to achieve greater efficiency and coordination. In addition to its large civilian workforce, the Department is responsible for 1.5 million active-duty military personnel, and another 1.2 million in the Guard and Reserve.

Department of Justice

The Office of Attorney General was created in 1789 as an adviser to the president, and in 1870 was elevated to cabinet-department status as the Department of Justice (DOJ). The role of the DOJ is to prevent and control crime, to punish those who are guilty of unlawful behavior, to enforce the nation's immigration laws, and to administer the justice system. The DOJ employs U.S. attorneys who prosecute offenders and represent the U.S. government in court. It also oversees the Federal Bureau of Investigation, the Drug Enforcement Administration, the Bureau of Prisons, and the United States Marshals Service, which protects the federal judiciary, apprehends fugitives, and detains people in federal custody.

Department of the Interior

The Department of the Interior (DOI), created in 1849, is responsible for maintaining and managing federally owned land, which includes about 20 percent of the nation's landmass. It maintains 900 dams and reservoirs that provide water to more than 30 million Americans. The department also handles federal relations with Native American tribes. Located within the department, the Bureau of Indian Affairs manages nearly 60 million acres of land held in trust by the United States. Finally, the DOI manages the national park system, which includes 388 parks and 540 wildlife refuges.

Department of Agriculture

The U.S. Department of Agriculture (USDA) was created in 1862 by Congress at the request of President Abraham Lincoln. At the time, nearly half of all U.S. workers were employed in farming. The USDA originally was created to provide farmers with seeds and information for improving farm production and services. Today, the USDA runs the school lunch, school breakfast, and food stamp programs; brings housing, telecommunications, and safe drinking water to rural farmland areas; is responsible for the safety of meat, poultry, and egg products; and provides research on farm technologies and safe food-handling practices.

Department of Commerce

The U.S. Department of Commerce and Labor was created in 1903 and was renamed the Department of Commerce (DOC) in 1913. Today, the DOC provides comprehensive statistical analysis of economic conditions in the United States, manages patent and trademark protection programs, and is responsible for conducting the U.S. Census. The department also provides grants to economically distressed areas for business and job development, promotes exports of U.S. manufactured goods, promotes the growth of minority-owned businesses, and runs the National Oceanic and Atmospheric Administration, which forecasts weather and environmental conditions.

Department of Labor

The Department of Labor was a bureau within the U.S. Department of Commerce and Labor and became a cabinet-level department in 1913. Its mission is to promote the welfare of the job seekers, wage earners, and retirees of the United States by improving their working conditions, advancing their opportunities for profitable employment, protecting their retirement and health care benefits, helping employers find workers, strengthening free collective bargaining, and tracking changes in employment, prices, and other national economic measurements. The department administers a variety of federal labor laws, including those that guarantee workers' rights to safe and healthful working conditions; a minimum hourly wage and overtime pay; freedom from employment discrimination; unemployment insurance; and other income support.

Department of Housing and Urban Development

The Department of Housing and Urban Development (HUD), created in 1965, is the federal department primarily responsible for dealing with the nation's housing needs. It administers programs that help cities and communities develop and rehabilitate. Many of HUD's activities focus on the nation's urban areas, providing housing assistance and public housing projects in many cities.

Department of Transportation

The Department of Transportation (DOT), established in 1966, sets federal transportation policy and works with state and local governments along with private-sector partners to promote a safe, secure, efficient, and interconnected national transportation system of roads, railways, pipelines, airways, and seaways. The DOT is responsible for managing more than a dozen agencies, including the Federal Aviation Administration, the Federal Highway Administration, the National Highway Traffic Safety Administration, and the Federal Railroad Administration.

Department of Energy

The Department of Energy (DOE) was created in 1978 in response to an energy crisis spawned by a reduction in Middle East oil production. Today the DOE helps protect national security by applying advanced science and nuclear technology to the nation's defense, manages programs to promote diverse energy sources, and is responsible for disposal of the nation's high-level radioactive waste.

Department of Education

The U.S. Department of Education, created in 1978, was originally one part of the Department of Health, Education, and Welfare. The department is responsible for administering a variety of federal programs supporting aid to local public schools and college tuition loan programs. The Office of Civil Rights within this department is responsible for administering Title IX of the Education Amendments of 1972 to the Civil Rights Act of 1964, which requires that educational institutions receiving federal funds maintain policies, practices, and programs that do not discriminate on the basis of sex. In accordance with Title IX, colleges must provide the same opportunities for sports-team participation by women as they do for men.

Department of Health and Human Services

Created in 1978, the Department of Health and Human Services (HHS) administers more than three hundred federal programs, covering a wide range of health and human services topics. These programs focus on medical and social science research, prevention of infectious disease outbreaks, immunization services, food and drug safety, financial assistance and services for low-income families, maternal and infant health, prevention of child abuse and domestic violence, substance abuse treatment and prevention, services for older Americans such as home-delivered meals, and comprehensive health services for Native Americans. HHS has the largest of the cabinet department budgets, over $500 billion for 2006.

Department of Veterans Affairs

This department, created in 1988, is charged with overseeing programs that promote the interest and general welfare of veterans of the U.S. military. The department operates the Veterans Health Administration and the Veterans Benefits Administration.

Department of Homeland Security

Created in 2002, the Department of Homeland Security (DHS) is the newest of the cabinet departments. It was created in response to the terrorist attacks of September 11, 2001. The department's main role is to protect the nation against further terrorist attacks within the nation's borders.

Source: © Cengage Learning

Special situations, and particularly crises, have led the U.S. government to create cabinet-level departments to deal with large-scale national problems. The creation of the Department of Defense in 1947, for example, was in response to large and costly inefficiencies in military operations during World War II. The Department of Energy was established in 1977 in response to the severe energy crisis and gasoline shortage that plagued the country during the 1970s. President Reagan successfully pressed for the creation of a Veterans Affairs Department in 1988 in order to promote his administration's appreciation of those who served in the U.S. military. The newest cabinet department is the Department of Homeland Security (DHS), established in 2002.

The Department of Homeland Security

The terrorist attacks of September 11, 2001, led to President George W. Bush's request to Congress to create the new department. At first, Bush resisted calls for another large unit in the federal bureaucracy. But given strong support in Congress and in the public for a unit to be in charge of the nation's security, he soon became an advocate of its creation. The DHS represents a reorganization of 22 existing federal agencies into one cabinet department. The reorganization was intended to improve the coordination and operations of these agencies in protecting the nation against threats to the homeland.

The primary areas of the DHS are the following:

- **Border and transportation security.** This includes the U.S. Customs Service (previously part of the U.S. Department of Treasury) and the former Immigration and Naturalization Service (previously part of the U.S. Department of Justice).

- **Emergency preparedness and response.** This includes the Federal Emergency Management Agency, formerly an independent agency, and the National Domestic Preparedness Office (previously in the Federal Bureau of Investigation).

- **Science and technology.** This includes a variety of scientific research offices formerly part of the U.S. Departments of Energy, Defense, and Agriculture.

- **Information analysis and infrastructure protection.** This includes the Federal Incident Computer Response Center, which was previously part of the General Services Administration, and the National Incident Protection Center (formerly in the Federal Bureau of Investigation).

- The Secret Service, which was previously in the Treasury Department.

- The U.S. Coast Guard.

In addition to maintaining the authority to carry out many of the nation's laws, the cabinet also plays a symbolic role in the political system. Many interest groups provide input to the president through leaders in the cabinet, and the voices of community and business leaders are often heard first by cabinet-department officials. As the highest-level units in the bureaucracy, cabinet departments theoretically represent the most important policy areas. Increasingly, presidents have used their cabinet secretary appointments to demonstrate diversity in government. For nearly two centuries, cabinet secretaries were almost exclusively white men, but over the last 20 years presidents have used race and gender as factors influencing their appointments. President Clinton made history by naming women to the inner cabinet for the first time: Janet Reno as attorney general in 1993 and Madeleine Albright as secretary of state in 1997. President George W. Bush then made history by appointing the first African American to the inner cabinet—Colin Powell as secretary of state in 2001, and then an African American woman, Condoleezza Rice, as Powell's replacement in 2005; he also appointed the first Hispanic to the inner cabinet when he named Alberto Gonzales as the nation's attorney general during his second term in office. President Obama's cabinet is also diverse, featuring in prominent positions four women (Secretary of State Hillary Clinton, Secretary of Health and Human Services Kathleen Sebelius, Secretary of Homeland Security Janet Napolitano, and Secretary of Labor Hilda Solis) and two African Americans (Attorney General Eric Holder and U.S. Trade Representative Ron Kirk).

THE MORE THINGS CHANGE, THE MORE THEY STAY THE SAME

Conflicts Within the President's Cabinet

Presidents choose the leaders of their cabinets, and those chosen are most often high-level political supporters and friends of the president, as well as those who agree with the chief executive on key issues of public policy. Even though the president makes all of these high-level appointments, conflicts between department heads are not uncommon. Discord among high-ranking officials may sometimes play out in the media and become a source of embarrassment to presidents. A 2010 book by Bob Woodward entitled *Obama's Wars* depicts top White House officials in conflict over how to resolve the war in Afghanistan. Yet cabinet leaders' differences of opinion on key policy matters may not always be a bad thing, because they give the president a variety of perspectives from which to make a choice.

From 1789 through 1793, President George Washington's cabinet included Secretary of State Thomas Jefferson and Secretary of the Treasury Alexander Hamilton. Washington's desire for his cabinet officers to work closely with each other and provide coordinated advice to him was soon dashed as severe conflicts broke out between these two men. Their primary disagreement was over Hamilton's proposal to create a central national bank. Hamilton believed that the federal government had the authority to establish such a bank, which he saw as necessary to solve the nation's economic problems. For Jefferson, the creation of a central bank exceeded the authority of the central government. The conflict between these top two cabinet officials reflected a battle between Jefferson's "states' rights" beliefs and Hamilton's "strong central government" views. In the end, Washington sided with Hamilton, and a central bank was created.

From 1977 through 1979, President Jimmy Carter's foreign policy team included Secretary of State Cyrus Vance and National Security Advisor Zbigniew Brzezinski. Brzezinski was a close adviser to the president and over time came to take on more and more of the responsibilities normally under the purview of the Secretary of State. For example, Carter in 1978 sent Brzezinski to Beijing to help normalize China–U.S. relations. As an emissary for Carter, Brzezinski assumed state functions beyond those of a policy adviser. The role Brzezinski played caused mounting friction between himself and Vance. This friction came to a head in 1979 over the U.S. response to the Iranian hostage crisis. Vance favored a policy of recognizing the Ayatollah Khomeini and negotiating with him, whereas Brzezinski favored U.S. military action to remove Khomeini. When Brzezinski convinced Carter to approve a plan to rescue the hostages by force (which failed), Secretary of State Vance resigned.

In 2003, George W. Bush found two of his inner-circle cabinet secretaries locked in a profound battle over the question of whether or not the United States should militarily intervene in Iraq. Iraqi leader Saddam Hussein had continuously defied United Nations (UN) resolutions regarding inspections to locate sites used for the development of weapons of mass destruction. Secretary of State Colin Powell advocated a diplomatic solution, threatening the use of the U.S. military only if the UN would endorse such action. Secretary of Defense Donald Rumsfeld argued for U.S. military action even without UN approval (France, Germany, Russia, and members of the UN Security Council had refused to support military intervention). In the end, President Bush sided with Rumsfeld, and the United States went to war with Iraq without the UN's full support. These conflicting positions between the president's top two foreign policy advisers reflect Rumsfeld's "hawkish" military perspective and Powell's more "realist" perspective. Powell resigned after President Bush's reelection in 2004; Rumsfeld remained defense secretary until December of 2006, resigning soon after the 2006 midterm elections.

For Critical Thinking and Discussion

1. Should differences among the president's top advisers be aired in public, or should they be resolved quietly behind the scenes?

2. Are there disadvantages to offering absolute transparency under these circumstances?

NASA is an independent agency with a highly trained technical and scientific staff. Pictured above is the NASA control room in Houston, Texas.

independent agency: A department that focuses on a narrower set of issues than do higher-status Cabinet departments.

regulatory agency: A government body responsible for the control and supervision of a specified activity or area of public interest.

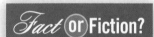

The president is the nation's chief executive, and so all of the agencies in federal bureaucracy report to the president.

Fiction.

Regulatory agencies do not report to the president. Commissioners of these agencies are nominated by the president and confirmed by Congress, but work independently in directing the affairs of those agencies. The president and Congress exert influence over these agencies through the nomination and confirmation of commission members.

Independent Agencies

A number of units in the federal bureaucracy do not have the high status of a cabinet department but do report directly to the president. Whereas cabinet departments tend to concentrate on broad areas, such as labor, energy, defense, or education, these **independent agencies**, which are not part of any executive cabinet department, tend to focus on a narrower scope of issues. NASA, for example, focuses on the U.S. space program, whereas the Small Business Administration concentrates on low-cost loans and support to encourage the development of small businesses. Independent agencies tend to be smaller than cabinet departments. The heads of these agencies are appointed by and report to the president.

Regulatory Agencies

Regulatory agencies are responsible for implementing rules and regulations with respect to individual or corporate conduct related to some aspect of the economy. Such agencies are supposed to be staffed by nonpartisan individuals who are entrusted to make sound decisions that promote fairness and weed out corrupt practices on fiscal matters. To accomplish this, regulatory agencies (unlike cabinet departments and independent agencies) are not under the direct control of the president. They are created by Congress and are run by independent boards or commissions that are not supposed to exert partisan influence.

The first regulatory agency was the Interstate Commerce Commission (ICC), created by Congress in 1887.[10] As with the creation of most regulatory agencies, the ICC was the federal government's response to widespread corruption. In the case of the ICC, the target was corruption in the railroad industry, which led to the high cost of railroad transportation. The ICC's scope of responsibility extended to regulation of commerce via not only railroad, but also pipeline, barge, automobile, and aircraft. The ICC established a complex set of rates for both passenger and freight transportation via the various modes of transport. ICC rules were intended to guarantee that transportation companies pay a fair fee on the value of property they used in carrying out their services. Congress abolished the ICC in 1995 because it determined that the agency was overregulating and thus stymieing growth in certain business sectors.

Today's federal bureaucracy includes a number of important regulatory agencies:

The Federal Trade Commission (FTC). The FTC was established in 1914 and has the authority to develop and implement rules and regulations to encourage competition in industry. Over the years, the FTC has played an instrumental role in preventing "price-fixing" policies of corporations.

The Federal Communications Commission (FCC). The FCC was established in 1934 with the authority to regulate radio, television, and interstate telephone companies. Unlike newspapers, which are not regulated, radio and TV stations use public airwaves, making them subject to regulations developed and administered by the FCC.

The Securities and Exchange Commission (SEC). The SEC is responsible for rule making with respect to the stock market and corporate bookkeeping practices. It was created in 1934 in response to the stock market crash of 1929.

The Equal Employment Opportunity Commission (EEOC). Created by Congress to help administer the Civil Rights Acts of 1964, the EEOC is charged with investigating violations of the act.

The Environmental Protection Agency (EPA). The EPA was created in response to the environmental protection movement of the 1960s and 1970s. Concerns about air and water quality, as well as hazardous-waste materials, led Congress to pass a number of important laws that addressed antipollution measures and empowered the EPA (in 1970) to implement environmental regulations. The EPA is the largest of the regulatory agencies.

The Consumer Product Safety Commission (CPSC). Consumer advocacy was another movement that gained steam in the 1960s and 1970s. Efforts to make manufacturers produce products that were safer for consumers were an important feature of that movement. The CPSC was created in 1972 to protect the public against risks associated with consumer products.

Government Corporations

A small number of units in the federal bureaucracy are set up to run like private companies even though they serve an important public purpose. These are called **government corporations**. The idea behind a government corporation is that there is a market of customers who are willing to pay individually for the services provided by the corporation. The revenue on which the government corporation relies comes primarily from citizens paying for the service provided by the corporation. Unlike private corporations, government

Ben Bernanke, Chairman of the Federal Reserve Board, testifies before a Senate Budget Committee Hearing.

The SEC, a regulatory agency, regulates the activities of traders on the busy floor of the New York Stock Exchange, pictured above.

has a special interest in the solvency of government corporations because they serve an important public purpose. Consequently, when the revenue of a government corporation falls short of meeting expenses, government often will intervene to keep the unit in business.

The most widely known and used government corporation is the U.S. Postal Service (USPS), which employs nearly 1 million workers. The primary source of funds for the USPS comes from the sale of U.S. postage stamps. Similar to a private business, the USPS has a product to offer (mail delivery) and charges a fee (the cost of postage) for use of that service.

Another government corporation is the Tennessee Valley Authority (TVA), which serves the power needs of seven states in the Tennessee Valley and operates the system for navigation and flood control of the Tennessee River. Users of TVA's generated power pay for service, as do those who navigate on the Tennessee River. Another well-known government corporation is Amtrak, a railroad service operated by the National Railroad Passenger Corporation. Amtrak maintains more than 20,000 miles of track and operates 500 stations across the nation. Its revenue is largely derived from the sale of passenger tickets; however, in recent years low ridership has forced Congress to subsidize Amtrak from the general revenue fund.

The Executive Office of the President

The president of the United States has an office staff that reports directly to the president, provides advice and counsel, and helps the president manage the rest of the federal bureaucracy. The **Executive Office of the President** is managed by the White House Chief of Staff and includes a Communications Office, a press secretary, a Council of Economic Advisors (to provide advice and management of the bureaucratic agencies responsible to the economy), a National Security Council (to provide advice on foreign and military affairs), an Office of Management and Budget (to coordinate and provide data on the national budget), a White House Counsel (to provide legal advice to the president), an Office of Science and Technology, an Office of the U.S. Trade Representative, and an Office of National Drug Control Policy, among others.

THE FEDERAL WORKFORCE

The federal bureaucracy encompasses an immense workforce. Currently it employs approximately 2.8 million civilian personnel, 85 percent of whom work outside of Washington, D.C.[11] In addition, there are about 1.6 million U.S. military personnel. Although the federal government remains the single largest employer in the United States, Figure 8.2 shows that the total number of federal employees has actually declined over the past half-decade, despite the fact that the total population has nearly doubled (from 179 million to 310 million).

Political Appointees and Career Professionals

About 8,000 members of the federal workforce are presidential appointees, some of whom must be confirmed by the Senate. Those requiring Senate confirmation include cabinet secretaries and the attorney general, heads of independent agencies, ambassadors, U.S. attorneys, and other high-level officers who have administrative responsibility. When a president's term of office expires, the new president generally fills these positions with new appointees. Presidential appointees are frequently referred to as "political" appointees because the job often represents a political reward for past service to the president or the president's political party.

Another 7,500 civilian federal employees are part of what is called the **Senior Executive Service (SES)**. These are senior officers in the federal bureaucracy who are career professionals. Those in the SES do not leave their positions when a new president takes office but work closely with presidential appointees and provide continuity in the operations of the federal bureaucracy from one presidential administration to the next. Congress established the SES in the late 1970s as a means of providing this continuity in leadership. Congress also spelled out a nonpartisan process for hiring SES officers based on educational background, work experience, and other qualifications.

FIGURE 8.2 Changes in Numbers of Federal Workers, Civilian and Military, 1960–2010

Source: U.S. Bureau of Labor Statistics.

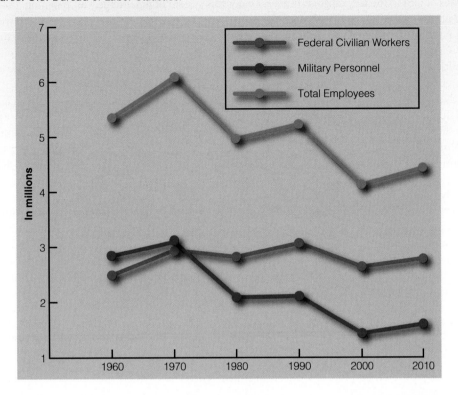

Presidential appointees are largely selected to reflect the political orientation of the president, and senior executives are selected primarily to find highly qualified career professionals who will maintain stability in the operations of the bureaucracy. Together, these groups of employees provide leadership and senior management of the units in the federal bureaucracy.

The Civil Service

The vast majority of the federal bureaucracy workforce is known as the **civil service**. Similar to the SES, civil service workers in the federal bureaucracy are theoretically hired for their position based on their qualifications, and remain employees beyond the term of a particular president. Thus they are supposed to be immune from partisan political maneuvering. Civil service jobs were not always insulated from partisan politics, as they are today. To understand the rules and processes for employment in the federal bureaucracy, it is useful to examine how employment in the federal workforce has changed over the years.

During the early years of the American republic, continuous recruitment of well-educated, upper-middle-class men characterized the development of the federal bureaucracy. Presidents Washington, Adams, and Jefferson hired political, business, and social elites to carry out the activities of the federal bureaucracy. With the exception of top posts in government such as cabinet secretaries, those in federal jobs usually remained from one presidential administration to the next. This tradition ensured an able and effective federal workforce, albeit a nondiverse one.

President Andrew Jackson, elected to office in 1828, undertook a massive restructuring of the federal workforce. Jackson ran for the presidency as a populist advocating for the interests of the "common man." Upon taking office, he chose to remove individuals in the bureaucracy who were not at all "common" and who found themselves politically at odds with the new president. Resistance among many in the bureaucracy to follow Jackson's orders, along with the president's own desire to see that the bureaucracy more closely reflected the demographics of American society, led Jackson to undertake a major overhaul of the bureaucratic workforce.

civil service: The system whereby workers in the federal bureaucracy are supposed to be immune from partisan political maneuvering.

spoils system: The postelection practice of rewarding loyal supporters of the winning candidates and party with appointive public offices.

patronage: The act of appointing people to government positions in return for their partisan and/or political support.

Jackson replaced the long-term, upper-middle-class bureaucrats with political supporters and friends who came from many walks of life. This **spoils system** of hiring federal workers quickly became a steadfast American tradition. To the victors of presidential elections went the spoils of jobs in the federal government. Under this system of **patronage**, campaigning, political party activities, and governing became intertwined. Political parties enticed people to work on political campaigns by promising the payoff of a good federal job with an electoral victory. Often, those who were given a job were expected to return a percentage of their salary to the political party—a very clever fundraising strategy. Strength of partisan support became the key criterion for landing and maintaining a good job.

Needless to say, this system of hiring workers produced a number of problems. Because qualifications to do the job were not important in the hiring decision, the bureaucracy became inefficient. Bureaucrats were more concerned about campaigning and supporting the political party than they were about doing their job. Further, the bureaucracy lacked any sort of continuity—for when the partisan control of the presidency changed hands, federal workers were fired en masse and replaced by a new set of underqualified political appointees.

By the time of the Civil War, the spoils system was entrenched and the bureaucracy was thoroughly corrupt. A civil service reform movement arose in the post–Civil War era, advocating an end to the spoils system and the development of a "professionalized" bureaucracy. Strong resistance from the political party bosses stalled the reform movement's agenda. But the 1881 assassination of President James Garfield by a disgruntled party worker who did not receive the federal job he thought he deserved gave strength to the movement. In 1883, Congress passed the **Pendleton Civil Service Reform Act**, which did the following:[12]

Pendleton Civil Service Reform Act: The 1883 law that created a merit system for hiring many federal workers, protected them from being fired for partisan reasons, and set up a Civil Service Commission to oversee the hiring and firing process.

- It created a **merit system** for hiring many federal workers based on qualifications for the job, including educational background, related job experience, and performance on civil service tests.

- It prevented employees from losing their federal jobs when the presidency changed hands.

- It set up a Civil Service Commission to oversee federal hiring and firing practices.

merit system: A system of appointing and promoting civil service personnel based on merit rather than political affiliation or loyalty.

Initially, the Pendleton Act applied only to a limited portion of the federal workforce, but it provided the basis for Progressive Era reformers of the early 1900s to develop a more professional bureaucracy through additional reform legislation. Today job qualifications in federal hiring and federal worker immunity from patronage are firmly rooted in the federal bureaucracy's employment practices. These principles now apply to more than 90 percent of federal workers.

The **Hatch Act of 1939** further insulated the civil service from partisan politics by (1) prohibiting the dismissal of an employee for partisan reasons (with the exception of certain high-level political appointments) and (2) prohibiting federal workers from running for office or actively campaigning for a political candidate. In the early 1990s, revisions to the Hatch Act relaxed some of the more stringent requirements of the law and allowed federal workers more flexibility in engaging in political activities. Those in the civil service can now participate in campaigns outside of their work hours, contribute money to a candidate or party, express partisan opinions, and wear campaign buttons, among other activities. However, under the current law, federal workers still cannot be candidates in a partisan election or use their official position to raise money or influence votes.

Hatch Act of 1939: The 1939 law that insulated the civil service from partisan politics by prohibiting employee dismissals for partisan reasons and by prohibiting federal workers from participating in political campaigns.

The **Civil Service Reform Act of 1978** replaced the Civil Service Commission with the Office of Personnel Management (OPM) and the Merit Systems Protection Board (MSPB). OPM and MSPB, bureaucratic agencies themselves, manage the civil service system today. Their functions include administering the system of federal hiring, protecting the rights of federal employees, conducting hearings and deciding cases where there are charges of wrongdoing in hiring and firing of employees, evaluating the effectiveness of federal hiring and retention practices, and regulating the ways in which federal workers can participate in politics.

Civil Service Reform Act of 1978: The federal act that replaced the Civil Service Commission (the agency that oversaw federal hiring and firing practices) with the Office of Personnel Management (OPM) and the Merit Systems Protection Board (MSPB).

FROM YOUR PERSPECTIVE

You, Your Parents, and the Dreaded FAFSA Form

You have probably seen it. Your parents or legal guardians have seen it. Most of your college friends have seen it too. It is the dreaded "FAFSA" (Free Application for Student Aid) form. The joy and satisfaction of getting accepted into college are often met with the red tape and complexity of applying for student financial aid. The FAFSA form must be filled out by all students applying for federal support to offset the increasingly high costs of college tuition. Most states and colleges also require the FAFSA to help make their own decisions about a student's financial need and thus the aid that may be required. The U.S. Department of Education begins accepting FAFSA applications on January 1 for eligibility during the school year that begins the following fall. FAFSA requires documentation for a myriad of financial information about college students and their legal guardians. If you have never seen the form, either because your parents have done the legwork for you or because you haven't applied for financial aid, take a look at it at on the web at www.fafsa.ed.gov.

Financial planners and other consultants have built an industry out of aiding college students and their families in their efforts to navigate the cumbersome FAFSA form.

The detailed financial information that FAFSA requires is not always handy—gathering that information can be an especially time-consuming and aggravating task. However, the goal of FAFSA remains a laudable one: to fairly and equitably distribute aid to college students based on documented financial need. Still, the challenge of filling out FAFSA and meeting all its requirements can offer a rude awakening indeed to prospective and returning students who have never before confronted the federal bureaucracy in all its glory.

For Critical Thinking and Discussion

1. What do you think about the FAFSA form? Is it too cumbersome or tedious?

2. Is the federal government transforming a simple process into one that is too complex to be effective? Or do you believe this form of red tape is necessary to ensure that colleges and universities can make fair decisions about financial aid for the nation's college students?

 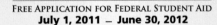 

FREE APPLICATION FOR FEDERAL STUDENT AID
July 1, 2011 — June 30, 2012

Use this form to apply free for federal and state student grants, work-study and loans.

Or apply free online at
www.fafsa.gov.

Applying by the Deadlines

For federal aid, submit your application as early as possible, but no earlier than January 1, 2011. We must receive your application no later than June 30, 2012. Your college must have your correct, complete information by your last day of enrollment in the 2011-2012 school year.

For state or college aid, the deadline may be as early as January 2011. See the table to the right for state deadlines. You may also need to complete additional forms.

Check with your high school guidance counselor or a financial aid administrator at your college about state and college sources of student aid and deadlines.

If you are filing close to one of these deadlines, we recommend you file online at **www.fafsa.gov**. This is the fastest and easiest way to apply for aid.

Using Your Tax Return

If you are supposed to file a 2010 federal income tax return, we recommend that you complete it before filling out this form. If you have not yet completed your 2010 tax return, you can still submit your FAFSA using best estimates. After you submit your tax return, correct any income or tax information that is different from what you initially submitted on your FAFSA.

Filling Out the FAFSA™

If you or your family has unusual circumstances that might affect your financial situation (such as loss of employment), complete this form to the extent you can, then submit it as instructed and consult with the financial aid office at the college you plan to attend.

APPLICATION DEADLINES
Federal Deadline - June 30, 2012
State Aid Deadlines - See below.

Check with your financial aid administrator for these states and territories:

AL, AS *, AZ, CO, FM *, GA, GU *, HI *, MH *, MP *, NC, NE, NM, NV *, PR, PW *, SD *, TX, UT, VA *, VI *, VT *, WA, WI and WY *.

Pay attention to the symbols that may be listed after your state deadline.

AK	AK Education Grant - April 15, 2011 *(date received)* AK Performance Scholarship - June 30, 2011 *(date received)*
AR	Academic Challenge - June 1, 2011 *(date received)* Workforce Grant - Contact the financial aid office. Higher Education Opportunity Grant - June 1, 2011 *(date received)*
CA	Initial awards - March 2, 2011 + * Additional community college awards - September 2, 2011 *(date postmarked)* + *
CT	February 15, 2011 *(date received)* # *
DC	June 30, 2011 *(date received by state)* # *
DE	April 15, 2011 *(date received)*
FL	May 15, 2011 *(date processed)*
IA	July 1, 2011 *(date received)*; earlier priority deadlines may exist for certain programs.
ID	Opportunity Grant - March 1, 2011 *(date received)* # *
IL	As soon as possible after January 1, 2011. Awards made until funds are depleted.
IN	March 10, 2011 *(date received)*
KS	April 1, 2011 *(date received)* # *
KY	As soon as possible after January 1, 2011. Awards made until funds are depleted.
LA	June 30, 2012 (July 1, 2011 recommended)
MA	May 1, 2011 *(date received)* #
MD	March 1, 2011 *(date received)*
ME	May 1, 2011
MI	March 1, 2011 *(date received)*
MN	30 days after term starts *(date received)*

STATE AID D

Courtesy U.S. Department of Education

The federal bureaucracy has grown dramatically, particularly since the New Deal era of the 1930s. As new presidents seek to advance new policy goals, federal departments and agencies have been created and expanded. These agencies have aided presidents in accomplishing new feats and bringing the United States to world "superpower" status. These include Lincoln's efforts to withstand the secession of the Southern states and preserve the Union; Theodore Roosevelt's drive to tame the corporate monopolies; Franklin Roosevelt's priming of the federal workforce to tackle the Great Depression; and Barack Obama's attempt to jumpstart the economy through a major stimulus spending plan. Over the centuries, presidents, with the support of the American people, have used the bureaucracy to accomplish important policy goals. The bureaucracy has also served as the "whipping boy" in rhetorical campaigns for political office. In many instances the bureaucracy has earned its reputation as wasteful, inefficient, and bloated. But without the federal bureaucracy, the most important national initiatives could not have been realized. Even those presidents who campaigned on a platform to cut the bureaucracy ended up using it to advance important initiatives. The federal bureaucracy is an easy target of criticism, yet there is no denying the fact that it has contributed as much to the development of the American political system as any other part of the political system.

SUMMARY: PUTTING IT ALL TOGETHER

WHAT IS BUREAUCRACY?

- Though the term *bureaucracy* often conjures up negative images, the government could not function effectively without bureaucratic organizations.

- Most units in the vast federal bureaucracy are located within the executive branch of government, and most engage primarily in policy implementation. Such implementation begins with the development of regulations that guide employees of the agency in carrying out particular programs or services.

Test Yourself on This Section

1. Which of the following is NOT one of the characteristics of successful bureaucracies that were identified by Max Weber?
   a. Power is distributed across all levels of the organization.
   b. They are organized on the basis of specialization, expertise, and division of labor.
   c. They maintain good records of actions taken.
   d. There is a common set of rules for carrying out functions.

2. The vast majority of federal bureaucratic organizations may be found in which branch of government?
   a. legislative   **c.** judicial
   b. executive   **d.** parliament

3. Despite the negative connotations of the term "bureaucracy," why is the federal bureaucracy essential?

WHAT DOES THE FEDERAL BUREAUCRACY DO?

- Because Congress lacks technical expertise, it often gives agencies wide administrative discretion to decide how to implement laws. Sometimes Congress also delegates important programs to agencies because it wants to avoid thorny political issues.

- Congressional oversight of executive agencies may occur through legislative hearings or through the use of congressional agencies such as the CBO and GAO. Congress may threaten poorly performing agencies with reduced funding, a refusal to confirm appointments to the agency, or (in some extreme cases) the elimination of the agency altogether.

- Congress has placed judicial power in some bureaucratic agencies to help determine the rights and duties of parties within the scope of an agency's authority.

Test Yourself on This Section

1. Bureaucracies are primarily responsible for
   - **a.** adjudication.
   - **b.** legislation.
   - **c.** implementation.
   - **d.** evaluation

2. Which of the following is the journal that publishes all of the rules and regulations promulgated by the bureaucracy?
   - **a.** *Congressional Record*
   - **b.** *Book of Rules*
   - **c.** *Federal Register*
   - **d.** *U.S. Reports*

3. The freedom of agencies to decide how to implement a vague law is known as
   - **a.** administrative law.
   - **b.** delegated power.
   - **c.** bureaucratic adjudicating.
   - **d.** administrative discretion.

4. How does Congress go about exercising its "oversight" function?

THE DEVELOPMENT OF THE FEDERAL BUREAUCRACY

- The size of the federal bureaucracy exploded as the federal government played an increasingly active role in regulating the U.S. economy, overseeing new territories, and conducting overseas military operations. After FDR's New Deal was enacted during the 1930s, the federal government accounted for a sizeable portion of the nation's economy as a whole. The bureaucracy continued to expand in the 1960s and beyond to meet the needs of President Lyndon Johnson's Great Society program and to compete with the Soviet Union in the Cold War.

Test Yourself on This Section

1. The first three departments in the federal bureaucracy created in the Washington administration included the
   - **a.** Department of Education.
   - **b.** Department of the Treasury.
   - **c.** Environmental Protection Agency.
   - **d.** Department of Veterans Affairs.

2. How did FDR's New Deal contribute to the rapid growth of the federal bureaucracy?

GETTING CONTROL OF THE GROWING BUREAUCRACY

- Beginning in the 1980s, some administrations attempted to reduce the size of the federal bureaucracy through (1) the privatization of certain government-provided services, (2) the deregulation of some federal activities, (3) the devolution of various powers and responsibilities back to the states, and (4) efforts to promote greater bureaucratic accountability through initiatives such as the Government Performance and Results Act.

Test Yourself on This Section

1. The elimination of government oversight of certain activities is known as
   - **a.** privatization.
   - **b.** deregulation.
   - **c.** devolution.
   - **d.** reinventing government.

2. The transfer of power for certain programs from the federal government to state governments is known as
   a. privatization.
   b. deregulation.
   c. devolution.
   d. reinventing government.

3. What did the Government Performance and Results Act of 1997 require of bureaucratic agencies?

THE ORGANIZATION OF THE FEDERAL BUREAUCRACY

- The federal bureaucracy is organized into 15 cabinet departments, including the recently created Department of Homeland Security, numerous independent agencies that focus on a narrower scope of issues, regulatory agencies that implement rules and regulations of private conduct, government corporations, and the Executive Office of the President.

Test Yourself on This Section

1. Which of the following type of units do not report directly to the president, but are run by independent boards or commissions?
   a. independent agencies
   b. cabinet departments
   c. regulatory agencies
   d. government corporations

2. Which of the following is an "independent agency"?
   a. Justice Department
   b. Federal Trade Commission
   c. Small Business Administration
   d. Interstate Commerce Commission

3. "Secretary" is the given to head of what type of bureaucratic unit?
   a. regulatory agency
   b. independent agency
   c. government corporation
   d. cabinet department

4. What distinguishes a "government corporation" from other types of bureaucratic units?

THE FEDERAL WORKFORCE

- The federal workforce includes 8,000 presidential employees who received their positions through political patronage, a Senior Executive Service consisting of approximately 7,500 senior career professionals, and a vast number of civil service workers whose jobs are immune from partisan politics. Today most lower-level federal workers are hired through a merit system, rather than through the spoils systems that prevailed throughout much of the nineteenth and early twentieth centuries.

Test Yourself on This Section

1. Which of the following laws instituted a merit system for hiring federal employees?
   a. Pendleton Act
   b. Hatch Act
   c. Civil Service Reform Act
   d. Glidden Act

2. The "spoils system" is the product of which U.S. president?
   a. Thomas Jefferson
   b. Andrew Jackson
   c. George Washington
   d. John Adams

3. Why was the Senior Executive Service established?

KEY TERMS

administrative discretion (p. 206)

administrative law (p. 207)

bureaucracy (p. 204)

bureaucratic adjudicating (p. 209)

cabinet departments (p. 212)

civil service (p. 221)

Civil Service Reform Act of 1978
(p. 222)

congressional oversight (p. 207)

delegation of congressional power
(p. 207)

deregulation (p. 211)

devolution (p. 211)

Executive Office of the President
(p. 220)

Federal Register (p. 206)

government corporations (p. 219)

Hatch Act of 1939 (p. 222)

independent agency (p. 218)

merit system (p. 222)

patronage (p. 222)

Pendleton Civil Service Reform
Act (p. 222)

policy implementation (p. 206)

privatization (p. 211)

regulations (p. 206)

regulatory agency (p. 218)

Senior Executive Service (SES) (p. 220)

spoils system (p. 222)

9 THE JUDICIARY

Learning Objectives

Types of Law

- Compare the different categories of law

The Structure of the U.S. Legal System

- Trace the development of the American legal system, including the role played by the 50 state judicial systems within that larger system today

The Adversarial System of Justice

- Contrast the inquisitorial system of justice with the adversarial system in the United States
- Compare the process by which civil litigation proceeds from complaint to settlement or verdict to the criminal justice system

Judicial Review and Its Implications

- Define the power of judicial review

Limitations on Courts

- Describe the structural limitations on courts

Electing and Appointing Judges

- Learn how federal and state judges are selected

How a Case Proceeds Within the U.S. Supreme Court

- Trace a Supreme Court case as it proceeds from writ of certiorari to final opinion

Why the Justices Vote the Way They Do

- Identify the factors that influence judges

Current Debates over the Exercise of Judicial Power

- Describe some of the recurring debates about the proper role of courts

rticle III of the U.S. Constitution vests in the Supreme Court the power to decide legal cases or controversies that come before it. As one of the three primary branches of the federal government, the judiciary enjoys a special status in our constitutional system. Many scholars have suggested that courts enjoy heightened prestige over other actors in government as a result of their own conscious efforts to foster the perception that they somehow stand "above the political fray." The solemn formalities that pervade so many judicial proceedings conducted by "high priests of the law"—the black robes, the prohibition of cameras in the U.S. Supreme Court, and the general reluctance of judges to seek out publicity—contribute to a mythology about courts in general and to a "cult of the robe" that carries credence with many Americans.[1] This chapter explores the nature of the federal judiciary and the specific role it plays in the U.S. political system by examining types of law and the manner in which the legal system in the United States is organized. It also explores the role state courts play in the political system and then focuses on the U.S. Supreme Court more closely, with an eye toward understanding how that court is confronting some of the great issues of the day.

The "Connections App" is an interactive web app that helps you better understand the relationship between historical and current events with basic concepts.

1975   1980   1985   1990   1995

1967

Then

Solicitor General Thurgood Marshall, preparing to testify at his Supreme Court confirmation hearings in 1967.

Source: AP Photo/John Rous

To millions of Americans, the Supreme Court is not just another branch of government: it serves as a symbol of justice, able to rise above the political squabbles that plague the other branches. Of course to serve that symbolic role, the High Court must appear to represent more than just a narrow slice of the polity. That logic did not escape the 36th president of the United States, Lyndon Baines Johnson. As a product of the rough-and-tumble, often racist world of Texas politics, few would have predicted that Johnson would one day secure a legacy as the president responsible for shepherding major civil rights and voting rights legislation through a resistant Congress. Yet even with that legacy secure, President Johnson went a step further in 1967, appointing the first African Ameri-can justice, Thurgood Marshall, to what had been an all-white U.S. Supreme Court. Marshall's credentials seemed impeccable: a former federal appeals judge, he first made his name as chief Supreme Court advocate on behalf of the National Advancement for the Association of Colored People (NAACP), successfully arguing the landmark case of *Brown v. Board of Education*, among other cases. Eleven Southern senators opposed Marshall's appointment, but those detractors were vastly outnumbered, and he coasted to confirmation by a 69–11 vote. Was Marshall's voting record as a Supreme Court justice in the years that followed influenced by his race and background? On this one point, Marshall's enemies and supporters would both answer in the affirmative.

2009

Now

Judge Sonia Sotomayor, nominated to the U.S. Supreme Court, testifying at her Senate confirmation hearings in July 2009.

Source: Christy Bowe/Corbis

President Barack Obama's ascension to the Oval Office broke perhaps the most visible racial barrier in American politics: the election of an African American to the presidency. Building on themes from his election campaign, Obama did not downplay the potential significance his own victory offered for race relations in America. And yet other racial barriers remained: consider that every session of the U.S. Supreme Court between 1967 and 2008 featured a bench made up of eight Caucasians and just one African American. President Obama altered that landscape when he nominated Judge Sonia Sotomayor, a woman of Puerto Rican descent, to the Supreme Court on May 26, 2009. Once confirmed, her appointment promised to diversify the High Court; not incidentally, it also gave Obama instant credibility with a large and powerful ethnic group. The road to Sotomayor's confirmation was rocky at times: Senate Republicans complained of comments she made about how the experiences of a "wise Latina woman" might help her reach better conclusions than a "white male who hasn't lived that life." But Sotomayor's strong academic pedigree, her extensive prosecutorial experience, and her significant judicial experience won her the votes of every Senate Democrat and over 20 Senate Republicans. Would Sotomayor's ethnic background give her a different perspective on the hardest cases? Debates over that question would be waged in the years to come.

civil law: This term has two meanings: (1) legislative codes, laws, or sets of rules enacted by duly authorized lawmaking bodies such as Congress, state and local legislatures, or any executive authority entrusted with the power to make laws; (2) the body of noncriminal laws of a nation or state that deal with the rights of private citizens.

common law: Judge-made law handed down through judicial opinions, which over time establish precedents.

The concept of law defies simple understanding. Although law is normally defined simply as "authoritative rules made by government," the philosopher John Locke argued that certain laws precede society and government. These natural laws are god-given, exist within human beings from the time they are born, and are intrinsic to the nature of individuals. Locke's notions of natural law (as distinguished from human-made or government-issued law) have influenced the legal systems of many nations, including the United States. Prior to the Civil War, opponents of slavery challenged its legitimacy with the claim that it ran counter to natural law. During the 1960s, civil rights advocates seeking to overhaul discriminatory practices presented similar arguments.

Still, even the foremost advocates of natural law concede that the rules imposed by sovereign governments enjoy some measure of legitimacy in most instances. Those rules and laws may be created and passed down in different ways. **Civil law** (also called "statutory law") refers to legislative codes, laws, or sets of rules that are enacted by authorized lawmaking bodies such as Congress, state and local legislatures, or any executive authority entrusted with the power to make laws.[2] **Common law** refers to judge-made laws handed down through judicial opinions, which establish slowly evolving precedents over time. Many European legal systems, such as those in France, Germany, and Italy, are characterized as primarily "civil law systems" due to their extensive reliance on detailed legislative codes. The legal system in Britain, by contrast, is recognized as mainly a common law system. The modern U.S. legal system features a combination of these two approaches: although the common law held sway for most of the nation's history, legislatures in all 50 states and Congress during the past century have replaced many traditional common law rules with detailed legislative codes on a number of important topics, including commercial law, probate law, and various aspects of criminal law. Other categories of law include the following:

- *Criminal law* is the body of rules and regulations that declare what types of conduct constitute an "offense against society," and that prescribe the punishment to be imposed for those offenses. Criminal laws against murder, rape, and burglary can be found in almost any legal system. The body of noncriminal law—which includes the law of property, contracts, and other issues dealing with the private rights of citizens—is sometimes referred to as "civil law." (Be careful not to confuse references to "civil law" in this context with the "civil law" referenced earlier, which primarily concerns the enactment of statutes and codes.) Serious criminal offenses may lead to jail time; by contrast, those who violate noncriminal laws can be fined, but not imprisoned. Of course criminal law and civil law may touch on the same events—for example, a person alleged to have killed someone may be criminally prosecuted for murder and also separately sued in a "wrongful death action" for the same incident. The two sets of proceedings are distinct and separate: The former football star and television personality O. J. Simpson was acquitted of criminal murder charges brought against him by the Los Angeles County district attorney, but subsequent civil suits were successfully brought against him by the victims' families.

- *Constitutional law* is the body of rules and judicial interpretations of rules found in the fundamental law of the nation or state, such as the Constitution of the United States. Normally constitutional law is considered "supreme" and overrides any statutes or executive decisions with which it comes into conflict.

- *Administrative law* is the body of rules, regulations, orders, and decisions issued by administrative agencies of a government, such as the Federal Trade Commission, the Environmental Protection Agency, or a state department of health.

- *Public law*, a term used more by academics than practitioners, refers to the laws and rules that govern disputes and issues involving the government directly acting in its official capacity. Constitutional, administrative, and criminal laws are all subcategories of the general rubric of public law.

- *Private law* refers to all parts of the law concerned with the definition, regulation, and enforcement of rights in cases where either (1) all the parties directly implicated are private individuals (such as a divorce settlement) or (2) the government is acting like any other private citizen when it sues or is being sued. For example, when a private person crashes his car into a government mail truck, the government's lawsuit against that person is usually a matter of private law rather than public law.

Significant overlap exists among all these categories of law. Knowing something about the different types of law is useful in helping to understand courts and the functions they serve in the American political system.

THE STRUCTURE OF THE U.S. LEGAL SYSTEM

Every court occupies a unique position within the larger hierarchy of state and federal courts. As a result, each court performs a variety of specific roles dictated by where it happens to be situated within the larger court structure.

State Legal Systems and State Courts

Most criminal and civil law matters in the United States first find their way into one of the 50 states' legal systems. Together, the state governments process nearly 35 million cases per year, more than 95 percent of the nation's litigation. About a third of the cases in state legal systems involve criminal matters. Each state system features its own unique characteristics and different nuances, an outgrowth of the states' different historical origins and significant population differences. Still, as shown in Figure 9.1, some common elements exist across the vast majority, if not all states.

Every state maintains trial courts, which do the bulk of work processing cases at the lower levels of the state legal system. These trial courts (often called "district courts" or "circuit courts" depending on the state or locality) may hear appeals from subordinate courts such as traffic courts; they also serve as sites for trials of more significant crimes. Thirty-nine of the 50 states have intermediate appellate courts, to which all appeals from trial courts must first be directed. All 50 states maintain at least one high supreme court. (Texas and Oklahoma have separate supreme courts for criminal and civil cases.) State supreme courts (or their equivalent of a different name) generally provide the final source of appeal for each state legal system.[3] To appeal beyond the state supreme court directly to the U.S. Supreme Court, a losing party must first exhaust all the remedies available at the state level, including losing his or her case at the state system's court of final appeal. He or she must also demonstrate there is a federal question at issue, whether based on the interpretation of a federal statute or of the U.S. Constitution.

In theory, state courts must comply with pronouncements from the U.S. Supreme Court over the meaning of the federal Constitution. The reality is much more complicated. During various periods of American history, rebellious state courts tried to evade certain Supreme Court pronouncements by distinguishing or limiting the Supreme Court ruling, and on occasion even by denying the Supreme Court's jurisdiction over the matter. The Virginia Supreme Court resisted various pronouncements of the U.S. Supreme Court in the early part of the nineteenth century; more than a century later, state courts sometimes ignored U.S. Supreme Court decisions protecting the accused. Although the Supreme Court can usually exert its will over defiant state courts, it must be willing to expend key institutional resources and prestige to do so.

The Supreme Court building in Washington, D.C.

Pat Benic/Associated Press

FIGURE 9.1 Common Features of a State Court System

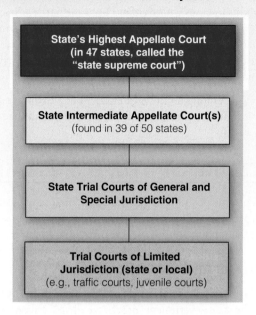

State's Highest Appellate Court
(in 47 states, called the
"state supreme court")

State Intermediate Appellate Court(s)
(found in 39 of 50 states)

State Trial Courts of General and
Special Jurisdiction

Trial Courts of Limited
Jurisdiction (state or local)
(e.g., traffic courts, juvenile courts)

Development of the Federal Court System

Article III of the Constitution establishes a Supreme Court and any "inferior courts" that Congress may wish to create. Accordingly, Congress provided at the nation's outset for the creation of district and circuit courts, the latter of which bear little resemblance to modern circuit courts. Specifically, these early federal circuit courts were staffed by Supreme Court justices and district court judges, and they performed both trial and appellate functions. Thus in addition to their formal duties on the High Court, Supreme Court justices in the early days of the Republic were also required to "ride circuit," traveling to their assigned circuits on a regular basis. (This practice formally ended when Congress reestablished the U.S. Courts of Appeals in 1891.)

During the nation's early history, the Supreme Court was seen as a weak third branch of government, with limited enforcement powers. With his ruling in *Marbury v. Madison* (1803),[4] Chief Justice John Marshall established the Court's power to review all acts of Congress for their constitutionality; even so, during Marshall's 34-year reign as chief justice the Court struck down just one act of Congress as unconstitutional.

The Constitution makes no reference to the specific size of the Supreme Court. Thus Congress during the eighteenth and nineteenth centuries altered the size of the Court to consist of one chief justice and anywhere from five to nine associate justices serving on the Court at one time. Occasionally the issue of Court size comes up as a matter of strategic politics: In 1937 President Franklin Delano Roosevelt's ill-fated plan to expand the size of the Court (to up to 15 members depending on the age of the sitting justices) was driven by the president's desire to appoint new justices who would support his New Deal program. Yet even some of President Roosevelt's own Democratic supporters opposed the plan. Since 1869 the Court's composition of nine members (one chief justice and eight associate justices) has remained essentially unchanged. Meanwhile, Congress has been active in creating, disbanding, and modifying the number of other judges who serve throughout the federal court system.

Cases today begin in the federal court system, rather than the state court system, only when they fit into one of three categories: (1) the lawsuit requires interpretation of the U.S. Constitution, a federal law, or a treaty of the United States; (2) the federal government is suing or prosecuting someone, or is itself being sued; or (3) the lawsuit is between two citizens of different states suing for an amount of more than $75,000. Many of the highest-profile legal cases in recent years became federal cases because they featured defendants accused of committing

FIGURE 9.2 The Federal Court System*

*Chart does not include specialized courts, including courts of international trade, tax courts, claims courts, etc.

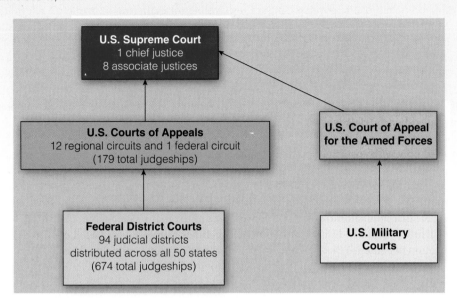

federal crimes. Included on this list are the trial of Oklahoma City bomber Timothy McVeigh and the prosecution of some of the terrorists involved (directly or indirectly) in the attacks of September 11, 2001. In recent decades Congress has become increasingly active in passing legislation to declare new federal crimes. Thus carjacking, the sale or possession of many types of illegal drugs, money laundering, and various other offenses are now considered federal crimes, and defendants who commit such offenses may face prosecution in federal courts.

The federal judicial system today also features a number of specialized courts, including tax courts, bankruptcy courts, and military courts. Most parties to a federal case start out in one of the 94 federal district courts located throughout the country. Federal district court judges have original jurisdiction (the power to rule in the first instance) over criminal and civil trials, and along with federal magistrates, they provide the initial sources of potential legal relief available in the federal judicial system.

Figure 9.2 above depicts the flow of cases in the federal system. After the federal district court has rendered its judgment, appeal is available to one of the 13 federal appeals courts (also referred to as "circuit courts of appeals") across the country. With some exceptions, federal appeals are normally decided by a panel of 3 judges selected at random from the pool of 10 or more judges authorized to serve on that court. In some cases, litigants can appeal from the three-judge panel to the full circuit court—this type of hearing is called "en banc." Because the San Francisco–based Ninth Circuit maintains a roster of 47 judges (spread out from Hawaii and California in the west, to Arizona, Nevada, Montana, and Idaho in the east), the phrase "en banc" on that court refers to 11-judge panels that perform essentially the same function as en banc panels in other circuits.[5]

Litigants who receive an adverse judgment in the federal appeals court and wish to be heard in the U.S. Supreme Court may petition for a *writ of certiorari*, which is the pleading of a losing party's files with the Supreme Court asking it to review the decision of a lower court. Currently the Supreme Court enjoys near absolute discretion over its docket, and so it remains a long shot (less than 3 percent) that it will even grant the writ of certiorari in the first place.

Petitioning the U.S. Supreme Court for review is the final option available to state court litigants who suffer adverse decisions in the highest state court, and to federal court litigants who suffer adverse decisions after exhausting all forms of appeal in the federal court system. In a normal year, approximately half of the cases heard by the Supreme Court come from federal appellate courts and the other half from the 50 state court systems.

THE ADVERSARIAL SYSTEM OF JUSTICE

Some European legal systems are based on an *inquisitorial system* of justice, in which judges, working on behalf of the government, are responsible for gathering information relevant to the disposition of a particular case. For example, in France—which adheres to the inquisitorial model—judges may initiate a criminal investigation against an individual, commission experts to investigate and report on special aspects of the crime, and even call witnesses and question them intensely. By contrast, the American legal system is primarily an *adversarial system* of justice, in which opposing parties contend against each other for a result favorable to themselves. In jury trials judges act merely as independent referees overseeing the contest; in so-called bench trials where no jury is present, judges must still remain objective arbiters as they prepare to make final decisions on the merits.[6] In an adversarial system, the judge is entrusted only with ensuring that the litigants achieve procedural fairness and plays no active role in evidence gathering or in the advocacy of one side over the other. Supporters of this system contend that adversarial proceedings pitting zealous representatives of parties against one another offer the best prospect of allowing the judge or jury to determine the truth. Critics counter that inquisitorial systems tend to be free of the many strategic "maneuvers" parties so frequently practice in U.S. courtrooms, such as the withholding of crucial evidence or the presentation of evidence that bears only a minimal relationship to the actual facts at issue.

Elements of Civil Litigation

Countless disputes among individuals or entities are resolved quietly, long before the threat to litigate is even invoked. Still, whenever one private party contests another over the definition or enforcement of certain legal rights or the legal relationship that may exist between them, the disagreement may wind up in the form of a lawsuit brought before a judge in a court of law. Any such judicial contest, including all the events that lead up to a possible court event, is referred to as **litigation**. Although the procedural rules governing such private disputes vary widely from state to state and system to system, some elements of civil litigation are common among all systems. Normally the complaining party who chooses to initiate formal legal proceedings (usually called the **plaintiff**) does so by filing a **complaint**, which is a written document justifying why the court is empowered to hear the case and explaining why the plaintiff is entitled to some form of relief (usually an amount of money) under the current law. The target of the complaint, the **defendant**, normally must respond to the complaint with a formal written defense, in which he or she either admits to or denies what the plaintiff has said.

If the defendant convinces the judge either that the court has no power to hear the case (perhaps it was filed in the wrong court) or that there is no law that provides a remedy to the plaintiff, the case may be dismissed. If the defendant's argument is unsuccessful, the case then moves forward to the stage of pretrial litigation normally referred to as **discovery**. During discovery, each side has the right to find out what information the other side has about the case by requesting documents or materials, access to property, and/or examinations, or by offering answers to questions about the litigation either in written form or verbally at a deposition. Although the judge may play some role in supervising discovery at pretrial conferences, almost all such discovery occurs outside of the courtroom. Following the discovery stage of the proceedings, each side may file new written documents to the court contending that it now has overwhelming evidence in its favor or that the other side has discovered no evidence to prove its own contentions.

litigation: Any judicial contest, including all the events that lead up to a possible court event.

plaintiff: The party that chooses to initiate formal legal proceedings in a civil case.

complaint: A document written by the plaintiff arguing why the court is empowered to hear the case and explaining why the plaintiff is entitled to some form of relief under the current law.

defendant: The target of a plaintiff's complaint.

discovery: A stage of pretrial litigation in which the plaintiff and defendant have the right to learn what information the other side has about the case by requesting documents or materials, access to property, and/or examinations, or by offering answers to questions about the litigation either in written form or verbally at a deposition.

A jury listens to an attorney present her case.

The vast majority of civil disputes never make it to trial. In some cases, one party may succeed in convincing the judge that no trial is necessary and that the judge should rule in that party's favor immediately. Far more often, the sides agree to a legally binding "settlement" of claims made against each other, in which one side pays money to the other side, or agrees to cease and desist a certain practice in order to avoid the costs and uncertainties of trial. In civil litigation, judges often play an active role in encouraging the two parties to settle their differences out of court, saving resources for them and the judicial branch that would have been wasted in a long, drawn-out trial.

In some instances, the parties are not able to reach an out-of-court settlement, and a formal trial becomes necessary. In a "bench trial," the parties present evidence to a judge, rather than a jury of citizens. A jury trial usually takes far longer than a bench trial because of the many procedures required to prevent undue prejudice of the jury. Even if a jury trial is necessary, the judge still plays a role in the courtroom by ensuring that the jury is properly selected and that fair procedures are adhered to during the trial. One of the most crucial roles played by a judge in either type of trial is to rule on the admissibility of evidence that may be used to reach a decision. Only relevant evidence, which logically tends to prove or disprove a disputed fact, may be admitted into the trial proceedings. In civil cases, the complaining party is obligated to prove its allegations by a "preponderance of the evidence," which is generally thought to be anything greater than 50 percent. Although there is widespread disagreement on what this standard exactly means, it is clearly well below the high standard imposed on prosecutors in criminal cases to prove guilt "beyond a reasonable doubt."

Once the judge or jury has reached a final decision on the case, normally called the "verdict" in the case of a jury trial or the "judgment" in a bench trial, and the judge or jury has settled on a monetary amount to be awarded, the trial stage of the process comes to an end. Some posttrial motions may be available, and a dissatisfied party is also free to appeal the decision to a higher court.

The Criminal Justice System at Work

Although the rules of criminal procedure also vary widely, most criminal prosecutions begin with the arrest of a suspect by some law enforcement official at the federal, state, or local level. Once the suspect is formally accused, he or she is also referred to as the "defendant." Because some criminal charges may be later revealed as groundless or unsubstantiated, the government must quickly demonstrate in one of two ways that the charges against the defendant are valid. Some prosecutors elect to present initial evidence at a preliminary hearing held before a magistrate or trial judge, where they must demonstrate that there is probable cause to proceed to trial against the suspect. Far more often the prosecutor convenes a **grand jury**, whose duty it is to receive complaints, hear the evidence offered by the prosecutor, and determine whether a trial is justified. Grand juries comprise a greater number of jurors than an ordinary trial jury. Unlike regular juries, which hear only one case, grand juries may be asked to hear evidence on numerous cases over a period of several weeks or even months. Because the grand jury process is supervised entirely by the prosecutor, he or she maintains a distinct advantage—some say a prosecutor could get the grand jury to "indict a bologna sandwich." In the overwhelming majority of cases, the grand jury does indeed return a bill of **indictment** authorizing the government to proceed to trial against the defendant.

Whereas discovery is far-ranging and extensive in civil litigation, it is far more limited in criminal trials. Defense attorneys are usually under little or no obligation to provide any evidence at all to prosecutors; as a general matter, prosecutors are under an obligation to provide defense attorneys only with evidence that tends to "clear" the accused from alleged fault or guilt, although some states and localities provide additional discovery rights to the accused.

Most criminal prosecutions in the United States are resolved through a negotiated **plea bargain** between the defendant and the prosecutor.[7] Indeed, over 90 percent of convictions are the direct product of negotiated plea bargains. Many defendants seek to reduce their jail sentences by entering plea agreements that lead to lesser punishments. Much of the negotiation that occurs between prosecutors and defense attorneys is over the appropriate charges that

Murder defendants are under no obligation to turn over to the prosecutor a murder weapon or any other evidence that may be extremely important to determining their guilt or innocence.

Fact.

As a general matter, defense attorneys are under little or no obligation to provide any evidence at all to prosecutors, no matter how relevant.

grand jury: A jury whose duty it is to hear the evidence offered by a prosecutor and determine whether a trial is justified.

indictment: A decision by a grand jury authorizing the government to proceed to trial against the defendant.

plea bargain: A pretrial negotiated resolution in a criminal case in which the defendants seek to reduce their jail sentences by pleading guilty and in return prosecutors are willing to trade down the severity of the punishment.

will be formally filed, as most courts have adopted the equivalent of "going rates" for particular crimes.[8] Prosecutors willingly trade down penalties for crimes either because they are seeking that defendant's cooperation at another trial or because they wish to avoid the uncertainty and huge expenditure of resources that come with a trial.

In criminal cases that do go to trial, the burden rests squarely on the prosecutor to prove that the defendant committed the crime "beyond a reasonable doubt." Defendants, by contrast, do not have to prove their innocence. Unless a defendant waives the right to a jury trial, she or he must be tried by a jury of peers. State courts require anywhere between 6 and 12 jurors, whereas the federal court system requires 12 jurors in all cases where a jury is present. Defendants, shielded by the Fifth Amendment privilege against self-incrimination, are under no obligation to testify. Numerous other constitutional safeguards are available to the defendant, including the right to a public and speedy trial and the right to directly confront witnesses. If the jury renders a "not guilty" verdict, the double jeopardy clause of the Fifth Amendment generally forbids the government from trying the defendant again for the same crime. A defendant who is convicted has a constitutional right to appeal the conviction or the resulting sentence to a higher court.

Although the burdens at trial appear to favor the accused, prosecutors generally have the benefit of experience in prosecuting many other defendants in the same court and can draw on a relatively large pool of resources (such as government investigators or medical examiners) to aid them in securing a conviction.

The Sixth Amendment has been interpreted to guarantee each indigent defendant the right to a government-provided lawyer in any instance where he or she faces the possibility of jail time. Unfortunately, many public defenders' offices are overworked and underfunded, placing defendants at a relative disadvantage. By comparison, wealthy or well-connected defendants who do enjoy access to top legal talent and other resources at trial often fare much better. For example, in 2005 the late recording star Michael Jackson was acquitted on charges of child abduction, molestation, and attempted molestation of several minor boys at his Neverland Ranch in Southern California. That result was due in no small part to the efforts of some of the nation's most well-known lawyers, including celebrity lawyers Susan Yu, Mark Geragos, and Benjamin Brafman. Clearly the American legal system does not always offer the same types of outcomes to those who are not similarly situated or well connected. For the vast majority of defendants, "justice" in the courtroom is meted out at lightning speed, with judges and prosecutors running through multiple criminal trials in a matter of hours with little opportunity to understand all the facts of a particular case. Public defenders only rarely have the chance to contest these trials with witnesses and evidence, lest they ignore all the other defendants under their charge. In sum, the picture of drama-filled trials seen so often on television or in the movies hardly depicts the reality of what goes on in this nation's criminal courtrooms.

The late recording star Michael Jackson was prosecuted in 2005 for various crimes related to several alleged incidents of child molestation. His high-priced legal team (including Thomas Mesereau, Jr., seen conferring with Jackson above) helped secure Jackson's acquittal on all charges.

EPA/Robyn Beck/Newscom

JUDICIAL REVIEW AND ITS IMPLICATIONS

Courts in general, and judges in particular, serve in a variety of capacities: supervising the disposition of legal controversies between private parties, overseeing preliminary hearings or trials of criminal defendants, and ruling on important issues concerning the procedures to be followed or the evidence to be introduced at trial. Indeed, the role many judges play as "independent magistrates" is fundamental to the effective functioning of the American legal system. But courts and judges also play a significant and far-reaching role in overseeing the operations of the other branches of government, both by supervising conflicts between those branches and by protecting citizens against government action that may violate the Constitution.

This judicial authority has been magnified by the general recognition that American courts enjoy the added power of **judicial review**, by which they may declare acts of the other branches of the federal or state governments unconstitutional and thus invalid. This dimension of judicial authority is not mentioned anywhere in the U.S. Constitution. Although Article VI of the Constitution declares the Constitution of the United States to be the "supreme law of the land . . . anything in the Constitution or laws of any state to the contrary notwithstanding," nowhere does the document explicitly vest any specific court (including the U.S. Supreme Court) with the authority to determine whether state laws are unconstitutional. Nor does the Constitution authorize the Supreme Court to serve as the authoritative interpreter of the document over the president, Congress, and other federal officials, all of whom are equally sworn to uphold the Constitution. In fact, scholars of the early constitutional period believe the drafters of the Constitution were unable to reach any consensus at all on this issue. How, then, did the power of judicial review arise?

judicial review: The power of a court to declare acts of the other branches of government or of a subordinate government to be unconstitutional and thus invalid.

The power of the Supreme Court to exercise judicial review was first established by the fourth chief justice of the United States, John Marshall, in the highly controversial case of *Marbury v. Madison* (1803).[9] With Thomas Jefferson's victory in the presidential election of 1800 and the Jeffersonian Republicans' rise to power in both houses of Congress the following year, nearly all of the nation's most powerful Federalists, including John Adams, Alexander Hamilton, and John Jay, were soon to be relegated to outsider status in the federal government. In his final hours as president, however, Adams appointed 16 circuit court judges and 42 new justices of the peace for the District of Columbia (all loyal Federalists); these positions were fully authorized by Congress, and each of the individuals chosen for the posts was confirmed by the lame-duck Federalist Congress that remained loyal to Adams. President Adams also named John Marshall as chief justice of the United States. Although surrounded by partisan opposition in Washington, Marshall made the Supreme Court into the Federalist Party's beachhead, from which that party's judicial holdovers, enjoying the benefit of life tenure, could continue to espouse their vision of a powerful central government. Immediately after Thomas Jefferson and his Secretary of State James Madison formally took office in March 1801, they learned that several of the commissions for the new justices of the peace appointed by Adams had never been delivered—including one for William Marbury. When Jefferson ordered Madison to withhold the commissions, Marbury asked the Supreme Court to issue a *writ of mandamus*, a judicial order commanding an official (in this case, Madison) to perform a ministerial duty over which his or her discretion is limited (namely, the formal delivery of a duly signed and sealed commission). As authority for the Supreme Court's power to issue such a writ, Marbury cited the Judiciary Act of 1789, which appeared to give the U.S. Supreme Court exactly that authority.

Marbury was seeking to have the Supreme Court decide the case immediately, without first having to suffer a loss in a lower court. Because Chief Justice Marshall was an ardent Federalist, Marbury further assumed the Court would be sympathetic to his plight. In truth, it was Marshall who was really at fault in the case—as Adams's Secretary of State, he had failed to properly mail the commission. Indeed, given his intimate knowledge of the facts, Marshall should have recused himself from the case, refusing to participate as a judge in the first place. Yet Marshall's Supreme Court rejected Marbury's request. Recognizing the tense political situation that surrounded the case—and all too aware that Jefferson might not abide by court order—Marshall lambasted the Jefferson administration for its refusal to perform its statutorily mandated duty, but denied that the Supreme Court possessed the power to issue the writ as requested.

Why the refusal to help his fellow Federalist? Marshall acknowledged that the 1789 law did in fact authorize the Court to issue such a writ in "original jurisdiction." But, Marshall ruled, that law was in explicit violation of Article III, Section 2, Clause 2, which did not specifically list "writs of mandamus" among the types of cases over which the Supreme Court had original jurisdiction. Nor could Congress extend the Court's original jurisdiction by mere statute. Thus, Marshall decided, the 1789 law was repugnant to the Constitution and was therefore null and void. With this decision, Marshall seized for the Court a power of judicial review over congressional laws that is unmentioned in the Constitution. The Supreme Court exercised this power only once more before the Civil War, although it has struck down well over 150 acts of Congress since then.

CHECK **THE LIST**

Five Justices Who Received No Formal Legal Education at a College or University

Although all members of the U.S. Supreme Court have been lawyers, more than a third of the justices lacked formal law school degrees. Some attended law school for a time, but did not graduate. Still others—following a pattern common to many lawyers prior to the twentieth century—read law and apprenticed under practicing lawyers after securing an undergraduate degree that featured some legal education. Finally, there have been at least five Supreme Court justices who received no legal education in either a graduate or undergraduate setting. Each of them was trained either entirely at home or through apprenticeships. Those five justices are:

Justice James F. Byrnes

Justice Samuel Chase

1. **James F. Byrnes (1882–1972)**—Byrnes served as U.S. senator from South Carolina for over a decade before Franklin Roosevelt appointed him to the Supreme Court in 1941 (he lasted just one term before taking a position in the Roosevelt administration). Amazingly, Byrnes quit school at the age of 14 and never attended high school, college, or law school, though that did not stop South Carolina Governor Miles B. McSweeney from appointing him as a clerk for state judge Robert Aldrich in 1900; after apprenticing to a lawyer, he was admitted to the bar for the first time in 1903.

2. **Samuel Chase (1741–1811)**—Chase holds the dubious distinction of being the only Supreme Court justice in history (he served from 1796 to 1811) to be formally impeached by the House of Representatives. Later acquitted by the Senate, Chase's alleged wrongdoing (critics claimed he let his partisan leanings affect his decisions) had little to do with his quaint educational background: Chase was tutored at home by his father until he was 18. At that point he moved to Annapolis, Maryland, where he studied law under attorney John Hall. Two years later, in 1761, he was formally admitted to the bar.

3. **John Hessin Clarke (1857–1945)**—President Woodrow Wilson appointed Clarke first to the federal district court in 1914, and then later to the U.S. Supreme Court in 1916. Clarke attended Western Reserve College, which offered no legal education. After graduating from college in 1877, Clarke chose to study law under his father rather than to attend law school; he passed the Ohio Bar exam cum laude in 1877.

4. **James Iredell (1751–1799)**—One of the first justices, George Washington appointed him to the U.S. Supreme Court in 1790. Lacking any formal education, Iredell began his career working at a customs house in North Carolina as deputy customs collector. Later, Iredell read law under Samuel Johnston, who became governor of North Carolina. He was admitted to the bar in 1771.

5. **Thomas Johnson (1732–1819)**—Considered one of the original Founding Fathers, Thomas was educated entirely at home. After studying law under Stephen Bordley, he passed the Maryland bar in 1753, and was later named a delegate to the Continental Congress. Eventually he became Maryland's first state governor in 1777. Washington appointed Johnson to the High Court in 1792.

▶**POINT TO PONDER:** Critics today complain that law schools do not provide enough useful training for lawyers, focusing on century-old cases over more current rules and practices. Given how many previous justices served without the benefit of a formal legal education, should we reconsider the more modern practice of only appointing justices who attend the most prestigious law schools? Is pedigree really as important as experience?

Source: Gathered by the authors from various sources, including Melvin Urofsky, Ed., *Biographical Encyclopedia of the Supreme Court*, CQ Press, 2006.

Two rulings more than a decade later further established the Supreme Court's authority in interpreting the Constitution. In *McCulloch v. Maryland* (1819),[10] the Court upheld the constitutionality of the Bank of the United States, thereby establishing the precedent that congressional power extends beyond those powers specifically listed in Article I of the Constitution. In *Martin v. Hunter's Lessee* (1816),[11] the Supreme Court ruled that the power of federal courts to review government actions for their constitutionality was not just applicable to other federal institutions; the supremacy clause ("The Constitution . . . shall be the Supreme Law of the Land") meant that the Supreme Court could also invalidate any actions of state governments that it believed to be in conflict with the U.S. Constitution. During his 34 years as chief justice, Marshall wrote 519 opinions, many of which remain influential commentary on constitutional power and authority. Under Marshall's leadership, the Court consistently rejected claims of state sovereignty that conflicted with federal interests. It was the special duty of the Supreme Court, Marshall believed, to make difficult judgments on the Constitution that either limited or affirmed the exercise of federal authority. In doing so, Marshall's court defined a strong role for the federal government, which was more clearly realized beginning in the twentieth century.

In the two centuries since Marshall served as chief justice, the Supreme Court has invalidated more than 1,200 state laws. In 1958, it once again reaffirmed the principle of judicial supremacy in *Cooper v. Aaron*[12] in response to official defiance of a lower court's desegregation rulings: governors and state legislatures were bound to uphold decisions of the Supreme Court just as they were bound by oath to uphold the Constitution. At times the exercise of judicial review has been extremely controversial. For example, the Supreme Court in *Dred Scott v. Sandford* (1857)[13] ruled that slaves were forever the property of their owners, even when they were brought temporarily into free states. The decision overturned a congressional law regulating the extension of slavery in the territories and may have helped to precipitate the Civil War four years later. During the Great Depression, the Supreme Court's rulings that many of FDR's New Deal proposals were unconstitutional instigated another constitutional crisis. More recently, President Obama suggested that if the Court invalidated his administration's signature health care reform legislation, it would be engaging in improper "judicial activism." As it turned out the Supreme Court in June 2012 modified just one aspect of the legislation (the medicare funding provision), leaving the rest of the Patient Protection and Affordable Care Act of 2010 intact. Despite the uncertain beginnings that led to this practice and the tense moments in the nation's history that it has given rise to, judicial review of federal and state laws has become an unchallenged dimension of judicial power within the U.S. political system.

Supporters of the Affordable Care Act celebrate in front of the U.S. Supreme Court building on June 28, 2012, after learning that the Court had affirmed the constitutionality of the controversial law by a 5-4 margin.

LIMITATIONS ON COURTS

In Federalist No. 78, Alexander Hamilton deemed the judiciary "the least dangerous" branch because it had "no influence over either the sword or the purse . . . and can take no active resolution whatsoever." Despite Hamilton's opinion, courts have played a critically influential role in the American political system. When the Supreme Court aggressively interposes itself between aggrieved citizens and the government, as it did when it ordered desegregation of public schools in *Brown v. Board of Education* (1954),[14] or when it helps resolve some great political crisis, as it did when it ordered President Richard Nixon to hand over controversial tapes of White House conversations in *United States v. Nixon* (1974),[15] the judiciary appears more like an all-powerful branch than one that is weak and inconsequential.

The power of American courts is great, but the method by which courts participate in the political system is far more circumscribed than that of the other two branches. The limitations that courts must adhere to include the following:

1. **Courts cannot initiate or maintain lawsuits.** Unlike legislatures, which can propose and pass bills on their own initiative, judges in the United States cannot decide issues that are not currently before them in a legitimately filed lawsuit. If none of the actors in a controversy elects to involve the courts directly, the court has no role whatsoever in resolution of the conflict.

2. **Courts can hear only those lawsuits that constitute true "cases" or "controversies."** Article III imposes on the Supreme Court and all federal courts the same type of limitation that applies to nearly all other courts: judges may hear and resolve only those lawsuits that amount to legitimate "cases" or "controversies" and must ignore mere "hypothetical" or "theoretical" conflicts. Although most of these terms are fuzzy enough to give courts room to maneuver, in practice courts tend to refuse to decide lawsuits that are moot (that is, it is too late to provide any effective remedy), including lawsuits involving affirmative action programs and policies brought against educational institutions by applicants who have since enrolled in (and in many cases, graduated from) another institution. Courts are equally reluctant to decide cases that are not yet ripe (that is, the actual conflict is still sometime in the future). Accordingly, courts normally refuse to provide executives with what amounts to "legal advice" about future controversies that have not yet occurred. Courts similarly refuse to hear cases that were contrived by the parties in the form of collusion, or cases in which jurisdiction has not been properly invoked.

   The courts have also maintained a long-standing tradition of refusing to decide cases where the Constitution has explicitly entrusted the issue to be decided by one of the other branches of government; such issues are generally referred to as "political questions." Of course when attempting to justify its refusal to take on a political question, the Supreme Court often engages in such extensive analysis of the underlying issues that it is hard to distinguish those opinions from analysis of the merits of the case itself. For example, in *Nixon v. United States* (2003),[16] the Supreme Court explained its refusal to reconsider the Senate's process of trying the impeachment of a federal judge, Walter Nixon, by issuing a lengthy opinion that reviewed in considerable detail the constitutional provisions entrusting the Senate with the "sole power" of trying impeachments. Related to the "case or controversy" rule is a requirement that courts impose on the parties themselves: courts will hear lawsuits only from parties that have proper **standing**, meaning that they are "uniquely" and "singularly affected" by the controversy. For example, courts usually reject lawsuits brought by individuals who are frustrated with the allotment of their tax dollars, because those individuals are not "singularly affected." Nor are individuals with a mere academic or political concern in a conflict allowed in court as parties to a case unless they have suffered some unique economic or physical burden related to the issue being decided. In the mid-twentieth century, Congress and many state legislatures loosened these harsh standing requirements by authorizing lawsuits brought by large numbers of people with clearly defined common interests. Such **class action lawsuits** can proceed through the legal system even when not every member of the class has formally signed on. High-visibility class action lawsuits in recent years include those brought by tobacco users across the country and those by people who have suffered from the effects of asbestos.

3. **Courts must rely on other branches for enforcement.** Unlike the other branches of government, courts rely on other political institutions to put their opinions or orders

standing: The requirement that a party must be uniquely or singularly affected by a controversy in order to be eligible to file a lawsuit.

class action lawsuit: A lawsuit filed by a large group of people with clearly defined common interests.

into direct effect—police officers, marshals, and executive branch officers, among others, must carry out the courts' mandates. Whereas Congress can cut off funding to executive agencies that ignore its dictates, no similar tool is available to the judiciary. In the vast majority of instances, disobedience of the court is not in question. Yet when a court makes a controversial pronouncement, officials may be reluctant to adhere to the court's decision. In some rare cases, a court's decisions may be met with outright disobedience. Sometimes courts even may react negatively to another court's rulings: In July 2001, Chief Justice Roy Moore of the Alabama Supreme Court authorized the installation of a monument to the Ten Commandments in the Alabama state judicial building. Even after a federal district court ruled that the monument violated the separation of church and state, Moore refused to remove it; more than two years after installation of the monument, Moore was removed from office for defying the federal court's order.

In 1832, President Andrew Jackson declined to enforce the Supreme Court's decision in *Worcester v. Georgia*,[17] which ordered that a white Christian missionary be freed from a Georgia prison. Chief Justice Marshall had ruled that the Georgia law imprisoning the missionary for residing on Cherokee Indian property without permission violated a U.S.–Cherokee treaty; yet President Jackson declared—perhaps apocryphally—that "John Marshall has made his decision…now let him enforce it." (The missionary served his entire four-year mission in jail.) Sometimes even popular Supreme Court decisions face the threat of resistance. President Richard Nixon considered refusing to comply with the Supreme Court's 1974 decision in *United States v. Nixon* ordering him to hand over the secret tapes he made of conversations in the Oval Office.[18]

Controversial Supreme Court decisions in the 1950s and 1960s occasionally led to significant resistance on the part of ordinary citizens as well.[19] The landmark decisions in *Brown v. Board of Education*,[20] which first held that segregated public schools violated the equal protection clause and then commanded that public schools be desegregated "with all deliberate speed," met with violent reaction in the South. Ultimately, President Dwight Eisenhower sent U.S. marshals to the South to enforce the desegregation decrees; otherwise, there might have been even greater resistance to the Court's controversial decision. The Supreme Court's 1962 decision invalidating school-sponsored religious prayer in public schools (*Engel v. Vitale*[21]) goes ignored in many parts of this country even today—in one instance, a federal district court in Alabama was forced to prohibit prayer in public schools throughout the state in response to reports of widespread defiance.

In addition to these limitations, courts must also adhere to limitations that arise from constitutional or statutory law. For example, Congress can by statute alter the Supreme Court's **appellate jurisdiction**, which is the power to review prior decisions handed down by state and lower federal courts. Thus Congress could in theory declare that federal courts as a whole are not empowered to hear abortion cases. In fact, foes of the Supreme Court's abortion decisions proposed just such a bill in the 1980s, but it was never passed. However, Congress cannot alter the Court's **original jurisdiction**, which is the power to hear a lawsuit at the outset. Article III authorizes the Court's original jurisdiction in cases involving ambassadors and cases in which states are the only parties.

One final limitation on courts is harder to see, but is no less significant. Because judges and justices are normally appointed by politically accountable entities such as executives and legislatures, or in some states elected by the public itself, courts in general rarely stray too far from the reigning political majority. Social scientist Robert Dahl affirmed this hypothesis in his landmark 1957 article, "Decision-making in a Democracy."[22] Dahl's study of Supreme Court opinions revealed that although the Supreme Court often defies public opinion in the short run, its opinions usually fall in line with the dominant national majority coalition in the long run. The Court's eventual adaptability to shifts in the national mood, though much more subtle and slow-moving than the more political branches of government, has helped sustain it as a vital force in the American political system.

appellate jurisdiction: The authority of a court to review decisions handed down by another court.

original jurisdiction: The authority of a court to be the initial court in which a legal decision is rendered.

Electing and Appointing Judges

The state and federal court systems differ dramatically in the way judges are selected. State court judges tend to be selected in one of five ways. Partisan elections are utilized in some states, with prospective and sitting justices required to campaign for their party's nomination and then to run in a general election. Nonpartisan elections, held in many other states, eliminate party designations from the election process. The "Missouri Plan" or merit plan selection process features a three-step process by which a judicial nominating commission initially screens candidates and then submits a list of three potential nominees to the governor, who then selects the judge from the list. Shortly thereafter, the new judge must then secure voter approval in a nonpartisan retention election.[23] Several other states authorize gubernatorial appointment of judges, in which the governor appoints judges, subject to approval of the state senate. Finally, a handful of states require that the state legislature appoint judges.

The selection of federal judges follows a more universal formula: all federal district court judges, federal appeals court judges, and Supreme Court justices are appointed by the president, subject to confirmation by a majority vote in the U.S. Senate. Whereas the Constitution dictates this formula for appointment of Supreme Court justices, Congress in its discretion authorized the appointment of lower federal court judges to require the Senate's advice and consent as well. Because all federal judges and Supreme Court justices hold their offices during "good behavior"—the functional equivalent of life tenure—they are thought of as more independent than those state judges who must run for reelection. In fact, the retention rate for state judges is often so high (due to low voter turnout and other factors) that even elected state judges tend to enjoy a large degree of independence in rendering decisions.

The Nomination Process

During a single term in office a president can expect to make hundreds of federal judicial appointments. The Constitution does not limit impose any requirements or limits on those who aspire to membership on a federal courts or even on the U.S. Supreme Court; it left the question of qualifications—whether education, experience, or anything else—to the political actors who control the process. In practice, a tradition of deference to home-state senators (often called "senatorial courtesy") provides legislators in the upper chamber—especially those hailing from the president's party—with considerable influence over the selection of district court judges in their own states. (Senatorial courtesy also has a more limited impact on the selection of appeals court judges, as circuits cross individual state boundaries.) In recent decades, presidents have not only relied on senators' recommendations to generate nominees for judgeships; they also consider ideological factors and the personal characteristics of potential nominees.

Some modern presidents have sought to place their own ideological stamp on the lower courts (whether liberal or conservative) by utilizing a committee of White House and Justice Department attorneys to screen and suggest candidates.[24] The Reagan and George W. Bush administrations were especially active in seeking to use the appointment of lower court judges as a means of moving the constitutional landscape in a conservative ideological direction. When the presidency and the Senate are held by different parties, battles over judicial nominees may become especially fierce. In 2002 and 2007–2008, the Democrat-controlled Senate Judiciary Committee gave heightened scrutiny to President George W. Bush's more conservative nominees. Though in the minority, Senate Republicans sought to return the favor to President Obama, delaying many of his court nominees in 2009 and 2010.

Given its place atop the U.S. legal system, vacancies on the U.S. Supreme Court tend to draw far more political attention than do other judicial vacancies. Because the president, the U.S. Senate, and the media follow personnel changes on the Supreme Court more closely, the process by which justices are nominated and confirmed is a major news event. A president may have the opportunity to appoint several Supreme Court justices—Presidents George H. W. Bush and Bill Clinton appointed two justices each, whereas President Ronald Reagan appointed three associate justices and promoted one associate to chief justice (the justice responsible for administering the Court's affairs and heading the federal justice system as a whole) during his eight years in office. President George W. Bush appointed no justices during his first

President Barack Obama introduces his second nominee to the U.S. Supreme Court, Elena Kagan, in 2010.

term, but filled two vacancies (including the chief justiceship) during the latter half of 2005. Bush's reelection helped him escape the fate suffered by President Carter, whose lone term in office witnessed no Supreme Court vacancies at all.

If a vacancy occurs in the position of chief justice, the president may choose to promote one of the eight associate Supreme Court justices to this prestigious position, as President Reagan did when he promoted William Rehnquist to the Court's center seat in 1986. More often, presidents reach outside the confines of the current Supreme Court for someone to take the position of chief justice. Chief Justice Earl Warren, for example, served as governor of California immediately prior to becoming chief justice in 1953. President George W. Bush also named an outsider, Judge John Roberts of the U.S. Court of Appeals for the D.C. Circuit, to succeed Rehnquist.

The court's current membership is listed in Table 9.1. In choosing nominees to the High Court, presidents in recent decades have considered several factors:

The nominee's ideological and policy preferences. This factor has enjoyed a place of special importance in presidential calculations. A nominee's views on abortion, school prayer, and other hot-button issues may well tip the balance of the Court in favor of the president's stated views. Certainly there exists little evidence that presidents employ "litmus tests" on nominees, by which they might refuse to appoint individuals unless they explicitly state their views on such issues to the president in advance. President Dwight Eisenhower allegedly referred to his appointments of Chief Justice Earl Warren and Justice William Brennan as the "two biggest mistakes" of his presidency, because both men decided cases in a far more liberal direction than Eisenhower would have preferred. More recently, the elder George Bush may have been frustrated by the pro–abortion rights opinions of Justice David Souter, his first appointment to the Supreme Court. Still, most modern presidents have mobilized White House and Justice Department resources to conduct extensive research on each candidate's past writings and opinions in hopes of eliminating any surprises.

TABLE 9.1 Current Membership of the U.S. Supreme Court

Member	Gender	Position	Date Born	Year Appointed (President)	Law School	Party	Religion
John Roberts	M	Chief Justice	1/27/55	2005 (Bush II)	Harvard	Republican	Roman Catholic
Antonin Scalia	M	Associate Justice	3/11/36	1986 (Reagan)	Harvard	Republican	Roman Catholic
Anthony Kennedy	M	Associate Justice	7/23/36	1988 (Reagan)	Harvard	Republican	Roman Catholic
Clarence Thomas	M	Associate Justice	6/23/48	1991 (Bush I)	Yale	Republican	Roman Catholic*
Ruth Bader Ginsburg	F	Associate Justice	3/15/33	1993 (Clinton)	Harvard/ Columbia	Democrat	Jewish
Stephen Breyer	M	Associate Justice	8/15/38	1994 (Clinton)	Harvard	Democrat	Jewish
Samuel Alito	M	Associate Justice	4/1/50	2006 (Bush II)	Yale	Republican	Roman Catholic
Sonia Sotomayor	F	Associate Justice	6/25/54	2009 (Obama)	Yale	Democrat	Roman Catholic
Elena Kagan	F	Associate Justice	4/28/60	2010 (Obama)	Harvard	Democrat	Jewish

*At the time of his 1991 appointment, Clarence Thomas regularly attended an Episcopal church but he later returned to Roman Catholicism, the faith in which he had been raised.

Source: © Cengage Learning

Judicial competence. Most presidents have an interest in appointing especially qualified candidates for the High Court, if only because it assists in speeding along the confirmation process. The American Bar Association (ABA), an interest group of lawyers, rates candidates for every federal judicial vacancy on a scale from "highly qualified" to "not qualified" on the basis of their legal background and accomplishments. Ethical considerations may also be considered, because the ABA may be reluctant to approve candidates who have previously been convicted of crimes, for example. Although a negative rating from the ABA does not always eliminate a candidacy, it may present significant obstacles in the Senate confirmation process. Early in his first term, President George W. Bush announced that he would no longer vet judicial candidates through the ABA prior to their formal nomination. Still, the ABA continued to rate those candidates after their nominations were submitted to the Senate. Two of President Bush's first three nominees for the High Court, John Roberts and Samuel Alito, received the highest rating of "well qualified" just prior to their appearance before the Senate Judiciary Committee. (Bush's other nominee, Harriet Miers, withdrew her name from consideration before the ABA released its rating of her candidacy.)

Political loyalty. Although loyalty has diminished somewhat as a priority in recent years, presidents still occasionally practice old-fashioned politics in the selection of Supreme Court nominees, choosing a justice based on a background of service to the president's party or to the president. During the twentieth century, well over 90 percent of all Supreme Court nominees were members of the president's political party. Of these, many emerged from the president's cabinet, from the members of Congress loyal to the president's legislative program, or from other positions close to the chief executive or his subordinates at the time the appointment was made. Certainly the former president of the United States, William Howard Taft, was well positioned to tout his own appointment as chief justice of the United States; President Warren Harding placed Taft on the High Court just seven years after Taft had left the White House.

Demographic factors. A president may choose a candidate for the diversity the nominee adds to the demographics of the current Supreme Court.[25] As was noted at the outset of this chapter, Lyndon Johnson appointed Thurgood Marshall as the first African American to the Court in 1967; Ronald Reagan appointed Sandra Day O'Connor as the first female justice in 1981; and President Obama appointed Sonia Sotomayor as the first Latina justice in 2009. Obama also appointed a second female, Elena Kagan, to the Court the following year, bringing the number of women on the Court up to three for the time being. The selection of nominees who can diversify the Court may pay political dividends for the White House as well: the president may be counting on such nominations to build support among certain groups.

The U.S. Supreme Court justices, as pictured at the start of the Court's Fall 2010 term. Standing, from left to right: Sonia Sotomayor, Stephen Breyer, Samuel Alito, and Elena Kagan. Seated, from left to right: Clarence Thomas, Antonin Scalia, John Roberts (Chief Justice), Anthony Kennedy, and Ruth Bader Ginsburg.

Steve Petteway, Collection of the Supreme Court of the United States

The current political environment. Supreme Court vacancies do not occur in a vacuum; presidents are well aware of the political conditions that surround a particular court vacancy, and more often than not they respond to it through their nomination choices. Such factors as low presidential approval ratings, a Senate controlled by the political opposition, or the need to achieve other legislative proposals may convince the president to select a more moderate or less controversial nominee. Thus President Bill Clinton—facing a challenging political environment during his first two years in office—chose two Supreme Court nominees during that period (Ruth Bader Ginsburg and Stephen Breyer) who were deemed acceptable by the ranking Republican member of the Senate Judiciary Committee, Senator Orrin Hatch (R-UT). On the other hand, a president who enjoys a strong political position may decide to name a more controversial Supreme Court nominee.

The Confirmation Process

Until the late 1960s, most confirmation processes tended to be little-noticed events, drawing scarce public attention or press coverage. Beginning at that time, however, with the growth of federal regulatory schemes placing more and more cases in the federal courts, presidents began to routinely utilize judicial appointments as a means of shaping public policy. The confirmation process for those nominees was simultaneously opened up to unprecedented high levels of public scrutiny. All hearings for Supreme Court nominees have been televised live on C-SPAN since 1981. Interest groups have become increasingly active in confirmation proceedings, lobbying senators directly and testifying in favor of or against particular nominees. With the ideological stakes raised, presidents and their aides have become increasingly active in lobbying for their nominees.[26]

The Senate confirms the vast majority of Supreme Court nominees; between 1900 and 2010, 59 of the 63 Supreme Court candidates who came up for a formal Senate vote on their respective nominations were confirmed. Nevertheless, as shown in Table 9.2, controversial nominees

TABLE 9.2 Failed Supreme Court Nominees Since 1900

Nominee	Year Nominated	Nominating President	Result
John J. Parker	1930	Hoover	Rejected, 39–41
Abe Fortas	1968	L.B. Johnson	Withdrawn*
Homer Thornberry	1968	L.B. Johnson	Nullified**
Clement Haynsworth	1969	Nixon	Rejected, 45–55
G. Harrold Carswell	1970	Nixon	Rejected, 45–51
Robert H. Bork	1987	Reagan	Rejected, 42–58
Douglas H. Ginsburg	1987	Reagan	Withdrawn
Harriet Miers	2005	G.W. Bush	Withdrawn

*Nomination for chief justice withdrawn
**Nomination for associate justice voided by withdrawal of Fortas nomination

Source: © Cengage Learning

in recent decades have experienced their share of public scrutiny—and in some cases, outright rejection by the Senate—when subjected to the glare of the confirmation process. One of Richard Nixon's nominees to the Supreme Court in 1970, Court of Appeals Judge G. Harrold Carswell of Florida, was rejected by the Senate in part because of his alleged links to white supremacist groups. Carswell was also dogged by charges that he was not competent to serve on the bench; to that came the deadly retort of one Senate supporter that "even the mediocre deserve some representation on the Supreme Court too." Despite all these obstacles, Carswell nearly survived Senate confirmation anyway—he was rejected by a six-vote margin. Frustrated by his defeat, Carswell resigned from the bench a few months later and ran unsuccessfully for the U.S. Senate in 1972.

Ronald Reagan's nomination of Judge Robert Bork to the Supreme Court in 1987 was defeated in the Senate amid a cloud of interest-group cries that Bork would reverse liberal precedents on free speech and abortion.[27] Bork, a former Yale law professor, sported a record of opposition to many Supreme Court doctrines supported by political liberals, including the doctrine of constitutionally protected abortion rights that the Court articulated in *Roe v. Wade* (1973).[28] In his award-winning book *The Selling of Supreme Court Nominees* (1994), University of Georgia Professor John Maltese notes that liberal interest groups that were determined to defeat Bork employed "a wide variety of tactics, including advertising, grass roots events, focus groups and polling" to increase public awareness of Bork's controversial positions.

The Reagan White House was caught off guard by the groundswell of opposition to Bork's nomination generated by the intense interest group–driven media campaign. By the time Senate confirmation hearings were held at the end of the summer, the campaign had taken its toll on Bork's candidacy: several senators, including Joseph Biden (D-DE), chairman of the Senate Judiciary Committee, had already been persuaded to oppose the appointment. The Senate eventually defeated Bork's nomination by a 58–42 vote. Presidents since then have come to understand the new politics of judicial confirmations, working closely with interest groups to mount their own campaigns in favor of judicial nominees. The Bork nomination gave rise to a new term in Washington's political lexicon—"to Bork," which defines the act of challenging a president's nominee through well-financed and organized interest-group opposition.

The Bork confirmation fiasco also encouraged subsequent presidents to favor nominees who either possess no paper trail at all or who would be far more circumspect than Bork in their willingness to engage the Senate on constitutional issues. Accordingly, in 1990 the first Supreme Court vacancy of George H. W. Bush's presidency went to David Souter, a little-known federal appeals judge who had logged most of his judicial career on the New Hampshire Supreme Court deciding technical issues of state law. Souter's position on issues such as abortion and the establishment clause were never really tested in the state court system, and senators on both ends of the political spectrum thus had little to work with when interrogating Souter. (He was confirmed easily by a 90–9 Senate vote.)

In recent years, the confirmation process for lower court nominees has been politicized as well, with battles being waged with extra ferocity over appointments to the U.S. courts of appeals. During the Clinton administration, Senate Republicans in control of that chamber often delayed nominees they felt were too liberal; Senate Democrats did the same to President George W. Bush's nominees in 2001. Before the Democrats regained control of Congress in the 2006

John Roberts, nominee for chief justice of the United States, testifying before the Senate Judiciary Committee in September 2005.

midterm elections, Senate Democrats opposed to some of George W. Bush's nominees on ideological grounds began to take advantage of Senate rules to stop votes on contested nominees. Specifically, they utilized the filibuster to block 10 of President Bush's appellate court nominees during his first term in office. Bush renominated nine of those blocked nominees at the start of his second term, and a frustrated Republican Senate leadership began to consider rule changes to foreclose the use of filibusters against future nominees. Senate Democrats referred to any such rule change as the "nuclear option," because they were prepared to respond by shutting down Senate business through use of the filibuster rule in all other instances. On May 24, 2005, this growing crisis was averted, as a group of 14 moderate senators (7 Republicans and 7 Democrats) settled on a plan to allow several of Bush's most controversial nominees to be confirmed, in return for the promise that the filibuster would be reserved for use against judicial appointments when there are "extraordinary circumstances."

writ of certiorari: The formal term for an order by which the Supreme Court acts in its discretion to review a case from a lower court.

HOW A CASE PROCEEDS WITHIN THE U.S. SUPREME COURT

The vast majority of cases that come before the U.S. Supreme Court arrive by a **writ of certiorari**, the formal term for an order by which the Court acts in its discretion to hear a case on appeal. Losing parties in the highest state court, a federal circuit court, or (in extremely rare cases) a federal district court can properly file a "cert petition" with the Supreme Court, asking the Court to hear its case. Decisions to grant a writ of certiorari generally follow the *Rule of Four*—if four of the nine justices vote to hear the case, it is placed on the Court's official docket of cases that it will hear during the coming year. Of the many thousands of cert petitions that arrive at the Court during a given year, barely more than 1 percent (fewer than 90 overall) are normally granted.

In theory, the justices decide to hear only those cases that are considered so important that they justify intervention at such a high level. Two other factors may also increase the likelihood that the Supreme Court will grant a writ of certiorari: (1) when the federal government intervenes in the case; or (2) when there is a split among two or more of the U.S. circuit courts of appeals on a similar issue. Additionally, some justices as a matter of strategy may vote to deny the petition for cert, even when they think the lower court case was wrongly decided, because they do not want their colleagues to transform the lower court precedent into a Supreme Court edict applicable throughout the land. Regardless of the justices' many motives, denial of a cert petition theoretically casts no aspersions whatsoever on whether a case has been wrongly or

Fact or Fiction?

Outside interest groups (such as the American Medical Association) may formally participate in a Supreme Court case even when those groups are not actually parties to the lawsuit.

Fact.

Outside parties such as the American Medical Association with an interest in the litigation may elect to file briefs, known formally as amicus curiae briefs (*amicus curiae* is Latin for "friend of the court"), expressing their own views on how the Court should decide a particular case.

rightly decided, although it does allow the lower court decision to stand as the controlling legal decision for the parties in that case. For example, the Supreme Court's 1997 denial of a cert petition in a case concerning affirmative action at the University of Texas did not necessarily imply High Court dissatisfaction with affirmative action; rather, it simply left intact a U.S. court of appeals decision that applied only to the three states in that circuit: Texas, Mississippi, and Louisiana. The U.S. Supreme Court waited until six years later to articulate new rules for affirmative action that would become applicable in all 50 states.

As shown in Figure 9.3, if the Court elects to issue a writ of certiorari and hear a case, both the losing and winning parties in the lower court file written documents called **briefs** arguing why constitutional or federal statutory law weighs in favor of their respective positions. Outside parties with an interest in the litigation may also elect to file briefs, known formally as **amicus curiae briefs** (*amicus curiae* is Latin for "friend of the court"), expressing their own views on how the Court should decide a particular case. Interest groups frequently file amicus briefs in Supreme Court cases that affect their members; in doing so, they offer a version of "expert testimony" on the law, albeit with their own strategic bent on the issue in question. The American Medical Association, for example, routinely files amicus briefs in abortion cases; the American Trial Lawyers Association may express its opinion in cases interpreting rules of trial procedure through amicus briefs as well. In some of the more high-profile cases, literally hundreds of such briefs may be filed, offering the Court an admittedly informal tally of the state of public opinion on the issue.

briefs: Written documents filed by parties in an appealed case arguing why constitutional or statutory law weighs in favor of their respective positions.

amicus curiae briefs: Written documents filed by outside parties in the case with an interest in the outcome of the litigation expressing their own views on how the Court should decide a particular case.

FIGURE 9.3 From Cert Petition to Final Judgment in the U.S. Supreme Court

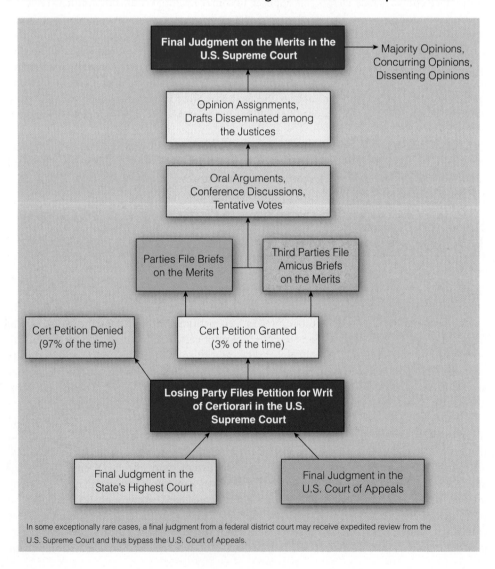

In some exceptionally rare cases, a final judgment from a federal district court may receive expedited review from the U.S. Supreme Court and thus bypass the U.S. Court of Appeals.

The **solicitor general** argues on behalf of the U.S. government in most cases where the federal government is a party. That office also stands among the most influential "friends of the court," filing amicus briefs on behalf of the federal government in approximately a quarter of all cases heard by the Supreme Court each year. Acting through the solicitor general, the U.S. government has enjoyed a disproportionate share of success in affecting Supreme Court case discretionary grants of review and case outcomes.[29]

After all party and amicus briefs have been filed, the Supreme Court justices normally hear oral arguments from opposing counsel in the Supreme Court's chamber. Attorneys licensed to practice before the Supreme Court present their clients' view of the law and facts within an allotted period of time (normally 30 minutes); most of that time is actually spent answering questions and inquiries from the justices. If a justice is truly undecided, he or she may be affected in the margins by the positions of advocates at oral arguments; the give-and-take with the lawyers may also suggest ways to more effectively draft the final opinion. Still, there remains little evidence that the oral arguments actually shift the votes of most justices. Regardless, the hearings in the Supreme Court chamber can still offer moments of high drama, such as when Richard Nixon's attorneys argued for an especially broad interpretation of executive privilege in the 1974 Watergate tapes case. Their argument was ultimately rejected, and Nixon resigned just days after the Court's decision was handed down.

Shortly after the oral arguments are completed and the case has been formally submitted, the justices meet in conference to discuss the case, offer initial votes, and assign opinions. The chief justice presides over all conferences, which culminate in the assignment of opinions to be researched and written by individual justices in accordance with the conference discussions. Each justice employs four clerks—selected from a pool of the top law school graduates from across the country—who work behind the scenes researching the law and creating initial drafts of written opinions according to the justice's specific wishes. In some cases clerks enjoy even more influence over the justices they work for, assisting them as they sort through competing legal arguments.

A **majority opinion** requires agreement of at least five of the Court's nine members; only a majority opinion carries the force of law. The chief justice has just one vote like his colleagues, but if he is in the majority, the chief justice also has the crucial power to choose who will write the Court's main opinion. (If the chief justice is not in the majority, the senior-most associate justice in the majority retains that power of assignment.) Individual justices may choose to write other opinions either on their own or on behalf of a minority of justices. A **concurring opinion** agrees with the end result reached by the majority but disagrees with the reasons offered for the decision. A **dissenting opinion**, on the other hand, disagrees with the result reached by the majority. Justices write concurring and dissenting opinions both to register their differences with the majority and to lay the groundwork for the future, when those alternate grounds may one day secure the support of a Court majority.

The dissents written by Oliver Wendell Holmes Jr., who served on the U.S. Supreme Court from 1902 to 1932, established him as one of the most important legal thinkers in American history. When President Theodore Roosevelt appointed Holmes to the U.S. Supreme Court in 1902, the Court majority at the time appeared to be favorably disposed to protect the rights of big business. Armed with his own "realist" view of law that emphasized the "necessities of the time," Holmes dissented vigorously from the Court's majority opinions invalidating industrial reform laws and other progressive legislation. With speech restrictions on the rise in America during and immediately after World War I, Holmes eventually adjusted his own philosophy to promote a broader conception of free speech under the Constitution. Along with fellow justice Louis Brandeis, Holmes dissented from the majority's opinions allowing the government to punish minority views. (Holmes also made famous the metaphor

solicitor general: The lawyer representing the U.S. government before the U.S. Supreme Court.

majority opinion: The opinion of a majority of members of the U.S. Supreme Court, which carries the force of law.

concurring opinion: The opinion of one or more justices that agrees with the end result reached by the majority but disagrees with the reasons offered for the decision.

dissenting opinion: The opinion of one or more justices who disagree with the result reached by the majority.

MPI/Getty Images

The Great Dissenter, Justice Oliver Wendell Holmes Jr., was appointed to the Supreme Court by President Theodore Roosevelt in 1902. Holmes's dissenting opinions on behalf of the freedom of expression would garner the support of Supreme Court majorities several decades later.

of a "marketplace of ideas" and cautioned that even liberal protections of free speech would not protect a man from "falsely shouting 'fire!' in a crowded theater.") For Holmes, "the life of law" was never logic; rather, it was "experience." Justices after Holmes came to embrace his practical, real-world approach to the law. For instance, in *New York Times v. Sullivan* (1964),[30] the Supreme Court built on Holmes's theories about the First Amendment to apply a more protective approach to libel law, making it harder for public officials to sue newspapers that criticized their actions.

Once drafts of the justices' opinions in a case have been circulated and finalized, the decision can be announced. Occasionally the justices can shift their votes near the end of the process. For example, in 1986 Justice Lewis Powell seemingly resolved his own inner struggles over the scope of privacy rights when he chose to join Justice Byron White's four-person opinion in *Bowers v. Hardwick*.[31] Powell's vote gave White the slim majority and determined that the right to homosexual sodomy would not receive constitutional protection until 2003, when the Court overturned *Bowers* in *Lawrence v. Texas*.[32] Powell later publicly recanted his support of *Bowers*, proving that his inner struggle had actually continued. Normally the justices issue written opinions only, but on special occasions, the justices may even decide to read from key passages of the opinions they authored.

WHY THE JUSTICES VOTE THE WAY THEY DO

Although it is difficult to determine what causes Supreme Court justices to vote as they do on certain issues, social scientists and legal scholars have identified a number of factors that may play a role in a judge's decision making:

- **Legal rules and precedents.** The law itself—including constitutional law, statutes, rules and regulations, and past court decisions interpreting those sources—may be unambiguous enough to counsel one particular application to the case at hand. Previous court decisions are especially hard to avoid—when judges follow the decisions of past judges' rulings in similar cases, they are adhering to the long-standing doctrine of "stare decisis," which is Latin for "stand by the decision" that has already been settled. For example, though Justice Byron White dissented from the original decision in *Miranda v. Arizona* (1966)[33] providing unprecedented rights to the accused, in later decisions he actively applied the *Miranda* holding to other cases, deferring to a High Court precedent that he personally opposed. Although the language of Supreme Court opinions suggests that stare decisis is always at work, often more than one reasonable interpretation of a law or legal opinion exists. In recent years, some judges have turned to international law and judicial opinions handed down in foreign courts as well. Most notably, Justice Anthony Kennedy in *Lawrence v. Texas* (2003) cited the European Court of Human Rights in support of the Court's protection of homosexual privacy rights. Defenders of this practice claim that because Americans share some values with the wider civilization, judges should be able to cite any and all sources of law in rendering their decisions; critics respond that there is no basis for U.S. judges to impose foreign "moods or fads" on Americans.

- **Changes in circumstances.** Sometimes changes in real-life conditions and circumstances may influence how laws are interpreted. In the school desegregation cases of the 1950s, the Supreme Court openly considered the newly discovered harmful effects of segregation on African American children. Similarly, in 1973, the Supreme Court took into account changes in modern medicine when it formulated the definition of constitutionally protected abortion rights in *Roe v. Wade*. Some jurists and scholars believe such changes in circumstances are irrelevant—rather, they view the Constitution as fixed in time and thus limited in scope to what the Framers envisioned. The search for the Framers' original intent about the Constitution is often referred to as "originalism." By contrast, other judges and scholars advocate the more flexible view of the Constitution as a "living, breathing document," which must adapt to changing circumstances and conditions.

- **Ideological "attitudes."** Many political scientists argue that Supreme Court justices' personal attitudes (liberal or conservative on law enforcement issues, free speech, and so forth)

THE MORE THINGS CHANGE, THE MORE THEY STAY THE SAME

"Swing Justices" Who Kept a Nation on Edge

Many of the Court's high-profile decisions have been decided by quite narrow margins. For example, the recent Supreme Court decision addressing the constitutionality of campaign finance laws—the decision in *Citizens United v. FEC* (2010)—was decided by just a 5–4 margin. Perhaps the passion expressed by interests on both sides of that decision was fueled by the reality that a shift in just one justice's thinking could change the decision's outcome. It is no wonder, then, that advocates before the Court tend to direct their arguments at so-called "swing justices" who provide the pivotal vote in the cases. Consider three justices who have managed to keep the Court (and the nation) continually on edge:

In 1937, an emboldened President Franklin Delano Roosevelt, fresh off his reelection landslide, turned his attention to the U.S. Supreme Court that had gutted many of his New Deal initiatives and more progressive state laws by 6–3 or 5–4 votes. Although the so-called "center of the Court" consisted of two justices—Chief Justice Charles Evans Hughes and Associate Justice Owen Roberts—Hughes had given key parts of the New Deal his blessing the previous year, leaving Owen Roberts as the all-important "swing justice" on the Supreme Court. As Roosevelt prepared to unveil his controversial "court-packing plan" that would have potentially increased the size of the Court to 15 (thus giving FDR the power to create a pro–New Deal majority), Owen Roberts showed signs of swinging once again. In the spring of 1937, the same Justice Roberts who

had joined a four-person conservative bloc to strike down the Bituminous Coal Conservation Act and the Agricultural Adjustment Act in 1936 now reversed course, voting in favor of broad interpretations of government power in 1937. Thus Roberts will forever be known as the swing justice whose "switch in time saved nine," as the court-packing bill soon failed for lack of necessity, leaving nine Supreme Court justices as the standard that remains in place even today.

In 1978 and then again in 1986, Associate Justice Lewis Powell cemented his reputation as the quintessential "swing justice" of the Burger Court. As a Virginia Democrat appointed by a Republican President (Nixon), Powell arrived at the Court with a stake in different political camps, and he often ruled as a justice in the middle. In the landmark affirmative action precedent of *Regents of California v. Bakke* (1978), Powell was essentially a one-man court: his ruling that hard racial quotas were unconstitutional drew support from the four more conservative justices, whereas his holding that race could be used as a "flexible" factor in admissions drew support from the four High Court liberals. Less than a decade later in *Bowers v. Hardwick* (1986), Powell than cast the deciding vote upholding state laws criminalizing homosexual sodomy. Powell had initially voted to strike down the sodomy law in conference, but then changed his mind after a few days. Later, after leaving the Court, Powell would come to regret his decision in public statements. More likely he regretted his status as the

Justice Owen Roberts

Justice Lewis Powell

(*Continued*)

THE MORE THINGS CHANGE,
THE MORE THEY STAY THE SAME

"Swing Justices" Who Kept a Nation on Edge (continued)

court's "swing justice" and the pressures that weighed on him as the one who earned so much attention.

In 1992, Justice Anthony Kennedy first established his reputation as a swing justice who was impossible to pigeonhole when—after routinely upholding restrictive abortion laws in previous cases—he helped forge a judicial compromise on abortion in *Planned Parenthood v. Casey* (1992). Although a conservative on most issues, Kennedy spent his subsequent years on the Court shifting over to the liberal justices' bloc at opportune times. Thus in *Lawrence v. Texas* (2003) he joined the liberals to reverse the *Bowers* decision and craft a right to sexual privacy. Even more

surprising, Kennedy's consistent position in favor of the government in criminal cases did not stop him from casting the deciding vote banning application of the death penalty to the mentally ill and those who are under the age of 18. Given Kennedy's propensity to shift back and forth, many were surprised when in 2012, his role as "swing Justice" was usurped temporarily by Chief Justice John Roberts, who cast the crucial fifth vote to save President Obama's health care reform initiative. Obviously "swing Justices" can emerge from unexpected places, depending on the facts and circumstances of the case at hand.

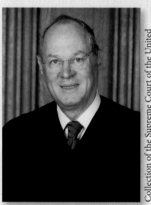

Collection of the Supreme Court of the United States; photographer: Robin Reid

Justice Anthony Kennedy

For Critical Thinking and Discussion

1. Is a Supreme Court justice who shifts back and forth between competing constitutional positions a "fair and open-minded" jurist, or a whimsical, unprincipled court politician?

2. If so-called "swing justices" bring an element of unpredictability to the Court's decision-making outcomes, is that a positive or negative development? Do we want the Court to be predictable? Why or why not?

influence their judicial decision making. This model of understanding how justices decide cases has been labeled "the attitudinal model." Defenders of the model cite numerous statistics that support their understanding of the way judges decide cases. For example, William O. Douglas was a New Deal liberal who voted in the liberal direction in criminal procedure cases nearly 90 percent of the time and in civil rights cases 93 percent of the time.[34]

- **Personal traits and characteristics.** Males and females may approach political events differently; accordingly, the gender of a Supreme Court justice affects his or her reaction to legal issues and cases to some degree. Just as some demographic groups tend to be more conservative, justices who fit into those groups may be expected to vote accordingly. A justice's personal experiences may also play a role in how he or she judges. Biographers of Justice Oliver Wendell Holmes, for example, contend that Holmes's near-death experiences as a soldier in the Civil War colored his approach to judging.[35]

- **Intra-Court politics.** A justice's interest in maintaining good relations with fellow justices may push him or her to vote in a certain way; behind-the-scenes bargaining and negotiating have also been features of Supreme Court politics throughout its history. In the late 1950s and early 1960s, Chief Justice Earl Warren and Justice William Brennan were famed for their ability to sway undecided justices in their favor; by contrast, Justice Felix Frankfurter's condescending attitude toward his fellow justices persuaded few and alienated many.

- **External political pressures.** Although Supreme Court justices enjoy life tenure and are thus theoretically immune to outside political pressures, the reality is much more complicated. Aware that the Court's prestige often rests on its ability to persuade the other branches, as well as the public, to comply with the Court's decisions, justices often react to the political environment that surrounds the Court when issuing legal opinions. *Roe v. Wade* survived its widely predicted demise in 1992 because at least two conservative justices feared its reversal would deal a blow to the Supreme Court's prestige. Chief Justice Roberts' concern with threats to the Court's prestige may have led him to defer to the political branches in the health care case of *NFIB v.* Sebelius (2012). Public opinion may thus play a role in determining the language of opinions and even the outcome of some cases.

CURRENT DEBATES OVER THE EXERCISE OF JUDICIAL POWER

American courts often find themselves the subject of controversy. Many of the recurring debates over the proper role of courts include the following:

- **Judicial restraint versus judicial activism.** The Supreme Court struck down several New Deal statutes in the 1930s; a few decades later, it invalidated state laws banning the use of contraceptive devices (in 1965) and state laws restricting the right to abortion (in 1973). Critics of those decisions protested the exercise of judicial activism by the High Court. Specifically, they charged that rather than deferring to the elected branches of government as a general matter, the justices responsible for those controversial decisions had effectively turned the Court into a "super legislature" that makes social policy. More recent cases such as *Citizens United v. FEC* (2010), in which the Court struck down a federal law banning corporations from most forms of participation in election campaigns, have revived those charges once again. Critics of judicial activism argue in favor of a philosophy of judicial restraint by which judges act more slowly and incrementally, affording the democratically elected branches considerable discretion to enact whatever laws they choose, so long as there is no clear and unambiguous prohibition against those laws in the Constitution itself. (Given the "elegant vagueness" of the Constitution's language, advocates of judicial restraint believe those instances are rare indeed.)

- **Electing judges versus appointing judges.** Federal judges are appointed by the president with the advice and consent of the Senate and then serve for life. Many state judges are appointed as well, for either fixed or indefinite terms; others must run for election and then must seek reelection to stay on the bench. These varying methods of judicial selection may have significant implications on judicial decision making. Appointed judges no longer accountable to the public or to any political processes enjoy increased independence in their decision making. Although many judicial elections pose little or no challenge to the incumbents, these election contests have become dramatically more contested in recent decades. For instance, in 1986 conservative groups disgruntled with liberal decisions rendered by the highest state court in California campaigned successfully to defeat three of its more liberal justices in recall elections, including Chief Justice Rose Bird. What elected judges may lack in independence they make up for in accountability; unlike judges appointed for life, elected judges should

Supreme Court Justice Antonin Scalia, speaking at a Federalist Society Gala in 2007.

Is Law School the Right Choice for You, and If So, When Should You Apply?

Currently there are almost two hundred law schools in the United States accredited by the American Bar Association (ABA) that award juris doctor degrees to students upon completion of three years or more of legal education. You are no doubt familiar with the names of many of these schools: Harvard, Yale, Columbia, the University of Chicago, and several others that enjoy sterling reputations and are well known around the world. Many graduates of these schools work in prestigious short-term clerkships for judges and then go on to enjoy their pick of legal jobs at extremely high starting salaries. Other law school graduates are not so fortunate, however. According to lawjobs.com, graduates of law schools ranked below the top 25 have a less than one-in-five chance of beginning their careers at a large law firm with relatively high starting salaries; and nearly 15 percent of all students at ABA-accredited schools either flunk out or are unemployed

for at least nine months after graduation. Moreover, at 44 ABA-accredited schools, fully 20 percent of students have flunked out or remain unemployed. Considering the high price of law school today (many students graduate with debts of $100,000 or more), these are daunting figures indeed.

Of course, for many college graduates who attend the right law school at the right moment in their young careers, legal education offers significant benefits, including the prospect of an exciting and lucrative career. Because the average age of entering law students across the nation is 25 years old (the average age is higher at some top-ranked schools), most college graduates will consider other post-graduation opportunities before law school, both to prepare them for the rigors of law school and to enhance their chances of admission at top schools.

© Sally and Richard Greenhill/Alamy

A law professor lectures to a large class of first-year law students.

For Critical Thinking and Discussion

1. Can you think of any benefits that accrue to law students who take time off after college?

2. Many college graduates apply to law school not so much because they dream of a legal career, but because they are unaware of any other promising options. What other types of graduate schools might be of interest to students who enjoy crafting arguments and debating public policy?

3. Law school applications tend to rise during difficult economic times. Why do you think that is true?

---

be more responsive to the public as a whole. The debate over judicial selection mechanisms often boils down to a question of how to strike the proper balance between the competing interests of judicial independence and accountability to the public.

- **Law versus politics.** Do judges sit on a court of law, or is their institution simply another political body exercising its political will? Certainly the judicial process is fashioned to trumpet the court's role as a legal body that transcends ordinary politics. The judicial robes, magisterial courtrooms, and reliance on formality give rise to this "cult of the robe" as the "apolitical" branch. Canons of judicial ethics require that judges avoid even the appearance of impropriety by not participating in political debates and lobbying other branches on various matters. At the same time, the U.S. Supreme Court in particular often finds itself at the storm center of American politics. In some instances the other branches actually come to the Court in search of legal answers to what are essentially political problems. The Court's 5–4 decision in *Bush v. Gore* (2000),[36] which ended the manual recounts for the 2000 presidential election in Florida and made George W. Bush the president-elect, illustrates just one way that law and politics can become intertwined. Over a decade later, the Supreme Court's decision to uphold President Obama's health care reform legislation offered political fodder for both sides of the political spectrum in the months leading up to the 2012 presidential election. In extremely rare cases, the elected branches essentially abdicate their responsibility to act altogether, forcing the courts to step in by enforcing judicial decrees. For example, federal courts have on rare occasions supervised the construction of prisons and the implementation of busing programs. The highly political manner in which judges are chosen and the ambiguous nature of so many legal provisions mean that the tension between law and politics is perhaps inevitable in the U.S. political system.

- **Cameras in the courtroom.** The Constitution guarantees to every criminal defendant a public trial; courts can satisfy that requirement by allowing the media and some members of the public access to the trial. Many states go a step further, allowing television cameras in state courtrooms, but the federal judicial system has so far resisted any such development. Do lawyers play up to the television cameras, undermining the interests of justice? It's hard to say. When Casey Anthony was tried for the murder of her two-year-old daughter in a Florida courtroom in 2011, the trial received gavel-to-gavel television coverage. In April 2005, Senator Charles Grassley (R-IA) introduced in Congress the so-called Sunshine in the Courtroom Act, which would allow cameras into federal courtrooms. Specifically, the bill would give the presiding federal judge in every case the authority to determine whether cameras would be permitted, and if so, for how long. Even if such legislation one day passes, it is unlikely that cameras will appear any time soon in the U.S. Supreme Court, where Chief Justice John Roberts continues to defer to a handful of older justices who remain adamantly opposed to television coverage. (See the timeline in Figure 9.4). Justices Stephen Breyer and Antonin Scalia have both spoken publicly against the move. Indeed, Scalia noted his objection in especially stark terms during a 2005 interview: "I think there's something sick about making entertainment out of other people's legal problems . . . I don't like it in the lower courts, and

FIGURE 9.4 A Timeline of Cameras in the Federal Courts

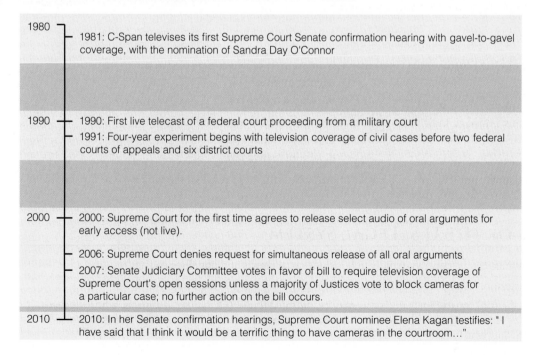

1980
— 1981: C-Span televises its first Supreme Court Senate confirmation hearing with gavel-to-gavel coverage, with the nomination of Sandra Day O'Connor

1990
— 1990: First live telecast of a federal court proceeding from a military court
— 1991: Four-year experiment begins with television coverage of civil cases before two federal courts of appeals and six district courts

2000
— 2000: Supreme Court for the first time agrees to release select audio of oral arguments for early access (not live).
— 2006: Supreme Court denies request for simultaneous release of all oral arguments
— 2007: Senate Judiciary Committee votes in favor of bill to require television coverage of Supreme Court's open sessions unless a majority of Justices vote to block cameras for a particular case; no further action on the bill occurs.

2010
— 2010: In her Senate confirmation hearings, Supreme Court nominee Elena Kagan testifies: " I have said that I think it would be a terrific thing to have cameras in the courtroom..."

I don't particularly like it in the Supreme Court."[37] Until the makeup of the current Court changes significantly, Supreme Court observers unable to observe oral arguments in person will have to settle for audiotapes of the oral arguments made available a short time later.

Since the outset of the republic, U.S. presidents have pursued diversity for the High Court. During the nineteenth century the diversity they looked for was mostly geographical, as they sought representation for different regions; in the early part of the twentieth century, presidents sought to have different religions represented on the High Court. In recent decades presidents have occasionally emphasized ethnic and racial diversity as well. It may be impossible to prove that demographic traits and characteristics systematically affect the way a justice approaches a Supreme Court case, but presidents and senators clearly assume they will have some effect. Politicians also understand the symbolic importance certain appointments carry as well. Hoping to move the Court beyond its history as an all-white tribunal, President Lyndon Johnson named the first African American (Thurgood Marshall); more than four decades later, President Barack Obama named the first Latina (Sonia Sotomayor). Both nominations generated some controversy, but both were eventually confirmed by comfortable margins. As a result, the Court would look different and—in the eyes of many—the Court's decision making would be influenced by the addition of new and unique perspectives.

SUMMARY: PUTTING IT ALL TOGETHER

TYPES OF LAW

- Law encompasses the authoritative rules made by government. The term *civil law* refers to statutes enacted most often by legislative bodies; common law consists of the rulings handed down by judges that establish precedents. Other types of law include criminal, civil, constitutional, and administrative law.

Test Yourself on This Section

1. A rule or regulation issued by the Federal Trade Commission is an example of which type of law?
   - **a.** civil law
   - **b.** common law
   - **c.** constitutional law
   - **d.** administrative law

2. Judge-made law handed down through judicial opinions that over time establish precedents is
   - **a.** civil law.
   - **b.** common law.
   - **c.** constitutional law.
   - **d.** administrative law.

3. Do generalist courts that handle criminal, civil, and constitutional cases still make sense in the modern era? Or should more courts specialize in different areas of the law?

THE STRUCTURE OF THE U.S. LEGAL SYSTEM

- Each of the 50 states maintains its own court system, which includes trial courts and appellate courts.
- Article III of the U.S. Constitution established the judicial branch, including the U.S. Supreme Court.
- Federal district courts are the trial courts. Their decisions may be appealed to the U.S. courts of appeals, whose decisions may be reviewed by the U.S. Supreme Court. The decision of a state supreme court that raises federal issues may also be brought directly to the U.S. Supreme Court.

Test Yourself on This Section

1. The U.S. Constitution specifically establishes which of the following?
   a. federal district courts
   b. U.S. courts of appeals
   c. the U.S. Supreme Court
   d. all of the above

2. Frustrated by a Supreme Court that struck down a number of his policies as unconstitutional, which president unsuccessfully attempted to add new justices?
   a. Abraham Lincoln
   b. Franklin Roosevelt
   c. John Kennedy
   d. Ronald Reagan

3. Under what circumstances would a party in a legal case file a writ of certiorari?

THE ADVERSARIAL SYSTEM OF JUSTICE

- The U.S. legal system is an adversarial system of justice, in which opposing parties contend against each other for a result favorable to themselves, and judges act merely as independent referees.

- In the United States, disputes between parties may be settled through civil litigation. Those accused of crimes are prosecuted through a criminal law system. The vast majority of criminal prosecutions are settled by plea bargaining.

Test Yourself on This Section

1. A party that initiates a formal legal proceeding in a civil case is referred to as a
   a. defendant.
   b. plaintiff.
   c. defense attorney.
   d. prosecutor.

2. An indictment is authorized by which of the following?
   a. grand jury
   b. trial jury
   c. judge
   d. prosecutor

3. The vast majority of criminal cases are resolved by which of the following methods?
   a. jury conviction
   b. jury acquittal
   c. hung jury
   d. plea bargain

4. One stage of the pretrial process is known as "discovery." What occurs at this stage?

JUDICIAL REVIEW AND ITS IMPLICATIONS

- Chief Justice John Marshall's opinion in *Marbury v. Madison* (1803) established the Supreme Court's authority to review the constitutionality of any act passed by Congress.

Test Yourself on This Section

1. The power of the Court to review a law passed by Congress as "unconstitutional" was established in which of the following decisions?
   a. *Marbury v. Madison*
   b. *McCulloch v. Maryland*
   c. *Martin v. Hunter's Lessee*
   d. *Dred Scott v. Sandford*

2. The authority of the Supreme Court to determine the scope of congressional power under the "necessary and proper clause" was established in
   a. *Marbury v. Madison*.
   b. *McCulloch v. Maryland*.
   c. *Martin v. Hunter's Lessee*.
   d. *Dred Scott v. Sandford*.

3. The power of the Supreme Court to exercise judicial review over coordinate branches is not found in the Constitution itself. How, then, did it become so firmly established?

LIMITATIONS ON COURTS

- Courts in the United States cannot initiate lawsuits, they can only hear true controversies, their decisions affect only those parties that are part of a case, and they have no ability to enforce their decisions.

Test Yourself on This Section

1. The authority of a court to review decisions handed down by another court is called
   a. standing.
   b. appellate jurisdiction.
   c. original jurisdiction.
   d. judicial review.

2. What are the limitations of judicial power that do not present such limitations for the other branches of government?

ELECTING AND APPOINTING JUDGES

- State judges are selected in various ways depending upon the jurisdiction: some are appointed by governors or legislatures; others must run in an election; still others are chosen by a merit plan system.
- All federal court judges are nominated by the president and must be confirmed by the U.S. Senate.

Test Yourself on This Section

1. Who nominates federal district judges?
   a. the president
   b. senators
   c. the Supreme Court justices
   d. the Speaker of the House

2. The current chief justice of the U.S. Supreme Court is
   a. Sonja Sotomayor.
   b. Elena Kagan.
   c. John Roberts.
   d. Ruth Bader Ginsburg.

3. What are the various factors that presidents consider when nominating an individual to serve on the Supreme Court?

HOW A CASE PROCEEDS WITHIN THE U.S. SUPREME COURT

- In order to grant a writ of certiorari to review a case, four of the nine justices must approve.
- After briefs are filed and oral arguments are heard, the justices vote on the merits and issue their majority opinion accordingly. Concurring and dissenting opinions may also be issued.

Test Yourself on This Section

1. A minimum of how many Supreme Court justices is required for a case to be added to the docket?
   a. two
   b. four
   c. five
   d. six

2. Who normally represents the U.S. government when arguing a case before the Supreme Court?
   a. the attorney general
   b. the president's chief counsel
   c. the solicitor general
   d. any member of the Washington, D.C., bar

3. The judicial principal of adhering to long-standing doctrinal decisions is known as
   a. amicus curiae.
   b. stare decisis.
   c. nolo contende.
   d. cogito ergo sum.

4. Distinguish between a "concurring" opinion and a "dissenting" opinion.

WHY THE JUSTICES VOTE THE WAY THEY DO

- Various factors influence a judge's decision making, including legal precedents, new circumstances, ideological attitudes, personal traits, intracourt politics, and external pressures.

Test Yourself on This Section

1. Which justice was particularly effective at swaying his judicial colleagues to vote with him in landmark cases such as *Brown v. Board of Education*?
   a. Oliver Wendell Holmes
   b. Felix Frankfurter
   c. Anthony Kennedy
   d. Earl Warren

2. What kind of external political pressures led two conservative justices to uphold *Roe v. Wade* in 1992?

CURRENT DEBATES OVER THE EXERCISE OF JUDICIAL POWER

- Justices who frequently overturn state and federal laws may be accused of judicial activism; critics of such activism advocate judicial restraint, deferring to democratically elected legislatures.

- State judges who must run for election occasionally face some opposition, which forces them to be more responsive to the public. Appointed judges, by contrast, enjoy more independence.

- A majority of justices continues to oppose allowing television cameras to cover oral arguments.

Test Yourself on This Section

1. What kind of judges may be elected?
   - **a.** federal district court judges
   - **b.** state superior court judges
   - **c.** judges on the U.S. Court of Appeals
   - **d.** U.S. Supreme Court justices

2. Distinguish between judicial activism and judicial restraint. Did the Court's 2003 *Lawrence v. Texas* decision represent activism or restraint?

KEY TERMS

amicus curiae briefs (p. 250)
appellate jurisdiction (p. 243)
briefs (p. 250)
civil law (p. 232)
class action lawsuit (p. 242)
common law (p. 232)
complaint (p. 236)
concurring opinion (p. 251)

defendant (p. 236)
discovery (p. 236)
dissenting opinion (p. 251)
grand jury (p. 237)
indictment (p. 237)
judicial review (p. 239)
litigation (p. 236)
majority opinion (p. 251)

original jurisdiction (p. 243)
plaintiff (p. 236)
plea bargain (p. 237)
Solicitor General (p. 251)
standing (p. 242)
writ of certiorari (p. 249)

LEARNING OBJECTIVES

PUBLIC OPINION IN AMERICAN POLITICS

- Appraise the role that public opinion plays in American democracy and the policy-making process

HOW IS PUBLIC OPINION EXPRESSED?

- Compare and contrast the different ways in which public opinion may be expressed.

THE LEVELS OF PUBLIC OPINION

- Distinguish between the different levels of public opinion, from broad values and beliefs, to partisan and ideological orientations, to attitudes and opinions on specific items

HOW INFORMED IS PUBLIC OPINION?

- Assess the mass public's level of knowledge about American politics and the capacity of the public to contribute to the political process

HOW DOES PUBLIC OPINION FORM?

- Assess the political socialization process and identify the important factors (such as the family, schools, friends, religion) that contribute to the development of political opinions

HOW IS PUBLIC OPINION MEASURED?

- Differentiate between a scientific poll and an unscientific poll
- Apply the criteria for asking unbiased poll questions

INTERPRETING PUBLIC OPINION DATA

- Analyze the findings from a poll along the dimensions of direction, intensity, and stability of public opinion

For political leaders and citizens alike, the appetite for information on what the public thinks has always been hearty. Today, this appetite is fed through the large number of opinion polls whose results are disseminated through newspapers, magazines, television, radio, and the Internet. The methods of gauging public opinion have advanced quite dramatically over the nation's history, and this advancement has been driven in no small part by the obsession to know "what Americans think." The nation's democratic roots, featuring a commitment to majoritarian rule and the notion of "consent of the governed," raise public opinion to a lofty status in the workings of American politics. Indeed, the willingness of officials to heed the people's voice has become firmly entrenched in American political culture. A president's authority to govern is, in part, influenced by his standing in the polls. When public support is high, a president enjoys a great deal of persuasive power. When public support for the president is low, the nation's leader may be reduced to a weak lame duck with little or no power to influence American politics. Modern presidential candidates invest heavily in conducting significant numbers of public opinion polls throughout their election campaigns. Even when they are victorious, presidents continue to invest in conducting polls while in office. Scientific measurement of public opinion is a relatively recent phenomenon in American politics. But the significant role that public opinion plays in the formulation of policy is as old as American democracy itself. Understanding what public opinion is, how it is expressed, how it forms, and how it is measured in contemporary politics is critical to understanding how American government works.

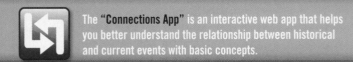

1975   1980   1985   1990   1995

1993–94

Then

President Bill Clinton

Source: Universal History Archive/Getty Images

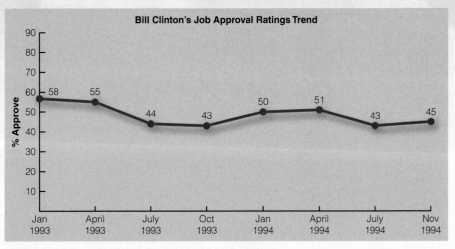

Bill Clinton's Job Approval Ratings Trend

Source: The Gallup Presidential Job Approval Center.

Public opinion concerning the president's job performance influences presidential power in significant ways. The higher the public approval, the more power the chief executive has to influence others within the political system, including Congress. Presidents generally begin their terms with high levels of public support. Certainly that was case with President Bill Clinton, when he first took office in January 1993. Clinton won the 1992 election with only 43% of the vote, but the first Gallup poll taken during his presidency measured public approval at 58%, 15 points higher than his vote total. The so-called "honeymoon period" for the young president, however, proved short-lived as partisan tensions exploded over Clinton's tax increase proposals and his ambitious plans for health care reform. By the summer of 1993, partisan outrage over the Clinton administration's tax increase (which passed) and his administration's controversial plans for health care reform effectively ended Clinton's honeymoon with the

public, as his approval dipped below the 50% mark for the first time. By the summer of 1994, Clinton's approval rating had stabilized in the 40 percent range, a rating which held through that year's November midterm elections. Clinton's low approval rating not only killed any possibility of health care reform; it also influenced the outcome of the 1994 midterm elections, as Republicans picked up 54 House seats and took control of that chamber for the first time in 30 years. It ushered in a period of divided government and political gridlock for the remainder of his first term in office.

2009–10

Now

President Barack Obama

Source: Pete Souza/Obama Transition Office via Getty Images

oneymoons between new presidents and the public are not uncommon. In 2009, the youthful new President Barack Obama, like Bill Clinton nearly two decades earlier, found himself riding high with impressive approval ratings during his initial days in office. Indeed, Obama managed a 69% public approval during this early period—17 points higher than the percentage of votes he

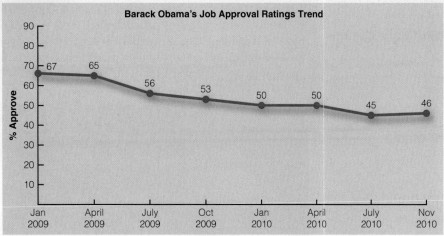

Barack Obama's Job Approval Ratings Trend

Source: The Gallup Presidential Job Approval Center.

had received in the November 2008 election. Obama's honeymoon with the also ended with the passing of his first year in office. Partisan wrangling over Obama's $787 billion stimulus spending plan and his own ambitious health care reform plans took its toll on Americans' opinion of their President throughout 2009. By the end of the year, the GOP had effectively tagged Obama's stimulus spending as a source for the rapidly exploding national debt. Controversy over the health care plan pushed

Obama's public approval down below the 50% mark for the first time in his presidency. By the summer of 2010, Obama's approval had stabilized in the low 40's. And by the November 2010 midterm elections, the drop in public support for Obama contributed heavily to the Republicans' 63-seat pickup in the House, giving the GOP control of that chamber, and helping to set the stage for partisan gridlock for the remaining two years of Obama's term.

PUBLIC OPINION IN AMERICAN POLITICS

The concept of public opinion is central to the American system of government. But the way in which public opinion is gauged and its relevance and uses in American politics has changed over the nation's history. The U.S. Constitution begins with the words "We the People," highlighting the important role of the *public* in the creation of the government. Nonetheless, there is no mention of the term *public opinion* in the Constitution. The word *democracy* literally translated (from its Greek roots *demos* and *kratos*) means "rule by the people," and thus the opinions of the public take on a particularly important role in governing. The American system of government was founded on a set of democratic principles, first articulated by Plato and Aristotle and later popularized by political philosophers of the eighteenth-century Enlightenment, such as Montesquieu.[1] These principles herald the role of the public in governing and in consenting to what government does.

From the time of the Founders up through the present day, the virtues of public opinion and its role in American democracy have been continually extolled. James Madison argued that the "public voice" and its formal role in voting provided primary justification for adopting the proposed Constitution. Borrowing from the political theories of John Locke, Madison acknowledged that government must serve the "will of the people." Andrew Jackson's presidency encouraged and empowered the rise of the "common man" to express his opinion for the purpose of influencing government.

Political leaders recognize that public opinion plays not only a theoretically important role in our democratic form of government, but an important tactical role as well. Political scientist E. E. Schattschneider, in an influential book titled *The Semisovereign People*, argued that "public opinion can emerge as a key factor in any political context," and that public opinion often is responsible for determining the outcome of important political battles. Long before Schattschneider, President Abraham Lincoln expressed this idea based on his own experiences, saying: "Public sentiment is everything. With public sentiment, nothing can fail; without it, nothing can succeed."[2]

Though most scholars, elected leaders, and everyday citizens would agree that **public opinion** is and should be very important in our system of government, the concept remains hard to define and measure. Many scholars regard public opinion as simply the summation of individual opinions on any particular issue or topic. Political scientist V. O. Key Jr., however, defined public

Protesters at an April 2006 rally in Washington, D.C., calling for American intervention to stop genocide in Darfur. Protests are an important expression of public opinion in the United States.

opinion more specifically as "those opinions held by private persons which government finds it prudent to heed." As an input in the American political system, public opinion must not only exist, Key argued, but it must also be "heeded" or at least heard by those making policy decisions.[3]

Public opinion is a vague, though important, concept. It is regularly used by presidents to justify their policies, by political candidates to mount campaigns, by interest groups to promote their causes, by journalists to describe public preferences, and by scholars to understand the American government. Today opinion polls—for better or worse—have become the yardstick through which public opinion is understood and evaluated. The barrage of polls released daily by major media organizations provides a plethora of data describing the American psyche. There are, however, numerous practices in addition to polling through which public opinion in America may be expressed.

HOW IS PUBLIC OPINION EXPRESSED?

The formal constitutional mechanism by which public opinion influences the federal government is the free, open, and regular election of House members. Since ratification of the Seventeenth Amendment in 1913, the direct election of U.S. senators has served as yet another constitutional means for the expression of public opinion. Chapter 14 covers this form of expressing public opinion in detail. Voting is one important expression of public opinion and provides guarantees that officials are responsive to voters. In many state and local elections, voters are asked to respond to referendum questions, which empower the public to directly resolve policy issues. But there are a number of additional ways beyond voting in which public opinion has an influence on government. The First Amendment's guarantees that the people have the right to free speech, to peaceably assemble, and to petition their government pave the way for political rallies and protest rallies, which are important manifestations of public opinion.

Supporting a candidate and engaging in attempts to elect an individual or political party to office through a monetary contribution or a contribution of time and effort is another way that public opinion is expressed. Likewise, contributing time or money to an interest group or political action committee enables individuals to express their opinion indirectly and may have a significant impact on what government does.

Public opinion is also expressed through the news media. Journalists often provide commentary on politics and public issues through talk radio shows, Web sites, editorial pages, and

Blogs have become an important medium through which many Americans express their political opinions. Pictured here is "The Daily Kos," a popular blog that many left-leaning ideologues use to express how they feel.

television news talk shows that provide perspectives on public opinion. Individual citizens may also use the media to express their opinion, by writing letters to the editor. In addition, members of the public often choose to express their opinion directly to elected officials by contacting them, via either a letter or e-mail, a phone call, or the Internet, for their views on a particular issue. Though many politically aware Americans still express their opinions on politics in these "traditional" ways, millions of others now take advantage of their laptops and smartphones to post comments on "blogs." Blogs vary widely in form, but most feature some form of personal commentary, references to data, and links to other sources on the Internet related to a topic of political discussion. Most bloggers don't aspire to the goal of providing "objective" commentary. Rather, they aim to provide up-to-date, personal, and often partisan perspectives on current political topics. Many liberals tend to flock to more left-leaning blogs such as *The Daily Kos* and *Talking Points Memo*, whereas conservatives frequent conservative blog sites, such as *Powerline* or the blog of conservative author Michelle Makin.

Perhaps the most visible and widely used expression of public opinion in contemporary politics is the public opinion poll. Most major and many smaller media organizations today regularly conduct polls on politics and policy issues, and publish the results of those polls in the form of news stories. The *USA Today*/Gallup Poll, the CBS/*New York Times* poll, the Fox News/Opinion Dynamics poll, and the NBC/*Wall Street Journal* poll are only a few examples of media-based polls that, on a regular basis, provide data on American public opinion.

values and beliefs: The broad principles underlying the American political culture that citizens support and adhere to.

Kindergarten students in a Maryland classroom learn to appreciate the values associated with the American flag.

Mark Wilson/Getty Images

THE LEVELS OF PUBLIC OPINION

Public opinion exists at three basic levels—the broad level of values and beliefs, an intermediate level of political orientations, and the specific level of preferences about particular topics.

Values and Beliefs

At the highest, most abstract level are the **values and beliefs** of the American people. Values are the broad principles underlying the American political culture that most citizens support and adhere to; they represent that which people find most important in life. Beliefs are the facts derived from values that people take for granted about the world. Although there are a number of values that Americans hold dear, political scientist Samuel Huntington[4] has identified four politically relevant values that are widely accepted in the American political culture and serve as the basis for defining political beliefs on which there is great consensus in America: liberty, equality, individualism, and the rule of law.

The vast majority of Americans support the idea of basic freedoms and liberties, such as freedom of religion and freedom of speech. These liberties are embedded in our political culture and serve as the basis for many government policies. Because Americans value liberty, for example, they believe that people should have the right to choose a religion or not to choose a religion, the right to publicly disagree with the president or the party in power, and the right to publish articles or news stories without government retribution.

Likewise, a majority of Americans firmly values the concept stated in the Declaration of Independence that "all men are created equal." Regardless of economic status, race, or gender, the American public on the whole subscribes to the belief that all people should be treated equally under the law and that all people should have equal opportunities for economic success.

Americans also show a strong propensity to support the value of individualism. Over the years, Americans have consistently shown a preference for rewarding individual hard work and for limiting the role of government.[5] Jefferson's maxim that "that government is best which governs the least" presumes that society will advance by encouraging individuals to succeed and leads to a belief in capitalism and free enterprise as the optimal economic system. Also, the Puritan work ethic that served as an important value in early American society continues to be reflected in Americans' affinity for the value of individualism.

Finally, the value of the "rule of law" encourages a strong belief in the legitimacy of the U.S. Constitution, in the importance of elections as a way to configure government, and in the beliefs that the opinion of the majority should prevail, that those in the minority should have the right to challenge the majority, and that those accused of a crime should be entitled to fair procedures.

Unlike other levels of public opinion, values and beliefs are unique in that they generally receive a high level of support and consensus. Whether individuals are Democrats or Republicans, from the far right or the far left, elites or more representative of the masses—the vast majority generally subscribes to these broad values. Accordingly, values are the level of public opinion that define our political culture; widespread agreement and support for them is thus critical to the maintenance of the American political system.

Political Orientations

Values and beliefs are very broad and abstract notions held by Americans that provide general guidance to people in thinking about politics. **Political orientations** are the translation of these values and beliefs into a systematic way of assessing the political environment. Although there may be broad consensus about values and beliefs among Americans, the translation of these values into an organized way of thinking about politics and issues is considerably more varied.

The two primary ways in which Americans orient themselves toward political topics and issues are partisanship (see Figure 10.1) and political ideology. Partisanship, which is discussed

political orientations: The translation of values and beliefs into a systematic way of assessing the political environment.

FIGURE 10.1 **Partisanship in America**

Source: http://www.people-press.org/party-identification-trend/

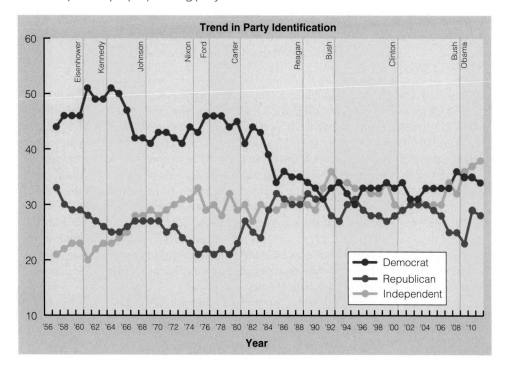

in a later chapter, features a psychological attachment to one of the main political parties, generally either the Democrats or the Republicans.[6] A partisan identification provides an orientational mechanism for understanding how to apply one's values and beliefs to the political world. Consider, for example, the political debate over affirmative action policies. A Democratic orientation largely applies the value of equality and the belief that people of all races and creeds should enjoy equal opportunities, therefore suggesting support for affirmative action programs, which attempt to level the playing field and make corrections for policies that have historically benefited white males. A Republican orientation, on the other hand, generally places a higher priority on the value of individualism and the belief that government should not interfere with individual initiatives to succeed, thus suggesting opposition to affirmative action programs. Partisan orientation often helps people translate values into specific opinions.

Likewise, political ideology provides an orientation for translating values into specific opinions. **Political ideology** is a philosophical guide that people use to help translate their values and beliefs into specific political preferences. The dominant ideologies in America are liberalism and conservatism. The contemporary **liberal ideology**, which is more closely associated with the modern Democratic Party, prefers that government take a more assertive role in the redistribution of economic resources, but that government advocate positions that emphasize individual freedom on a range of social issues. Today's **conservative ideology**, which is more closely identified with the Republican Party, favors government activism in defense of more traditional values on social issues, but prefers government restraint in economic redistribution.

The liberal and conservative camps largely agree on the basic values and beliefs of the American political culture—in the rule of law and majority rule and minority rights and in the idea that the free enterprise system will generally guarantee the most robust economy. But liberals and conservatives often differ when seeking to translate these values and beliefs into actual policies.

Partisanship and political ideology are two very important topics in the study of American public opinion. They provide a framework for individuals to translate broad values and beliefs into preferences for issue positions and political candidates. These orientations help people to efficiently form opinions and express those opinions. Partisanship and political ideology also enable both political leaders and scholars to better understand why Americans think what they think about particular issues and vote the way they vote in elections.

The political orientations of Americans tend to be quite stable and lasting[7]—more so than the specific preferences that people have toward policies and political actors. The stability in American political orientations provides an order and consistency to American public opinion, which ultimately promotes stability in the political system as a whole.

Political Preferences

The most discussed level of public opinion is the particular **political preferences** that Americans have on policy issues, their attitudes regarding the performance of political leaders and institutions, and their candidate preferences in elections. Support for the minimum wage, gun control proposals, the use of U.S. troops in fighting terrorism, abortion policy, campaign finance reform proposals, tax increases, or tax cuts are all specific policy issues on which the American public expresses opinions. In addition to policies, Americans also hold specific opinions about the performance of their elected leaders such as the president, as well as their confidence in institutions such as Congress, the U.S. Supreme Court, and the military.

What Americans think about the minimum wage, the performance of the president, or the candidates in a political campaign is highly influenced by their political orientations. For example, an individual who identifies as a Republican and considers herself ideologically conservative is much less likely to say she approves of President Obama's performance than would a Democrat who considers himself to be liberal.

Figure 10.2 depicts public opinion on two preference questions that have experienced considerable change in the recent past: attitudes about gay marriage (for which public support has increased) and the percentage saying that the most important problem in America relates to economic conditions (which spiked from late 2007 through 2009 during the recession).

---

political ideology: A philosophical guide that people use to help translate their values and beliefs into political preferences.

liberal ideology: A political orientation that favors a more assertive role in the redistribution of economic resources, but emphasizes individual freedom on a range of social issues.

conservative ideology: A political orientation that generally favors government activism in defense of more traditional values on social issues, but favors government restraint in economic redistribution.

political preferences: The attitudes people maintain regarding the performance of political leaders and institutions, their candidate preferences in elections, and specific policy issues.

Fact or Fiction?

Public support and opposition for gay marriage have remained equally divided over the past 15 years.

Fiction.

Fifteen years ago, opposition to gay marriage was significant. However, today a majority of Americans supports gay marriage.

FIGURE 10.2 Preferences of Americans

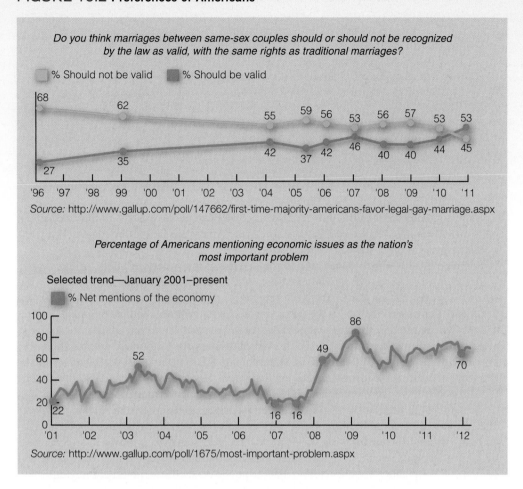

Do you think marriages between same-sex couples should or should not be recognized by the law as valid, with the same rights as traditional marriages?

□ % Should not be valid   ■ % Should be valid

Source: http://www.gallup.com/poll/147662/first-time-majority-americans-favor-legal-gay-marriage.aspx

Percentage of Americans mentioning economic issues as the nation's most important problem

Selected trend—January 2001–present

■ % Net mentions of the economy

Source: http://www.gallup.com/poll/1675/most-important-problem.aspx

HOW INFORMED IS PUBLIC OPINION?

As discussed earlier in this chapter, American democracy relies on public opinion to choose leaders and inform public policy. This reliance is based on an important assumption about democracy—that citizens have the necessary information and skills to be able to understand political issues and provide informed input. Since the time of Plato and Aristotle, political philosophers have dealt with questions about this important assumption: is the public capable of democracy?

In the Federalist Papers, Alexander Hamilton and James Madison expressed concerns about the fickleness of public opinion and the potential "tyranny of the masses," which could lead to instability in governance.[8] Hamilton's solution for this problem was a republican form of government, in which the public chooses leaders who run the government, rather than a direct democracy, in which the public rules directly.

Suspicions about the capacity of the public for meaningful contributions to governance were also articulated quite well by Walter Lippman in the early twentieth century.[9] Lippman, a well-known public opinion scholar, delivered withering attacks on ordinary citizens' lack of knowledge regarding politics. He argued that citizens invest very little energy and effort in acquiring information about politics, and as a consequence, the public lacks the necessary knowledge for their opinions to provide value. Subsequent research in the 1960s and 1970s, most notably by Philip Converse and his colleagues in *The American Voter*, used scientific surveys to support the argument that ordinary citizens tend to be ill-informed about political issues, ill-equipped to understand politics, and quite fickle in how they stand on issues.[10]

FIGURE 10.3 American Lack of Political Knowledge

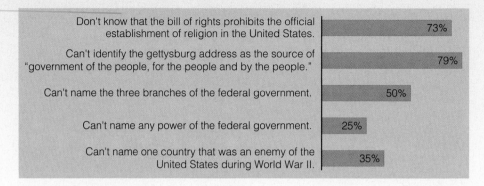

More contemporary studies indicate that the American public today is uninformed about politics. For example, Figure 10.3 depicts how many Americans lack knowledge on some important aspects of the American political system:[11]

Some political scientists have come to the defense of the American public in this regard. V. O. Key Jr., in his work *The Responsible Electorate*,[12] stated that although "many voters act in odd ways indeed," if one studies the electorate more carefully one would find that "voters are not fools." Key observed that "in the large, the electorate behaves about as rationally and responsibly as we should expect, given the clarity of the alternatives presented to it and the character of the information available to it." If political leaders don't rationally discuss issues and provide a framework for voters to use to understand politics, it is not the voters who should be blamed, but rather the leaders. Considering this caveat, Key extolled the capacity of the public to form stable, responsible opinions and to contribute to the governing process.

Benjamin Page and Robert Shapiro extended Key's ideas in their book *The Rational Public*.[13] They used decades of public opinion poll data to show that over the long haul, public opinion on many issues does remain fairly stable, and when it does change, it moves in logical directions. The aggregate responses of the public in polls, Page and Shapiro found, make sense and demonstrate rationality. They also found that the public makes distinctions between important policy areas and that public opinion tends to form meaningful patterns, consistent with a set of underlying beliefs and values.

The link between public opinion on an issue and public policy is a difficult one to establish. Page and Shapiro report that over the long haul, there does seem to be a relationship between public attitudes on policy issues and the public policies that emerge from government. These researchers also argue that when public opinion shifts, a corresponding shift in public policy is likely to follow.

Political scientist Samuel Kernell has noted a more indirect link between public opinion and public policy:[14] political actors (most notably the president) who have high levels of public support are generally better able to get legislation passed. President Bush, for example, in 2003 was able to get Congress to pass a new tax cut package in part because of the high job performance ratings Americans gave him at that time. High levels of public support may be translated into an officeholder's greater political power to influence the legislative process.

HOW DOES PUBLIC OPINION FORM?

Through voting, opinion polls, protest rallies, communications with leaders, and newspaper editorials, public opinion is expressed and provides an important input for public policymaking. But how do individuals develop their particular political orientations, and how do they come to hold their specific political preferences? How do the more deep-seated values and beliefs form? What influences the values that people hold, their partisan and ideological orientations, and their opinions on specific issues?

Political socialization is the process by which an individual acquires values, beliefs, and opinions about politics. Political socialization is a lifelong process, beginning in early childhood and continuing throughout an individual's life. The learning process that leads to the

political socialization: The process by which an individual acquires values, beliefs, and opinions about politics.

acquisition of values and opinions not only applies to politics—it also applies to other orientations of people, including their beliefs about religion and culture.

Just as there are a number of factors and influences that lead individuals to consider themselves Democrats or Republicans or supporters of gun control or gun rights, there are also numerous factors and influences that lead people to choose a particular religion, such as Protestant or Catholic, or to choose no religion at all. Socialization is important not only in the development of political learning for individuals, but also in the transmission of the fundamental beliefs and values of the American political culture from one generation to the next.

Though political socialization is a lifelong process, there are certain times in life when political learning is greater. For example, the political socialization that occurs early in life has a more profound impact on political orientations than learning that occurs in adulthood. The impressions and information that are acquired while the individual is younger tend to be most influential and the longest lasting. Psychologists refer to this as the **primacy tendency**.

Though early political learning tends to be most profound, socialization to politics remains at work through a number of influences over the course of a person's life. A number of factors and institutions, known as **agents of political socialization**,[15] have been identified as having a particularly relevant impact on one's socialization to politics.

Certainly demographic factors such as race, ethnicity, gender, age, and economic status go a long way toward defining individuals' identities, and can influence their political values. But a list of the most important agents of political socialization also includes such influences as family, friends and peer groups, schools, the media, and religion. Collectively, these agents promote the acquisition of the political values, beliefs, and opinions that an individual comes to hold.

primacy tendency: The theory that impressions acquired while an individual is younger are likely to be more influential and longer lasting.

agents of political socialization: Factors that have a significant impact on an individual's socialization to politics.

Family

Because much of the early years in a person's life is dominated by experiences with the family, the primacy tendency leads many to develop values and beliefs consistent with parents' values and beliefs. Parents begin to teach their children about the political world early in the child's life. They transfer feelings about such concepts as authority, freedom, democracy, and racial prejudice to their children in both formal and informal ways. By standing at attention during the playing of the national anthem or attending a Memorial Day service, parents are informally communicating important values about politics. Telling children that skin color should not affect how to think about a particular person or explaining why it is important to vote in an election are formal ways political information is communicated.

These early formal and informal cues from parents have a long-term and lasting impact on a child's political socialization. Over the years, researchers have found that children whose parents are more involved in politics tend to be more involved in politics themselves. The transference of party identification from parent to child is also significant. Children who grew up in homes where parents regard politics as important also tend to regard politics as important throughout their lives. Because children generally want to be like their parents, the many cues, both formal and informal, that they receive from their parents are a strong influence on the formation of political orientation.

Parents provide an important influence in socializing their children to appreciate American political values. Above, a father teaches his son to appreciate the values associated with Independence Day.

Friends and Peer Groups

As children grow older, they begin to interact with people outside of their immediate family. They seek friendships with others and show a desire to get along in social groups. Children acquire a great deal of new political learning through their friends and associates, as well as from the social groups that they seek to join. Often, the values, beliefs, and opinions of social peers are the same as or similar to those of the family, so friends and peers reinforce what was learned from parents. For example, wealthy people tend to live together in particular neighborhoods, and so as children from wealthy families find friends and peers, they are likely to find people who have been socialized by their parents in ways similar to themselves.

By the fifth or sixth grade, children become cognitively equipped to better understand the world of politics. Whereas previous learning tends to be based on unquestioned acceptance of what is being communicated, young adults have the ability to critically analyze new information. This cognitive skill development comes at a time in life (young adolescence) when friends and peer groups are particularly influential. Thus the desire to get along and to form social relationships has an important influence on political learning at this point in life.

The Schools

Part of the curriculum in many school systems across the United States focuses on the development of political values, such as respect for authority, the legitimacy of our political institutions, patriotism, and capitalism. Classes in civic education and American government, the daily morning pledge of allegiance to the flag, and pictures of American presidents are just some of the mechanisms by which schools act as an agent of socialization.

Schools serve as an important mechanism for the positive development of attitudes about basic American democratic values, thus promoting general positive attitudes about the legitimacy of the democratic system. Research conducted by David Easton and his colleagues in the 1950s and 1960s demonstrated that schools promoted a positive affective attachment to the concept of "democracy" by the third grade.[16] During the early grades, children acquire beliefs regarding a citizen's role in politics—obeying laws, voting, and paying attention to political events.

Political socialization from the school is not limited to elementary and high school. The college experience also has an important socializing effect on citizens' political development. College graduates tend to be more likely to vote and participate in politics, they are more

High schools, such as this one in Austin, Texas, help to teach the values of the democratic process by providing mock trials in which students learn how our legal system works.

likely to follow news and political campaigns, and they are better able to understand the political world in which they live. The effects of formal education, even beyond the specific civics education curriculum of the earlier grades, make an important positive contribution to an individual's political socialization.

The Media

Americans spend a great deal of time accessing news information and being entertained by the mass media. It is not surprising, then, that the media act as an important agent of political socialization as well. Information that citizens glean from media news coverage about political events and political campaigns has an impact on their values, beliefs, and opinions. Research has shown that heavy users of the news media are more politically informed than lighter users;[17] they are also more supportive of basic American values, such as individualism, equality, and free speech rights.

Stephen Colbert, of TV's popular Colbert Report, *uses the medium of cable television to provide political humor.*

Associated Press

The media's impact as a socialization agent extends beyond the provision of news information. Entertainment television, the movies, talk radio, and other media forms also inspire various types of political learning. Studies have shown, for example, that entertainment television tends to promote negative stereotypes of women and minorities, which may reinforce negative attitudes about race or affirmative action. Use of Internet Web sites and blogs may also help shape a person's political outlook.

Religion

Throughout American history, religious organizations have played an important role in the political socialization process. The values of individualism and hard work were important influences in establishing a capitalist economy and continue to underpin economic policy in the United States. These values, based on the Protestant work ethic, continue to influence the socialization process. More recently, the Christian-based fundamentalist movement has utilized religious teaching to influence opinions about political issues. The Catholic Church's opposition to abortion affects many Catholics' position on that issue.

How Is Public Opinion Measured?

When Americans think about the term *public opinion* in contemporary politics, they often focus on the results of public opinion polls. A **public opinion poll** is a method of measuring the opinions of a large group of people by selecting a subset of the larger group, asking them a set of questions, and generalizing the findings to the larger group.

Public opinion polls are not the only way that public opinion in America is either expressed or understood, but polls have become the most obvious and important instrument for gauging public opinion. Polls provide information that elected leaders use in making public policy, thus providing an important way for public sentiment to influence public policy. Polls have also become a centerpiece of elections, used both by the candidates to shape a winning strategy and by journalists to provide news coverage of campaigns.

Polling has become a huge industry in the United States. To the public, the most visible polls are those that are regularly conducted by media organizations, asking Americans what they think about a variety of topics, such as whom they plan to vote for in an upcoming election, how they rate the job the president is doing, how they feel about the condition of the economy, and many other topics. Media polls are conducted with the purpose of broadcasting results as

public opinion poll: A method of measuring the opinions of a large group of people by asking questions of a subset of the larger group and then generalizing the findings to the larger group.

news stories. However, the polling industry extends far beyond media polls. Candidates at all levels conduct polls to identify strategies for waging a successful election campaign. Federal, state, and local government agencies conduct polls to evaluate the successes and failures of public programs. Interest groups conduct polls to promote their agendas.

Even though polls have come to play an important and visible role in American politics, the manner in which they are conducted is often misunderstood, and questions about their accuracy are often raised. What makes a poll "scientific"? How is it possible to interview 1,000 Americans and conclude how more than 200 million Americans think? How can two polls be conducted on the same topic and produce different findings? An understanding of polling techniques can help answer these questions.

The History of Political Polling

The immediate predecessor to modern scientific polling in the United States dates back to the 1824 presidential campaign. Newspapers such as the *Boston Globe*, *New York Herald*, and *Harrisburg Pennsylvanian* attempted to gauge voter attitudes about the presidential candidates and predict the election outcome that year by conducting what has come to be known as the **straw poll**. A straw poll gathers the opinions of people who are conveniently available in a particular gathering place. (Today, many refer to these polls as "convenience" polls.) Back in 1824, the newspapers sent "counters" to public places (such as taverns and public meetings) to ask patrons and attendees whom they planned to vote for in the upcoming election. Newspaper publishers quickly found a hearty appetite among readers for stories that attempted to predict the outcome of political races—an appetite modern media executives continue to find quite strong today.

Early straw polls assumed that the accuracy of polls was based on the total number of respondents included in each poll. The larger the number of respondents, the more accurate the results, so it was thought. Straw polls remained the basic methodology for conducting polls for more than a century.[18]

By the early 1930s, the most famous national straw poll was the *Literary Digest* poll. In addition to conducting straw polls on policy issues, this poll correctly predicted the winners of the 1920, 1924, 1928, and 1932 presidential elections. The *Literary Digest* conducted its polls by mailing ballots to millions of people. Mailing addresses were obtained from the *Digest*'s own readership lists as well as telephone directories and automobile registration lists. The *Digest* assumed its accuracy in predicting election outcomes was based on the large number of ballots that it counted from voters across the country.

In the 1936 election between Franklin Roosevelt and Alfred Landon, the *Literary Digest* collected ballots from more than 2 million people and confidently predicted that Landon would receive 55 percent of the vote, Roosevelt would get 41 percent, and the remaining 4 percent would go to Union Party candidate William Lemke. The actual election results stunned the *Literary Digest* and its many readers. Roosevelt won the election with a whopping 61 percent of the popular vote. Landon garnered 36.5 percent, whereas Lemke won less than 2 percent. The missed projection put the *Literary Digest* out of business.

This widely publicized missed call by the *Literary Digest* is explained by the faulty assumption of the straw-poll methodology—the assumption that the greater the number of respondents, the more accurate the poll. The number of interviews in a poll is only one of a number of factors that affect poll accuracy. In 1936, the United States was still fighting the effects of the Great Depression, when many Americans had difficulty making ends meet. Those Americans with telephones, automobiles, and subscriptions to the *Literary Digest* (the sources of the mailing addresses for the ballots) tended to be wealthier, less affected by the Depression, and disproportionately less likely to support the liberal economic policies of FDR's New Deal.

At the time, the *Literary Digest* debacle was aptly explained by several researchers who had already begun to conduct polls with more accurate methodologies. Chief among these was Dr. George Gallup, who was applying probability sampling methods to the polls he conducted. During the 1936 campaign, Gallup argued that the *Literary Digest* methodology was producing faulty results. His cries fell on many deaf ears until after the election, when his advice sowed the seeds for a healthy polling industry based on more scientific methods. However,

THE MORE THINGS CHANGE, THE MORE THEY STAY THE SAME

Polling Problems in Presidential Elections

"Dewey Defeats Truman"? "Gore Defeats Bush"? Not so, as it turned out. Still, that didn't stop public opinion pollsters from convincing many in the media that Thomas Dewey would be elected president in 1948, and that Al Gore would be the winner in 2000. More than 50 years apart, the polls played an important role in two predictions that caused considerable confusion. Then, in 2008, the pollsters struck again. . . .

In 1948, polls leading up to Election Day predicted that New York Governor Thomas Dewey would soundly defeat President Harry S Truman. The Gallup Poll, the Roper Poll, and other opinion polling organizations consistently found Dewey ahead throughout much of the fall campaign. The scientific sampling methods they employed had been used by these same organizations in successfully calling the winner of every presidential race since 1936. The problem? All the major pollsters stopped their preelection polling at least two weeks before Election Day. In fact, Dewey did maintain a large lead throughout the campaign, a lead that had not changed up through mid-October. So the pollsters

The polls projected Thomas Dewey would defeat President Harry Truman in 1948. The polls were wrong, but they led many newspapers across the country to prematurely project Truman's defeat as they went to press.

just stopped polling. Then, in the final weeks of the campaign, Truman's furious and aggressive campaign schedule began to make a difference, and voter opinions began to shift in favor of the incumbent president. Yet the pollsters didn't pick up these changes. Thus their confident prediction that Dewey would win proved wrong, and the *Chicago Daily Tribune* became famous for running the presses with its premature headline: "Dewey Defeats Truman."

In 2000, the presidential election between Republican George W. Bush and Democrat Al Gore proved once again the pollsters could be fallible. In the last few weeks of the campaign, many respected polling organizations showed a tight race between the two candidates. The Voter News Service (VNS), a company that conducted polls of voters almost immediately after they exited voting booths (aptly termed "exit polls"), was supported in 2000 by ABC, CBS, NBC, CNN, Fox, and the Associated Press. On Election Day that year, VNS conducted exit polls in each of the 50 states as a way of predicting the winner in each state, thus facilitating an accurate prediction of the electoral college outcome. For each of the 50 states in the previous seven presidential elections, network exit polling correctly predicted the presidential winners. When the polls in Florida closed at 8 PM, VNS began tabulating its results, including its results in Florida, and sent the results to the media organizations that supported VNS. Based on the Florida exit poll data, the networks declared Gore the winner in Florida, which gave him enough electoral college votes to win the election. Unfortunately, Florida was so close, and balloting was so complicated in that state, that the exit-poll call was problematic. The flawed exit-poll prediction complicated an already confusing election night for the television networks. It would take more than five weeks after Election Day, and a U.S. Supreme Court decision, to declare George W. Bush the winner in Florida, and thus the winner of the presidential election.

In 2008, preelection pollsters struggled to accurately project the outcome of several Democratic Party primaries. Most notable were the polls associated with the New Hampshire primary. *USA Today*/Gallup, CBS,

(Continued)

THE MORE THINGS CHANGE,
THE MORE THEY STAY THE SAME

Polling Problems in Presidential Elections (continued)

Fox, and a number of other organizations conducting polls in New Hampshire all concluded that Barack Obama would win the Democratic primary. Some of the polls indicated that Obama would defeat Hillary Clinton by more than 10 points. The nation and particularly the pollsters were surprised to find on election night that Clinton had defeated Obama. Clinton's surprise win in the nation's first primary came days after Obama's defeat of Clinton in the first caucus in Iowa and helped fuel a long and bitter battle for the Democratic presidential nomination.

For Critical Thinking and Discussion

1. Polls, for the most part, have been quite successful in predicting the outcome of elections, despite the snafus just listed. Do you think that these highly visible, though infrequent, instances of incorrect poll projections should make journalists more cautious in relying on polls to report on any particular race?

2. The publication of poll results in the days before an election is often criticized because some say that voters are influenced to vote for the "leader" in the poll—the so-called 'bandwagon effect. Do you think that there is any merit to this criticism?

his scientific methods of polling would quickly become adopted as standards of the polling industry in the decades to come. Figure 10.4 shows the remarkable accuracy of the Gallup Poll in predicting winners of presidential elections over the past eight decades.

Scientific Sampling

The polling procedures popularized by Gallup in the aftermath of the 1936 election relied on the principles of probability theory, and focused on the sampling of the population under study.[19] A *sample* is a subgroup of people from a population who are studied for the purpose of learning something about the whole population. Based on the laws of probability, it is possible to draw a sample from a population, administer a set of questions to those in the sample, and understand something about the entire population, within a known level of error.

A **scientific sample** is one that uses probability theory as a guide to selecting people from the population who will compose the sample. Random selection of respondents in the sample is key to achieving a scientific, or representative, sample. *Random sampling* is achieved by giving each possible respondent in the population a known chance of being selected in the sample. There are a number of ways of achieving a random sample.

Unscientific Polls

In a scientific poll, the results of the poll are generalizable to a population that is represented by the sample of people who are interviewed. **Unscientific polls** differ from scientific ones in that the sample of people who are interviewed is not representative of any group beyond those who register their opinion. There

An NBC News exit pollster interviews a voter shortly after she casts her ballot. Exit polls allow the networks to project winners and losers before the polls close.

Billy E. Barnes/PhotoEdit

FIGURE 10.4 Accuracy of the Gallup Poll in Predicting Voter Behavior

Preelection polls offer candidates, journalists, and voters detailed information on the dynamics of an election contest. How well the polls actually predict vote choices is a frequently voiced concern. One of the best-known opinion polls in the United States is the Gallup Poll, which has been conducting preelection polls since the 1936 presidential election. This figure shows Gallup's prediction for the percentage of the vote that the winner would receive in each presidential election from 1936 to the present, along with the actual percentage of the vote that the winner got on Election Day. Gallup made incorrect predictions of the winner in two elections—in 1948, it predicted that Dewey would defeat Truman and in 2012 it predicted Romney would defeat Obama.

Source: The Gallup Organization. © 1936–2012 The Gallup Organization

scientific sample: A randomly selected subgroup drawn from a population using probability theory.

unscientific poll: A poll in which the sample of people interviewed is not representative of any group beyond those who register their opinion.

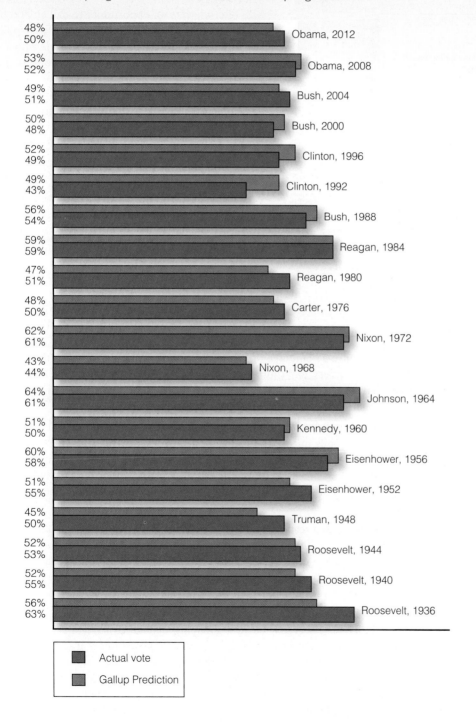

■	Actual vote
■	Gallup Prediction

Fact or Fiction?

The Gallup Poll has correctly predicted the winner of every presidential election contest since its first projection in 1936 that Franklin D. Roosevelt would defeat Alf Landon.

Fiction.

Although the Gallup Poll has an impressive record of predicting elections, it erred in 1948 when it predicted that Thomas Dewey would defeat Harry Truman. This has been the only Gallup "missed call" in a presidential election since 1936.

An unscientific poll as it appears to those who visit CNN's Web site.

CNN

are many examples of unscientific polls in politics. What makes a poll unscientific is the way respondents are selected for the sample. If the vast majority of people in a population are given a chance of being sampled, then the poll is scientific. If not, then the sample represents nothing beyond itself. In an unscientific sample, some individuals in the population have no chance of being included. Many unscientific polls are conducted even today. A good example is the television call-in poll. Often television news shows that deal with political topics will offer viewers an opportunity to call an 800 or 900 number to answer a poll question. These polls are unscientific because only those people who are viewing the show have an opportunity to respond. E-mail surveys conducted by CNN.com and ESPN.com are similarly unscientific surveys. The sample of people who call in is not representative of any group beyond the callers themselves. Other examples of unscientific polls include the following:

- **Log-in polls.** A poll question pops up as you enter your computer's Web browser with the question: Do you think Sarah Palin would make a good president? Click here for "yes" or click here for "no." Many services, such as Yahoo!, Netscape, and MSN, include questions such as these on their home page, and then present a tally of the results. This type of poll is an unscientific one, because only those people who click on the browser and decide to take the time to answer the question have their opinion registered.

Those who don't have a computer (for example, poorer and older people), those who don't have Internet access, and those who are less interested in politics have no chance or far fewer chances of being selected for such a poll. The results of those polls represent nothing more than the people who answer the question.

- **SLOPs, or self-selected listener opinion polls.** Television and radio news/talk shows sometimes conduct polls during the course of a broadcast by offering an 800 or 900 phone number for registered listeners to call and express their opinion on some topic. SLOPs are also known as "call-in" polls. These polls are unscientific because only those people who happen to be tuned in to the broadcast have any opportunity to be included in the sample.

- **CRAPs, or computerized response audience polling.** This kind of poll is often used by local news organizations. Telecommunications equipment places a call, and automated voice systems ask the poll questions. Respondents are asked to use the keypad of their telephone to register their answers to the questions. The extremely high rate of refusal (for example, most people hang up when they hear the automated voice) renders them highly unscientific.

- **Intercept polls**. Have you ever been in a shopping mall when someone with a clipboard comes up to you and asks if you would answer some questions? If so, you've been solicited to participate in an intercept poll (that is, an interviewer "intercepted" you). Respondents in such polls are conveniently selected into the sample because they are spotted by the interviewer. Because people who are at shopping malls or other public places are not representative of all people, this is regarded as an unscientific type of poll.

The *Literary Digest* mishap highlights the problem with unscientific samples—those people who have no chance of being included in the sample may be very different from those who are included. Voters who had no car or published telephone number had no chance of being selected in the *Literary Digest* sample described earlier. Even though the total number of people in the sample was quite high (more than 2 million), it was not representative of the population of voters because less-well-off people had little to no chance of being included in the sample. Today's reliance on telephone surveys to gauge public opinion has come under attack on the basis that cell phone numbers are not sampled and thus systematically exclude younger Americans from the sampling (because younger people are more likely to rely on cell phones).

Pseudo-Polls

Recently, some unscrupulous political campaigns and political action committees (PACs) have been disguising themselves as pollsters for the purpose of planting messages with voters, rather than measuring public opinion. Some of these campaigns or PACs present themselves as pollsters for the purpose of fundraising as well. These phone calls have come to be known as **pseudo-polls**. As the term implies, there is no polling going on with a pseudo-poll. Pretending to be pollsters, callers often contact tens of thousands of voters and ask hypothetical (that is, untrue) questions about their political opponents—such as "Did you happen to know that John Smith is reported to have beaten his wife in the past—does this make you any less likely to support him in his race for senator?" Respondents to the call believe they are being interviewed by a legitimate polling firm and take away from the conversation a contrived and false message about a political candidate. This type of pseudo-poll is called a "push poll," because the intention of the call is to "push," or influence, people to vote a particular way.

Another type of pseudo-poll is referred to as "FRUGing," or fundraising under the guise of polling. This is an unethical practice that tricks people into thinking they are being polled by a legitimate organization, when they are really being set up for a fundraising attempt. "SUGing," or selling under the guise of polling, is a pseudo-poll that engages in telemarketing. The individual—who will ultimately receive a sales pitch at the end of the call—believes that she or he is answering a legitimate poll.

pseudo-poll: Phone calls from members of political campaigns or PACs who present themselves as pollsters for the purpose of planting messages with voters rather than measuring public opinion.

Sample Size

A fundamental characteristic of a scientific public opinion poll is the nature of the procedures used to draw a sample from the population. The size of the sample is also a factor in poll quality. **Sampling error** is the term used to indicate the amount of error in the poll that results from interviewing a sample of people rather than the whole population under study. Sampling error is largely a function of sample size: the larger the sample size, the less sampling error with the poll. However, there is a law of diminishing returns associated with increasing the size of the sample.

For example, a national scientifically drawn sample of two hundred Americans has a sampling error of about $+/-7$ percent at the 95 percent level of confidence. This means that with a sample of 200, chances are 95 in 100 that the sample will produce results within 7 points above or below the survey result. By increasing the sample size by 400 respondents, from 200 to 600, the sampling error is reduced to $+/-4$ percent. An additional 600 respondents in the sample, bringing the sample size to 1,200, reduces the sampling error to $+/-3$ percent.

Media organizations that report poll findings often attempt to convey information about the poll to help the reader/audience understand the sampling error associated with the results. Typically, a news report on a poll will include a statement like this: "The survey was conducted by telephone with a random sample of 1,200 American adults. Sampling error for the survey is $+/-3$ percent at the 95 percent level of confidence."

What does this statement mean? Suppose the poll found that 60 percent of the respondents approved of the job that Barack Obama was doing as president. The statement indicates that

sampling error: The amount of error in a poll that results from interviewing a sample of people rather than the whole population under study; the larger the sample, the less the sampling error.

random-digit dialing (RDD): A probability technique for scientific telephone polling that randomly assigns the last four digits to known information about telephone area codes and exchanges.

there was a "random sample" of American adults. This means that the poll was a scientific poll, and the results can be generalized to the full American adult public.

With any scientific poll, there is sampling error, and probability theory allows us to calculate what the sampling error might be. This calculation is thus expressed as a "confidence interval," or range, which is reported to be $+/-3$ percent of the poll result (or a 6-point range). The level of confidence typically reported is at the "95 percent level of confidence" (meaning that 95 out of 100 similarly conducted polls would produce results in this range). Thus what the statement says, then, is that we can be 95 percent confident that the approval rating for President Obama is somewhere between 57 and 63 percent.

In addition to random selection and sample size, the quality of the sample is affected by "nonresponse" error. Once a sample is selected, it is necessary to contact and conduct interviews with those in the sample. Rarely is it possible to obtain an interview with 100 percent of those sampled. Some people refuse to be interviewed, some are not home when contacts are made, and others screen their phone calls through an answering machine or caller ID system. Nonresponse is problematic when those who do not respond tend to answer the questions differently than those who do respond. The goal is to achieve as high a response to the poll as possible in order to limit possible nonresponse error.

Modern-day scientific polls of Americans and voters typically use a probability technique known as **random-digit dialing (RDD)** to obtain scientific telephone samples. RDD uses known information about telephone area codes and exchanges and randomly assigns the last four digits to these. Because about 90 percent of the households in the United States have active telephone lines, almost everyone living in a house with a telephone has some chance of being selected in the sample.

Asking Questions on Polls

Accurate and reliable polls require not only scientific sampling procedures, but also significant attention to the way in which polling questions are asked. The way in which a question is worded can have a large impact on the type of answers that are given by survey respondents. Consider the following example of a question asked on a national survey conducted by the Roper Organization in 1993: "Does it seem possible or does it seem impossible to you that the Nazi extermination of the Jews never happened?" More than one in five respondents to the poll indicated that they thought it was possible that the Holocaust never happened. The results from this question led to a series of news stories expressing concern that nearly one-quarter of the American public questioned the reality of the Holocaust. However, researchers noted an important problem with the wording of the question; namely, it included a double negative. It is difficult for respondents, particularly in a telephone interview (where they are not looking at the words of the question), to interpret what it means to "seem impossible" that something "never happened." The confusing question led to the exaggerated survey result. To test the notion that the question was confusing, the Gallup organization instead asked this question in a 1994 survey: "In your opinion, did the Holocaust definitely happen, probably happen, probably not happen, or definitely not happen?" In this form of the question, only 2 percent said that the Holocaust probably did not happen, and 0 percent said that it definitely did not happen.

Another example of how wording can influence the responses to a question involves two questions, on separate surveys, intended to measure attitudes about the legality of flag burning. A CBS/*New York Times* poll asked, "Should burning or destroying the American flag as a form of political protest be legal or should it be against the law?" Fourteen percent said it should be legal, and 83 percent said it should be against the law. A Gallup Poll asked the question this way: "The Supreme Court ruled that burning the American flag, though highly offensive, is protected under the free speech guarantee of the First Amendment to the Constitution. Do you agree or disagree?" Thirty-eight percent agreed that flag burning should be legal based on this question—fully 24 percentage points higher than what was found with the CBS/*New York Times* question. In this case, the context in which Gallup framed the question—that the Supreme Court said flag burning was legal based on the First Amendment—produced the different result.

CHECK **THE LIST**

Items That Should be Disclosed About Any Publicly Released Poll

Many polls conducted in the United States are intended to provide information for public consumption. These polls are referred to as "public polls." The *USA Today*/CNN/Gallup Poll, the *New York Times*/CBS Poll, and the Harris Interactive Poll are just a few of the organizations that regularly conduct polling intended for public consumption.

There are so many polling organizations, people often have a hard time ascertaining the quality of a poll. The National Council on Public Polls (NCPP) is an association of organizations that regularly conduct public polls. Members of NCPP have articulated the following list of items that should be disclosed about any poll that is released publicly, as a way to help the poll consumer evaluate the quality of the poll:

- ✓ The name of the organization that sponsored or paid for the poll
- ✓ The dates of interviewing
- ✓ The method for obtaining the interviews (for example, telephone, e-mail, in-person)
- ✓ A definition of the population that was sampled
- ✓ The size of the sample (that is, the number of interviews conducted)
- ✓ The size and description of subsamples, if the poll relies primarily on less than the total sample
- ✓ The complete wording of questions on which the poll results are based
- ✓ The percentages from the poll on which conclusions are based

▶ **POINT TO PONDER:** Do these questions address the average citizen's concerns about the use of polls in modern election campaigning? Is there more that you would need to know to judge the validity of polls, and if so, what?

Source: A list articulated by members of the National Council on Public Polls.

The polling community of practitioners and scholars has, over the years, conducted a number of experiments to test how question wording can influence the results of polls. Listed here are of some of the key recommendations for guidelines in constructing good poll questions:[20]

1. **Avoid double negatives in questions (as in the Holocaust question example cited earlier).**

2. **Keep the question as simple as possible, using words that people with a limited vocabulary might understand.**

3. **Don't include more than one question within a question—such an error is called a double-barreled question.** An example of a double-barreled question is, "Do you approve or disapprove of the job that President Obama is doing in handling the economic and domestic affairs of the nation?" Respondents might have different answers to the president's performance in economic versus other domestic affairs.

4. **The questions should not lead the respondent to a particular answer.** The following is an example of a leading question: "Do you approve of the job that Barack Obama is doing as president?" Because only the "approve" option is stated in the question, some respondents might likely answer "yes, they approve," when they might have answered that they "disapprove" had that option been provided as well.

5. **Don't expect honest answers to socially unacceptable response questions.** For example, using illegal drugs is not only illegal but regarded as socially unacceptable. So one should not necessarily expect all drug users to answer honestly a question about their own use of drugs.

INTERPRETING PUBLIC OPINION DATA

Understanding public opinion requires attention not only to the scientific aspects of sampling and the wording of questions, but also to the analysis and interpretation of the results of a poll. In assessing results, analysts are concerned with three important characteristics of public opinion data: direction, intensity, and continuity.[21]

direction (of public opinion): A tendency toward a particular preference, usually (though not always) characterized as either positive or negative.

To understand the **direction** of public opinion, the analyst seeks to find which position or preference a majority of people hold as their opinion. On most topics, there are two possible directions in which public opinion might lean—a positive direction or a negative direction. For example, with respect to presidential approval, respondents might either approve or disapprove of the job the president is doing. Similarly, the public might either trust or distrust their political leaders; or they might support or oppose a proposal for a policy that makes it more difficult to buy a handgun. On any given opinion question, direction is a basic characteristic that the analyst seeks to gauge.

intensity (of public opinion): The degree of strength or commitment the public feels about the opinion it holds.

Intensity is also an important characteristic of public opinion. Often, the analyst seeks not only to find the direction of opinion but also to determine how strongly or how committed the public feels about the opinion that it holds. Consider the responses to the following question asked to a national sample of Americans in 2000: "Do you agree or disagree with this statement—companies should be allowed to advertise tobacco products on television?" Those polled were asked a follow-up question: "Do you strongly or mildly (agree/disagree) with this?" The results are shown in Figure 10.5.

The direction of opinion in this case only marginally swings in agreement that companies should be able to advertise tobacco on TV. Fifty-one percent, a bare majority, agreed with this statement, and 47 percent disagreed. The direction of opinion only modestly endorses the statement. However, the follow-up question sheds additional light on the intensity of opinion. Among those who agree, they are about evenly divided, 24 percent to 27 percent, between strongly and mildly agreeing. Those who disagree are much more intense in their feelings, with 37 percent strongly and only 10 percent mildly disagreeing.

continuity (in public opinion): A tendency for political preferences to remain generally stable over time.

Continuity is a third important characteristic of public opinion. Political preferences may remain very stable over time, they may gradually change, or they may fluctuate wildly over short periods of time. Continuity (or "changeability," its opposite) is often an important dimension of public opinion. The presidential approval rating is often analyzed from the context of the continuity/change dimension. When major political events occur, we often see change. Figure 10.6 shows the changing views of Americans on their concerns about environmental protection from 2007 through 2011. The decline in the percentage who feel that environmental issues are "very serious and should be a priority for everyone" decreased over this period, the likely result of enhanced concerns about the American economy through the recessionary years.

FIGURE 10.5 Attitudes About TV Tobacco Advertising

Source: State of the First Amendment: 1999, report, prepared by the First Amendment Center. url: http://www.firstamendmentcenter.org/madison/wp-content/uploads/2011/03/sofa1999report.pdf

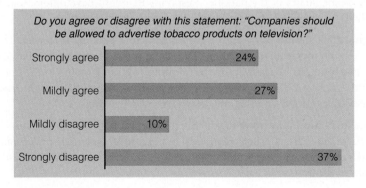

FIGURE 10.6 Change in Attitudes About the Environment

Source: Survey conducted by GfK-Roper for the Robert Wood Johnson Foundation

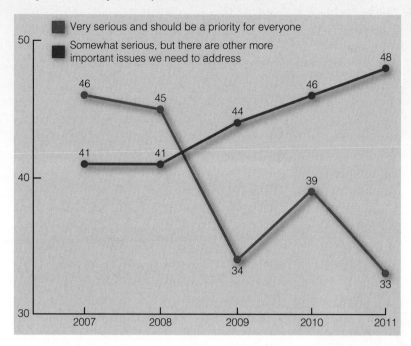

Public opinion plays an important role in any system of government. Even authoritarian regimes such as the French government under King Louis XVI in the late eighteenth century, the Soviet Union in the late twentieth century, and the Egyptian dictatorship of Hosni Mubarek in 2011 were susceptible to being overthrown by the forces of the popular will. But in a democratic society, public opinion is freely expressed and willingly heeded by those running the government. In contemporary American politics, there are a variety of ways in which public opinion may be expressed. Presidents have learned that public opinion can change drastically over the course of their term in office, keeping chief executives and other public officials continuously accountable to the popular will. In 2010 President Obama's deteriorating approval rating contributed to a GOP takeover of the House in the midterm elections. However, by 2012, a rebounded approval rating helped him earn a resounding reelection victory. Modern technology and the advancement of social science research have enabled political scientists, journalists, political candidates, and elected leaders to measure accurately and understand better not only what public opinion is, but also how and why it changes. Modern presidents have the resources of scientific public opinion polls at their disposal and use them quite extensively. But although the scientific opinion poll is a modern phenomenon, the importance of public opinion has always been central to the life of American politics.

FROM YOUR PERSPECTIVE

College Students Making Their Voices Heard in Occupy Wall Street

The economic recession of 2007–2010 slammed virtually all sectors of the American economy. College students seeking part-time summer jobs to help support their education and new college graduates seeking to enter the world of work were perhaps hit the hardest. Thus, many students were drawn to the Occupy Wall Street movement, which sought to focus public attention on the growing trend of income inequality and the excesses of Wall Street. On October 14, 2011, rallies were held on 100 campuses across the nation to show college student unity with the broader Occupy Wall Street movement that was sweeping the nation. Demonstrators on and off campuses voiced their concerns with lack of jobs, the high cost of college tuition, and the mounting debt from student loans.

AP Photo/Jeff Chiu

Pictured above is an October 14, 2011 "Occupy" rally on the Berkeley campus at the University of California.

For Critical Thinking and Discussion

1. Have you ever participated in a protest rally or march on campus? If so, what spurred you to do so? If not, what would it take to incite you to join such a protest?

2. Marches and protests are more common expressions of public opinion among college and university students than they tend to be among other groups of like-minded citizens. How, if it all, do you think colleges and universities tend to foster this form of expression in particular?

SUMMARY: PUTTING IT ALL TOGETHER

PUBLIC OPINION IN AMERICAN POLITICS

- Public opinion plays an important role in ensuring that citizens' beliefs are embraced in a democracy; public opinion also plays a tactical role for political officials, influencing the outcome of many important political battles.

Test Yourself on This Section

1. Which of the following people argued in an influential book entitled *Semisovereign People* that "public opinion can emerge as a key factor in any political context"?
   a. James Madison
   b. V. O. Key
   c. E. E. Schattschneider
   d. Abraham Lincoln

2. V. O. Key argued that "public opinion" is not merely the summation of individual opinions. What else, according to Key, was necessary for "public opinion" to be present?

HOW IS PUBLIC OPINION EXPRESSED?

- Public opinion may be expressed through a variety of means, including public opinion polls, voting, free speech and assembly, political blogging, the support of particular candidates for political office, and the contribution of time and effort to interest groups.

- The news media also serve as an outlet for public opinion, whether by publishing articles about important individuals' opinions or by sponsoring their own public opinion polls on politics and policy issues. Still, many members of the public prefer to express their opinions directly to elected officials through letters, phone calls, or e-mails. Blogs have become an increasingly popular way for individuals to express their views on issues.

Test Yourself on This Section

1. The legal guarantees protecting protests as a form of public opinion may be found in the
   a. Declaration of Independence.
   b. Preamble to the Constitution.
   c. First Amendment.
   d. Fourth Amendment.

2. Elections are an expression of public opinion. When the Constitution was first adopted, which of the following provided a direct link between popular preferences and federal officeholders?
   a. presidential elections
   b. Senate elections
   c. House elections
   d. elections of Supreme Court justices

3. Identify five specific ways that public opinion may be expressed in the American political system.

THE LEVELS OF PUBLIC OPINION

- Public opinion exists at its most abstract level in the form of values and beliefs; it exists in a more specific form through political orientations, which translate values and beliefs into a systematic way of assessing political realities, and in an even more specific way in the form of particular political preferences.

Test Yourself on This Section

1. Over the past 50 years, which of the following partisan groups has increased proportionately?
   a. Democrats
   b. Independents
   c. Republicans
   d. Socialists

2. The broadest and most abstract level of public opinion that forms the basis for American political culture is
   a. values and beliefs.
   b. political orientations.
   c. preferences on policy issues.
   d. preferences for political candidates.

3. Distinguish between the "liberal" and "conservative" ideologies in contemporary politics.

HOW INFORMED IS PUBLIC OPINION?

- Many noted scholars in the early and mid-twentieth century argued that the public lacks the necessary knowledge for their opinions to provide value. Contemporary surveys continue to confirm that the public maintains a low interest in politics generally, and that most Americans are uninformed about basic political facts.

- By contrast, numerous other scholars, beginning with V. O. Key Jr. in the 1960s, have argued that regardless of its specific knowledge of politics, the public as a whole behaves quite rationally over the long haul, expressing stable opinions that move (if at all) in logical and meaningful directions based on their values and beliefs.

Test Yourself on This Section

1. Which of the following books used scientific surveys to document the low level of political knowledge among ordinary American citizens?
   a. *Federalist Papers*
   b. *The American Voter*
   c. *The Decline of America*
   d. *Jay-Walking in America*

2. Despite low levels of political knowledge among Americans, V. O. Key argued that "voters are not fools." How does he justify this claim?

HOW DOES PUBLIC OPINION FORM?

- Individuals' opinions are shaped in part by political socialization; impressions formed during youth often last well into adulthood. Opinions are also shaped by demographics (race, ethnicity, gender, age, and so on), family members, friends and peer groups, schools, the media, and religious organizations.

Test Yourself on This Section

1. The "primacy tendency" has its greatest impact through which of the following agents of political socialization?
   a. family
   b. friends
   c. religion
   d. the media

2. How does entertainment television programming act as a factor that influences one's socialization to politics?

HOW IS PUBLIC OPINION MEASURED?

- Public opinion polls measure the opinions of a large group of people by selecting a subset of the larger group and then generalizing the findings from the small group back to the large group. To ensure that the poll is scientific, the sample must be chosen randomly using probability theory through techniques such as random-digit dialing. Unscientific polls can produce misleading results.

- The way in which questions on a poll are worded is also an important factor in assessing the quality of a poll. Misleading questions, whether intentional or unintentional, may produce faulty results.

Test Yourself on This Section

1. Phone calls initiated by political campaigns that pretend to be conducting a poll but actually intend to send negative messages about political opponents are known as
   a. intercept polls.
   b. push polls.
   c. log-in polls.
   d. self-selected listener opinion polls.

2. Most scientific telephone opinion polls use which of the following techniques in selecting a sample of respondents?
   a. random sampling from phone directories
   b. Internet recruiting via e-mail
   c. call-ins from news television shows
   d. random-digit dialing

3. What distinguishes a scientific poll from an unscientific one?

INTERPRETING PUBLIC OPINION DATA

- The proper interpretation of public opinion data requires attention to the direction, intensity, and continuity of the public's expressions. With regard to the third characteristic, political preferences may fluctuate wildly over short periods of time.

Test Yourself on This Section

1. The strength of commitment that the public feels about the job performance of the president is a measure of
   a. the direction of opinion.
   b. the Intensity of opinion.
   c. the continuity of opinion.
   d. change in opinion.

2. How has public opinion changed regarding concerns about the environment from 2007 through 2011? Why has this change occurred?

KEY TERMS

agents of political socialization (p. 273)

conservative ideology (p. 270)

continuity (in public opinion) (p. 284)

direction (of public opinion) (p. 284)

intensity (of public opinion) (p. 284)

liberal ideology (p. 270)

political ideology (p. 270)

political orientations (p. 269)

political preferences (p. 270)

political socialization (p. 272)

primacy tendency (p. 273)

pseudo-poll (p. 281)

public opinion (p. 266)

public opinion poll (p. 275)

random-digit dialing (RDD) (p. 282)

sampling error (p. 281)

scientific sample (p. 278)

straw poll (p. 276)

unscientific poll (p. 278)

values and beliefs (p. 268)

INTEREST
GROUPS

Learning Objectives

Pluralism and the Interest-Group System

- Assess the function of interest groups as a mechanism by which groups of people attempt to influence government to advance shared goals

- Define pluralism as the theory that public policy is largely the product of a variety of different interest groups competing with one another to promote laws that benefit members of their respective groups

- Compare and contrast both the benefits and criticisms of the interest-group system in the United States

Interest Groups in Action

- Identify the reasons for the growth of interest groups in the United States over the past few decades

- Evaluate the critical role interest groups play in influencing policymaking through iron triangles and issue networks

- Distinguish between the three types of benefits that are derived from group membership: material, solidary and purposive

- Assess the factors that contribute to each interest group's level of influence on policy

Types of Interest Groups

- Distinguish between economic interest groups and noneconomic interest groups according to their primary purpose

- Explain the "free rider" problem that many interest groups face

How Interest Groups Achieve Their Goals

- Identify the activities interest groups engage in to achieve their goals and influence public policy

The U.S. political system provides numerous opportunities for people to influence public policy. Voting in elections to choose leaders offers one such opportunity. The guarantees of freedom of speech to speak one's mind about political issues and freedom of the press to critically assess issues and leaders' performance are others. Public opinion polls are yet another mechanism that solicits input from the masses. But perhaps the most natural—and arguably the most influential—form of public input arrives by way of the activities of interest groups. Interest groups today play a central role in making laws, regulating industries, and even influencing court decisions. The vast influence of interest groups makes them a target of criticism, particularly when scandals emerge. Thus, a persistent issue regarding interest-group activities is just how far we should allow such groups to press their interests. At what point do interest groups become a negative force in democracy? This chapter assesses the workings and performance of American politics from the perspective of interest-group activity. What are interest groups? How do they work? Who belongs to them? Which ones are more and less powerful? How do they exert influence on what government does?

William Thomas Cain/Getty Images

1860   1870   1880   1890   1900

1872

Then

Rep. Oakes Ames (R-MA) served in Congress from 1863 to 1873.

Source: Library of Congress Prints and Photographs Division Washington, D.C

Scandalous activities of lobbyists contribute to the skepticism that many Americans hold regarding the role of interest groups. One such scandal plagued U.S. politics in the post–Civil War era, when railroads were the dominant economic interest in Washington, D.C. Seeking legislative support, the Union Pacific Railroad in particular exerted pressure on Congress. Oakes Ames (R-MA), a congressman himself, also lobbied for his family firm for the construction of the Union Pacific; he even installed his brother Oliver Ames as president of the railroad in 1866. In 1872 the railroad established a front company, known as Crédit Mobilier, as part of a financial scam to funnel money back to the railroads through their own construction contracts. Ames then allowed members of Congress to purchase railroad shares at face rather than market value; in return, the members agreed to ignore illegal corporate transactions and to help produce dividends for the railroads they now owned. Ames's scheme was eventually exposed, and he was censured after a House investigation. In addition, Ames's actions nearly ruined the Union Pacific railroad, which went bankrupt in the 1870s. But at a time when corruption laws were still in their infancy, many politicians escaped with nothing more than "the embarrassment of public exposure."

1980   1990   2000   2010   2020

2006

NOW

Former lobbyist Jack Abramoff.

Source: AP Photo/Gerald Herbert

Although the legal rules governing lobbying activities have been significantly strengthened since the Credit Mobilier scandal, transgressions continue to discredit the influence of interest groups. One such transgression was orchestrated by the now infamous Jack Abromoff, who lobbied on behalf of Native American tribes in their efforts to promote Indian-run casinos. Many Native American tribes benefited from the 1988 Indian Gaming Regulatory Act, which permitted casinos on tribal lands. Several tribes hired Abramoff to represent them before Congress to further promote casino development into the twenty-first century. Abramoff proved especially effective in this role, helping to defeat federal legislation that would have assessed a federal tax on Native American casinos. House Majority Leader Tom DeLay (R-TX) was one of many House members who played a role in this and other victories. Abramoff did more than just "argue forcefully" on the tribes' behalf: he spent millions of dollars to illegally influence politicians by offering many members of Congress free meals at his restaurant, free seats in his skyboxes at major sports arenas, and free vacations. Joining Abramoff on one vacation in 2000 was DeLay, whose airfare was charged to Abramoff's credit card. Abramoff's illegal acts did not end at bribery; he also defrauded the very Native American tribes he had been hired to serve by overbilling them and orchestrating lobbying activities against them. Once exposed, he was prosecuted by the federal government and he eventually pleaded guilty to numerous charges. The scandal also led to the downfall of House Majority Leader DeLay and many other members of Congress and their aides. Scandals such as this one continue to fuel arguments against the role of interest groups in America politics.

PLURALISM AND THE INTEREST-GROUP SYSTEM

interest group: An organization of people with shared goals that tries to influence public policy through a variety of activities.

Perhaps the most natural—and arguably the most influential—form of public input into government arrives by way of the activities of interest groups. James Madison, in Federalist No. 10, admonished that "the latent causes of faction are thus sown in the nature of man."[1] By faction, Madison was referring to what we now term interest groups. Madison was concerned about the potential influence of factions on the government. But at the same time, he understood that people were by nature drawn toward the organization of collective interests and the use of that organization to influence government action. Madison expected that if enough interest groups vied to influence policy, they would cancel each other out.

What Is an Interest Group?

An **interest group** (also referred to as a "pressure group" or "organized interest") is an organization of people with shared goals that tries to influence public policy through a variety of activities. Every individual has interests, and interest groups are a mechanism for people with shared goals to protect or advance their own interests. People can try to influence government on their own—such as by calling or writing their elected representatives to voice their opinion, or by voting in an election. Another way that people can influence government is by joining a group that is organized to accomplish an objective.

Senior citizens, for example, have a shared interest in securing cost-of-living adjustments (COLAs) in the Social Security system that disburses checks to them each month. Each year, the president and Congress determine the percentage rate increase in the COLA. The larger the increase, the higher will be an individual's monthly Social Security check. Each individual senior citizen might call his or her representatives in Congress to try to influence the vote for a larger COLA increase. Another way senior citizens may try to influence government is by joining and supporting AARP (formerly the American Association for Retired People), an interest group that, among other activities, tries to influence government to approve large increases

GOP Presidential candidate Rick Santorum addresses the Conservative Political Action Conference (CPAC) during his nomination campaign. CPAC and Santorum have been big advocates for conservative social policies.

Kevin Dietsch/UPI/Landov

in the annual COLA for Social Security. AARP is large, with many resources and lobbyists to influence legislators. Though an individual citizen's call to a representative may carry some weight, it is no match for the vast resources and activities of the AARP.

Interest groups link people with government policies. The linkage created by interest groups is constitutionally protected by the First Amendment, which guarantees the people's right "to peaceably assemble and petition the government for redress of grievances." People assembling in groups that carry out activities to foster group members' goals is a common activity in Washington, in the 50 state capitals, and in thousands of local governments.

Alexis de Tocqueville, a Frenchman who toured the United States in the early 1830s and observed the early workings of the U.S. political system, was struck by the extent to which group association and activity dominated the American system. In his now-classic 1835 book titled *Democracy in America*,[2] de Tocqueville praised the extent to which group activity underpins American democracy:

> *The [citizen] of the United States learns from birth that he must rely on himself to com-*
> *...t the ills and trials of life. . . . If some obstacle blocks the public road halting . . . traffic,*
> *...ody; this improvised assembly produces an authority*
> *...ne has thought of the possibility beyond that of those*
> *...to combat moral troubles. Public security, trade and*
> *...rovide the aims for associations in the United States.*
> *...vill despair of attaining by the free action of the col-*
>
> *...d to form centers of action at certain important places*
> *...eater and its influence more widespread.*

Interest Group
- is An Organization of people with shared goals that tries to influence public policies through a variety of activities

Pluralism
- The theory that public policy largely results from a variety of interest groups competing with one another to promote laws that benefits members of their respective groups

...ınd other Europeans that he observed, de Tocqueville ...y prone to organize in groups and use their associations

...t public policy largely results from a variety of interest ...to promote laws that benefit members of their respec... ...**nism** refers to the theory that public policy is a product ...Whereas the majoritarian perspective focuses on public ...resentation to describe how democracy in America actu... ...uggests that in fact "the majority rarely rules."

...n architect of pluralist ideas, suggested in *A Preface to* ...rican people are represented in government primarily ... products of public policy are largely a function of sup... ...st groups that compete for influence through activities ...l system, according to Dahl, offers a number of "access ...vide input. These access points include Congress, execu... ...ctions, and the news media. David B. Truman, another ...e notion that group activity and mobilization are natural ...[4] The free and open competition among groups advances ...ree and open marketplace of ideas promotes the adoption

Fact or Fiction?

The First Amendment guarantees the right of interest groups to function in the political system.

Fact.

Two of the rights listed in the First Amendment protect the function of interest groups: the right to peaceably assemble, and the right to petition government for a redress of grievances.

pluralism: The theory that public policy largely results from a variety of interest groups competing with one another to promote laws that benefit members of their respective groups.

majoritarianism: The theory that public policy is a product of what majorities of citizens prefer.

The Pros and Cons of Interest Groups

The political power that emanates from groups of people organizing for the purpose of influencing government outputs can be quite strong. "Are interest groups good or bad for American democracy?" is a question akin to the old cliché "Is the glass half full or half empty?" The answer, of course, depends on one's perspective. Madison himself recognized that interest groups were powerful and that they could be dangerous. But he also acknowledged that factions could not be eliminated. Channeling them into productive devices for promoting public input was a primary challenge his generation faced in framing the government.

2012 GOP presidential contender Newt Gingrich was criticized by fellow GOP candidates for being a lobbyist for the controversial Fannie Mae. Gingrich, shown above, dismisses these criticisms at a Republican debate, claiming that he was not a lobbyist, but rather a "historian" for Fannie Mae.

Interest groups in America invite criticism from some circles and praise from others. Listed below are the primary arguments regarding the advantages and disadvantages of interest-group activity:

The Pros. Many observers today sing the praises of an interest-group system that advances the interests of the people. Their arguments in support of interest groups include the following:

- Interest groups provide all groups in society with an opportunity to win support for their ideas and positions. The vast number of interest groups represents a wide array of political opinions, economic perspectives, and social class differences.

- By their very nature, humans seek out others who have ideas similar to their own. Joining groups and working for the interests of the group is a natural inclination of citizens and should be encouraged as a method of representation in our democracy.

- The right of association is a basic right protected implicitly by the First Amendment to the U.S. Constitution, which affords individuals the right "peaceably to assemble."

- A wide array of diverse groups in society—rich and poor, urban and non-urban, male and female, northern and southern, liberal and conservative—potentially may organize and attempt to influence government. The system is fair in that it gives all groups an equitable opportunity to compete.

The Cons. Many other observers of the U.S. political system are quite critical of the power exerted by interest groups. In *The Power Elite*, C. Wright Mills[5] characterizes interest groups as a tool of the political elite rather than a system that enables broad participation in influencing public policy. Along this line, many criticize the ability of wealthy corporations and individuals to exert disproportionate influence on government through well-financed interest-group activities. John Heinz and his colleagues argue further that the influence of interest groups is contingent on a number of factors and that their influence may be quite limited.[6] Other criticisms of interest groups include the following:

- Use of interest groups to make public policy is unfair because groups supported by the wealthy have far greater resources to promote their interests in the political system.

- Large corporations exist to maximize profits. They dominate the interest-group system and tend to be ruthless in achieving their policy goals. The interest-group system thus promotes the advancement of interests that do not always strive for the common good.

- The amount of interest-group activity is so great that it has made it difficult to get things done in government. Too many groups are operating, slowing down the policymaking process to a state of gridlock in many arenas.

- Interest-group leaders are not elected, distinguishing them from many of the policymaking institutions that have been constitutionally ordained—such as Congress and the executive branch. Thus interest-group dominance of the political system is an affront to democracy.

- Interest groups work to concentrate benefits for the few while distributing costs to the many.

Interest Groups versus Political Parties

Political parties also link people to government policies. However, parties differ from interest groups in two important ways. First, parties today mainly focus on elections by endorsing candidates and working for their election to office. Most interest groups do not run candidates for office as parties do (although interest groups often endorse candidates). Interest groups commonly find other access points of government to accomplish their goals—access points such as the courts, the committee system in Congress, and executive agencies.[7]

A second important difference between interest groups and political parties is that groups tend to focus narrowly on special issues or sets of issues (hence the term *special interests*), whereas major parties are generally all-encompassing and are guided by broader ideological approaches to governing, rather than by a specific policy position. In short, the major parties are generalist whereas interest groups are focused. Consequently, there are few political parties, but many, many interest groups. Groups do not try to appeal to as many individuals as possible; rather, they appeal to those whose special interests are advocated by the group. For example, the National Rifle Association (NRA) does not try to recruit gun control advocates because they are less likely to help promote the group's interests. Conversely, parties try to appeal to as many people as possible to optimize their electoral success.

Interest Groups and Social Movements

Numerous **social movements** have been identified in American history, such as the civil rights, consumer safety, women's rights, and environmental movements of the 1960s and 1970s. These large informal groupings of individuals were often spawned directly from particular interest groups. The consumer protection movement, for example, was driven by the activities of the group Public Citizen, formed by consumer activist Ralph Nader. The American drive toward equality has produced a number of important social movements that utilized organized interests.

Movements have been political (for example, women's suffrage in the early 1900s), economic (for example, labor rights in the late 1800s and early 1900s), and social (for example,

social movement: A large informal grouping of individuals and/or organizations focused on specific political or social issues.

Lewis W. Hine/Time Life Pictures/Getty Images

Women and children in 1890 labor at a food processing plant.

the civil rights movements of the 1960s). These movements have all been propelled by the activities of interest groups.

INTEREST GROUPS IN ACTION

Interest groups have always played an important role in American politics. Even in the colonial period, groups such as the Sons of Liberty gathered members, collected donations, and organized protests to achieve the goal of American freedom from British taxation. The Sons of Liberty were successful in their aims because they tied their actions to the economic interests of their members. As Madison acknowledged, economic interests tend to be the type of concerns that are most salient to people and thus move them to collective action.

In 1886, the American Federation of Labor (AFL) was formed as the first broad-based national labor union. The AFL was originally established to advocate the rights of craft unions and ensure the terms of union contracts. Organized and led by Samuel Gompers for 40 years, it attracted many members and raised funds to promote laws benefiting organized labor. The AFL was the principal advocate for establishing a cabinet department, the U.S. Department of Labor, to administer labor programs. This department continues to serve as one of the largest executive departments in the nation. In the 1950s, the AFL merged with the Congress of Industrial Organizations (CIO) to create the AFL-CIO, an interest group still very active in promoting the labor agenda.

The National Association of Manufacturers (NAM) was organized in 1885 for the purpose of advancing the interests of the manufacturing businesses. Though setting protective tariffs was its core objective, the NAM also became a primary opponent of the AFL and other labor interest groups. The goals of organized labor (such as higher wages for workers, better working conditions, increased benefits, and job security) and the goals of business owners (maximizing profits) often came into conflict.

Tensions between labor and business interests intensified with the tremendous growth of the American economy beginning in the late 1800s and continued to mount as the economy expanded. Large companies, focusing on maximizing profits (which in turn appealed to shareholders), opposed laborers' demands for increased wages, better working conditions, and worker benefits. Today, labor and business interest groups continue to be among the largest and most powerful interest groups in the nation.

The Growth of Interest Groups

The U.S. Supreme Court has ruled that corporations and unions have the same rights as citizens to make contributions to interest groups.

Fact.

The 2010 Supreme Court decision in *Citizens United v. F.E.C.* ruled that unions and corporations enjoy the same First Amendment rights as individuals, and thus may contribute to PACs under certain conditions.

Perhaps the most significant factor leading to an increase in the number of interest groups has been the overall growth in government. Interest groups attempt to advance their agenda by influencing various aspects of government. As the number of government programs and agencies has expanded, along with their reach, opportunities for influencing what government does through interest-group activities have expanded as well.

The New Deal programs of the 1930s and the Great Society programs of the 1960s led to tremendous growth in the federal government and huge increases in the federal budget. Government began to assume a more active role not only in promoting its economic policies but in promoting social policies as well. In response, a vast number of interest groups formed. Both proponents and opponents of a more active government organized interest groups to advocate their views. As the number of interest groups advocating economic issues expanded, so too did the number of groups promoting ideological perspectives, positions on single issues, and political reforms.

Although interest groups have been part of the American system since its beginning, the number of groups has increased dramatically over the past half-century. Between 1960 and 2000, the number of official associations increased by 400 percent (from 5,843 to 23,298); the total amount of lobbying spending in Washington increased from $1.43 billion in 1998 to $3.47 billion in 2009; and from 1998 through 2009 the total number of registered lobbyists in Washington, D.C., increased from 10,403 to 13,739.[8] Major political developments, such as the antiwar movement, the civil rights movement, and the Watergate scandal of the Nixon administration, mobilized a better-educated mass public to become increasingly concerned about political issues. This heightened concern about social and political issues fostered a significant amount of new interest-group activity. The sophisticated use of mass-media technologies such as television, the computer, and the Internet has facilitated the ability of groups to emerge and flourish.

Another factor contributing to the increase in interest-group activity has been the escalating cost of financing political campaigns. As costs have increased, interest groups have come to play a greater role in supporting political parties and the election of candidates. The Federal Election Campaign Act of 1971 placed limits on individual and corporate contributions to political campaigns. As a means of financing campaigns through alternative methods, interest groups have formed **political action committees (PACs)**, which raise money from individuals and provide a source of funding for candidates and political parties. PACs also engage in "soft money" spending on advertising and other political work independent of candidates and parties. Recently the Supreme Court ruled in *Citizens United v. Federal Election Commission* (2010) that corporations, like individuals, may make contributions to PACs, which has in 2012 facilitated the rise of the so-called "super-PACs." As we will see in Chapter 14, PACs are a source of much controversy.

political action committee (PAC): The political arm of an interest group that promotes candidates in election campaigns primarily through financial contributions.

Iron Triangles, Issue Networks, and the Influence of Groups

The influence of interest groups is buoyed by the process in which public policy is created and modified. As shown in Figure 11.1, in any policy area, three key sets of actors interact to produce public policy: (1) congressional committees and subcommittees assigned to a specific policy area, (2) executive agencies of government that have the authority to administer policies in a particular area, and (3) private interest groups that have an interest in influencing that policy area. Members of congressional committees, managers of agencies, and leaders of interest groups all have vested interests in the specific policy area. As political scientist Theodore Lowi has noted, although these parties may not always agree on particular positions, they all seek to promote policies favorable to their interests, and they come to depend on one another for support and influence. Together, this network of actors dominates the development of public policies. This durable and seemingly impenetrable three-sided network has come to be known as the **iron triangle** of policymaking.[9]

The development of U.S. defense policy illustrates how iron triangles work. The armed services and defense committees and subcommittees in Congress are responsible for appropriating

iron triangle: A three-sided network of policymaking that includes congressional committees (and subcommittees) in a specific policy area, executive agencies with authority over that area, and private interest groups focused on influencing that area.

FIGURE 11.1 The Iron Triangle of Policymaking
Source: © Cengage Learning

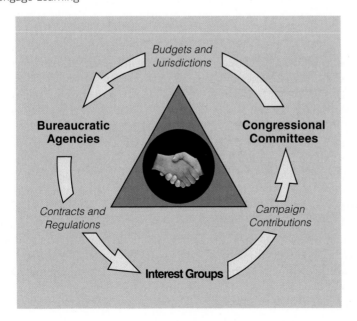

funds for defense contracts (such as for the building of new military aircraft). Members of Congress on these committees are committed to maintaining a strong national defense, and they control the purse strings for developing new defense systems. Leaders in the U.S. Department of Defense are responsible for implementing defense systems under the orders of the president and rely on congressional committees to fund strong systems. Private contractors such as Pratt & Whitney (an airplane engine manufacturer) employ the engineers and researchers to design superior systems and provide valuable information to the congressional committees and the defense department.

The committees and the Department of Defense depend on Pratt & Whitney for advanced engine technologies, advice on aircraft design, and the capacity to produce cutting-edge aircraft engines. Pratt & Whitney benefits from winning federal contracts to produce defense systems. The congressional committees, Defense Department managers, and corporate leaders and lobbyists from Pratt & Whitney are familiar with one another, depend on one another, and use one another in the development of defense systems. The iron-triangle approach to public policymaking has institutionalized the role of interest groups in the exercise of American democracy.

Although an iron triangle refers to the interdependent relationship between legislators, bureaucrats, and lobbyists in a particular policy area, it is also possible to identify a broader set of actors who all have a vested interest in an area of public policy and try to collectively influence their policy area. Political scientists have used the term **issue networks** to describe this broader array of actors beyond legislators, bureaucrats, and lobbyists who try to influence a particular policy area. These include congressional staff people, journalists or other members of the media who often report on the policy area, and researchers who have done work on and are experts in the policy area.[10]

issue network: The broad array of actors (beyond just the iron triangle) that try to collectively influence a policy area in which they maintain a vested interest.

Membership in Groups

Many Americans belong to interest groups, and many businesses, nonprofit organizations, and public entities belong to interest groups as well. It is estimated that about four in five citizens belong to at least one interest group. Many of the more common groups Americans belong to include labor unions (such as the AFL-CIO, which boasts a total of about 11 million members), professional associations (such as the 240,000 physicians and medical students who belong to the American Medical Association), and organizations such as the AARP to which many of the nation's senior citizens belong. As many as 3 million businesses across the United States belong to the U.S. Chamber of Commerce.[11]

Although the number of Americans who belong to interest groups is high, certain types of people are more likely than others to engage in interest-group activity. Americans with higher incomes and greater resources, and those who are better educated and employed in professional occupations, are much more likely to belong to groups. Those with more financial resources tend to better appreciate the utility of group membership and interest groups' impact on the political process; wealthier individuals are also more likely to have the resources to support interest-group activities. Thus many critics of interest-group politics charge that the pluralist model of democracy favors the upper middle class and upper class of society. Because those with more resources can and do support interest groups, they are more likely to influence public policy to their financial advantage.

Various reasons have been proposed to explain why people or organizations might join and support certain interest groups. One is that they receive specific, tangible benefits from membership. These are referred to as **material benefits**[12] of group membership. For instance, local units of the National Education Association (NEA) work for its teacher members to win salary increases, and so the benefits of membership often produce a favorable material benefit to teachers in the form of higher wages. Many interest groups provide their members with other material benefits such as health and auto insurance discounts, magazine subscriptions, and free products.

Another reason why interest groups are appealing is the **purposive benefits** (or expressive benefits) of membership.[13] Purposive rewards are those that do not directly benefit the

Less than half of all American adults are members of an interest group.

Fiction.

The vast majority of Americans—about four out of five—belong to at least one interest group.

material benefits (of group membership): The specific, tangible benefits individuals receive from interest-group membership, such as economic concessions, discounts on products, and so forth.

purposive benefits (of group membership): Rewards that do not directly benefit the individual member, but benefit society as a whole.

individual member, but benefit society more generally. Some interest groups, for example, are committed to the goal of improving the environment and promoting policies that better protect the natural environment. The Sierra Club is one such organization that endorses these goals, and members of the Sierra Club receive purposive benefits from membership and support of the group's activities.

A third type of incentive for interest-group membership is the **solidary benefits**[14] of membership, or the satisfaction that individuals receive from interacting with like-minded individuals for a cause. Solidary rewards derive less from the interest group's goals and more from the process of interacting with others to achieve a goal. For example, a union worker who attends a labor rally to support increases in a new contract may receive satisfaction from simply being with colleagues in support of a cause.

solidary benefits (of group membership): Satisfaction that individuals receive from interacting with like-minded individuals for a cause.

What Makes Some Groups More Powerful Than Others?

Although there are thousands of interest groups operating in the United States, some groups are more successful than others in promoting their cause and affecting public policy. There are three general characteristics of an interest group, which may have significant bearing on how powerful that group's influence will be in Washington:

1. **The size of the membership.** There is, undoubtedly, power in numbers. The larger the number of members of an interest group, the more powerful that group will be in affecting public policy. Large membership alone makes elected leaders responsive to a group's concerns. An interest group with a large number of members can increase its power and influence by convincing its members to vote for a candidate or candidates. The Christian Coalition of America (CCA) is a Christian political advocacy group that includes fundamentalists, evangelicals, Pentecostals, and many members of mainline Protestant churches as well. Officials of the CCA often communicate with the organization's huge membership regarding the endorsement of candidates. Not surprisingly, the CCA attracts the attention of candidates as well as officeholders who plan on running for another term. Groups with large numbers of members also have an advantage in raising funds to support their activities. With many members, the potential for fundraising is great. And funding goes a long way in advancing the effectiveness of interest-group activities. A good example of a group that exhibits strength through numbers is the American Farm Bureau Federation (AFBF), which boasts 4.7 million members and has proven especially effective at promoting policies that provide large subsidies and other benefits to American farmers. A bilateral trade agreement between the United States and Russia in late 2006 was a testament to AFBF influence, as it substantially expanded the export market for U.S. farmers.

2. **The wealth of the members.** The number of members is an important indicator of the potential amount of money that interest groups might be able to raise. But just as important is the wealth of the membership. Certain interest groups enjoy a huge advantage when it comes to the average wealth of members. For example, the American Trial Lawyers Association (ATLA) is made up of trial lawyers who, by virtue of their occupation, are quite wealthy when compared to average Americans. Thus, whereas the number of members of the ATLA is only about 60,000, the wealth of its membership and the consequent level of financial contributions from members provide sufficient resources to make it an especially powerful interest group in Washington.

3. **The dedication of members to the goals of the group.** In addition to the number of members and wealth of members, groups that have a loyal following based on member commitment to the cause of the group can be a powerful resource.[15] The National Right to Life Committee (NRLC) is a good example. The NRLC organized and began to solicit members and contributions in 1973, after the *Roe v. Wade* decision legalized abortion. NRLC's members tend to be dedicated to right-to-life positions and willing to contribute much time, effort, and resources to advance its pro-life agenda.

CHECK **THE LIST**

The Top 10 Most Influential Interest Groups

Each year, *Fortune* magazine lists the 10 most influential interest groups in the nation based on a survey of Washington, D.C., political players. The following groups made a recent top 10 list.

✓ 1. AARP. The AARP provides services for senior citizens, including consumer and policy advocacy, health care information, and tax counseling.

✓ 2. The National Rifle Association (NRA). The NRA is dedicated to preserving the rights of law-abiding citizens to purchase, own, and use their own firearms. The Institute for Legal Action is the lobbying arm of the NRA.

✓ 3. The National Federation of Independent Businesses (NFIB). This is the largest advocacy group in the nation that represents small businesses. Among other things, the NFIB supports a simpler tax system and lower taxes on businesses, and it opposes minimum-wage increases and the expansion of the Family Medical Leave Act.

✓ 4. American Israel Public Affairs Committee (AIPAC). The AIPAC is a strong advocate of a pro-Israel foreign policy for the U.S. government.

✓ 5. The American Federation of Labor–Congress of Industrial Organizations (AFL-CIO). The goal of the AFL-CIO is to empower working people by giving them a strong voice in the workplace and in government policymaking.

✓ 6. The Association of Trial Lawyers of America (ATLA). ATLA, the world's largest trial lawyers association, promotes policies that enhance fairness for injured persons in the judicial process and aid lawyer effectiveness in pursuing such claims.

✓ 7. The U.S. Chamber of Commerce. This is the world's largest federation of businesses. Among other things, it lobbies to reduce government's regulation of businesses and improve trade opportunities for U.S. firms doing business abroad.

✓ 8. National Right to Life Committee (NRLC). The NRLC was formed in response to the *Roe v. Wade* decision in which the Supreme Court protected abortion under certain circumstances from government regulation. The NRLC has lobbied to make abortion laws more stringent.

✓ 9. The National Education Association (NEA). The NEA focuses on advancing public education in the United States. It lobbies for improved teacher preparation, better working conditions for teachers, and increased resources for the nation's schools.

✓ 10. The National Restaurant Association. This is the leading business association for the restaurant industry.

▶ **POINT TO PONDER: The AARP, ranked number one in the Fortune list, is generally regarded as one of the most effective interest groups in Washington. The AARP's well-funded and active program to keep Congress from changing Social Security (a program that many analysts think will be bankrupt by 2020) has effectively maintained benefits for seniors, but at the same time puts the program at risk of collapse in the long run. Do you think the AARP is effectively defending Social Security by encouraging Congress to keep its "hands off"?**

TYPES OF INTEREST GROUPS

Although interest groups represent a wide array of interests in American society, there are two basic types of interest groups—economic groups and noneconomic groups. Many groups engage in both economic and noneconomic pursuits, but most can be classified as either primarily economic or noneconomic in nature.

Economic Groups

Although the specific goals of different interest groups vary greatly, the vast majority of groups in America have goals that are economic in nature. Two out of every three interest groups in America are **economic interest groups**, or groups that exist to promote favorable economic conditions and economic opportunities for their members. Economic groups also tend to be the largest and most powerful groups because members of such groups maintain a vested personal financial stake in having the group achieve its goals.

As well as being the most numerous, economic groups also tend to be the best organized and most influential interest groups. Because economic interests are those that generally inspire more concern from businesses and citizens alike, they tend to feature greater individual involvement, commitment, resources, and organization.

There are thousands of interest groups that focus primarily on advancing the economic goals of members. These groups include private businesses, labor unions, business and industry associations, and professional associations.

Business Groups. The largest companies in the nation and the world typically maintain internal units that function as an interest group for the company. Very large companies, such as General Motors (GM) and IBM, for example, have their own interest groups. Such companies typically have wide and varied interests. GM, for example, is affected by environmental laws (tougher air pollution laws often require GM to spend more on technologies to reduce emissions from its cars), labor laws (increases in the minimum wage require higher pay for some workers), and product safety laws (increased safety standards might increase the cost of assembling a car). GM needs a well-staffed interest group to try to influence these and many other types of legislation.

Most businesses belong to associations, and often these associations engage in interest-group activities to advocate for the interests of their members. Some associations are very broad in scope, such as the U.S. Chamber of Commerce, with its 3 million members. These businesses range from small neighborhood auto mechanics to large billion-dollar financial institutions. The Chamber seeks to broadly advance the interests of business owners.

Another type of business association is a **trade association**. A trade association typically focuses on one particular industry, and members of the association are drawn exclusively from that industry. Businesses in a particular trade often face similar types of concerns, and the trade association looks out for the specific interests of a classification of businesses. For example, the American Society of Travel Agents (ASTA) is a trade association whose 24,000-member institutions include travel agencies, hotels, airlines, car rental agencies, and the like. ASTA promotes legislation and regulations favoring the travel industry.

Businesses, business associations, and trade associations have an advantage over associations and other organizations whose members are individual citizens or consumers. Businesses quickly see the advantage of joining an association, which collectively advocates for the interests of like businesses. Individuals, however, are less likely to join and contribute to an association that advocates for such things as consumer protection. Because there are so many consumers, an individual consumer is less likely to see a benefit in his or her own contribution. But because there are fewer businesses that belong to any given trade association, businesses are more likely to perceive a benefit from participating in the organization. As Mancur Olson, a well-known scholar on interest groups, put it, smaller groups are more likely to organize and associate because members can more readily see the benefits and "logic of collective action."[16] That is, people with common interests working together in groups are more effective than the same number of people working independently.

economic interest group: An organized group that exists to promote favorable economic conditions and economic opportunities for its members.

trade association: A business association that focuses on one particular industry, with membership drawn exclusively from that industry.

Certainly members of smaller groups are more likely to perceive direct benefits from their membership; smaller groups are also less likely to suffer from the free rider problem. **Free riders** are those individuals who do not join or contribute to an interest group that is representing their interests. Thus, they enjoy the benefits of membership without paying for the costs. The free rider problem is more common in larger groups, which may have trouble convincing individuals to contribute due to each individual's perception that others will work to achieve the group's goal.

Labor Unions. Whereas business groups promote the interests of companies and corporations, labor unions promote the interests of American workers. Initially, labor unions emerged from the expansion of the U.S. economy in the late 1800s and early 1900s. The new technologies that resulted from the Industrial Revolution led to the rapid growth of large-scale farming and manufacturing and created many new jobs. Many business owners exploited their laborers, providing low pay, few benefits, and often poor and unsafe working conditions. Workers then organized into unions, using the threat of a strike to improve their conditions.

In the early 1940s, as many as 35 percent of workers in America were union members. Over the years, however, the percentage of union workers has declined. Today only about 13 percent of workers belong to a union. An important reason for this decline relates to changes in the type of jobs that Americans hold. Skilled and unskilled laborers are most likely

newscom

Pictured above are railroad workers on strike in southeastern Pennsylvania in November 2009. The strike shut down bus, train, and trolley service in Philadelphia.

to be unionized, but these types of jobs represent an increasingly smaller proportion of the workforce. Professional and service jobs, which are less likely to be unionized, now dominate the American workforce, and so union membership has declined. Rather than unionizing, professionals tend to organize and join professional associations. Some professionals, however, have unionized. The largest union in the United States today is a teachers' union, the National Education Association.

Unions differ from professional associations in that the laws provide certain bargaining rights to unions. Union membership may be required for all employees as well. State laws vary on this issue. Some states are **open shop**, which means that employees in that state maintain the option of whether or not to join a certified union. Of course in open-shop states, workers who do not join the union may benefit from union activities without "paying the price"— another form of the "free rider" problem. Since 1947, the federal Taft-Hartley Act has technically banned the **closed shop**, which requires union membership as a condition of employment in a unionized workplace. Still, unions have successfully convinced some state legislatures that because all workers enjoy the benefits of union advocacy (for example, promoting pay increases and so on), all workers should at least be required to pay dues to the union. Thus many states allow so-called **union shops**, which require that employees in unionized workplaces either join the union or pay the equivalent of union dues to it after a set period of time.

Professional Associations. Higher levels of education and advances in technology have transformed the American workforce over the past half-century. One of the major changes has been an increase in professional, technical, and service jobs, and a decrease in the number of skilled and unskilled labor jobs. Professionals have organized to promote and protect their economic interests through membership in professional organizations, which lobby on their behalf.

Two large and growing classes of professionals are lawyers and medical doctors, both of which have high-profile and powerful interest groups—the American Bar Association (ABA) for lawyers and the American Medical Association (AMA) for doctors. The medical and legal professions are regulated by state governments, and the AMA and ABA have been quite

open shop: The law that allows employees the option of joining or not joining the certified union at a unionized workplace.

closed shop: The law that requires employees to become members of the union as a condition of employment in unionized workplaces.

union shop: The law that requires that employees in unionized workplaces either join the union or pay the equivalent of union dues to it after a set period of time.

A meeting of the Airline Pilots Association in Atlanta, Georgia, where union organizers discuss concerns of the pilots.

successful in influencing the regulatory process—for example, by establishing licensing requirements for doctors and lawyers.

Another large and influential professional association is the National Association of Realtors (NAR), with a total membership of over 700,000, an annual budget of over $60,000,000, and an organizational staff of more than 400 people. The size, budget, and organization of the NAR provide it with ample resources to advocate the interests of the nation's real estate agents.

Noneconomic Groups

noneconomic interest group: An organized group that advocates for reasons other than its membership's commercial and financial interests.

Economic groups exist primarily to advance the commercial and financial interests of their members. Whereas economic interests (as demonstrated in Table 11.1) dominate pluralist activities, many other interest groups advocate for primarily noneconomic concerns. Three general categories of **noneconomic interest groups** are public-interest groups, issue or ideological groups, and government groups.

TABLE 11.1   Who Spends the Most on Lobbying?

In 2011, interest groups spent more than $3 billion on lobbying activities in Washington, D.C. This table shows the biggest spenders from 1998 through 2011.

Organization	Total
U.S. Chamber of Commerce	$805,535,680
American Medical Association	$264,747,500
General Electric	$262,920,000
American Hospital Association	$214,818,936
Pharmaceutical Research and Manufacturers of America	$214,053,920
AARP	$212,922,064
Blue Cross/Blue Shield	$179,500,520
National Association of Realtors	$178,352,843
Northrop Grumman	$171,945,253
Exxon Mobil	$169,422,742
Verizon	$164,424,841
Edison Electric Institute	$159,395,999
Business Roundtable	$157,510,000
Boeing	$155,484,310
Lockheed Martin	$150,411,138
AT & T	$134,898,336
Southern Co.	$130,700,694
General Motors	$127,279,170

Source: Center for Responsive Politics, http://www.opensecrets.org

Public-Interest Groups. Public interest groups promote the broad, collective good of citizens and consumers. Many public-interest groups seek to promote political reforms that enhance the role of the public in the political process. The League of Women Voters is one such group. Initially formed as an interest group that promoted women's suffrage, the League has become a leading advocate for improving turnout among all citizens in elections. The League of Women Voters has also taken the lead in promoting candidate engagement on issues of importance to the voters by sponsoring campaign debates.

Another highly active public-interest group is Common Cause. This group's literature escribes itself in the following way: "Common Cause is a nonprofit, nonpartisan citizen's lobbying organization promoting open, honest and accountable government. Supported by the dues and contributions of over 200,000 members in every state across the nation, Common Cause represents the unified voice of the people against corruption in government and big money special interests."[17]

Common Cause promotes reforming the political system in ways that enhance the role of the average citizen. Thus it supports laws limiting elected officials from taking gifts from special interests, banning large speaking honoraria for members of Congress, and reforming the presidential campaign finance system. Ironically, Common Cause also tries to limit the role interest groups play in the electoral process.

Ralph Nader and the various citizens' advocacy groups he helped to start (including Public Citizen and the Center for Auto Safety) are among the nation's leading public-interest groups. Nader's best-selling book *Unsafe at Any Speed: The Designed-in Dangers of the American Automobile* forced the president of General Motors to publicly admit to the U.S. Senate that the company ignored automobile safety problems. Nader's Raiders, the name later given to the hundreds of young activists who arrived in Washington, D.C., to help Nader investigate government corruption, were highly influential in pushing automobile safety legislation in the late 1960s, which dramatically raised safety standards for cars and trucks. Their efforts effectively launched a widespread consumer movement, which remains strong. Today these groups advocate campaign finance reform, monitor the health care industry, and promote consumer safety and consumer rights, among other public-interest activities.

Issue and Ideological Groups. Interest groups that focus on specific issues and ideological perspectives are known as **issue and ideological groups**. Abortion, women's rights, and the environment are just a few of the policy issues that have produced interest groups such as the National Right to Life Committee (pro-life), Americans for Free Choice (pro-choice), the National Organization for Women (NOW; women's rights), and the Sierra Club and the Nature Conservancy (both environmental groups). Each of these groups maintains effective lobbies on behalf of its positions.

Some groups have a broader focus than a particular issue or set of policy issues. These are known as ideological groups, and they promote a more general ideological approach on how government should deal with a host of issues. Both liberal and conservative ideological groups operate in the American pluralist system. Americans for Democratic Action (ADA), for example, is an interest group that promotes government policies with a liberal orientation. Since 1947, the voting records of members of Congress on certain issues have served as the standard measure of political liberalism. The ADA supports candidates for office whose votes on key issues score a high "liberal quotient."

The American Civil Liberties Union (ACLU) is an interest group that advocates for the civil rights and liberties of American citizens. Specifically, the ACLU adamantly supports the rights of the accused, free speech rights, free press rights, religious liberty rights, and many other liberties guaranteed by the Bill of Rights. The ACLU has also become a strong advocate for students' rights, the rights of workers, lesbian/gay rights, and immigrants' rights.

The Christian Coalition of America (CCA) is another ideological group that has become a lobbying powerhouse in recent decades; it offers a vehicle to become involved in influencing public policy. The CCA's agenda advocates pro-life positions, promotes the role of religion as a part of what government does, favors reducing tax burdens on families, and supports victims' rights.

public interest group: An organized group that promotes the broad, collective good of citizens and consumers.

issue and ideological group: An organized group that focuses on specific issues and ideological perspectives.

Government Interest Groups. Most interest-group activity organizes private concerns (of either individuals or businesses) for the purpose of influencing public policy. But private interests are not the only ones represented in the pluralist system. Groups representing the interests of governments also operate in this complex system.

Cities and states across the nation have organized to exert influence on the federal government. Most states and large cities employ their own lobbyists in Washington, D.C. But states, cities, and other governments also organize collectively through a variety of interest groups, which are generally referred to as **intergovernmental lobbies**. The National League of Cities, for example, is an interest group that advocates for the broad interests of local governments. Another intergovernmental lobby advancing the cause of the nation's cities is the U.S. Conference of Mayors. The Council of State Governments and the National Governors Association lobby on behalf of the states' interests.

Not only do state and local governments lobby in Washington, D.C., but foreign governments also organize and lobby. Many nations have embassies in the Washington, D.C., area, and many of these embassies engage in interest-group activities of their own.

intergovernmental lobby: Any interest group that represents the collective interests of states, cities, and other governments.

HOW INTEREST GROUPS ACHIEVE THEIR GOALS

Interest groups engage in a number of activities to advance the goals of the group and influence public policy. These activities usually involve lobbying, supporting candidates and parties in election campaigns, mounting persuasion campaigns, and litigating.

Lobbying

Interest groups attempt to influence elected and other public leaders to make decisions that are favorable toward the group's goals. **Lobbying** is the term used to describe how interest groups go about influencing government officials. Lobbyists are the professionals who do the lobbying.

Lobbyists provide information to public officials, with the hope that the information will convince the official to vote or act in a manner favorable to the group's interest. Lobbyists perform a valuable function to public officials by providing not only information and perspectives on issues, but expertise as well. In the iron triangle system, lobbyists seek access to members of Congress and to managers in executive agencies in a particular policy area. Public officials come to depend on the lobbyists for information and knowledge. For example, managers in the Department of Defense and members of Congress on the Armed Services Committee rely on lobbyists from Pratt & Whitney for information on emerging jet engine technologies, engine performance data, and other information, which allows the military to plan and improve the nation's defenses.

Similarly, the congressional committees responsible for workplace safety standards and the Occupational Safety and Health Administration (OSHA), the executive agency responsible for administering those standards, depend on the lobbyists representing labor unions and product safety groups for data and information on workplace hazards, and recommendations for remediation. Of course, these same public officials are likely to be lobbied by business interests concerned about the increased costs associated with remediation of hazards.

Lobbyists communicate with public officials in many different ways, including formal presentations, written memos and policy papers, informal e-mails or notes, face-to-face meetings, and informal discussions over a meal or a drink. The most effective lobbyists are those who provide valuable, truthful information on policy issues and who make persuasive arguments. Having a good working relationship with public officials and a quality reputation provides the lobbyist with access to officials, which is crucial to the lobbyist's success.

A common depiction of lobbying is that of an individual offering money, gifts, trips, or other goods in return for a favorable action, such as a congressperson's vote on a particular bill. Though such activities do take place, in modern times they have become the exception rather than the rule. The activities of lobbyists today are strictly regulated by federal and state governments. Lobbyist gift-giving and bribery of public officials is illegal in most states and can be prosecuted.

lobbying: The means by which interest groups attempt to influence government officials to make decisions favorable to their goals.

THE MORE THINGS CHANGE,
THE MORE THEY STAY THE SAME

High-Powered Lobbyists in American History

Today lobbyists are as important in policymaking as members of Congress themselves. But this is nothing new in American politics. Lobbying has been part of the American political system since the colonial era. Some of the nation's most successful lobbyists over time include the following:

Benjamin Franklin, whom most students of American history recognize as a Founding Father, political philosopher, and inventor/scientist, was also a lobbyist and quite a successful one. The colonies of Pennsylvania, Georgia, and Massachusetts hired him to lobby on their behalf before the British Parliament from 1757 to 1770. Franklin's greatest lobbying success was securing the repeal of the Stamp Act in 1766.

Tommy Corcoran, or "the Cork," as he was known in Washington circles, set the mold for today's most successful lobbyists. He was a trusted friend and adviser to President Franklin Delano Roosevelt during the New Deal era, when Corcoran successfully lobbied Congress on behalf of the White House for many new government programs, including the Securities and Exchange Commission, the Tennessee Valley Authority, and the Federal Housing Administration. He also placed hundreds of attorneys in jobs to run these New Deal agencies. A well-connected insider, The Cork established a private lobbying practice in 1942, where his many connections in government proved valuable for his private-sector clients. From the 1940s until the 1960s, he was the most powerful and influential lobbyist in Washington.

Robert Packwood, a Republican from Oregon, served nearly three decades in the Senate. He was regarded as a shrewd, legislatively accomplished liberal on many social issues, such as abortion rights and family planning. Immediately after he won reelection to a fifth term in the Senate, a story appeared in the *Washington Post* accusing him of sexual harassment. Packwood's strong record of support for feminist issues made the charges of harassment, and his denial of them, especially controversial. Packwood resigned from the Senate in 1995 after an ethics committee recommended his expulsion for sexual misconduct. The cloud of controversy surrounding his departure from the Senate, however, did not diminish his potential for a career as a lobbyist. One year to the day after his resignation, he became a lobbyist with the Sunrise Research Group. Packwood's clients include Northwest Airlines, Verizon Communications, and the National Association of Real Estate Investment Trusts.

Tom Daschle, a Democrat from South Dakota, served as Senate majority leader from June 2001 through January 2003. Daschle was first elected to the Senate in 1986 and became the Senate minority leader just eight years later—in the history of the U.S. Senate, only Lyndon Johnson served fewer years before being elected to lead his party. When Daschle lost his reelection bid in 2004, he immediately took a job with the lobbying arm of the law firm Alston & Byrd. Health care clients including CVS, Abbott Laboratories, and HealthSouth soon flocked to the firm: eventually 60 percent of the firm's lobbying receipts came from that one industry alone.

Mark Wilson/Getty Images

Former Senator Tom Daschle

For Critical Thinking and Discussion

1. "Revolving door" laws prohibit public officials from lobbying activities for one year after they leave office. Do you think one year is a sufficient period of time to discourage public officials from making decisions in office that might affect their future financial gain?

2. Who are the former senators who have represented your state? What are they doing now? Are they lobbyists?

States require lobbyists to provide financial statements, report expenses, and maintain official registration for interest groups and individuals who provide lobbying services.

Lobbyists are regularly seen in the halls of the Capitol building and the House and Senate office buildings. They are also common fixtures in the halls and offices of the state capitol buildings. Many lobbyists own their own lobbying firms and contract with interest groups to provide services, similar to the way that an organization might hire a law firm to conduct legal work. More commonly, however, lobbyists are employed by businesses, associations, or other organizations to lobby for that employer alone. Large organizations and businesses have the resources to hire full-time lobbyists; contract lobbyists often work for smaller organizations that do not have the resources to hire their own full-time lobbying staff.

A form of lobbying that has been used more frequently in recent years is known as **grassroots lobbying**. The idea behind grassroots lobbying is that interest groups communicate with government officials by mobilizing public opinion to exert influence on government action. Because elected leaders are often quite sensitive to the opinions of voters, if a group can demonstrate that public opinion supports a particular position or that the public is willing to contact officials to express their view, officeholders will respond favorably because they want to enhance their chances of being reelected to office. Interest groups with a large number of members are particularly effective at grassroots lobbying, mainly because they can produce large numbers of potential votes in a given election. The AARP, with more than 40 million members, has successfully used grassroots methods of lobbying to put pressure on Congress to protect the Social Security and Medicare systems—two primary goals of the AARP.

grassroots lobbying: Communications by interest groups with government officials through the mobilization of public opinion to exert influence on government action.

Supporting Candidates and Parties in Elections

Interest groups are also quite active in electoral politics, providing resources for candidates and parties that support the interest groups' goals. Table 11.2 lists the groups that have contributed the most money to political campaigns over the past quarter century. PACs, described earlier in this chapter, are an important instrument through which interest groups provide financial support to candidates and political parties.

TABLE 11.2   Big Givers to Campaigns

These 10 organizations were the biggest contributors to American political campaigns between 1989 and 2012. AT & T, the National Association of Realtors and Goldman Sachs gave about equally to Democrats and Republicans, whereas the remaining top 10 givers heavily tilted toward giving to Democratic Party candidates. None of the top 10 tilted toward the GOP.

Organization	Contributions
ActBlue	$58,511,226
AT & T, Inc.	$48,196,209
American Federation of State, County and Municipal Employees	$47,347,798
National Association of Realtors	$41,687,376
Service Employees International Union	$38,083,375
National Education Association	$37,937,019
Goldman Sachs	$37,343,517
American Association for Justice	$35,673,179
International Brotherhood of Electrical Workers	$34,821,537
American Federation of Teachers	$32,833,966
Laborers Union	$32,409,200

Source: Center for Responsive Politics, February, 2012.

In addition to providing financing to support candidates, groups can play an important role in campaigns in other ways as well. For example, a labor union might endorse a candidate and communicate that endorsement to its members, urging members to vote for the candidate. A group might also use its resources to hire a phone bank to make "get out the vote" phone calls on behalf of a candidate or slate of candidates. Groups have also provided support by drafting speeches for candidates on policy matters or hosting rallies for office seekers.

Business groups tend to support Republican candidates, largely because Republicans are more likely to agree with their goals. Similarly, labor unions tend to support Democratic candidates because Democrats are likely to support labor's positions on many issues, such as increases in the minimum wage and family leave laws. On social issues, Republican candidates tend to receive the support of conservative groups, such as pro-life groups and groups advocating stiffer crime control measures. Groups that advocate a more liberal social agenda (such as the ACLU and Sierra Club) tend to support Democratic candidates, whose issue agenda is more consistent with the groups' goals.

ACLU attorney Ruth Bader Ginsburg in 1977. Sixteen years later Ginsburg became an associate justice on the U.S. Supreme Court.

Litigation

Interest groups have also become quite adept at using the court system as a means of achieving their goals. Groups regularly initiate lawsuits, request injunctions, defend members, and file briefs. Consumer product safety groups, for example, regularly file for injunctions in courts seeking to order companies to cease the sale of products that are unsafe.

Some interest groups focus primarily on the courts to achieve their goals. For example, the ACLU regularly initiates lawsuits in circumstances in which it believes the government is compromising individual civil liberties. The ACLU is very active in litigating gender discrimination cases. One of the advantages of interest-group litigation is its capitalization of interest groups' financial resources; average citizens do not have sufficient resources to initiate so many lawsuits. Also, because interest groups often specialize in particular kinds of lawsuits, they are able to litigate more skillfully.

Another way interest groups use the court system to exert influence is by the filing of amicus curiae ("friend of the court") briefs, which are companion briefs supporting an argument or set of arguments in an existing Supreme Court case.[18] Although the interest group is not a direct litigant in a matter, it can use an amicus brief to further or better articulate a position and thus aid litigants in their respective case.

Interest groups have also influenced the court system by engaging in lobbying activities to influence the appointment of judges. Pro-life and pro-choice groups are very active in supporting or opposing particular judicial nominees, based on the nominees' position and past decisions on abortion cases. The American Bar Association uses a rating system to rank individuals nominated for federal judgeships that has become extremely influential in the appointment process.

Persuasion Campaigns

Many interest groups run media campaigns to persuade the public to support their position on issues. Some of this persuasion occurs during election campaigns when groups create and place ads intended to help a political candidate or political party achieve victory. But increasingly, groups have run such campaigns outside of election campaigns to persuade or educate others to the group's way of thinking.

Groups have developed sophisticated public relations operations to communicate their positions. They use tactics such as "targeted mass mailings," in which they mail a pamphlet or other document to a large list of individuals that the group is attempting to influence. For example, the Americans for Democratic Action maintains a list of voters who are not registered with any particular political party. The ADA often sends mailings to those on the list to try to persuade them to support the ADA's position on a particular issue. In addition to mass mailings, groups regularly use television, radio, newspapers, magazines, or even billboards to communicate positions and try to persuade. They also use the Internet to send messages to the wider public.

"Before the Lecture Begins, Students from PIRG Have an Announcement . . ."

If you have spent significant time on a college campus, you have probably heard about PIRG (Public Interest Research Group). PIRG is a federation of state-based public interest groups that, in the words of its Web site, "stand up to powerful special interests on behalf of the American public" (see http://www.uspirg.org/about-us).

The PIRG model of a national campus network was proposed by public interest advocate Ralph Nader in 1970, and now had expanded to include 30 state-based organizations.

State PIRGs are particularly active in recruiting students on college campuses. At the start of the semester, student members of PIRG ask professors for a few minutes of class time to pitch PIRG-related activities to the class. For many students, this is their first exposure to an interest group. Those who join will quickly get involved in PIRG's public-interest causes and sometimes even become interns and get course credit for the experience.

Jeff Greenberg/Alamy

A college student in Florida solicits signatures on a petition for Florida PIRG.

For Critical Thinking and Discussion

1. Does PIRG operate on your campus? If so, how effective has it been in influencing state legislative decisions?

2. Take a look at your campus PIRG's Web site. What positions does it advance on which issues? Do you personally support its lobbying efforts, or do you oppose its lobbying efforts?

Interest groups have become firmly entrenched within the American political landscape. Their influence is both certain and controversial. More than two centuries ago, James Madison expressed concerns about the influence of "factions." Today, many observers of American politics continue to express concerns about the influence of groups and the value of pluralism as a mode of governance. Nevertheless, interest groups offer an important and unique linkage between American citizens' varied interests and public policy. This does not diminish the importance of other linkages, such as free and open elections. But the linkage offered by interest groups is unique in that it allows citizens to exert influence by interacting with one another and collectively attempting to influence what government does. Few would argue with the premise that interest groups have been responsible for leading the charge in promoting political and social policies that have significantly improved the lot of millions of Americans.

SUMMARY: PUTTING IT ALL TOGETHER

PLURALISM AND THE INTEREST GROUP SYSTEM

- Interest groups are a popular mechanism by which groups of people attempt to influence government to advance their shared goals.

- Pluralism is the theory that public policy largely results from a variety of interest groups competing with one another to promote laws that benefit members of their respective groups.

- Many praise the interest-group system in the United States because it provides all groups in society with access and a fair opportunity to compete for influence over public policy.

- The interest group system is also criticized for allowing wealthy corporations and individuals a disproportionate influence on public policy, encouraging many groups to promote their own causes even if they run counter to the public interest, and significantly slowing down the policymaking process.

- Unlike political parties, interest groups usually do not run their own candidates for public office, and they tend to focus more narrowly on special issues or sets of issues.

Test Yourself on This Section

1. What theory suggests that the competition between interest groups is responsible for policymaking?
   a. elitism
   b. majoritarianism
   c. pluralism
   d. liberalism

2. The argument that interest groups are a tool of the political elite and are thus used to advance the views of the wealthy and powerful was first advanced by
   a. C. Wright Mills.
   b. Robert Dahl.
   c. Alexis de Tocqueville.
   d. David Truman.

3. What distinguishes an interest group from a political party?

INTEREST GROUPS IN ACTION

- The growth of interest groups in the United States during the twentieth century was a product of the tremendous growth of government in general over that same period and the increased concerns about political issues that are expressed by a better-educated mass public.

- Interest-group influence over public policy is theoretically informal; in reality, interest-group participation has become ingrained in the process through structures such as iron triangles and issue networks.

- Individuals tend to join or support interest groups in order to receive material benefits, purposive benefits (those that benefit society more generally), and solidary benefits based on individuals' satisfaction from interacting with like-minded people in pursuit of a goal.

- Large interest groups must always concern themselves with the problem of "free riders," those who benefit from interest-group activities on their behalf without ever joining or contributing to that interest group.

- The most successful interest groups tend to maintain a large membership of individuals, at least some of whom are wealthy, as well as a loyal following based on members' commitment to the cause.

Test Yourself on This Section

1. If an individual joins an interest group as a way of advancing his or her own economic interests, what type of benefits is that individual seeking?
   a. material
   b. purposive
   c. solidary
   d. instrumental

2. An "iron triangle" does NOT include which of the following entities?

   a. a federal court

   b. an Interest group

   c. a bureaucratic agency

   d. a congressional committee

3. The American Trial Lawyers Association is a successful interest group primarily because

   a. its members are dedicated to a cause.

   b. it contains millions of members.

   c. its members tend to be quite wealthy.

   d. most members of Congress are lawyers.

4. Distinguish between an "iron triangle" and an "issue network."

TYPES OF INTEREST GROUPS

- Economic interest groups that pursue favorable monetary benefits for their members include business groups such as industry trade associations, labor unions, and professional associations. Noneconomic interest groups that pursue goals other than the commercial interests of their members include public-interest groups, issue or ideological groups, and government interest groups.

Test Yourself on This Section

1. Two out of every three interest groups are

   a. public-interest groups.

   b. economic-based groups.

   c. single-issue groups.

   d. ideological groups.

2. A unionized workplace that requires employees to join the union by state law is known as a(n)

   a. closed shop.

   b. open shop.

   c. union shop.

   d. mixed shop.

3. What type of interest group is the PIRG on your campus? Why would you classify it that way?

HOW INTEREST GROUPS ACHIEVE THEIR GOALS

- Interest groups achieve their goals through lobbying activities, supporting candidates in election contests, litigating, and mounting persuasion campaigns.

Test Yourself on This Section

1. If an interest group files an "amicus curiae" brief, it is engaging in what type of activity?

   a. persuasion campaign — _mass measure._

   b. litigation

   c. election support

   d. grassroots lobbying

2. Which of the following Supreme Court justices was once an important official with the ACLU?

   a. Antonin Scalia

   b. Anthony Kennedy

   c. Clarence Thomas

   d. Ruth Bader Ginsburg

3. Why is the AARP so successful at using grassroots lobbying campaigns to achieve its goals?

KEY TERMS

closed shop (p. 305)
economic interest group (p. 303)
free rider (p. 304)
grassroots lobbying (p. 310)
interest group (p. 294)
intergovernmental lobby (p. 308)
iron triangle (p. 299)
issue and ideological group (p. 307)
issue network (p. 300)

lobbying (p. 308)
majoritarianism (p. 295)
material benefits (of group membership) (p. 300)
noneconomic interest group (p. 306)
open shop (p. 305)
pluralism (p. 295)
political action committee (PAC) (p. 299)

public-interest group (p. 307)
purposive benefits (of group membership) (p. 300)
social movement (p. 297)
solidary benefits (of group membership) (p. 301)
trade association (p. 303)
union shop (p. 305)

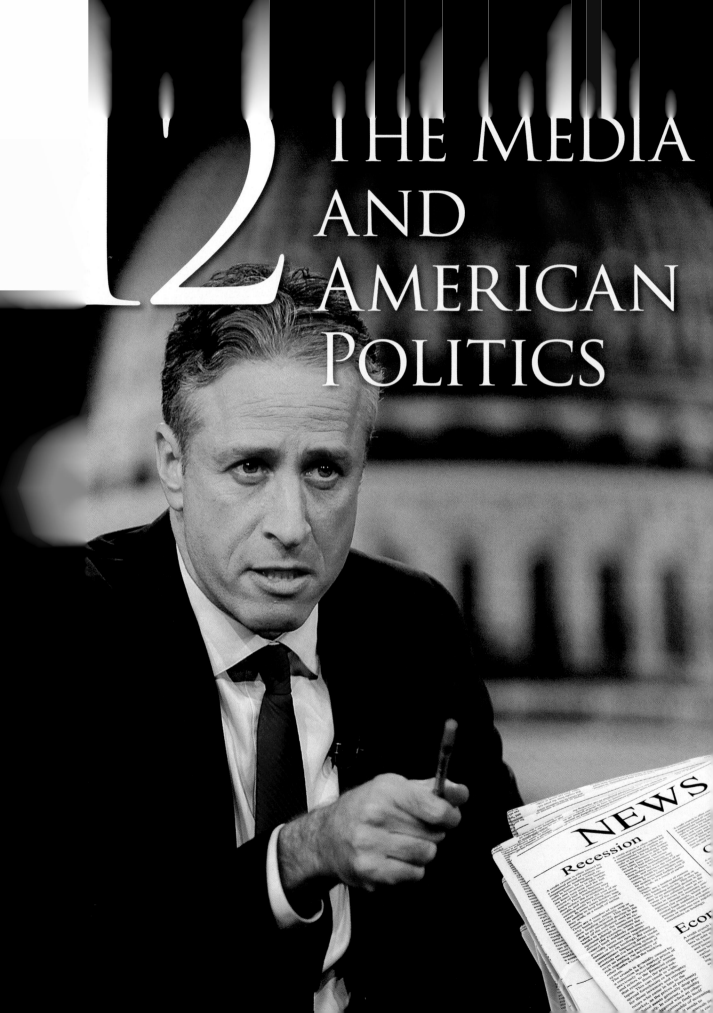

12

THE MEDIA AND AMERICAN POLITICS

LEARNING OBJECTIVES

THE MEDIA IN AMERICAN POLITICS

- Describe the purpose and evolution of the Federal Communications Commission
- Compare and contrast the various functions that the media serve in the American political system

HISTORICAL DEVELOPMENT OF THE MEDIA

- Assess the evolution from a partisan press to a media focused on objectivity
- Explain how changes in technology have transformed the nature of the media

THE MASS MEDIA TODAY

- Identify the large variety of media that cover news and provide opinion about government and politics, including both traditional media and "new" media
- Appraise changes in audience and readership patterns, and the impact of those changes on news coverage
- Describe how the ownership of media organizations is concentrated in large corporations

THE EFFECTS OF THE MEDIA

- Compare and contrast the different theories that have been developed to explain the effect that exposure to news has on viewers/readers

CRITICISMS OF THE NEWS MEDIA

- Critique media coverage of politics, including bias, sensationalism, and the concentration of corporate ownership

The news media serve a number of important political functions in the United States, operating through a large and growing number of outlets. Voters' primary source of information about political candidates and political issues is the news media, and political leaders constantly monitor and attempt to influence the content of news stories to their political advantage. The technologies of television and the Internet both allow citizens to observe events on the battlefield, look into the eyes of presidential candidates, and watch tragedies unfold. Consider the devastation unleashed on New Orleans and other parts of the Gulf Coast by Hurricane Katrina in 2005—the hurricane itself and the government's reaction to the event unfolded live before a worldwide audience sitting in their own homes. Not only do the media serve as an important information source, but they also help set the political agenda, provide perspective and commentary on issues and political candidates, and help keep the government accountable to the people.

1940   1950   1960   1970   1980

Then

1964

A still shot from a television report showing a Birmingham fireman hosing down protesters in 1963.

Source: Charles Moore/Black Star/Alamy

In 1964, President Lyndon Johnson used the relatively new medium of television to accomplish civil rights reforms that had eluded his predecessors. Past presidents had tried and failed to pass civil rights laws: In 1947 President Truman was rebuffed in his hopes for legislation that addressed segregation. President Eisenhower pursued a centrist agenda on civil rights, but the best he could achieve was to establish a bipartisan civil rights commission and a civil rights division in the Justice Department; the 1957 Civil Rights Act had such a narrow impact that it proved a disappointment to civil rights leaders. Johnson's ambitious civil rights agenda might have met a similar fate had the plight of African Americans in the South not been seen by the rest of the nation through extensive and unprecedented television coverage. Footage from television cameras allowed viewers at home to witness police officials directing full-pressure water hoses on African American school children, police dogs set loose on civil rights demonstrators, and numerous brutal beatings. Donations to the civil rights movement increased dramatically once the public outside the South became an eyewitness to these dramatic events, and legislative leaders from both parties soon felt public pressure to overcome the objections of opponents. After waiting out a 54-day filibuster, the Senate eventually joined the House in approving major civil rights legislation. On July 2, 1964, President Lyndon Johnson signed the Civil Rights Act into law. Clearly the "small screen" had played a large role in the process.

Now

The Obama White House web page in 2009, promoting the Health Care Reform bill.

Source: Courtesy of Whitehouse.gov

Civil rights reform was not the only legislation that benefitted from a president's use of a new communications medium. Early in his presidency, Barack Obama was determined to achieve legislative success on a subject that had proved elusive to so many of his predecessors: comprehensive health care reform. Franklin Roosevelt in 1935, Harry Truman in 1951, and Bill Clinton in 1994 all saw their major health care reform proposals defeated by well-organized opposition. In these earlier battles, the American Medical Association and other opponents used media campaigns to prey upon public fears that the legislation might separate individuals from their own doctors. The Obama administration's efforts to pass health care reform would overcome similar opposition campaigns by embarking on a successful media effort of its own, using the Internet. Obama's forces effectively used the newest communications medium to bring the full debate over health care out into the open, exposing backroom deals and revealing opponents' exaggerations about negative consequences of the reform proposals. Through a continuous bombardment of information released over the Internet, Obama successfully justified the plan to many of the millions of Americans lapping up news on the Internet. The legislation eventually overcame all obstacles in its path, including a Republican party-line filibuster. Had the public not been privy to the immense amounts of information pouring forth from the Internet, the arguments against the administration's plan might once again have proven too difficult to overcome.

THE MEDIA IN AMERICAN POLITICS

Consider the following facts about media use in the United States: More than 170 million Americans use Facebook, and each user has an average of 130 "friends"; the average American spends more time watching television than working or going to school; all forms of media considered, the average person is engaged in media consumption for 3,500 hours each year—that's almost 40 percent of the 8,760 hours that exist in a year. There are even more TV sets per household than there are toilets. The media clearly have a pervasive presence in the everyday life of most Americans. From watching the political comedy of Jon Stewart's *The Daily Show*, to listening to the political commentary of Rush Limbaugh, to catching up on the latest news from around the world on cable TV's CNN or Politico on the Internet, Americans make ample use of media sources available to them for getting political information.

Most news media organizations in the United States are owned by private companies, which, like most other private companies, seek to make a profit. Unlike other industries, however, the media enjoy a special constitutionally granted protection. The First Amendment to the U.S. Constitution specifically provides that "Congress shall make no law . . . abridging the freedom . . . of the press." When the First Amendment was adopted in 1791, the press was mostly a small collection of newspapers and magazines. Over the years, the press, now more commonly referred to as the media, has expanded to include radio, television, book publishers, music producers, the Internet, and motion pictures.

One early event that helped shape America's perspective on freedom of the press was the trial in 1735 of newspaper printer Peter Zenger, who in the *New York Weekly Journal* published a series of articles highly critical of the British-appointed governor of New York. Zenger was arrested on charges of criminal libel. He was defended by Philadelphia lawyer Andrew Hamilton, who won the case with his argument that Zenger had printed the truth and the truth cannot be considered libelous. Hamilton's argument thus established the principle of truth as a defense against libel.

The argument for a free press in United States today largely rests upon the concept of the "free marketplace of ideas," a phrase coined by Supreme Court Justice Oliver Wendell Holmes in his dissenting opinion in *Abrams v. United States* (1919), which suggests that allowing people to freely communicate their ideas will provide a larger variety of ideas to consider. Encouraging the publication and dissemination of a wide variety of political ideas offers citizens a diversity of opinions and perspectives and facilitates the free flow of information about local, national, and global events. Of course, for ideas to flow freely, government must be prevented from using its power to stifle perspectives with which it disagrees.

Government Regulation of the Media

Congress created the Federal Communications Commission (FCC) in 1934 to regulate the electronic media (primarily radio and eventually television) through the licensing of broadcasters and creating rules for broadcasters to follow. The FCC does not have authority to regulate the print media, such as newspapers. In fact, regulation of print media is rare, and courts have consistently treated the right of print media to publish free of government regulation. Some electronic media require broadcast frequencies that are scarce and thus need to be regulated to ensure the orderly transmission of programs.

Among the tools that the FCC may employ to regulate the activities of broadcasters is the threat of revoking a license or fining a station for violating its rules. The FCC has used these tools to limit the language and type of sexual material that broadcasters might use. For example, the FCC imposed fines on the owners of radio stations that broadcast "shock jock" Howard Stern. Stern's program often included graphic descriptions of sexual acts and sex games, as well as language that the FCC deems unacceptable. Some of those stations fined then dropped the Stern show from their program schedule. To avoid further legal battles with the FCC, in 2005 Stern moved his show to a satellite radio station, which is not subject to FCC regulations because satellite radio is purchased by users and does not rely on the publicly controlled airwaves.

One of the most celebrated instances of the FCC clamping down on material in broadcast transmission involved comedian George Carlin's "Seven Dirty Words" skit, which satirized attitudes toward vulgar language. In the skit, Carlin continually repeated the seven words that you can't say on TV or radio. The piece was played on a radio station licensed to the Pacifica Foundation. Prior to playing the piece, the announcer warned the audience about its content. Nevertheless, a listener complained to the FCC, and the FCC in turn warned the radio station not to replay the piece. The station challenged the FCC's authority to regulate programming content, and the case made its way to the U.S. Supreme Court in *FCC v. Pacifica Foundation* (1978).[1] In that case the Supreme Court upheld the FCC's power to regulate the broadcast media on the criteria of indecent material.

The FCC's **equal time rule** mandates that radio and TV stations must offer equal amounts of airtime to all political candidates who want to broadcast advertisements. This rule also now includes a provision requiring that if a station broadcasts the president's State of the Union message, then that station must also provide free airtime for the opposing political party to broadcast a response.

> **equal time rule:** The FCC mandate that radio and TV stations offer equal amounts of airtime to all political candidates who want to broadcast advertisements.

From 1950 through the late 1980s, the FCC also enforced the so-called fairness doctrine, requiring broadcasters to set aside time for public affairs programming. The proliferation of news sources and technologies for transmitting electronic messages during the 1980s effectively ended the FCC's fairness doctrine requirements. These changes in technologies also resulted in the passage of the 1996 Telecommunications Act, which shifted the emphasis of government policy from regulating to facilitating competition. This law deregulated cable television providers, eliminated monopolies held by local phone companies, and allowed local phone companies to provide long-distance phone services. The Telecommunications Act transformed the FCC from a regulator of the telecommunications industry into an aggressive supporter of competition within that industry.

Functions of the Media in American Politics

Throughout the history of the United States, the media have come to serve a number of functions in the political system, all of which promote the free flow of information to the public. Principal functions of the media include (1) providing objective coverage of events, (2) facilitating public debate, and (3) serving as government watchdog.

Providing Objective Coverage of Events. The media's most basic role involves monitoring events around the nation and the world and communicating those events to the public. Through modern communications technologies, the media have become proficient at reporting major events as they happen. Live coverage of presidential addresses, campaign debates, war operations, prominent trials, natural disasters, and other important world events have made their way almost instantaneously onto front-page headlines and into television's round-the-clock news coverage.

Providing information about news and events is perhaps the most basic and most important function of the media. Factual news information is an essential component of evaluating events and forming political opinions. Operating free of government control, the U.S. media can provide objective coverage of events to the American public. **Objectivity** refers to the media reporting events factually, accurately, fairly, and equitably—an important goal for many journalists. In addition to providing factual information about events, objective journalism requires signaling when important events occur and providing perspectives on all sides of an issue or policy debate. The goal of objectivity, however, is itself the subject of some debate. Objectivity is hard to define and measure, and journalists sometimes take a shortcut by trying to give equal weight to all sides without making any judgments of their own. This approach permitted Senator Joseph McCarthy to falsely but very publicly accuse people of being communists in the 1950s; it let cigarette companies get away with denying that smoking causes cancer; and it prolonged the current national debate on global warming. Journalism professor Philip Meyer has advocated for a science-based definition of objectivity by getting journalists to seek more independent verification of facts.[2]

> **objectivity:** The journalistic standard that news reporting of events must be factual, accurate, fair, and equitable.

CHECK **THE LIST**

Top 10 Political Blogs, as of April 2012

1. The Huffington Post (www.huffingtonpost.com)
2. BuzzFeed (www.buzzfeed.com)
3. The Daily Beast (www.dailybeast.com)
4. Ars Technica (www.arstechnica.com)
5. Think Progress (www.thinkprogress.org)
6. Jezebel (jezebel.com)
7. Mediaite (www.mediaite.com)
8. Hot Aire (www.hotair.com)
9. Business Insider (www.businessinsider.com)
10. L.A. Now (www.latimesblogs.latimes.com/lanow)

▶**POINT TO PONDER:** The Huffington Post, launched by Arianna Huffington in 2005, was founded as a left/liberal leaning Internet commentary outlet. Acquired by AOL in 2011, the Huffington Post is by far the leading blog in terms of Internet traffic, with nearly three times the total number of visitors in April 2012 than the second-place TMZ, the celebrity gossip blog. Visit that blog at www.huffingtonpost .com. Why do you think the Huffington Post blog has been so successful?

Source: http://technorati.com/blogs/top100/

Numerous media formats strive to provide objective coverage of news information. Most of the content of newspapers (with the notable exception of the editorial pages) is aimed at objectively covering news events and politics at the global, national, and local levels. The 24-hour cable news channels, such as CNN, Fox News, and MSNBC, provide news of events on a continuous basis. Many other formats are aimed at providing an objective look at news information to readers and viewers.

Moreover, the proliferation of cable television has broadened the role of the media as provider of information. Channels like the Biography Channel, the History Channel, local government access channels, and C-SPAN now offer programming that gives historical context to local, national, and international events.

Facilitating Public Debate. In addition to monitoring and reporting events, the media also facilitate public dialogue and debate on important political issues. By helping frame issues, offering perspectives on how a problem might be solved, and providing context and commentary on political campaigns, the media serve a vital role in a democratic system that depends heavily on voters to make informed choices in elections.

The media facilitate public debate through a variety of forms, both print and electronic. Newspaper editorials provide perspectives on policy debates and political candidates. Syndicated columnists, such as conservatives Charles Krauthammer and George Will and liberals such as Thomas Friedman and Mark Shields, publish columns in numerous newspapers around the nation on a regular basis, presenting their own perspectives on issues. Most newspapers dedicate space on their editorial pages for citizens to write opinion pieces ("op-eds") and letters to the editor offering their point of view. Many news magazines adhere to a liberal or conservative approach to discussing issues or evaluating candidates for office. *The Nation*, for example, has a liberal perspective, whereas *The National Review* presents a conservative perspective. Even magazines devoted to one perspective or another, however, usually offer a forum for readers to assess issues. Radio talk shows that offer perspectives on politics, such as those of conservative radio talk show host Rush Limbaugh or liberal political commentator Ed Schultz, also facilitate public debate, as do television programs like MSNBC's *Hard Ball with Chris Matthews* and Fox News' *Hannity's America*, which often feature debates between the anchors and their ideological opponents.

These media formats go beyond objectively reporting news to analyzing events and presenting arguments from varying ideological perspectives that readers and viewers can evaluate and use in forming their own opinions about public policies and political candidates.

Liberal commentator Chris Matthews hosts "Hardball" on MSNBC.

Government Watchdog. Since the founding of the nation, American political culture has been characterized by a healthy skepticism about government. To govern is to have power, and power (in the minds of many) corrupts. The federal system that divides power between the federal government and state and local governments; the system of shared power among the legislative, executive, and judicial branches of government; and the system of checks and balances among these three branches are mechanisms that help guard against the potential abuse of government power. The news media also help prevent the abuse of government power through their role as government watchdog. In this role, the media are sometimes referred to as the fourth branch of government, or the "fourth estate," checking the power of the other branches. Rooting out corruption and abuses of power through investigative journalism is a core function of the American media, no less important today than it was two centuries ago.

More than a century ago, a group of journalists, who came to be known as "muckrakers"[3] (they were given this name by President Theodore Roosevelt), investigated and exposed corporate and political corruption in American life, including the corrupting effect of corporate contributions on presidential candidates who won office. In the late 1800s, corporate wealth was concentrated in a handful of companies in the railroad and banking industries, and those companies bought favors and influence with various presidential administrations. The muckrakers exposed the rash of influence peddling and by doing so helped spawn new laws curbing corporate contributions to federal campaigns.

Perhaps the most well-known case of the media uncovering and exposing government corruption was the investigative reporting of *Washington Post* reporters Bob Woodward and Carl Bernstein in the early 1970s concerning the Watergate corruption scandal of President Richard M. Nixon's administration. Their work led in part to the resignation of President Nixon in 1974 for his role in covering up the details of the Republican-led break-in of Democratic National Headquarters in the Watergate Hotel during the 1972 presidential campaign.[4] Woodward and Bernstein largely depended on an anonymous administration source, who came to be known as "Deep Throat," for information that ultimately exposed the White House cover-up of a number of criminal activities in Nixon's 1972 campaign for reelection. It was not until 30 years later, in 2005, that Mark Felt, who at the time of the Watergate break-in was deputy director of the FBI, publicly announced that he was in fact "Deep Throat."

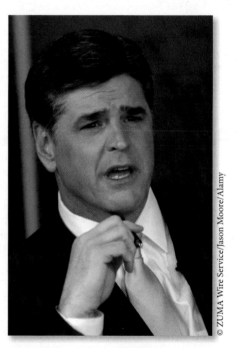

Conservative Sean Hannity hosts "Hannity's America" on the Fox News Channel.

The media also exercise their watchdog function through television programs such as *60 Minutes*, *Dateline*, and *Meet the Press* and through Internet Web sites set up by groups like Common Cause, which provides data on the negative influence of corporate donations on political campaigns. The media also carry out their watchdog function through books. For example, the 2008 book *What Happened* by Scott McClellan, former press secretary to President

Pulitzer Prize–winning investigative reporters Carl Bernstein and Bob Woodward in 1973. Woodward and Bernstein investigated the Watergate scandal of the Nixon administration from 1972 through 1974 for the Washington Post.

Bettmann/CORBIS

George W. Bush, severely criticized the president and top Bush administration officials for waging a propaganda campaign to convince the American public that war with Iraq was necessary.

HISTORICAL DEVELOPMENT OF THE MEDIA

Before the American Revolution, the news media consisted of a handful of newspapers that were published by printers.[6] The main job of the printer was not to publish a newspaper, but rather to prepare official documents (such as marriage licenses, deeds to land, and government documents), political pamphlets, and religious books. Newspapers of the time mostly featured notices of public events and advertisements for local merchants. These early newspapers carried little information about politics or news events.

The political events that led up to the American Revolution and the events of the Revolution itself changed the nature and functions of the colonial newspapers. Many colonists were intensely interested in the disputes with Great Britain and eager for news about the battles of the Revolution. Newspapers responded to these interests with news stories about the events. Stories about the economic turmoil of the post-Revolution period, particularly the bitter partisan fight between the Federalists and Anti-Federalists over ratification of the Constitution, also appeared in the nation's early newspapers.

The Era of the Partisan Press

partisan press era: The period from the late 1700s to the mid-1800s when newspapers typically supported a particular political party.

The Federalist/Anti-Federalist battle ushered in the **partisan press era**, a period characterized by newspapers supporting a particular political party. This period lasted from the 1700s through the mid-1850s. Newspapers advocating the Federalist position that favored a stronger central government included John Fenno's *Gazette of the United States* and Noah Webster's *American Minerva*. The Anti-Federalists and later the Jeffersonian-Republicans, who supported states' rights, had their own partisan newspapers, such as the *National Gazette* and the *National Intelligencer*.

Partisan newspapers appealed mostly to readers who already agreed with the political positions advocated by those publications. Partisan-oriented news eventually became big business, and government printing contracts to partisan publications became a regular part of the spoils system.

During the early nineteenth century, a number of technological developments had a significant impact on the newspaper business. The invention of the rotary press in 1815 enabled the mass production of newspapers. The invention of the telegraph and the development of the telegraph system across the United States in the 1840s provided for the widespread electronic dissemination of news information. The expansion of the railroad system across the nation facilitated the mass distribution of newspapers across the continent. These developments allowed newspapers to print news events more quickly and distribute their publications to a larger number of people in a shorter period of time. These technologies also helped reduce production costs, making newspapers affordable for most Americans. The term *penny press* aptly described the low cost of newspapers during the early to mid-nineteenth century.

By the 1850s, newspapers found that they could increase their circulation by distancing themselves from particular partisan positions. Eyeing ever-larger markets, newspapers began

Up until the Civil War period, most American newspapers advocated perspective of a particular political party.

Fact.

The initial commercial successes of newspapers in the United States were based on partisan content that appealed to their readers.

to appeal to all Americans. Journalists began to tout the goals of objective reporting of the facts, rather than providing a biased or partisan perspective on events. By the end of the nineteenth century, the technological innovations and the desire of newspaper publishers to reach larger numbers of readers and maximize profits through the selling of advertisements had transformed the newspaper industry from a mostly partisan press to one focused on objective reporting of the news.

The Emergence of Electronic Media

The development of the radio in the early twentieth century provided a new means for Americans to get information about politics. Most notably, communication from the media source to the audience was instantaneous. In addition, the technology allowed political leaders to directly communicate with the American people. The first radio station was KDKA in Pittsburgh, established in 1923. The first network of radio stations, which was established in 1926 as the National Broadcasting Company (NBC), provided common programming and newscasts that were made available to the first truly mass audiences.

President Franklin Delano Roosevelt, delivering one of his famous "fireside chats" in 1933.

Franklin Delano Roosevelt, elected president in 1932, used the radio to deliver comforting and inspiring messages to the nation, then suffering in the midst of the Great Depression. FDR's weekly radio addresses, which the president called "fireside chats," represented the first significant use of this medium by a political leader to communicate to the nation's people. In addition to FDR's fireside chats, radio commentators such as Father Charles Coughlin (Detroit's anti-Semitic "fighting priest") and Louisiana Senator Huey Long popularized radio as a medium that could provide a great deal of political commentary and debate. During World War II, Americans eager for news about the progress of the war turned to the radio for information. Edward R. Murrow's live radio reports from London during the Nazi bombings of that city and from other battle sites captivated the nation.

In the 1950s, Joe Pyne of radio station KABC hosted the first political talk radio show. Pyne challenged the status quo political views of the times, invited call-in questions from listeners, and promoted confrontation and debate. Pyne's style and format laid the foundation for many of today's popular political talk radio shows.

CBS news anchor Walter Cronkite, pictured here in 1969, was a very popular and trusted newsman for CBS news.

Numerous technological advancements have had a large impact on the scope and importance of the news media through American history, but none has had a more profound influence than the invention of television. In the post–World War II boom of the American economy, the nation quickly adopted TV as its primary medium for getting news about politics and the world. NBC and CBS developed the standard TV news show format in the early 1950s with a 15-minute daily news program. The program featured a news anchor reading the news, supported by film footage and reporters. This format—now modified into a half-hour program produced each evening—continues to be widely used today by all the major networks. In the 1950s, TV networks broadcast the Army–McCarthy hearings of the U.S. Senate that exposed Senator Joseph McCarthy as a crude bully and resulted in his censure for ethical misconduct. Live television coverage of the Republican and Democratic national conventions set the standard for live broadcasts of major political events. The networks also sold advertising time to the major party candidates in the presidential election of 1952, revolutionizing the way in which candidates would wage their bids for elective office.

Presidential Debates and the Power of Television. A defining moment in revealing the political power of electronic media was the live television broadcast of the debates between Republican Richard Nixon and Democrat John

Brian Williams, NBC's evening news anchor.

Kennedy, candidates in the presidential election of 1960. For the first time, all Americans were able to watch a live debate between the candidates. Many observers credit Kennedy's favorable TV performance as an important factor contributing to his razor-thin victory over Nixon in the November election. During the first of three televised debates, Kennedy won over the audience with his relaxed and self-assured manner before the camera; by contrast, Nixon seemed nervous and uncomfortable. Nixon prepared for the debate by studying briefing documents, but spent little time practicing debate style. Kennedy, on the other hand, spent a great deal of time practicing answers to questions out loud. For the two days prior to the first debate, Kennedy and his inner circle of advisers didn't leave the practice session in their hotel room. On the night of the debate, a tanned Kennedy looked strong and healthy. He wore a navy blue suit that contrasted sharply with the light walls of the TV studio. Nixon, on the other hand, looked ill and underweight. Just before the debate he had been hospitalized with an infection, exhausted from a hard week of campaigning. He wore makeup to cover up his five o'clock shadow and dressed in a light gray suit that blended into the background.

The candidates debated the important issues and both did well in articulating their positions. But TV analysts reported that Kennedy won the debate. His stage presence, practice addressing the camera, tanned complexion, hand gestures, and commanding appearance compared favorably to the somber, pale Nixon. It was a lesson that no future presidential candidate would forget.

Interestingly, research on this debate[7] reveals that those who listened to the debate on the radio thought Nixon won, whereas those who watched the debate on TV tended to think that Kennedy won, proving that the medium through which events are communicated can indeed influence the way in which people evaluate those events. That the medium itself may have an important effect on the way in which people receive and perceive news was suggested by communications researcher Marshall McCluhan, who summarized this idea with his memorable phrase "the medium is the message."[8]

Live televised debates between the candidates for president did not occur again until 1976, when Republican President Gerald Ford and Democratic challenger Jimmy Carter met. This time both candidates were well prepared to convey the image they wanted to the American viewing audience. Dressed to coordinate with the set background, prepped with numerous practice sessions, and made up to ensure a favorable skin color tone, both Carter and Ford

President Barack Obama and Governor Mitt Romney spar at the second presidential debate of the 2012 race. This debate used the town meeting format.

sought to communicate a positive image. Live broadcasts of presidential campaign debates have been a part of every presidential election contest since 1976.[9]

Television has transformed virtually every aspect of political campaigns and government policymaking. Prior to TV, the vast majority of voters never saw more than a still picture of the candidates, and most learned about them from reading newspaper accounts of their statements, speeches, and activities. Television, however, has allowed viewers to observe candidates live and in action, and to see how they deliver a speech and respond to questions. Television has also given candidates the opportunity to develop an "image" through carefully planned media appearances and strategically designed political advertisements.

Presidential Press Conferences. The power of televised images has also altered the governing process. Whereas President Woodrow Wilson was the first to hold regular and formal presidential news conferences, President Dwight D. Eisenhower was the first to hold regular news conferences as we know them today, as a means of explaining his administration's policies and appealing directly to the public for support. Before Eisenhower, the news media's access to the president was primarily through appointments that the chief executive would give to favored reporters. Eisenhower opened up the press conference to reporters from all types of news organizations. The questions were not prescreened, and Eisenhower addressed whatever topics were on reporters' agendas. This format for addressing the nation, coupled with the capability of television to show Americans the event, opened up the presidency to the public.

Eisenhower's successor, President John F. Kennedy, quickly mastered the art of the presidential press conference. He made events seem even more dramatic and intriguing by allowing TV to broadcast them live. Kennedy's preparedness on issues, strong intellect, charismatic personality, and sense of humor made his press conferences interesting and successful events. President Lyndon B. Johnson continued the press conference tradition set by his predecessors, but such events became more difficult for Johnson as America's involvement in the Vietnam War escalated, with press questions increasingly focused on war casualties and military ineffectiveness.

Eisenhower, Kennedy, and Johnson averaged about two press conferences every month, but Presidents Nixon, Ford, Carter, and Reagan held fewer—less than one per month. Nixon, Ford, and Carter each dealt with crisis situations (Vietnam, Watergate, a severe energy crisis, and the Iranian hostage crisis), which led to uncomfortable open questioning from journalists, and so each president cut back on the number of conferences. Reagan, despite his acting background

President Obama holds a press conference at the White House in 2012.

and ease in front of a camera, had a difficult time dealing with reporters' questions in a press conference setting, and so he began a weekly radio address as a regular means of communicating with the American public. All presidents since Reagan have used this form of weekly address to speak to the nation.

President Bill Clinton increased the number of presidential press conferences to an average of two per month, based on his ability to use this format quite effectively. However, the number of Clinton press conferences was reduced sharply during the period when he faced his biggest crisis in office, over his relationship with White House intern Monica Lewinsky. President George W. Bush, who like Reagan was often ill at ease at responding to questions in a press conference situation, averaged only one press conference per year. Staged events, one-on-one interviews with reporters, televised speeches, and the weekly radio address were Bush's preferred means of communicating to the public through the media. Like his predecessor, President Obama has also held few press conferences, preferring public appearances, staged events, and use of his White House Web page to communicate with the public. As indicated at the opening of this chapter, Obama's use of the Internet to influence both public and elite opinion is credited with the passage of the Health Care Reform law passed in 2010.

With each successive presidential administration, White House staffs have become better equipped at using the media to influence the public through direct communication. Press conferences, presidential addresses, and carefully staged presidential appearances are typical of the means by which the White House uses the media to muster support for the president's agenda.

THE MASS MEDIA TODAY

Today's mass media include a variety of channels of communication through which news content is disseminated to audiences. Channels of communication may be either print or electronic. Print media largely include newspapers, magazines, and books. Electronic media include television, radio, the Internet, and movies. In addition, forms of content on any medium may be classified as either news or entertainment. In newspapers, for example, the first section of most publications is entirely devoted to news stories and editorials. Subsequent sections might include other news such as sports news or business news. Typically there is an entertainment section that includes movie reviews, comics, crossword puzzles, recipes, and so forth. Television stations also provide news programming in the forms of news broadcasts, investigative reporting shows, and political talk shows, and entertainment programming in the form of sitcoms, soap operas, reality TV programs, and drama shows.

Christina Aguilera lends her familiar face to a Rock the Vote poster. MTV, a popular media outlet for young people, airs this campaign prior to major elections.

THE FUTURE IS IN OUR HANDS

IT'S TIME TO ROCK THE VOTE

REGISTER TO VOTE AT ROCKTHEVOTE.COM

©2008 CHRISTINA AGUILERA AND SON FOR ROCK THE VOTE

ROCKTHEVOTE.COM

THE MORE THINGS CHANGE, THE MORE THEY STAY THE SAME

Political Satire Throughout the Years

Political satirists attempt to derive entertainment from politics. In theory, they seek to entertain rather than to fulfill any specific political agenda. Of course that distinction is more theoretical than real, as the line between hard-hitting satire and passionate political argument is often difficult to draw. Moreover, as the three following examples illustrate, some of the most famous American political satirists are hardly shy about using satire to make a partisan political argument:

In 1905, Mark Twain—better known for his earlier fiction works such as *The Adventures of Tom Sawyer* (1876) and *The Adventures of Huckleberry Finn* (1885)—cemented his standing as one of the great political satirists in America as well. That year in his pamphlet titled *King Leopold's Soliloquy,* Twain wrote in the voice of a fictional "King Leopold," who raves madly about the good things that he says he has done for the people of the Congo Free State, including the disbursement of millions for religion and art. Leopold claimed that he had come to the Congo with piety "oozing" from "every pore," that he had only wanted to convert the people to Christianity, and that he had wanted to stop the slave trade. By effectively using satire, Twain was able to make an especially effective (and condemnatory) attack on imperialism.

In 1970, Garry Trudeau launched his daily comic strip "Doonesbury," which chronicled the adventures and lives of many characters of different ages, professions, and backgrounds, from the president of the United States to the title character, Michael Doonesbury. Trudeau's use of real-life politicians as characters often proved controversial, and in the eyes of his critics, revealed some of his more "liberal leanings." For example, he often portrayed George W. Bush with a Stetson hat sitting atop a Roman military hat representing imperialism. When Doonesbury ran the names of soldiers killed in Iraq in 2003, many newspapers responded by moving the strip from the comics page to the editorial page. Still, even some of the most conservative newspapers refused to cancel the comic strip outright, as Trudeau's brand of satire proved just as popular to readers as Mark Twain's had a century earlier.

Shown above is an early edition of Mark Twain's "King Leopold's Soliloquy."

A clip of Gary Trudeau's "Doonesbury" comic strip featuring commentary on President George W. Bush.

In 2005, the comedian Stephen Colbert launched his half-hour show *The Colbert Report*, in which he played a caricatured version of conservative political pundits, including the extremely popular Fox News personality Bill O'Reilly. Far from the real Stephen Colbert's roots in improvisational theater in Chicago, Colbert's alternate persona was raised in South Carolina and was the youngest

(Continued)

Political Satire Throughout the Years (continued)

of 11 siblings. Colbert mocked the political process and its campaign finance system by using the show as a vehicle to start campaigns on behalf of himself and his super-PAC, the "Definitely Not Coordinating with Stephen Colbert super-PAC." Real-life politicians ignored Colbert and the people of "Colbert Nation" only at great political cost.

Stephen Colbert of The Comedy Channel's "The Colbert Report."

For Critical Thinking and Discussion

1. Does political satire that mocks politicians and the political process contribute positively to our political discourse, or does it simply add to the incivility that already exists?

2. Are there any issues that you consider so serious that they should essentially be off limits to political satirists or humorists? Child molestation? The Holocaust? Or is that simply the price we must pay in a free society?

Even media sources that are intended primarily to provide entertainment programming sometimes include content that may fall within the realm of politics. One very popular show that combines news with comedy is *The Daily Show*, hosted by political comedian Jon Stewart. During recent presidential elections the cable television station MTV broadcast programming that attempted to increase voter turnout among young people.

The Print Media

The modern print media mostly include newspapers, magazines, and books. Use of these print media has declined in recent decades. *Time* and *Newsweek* are popular weekly magazines devoted to providing in-depth coverage of current events, though their readership too has declined as consumers of news increasingly turn to electronic sources of information. These and other news magazines often rely on photojournalism to support their longer stories to engage readers.

Books also enjoy an important place in American journalism. *Plan of Attack*, a 2004 book by Bob Woodward, documented the role of the Bush administration in preparing for the second Iraq War. Woodward, through interviews with top White House sources, including the president and the secretary of state, concluded that the Bush administration had actively begun preparations for war long before the U.S. invasion and well before

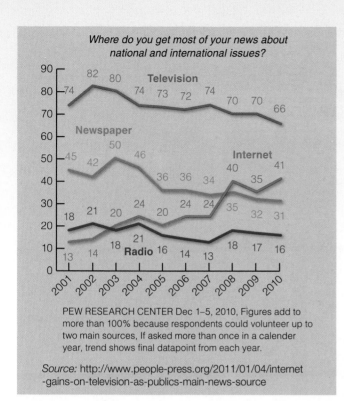

FIGURE 12.1 Americans' Primary News Sources

Where do you get most of your news about national and international issues?

PEW RESEARCH CENTER Dec 1–5, 2010, Figures add to more than 100% because respondents could volunteer up to two main sources, If asked more than once in a calender year, trend shows final datapoint from each year.

Source: http://www.people-press.org/2011/01/04/internet -gains-on-television-as-publics-main-news-source

notifying Congress of its intentions. Woodward's work became an important topic during the 2004 presidential campaign. Thirty years earlier in a book called *All the President's Men*, co-written with Carl Bernstein, Woodward documented the Nixon administration's role in the Watergate affair.

A century ago there were about 2,200 newspapers published daily; today there are only about 1,500 daily newspapers—a 30 percent decline—purchased by about 76 million readers. Once the prime source of news for Americans, newspapers now take a backseat to television as the nation's main news source (see Figure 12.1). Just as the number of newspaper readers has declined steadily since the 1950s, today the Internet seems to be becoming a more popular source of news and, as a result, the number of newspaper readers is falling at an even greater rate than before. The youngest generation of news consumers—those in high school—are most likely to be using digital media to get their news and information, as demonstrated in Figure 12.2. As the American population ages, it is likely that the trend toward greater use of the Internet and lesser us of traditional media such as newspapers will continue.

The vast majority of newspapers are regional metropolitan and suburban publications. They range from those that cover large metropolitan areas, such as the *Chicago Tribune*, the *Miami Herald*, the *Dallas Morning News*, and the *San Francisco Chronicle*, to those covering much smaller towns. A handful of newspapers such as the *New York Times*, the *Wall Street Journal*, and *USA Today* are considered national dailies and are designed to appeal to a national readership. The *New York Times* trumpets its supposed status as the "paper of record" of events from around the world; the *Wall Street Journal* has the niche of being the nation's leading newspaper on financial markets and commerce; *USA Today*'s format of brief stories along with colorful graphics and pictures has helped it attract a nationwide following.

Wire services provide a clearinghouse for news as it is occurring. The largest wire service by far is the Associated Press (AP). The AP employs a large number of reporters throughout the nation and around the world to write stories on news events. Newspapers and television and radio stations that are members of the AP share the news services it produces. Using the AP as their news source allows smaller regional newspapers and local TV and radio stations to cover events from around the world in an efficient, informative, and cost-effective manner.

Fact or Fiction?

Newspapers are the number one source of news for Americans today.

Fiction.

Since the advent of the TV news broadcast, newspapers have always lagged behind television as the primary source of news. More recently, the Internet has surpassed newspapers as a prime news source as well.

FIGURE 12.2 The Generational Divide in Use of Digital Media to Get News

Source: 2011 survey commissioned by the Knight Foundation.

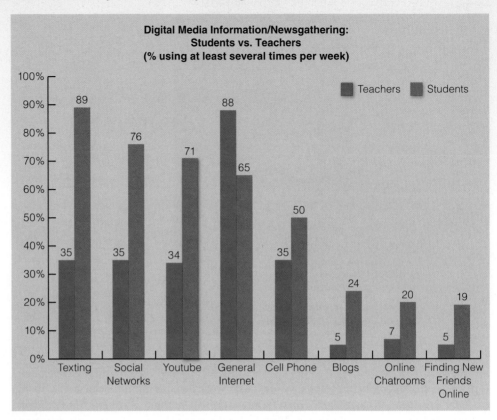

Digital Media Information/Newsgathering:
Students vs. Teachers
(% using at least several times per week)

Legend: Teachers, Students

Category	Teachers	Students
Texting	35	89
Social Networks	35	76
Youtube	34	71
General Internet	88	65
Cell Phone	35	50
Blogs	5	24
Online Chatrooms	7	20
Finding New Friends Online	5	19

The Electronic Media

The major electronic media are television, radio, and the Internet. Television and radio have played an important role in American politics for many decades, and the Internet has been responsible for more recent changes in the news and the way in which Americans use the news. The Internet, along with other relatively new media technologies such as DVDs, fax machines, cell phones, satellites, and cable TV, have come to be known as the **new media** (or "digital media"), which have revolutionized the news business at every level.

new media: Media outlets that rely on relatively newer technologies for communicating, such as the Internet, DVDs, fax machines, cell phones, satellites, cable TV, and broadband.

Television. With its mass adoption by households in the early 1950s, television became and has remained the primary source of news for most Americans. More than 98 percent of households in the United States report having at least one television set. News programming on TV is provided mostly by broadcast television networks and their local affiliates. The broadcast networks include ABC, CBS, and NBC. Cable television stations, such as CNN, Fox News, and MSNBC, provide 24-hour news programming as well. Other cable stations, such as C-SPAN and local public access stations, provide specialized coverage—for example, the live broadcast of congressional debates and committee meetings.

The defining characteristic of television is its visual nature.[10] The implied "reality" of seeing video of events, or live broadcasts of events, can be quite powerful, as civil rights demonstrators learned in the mid-1960s. Compared to the written word, the spoken word, or even still pictures, video communicates events "as they are," and so is regarded by viewers as more trustworthy and "real." Many argue that film footage of reporters covering the Vietnam War contributed to the erosion of public support for America's involvement there. The daily barrage of video showing dead soldiers brought new meaning to Americans' understanding of war and helped influence President Lyndon Johnson's decision not to seek reelection in 1968. In 2004, video of Americans captured and mutilated by Iraqi insurgents as a protest against the U.S.

military occupation of Iraq captured a great deal of attention and reduced support for the Bush administration's policy. Likewise, vivid pictures of American mistreatment of Iraqi detainees at Abu Ghraib prison did not help the Bush administration's effort to defeat the Iraqi insurgents.

New satellite technologies further facilitate the live and instantaneous coverage of events not only around every corner of the globe, but also from the moon, Mars, and Jupiter. The new high-tech satellites provide an opportunity for people to view events as they occur even from the outer reaches of the universe, such as the live pictures sent back from satellites on the 2004 U.S. spaceship mission to Mars.

Fox News conservative talk show host Bill O'Reilly draws a very high audience for his nightly cable TV show, The O'Reilly Factor.

Radio. Contemporary radio largely programs commercial music, with several minutes of each hour allotted for news, sports, traffic reports, and weather forecasts. These short news reports are an important source of information (particularly for commuters who use their cars to get to and from work or school) about news events and politics. Many radio stations carry a specialized form of radio programming referred to as **talk radio**, in which one or more hosts provide commentary and often invite listeners to call in to the show and offer their own opinions. Talk radio steadily gained popularity in the late 1980s and early 1990s, marked by a growing interest in political talk shows, as increasing numbers of commuters with cell phones began to take time while sitting in traffic to listen to these shows and call in to offer their own views.

talk radio: A specialized form of radio programming on which one or more hosts provide commentary and often invite listeners to call in to the show and offer their own opinions.

Some of the more popular call-in shows focus on politics. The hosts often provide an ideological perspective on policies, issues, and political candidates and campaigns. Listeners of a particular ideological persuasion enjoy hearing what the host and others have to say, and small numbers call in to offer their own views. Many local radio stations provide political talk radio programs, ranging from very modestly ideological debates to extremely partisan ones. Several nationally syndicated shows have also attracted an especially large listening audience, such as conservative commentator Rush Limbaugh's show.

A trend in ownership of radio is the purchase of smaller, local radio stations by large media organizations. Critics of this trend contend that the large corporate owners typically impose standardized programming through satellite feeds, thus depriving them of their local character.

The Internet. In 1993, a group of students at the University of Illinois developed MOSAIC, the first graphical Internet browser. MOSAIC allowed users to view pictures and color images on the World Wide Web. MOSAIC soon went commercial and became Netscape, and by the mid-1990s it was attracting tens of millions of users. Coupled with huge worldwide increases in sales of personal computers through the 1990s, the ease and user-friendliness of accessing the Internet made the medium an attractive source of news and information for people around the world.

The Internet's rise as a mass medium has many implications for news, information, and the American political system. One such effect is the way in which people use the Internet compared to other news sources. From the viewers' perspective, television watching is a passive activity. Once they've tuned into a particular channel, viewers have no other choice but to get whatever news is being presented. They cannot ask questions or seek specific answers to questions they might have. Likewise, listening to a radio broadcast is a fairly passive activity for listeners unless, of course, they choose to call in to the show. While reading a newspaper, people can pick and choose the articles they prefer to read. However, newspapers are also limited in the amount of content they can provide, and readers cannot query a newspaper to get answers on specific questions they might have.

The Internet, however, allows users to pursue exactly the kind of news and information they are interested in. Search engines such as Google and Yahoo allow Internet users to find whatever they are looking for. Furthermore, most news Web sites include a "search" feature that allows users to search the Web site and/or newspaper database for information relevant to a particular query.

Unlike other media, the Internet also enables individual users to be their own mass publisher. Most word processing packages include the option of "save as Web page." A simple set of keystrokes enables users to place information, data, and graphics on their own Web page. Web design software enables users to put a Web page on a server and thus make that page available to millions of other Internet users to access. In this way, Internet users can publish material that is accessible to a mass audience.

Most newspapers and television stations maintain Web sites that include the organization's news content, and links to other sources, such as the Associated Press. Many of these sites also include a searchable database of archived news stories. Some of the most used news Web sites are CNN (http://www.cnn.com) and the *New York Times* (http://www.nytimes.com). With searchable indices to past stories, links to other sites, online forums, and audio and video files, these sites offer a broad array of content that users can easily access.

The Internet has transformed the flow of news and information about politics in other ways as well. It has become a common source of information about political campaigns, because candidates for office often create a Web page and post it on a server for voters to access. Widely varying "chat rooms" and online forums serve as venues for users to post their opinions, ask questions, and engage in dialogue on political issues. **Blogs** (derived from the term *weblogs*) are also becoming popular among many Internet users. In 2008, for example, the significant amount of fundraising and voter communication by Obama supporters substantially buoyed that campaign's success. Blogs provide a combination editorial page, personal Web page, and online diary offering personal observations in real time about news events and issues. Some of the more popular blogs are published by journalists and political commentators.

About 65 percent of Americans report that they use personal computers on a regular basis, and most of these PCs are connected to the Internet. Those who use the Internet are more likely to be younger, middle and upper class, better educated, and nonminority—a disparity that has been referred to as the **digital divide**. Greater access to the Internet facilitates access to news and information, and those who have access clearly enjoy an advantage. However, as computers and Internet access costs decline, and as younger generations with computer skills replace older generations, the digital divide is likely to become less and less pronounced. Public libraries have provided another remedy to the digital divide. In 1996, 28 percent of all libraries had public access to the Internet. Today, 95 percent of libraries offer Internet access to patrons. Because they are eager to gain access, the number of visitors to public libraries has increased by nearly 20 percent over the past six years.

Ownership of the Media

The Framers of the Constitution were clearly committed to the freedom of the press. Government ownership of the press was then and is today regarded as a threat to the basic freedoms that Americans enjoy. If government controls the news and the flow of information to citizens, it holds too much power. Private ownership of the media allows for the free and open exchange of ideas. Ironically, some today argue that the concentration of ownership of the news media by large nonmedia corporations, such as General Electric and the Disney Corporation, has stifled diversity in news content and blurred the line between what is news and what is entertainment. One large corporation that owns multiple media outlets has become the norm, whereas in the past most media outlets were independently owned. It is also argued that ownership of media organizations by a conglomerate such as GE might compromise the objectivity of the news. When NBC, which is owned by GE, reports on a story about GE, might that story be biased?

The big three television networks—ABC, CBS, and NBC—have dominated television viewership since the early 1950s. By 1956, more than 9 in 10 stations were affiliated with one of these networks. Over the past several decades, the growing popularity of cable and satellite TV challenged the predominant position of the three networks. With hundreds of channels now available, the three networks' share of the viewing market continues to shrink. This competition led the networks to focus on greater efficiencies in the day-to-day operation of their businesses. By the mid-1980s, all three networks had experienced a change in corporate

blogs: Internet sites that include a combination of editorial page, personal Web page, and online diary of personal observations in real time about news events and issues.

digital divide: The large differences in usage of the Internet between older and younger people, lower- and middle-/upper-class people, lesser and better educated people, and minority groups and nonminority groups.

ownership, and all three now are part of "vertically integrated" corporations that are involved in video production as well as national and local distribution. In the late 1980s, competition between the networks further increased with the addition of the Fox Network.

NBC is currently owned by the megacorporation General Electric (GE); the CBS network, formerly owned by Viacom, is now its own corporation; the Disney Corporation owns and operates the ABC network; and Fox, the newest of the major networks, is owned by the News Corporation. Table 12.1 suggests the extent to which these four corporate owners control the nation's media.

Not all television and radio stations in the United States are privately owned. The Public Broadcasting Act of 1967 created the Corporation for Public Broadcasting (CPB), which is responsible for distributing federal funds to support public, noncommercial radio and television stations. These stations have had a difficult time surviving economically in a marketplace dominated by commercial interests. CPB funds the Public Broadcasting Service (PBS), which was formed in 1969 to distribute programming to the nation's public television stations. CPB-funded radio programs are distributed by National Public Radio (NPR), American Public Media, and Public Radio International to member stations.

The 1967 law provided much-needed support for noncommercial TV and radio and has established a rather impressive network of stations that provide some very popular programming. *Morning Edition* and *All Things Considered* are highly regarded radio news shows with a very loyal following; the same goes for the PBS-supported *News Hour with Jim Lehrer*. *Frontline* is a popular, award-winning investigative reporting program supported by PBS. Documentary series on the Civil War, produced by Ken Burns, and other such topics have been well received by large audiences. PBS has also supported a significant amount of children's educational programming, including *Sesame Street*.

PBS and NPR member stations do not generally engage in commercial advertising. They rely instead on funds from the CPB and on donations from businesses and individuals to support their broadcasting operation. For example, in 1999 General Motors provided a major

All of the news media organizations in the United States are privately owned and operated.

Fiction.

The Broadcasting Act of 1967 initiated federal government support for publicly funded television and radio broadcasting. Although such funding has been provided since the act was passed, federal funding for CPB and NPR remains politically controversial.

TABLE 12.1   Corporate Ownership of the Four Major Television News Outlets

Corporate Owner	General Electric (GE)	CBS Corporation	Disney Corporation	News Corporation
Network TV Affiliates Owned	10	16	10	25
Cable TV Channels Owned	MSNBC, CNBC, Bravo, the Weather Channel, Oxygen, Telemundo	Showtime, CBS College Sports Network	Disney Channel, ESPN, ABC Family	Fox Sports, Fox Family, Fox Kids, FX, Fox News, Fox Movie Channel, Fox Business Network, Fox Classics, Fox College Sports, FX Networks, Speed Channel, FUEL TV, National Geographic Channel
Other Holdings	Manufactures electrical appliances, electrical power equipment	Simon & Schuster (book publisher)	ESPN magazine, Disneyland, Disneyworld	HarperCollins (book publisher), newspapers

Source: © Cengage Learning

10-year commitment of support to PBS to finance productions by Burns, including documentaries on major league baseball and jazz music. Individual pledges of support are typically solicited through on-air membership drives and corporate underwriting of programming. There are nearly 400 PBS television stations, many of which are aligned with communications departments in colleges and universities across the nation.

An important assumption underlying federal support for public broadcasting is that government is obligated to ensure that offerings are diverse and that ample numbers of educational programs are developed. Federal support for public TV and radio, however, is often a political hot potato. Conservatives claim that public television has a liberal bias, and many have attempted, unsuccessfully, to curb federal funding for CPB.

THE EFFECTS OF THE MEDIA

There is no doubt that Americans rely on the media for news and information about politics. What is less clear is the influence that media exposure has on citizens' opinions (Does watching a news story on the increase in crime rates make the viewer more fearful of crime?) and behavior (Does reading an article about Barack Obama's community organizing experiences lead a reader to vote for or against him on Election Day?).

Researchers can quite easily gauge the exposure and use of the media. It is much more difficult, however, to identify the impact of media exposure on opinions and behavior. Citizens are constantly bombarded by news stories from a variety of different media. Isolating how one news story, or even several stories in one medium, influences opinions or behaviors is very hard to determine.

Despite the difficulty of proving media effects, political leaders and candidates for election certainly act as though the effects are powerful. Leaders constantly try to influence campaign stories and news stories to favor their own positions. Presidents use press conferences to send messages and attempt to win public support. Candidates buy advertising time to try to influence voters. Political parties orchestrate events at party conventions to send favorable partisan messages to voters.

minimal effects theory: The theory that deep-seated, long-term political attitudes have much greater influence on an individual's vote decisions than does news media coverage.

Early research studies of media effects examined how citizen exposure to media content during a campaign influenced how they voted. In classic books on the subject (such as *The Voter Decides* and *The American Voter*), the media were credited with having little or no effect on voters' decisions. These studies, which led to a theory known as **minimal effects theory**, found that deep-seated, long-term political attitudes had a much greater influence on the vote decision.[11] Such enduring and preexisting attitudes lead to selective perception and retention of news content. People evaluate news material from their own partisan perspective (selective perception) and tend to process and remember the material more consistent with their preexisting attitudes (selection retention).[12]

Moreover, preexisting attitudes often influence what kinds of news people choose to pay attention to in the first place (selective exposure). Psychologists suggest that people's desire to achieve cognitive consistency

President Obama appears on the Tonight Show with Jay Leno *in an effort to promote his administration's legislative agenda in March 2009.*

and avoid cognitive dissonance explains why they process new information in such a way as to assimilate with existing attitudes. These early studies that found "minimal effects" were largely focused on partisan elections and attempted to evaluate the effects of media exposure on the vote decision.

Subsequent research, though not refuting the findings of the media's minimal effects on partisan behavior, examined other areas where media exposure might have an impact. **Social learning theory**, for example, argued that viewers imitate what they view on television through observational learning.[13] Television's focus on sex and violence has led to a large number of studies that try to assess whether exposure to such material leads viewers to become more violent, with reduced moral standards. Some of this research suggests that viewers do learn negative, antisocial behavior from TV.

social learning theory: The theory that viewers imitate what they view on television through observational learning.

Some communications researchers have advanced the notion of *priming*,[14] which suggests that the activation of one thought also activates other thoughts, and exposure to media provides cues to people on this thought-activation process. For example, watching the Road Runner beat up on Wile E. Coyote in the old Warner Brothers cartoon may make one child act violently against another child after watching the cartoon. The rash of injuries related to the show *Jackass* is another example of the priming theory in action.

Critics of media often use social learning and priming theories to advocate for government controls of the media. The Telecommunications Act of 1996, for example, required television set manufacturers to include a V-chip in new units to allow parents to block programs they did not wish their children or families to view. Another law passed in 1997 required the television industry to develop a rating system for television shows based on the show's level of sex, violence, and profanity. Studies that demonstrated a connection between TV exposure and negative behavior were important pieces of evidence used to promote support for the V-chip requirement and the TV ratings system.

The **cultivation theory** of media effects suggests that heavy television exposure helps develop an individual's overall view of the world.[15] According to this theory, the emphasis on violence and crime in both news and entertainment programming would lead the heavy viewer to overestimate and be disproportionately concerned about the extent of crime and violence.

cultivation theory: The theory of media effects that suggests that heavy television exposure helps develop an individual's overall view of the world.

A final theory of media effects is best known as **agenda setting**. This theory suggests that although the effects of exposure may be minimal or difficult to gauge, the media are quite influential in telling the public what to think about. For example, Monica Lewinsky's affair with President Bill Clinton was a lead story in the news throughout 1998, and the prominent placement of that story in numerous media outlets helped to keep it a popular topic of conversation. Daily news coverage of the number of soldiers and civilians killed in Iraq focuses public attention on the U.S. military engagement there.

agenda setting theory: The theory holding that although the effects of television exposure may be minimal or difficult to gauge, the media are quite influential in telling the public what to think about.

The media set the public agenda for the issues and activities that many Americans choose to think about and talk about. Prominently placed and frequently repeated headlines in newspapers, lead stories on television news shows and on talk radio, and highlighted stories on well-trafficked Web sites set the stage for public discourse. Citizens pick up a newspaper or flip on an all-news TV station to become informed about what is happening in their community, the nation, and the world. In this sense, the news media have a powerful impact on public debate.[16] As news media scholar Doris Graber has noted, "When media make events seem important, average people as well as politicians discuss them and form opinions. This enhances the perceived importance of these events and ensures even more public attention and, possibly, political action."[17]

CRITICISMS OF THE NEWS MEDIA

Though Americans rely on the media for information about what is going on in the nation and around the world, the news media are also the subject for a number of criticisms. For example, despite the vast array of news sources available, most news programming follows a standard format that makes it appear the same to the public. Many newspapers are owned by a handful of publishers (such as the Tribune Company and Gannett) and follow a standard format for news. Similarly, just a few companies own many of the nation's radio stations and TV stations

FIGURE 12.3 Perceptions of Fairness and Accuracy in the Media

Source: http://www.people-press.org/2009/09/13/press-accuracy-rating-hits-two-decade-low/

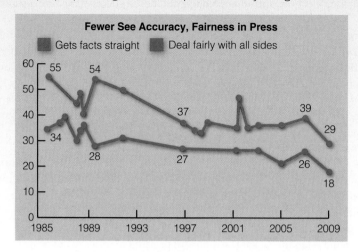

and employ a similar format in their programming. Critics charge that this concentration in ownership could result in a handful of companies promoting their own political objectives.

Polls have also demonstrated that there has been a decline in the percentage of Americans who say that news reporting is fair and accurate. Figure 12.3 demonstrates this erosion in public sentiment over the past three decades.

Another criticism of the private ownership of the media stems from the premise that the media, like most other privately owned companies, are in business primarily to make money. For the media, increasing profits requires attracting larger audiences and more readers, and as many media companies have found, providing higher-quality news programming on politically important topics does not always guarantee increased audience ratings or numbers of readers. Rather, news that provides more entertainment tends to get larger audience shares.

Often, the result is news that is characterized by "sensationalized" content. Stories that highlight or exploit crime, violence, disasters, personal conflicts, competition, and scandals tend to increase the sale of newspapers and improve the ratings of TV news programs. Thus the profit motive of private ownership drives companies in the news business to disproportionately cover events that include sensationalized content. Stories like the untimely deaths of Michael Jackson and Whitney Houston, and the extramarital affairs of John Edwards, Tiger Woods, New York Governor Elliot Spitzer, and South Carolina Governor Mark Sanford, all received a tremendous amount of coverage at the expense of other, more important and politically relevant stories.

Sensationalism extends to coverage of elections as well. Studies of election coverage have found that most news dwells more on stories about the candidates' personal background than on their positions on the issues. Political scientists note that this emphasis on covering "character" issues rather than policy positions characterizes modern presidential election campaign news. In 2000, for example, much of the coverage of candidate George W. Bush in the final week before the election focused on a drunk-driving charge that occurred while he was young. In 2004, significant coverage targeted the military service of the candidates, including Bush's "questionable" military record in the Alabama Air National Guard and John Kerry's record as a Vietnam War soldier and protester. More recently in 2008, a significant amount of coverage focused on Barack Obama's association both with his outspoken pastor Jeremiah Wright and with William Ayers, a cofounder of the Weather Underground, a radical leftist organization. Critics of election coverage also charge that there is too much focus on preelection polls and the competitiveness of the "horse race," which crowds out the more substantive coverage of the issues and the candidates' positions on them.

FROM YOUR PERSPECTIVE

Are You a Blogger?

Political blogs have significantly changed the way that people across the country participate in American politics. They offer anyone with a computer and access to the Internet the opportunity to publish their political opinions in the mass media, to share ideas and perspectives with others, to recommend the views of others by providing cross-links, and to debate and challenge the positions of those with whom they disagree. Of the literally millions of political blogs to be found on the Internet, most are associated with a particular partisan or ideological perspective.

Although political bloggers may be found all around the world, Americans between the ages of 18 and 35 have been especially active in contributing their ideas in this particular marketplace, sometimes termed the "blogocracy." Some of their efforts have had a significant impact on political events. For example, during the 2006 Virginia Senate campaign, a supporter of Democratic candidate Jim Webb was following Webb's opponent, incumbent Senate George Allen, with a video camera. Annoyed at being followed, Allen referred to the Webb supporter as a "Macaca," which is a term that refers to a species of monkey and is considered an ethnic slur. The videotaper, S. R. Sidarth, was also a blogger, and immediately posted the video of Allen's slur on YouTube. Many other blogs and national news organizations began to cover the clip of Allen's slur. The posting is credited both with clinching Webb's narrow victory in the race, and in stifling Allen's presidential ambitions for 2008.

Another way some bloggers have influenced politics is through the "moneybomb," a blog-driven grassroots fundraising campaign that is usually generated over a short period of time: supporters use the blogs to create a frenzied atmosphere to quickly raise money. Bloggers who supported Massachusetts GOP senate candidate Scott Brown initiated a moneybomb for him in his 2010 special election once Brown came within striking distance of winning Ted Kennedy's reliably Democratic seat. The effort raised $10 million.

ML Harris/Getty Images

College students, like the one pictured, can publish blogs from anywhere on campus.

For Critical Thinking and Discussion

1. Search for a blog that aligns with your own political interests or attitudes and read at least a week's worth of posting and comments. What do you notice? Do opinions tend to get debated or echoed within that blog?

2. What are the advantages and disadvantages of engaging in this form of political participation?

Another common criticism of the news media is that they are politically biased. Some critics, for example, charge that corporate owners of media organizations are more likely to hold a conservative ideology, which is reflected in their news products. Others cite studies indicating that journalists and reporters tend to hold a more liberal philosophy, and that this orientation seeps into their stories. Certainly there is evidence to support the assertions that owners and managers are more conservative than the citizenry as a whole, and that journalists are more liberal. But the issue of whether personal ideology or partisanship is reflected in news stories is less clear. In some elections, research has demonstrated that newspapers and TV news programs have shown a pro-Republican bias, whereas in others it has found a pro-Democratic bias.[18]

The media serve a number of important functions in the American political system. In addition to providing information, signaling events, and "watchdogging" what government does, the media also provide an infrastructure that leaders use to communicate with citizens. In the examples used at the outset of this chapter, we saw how Presidents Johnson and Obama took advantage of relatively new media (television and the Internet, respectively) to successfully win long-term political struggles to pass civil rights and health care reform legislation. Technological innovations have served to change the forms and nature of the media throughout the course of American history. These changes have opened up new opportunities for presidents and other leaders to help shape a political agenda and successfully bring an important policy idea to fruition. These changes have also had the effect of bringing news and information to audiences with more and more speed and efficiency. The America media remain as important a political institution as any in our system of government. Americans' demand for information, the appetite of journalists to keep tabs on government performance, and political leaders' reliance on the media to communicate with citizens all serve to make the media stronger today that they have ever been.

SUMMARY: PUTTING IT ALL TOGETHER

THE MEDIA IN AMERICAN POLITICS

- The media serve a number of important functions in the political system, all of which promote the free flow of information to the public. These functions include providing objective coverage of events, facilitating public debate, and serving as government watchdog.

- Congress created the Federal Communications Commission (FCC) in 1934 to regulate the electronic media through licensing of broadcasters and creating rules for broadcasters to follow. The FCC does not have authority to regulate the print media, because the courts have consistently treated the right of print media to publish free from government regulation.

Test Yourself on This Section

1. The FCC has the authority to regulate all of the following, EXCEPT
   a. political stories in the *New York Times*.
   b. NBC entertainment shows.
   c. your local radio station.
   d. ABC's political talk shows.

2. The FCC's "equal time rule" applies to
   a. newspapers.
   b. the Internet.
   c. magazines.
   d. television networks.

3. What are the primary functions that the news media provide in American democracy?
   providing objectivefg coverage of events

HISTORICAL DEVELOPMENT OF THE MEDIA

- From the nation's founding through the 1850s, news in America was largely provided by a partisan press, made up of newspapers supported by a particular political party.

- Over the past 150 years, the standards for news reporting have become less focused on serving political party interests and more focused on "objectivity."

- Technological change has greatly altered the news media. The invention of the rotary press in 1815 facilitated the mass printing of papers; the railroad system provided for speedy distribution of papers; the invention of the radio provided instantaneous coverage of events as they unfolded; and television brought taped and live footage of news events into people's homes.

Test Yourself on This Section

1. The "partisan press era" refers to
   - **a.** the post–Revolutionary War era through the mid-1800s.
   - **b.** the Civil War through the Industrial Revolution.
   - **c.** World War I and World War II.
   - **d.** the modern era of cable news shows.

2. The president who most effectively communicated his positions through press conferences was
   - **a.** Franklin Roosevelt.
   - **b.** John Kennedy.
   - **c.** George W. Bush.
   - **d.** Barack Obama.

3. What did Marshall McCluhan mean when he penned "the medium is the message"?

THE MASS MEDIA TODAY

- Politics and political events, such as presidential campaigns, debates, and news conferences, are widely covered by media organizations.
- Today's mass media comprise large and varied types of news outlets, including radio, television, books, newspapers, and magazines. They also include the so-called new media facilitated by the Internet, satellites, cell phones, broadband, and other newer technologies.
- Corporate ownership of news media outlets today is characterized by large nonmedia corporations, such as General Electric and the Disney Corporation. Some argue that this concentration of large corporate ownership has stifled diversity in news content and blurred the line between what is news and what is entertainment.
- Although the big three television networks—ABC, CBS, and NBC—have dominated television viewership since the early 1950s, the growing popularity of the Fox network, as well as cable and satellite TV, have begun to offer stiff competition.
- The Public Broadcasting Act of 1967 created the Corporation for Public Broadcasting (CPB), which is responsible for distributing federal funds to support public, noncommercial radio (NPR) and television (PBS) stations.

Test Yourself on This Section

1. The medium that most Americans say is their primary source of news is
   - **a.** newspapers.
   - **b.** the Internet.
   - **c.** radio.
   - **d.** television.

2. MOSAIC, the first graphical Internet browser, was developed by
   - **a.** Microsoft.
   - **b.** IBM.
   - **c.** students at the University of Illinois.
   - **d.** the Central Intelligence Agency.

3. Which of the following is a news program produced by the Corporation for Public Broadcasting?
   - **a.** the *News Hour with Jim Lehrer*
   - **b.** *Hannity's America*
   - **c.** *Hard Ball with Chris Matthews*
   - **d.** the *Nightly News with Brian Williams*

4. What do critics cite as a problem with the concentration of media outlets owned by a few large corporations?

THE EFFECTS OF THE MEDIA

- The effects of exposure to news on readers/viewers are the subject of much debate. A number of theories—including social learning, minimal effects, cultivation, and agenda setting—seek to explain how the news media influence what people think about politics.

Test Yourself on This Section

1. The theory of media effects suggesting that viewers imitate what they view on television through observational learning is
   a. agenda setting.
   b. cultivation.
   c. minimal effects.
   d. social learning.

2. The theory of media effects suggesting that the media are influential in telling people what to think about is
   a. agenda setting.
   b. cultivation.
   c. minimal effects.
   d. social learning.

CRITICISMS OF THE NEWS MEDIA

- Media performance is often the subject of criticism. Some of the major sources of discontent with media performance include the concentration of corporate ownership of media outlets, sensationalized coverage of relatively unimportant events, and ideological bias in news reporting.

Test Yourself on This Section

1. Media coverage of which presidential candidate focused a great deal of attention on his association with the controversial Reverend Jeremiah Wright?
   a. Bill Clinton
   b. George W. Bush
   c. John McCain
   d. Barack Obama

2. What are the main criticisms of the media in their coverage of politics in America?

KEY TERMS

agenda setting theory (p. 337)
blogs (p. 334)
cultivation theory (p. 337)
digital divide (p. 334)

equal time rule (p. 321)
minimal effects theory (p. 336)
new media (p. 332)
objectivity (p. 321)

partisan press era (p. 324)
social learning theory (p. 337)
talk radio (p. 333)

13 POLITICAL PARTIES AND VOTING

LEARNING OBJECTIVES

THE DEVELOPMENT OF POLITICAL PARTIES IN THE UNITED STATES

- Explain the historical development of the modern Democratic and Republican Parties
- Define "critical elections" and party realignment and dealignment in the United States and cite examples of their occurrence

THE FUNCTIONS OF POLITICAL PARTIES

- Identify and explain the four broad functions of political parties

WHY A TWO-PARTY SYSTEM?

- Describe the historical and legal factors that contributed to the development of the two-party system in the United States
- Assess the role that third parties have played in U.S. elections

PARTY ORGANIZATIONS

- Illustrate how party organizations operate at the national, state, and local levels and how they help their candidates win elections

ARE PARTIES IN DECLINE?

- Analyze the decline in political parties over the past few decades and assess the future prospects for the parties

VOTING

- Assess the role of state governments in managing elections
- Evaluate the effect of constitutional amendments on the expansion of voting rights in the United States
- Distinguish between the wide array of voter registration systems implemented in the 50 states

EXERCISING THE FRANCHISE

- Assess the influence of different factors in influencing voter turnout, including personal demographics and the type of election contest
- Analyze the trends in U.S. voter turnout over time and how turnout in the United States compares to that in other democracies

PARTICIPATION BEYOND THE VOTING BOOTH

- Explain the many forms of political participation beyond voting

Campaign buttons: © Lynne Fernandes/The Image Works; Elephant background image: Joe Raedle/Newsmakers/Getty Images

Though they merit no mention at all in the Constitution itself, political parties have become the lifeblood of American politics. New laws are enacted through the debate and negotiation of party leaders in government, and individuals are recruited and promoted as political candidates through the apparatus of the political party structure. At the national, state, and local levels, the two major political parties set the tone, control the agenda, and run the government. The electoral successes and failures of the Democrats or the Republicans, and competition within the majority party to set the national agenda, define the nature of public policy. Further, political parties provide the framework through which citizens participate in American politics; they remain the primary cue that voters use to understand and participate in politics.

The "Connections App" is an interactive web app that helps you better understand the relationship between historical and current events with basic concepts.

1870   1880   1890   1900   1910

1892

Then

A rally of the Populists' movement in Willowdale Township, Kansas, during the early 1890s.

Source: Fotosearch/Getty Images

Radical political movements within a political party can provide a boost to electoral success; at the same time, they also present governing challenges once in office. The successes of the GOP in 1888 provided that party with an opportunity to leave an indelible impact on the course of policymaking. However, Democratic resistance to the GOP gained a voice of its own as a result of its own losses that year: the Democrats then used that new voice to resurge shortly thereafter. Thus even after winning the White House and securing majorities in both houses of Congress in the 1888 elections, Republicans looked to the upcoming elections of 1890 and 1892 with considerable trepidation. Republican President Benjamin Harrison and his administration had significantly expanded the federal government's powers: the Republicans raised import duties to protect American businesses against global competition, expanded the money supply through the issuance of certificates backed by silver, increased pensions for military veterans, and passed the Sherman Anti-Trust Act to regulate the power and growth of monopolies. In response, Democrats became the party of "No!" With the 1890 elections approaching, they berated the "billion-dollar" Congress for raiding the treasury, and voters quickly took to the Democrats' anti-silver, small government message to give them back control of Congress. Eventually, the arrival of the "People's Party," known also as "Populists," would complicate matters substantially for Democrats eager to oust Harrison from office in the 1892 election. The Populists were radicals who crusaded against banks, railroads, and elites in general, and their natural allies were the Democrats.

2010

Now

Tea Party activists wearing themed costumes march in a tax-revolt rally in 2009.

Source: Phil McCarten/Reuters /Landov

In 2008, the Democrats scored major gains in the congressional and presidential elections. With these majorities, President Barack Obama and the Democrats muscled through an economic stimulus bill and landmark legislation addressing health care and financial reforms. The Republican minority held firm in its opposition to unprecedented spending, happily embracing their status as the party of "No." As deficits ballooned, the Republicans viewed the 2010 elections as an opportunity to reverse their electoral misfortunes in 2006 and 2008. At the same time, a political movement known as the "Tea Party" arrived on the political scene. Espousing principles of "fiscal responsibility," "adherence to the Constitution," and limited government, the Tea Party opposed what it regarded as excessive government spending by both major parties. The Tea Party movement had aided the cause of the more extreme conservative GOP contestants in primary contests, as its energetic band of followers occasionally frustrated Republican moderates. Still, the vast majority of Tea Party movement supporters were Republicans, and in the 2010 midterm elections the GOP recaptured the House and reduced the Democratic margin in the Senate. Tea Party candidates, such as Rand Paul of Kentucky, celebrated their Senate election victories with warnings that the Republican Party could not take their support for granted. The Republican congressional leaders in the new 112th Congress were quickly forced by its Tea Party members to stand firm in opposition to President Obama's agenda for change.

THE DEVELOPMENT OF POLITICAL PARTIES IN THE UNITED STATES

More than 60 years ago, the American Political Science Association (APSA) focused the scholarly community's attention on what it referred to as responsible party government.[1] The "responsible party government" model depicts the proper role of parties as organizations that offer clear programs and policy positions to voters. Voters make choices on the basis of those programs, and when victorious in elections, the party works toward achieving those programs and policies. At the time of the next election cycle, voters hold the party accountable for what it has accomplished.

The extent to which parties actually resemble the responsible party model has been the subject of much debate over the past half-century. Moreover, despite the large role parties play in the American political system, many observers argue that parties are organizationally weak, particularly when compared to parties in other democracies around the world. Whereas most European parties have clearly defined constituencies based on social class, regional, ethnic, or religious divisions, American political parties are often ideologically vague, aligning with broader constituencies and gravitating toward more centrist positions on issues. And despite their prevalence in politics, there are indications that the influence of parties is on the decline.

The Founders who drafted the Constitution designed a federal system without political parties. They envisioned a system that would be run by independent-minded people who served out of a sense of civic virtue. James Madison's famous Federalist No. 10 deplores "factions," as he calls them. Madison and his colleagues largely looked upon parties (the equivalent of extremely large factions) as tools of the politically ambitious that would tend to promote corruption and bias in the political system.

Despite the Founders' disdain for political parties, they have become central to the American political system. E. E. Schattschneider, a well-regarded student of American politics, observed in 1942 that "democracy is unthinkable, save in terms of the parties."[2] The Democratic and Republican Parties not only have become important political institutions in their own right, but they play a central role in running government at all levels, and they organize and provide context to voters.

Political parties are organizations that seek to win elections for the purpose of influencing the outputs of government. They are typically guided by a political philosophy, rooted in particular values and an ideological approach to governing. The philosophy, values, and ideological approach generally lead to specific issue positions espoused by leaders of a party and the candidates who run for office under a party's label. Some minor parties focus less on the unrealistic assumption that they might win elections and more on articulating an ideological approach to governing and supporting particular issue positions. As in any organization, parties include leaders as well as citizens. In American politics, parties provide an important link between citizens and their leaders, playing a key role in recruiting citizens and relying on them for support at election time.

Even though the Founders frowned on political parties and made no provision for them in the federal government they designed, not long after the first government

Political parties: Political parties are organizations that seek to win elections for the purpose of influencing the outputs of government.

Parties are also important in other democracies around the globe. Left: British Prime Minister David Cameron of the Conservative Party. Right: Israeli Prime Minister Benjamin Netanyahu of the Likud Party.

under the new U.S. Constitution took office in 1791, some of the architects of the Constitution became strong advocates of particular parties.[3] Perhaps more than anything else, this contradiction serves to highlight not only the importance of political parties to the practice of democracy, but also the necessity of parties. In the United States, competition between the political parties has kept any one group or "faction" from becoming too powerful for too long. The Constitution provides various safeguards against the accumulation of power in the form of checks and balances. Paradoxically, although parties are not mentioned at all in the Constitution, competition between political parties has proven to be a significant check against tyranny.

The First Parties in America

The history of political parties in the United States traces back to colonial America, when supporters of the English Crown aligned with the British Tory Party, and advocates of a new independent American nation aligned themselves with the British Whig Party. Benjamin Franklin and other founders still considered themselves Tories up through the early 1770s, and during the American Revolution colonists who supported Britain were called Tories or Loyalists. The period following the war ushered in new challenges as leaders of the new American nation debated the relationship that should exist between the national government and the state governments. Ultimately this debate created two new parties (or "factions" as many still called them in the eighteenth century). The U.S. Constitution that replaced the Articles of Confederation significantly enhanced the structure, power, and importance of the national government. The debate over ratification of the new Constitution pitted the Federalists, who supported a stronger federal government, against the Anti-Federalists, who opposed a strong federal government and supported state sovereignty.[4]

More formal, identifiable political parties emerged and began to assume the critical function of supporting candidates for elective office during the first administration of George Washington. Once again, the issue that spurred the emergence of parties as vehicles for nominating candidates was the distribution of power between the federal and state governments under the Constitution. The Federalists continued to support a stronger federal government and the policies of the Washington administration, which promoted the power of the national government. Most Federalists also favored maintaining close ties with Great Britain. President Washington did not consider himself a member of the Federalist Party; he despised parties and refused to endorse their presence in the politics of the new country. Yet many of Washington's supporters, led by Alexander Hamilton, organized the Federalist Party and used the organization to recruit candidates for office.

The Federalist Party was soon challenged by the Democratic-Republican Party, which asserted that the Washington administration was assuming greater powers than those the Constitution granted the federal government. It also criticized the federal government's favorable relations with Britain, preferring France as a closer European ally. As early as 1792, the Democratic-Republicans were organized and led by Thomas Jefferson and James Madison—the same Madison who 10 years earlier had authored in Federalist No. 10, perhaps the most eloquent argument *against* factions that has ever been written. In the congressional elections of 1792, Democratic-Republican candidates won a majority of seats in the House

Thomas Jefferson (left) of the Democratic-Republican Party and Alexander Hamilton (center) of the Federalist Party, speaking to President George Washington (right).

MPI/Archive Photos/Getty Images

of Representatives. George Washington was unopposed for president, but the Democratic-Republicans backed George Clinton against Federalist John Adams for the vice presidency. Adams, however, won reelection to the vice presidency by an electoral-vote margin of 77 to 50.

Every presidential and congressional election since 1796 has featured some form of party competition. In this early period of American political parties, the Federalists drew most of their support from the northern states, whereas the Democratic-Republicans had greater support in the southern and mid-Atlantic states. Sectional differences in partisan support have characterized American politics for much of the nation's history. In the first competitive presidential election of 1796, the Federalists endorsed John Adams and the Democratic-Republicans endorsed Thomas Jefferson. Adams won 71 electoral votes and Jefferson won 68 votes, making Adams president and Jefferson vice president. Not anticipating political parties, the Constitution allowed for the election of a president and vice president who stood very far apart on critical issues of the day.

By the time of the election of 1800, the parties were highly organized. Each of the two political parties endorsed a slate of candidates for president and vice president to avoid the problem of having two separate parties occupy those offices. The party organization selected presidential electors, who dutifully cast their constitutionally granted two votes to their party's candidates. The Federalists nominated both John Adams and Charles Pinckney, whereas the Democratic-Republicans endorsed Thomas Jefferson and Aaron Burr. Jefferson and Burr each received 73 electoral votes, thus producing an electoral college tie for the presidency. By the provisions of the Constitution, the election was then to be decided by the House of Representatives. After a fair amount of debate and politicking, the House eventually selected Jefferson on the 36th ballot. Clearly the system of selecting the president needed to be modified from one that did not recognize the importance of political parties in the electoral process to one that did.

The Twelfth Amendment deferred to the reality of parties in presidential elections. Ratified prior to the election of 1804, this amendment formally separated the electoral college vote for president and vice president. Rather than having electors cast two ballots for president, electors were now to cast separate votes for president and vice president. This modification in the electoral process helped avoid the problem that had occurred in 1796 of having a president and vice president locked in partisan struggle, as well as the problem in the 1800 election that resulted in two candidates from the same party tied for the presidency.

The election of 1800 marked the beginning of the end for the Federalist Party. The Federalists would never again win a presidential election, and their strength in Congress diminished steadily over the next two decades. The Democratic-Republicans enjoyed party dominance to such an extent that the Federalists were virtually extinct after the election of 1820. Interestingly, this lack of competition from the Federalists during the first two decades of the nineteenth century had the effect of fragmenting the Democratic-Republicans. In 1824, the Democratic-Republican Party put forth several sectional candidates, but no candidate received a majority of electoral votes. (Andrew Jackson won 99 votes, John Quincy Adams took 84, and another 74 votes were

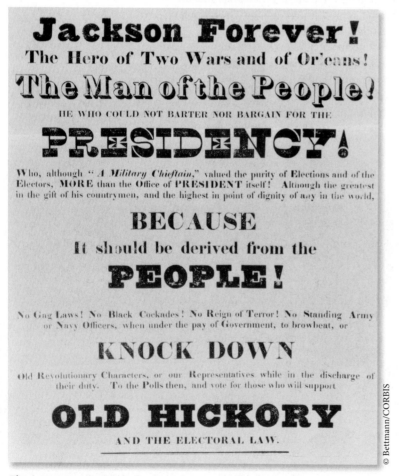

Election poster in 1828 for Andrew Jackson's presidential campaign. Jackson is the founder of today's Democratic Party.

scattered among other candidates.) Eventually, the House of Representatives decided in favor of Adams. The result was a Democratic-Republican Party in disarray.

A Second Party System Emerges

Disillusioned by the outcome of the 1824 election, Andrew Jackson eventually formed a new political party, the Democratic Party, which remains one of the two major parties still competing in American politics today. Jackson's support in 1824 derived from many of the new states that had been added to the Union as a result of westward expansion. Many such states, including Jackson's home state of Tennessee, allowed voters to choose presidential electors directly, rather than following the traditional practice of authorizing the state's congressional delegation (known as the "congressional caucus") to choose electors. Because he received more popular votes than John Quincy Adams in 1824, Jackson felt the presidency was rightfully his that year. However, Henry Clay, the fourth-place candidate, allied himself with Adams, thereby giving Adams enough votes for victory. When Adams became president he appointed Clay as secretary of state. Jackson and his supporters accused Clay of making a "corrupt bargain" by trading his votes to Adams in exchange for his appointment as secretary of state. Those who remained loyal to John Quincy Adams began calling themselves the National Republicans. The next presidential election would be a contest essentially between two splinter groups (Democrats and National Republicans) of the now defunct Democratic-Republicans.[5]

Jackson took his case directly to the people and ran for president again in 1828, this time as a Democrat. He ran a populist campaign, arguing that the people should have a greater say in selecting the president, and developed his campaign theme around the Adams–Clay "corrupt bargain." Jackson's theme caught fire with the voters, and the nation's continuing westward expansion, along with voting reforms and increased suffrage in eastern states, suddenly expanded the role of voters in selecting presidential electors. Thus, in a campaign that was essentially decided by the people, puritanical John Quincy Adams proved no match for the flamboyant Jackson, still revered as the general who led American forces to victory in the Battle of New Orleans, the final military engagement of the War of 1812. And Jackson's newly established Democratic Party emerged as a national force to be reckoned with.

The election of 1828 also permanently changed the nature of campaigns, and with them, the nature of parties. The precedent for a presidential election influenced by the masses was now set, and the era of congressional delegations selecting presidential electors was over. Parties quickly recognized the need to organize in states and localities to accommodate the new process of selecting presidential electors. Party organizations became larger and more powerful as they developed into critical instruments in campaigns. This era also established the tradition of holding **national party conventions**. These conventions drew together party delegates from across the states for several purposes. First, the delegates were responsible for choosing the party's presidential candidate and vice presidential candidate. Second, the delegates articulated their **party platform**, a document outlining the party's position on important policy issues. Third, the conventions coordinated the activities of parties across the states. National party conventions remain a central event both in the presidential selection process and in the organization of modern political parties in general.

The Democratic Party held its first national party convention in 1832, once again nominating Andrew Jackson for president. The National Republicans again nominated Henry Clay, who lost to Jackson in the November election. Several years later a new political party, the Whigs, which was made up of a coalition of National Republicans and other groups, emerged as a principal competitor to the Democrats. By the 1840s, the Democrats and Whigs dominated not only election contests, but also leadership and committee assignments in Congress. Soon those two parties became the primary vehicles through which legislation was sponsored and then shepherded through the Congress.

From 1836 through 1856, the Whigs and the Democrats shared the presidency and the vast majority of seats in Congress. Both parties were truly national parties, with organizations in each of the states. The issue of slavery, however, soon became the principal issue on the American political agenda. The Civil War would transform American politics forever, and a product of this transformation was the demise of the Whig Party. Within the Whigs, there were strong

national party convention: A large meeting that draws together party delegates from across the nation to choose (or formally affirm the selection of) the party's presidential and vice presidential candidates.

party platform: A document outlining the party's position on important policy issues.

critical election: An election that produces sharp changes in patterns of party loyalty among voters.

differences of opinion over the slavery issue, which led to the decline of the Whigs as a national force by the late 1850s. New, smaller parties emerged, such as the Free Soil and Know-Nothing parties, but none of those parties was able to attract large numbers of voters over an extended period of time. By the late 1850s, a new Republican Party had emerged to absorb these smaller parties and replace the Whigs as the major opposition party to the Democrats.

The Modern Party System in America: Democrats versus Republicans

The year 1856 marked the first presidential election when the precursors to the modern Democratic and Republican parties faced off for office. Democratic nominee James Buchanan defeated Republican candidate John Fremont by 174 to 114 electoral votes. Since 1856, every presidential election but one has featured the Democrats and Republicans as the only two major political parties in serious contention for the White House.

Campaign buttons and a "bull moose" keychain used by Theodore Roosevelt in his 1912 bid for the White house as the Bull Moose party candidate.

In 1860, Democratic Party support for states' rights and Republican Party support for national power and preservation of the Union divided the parties over the issue of slavery. Republican Abraham Lincoln's successful campaign that year helped his party capture the presidency and a majority in both houses of Congress. It also precipitated the Civil War. With the eventual secession of 11 Democrat-heavy states in the South, the Republican Party came to dominate politics for the next decade.

Like the election of 1828, the election of 1860 is considered by many scholars to be a **critical election** in the modern era of American parties. The theory of critical elections, developed by political scientist V. O. Key Jr., posits that certain elections can be characterized as producing sharp changes in patterns of party loyalty among voters.[6] This occurred in 1860 when voter support for parties realigned along the issue of slavery, based primarily on a North-versus-South division. Until 1860, the Democratic Party had enjoyed support from urban and industrial areas in both the North and the South and the demographic and social groups associated with those regions. The Civil War shifted these alignments to a North–South division, thus rendering the 1860 contest a critical election. The theory of critical elections suggests that every such election is accompanied by some type of electoral realignment,[7] a lasting reconfiguration of how certain groups of voters align with the parties.

When the last of the former Confederate states was readmitted to the Union in 1870, the Democratic Party once again began to assert itself in national politics. The Civil War had cemented a "solid South" stronghold for the Democratic Party that would continue for a century. Republicans remained the favored party in the northern and midwestern states, although some major cities in the North (including New York City) tended toward the Democratic Party. Republicans dominated the presidency for the remainder of the century, winning six of the next eight presidential contests.

A third realigning election in the modern party era occurred in 1896. That election did not result in a clear shifting of voter preferences from one party to another; rather, it marked the rise of the Republican Party to a near total consolidation of power and voter support in the northern and western states, as well as the continued Democratic Party dominance in southern states. Republican candidate William McKinley won the 1896 election, and with it a realignment of new allegiances to the Republican Party. Indeed, the only Democrat to capture the presidency between 1896 and 1932 was Woodrow Wilson, and Wilson's initial success was more a consequence of Theodore Roosevelt's split with the Republican Party than it was a result of an expanded Democratic base. Roosevelt, a Republican president from 1901 to 1909, formed the Progressive "Bull Moose" Party and ran as its presidential candidate in 1912. He in effect split the Republican vote, handing Democrat Woodrow Wilson an electoral college victory.

In 1912, the Republican Party's progressive and conservative wings split, giving the Democrats the White House and a majority in both houses of Congress. Within six years, however, Republicans regained control of Congress and were well positioned to retake the White House in 1920. During the 62-year period from 1870 to 1932, the two major parties developed their party organizations and shored up their voting coalitions. They institutionalized their power in Congress by creating the party caucuses and electing party leaders. Also, during this period the Democrats and Republicans developed party organizations so strong that the two-party Democrat–Republican system would become permanently institutionalized in American politics.

A fourth realigning election in the modern party era resulted from shifting party allegiances in the midst of the Great Depression. Republican President Herbert Hoover was elected in 1928, less than a year before the stock market crash of 1929 sent the economy into a tailspin. Hoover and the Republicans adopted some limited measures to deal with the economic disaster, but they maintained their party's traditional conservative faith in the dynamics of the market to solve economic problems. Franklin Delano Roosevelt, the Democratic candidate opposing Hoover in 1932, advocated a substantially larger and more activist role for government in dealing with the Depression. Roosevelt's pledge of a "New Deal" and an activist government won the support of the urban working class, people of lower socioeconomic status, new immigrants, and many Catholics and Jews. The shift in allegiances from the Republican Party to the Democratic Party in 1932 (FDR carried 42 states and 60 percent of the vote) had a lasting impact on voters. Adding the "New Deal coalition" to the "solid Democratic South" resulted in Democratic Party domination of American politics for at least the next 36 years. The policies of Democratic Presidents Roosevelt, Harry Truman, John F. Kennedy, and Lyndon Johnson

The first candidate to win the presidency as the Republican Party's nominee was Abraham Lincoln in 1860.

Fact.

The first GOP president was Abraham Lincoln, and the first Democratic president was Andrew Jackson, who was first elected in 1828.

President Franklin Delano Roosevelt, a Democrat, campaigning for reelection in Hartford, Connecticut, in 1936.

during this era, supported by large Democratic majorities in Congress, were the product of the powerful New Deal coalition established in 1932.

Since 1968, however, both the New Deal coalition and the Democrats' solid grip on the South have declined.[8] At the same time, the century-long southern hostility toward the Republican Party of Abraham Lincoln has diminished, as many conservatives in the South have become attracted to the Republican Party and its socially conservative agenda. Between 1969 and 2013, the Democrats controlled the White House for just 16 years, whereas the Republicans held the White House for 28 years. During that same period, the Democrats controlled both chambers of Congress for 24 years and the Republicans for 10 years, with 10 years of split majorities in the House and Senate. No clear critical elections appear to have occurred over this time frame, and few patterns in voter realignment are obvious. Indeed, some political scientists have argued that the term **dealignment**[9] best describes the behavior of voters since the 1960s. Dealignment refers to the decline in voter attachment to both parties.

The 2010 and 2012 election results provided new evidence of the electorate's lack of attachment to either of the two major political parties. After successive election cycles in which the Democratic Party took significant strides toward reestablishing itself as a lasting majority, many independents and disaffected Republicans who had voted for Democrats in 2006 and 2008 returned to the Republican fold in 2010. As a result, the Republicans retook control of the House and reduced the Democrats' margin of control in the Senate to just six seats. Yet the pendulum swung back once again in 2012, as voters opted for divided government: They returned President Obama to the White House, gave the Democrats a slightly expanded majority in the Senate, and maintained the GOP's sizeable majority in the House. As the Democrats and Republicans struggle with their long-term political identities, conflicting electoral outcomes will continue to hold their feet to the fire, threatening the long-term party attachments that had been so prevalent in the past.

dealignment: A decline in voter attachment to parties and in clarity of party coalitions.

THE FUNCTIONS OF POLITICAL PARTIES

Political parties serve a number of critical functions in the American political system at the national, state, and local levels of government. They give organizational coherence to both the operations of popular elections and the management of government. The functions that political parties serve have become inseparable from the principles that define how Americans choose leaders and how elected leaders formulate and administer public policies.

Contesting Elections

Free and open elections are the hallmark of the American republican form of government. With winning elections as their principal goal, political parties promote the prominence, competitiveness, and significance of elections in America. By winning elections and occupying seats in the government, members of the party can influence public policy. The larger the number of elective seats that a party controls, the greater the party's potential influence on policy outcomes. Thus contesting elections lies at the core of a political party's functions.

To contest elections most effectively, the two major parties in the United States have developed a large set of party organizations. These organizations, which operate at the national, state, and local levels, are engaged in a number of activities directed toward winning elections. These activities include fundraising, organizing events and meetings, providing funding to candidates who are running for office, recruiting and organizing volunteers who want to work for the election of candidates, and purchasing services (for example, polling services, political advertisements, campaign materials such as bumper stickers, direct mail to homes, and so forth) to promote the election of candidates. Many election contests feature a candidate from the party currently in office (the incumbent candidate) defending his or her record against an alternative candidate from the party out of power. The fact that political parties are organized to contest elections and offer alternative proposals for making public policy promotes the responsiveness of elected officials to the voters: by offering voters alternative candidates more in line with public opinion, parties provide an effective mechanism for voters to remove leaders from office through elections. The alternative candidates offered by the Democratic and

Republican parties also serve to organize the process of competitive elections in the United States, because the vast majority of elections feature a Democratic candidate and a Republican candidate running against each other. Some elections include independent or third-party candidates, and in some elections a Democratic candidate or a Republican candidate runs unchallenged. But most election contests feature some form of competition between candidates from the two major parties.

Recruiting and Nominating Candidates

Political parties are the main vehicles through which candidates for office are recruited and screened. The fact that parties exist to win elections gives them the incentive to recruit candidates to run for office under the party label. Parties want to find candidates who will represent the party well, and thus they provide a "weeding out" process that results in higher-quality candidates.

Most recruiting and promoting of candidates begins at the local party level. Individuals interested in politics often donate their time and efforts to working for political parties by, among other things, attending and participating in party meetings, distributing campaign literature, and driving candidates to campaign events. Local organizations tend to reward this service work with nominations for local offices, such as a seat on a local school board or a planning and zoning board. Successful candidates for these local offices often move up through the ranks of the local party organization to earn the endorsement and nomination of their party for higher office.

Through the winter and spring of 2012, former Massachusetts Governor Mitt Romney (left) and former House Speaker Newt Gingrich (right) were two of the leading candidates vying for the GOP Party presidential nomination.

Providing a Framework for Voters to Make Vote Choices

Political parties also provide a useful framework for voters who must choose among candidates for elective office. Without even knowing the names of particular candidates for office, voters may be cued in to those candidates' political, ideological, and policy perspectives on the basis of a candidate's party. Most voters associate the political parties with at least broad approaches to governing, if not positions on specific policy issues. For example, on the role that government should play in fixing economic problems, most voters perceive the Democratic Party to be more likely to support an active role for government, whereas Republicans are perceived as having a more "hands-off" approach, preferring economic problems to correct themselves through the free market.

The organizational framework for voters to assess candidates is the political party. This framework helps voters more easily process and evaluate campaign information. Party labels thus offer voters an efficient shortcut mechanism for choosing among candidates. For instance, the Democratic Party and candidates running under that label are often regarded by

Senators Hillary Clinton (D-NY) and Barack Obama (D-IL) waged a long battle for the 2008 Democratic presidential nomination.

voters as being more liberal or left of center in their position on issues, whereas candidates under the Republican Party label are viewed as being more conservative or right of center. Party identification is the psychological connection that voters have with a political party that influences other attitudes (such as one's position on gun control) as well as voting behavior. **Party identification**, an individual's feeling of attachment to a particular political party, is a political attitude that begins to form early in a person's life and generally remains quite stable throughout his or her lifetime. The authors of *The American Voter*,[10] a classic book on American voting behavior, described party identification as "generally a psychological identification which can persist without legal recognition or evidence of formal membership." Party identification serves an important role in forming attitudes on particular issues and making vote decisions.

Scientific surveys usually measure party identification by asking questions such as: "Generally speaking, do you think of yourself as a Republican, a Democrat, an independent, or what?" Scholars began measuring party identification in the 1950s, and research on the concept has revealed several important findings. First, although the number of independents has grown slightly over the years, there are many more party identifiers than there are independents. Indeed, the majority of Americans today identify with a political party. Second, whereas the Democratic Party had more identifiers than the Republican Party from the mid-1940s to the 1980s, the number of Democrats and Republicans is nearly equal today. As a consequence, the two major parties enjoy pretty much equal amounts of support from the American public. Third, despite these shifts, party identification in the electorate is quite resistant to change. Thus, from one election to another, voting patterns remain remarkably stable and rarely deviate from either a Democratic or Republican victory. Fourth, party identification plays a very important role in helping voters make voting decisions: as shown in Figure 13.1, the vast majority of Republican identifiers vote for Republican candidates and the vast majority of Democratic identifiers vote for Democratic candidates.[11]

In addition to providing an important cue to voting habits, party identification also serves as an important influence on the policy positions that individuals hold. Figure 13.2 shows that Americans who consider themselves Democrats tend to have different perspectives on social issues than those who consider themselves Republicans. For example, the following data from a Gallup Poll depict the stark differences in partisan groups on what is considered to be "morally acceptable."

Party identification is also an important concept for candidates and party leaders in plotting campaign strategies and contesting elections. As political scientist Phillip Converse has noted, a **normal vote**[12] can be expected for any given election contest. That is, a certain percentage of voters can be expected to cast a ballot for the Democrats, whereas another predictable percentage can be expected to vote for the Republicans. The strategy designed to win an election, and the chances that the strategy will result in a victory, largely depend on the normal vote distribution. The larger the margin of one party's normal vote, the less competitive the race. The competitiveness of the race can also be influenced by the number of the nonpartisan voters.

party identification: The psychological attachment that an individual has to a particular party.

normal vote: The percentage of voters that can be expected with reasonable certainty to cast a ballot for each of the two major political parties.

FIGURE 13.1 Party Identifiers Who Say They Will Support the Party Line

Source: Fox News/Opinion Dynamics Poll, September 2008.

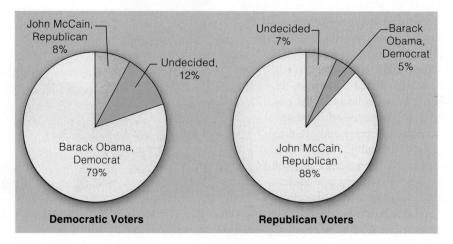

Source: Gallup Poll, May 2010. © 2010 The Gallup Organization.

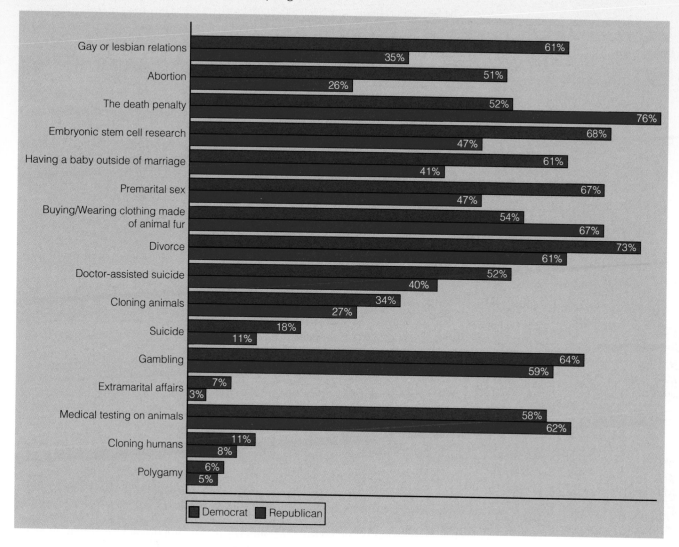

An important caveat about the "normal vote" is that states vary widely in their distribution of Democrats and Republicans. In other words, what is normal for one state may be very abnormal when compared to another state. Figure 13.3 depicts the large variety in Democratic and Republican Party identifiers from state to state. For example, whereas in Rhode Island, Massachusetts, Hawaii, and Vermont Democratic party identifiers largely outnumber Republicans, the opposite is especially true in Utah, Wyoming, Idaho, and Alaska.

Though party identification is defined as a psychological attachment that an individual has to a particular political party and is regarded by political scientists as an attitude, formal membership in a political party is generally associated with the process of voter registration. In addition to making a citizen eligible to vote, the voter registration process in many states includes registering as a member of a political party. In some states, membership in a political party is a necessary precondition for voting in that political party's primary elections to select the candidates who will represent the party in a general election. States with open primaries do not limit the nomination process to voters of one party. State laws govern how a citizen becomes a member of a political party and thus eligible to vote in the party's primary election contests. In most states, it is possible to register to vote without being a member of any particular party. The rules for becoming a member of a party vary widely from state to state.

FIGURE 13.3 Party Identification: The Most Democratic States and the Most Republican States

Source: The Gallup Poll, http://www.gallup.com/poll/114016/state-states-political-party-affiliation.aspx.

Top 10 Democratic States		Top 10 Republican States	
State	**Democratic advantage**	**State**	**Democratic advantage**
	Pct. pts.		Pct. pts.
District of Columbia	75	Utah	–23
Rhode Island	37	Wyoming	–20
Massachusetts	34	Idaho	–15
Hawaii	34	Alaska	–11
Vermont	33	Nebraska	–7
New York	27	Kansas	–2
Connecticut	26	Alabama	–1
Maryland	26	Arizona	0
Illinois	24	South Carolina	0
Delaware	23	Three tied at	1

Providing Organization for the Operations of Government

The majority party organizes its respective institution to accomplish the task of governing.[13] The leadership organization in the House and Senate is based primarily on majority-party leadership. The top leadership position in the House of Representatives is the Speaker of the House, who is always chosen by the majority-party caucus of the House. The chief leadership position in the Senate is the majority leader, who is selected by the majority-party caucus in the Senate. Members of the majority party chair committees in both houses of Congress. Leaders in Congress then try to implement the campaign pledges and platforms advocated by their party during the previous election campaigns. The executive branch, headed by the president, includes various departments and agencies that conduct the work of the federal government. Partisanship and loyalty to the president's political party are important factors that influence whom the president appoints to lead these agencies and departments.

The policy agenda and important policy decisions are largely the result of the political party organization and partisan leadership of these key branches of government. The greater a party's control over the key governing institution, the more power that party has in influencing public policy. When the Democratic Party has a majority in both the House and the Senate and occupies the presidency, the Democratic Party has virtual control over what laws get passed. For example, the 1932 elections brought FDR, a Democrat, into the White House and resulted in increased Democratic majorities in both houses of Congress. The result of this dominance was passage of numerous laws promoting active government involvement in dealing with the Great Depression.

Justin Sullivan/Getty Images

Bill Clark/Roll Call

In 2012, the Chair of the Republican National Party was Reince Priebus (left) and the Chair of the Democratic National Party was Debbie Wasserman-Schultz (right).

Divided government,[14] on the other hand, refers to split-party control of Congress and the presidency. Because both houses of Congress are required for passing new laws, when the majority party in at least one house of Congress differs from the party occupying the presidency, a form of divided government exists. For example, beginning in January 2011 the Republicans controlled the House of Representatives while the Democrats retained control of the Senate and Democratic President Barack Obama was still in the White House. The presence of divided government often makes it difficult for either party to advance its policy goals and objectives.

Whereas the first 150 years of the republic was mostly characterized by one party controlling both branches of government, the last half-century has been dominated by divided government. For example, during the eight years that Republican Ronald Reagan was president, the Democrats held a majority of seats in the House of Representatives, and they continued to do so through Republican George H. W. Bush's administration that followed. During the administration of Democratic President Bill Clinton, the Republicans maintained a majority of seats in both houses for the last six of Clinton's eight years in office. For the first six months of George W. Bush's presidency, the Republicans held control of the House, while the Senate was split 50–50 among Democrats and Republicans. The defection of Vermont Senator James Jeffords from the Republican Party in mid-2001 gave the Democrats a majority in the Senate, resulting in a divided government. After the 2002 elections, Republicans reasserted control over the Senate, and united government under Republican control was established for the next four years. Yet with a Democratic sweep of the House and Senate in November 2006, President Bush was forced to navigate through the perils of divided government for the remainder of his time in office.

The Democratic Party ended divided government for a two-year period with Barack Obama's 2008 presidential election victory over Republican challenger John McCain. In addition, the Democratic Party caucuses increased their margins in both the House of Representatives and the Senate for the 111th Congress. Those large margins of control proved short-lived, however, as the Republicans in 2010 gained over 60 House seats to retake the majority in that chamber and reduced Democratic margins in the Senate as well. Divided-party government thus returned to Washington once again in 2011.

Little changed as a result of the 2012 elections with the reelection of President Obama, and the maintenance of a Democratic majority in the Senate and a GOP majority in the House.

Many observers of American politics question the rationality of an American electorate that so often sends one party to the presidency, yet keeps the opposite party in control of Congress. The stalemate or gridlock that may result from divided government is problematic to some. Still, many Americans believe that divided government has its benefits; certainly divided control tends to intensify the checks and balances on power envisioned by the framers of the Constitution.

WHY A TWO-PARTY SYSTEM?

Political parties are an integral part of many of the world's democracies. Contemporary party systems are largely a product of the unique characteristics, history, issues, and social class structure of any given nation.

Though party systems in a democracy vary in numerous ways, they may generally be classified into one of two types: (1) **two-party systems** and (2) **multiparty systems**. The United

FIGURE 13.4 Partisan Voting in Congress

Every year, *Congressional Quarterly* measures the percentage of partisan votes taken in the House and Senate. A roll-call vote is considered partisan if a majority of one party votes against a majority of the other. The percentage of partisan voting has hovered around a relatively high 50 percent in the House for the past two decades and stayed there during 2009, at 51 percent. But in the Senate, it was a whopping 72 percent—the highest percentage of partisan votes ever tallied in that chamber.

Source: Congressional Quarterly.

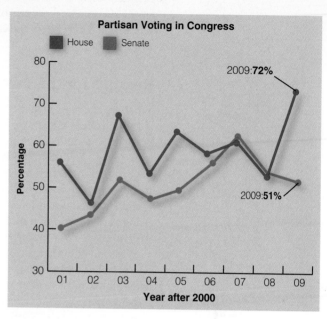

divided government: Split-party control of Congress and the presidency.

two-party system: A party system dominated by two major parties that win the vast majority of elections.

multiparty system: A political system in which many different parties are organized on the basis of political ideologies, economic interests, religion, geography, or positions on a single issue or set of issues.

States features a two-party system, dominated by the Democratic and Republican Parties.[15] The vast size and organizational structure of the two major parties, coupled with the fact that these two parties win the great majority of elections, appropriately classifies the United States as a two-party system. Other democracies feature as many as 10 parties of relatively equal stature. The nations with multiparty systems typically include parties organized on the basis of political ideologies (such as the Socialist Party or Conservative Party), particular economic interests (such as the Agricultural Party or the Industrial Party), religion, geography, or positions on a single issue or set of issues.

In the United States, there is a wide range of ideological views, economic interests, religious orientations, ethnic groups, and geographic disparities. Other nations with such a wide diversity of interests typically rely on multiple parties to represent these different components of the population. However, in the United States a two-party model has persisted now for more than two centuries.

Reasons for the Two-Party System in the United States

What are the factors that contribute to the American two-party model? A key factor is the electoral college system for selecting the president of the United States. In order to win the presidency, a candidate must obtain a majority, not simply a plurality, of votes in the electoral college. Naturally, this requirement encourages groups of voters to align with one of the major political parties, lest their votes be wasted. Minority groups, such as blue-collar union members, which have no chance of achieving a majority of votes as a single unified party, have found it in their best interest to support one of the two major parties in a presidential election. Being part of a winning coalition yields more influence than being in a smaller unified group with no chance of winning.

A second important factor that promotes the two-party system is the winner-take-all process that prevails in selecting members of Congress. In U.S. congressional elections, only the candidate with the most votes in a single district wins the seat. For example, in a race for a Senate seat, if the Democratic candidate receives 40 percent of the vote, the Republican 35 percent, the Reform Party candidate 15 percent, and the Green Party 10 percent, the Democratic candidate with the 40 percent plurality is elected to Congress. By contrast, in other democracies, such as Israel, France, and Germany, forms of **proportional representation** are used. Under this system, the percentage of the vote that a party receives is reflected in the number of seats that that party occupies in the national legislature. In Israel, for example, a party that receives as little as 1.5 percent of the vote nationally is entitled to at least one seat in the 120-seat Knesset (the Israeli legislature). Whereas a proportional representation system gives minor parties representation in the legislature, the winner-take-all system does not. A third party must win the most votes in any given election contest to win a seat. The winner-take-all system promotes the two-party system and prevents smaller parties from achieving even minimal representation in the national legislature.

A third factor promoting the two-party system is the ideological nature of public opinion in America. Most Americans are ideologically centrist, or moderate, with few considering themselves strong ideologues. The lack of strong ideological differences helps explain why only two parties dominate American politics. Neither the Democratic nor the Republican Party can afford to be too strongly ideological because to be so would risk building a winning coalition in elections.

A fourth factor promoting the two-party system are the laws and regulations that govern campaigns in United States, which tend to benefit the major parties at the expense of third parties. For example, in order to qualify for matching federal funds for presidential campaigns and many state gubernatorial campaigns, candidates must demonstrate a minimum level of support in prior elections and/or primary elections. Most minor parties, however, are eligible to receive such funds only after the election is over. They receive public funding in federal elections, for example, if (1) they receive 5 percent of the popular vote and (2) they appear on the ballot in at least 10 states. Because money to finance a campaign is necessary during, rather than after, the campaign, third parties are at a serious disadvantage. The lack of a history and lack of public interest in third-party primary elections precludes most from receiving federal or state funding in these elections. For a third party's candidate to appear on election ballots in the states, the party must meet a number of criteria, including petitions supporting the candidate and often significant fees.

proportional representation: A system of electing a national legislature in which the percentage of the vote that a party receives is reflected in the number of seats that the party occupies.

Former Pennsylvania Senator Rick Santorum, a favorite of social conservative voters, waged a campaign for the GOP presidential nomination in 2012. Santorum was the last candidate to exit the GOP race once it became clear that Mitt Romney would win a large enough number of delegates to claim victory.

Minor and Third Parties

Despite the dominance of the Republican and Democratic Parties over the past century and a half, third parties occasionally have contested elections in the United States. The most recent third party of note was the Green Party, from which Ralph Nader launched his presidential campaign during the 2000 election.* Most third-party candidates fail to register even one percentage point of the popular vote in presidential elections, and few third-party candidates are found in the U.S. Congress, in state legislatures or governorships, or in local government. For the past 160 years, not one president has been elected who did not run as either a Democrat or Republican.

Even the few-and-far-between third-party candidacies that have attracted a sizeable percentage of popular votes in presidential elections have experienced only short-lived success (see Table 13.1). The Progressive or "Bull Moose" Party of Theodore Roosevelt, for example, garnered 27 percent of the vote in 1912, but failed to establish itself as a permanent threat to the two major parties. Its success was largely based on Roosevelt's personal stature and popularity, and by 1916 Roosevelt had returned to the Republican fold. Likewise, Ross Perot, running as an independent in the 1992 presidential race, captured nearly 20 percent of the popular vote. But his attempt to match his 1992 success met with disappointment in his 1996 bid, when he took only 9 percent of the popular vote. By 2000, Perot's Reform Party showed up as barely a blip in the vote totals.[16]

Third parties face a number of obstacles in their attempt to become viable. First, their mostly negligible chance of winning at the outset leads many voters to sense that a vote for a third party would be wasted. The strong historical and cultural institutionalization of the American two-party system is another obstacle third parties face. The sizeable number of voters who identify themselves as either a Democrat or Republican inclines most voters to support major-party candidates in elections. In addition to the legal barriers already discussed, media coverage of campaigns also plays a role; the media tend to focus most coverage on the two major parties, with little attention given to third-party candidacies.

Still, third parties persist. Table 13.2 lists and describes the most active third parties in the U.S. today. Despite their limited success in winning important government positions, they often have substantial influence on the outcome of elections. Third-party candidates in hotly contested presidential races have on occasion siphoned off enough votes from one of the major-party

---

*Nader was technically the Green Party candidate for president in 1996 as well, but he was only on 22 state ballots that year, and his candidacy labored under a self-imposed spending limit of $5,000. In the 2004 presidential election the Green Party candidate was Texas attorney David Cobb; Nader ran as an independent in 2004.

TABLE 13.1 Important Third-Party Candidacies in Presidential Races

Third parties are by no means a new phenomenon in American politics. Despite their tendency to be short-lived and their relative lack of success in capturing elective office, third-party movements endure, often affecting which major-party candidate wins office. The following is a select list of third parties, their respective candidates, and their vote totals in presidential elections.

Year	Party	Candidate	% of Popular Vote
1832	Anti-Masonic	William Wirt	8
1856	Know-Nothing	Millard Fillmore	22
1892	Populist	James Weaver	9
1912	Bull Moose	Theodore Roosevelt	27
1912	Socialist	Eugene V. Debs	6
1924	Progressive	Robert La Follette	17
1948	States' Rights	Strom Thurmond	2
1948	Progressive	Henry Wallace	2
1968	American Independent	George Wallace	14
1980	National Unity	John Anderson	7
1992	United We Stand America	Ross Perot	19
1996	Reform	Ross Perot	9
2000	Green	Ralph Nader	3
2004	Independent	Ralph Nader	1

*Nader was technically the Green Party candidate for president in 1996 as well, but he was only on 22 state ballots that year, and his candidacy labored under a self-imposed spending limit of $5,000. In the 2004 presidential election the Green Party candidate was Texas attorney David Cobb; Nader ran as an independent in 2004.

Source: © Cengage Learning 2012

candidates to provide an electoral college victory to the other major party. Twice since 1832 a third party has won more than 20 percent of the popular vote in a presidential race, and five times during this period a third party has won at least 10 percent of the popular vote.

PARTY ORGANIZATIONS

Political parties exist through party organizations at the national, state, and local levels. Though most elected government officials are members of the Democratic or Republican Parties, political parties also exist as organizations outside of the government. These party organizations, which often count millions of volunteers among their members, articulate positions on issues; enlist members from the public at large; recruit candidates who will run under the party label for elective office; raise money from individuals, corporations, and interest groups; and provide organizational and campaign services to candidates who are running for office.

Andrew Jackson is regarded as the father of the **national party organization**. Up until the election of 1828, a party's candidates for president and vice president were nominated by the party congressional caucus. Jackson changed this process by establishing a national party convention to be held several months before a presidential election. The convention brings together state and local party leaders to nominate the party's candidates for president and vice president. In addition to party leaders, the national conventions today include delegates from the states elected by members of the party in presidential primary elections.

national party organization: The institution through which political parties exist at the national, state, and local levels, primarily focused on articulating policy positions, raising money, organizing volunteers, and providing services to candidates.

TABLE 13.2 Third Parties Today

Despite the lack of electoral success by third parties, many continue to operate in the United States today. Listed here are a few of them, along with a description of their reason for being.

Party	Description
1. Natural Law Party	This party advocates "all-party" government, which it defines as "bringing together the best ideas, programs, and leaders from all political parties and the private sector to solve and prevent problems." The party argues that bringing the individual lives of people and national policies into harmony with the "natural law" will best solve the nation's problems.
2. Constitution Party	This party bases the foundation of its political activities on religious principles of Christianity. It argues that the U.S. Constitution established a "republic under God, rather than a democracy."
3. Reform Party	Ross Perot ran as a candidate in the 1992 presidential election under the organization "United We Stand America." He ran to protest the leadership of both the Republican and Democratic parties and won 19 percent of the popular vote. In 1996, Perot reorganized under the Reform Party name and won 9 percent of the popular vote. Former Republican Pat Buchanan was a Reform Party candidate for president in 2000, receiving 0.5 percent of the popular vote.
4. Libertarian Party	This party endorses the notion that government should be small and limited, interfering as little as possible with the lives of citizens. The Libertarian Party argues that "individuals have the right to exercise sole dominion over their own lives [and] they have the right to live in whatever manner they choose so long as they do not interfere with the rights of others." Libertarians place a premium on individual liberties and personal responsibility.
5. Socialist Party	Whereas the Libertarians support a very limited role for government, the Socialist Party supports active government involvement in providing equitable distributions of resources in society. Socialists endorse a strong government role in providing health care, jobs, housing, and education, among other public programs. Although Bernie Sanders won election in 2006 as a U.S. senator from Vermont running as a self-described "Democratic Socialist," he does not belong to the Socialist Party.
6. Green Party	The foundation of the Green Party rests on pro-environmentalist positions like "Green" parties in other democracies, such as Germany and France. In the United States, the Green Party is also identified with a number of social justice causes, including feminism, promotion of diversity, and global responsibility. Green Party candidate Ralph Nader took 2.7 percent of the popular vote in the 2000 election, finishing in third place.

Source: © Cengage Learning 2012

Since the middle of the nineteenth century, both the Democratic and Republican national party organizations have been run by a **national committee**, which oversees the conduct of the presidential campaign and develops strategy for each party's congressional elections as well. The national committees, consisting of state and local party representatives, are run by a **national committee chair** chosen soon after the presidential election has concluded.

At the national level, the committees, chairs, and party organization largely provide a supportive role during the presidential campaign. Once providing a core advisory role to a presidential candidate, the national organizations today are more involved in helping their candidate raise money and campaign for office. Strategy, planning, and advising are now handled mostly by the candidate's own campaign staff, which typically includes a media consultant, a pollster, a campaign manager, and various other campaign consultants. The modern-day national party organization is also less influential in determining who the nominee will be and more responsive to the victorious candidate's personal campaign staff. They do maintain greater influence in assisting state and local party efforts to win elections by providing polling and media consulting services, campaign management services, and financial resources.

In the modern era, state and local party organizations tend to be more influential in the nomination of candidates, in developing and organizing campaigns, and in providing a cue to

national committee: The committee that oversees the conduct of a party's presidential campaign and develops strategy for congressional elections.

national committee chair: The head of the national committee for one of the two major parties.

voters about their vote selections. Voters pay less attention to campaigns in state and local elections and therefore depend more on partisan cues in their choice of candidates. State legislative and local election campaigns generally have limited resources to mount significant image-building campaigns for candidates. Candidates are thus more dependent on the resources of the state and local party organizations for financing. Local party organizations provide "get out the vote" services by funding phone banks to contact voters directly. State and local organizations also fund and make available polling services and media consulting services to candidates in less visible races. Because they benefit from these services, candidates for local and state offices may feel the need to be more responsive to the party organizations.

Local party organizations also provide the grassroots manpower for soliciting mass participation in political activities. These activities include implementing voter registration drives, organizing political fundraisers and rallies, and staffing phone banks to make direct contact with voters urging them to vote for their party's candidates. Local organizations also provide the mechanism for identifying and recruiting talented citizens to become candidates for elective office. They provide the "farm team" for potential candidates for higher offices, such as governor, member of Congress, and senator.

ARE PARTIES IN DECLINE?

Many political scientists contend that the political party is in a state of decline in America. Bolstering this claim is the dealignment thesis described earlier in this chapter, which holds that voters today are less attached to parties and tend to be more independent-minded than they were up through the 1960s. Political scientist Martin Wattenberg[17] argues that increased negativity toward the parties has contributed to party decline. Wattenberg suggests further that the mass media have contributed to this decline by neglecting to cover parties. Prior to the 1960s, voters depended mainly on parties to provide information about political issues and candidates; now voters turn to the media as the prime information source. Furthermore, the medium of television allows candidates today to bypass parties and appeal directly to the public for support. Many candidates now run campaigns that de-emphasize parties and focus primarily on the candidate's image.

© ZUMA Press, Inc./Alamy

Mitt Romney making his acceptance speech as the Republican party's nominee at the national convention in Tampa in August 2012.

Scholars have also noted a decline in the organizational linkages between officeholders and the political parties. Patronage, the practice by which victorious parties offer loyal party members jobs in government, declined substantially during the past century. Under the patronage system, parties were able to retain the strong support of many of their members by offering the prospect of a good government job if the party was victorious. The civil service and other reforms seriously limited a political party's ability to offer jobs or other favors in return for supporting the party. Although these reforms have eroded the power of parties, they have also improved the quality of government officials and reduced corruption in government affairs.

Changes in the way candidates are nominated by a party have also reduced the power of party organizations. Until recently, parties exerted powerful control over the process by which an individual becomes a candidate wearing the party label in a general election. Without endorsement of the party organization, candidates for president, Congress, and state and local office once were virtually precluded from running under the party label. However, reforms in the 1960s and 1970s reduced the party organization's role in the nomination process. The **direct primary election**, which provides for the nomination of a candidate based on an open election among all party members, has empowered rank-and-file party members rather than party leaders to choose the party's nominees. Direct primaries make it easier for candidates who are not necessarily approved by the party organization to wear the party label in a general election.

direct primary election: An open election, rather than an election by party leaders, to choose candidates for the general election.

Some scholars, however, are not so convinced that parties are on the decline. They argue that although certain aspects of parties are declining, in other ways parties are showing a resurgence in relevance.[18] For example, parties have adapted quite well to candidate-centered campaigns by servicing candidate organizations. In 2006, the Democratic Party supported some candidates who actually de-emphasized their party identification, and thus helped forge victories for Democrats in congressional districts that were considered moderate-to-conservative. Additionally, party-line voting in the House and the Senate has been highly disciplined in recent years. In the 110th Congress (2007–2008), for example, senators voted with their party's position on legislation an average of 83 percent of the time. Not much changed during the 111th Congress: when health care reform came up for a series of final votes in the Senate in late 2009 and early 2010, all 100 senators voted down the line with their party leadership's position on the issue.

Whether they are declining or not, at the moment parties remain alive and quite active in American politics. Even though voter partisanship may have waned, party identification still remains a strong determinant of vote choice. Although the parties may be less visible to voters, they continue to exert considerable influence over voting decisions. The Democratic and Republican Party organizations are well funded and include millions of party workers. Party organizations provide money and expertise to candidates to help them achieve electoral success. The president remains the recognized leader of the party label he wears, and the party with a majority of seats in each house of Congress maintains clear control of the legislative agenda. Although the power of the party may have declined, it is clear that "the party" is far from over in American politics.

VOTING

Political participation takes many forms in American politics, as shown in Figure 13.5.[19] At the core of participation is the act of voting. Open and free elections held on a regular basis are the hallmark characteristic of a democratic government. Voting provides the critical linkage between citizens' preferences and governmental authority. The United States is not a direct democracy in which every citizen is invited to deliberate the issues and vote on public policy. Rather, the U.S. system is a **representative democracy**, sometimes referred to as an indirect democracy or republican form of government, in which citizens choose the individuals who are then responsible for making and enforcing public policy. The people do not directly rule, but they have the opportunity to exercise power vicariously by choosing as their leaders those whom they prefer.

representative democracy: System of government in which citizens elect the individuals who are responsible for making and enforcing public policy.

The core principle underlying representative democracy is **majoritarianism**, or majority rule, which means that among the choices presented to voters, the choice that is supported by

majoritarianism: The principle that the choice that is supported by the most voters is the choice that prevails.

President Barack Obama, campaigning for votes in June 2012, in Cleveland Ohio.

the most voters (that is, receives the most votes) is the choice that prevails. When a majority makes its choice, the consent of the governed is satisfied. Given the diversity of opinions and interests among people in our society, it is unrealistic to assume that all, or even most, voters will agree on one choice. But the will of the people is accomplished when the majority decides.

voting: The political mechanism that ensures that the majority will rule.

Voting is the mechanism that ensures that the majority will rule. Times change, and so do people's opinions and preferences. Therefore, representative democracy not only requires an election in the selection of leadership, but also requires that elections occur on a regular basis so that the government's authority reflects changing majority views. Regular and periodic elections allow the majority of voters to continue to exercise ultimate control over the direction of public policy.

The Legal Structure for Voting in the United States

franchise: The right to vote.

The **franchise**, or suffrage, is the right to vote. When speaking about majority rule, it is important to ask, "majority of whom?" Article I, Section 4 of the U.S. Constitution assigns the system of voting, including the definition of who is granted suffrage, to the states. Voting registration, voter eligibility, methods of casting ballots, and the tallying of official results are all functions reserved for states. The original Constitution prescribes eligibility requirements for federal officeholders (representatives, senators, and the president) and lays out the system for selection of the president and vice president, but it says nothing about who can vote in the elections for these officials. Constitutional amendments have been ratified and federal laws have been passed that prevent states from discriminating in granting suffrage rights; but technically, there exists no absolute constitutional right to vote in the first place.

Toward Universal Suffrage

The states have exercised significant authority in defining who is eligible to vote. For many years states regularly denied minorities, women, young adults, Native Americans, and the poor the right to vote for officeholders at the local, state, and national levels of government. In addition, a number of states prescribed property ownership requirements that prevented many people from being eligible to vote. Some states at various points in the nation's early history

FIGURE 13.5 The Ways in Which Americans Participate in Politics

Americans participate in politics in a number of different ways. The following chart lists some of the more common methods of political participation, along with the percentage of Americans who have engaged in each type of activity.

Source: 2008 national survey of 2,500 American adults, conducted by Intercollegiate Studies Institute (ISI).

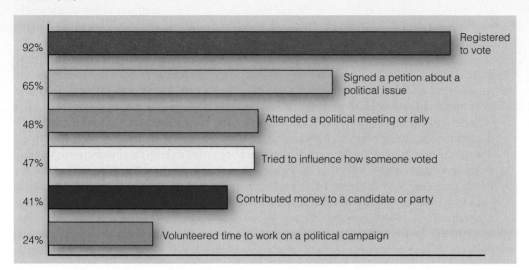

sought to broaden the right of suffrage. New Jersey, for example, allowed women the right to vote in the early 1800s, and some northern states provided for black suffrage prior to the Civil War.[20] But the goal of **universal suffrage**—or the right of all citizens to vote—has been an elusive one throughout American history. Restrictions on voting rights have systematically denied the right of particular groups of people to participate in choosing their leaders.

Two centuries of government under the Constitution, however, have been marked by steady progress toward the goal of extending the franchise to all Americans. In the first federal elections in 1788, voting rights were limited to white men who owned property, whereas in the most recent federal elections of 2012, all citizens of the United States aged 18 or older (who were not otherwise prohibited from voting due to a felony conviction or some similar offense) enjoyed the legal right to vote. Enfranchisement was not achieved quickly, nor did it happen as the result of one or two events. Rather, the process of extending the right to vote to all American adults occurred over centuries of time, and with much opposition.

The Civil War presented the first major challenge to the disenfranchisement of a particular class of people, namely, African Americans. Prior to the Civil War, African American slaves not only did not have the right to vote, they had no rights at all. In the infamous U.S. Supreme Court decision *Dred Scott v. Sanford* (1857), the Court ruled that slaves were property, that they had no rights under the law, and that they were not and could never become legal citizens of the United States. Immediately after the surrender of Confederate forces in 1865, President Abraham Lincoln gave an address suggesting that freed slaves be given the franchise. The idea met with some resistance, even among the Northern states. However, the so-called Civil War amendments to the Constitution not only ended the institution of slavery (the Thirteenth Amendment) and granted citizenship to former slaves (the Fourteenth Amendment), but the **Fifteenth Amendment**, passed in 1870, guaranteed that "the right of citizens of the United States to vote shall not be abridged by the United States or any state on account of race, color, or any previous condition of servitude." The Fifteenth Amendment was the first formal action granting the federal government the power to enforce voting rights over the states.

The Fifteenth Amendment, however, did not deter some officials from the former Confederate states from finding ways to deny African Americans their newly won voting rights after Reconstruction ended in 1877. Threats, beatings, destruction of property, and other intimidation tactics, often ignored by local police, effectively kept blacks from coming to the polls on Election Day.[21] In addition, some states sought legal means to prevent blacks from voting. They

universal suffrage: The idea that all citizens in a nation have the right to vote.

Fifteenth Amendment: The amendment to the Constitution that guaranteed the franchise regardless of race, color, or any previous condition of servitude.

Twenty-fourth Amendment: The constitutional amendment that outlaws poll taxes.

Nineteenth Amendment: The constitutional amendment that guarantees women equal voting rights.

Twenty-third Amendment: The constitutional amendment providing electoral votes to the District of Columbia, thus giving District residents the right to vote in presidential elections.

Twenty-sixth Amendment: The constitutional amendment that lowered the voting age to 18 in all local, state, and federal elections.

passed laws instituting a **poll tax** that required individuals to pay a fee before being allowed to vote; they required potential voters to pass a **literacy test** to prove that they could read and write. Because most blacks were poor, they were often unable to pay the poll tax (usually about $30). Blacks also tended to have less education (in some states it had been illegal to teach slaves to read and write), so they frequently could not pass the literacy tests, which were often deliberately difficult and unfairly applied to minorities to prevent them from voting. From the late 1800s through the first half of the twentieth century, these methods posed a substantial barrier to black turnout in federal elections, which typically was about 10 percent. These laws also depressed turnout of poor people in general.

The civil rights movement of the 1960s addressed the problems associated with the disenfranchisement of blacks. Two important products of this movement were the Twenty-fourth Amendment and the Voting Rights Act of 1965. The **Twenty-fourth Amendment**, passed in 1964, outlawed poll taxes by making unconstitutional any law that made payment of a tax a voting eligibility requirement in federal elections.[22] The Voting Rights Act of 1965 denied states the right to use literacy tests as a requirement for voting; it also provided African Americans with protection from intimidating tactics that had been used to keep them away from the polls.

The past century also witnessed the enfranchisement of women. Though passage of the Fifteenth Amendment in 1870 granted African American men the legal right to vote, women would not receive the same constitutional guarantee until 1920 with the passage of the **Nineteenth Amendment**. In 1848, some 200 delegates—women and men—met in Seneca Falls, New York, to issue a call for women's rights, including the right to vote. The Civil War years diverted the nation's attention from women's rights to other pressing problems.[23] Attempts to include a women's right to vote in the Fifteenth Amendment proved unsuccessful, although women began voting in some states well before passage of the Fifteenth Amendment. By the late nineteenth century, some of the new western states, such as Utah, Wyoming, Colorado, Idaho, Washington, and California, enacted women's suffrage laws. Despite continued opposition from leaders, including President Woodrow Wilson and many states in the Northeast, popular sentiment and a well-organized lobbying effort eventually led to the passage of the Nineteenth Amendment.

Three other groups have successfully won the right to vote through federal legislation and constitutional amendment. Until the early twentieth century, Native Americans had neither citizenship nor voting rights; but federal laws passed in 1924 made it illegal for states to deny Native Americans the franchise. In 1961, the **Twenty-third Amendment** to the Constitution gave residents of the District of Columbia the right to vote in presidential elections. Because the District is not a state, its residents had not been allowed to participate in presidential elections. The Twenty-third Amendment allocates electoral votes to the District using the same formula by which electoral votes are allocated to a state: the total number of representatives it would have in the House, if it were a state, plus two. Today, the District of Columbia has a total of three electoral votes. In 1971, in the midst of the Vietnam War when many young Americans were dying in battle, Congress passed and the states ratified the **Twenty-sixth Amendment**, which lowered the voting age to 18 in all local, state, and federal elections.

Although the administration of election and voting rules is largely controlled by the states, significant numbers of federal laws and constitutional amendments have extended voting rights in the United States. Collectively, these laws prevent states from discriminating against particular groups of citizens with respect to their right to vote. Unfortunately, racism and other forms of discrimination continue to exist and thus continue to affect voting rights in America. Subtle forms of discrimination, including intimidation tactics by groups such as the Ku Klux Klan, may scare individuals into not voting. But more overt discriminatory tactics, supported by some state and local laws, have largely been erased. As a society the United States, over many years, has progressed toward the democratic ideal of universal suffrage. Today in the United States, the only adults legally disenfranchised are convicted felons in prison (47 states), on probation (29 states), and on parole (32 states).

Voter Registration Laws

Just as the extension of the franchise has evolved over the years, so has the system of voter registration. Most states today have voter registration systems in which individuals must qualify

THE MORE THINGS CHANGE, THE MORE THEY STAY THE SAME

Breaking Down Traditional Barriers to Winning the White House

The breaking down of institutional barriers to voting has significantly opened up opportunities for more Americans to make runs for all types of political offices, including even the presidency. Andrew Jackson's successful bid for the White House in 1832, for example, reflected a voting population that included broader participation from the common man. The drive toward universal manhood suffrage through the post–Civil War amendments and laws and amendments passed since then substantially changed opportunities for Americans who typically could not compete for the White House. Two presidential elections in particular represented landmark victories, as voters opted for candidates who belonged to a demographic group that never before made it to the highest elective office in America:

In 1960, Senator John F. Kennedy exploded onto the nation's political map. Voters in the Democratic Party were attracted to his youthful and charismatic personality, and nominated him to wear their party's banner in the 1960 presidential election. They stormed to his campaign despite the fact that he was a Catholic and no Catholic before had ever won a presidential election. In fact, the last Catholic nominee, Democrat Al Smith, had carried just eight states (all in the South and New England) in 1928. During his own general election campaign more than three decades later, Kennedy drew large crowds at political rallies. His campaign mobilized many new voters in the process—and his victory in November changed presidential history by breaking the glass ceiling that Catholicism once represented.

Barack Obama in 2008, campaigning as an African American candidate for the presidency.

took notice of the youthful senator, though some remained wary that an African American candidate could not win a major-party nomination, let alone the presidency. The last serious African American candidate, the Reverend Jesse Jackson, won just 10 democratic primary contests in 1988. Overcoming all doubts, Obama's campaign attracted record numbers of new voters. These voters supplied all the votes Obama needed to win the party nomination. Voters were attracted to something new and different in Obama, and thus helped to break an age-old glass ceiling for racial minorities in the presidential selection process.

John F. Kennedy, campaigning in 1960 as a Catholic running for the presidency.

In 2008, Senator Barack Obama burst on the political scene as a young, gifted, charismatic orator, vying for the Democratic Party's presidential nomination. Primary voters

For Critical Thinking and Discussion

1. Although the elections of Kennedy and Obama opened up opportunities for Catholics and African Americans, many demographic groups have still never achieved the presidency. In thinking ahead to the elections of 2016 and 2020, can you identify any possible candidates from these other groups—perhaps women, Asians, or Jewish candidates—who might break through yet another glass ceiling?

2. The elections of Kennedy and Obama have been touted as important symbolic victories for Catholics and African Americans, respectively, demonstrating that non-Protestant and non-white candidates can achieve the nation's highest office. Do you think Obama's victory has also changed the way nonwhite voters think about American government? How does a demographic group's success in achieving the high office impact the group's views on policymaking and government in general?

in order to become eligible to vote. The responsibility for qualifying lies with the individual. States do not compile and maintain a list of individuals who are eligible to vote. Rather, individuals must take it upon themselves to demonstrate their qualifications and file the appropriate paperwork to become eligible.

Massachusetts, in 1800, was the first state to require individuals to register to vote.[24] A handful of states followed Massachusetts's lead, but not until after the Civil War did most states adopt voter registration systems. Many of the voter registrations systems that were adopted between the 1870s and the early 1900s made it harder for immigrants, the less educated, and those less familiar with the political system to vote. A leading force behind the institution of voter registration systems was the populist movement of the late nineteenth century, which largely included white, middle-class, native-born Americans. In the northern states, registration laws were intended to make it more difficult for new European immigrants to vote; in the West, the intention was to make voting by new Chinese and Japanese immigrants more difficult; in the South, registration was aimed at limiting the black vote; and the source of concern in the Southwest was Mexican immigrants. Most states today still rely on some form of self-initiated voter registration, which continues to present an obstacle to voting for some people. A person must first find out how to register, remember to register in advance of Election Day, and then spend time registering. Many states require proof of age and citizenship, and many also impose a length-of-residence qualification, requiring a potential voter to prove that he or she has resided in the state for a specified period of time.[25]

Numerous organizations and public-interest groups have lobbied state legislatures and Congress to simplify and ease voter registration requirements in order to allow more people to vote on Election Day, including those who fail to register in advance of the election. North Dakota is the only state that does not currently require registration, and three states—Maine, Minnesota, and Wisconsin—permit voters to register on Election Day. The National Voter Registration Act of 1993, often called the **Motor Voter law**, mandates that when an individual applies for or renews a state driver's license, the state must also provide that individual with voter registration materials. The idea behind the law is that combining the process of registering to vote with the more routine task of obtaining a driver's license makes voter registration easier. Research suggests that although this law has increased voter registration, it has not increased actual turnout.[26]

Motor Voter law: The federal law mandating that when an individual applies for or renews a state driver's license, the state must also provide that individual with voter registration materials.

EXERCISING THE FRANCHISE

A number of factors explain why people decide to cast a ballot on Election Day. An individual's interest in politics is one important factor. People who are more interested in politics tend to follow news about campaigns to a much greater degree than those who are less interested, and those who are more interested are more likely to vote.

Interest in politics, however, is only one factor that leads people to vote. Another is a person's sense of "civic duty," or the belief that being a good citizen requires one to vote. Many people who are not very interested in politics show up to vote nonetheless because they have a sense of civic duty.[27] From a young age, most Americans are socialized to believe that participating in elections is characteristic of the good democratic citizen, and so they feel an obligation to cast a vote even though they may not be particularly interested in elections and campaigns.

Another factor that influences some people to vote is the perception that their vote can have an impact on the outcome of an election. Individuals who feel strongly about a particular issue, set of issues, or a candidate may want to vote on the theory that if the election is close, their vote might actually make a difference in the outcome. Indeed, the sense that one's vote can make a difference contributes to higher turnout in elections that are perceived to be close.

Finally, for some people social group pressure can be a motivating factor in deciding to vote. Voting is often regarded as the "right" thing to do, and some people feel that casting a ballot is expected of them by others. This sense of social pressure to do what is acceptable by society's standards can increase the likelihood that a person will vote.

Who Turns Out to Vote?

An individual's interest in politics and attentiveness to news about politics and campaigns, sense of civic duty, and sense of political efficacy (that is, the belief that one's vote can make a difference) all lead to higher rates of **voter turnout**, which is the percentage of eligible voters who show up to vote on Election Day. In addition to these "political" factors that help to distinguish between citizens who are more or less likely to vote, there are a number of demographic characteristics that also help to explain turnout. A person's gender, age, and level of education are all related to the decision to vote (see Figure 13.6).

In many elections, younger people tend to pass up the opportunity to vote at greater rates than middle-aged and older people do. Youth nonvoting is often attributed to the more transient nature of younger people's lives.[28] At about age 18, many young people leave their parents' home to go to college or to take a job or to start their careers. Younger Americans are less rooted in a community, have had less time to register to vote, and are experiencing major changes in their social and personal situation. Voting tends to be less of a priority under these changing circumstances. As people age, buy a home, have a family, and reside in a particular community for a period of time, they become more socially attached and are more likely to vote.

Two other demographic groups are substantially more likely to vote—better-educated Americans[29] and wealthier Americans.[30] These two factors are related, because higher levels of education also lead to higher relative affluence and social status. The process of being educated sharpens a person's mind, improves the individual's ability to understand problems in society, and equips him or her to deal with complex information, such as the issues discussed in political campaigns. Education also enhances a person's appreciation for democracy and sense of civic duty. A better understanding of the issues and appreciation for the democratic process encourage higher levels of voter participation.

voter turnout: The number of people who turn out to vote as a percentage of all those eligible to vote.

How Do They Vote? Methods of Casting a Ballot

Once a person decides to vote, there are several different ways in which a ballot can be cast. In the United States, five different methods of voting are generally used: (1) hand-counted paper

FIGURE 13.6 Differences in Voter Turnout Among Demographic Groups in the 2008 Presidential Election

Source: Current Population Survey, U.S. Bureau of the Census 2008.

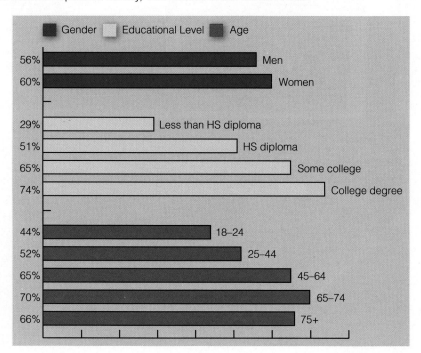

ballots, (2) mechanical lever machines, (3) computer punch cards, (4) optical scan cards, and (5) electronic voting systems. Each of the 50 states has the authority to administer elections, and most states delegate most of the work to counties or other localities. In all, more than 10,000 jurisdictions at the county level or below are responsible for carrying out the important task of collecting and tabulating votes.

Paper ballots were the only method of voting used in the United States during the first 100 years of the nation's history. Originally the paper ballots used were produced by a political party and listed only the candidates belonging to the party that produced the ballot. On Election Day, the party would make the ballot available to the voter, who would then place it in the ballot box. In 1856, many jurisdictions began using a form of the paper ballot known as the "Australian secret ballot," which lists all the candidates for each office being contested, and voters then choose which candidate they prefer. (The other four methods of voting also employ the characteristics of the Australian ballot: all possible choices are displayed for all offices, the voter marks choices through some mechanism, and those choices are secret.) Paper ballots are still currently used in about 3 percent of precincts, mostly in rural areas.

The first real technological advance in voting technologies came with the introduction of the *lever voting machine* in 1892. A voter enters a voting booth and chooses candidates listed on a posted ballot by pulling a lever. The votes are recorded by advances in a counting mechanism that are made when the voter leaves the booth. The lever machine does not require a paper ballot and does not require (or allow) manual counting of ballots. When the polls close, poll workers simply read the numbers recorded by the counters. About 22 percent of precincts currently use lever machines.

Clockwise from top left: the traditional paper ballot method of casting a vote, a mechanical voting lever machine, the computer punch card method of voting, the touch-screen computer ballot, and optical scanning card technology.

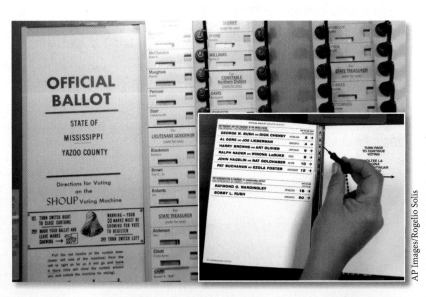

Punch cards, which debuted in 1964, were the first computerized method of vote counting. Voters record choices by punching holes in appropriate locations on a card. These cards are computer readable. The piece of card that is punched out is called the *chad*. Unlike lever machines, the punch cards may be saved as a record of the vote, and manual recounts of the actual votes are possible. The punch card system is the most widely used in the United States, with about 37 percent of precincts using this method. Much of the controversy regarding the Florida vote for president in 2000 dealt with the issue of whether a "hanging" chad (a chad that had been punched but was still clinging to the punch card by a fiber) should be counted as a legal vote.

Optical scan ballots are a method of voting based on the same technology as that used to grade standardized tests such as the SAT. Given a paper card and a pencil, voters mark their selections by filling in boxes or ovals on the card. The ballots are then scanned by a computer for vote tabulation. As with punch cards and paper ballots, a permanent record of the vote is kept and is available for manual counting. About 25 percent of precincts use optical scan voting systems.

Electronic voting is similar to lever machine voting in that it involves no paper record of the individual votes; however, the technology is much more sophisticated. Voters select candidates from a ballot, which may be posted on the voting machine or displayed on a computer screen. Typically, voters make their choices by pushing a button or touching the computer screen, then submit their selections by pushing a specific button. The votes are stored in the computer. Write-in votes are entered via a keypad. About 7 percent of precincts use electronic voting systems.

In addition to these five main voting methods, several other methods are currently under development. One is Internet voting, which would allow voters to cast their ballots online using their personal computer (as long as the computer had online access) to vote. At present, the biggest obstacle to implementing Internet voting systems is ensuring authenticity and anonymity in the voting process.

Why Don't More People Vote?

Despite the numerous factors that motivate people to vote, many in fact do not vote. Voter turnout is a measure of how engaged Americans are in voting in any given election contest. High turnout is considered a healthy sign for a democratic system. It implies that people are engaged in political issues, spend the time to contribute to the system, and take responsibility for selecting leaders. Lower turnout is often viewed as a by-product of alienation, mistrust, and lack of confidence in the political system.

Economist Anthony Downs originally offered an explanation for nonvoting based on a theory known as *rational choice*.[31] He argued that voters might decide not to vote because they reason that the costs of obtaining and understanding information about candidates and campaigns outweigh the benefits of making a vote choice. It is a rational choice, therefore, to decide not to vote, or to vote on the basis of certain "shortcuts" such as a candidate's political party.

Elections are plentiful in the United States and are held for many different offices at many different levels of government. Turnout varies from one type of election to another. Some elections draw much more media attention and thus engender more interest than others. Some feature much more political advertising and so provide more cues to voters. Some elections are inherently viewed as more important and so inspire a greater sense of civic duty among voters.

In 1966, political scientist Angus Campbell and his colleagues identified five factors that distinguish between "high-stimulus" elections (in which turnout tends to be higher), and "low-stimulus" elections (in which turnout is generally lower).[32] The factors that characterize a high-stimulus election are (1) greater levels of media coverage, (2) higher significance of the office, (3) campaigns in which voters assign high importance to an issue, (4) more attractive candidates, and (5) perceptions of a close race. Campbell and his colleagues argue that events external to voters may stimulate interest in elections and thus increase the likelihood that individuals will turn out to vote on Election Day. For example, when big issues such as war and peace are at stake, people are more likely to take an interest in the election and vote.

Presidential elections tend to produce the highest levels of turnout because (1) they are heavily covered by the media; (2) there is more spending on political advertisements, particularly on television, thus making the campaign more visible to voters; and (3) the presidency is the most significant office in the U.S. political system. In presidential races where an issue important to many voters is at stake, such as problems with the economy in 1992 or the Vietnam War in 1968 or the war with Iraq and terrorism in 2004, turnout tends to be especially high. Races for higher office typically deal with bigger issues and feature candidates who are more attractive to voters. For these reasons, turnout in presidential races, and to a lesser extent in contests for U.S. senators and state governors, tends to be higher than turnout in elections for lower state offices and local races.

A well-documented trend from 1960 through 2000 was the declining rate of voter turnout in U.S. elections. Prior to 2004, turnout hovered around 50 percent for eight presidential elections. In fact, the election of 1996 marked the first time since 1908 that turnout actually dipped below the 50 percent mark, with only 49.1 percent of Americans of voting age going to the polls. For the past three presidential elections, however, voter turnout has trended upward (60 percent in 2004, 61 percent in 2008, and approximately 58 percent in 2012.). Voter turnout is usually much lower in midterm congressional elections (that is, the congressional elections that occur midway through a president's term). Forty-one percent of American adults cast a ballot in the 2006 elections.

Figure 13.7 depicts the trend in voter turnout for presidential elections covering the past half-century. It shows that the downward trend in turnout from 1960 through 2000 has been reversed, with turnout in 2004 reaching the 60 percent level.

Voting in the United States Compared with Other Democracies

Many observers of elections note that voter turnout rates are lower in the United States than they are in other democracies. From 1992 through 2000, the average turnout rate in the United States for presidential elections was 52 percent. Over the same period, the average turnout rate in all federal elections (including midterm congressional races) was 45 percent. During

FIGURE 13.7 Voter Turnout in U.S. Congressional and Presidential Elections

The following shows trends in voter turnout from 1960 through 2012 for presidential year elections and midterm congressional elections.

Source: © Cengage Learning

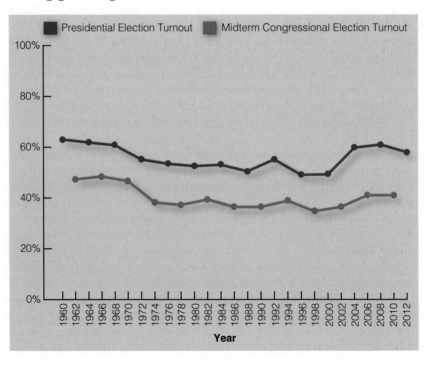

roughly the same period of time, turnout in other nations, as shown in Figure 13.8, was much higher.[33]

Several explanations have been offered to account for both the lower turnout rates in the United States compared to other democracies as well as the trend toward declining rates of turnout in the United States over the past half-century:

1. **There are a large number of elections in America, making the opportunity to participate less of a novelty.** U.S. turnout rates may be lower than those in other democracies of the world simply because there are so many elections held in the United States.[34] The U.S. system of federalism produces several layers of government—national, state, and local. At the federal level, elections are held for president, the Senate, and the House of Representatives. At the state level, there are gubernatorial races as well as elections for other statewide offices, including attorney general, state treasurer, and other state agency heads. At the local level, there may be elections for mayor, city council, sheriff, local judges, and so on. Furthermore, for many of these offices there are two elections: a primary election to elect the party candidate and a general election to determine the office winner. Also, in many states and localities there are often special elections on referendum questions and bond issues. Opportunities for participation in elections in the United States are so plentiful that they have become commonplace events. The vast number of elections may help explain lower rates of voting in any one contest. Switzerland, which also has a large number of elections, also has relatively low turnout compared to other democracies.

2. **Tuesdays are workdays.** Traditionally, most elections in the United States have been held on Tuesdays. Most working people work on Tuesday, and so it may be inconvenient or difficult for many voters to find the time to vote on this day. People report having less and less free time in our society, which can account in part for declining turnout. In many other countries, elections are held on weekends or over a period of a number of days, making it easier for people to find the time to cast a vote.

3. **Voting in the United States usually requires advance registration.** As described earlier in this chapter, voters in most U.S. states are required to register to vote prior to Election Day. In other countries, voter registration is often automatic; that is, citizens of legal age are automatically registered to vote. Thus voters simply need to show up at the voting place on Election Day. In countries where registration is automatic,

FIGURE 13.8 Voter Turnout Around the World

Voter turnout varies a great deal from one country to another. This figure depicts average voter turnout from 1991 through 2000 in a number of the world's democracies. The turnout rates are expressed as the percentage of the voting-age population that actually voted in national elections. For the United States, the percentage includes both presidential and midterm congressional elections.

Source: International Institute for Democracy and Electoral Assistance.

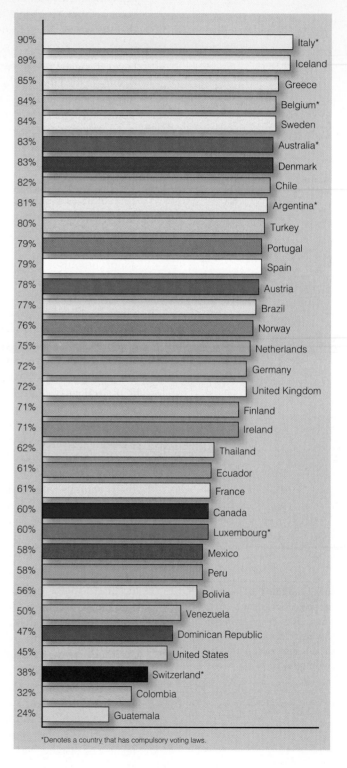

Percentage	Country
90%	Italy*
89%	Iceland
85%	Greece
84%	Belgium*
84%	Sweden
83%	Australia*
83%	Denmark
82%	Chile
81%	Argentina*
80%	Turkey
79%	Portugal
79%	Spain
78%	Austria
77%	Brazil
76%	Norway
75%	Netherlands
72%	Germany
72%	United Kingdom
71%	Finland
71%	Ireland
62%	Thailand
61%	Ecuador
61%	France
60%	Canada
60%	Luxembourg*
58%	Mexico
58%	Peru
56%	Bolivia
50%	Venezuela
47%	Dominican Republic
45%	United States
38%	Switzerland*
32%	Colombia
24%	Guatemala

*Denotes a country that has compulsory voting laws.

100 percent of eligible voters are thus registered; in the United States, where registration is usually a separate process, typically about 70 percent of eligible individuals have registered to vote.

4. **Over the past 50 years, perceptions both that participation can make a difference in what government does (that is, voters' sense of "internal efficacy") and that government is responsive to the people ("external efficacy") have declined.** Many researchers have concluded that the decline in political efficacy,[35] which is accompanied by declines in political trust and in confidence in political institutions, has produced lower rates of voter turnout. As people come to feel that they are less able to influence the system and that the system is less responsive to them, they may become less likely to vote.

5. **Extensions of the franchise lead to short-term declines in turnout.** Ironically, events that have expanded the franchise have been followed by lower rates of voter turnout. Following passage of the Fifteenth Amendment in 1870, which enfranchised former male slaves, the turnout rate dropped in 1872; passage of the Nineteenth Amendment in 1920, granting women the right to vote, led to an overall drop in turnout; and passage of the Twenty-sixth Amendment in 1971 that lowered the voting age to 18 led to lower turnout rates. One explanation for this phenomenon is that many newly eligible voters are not yet registered to vote and may require some time and socialization to get into the habit of voting.

6. **Voting in the United States is not compulsory.** Some democracies, including the United States, regard the franchise as a right. Accordingly, citizens have the opportunity to exercise their right to vote or they may choose not to vote. By contrast, some democracies have compulsory voting laws requiring citizens to vote. These nations assert that voting is a citizen's responsibility. Belgium, in 1892, was the first country to adopt compulsory voting. According to the International Institute for Democracy and Electoral Assistance, 32 countries have compulsory voting laws on the books. Twenty-four countries enforce these laws to some degree, and of them, nine—Australia, Belgium, Cyprus, Fiji, Luxembourg, Nauru, Singapore, Switzerland, and Uruguay—have strict enforcement policies.

   Punishments for not voting in countries with compulsory voting laws include large fines, possible imprisonment (although imprisonment is generally the punishment for not paying a fine), and disenfranchisement. In Belgium, individuals who do not vote in four elections over a 15-year period are stripped of their voting rights. In Bolivia, voters are given vouchers after they vote, and these vouchers are needed to receive a salary from a bank during a three-month period after an election. In Greece, it is very difficult to get a passport or driver's license without showing proof of having voted.

   Many arguments can be made in favor of or against compulsory voting laws, but one thing is certain: countries with compulsory voting laws have much higher turnout rates than countries without such laws. In Italy, for example, where lists of nonvoters are publicized, turnout has been around 90 percent. Though compulsory voting laws certainly increase turnout, many critics argue that the right to vote implicitly includes the right not to vote, just as the right to practice the religion of one's choice also includes the right not to practice a religion.

7. **The decline in "social capital."** Political scientist Robert Putnam has noted a general decline in **social capital**, which is the extent to which individuals are socially integrated into their community.[36] Over the past half-century, Americans have become less socially connected because they are not as likely to be members of organizations such as political parties, labor unions, civic groups, or even bowling leagues. As reasons for this decline, Putnam cites the increase of women in the workforce and corresponding reduction in the amount of time that women have available to spend on social and community activities. Other factors for the decline include the increase in residential mobility, and technological innovations such as radio, television, and the Internet. People today are more likely to stay home and watch TV or surf the Internet and less likely to engage in social activities with other people. Voting is, in part, a social activity. The decline in social capital may be responsible, at least in part, for the general decline in voting.

social capital: The "social connectedness" of a community, or the extent to which individuals are socially integrated into their community.

Is Nonvoting a Problem?

Although turnout has declined, the American political culture encourages people to vote. Over the years, voting has evolved from a privilege offered to a relatively few number of people to a right enjoyed by all. The League of Women Voters, Common Cause, and other groups regularly engage in campaigns to increase voter registration and stimulate turnout on Election Day. Candidates often stress the importance of voting, and the nation's educational system promotes the values of exercising the franchise, even to those not yet of age to vote. Even the

CHECK THE LIST

The Top 10 and Bottom 10 Popular Vote Winners in Presidential Elections

The 10 presidential election winners who received the highest percentage of the popular votes:

✓ 1.	Lyndon Johnson	Democrat	1964	61.3%
✓ 2.	Franklin Roosevelt	Democrat	1936	60.8%
✓ 3.	Richard M. Nixon	Republican	1972	60.6%
✓ 4.	Warren G. Harding	Republican	1920	60.4%
✓ 5.	Ronald Reagan	Republican	1984	59.0%
✓ 6.	Herbert Hoover	Republican	1928	58.2%
✓ 7.	Franklin Roosevelt	Democrat	1932	57.4%
✓ 8.	Theodore Roosevelt	Republican	1904	57.4%
✓ 9.	Andrew Jackson	Democrat	1828	56.0%
✓10.	Ulysses S. Grant	Republican	1872	55.6%

The 10 presidential election winners who received the lowest percentage of the popular vote:

✓ 1.	John Quincy Adams	National Republican	1824	30.5%
✓ 2.	Abraham Lincoln	Republican	1860	39.8%
✓ 3.	Woodrow Wilson	Democrat	1912	41.9%
✓ 4.	Bill Clinton	Democrat	1992	43.2%
✓ 5.	Richard Nixon	Republican	1968	43.4%
✓ 6.	James Buchanan	Democrat	1856	45.3%
✓ 7.	Grover Cleveland	Democrat	1892	46.1%
✓ 8.	Zachary Taylor	Whig	1848	47.4%
✓ 9.	Benjamin Harrison	Republican	1888	47.9%
✓10.	Rutherford B. Hayes	Republican	1876	48.0%

▶ **POINT TO PONDER:** Does the size of a president's victory, as measured by the percentage of the popular vote achieved, have some bearing on the success that president enjoys during his initial months in office? In other words, does greater support from Americans at the polls translate into greater opportunities for a successful administration? Are those presidents who have garnered a higher share of the popular vote regarded as more successful chief executives?

television station MTV invested time and money into the popular "Rock the Vote" campaign to encourage young people to vote. These efforts are predicated on the assumption that voting is important and that, conversely, nonvoting is problematic.

So to what extent is low voter turnout a problem in our democracy? Two main arguments support the contention that nonvoting is problematic. The first holds that low voter turnout rates are a symptom of a weak democracy. The essence of what makes a democracy is the link between what a majority of citizens prefer and those who are given the authority to govern. Voting is the mechanism that creates this link. With low turnout, majorities of all citizens do not rule. When barely 50 percent of eligible voters cast ballots, successful candidates can hardly claim to have captured majority support. George W. Bush won the 2000 presidential election, for example, but less than 25 percent of all American adults voted for him.

The second argument contends that low turnout awards distinct advantages to the affluent, higher-socioeconomic groups in our society. As we have seen, turnout rates are lower among less educated and lower-income groups. Thus, nonvoting affords better-educated and wealthier groups of people more power in determining the winner of a political race.

There are also reasons, however, as to why nonvoting may not be a cause for concern. Perhaps nonvoting produces an electorate that is more informed, more aware of the important issues, and better able to make vote choices for the candidates who most deserve election to office. Former Senator Sam Ervin once said, "I don't think it's a problem that apathetic, lazy people don't vote." Voting simply for the sake of voting may not produce good choices. Though ideally all citizens should become informed and cast a vote based on their information, many people lack the capacity or interest to cast a truly meaningful vote.

Another reason why nonvoting may not be a problem rests on the premise that voting is a voluntary right, just as the rights of free speech, religious choice, and peaceful assembly are voluntary. Our society does not compel citizens to speak out on issues, to declare a religious affiliation, or to contribute time or money to any particular cause or political party. So why should it expect people to exercise their right to vote? Furthermore, for many people nonvoting may be their expression of satisfaction with the status quo.

PARTICIPATION BEYOND VOTING

One recent protest movement that gained a national following is the so-called Tea Party movement. Beginning in early 2009, a series of anti-tax protests emerged in response to the federal government's increase in spending to combat the economic recession. The Tea Party protests challenged the Barack Obama–Democratic Party policies of deficit spending and proposals to reform the nation's health care insurance system. The term *Tea Party* was chosen strategically to reference the Boston Tea Party, whose goal was to protest Britain's taxation policies toward the colonies during the American Revolutionary period. "TEA" is also used as an acronym for "taxed enough already." In addition to organizing protest rallies across the nation (annually on April 15, or "tax day," for example), Tea Party organizers were particularly active during the 2010 midterm elections, and are credited with the large-scale GOP victories in the 2010 congressional contests.

Another protest movement that became popular in 2011 was the "Occupy Wall Street" protest movement. Beginning as a protest rally in New York City's financial district near Wall Street, many supporters of the movement organized rallies around the nation to voice their concerns about the growing division in economic equality between the top 1 percent of wealth and the remaining 99 percent. They blame the growing economic inequality on the greed and corruption of large financial institutions, and demand reforms in public policy to reverse this inequality.

Protests can take one of three forms: legal protests in which citizens play by the "rules of the game" to speak out against a government policy, acts of nonviolent civil disobedience, and illegal protest activities that often include violence.

Occupy Wall Street demonstrators march outside of the New York Stock Exchange in November 2011.

Marches, sit-ins, and rallies are forms of legal protests; such activities are designed to call attention to an issue that the protesters feel is not receiving adequate attention in the standard political process. Protesters are exercising their First Amendment right "peaceably to assemble and to petition the government for a redress of grievances." Many legal peaceful protests have raised awareness of an issue to a level that forces the normal legislative process to address it. A number of protest movements paved the way for substantial changes in public policy. Protests against the Vietnam War, for example, during the late 1960s and early 1970s led, in part, to American withdrawal from the Vietnam War. After World War I, protests among women's groups demanding the right of women to vote led to the adoption in 1920 of the Nineteenth Amendment granting women suffrage. Successful protests are often begun by small groups of individuals who feel strongly about an issue and are willing to spend the time and effort to make their case.

Protests make for good television because they generally feature conflict, a grievance, and individuals who are outspoken about the particular cause. Well-organized groups that engage in protests on hot-button issues, such as environmental groups, pro-life or pro-choice groups, and anti–death penalty groups, have become adept at informing the news media about the protests ahead of time and engaging articulate speakers to make their case. The media attention often provides protesters an opportunity to ensure that their causes reach the policy agenda of governing institutions.

The second type of protest behavior, *civil disobedience*, involves protesters engaged in illegal but nonviolent activity. The goal of the protesters is to break laws that they feel are unjust, and the protesters willingly accept the consequences for breaking the law. Blacks protesting segregation laws in the southern states during the 1950s and 1960s would intentionally break those laws as a way of drawing attention to the problem of segregation.

Finally, a third type of protest behavior involves violent protests. In 1992, a number of rioters in south central Los Angeles took to the streets after a jury acquitted several white police officers in a case where the officers had been caught on videotape brutally beating a black man they had stopped for a traffic violation. The rioters were protesting accusations of racial bias in the Los Angeles criminal justice system. The protesters looted businesses, stopped traffic, pulled a white truck driver out of his vehicle and severely beat him, and caused much damage to property.

How Might Television Shape Your Own Views of What Is Politically Possible?

When Barack Obama became the first African American to take the oath of office as U.S. president in 2009, he overcame racial barriers thought to be impenetrable just two decades earlier, when many voters dismissed Jesse Jackson's run for the presidency as a sideshow. Still, those among the tens of millions who watched Obama's inauguration as the 44th president should be forgiven if the whole thing seemed a bit...*familiar*. Consider that on October 29, 2002, almost six years before Obama's election victory, viewers of the popular Fox series *24* were greeted by a television breakthrough of sorts, when African American character actor Dennis Haysbert was introduced in his new role as U.S. President David Palmer. More than four years later, on January 14, 2007, *24* fans were introduced to the sight of yet another African American president: this time it was David Palmer's brother Wayne (played by D. B. Woodside).

Other historical breakthroughs in television's depiction of the American presidency are notable as well. On May 14, 2007, the fictional Latin American Congressman Matthew Santos (played by Jimmy Smits) was sworn in as the new U.S. president in the final episode of the critically acclaimed drama series *The West Wing*. Women presidents have also appeared in prime time, both in the short-lived 2005 drama series *Commander in Chief* (Academy Award–winning actress Geena Davis played President Mackenzie

Isabella Vosmikova/AFP/Getty Images/Newscom

Pictured above is Dennis Haysbert, playing President David Palmer, on the TV show "24."

Allen), as well as in the seventh season of *24*, when Allison Taylor (played by Cherry Jones) became the latest fictional chief executive.

For his part, Dennis Haysbert has argued that his role as an African American president may have actually benefited Barack Obama: "If anything, my portrayal of David Palmer, I think, may have helped open the eyes of the American people." This may be a case of reality not so much mimicking popular culture as being influenced by its more open-minded mores. Keep that in mind the next time you are using your remote control to flick through shows featuring fictional political leaders.

For Critical Thinking and Discussion

1. What role does race or gender play in voters' assessments of candidates?

2. Can a fictional television series influence the way voters think about real-life candidates and their political viability? If so, how?

3. Do historical electoral breakthroughs (such as the election of the first African American or woman as president) require that voters first undergo a fundamental change in attitudes?

Warner Bros./Getty Images

Above is Jimmy Smits playing President Matthew Santos on the TV show "The West Wing."

Source: Simon Reynolds, "Haysbert: '24' President Helped Obama," Digitalspy.com, July 2, 2008.

The Founders never intended for a two-party system to take hold in the republic they so carefully designed; and yet two-party systems have dominated U.S. politics for over two centuries, beginning with the rivalry between Federalists and the Democratic-Republicans in the 1790s, and extending all the way up to the present, when the Democrats and modern-day Republicans take turns controlling our government. Sometimes both major parties—despite all their built-in political advantages—lose touch with passionate strains of popular opinion. This is most likely to occur when the public grows increasingly skeptical about government as a whole. In such instances, an upstart political movement may suddenly arrive on the scene, connecting with the interests of a segment of the electorate that seeks a brand new means of influencing government. In the 1890s it was the "People's Party" (also known as the Populists) that made its voice heard; in 2010 the Tea Party movement lent its support to numerous anti-government candidates and helped to shift party control of Congress in the process. If history is a guide, those movements tend to be short-lived, exerting significant influence in a series of election cycles before one or both of the major parties bring the movement's energetic set of followers into their own party's fold. Will the major political party that is most successful in this regard be willing to incorporate the upstart movement's ideas into its policy agenda as well? That was the dilemma that faced the Democratic Party in the 1890s, and that faces the Republican Party today.

SUMMARY: PUTTING IT ALL TOGETHER

THE DEVELOPMENT OF POLITICAL PARTIES IN THE UNITED STATES

- Because many of the founders frowned on parties and other factions, the Constitution nowhere mentions or contemplates parties. Nevertheless, the debate over ratification of the Constitution gave rise to two parties: the Federalists and the Anti-Federalists. The United States has had a two-party system ever since.

- Every presidential and congressional election since 1796 has featured some form of party competition. National party conventions and national party organization originated during Andrew Jackson's presidency. The Democratic and Republican Parties have dominated since 1856.

- Certain elections, such as those of 1860, 1896, and 1932, are considered "critical elections" because they produced sharp and lasting changes in patterns of party loyalty among voters.

- Some political scientists have termed the era since 1968 as a period of dealignment, characterized by a decline in voter attachment to parties and in clarity of party coalitions.

Test Yourself on This Section

1. In 1796 and 1800, Thomas Jefferson ran for president as a candidate from which political party?
   a. Federalists
   b. Democratic-Republicans
   c. Republicans
   d. Whigs

2. The modern Democratic Party's first successful attempt to win the presidency occurred in
   a. 1796 with the victory of John Adams.
   b. 1824 with the victory of John Quincy Adams.
   c. 1828 with the victory of Andrew Jackson.
   d. 1932 with the victory of Franklin Roosevelt.

3. All of the following are considered to be critical realigning elections EXCEPT
   a. Jefferson's victory in 1800.
   b. Lincoln's victory in 1860.
   c. McKinley's victory in 1896.
   d. Roosevelt's victory in 1932.

4. Distinguish between a "realigning" election and a "dealignment."

THE FUNCTIONS OF POLITICAL PARTIES

- The two major parties have developed large organizations that exist at the national, state, and local levels. They assist in fundraising for candidates, recruiting and organizing volunteers to work for candidates, and purchasing political services to promote the election of candidates.

- Party identification develops early in a person's political life, psychologically connecting the individual to a political party, which in turn influences other attitudes and voting behavior.

- Majority-party leadership in Congress organizes that branch to accomplish the task of governing. Partisanship also influences a president's policy positions and appointments.

- When divided-party government exists, it becomes difficult for either party to advance its policy goals and objectives.

Test Yourself on This Section

1. Party identification is measured by asking voters
   - **a.** which party they are registered with.
   - **b.** whether they belong to a third party.
   - **c.** which party best represents their issue preferences.
   - **d.** which party they support.

2. The condition when American government is characterized by split-party control of Congress and the presidency is known as
   - **a.** gridlock government.
   - **b.** partisan government.
   - **c.** divided government.
   - **d.** locked government.

3. What are the implications of the "normal vote" concept for presidential candidates as they try to develop winning strategies?

WHY A TWO-PARTY SYSTEM?

- The U.S. party system has been dominated by Democrats and Republicans since the election of 1856. This two-party system is perpetuated by several factors, including the need for a majority of electoral college votes (not just a plurality) to win the presidency outright, and a winner-take-all system that makes it especially hard for third parties to succeed to any degree.

- Third-party candidates rarely attract a significant percentage of popular votes in presidential elections because voters perceive that votes for such a candidate would be wasted and because various legal barriers make it hard for third-party candidates to receive government funding.

Test Yourself on This Section

1. Governments that rely on proportional representation as a means of selecting a national legislature and ruling government most typically have what type of party system?
   - **a.** single-party system
   - **b.** two-party system
   - **c.** multiparty system
   - **d.** no party system

2. The most successful third party in U.S. presidential election history, whose candidate received more votes that the Republican Party candidate, was
   - **a.** Ross Perot's Reform Party in 1996.
   - **b.** Ralph Nader's Green Party in 2000.
   - **c.** Theodore Roosevelt's Bull Moose Party in 1912.
   - **d.** George Wallace's American Independent Party in 1968.

3. What are the factors that contribute to the fact that the United States is dominated by a two-party model?

PARTY ORGANIZATIONS

- The two major political parties have organizations at the national level, at the state level in all 50 states, and at the local level in most cities and towns across the nation. These organizations are active in developing party platforms, recruiting candidates to run for office, and providing financial support and other resources to aid the candidates electorally.

1. In the modern era of elections, which level of party organization has the least amount of influence in nominating candidates for office?
   a. national parties
   b. state parties
   c. county/parish parties
   d. local parties

ARE PARTIES IN DECLINE?

- The decline of patronage and the prevalence of the direct primary election have contributed to the belief that parties are now in decline. Regardless, party identification remains an especially strong determinant of vote choice in America today.

Test Yourself on This Section

1. Which of the following makes it easier for candidates to bypass the parties in a pathway to the party nomination?
   a. party caucuses
   b. direct primary elections
   c. political party machines
   d. state election laws

2. What evidence has been used recently to suggest that political parties are not in a state of decline?

VOTING

- Traditionally, the states and not the federal government have had authority in running elections. However, state attempts to disenfranchise certain groups have been thwarted by constitutional amendments and federal laws. Although the goal of universal suffrage may not be fully realized today, over the centuries the United States has moved closer to this goal.

- The constitutional amendments that have limited states' ability to disenfranchise voters include the Fifteenth Amendment (guaranteeing African American men the franchise), Nineteenth Amendment (women's suffrage), Twenty-fourth Amendment (outlawing poll taxes), and Twenty-sixth Amendment (guaranteeing the vote to those eighteen years of age).

- States are responsible for maintaining a system of voter registration, and the systems vary widely from state to state. Only one state (North Dakota) does not require voters to register to vote as a prequalification to voting. Through the Motor Voter law, the federal government has tried to encourage higher levels of voter registration.

Test Yourself on This Section

1. Which Amendment to the U.S. Constitution declares "the right of citizens of the United States to vote shall not be abridged by the United States or any state on account of race, color, or any previous condition of servitude?
   a. Tenth Amendment
   b. Thirteenth Amendment
   c. Fifteenth Amendment
   d. Twentieth Amendment

2. The 1857 U.S. Supreme Court ruling that slaves were property and could not become legal citizens of the United States, thus precipitating the Civil War, was
   a. *Scott v. Sanford.*
   b. *Plessy v. Ferguson.*
   c. *McCulloch v. Maryland.*
   d. *Brown v. Board of Education.*

3. What is the "Motor Voter" law, and how does it improve voter registration?

EXERCISING THE FRANCHISE

- Among the factors that have been identified as relating to a citizen's propensity to vote are interest in politics, sense of civic duty, the perception that one's vote can make a difference, level of education, level of income, age, and social group pressure.

- The nature of the times and type of political campaign can also influence turnout. High-stimulus elections, in which the issues are very important or the races are more visible, tend to produce higher voter turnout. Presidential elections generally promote the highest levels of turnout, and the less visible local races inspire the lowest levels of turnout.

- Although there has been a general declining trend in voter turnout in the United States over the past six or seven decades, recent presidential and midterm congressional elections have seen a modest increase in voting. This may be the result of voter concerns about U.S. military involvement in Iraq.
- Voter turnout in the United States tends to be lower than turnout in other democracies. Reasons that account for the lower U.S. turnout are the fact that there is no compulsory voting in the United States, the wide variation in states' voter registration requirements, the vast number of U.S. elections, and the tradition of holding elections on one weekday.

Test Yourself on This Section

1. Members of which one of the following demographic groups are most likely to turnout to vote in an election?
   a. men
   b. women
   c. 18- to 24-year-olds
   d. 65- to 75-year-olds

2. Which of the following is NOT an example of a "high-stimulus" election?
   a. a race believed to be very close
   b. a presidential race
   c. a mayoral race
   d. a race with a high level of media coverage

3. What are the explanations for why voter turnout in the United States tends to be lower than voter turnout in other democracies?

PARTICIPATION BEYOND THE VOTING BOOTH

- Americans participate in politics in many ways beyond voting, including contributing time and money, participating in rallies and protests, and contacting their elected officials.

KEY TERMS

critical election (p. 352)
dealignment (p. 354)
direct primary election (p. 365)
divided government (p. 359)
Fifteenth Amendment (p. 367)
franchise (or suffrage) (p. 366)
literacy test (p. 368)
majoritarianism (p. 365)
Motor Voter law (p. 370)
multiparty system (p. 359)

national committee (p. 363)
national committee chair (p. 363)
national party convention (p. 351)
national party organization (p. 362)
Nineteenth Amendment (p. 368)
normal vote (p. 356)
party identification (p. 356)
party platform (p. 351)
political party (p. 348)
poll tax (p. 368)

proportional representation (p. 360)
representative democracy (p. 365)
social capital (p. 376)
Twenty-fourth Amendment (p. 368)
Twenty-sixth Amendment (p. 368)
Twenty-third Amendment (p. 368)
two-party system (p. 359)
universal suffrage (p. 367)
voter turnout (p. 371)
voting (p. 366)

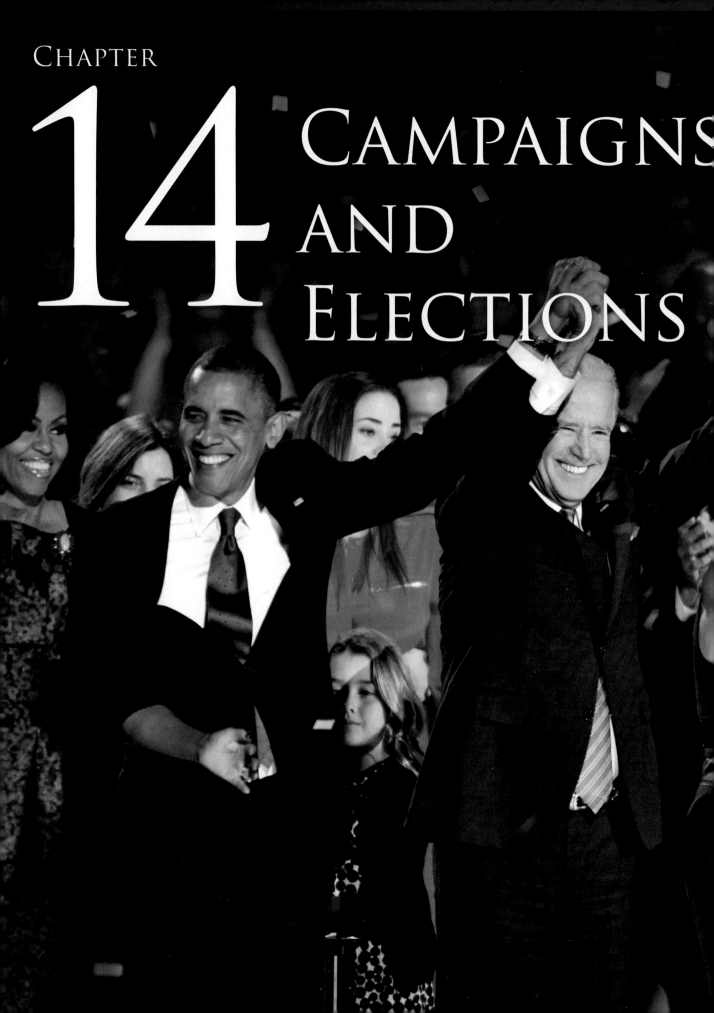

14 CAMPAIGNS AND ELECTIONS

LEARNING OBJECTIVES

AMERICAN PRESIDENTIAL ELECTIONS IN HISTORICAL PERSPECTIVE

- Describe the historical development of the presidential selection process

THE PRENOMINATION CAMPAIGN

- Describe the activities of presidential candidates as they compete for the "invisible primary"

THE NOMINATION CAMPAIGN

- Distinguish between primaries and caucuses, and assess how the timing of those contests plays a role in the outcome of the nomination process
- Assess the role of national party conventions

THE GENERAL ELECTION CAMPAIGN

- Compare and contrast incumbent races and open elections
- Describe the strategies that candidates use to win elections
- Critique the electoral college system

MAKING A VOTE CHOICE

- Compare and contrast the factors that explain vote choices

CAMPAIGN FUNDING

- Assess the impact of money on presidential campaigns, and describe the laws governing campaign finance

CONGRESSIONAL CAMPAIGNS AND ELECTIONS

- Define the power of incumbency, turnout levels, and presidential coattails in congressional elections

The U.S. Constitution calls for a presidential election every four years and congressional elections every two years. Without skipping a beat, the United States has met this constitutional requirement for 225 years. Through a Civil War, two world wars, and several major economic depressions, elections—the hallmark of American democracy—have taken place like clockwork. In designing this representative democracy, the Founders intended a system that demanded accountability from elected officials. Elections for president and Congress provide this accountability. Regular and free elections are the linchpin underlying democracy in America. Every year Americans are invited to cast ballots in elections for many local, county, and statewide races, but no election receives more attention than the race for the presidency.

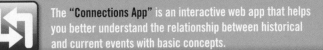

1960   1970   1980   1990   2000

1984

Then

President Ronald Reagan (right) and former Vice President Walter Mondale (left) square off in the first presidential debate of 1984. Reagan's performance in the debate was lackluster.

Source: © Bettmann/CORBIS

Modern presidential campaigns are highly staged affairs: campaign managers and strategists leave nothing to chance, scripting every speech, obsessing over every television ad, and planning every moment of the national party convention. For that reason, the presidential debates that occur in the weeks leading up to election day are a source of considerable anxiety for campaign staffs. After all, tens of millions of Americans tune into these debates precisely because they cannot be so easily scripted. An ill-timed gaffe or misstep may shift the entire tenor of the campaign. Consider the challenge facing President Ronald Reagan as he prepared to square off in two presidential debates against his Democratic challenger, Walter Mondale, in September of 1984. Now the oldest president in history at 73, Reagan's capacity to endure the grueling demands of the presidency had been openly questioned. In fact, the first debate on September 7, 1984 proved disastrous for the incumbent: Mondale was the far more effective speaker, while Reagan appeared tired and often confused by the moderator's questions. The uneven debate boosted Mondale's prospects in the short term, helping to narrow what had been a large, double-digit lead for Reagan in the polls. Of course, one night does not define an entire election campaign. Reagan recovered in the second debate two weeks later, diffusing the age issue with a quip about how he would not "exploit, for political purposes, my opponent's youth and inexperience." Boosted by a strong economy and high approval ratings, Reagan rebounded from his poor performance in the first debate and never looked back on the way to a resounding reelection victory. Given the stakes, the American electorate would not allow one bad night to cloud its judgment about which candidate belonged in the White House.

2012

Now

Former governor Mitt Romney (left) and President Obama (right) during the first debate in the 2012 campaign. Obama's performance fell far short of expectations.

Source: Chip Somodevilla/Getty Images

President Barack Obama lacked many of Ronald Reagan's political assets when he stood for reelection in 2012. Following the great recession of 2008-2009, the economy remained stagnant; Obama's approval ratings hovered at or below the 50 percent mark, and many of his administration's signature achievements (such as the passage of health care reform) did not enjoy widespread popularity. And yet Obama capitalized on his inherent advantages as the sitting commander-in-chief and his personal strengths as a campaigner to build a consistent (if narrow) lead in the polls over his Republican challenger, Mitt Romney, during the late summer and early fall. By the end of September, President Obama appeared to be coasting to victory in the Electoral College. Unfortunately for the incumbent, the fundamental dynamics of the campaign were altered significantly as a result of the first presidential debate on October 3, 2012. That

night Romney was energetic and forceful in listing his grievances with the current administration; Obama appeared listless and offered a less-than-passionate defense of his record. In the two weeks following that first debate, Romney caught up to President Obama in public opinion polls, offering the prospect of a dead heat contest on election day. And yet, by the end of October, President Obama was able to stabilize the race just as Reagan had done more than a quarter century earlier. He turned in two stronger debate performances in mid-to-late October, and by the time election day rolled around, President Obama had re-energized his followers enough to help him secure another four years in office. One bad debate altered the campaign's dynamics, but not the ultimate outcome of the race. When the stakes are so great, short-term campaign missteps cannot so easily erase the larger landscape of a presidential campaign.

AMERICAN PRESIDENTIAL ELECTIONS IN HISTORICAL PERSPECTIVE

The U.S. Constitution says nothing about political parties or the process by which individuals become candidates for the presidency. The Founders assumed that electors, chosen by the states (and heavily influenced by the House of Representatives), would identify and evaluate potential candidates, and then the electoral college would select the chief executive.[1] Parties, or "factions," were frowned upon; the selection of president was intended to be the product of a select group of rational, wise men making choices at a lofty level above partisan politics.

Although their intentions for presidential selection were noble, the Founders' expectations about how a president would actually be chosen proved to be quite naïve. Political parties, though weaker today than in the past, have provided the framework for every presidential election since 1796. Each of the two major parties holds nomination contests in the 50 states to select the party's candidate in the general election; the party nominees then compete in the general election.

The presidential selection process that has evolved over the past two centuries of U.S. nationhood is long and complex. The manner in which the 2012 selection process occurred was not based on some elaborate constitutional design. Rather, this complicated and quirky process is the result of more than 200 years of modification and evolution. Over the years, two distinct phases of the presidential selection process have developed: the nomination phase and the general election phase.

The Nomination Phase

In the nomination phase of the presidential election process, the political parties select specific people to run as the presidential and vice presidential candidates in the general election. This duo is referred to as the "party ticket." The Constitution did not account for a nomination phase because the Founders did not anticipate that a two-party system would emerge. The first two presidential elections did not even include political parties. Rather, the electors from the states all agreed that George Washington should be president in 1789 and again in 1792. Nevertheless, divisions within the federal government erupted and political alliances began to form during Washington's administration. These alliances resulted in the first two major political parties, the Federalists and their opponents, who eventually became known as the Democratic-Republicans. In 1796, when Washington decided not to seek a third term, each of these parties sought to win the presidency by recruiting and supporting candidates.[2]

The Federalists in Congress supported John Adams and the Democratic-Republicans threw their support to Thomas Jefferson. Electors, who were largely chosen by state legislatures, followed the cues of their partisan leadership in casting their electoral votes, and Adams, the Federalist-supported candidate, won the general election with 71 electoral votes, whereas Jefferson received 68 electoral votes. The nomination process in 1796 reflected a significant level of party discipline in the casting of ballots among electors. In the elections of 1800, 1804, and 1808, both the Federalists and the Democratic-Republicans used informal meetings and discussions to choose a party nominee. Democratic-Republicans dominated electoral politics from 1812 through 1828, as the Federalist Party eventually disappeared.

In 1824, however, a significant split occurred within the Democratic-Republican Party. Andrew Jackson, who had the support of many common people, challenged party favorite John Quincy Adams. Jackson won both the popular vote and a plurality of the electoral vote, but no candidate received a majority of electoral votes. By constitutional provision, the election was sent to the House of Representatives, which voted Adams the victor. Jackson then founded a new party, the Democratic Party,[3] which is, of course, one of the two major parties still in existence today. Jackson and his followers believed in the enfranchisement of all white men, rather than just the propertied class—during what became known as the Jacksonian era, white male suffrage was dramatically expanded throughout the country. Specifically, more and more state political parties adopted open caucuses, in which party members formally met to provide input as to who their party should nominate for elective office.

Former Pennsylvania Senator Rick Santorum was a candidate for the GOP nomination in 2012. He was a favorite of many social conservatives in the Republican Party.

Electoral reforms during the Progressive era of the early 1900s opened participation in the nomination process to a greater number of Americans. The direct primary gave voters an opportunity to cast a ballot for delegates, who would in turn be sent to a national convention for the purpose of choosing a presidential nominee. The state of Florida was the first to hold a direct primary in a presidential election, in 1900. Although direct primaries did allow greater numbers of people the opportunity help select delegates, until the 1960s it was still the political elite of a party (governors, mayors, party chairs, and other officials) that selected most of the delegates and thus had the most input in choosing the party's presidential nominee.

The political unrest of the 1960s, spurred by anti–Vietnam War activism, led to further changes that gave voters in primaries even more weight in selecting party nominees. Benefiting from the increased percentage of convention delegates chosen through open primaries, Jimmy Carter, the little-known governor of Georgia, won the Democratic Party's nomination in 1976. A political outsider, Carter was able to appeal directly to average voters. Carter not only won the nomination, but he also went on the win the presidency that year. His victory demonstrated to candidates in both the Democratic Party and the Republican Party that securing sufficient numbers of delegates to win the nomination requires direct appeals to voters, whether through party caucuses or, more likely, through party primary contests. Today this pattern persists: to win a party's nomination, a candidate must win a majority of delegates who are primarily chosen by voters in the state primaries and caucuses.

The General Election Phase

The unanticipated emergence of political parties not only established a party nomination process, but it also forced a change in the Founders' design for selecting presidents from among the party nominees. The Founders intended the state legislatures to pick well-qualified "electors," who would meet on a specified day in their state to decide who was the best choice to become president. At the end of the day, these electors would then cast votes for president. The states then sent their vote totals to the president of the U.S. Senate (the sitting vice president), who counted the votes before Congress. The candidate with a majority of votes became president, and the second-place finisher became vice president. If no one candidate received a majority of the votes, the election was to be decided by the House of Representatives, with each state delegation having one vote to select the new president. The Senate was to select the vice president.

In the 1800 presidential race, nearly all of the Federalists voted for John Adams and Charles Pinckney (65 and 64 votes, respectively), and all of the Democratic-Republicans voted for Jefferson and Aaron Burr, each of whom received 73 votes. Although it was generally agreed that Jefferson was the leader of the Democratic-Republican ticket, Burr challenged Jefferson in the House (because the election was a tie, the House state delegations had to choose the new president). Ultimately the House decided in favor of Jefferson, who became president, with Burr then becoming vice president. It was clear that the presidential election system needed fixing.[4]

The Twelfth Amendment to the Constitution, passed in 1804, provided for separate balloting for president and vice president by requiring that electors designate one of their two votes for president and the second of their two votes for vice president. This amendment greatly reduced the possibility that future elections would end in a tie.

Several other amendments to the Constitution have altered the presidential selection process. The Twenty-second Amendment, ratified in 1951, limits presidents to two 4-year terms in office (or 10 years if a vice president serves out the term of a president). The Twenty-third Amendment, ratified in 1961, provides the District of Columbia with three electoral votes. Because the District is not a state, it previously had no electoral votes.

The modern presidential selection system, then, is an amalgamation of the Founders' design, modified by constitutional amendments and changes that occurred over time. This all makes for a complex system of picking a president. Although there are many caveats and exceptions to the rules, the contemporary presidential selection process generally consists of five stages:

1. **The prenomination campaign.** After a new president is selected, potential candidates for the next presidential election (four years hence) begin to explore the possibility of running. The ability to raise money, garner support from key leaders in the party, and attract the attention of the news media all contribute to each candidate's decision of whether to enter the race.

2. **The nomination campaign.** From January through June of the presidential election year, parties in each state hold either a primary or caucus in which the party delegates from the state commit to candidates. Each party has different criteria for allocating the number of delegates that a state will get. The candidate who receives a majority of delegates wins the party nomination.

3. **The national conventions.** Each political party holds a national convention during the summer to showcase its candidate. Prior to the convention, the party nominees select their vice presidential running mates. Although the conventions used to play an important role in defining the party platform and selecting the party's nominee, today the conventions are largely publicity events for the ticket and other stars in the party, as well as an opportunity to critique the opposing party.

4. **The general election campaign.** Because national party conventions today generally affirm rather than choose party nominees, presidential candidates usually begin waging their general election campaigns before the conventions, as soon as it becomes clear who the two major-party nominees will be. (These decisions generally occur in the spring of the election year.) Most recent campaigns have included a series of televised debates between the presidential and the vice presidential candidates, a significant amount of advertising and campaigning in key states, and, more recently, strong efforts to appeal to voters through the social media.

5. **The electoral college decision.** The winner of the presidential election is decided on the basis of the vote count in the electoral college. The number of electoral votes for each state is equivalent to the state's allotment of House members plus two (for the state's two U.S. senators). In all but two states, the candidate who wins the popular vote automatically receives all of the electoral votes from that state. (Currently in Maine and Nebraska,

the votes for president are counted for each congressional district; candidates get one elector for each district they win, and the candidate who wins the state overall gets an additional two electors.) Nationwide, the candidate who receives an outright majority of electoral votes wins the election.

THE PRENOMINATION CAMPAIGN

Although the presidential campaign officially begins with the first state contest for delegates in January of the election year, the real campaign for president actually begins much earlier, soon after the previous presidential election has concluded. As part of the **prenomination campaign**, behind-the-scenes candidates who are thinking about making a run often begin to "test the waters" by talking to party insiders, shoring up early commitments of support, lining up a campaign staff, beginning a fundraising operation, traveling around the country making speeches and appearances, setting up "exploratory committees" to assess the feasibility of making a formal declaration of official candidacy, and then making the official announcement. Shortly after the 2008 election, former Governor Mitt Romney, Congresswoman Michele Bachmann, former Senator Rick Santorum, businessman Herman Cain, Governor Rick Perry, and Congressman Ron Paul, among others, all established exploratory committees and began testing the waters to wage a bid for the GOP nomination. On the Democratic side, no serious challenger to first-term incumbent Barack Obama emerged.

The prenomination campaign also marks the beginning of the "weeding-out" process. Early on, many would-be candidates find insufficient support from party insiders. Others cannot raise sufficient funds to be competitive. Some tire too quickly of the arduous and time-consuming schedule necessary for launching a run for the presidency. These and other obstacles begin the process of narrowing the field of candidates.

The **invisible primary** is the competition between candidates seeking the party nomination for frontrunner status. A candidate gains frontrunner status by winning broad support from important people within the party, raising more money than others, and achieving the top position in the public polls conducted by leading news organizations. Frontrunners tend to receive more coverage in the news, thus promoting their name recognition and popularity as candidates.

Within the Republican Party in 2012, the invisible primary began as a battle primarily among Romney, Bachmann, Cain, and Perry. At one point prior to the first contest in Iowa,

> **prenomination campaign:** The political season in which candidates for president begin to explore the possibility of running by attempting to raise money and garner support.

> **invisible primary:** The competition among candidates seeking the party nomination for frontrunner status prior to the primaries and caucuses.

GOP presidential candidates, from left to right, Rick Santorum, Ron Paul, Thaddeus McCotter, Herman Cain and Michele Bachmann gather before the Iowa "straw poll" in August 2011.

THE MORE THINGS CHANGE, THE MORE THEY STAY THE SAME

New Romances and Old Horses in the Race for the Presidential Nomination

When a political party does not have a sitting incumbent seeking reelection, the competition for that party's nomination can become intense. In addition, the race can be quite volatile, as voters consider possible candidates, and then reconsider their choices:

In 1964, the race for the GOP nomination featured a crowded field of candidates prepared to take on the unelected presidential incumbent, Democrat Lyndon Baines Johnson. Senator Barry Goldwater, a conservative from Arizona, and Governor Nelson Rockefeller, a moderate from New York, led the pack at the start of the primaries. However, Governor William Scranton of Pennsylvania, Senator Margaret Chase Smith of Maine, Governor Harold Stassen of Minnesota, and James Rhodes of Ohio all found themselves with shifting support and momentum at one point or another during this volatile race. The party thus found itself divided between the more conservative forces and the liberal-to-moderate Republicans. When the moderate Rockefeller gave way to Goldwater (amid news that Rockefeller was divorcing his wife and marrying a much younger woman), many moderates shifted their support to Scranton, whose support suddenly surged. At various points during the race, party leaders encouraged Governor George Romney of Michigan (father of 2012 GOP nominee Mitt Romney), former GOP nominee Richard Nixon, and Oregon Governor Mark Hatfield to throw in their hats as well to break the conservative-moderate logjam . . . but all declined. Complicating matters further was former Massachusetts Senator (and 1960 vice presidential candidate) Henry Cabot Lodge Jr., who won the New Hampshire and New Jersey primaries, but then decided to quit the race. Ultimately, Goldwater prevailed, but only after many ups and downs, including a party convention where Romney led a walk-out of his own delegates in protest of the extremely conservative nominee chosen.

In 2012, the race for the GOP nomination also featured a crowded field of candidates who wanted to take on incumbent Democrat Barack Obama. At the start of the primaries, two candidates found themselves at the top of the national polls: former Massachusetts Governor Mitt Romney and former House Speaker Newt Gingrich. Romney was the favorite of the moderates and Gingrich appealed to conservatives. Throughout the prenomination and early nomination process, a number of other candidates found themselves with surging support, including businessman Herman Cain, billionaire Donald Trump, libertarian Ron Paul, Minnesota Congresswoman Michele Bachmann, former Pennsylvania Senator Rick Santorum, and Texas Governor Rick Perry. At times, GOP insiders encouraged Sarah Palin and Governors Chris Christie (NJ) and Mitch Daniels (IN) to enter the race, though none ever did. When Gingrich began to lose support after his South Carolina primary win (his decline was hastened by questions about his lobbying activities as well as circumstances surrounding the divorce of his former wife), former Pennsylvania Senator Rick Santorum became the latest darling of conservative voters. Romney's organization and funding in the end proved too large for Santorum to overcome, and ultimately Romney won a race that had many ups and downs.

For Critical Thinking and Discussion

1. In running for the party's nomination, what are the advantages and disadvantages of a candidate who has a stronger ideological record? For example, in the 2012 GOP nomination race, what advantages did Rick Santorum (the stronger socially conservative candidate) have as compared to Mitt Romney?

2. Under what circumstances and conditions is a party's presidential nomination race more likely to be characterized by a large field of candidates and volatility in the lead?

each one of these candidates held a lead in the national polls—as did (briefly) business magnate Donald Trump as well. Despite their poor showing in the polls during the invisible primary season, Santorum, Gingrich, and Paul stayed in the race. Others who were considering a run (such as Governors Chris Christie and Mitch Daniels) decided not to run. Still others, such as Governor Tim Pawlenty and Herman Cain, bowed out the race before the end of 2011.

THE NOMINATION CAMPAIGN

The invisible primary may go a long way toward winnowing the field down to a handful of realistic contenders for major-party nominations. Still, contenders for the party nomination must ultimately deliver victories in state primaries and caucuses or risk seeing their financial and volunteer support dry up in a hurry. Given the reduced importance of party conventions in influencing nomination decisions in the modern era, success in the early primaries and caucuses is crucial.

Primaries and Caucuses

The nomination of a candidate by a political party is the product of state-to-state contests in which delegates are committed to those candidates seeking the party's nomination. There are two basic methods by which states allocate delegates: presidential primary elections and caucuses.[5] A **presidential primary** is a statewide election to select delegates who will represent a state at the party's national convention.[6] In this election, voters choose among delegates who are committed to a particular candidate. The delegates who win go to the national convention and cast their vote for a party nominee to run in the general election. In 2012, 45 states used the presidential primary method of delegate selection. There are two types of primaries held by states. The less common approach is the **open primary**,[7] in which voters can show up at the voting booth on the primary Election Day and declare whether they want to vote in the Democratic Party primary or the Republican Party primary; they then cast their vote in the primary they have chosen. A **closed primary**[8] election, by contrast, requires voters to declare a party affiliation ahead of time. When the voters show up to vote on primary Election Day, they are eligible to vote only in the party in which they are registered. Many states that use the closed primary have modified their requirements by allowing voters who have previously declared no party affiliation to show up at the polls on Election Day and declare a party, and thus vote in that party's primary.

A handful of states, including Iowa, Nevada, and Maine, do not hold presidential primary elections; instead they use the caucus method to select delegates for the national party convention. In the **caucus** method, party members are invited to attend local meetings at which they choose delegates who make a commitment to a candidate for the party nomination. These

presidential primary: A statewide election to select delegates who will represent a state at the party's national convention.

open primary: An election that allows voters to choose on the day of the primary election the party in which they want to vote.

closed primary: An election that requires voters to declare their party affiliation ahead of time.

caucus: A method of choosing party nominees in which party members attend local meetings at which they choose delegates committed to a particular candidate.

T.J. Kirkpatrick/Getty Images

GOP presidential candidate and former House Speaker Newt Gingrich, with his wife Callista, declaring victory in the South Carolina primary in January 2012.

Harold Stassen holds the record for most attempts to win a party nomination—10. Stassen, a Republican governor of Minnesota, first attempted to win the Republican nomination in 1948. His 10th and final attempt was in 1992. In only two elections (1956 and 1972) between his first and last attempts was Stassen not a contender for the Republican nomination. Pictured here are Stassen supporters at the 1948 Republican convention.

nomination campaign: The political season in which the two major parties hold primaries and caucuses in all the states to choose party delegates committed to specific candidates.

delegates in turn attend more regionalized meetings and select delegates from that group. Depending on the size of the state and the number of regions, this process continues until a slate of delegates attends a statewide convention, or caucus. At this statewide caucus, attendees again vote for a slate of delegates, who are committed to a candidate, to send to the party's national convention.

The first state contest for delegates, normally the Iowa caucus, launches the process by which delegates from the states commit to candidates for the party nomination. About one week after the Iowa caucus comes the New Hampshire primary,[9] which has traditionally been the first state primary election in which delegates commit to candidates.[10] Each of the 50 states (along with the District of Columbia, the U.S. Virgin Islands, American Samoa, and Guam) holds either a caucus or primary election, and in each of these contests delegates commit to candidates. The calendar of state caucuses and primaries, beginning in January and extending into July, is referred to as the nomination campaign. Through the **nomination campaign**, a candidate attempts to win a majority of delegates in the caucus and primary contests to lay claim to be the winner of the party's nomination.

The Traditional Importance of the Iowa and New Hampshire Contests

Iowa and New Hampshire are small states with relatively few delegates. The Iowa caucus in 2012 had just 28 delegates at stake, and the 2012 New Hampshire primary had a mere 23 delegates at stake. To win the nomination campaign, the successful Republican candidate needed to amass support from at least 1,144 of the 2,286 total delegates. In pure delegate count, larger states, such as California with 172 delegates and New York with 95, are of course much more important. Why, then, do Iowa and New Hampshire enjoy such disproportionately great influence in the nomination process? The answer is timing: Iowa and New Hampshire have traditionally been the first two contests held. The news media thus focus a tremendous amount of attention on these initial competitions. Winners of the Iowa and New Hampshire contests receive a great amount of attention in the news, whereas losers tend to get written off as "unelectable."

frontloading: The recent trend of states moving their primaries and caucuses earlier in the year to attract greater attention from the candidates and the media.

The importance of the early contests has led to a phenomenon known as **frontloading**,[11] a trend that has occurred over the past five or six presidential elections in which states have moved their primary or caucus contests earlier in the year to attract greater attention from the candidates and the media. A state that holds its contest early makes itself more important in the nominee selection process. In 1988, the time between the Iowa caucus and the date by which most states had chosen their convention delegates was more than 20 weeks.

In 2008, most delegates from both parties were selected within a four-week period, from January 3 to February 5. This rush to move the contests earlier caused considerable confusion in the Democratic nomination race that year. In an attempt to ensure that New Hampshire would remain the first contest, the Democratic National Committee had passed a rule that any state that moved its primary earlier than February 5 (Super Tuesday) would forfeit its delegates. Nevertheless, the states of Michigan and Florida both moved their primaries to January,

Roy Dabner/EPA /Landov

GOP candidates Ron Paul, Rick Santorum and Mitt Romney at a debate in Arizona before that state's primary in February 2012.

disqualifying both states' primary outcomes, which had favored frontrunner Hillary Clinton. Ironically, the closeness of the ensuing race between Barack Obama and Clinton throughout the spring of 2008 meant that considerable attention would be paid to later contests held in Pennsylvania, North Carolina, and Indiana.[12]

In 2012, both major political parties agreed to stall, if not reverse, the frontloading process. Thus, no primary or caucus occurred prior to the Iowa caucuses on January 3. Also, only Iowa, New Hampshire, South Carolina, and Florida were allowed to hold contests before February. States that allocated their delegates proportionate to the vote outcome were permitted to hold contests as early as the first Tuesday in March, as a way to encourage greater voter turnout. States that allocated all delegates to the contest winner (the "winner-take-all" states) were allowed to hold contests beginning on the first Tuesday in April. This plan was intended to spread out the primaries and caucuses, giving candidates more time to campaign in more states, and at the same time preserve the unique role that Iowa and New Hampshire have played in the nomination process.

Still, by "Super Tuesday" on March 6, 2012 (dubbed "super" because nine states all held their contests on that day), the GOP nomination race was all but formally won by Mitt Romney. Thus while Gingrich and Santorum were able to score some early victories in Iowa (Santorum) and South Carolina (Gingrich), Romney's early victories in New Hampshire, Florida, and Nevada—coupled with his significant campaign war chest and organization—provided a Super Tuesday set of victories that made it clear that Romney would win the nomination. By early May, Romney was the only candidate left standing even though the last primary would not occur until July 14.

AP Photo/Stephan Savoia

On "Super Tuesday" Mitt Romney declares victory, and goes on to capture the GOP nomination.

The Nominating Conventions

The national conventions for the Democratic and Republican Parties were once used to discuss the party platform and, most important, to choose the candidate who would represent the party in the general election. The images of the smoke-filled back rooms where deals were cut and delegates were lobbied to throw their support behind a particular candidate were very real. For most of our nation's history, the major parties selected candidates for the presidency in this way. Much of the brokering and deal making took place by skilled political operators at the national conventions.

The 1968 Democratic national convention, held in Chicago, was characterized by a great deal of divisiveness and discord, much of which was captured on national network television. Vietnam War protesters outside of the convention hall were beaten by Chicago police under the direction of Chicago mayor and "political boss" Richard J. Daley. Tension reigned inside the convention center as well, with antiwar supporters of Eugene McCarthy and George McGovern clashing with the party regulars supporting Hubert Humphrey. Television brought the negative images of the divided Democratic Party into American homes, seriously damaging the Democratic ticket. Four years later, television coverage again captured a disunited Democratic Party at the national convention in Miami, where delegates fought into the wee hours of the morning to nominate a party nominee (George McGovern finally won the nomination). The Democrats were not the only party to suffer discord and division. In 1976, grassroots support for Ronald Reagan spoiled any momentum incumbent President Gerald Ford hoped to generate at the Republican national convention.

By the mid-1980s, both major political parties, recognizing the influential role that television was playing in election politics, had begun to adjust their agenda for the national conventions. With the frontloading process allowing candidates to capture a majority of delegates prior to the national convention, the parties began to choreograph their conventions and use them as advertisements for the party ticket. Today's conventions tend to avoid airing any intraparty differences. Instead, they are "anointing" ceremonies for the party ticket. They feature popular members of the party endorsing the nominees and include prerecorded videos highlighting the nominees' record of public service and family values.[13]

At the 2008 Democratic national convention, for example, a video of Barack Obama's life highlighted his experience as a community organizer in Chicago and his commitment to his family. His wife and brother-in-law spoke on his behalf. Former President Bill Clinton and Senator Hillary Clinton added words of praise for the ticket, and vice presidential candidate Joe Biden delivered his own "prime-time" speech promoting Obama. Likewise, speakers at the Republican national convention touted John McCain's military service. His wife, Cindy McCain, offered a brief testimonial on his behalf as well, and McCain's vice presidential running mate, Sarah Palin, gave a stirring speech that was widely regarded as the highlight of the convention.

The 2012 GOP and Democratic nominating conventions were important political events. Rather than playing a crucial role in selecting the party nominee and debating the policy positions of the party, however, these conventions provided a

Chicago has been a frequent host to national party conventions. Twenty-five national conventions have been held in the Windy City, 11 Democratic and 14 Republican. The second most frequent hosting city is Baltimore, which has seen 10 conventions. The 1968 Democratic convention in Chicago was characterized by violent protests over the Vietnam War.

AP Images

President Barack Obama delivers a "prime time" speech at the 2012 Democratic National Convention.

week-long forum for the parties and their nominees to introduce themselves to voters and to formally kick off the general election campaign.

The GOP convention in August 2012 was held in Tampa, Florida. Delayed one day by a hurricane, it prominently featured speeches by Ann Romney, the candidate's wife, popular New Jersey Governor Chris Christie, and Vice Presidential nominee Paul Ryan. Romney's acceptance speech on the last night of the convention was somewhat obscured by a quirky introduction from Hollywood actor Clint Eastwood (who spoke to an empty chair that Eastwood pretended to be occupied by President Obama).

Most analysts agreed that the Democratic convention, held one week later, was better staged and choreographed. First lady Michelle Obama and former President Bill Clinton were featured speakers and gave passionate speeches endorsing the incumbent. Vice President Joe Biden and Obama himself delivered addresses to a large national audience on the last night of the convention.

THE GENERAL ELECTION CAMPAIGN

A number of factors provide context for understanding general election campaigns in the American political system. These include whether or not an incumbent is running, the candidate's pick for the number-two spot on the ticket, the strategy for achieving a winning coalition of states, the presidential debates, political advertisements, and finally the vote in the electoral college.

Incumbent Race versus Open Election

General election campaigns for president are highly visible, very well funded, and among the most noteworthy of events in the American political system. Sometimes the contest is an **incumbent race** pitting a sitting president against a challenger, such as the 2012 contest between President Obama and challenger Mitt Romney. In an incumbent race, the focus of the campaign tends to revolve around the performance of the incumbent over the past four years. In this sense, incumbent races are often viewed as a referendum on the performance of the current occupant of the White House.

incumbent race: General election race pitting a person currently holding the office against a challenger.

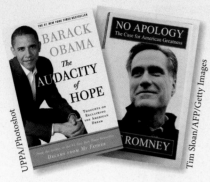

Stump speeches, advertisements, and visits to the county fair have been staples in presidential campaigns for a long time. More recently a new item has been added to the list: writing a book. Barack Obama wrote two books in 2008, The Audacity of Hope *and* Change We Can Believe In. *In 2010, Mitt Romney published* No Apology: The Case for American Greatness.

open election: General election race in which neither candidate is the incumbent. (Open elections for Congress are normally called "open-seat elections.")

In all, there have been 11 incumbents who lost their bids for another term. Five of these incumbent losses occurred over the past 100 years: in 1912 Woodrow Wilson defeated President William Howard Taft; in 1932 Franklin Delano Roosevelt defeated President Herbert Hoover; in 1976 Jimmy Carter defeated President Gerald R. Ford; in 1980 Ronald Reagan beat President Carter; and in 1992 Bill Clinton defeated President George H. W. Bush.

In 2004, incumbent President George W. Bush touted his accomplishments and tried to convince voters that he was best able to lead in the war on terrorism, based on his response to 9/11 and military actions in Afghanistan and Iraq. Bush also claimed that the tax cuts he signed earlier in his term set the stage for a rebound to the national economy. In his campaign, Kerry harshly criticized Bush's "rush to war" in Iraq without building international support and without establishing a connection between Al Qaeda and Saddam Hussein. Kerry also blamed the policies of the Bush administration as the reason why the economy was still performing poorly. In incumbent races, the outcome often is determined on the basis of public evaluations of the incumbent. In the end, Bush's defeat of Kerry in 2004 was based on the president's ability to convince voters that he deserved another term in office.

The 2012 contest featured President Obama, the incumbent, against GOP challenger Mitt Romney. Obama was forced to defend his four-year performance as chief executive against the background of an economy that showed only marginal signs of recovery from the great recession of 2008-2009. Also at issue was Obama's signature accomplishment, comprehensive health care reform legislation. Throughout the campaign, the incumbent touted his primary foreign policy accomplishment: the assassination of Osama bin Laden. In a close popular vote, the electorate ultimately returned the incumbent to office.

In **open elections,** neither candidate is an incumbent. Accordingly, they tend to be far less focused on the past. In 2008, for example, neither the incumbent president of the United States nor the incumbent vice president was actively seeking to win the White House. Because President George W. Bush was constitutionally prohibited from seeking a third term, and Vice President Dick Cheney declined to make a bid for the White House in his own right, the 2008 presidential election became the first in 80 years to feature a truly open-ended contest for the presidency. (Although neither President Harry Truman nor Vice President Alben Barkley was a major-party nominee in 1952, both pursued the Democratic nomination for a short period of time before dropping out of the race.) The last open-ended election before 2008 occurred in 1928, when neither President Calvin Coolidge nor Vice President Charles Dawes was ever a serious candidate for their party's nomination.[14]

The Choice of a Vice Presidential Candidate

Another important aspect of campaign strategy is the selection of the vice presidential running mate. Significant amounts of thought and fanfare go into the selection. Vice presidential candidates are quite visible on the campaign trail and can provide a boost to the ticket. The choice of running mate often attempts to balance the ticket geographically; John Edwards, for example, was from the southern state of North Carolina, a factor deemed important by the 2004 Democratic nominee, John Kerry, who was from Massachusetts, a New England state. Vice presidential candidates are often chosen on the basis of their ideological leanings. In 1980 Ronald Reagan selected George H. W. Bush as his running mate in part because Reagan was viewed as far to the political right and needed a running mate who was more moderate. By contrast, the more moderate Bob Dole chose the ideologically conservative Jack Kemp as his choice for vice president in 1996 to mobilize conservative Republican voters.

A fair amount of scrutiny goes into the process of selecting a vice presidential running mate, because some have turned out to be liabilities for the ticket. In 1972, when it was revealed that Senator Thomas Eagleton had been hospitalized for nervous exhaustion and had received electroshock therapy, an embarrassed George McGovern quickly replaced him on the ticket with the former U.S. Ambassador to France, Sargent Shriver. Similarly, it became clear in 1988 that George H. W. Bush's selection of Dan Quayle as his running mate was problematic after disclosure of Quayle's attempts to avoid the military draft during the Vietnam War. Bush kept Quayle on the ticket, however, and went on to win the 1988

Incumbent Vice President Joe Biden (left) once again rounded out the Democratic ticket in 2012. Wisconsin Representative Paul Ryan (right) was Mitt Romney's selection for the second spot on the GOP ticket.

election. Many observers questioned George W. Bush's decision to keep Vice President Dick Cheney on the ticket in 2004, given the perception that Cheney was the driving influence behind the decision for early and swift American military action in Iraq, where weapons of mass destruction were never found.

In 2008, John McCain's selection of the relatively unknown Alaska governor, 44-year-old Sarah Palin, earned him plaudits from social conservatives. But the choice also led to excessive scrutiny of McCain's selection process for the vice presidential slot after Palin stumbled in several interviews with the mainstream media. Palin was also regarded by some as being too inexperienced to sit just "a heartbeat away" from the presidency. By comparison, Barack Obama's selection of Senator Joseph Biden of Delaware received relatively little scrutiny.

In 2012, Mitt Romney selected Wisconsin Representative Paul Ryan as his running-mate. Ryan, the chair of the House Budget Committee, was an outspoken critic of the Obama Adminstration's handling of the national debt crisis.

Gathering a Winning Coalition of States

A central feature of any general election campaign is each candidate's plan to put together a coalition of states sufficient to win a majority of electoral votes. At the outset of the campaign, states may be divided into three categories: reliably Republican states, reliably Democratic states, and the so-called **battleground** (or "swing") **states**, those that either candidate has a reasonable chance of winning. The map in the "Check the List" feature depicts this categorization of states for the 2012 presidential campaign. The blue states were considered safely Democratic and the red were considered safely Republican; the gold states were the ones up for grabs.

battleground states: States identified as offering either major-party candidate a reasonable chance for victory in the electoral college.

In 2012 both the Republican nominee, Mitt Romney, and the Democratic nominee, Barack Obama, set their sights on 12 battleground states in particular: Colorado, Florida, Iowa, Michigan, Nevada, New Hampshire, New Mexico, North Carolina, Ohio, Pennsylvania, Virginia, and Wisconsin. On election day 2008, Obama's strategy of focusing on battlegrounds reaped rewards for the Democratic ticket: Obama won a clear majority of the 12 battleground states and thus coasted to victory in the electoral college. President Obama was also quite successful in capturing those same battleground states in 2012: on election day he won every swing state but North Carolina, and thus coasted to a comfortable victory in the Electoral College.

CHECK THE LIST

Top Battleground States in 2012

In the presidential campaign of 2012, the vast majority of states saw relatively little activity in terms of candidate appearances and television advertising. Instead, the candidates for both major parties targeted a few select states for concentrated activity. They spent most of their resources of time and money on these battleground states because, as each candidate knew well ahead of time, these were where the election outcome would be decided.

Popular Vote Outcomes in the 2012 Presidential Election

State	Obama (D)	Romney (R)
✓ Colorado	51%	47%
✓ Florida	50%	49%
✓ Iowa	52%	47%
✓ Michigan	54%	45%
✓ Nevada	52%	46%
✓ New Hampshire	52%	46%
✓ New Mexico	53%	43%
✓ North Carolina	48%	51%
✓ Ohio	50%	48%
✓ Pennsylvania	52%	47%
✓ Virginia	51%	48%
✓ Wisconsin	53%	46%

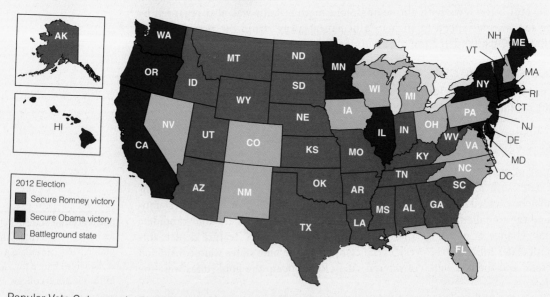

Popular Vote Outcomes in the 2012 Presidential Election.

▶ **POINT TO PONDER:** The majority of campaign spending and candidate appearances in 2012 occurred in these battleground states. Do you think that voters in states where the race is not close have less of an opportunity to make an informed vote choice?

The Presidential Debates

The media and the public have come to expect that a presidential campaign will feature debates between the presidential candidates, and sometimes between the vice presidential candidates as well. Candidates may not believe it is in their strategic interest to debate their opponents (for example, a candidate who is ahead in the polls might prefer to play it safe and not run the risk of losing a debate and perhaps the lead in the campaign). Still, both major-party candidates usually agree to debate so that they aren't portrayed as being "afraid" to do so. The expectation of a set of debates, however, is a relatively recent phenomenon in presidential elections. The first debates that generated a high level of interest and scrutiny were those between John F. Kennedy and Richard M. Nixon in the 1960 election campaign. Some political scientists today credit Kennedy's victory as partly the result of his strong performance in the debates.[15]

The next set of debates occurred in 1976, between Gerald Ford and Jimmy Carter. Each presidential campaign since then has included debates between the presidential candidates and sometimes also between the vice presidential candidates. (The presidential debates are discussed in further detail in Chapter 12.) The schedule of debates and the rules governing their conduct are the product of intense negotiation between the campaigns. In 2008, the detailed set of rules for the four debates included instructions that the candidates could not cross over a line on the stage separating them, time limits on answering questions and offering rebuttals, and a restriction for the final two debates that the candidates could not ask questions of each other.

The candidates shake hands at the start of the first presidential debate in the 2012 general election campaign. Romney, who had been trailing in the polls, was widely regarded as the winner of this debate, thus closing the gap and heightening interest in the second and third debates.

Despite the large amount of attention both the campaigns and the media pay to the debates, the impact that debates have on the election outcome is unclear. Many researchers have documented that those who tend to watch the debates already have moderate to strong convictions regarding who they want to win, and these convictions often shape how an individual voter evaluates the candidate's performance in the debates. Though polls sometimes show that the voters tend to identify a debate "winner," there is far less evidence to show that this has any impact on voter intentions. The first of the debates often gets the most attention, and yet many of the media-dubbed "winners" of first debates, whether Walter Mondale in 1984, Michael Dukakis in 1988, Ross Perot in 1992, or John Kerry in 2004, have ended up on the short side of the electoral vote count on election day. Evidence of this pattern was especially clear in the 2012 race, as Republican challenger Mitt Romney was widely regarded as the winner of the first debate against President Barack Obama. Yet it was Obama who secured the overall victory on election day. Some observers of elections indicate that although debates may not have a direct impact on vote intentions, they can change the dynamics of a campaign, which in turn may influence the outcome.[16]

Above is a still shot from a TV ad run by the Obama campaign in 2012. The ad attempts to paint Romney as a businessman who was responsible for shipping U.S. jobs overseas.

The Advertising

Television advertisements have become a staple of presidential campaign strategies.[17] They are used to heighten name recognition, communicate core messages to voters, and offer reasons why one should vote for (or against) a particular candidate. Television advertising uses a variety of different techniques to accomplish these goals. The most controversial of these techniques is the attack or "negative" ads that candidates often use to portray their opponents in a bad light.[18] Television ads can be very effective at convincing voters to support a candidate—particularly voters who are undecided on any particular candidate or who are politically independent rather than identifying themselves as a Democrat or a Republican. Whereas other forms of campaign communication (such as televised debates, political news columns, political talk shows on radio and TV, and news broadcasts) are provided in formats that appeal to voters who are interested in the campaign and have already made up their minds about who they will vote for, televised advertisements may be placed during certain shows or at certain times when independents and undecided voters are tuning in. The unsuspecting audience is captive to the short advertisement, which provides a unique opportunity for a campaign to attract votes.

The Electoral College Vote

Unlike elections for most public offices in the United States, the outcome of the popular vote does not determine who wins the presidential election. The winner of the presidential election is the candidate who receives a majority of the 538 votes in the **electoral college**. In the highly controversial 1876 and 2000 presidential elections the popular vote winner lost the presidential race. Similarly, John Quincy Adams won the 1824 election despite losing the popular vote, as did Benjamin Harrison in 1888.

How does the electoral college work? The Constitution allocates each state a certain number of electoral votes, based on the sum of the number of senators (two) plus representatives (currently anywhere from 1 to 53) that a state has in the U.S. Congress. The Twenty-third Amendment to the Constitution allocated three electoral votes to the District of Columbia. The number of seats a state has in the House of Representatives may change as a result of the official census conducted every 10 years. Thus the number of electoral votes that a state has may change as well. The total number of electoral votes remains fixed at 538, and a candidate must receive a majority—270—to win the presidency (see Figure 14.1).

The minimum number of electoral votes possible for any one state is three because the Constitution guarantees to each state two senators and one House member. Vermont, Wyoming, North Dakota, South Dakota, Alaska, Montana, and Delaware have three votes. California currently has the largest number of electoral votes with 55 (53 members of the House and 2 senators).

Even small states with as few as three electoral votes can influence the outcome of an election. In 2000, George Bush received 271 electoral votes, only one vote more than the 270 majority he needed to win. Had just one of the small states that gave Bush its three electoral votes voted for Gore, Bush would not have won the election.

Over the past 60 years the U.S. population has shifted, with the southern and western states gaining population and the northeastern and midwestern states losing. Consequently, the numbers of electoral votes in states such as Florida, California, Texas, and Arizona have grown, and the number of votes allocated to states such as New York, Pennsylvania, Ohio, and Illinois has declined. Based on figures from the 2010 U.S. Census, the 2012 electoral vote count in Texas swelled from 34 to 38. Florida gained two electoral votes, and a number of states gained at least one electoral vote: Arizona, Georgia, Nevada, South Carolina, Utah, and Washington. By contrast, each of the following states lost at least one electoral vote: Illinois, Iowa, Louisiana, Massachusetts, Michigan, New Jersey, and Pennsylvania. Ohio and New York lost two each.

electoral college: The constitutional mechanism by which presidents are chosen. Each state is allocated electoral college votes based on the sum of that state's U.S. senators and House members.

The presidential election of 2000 was the only election in American history when the winner of the popular vote (Al Gore) was defeated in the electoral college (by George W. Bush)

Fiction.

There have been four presidential elections in all when the popular vote winner was not the winner in the electoral vote count.

FIGURE 14.1 The Electoral College Map

This map of the states depicts the number of electoral votes each state has as a result of the 2010 U.S. Census. The states shaded in red are those states whose electoral votes were cast for Republican Mitt Romney in 2012. The blue states' electoral votes went to Democrat Barack Obama.

Source: http://www.270towin.com/.

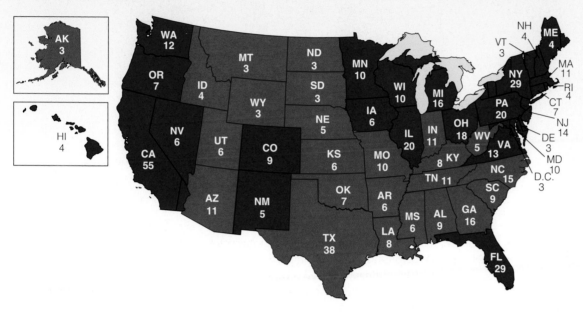

Article II of the Constitution gives the state legislature of each state the authority to appoint **electors**, one for each electoral vote that a state has been allocated. During the first few presidential elections, most states used the state legislature to select the individuals who would be the state's electors.[19] By 1860, however, states gradually shifted to using the popular vote outcome in the state to allocate electors, or the so-called **unit rule**. The unit rule (or "winner-take-all" system) means that the candidate who receives the most votes among the popular votes cast for president in a state will receive all the electoral votes from that state. At present only two states, Maine and Nebraska, do not use the unit rule. Rather, in those states the popular vote winner in each congressional district receives the electoral vote from that district, and the two votes that derive from the state's Senate seats are awarded to the statewide popular vote winner. In 2004, voters in Colorado defeated a referendum to allot electoral votes as Maine and Nebraska currently do.

In practice, the voters in a presidential election vote not for the actual candidate but for the slate of electors who commit to the candidate for whom the voters cast their ballots. Interestingly, the electors who pledge themselves to a candidate are under no legal obligation to actually cast their electoral vote for that candidate. In fact, electors do sometimes break their pledge. In 7 of the last 15 presidential elections, at least one individual elector has not voted for the candidate who won the popular vote in his or her state.

The most recent deviation occurred in 2004, when a Minnesota elector pledged to vote for John Kerry cast his presidential vote for "John Ewards" [sic] instead. That misvote may have been an accident. By contrast, in 2000, Washington, D.C., elector Barbara Lett-Simmons, while pledged to vote for Democrats Al Gore and Joe Lieberman, intentionally cast no electoral votes as a protest against the District of Columbia's lack of statehood. To date, however, these rare broken promises (or mistakes) have not had an impact on an election outcome—and only 9 of the 21,829 electoral votes cast since 1796 deviated from the vote that was expected of an elector.[20]

The significance of the unit rule is illustrated by the outcome of the 2000 presidential election. In Florida, which had 25 electoral votes, the popular vote distribution between Bush and Gore was very close. For nearly one month after the election, controversies surrounding the vote count and the ballot in Florida left uncertain which candidate won the most popular votes in the state. What loomed in the balance was all of Florida's 25 electoral votes—and the election

electors: Individuals appointed to represent a state's presidential vote in the electoral college; in practice, voters in presidential elections vote for a slate of electors committed to a particular candidate, rather than voting directly for the candidate.

unit rule: The system in 48 states by which the candidate who wins the most votes among popular votes cast for president in a state receives all the electoral votes from that state; also known as the "winner-take-all" system.

FIGURE 14.2 Americans Support Using Popular Vote to Select the President

Source: Gallup Polls conducted in 2000, 2002, 2004, and 2011.

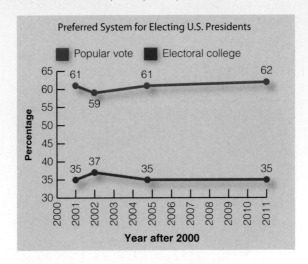

victory. Without Florida, Gore had 267 electoral votes—just 3 votes shy of victory, whereas Bush had 246. Because the unit rule applied to Florida's 25 votes, all 25 would be allocated on the basis of which candidate received the most popular votes.

The Founders' original intent in creating the electoral college was to keep the presidential selection process out of the direct hands of the people. They felt that the people were best represented by the House of Representatives, whose members were elected directly by voters. But the Founders questioned the ability of the general public to select the chief executive. Rather, they believed that the more knowledgeable, wise, and politically thoughtful members of each state's legislature should be empowered with the authority to appoint electors who would choose from the best of the best.

But as the meaning of democracy changed and as American politics opened up to greater political participation, states began to use the popular vote as a means of allocating their electoral votes. Further, as seen in Figure 14.2, public opinions polls strongly endorse presidential selection based on the national popular vote, rather than the electoral vote.

If Americans strongly prefer the selection of a president based on the total national popular vote rather than by the electoral vote, why, then, do we continue to use this rather complicated, indirect system for voters to choose their president? Why not simply use the sum total of the popular vote to choose a winner? The most basic answer is explained by politics, not necessarily logic. The electoral college system benefits smaller states. For example, Wyoming's population of approximately 500,000 represents 0.17 percent of the potential popular vote. But its three electoral votes still constitute 0.56 percent of the electoral vote total. Because every state starts off with two electoral votes (for its two U.S. senators), smaller states end up with disproportionately more voting power in the electoral college than in the popular vote. In recent years, the states that benefit from the electoral college system have tended to be dominated by Republican legislatures. Because changing the electoral college system requires a constitutional amendment, and because amendment procedures require approval by three-fourths of the state legislatures, any attempt to change the system is unlikely to win the support of a sufficient number of state legislatures, enough of which are small enough to benefit from the electoral college. Despite the many proposals that have been offered to reform or eliminate the electoral college, it seems likely, at least for the foreseeable future, that the electoral college is here to stay.

MAKING A VOTE CHOICE

Although the electoral college system muddies the connection between popular vote choice and the election outcome, voter decisions are still the basis upon which candidates win. It's not so surprising, then, that in covering American politics the news media spend a tremendous

The individuals selected by states to vote in the electoral college are not constitutionally required to cast their ballots for the candidate who wins the popular vote in the state that the electors represent.

Fact.

Under the Constitution, electors are free to vote as they choose, though few in history have actually voted against the popular vote outcome of their respective states.

amount of time and resources analyzing how voters will vote in a contest, particularly in presidential elections. For this reason, preelection polling has become a centerpiece of American political campaign strategy as well as news coverage. Years before a presidential election takes place, media polls query American voters on the potential candidates and assess the level of support voters offer these candidates. Months before the election, daily tracking polls monitor how voters are thinking and how opinions are changing from day to day.

Likewise, political scientists' primary focus of research on American political behavior is on how voters make up their minds about who they will vote for. Research has identified a number of different factors that act as cues to individual voters in helping them make a vote decision. Collectively, these factors are referred to as "determinants of vote choice."

Candidate Familiarity

The most basic voting cue is simple name recognition and familiarity with a candidate. Many voters pay little attention to politics and political campaigns. Recognizing the name of a candidate on a ballot, then, offers an important voting cue. If voters recognize one candidate's name and no others, they are much more likely to vote for the name they recognize. Likewise, the more familiar voters are with a candidate, the more likely they are to vote for that candidate. In lower-visibility elections, such as primaries and local elections, name recognition plays a large role in the voting decision. However, even in statewide and presidential races (particularly presidential primaries), familiarity with a candidate can be an important cue to voters. High name recognition and voter familiarity propelled George W. Bush to the top of the pack in the Republican presidential primaries during the 2000 campaign. High name recognition of former first lady Hillary Clinton allowed her to gain frontrunner status early on in the race for the 2008 Democratic presidential nomination. In many congressional House races, incumbents tend to win reelection at rates in excess of 90 percent in large part because voters recognize their names and are less familiar with the challengers.

Party Identification

Political parties play many important roles in the American political system. Often voters form a psychological attachment to a party that helps them organize their political information and offers an important cue to vote choice. As discussed in Chapter 13, party identification is the term for this psychological attachment to a political party. Party identification tends to be a long-term predisposition—once it is formed, it usually remains with an individual over the course of his or her life. Party identification, then, is an important determinant of vote choice.[21]

Party identification is particularly powerful in influencing a vote decision in lower-profile political races: those in which no particularly serious issues are at stake, the candidates are not well known, and the news media pay little attention to covering the race. In such contests, those who identify with a political party are most likely to turn out to vote, and those who turn out usually vote for the candidate associated with their political party.[22]

For example, elections for the House of Representatives tend to be lower profile than presidential or Senate races. Among the 435 congressional districts across the country, more than 350 are considered to be "safe seats" for one of the two major parties. Safe seats are districts where the party affiliation of the voters is so one-sided that the candidate who wears that party's label is virtually assured of victory.

It should be noted, however, that overall party identification and its impact on vote choice have been in a state of decline.[23] Over the past 50 years, voters have become less likely to identify as either a Democrat or a Republican, and more likely to say that they are independent. Decline in confidence in the political parties, campaigns that are more focused on the candidates than on the candidate's party, and increased television news coverage of campaigns are cited as primary reasons for the drop in party identification.

Still, two-thirds of voters continue to identify with one of the major parties, and thus party identification remains the single best predictor of how an individual might vote in an election. Identifying with a partisan perspective provides a shortcut for voters in making candidate choices. More broadly, party identification enables people to more readily make sense of their political world.

Issue Voting

For voters who identify themselves as Democrats, the Democratic Party's candidate is likely to hold an issue position that they favor; the same is true for voters who identify as Republicans. For voters who identify themselves as independents, however, a candidate's party does not serve as a determinant of vote choice. For these voters, a candidate's position on a particular issue or set of issues is a voting cue.

Voting on the basis of issues is more likely to occur in certain types of elections.[24] First, when a particular issue captures the attention of many people in the electorate, voters are more likely to use a candidate's position on that issue to form a vote decision. For example, in the 1968 presidential race, American involvement in the Vietnam War was a central concern for many voters, and many voted on the basis of the two candidates' positions on the war.[25]

Second, issue voting occurs more often when an issue is of particular personal concern to a voter. In 2012, for example, American voters were concerned about a poorly performing economy, and thus many cast a vote on the basis of President Obama's performance in dealing with the "Great Recession" and Mitt Romney's proposed alternatives for addressing the economic crisis. Third, issue voting is much more likely to occur when the candidates hold clearly distinct positions on issues.

Anthony Downs's rational-choice approach to understanding voting turnout also applies to making a vote choice. Downs suggested that in making a choice, voters examine the issue positions of the candidates and assess how close they are to the voters' own positions? The candidate whose positions on the issues are closer to the voter's earns the vote.

Issue voting is often regarded as the most sophisticated type of voting behavior. Notions of the "ideal democratic citizen" describe such a person as someone who is informed about issues, has developed a position on those issues, and then compares that position to the positions of the candidates. Voting on the basis of such a calculation requires political knowledge and attentiveness to campaigns. Although issues remain important to many voters and take on higher levels of importance under certain circumstances, most research indicates that other shortcut factors, such as party identification, are more commonly used to make choices.

Retrospective Voting

retrospective voting: A theory on voting behavior that suggests voter evaluations of an incumbent's past performance provide important cues to voters in deciding whether to vote for that incumbent again.

In issue voting, a voter assesses the candidates' issue positions and casts a vote based on which candidate the voter thinks will do a better job in dealing with that issue in the future. However, a voter's past experience with a candidate or a political party also can be an important determinant of vote choice. **Retrospective voting**, a concept developed by political scientist Morris Fiorina, posits that evaluations of incumbents' past performance in office provide important cues for voters in deciding whether to vote for that incumbent.[26] Voters who believe that an incumbent has done a good job are likely to vote for the officeholder, whereas if they judge that an incumbent's job performance has been poor, they are likely to vote against the officeholder. Voter assessments of the economy and the performance of the president in handling economic conditions are especially important in a voter's retrospective evaluation of an incumbent. Bill Clinton's victory over incumbent George H. W. Bush in the 1992 presidential election was largely the result of voters' negative evaluations of Bush's handling of the nation's economy. Likewise, Ronald Reagan's defeat of incumbent President Jimmy Carter in 1980 was based on voters' perception that Carter performed poorly in dealing with economic problems and the Iranian hostage crisis.

In retrospective voting, the evaluation of the incumbent provides the determination of vote choice. In other words, a voter's assessment of the incumbent's job performance provides a shortcut decision rule on voting for or against the incumbent. Pollsters often measure this assessment through a question on "job approval rating." The percentage of voters who approve of the incumbent's job performance often reflects the percentage of the vote that the incumbent receives in a reelection bid.

Candidates for office often try to encourage voters to think retrospectively, if it is in their strategic interest to do so. In the 1980 presidential campaign, while the nation was experiencing economic problems and an extended international crisis with hostages being held in Iran, challenger Ronald Reagan defeated incumbent Jimmy Carter in part by asking the voters, "Are you better off today than you were four years ago [before Carter took office]?" Similarly, in 1992, challenger Bill Clinton questioned the integrity of President George H. W. Bush by repeating a TV clip of the president saying "Read my lips, no new taxes"—a pledge Bush had made in 1988 but did not keep.

Candidate Image Voting

The image, personal traits, and other characteristics of the particular candidates in a campaign can also influence the way people vote. Especially in higher-stimulus elections, where candidates make ample use of television advertisements to build an image, voter perceptions of candidates' qualities are important. Perceptions of candidate image include such characteristics as honesty, trustworthiness, leadership ability, concern for voters, integrity, intelligence, and sense of humor.

Candidates for office who have more favorable images than their opponents among voters tend to fare much better in election contests. In 11 of the 13 presidential elections between 1952 and 2000, the candidate who had the higher "image score" from questions asked on the American National Election Survey won the election. The two exceptions were 1960, when John Kennedy and Richard Nixon shared an identical score in a very close election that Kennedy won, and in 1984 when Walter Mondale and Ronald Reagan shared an identical score (Reagan went on to a decisive victory).

In today's media age, candidates have found that image development is an efficient means of persuading swing voters how to vote. Thus, candidates often use television advertising to build their own favorable image or, conversely, to depict their opponents as having negative image characteristics. Visual images on television are useful in conveying symbolic, image-oriented messages. Bill Clinton in 1996 built a successful campaign around a theme that he would continue to improve the nation's economic future (his theme was captured in the slogan "building a bridge to the twenty-first century"). Ronald Reagan in 1984 cemented his strong leadership image in his campaign for reelection (with the TV ad slogan "It's morning again in America").

CAMPAIGN FUNDING

Waging a political campaign, particularly a presidential campaign, is becoming increasingly expensive.[27] In 2012 the campaigns of President Barack Obama and Governor Mitt Romney combined to raise about $2 billion. That figure does not include money raised or held by the two candidates' "victory funds," which are joint fund-raising committees that distribute funds to the campaigns and party committees. President Obama, in particular, focused on individual contributors for support, even though their individual donations were limited to $2500 by campaign finance laws. The 2012 figures thus dwarfed all previous figures. In 2008, all the candidates together raised more than $1.7 billion, nearly double the amount raised in 2004, and more than four times the amount raised in 2000 (see Figure 14.3). Barack Obama's campaign alone raised $745 million.

Campaign financing, then, is one of the most important functions of a political campaign. Hiring a professional staff to develop and implement a successful campaign, producing and airing TV commercials and radio spots, renting campaign headquarters office space, conducting polls to monitor the course of the campaign, and producing buttons, bumper stickers, and signs all cost money. Good candidates have demonstrated a high capacity for raising money to wage a campaign.

Sources of Funding

Where do campaigns find financial support? They find money from individual citizens, from interest groups and political action committees, and from political parties. Companies, groups, and individuals all have vested interests in the political system, and each may provide support (including monetary contributions) to promote candidates who advocate their own positions on issues. Our system of politics encourages people and groups to participate in the political process, and this participation includes financial contributions to campaigns. Indeed, giving money to candidates may be seen as a healthy sign that people are engaged in the political process and want to participate in making a difference.

Total fundraising by all presidential candidates nearly doubled from 2004 to 2008.

Fact.

Prior to 2000, total presidential candidate fundraising never exceeded a half billion dollars. In 2008, fund raising topped $1.7 billion, nearly double the amount from four years earlier. Early estimates are that total fundraising in 2012 hit the $2 billion mark.

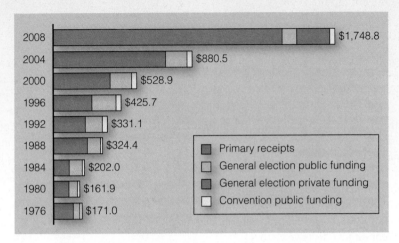

FIGURE 14.3 Fundraising by Presidential Candidates, 1976–2008

Source: http://www.opensecrets.org/pres08/totals.php?cycle=2008.

Year	Amount
2008	$1,748.8
2004	$880.5
2000	$528.9
1996	$425.7
1992	$331.1
1988	$324.4
1984	$202.0
1980	$161.9
1976	$171.0

- Primary receipts
- General election public funding
- General election private funding
- Convention public funding

Beginning in the 1970s, parties and candidates turned to political action committees (PACs) to address the new realities of political campaigns, particularly regarding fundraising and limits on individual contributions. PACs are the arms of interest groups that raise and give money to political candidates. Any group that wishes to participate in financing campaigns must create a PAC and register it with the Federal Election Commission (FEC). There are more than 4,000 PACs currently registered with the federal government (see Figure 14.4). Of the $1 billion raised by House and Senate campaigns in 2004, about 30 percent came from the fundraising efforts of PACs.

In addition to individual and PAC contributions, the political parties play an important role in financing political campaigns. Both major parties have national and statewide committees, which raise money and give money to candidates to fund campaigns. In 2000, the national party committees each collected and spent about $200 million to help fund their candidates. Typically, the parties support House and Senate candidates, particularly those who have a competitive chance of winning.

Another important source of campaign funding comes from the individual candidates' House and Senate campaigns. Members of Congress who hold safe seats are very effective at raising money for their own campaigns. These campaigns, because they are for safe seats, tend not to need a great deal of funding. So the incumbents use their campaign war chests to help fund the campaigns of their colleagues in more competitive races. Often they do so through the formation of a PAC.

Though not the norm, some federal candidates for office use their own personal wealth to fund their campaigns. In 1992 and 1996, independent presidential candidate Ross Perot spent millions of dollars of his own personal fortune (Perot's personal wealth is in the billions of dollars). Similarly, Democratic Senator Jon Corzine from New Jersey spent more than $50 million of his own money to win a Senate seat in 2000 (his Republican competitor spent over $30 million of his own money).

The federal government and a handful of state governments (including Arizona, Connecticut, North Carolina, and Maine) maintain some form of public campaign financing as well. Although candidates cannot be forced to participate in public financing schemes, which restrict their expenditures, the government may entice their participation by offering them significant public funds in return for their agreement to abide by personal campaign spending limits. The federal government's presidential election financing system allows major-party candidates to draw on funds received when taxpayers check a box on their tax returns agreeing to donate to the fund. In 2004, presidential candidates were eligible to receive approximately $70 million each if they agreed to limit their campaign expenditures. Yet neither of the two major-party candidates in 2004, George W. Bush and John Kerry, elected to participate in the federal financing scheme. By rejecting the use of such public financing, they were able to freely spend throughout the primaries and general election campaign without regard to any federally imposed limits. In 2008, John McCain accepted the $85 million he qualified for in public financing to fund his general election campaign. Barack Obama, however, declined public financing and continued to privately raise funds through the general election—a decision based on his widespread success in raising campaign money during the primaries. The 2012 general election between Barack Obama and Mitt Romney marked the first time that *both* major candidates turned down public financing so they could continue unlimited fundraising activities after their respective conventions.

In recent presidential election cycles, candidates have been able to take advantage of the Internet as yet another means of fundraising. In 2000, Bill Bradley raised more than $2 million via the Internet for his campaign for the Democratic presidential nomination. (He ended up losing his bid for the nomination to Al Gore.) Then, in the 2004 race for the Democratic presidential nomination, a little-known former governor from the small state of Vermont, Howard Dean, waged an impressive campaign by tapping into the vast potential of the Internet and online fundraising. His followers, who came to be known as "Deaniacs," tended to be younger Americans, a group much more inclined to use the Internet, to IM (instant message), and to blog. The Dean campaign translated this orientation of his followers into the most successful Internet fundraising campaign that American politics had ever seen.

Dean raised an unprecedented $40 million in his campaign for the nomination. This amount exceeded that of all his competitors for the nomination, and the vast bulk of his campaign war chest was derived from small, individual donations solicited through the Internet. Although Dean's campaign collapsed after the candidate suffered unexpected losses in Iowa and New Hampshire and though most of his $40 million war chest was depleted by the first primary contest, Dean's success at Internet fundraising was nonetheless quite impressive. Then in 2008 Barack Obama's campaign substantially raised the stakes in fundraising through the Internet by raising over $200 million through that medium, and in 2012 the Obama re-election campaign proved groundbreaking in this regard, leveraging micro-donations by raising money on-line from over 3 million separate donors. His appeal to voters through the Internet represents a significant achievement in the use of this new technology in campaign politics. As Americans increasingly come to

FIGURE 14.4 The Growth of Political Action Committees

The federal campaign finance legislation of the 1970s was the first vigorous attempt to monitor and regulate the money that was raised and spent on political campaigns. These laws applied to the regulation of hard money, which was money raised directly by and spent by the political candidates. They influenced the creation of political action committees (PACs), which raise and spend soft money—funds for political campaigning independent of the political candidates. In 1974, there were only 608 PACs registered with the federal government; by 2002, 4,027 PACs were registered. This figure shows the total amount of receipts and expenditures of all PACs registered with the federal government from the 1975–1976 election cycle to the 2007–2008 election cycle.

Source: Harold W. Stanley and Richard G. Niemi, *Vital Statistics on American Politics 2004–2005* (Washington, DC: CQ Press, 2006), 103. Copyright 2006 CQ Press, a division of Sage Publications. Data for 2005–2008 are from http://www.fec.gov/press/press2009/20090415pac/20090424pac.shtml.

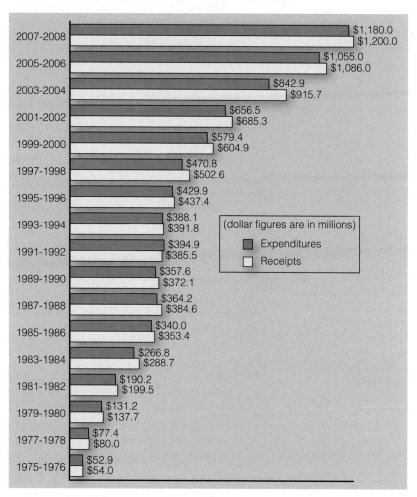

In the 2008 Democratic nomination race, the Obama campaign perfected the art of Internet fundraising. The site pictured here was used by the successful Obama to raise more than $100 million in small donations during that race.

Andrew Harrer/Bloomberg via Getty Images

rely on the Internet, it is likely that political candidates will follow Dean's and Obama's examples and harness this technology for fundraising and other campaigning.

Regulating Campaign Financing

Congress and the states have passed many and varied laws to regulate the conduct of campaign contributions. These laws are not intended to prevent individuals or groups from giving money. Rather, they attempt to prevent a "quid pro quo," or a donation in return for an elected official voting or acting in a certain way in direct response to accepting the campaign gift.

The first significant piece of federal legislation aimed at regulating campaign financing was the **Federal Election Campaign Act (FECA)**, passed in 1971 and amended in 1974. The law required that all federal candidates accurately disclose campaign contributions and document all campaign expenditures. Subsequent amendments to FECA imposed legal limits on campaign contributions by individuals ($1,000 to each candidate per election cycle; $5,000 to PACs per year; and $20,000 to national party committees per year). Additionally, FECA imposed an outright ban on certain campaign contributions by corporations, unions, national banks, and foreign nationals, among others.

All these provisions targeted so-called **hard money** contributions that go directly to candidates and their campaign committees. FECA did little to stem the influx of **soft money** funds to political parties and political advocacy groups that are not contributed directly to candidate campaigns and that do not expressly advocate the election of a particular candidate. In the two decades following FECA, the two major political parties have strategically spent soft money on administrative and party-building activities, as well as on issue ads that do not specifically promote an individual candidate, but that nevertheless attempt to affect the election outcome.

The **Federal Election Commission (FEC)** was established in 1974 to enforce all campaign financing rules and regulations, including limits on campaign contributions. Today, the FEC is the federal agency in charge of enforcing election laws. Provisions for public funding of presidential campaigns were subsequently passed in 1976 and 1979.

Critics have voiced a number of complaints about the system of campaign finance regulations. For one thing, the original limits on individual contributions—fixed by legislation in the 1970s—were never indexed to inflation. This oversight was addressed in legislation in 2002 mandating

Federal Election Campaign Act (FECA): The federal legislation passed in 1971 that established disclosure requirements and restricted individual campaign contributions.

hard money: Donations made directly to political candidates and their campaigns that must be declared with the name of the donor (which then becomes public knowledge).

soft money: Money not donated directly to a candidate's campaign, but rather to a political advocacy group or a political party for "party-building" activities.

Federal Election Commission (FEC): The agency created in 1974 to enforce federal election laws.

that limits be indexed for inflation every two years. For example, in 2005–2006 individuals were able to give up to $2,100 to candidates and up to $26,700 to national party committees.

Another complaint concerns the failure of the system to adapt to modern campaign dynamics. As a result of frontloading, presidential primary elections are now bunched up earlier and earlier in the general election campaign; yet the strict limits on expenditures imposed on those who accept public financing do not really account for these new campaign realities, which compel candidates to spend a considerable amount of their money during a relatively short period of time.

In recent years, advocates of campaign finance reform have focused their greatest criticism on soft money in the form of **independent campaign expenditures**. These are monies that PACs or individuals spend to support political campaigns but that do not directly contribute to them. FECA banned the unlimited use of independent expenditures to directly support the election of one candidate or the defeat of another candidate, but those funds could still be used to build the party as a whole. For example, a PAC can produce and support a political advertisement that endorses a particular party's position on an issue and pay for the airtime to broadcast that ad on television. The money for the ad is not donated to a campaign per se, but instead is spent on services that support the campaign; thus, the money spent is considered an "independent" expenditure. The U.S. Supreme Court in *Buckley v. Valeo* (1976)[28] ruled that Congress could limit campaign contributions consistent with the First Amendment, but that it could not limit independent campaign expenditures or personal money spent by candidates on behalf of their own campaigns. Twenty years later in *McConnell v. F.E.C.* (2003),[29] the Court extended that ruling to apply to spending by political parties as well. Thus political parties themselves often sponsor television ads that talk more generally about issues facing the country without mentioning any individual candidate or race; of course most political experts acknowledge that these ads may have a significant impact on individual campaigns.

The most recent reform attempts have focused on soft money and independent campaign expenditures. Senators John McCain (R-AZ) and Russell Feingold (D-WI) were particularly critical of the loopholes in campaign financing that have allowed soft money to go unregulated by the FEC. They cosponsored legislation designed to better regulate the way campaigns are financed and how the money is spent. In 2002, Congress passed the **Bipartisan Campaign Reform Act (BCRA) of 2002**, popularly known as the McCain-Feingold Act, which prohibited national parties and candidates for federal office from accepting soft money (i.e., that which is not subject to regulation by the FEC). The BCRA also raised limits on contributions to a particular candidate for federal office from $1,000 to $2,000. The U.S. Supreme Court, in 2010, struck down as unconstitutional several other provisions of the BCRA, including certain limits on corporate and union funding of broadcast ads right before an election. Though President Obama has been openly critical of that Supreme Court opinion, his 2012 presidential campaign benefitted to a degree from the new rules, as labor unions helped to bankroll super PACS that favored his reelection. And while the Obama campaign refused to accept corporate or PAC donations for the Democratic party convention, the president's advisors pressed labor unions to help close financial shortfalls stemming from the convention.

CONGRESSIONAL CAMPAIGNS AND ELECTIONS

Although presidential elections typically receive the most attention from the media and the public, many other elections also occur regularly, including those that send members to the two houses of Congress. In each presidential election year, all 435 seats in the House of Representatives are contested, as are one-third of the seats in the Senate. Midway between successive presidential elections are the **midterm congressional elections**, in which all 435 House seats are contested again and another one-third of the Senate seats are voted on (senators serve six-year terms, and the 100 Senate elections are staggered so that about one-third of the seats are contested every two years).

Midterm elections for Congress differ from presidential-year elections in important ways.[30] First, voter turnout tends to be lower in the midterm contests. Without the large-scale attention

independent campaign expenditures: Political donations that PACs or individuals spend to support campaigns, but do not directly contribute to the campaigns.

Buckley v. Valeo (1976): The 1976 Supreme Court opinion that held that spending money to influence elections is protected First Amendment speech, and that prohibited limitations on independent expenditures or personal money spent by candidates on their own campaigns.

Bipartisan Campaign Reform Act (BCRA) of 2002: Also called the McCain-Feingold Act, the federal legislation that (1) restricted soft money spent by political parties, (2) regulated expenditures on ads that refer to specific candidates immediately before an election, and (3) increased limits on hard money donated directly to candidates and their campaigns.

midterm congressional elections: Congressional elections held midway between successive presidential elections.

One of the most hotly contested Senate races in 2012 was the contest in Massachusetts between GOP incumbent Scott Brown (left) and Harvard professor Elizabeth Warren (right). Warren eventually defeated Brown in November.

AP Photo/Cliff Owen

John Suchoki/The Republican /Landov

the presidential race receives, voter interest and engagement in the midterm elections are lower, and thus turnout tends to suffer. Even in the highly charged midterm elections of 2010, voter turnout was just 43 percent, almost 15 percentage points below voter turnout figures for the preceding presidential election.

coattail effect: The potential benefit that successful presidential candidates offer to congressional candidates of the same political party during presidential election years.

Second, midterm elections fail to offer congressional candidates what has come to be known as the **coattail effect**. In a presidential election year, the names of candidates for Congress typically are listed below the name of their party's candidate for president on the ballot. Thus, voters' selection of congressional candidates may be influenced by their choice for president. The congressional candidates, in effect, ride the coattails of the presidential candidate.[31] For the coattail effect to be apparent, the outcome of the presidential race typically needs to be a landslide victory for the winner, such as in 1984 when President Ronald Reagan soundly defeated Democrat Walter Mondale. For the first time in decades, the 1984 elections ushered in a Republican majority to the U.S. Senate. By contrast, George W. Bush's narrow victory in 2004 did not appear to produce a coattail effect.

Third, in midterm elections there has been a discernible trend—though often not very strong—that favors congressional candidates in the party opposite the president's party in midterm contests. When a president wins, especially by a large margin, the coattail effect distorts what would normally occur in any given congressional race. Yet in midterm elections, without the president's name at the top of the ballot, the absence of the coattail gives the advantage to the opposing party. In the modern era, the party in opposition to the president has managed to regain control of Congress only in the midterm elections when the president's popularity is waning. Thus in 1946 and then in 1994, the Republicans wrestled both houses of Congress back from the Democrats at midterm elections during the presidencies of Democrats Harry Truman and Bill Clinton, respectively. In 2006, voters upset about the state of the war in Iraq dealt a devastating blow to the Republicans' control of Congress: although many Republican incumbents in the House and Senate were ousted from office that year, not one Democratic House member or Senator lost a seat in the 2006 midterm elections. The Democrats successfully rode the public's antiwar sentiment to regain control of both houses of Congress midway through the second term of Republican President George W. Bush.

True to form, the 2010 midterm elections once again offered a rebuke to the political party holding the White House. Running on a platform that opposed Democratic spending initiatives and promised to rein in the size of government, Republican House candidates transformed a 178-seat minority into a 240-seat majority. By taking more than 60 seats away from the Democrats, Republicans enjoyed a level of midterm election success not seen by either party in decades. Republicans were also successful in the Senate, shrinking the Democrats' 18-seat margin of control down to just 6 seats.

power of incumbency: The phenomenon by which incumbent members of Congress running for reelection are returned to office at an extremely high rate.

More important than presidential coattails or any other factor in congressional elections, however, is the **power of incumbency**. Incumbent members of Congress, particularly those in the House, are returned to office by voters at amazingly high rates. In a normal year of House races, an incumbent who is running for reelection stands a better than 90 percent chance of being returned to office.[32] What accounts for such a high return rate? First, name recognition of the candidate is a significant factor in lower-profile congressional races, and incumbents, because they have been in office, tend to have higher name recognition than do challengers. Second, the vast majority of congressional districts and thus the vast majority of seats in Congress are dominated by either the Republican Party or the Democratic Party. Congressional seats from districts that include either a high percentage of Democratic voters or a high percentage of Republican voters are dominated by their respective majority party and are referred to, as noted earlier, as **safe seats**. A far smaller number of districts tend to have similar numbers of Democratic and Republican voters and are known as **marginal seats**. In the redistricting of congressional districts that periodically takes place, the political parties try to configure districts to their own partisan advantage. This maneuvering tends to create a large number of safe seats and often very few marginal seats (see Table 14.1).

safe seat: A congressional seat from a district that includes a high percentage of voters from one of the major parties.

marginal seat: A seat in a congressional district that has relatively similar numbers of Democratic and Republican voters.

TABLE 14.1 Safe Seats in Congress

The vast majority of the 435 seats in the House of Representatives, each of which is contested every two years, and the 100 U.S. Senate seats, each of which is contested every six years, are safe seats for incumbents who are running for reelection. Even if there is not an incumbent running for reelection, most of these seats tend to be safe for one of the two major political parties. The 2010 midterm elections proved to be a bit of an anomaly, as 51 Democratic House incumbents in all lost their general reelection bids.

The following table below shows the number of incumbents defeated and the number of seats that switched from one party to another in each congressional election since 1980.* Keep in mind that in each election year, 435 House races and 33 or 34 Senate races are usually contested.

Year	Incumbents Defeated	Open Seats Where Party Changed	Total Changes	Incumbents Defeated	Open Seats Where Party Changed	Total Changes*
	House of Representatives			Senate		
1980	30	11	41	9	3	12
1982	23	8	31	2	2	4
1984	16	6	22	3	1	4
1986	6	15	21	7	3	10
1988	6	3	9	4	3	7
1990	15	6	21	1	0	1
1992	24	19	43	4	0	4
1994	35	26	61	2	6	8
1996	21	14	35	1	3	4
1998	6	11	17	3	3	6
2000	6	12	18	6	2	8
2002	4	8	12	3	1	4
2004	5	5	10	1	7	8
2006	22	9	31	6	0	6
2008	17	13	30	5	3	8
2010	53	10	63	2	4	6

*Figures include only shifts from one major party to the other party.

Source: Harold W. Stanley and Richard G. Niemi, *Vital Statistics on American Politics 2005–2006* (Washington, DC: CQ Press, 2006), 48–49. Copyright ©2006 CQ Press, a division of Sage Publications; updated by authors.

franking privilege: The traditional right of members of Congress to mail materials to their constituents without paying postage.

Finally, incumbent members of Congress enjoy financial advantages, such as the **franking privilege**, which allows members to mail materials to their constituents without paying postage.

Elections and campaigns are central features of the republican form of government in the United States. The number of elections is many, the cost of campaigns is high, and the process for selecting the nation's chief officeholder, the president of the United States, is long and complex. Several times in the nation's history the complicated procedure for selecting a president has resulted in considerable controversy, as in the elections of 1876 and 2000. Yet through these controversies and many others, the U.S. political system has maintained free, open, and regular elections since George Washington was unanimously chosen as the nation's first president in 1789. U.S. presidential elections evoke a great deal of passion, engage the interest of millions of voters, persuade vast numbers of citizens and groups to contribute large amounts of money, and focus attention on the great issues of the day. Thus campaigns and elections duly serve their purpose in providing an important connection between Americans and their government.

FROM YOUR PERSPECTIVE

Getting Involved in Political Campaigns

Politics is very much on the minds of college-age Americans today. In 2008, a record 35.6 percent of first-year college students said that they had frequently discussed politics in the past year. (The previous high was 33.6 percent in 1968, at the height of the Vietnam War.) In the most recent presidential campaign, college students were more interested and more active than ever before. Students who work on election campaigns may find themselves performing such simple tasks as stuffing envelopes or walking door-to-door to distribute leaflets. Those who are technologically savvy may assist campaigns in other ways—for example, by helping to create Facebook profiles or fan pages on the Internet. In 2008, college Republicans nationwide socially networked through a Web site called Student Tools for Online Republican Mobilization, or STORM. Have you ever volunteered time to work on a political campaign? About 11 percent of first-year college students in 2008 said they did. (This figure was up by about three percentage points from 2004.) More first-year college students also report that they are likely to engage in a political protest (6.1 percent in 2008, as compared to 4.9 percent in 1966).

For Critical Thinking and Discussion

1. Why do you think your peers were so energized about the 2008 presidential election?

2. Do you think college students' participation made a difference in 2008?

Note: Data presented are from Mary Beth Marklein, "Presidential Race Raised Student Political Involvement," *USA Today*, January 22, 2009.

Chris Hondros/Getty Images

Students at Ohio State University volunteer their time to support the candidacy of Barack Obama.

SUMMARY: PUTTING IT ALL TOGETHER

AMERICAN PRESIDENTIAL ELECTIONS IN HISTORICAL PERSPECTIVE

- The system for choosing U.S. presidents includes two distinct phases: a nomination phase (during which major-party nominees are chosen) and a general election phase (in which a new president is selected).

- From 1796 up through the 1830s, the nomination process was dominated by officials of the two major parties who chose party nominees based on informal discussions.

- Andrew Jackson and the Democratic Party he founded gave the "common man" increased influence in choosing nominees; by the twentieth century, electoral reforms such as the direct primary gave voters in many states a formal opportunity to cast a ballot for delegates, who would in turn choose their party's nominees at a national convention.

Test Yourself on This Section

1. In the presidential election of 1800, Thomas Jefferson and which other candidate had the same number of electoral votes, thus sending the election to the House of Representatives?
   a. John Adams
   b. Alexander Hamilton
   c. Aaron Burr
   d. Andrew Jackson

2. The state that held the first direct primary election for the party nomination was
   a. California.
   b. New York.
   c. Texas.
   d. Florida.

3. Which of the following amendments to the Constitution limits the office of president to two terms?
   a. Thirteenth Amendment
   b. Fifteenth Amendment
   c. Twenty-second Amendment
   d. Twenty-seventh Amendment

4. What are the five discernable stages in modern presidential election races?

THE PRENOMINATION CAMPAIGN

- Modern presidential elections begin with a prenomination campaign waged by potential candidates to raise money and gain the support of key party leaders. A candidate's failure to raise sufficient funds in this "invisible primary" may cause him or her to drop out of the race before any formal primaries or caucuses have been held.

Test Yourself on This Section

1. The 2012 prenomination campaign for the GOP included all of the following candidates, EXCEPT
   a. Mitt Romney.
   b. John McCain.
   c. Rick Santorum.
   d. Newt Gingrich.

2. Why is the invisible primary called the "invisible" primary?

THE NOMINATION CAMPAIGN

- Nomination campaigns focus on attaining victories in presidential primaries and caucuses. The Iowa caucus and the New Hampshire primary have traditionally come at the beginning of the nomination calendar, and so they tend to disproportionately influence final outcomes. In recent elections, many states have attempted to move their primaries and caucuses up on the calendar in a process known as frontloading.

- National party conventions used to play an important role in helping choose party nominees; today they are mostly made-for-television affairs, anointing the party ticket with speeches offering testimonials to the nominees.

Test Yourself on This Section

1. A state nomination contest in which party members are invited to attend local meetings at which they choose delegates who make a commitment to a candidate for the party nomination is a(n)
   a. open primary.
   b. closed primary.
   c. caucus.
   d. general election.

2. Which of the following states holds the first caucus of the presidential nominating process?
   a. Iowa
   b. New Hampshire
   c. Florida
   d. South Carolina

3. Who was the political boss in Chicago who used police force against protesters during the 1968 Democratic national convention?
   a. Hubert Humphrey
   b. George McGovern
   c. Rahm Emanuel
   d. Richard Daley

4. Distinguish between an open primary and a closed primary.

THE GENERAL ELECTION CAMPAIGN

- General election races may be either incumbent races (pitting a sitting president against a challenger) or open elections (with no incumbent in the race). In the former, the election often amounts to a referendum on the performance of the president over the previous four years.

- Presidential candidates choose their running mates (the vice presidential candidates) strategically to address specific weaknesses of the presidential candidate or to boost the ticket's prospects in certain geographical areas.

- To win the presidency, a candidate must put together a coalition of states sufficient to win a majority of the 538 electoral college votes, which are allocated to each state based on the sum of the number of senators and the number of representatives. The candidate who does well in battleground states will normally win the 270 or more votes necessary to secure a majority.

- Televised presidential debates between major presidential candidates occurred for the first time in 1960 and have been held in every presidential election since 1976. These debates tend to receive a large amount of attention from the press and the public, but their impact on the final election outcome remains unclear.

Test Yourself on This Section

1. The vice presidential candidate chosen to run with President Barack Obama was
   a. Sarah Palin.
   b. Dick Cheney.
   c. Al Gore.
   d. Joe Biden.

2. Which of the following was a battleground state in the 2012 presidential election?
   a. Texas
   b. Ohio
   c. New York
   d. California

3. Which of the following states gained the most net votes in the electoral college as result of the 2010 census?
   a. Texas
   b. Florida
   c. Ohio
   d. Pennsylvania

4. What is the "unit rule," and how does it impact presidential elections?

CAMPAIGN FUNDING

- Campaign funding is critical to the success of individual candidates. Election laws since 1974 have limited the amount individuals or organizations can give to candidates (hard money). The Bipartisan Campaign Reform Act (BCRA) of 2002 went a step further, restricting expenditures to political parties or advocacy groups that are theoretically independent of specific candidates or campaigns (soft money). The Federal Election Commission enforces all such limitations that have been upheld as constitutional by the U.S. Supreme Court.

Test Yourself on This Section

1. Donations made directly to political candidates and their campaigns that must be declared with the name of the donor are known as
   a. hard money.
   b. soft money.
   c. hot money.
   d. cold money.

2. What did the Bipartisan Campaign Reform Act accomplish, and which provision of it was struck down as unconstitutional by the Supreme Court?

CONGRESSIONAL CAMPAIGNS AND ELECTIONS

- In congressional elections, the power of incumbency is more important than any other factor. Unlike midterm elections, congressional elections that coincide with presidential elections tend to garner greater voter turnout, and members of the successful presidential candidate's party sometimes benefit from the coattail effect.

Test Yourself on This Section

1. An incumbent member of Congress who is running for reelection on average stands about what chance of being reelected?
   a. 30 percent
   b. 50 percent
   c. 70 percent
   d. 90 percent

2. The electoral benefit that a presidential candidate provides to congressional candidates of the same party during a presidential election is known as the
   a. executive effect.
   b. incumbency effect.
   c. safe-seat effect.
   d. coattail effect.

3. What factors contribute the power of incumbency?

KEY TERMS

battleground states (p. 401)
Bipartisan Campaign Reform Act (BCRA) of 2002 (p. 413)
Buckley v. Valeo (1976) (p. 413)
caucus (p. 395)
closed primary (p. 395)
coattail effect (p. 414)
electoral college (p. 404)
electors (p. 405)
Federal Election Campaign Act (FECA) (p. 412)

Federal Election Commission (FEC) (p. 412)
franking privilege (p. 416)
frontloading (p. 396)
hard money (p. 412)
incumbent race (p. 399)
independent campaign expenditure (p. 413)
invisible primary (p. 393)
marginal seat (p. 415)
midterm congressional elections (p. 413)

nomination campaign (p. 396)
open election (p. 400)
open primary (p. 395)
power of incumbency (p. 414)
prenomination campaign (p. 393)
presidential primary (p. 395)
retrospective voting (p. 408)
safe seat (p. 415)
soft money (p. 412)
unit rule (p. 405)

15

AMERICAN DOMESTIC POLICY

Federal Reserve Chairman Ben Bernanke (back to camera) testifies before the U.S. Congress Joint Economic Committee in October 2011.

LEARNING OBJECTIVES

AN OVERVIEW OF THE POLICYMAKING PROCESS

- Describe the various stages in which the public policymaking process unfolds, as well as the various players involved

THEORIES AND PRACTICE IN FISCAL POLICY

- Recognize the different theories that justify decisions to craft fiscal policy
- Trace the budget-making process, how it unfolds, and the roles played by Congress and the president in the process
- Define the different categories of tax policy and assess the differences between mandatory and discretionary spending by government

THEORIES AND PRACTICE IN MONETARY POLICY

- Trace the development of the Federal Reserve System in the United States

THE NATURE AND PRACTICE OF CRIME POLICY

- Compare and contrast the prevailing models of criminal justice policymaking

THE WELFARE STATE AND PROGRAMS FOR THE POOR

- Contrast the U.S. welfare state model to that found in other Western democracies

THE SOCIAL SECURITY SYSTEM

- Assess the state of the Social Security system, its prospects, and reforms
- Contrast the various tax-favored investment vehicles that supplement retirement savings

HEALTH CARE POLICY

- Compare America's health care system to European systems that feature universal care

I n the 1950s, Yale Professor Charles E. Lindblom described U.S. domestic policymaking as the "science of muddling through."[1] Lindblom's view challenged what had been the prevailing model of policymaking: a rational and comprehensive process in which decision makers utilized scientific analysis and logic to develop public policy. Lindblom's theory introduced the human element and expressly partisan factors into the process. Today we view public policy—whether in the form of small, incremental shifts, or in the form of landmark sweeping legislation—as the product of reluctant compromises entered into between the president, Congress, and other political actors based on the immediate political environment. Indeed, the very term "public policy" in the United States has come to be associated today with the coordinated response of public institutions to immediate events and conditions, a nod to the often messy reality of modern policymaking. Whether the government is enacting economic policy, social policy, or foreign policy, imperfect solutions to significant problems are a given, and the final outcome rarely garners widespread satisfaction. So long as the political (and often highly partisan) branches of government engage in some form of conflict, such "muddling through" to landmark legislation may offer the best policy process to which we can realistically aspire.

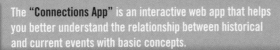
1880   1890   1900   1910   1920

Then

1905

President Theodore Roosevelt at Yosemite National Park's Glacier Point.
Source: © CORBIS

In the early 20th century, Congress muddled through President Theodore Roosevelt's aggressive agenda to protect the nation's natural resources. Roosevelt's romanticism about nature and the wilderness dated back to his childhood obsession with zoology, and then later to his experience as an amateur rancher in the badlands of North Dakota during the late 1880s. As his political career progressed, he watched with frustration as conglomerate trusts abused the environment in the name of industrial progress. He believed that natural resources were like a family trust—they existed to be used, but they had to be used wisely. At the outset of his administration, Roosevelt announced that the conservation of forest and water resources would be considered a national issue of vital importance.[2] By executive order he designated many federal tracts as game reserves, and he reserved more than 150 million acres in all as national forest reserves protected from unregulated strip mining. Yet to effectively conserve resources, there was only so much the president could do without Congress; business interests had successfully lobbied the legislative branch to go slow in protecting many aspects of the environment. Roosevelt prevailed to a degree when Congress passed the Transfer Act of 1905, moving the management of forest reserves over to the Bureau of Forestry, where it became known as the U.S. Forest Service. But he was frustrated in other ways, as Congress refused his entreaties to pass laws protecting the nation's water resources. Roosevelt moved his environmental agenda forward, but he was denied more comprehensive forms of reform. So goes the plight of the nation's chief executive, who must accept significant compromises when he pushes for landmark legislation.

1980   1990   2000   2010   2020

2010

Now

President Barack Obama at a rally celebrating passage of the Patient Protection and Affordable Care Act in March 2010.

Source: Jewel Samad/AFP/Getty Images

President Obama's health care reform agenda in 2009 similarly became the product of a "muddling-through" process. America's health care system had been an issue of growing national concern for decades. Spiraling costs and widespread complaints about limited access to care forced the issue to the forefront of the political agenda once again in 2009. Approaching the issue from a position of considerable political strength, Obama argued for an expansion of health insurance to cover all of the uninsured, caps on premium increases, and provisions that allowed people to retain their coverage when they left or changed jobs. In addition to universal coverage, a centerpiece of his proposed reform was the promise of a government insurance plan, known as the "public option," to compete with the corporate insurance sector to reduce costs. However, Obama soon met opposition not just from Republicans across the board, but from moderate Democrats as well, who believed the costs of universal coverage and the public option proposal made health care reform less attractive. To achieve the votes needed to overcome a Republican filibuster in the Senate, disappointed House leaders and a frustrated White House soon deferred to political reality: on March 23, 2010, President Obama signed into law health care reform legislation that followed the more moderate Senate model almost exactly; it lacked universal coverage and featured no public option. Still, the legislation amounted to a sweeping overhaul of the U.S. health care system aimed at mandating coverage and lowering costs. From the perspective of the White House, it was better to pass significant legislation that met many of President Obama's goals than to do nothing at all.

AN OVERVIEW OF THE POLICYMAKING PROCESS

public policy: The set of laws, regulations, and rules that affects the whole of society.

social policy: Rules, regulations, and policymaking pertaining to the quality of life, welfare, and relations of human beings in the United States.

Public policy refers to the set of laws, regulations, and rules that affect the whole of society. Because the responsibilities and interests of private and public institutions often overlap, some battles that are waged primarily among private parties may still fall under the general subject of public policy—after all, government may seek to enact laws or regulations aimed at monitoring such disputes. Antitrust laws, for example, offer a public policy response to disputes that arise between competing private companies such as Amazon and Apple. In April 2012, the Department of Justice brought an antitrust action against Apple and five major book publishers for allegedly colluding to raise prices for e-books after Apple had launched its iPad. Amazon wanted to charge $9.99 for most e-books available on its Web site; the Justice Department claimed that Apple and the publishers secretly agreed to adopt a model of higher prices in retaliation against Amazon. More than anything, the government regulators feared that such collusive practices had prevented market forces from establishing what should be the fair price for digital books. Thus the regulation of Apple and the book publisher defendants became a matter of public policy, even though the alleged agreement to raise prices was entered into by private entities. Meanwhile, **social policy**—a subset of public policy—refers to the rules, regulations, and policymaking pertaining to the quality of life, welfare, and relations of human beings in the United States. There are many different types of social policy, and this chapter will review some of the major ones: crime policy, welfare policy, Social Security policy, and health care policy.

Although the policymaking process tends to vary considerably from one subject area to another, most policies unfold in five separate stages:

- The recognition/definition stage, in which objectives to be fulfilled and goals to be pursued through policy are first identified and defined according to how the problem fits within existing policy categories, and then prioritized;

- The formulation stage, in which various alternative courses for this policy are considered, and a preferred course is selected;

- The adoption (or legitimation) stage, in which the policy under consideration assumes the authority of law through ratification by Congress or through regulations issued by the relevant administrative agencies;

- The implementation stage, in which a bureaucratic agency translates law into action though the adoption of administrative regulations and the dedication of agency resources to carry out the policy; and

- The evaluation stage, in which the policy is assessed for its worth and effectiveness in meeting its original objectives and goals.

Numerous actors and institutions are involved in making policy in the United States. Bureaucrats in administrative agencies often play a key role at every stage of the policymaking process, helping to define the problem and identify the possible options, proposing alternatives and implementing the preferred course, and assisting in collecting information necessary to evaluate the policy.[3] The Department of Commerce, for example, in addition to the Secretary of Commerce, employs at least six undersecretaries responsible for overseeing the formulation of numerous policy initiatives on behalf of the agency. Just one of those commerce officials, the Undersecretary for the National Oceanic and Atmospheric Administration, oversees a $5.54 billion bureaucracy that supervises the National Marine Fisheries Service, the National Ocean Service, and the National Weather Service, among other ocean-related agencies.

Congress and the president are most directly involved in the recognition, formulation, and adoption stages of policymaking, when media attention is most intense; their influence over the other stages is limited by the practical need to delegate administrative details to agencies with the resources and expertise to handle such matters. The courts may play a role in ensuring that all proper procedures are followed in the formulation of policy and in interpreting rules, regulations, and policies that emerge from the policymaking process.[4]

Interest groups and think tanks (policy research institutes) tend to focus on influencing program choices and decisions, where they have the opportunity to make significant gains on behalf of their members.[5] For example, the Sierra Club lobbies bureaucrats at the Environmental Protection Agency (EPA) and members of Congress on environmental committees to ensure that the Clean Air Act is successfully updated to meet new challenges. The specialized committee structure of Congress encourages interest groups to focus their resources on those legislators and members of legislative staffs who have authority over relevant issue areas. Think tanks are organizations that do intensive research and problem solving, either on behalf of other entities or on their own (see Table 15.1). Normally, a think tank staffed by researchers and policy analysts will produce an elaborate report detailing the implications of the problem it has studied; as with interest groups, it then seeks to publicize its findings, whether by holding a press conference, sponsoring a symposium or panel discussion, or some other means.

Economic policymaking encompasses all the legislative and rule-making initiatives that affect the management of wealth and resources within this country. For much of its history, the United States maintained one of the world's most entrepreneurially free economies, with minimal government regulation. The government's mostly hands-off approach to economic matters survived until the early part of the twentieth century, when the federal government began to insert itself more regularly in the economy. At first, government involvement was directed at antitrust matters and corporate abuses such as the employment of child labor; by the 1930s government involvement had begun to take a variety of new forms, as federal agencies actively oversaw the monetary system, supported struggling businesses, regulated the stock and bond markets, and otherwise reinforced the economic infrastructure as a whole. Indeed, immediately following the frightening events on Wall Street that occurred in September 2008, few from either political party questioned the wisdom of increasing government oversight of Wall Street. Today the government's role in managing the economy is significant—elections are

TABLE 15.1 Influential Policy Think Tanks

Institute	Date Established	Philosophy/Goals
American Enterprise Institute	1943	A conservative think tank dedicated to preserving "limited government, private enterprise . . . and a strong foreign policy and national defense."
The Brookings Institution	Roots trace back to 1916	A more liberal policy institute (once targeted by the Nixon administration) that aims to improve "the performance of American institutions and the quality of public policy" through the use of social science.
The Cato Institute	1977	Mostly libertarian; seeks to broaden the parameters of public policy debate to allow consideration of "the traditional American principles of limited government, individual liberty, free markets, and peace."
The Heritage Foundation	1973	Seeks "to formulate and promote conservative public policies based on the principles of free enterprise, limited government, individual freedom, traditional American values, and a strong national defense."
The Rand Corporation	1945	Seeks to provide policy analysis and solutions that address challenges facing the nation and the world, including education, poverty, crime, and the environment, as well as a range of national security issues.
The Progressive Policy Institute	1989	Affiliated with the Democratic Leadership Council maintains as its mission the definition and promotion of a new progressive politics in America. Its work rests on three ideals: equal opportunity, mutual responsibility, and self-governing citizens and communities.

Source: © Cengage Learning

often decided by voter perceptions of success or failure in this area. Overseeing the economy includes two distinct forms of policymaking: fiscal policymaking and monetary policymaking.

THEORY AND PRACTICE IN FISCAL POLICY

fiscal policy: Decisions by the federal government that relate to raising revenue through taxation and spending the revenue that is thereby generated.

inflation: The overall general upward price movement of goods and services in an economy, normally measured by the consumer price index (CPI).

laissez-faire economics: Fiscal policy theory that favors minimal intervention in the nation's economy.

Fiscal policy is concerned with how to raise revenue through taxation and how to spend the revenue generated. Many economists believe that the nation's fiscal policy has direct implications for unemployment, measured as the percentage of the workforce that wants to work and is not currently employed, and **inflation**, or consistent increases in the prices of goods and services. The primary instrument by which the federal government manages fiscal policy is the *federal budget*, a comprehensive plan laying out what the government will spend for its various programs during the coming fiscal years and how it expects to raise the money to pay for them.

Fiscal policy can be thought of as lying on a spectrum. At one end of the spectrum is the policy of minimal government interference in the economy, in which the government exercises little or no budget-making power by authorizing only minimal spending, taxation, and regulation of private business practices. At the opposite end of the spectrum is the policy of considerable government intervention in the economy, perhaps by taxing citizens or by offering subsidies to farmers in return for their agreement not to overproduce certain commodities.

Various economic theories explain the decision to craft fiscal policy at a given point along the fiscal policy spectrum. For example, the economic doctrine known as **laissez-faire** (a French phrase meaning literally "leave us alone") **economics** guided the fiscal policy that prevailed for much of the eighteenth and nineteenth centuries in the United States.[6] Laissez-faire favors less intervention in the economy, allowing businesses to conduct their affairs more or less free from governmental regulation. The theory came under attack toward the end of the 1800s, when increasing industrialization led to more frequent financial panics, bouts of severe unemployment, corrupt business practices, and the abuse of workers, especially in big cities. Government's involvement in the economy gradually increased, and in the 1930s widespread public support for President Franklin Roosevelt's New Deal programs, enacted to address the problems of the Great Depression, effectively spelled the end of laissez-faire theory as the guiding principle for the nation's fiscal policy.

Keynesian economic theory: Fiscal policy theory that favors government taxation and spending during difficult economic times.

Many of FDR's New Deal policies were based on **Keynesian economic theory**, named for the British economist John Maynard Keynes. Keynesian theory argues that the government should increase spending when economic times are bad as a way of raising total demand. Total demand for goods and services, according to this theory, is the key determinant of whether the economy is performing well.[7] The economic recovery that occurred during World War II, when federal military spending increased significantly, is often used to support the validity of Keynesian theory. Administrations that attempted to draw on the theory quickly learned that although government spending may forestall or even end a **recession**—defined as an economic slowdown characterized by higher unemployment, reduced productivity, or some other negative economic indicators—it may also bring about other economic problems such as inflation and chronically high deficits. Barack Obama's administration also adopted a Keynesian approach to addressing the financial crisis of 2007–2010. President Obama adopted that approach while aware of the risks that higher deficits might pose to his reelection chances in 2012.

recession: An economic slowdown characterized by high unemployment, reduced productivity, or other negative economic indicators.

supply-side economics: Economic theory that favors cutting taxes as a way of increasing economic productivity.

Supply-side economics is an alternative to Keynesian economics, arguing that rather than increasing government spending, cutting taxes (and cutting the government spending such taxes help to fund) is the preferred way to increase economic productivity and spur the economy. According to supply-side theory, high taxes take money out of the economy that would otherwise be invested in goods and services; thus by decreasing taxes, money flows back into the economy, stimulating business, new jobs, and overall productivity. While campaigning for the presidency in 1980, Ronald Reagan seized on this theory to propose that a program of tax cuts, spending cuts, and balancing the budget was the best means to get the economy out of recession. (As president, Reagan did secure passage of a large tax cut, but federal spending and deficits also multiplied during his eight years in office.[8])

Assessing the Economy's Performance

Just as different economic theories guide the crafting of fiscal policy, different measures are used to assess whether the nation's fiscal policy has been a success. Following are several economic measures regarded as especially significant indicators of general economic performance:

- **Gross domestic product (GDP)** is an estimate of the total money value of all the goods and services produced in the United States in a given one-year period. When GDP improves, workers are producing more in fewer hours, allowing employers in turn to increase wages without raising prices. By contrast, declining productivity signals higher labor costs and, ultimately, higher prices for consumers. Measured in constant dollars (that is, adjusting for inflation), the GDP enjoyed its highest one-year increase during the past half-century in 1984, when it rose by 6.8 percent. The GDP has actually fallen in constant dollars in five separate years over that same 50-year time span.

- The **consumer price index (CPI)** is an index of prices for goods and services regularly traded in the U.S. economy. A sustained rise over time in the CPI indicates that inflation is on the rise and consumers' buying power is on the decline. Although critics argue that the CPI overstates inflation by at least 1 percent per year, the government still heavily relies on the CPI in defining tax brackets and spending for certain entitlement programs, such as cost-of-living adjustments for Social Security recipients. In 1980, the CPI increase for urban consumers was 13.5 percent, the highest figure recorded in more than three decades. Since 1983, the CPI has not increased by more than 6 percent in any given year.

- The unemployment rate measures the percentage of people unemployed and actively looking for work in the U.S. labor market. Although a major goal of the economic programs of most Western governments (including the United States) is to keep

gross domestic product (GDP): An estimate of the total money value of all the goods and services produced in the United States in a one-year period.

consumer price index (CPI): An index of prices for goods and services regularly traded in the U.S. economy.

Yellow Dog Productions/The Image Bank/Getty Image

The Great Recession of 2007–2010 claimed many workers' jobs. Here, individuals wait their turn to claim unemployment benefits in early 2010.

The federal government has run up budget deficits every year during the past two decades.

Fiction.

The federal government actually posted annual budget surpluses for four straight years from 1998 through 2001.

---

budget deficit: The amount of money spent by the U.S. government beyond that which it collects in taxes and other revenue in a single year.

---

budget surplus: The amount by which the U.S. government's revenue exceeds its spending in a given fiscal year.

---

national debt: The total sum of the federal government's outstanding debt obligations.

unemployment relatively low, full employment remains an elusive goal due to seasonal factors, voluntary job changes, and routine shifts in economic conditions (such as the rise in interest rates) that assist some businesses (e.g., apartment rental firms) and hinder others (e.g., construction companies and home loan financing companies). In recent years, a rate of 5 percent has been considered a realistic minimum for unemployment in the United States. That rate is certainly better than the unemployment rate of about 10 percent recorded for a short period during 2009.

- The **budget deficit** is the amount of money spent by the U.S. government over and above what it collects in taxes and other revenue in a single year. A **budget surplus**, on the other hand, is the amount by which the U.S. government's revenue exceeds its spending in a given fiscal year. The federal government has posted annual budget surpluses just 11 times since 1931, including four straight years from 1998 through 2001. Prior to 1998, the last surplus recorded was in 1969, the first year of Richard Nixon's presidency. Although budget deficits are often compelled by national crises that require the quick allotment of funds for some specific purpose (such as responding to the September 11, 2001 terrorist attacks), critics argue that continued budget deficits beyond a short period of time can lead to politically unpopular remedies such as tax increases or spending cuts, or, alternatively, to a burgeoning national debt that can slow economic growth in the long run. The Obama administration's attempts to address the nation's economic problems in 2009 contributed to record deficits. According to the Congressional Budget Office, the deficit forecast for fiscal year 2013 will exceed $987 billion.

- The **national debt** is the total sum of the outstanding debt obligations of the U.S. government, largely generated through the sale of interest-bearing U.S. savings bonds, U.S. treasury notes, and U.S. treasury bills to individuals or organizations. It represents the accumulated total of all government budget surpluses and deficits of past years as well.[9] In 2012 the debt reached the 15-trillion-dollar mark and will likely escalate by at least 1 trillion per year for the foreseeable future. Thus the government must pay in excess of $350 billion per year in interest costs alone. That means to meet interest obligations on the debt, the government must annually pay out the equivalent of more than $1,300 for every man, woman, and child in the country.

- The Dow Jones Industrial Average is perhaps the most widely used indicator of the overall condition of the stock market, where publicly owned companies are actively traded each business day. "The Dow" is actually just a price-weighted average of 30 actively traded blue-chip stocks (that is, from large companies), but its prominence on network newscasts each evening testifies to the important status it holds in the minds of consumers. Other stock market indexes include the Standard & Poor's 500 Index, which encompasses a broader range of large company stocks, and the NASDAQ, an index of high-tech company stocks.

- Housing starts are a measure of the number of U.S. residential building construction projects begun during a specific period of time. Many experts believe that a decline in housing starts is one of the first signs of an approaching economic downturn, and thus it is one of the first indicators consulted by those trying to assess the overall direction of the economy.

- The consumer confidence index (CCI) measures the public's evaluation of the economy by asking a representative sample of Americans how they feel about the current condition of the economy, their personal financial situation, and their prediction about the future of the economy. As shown in Figure 15.1, the CCI underwent dramatic changes between June of 1997 and the beginning of the Great Recession of 2007–2010.

- Balance-of-trade figures (also called net exports) measure the sum of the money gained by a given economy by selling exports, minus the cost of buying imports. When a country exports more than it imports, the country has a trade surplus, whereas the reverse situation denotes a trade deficit. The United States has posted an annual trade deficit dating back to the 1970s; this is perhaps a testament to the rising purchasing power American consumers enjoy around the world. Economists often debate whether such

FIGURE 15.1 Consumer Confidence in the United States, 2000–2012

Source: The Conference Board's CCI, 2000–2012; chart from http://www.tradingeconomics.com/united-states/consumer-confidence

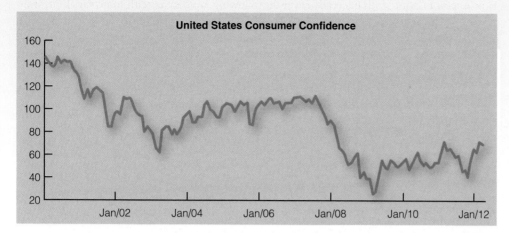

chronic trade deficits are a bad thing; regardless, because especially large trade deficits or surpluses may be a sign of some other economic problems, economists keep a watchful eye on these measures.

In an effort to gauge the state of the economy as a whole, economists have attempted to combine these measures and others into some all-purpose economic indicator. For example, the misery index, measured by adding the inflation rate to the unemployment rate, is a rough indicator of how badly the economy is performing. Jimmy Carter capitalized on an exceedingly high misery index for 1975 to defeat incumbent President Gerald Ford, only to be victimized by an even higher misery index in 1979, which may well have cost Carter reelection in 1980.

Although most observers agree that presidents actually exert only a marginal impact on the economy, economic performance can still be a crucial factor in determining which party wins a presidential election.[10] The U.S. economy normally runs in cycles. The onset of a recession tends to deliver a "one-two punch" against the economy: first, federal revenues decline as profits decrease and fewer people work; then federal expenditures increase as people claim more and more *entitlements* (guaranteed government benefits such as food stamps and welfare) to get them through the jobless period. A recession is eventually followed by an economic recovery, marked by an upswing of positive economic indicators.

The Federal Budget-Making Process

Once considered to be little more than a document detailing sums of money to be spent for particular purposes, the federal budget today has become the primary instrument of federal fiscal policy. The Budget and Accounting Act of 1921 made the president formally responsible for initially formulating the national budget. Today, the president's budget establishes the position around which all subsequent budget battles will be fought. With passage of the Employment Act of 1946, Congress permanently committed the federal government to use the budgetary process to promote maximum employment, production, and purchasing power. Together, these two acts obligate the president to craft budgets strategically to strengthen the economy.

The budget process begins when federal agencies formulate their budget requests and pass them on to the Office of Management and Budget (OMB). A part of the Executive Office of the President, the OMB determines whether the agency's budget proposals are in accord with the president's program and then uses those proposals to prepare an overall budget for the coming fiscal year, setting guidelines for estimating revenue and allotting spending.[11]

After receiving the president's proposals, Congress offers its own budget resolution for the fiscal year, based on its own projections for revenue. The appropriations committees of the House and the Senate are primarily responsible for such budget formulation. Each of the two committees plans overview hearings during which the OMB director and representatives of federal agencies discuss the president's budget priorities. Each of the appropriations committees must eventually pass 10 to 12 appropriations bills to keep the government running. House appropriations bills generally cover the following topic areas, with some variations from year to year:

1. Agriculture, rural development, and related agencies

2. Science, the Departments of State and Justice, and related agencies

3. Defense

4. Transportation, Treasury, Housing and Urban Development, the Judiciary, the District of Columbia

5. Energy and water development

6. Foreign operations, export financing, and related programs

7. Homeland Security

8. Interior, Environment, and related agencies

9. Labor, Health and Human Services, and Education

10. Military Quality of Life and Veterans Affairs

All appropriations bills originate in the House; after the House Appropriations Committee has reported the bills to the full House, and after the full House has passed each measure, the Senate Appropriations Committee takes its turn revising the House version. After Senate subcommittee work has been completed on the House bills, the Senate Appropriations Committee marks up its own versions of the bills and reports them to the Senate for floor action.

Congress created separate House and Senate budget committees during the 1970s to oversee the budget process. The Budget and Impoundment Act of 1974 required Congress to set a maximum spending figure for the total budget and for each of several broad funding categories based on projections of future revenue. These figures are prepared by the Congressional Budget Office (CBO), which reports to Congress, and the OMB, which reports to the president. When the CBO and the OMB differ widely on estimates, as has happened frequently in recent years, Congress tends to side with its own agency. The House and Senate budget committees may require cuts in spending to ensure that the overall budget targets can be reached. Eventually the House and Senate must reconcile their competing versions of the budget and secure additional votes from their members for approval of the final budget bill, which is then presented to the president for signature.

All these legislative obstacles must be navigated over a period of eight months, extending from the first Monday in February (when the president's budget proposal is delivered to Congress) through October 1, when the new fiscal year begins. If Congress and the president cannot agree on a final budget over this period of time, Congress may be forced to pass "continuing resolutions" to allow the government to keep running while final budget negotiations continue.[12] Occasionally, Congress and the president are at such loggerheads that a budget showdown becomes inevitable. In late 1995 the Republican Congress, led by House Speaker Newt Gingrich, insisted that President Bill Clinton sign a budget bill with spending cuts that Clinton's administration had strenuously opposed. When Congress refused to keep passing continuing resolutions, the resulting impasse led to two government shutdowns totaling 27, during which all federal government institutions and buildings were forced to close.[13] President Barack Obama and the Republican-controlled House of Representatives underwent a similar battle over proposed budget cuts in April of 2011. Yet although the 2011 battle proved to be highly contentious, the two sides narrowly averted a government shutdown with a last-minute compromise that cut over $38 billion from the original budget.

Even though the Senate and House budget committees have brought more fiscal restraint to the budget process, some within and outside Congress attempted to introduce bolder budgetary reforms in response to the $200-billion deficits of the mid-1980s. The Gramm-Rudman-Hollings Act of 1985 set annual targets for reducing the deficit and required the General Accounting Office (GAO) to determine whether automatic spending cuts would take effect

House Speaker John Boehner, surrounded by fellow Republican Congressional leaders, announces the details of a budget compromise which helped avert a government shutdown on April 8, 2011.

if Congress passed budgets that missed the established deficit target. In 1986, the Supreme Court struck down the act as unconstitutional because the GAO, accountable only to Congress, could not legally perform what were essentially "executive" acts.[14] The Budget Enforcement Act of 1990 set deficit targets that could be adjusted due to unforeseen economic changes; however, the act did not compensate for unexpected spending increases by requiring offsetting cuts elsewhere.

Of course the central problem of the budget process—that it allows the federal government to spend more money than it takes in—remained in place even with such reforms. Thus, as shown in Figure 15.2, the total U.S. debt continues to grow by leaps and bounds, with little end in sight. In recent years, Congress has debated passing a balanced budget amendment to the Constitution, which would at least require that annual federal spending be kept at or below revenue collected during the year. Proponents of the amendment argue that it would force free-spending lawmakers to become accountable: just as many taxpayers must live off their income (or even considerably less), the government should be expected to do likewise. Opponents of the amendment counter that the government might—in accordance with Keynesian principles—want to engage in deficit spending during times of recession as a method of economic stimulation. They also note that the federal government must be able to spend freely to defend the national security of the United States, even if that means running up large deficits. (Although recent versions of the amendment would allow Congress to waive the requirement in case of war or military conflict, critics argue that even more flexibility is necessary.) The Balanced Budget Amendment has been passed in one house but defeated in the other on five separate occasions since 1982. In 1995 and again in 1997, the amendment failed by a single vote in the U.S. Senate.

Taxation Policy

Taxation policies tend to fall into one of two general categories. **Redistributive tax policies** aim to provide a social safety net to meet the minimum physical needs of citizens. Such policies accomplish this end by following Robin Hood's principle of "taking from the rich and giving to the poor." For example, taxes that are channeled directly into public assistance programs are redistributive. **Distributive tax policies**, on the other hand, are intended to promote the interests of all economic classes equally. Taxes that are directed toward the maintenance of national parks or the national highway system theoretically benefit all citizens.

redistributive tax policies: Taxation policies that aim to provide a social safety net to meet the minimum physical needs of citizens.

distributive tax policies: Taxation policies intended to promote the interests of all classes equally.

FIGURE 15.2 Total U.S. Debt by Fiscal Year

Source: http://www.babylontoday.com

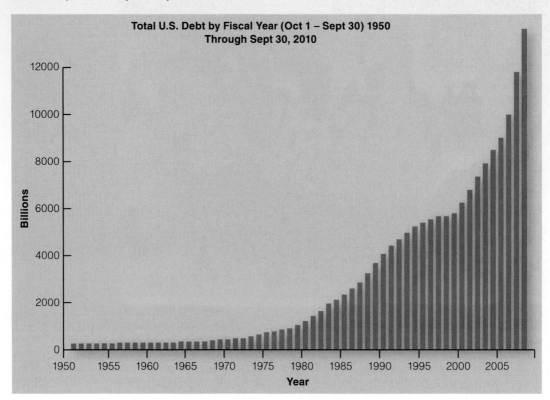

All governments need revenue to pay the salaries of government workers and to fund its various activities. In July 1789, just four months after the creation of a new government, Congress passed its first revenue-raising bill: specifically, it levied tariffs, which are taxes on imported foreign goods. Up until the Civil War, tariffs provided approximately 90 percent of the federal government's revenue; yet as that war evolved into a long-lasting conflict, the Union needed far greater revenues than even high tariffs could provide. The exponential growth of the federal government after the Civil War exacerbated these demands further. Thus in the late nineteenth and early twentieth centuries, the federal government was forced to look elsewhere for major sources of funding. Eventually it started to draw more heavily on internal sources of revenue, including payroll taxes, corporate income taxes, and individual income taxes.

The Sixteenth Amendment to the U.S. Constitution authorizes Congress to tax an individual's increase in wealth, whether that wealth comes from wages, benefits, bonuses, or any other form of income. The fairness of individual income taxes, which now provide nearly half of all revenue that flows into the U.S. treasury, remains a subject of contentious debate. The federal government has traditionally imposed a **progressive tax** on incomes. With a progressive tax, the tax rate on an individual's income increases as the amount of income gets larger. Though President Reagan signed tax reform legislation in 1986 to cut top rates and close various loopholes, the personal income tax system still remained mostly progressive—in 2012 the tax system featured rates that go up in several stages to a high of 35 percent for all wages earned over $388,350.

progressive tax: A tax whose effective rate on an individual's income increases as the person's income rises.

Conversely, a tax that charges all individuals the same amount, regardless of income, is called a **regressive tax** because it exacts a larger percentage of income from the lower-wage earner than it does from the high-income earner. Most state sales taxes are regressive, because they apply equally to every purchaser: for example, both a poor person and a wealthy person pay the same amount of sales tax for a gallon of gasoline, but that amount constitutes a higher percentage of the poor person's income.

regressive tax: A tax that charges individuals the same amount, regardless of income.

Some people confuse regressive taxes with **flat taxes**. Unlike regressive taxes, flat taxes tax all entities at the same rate *as a proportion of income*. Thus with a flat tax, a rich person may

flat tax: A tax policy that draws money from all entities at the same proportion of their income.

pay far more in total taxes than a poor person, although the two are still being taxed at the same percentage rate. In 1996 and 2000, presidential candidate Steve Forbes proposed that the federal government impose a flat tax of 15 percent on all income earned in the United States. Forbes argued that such a system would spread the tax burden more evenly, stop penalizing Americans for working harder to earn more, and dramatically simplify the current system.[15] Forbes's proposals have not fared well in the political arena; currently, neither of the two major parties is putting its weight behind a truly flat income tax for Americans.

Social Security taxes (a tax on personal income and on employers) contribute on average 35 percent to the federal government's overall revenues. Created in 1935, the Social Security system is primarily a self-supporting, "pay-as-you-go" program: payments to current retirees come from current worker payments (dedicated payroll taxes taken directly out of workers' paychecks). In recent decades Social Security has become the largest expenditure in the federal budget. If and when near-term revenue from payroll taxes proves insufficient to fund near-term benefits, the government may eventually be forced to alleviate the shortfalls either by cutting benefits payments or by passing tax increases. Neither approach would be popular with the public.

During the past century Congress has also imposed corporate income taxes, which today make up just less than 10 percent of the government's revenues. Other important revenue sources include federal taxes on gasoline, communications services, estates, large financial gifts, and customs duties. And if these revenue sources fall short of projected expenditures in the form of a deficit, the federal government must make up the difference by borrowing money in the form of issuing U.S. savings bonds, treasury bills, and the like.

Americans commonly complain about the high taxes they pay, and politicians do not like to be perceived as favoring tax increases; in 1984, Democratic presidential candidate Walter Mondale promised to raise taxes in response to skyrocketing deficits, a promise that all but doomed his hopes of unseating President Ronald Reagan, the candidate more closely identified with lower taxes.

At the Republican national convention in 1988, Vice President George H. W. Bush—having just been named his party's presidential nominee for the upcoming fall—sought to associate himself with the economic policies of the Reagan administration and its emphasis on tax cutting. In his speech accepting the nomination, Bush predicted that if elected president, the Democratic Congress would come to him, pushing him to raise taxes . . .

> . . . and I'll say no, and they'll push, and I'll say no, and they'll push again, and I'll say to them: "READ MY LIPS: NO NEW TAXES."

Bush's promise seemed politically astute at the time it was issued, and he coasted to victory that fall. But in 1990, with an economic recession firmly in place, Bush signed the Revenue Reconciliation Act, which aimed to reduce the federal deficit by $500 billion over the next five years. To accomplish that goal, the act called for $125 billion in new taxes, inviting charges that the president had flip-flopped on his 1988 pledge of "no new taxes." In the 1992 presidential campaign, Democratic candidate Bill Clinton attempted to capitalize on the flip-flop. Bush's defeat in the 1992 election was attributed in part to the lack of enthusiasm his candidacy had generated among conservatives, many of whom were still frustrated by the president's decision to sign that infamous tax bill in the first place. James Carville, chief political consultant to Clinton's 1992 presidential campaign, called it "the most famous broken promise in the history of American politics."

Despite all the complaints about high taxes, Americans' tax burden is quite low when compared with the tax burdens of other developed countries. Although U.S. citizens pay an income tax rate somewhere between 10 percent and 35 percent, citizens of Sweden pay twice that amount—between 33 percent and 60 percent of their income—to the Swedish government. Taxes paid by citizens in France, Germany, and Great Britain also tend to be higher (as a percentage of their income) than those paid by citizens of the United States. Of course such comparisons are not altogether fair—for example, Sweden, as part of its welfare system, provides all its citizens with an extensive tax-funded public child care system, dental care, and a ceiling on health care costs. England's tax-funded national health care service offers its citizens "free" services as well.

Still, politicians are reluctant to ignore perceptions that the American tax system is overly burdensome or unfair. In the run-up to the 2012 election, President Barack Obama sought to

President Barack Obama and New Jersey Governor Chris Christie visit the Jersey Shore to witness first hand the devastation caused by Hurricane Sandy in October 2012. Since 2008, Congress has allotted to the Federal Emergency Management Agency (FEMA) nearly $6 billion per year in disaster relief funds. FEMA then dispenses those funds to victims of natural disasters across the United States.

redirect the issue to tax fairness, arguing that the highest income earners—many of whom take advantage of tax breaks on real estate and capital gains to pay an "effective tax rate" considerably lower than 35 percent—should pay the same or a higher rate than lower-income earners. His administration thus proposed the so-called "Buffet plan" named after wealthy investor Warren Buffet, who had argued publicly for higher income tax rates on wealthy individuals such as himself. The Buffet plan would have applied an absolute minimum effective tax rate of 30 percent on earnings of more than $1 million annually. High-profile Republicans, including House Budget Chairman Paul Ryan and Republican presidential candidate Mitt Romney, criticized the proposal as a form of "class warfare" that would negatively impact job creation and investment. Tax fairness promises to be a front-burner issue in national elections for the foreseeable future.

Spending Policies—Dividing the Pie

Budget surpluses are a rarity in modern American politics because the federal government has demonstrated time and again its capacity to spend taxpayer money—U.S. government spending topped $3.8 trillion in fiscal year 2012 alone. Although the president is legally responsible for proposing budgets and has the power to veto spending decisions, Article I of the Constitution grants the Congress exclusive power to lay and collect duties "to pay the debts and provide for the common defense and general welfare of the United States." In reality, Congress allots funds from the U.S. treasury to federal departments and agencies and then gives them **budget authority**, which allows them to incur obligations to spend or lend that money. Budget authority for a fiscal year is essentially like the permission for an agency to enter a contract; it is not the same thing as how much the agency will spend in that fiscal year—that amount is called **outlays**.

Where does taxpayer money go? The truth about government spending might surprise you. Spending tends to fall into two general categories. **Mandatory spending** refers to spending not controlled by annual budget decisions—these funds are automatically obligated by virtue of previously enacted laws and may not be modified by annual budget decisions (although they can be modified by repeal or modification of the original legislation). Most mandatory spending occurs in the form of entitlements: government spending such as Social Security, Medicare (national health insurance for seniors), and veterans benefits that must be paid to anyone meeting specific eligibility requirements. President Franklin Roosevelt's New Deal programs and President Lyndon Johnson's Great Society programs substantially expanded the number of entitlements, forcing future lawmakers to grapple with those entitlements when they considered reforms of their own. Since 1995, nearly two-thirds of all government spending has been mandatory, almost double the percentage of mandatory spending outlays of the early 1960s (see Figure 15.3).

Discretionary spending encompasses all those spending categories that Congress does have the power to modify or eliminate in a given year. Budgeting is normally a give-and-take process between Congress and the president concerning the most appropriate levels of discretionary spending. Most federal spending on education, the environment, and national defense is based on discretionary spending outlays. When an administration's critics accuse the president of not being fiscally conservative enough with government spending, their criticisms usually focus on government spending as a whole; in fairness, however, only discretionary spending really lies within the president's immediate influence. In the eight years the Clinton administration was responsible for the federal budget (1994 through 2001), discretionary spending increased by an annual average of 3.4 percent; during the George W. Bush

budget authority: The power of federal departments and agencies to incur obligations to spend or lend money.

outlays: The amount of money a government agency will actually spend during a fiscal year.

mandatory spending: Federal government spending that is not controlled by annual budget decisions; includes entitlements such as Medicare and Social Security.

discretionary spending: Forms of federal government spending that Congress can modify or eliminate in any given year, including spending on education, the environment, and national defense.

FIGURE 15.3 Where Do Federal Tax Dollars Come from and Where Do They Go?

Mandatory spending (required by law) represents such a large percentage of the budget (approximately two-thirds of all government spending) that lawmakers often complain that their hands are tied as they wrestle with ways to cut costs. Unlike most spending on our national defense, which Congress authorizes each year at its discretion, entitlements such as Social Security, Medicare, and the food stamp program are examples of mandatory spending categories. The two pie charts shown here illustrate sources of federal revenues and the allocation of federal spending in fiscal year 2011.

Source: Office of Management and Budget, Budget of the U.S. Government Historical Tables.

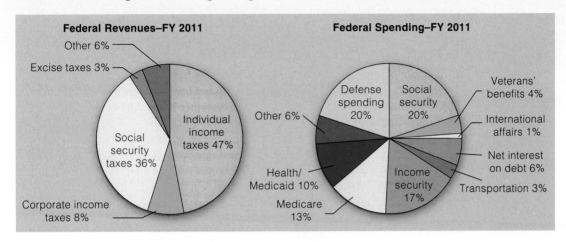

administration, discretionary spending increased by an average of 10.5 percent annually. Currently discretionary spending under the Obama administration amounts to about 15% of the overall budget.

Year in and year out, one particular mandatory spending category—Social Security spending—tops all the other categories. In fiscal year 2011, the federal government spent over $720 billion on the program, and Social Security expenditures of over $820 billion are anticipated by fiscal year 2013. Among the discretionary program outlays, national defense has traditionally constituted the largest part of the budget. In 1962, the federal government allotted $52.4 billion to defense, almost 10 times the amount earmarked to any other discretionary program category. Nearly a half-century later, in 2011, over $838 billion was allotted to national defense. The growth in discretionary spending during the past decade can be attributed in part to the George W. Bush administration's desire to increase spending on defense and homeland security in the wake of the terrorist attacks of September 11, 2001, as well as to the Obama administration's willingness to continue most of those same defense policies and to increase military spending in Afghanistan.

THEORIES AND PRACTICE IN MONETARY POLICY

Monetary policy is the means by which the government controls the supply and price of money in the economy. Although this may seem like a nonpolitical, technical function, the exercise of monetary policy can have profound implications on unemployment rates and inflation, and thus is the focus of considerable political interest.

With few exceptions, the **Federal Reserve System**, which is headed by the **Federal Reserve Board** ("the Fed"), determines monetary policy in the United States. Since 1913, this independent agency has acted as the nation's central bank, supervising and regulating all of the nation's banks, and providing financial information to the public. In addition to the Federal Reserve Board, Congress established 12 nonprofit Federal Reserve Banks to serve as the operating arms of the central banking system. By law, all "member banks" in the United States (which includes all national banks and many state banks) must maintain fractional reserves—a portion of their deposits that must be kept on hand or at the Fed to satisfy any demands for withdrawal. (Most fractional reserves are kept in accounts at the Federal Reserve Banks.) The Federal Reserve

monetary policy: Regulation of the money supply and interest rates by a central bank, such as the U.S. Federal Reserve Board, in order to control inflation and stabilize the currency.

Federal Reserve System: The central banking system of the United States, which controls the nation's money supply.

Federal Reserve Board: The Federal Reserve System's Board of Governors, which votes on monetary policy in the United States, supervises the nation's banks by setting rules for the 12 Federal Reserve Banks, and engages in open market operations.

discount rate: The rate (expressed as a percentage) that all Federal Reserve member banks and other depository institutions will be charged by the Federal Reserve Banks to borrow short-term funds.

open market operations: The buying and selling of government securities by the Federal Reserve Board as a means of controlling the national money supply.

reserve requirement: The minimum liquid assets each bank must keep on hand to back customer loans.

Fact or Fiction?

On average, Americans have a far higher tax rate than citizens in most other Western democracies.

Fiction.

The four Western European nations in the G-7 all impose higher tax burdens on their citizens than does the United States on its own states.

Banks in turn issue stock and pay dividends to member banks as partial compensation for the lack of interest they pay on member banks' required reserves. The Federal Reserve Board sets all rules and regulations for the Federal Reserve Banks.[16]

Perhaps the single most important responsibility of the Federal Reserve is to set the **discount rate** that all member banks and other depository institutions will be charged to borrow short-term funds. A high discount rate makes it more expensive for member banks to borrow money from the Federal Reserve Banks, but more profitable for banks to lend money (because they'll secure a greater interest on their investment). The opposite is true when the Federal Reserve lowers the discount rate: banks are more apt to borrow money because it is cheaper, whereas lending money to others becomes less profitable. A second important function of the Federal Reserve is engaging in **open market operations**, in which it buys and sells government securities as a means of controlling the national money supply—buying bonds increases the amount of money in circulation, whereas selling has the opposite effect. Finally, the Federal Reserve sets the **reserve requirements** of member banks, determining the minimum liquid assets each bank must keep on hand to back customer loans. Any of these actions has the effect of either tightening or loosening the overall money supply.

In recent years, it has become common for investors to eagerly anticipate the Federal Reserve's next announcement that it plans to adjust the interest rate up or down.[17] Although hardly an exact science, the Federal Reserve's setting of a new discount rate can affect the economy in profoundly important ways. Why would the Federal Reserve choose to raise the discount rate? The primary goal of the Federal Reserve is to stabilize the economy and prevent dangerously wide fluctuations that can upset the economy. Although politicians may benefit in the short run from a quickly growing economy, the Federal Reserve may fear the eventual onset of high inflation. Under such circumstances, it may seek to tighten the money supply (the total amount of money available in the economy at a particular point in time) by increasing the discount rate. Such a move may be politically unpopular, because interest rates throughout the economy tend to rise along with the discount rate, making it harder for individuals to borrow money for houses and consumer goods. Investments by businesses may similarly be curtailed.

On the flip side, the Federal Reserve may choose to lower the discount rate as a way to stimulate investment and spur the economy forward. Lower interest rates allow individuals to borrow and invest more for consumer goods and real estate and businesses to borrow more money for capital investment. Some economists believe lower interest rates also keep unemployment at a minimum, because businesses are better able to maximize their production capacity.

When Congress enacted the Federal Reserve Act in 1913, it sought to ensure that the Federal Reserve could act independently of partisan political considerations, which often demand short-term fixes to the economy. Each of the Fed's seven members serves a term of 14 years. Once appointed and confirmed, a board member may not be removed from office except through a cumbersome impeachment process for serious criminal violations. The president also determines (with the consent of the Senate) who will serve as Federal Reserve Chair for a period of four years, although in practice the chair is often reappointed several times.

Few officials in history have faced a more daunting challenge than Ben Bernanke, the current Federal Reserve Chair who was first appointed by President George W. Bush in January 2006. Bernanke replaced Alan Greenspan, the legendary chairman who presided over an unprecedented period of high economic growth and low inflation during his 19 years at the helm of the Fed.

Bernanke's challenge grew significantly in late 2008 when, during his first term as Federal Reserve Chairman, he presided over the biggest economic collapse since the Great Depression. Bernanke approached the crisis by proposing initiatives designed to save the world economy rather than simply to shape U.S. monetary policy. Under his leadership the Federal Reserve Bank ratcheted interest rates down to zero; lent money to mutual funds, hedge funds, foreign banks, investment banks,

Former Federal Reserve Chairman Alan Greenspan, left, confers with his successor, Federal Reserve Chairman Ben Bernanke, in 2007.

AP Photo/Kevin Wolf

CHECK THE LIST

The G-7 Nations, Ranked According to Income Tax Rates Imposed on Their Citizens

Nobody likes to pay taxes, and Americans frequently complain about how much they have to pay to the government. Are such complaints justified? One way to assess the fairness of the U.S. income tax burden is to compare it to the tax burdens of other countries around the world. Perhaps the best comparison is with the so-called G-7 nations, a group of seven large industrialized nations that share information on economic policies. The Organization for Economic Cooperation and Development (OECD) collects data on state and federal wage taxes for the G-7, and its most recent analysis shows that the top rate for American taxpayers is actually toward the lower end of the pack. Whereas the wealthiest citizens in France and Italy have a somewhat lower income tax burden, the four other nations in the G-7 all impose higher tax burdens on their citizens. Britain, in particular, stands out as maintaining the largest top tax rate by far among the G-7 nations. (Among other countries, Sweden is notable for its top income rate of 56.5 percent.)

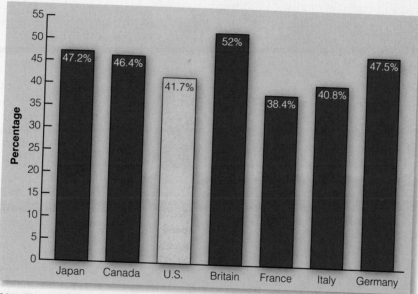

2011 Top Personal Income Tax Rates (State and Federal Rates Combined), by Country

▶ **POINT TO PONDER:** Why do you think there is such a disconnect between Americans' perceptions of their tax burdens and the reality of where our tax burden stands relative to other nations? Given these statistics, why do you think politicians remain so reluctant to suggest income tax increases?

Source: http://www.oecd.org/dataoecd/46/18/2506453.xls

manufacturers, insurers, and other borrowers; and jump-started stalled credit markets and revolutionized housing finance in the United States by purchasing mortgage bonds in bulk. *Time* magazine named Bernanke its "Person of the Year" in 2009 for these efforts, and President Obama reappointed Bernanke to a second term in 2010, though not without overcoming resistance from senators who feared the Federal Reserve Bank had grown too powerful under Bernanke's leadership.

THE NATURE AND PRACTICE
OF CRIME POLICY

crime control model: Criminal justice policymaking model that views the controlling of criminal behavior as the system's most important function.

Perhaps the most fundamental way in which modern societies manage relations among human beings residing within their jurisdictions is through the use of a comprehensive criminal justice system. Democratic systems must strike a careful balance between maintaining public order and protecting individual freedom—the rules and practices of the criminal justice system determine where and how that balance will be struck. For example, especially severe and strict forms of law enforcement could prove effective at making citizens safe, but only at a very high cost in taxpayers' money and possibly some loss of individual freedom as well.

A defendant being arraigned in one of the nation's criminal courtrooms.

In 1968, social scientist Herbert Packer defined two different models of criminal justice policymaking: the "crime control model" and the "due process model."[18] The **crime control model** views the controlling of criminal behavior as the most important function of criminal justice. Packer depicts the crime control model as a type of "assembly line justice" because it tries to move cases quickly and efficiently though the system. The process requires that police and prosecutor make crucial judgments about defendants' guilt early in the process; the crime control model thus relies extensively on negotiations between defense attorneys and state prosecutors early on, to avoid the uncertainty and high costs associated with a full-blown trial. In theory, the guilty will be routinely pressed to enter plea bargains, whereas the innocent should hope to see their indictments dismissed early in the process. Of course, the quick nature of this process increases the likelihood that public officials and defense attorneys will not always make the best judgments.

due process model: Criminal justice policymaking model that views the attainment of justice—which includes protection of the innocent—as the principal goal of the system.

By contrast, in the **due process model** the principal goal is justice, which focuses just as much on acting to protect the innocent as it does on convicting the guilty. Stressing the adversarial process and the need for hearings, the model endeavors to guarantee that all criminal justice decisions will be based on reliable information at every stage of the process, with the government forced to meet far higher standards than the accused along the way. By placing a premium on protecting the rights of individuals, some guilty defendants may go free simply because the state has not met its high burden of proving guilt "beyond a reasonable doubt."[19]

The American system of criminal justice can be characterized as a tug-of-war between both these models, with no-name, relatively run-of-the-mill, usually poor defendants generally falling into the crime control "assembly line," whereas bigger-name, higher-profile, and wealthy defendants are far more likely to experience the due process model.

Critics of the criminal justice system charge that racial disparities have become the norm, with African Americans, Hispanic Americans, and other racial and ethnic minorities entering the system in numbers disproportionate to their representation in the general population.[20] They point also to the controversy surrounding police use of racial profiling, in which African Americans in particular are often stopped and interrogated simply because they possess the same racial characteristics as others who have committed crimes. Defenders of the system contend that racial minorities commit a larger percentage of crimes, perhaps a product of their relative economic disadvantage in society as a whole. That defense does not take into account alarming statistical trends showing that race figures directly into sentencing decisions.

For example, a famous 1990 study demonstrated that killers of whites in Georgia were 4.3 times more likely to be sentenced to death than killers of African Americans.[21] Because racism remains a problem in American society as a whole, judicial sentencing and racial stereotyping may well be tainted by feelings of racism that lie below the surface.

Up through the 1980s, criminal justice policymaking mostly occurred within state and local governments. In recent decades, however, Congress has acted to criminalize and/or increase sentences for a host of unlawful activities at the federal level.[22] Passage of the federal Gun-Free School Zones Act of 1990 outlawing the possession of guns within a specified proximity of a school building, a 1996 federal carjacking statute, and federal crime bills that expand the death penalty to cover certain federal crimes are all representative of this modern policymaking trend.[23] Congress has also been actively involved in the "war on drugs," passing numerous statutes outlawing the possession, use, and sale of certain illegal drugs. As a result, federal drug laws today account for over 30 percent of all drug offenders sentences.

An African American man being arrested. Racial profiling authorizes the stopping and interrogating members of racial minorities simply because their racial characteristics are similar to those of others who have committed crimes.

Occasionally Congress has overstepped its constitutional bounds in passing crime laws—in 1995 the Supreme Court struck down the Gun-Free Schools Zones Act as an unconstitutional usurpation of each state's prerogative to criminalize acts that take place solely within its jurisdiction.[24] Additionally, many of these federal laws duplicate existing state criminal laws. Still, given the public's favorable response to such laws, it is tough to imagine Congress withdrawing from this area of policymaking any time soon.

THE WELFARE STATE AND PROGRAMS FOR THE POOR

The term **welfare state** refers to a social system in which the state assumes a considerable degree of responsibility for citizens in matters of health care, employment, education, and retirement income. In its ideal form, a welfare state is expected to do more than merely guarantee a minimum level of subsistence in these matters; thus welfare states do not simply ensure a "safety net" for their citizens. (Naturally, these welfare states require higher levels of taxation than do more strictly capitalist systems.) The actual amount of welfare provided varies widely from nation to nation. Nearly all modern welfare states sit somewhere on a spectrum between pure **capitalism** (an economic system in which all or most of the means of production are privately owned under competitive conditions) and **socialism** (an economic system in which all or most of the means of production are owned by the community as a whole). Most welfare states have this much in common: they ensure that whatever welfare is provided is done so in universal fashion—in short, they tend to cover every person who meets welfare standards as a matter of right, rather than discretion.

The form of the modern welfare state dates back to the late nineteenth and early twentieth centuries. Germany under Chancellor Otto von Bismarck in the 1880s was the first nation in history to provide social insurance for its citizens.[25] In the early part of the twentieth century, Scandinavian countries were among the first to establish comprehensive welfare states—Sweden, for example, provided for child care, maternity and paternity leave, a ceiling on health care costs, free education at all levels, and retirement pensions. Many other Western European nations, including Ireland, Britain, and France, soon followed suit.

welfare state: Social system in which the state assumes a considerable degree of responsibility for citizens in matters of health care, employment, education, and retirement income.

capitalism: Economic system in which all or most of the means of production are privately owned under competitive conditions.

socialism: Economic system in which all or most of the means of production are owned by the community as a whole.

Long lines of people in New York City waited patiently for handouts during the Great Depression.

Fiercely protective of its capitalist origins, the U.S. government vigorously resisted assuming broad welfare state functions up until the 1930s, when the Great Depression exposed the harsh realities that unfettered capitalism can occasionally impose on the masses. Still, though Franklin Delano Roosevelt's New Deal is accurately credited with establishing the modern welfare state in America with its provisions for assisting the poor, his program actually featured few express provisions that directly ensured better education or health care for the masses, to name just two examples.[26] Even the Social Security Act of 1935, which established the Social Security system, was billed at the time not as a welfare program, but as a system of forced savings that would benefit only those in wage-earning families. It wasn't until the Great Society legislation of the mid-1960s that the federal government actively expanded the reach of the welfare state to include the provision of education, health care, and assistance to the poor.

Compared with other Western democracies in Europe and elsewhere that have embraced the welfare state on behalf of their citizens, the U.S. welfare state model is far less comprehensive and ambitious. Why the reluctance to go further? Welfare continues to be seen as "taking something" without contributing in return, so the notion of a state built around this premise remains objectionable to many Americans. Indeed, many Americans (and the political parties that curry favor with them) view welfare recipients as going against the grain of the work ethic, and thus getting a "free ride" based on the efforts of others. Although the miserable conditions associated with the Great Depression went a long way toward debunking the belief that the poor are always responsible for their own plight, Americans are still reluctant to see the federal government install a system of social welfare similar to what has been established in many European democracies.

Poverty has always been a problem in the United States, but until the middle part of the twentieth century, true welfare programs—defined as those programs that maintain the economic and physical well-being of society's poorest members—were primarily the responsibility of local communities and private organizations, including churches. The federal government acted only when circumstances seemed to dictate a potential crisis: for example, the Freedmen's Bureau provided rudimentary education and work opportunities for former slaves in the late 1860s and early 1870s; similarly, industrial abuses led to limited federal aid to poor mothers and children during the initial decades of the twentieth century. But in general, public resistance to a substantial federal welfare role held fast, at least up until the 1930s.

The Great Depression created a significant change in attitudes about welfare programs and led directly to broader government involvement. New Deal programs such as the Works Progress Administration and the Federal Emergency Relief Administration provided public jobs and emergency aid. Aid to Dependent Children (later called Aid to Families with Dependent Children, or AFDC) supplemented existing state programs by providing money to poor single mothers unable to work and partake in federal jobs programs.[27] More a public charity than an entitlement, AFDC money went to the extremely poor, and its benefits were often below prevailing minimum wages.

President Lyndon Johnson's Great Society program of the mid-1960s substantially expanded federal welfare programs. As part of his administration's "war on poverty," a federal food stamps program was initiated in 1964; the federal government also gave money to community service programs such as Legal Aid, medical clinics in poor neighborhoods, and the Head Start preschool education program for disadvantaged children. The **Medicare** program was created to provide health insurance for the elderly in general, whereas **Medicaid** became the first federal program to provide limited health care services to the poor.[28] Mismanagement slowed the progress of the war on poverty; the outbreak of riots and crimes in the inner cities—where much of the antipoverty legislation was targeted—further doomed legislative support for the expansion of such programs.

Once established into law, the welfare reforms of the mid-twentieth century were not free of controversy. Activists complained that AFDC benefits were not high enough to bring poor families out of poverty, trapping them in their economic plights for the foreseeable future. Additionally, approximately 25 percent of those defined as poor by federal law were still not receiving any form of federal benefits under the current program. Conservatives were also frustrated, charging that the incentives of the welfare system encouraged poor mothers to stay home without actively seeking employment, or even to have more children as a means of increasing government payments.

As a presidential candidate in 1992, Bill Clinton promised to "end welfare as we know it"; four years later, with the Republicans firmly in control of Congress, President Clinton was presented with legislation that held him to those very words. In 1996, Congress passed and Clinton signed into law the Personal Responsibility and Work Opportunity Reconciliation Act, which replaced AFDC with the TANF (Temporary Assistance to Needy Families) program. TANF devolved much of the former AFDC program back to the states, scaled back the food stamps program, and required welfare recipients to work, or at least actively look for work. The law also imposed a five-year limit on receiving benefits, overthrowing the previous system of providing indefinite benefits to those who met federal eligibility requirements.[29] In its first few years, the program succeeded in decreasing state caseloads by as much as 50 percent. Still, critics charged that it penalizes the truly needy; additionally, because "last hired" individuals tend to be the first ones fired during more difficult times, many have returned to welfare in the last 15 years, increasing caseloads for state governments to manage.

Medicare: Federal program that provides health insurance for the elderly.

Medicaid: Federal program that provides limited health care services to the poor.

The Social Security System

Social Security has frequently been called the "third rail" of American politics—any politician who touches it is sure to get shocked into submission.[30] The specter of millions of older Americans living in poverty as a result of the Great Depression led to the establishment of Social Security in 1935 as a sort of national pension system. The system was originally intended to be a self-sufficient "pay-as-you-go" system: workers and their employers would pay dedicated Social Security taxes, and these funds would then be disbursed in the form of pension payments to current retirees. During its early years the Social Security system often ran surpluses, because the ratio of workers to beneficiaries remained high. In the 1950s, Congress even broadened the system's coverage and raised minimum benefits to lower-income contributors.

Unfortunately, the severe economic strains of the 1970s, including high inflation, substantially eroded the Social Security trust fund, which contains securities redeemable to make payments to retirees whenever contributions are not sufficient to pay benefits. Minor reforms have been implemented to increase Social Security taxes and raise the retirement age, shoring up the trust fund for the time being. Still, some economists fear that the Social Security system will become weaker in the years ahead, as a greater percentage of the disproportionately large baby boom generation (those born between 1946 and 1964) reaches retirement age during the first decade of the twenty-first century.[31] By the year 2025, when all baby boomers are eligible for Social Security, the system may face serious solvency issues. In fact, substantial numbers of

Fact or Fiction?

Through the use of tax incentives, the federal government encourages people to put aside their own savings for retirement, rather than simply have them rely on social security.

Fact.

Encouraged by tax breaks, millions today invest a substantial portion of their savings in the stock market through the use of tax-favored retirement vehicles such as individual retirement accounts (IRAs) and 401(k) plans.

THE MORE THINGS CHANGE,
THE MORE THINGS STAY THE SAME

States as "Laboratories of Democracy" That Point the Way for National Domestic Policy

State legislators who sponsor innovative new programs in their respective jurisdictions may—if the programs are successful—start a movement of similar initiatives in other states. They may also offer a model of sorts for the federal government to enact a similar program on a national scale some time later. In this way, state governments and their laws can fulfill an even greater purpose in a democracy: As Supreme Court Justice Louis Brandeis argued in 1932, states provide the nation as whole with true "laboratories for democracy." Consider two such laboratories in action:

In 1930, with a severe economic crisis bearing down on states across the country, New York Governor Franklin Delano Roosevelt urged passage of legislation to provide so-called "old-age pensions." Such laws had been practically nonexistent before the onset of the Great Depression; yet 30 separate states passed some form of elderly assistance legislation between 1930 and 1935, including legislatures in California, Massachusetts, and New York. Thus when President Franklin Roosevelt proposed the national system of Social Security legislation in 1935, he was able to learn and borrow from states' experiences, including his own. Unlike failed programs in other states, California and Massachusetts did not require counties to "opt in" to the program to participate; all counties were enrolled automatically. Roosevelt also learned that many of the failed state programs had trouble enrolling older citizens who were reluctant to "go on welfare"; the more successful state policies billed themselves instead as variations on employee savings programs. Accordingly, the national Social Security program passed in 1935 was mandatory, and it too would be financed by payroll taxes, distinguishing it further from more traditional welfare programs. The state governments had performed a valuable service with their experimental policies, pointing the way to a national program that survives nearly 85 years later. Roosevelt must have been especially proud, as the Old Age Pension Act of New York that he had signed into law as governor of that state helped pave the road to the Social Security Act he signed into law as president just a few years later.

In 2010, the Obama administration settled for half a loaf rather than no loaf at all. Although the comprehensive health care policy passed by Congress and signed into law on March 23, 2010, significantly expanded health care coverage to uninsured individuals across the country, it stopped short of the "universal coverage" Obama and Democratic leaders had once advocated. Supporters of universal health care coverage should have been forewarned: progressive state legislatures had debated the merits of their own health care initiatives in recent decades, and a handful had even made significant strides, but none had succeeded in guaranteeing complete universal coverage. Hawaii was the true pioneer in this regard: in the 1970s its legislature enacted a law that mandated employer-based health insurance for all employees not covered by collective bargaining. Later, in 1989, the Aloha state went a step further, subsidizing insurance coverage for Hawaiians unable to pay. Even so, 5 percent of Hawaii's population remained uninsured. Five thousand miles away in Boston, Massachusetts, the state legislature in 2006 passed legislation requiring all residents to purchase health insurance or face stiff legal penalties. Once again, however, ambiguous

Massachusetts Governor Mitt Romney, flanked by state leaders (including U.S. Senator Edward M. Kennedy), signs into law the state's new comprehensive health care legislation in April 2006.

THE MORE THINGS CHANGE,
THE MORE THINGS STAY THE SAME

States as "Laboratories of Democracy" That Point the Way for National Domestic Policy (continued)

definitions of the term *affordable* meant that at least some Massachusetts residents would continue to be uninsured. Several state governments had expanded health care coverage, but they had failed to enact universal coverage for their populations. Like its state forbearers, the national government's health care reform plan similarly expanded coverage for millions, but it too failed to provide universal coverage.

For Critical Thinking and Discussion

1. Are some states so different in culture and character from the nation as a whole that they make poor "laboratories" for experimentation? In considering national legislation, can we really learn much from Hawaii, Alaska, or Wyoming, to name just a few places?

2. How can the federal government do more to encourage state-level policy innovations?

---

baby boomers are not all that optimistic about their prospects of receiving Social Security: in one poll conducted for the AARP (formerly the American Association of Retired Persons), just 54 percent felt very or somewhat confident that Social Security would even be around when they retire.[32]

Social Security thus represents a conundrum for politicians: many recognize the need for large-scale reform of the system, but public opinion and interest groups that favor the current system have proven just as stubborn. The broad political support Social Security enjoys is based largely on the premise that the system is not simply another form of welfare; although lower-income contributors do receive some breaks, rich and poor employees alike pay into the system and receive its benefits.

Because of the concern over the long-run solvency of the Social Security system, many future retirees have been forced to adjust their savings strategies to plan for a future without any guarantee of Social Security. Traditionally, government employees and people who work for larger companies or organizations have enjoyed conventional pension plans that guarantee a monthly benefit after retirement. Unfortunately, employees normally have no control over the investment of pension funds—many employees learn that their company's pension fund has been depleted by unwise investments only after the damage has been done. Additionally, most pension plans provide significant benefits only for employees who work at a particular organization for the long haul—perhaps for 25 or 30 years. In an increasingly mobile economy such as ours, fewer and fewer workers fit this description.

Through the use of tax incentives, the federal government has recently played a role in encouraging people to put aside extra savings for retirement. As a result, millions today directly invest a substantial portion of their savings in the stock market through the use of tax-favored retirement vehicles such as individual retirement accounts (IRAs) and 401(k) plans. Not only do such vehicles help provide an extra retirement cushion, they also have helped to ensure that a stream of investment capital continues to flow into publicly traded companies on the stock market, which in turn contributes to the well-being of the economy.

HEALTH CARE POLICY

The U.S. health care system differs in important ways from the public-run systems found in other modern industrial nations. France, Great Britain, and other European democracies have all adopted systems of **universal health care**, in which full access to health care is provided to citizens at government expense. In the United States, health care has remained a privately operated activity, in which patients secure health care insurance and enter into relationships with physicians largely outside of government control. The **Patient Protection and Affordable Care Act of 2010 (PPACA)** and subsequent legislation passed by Congress (most notably the Health Care and Education Reconciliation Act of 2010) features an "individual mandate" which penalizes most citizens who do not obtain health care insurance. Still, the recent legislation does not provide any form of public-sponsored health care plans (other than "health insurance exchanges" that organize the marketplace for the purchase of private health insurance in more cost-efficient ways), and federal laws do not assign doctors to patients. Consequently, Americans still have more choice in doctors and facilities than do citizens in most other parts of the world.

Ensuring that society's oldest and poorest citizens receive adequate health care was a primary concern of U.S. health care laws even before the 2010 legislative reforms. Since 1965, the Medicare program has provided health insurance as a Social Security benefit to retirees; amendments to the program in 2003 limited the costs of prescription drugs for seniors. More recently, the federal government extended the reach of Medicare to small, rural hospitals and facilities. The poor sometimes receive health insurance through grants to the states as part of the Medicaid program; the PPACA expanded Medicaid eligibility as well. Beginning in 2014, persons with income levels up to 133 percent of the poverty line will qualify for coverage. Additionally, federal legislation dictates the rules to be followed by **health maintenance organizations (HMOs)**, which are prepaid group practice arrangements that attempt to limit costs through flat monthly rates.[33] Yet the defining characteristic of health care in the United States—patients' reliance on private, voluntary health plans—continues, with government incentives and penalties playing a major role in the process.

Significant criticisms of the health care system in the United States remain. Most of those who do have health insurance receive it through group plans offered by their employers, and the 2010 legislation did little to reverse that reality. Thus when employees change jobs, their health insurance coverage is normally disrupted. Additionally, in 2009 one in seven Americans under age 65 still did not have health insurance. Although the PPACA is expected to significantly lower this figure, it will not guarantee universal coverage by any means.

Finally, health insurance is not the same as actual health care. Many continue to be hindered by a lack of access to primary care: more than 20 million people in the United States live in rural areas or inner-city neighborhoods that have a shortage of physicians to meet their basic health care needs.[34] Rural residents are particularly disadvantaged; according to the U.S. Department of Health and Human Services, residents of rural areas maintain the highest death rates for unintentional injuries generally and for motor-vehicle injuries specifically, due in large part to the shortage of physicians in such areas. Thus health care delivery practices will continue to be a problem, no matter how far government extends the scope of health care insurance coverage.

Domestic policy in the United States has been a source of continued frustration for many. This nation's status as one of the richest nations in the world over the past century might imply a responsibility on the part of the government to spread around those riches so that each person is assured at least a minimum level of subsistence and welfare. At the same time, the U.S. capitalist system tends to foster a culture of "pull yourself up by your bootstraps," which is at odds with policy efforts leading to the systematic provision of goods and services to needy people. In the modern era, the U.S. government has attempted to strike a balance between these two positions, to the satisfaction of few. Prior to the New Deal, the government's role in providing social welfare was quite limited. Since the 1930s, and especially since the 1960s, the government's social welfare functions have increased substantially. Of course, innovative social welfare policies do not emerge overnight. The controversy that surrounds governmental welfare schemes often invites as much resistance as it does cheerleading, and presidents must learn to scale back their dreams to ensure some form of victory in the short term. Theodore Roosevelt's attempt to establish landmark environmental conservation policies met with resistance in Congress; his administration managed to create 150 million acres of national forest reserves and a national forest service to look out for them, but little else. President Barack Obama entered office in 2009 with hopes of passing comprehensive health care reform featuring universal coverage and a government-run public option; by the time the smoke cleared in March 2010, his administration had managed to transform the system in significant ways, yet universal coverage and a "public option" were nowhere to be found in the final legislation. Roosevelt and Obama—even with a generally supportive Congress on their respective sides—had to scale back their goals . . . or risk achieving nothing at all. Clearly Charles Lindblom's "science of muddling through" is a policymaking process for the patient only, even in the case of policy reforms that are considered groundbreaking in many respects.

FROM YOUR PERSPECTIVE

Realistic Options for National Service

In the early 1960s, young people in the United States who wanted to help change the world considered joining the Peace Corps, a government agency charged with "increasing international mutual understanding." More than 200,000 have taken up that call, working for the Peace Corps in 139 different countries. But for all the opportunities the Peace Corps provided for international service, it lacked an outlet to serve the United States at home. That changed in 1993 when the National Community and Service Trust Act created AmeriCorps. Since its creation, AmeriCorps has sent over a quarter of a million young people to communities in the United States to support the start-up of innovative new national programs, including City Year, Public Allies, and Teach for America. It also brought vital resources to established programs, including the Boys and Girls Club, Big Brothers and Big Sisters, Justicecorps, and the American Red Cross.

Like any government program, AmeriCorps has its share of critics. Some have alleged that the program diverts young people participating in the program from attaining higher levels of education on their own behalf or that it delays the start of their careers. Critics also charge that AmeriCorps sends the wrong message by implying that volunteers should be paid for community service work (full-time members who complete their service earn a Segal AmeriCorps Education Award of $4,725).

© Jim West/Alamy

A volunteer for Habitat for Humanity pitches in to rebuild a house in New Orleans in the wake of Hurricane Katrina.

For Critical Thinking and Discussion

1. Would you consider joining AmeriCorps or some other form of national service before embarking on your own career? Why or why not?

2. Should AmeriCorps "volunteers" be paid even a minimal scholarship amount? How would such payments influence the makeup and character of students attracted to the program?

SUMMARY: PUTTING IT ALL TOGETHER

AN OVERVIEW OF THE POLICYMAKING PROCESS

- The policymaking process generally unfolds in five stages: a recognition/definition stage, a formulation stage, an adoption stage, an implementation stage, and an evaluation stage.
- Bureaucrats in administrative agencies, interest groups (including think tanks), Congress, and the president are all actively involved throughout the process.

Test Yourself on This Section

1. The stage of the policymaking process where the proposed policy assumes the authority of law is the
   a. definition stage.
   b. formulation stage.
   c. adoption stage.
   d. implementation stage.

2. The federal bureaucracy is primarily responsible for which stage of the policymaking process?
   a. definition stage
   b. formulation stage
   c. adoption stage
   d. implementation stage

3. What are the various stages of policymaking process, and do they oversimplify the actuahl process in practice?

THEORIES AND PRACTICE IN FISCAL POLICY

- Fiscal policy is concerned with the raising of revenue through taxation and the spending of whatever revenue has been generated. The federal budget, which lays out a comprehensive plan of government spending, is the primary means by which government carries out fiscal policy.
- Laissez-faire capitalism, which favors minimal government interference in the economy, dominated the U.S. economy for much of the eighteenth and nineteenth centuries; however, beginning in the 1930s, the government began to apply the principles of Keynesian economic theory, which favors government spending during difficult economic times.
- During the past quarter century, some presidents have turned to supply-side economics, which favors cutting taxes as way of increasing economic productivity, whereas others have returned to Keynesian economic theory once again.
- The most significant indicators of U.S. economic success or failure include the nation's gross domestic product, the consumer price index, the unemployment rate, the budget deficit, and the Dow Jones Industrial Stock Average.
- Today's budget-making process is dominated by the president, who proposes an initial budget that will serve as the framework for all budget negotiations. Congress responds initially through its appropriations and budget committees, which in turn formulate budget proposals based on their own projections for future revenue. Occasionally Congress and the president struggle to find a compromise, and in some extreme cases the federal government has been forced to shut down until middle ground can be reached.
- Taxation policies may be redistributive (benefiting the poor at the expense of the rich) or distributive (promoting the interests of all economic classes equally).
- A large percentage of taxpayer funds goes to mandatory spending (usually in the form of entitlements such as Medicare and Social Security) that is unaffected by annual budget decisions. Discretionary spending categories include defense, education, and the environment.

Test Yourself on This Section

1. The fiscal theory that favors stimulus spending by government as a way to spark economic activity is
   a. supply-side economics.
   b. Keynesian economics.
   c. laissez-faire economics.
   d. Reaganomics.

2. The total money value of all goods and services produced in the United States in a given one-year period is the
   a. gross domestic product.
   b. consumer price index.
   c. consumer confidence index.
   d. Dow Jones industrials.

3. A tax that exacts a larger percentage of income from lower-wage earners than higher-wage earners is a

    a. progressive tax.

    b. regressive tax.

    c. flat tax.

    d. unfair tax.

4. Distinguish between federal "mandatory" spending and "discretionary" spending, and give an example of each.

THEORIES AND PRACTICE IN MONETARY POLICY

- The Federal Reserve supervises the nation's monetary policy by setting the discount rate that its Federal Reserve Banks may charge member banks to receive loans and by determining the minimum assets banks must keep in hand, called the reserve requirements. When the Federal Reserve lowers the discount rate, it may stimulate economic investment, but it risks setting off higher inflation rates.

Test Yourself on This Section

1. Which of the following determines monetary policy?

    a. Office of Management and Budget

    b. Department of Treasury

    c. Congressional Budget Office

    d. Federal Reserve Board

2. The minimum liquid assets that banks must keep on hand to back customer loans is called the

    a. discount rate.

    b. open market mandate.

    c. savings rate.

    d. reserve requirement.

3. How is the Federal Reserve designed to operate independent of partisan politics?

THE NATURE AND PRACTICE OF CRIME POLICY

- Democratic governments must strike a delicate balance between maintaining public order and protecting individual freedom. Especially severe and strict forms of law enforcement would make citizens safe, but with a very high cost to taxpayers and possibly some loss of individual freedom as well.

- Though criminal justice policymaking has been an area of law reserved primarily for state governments, the federal government has recently become more proactive in legislating such areas as gun control, drug trafficking, and carjacking.

Test Yourself on This Section

1. The model of criminal justice policymaking that emphasizes rights of the accused is the

    a. crime control model.

    b. First Amendment model.

    c. due process model.

    d. equal protection model.

2. What are the most common criticisms leveled at the criminal justice system today?

THE WELFARE STATE AND PROGRAMS FOR THE POOR

- The welfare state is a social system in which the state assumes a considerable degree of responsibility for citizens in matters of health care, employment, education, and retirement income. The actual amount of welfare provided varies widely from nation to nation. Most modern welfare states sit somewhere on a spectrum between pure capitalism and pure socialism.

- The United States generally resisted any meaningful attempt to provide welfare benefits to all citizens until the 1930s. In response to the severe economic depression, President Franklin D. Roosevelt proposed—and Congress passed—a "New Deal" of programs that provided certain welfare services, such as Social Security.

- President Lyndon Johnson's Great Society programs of the mid-1960s further advanced welfare programs in the United States, introducing such programs as Medicare and Medicaid.

Test Yourself on This Section

1. Which of the following is true of the Medicaid program?
   a. Its funding comes exclusively from the federal government.
   b. People become eligible for benefits at age 65.
   c. It is a health insurance system.
   d. It provides money for health services for those in poverty.

2. The 1996 Welfare Reform Law that replaced AFDC with TANF did which of the following?
   a. placed a five-year limit on welfare payments
   b. required welfare recipients to work
   c. scaled back the food stamps program
   d. all of the above

3. What distinguishes a capitalist economic system from a socialist economic system?

THE SOCIAL SECURITY SYSTEM

- Social Security is a retirement benefit program for members of the U.S. workforce. Though it has provided retirement income for millions of retirees since 1935, many economists predict that the system will eventually be forced to pay out significantly more than it brings in.
- Numerous proposals to privatize Social Security have been suggested; however, to date the U.S. Congress has enacted no major policy changes, and the crisis on Wall Street in September 2008 put off all discussion of privatization for the time being.
- The U.S. government encourages private retirement investing through tax-free investment vehicles such as IRAs and 401(k) plans.

Test Yourself on This Section

1. The Social Security system was created under the administration of which president?
   a. Franklin Delano Roosevelt
   b. Lyndon Baines Johnson
   c. Ronald Reagan
   d. Bill Clinton

2. The Social Security system is funded through
   a. payroll taxes on employers and employees.
   b. taxes on individuals earning over $1 million annually.
   c. corporate income taxes.
   d. taxes on imported goods.

3. Beyond Social Security, what programs has Congress put in place to encourage American workers to save money for retirement?

HEALTH CARE POLICY

- The U.S. health care system contrasts sharply with systems found in other Western democracies that feature universal health care.
- Criticisms of the U.S. system focus on limitations on access and excessively high costs. The 2010 federal legislation addressed various inequities in the insurance industry, but it did not address these access-to-care issues.

Test Yourself on This Section

1. The element of the 2010 health care reform laws that requires the purchase of health insurance is known as the
   a. universal requirement.
   b. individual mandate.
   c. single-payer duty.
   d. public option.

2. What are HMOs, and how do they control health care costs?

KEY TERMS

budget authority (p. 434)
budget deficit (p. 428)
budget surplus (p. 428)
capitalism (p. 439)
consumer price index (CPI) (p. 427)
crime control model (p. 438)
discount rate (p. 436)
discretionary spending (p. 434)
distributive tax policies (p. 431)
due process model (p. 438)
Federal Reserve Board (p. 435)
Federal Reserve System (p. 435)
fiscal policy (p. 426)
flat tax (p. 432)

gross domestic product (GDP) (p. 427)
health maintenance organizations (HMOs) (p. 444)
inflation (p. 426)
Keynesian economic theory (p. 426)
laissez-faire economics (p. 426)
mandatory spending (p. 434)
Medicaid (p. 441)
Medicare (p. 441)
monetary policy (p. 435)
national debt (p. 428)
open market operations (p. 436)
outlays (p. 434)

Patient Protection and Affordable Care Act of 2010 (PPACA) (p. 444)
progressive tax (p. 432)
public policy (p. 424)
recession (p. 426)
redistributive tax policies (p. 431)
regressive tax (p. 432)
reserve requirement (p. 436)
social policy (p. 424)
socialism (p. 439)
supply-side economics (p. 426)
universal health care (p. 444)
welfare state (p. 439)

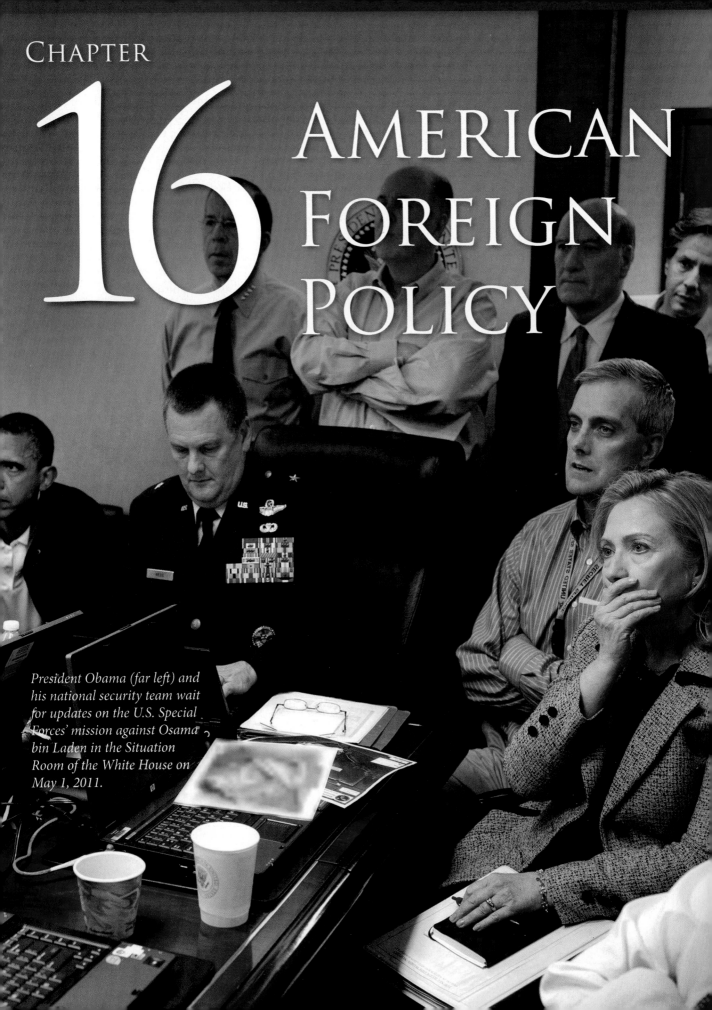

16

AMERICAN FOREIGN POLICY

President Obama (far left) and his national security team wait for updates on the U.S. Special Forces' mission against Osama bin Laden in the Situation Room of the White House on May 1, 2011.

LEARNING OBJECTIVES

THE CONSTITUTIONAL FRAMEWORK OF AMERICAN FOREIGN POLICY

- Discuss the formal powers of Congress and the president to conduct foreign policy under the Constitution

THE ROOTS OF AMERICAN FOREIGN POLICY

- Trace the history of U.S. foreign policy from American independence to the present
- Compare different approaches to foreign policy, including isolationism, pacifism, and expansionism
- Describe America's approach to the Cold War, including theories of containment
- Discuss current foreign policy in the Middle East, including the ongoing war on terrorism

THE STRUCTURE OF AMERICAN FOREIGN POLICYMAKING

- Explain how foreign and military policy is conducted by the president, the State Department, the National Security Council, and various intelligence agencies
- Describe how members of Congress, interest groups, and public opinion influence foreign policy

FOREIGN POLICY DILEMMAS FOR THE TWENTY-FIRST CENTURY

- Define the preemption doctrine and explain how it has been used to justify aggressive military actions in the Middle East
- Evaluate the state of Russian–U.S. relations, the nature of U.S. foreign aid, and the role of the United Nations

U.S. foreign policy comprises all of the nation's activities directed at conducting relations with other countries, including military operations and diplomatic activities. The establishment of trade practices, the entering of treaties, and the decision to lend arms to another country in battle are but some of the many elements that make up the nation's extensive foreign policy apparatus. Unlike other types of government authority that are subject to frequent jurisdictional squabbles, few dispute the federal government's status as the sole authority in charge of U.S. foreign policy. Of course with that undisputed power comes significant responsibility and accountability. In fact, the list of presidential administrations that have seen their domestic policy successes overshadowed (if not outright negated) by foreign policy failures is a long one indeed. No president can afford to ignore the importance that Americans place on the country's leading role in the world as an economic and military superpower.

REUTERS/White House/Pete Souza /LANDOV

The **"Connections App"** is an interactive web app that helps you better understand the relationship between historical and current events with basic concepts.

1965   1970   1975   1980   1985

1975

Then

Left: The evacuation of CIA station personnel by a U.S. military helicopter on April 29, 1975, the day before Saigon fell to North Vietnamese forces. Right: The family of Major Wesley D. Schierman greets him upon his return from Vietnam in 1973.

Source: Left: © Bettmann/CORBIS, Right: Bettmann/CORBIS

Several presidents have faced the unfortunate reality that "wars are easy to start, but impossible to finish." Consider the challenge facing President Gerald R. Ford in 1975. Ten years earlier, when Ford was in his first year as House minority leader, President Lyndon Johnson committed to a vast expansion of troops for the Vietnam conflict. By 1973 Congress had stopped funding the war effort and President Nixon signed the Paris Accords declaring a ceasefire in Vietnam. Still, it was left to Ford, who became president in 1974 after Nixon resigned, to manage the difficult politics of withdrawing the last American troops out of South Vietnam the following year. Although still relatively new to the presidency, Ford faced a constellation of factors that threatened U.S. interests in that region at that time: (1) In addition to cutting off military aid, Congress dramatically cut all foreign aid to South Vietnam in 1974, with plans for a total cut-off in 1976; (2) North Vietnamese offensives continued after the ceasefire, threatening lands tenuously held by the South; and (3) rising worldwide oil prices had rendered South Vietnam's military advantage in tanks and armored cars all but useless. Still, the American public had soured on the conflict and offered no support for continuing the battle, even if it meant the capital of South Vietnam would fall to the communists. Thus what started as an orderly evacuation of U.S. troops and foreign nationals quickly devolved into an atmosphere of desperation. When Saigon fell for good on April 30, 1975, America suffered a psychological defeat that would haunt its political leaders for decades afterward.

2011

Now

The last American military convoy to depart Iraq drives through Camp Virginia after crossing over the border into Kuwait on December 18, 2011.

Source: Mario Tama/Getty Images

Upon taking office in 2009, President Barack Obama faced the difficult challenge of executing his promise to end the war in Iraq. The war had been launched under the order of President George W. Bush six years earlier in an attempt to thwart Iraqi dictator Saddam Hussein's development of weapons of mass destruction and of harboring and supporting terrorist elements in Al Qaeda. Though neither of those accusations proved to be indisputably correct, the invasion did result in the deposition of Hussein and the occupation of Iraq amid widespread violence among sectarian groups and a civil war. By 2009 when Obama became president, Americans had grown tired of the long, costly battle. In February of 2009, he announced an 18-month withdrawal window for all but 50,000 U.S. troops, who would remain in the country to advise and train Iraqi security forces. The Obama administration feared that a complete withdrawal would lead to increased violence from insurgents; but the Iraqi government refused to extend any further immunity to U.S. forces who killed civilians, and that effectively ended all talk of an extension for limited troop deployments. Thus the objective of full withdrawal of all U.S. troops was finally achieved on December 18, 2011. An upsurge of violence immediately followed, offering a sobering reminder of the inherent fragility of American gains in the region.

- Congress must approve of the use of the U.S. military before the president can deploy troops abroad.

- The U.S. Congress never ratified the peace treaty to end World War I.

- In the event of a terrorist threat within U.S. borders, the Defense Department is primarily responsible for formulating a comprehensive response to the threat and recovery plan.

THE CONSTITUTIONAL FRAMEWORK OF AMERICAN FOREIGN POLICY

Two of the three original cabinet departments created by Congress in 1789 were the Department of State and the Department of War, a sign of just how important these two functions would be to the young nation. Article I of the Constitution gives Congress the exclusive power to declare war, raise armies, punish maritime crimes, and regulate foreign commerce. Under Article II, the president is empowered as commander in chief to conduct the course of war. The Founders' intent in separating the power to command from the power to fund the military was to check the war power from being abused. The Constitution also gives the president the authority to negotiate treaties and to appoint and receive ambassadors.

Perhaps the most basic elements of foreign policy during the eighteenth and nineteenth centuries were the treaties the United States entered into with foreign nations. Because the Senate alone was vested with the authority to ratify such treaties (by a two-thirds vote), many expected that this small legislative body (there were just 26 senators at the outset) would exert a strong influence over the nation's foreign policy.

Within the next two centuries, control over foreign affairs, including the power to make war, would shift from Congress to the White House. Fundamental changes in America's role in world affairs during the twentieth century spurred this transfer of power. America's ascendancy to superpower status in the early part of the twentieth century led to U.S. involvement in world affairs. The presidency was well suited to respond to these new demands on America's attention; within the three branches of government, the single chief executive is best positioned to respond to sudden changes in circumstances around the globe in a quick and forceful manner. Unlike Congress, the president can use the "bully pulpit" of the office to communicate policies and generate support for the administration's goals. Highly activist presidents, including Theodore Roosevelt, Woodrow Wilson, and Franklin Delano Roosevelt, capitalized on these assets by communicating frequently with world leaders and their own publics on pressing affairs around the world.

Although the Constitution appears to give Congress primary authority over foreign and military affairs, the large and often unwieldy Congress has proven no match for modern presidents on the world stage. Political scientist Aaron Wildavsky's **two presidencies theory** posits the existence of a more powerful presidency in foreign affairs and a more limited presidency in the domestic sphere. Of course the president's dominance over foreign affairs hasn't stopped Congress from at least trying to reassert its authority in this realm.

In 1973, with public opinion shifting against military involvement around the globe, Congress passed the **War Powers Resolution**, overriding President Richard Nixon's veto in the process. The resolution theoretically restricted the president's power to engage in war to instances in which Congress had declared war or specifically granted the president permission to use armed forces, or to cases where the nation was under attack. The resolution required the president to report to Congress whenever American forces were entered into hostilities and attain congressional permission to engage those forces for more than 60 days. Every president since Nixon has either evaded or ignored the War Powers Resolution, arguing that it unconstitutionally infringes on the president's war powers. In fact, no court to date has ever ruled definitively on whether the president must comply with the law's provisions.

With some exceptions, the rise of the president to become the key actor in foreign affairs was a twentieth-century development. Initially, the Founders' hopes for an American foreign policy built on consensus among the political branches of government were for the most part realized. But this new decision-making apparatus faced severe tests in the decades following the American Revolution.

THE ROOTS OF AMERICAN FOREIGN POLICY

As a new nation with a limited military, the United States was at first heavily dependent on maintaining good foreign relations to avoid disadvantageous military engagements. Fortunately, the great distance that separated America from Western European superpowers

two presidencies theory: Theory articulated by political scientist Aaron Wildavsky that posits the existence of a more powerful presidency in foreign affairs and a more limited presidency in the domestic sphere.

War Powers Resolution: Largely ignored congressional policy that restricts the president's power to engage in war except (1) when Congress has declared war, (2) when Congress has specifically granted the president permission to use armed forces, or (3) when the nation is under attack. The resolution further requires the president to report to Congress whenever American forces are entered into hostilities.

A napalm strike erupts in a fireball near U.S. soldiers in Vietnam in 1966.

provided a measure of protection from frequent threats and incursions. More than two centuries later, the nation's status as a military superpower affords it far more leverage in its relations with foreign powers. Still, with advances in communications and transportation effectively shrinking the size of the global community, the United States must expend considerable resources and energy to successfully navigate through an increasingly complex foreign policy landscape. American foreign policy has always stood front and center in the list of U.S. government priorities.

The Isolationist Tradition and the Monroe Doctrine

The successful transition of the former British colonies in America into an independent nation was the product of astute foreign policy initiatives by some high-profile figures. George Washington's Continental army struggled for victories throughout the war for American independence; American fortunes in the war were raised only after Benjamin Franklin helped convince France in 1778 to join the war on the side of the colonies. Indeed, many historians and analysts attribute the Americans' victory over Britain to this crucial Franco-American alliance, which provided the colonies with resources to threaten British ships off the waters near the Atlantic Coast. However, under the leadership of President George Washington, the newly formed United States of America set aside the alliance with France and declared formal neutrality when England and revolutionary France went to war in 1793. In his farewell address to the nation in 1796, Washington urged his fellow Americans to steer clear of permanent alliances of any kind.

During the nation's early years, the United States maintained a foreign policy marked by **isolationism**, defined as opposition to both (1) interventions in distant wars (that is, outside

Congress must approve of the use of the U.S. military before the president can deploy troops abroad.

Fiction.

Though the president cannot declare war, he can deploy troops abroad without permission from Congress. Even the War Powers Resolution, which is of questionable constitutionality, only requires that the president attain permission for such continued deployments after 60 days have passed.

isolationism: Foreign policy doctrine that opposes intervention in distant wars and involvement in permanent military alliances.

pacifism: Doctrine of foreign relations that refuses to sanction any military conflict and that opposes all war making.

Monroe Doctrine: U.S. foreign policy that proclaimed North and South America unavailable for future colonization by any European power and that declared that any such colonization would be viewed as an act of war on the United States.

the Western hemisphere) and (2) involvement in permanent military alliances. The policy of isolationism dominated America's foreign affairs for nearly a century and a half, preserving America's freedom to refuse to act until the very last minute, and in most cases allowing it to forgo intervention altogether. Isolationism is distinguished from **pacifism**, a policy that refuses to sanction *any* military conflict and opposes all war making. Consistent with its general policy of isolationism, during the nineteenth century the United States fought wars in lands that bordered the nation or lay within U.S. boundaries in 1812 (against Britain), in 1846 (against Mexico), and in 1898 (against Spain in the Caribbean). Finally, the policy of military isolationism did not mean complete isolation from the world's culture or commerce, as Americans enthusiastically learned from other nations and welcomed visitors and products from abroad throughout this period.

America's brand of military isolationism never applied to the Western hemisphere. On December 2, 1823, President James Monroe declared the nation's commitment to a foreign policy that would eventually become known as the **Monroe Doctrine**. Specifically, Monroe proclaimed that both North and South America should not be considered "as subjects for future colonization by any European power," and that the United States would consider any efforts by Europeans to colonize these areas "as dangerous to our peace and safety." The implications of the Monroe Doctrine were profound: America would consider any new colonization efforts on its side of the Atlantic Ocean as tantamount to an act of war against the United States. This doctrine did not cause much controversy for most of the nineteenth century. Yet the degree to which European nations actually deferred to the United States because of the doctrine (as opposed to deferring because it was in their interests to do so) is difficult for historians to assess.

With the rise of European imperialism at the end of the nineteenth century, the United States eventually took action on its own to invoke the Monroe Doctrine. In 1895, the United States intervened in a dispute between Great Britain and Venezuela over the boundaries between Venezuela and British Guiana (present-day Guyana). In the early twentieth century, the United States prevented European nations from interfering in the affairs of debt-ridden Latin American countries by taking over the struggling economies of the Dominican Republic (1907) and Nicaragua (1911). Concerned about German influence over the Republic of Haiti, the United States even occupied that small country in 1915. The United States also actively encouraged the revolt of Latin American nations against Spain in the early part of the twentieth century, even though Spanish possession of these territories predated the Monroe Doctrine.

Expansionism and the Birth of a Superpower

expansionism: Doctrine that favors a country expanding its own territory and influence.

manifest destiny: U.S. policy of the mid-nineteenth century that advocated acquiring lands and occupying the entire American continent from one ocean to the other.

U.S. opposition to further European colonization in the Western hemisphere helped the nation to establish itself as the preeminent power in the Americas. Meanwhile, the United States practiced a policy of expansionism on the North American continent. **Expansionism** is the doctrine of expanding the territory or economic influence of one's own country. The policy began as a systematic effort to pursue what many American officials viewed as the nation's defining ideology: its **manifest destiny** to acquire lands and occupy the entire continent from the Atlantic to the Pacific Ocean. America's purchase of the massive Louisiana Territory from the French in 1803 more than doubled the land size of the United States at the time. The federal government went on to annex Florida after conquering Spanish holdings there between 1817 and 1819. Resolution of border conflicts with Great Britain in the 1840s established the northeastern boundary of Maine and of the Oregon territory. The United States annexed the independent Republic of Texas in 1845, and following a successful war against Mexico in 1846–1848 gained all of present-day California, Nevada, and Utah and parts of present-day Arizona, New Mexico, Colorado, and Wyoming.

Adherence to isolationism in principle also did not preclude the United States from setting its imperial sights on territories in the Pacific Ocean and the Caribbean Sea. In the late 1890s, Congress annexed Hawaii around the same time that it fought the Spanish-American War to free Cuba from Spain. The United States gained possession of the Philippine Islands as a result of the Philippine–American War of 1898–1902. Although the United States mostly discontinued its quest for territorial acquisitions abroad after the turn of the century, it continued to play an active role in opposing the imperialist designs of other nations.

America's increasing willingness to intervene militarily in foreign affairs signaled a potential shift in the traditional balance of powers, as the United States increasingly found itself a major player on the world stage. Nevertheless, up until World War I the United States remained primarily separate from the rest of the world militarily. Even the outbreak of World War I in 1914 produced no immediate change in U.S. foreign policy; President Woodrow Wilson openly proclaimed U.S. neutrality in the

A cartoon satirizing President Theodore Roosevelt's approach to foreign policy: "Speak softly and carry a big stick."

dispute and between 1915 and 1917 continually attempted mediation among the warring parties. Only when those efforts to settle the war failed, and Germany began to relentlessly attack U.S. vessels in 1917, did America enter the war on the side of the Allies—Great Britain, France, Italy, and Russia.

By the end of World War I, the European Allies owed more than $11 billion to the United States, making America a creditor nation for the first time in its history. Other world powers looked to the United States for guidance and resources to help construct a new international order, and together with President Wilson, in 1919 they drafted the Treaty of Versailles, which established a system of reparations and called for the creation of a League of Nations, which was intended to arbitrate international disputes and thereby avoid future wars. Yet preferences for a policy of isolationism still ran strong throughout America. After an overconfident Wilson engaged in a series of political missteps in selling the Treaty of Versailles to the public, the Republican-controlled U.S. Senate balked at the risk that the League of Nations might force the U.S. president to engage in military action; the Senate wanted Wilson to modify those aspects of the League covenant, but he refused. Facing an unyielding president on the issue, the Senate voted against U.S. membership in the League, which thereafter proved ineffective in maintaining peace and preventing aggression and was eventually dissolved in 1946. Thus American isolationism continued to prevail in the years between the two world wars.

As a second world war approached in the late 1930s and early 1940s, President Franklin Roosevelt made clear where the sympathies of the U.S. government lay, first by utilizing a lend-lease program with Britain that supplied that country with arms at little or no cost, and later, by increasing economic pressures on the Japanese in the Pacific.[1] The Japanese attack on Pearl Harbor on December 7, 1941, propelled the United States into the war against Germany, Japan, and Italy.

U.S. involvement in World War II proved critical to the final outcome: American manpower and resources were an important component in the success of the D-Day invasion of France and much of Western Europe in 1944. The United States detonated two atomic bombs over Japan in August 1945, forcing the Japanese to surrender. After the war, the European victors looked to the United States again to help keep international peace. This time they were not disappointed, as they had been when the U.S. Senate refused to support the League of Nations three decades earlier. In 1945, the United States joined the newly created **United Nations (UN)**, an international organization formed to promote and maintain international security and peace.

After World War II, America's prevailing foreign policy changed from one marked by isolationism to one featuring **internationalism**—the United States now actively participated in a

Fact **or** *Fiction?*

The U.S. Congress never ratified the peace treaty to end World War I.

Fact.

The U.S. Senate voted against joining the League of Nations, a central provision of the peace treaty negotiated by Woodrow Wilson in Paris.

United Nations (UN): International organization formed after World War II to promote and maintain international security and peace.

internationalism: Doctrine that favors active participation of the nation in collective arrangements that secure the political independence and territorial boundaries of other countries.

process that collectively secured the political independence and territorial boundaries of other countries by a system of economic and military sanctions against aggressor nations. In fact, America went even further than other nations in this regard. The **Marshall Plan** (formally the European Recovery Program) introduced by Secretary of State George Marshall in 1947 provided $13 billion in loans to Western European countries whose economies had been ravaged by World War II. Some countries used the money to combat inflation or retire state debts; others (defeated Germany, Austria, and Italy among them) used the assistance to buy food. Proponents of the plan deemed it a humanitarian policy intended to alleviate suffering, whereas critics argued that the aid had a more strategic purpose: to increase European dependence on the United States and discourage potential new alliances with the Soviet Union.[2]

Out of the wreckage of World War II emerged two global military and political superpowers, the United States and the Soviet Union, locked in what would become a half-century-long struggle called the **Cold War**.[3] This conflict over ideological differences (the promotion of democracy by the United States versus the promotion of communism by the Soviet Union) lasted from 1945 until the dissolution of the Soviet Union in 1991 and was carried on by a variety of methods, including economic warfare, arms buildups, and tense diplomacy. Postwar leaders in the United States believed that the nation had fought in World War II to protect self-determination and open trade, and together with other Western European nations, including Great Britain and France, it formed military, political, and, at times, economic alliances. Formally created in 1949, the **North Atlantic Treaty Organization (NATO)** bound the United States to the military defense of Western Europe. Meanwhile, the Soviet Union in the late 1940s dominated its Eastern European neighbors, including Poland and Romania. In 1955, those nations and others within the Soviet sphere formed the **Warsaw Pact**. Germany, divided in two following World War II, was split between the two alliances, with West Germany as a model democratic nation in NATO, and East Germany serving as a western outpost for Soviet communism in the Warsaw Pact.

In 1947, President Harry Truman articulated the **Truman Doctrine**, which provided money and resources to sustaining noncommunist governments in areas strategically vital to the United States, such as the Mediterranean and the Middle East. American foreign policy during the Cold War generally adhered to a policy of **containment**—restricting Soviet power to its current geographical sphere and resisting any efforts to expand communist influence. When the Soviets in 1949 blockaded the city of Berlin (a West German city located entirely within Soviet-controlled East German territory), the United States airlifted supplies to the city for nearly a year. Aerial reconnaissance allowed the Cold War adversaries to keep a more careful eye on each other beginning in the 1950s. It also led to the Cuban missile crisis in October 1962, when President John F. Kennedy's demands that the Soviet Union remove missiles from nearby Cuba led to a tense standoff with the Soviets and nearly ignited a nuclear war. U.S. military involvement in both the Korean and Vietnam Wars was spurred by U.S. government fears of a total communist takeover of those two countries. Most U.S. presidents during the Cold War subscribed to some version of the **domino theory**, which posited that communist takeovers of these Southeast Asian countries would be followed by takeovers of Taiwan, India, Iran, and possibly other nations as well.

A distraught President Ronald Reagan and Soviet leader Mikhail Gorbachev leaving their unsuccessful arms limitations talks in Reykjavik, Iceland, in October 1986.

The American military failure in the Vietnam War in particular led officials at every level of the American government to revisit some of the most fundamental premises of U.S. foreign policy, including the theory of containment.[4] The American phase of that war, extending from 1964 until 1973, proved longer lasting and more divisive than any other war involving the United States up to that point.[5] The conflict eventually left 58,000 Americans dead or missing and cost the U.S. government more than $167 billion. Despite all the bloodshed, none of the U.S. aims in the war—to repel North Vietnam aggression, help negotiate a lasting peace, and encourage South Vietnam as a self-sufficient republic—were accomplished. The final peace agreement allowed for extrication of U.S. forces and return of prisoners of war, but little else; and by 1975 South Vietnam had fallen to the communists.[6] The decade-long Vietnam quagmire struck a blow against the domino theory. Future military interventions would require that administrations present some additional evidence of a direct threat to America's strategic interests abroad or at home.

During the 1970s, the United States and the Soviet Union engaged in a period of somewhat eased tensions, or limited détente. During this time they agreed on several strategic arms limitation treaties (SALT I and SALT II) that set restrictions on nuclear missiles.[7] But such détente proved short-lived, as confrontations in underdeveloped Third World nations continued to inject tensions into the Cold War landscape. President Ronald Reagan, denouncing the Soviet Union as an evil empire, outlined a new defense plan, the controversial **Strategic Defense Initiative (SDI)**, an antimissile system based on the use of lasers and particle beams to shoot down Soviet nuclear missiles in outer space.[8]

East–West tensions eased with the ascension of reform-minded Mikhail Gorbachev to the leadership of the Soviet state in 1985. Gorbachev's reforms aimed at restructuring the faltering Soviet economy with greater competition and at liberalizing dissent by introducing press freedoms could not be reconciled with a continuation of the costly arms race with the United States. The Cold War formally came to a close in 1991, when Gorbachev resigned his position with the Soviet government amid extremely difficult economic times. In addition to the former Soviet-bloc countries, 10 former Soviet republics, including Russia, declared their independence.[9] Following the end of the Cold War, U.S. leaders redirected their foreign policy thinking toward a new world order characterized by conflicts in the Third World, a war on terrorism, and threats of nuclear attack from both terrorists and rogue nations.

New World Order and New World Disorder

U.S. responsibilities around the world have not decreased much at all in the aftermath of the Cold War. In his January 1991 State of the Union speech, President George H. W. Bush spoke of the onset of a **new world order**, in which numerous nations would work together for the purpose of securing collective peace, security, freedom, and the rule of law.[10] Maintaining this new world order has been a challenge for American political leaders ever since.

Further complicating the foreign affairs landscape was the looming presence of China. Still a communist nation, China is a crucial market for U.S. goods and products, given that it contains one-fifth of the world's population. In the 1990s, both Presidents George H. W. Bush and Bill Clinton emphasized the need for liberalization of global trade, and in 1993 Congress approved the North American Free Trade Agreement (NAFTA), which lifted trade barriers such as protective tariffs and investment restrictions between the United States and Canada and Mexico. With the U.S. economy increasingly intertwined with the global economy, economic relations with East Asia, Europe, and other countries in the Western hemisphere continue to be a central factor in American foreign policy. Of course economic concerns do not eliminate other interests—tragic human rights abuses in Somalia and Bosnia put pressure on the George H. W. Bush and Clinton administrations to

Warsaw Pact: Formal alliance of nations within the Soviet sphere during the Cold War.

Truman Doctrine: Doctrine articulated by President Harry Truman in the late 1940s by which money and resources were provided to support and sustain non-communist governments in areas strategically vital to the United States.

containment: U.S. foreign policy that sought to restrict Soviet power (and communist influence) to its existing geographical sphere.

domino theory: The theory that held that communist takeovers of countries in Southeast Asia and elsewhere would be followed by subsequent communist takeovers of nearby countries.

© Sean Adair/Reuters/CORBIS

The September 11 terrorist attacks on the World Trade Center towers shifted the focus of American foreign policy to fighting terrorism in the Middle East and elsewhere.

intervene on humanitarian grounds in those countries. The balance both presidents struck in those instances, providing limited aid but no military assistance, prompted criticisms that they had failed to wield America's superpower status in the most appropriate fashion.[11]

The U.S. Government Confronts the Middle East

Although the Cold War has ended, among the current generation of policymakers the specter of the Vietnam War continues to cast a large shadow on foreign policy deliberations. Discussions of American military intervention since the early 1970s have occurred with the lessons of the Vietnam War looming ominously in the background. Some hawkish conservatives even complain of what they call a "Vietnam syndrome," in which the problems of Vietnam produce an undesirable pacifism on the part of American leaders. Politicians live in fear of supporting yet another war in which public support is flimsy, the military objectives are unclear, and an exit strategy remains ill defined. American interventions in the Balkans and Somalia in the 1990s were limited by fears that increased U.S. involvement in those countries would escalate into another Vietnam. During the first Persian Gulf War of 1991, Joint Chiefs of Staff Chairman Colin Powell urged the nation to avoid Vietnam-like entanglements in which fear of escalation placed the military in an essentially unwinnable conflict.

President George W. Bush's administration faced inevitable comparisons between the Vietnam War and the U.S. intervention in Iraq in 2003. When the military failed to unearth the "weapons of mass destruction" cited as partial justification of the war, critics of the Iraqi intervention argued that U.S. interests in the region were just as unclear as they had been in Southeast Asia during the 1960s. Furthermore, the U.S. military's failure to contain rebel insurgents even after taking control of Baghdad invited comparisons to guerrilla war in North Vietnam. In response, President Bush proclaimed that the Iraqi invasion had both removed a brutal dictator, Saddam Hussein, from power and restored a democratic government, in the form of duly held elections, to the previously oppressed nation.

Militarily, the greatest threats to U.S. security during the first decade of the twenty-first century appear to be in two areas of the world: the Middle East and North Korea. More of the U.S. government's attention in recent decades has been focused on the former locus of conflict. Since it first recognized the newly created independent nation of Israel in 1948, the United States has been committed in its support for that country as a political haven for Jews. Meanwhile, Israel has emerged as a modernized democratic presence in a region of the world dominated by Arab countries largely hostile to Western economic power and its cultural domination. U.S. support for Israel has assured the United States of a friendly ally in the Middle East, yet it has also at times run counter to fundamental principles of self-determination, as U.S. officials have been forced to confront another dilemma—what to do with the tens of thousands of Palestinian refugees uprooted from their homes in the years following Israel's occupation of former Palestinian territory.

President Jimmy Carter's successful mediation of disputes between Israel and Egypt in 1978 demonstrated that the United States can play a role in resolving conflicts, but long-term peace between Israel and its neighbors has remained elusive despite such efforts. The George H. W. Bush administration encouraged negotiations between Palestinian Liberation Organization head Yasir Arafat and the Israeli government—the resulting Oslo accords of 1993 called for the exchange of Israeli territory and ultimate Palestinian self-determination for the guarantee of peace. Unfortunately, the accords left unclear the precise boundaries and the specific characteristics of Palestinian rule. Right-wing Israeli extremists murdered Israeli Prime Minister Yitzhak Rabin two years later, and both sides hardened against the accords. The Clinton administration attempted to renew negotiations between the two sides in the late 1990s, but the impasse continues today, with Palestinian suicide bombers and Israeli government bombings becoming a routine feature of Israeli and Palestinian daily life in the early part of the twenty-first century.

Distrust of the United States by many Middle East countries has intensified in the wake of recent administrations' overwhelming support for Israel, and the continued presence of the U.S. military in the Middle East, facilitated by the granting of military bases to the United States in Saudi Arabia and Kuwait. Activities by revolutionary forces have occasionally fomented in the region, threatening U.S. interests directly and indirectly. In 1979, the new fundamentalist Iranian regime under Ayatollah Khomeini seized the U.S. Embassy and held U.S.

THE MORE THINGS CHANGE, THE MORE THINGS STAY THE SAME

Assassinating Foreign Leaders

On December 4, 1981, President Ronald Reagan signed Executive Order 12333. Part 2.11 of that order reiterated a general prohibition on U.S. intelligence agencies sponsoring or carrying out assassinations. President Reagan's order reaffirmed several previous presidents' bans on assassinations in general, and the assassination of foreign leaders in particular. On one hand, the targeted assassination of a mass murderer or frequent violator of human rights might be justified as in the public interest. Still, two factors counsel in favor of such a prohibition: (1) The contradiction inherent in the U.S. trumpeting its efforts to serve as "moral conscience" of the world, while at the same time participating in the act of murder; and (2) the occasional failure of targeted assassinations (including even successful ones) to actually create positive regime change. That said, the U.S. government's involvement in past plots to assassinate foreign leaders is now a matter of public record:

In 1960, two CIA officials were asked by superiors to assassinate Patrice Lumumba, the prime minister of the Congo suspected of being a communist. (Lumumba denied having any communist ties.) Poisons were sent to the Congo and some exploratory steps were taken, but Lumumba was killed first by his own local Congolese rivals.

Between 1960 and 1965, according to a 1975 Senate Committee chaired by Senator Frank Church (D.-Id.), U.S. government personnel plotted to kill Cuban communist leader Fidel Castro on at least eight occasions. According to the Church committee, some of the plots were of the "James Bond variety": poisoned pills, an exploding seashell, and a planned gift of a diving suit contaminated with toxins. None proved successful, and Castro remained in power more than four decades later.

In 1961, Dominican Republic leader Rafael Trujillo was shot by Dominican dissidents supported by the U.S.

The Cuban Communist revolutionary and politician, Fidel Castro, survived at least eight CIA-led assassination plots.

Owen Franken/CORBIS

Al-Qaeda founder Osama bin Laden was killed by U.S. Special forces on May 2, 2011.

AFP/Getty Images

(*Continued*)

THE MORE THINGS CHANGE,
THE MORE THINGS STAY THE SAME

Assassinating Foreign Leaders (continued)

government (at least three carbines and three pistols were furnished by U.S. officials). Trujillo's government was charged with brutally oppressing actual or perceived members of the opposition. As worldwide opinion against Trujillo rose to a fever pitch in the 1950s, he became an embarrassment to the United States, which had initially supported Trujillo's anti-communist regime.

In 2011, Al Qaeda leader Osama bin Laden, mastermind of the 9/11 terrorist attacks, was killed by a U.S. special forces military unit pursuant to Operation Neptune Spear. Unlike the assassinations just described in which the United States sought to evade responsibility for the outcome, President Barack Obama authorized the killing through orders given to the Central Intelligence Agency (CIA). Amnesty International, among other organizations, questioned two aspects of the killing: (1) the decision not to take bin Laden into custody given that he was unarmed; and (2) the decision to not release any photographic or DNA evidence of bin Laden's death to the public. By contrast, the United Nations and the leaders of most other countries issued statements welcoming the news.

For Critical Thinking and Discussion

1. Can one justify the assassination of foreign leaders (military or otherwise) *other than* those recognized by the international community to be mass murderers? Are there any foreign leaders in place today whose assassination would be welcomed worldwide? Who are they?

2. Some defenders of selective assassinations contend that the trial of individuals like Castro or bin Laden would offer nothing more than a "show trial" with little hope of real justice. Do you think a prisoner of Castro's or bin Laden's infamy could ever hope to achieve justice in such a forum? What obstacles would he or she face?

Source: Senate Committee to Study Governmental Operations, Interim report on "Alleged Assassination Plots Involving Foreign Leaders," 94th Congress, 1st sess., November 20, 1975.

---

hostages for more than a year. In late 1990, Iraq President Saddam Hussein invaded Kuwait, threatening U.S. economic interests in the region and spurring the first Bush administration to militarily expel Hussein's army from Kuwait in early 1991.

Navigating the New World Order
After the September 11 Attacks

The events of September 11, 2001, refocused the U.S. government's foreign policy energies toward a global war on terrorism. After a short-lived war in Afghanistan that purportedly expelled the Al Qaeda terrorist network from that country, the George W. Bush administration turned its attention back to Saddam Hussein's government in Iraq, which it accused of supporting terrorism abroad and concealing weapons of mass destruction. After less than six weeks of fighting, American military forces liberated the country of Hussein's dictatorial government during the spring of 2003.

Yet the aftermath of the Iraqi invasion proved highly problematic, with insurgent forces in and around the nation's cities posing a threat to the more than 150,000 American troops who remained there for years as part of the occupation phase of the operation.[12] By early 2007, over 3,000 Americans had died in Iraq, and Congress began putting pressure on the Bush administration to lay out a timetable and plan for eventual American withdrawal. Rejecting those entreaties, in early 2007 President Bush increased by over 20,000 the number of troops deployed to Iraq in what came to be known as the "Iraq war troop surge of 2007." As one of the first moves of his young presidency, Barack Obama announced an 18-month withdrawal window for combat forces, with approximately 50,000 troops remaining in the country after 2011 "to advise and train Iraqi security forces and to provide intelligence and surveillance." Those final troops exited the country on December 18, 2011, marking the end of America's military presence in that country.

President Obama's announcement did not spell a pullback from the Middle East as a whole, however: In December 2009 he confirmed plans to escalate U.S. military involvement in Afghanistan by deploying an additional 30,000 troops. The Obama administration cited the recent strengthening of the Taliban, a Sunni Islamist political movement that has supported terrorist training camps in the region, as the reason for increasing its military presence in that country. Threats of nuclear and biological terrorism remain ever present in the Middle East, where terrorists continue to operate underground. In the past decade, North Korea has also emerged as a potential nuclear threat. Critics charge that the end of the Cold War has in fact ushered in a "new world disorder," featuring ever-shifting alliances and grave terrorist threats from entities not formally associated with any specific nation.

President Barack Obama welcomes Mexican President Felipe Calderon, on a state visit in May 2010.

Mandel Ngan/AFP/Getty Images

Within this constantly shifting international terrain, America continues to search for its role and identity in the twenty-first-century world. In *Colossus: The Rise and Fall of the American Empire*, British-born Harvard University Professor Niall Ferguson argues that like the great British empire of old, the United States needs to embrace its imperial character and commit to more securely establishing the types of democratic institutions around the world that foster long-term prosperity.[13] In another influential book, *Soft Power: The Means to Success in World Politics*, Joseph Nye argues that rather than relying on unilateralism and military power, the United States should endeavor to win the voluntary cooperation of foreign governments.[14] Is the United States an empire? Does it want to be? In light of the difficulties U.S. military forces have faced in postwar Iraq, many of these questions will continue to be debated in the years ahead.

THE STRUCTURE OF AMERICAN FOREIGN POLICYMAKING

The Constitution designates specific roles for the president and the Senate in making U.S. foreign policy. Yet over the course of two centuries, the president of the United States and the executive branch that reports to the president have assumed an increasingly significant role in the process, rendering Congress, interest groups, and citizens themselves less significant in foreign policymaking.

Many actors and institutions attempt either formally or informally to influence American foreign policy. The president of the United States sits squarely at the center of foreign policymaking—within the federal government, the president often dictates its terms with little interference from the other branches.[15] On the positive side, presidential dominance of foreign policy allows the U.S. government to act immediately and decisively in response to developments abroad. The quick responses to the bombing of Pearl Harbor, the threat of nuclear missiles in Cuba, and the 9/11 terrorist attacks might not have been possible had the principal decision makers been a legislative body or council. At the same time, more controversial foreign policy forays such as America's involvement in the Vietnam War, the trading of arms for hostages with Iran in the 1980s, and military intervention in Iraq without proof of weapons of mass destruction might well have been avoided had so much power not been vested in one individual. Although the president is at the center of foreign policymaking, other executive branch departments and agencies help formulate and implement foreign policy.

The **Department of State**, headed by the secretary of state, maintains primary responsibility for many foreign policy programs. State Department programs include diplomatic missions to other countries, foreign aid to developing nations, and contributions to **international organizations** (official entities of international scope or character, usually established by treaty, such as the World Bank and the International Monetary Fund). During the latter half of the twentieth century, the secretary of state emerged as a principal spokesperson for the U.S. government on all foreign policy matters.

In recent times, the position of secretary of state has been held by individuals with political star power that rivals that of the president. Colin Powell, the secretary of state during George W. Bush's first term in office, served a decade earlier as the first African American chairman of the Joint Chiefs of Staff under President George H. W. Bush. In that capacity, Powell articulated the framework for intervention in the first Gulf War, later termed the "Powell Doctrine": military action should be used as a last resort, and then only with clear popular support, overwhelming force, and a clear exit strategy. After flirting with a presidential run of his own, Powell eventually landed at the State Department, where he failed in his efforts to line up many of America's European allies behind the George W. Bush administration's threat to engage in a second Iraq war.[16] Hillary Rodham Clinton, a former first lady and runner-up to Barack Obama in the 2008 Democratic primaries, served as her former rival's first secretary of state. Performing in that role, she is credited with shifting America's foreign policy toward a greater emphasis on diplomacy and foreign aid, in line with President Obama's stated goals.

Military power is an important factor in U.S. foreign relations. The **Department of Defense** plays a critical role in helping formulate and implement U.S. foreign policy by managing the nation's military. The secretary of defense is the principal civilian adviser to the president on military matters. On the military side, the president is advised by the **Joint Chiefs of Staff (JCS)**, which consists of the chief officers of the four branches of the armed forces (army, navy, air force, and marines) as well as the JCS chair and vice chair. The JCS delivers the president's orders to the military commands involved in a particular operation. During the 2003 war in Iraq, Secretary of Defense Donald Rumsfeld emerged as the principal spokesman for the administration, holding frequent press conferences to report on the operation's progress and reaffirm the administration's objectives. Three years later, several retired army officers complained that when the decision was made to go to war in Iraq, Rumsfeld bypassed the advice of the Joint Chiefs of Staff. Rumsfeld resigned in November 2006, at which point he was already the second-longest-serving defense secretary in American history (only Robert McNamara, who served during the 1960s for the Kennedy and Johnson administrations, served longer).

In 1947, the National Security Act established the **National Security Council (NSC)** as an advisory body to the president, coordinating information about foreign, military, and economic policies that affect national security. By law the NSC must include the president, vice president, and the secretaries of state and defense. But recent presidents have also appointed a national security adviser to supervise the council and monitor the implementation of national security decisions made by the president. Dating back to the 1960s, the national security adviser has served as both a key adviser and policymaker for most modern presidents.[17]

With three executive branch officials (the secretary of defense, the secretary of state, and the national security adviser) in a position to advise the president on foreign policy, some conflicts are inevitable. During George W. Bush's first term as president, National Security Advisor Condoleezza Rice, Secretary of State Colin Powell, and Secretary of Defense Donald Rumsfeld all served as critical advisers in helping the president formulate national security policy in the wake of the 9/11 terrorist attacks. The war in Afghanistan that followed generated widespread support throughout the country, and among these officials as well. But when the Bush administration turned its attention to a possible war in Iraq, sharp divisions among the three officials emerged. Although such terms may be oversimplified, the administration's **hawks**— who called for aggressive military action wherever hostile forces might be found—were led by

---

Department of State: Executive branch agency that is primarily responsible for most foreign policy programs within the executive branch, including diplomatic missions, foreign aid, and contributions to international organizations.

---

international organization: Entity of international scope or character, usually established by treaty, such as the World Bank or the International Monetary Fund.

Department of Defense: Executive branch agency that is responsible for managing the nation's military and advising the president on all military matters.

Joint Chiefs of Staff (JCS): Group of chief officers of the four branches of the armed forces as well as a JCS chair and vice chair, which advises the president on military matters and delivers the president's orders to the military.

National Security Council (NSC): Advisory body to the president charged with coordinating information about foreign, military, and economic policies that affect national security.

---

hawks: Members of the president's administration who call for aggressive military actions wherever hostile forces may be found.

Rumsfeld, Rice, and Vice President Dick Cheney. On the other side of this divide were the **real-ists**, led by Powell, who counseled diplomacy as the primary means of protecting U.S. interests abroad. Powell was particularly concerned that a military attack on Iraq might reduce support for democratic reforms in Saudi Arabia and strain relationships with important Western European allies such as France and Germany. Ultimately the hawks won the day, because the Bush administration waged the 2003 war in Iraq without support from the United Nations and many of its allies. Powell resigned his position after the 2004 presidential election.

Although not directly responsible for formulating the administration's overall foreign policy direction, other agencies and executive branch officials also influence aspects of foreign policy. In the aftermath of the 9/11 terrorist attacks, the Bush administration sought to create a unified security structure to coordinate the protection of U.S. citizens against terrorist threats within the nation's own borders. Accordingly, Congress in 2002 established the **Department of Homeland Security (DHS)**. Various governmental divisions responsible for U.S. security have been brought under DHS control, including border and transportation security, infrastructure protection, the U.S. Coast Guard, the U.S. Secret Service, the Federal Emergency Management Agency (FEMA), and the Bureau of Citizenship and Immigration Services. The DHS secretary is responsible for overseeing the efforts of more than 180,000 government employees in the department's efforts to strengthen U.S. borders, provide for intelligence analysis and infrastructure protection, and improve the use of science and technology to combat terrorist threats. The DHS is also responsible for formulating a comprehensive response and recovery capability in the event of an unexpected threat.

The National Security Act of 1947 created the **Central Intelligence Agency (CIA)** to correlate, evaluate, and disseminate intelligence information from throughout the world that affects national security. Unlike the NSC, the CIA is also responsible for disseminating propaganda or performing public relations functions on behalf of the U.S. government, and for engaging in overt or covert activities at the direction of the president.

Since the fall of the Soviet Union in 1991, the CIA has struggled to define its role in the post–Cold War era, particularly with regard to the Middle East and the recent war on terrorism. The first CIA director during the George W. Bush administration, George Tenet, came under heated criticism both for the failure of his agency to coordinate information about the Al Qaeda terrorist network in advance of the 9/11 attacks and for mistakenly allowing President Bush to make false claims about Iraq's nuclear capabilities during a State of the Union address.

realists: Members of the president's administration who advocate diplomacy as the primary means of protecting U.S. interests abroad.

Department of Homeland Security (DHS): Executive branch agency established in 2002 to coordinate government entities in protecting U.S. citizens against terrorism within the nation's borders.

Central Intelligence Agency (CIA): Federal agency charged with evaluating and disseminating intelligence information, performing public relations functions that affect international perceptions of the United States, and engaging in overt and covert operations at the direction of the president.

Don Emmert/AFP/Getty Images

Secretary of State Hillary Clinton greets President Mohamed Magariaf, Libya's first elected leader following that nation's 2011 civil war, in September 2012.

With the continued need for information about activities in the Middle East, the Balkans, and North Korea, the CIA still plays a critical role in helping American leaders craft foreign policy.[18] Congress has increasingly pressed the agency to improve its operations and justify its specific operations. A House-Senate Intelligence Committee investigating the 9/11 attacks complained that the traditional post of Director of Central Intelligence was outdated and poorly suited to coordinate intelligence coming from so many different parts of government; accordingly, it recommended the establishment of a new cabinet-level post on intelligence matters. In 2004, the Bush administration created the new position of Director of National Intelligence, charged with leading the intelligence community across all government agencies.

Other Foreign Policy Actors and Interests

Although generally more oriented toward domestic affairs, Congress possesses various constitutional powers that give it some stake in crafting U.S. foreign policy. Although presidents have committed troops to battle more than a hundred times in our nation's history without a formal declaration of war from Congress—including most notably in Korea and Vietnam—modern chief executives have learned that there may be some political benefits to asking for a congressional resolution to support military action. Congressional approval of such actions can help rally public support and possibly provide some political cover should those military operations fail. In October 2002, for example, Congress passed a resolution backing the use of military force in Iraq. In the months that followed the invasion when guerrilla warfare continued to threaten American soldiers, many Democratic senators who voted for the resolution were hard-pressed to criticize the president's decision to invade.

Legislators on the Foreign Relations committees of the Senate and the House may take the lead in initiating investigations into a broad range of foreign policy initiatives undertaken by the executive branch.[19] The secretary of state reports regularly to both committees, which oversee relations with foreign nations, executive agreements in foreign affairs, international organizations, and foreign interventions. The secretary of defense reports regularly to the House and Senate Armed Services committees, which are responsible for overseeing defense and national security issues. The diffusion of power among so many separate committees and individual legislators tends to hamstring congressional efforts to encourage the executive branch to consult with the committees before taking some action. Further, the possibility that members of congressional committees might leak information provides the White House with the incentive to conceal information by claiming executive privilege. The Senate's constitutionally vested power to ratify all treaties may also thwart a president eager to move forward. For example, when the Senate in the late 1970s ratified two treaties guaranteeing that the United States would transfer control of the Panama Canal to Panama, senators offered no fewer than 145 amendments to the treaties.

Groups of legislators frequently tour other nations to learn firsthand the nature of particular foreign policy problems. In rare cases, individual legislators may choose to act on their own to influence foreign policy, sometimes causing headaches for White House officials determined to present a unified front to foreign nations. For example, during the 1980s, Representative Charlie Wilson (D-TX), a maverick congressman from East Texas, worked behind the scenes to help the CIA arm and sustain a rebel Afghanistan group, the Mujahidin, in its revolt against military occupation by the Soviet Union.[20] In November 2005, the late Congressman John Murtha (D-PA), a former Marine and noted war hawk, spoke out forcefully against the war in Iraq. After attempts to paint Murtha as an extremist failed, Bush administration officials, including Vice President Dick Cheney, scrambled to respond to Murtha's comments with specific plans for the occupation.

Certainly some private citizens may be in a position to pursue similar initiatives on their own; before making his first presidential bid in 1992, millionaire Ross Perot helped rescue two employees of his corporation from an Iranian prison.[21] Yet most Americans seeking to influence foreign policy organize themselves into special interest or "pressure" groups for the purpose of doing so. The power that the so-called pro-Israel lobby wields in Congress is well known: the American-Israel Public Affairs Committee (AIPAC) has influenced important appropriation decisions on Capitol Hill during the past 30 years, helping to ensure the continuation of American aid to Israel. AIPAC's tactics have included letter-writing campaigns and active involvement in election campaigns to assist members of Congress who it believes are sympathetic to Israel.

Private-sector interest groups have been especially active with regard to most aspects of general trade policy. Textile manufacturers' lobbies have fought to limit imports of foreign garments, whereas farmers' lobbies have pressured the government to pass tariffs on agricultural products imported from other countries. U.S. business interests seeking to export high-tech goods, such as computer and software firms and aerospace manufacturers, have opposed all efforts to impose trade restrictions and sanctions on large potential markets such as China. Is it appropriate for such interest groups to attempt to influence foreign affairs? Critics contend that the lobbying activities of these pressure groups may inadvertently undermine American foreign policy or even threaten American national security interests. Despite these concerns, interest groups continue to play an active and aggressive role in the process.

The term **military-industrial complex** refers to the vast network of defense industries in America, such as manufacturers of weapons, missiles, aircraft, submarines, and so forth, and their bureaucratic allies. The complex as a whole maintains a keen interest in foreign policymaking that is concerned with defense and national security. These industries expanded during the Cold War as U.S. defense budgets rose to as much as 40 percent of annual federal spending. In the late 1990s, defense spending amounted to just 15 percent of the budget, generating ever more feverish efforts by members of the military-industrial complex to either increase that allotment or shift the focus of defense spending to weapons and resources that meet their own areas of expertise. One of the by-products of the terrorist attacks of 9/11 was a renewed commitment to military and national security spending; 10 years after the tragedy, America's military spending had leveled to approximately 20 percent of the overall U.S. budget.

military-industrial complex: The vast network of defense industries in America (including manufacturers of weapons, missiles, aircraft, and so forth) and their allies in the federal bureaucracy.

American Foreign Policy and Public Opinion

Public opinion on foreign policy issues is a central concern for key actors in the U.S. foreign policymaking arena, including the president, in part because those actors won't keep their jobs for long if they ignore popular sentiments. When the public punishes officials at the polls for their ill-advised foreign policy decisions, observers are quick to criticize those officials for ignoring the will of the people.[22] Certainly when President George W. Bush ordered a "surge" of 20,000 more U.S. forces in Iraq in early 2007, he was not responding to public opinion as much as he was hoping to shift it in a pro-war direction. President Obama assumed the intervention in Afghanistan would be well received, although as shown in Figure 16.1, the public saw little success there occurring during President Obama's first term in office. Moreover, many political defeats occur because officials have misinterpreted public attitudes, rather than ignoring them outright. Even Lyndon Johnson, whose Vietnam policy proved so unpopular that he was forced to drop out of the presidential election race in 1968, was known to have carried in his pajama pockets the results of public opinion polls about foreign policy.

FIGURE 16.1 Failing to Win over the Public in Afghanistan

When President Barack Obama elected to turn the military's focus away from Iraq and toward Afghanistan, he expected the decision to be controversial. Still, the Obama administration could never have imagined that the decision to increase troops in that country would create perceptions of failure, rather than success in that region. To that end, consider the Pew Research center poll that asked: *"How well is the U.S. military effort in Afghanistan going: very well, fairly well, not too well, or not at all well?"*

Source: Pew Research Center, April 4–15, 2012, http://www.pollingreport.com/afghan.htm
N = 1,494 adults nationwide. Margin of error = ±3.

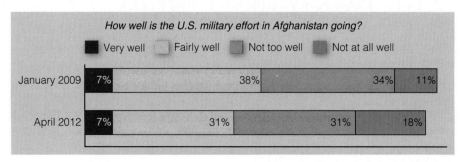

Part of the challenge facing U.S. officials is that public attitudes toward foreign affairs often defy easy analysis and interpretation. Modern presidents have managed to generate considerable public support for foreign policy objectives that protect American jobs, control illegal immigration, or counter the illegal drug trade. Foreign policy initiatives that promote human rights or advance democracy abroad have been far less likely to garner support. The 1991 Persian Gulf War generated public support from the outset because an adversary had engaged in aggressive military action against a U.S. ally. By contrast, the Clinton administration fought an uphill battle against public opinion in its Operation Restore Hope to counter widespread famine in Somalia and in its limited military interventions in Bosnia. Political scientist John Mueller offered the following four propositions to describe American public opinion concerning foreign policy:

1. Americans will tolerate a substantial loss of American lives only if the enemy is seen to be truly powerful and set on jeopardizing vital American interests;

2. The advantage to a president of a success in minor foreign policy ventures is marginal; the disadvantage to a president of a failure in such a venture is more than marginal;

3. If they are not being killed, American troops can remain in peacekeeping or other ventures virtually indefinitely with little public criticism; and

4. Although few concerns can turn the public's attention to foreign affairs, nuclear weapons retain the capacity to arrest the public's attention, and the same may hold for biological and chemical weapons.[23]

Once again it was the events of September 11, 2001, that turned the attention of Americans to foreign policy like few other events of the past 30 years. The George W. Bush administration sought to characterize its foreign policy initiatives in Afghanistan, Iraq, and elsewhere in terms designed to be acceptable to public opinion. The war on terrorism is framed in terms of a worldwide threat of seismic proportions. Officials may have delayed the 2003 war to lay the groundwork for clear-cut and unambiguous military success. Even after the formal military engagement of that war was concluded, President Bush continued to couch the threat in terms of intelligence received that Iraq possessed nuclear capabilities. More recently, President Obama faced an uphill battle in generating public support for his decision to increase troop levels for the war in Afghanistan: nearly a decade after the terrorist attacks of 9/11, the war no longer seemed so pressing to a majority of the American population. Indeed, polls indicated that the public remained split during the summer of 2010 on whether fighting that war was even "the right thing to do."

The thorny politics of foreign occupation that occurs following most military battles—when the victors must (at least temporarily) control the area that has been seized by military force—can weigh especially heavily in the court of public opinion. Public support for the war tends to tail off once the opposing armies have been defeated. If the occupation fails, the defeated or other hostile entities may seize the opportunity to reverse the war's outcome. America's military history features numerous successful military occupations, such as that over West Germany and Japan in the aftermath of World War II. By contrast, the George W. Bush administration invested more than $1 billion per day in the occupation of Iraq; yet far more American troops were killed during the occupation than during the brief six-week military conflict.

FOREIGN POLICY DILEMMAS FOR THE TWENTY-FIRST CENTURY

Some foreign policy dilemmas of the twenty-first century, such as the problematic occupation of Iraq by U.S. forces after the 2003 Iraq War, represent new versions of age-old challenges that the U.S. government has faced on an intermittent basis since the nation's founding. Others represent unforeseen obstacles produced by circumstances unique to the modern, post–Cold War world. Regardless, American officials must always be on the lookout for foreign policy challenges that arise with little or no warning and that can overshadow all other aspects of the federal government's agenda if they are not kept under control. Officials must also be prepared to justify their actions according to some theory or well-articulated rationale, lest they be accused of conducting foreign policy "on the fly" with little real reason for endangering American resources and, in some instances, for putting American troops in harm's way.

Is the "Preemption Doctrine" Justifiable?

Only a year after the collapse of the Soviet Union in 1991, the first hint of a dramatic transformation in America's foreign policy could be seen. In 1992, several Pentagon planners working in the George H. W. Bush administration drafted a policy statement asserting that the American government should assume a far more activist role in foreign affairs, especially in the Middle East. Their statement specifically reserved the right of the U.S. military to use advance strikes to stop rogue states from developing weapons of mass destruction. Later termed the **preemption doctrine**, this statement sparked considerable controversy after it was leaked to the *New York Times*. In 1997 one of its original authors, Paul Wolfowitz, joined Donald Rumsfeld and other conservative foreign policy advocates to warn President Bill Clinton that America's containment of Iraq had failed. They urged the government to shift its focus to the outright removal of Iraqi leader Saddam Hussein, who had remained in power even through the American military's conquering of his country during the Persian Gulf War of 1991.

preemption doctrine:
Doctrine of war making that reserves the right of the U.S. military to use advance strikes to stop rogue states from developing weapons of mass destruction.

With George W. Bush's election as president in 2000 and the more intense focus on international terrorism that followed the September 11, 2001, attacks, the emphasis on preemption became ingrained in U.S. policy. Rumsfeld, who had become secretary of defense, joined others in pressing the administration to exercise its military power, unilaterally if necessary, to confront hostile states bent on acquiring weapons of mass destruction. Bush named Wolfowitz as deputy secretary of defense, a platform from which he more forcefully stressed the merits of a strategic preemption doctrine.

Even advocates of this doctrine do not dispute that preemption carries with it some significant risks. The fundamental paradox of preemption is that it can be effectively applied only to a country that lacks the capacity to retaliate. Though Iraq suffered from preemptive American attacks in the spring of 2003, North Korea and Iran—two nations similarly charged with posing international threats—are less likely to be targets of a U.S. preemptive attack because neither is viewed as so weak or vulnerable as was Saddam Hussein's regime. Critics of the preemption doctrine also charge that although this policy may be justified in the rare instance when a rival power's attacks are imminent, it cannot be justified to prevent attacks in the distant and more ambiguous future.

Cultivating Relations with the New Russian Federation

Although many now view America as the world's lone remaining superpower, the fall of the Soviet Union did not by any means eliminate all threats to the United States from that part of the globe. The Russian Federation headed by Vladimir Putin controls a landmass of more than 6.5 million square miles, nearly twice the size of the United States. It also maintains one of the world's most powerful military threats, because most of the nuclear capabilities of the former Soviet Union were passed on to Russia. Though U.S. foreign policy must address each of the 12 independent nations of the former Soviet Union on its own merits, the Russian Federation continues to capture the bulk of attention from American foreign policymakers.

Concerns around the world have been raised about Russia's occasional use of military force: for example, it subdued the smaller Republic of Chechnya, the site of the bloody Chechen–Russian War of 1994–1996. More recently, in August 2008, Russia temporarily occupied the nearby country of Georgia by force after months of skirmishes and increasing tensions between the two nations. Both American and Russian officials have strong incentives to cultivate friendly relations with each other. Russia's efforts to establish itself as a member of the club of democratic nations in good standing require it to demonstrate to the world that it can conduct responsible foreign policy with the United States.

Meanwhile, the United States needs Russian cooperation to allow the stationing of U.S. forces in distant sites, such as the central Asian republic of Tajikistan, in order to combat terrorist threats in that part of the globe. President Barack Obama's election led to a breakthrough of sorts on U.S.–Russian relations, as : Obama and then Russian President Dmitri Medvedev promised a "fresh start" in U.S.–Russia relations in 2009. One year later, this rapprochement went a step further, as the United States and Russia reached an agreement to reduce their stockpiles of nuclear weapons. Putin's return to power in 2012 (he had previously served as President from 2000 to 2008) returned the two countries to a somewhat frostier relationship, with the leaders squaring off in recent meetings over how to address unrest in Syria and elsewhere. A stronger relationship between Russia and the United States would have important implications on American foreign policy: specifically, it might encourage some of America's allies, particularly France and Germany, to go along with American military operations. Russia's refusal to support the 2003 war in Iraq may have helped embolden those two Western European countries to withhold support for the American-led war.

What Role Does Foreign Aid Play in the New International Order?

The American government's legacy of providing monetary aid to struggling nations and allies was first established on a monumental scale with the Marshall Plan to help Western European nations recover after World War II. Although humanitarian concerns continue to influence such aid, U.S. economic and national security interests also affect foreign aid decisions. Expanded foreign markets would purchase domestic products and agricultural goods, boosting the U.S. economy. New states would also be more likely to join the expanding capitalist world economy if U.S. aid contributed to their recovery and encouraged them to reject anti-capitalist economic systems.

Because the dissolution of the Soviet Union has weakened some of the strategic rationale for foreign aid, there have been substantial reductions in such aid during the past decade. Critics of foreign aid also charge that much of the money provided by America goes to elites in the recipient nations, rather than to those who need help. Defenders of aid respond that even when elites control a sizeable portion of the aid, the recipient nation is able to expand its national output, which leads to higher living standards for all. But this "trickle-down" theory of foreign aid has been cast aside in recent years by experts such as economist Peter Boone of the London School of Economics. After assessing the experience of nearly 100 nations, Boone concluded that because foreign transfers only tend to increase government consumption (which has no positive effect on growth), foreign aid has had little or no impact on the recipient country's overall investment levels.[24]

The United States continues to be a leading contributor to such international aid institutions as the World Bank, which since 1945 has extended credit to nations for building and economic development. America also contributes substantially to the International Monetary Fund, which helps to maintain the value of foreign currencies during times of crisis. But the heyday of foreign aid—when it served as a critical instrument of U.S. foreign relations—appears to be a thing of the past.

Does the United Nations Still Serve an Important Function?

The United Nations, founded at the conclusion of World War II, is structured around five separate governing bodies: (1) the General Assembly, which is made up of all member states (at present there are 192 member states); (2) the Economic and Social Council, which is made up of 54 members chosen by the General Assembly and serves primarily an advisory body to the General Assembly on matters of international economic and social cooperation; (3) the Secretariat, which supports the other UN bodies and carries out tasks as directed by the other bodies; (4) the International Court of Justice, the UN's judicial organ that has jurisdiction to try certain international war criminals and settles disputes submitted to it by duly authorized international entities; and (5) the Security Council, which maintains peace and security among nations by issuing resolutions that (at least in theory) are binding on UN members. The separation of the Security Council from the larger General Assembly is significant. As currently constituted, the Security Council consists of 5 permanent members (China, France, the Russian Federation, the United States, and Great Britain) and 10 nonpermanent rotating members. Each of the five permanent members maintains the absolute right to veto decisions of the all-important council, the only UN body with the power to authorize economic sanctions or military force. However, the General Assembly retains the exclusive power to enforce Security Council decisions.

CHECK **THE LIST**

Who Is in the "Nuclear Club"?

The list of states that have successfully detonated nuclear weapons—often termed "the nuclear club"—continues to grow in the post–Cold War era. Only five members of the club are considered "nuclear weapon states" under the terms of the Nuclear Non-Proliferation Treaty (NPT), a landmark international treaty first established in 1970 between states that possess such weapons and 190 nations that do not. Four other states in the club do not subscribe to the NPT, but they are known or believed to possess nuclear weapons. Just one state (South Africa) has actually dropped out of the club, dissembling its arsenal before joining the NPT. The current list of states in the "nuclear club" is as follows:

Recognized nuclear weapon states under the terms of the NPT:

Year of first test:

1. The United States

   1945

2. Russia (successor state to the Soviet Union)

   1949

3. United Kingdom

   1952

4. France

   1960

5. China

   1964

Other states believed to have nuclear weapons (non-signatories to the NPT):

6. India

   1974

7. Pakistan

   1998

8. North Korea

   2006

9. Israel

   1979*

▶ **POINT TO PONDER:** When, if ever, should the testing of nuclear weapons by a non-signatory of the NPT be considered acceptable to the international community? Do you favor the U.S. government actively destroying large parts of its nuclear arsenal to set an example for other nations?

Source: Natural Resources Defense Council Archive of Nuclear data.

*Year is disputed; Israel neither confirms nor denies that it has conducted nuclear tests.

The United States dominated the UN on all security issues during its first 40 years, but as U.S. influence over the body has declined, calls have increased within Congress to reduce American aid to the organization and to ignore its dictates whenever American security interests are at issue. In 2003, America went to war in Iraq even though the UN Security Council was unwilling to offer advance authorization for any such military action. Yet immediately after the war with Iraq had concluded, the UN began relief and reconstruction activities in the war-torn nation, and began pushing for a resolution that would broaden international control over the region. Thus in the twenty-first century, the UN seems destined to play at least a limited role in international affairs, asserting its authority most strongly during peacekeeping and relief missions that follow military action.

President Obama delivers an address to the UN General Assembly on September 23, 2009.

©Todd Heisler/The New York Times

As much as individual presidents like to think that they control the military and foreign relations of their respective administrations, unforeseen events and crises have a tendency to scuttle even the most carefully laid plans and raise previously unforeseen issues. When President Johnson's administration increased America's military presence in Vietnam, he could not have imagined that such a decision would destroy his own presidency and create significant headaches for future presidents charged with managing the withdrawal of troops from an unpopular conflict. More than three decades later, George W. Bush moved ahead with his administration's war on Iraq; despite some early successes, the American public eventually soured on the conflict and elected a new president (Barack Obama) committed to withdraw U.S. troops from that war-torn country. Although it only takes a single president to commit American troops abroad, success is never guaranteed, and the public can turn on the war quite quickly. When that happens, withdrawing troops in a safe and politically expedient way is no simple matter—all the gains of previous years can be wiped away if the wrong strategies are employed. Certainly many presidents, including most recently Presidents Nixon and Clinton, found foreign policy to be a welcome diversion from the scandals that were rocking their respective presidencies. At the same time, many foreign policy issues—relations with Russia, the Arab–Israeli conflict, the military occupation in Iraq, to name just a few—are among the most complicated and difficult issues a president faces. As a result, although some presidents enjoy short-term successes in foreign affairs, few are able to offer long-term solutions, and many only tend to exacerbate the problems faced by their predecessors.

FROM YOUR PERSPECTIVE

Is the American Military Draft a Thing of the Past?

The U.S. government discontinued use of compulsory military service in 1973, much to the relief of a generation of young Americans that had grown increasingly hostile to America's military involvement in Vietnam. Since then Americans have marveled at the degree to which America's comparative advantage in military technology has helped to reduce (although certainly not eliminate) casualties of U.S. military incursions. Yet is the move to an all-voluntary military force permanent? Critics of the Bush administration's invasion of Iraq argue that America's active military force of nearly 1.5 million soldiers was stretched far too thin between 2003 and 2008. Several high-profile members of Congress at the time, including Charles Rangel (D-NY), even called for the draft to be reinstated as a means of ensuring that service would be spread equally between the rich and the poor (those from poor families are more apt than those from wealthier families to voluntarily enlist for military service). President Barack Obama's decision to upgrade the nation's military presence in Afghanistan reopened those same questions yet again.

Should college-age students anticipate that the draft might come again in the near future? On one hand, the political platforms of both parties have consistently opposed reinstatement of the draft. On the other hand, since 1980 all male U.S. citizens age 18 or older have been required by law to register with the selective service, in case emergency manpower needs in a time of national crisis require conscription once again.

© AFP/Getty Images

An official at Selective Service Headquarters in Washington D.C. draws labeled ping-pong balls to determine the rank order of birthdates in the first nationally televised draft lottery on December 2, 1969. All 19-year-old male citizens with birthdays chosen early in the process would become the first draftees in the Vietnam War.

For Critical Thinking and Discussion

1. Do you believe America's selective service system is unfair? Should it apply only to male U.S. citizens? (Consider that noncitizens and women can voluntarily serve in the armed forces.)

2. Given the advanced state of military technology, can conscription still be justified?

SUMMARY: PUTTING IT ALL TOGETHER

THE CONSTITUTIONAL FRAMEWORK OF AMERICAN FOREIGN POLICY

- The federal government maintains exclusive authority over foreign policy in the United States.
- The president is the commander in chief and has the power to negotiate treaties and appoint and receive ambassadors; Congress has the power to declare war, raise armies, and regulate foreign commerce, among its other functions.

1. The U.S. Constitution grants which of the following the power to declare war?
   a. the president
   b. Congress
   c. the U.S. Supreme Court
   d. the secretary of defense

2. The "two presidencies theory" suggests that presidents
   a. have more power in influencing domestic policy.
   b. have more power in influencing foreign policy.
   c. should have the power to declare war.
   d. lack the ability to negotiate treaties with other nations.

3. Why did Congress pass the War Powers Resolution in 1973?

The Roots of American Foreign Policy

- Over two centuries, the practical power to make war has shifted from Congress to the president, who, as commander in chief, is far better suited to respond to sudden changes in circumstances around the world. Thus the president has become even more powerful in foreign affairs than in domestic affairs.

- The United States adhered to a policy of isolationism from the time of its founding until the late nineteenth century, generally forgoing intervention in foreign wars during that period. However, in the mid-nineteenth century the U.S. government practiced aggressive expansionism in North America; near the end of the century it also annexed Hawaii and gained possession of the Philippine Islands.

- With its entry into World War I and World War II, the United States rose to the status of world superpower, with many smaller nations looking to the U.S. government to preserve international peace. America's foreign policy eventually shifted to an emphasis on internationalism, by which it participated in a system of collective security.

- The Cold War, pitting the United States against the Soviet Union from 1945 until 1991, was waged through economic warfare, arms buildups, and moments of tense diplomacy that fell short of direct military engagements between the two superpowers. The demise of Soviet-run regimes in Russia and elsewhere beginning in the late 1980s failed to decrease U.S. involvement around the world.

- The Middle East remains a source of great concern for U.S. foreign policy in the twenty-first century. After the 9/11 attacks, the federal government launched an aggressive war on terrorism. The U.S. military overthrew the governments of Afghanistan and Iraq in 2001 and 2003, respectively, as part of the war on terrorism.

- Although the continued occupation of Iraq by U.S. forces after the Iraqi war was a source of debate among political officials between 2003 and 2008, President Obama accomplished a drawdown of forces in Iraq; the Obama administration sought instead to redirect U.S. military strength to Afghanistan and elsewhere.

Test Yourself on This Section

1. Which of the following best characterizes U.S. foreign policy prior to the twentieth century?
   a. pacifism
   b. internationalism
   c. isolationism
   d. colonialism

2. The policy that the United States would consider any European colonization of the Americas as an act of war is known as
   a. the Marshall Plan.
   b. the Monroe Doctrine.
   c. the Truman Doctrine.
   d. manifest destiny.

3. The Cold War ended when
   a. the United States defeated South Vietnam in 1973.
   b. the United States forced the Soviets to withdraw missiles from Cuba in 1962.
   c. Soviet leader Mikhail Gorbachev resigned amid the economic collapse of soviet nations in 1991.
   d. President Nixon negotiated the SALT agreements with the Soviets in 1973.

4. What dangers would the U.S. government face if it were to move to a more isolationist policy in the modern era?

The Structure of American Foreign Policymaking

- In formulating foreign policy, the president is assisted by the secretary of state, the secretary of defense, the Joint Chiefs of Staff, the national security adviser, and the Director of National Intelligence.

- The Department of Homeland Security, created by an act of Congress in 2002, is responsible for border and transportation security, intelligence analysis, infrastructure protection, and all other government divisions that play a role in protecting against terrorist threats in the United States.
- Congress oversees foreign policy through its Foreign Relations committees, which receive regular reports from the secretary of state and the secretary of defense. Groups of legislators frequently travel overseas to learn firsthand about foreign policy problems.
- Public opinion concerning American foreign policy often defies easy interpretation. Many presidents have been punished at the polls for ill-advised foreign policy decisions, whereas others have essentially rescued their presidencies by engaging in successful foreign policy initiatives.

Test Yourself on This Section

1. The U.S. cabinet department primarily responsible for protecting the United States from a terrorist attack is the
   a. Department of State.
   b. Department of Defense.
   c. Department of Interior.
   d. Department of Homeland Security.

2. Those who advocate diplomacy as the initial means of protecting U.S. interests abroad are known as
   a. hawks.
   b. doves.
   c. realists.
   d. diplomats.

3. Which of the following presidents ordered a "surge" in U.S. military activities, despite opposition in the public opinion polls, to defeat insurgents in Afghanistan?
   a. George H.W. Bush
   b. Bill Clinton
   c. George W. Bush
   d. Barack Obama

4. What are the four propositions, developed by political scientist John Mueller, that describe public opinion about foreign policy?

FOREIGN POLICY DILEMMAS FOR THE TWENTY-FIRST CENTURY

- Foreign policy dilemmas facing American officials in the twenty-first century include questions about when (if at all) a preemptive military attack is justified, what role (if any) the United States should play in supporting the United Nations, and whether the United States should increase or decrease foreign aid in general.

Test Yourself on This Section

1. The modern foreign policy position that states the United States may use advance military strikes to prevent rogue nations from developing weapons of mass destruction is
   a. the advance option.
   b. the Clinton doctrine.
   c. containment.
   d. the preemption doctrine.

2. How is the United Nations structured, and which five nations have disproportionate power in that structure?

KEY TERMS

Central Intelligence Agency (CIA) (p. 465)
Cold War (p. 458)
containment (p. 459)
Department of Defense (p. 464)
Department of Homeland Security (DHS) (p. 465)
Department of State (p. 464)
domino theory (p. 459)
expansionism (p. 456)
hawks (p. 464)

international organization (p. 464)
internationalism (p. 457)
isolationism (p. 456)
Joint Chiefs of Staff (JCS) (p. 464)
manifest destiny (p. 456)
Marshall Plan (p. 458)
military-industrial complex (p. 467)
Monroe Doctrine (p. 456)
National Security Council (NSC) (p. 464)
new world order (p. 460)

North Atlantic Treaty Organization (NATO) (p. 458)
pacifism (p. 456)
preemption doctrine (p. 469)
realists (p. 465)
Strategic Defense Initiative (SDI) (p. 460)
Truman Doctrine (p. 459)
two presidencies theory (p. 454)
United Nations (UN) (p. 457)
War Powers Resolution (p. 454)
Warsaw Pact (p. 459)

APPENDIX

DECLARATION OF INDEPENDENCE

In Congress, July 4, 1776.

A DECLARATION

By the Representatives of the United States of America,

In General Congress Assembled.

When in the Course of human Events, it becomes necessary for one People to dissolve the Political Bands which have connected them with another, and to assume among the Powers of the Earth, the separate and equal Station to which the Laws of Nature and of Nature's God entitle them, a decent Respect to the Opinions of Mankind requires that they should declare the causes which impel them to the Separation.

We hold these Truths to be self-evident, that all Men are created equal, that they are endowed by their Creator with certain unalienable Rights, that among these are Life, Liberty, and the Pursuit of Happiness—That to secure these Rights, Governments are instituted among Men, deriving their just Powers from the Consent of the Governed, that whenever any Form of Government becomes destructive of these Ends, it is the Right of the People to alter or abolish it, and to institute new Government, laying its Foundation on such Principles, and organizing its Powers in such Form, as to them shall seem most likely to effect their Safety and Happiness. Prudence, indeed, will dictate that Governments long established should not be changed for light and transient Causes; and accordingly all Experience hath shewn, that Mankind are more disposed to suffer, while Evils are sufferable, than to right themselves by abolishing the Forms to which they are accustomed. But when a long Train of Abuses and Usurpations, pursuing invariably the same Object, evinces a Design to reduce them under absolute Despotism, it is their Right, it is their Duty, to throw off such Government, and to provide new Guards for their future Security. Such has been the patient Sufferance of these Colonies; and such is now the Necessity which constrains them to alter their former Systems of Government. The History of the present kind of Great Britain is a History of repeated Injuries and Usurpations, all having in direct Object the Establishment of an absolute Tyranny over these States. To prove this, let Facts be submitted to a candid World.

He has refused his Assent to Laws, the most wholesome and necessary for public good.

He has forbidden his Governors to pass Laws of immediate and pressing importance, unless suspended in their Operation till his Assent should be obtained; and when so suspended, he has utterly neglected to attend to them.

He has refused to pass other Laws for the Accommodation of large Districts of People, unless those People would relinquish the Right of Representation in the Legislature, a Right inestimable to them, and formidable to Tyrants only.

He has called together Legislative Bodies at Places unusual, uncomfortable, and distant from the Depository of their public records, for the sole Purpose of fatiguing them into Compliance with his Measures.

He has dissolved Representative Houses repeatedly, for opposing with many Firmness his Invasions on the Rights of the People.

He has refused for a long Time, after such Dissolutions, to cause others to be elected; whereby the Legislative Powers, incapable of Annihilation, have returned to the People at large for their exercise; the State remaining in the mean time exposed to all the Dangers of Invasion from without, and Convulsions within.

He has endeavoured to prevent the Population of these States; for that Purpose obstructing the Laws for Naturalization of Foreigners; refusing to pass others to encourage their Migrations hither, and raising the Conditions of new Appropriations of Lands.

He has obstructed the Administration of Justice, by refusing his Assent to Laws for establishing Judiciary Powers.

He has made Judges dependent on his Will alone, for the Tenure of their Offices, and the Amount and Payment of their Salaries.

He has erected a Multitude of new Offices, and sent hither Swarms of Officers to harass our People, and eat out their Substance.

He has kept among us, in Times of Peaces, Standing Armies, without the consent of our Legislatures.

He has affected to render the Military independent of and superior to the Civil Power.

He has combined with others to subject us to a Jurisdiction foreign to our Constitution, and unacknowledged by our Laws; giving his Assent to their Acts of pretended Legislation:

For quartering large Bodies of Armed Troops among us:

For protecting them, by a mock Trial, from Punishment for any Murders which they should commit on the Inhabitants of these States:

For cutting off our Trade with all Parts of the World:

For imposing Taxes on us without our Consent: For depriving us, in many Cases, of the Benefits of Trial by Jury:

For transporting us beyond Seas to be tried for pretended Offences:

For abolishing the free System of English Laws in a neighbouring Province, establishing therein an arbitrary Government, and enlarging its Boundaries, so as to render it at once an Example and fit Instrument for introducing the same absolute Rule into these Colonies:

For taking away our Charters, abolishing our most valuable Laws, and altering fundamentally the Forms of our Governments:

For suspending our own Legislatures, and declaring themselves invested with Power to legislate for us in all Cases whatsoever.

He has abdicated Government here, by declaring us out of his Protection and waging War against us.

He has plundered our Seas, ravaged our Coasts, burnt our Towns, and destroyed the Lives of our People.

He is, at this Time, transporting large Armies of foreign Mercenaries to compleat the Works of Death, Desolation, and Tyranny, already begun with circumstances of Cruelty and Perfidy, scarcely paralleled in the most barbarous Ages, and totally unworthy the Head of a civilized Nation.

He has constrained our fellow Citizens taken Captive on the high Seas to bear Arms against their Country, to become the Executioners of their Friends and Brethren, or to fall themselves by their Hands.

He has excited domestic Insurrections amongst us, and has endeavoured to bring on the Inhabitants of our Frontiers, the merciless Indian Savages, whose known Rule of Warfare, is an undistinguished Destruction, of all Ages, Sexes and Conditions.

In every stage of these Oppressions we have Petitioned for Redress in the must humble Terms: Our repeated Petitions have been answered only by repeated Injury. A Prince, whose Character is thus marked by every act which may define a Tyrant, is unfit to be the Ruler of a free People.

Nor have we been wanting in Attentions to our British Brethren. We have warned them from Time to Time of Attempts by their Legislature to extend an unwarrantable Jurisdiction over us. We have reminded them of the Circumstances of our Emigration and Settlement here. We have appealed to their native Justice and Magnanimity, and we have conjured them by the Ties of our common Kindred to disavow these Usurpations, which, would inevitably interrupt our Connections and Correspondence. They too have been deaf to the Voice of Justice and of Consanguinity. We must, therefore, acquiesce in the Necessity, which denounces our Separation, and hold them, as we hold the rest of Mankind, Enemies in War, in Peace, Friends.

We, therefore, the Representatives of the UNITED STATES OF AMERICA, in GENERAL CONGRESS, Assembled, appealing to the Supreme Judge of the World for the Rectitude of our Intentions, do, in the Name, and by Authority of the good People of these Colonies, solemnly Publish and Declare, That these United Colonies are, and of Right ought to be, FREE AND INDEPENDENT STATES; that they are absolved from all Allegiance to the British Crown, and that all political Connection between them and the State of Great-Britain, is and ought to be totally dissolved; and that as FREE AND INDEPENDENT STATES, they have full Power to levy War, conclude Peace, contract Alliances, establish Commerce, and to do all other Acts and Things which INDEPENDENT STATES may of right do. And for the support of this Declaration, with a firm Reliance on the Protection of divine Providence, we mutually pledge to each other our Lives, our Fortunes, and our sacred Honor.

John Hancock

Georgia:
Button Gwinnett
Lyman Hall
George Walton

North Carolina:
William Hooper
Joseph Hewes
John Penn

South Carolina:
Edward Rutledge
Thomas Heyward, Jr.
Thomas Lynch, Jr.
Arthur Middleton

Maryland:
Samuel Chase
William Paca
Thomas Stone
Charles Carroll of Carrollton

Virginia:
George Wythe
Richard Henry Lee
Thomas Jefferson
Benjamin Harrison
Thomas Nelson, Jr.
Francis Lightfoot Lee
Carter Braxton

Pennsylvania:
Robert Morris
Benjamin Rush
Benjamin Franklin
John Morton
George Clymer
James Smith
George Taylor
James Wilson
George Ross

Delaware:
Caesar Rodney
George Read
Thomas McKean

New York:
William Floyd
Philip Livingston
Francis Lewis
Lewis Morris

New Jersey:
Richard Stockton
John Witherspoon
Francis Hopkinson
John Hart
Abraham Clark

New Hampshire:
Josiah Bartlett
William Whipple

Massachusetts:
Samuel Adams
John Adams
Robert Treat Paine
Elbridge Gerry

Rhode Island:
Stephen Hopkins
William Ellery
Connecticut:
Roger Sherman
Samuel Huntington
Oliver Wolcott

New Hampshire:
Matthew Thornton

Federalist No. 10

November 23, 1787

TO THE PEOPLE OF THE STATE OF NEW YORK

Among the numerous advantages promised by a well-constructed Union, none deserves to be more accurately developed than its tendency to break and control the violence of faction. The friend of popular governments never finds himself so much alarmed for their character and fate, as when he contemplates their propensity to this dangerous vice. He will not fail, therefore, to set a due value on any plan which, without violating the principles to which he is attached, provides a proper cure for it. The instability, injustice, and confusion introduced into the public councils, have, in truth, been the mortal diseases under which popular governments have everywhere perished; as they continue to be the favorite and fruitful topics from which the adversaries to liberty derive their most specious declamations. The valuable improvements made by the American constitutions on the popular models, both ancient and modern, cannot certainly be too much admired; but it would be an unwarrantable partiality, to contend that they have as effectually obviated the danger on this side, as was wished and expected. Complaints are everywhere heard from our most considerate and virtuous citizens, equally the friends of public and private faith, and of public and personal liberty, that our governments are too unstable, that the public good is disregarded in the conflicts of rival parties, and that measures are too often decided, not according to the rules of justice and the rights of the minor party, but by the superior force on an interested and overbearing majority. However anxiously we may wish that these complaints had no foundation, the evidence of known facts will not permit us to deny that they are in some degree true. It will be found, indeed, on a candid review of our situation, that some of the distresses under which we labor have been erroneously charged on the operation of our governments; but it will be found, at the same time, that other causes will not alone account for many of our heaviest misfortunes; and, particularly, for that prevailing and increasing distrust of public engagements, and alarm for private rights, which are echoed from one end of the continent to the other. These must be chiefly, if not wholly, effects of the unsteadiness and injustice with which a factious spirit has tainted our public administrations.

By a faction, I understand a number of citizens, whether amounting to a majority or a minority of the whole, who are united and actuated by some common impulse of passion, or of interest, adversed to the rights of other citizens, or to the permanent and aggregate interests of the community.

There are two methods of curing the mischeifs of faction: the one, by removing its causes; the other, by controlling its effects.

There are again two methods of removing the causes of faction: the one, by destroying the liberty which is essential to its existence; the other, by giving to every citizen the same opinions, the same passions, and the same interests.

It could never be more truly said than of the first remedy, that it was worse than the disease. Liberty is to faction what air is to fire, an aliment without which it instantly expires. But it could not be less folly to abolish liberty, which is essential to political life, because it nourishes faction, than it would be to wish the annihilation of air, which is essential to animal life, because it imparts to fire its destructive tendency.

The second expedient is as impracticable as the first would be unwise. As long as the reason of man continues fallible, and he is at liberty to exercise it, different opinions will be formed. As long as the connection subsists between his reason and his self-love, his opinions and his passions will have a reciprocal influence on each other; and the former will be objects to which the latter will attach themselves. The diversity in the faculties of men, from which the rights of property originate, is not less an insuperable obstacle to a uniformity of interests. The protection of these faculties is the first object of government. From the protection of different and unequal faculties of acquiring property, the possession of different degrees and kinds of property immediately results; and from the influence of these on the sentiments and views of the respective proprietors, ensues a division of the society into different interests and parties.

The latent causes of faction are thus sown in the nature of man; and we see them everywhere brought into different degrees of activity, according to the different circumstances of civil society. A zeal for different opinions concerning religion, concerning government, and many other points, as well of speculation as of practice; an attachment to different leaders ambitiously contending for pre-eminence and power; or to persons of other descriptions whose fortunes have been interesting to the human passions, have, in turn, divided mankind into parties, inflamed them with mutual animosity, and rendered them much more disposed to vex and oppress each other than to co-operate for their common good. So string is this propensity of mankind to fall into mutual animosities, that where no substantial occasion presents itself, the most frivolous and fanciful distinctions have been sufficient to kindle their unfriendly passions and excite their most violent conflicts. But the most common and durable source of factions has been the various and unequal distribution of property. Those who hold and those who are without property have ever formed distinct interests in society. Those who are creditors, and those who are debtors, fall under a like discrimination. A landed interest, a manufacturing interest, a mercantile interest, a moneyed interest, with many lesser interests, grow up of necessity in civilized nations, and divide them into different classes, actuated by different sentiments and views. The regulation of these various and interfering interests forms the principal task of modern legislation, and involves the spirit of party and faction in the necessary and ordinary operations of the government.

No man is allowed to be a judge in his own case, because his interest would certainly bias his judgment, and, not improbably, corrupt his integrity. With equal, nay with greater reason, a body of men are unfit to be both judges and parties at the same time; yet what are many of the most important acts of legislation, but so many judicial determinations, not indeed concerning the rights of single persons, but concerning the rights of large bodies of citizens? And what are the different classes of legislators but advocates and parties to the causes which they determine? Is a law proposed concerning private debts? It is a question to which the creditors are parties on one side and the debtors on the other. Justice ought to hold the balance between them. Yet the parties are, and must be, themselves the judges; and the most numerous party, or, in other words, the most powerful action must be expected to prevail. Shall domestic manufactures be encouraged, and in what degree, by restrictions on foreign manufactures? are questions which would be differently decided by the landed and the manufacturing classes, and probably by neither with a sole regard to justice and the public good. The apportionment of taxes on the various descriptions of property is an act which seems to require the most exact impartiality; yet there is, perhaps, no legislative act in which greater opportunity and temptation are given to a predominant party to trample on the rules of justice. Every shilling with which they overburden the inferior number, is a shilling saved to their own pockets.

It is in vain to say that enlightened statesmen will be able to adjust these clashing interests, and render them all subservient to the public good. Enlightened statesmen will not always be at the helm. Nor, in many cases, can such an adjustment be made at all without taking into view indirect and remote considerations, which will rarely prevail over the immediate interest which one party may find in disregarding the rights of another or the good of the whole.

The inference to which we are brought is, that the *causes* of faction cannot be removed, and that relief is only to be sought in the means of controlling its *effects*.

If a faction consists of less than a majority, relief is supplied by the republican principle, which enables the majority to defeat its sinister views by regular vote. It may clog the administration, it may convulse the society; but it will be unable to execute and mask its violence under the forms of the Constitution. When a majority is included in a faction, the form of popular government, on the other hand, enables it to sacrifice to its ruling passion or interest both the public good and the rights of other citizens. to secure the public good and private rights against the danger of such a faction, and at the same time to preserve the spirit and form of popular government, is then the great object to which our inquiries are directed. Let me add that it is the great desideratum by which this form of government can be rescued from the opprobrium under which it has so long labored, and be recommended to the esteem and adoption of mankind.

By what means is this object attainable? Evidently by one of two only. Either the existence of the same passion or interest in a majority at the same time must be prevented, or the majority, having such coexistent passion or interest, must be rendered, by their number and local situation, unable to concert and carry into effect schemes of oppression. If the impulse and the opportunity be suffered to coincide, we well know that neither moral nor religious motives can be relied on as an adequate control. They are not found to be such on the injustice and violence of individuals, and lose their efficacy in proportion to the number combined together, that is, in proportion as their efficacy becomes needful.

From this view of the subject it may be concluded that a pure democracy, by which I mean a society consisting of a small number of citizens, who assemble and administer the government in person, can admit of no cure for the mischiefs of faction. A common passion or interest will, in almost every case, be felt by a majority of the whole; a communication and concert result from the form of government itself; and there is nothing to check the inducements to sacrifice the weaker party or an obnoxious individual. Hence it is that such democracies have ever been spectacles of turbulence and contention; have ever been found incompatible with personal security or the rights of property; and have in general been as short in their lives as they have been violent in their deaths. Theoretic politicians, who have patronized this species of government, have erroneously supposed that by reducing mankind to a perfect equality in their political rights, they would, at the same time, be perfectly equalized and assimilated in their possessions, their opinions, and their passions.

A republic, by which I mean a government in which the scheme of representation takes place, opens a different prospect, and promises the cure for which we are seeking. Let us examine the points in which it varies from pure democracy, and we shall comprehend both the nature of the cure and the efficacy which it must derive from the Union.

The two great points of difference between a democracy and a republic are: first, the delegation of the government, in the latter, to a small number of citizens elected by the rest; secondly, the greater number of citizens, and greater sphere of country, over which the latter may be extended.

The effect of the first difference is, on the one hand, to refine and enlarge the public views, by passing them through the medium of a chosen body of citizens, whose wisdom may best discern the true interest of their country, and whose patriotism and love of justice will be least likely to sacrifice it to temporary or partial considerations. Under such a regulation, it may well happen that the public voice, pronounced by the representatives of the people, will be more consonant to the public good than it pronounced by the people themselves, convened for the purpose. On the other hand, the effect may be inverted. Men of factious tempers, of local prejudices, or of sinister designs, may, by intrigue, by corruption, or by other means, first obtain the suffrages, and then betray the interests, of the people. The question resulting is, whether small or extensive republics are more favorable to the election of proper guardians of the public weal; and it is clearly decided in favor of the latter by two obvious considerations:

In the first place, it is to be remarked that, however small the republic may be, the representatives must be raised to a certain number, in order to guard against the cabals of a few; and that, however large it may be, they must be limited to a certain number, in order to guard against the confusion of a multitude. Hence, the number of representatives in the two cases not being in proportion to that of the two constituents, and being proportionally greater in the small republic, it follows that, if the proportion of fit characters be not less in the large than in the small republic, the former will present a greater option, and consequently a greater probability of a fit choice.

In the next place, as each representative will be chosen by a greater number of citizens in the large than in the small republic, it will be more difficult for unworthy candidates to practice with success the vicious arts by which elections are too often carried; and the suffrages of the people being more free, will be more likely to centre in men who possess the most attractive merit and the most diffusive and established characters.

It must be confessed that in this, as in most other cases, there is a mean, on both sides of which inconveniences will be found to lie. By enlarging too much the number of electors, you render the representatives too little acquainted with all their local circumstances and lesser interests; as by reducing it too much, you render him unduly attached to these, and too little fit to comprehend and pursue great and national objects. The federal Constitution forms a happy combination in this respect; the great and aggregate interests being referred to the national, the local and particular to the State legislatures.

The other point of difference is, the greater number of citizens and extent of territory which may be brought within the compass of republican than of democratic government; and it is this circumstance principally which renders factious combinations less to be dreaded in the former than in the latter. The smaller the society, the fewer probably will be the distinct parties and interests composing it; the fewer the distinct parties and interests, the more frequently will a majority be found of the same party; and the smaller the number of individuals composing a majority, and the smaller the compass within which they are placed, the more easily will they concert and execute their plans of oppression. Extend the sphere, and you take in a greater variety of parties and interests; you make it less probable that a majority of the whole will have a common motive to invade the rights of other citizens; or if such a common motive exists, it will be more difficult for all who feel it to discover their own strength, and to act in unison with each other. Besides other impediments, it may be remarked that, where there is a consciousness of unjust or dishonorable purposes, communication is always checked by distrust in proportion to the number whose concurrence is necessary.

Hence, it clearly appears, that the same advantage which a republic has over a democracy, in controlling the effects of faction, is enjoyed by a large over a small republic,—and is enjoyed by the Union over the States composing it. Does the advantage consist in the substitution of representatives whose enlightened views and virtuous sentiments render them superior to local prejudices and schemes of injustice? It will not be denied that the representation of the Union will be most likely to possess these requisite endowments. Does it consist in the greater security afforded by a greater variety of parties, against the event of any one party being able to outnumber and oppress the rest? In an equal degree does the increased variety of parties comprised within the Union, increase this security. Does it, in fine, consist in the greater obstacles opposed to the concert and accomplishment of the secret wishes of an unjust and interested majority? Here, again, the extent of the Union gives it the most palpable advantage.

The influence of factious leaders may kindle a flame within their particular States, but will be unable to spread a general conflagration through the other States. A religious sect may degenerate into a political faction in a part of the Confederacy; but the variety of sects dispersed over the entire face of it must secure the national councils against any danger from that source. A rage for paper money, for an abolition of debts, for an equal division of property, or for any other improper or wicked project, will be less apt to pervade the whole body of the Union than a particular member of it; in the same proportion as such a malady is more likely to taint a particular county or district, than an entire State.

In the extent and proper structure of the Union, therefore, we behold a republican remedy for the diseases most incident to republican government. And according to the degree of pleasure and pride we feel in being republicans, ought to be our zeal in cherishing the spirit and supporting the character of Federalists.

PUBLIUS

Federalist No. 51

February 8, 1788
TO THE PEOPLE OF THE STATE OF NEW YORK

To what expedient, then, shall we finally resort, for maintaining in practice the necessary partition of power among the several departments, as laid down in the Constitution? The only answer that can be given is, that as all these exterior provisions are found to be inadequate, the defect must be supplied, by so contriving the interior structure of the government as that its several constituent parts may, by their mutual relations, be the means of keeping each other in their proper places. Without presuming to undertake a full development of the important idea, I will hazard a few general observations, which may perhaps place it in a clearer light, and enable us to form a more correct judgment of the principles and structure of the government planned by the convention.

In order to lay a due foundation for that separate and distinct exercise of the different powers of government, which to a certain extent is admitted on all hands to be essential to the preservation of liberty, it is evident that each department should have a will of its own; and consequently should be so constituted that the members of each should have as little agency as possible in the appointment of the members of the others. Were this principle rigorously adhered to, it would require that all the appointments for the supreme executive, legislative, and judiciary magistracies should be drawn from the same fountain of authority, the people, through channels having no communication whatever with one another. Perhaps such a plan of constructing the several departments would be less difficult in practice than it may in contemplation appear. Some difficulties, however, and some additional expense would attend the execution of it. Some deviations, therefore, from the principle must be admitted. In the constitution of the judiciary department in particular, it might be inexpedient to insist rigorously on the principle: first, because peculiar qualifications being essential in the members, the primary consideration ought to be to select that mode of choice which best secures these qualifications; secondly, because the permanent tenure by which the appointments are held in that department, must soon destroy all sense of dependence on the authority conferring them.

It is equally evident, that the members of each department should be as little dependent as possible on those of the others, for the emoluments annexed to their offices. Were the executive magistrate, or the judges, not independent of the legislature in this particular, their independence in every other would be merely nominal.

But the great security against a gradual concentration of the several powers in the same department, consists in giving to those who administer each department the necessary constitutional means and personal motives to resist encroachments of the others. The provision for defense must in this, as in all other cases, be made commensurate to the danger of attack. Ambition must be made to counteract ambition. The interest of the man must be connected with the constitutional rights of the place. It may be a reflection on human nature, that such devices should be necessary to control the abuses of government. But what is government itself, but the greatest of all reflections on human nature? If men were angels, no government would be necessary. If angels were to govern men, neither external nor internal controls on government would be necessary. In framing a government which is to be administered by men over men, the great difficulty lies in this: you must first enable the government to control the governed; and in the next place oblige it to control itself. A dependence on the people is, no doubt, the primary control on the government; but experience has taught mankind the necessity of auxiliary precautions.

This policy of supplying, by opposite and rival interests, the defect of better motives, might be traced through the whole system of human affairs, private as well as public. We see it particularly displayed in all the subordinate distributions of power, where the constant aim is to divide and arrange the several offices in such a manner as that each may be a check on the other—that the private interest of every individual may be a sentinel over the public rights. These inventions of prudence cannot be less requisite in the distribution of the supreme powers of the State.

But it is not possible to give to each department an equal power of self-defense. In republican government, the legislative authority necessarily predominates. The remedy for this inconveniency is to divide the legislature into different branches; and to render them, by different modes of election and different principles of action, as little connected with each other as the nature of their common functions and their common dependence on the society will admit. It may even be necessary to guard against dangerous encroachments by still further precautions. As the weight of the legislative authority requires that it should be thus divided, the weakness of the executive may require, on the other hand, that it should be fortified. An absolute negative on the legislature appears, at first view, to be the natural defense with which the executive magistrate should be armed. But perhaps it would be neither altogether safe nor alone sufficient. On ordinary occasions it might not be exerted with the requisite firmness, and on extraordinary occasions it might be perfidiously abused. May not this defect of an absolute negative be supplied by some qualified connection between this weaker department and the weaker branch of the stronger department, by which the latter may be led to support the constitutional rights of the former, without being too much detached from the rights of its own department?

If the principles on which these observations are founded be just, as I persuade myself they are, and they be applied as a criterion to the several State constitutions, and to the federal Constitution it will be found that if the latter does not perfectly correspond with them, the former are infinitely less able to bear such a test.

There are, moreover, two considerations particularly applicable to the federal system of America, which place that system in a very interesting point of view.

First. In a single republic, all the power surrendered by the people is submitted to the administration of a single government; and the usurpations are guarded against by a division of the government into distinct and separate departments. In the compound republic of America, the power surrendered by the people is first divided between two distinct governments, and then the portion allotted to each subdivided among distinct and separate departments. Hence a double security arises to the rights of the people. The different governments will control each other, at the same time that each will be controlled by itself.

Second. It is of great importance in a republic not only to guard the society against the oppression of its rulers, but to guard one part of the society against the injustice of the other part.

Presidents of the United States

Name of President	Dates of Service	Political Party Affiliation	Vice President(s)	Major Party Candidate(s) Defeated in General Election
George Washington	1789–97		Adams	
John Adams	1797–1801	Federalist	Jefferson	Jefferson
Thomas Jefferson	1801–09	Democratic-Republican	Burr/Clinton	Adams, Pinckney
James Madison	1809–17	Democratic-Republican	Clinton/Gerry	Pinckney, D. Clinton
James Monroe	1817–25	Democratic-Republican	Tompkins	King
John Quincy Adams	1825–29	Democratic-Republican/Democratic	Calhoun	Jackson
Andrew Jackson	1829–37	Democratic	Van Buren	J. Q. Adams, Clay
Martin Van Buren	1837–41	Democratic	Johnson	Harrison
William Harrison	1841	Whig	Tyler	Van Buren
John Tyler	1841–45	Whig	vacant	
James Polk	1845–49	Democratic	Dallas	Clay
Zachary Taylor	1849–50	Whig	Fillmore	Cass
Millard Fillmore	1850–53	Whig	vacant	
Franklin Pierce	1853–57	Democratic	King/vacant	Scott
James Buchanan	1857–61	Democratic	Breckinridge	Fremont
Abraham Lincoln	1861–65	Republican	Hamlin/Johnson	Breckinridge, Douglas, McClellan
Andrew Johnson	1865–69	Democratic	vacant	
Ulysses S. Grant	1869–77	Republican	Colfax/Wilson/vacant	Seymour, Greeley
Rutherford B. Hayes	1877–81	Republican	Wheeler	Tilden
James Garfield	1881	Republican	Arthur	Hancock
Chester Arthur	1881–85	Republican	vacant	
Grover Cleveland	1885–89	Democratic	Hendricks/vacant	Blaine

Name of President	Dates of Service	Political Party Affiliation	Vice President(s)	Major Party Candidate(s) Defeated in General Election
Benjamin Harrison	1889–93	Republican	Morton	Cleveland
Grover Cleveland	1893–97	Democratic	Stevenson	Harrison
William McKinley	1897–1901	Republican	Hobart	Bryan
Theodore Roosevelt	1901–09	Republican	vacant/Fairbanks	Parker
William Taft	1909–13	Republican	Sherman/vacant	Bryan
Woodrow Wilson	1913–21	Democratic	Marshall	T. Roosevelt, Taft, Hughes
Warren G. Harding	1921–23	Republican	Coolidge	Cox
Calvin Coolidge	1923–29	Republican	vacant/Dawes	Davis
Herbert Hoover	1929–33	Republican	Curtis	Smith
Franklin D. Roosevelt	1933–45	Democratic	Garner/Wallace/ Truman	Hoover, Landon, Wilkie, Dewey
Harry Truman	1945–53	Democratic	vacant/Barkley	Dewey
Dwight Eisenhower	1953–61	Republican	Nixon	Stevenson
John F. Kennedy	1961–63	Democratic	Johnson	Nixon
Lyndon Johnson	1963–69	Democratic	vacant/Humphrey	Goldwater
Richard Nixon	1969–74	Republican	Agnew/vacant/Ford	Humphrey, McGovern
Gerald Ford	1974–77	Republican	vacant/Rockefeller	
Jimmy Carter	1977–81	Democratic	Mondale	Ford
Ronald Reagan	1981–89	Republican	G. H.W. Bush	Carter, Mondale
George H. W. Bush	1989–93	Republican	Quayle	Dukakis
William Clinton	1993–2001	Democratic	Gore	G. H. W. Bush, Dole
George W. Bush	2001–2009	Republican	Cheney	Gore, Kerry
Barack Obama	2009–present	Democratic	Biden	McCain, Romney

Different interests necessarily exist in different classes of citizens. If a majority be united by a common interest, the rights of the minority will be insecure. There are but two methods of providing against this evil: the one by creating a will in the community independent of the majority that is, of the society itself; the other, by comprehending in the society so many separate descriptions of citizens as will render an unjust combination of a majority of the whole very improbable, if not impracticable. The first method prevails in all governments possessing an hereditary or self-appointed authority. This, at best, is but a precarious security; because a power independent of society may as well espouse the unjust views of the major as the rightful interests of the minor party, and may possibly be turned against both parties. The second method will be exemplified in the federal republic of the United States. Whilst all authority in it will be derived from and dependent on the society, the society itself will be broken into so many parts, interests, and classes of citizens, that the rights of individuals, or of the minority, will be in little danger from interested combinations of the majority. In a free government the security for civil rights must be the same as that for religious rights. It consists in the one case in the multiplicity of interests, and in the other in the multiplicity of sects. The degree of security in both cases will depend on the number of interests and sects; and this may be presumed to depend on the extent of country and number of people comprehended under the same government. This view of the subject must particularly recommend a proper federal system to all the sincere and considerate friends of republican government, since it shows that in exact proportion as the territory of the Union may be formed into more circumscribed Confederacies, or States oppressive combinations of a majority will be facilitated: the best security, under republican forms, for the rights of every class of citizens, will be diminished; and consequently the stability and independence of some member of the government, the only other security, must be proportionately increased. Justice is the end of government. It is the end of civil society. It ever has been and ever will be pursued until it be obtained, or until liberty be lost in the pursuit. In a society under the forms of which the stronger faction can readily unite and oppress the weaker, anarchy may as truly be said to reign as in a state of nature, where the weaker individual is not secured against the violence of the stronger; and as, in the latter state, even the stronger individuals are prompted, by the uncertainty of their condition, to submit to a government which may protect the wear as well as the more powerful. It can be little doubted that if the State of Rhode Island was separated from the Confederacy and left to itself, the insecurity of rights under the popular form of government within such narrow limits would be displayed by such reiterated oppressions of factious majorities that some power altogether independent of the people would soon be called for by the voice of the very factions whose misrule had proved the necessity of it. In the extended republic of the United States, and among the great variety of interests, parties, and sects which it embraces, a coalition of a majority of the whole society could seldom take place on any other principles than those of justice and the general good; whilst there being thus less danger to a minor from the will of a major party, there must be less pretext, also, to provide for the security of the former, by introducing into the government a will not dependent on the latter, or, in other words, a will independent of the society itself. It is no less certain than it is important, notwithstanding the contrary opinions which have been entertained, that the larger the society, provided it lie within a practical sphere, the more duly capable it will be of self-government. And happily for the *republican cause*, the practicable sphere may be carried to a very great extent, by a judicious modification of mixture of the *federal principle*.

PUBLIUS

ANSWERS TO THE TEST-YOURSELF MULTIPLE-CHOICE QUESTIONS

CHAPTER 1

FORMS AND FUNCTIONS OF GOVERNMENT
1. (d)   2. (c)

AMERICAN GOVERNMENT AND POLITICS
1. (b)   2. (a)

AMERICAN POLITICAL CULTURE
1. (a)   2. (d)

IS AMERICAN DEMOCRACY IN DECLINE?
1. (c)   2. (a)

CHAPTER 2

THE BEGINNINGS OF A NEW NATION
1. (a)   2. (d)   3. (b)

THE CONSTITUTIONAL CONVENTION
1. (b)   2. (a)

THE NEW CONSTITUTION
1. (b)   2. (c)

THE RATIFICATION BATTLE
1. (a)   2. (b)   3. (d)

CHANGING THE CONSTITUTION
1. (c)

CHAPTER 3

WHAT IS FEDERALISM?
1. (b)   2. (a)   3. (d)

THE HISTORY OF AMERICAN FEDERALISM
1. (d)   2. (d)   3. (b)

WHY FEDERALISM? ADVANTAGES AND DISADVANTAGES
1. (c)   2. (a)

CHAPTER 4

THE BILL OF RIGHTS: ORIGINS AND EVOLUTION
1. (d)   2. (a)   3. (c)

FREEDOM OF RELIGION AND THE ESTABLISHMENT CLAUSE
1. (a)   2. (b)

FREE EXPRESSION RIGHTS
1. (b)   2. (d)   3. (b)

THE SECOND AMENDMENT RIGHT TO BEAR ARMS
1. (d)

THE RIGHTS OF THE CRIMINALLY ACCUSED
1. (c)   2. (b)   3. (d)

THE MODERN RIGHT TO PRIVACY
1. (c)   2. (a)

CHAPTER 5

TYPES OF EQUALITY
1. (b)   2. (a)

THE STRUGGLE FOR EQUALITY: APPROACHES AND TACTICS
1. (d)   2. (b)

THE AFRICAN AMERICAN STRUGGLE FOR EQUALITY AND CIVIL RIGHTS
1. (b)   2. (a)
3. (d)   4. (a)

THE WOMENÕS MOVEMENT AND GENDER EQUALITY
1. (b)   2. (c)

OTHER STRUGGLES FOR EQUALITY
1. (c)   2. (d)   3. (c)

CHAPTER 6

ARTICLE I AND THE CREATION OF CONGRESS
1. (c)   2. (a)   3. (c)

THE STRUCTURE AND ORGANIZATION OF CONGRESS
1. (d)   2. (a)   3. (b)

THE COMMITTEE SYSTEM
1. (c)   2. (a)   3. (b)

HOW A BILL BECOMES A LAW
1. (c)   2. (b)   3. (d)

OVERSIGHT AND PERSONNEL FUNCTIONS OF CONGRESS
1. (a)   2. (b)

CONSTITUENT SERVICE: HELPING PEOPLE BACK HOME

   1. (b)

CHAPTER 7

WHERE DO PRESIDENTS COME FROM? PRESIDENTIAL COMINGS AND GOINGS

   1. (b)   2. (c)

THE EVOLUTION OF THE AMERICAN PRESIDENCY

   1. (c)   2. (a)

EXPRESS POWERS AND RESPONSIBILITIES OF THE PRESIDENT

   1. (b)   2. (a)

IMPLIED POWERS AND RESPONSIBILITIES OF THE PRESIDENT

   1. (d)   2. (c)

PRESIDENTIAL RESOURCES

   1. (d)   2. (c)

IMPORTANT PRESIDENTIAL RELATIONSHIPS

   1. (c)   2. (d)

CHAPTER 8

WHAT IS BUREAUCRACY?

   1. (a)   2. (b)

WHAT DOES THE FEDERAL BUREAUCRACY DO?

   1. (c)   2. (c)   3. (d)

THE DEVELOPMENT OF THE FEDERAL BUREAUCRACY

   1. (b)

GETTING CONTROL OF THE GROWING BUREAUCRACY

   1. (b)   2. (c)

THE ORGANIZATION OF THE FEDERAL BUREAUCRACY

   1. (c)   2. (c)   3. (d)

THE FEDERAL WORKFORCE

   1. (a)   2. (b)

CHAPTER 9

TYPES OF LAW

   1. (d)   2. (b)

THE STRUCTURE OF THE U.S. LEGAL SYSTEM

   1. (c)   2. (b)

THE ADVERSARIAL SYSTEM OF JUSTICE

   1. (b)   2. (a)   3. (d)

JUDICIAL REVIEW AND ITS IMPLICATIONS

   1. (a)   2. (b)

LIMITATIONS ON COURTS

   1. (b)

ELECTING AND APPOINTING JUDGES

   1. (a)   2. (c)

HOW A CASE PROCEEDS WITHIN THE U.S. SUPREME COURT

   1. (b)   2. (c)   3. (b)

WHY THE JUSTICES VOTE THE WAY THEY DO

   1. (d)

CURRENT DEBATES OVER THE EXERCISE OF JUDICIAL POWER

   1. (b)

CHAPTER 10

PUBLIC OPINION IN AMERICAN POLITICS

   1. (c)

HOW IS PUBLIC OPINION EXPRESSED?

   1. (c)   2. (c)

THE LEVELS OF PUBLIC OPINION

   1. (b)   2. (a)

HOW INFORMED IS PUBLIC OPINION?

   1. (b)

HOW DOES PUBLIC OPINION FORM?

   1. (a)

HOW IS PUBLIC OPINION MEASURED?

   1. (b)   2. (d)

INTERPRETING PUBLIC OPINION DATA

   1. (b)

CHAPTER 11

PLURALISM AND THE INTEREST GROUP SYSTEM

   1. (c)   2. (a)

INTEREST GROUPS IN ACTION

   1. (a)   2. (a)   3. (c)

TYPES OF INTEREST GROUPS

   1. (b)   2. (a)

HOW INTEREST GROUPS ACHIEVE THEIR GOALS

   1. (b)   2. (d)

CHAPTER 12

The Media in American Politics
1. (a) 2. (d)

Historical Development of the Media
1. (a) 2. (b)

The Mass Media Today
1. (d) 2. (c) 3. (a)

The Effects of the Media
1. (d) 2. (a)

Criticisms of the News Media
1. (d)

CHAPTER 13

The Development of Political Parties in the United States
1. (b) 2. (c) 3. (a)

The Functions of Political Parties
1. (d) 2. (c)

Why a Two-Party System?
1. (c) 2. (c)

Party Organizations
1. (a)

Are Parties in Decline?
1. (b)

Voting
1. (c) 2. (a)

Exercising the Franchise
1. (d) 2. (c)

CHAPTER 14

American Presidential Elections in Historical Perspective
1. (c) 2. (d) 3. (c)

The Prenomination Campaign
1. (b)

The Nomination Campaign
1. (c) 2. (a) 3. (d)

The General Election Campaign
1. (d) 2. (b) 3. (a)

Campaign Funding
1. (a)

Congressional Campaigns and Elections
1. (d) 2. (d)

CHAPTER 15

An Overview of the Policymaking Process
1. (c) 2. (d)

Theories and Practice in Fiscal Policy
1. (b) 2. (a) 3. (b)

Theories and Practice in Monetary Policy
1. (d) 2. (d)

The Nature and Practice of Crime Policy
1. (c)

The Welfare State and Programs for the Poor
1. (d) 2. (d)

The Social Security System
1. (a) 2. (a)

Health Care Policy
1. (b)

CHAPTER 16

The Constitutional Framework of American Foreign Policy
1. (b) 2. (b)

The Roots of American Foreign Policy
1. (c) 2. (b) 3. (c)

The Structure of American Foreign Policymaking
1. (d) 2. (c) 3. (d)

Foreign Policy Dilemmas for the Twenty-first Century
1. (d)

GLOSSARY

A

administrative discretion The freedom of agencies to decide how to implement a vague or ambiguous law passed by Congress.

administrative law A law that relates to the authority of administrative agencies and the rules promulgated by those agencies.

affirmative action Programs, laws, or practices designed to remedy past discriminatory hiring practices, government contracting, and school admissions.

agenda setting theory The theory holding that although the effects of television exposure may be minimal or difficult to gauge, the media are quite influential in telling the public what to think about.

agents of political socialization Factors that have a significant impact on an individual's socialization to politics.

amendments Modifications or additions to the U.S. Constitution passed in accordance with the amendment procedures laid out in Article V.

amicus curiae briefs Written documents filed by outside parties in a Supreme Court case with an interest in the outcome of the litigation expressing their own views on how the Court should decide a particular case.

anarchy A state of lawlessness and discord in the political system caused by lack of government.

Anti-Federalists Those who opposed ratification of the proposed constitution of the United States between 1787 and 1789.

appellate jurisdiction The authority of a court to review decisions handed down by another court.

Articles of Confederation The document creating a "league of friendship" governing the 13 states during and immediately after the war for independence; hampered by the limited power the document vested in the legislature to collect revenue or regulate commerce, the Articles eventually proved unworkable for the new nation.

authoritarianism A form of government in which one political party, group, or person maintains such complete control over the nation that it may refuse to recognize and may even suppress all other political parties and interests.

authority The ability of public institutions and the officials within them to make laws, independent of the power to execute them.

B

bail An amount of money determined by a judge that the accused must pay to a court as security against his or her freedom before trial.

battleground states States identified as offering either major-party candidate a reasonable chance for victory in the electoral college.

bicameral legislature A legislature composed of two separate chambers.

bill A proposed law presented for consideration to a legislative body.

bill of attainder An act of a legislature declaring a person (or group) guilty of some crime, and then carrying out punishment without a trial. The Constitution denies Congress the ability to issue a bill of attainder.

Bill of Rights The first 10 amendments to the U.S. Constitution, which protect various rights of the people against the new federal government.

Bipartisan Campaign Reform Act (BCRA) of 2002 Also called the McCain-Feingold Act, the federal legislation that (1) restricted soft money spent by political parties, (2) regulated expenditures on ads that refer to specific candidates immediately before an election, and (3) increased limits on hard money donated directly to candidates and their campaigns.

block grants Grants from the federal government to the states that may be used at the discretion of states to pursue more generalized aims.

blogs Internet sites that serve as a combination editorial page, personal Web page, and online diary of personal observations in real time about news events and issues.

briefs Written documents filed by parties in an appealed case arguing why constitutional or statutory law weighs in favor of their respective positions.

***Brown v. Board of Education* (1954)** The 1954 U.S. Supreme Court decision that declared school segregation to be unconstitutional.

Buckley v. Valeo (1976) The 1976 Supreme Court opinion that held that spending money to influence elections is protected First Amendment speech, and that prohibited limitations on independent expenditures or personal money spent by candidates on their own campaigns.

budget authority The power of federal departments and agencies to incur obligations to spend or lend money.

budget deficit The amount of money spent by the U.S. government beyond that which it collects in taxes and other revenue in a single year.

budget surplus The amount by which the U.S. government's revenue exceeds its spending in a given fiscal year.

bureaucracy An organization set up in a logical and rational manner for the purpose of accomplishing specific functions.

bureaucratic adjudicating Determining the rights and duties of particular parties within the scope of an agency's rules or regulations.

C

cabinet departments Those federal agencies that qualify as the major administrative organizations of the executive branch.

cabinet The collection of the principal officers in each of the executive departments of the federal government who serve as key advisers to the president.

capitalism Economic system in which all or most of the means of production are privately owned under competitive conditions.

casework The direct assistance that a member of Congress provides to a constituent, community group, or a local or state official.

caucus A method of choosing party nominees in which party members attend local meetings at which they choose delegates committed to a particular candidate.

Central Intelligence Agency (CIA) Federal agency charged with evaluating and disseminating intelligence information, performing public relations functions that affect international perceptions of the United States, and engaging in overt and covert operations at the direction of the president.

checks and balances A system of limits imposed by the Constitution that gives each branch of government the limited right to change or cancel the acts of other branches.

civil law This term has two meanings (1) legislative codes, laws, or sets of rules enacted by duly authorized lawmaking bodies such as Congress, state and local legislatures, or any executive authority entrusted with the power to make laws; (2) the body of noncriminal laws of a nation or state that deal with the rights of private citizens.

civil liberties Those specific individual rights that are guaranteed by the Constitution and cannot be denied to citizens by government. Many of these rights are found in the first 10 amendments to the Constitution, known as the Bill of Rights.

Civil Rights Act of 1964 The federal law that banned racial discrimination in all public accommodations, including those that were privately owned; prohibited discrimination by employers and created the Equal Employment Opportunity Commission to investigate complaints of discrimination; and denied public funds to schools that continued to discriminate on the basis of race.

Civil Rights Act of 1968 The federal law that banned race discrimination in housing and made interference with a citizen's civil rights a federal crime.

civil rights Those positive rights, whether political, social, or economic, conferred by the government on individuals or groups.

Civil Service Reform Act of 1978 The federal act that replaced the Civil Service Commission (the agency that oversaw federal hiring and firing practices) with the Office of Personnel Management (OPM) and the Merit Systems Protection Board (MSPB).

civil service The system whereby workers in the federal bureaucracy are supposed to be immune from partisan political maneuvering.

Civil War Amendments The Thirteenth Amendment (ratified in 1865) banished slavery from all states and U.S. territories. The Fourteenth Amendment (ratified in 1868) granted full U.S. and state citizenship to all people born or naturalized in the United States and guaranteed to each person "the equal protection of the laws." The Fifteenth Amendment (1870) forbade the denial or abridgement of the right to vote by any government on account of race.

class action lawsuit A lawsuit filed by a large group of people with clearly defined common interests.

closed primary An election that requires voters to declare their party affiliation ahead of time.

closed rule A rule of procedure adopted by the House Rules Committee that severely limits the ability of members of Congress to amend a bill.

closed shop The law that requires employees to become members of the union as a condition of employment in unionized workplaces.

cloture A Senate debate procedure that permits that body to end debate and force a vote on a bill by a vote of 60 senators.

coattail effect The potential benefit that successful presidential candidates offer to congressional candidates of the same political party during presidential election years.

Cold War The nearly half-century struggle over ideological differences between the United States and the Soviet Union. Waged through economic warfare, arms buildups, and tense diplomatic talks, the Cold War never broke out into a sustained military engagement between the two nations and ended with the dissolution of the Soviet Union in 1991.

common law Judge-made law handed down through judicial opinions, which over time establish precedents.

complaint A document written by the plaintiff arguing why the court is empowered to hear the case and explaining why the plaintiff is entitled to some form of relief under the current law.

concurrent powers Those powers shared by the federal and state governments under the Constitution.

concurring opinion The opinion of one or more justices that agrees with the end result reached by the majority but disagrees with the reasons offered for the decision.

confederation A system of government (or "league") in which two or more independent states unite to achieve certain specified common aims.

conference committee A joint committee of Congress appointed by the House of Representatives and the Senate to resolve differences on a particular bill.

congressional agencies Government bodies formed by and relied on by Congress to support members of Congress in performing their functions.

congressional committee staff A group of workers assigned to congressional committees to support each committee's legislative work.

congressional district A geographic region (either a state itself or a region located entirely within one state) whose residents select one member to represent it in the House of Representatives.

congressional oversight Congress's exercise of its authority to monitor the activities of agencies and administrators.

congressional personal staff A group of workers who assist an individual member of Congress in performing his or her responsibilities.

conservative ideology A political orientation that generally favors government activism in defense of more traditional values on social issues, but favors government restraint in economic redistribution.

Constitutional Convention Meeting of delegates from 12 states in Philadelphia during the summer of 1787, at which was drafted an entirely new system to govern the United States.

consumer price index (CPI) An index of prices for goods and services regularly traded in the U.S. economy.

containment U.S. foreign policy that sought to restrict Soviet power (and communist influence) to its existing geographical sphere.

continuity (in public opinion) A tendency for political preferences to remain generally stable over time.

cooperative federalism The doctrine of federalism that affords Congress nearly unlimited authority to exercise its powers through means that often coerce states into administering and/or enforcing federal policies.

crime control model Criminal justice policymaking model that views the controlling of criminal behavior as the system's most important function.

critical election An election that produces sharp changes in patterns of party loyalty among voters.

cultivation theory The theory of media effects that suggests that heavy television exposure helps develop an individual's overall view of the world.

D

dealignment A decline in voter attachment to parties and in clarity of party coalitions.

Declaration of Independence Formal document listing colonists' grievances and articulating the colonists' intention to seek independence; formally adopted by the Second Continental Congress on July 4, 1776.

defendant The target of a plaintiff's complaint or a criminal complaint.

delegation of congressional power Congress's transferring of its lawmaking authority to the executive branch of government.

democracy Form of government in which the people, either directly or through elected representatives, hold power and authority. The word *democracy* is derived from the Greek *demos kratos*, meaning "rule by the people."

Department of Defense Executive branch agency that is responsible for managing the nation's military and advising the president on all military matters.

Department of Homeland Security (DHS) Executive branch agency established in 2002 to coordinate government entities in protecting U.S. citizens against terrorism within the nation's borders.

Department of State Executive branch agency that is primarily responsible for most foreign policy programs within the executive branch, including diplomatic missions, foreign aid, and contributions to international organizations.

deregulation The elimination of government oversight and government regulation of certain activities.

devolution The transfer of power and responsibilities for certain regulatory programs from the federal government back to the states.

digital divide The large differences in usage of the Internet between older and younger people, lower- and middle-/upper-class people, lesser and better educated people, and minority groups and nonminority groups.

direct democracy A system of government in which all citizens participate in making policy, rules, and governing decisions.

direction (of public opinion) A tendency toward a particular preference, usually (though not always) characterized as either positive or negative.

direct primary election An open election, rather than an election by party leaders, to choose candidates for the general election.

discount rate The rate (expressed as a percentage) that all Federal Reserve member banks and other depository institutions will be charged by the Federal Reserve Banks to borrow short-term funds.

discovery A stage of pretrial litigation in which the plaintiff and defendant have the right to learn what information the other side has about the case by requesting documents or materials, access to property, and/or examinations, or by offering answers to questions about the litigation either in written form or verbally at a deposition.

discretionary spending Forms of federal government spending that Congress can modify or eliminate in any given year, including spending on education, the environment, and national defense.

dissenting opinion The opinion of one or more justices who disagree with the result reached by the majority.

distributive tax policies Taxation policies intended to promote the interests of all classes equally.

divided government Split-party control of Congress and the presidency.

domino theory The theory that held that communist takeovers of countries in Southeast Asia and elsewhere would be followed by subsequent communist takeovers of nearby countries.

double jeopardy clause The constitutional protection that those accused of a crime cannot be tried twice for the same crime.

dual federalism The doctrine of federalism that holds that state authority acts as a significant limit on congressional power under the Constitution.

due process model Criminal justice policymaking model that views the attainment of justice—which includes protection of the innocent—as the principal goal of the system.

E

economic equality May be defined as providing all groups the equality of opportunity for economic success, or as the equality of results. In the United States, the latter has been the more common understanding of economic equality.

economic interest group An organized group that exists to promote favorable economic conditions and economic opportunities for its members.

electoral college The constitutional mechanism by which presidents are chosen. Each state is allocated electoral college votes based on the sum of that state's U.S. senators and House members.

electors Individuals appointed to represent a state's presidential vote in the electoral college; in practice, voters in presidential elections vote for a slate of electors committed to a particular candidate, rather than voting directly for the candidate.

enumerated powers Express powers explicitly granted by the Constitution, such as the taxing power specifically granted to Congress.

equal time rule The FCC mandate that radio and TV stations offer equal amounts of airtime to all political candidates who want to broadcast advertisements.

establishment clause The clause in the First Amendment that prohibits government from enacting any law "respecting an establishment of religion." Separationist interpretations of this clause affirm that government should not support any religious activity. Accommodationists say that support for a religion is legal provided that all religions are equally supported.

exclusionary rule The legal rule requiring that all evidence illegally obtained by police in violation of the Bill of Rights must be "excluded" from admission in a court of law, where it might have assisted in convicting those accused of committing crimes.

executive agreement A pact reached between the president and a foreign government that does not require the consent of Congress.

Executive Office of the President The staffers who help the president of the United States manage the rest of the federal bureaucracy.

executive orders Rules or regulations issued by the chief executive that have the force of law and do not require the consent of Congress.

expansionism Doctrine that favors a country expanding its own territory and influence.

ex post facto law A law that punishes someone for an act that took place in the past, at a time when the act was not illegal. The Constitution denies government the ability to write laws ex post facto.

F

Federal Election Campaign Act (FECA) The federal legislation passed in 1971 that established disclosure requirements and restricted individual campaign contributions.

Federal Election Commission (FEC) The agency created in 1974 to enforce federal election laws.

federalism The doctrine underlying a system of government in which power is divided between a central government and constituent political subunits.

Federalist Papers A series of articles authored by Alexander Hamilton, James Madison, and John Jay, which argued in favor of ratifying the proposed constitution of the United States; the Federalist Papers outlined the philosophy and motivation of the document.

Federalists Those who supported ratification of the proposed constitution of the United States between 1787 and 1789.

Federal Register The journal that publishes regulations that implement a federal program.

Federal Reserve Board The Federal Reserve System's Board of Governors, which votes on monetary policy in the United States, supervises the nation's banks by setting rules for the 12 Federal Reserve Banks, and engages in open market operations.

Federal Reserve System The central banking system of the United States, which controls the nation's money supply.

Fifteenth Amendment The amendment to the Constitution that guaranteed the franchise regardless of race, color, or any previous condition of servitude.

filibuster The action by a single senator or a minority of senators to block a bill from passage by refusing to end discussion.

fiscal policy Decisions by the federal government that relate to raising revenue through taxation and spending the revenue that is thereby generated.

flat tax A tax policy that draws money from all entities at the same proportion of their income.

franking privilege The traditional right of members of Congress to mail materials to their constituents without paying postage.

free exercise clause The religious freedom clause in the First Amendment that denies government the ability to prohibit the free exercise of religion. Debate over the clause has largely focused on whether government laws can force adherents of a certain religion to engage in activities that are prohibited by their religious beliefs or prevent them from performing acts that are compelled by their religious beliefs.

free rider An individual who does not join or contribute to an interest group that is representing his or her interests.

frontloading The recent trend of states moving their primaries and caucuses earlier in the year to attract greater attention from the candidates and the media.

full faith and credit clause The provision in Article IV, Section 1 of the Constitution that forces states to abide by the official acts and proceedings of all other states.

G

gerrymandering The drawing of House district boundaries to the benefit of one political party over another. The term is named for Elbridge Gerry, a Massachusetts delegate to the Constitutional Convention, who (as governor) redrew districts in this fashion to favor the Democratic-Republicans.

Gibbons v. Ogden (1824) The Supreme Court case that held that under the Constitution, a federal license to operate steamboats overrides a state-granted monopoly of New York water rights.

good faith exception An exception to the exclusionary rule stating that if a search warrant is invalid through no fault of the police, evidence obtained under that warrant may still be admitted into court.

government corporations Units in the federal bureaucracy set up to run like private companies that depend on revenue from citizens to provide their services.

government The collection of public institutions in a nation that establish and enforce the rules by which the members of that nation must live.

grand jury A jury whose duty it is to hear the evidence offered by a prosecutor and determine whether a trial is justified.

grants-in-aid Grants from the federal government to states that allow state governments to pursue specific federal policies, such as highway construction.

grassroots lobbying Communications by interest groups with government officials through the mobilization of public opinion to exert influence on government action.

Great Compromise A proposal also known as the "Connecticut Compromise" that provided for a bicameral legislature featuring an upper house based on equal representation among the states and a lower house whose membership was based on each state's population; approved by a 5–4 vote of the state delegations.

Great Society A set of aggressive federal domestic policies proposed by President Lyndon Johnson and passed by Congress in the 1960s that further enhanced the role of the presidency.

gross domestic product (GDP) An estimate of the total money value of all the goods and services produced in the United States in a one-year period.

H

hard money Donations made directly to political candidates and their campaigns that must be declared with the name of the donor (which then becomes public knowledge).

Hatch Act of 1939 The 1939 law that insulated the civil service from partisan politics by prohibiting employee dismissals for partisan reasons and by prohibiting federal workers from participating in political campaigns.

hawks Members of the president's administration who call for aggressive military actions wherever hostile forces may be found.

health maintenance organizations Prepaid group practice arrangements entered into by doctors and other health professionals that attempt to limit costs by charging customers flat monthly rates with little or no deductibles.

I

impeachment The first step in a two-step process outlined in Article II, Section 4 of the U.S. Constitution to remove a president or other high official from office. The House of Representatives, by majority vote, may impeach if the official has committed "treason, bribery, or other high crimes or misdemeanors." The second step requires a conviction in the Senate by a two-thirds vote.

incorporation The process by which the U.S. Supreme Court used the due process clause of the Fourteenth Amendment to make most of the individual rights guaranteed by the Bill of Rights also applicable to the states. Incorporation provided that state and local governments, as well as the federal government, could not deny these rights to citizens.

incumbent race General election race pitting a person currently holding the office against a challenger.

independent agency A department that focuses on a narrower set of issues than do higher-status Cabinet departments.

independent campaign expenditures Political donations that PACs or individuals spend to support campaigns, but do not directly contribute to the campaigns.

indictment A decision by a grand jury authorizing the government to proceed to trial against the defendant.

individualism The value that individuals are primarily responsible for their own lot in life and that promotes and rewards individual initiative and responsibility. This value underlies America's reliance on a capitalist economy and free market system.

inflation The overall general upward price movement of goods and services in an economy, normally measured by the consumer price index (CPI).

intensity (of public opinion) The degree of strength or commitment the public feels about the opinion it holds.

interest group An organization of people with shared goals that tries to influence public policy through a variety of activities.

intergovernmental lobby Any interest group that represents the collective interests of states, cities, and other governments.

internationalism Doctrine that favors active participation of the nation in collective arrangements that secure the political independence and territorial boundaries of other countries.

international organization Entity of international scope or character, usually established by treaty, such as the World Bank or the International Monetary Fund.

invisible primary The competition among candidates seeking the party nomination for frontrunner status prior to the primaries and caucuses.

iron triangle A three-sided network of policymaking that includes congressional committees (and subcommittees) in a specific policy area, executive agencies with authority over that area, and private interest groups focused on influencing that area.

isolationism Foreign policy doctrine that opposes intervention in distant wars and involvement in permanent military alliances.

issue and ideological group An organized group that focuses on specific issues and ideological perspectives.

issue network The broad array of actors (beyond just the iron triangle) that try to collectively influence a policy area in which they maintain a vested interest.

J

Jim Crow laws Laws used by some southern states that required segregation of blacks and whites in public schools, railroads, buses, restaurants, hotels, theaters, and other public facilities. The laws excluded blacks from militias and denied them certain education and welfare services.

Joint Chiefs of Staff (JCS) Group of chief officers of the four branches of the armed forces as well as a JCS chair and vice chair, which advises the president on military matters and delivers the president's orders to the military.

joint committee A committee composed of members of both the House and the Senate that is investigative in nature.

judicial review The power of a court to declare acts of the other branches of government or of a subordinate government to be unconstitutional and thus invalid.

K

***Katz* test** The legal standard that requires the government to attain a warrant demonstrating "probable cause" for any "search" that violates a person's actual and reasonable expectation of privacy.

Keynesian economic theory Fiscal policy theory that favors government taxation and spending during difficult economic times.

L

laissez-faire economics Fiscal policy theory that favors minimal intervention in the nation's economy.

layer-cake federalism Description of federalism as maintaining that the authority of state and federal governments exists in distinct and separate spheres.

legitimacy The extent to which the people afford the government the authority and right to exercise power.

Lemon test The legal test that determines if a government statute aiding public or private schools is an unconstitutional violation of the establishment clause. The statute is unconstitutional if the statute has no secular purpose, if its principal or primary effect advances or inhibits religion, or if it fosters "an excessive government entanglement with religion."

libel Printing or disseminating false statements that harm someone.

liberal ideology A political orientation that favors a more assertive role in the redistribution of economic resources, but emphasizes individual freedom on a range of social issues.

limited government The value that promotes the idea that government power should be as restricted as possible.

literacy test The requirement that individuals prove that they can read and write before being allowed to vote.

litigation Any judicial contest, including all the events that lead up to a possible court event.

lobbying The means by which interest groups attempt to influence government officials to make decisions favorable to their goals.

logrolling The trading of influence or votes among legislators to achieve passage of projects that are of interest to one another.

loose construction Constitutional interpretation that gives constitutional provisions broad and open-ended meanings.

M

majoritarianism The principle that the choice that is supported by the most voters is the choice that prevails.

majoritarianism The theory that public policy is a product of what majorities of citizens prefer.

majority caucus The members of the party that has the majority of seats in a particular chamber.

majority leader In the Senate, the controlling party's main spokesperson who leads his or her party in proposing new laws and crafting the party's platform. The Senate majority leader also enjoys the power to make committee assignments. In the House, the majority leader is the controlling party's second in command, who helps the Speaker to oversee the development of the party platform.

majority opinion The opinion of a majority of members of the U.S. Supreme Court, which carries the force of law.

majority rule The notion that the will of the majority should guide decisions made by American government.

mandatory spending Federal government spending that is not controlled by annual budget decisions; includes entitlements such as Medicare and Social Security.

manifest destiny U.S. policy of the mid-nineteenth century that advocated acquiring lands and occupying the entire American continent from one ocean to the other.

marble-cake federalism Description of federalism as intertwining state and federal authority in an inseparable mixture.

marginal seat A seat in a congressional district that has relatively similar numbers of Democratic and Republican voters.

Marshall Plan The 1947 U.S. policy that provided loans and aid to Western European countries whose economies had been ravaged by World War II.

***Martin v. Hunter's Lessee* (1816)** The Supreme Court case that established that state governments and state courts must abide by the U.S. Supreme Court's interpretation of the federal Constitution.

material benefits (of group membership) The specific, tangible benefits individuals receive from interest-group membership, such as economic concessions, discounts on products, and so forth.

***McCulloch v. Maryland* (1819)** The Supreme Court case that established that Congress enjoys broad and extensive authority to make all laws that are "necessary and proper" to carry out its constitutionally delegated powers.

Medicaid Federal program that provides limited health care services to the poor.

Medicare Federal program that provides health insurance for the elderly.

merit system A system of appointing and promoting civil service personnel based on merit rather than political affiliation or loyalty.

midterm congressional elections Congressional elections held midway between successive presidential elections.

military-industrial complex The vast network of defense industries in America (including manufacturers of weapons, missiles, aircraft, and so forth) and their allies in the federal bureaucracy.

minimal effects theory The theory that deep-seated, long-term political attitudes have much greater influence on an individual's vote decisions than does news media coverage.

minority caucus The members of the party that has a minority of seats in a particular chamber.

minority leader The leader of the minority party in each chamber.

***Miranda* warning** The Supreme Court's requirement that for a confession to be admissible in court, an individual who is arrested must be read a statement that explains the person's right to remain silent and the right to an attorney.

monarchy A form of government in which one person, usually a member of a royal family or a royal designate, exercises supreme authority.

monetary policy Regulation of the money supply and interest rates by a central bank, such as the U.S. Federal Reserve Board, in order to control inflation and stabilize the currency.

Monroe Doctrine U.S. foreign policy that proclaimed North and South America unavailable for future colonization by any European power and that declared that any such colonization would be viewed as an act of war on the United States.

Motor Voter law The federal law mandating that when an individual applies for or renews a state driver's license, the state must also provide that individual with voter registration materials.

multiparty system A political system in which many different parties are organized on the basis of political ideologies, economic interests, religion, geography, or positions on a single issue or set of issues.

N

national committee chair The head of the national committee for one of the two major parties.

national committee The committee that oversees the conduct of a party's presidential campaign and develops strategy for congressional elections.

national debt The total sum of the federal government's outstanding debt obligations.

national party convention A large meeting that draws together party delegates from across the nation to choose (or formally affirm the selection of) the party's presidential and vice presidential candidates.

national party organization The institution through which political parties exist at the national, state, and local levels, primarily focused on articulating policy positions, raising money, organizing volunteers, and providing services to candidates.

National Security Council (NSC) Advisory body to the president charged with coordinating information about foreign, military, and economic policies that affect national security.

national supremacy doctrine Chief Justice John Marshall's interpretation of federalism as holding that states have extremely limited sovereign authority, whereas Congress is supreme within its own sphere of constitutional authority.

natural law According to John Locke, the most fundamental type of law, which supersedes any law that is made by government. Citizens are born with certain natural rights (including life, liberty, and property) that derive from this law and that government cannot take away.

necessary and proper clause The clause in Article I, Section 8 of the Constitution that affords Congress the power to make laws that serve as a means to achieving its expressly delegated powers.

New Deal A set of aggressive federal domestic policies proposed by President Franklin Roosevelt in the 1930s and passed by Congress as a response to the Great Depression; it ultimately transformed the presidency into an institution marked by permanent bureaucracies and well-established repositories of power.

New Jersey Plan A proposal known also as the "small states plan" that would have retained the Articles of Confederation's principle of a legislature where states enjoyed equal representation.

new media Media outlets that rely on relatively newer technologies for communicating, such as the Internet, DVDs, fax machines, cell phones, satellites, cable TV, and broadband.

new world order President George H. W. Bush's description of the post–Cold War world, in which nations would work together for the purpose of securing collective peace, security, freedom, and the rule of law.

Nineteenth Amendment The constitutional amendment that guarantees women equal voting rights.

nomination campaign The political season in which the two major parties hold primaries and caucuses in all the states to choose party delegates committed to specific candidates.

noneconomic interest group An organized group that advocates for reasons other than its membership's commercial and financial interests.

normal vote The percentage of voters that can be expected with reasonable certainty to cast a ballot for each of the two major political parties.

North Atlantic Treaty Organization (NATO) A military, political, and economic alliance of nations formally bound to protect self-determination and open trade in Western Europe.

O

objectivity The journalistic standard that news reporting of events must be factual, accurate, fair, and equitable.

oligarchy A form of government in which a small exclusive class, which may or may not attempt to rule on behalf of the people as a whole, holds supreme power.

open election General election race in which neither candidate is the incumbent. (Open elections for Congress are normally called "open-seat elections.").

open market operations The buying and selling of government securities by the Federal Reserve Board as a means of controlling the national money supply.

open primary An election that allows voters to choose on the day of the primary election the party in which they want to vote.

open rule A rule of procedure adopted by the House Rules Committee that permits amendments to a bill.

open shop The law that allows employees the option of joining or not joining the certified union at a unionized workplace.

original jurisdiction The authority of a court to be the initial court in which a legal decision is rendered.

outlays The amount of money a government agency will actually spend during a fiscal year.

overriding (a veto) The power of the Congress to enact legislation despite a president's veto of that legislation; requires a two-thirds vote of both houses of Congress.

P

pacifism Doctrine of foreign relations that refuses to sanction any military conflict and that opposes all war making.

pardon The president's constitutional authority to relieve an individual of both the punishment and the guilt of violating the law.

partisan press era The period from the late 1700s to the mid-1800s when newspapers typically supported a particular political party.

party identification The psychological attachment that an individual has to a particular party.

party platform A document outlining the party's position on important policy issues.

Patient Protection and Affordable Care Act (PPACA) The main federal legislation passed in 2010 that overhauled the health care system by expanding Medicaid and guaranteeing health care coverage for select groups of citizens. The law was amended a week later as the Health Care and Education Reconciliation Act of 2010.

patronage The act of appointing people to government positions in return for their partisan and/or political support.

Pendleton Civil Service Reform Act The 1883 law that created a merit system for hiring many federal workers, protected them from being fired for partisan reasons, and set up a Civil Service Commission to oversee the hiring and firing process.

plaintiff The party that chooses to initiate formal legal proceedings in a civil case.

plea bargain A pretrial negotiated resolution in a criminal case in which the defendants seek to reduce their jail sentences by pleading guilty and in return prosecutors are willing to trade down the severity of the punishment.

***Plessy v. Ferguson* (1896)** The Supreme Court case that upheld a Louisiana segregation law on the theory that as long as the accommodations between the racially segregated facilities were equal, the equal protection clause was not violated. The Court's ruling effectively established the constitutionality of racial segregation and the notion of "separate but equal."

pluralism The theory that public policy largely results from a variety of interest groups competing with one another to promote laws that benefit members of their respective groups.

pocket veto The indirect veto of a bill received by the president within 10 days of the adjournment of Congress, effected by the president's retaining the bill unsigned until Congress adjourns.

policy implementation The process of carrying out laws, and the specific programs or services outlined in those laws.

political action committee (PAC) The political arm of an interest group that promotes candidates in election campaigns primarily through financial contributions.

political culture The values and beliefs about government, its purpose, and its operations and institutions that are widely held among citizens in a society; it defines the essence of how a society thinks politically and is transmitted from one generation to the next.

political equality A condition in which members of different groups possess substantially the same rights to participate actively in the political system. In the United States, these rights include voting, running for office, petitioning the government for redress of grievances, free speech, free press, and the access to an education.

political ideology A philosophical guide that people use to help translate their values and beliefs into political preferences.

political orientations The translation of values and beliefs into a systematic way of assessing the political environment.

political parties organizations that seek to influence government policy, usually by nominating candidates with aligned political views and attempting to place them in political office.

political preferences The attitudes people maintain regarding the performance of political leaders and institutions, their candidate preferences in elections, and specific policy issues.

political socialization The process by which an individual acquires values, beliefs, and opinions about politics.

politics The way in which the institutions of government are organized to make laws, rules, and policies, and how those institutions are influenced.

poll tax The requirement that individuals pay a fee before being allowed to vote.

popular sovereignty The idea that the ultimate source of power in the nation is held by the people.

pork-barrel legislation A government project or appropriation that yields jobs or other benefits to a specific locale and patronage opportunities to its political representative.

power of appointment The president's constitutional power to hire and fire those charged with administrative authority to help execute federal laws, such as ambassadors; federal judges, including those on the Supreme Court; and all other federal officers under the president's charge. Most of these appointments require the consent of the Senate.

power of incumbency The phenomenon by which incumbent members of Congress running for reelection are returned to office at an extremely high rate.

power The ability to get individuals to do something that they may not otherwise do, such as pay taxes, stop for red lights, or submit to a search before boarding an airplane.

preemption doctrine Doctrine of war making that reserves the right of the U.S. military to use advance strikes to stop rogue states from developing weapons of mass destruction.

preemption The constitutional doctrine that holds that when Congress acts affirmatively in the exercise of its own granted power, federal laws supersede all state laws on the matter.

prenomination campaign The political season in which candidates for president begin to explore the possibility of running by attempting to raise money and garner support.

presidential primary A statewide election to select delegates who will represent a state at the party's national convention.

president pro tempore In the absence of the vice president, the senator who presides over the Senate session. By tradition, this is usually the senator from the majority caucus who has served the longest number of consecutive years in the Senate.

primacy tendency The theory that impressions acquired while an individual is younger are likely to be more influential and longer lasting.

prior restraint The government's requirement that material be approved by government before it can be published.

privatization The process of replacing government-provided services with services provided by the private sector.

progressive tax A tax whose effective rate on an individual's income increases as the person's income rises.

proportional representation A system of electing a national legislature in which the percentage of the vote that a party receives is reflected in the number of seats that the party occupies.

pseudo-poll Phone calls from members of political campaigns or PACs who present themselves as pollsters for the purpose of planting messages with voters rather than measuring public opinion.

public interest group An organized group that promotes the broad, collective good of citizens and consumers.

public opinion poll A method of measuring the opinions of a large group of people by asking questions of a subset of the larger group and then generalizing the findings to the larger group.

public opinion The summation of individual opinions on any particular issue or topic.

public policy The set of laws, regulations, and rules that affects the whole of society.

purposive benefits (of group membership) Rewards that do not directly benefit the individual member, but benefit society as a whole.

R

racial profiling The law enforcement practice of taking race into account when identifying possible suspects of crimes.

random-digit dialing (RDD) A probability technique for scientific telephone polling that randomly assigns the last four digits to known information about telephone area codes and exchanges.

realists Members of the president's administration who advocate diplomacy as the primary means of protecting U.S. interests abroad.

reapportionment The allocation of a fixed number of House seats to the states.

recession An economic slowdown characterized by high unemployment, reduced productivity, or other negative economic indicators.

redistributive tax policies Taxation policies that aim to provide a social safety net to meet the minimum physical needs of citizens.

redistricting The act of redrawing congressional boundaries to achieve equal representation in each of the congressional districts.

regressive tax A tax that charges individuals the same amount, regardless of income.

regulations Rules or other directives issued by government agencies.

regulatory agency A government body responsible for the control and supervision of a specified activity or area of public interest.

reporting legislation The exclusive power of standing committees to forward legislation to the full House or Senate. Neither chamber can vote on a bill unless the committee votes to approve it first.

representative democracy A form of government designed by the U.S. Constitution whereby free, open, and regular elections are held to allow voters to choose those who govern on their behalf; it is also referred to as *indirect democracy* or a *republican* form of government.

representative democracy System of government in which citizens elect the individuals who are responsible for making and enforcing public policy.

reprieve The president's constitutional authority to reduce the severity of a punishment without removing the guilt for those who have violated the law.

reserved powers Those powers expressly retained by the state governments under the Constitution.

reserve requirement The minimum liquid assets each bank must keep on hand to back customer loans.

retrospective voting

Rules Committee A committee in the House of Representatives that determines the rules by which bills will come to the floor, be debated, and so on.

S

safe seat A congressional seat from a district that includes a high percentage of voters from one of the major parties.

sampling error The amount of error in a poll that results from interviewing a sample of people rather than the whole population under study; the larger the sample, the less the sampling error.

scientific sample A randomly selected subgroup drawn from a population using probability theory.

select committee A committee established by a resolution in either the House or the Senate for a specific purpose and, usually, for a limited time.

Senior Executive Service (SES) Since the late 1970s, a defined group of approximately 7,500 career professionals in the federal bureaucracy who provide continuity in the operations of the bureaucracy from one presidential administration to the next.

separation of powers The principle that each branch of government enjoys separate and independent powers and areas of responsibility.

Shays's Rebellion Armed uprising by debt-ridden Massachusetts farmers frustrated with the state government.

SLAPS test A standard that courts established to determine if material is obscene based in part on whether the material has serious literary, artistic, political, or scientific value. If it does, then the material is not obscene.

social capital The "social connectedness" of a community, or the extent to which individuals are socially integrated into their community.

social contract From the philosophy of Jean-Jacques Rousseau, an agreement people make with one another to form a government and abide by its rules and laws, and in return, the government promises to protect the people's rights and welfare and promote their best interests.

social equality Equality and fair treatment of all groups within the various institutions in society, both public and private, that serve the public at large, including in stores, theaters, restaurants, hotels, and public transportation facilities, among many other operations open to the public.

socialism Economic system in which all or most of the means of production are owned by the community as a whole.

social learning theory The theory that viewers imitate what they view on television through observational learning.

social movement A large informal grouping of individuals and/or organizations focused on specific political or social issues.

social policy Rules, regulations, and policymaking pertaining to the quality of life, welfare, and relations of human beings in the United States.

soft money Money not donated directly to a candidate's campaign, but rather to a political advocacy group or a political party for "party-building" activities.

solicitor general The lawyer representing the U.S. government before the U.S. Supreme Court.

solidary benefits (of group membership) Satisfaction that individuals receive from interacting with like-minded individuals for a cause.

***South Dakota v. Dole* (1987)** The Supreme Court Case that allowed Congress to coerce state governments to pass state laws by conditioning grants to those states, so long as the requirements are related to the overall spending in question.

sovereignty The supreme political power of a government to regulate its affairs without outside interference.

Speaker of the House The leader of the House of Representatives, responsible for assigning new bills to committees, recognizing members to speak in the House chamber, and assigning chairs of committees.

spoils system The postelection practice of rewarding loyal supporters of the winning candidates and party with appointive public offices.

standing committee A permanent committee that exists in both the House and Senate; most standing committees focus on a particular substantive area of public policy, such as transportation, labor, foreign affairs, and the federal budget.

standing The requirement that a party must be uniquely or singularly affected by a controversy in order to be eligible to file a lawsuit.

State of the Union address An annual speech that the president delivers to Congress laying out the status of the nation and offering suggestions for new legislation.

Strategic Defense Initiative (SDI) A theoretical anti-missile system based on the use of lasers and particle beams to shoot down Soviet nuclear missiles in outer space.

straw poll An unscientific poll that gathers the opinions of people who are conveniently available in a gathering place, such as a shopping center.

strict construction Constitutional interpretation that limits the government to only those powers explicitly stated in the Constitution.

strict scrutiny A legal standard set in *Brown v. Board of Education* for cases related to racial discrimination that tends to invalidate almost all state laws that segregate racial groups.

supply-side economics Economic theory that favors cutting taxes as a way of increasing economic productivity.

supremacy clause The provision in Article VI, Clause 2 of the Constitution that provides that the Constitution and federal laws override any conflicting provisions in state constitutions or state laws.

symbolic speech Nonspoken forms of speech that might be protected by the First Amendment, such as flag burning, wearing armbands at school to protest a war, or camping out in public parks to protest the plight of the homeless.

T

talk radio A specialized form of radio programming on which one or more hosts provide commentary and often invite listeners to call in to the show and offer their own opinions.

theocracy A form of government in which a particular religion or faith plays a dominant role in the government.

Three-Fifths Compromise A compromise proposal in which five slaves would be counted as the equivalent of three free people for purposes of taxes and representation.

Title IX The section of the Federal Educational Amendments Law of 1972 that prohibits the exclusion of women from an educational program or activity receiving financial assistance from the federal government. Courts have interpreted those

provisions to force colleges and universities to provide as many athletic teams for women as they do for men.

trade association A business association that focuses on one particular industry, with membership drawn exclusively from that industry.

Truman Doctrine Doctrine articulated by President Harry Truman in the late 1940s by which money and resources were provided to support and sustain non-communist governments in areas strategically vital to the United States.

Twenty-fourth Amendment A 1964 constitutional amendment that banned poll taxes in federal elections.

Twenty-fourth Amendment The constitutional amendment that outlaws poll taxes.

Twenty-second Amendment Passed in 1951, this constitutional amendment restricts any one person from being elected to the presidency "more than twice," or from acting as president for longer than two and a half terms.

Twenty-sixth Amendment The constitutional amendment that lowered the voting age to 18 in all local, state, and federal elections.

Twenty-third Amendment The constitutional amendment providing electoral votes to the District of Columbia, thus giving District residents the right to vote in presidential elections.

two-party system A party system dominated by two major parties that win the vast majority of elections.

two presidencies theory Theory articulated by political scientist Aaron Wildavsky that posits the existence of a more powerful presidency in foreign affairs and a more limited presidency in the domestic sphere.

U

union shop The law that requires that employees in unionized workplaces either join the union or pay the equivalent of union dues to it after a set period of time.

unitary system of government A system of government in which the constituent states are strictly subordinated to the goals of the central government as a whole.

United Nations (UN) International organization formed after World War II to promote and maintain international security and peace.

unit rule The system in 48 states by which the candidate who wins the most votes among popular votes cast for president in a state receives all the electoral votes from that state; also known as the "winner-take-all" system.

universal health care National health care system in which full access to health care is provided to citizens at government expense.

universal suffrage The idea that all citizens in a nation have the right to vote.

unscientific poll A poll in which the sample of people interviewed is not representative of any group beyond those who register their opinion.

V

values and beliefs The broad principles underlying the American political culture that citizens support and adhere to.

veto The constitutional procedure by which the president refuses to approve a bill or joint resolution and thus prevents its enactment into law.

Virginia Plan A proposal known also as the "large states plan" that empowered three separate branches of government, including a legislature with membership proportional to population.

voter turnout The number of people who turn out to vote as a percentage of all those eligible to vote.

Voting Rights Act of 1965 The federal law that invalidated literacy tests and property requirements and required select states and cities to apply for permission to the Justice Department to change their voting laws. As a consequence, millions of African Americans were effectively reenfranchised in the South.

voting The political mechanism that ensures that the majority will rule.

W

War Powers Resolution Largely ignored congressional policy that restricts the president's power to engage in war except (1) when Congress has declared war, (2) when Congress has specifically granted the president permission to use armed forces, or (3) when the nation is under attack. The resolution further requires the president to report to Congress whenever American forces are entered into hostilities.

warrant A document issued by a judge or magistrate that allows law enforcement to search or seize items at a home, business, or anywhere else that might be specified.

Warsaw Pact Formal alliance of nations within the Soviet sphere during the Cold War.

welfare state Social system in which the state assumes a considerable degree of responsibility for citizens in matters of health care, employment, education, and retirement income.

whip (majority and minority) Member of Congress elected by his or her party to count potential votes and promote party unity in voting.

White House chief of staff The manager of the White House staff, which serves the president's organizational needs, including speechwriting, advance work for presidential appearances, scheduling, congressional relations, public relations, and communications.

White House Office of Legislative Affairs A presidential office that serves as a liaison between the president and Congress. This office helps the president develop the strategy used to promote passage of the president's legislative agenda.

White House press secretary The person on the White House staff who plays an especially important role in briefing the press, organizing news conferences, and even briefing the president on questions that may be asked.

writ of certiorari The formal term for an order by which the Supreme Court acts in its discretion to review a case from a lower court.

Notes

Chapter 1

1. See Thomas Hobbes, *Leviathan* (London: A. Crooke, 1651).

2. For a collection of Rousseau's work, see Jean-Jacques Rousseau, *The Social Contract and Discourses,* translation and commentary by G. D. H. Cole (London: Guernsey Press, 1983).

3. Harold Lasswell, *Politics: Who Gets What, When and How* (New York: McGraw-Hill, 1936).

4. John Locke, *Two Treatises of Government,* ed. Peter Laslett (Cambridge: Cambridge University Press, 1960).

5. Alexis de Tocqueville, *Democracy in America, 1835,* ed. Richard Hefner (New York: Penguin Books, 1956).

6. Ruchir Sharma, *China Slows Down, and Grows Up* (*The New York Times:* April 26, 2012, page A23).

Chapter 2

1. Fred Anderson, *The War That Made America: A Short History of the French-Indian War* (New York: Viking, 2005).

2. Robert Middlekauff, *The Glorious Cause* (New York: Oxford University Press, 1982).

3. Events of these years are nicely recounted in Pauline Maier, *From Resistance to Revolution: Colonial Radicals and the Development of American Opposition to Britain, 1765–1776* (New York: W. W. Norton, 1992).

4. *The Political Writings of Thomas Paine, Vol. 1* (Boston: J. P. Mendum Investigator Office, 1870).

5. David McCullough, *John Adams* (New York: Simon & Schuster, 2001), 119; Joseph Ellis, *Founding Brothers* (New York: Knopf, 2000), 212–213.

6. Pauline Maier, *American Scripture: Making the Declaration of Independence* (New York: Vintage, 1998).

7. Merrill Jensen, *The Articles of Confederation: An Interpretation of the Social-Constitutional History of the American Revolution, 1774–1781* (Madison: University of Wisconsin Press, 1959).

8. For an account of Massachusetts public policy during this period, see Van Beck Hall, *Politics Without Parties: Massachusetts 1780–1791* (Pittsburgh: University of Pittsburgh Press, 1972).

9. Robert Gross, ed., *In Debt to Shays* (Charlottesville: University of Virginia Press, 1993).

10. Christopher Collier, *Decision in Philadelphia: The Constitutional Convention of 1787* (New York: Ballantine Books, 2007).

11. For a discussion of the Founders' silence on slavery, see Joseph Ellis, *Founding Brothers* (New York: Knopf, 2000), 81–119.

12. Jacob E. Cooke, ed., *The Federalist* (Middletown, CT: Wesleyan University Press, 1961).

13. Saul Cornell, *The Other Founders: Anti-Federalism and the Dissenting Tradition in America 1788–1828* (Chapel Hill: University of North Carolina Press, 1999).

14. Henry Mayer, *A Son of Thunder: Patrick Henry and the American Republic* (Charlottesville: University of Virginia Press, 1992).

15. Paul Murphy, *The Historic Background of the Bill of Rights* (New York: Taylor & Francis, 1990).

16. See Jefferson–Madison correspondence republished in Philip Kurland, ed., *The Founders' Constitution* (Indianapolis: Liberty Fund, 2000).

17. There may be numerous legal problems implicated by the holding of such a convention, as noted in Russell Caplan, *Constitutional Brinksmanship: Amending the Constitution by National Convention* (New York: Oxford University Press, 1988).

18. One of the better recent works on Marshall's tenure at the Court is R. Kent Newmyer, *John Marshall and the Heroic Age of the Supreme Court* (Baton Rouge: Louisiana State University Press, 2002).

19. 17 U.S. 316 (1819).

20. Robert Bork, *The Tempting of America* (New York: Simon & Schuster, 1990).

21. Justice Antonin Scalia, interview with *60 Minutes* (episode aired April 27, 2008), http://www.cbsnews.com/stories/2008/04/24/60minutes/main4040290.shtml.

22. Lawrence Tribe, *Constitutional Choices* (Cambridge, MA: Harvard University Press, 2004).

23. John Hart Ely, *Democracy and Distrust* (Cambridge, MA: Harvard University Press, 1980).

24. 5 U.S. 137 (1803).

Chapter 3

1. Stanley R. Sloan, *NATO, The European Union and the Atlantic Community: The Transatlantic Bargain Reconsidered* (New York: Rowman & Littlefield, 2002).

2. See *McCulloch v. Maryland*, 17 U.S. 316 (1819).

3. 14 U.S. 304 (1816).

4. For example, in *Supreme Court of New Hampshire v. Piper*, 470 U.S. 274 (1985), the Supreme Court interpreted the privileges and immunities clause of Article IV to forbid states from excluding nonresidents from admission to the practice of law.

5. See *New Jersey v. New York*, 523 U.S. 767 (1998).

6. Stanley Elkins and Eric McKitrick, *The Age of Federalism: The Early American Republic 1788–1800* (New York: Oxford University Press, 1995).

7. 17 U.S. 316 (1819).

8. 22 U.S. 1 (1824).

9. H. W. Brands, *Andrew Jackson: His Life and Times* (New York: Doubleday, 2005).

10. *Railroad Retirement Board v. Alton Railroad Co.*, 295 U.S. 330 (1935); Carter v. Carter Coal Co., 298 U.S. 238 (1936).

11. William E. Leuchtenburg, *The Supreme Court Reborn: The Constitutional Revolution in the Age of Roosevelt* (New York: Oxford University Press, 1995).

12. *Heart of Atlanta Motel v. United States*, 379 U.S. 241 (1964); *Katzenbach v. McClung*, 379 U.S. 294 (1964).

13. 483 U.S. 203 (1987).

14. For an application of the term to welfare policy, see Pamela Winston, *Welfare Policymaking in the States: The Devil in Devolution* (Washington, DC: Georgetown University Press, 2002).

15. David Savage, *Turning Right: The Making of the Rehnquist Supreme Court* (New York: Wiley, 1993).

16. 514 U.S. 549 (1995).

17. 529 U.S. 598 (2000).

18. John T. Noonan Jr., *Narrowing the Nation's Power: The Supreme Court Sides with the States* (Berkeley: University of California Press, 2003).

19. 372 U.S. 335 (1963).

20. *New State Ice Co. v. Liebmann*, 285 U.S. 262, 311 (1932).

21. See BEA News Release No. 08–11, "State Personal Income Tax 2007" (released March 26, 2008).

Chapter 4

1. Antonin Scalia, "Law and the Winds of Change." Remarks made at the 24th Australian Legal Convention, Perth, West Australia, September 21, 1987.

2. Alexander Hamilton, James Madison, and John Jay, *The Federalist Papers,* ed. Clinton Rossiter (New York: New American Library, 1971).

3. Jefferson–Madison correspondence in Philip Kurland, ed., *The Founders' Constitution* (Indianapolis, IN: Liberty Fund, 2000).

4. 32 U.S. 243 (1833).

5. Thomas Jefferson first coined that phrase in a letter he wrote as president to the Baptists of Danbury, Connecticut, in 1802. George Seldes, ed., *The Great Quotations* (Secaucus, NJ: Citadel Press, 1983), 369.

6. 319 U.S. 624 (1943).

7. 374 U.S. 398 (1963).

8. 406 U.S. 205 (1972).

9. 98 U.S. 145 (1878).

10. 494 U.S. 872 (1990).

11. Carolyn N. Long, *Religious Freedom and Indian Rights: The Case of* Oregon v. Smith (Lawrence: University Press of Kansas, 2000).

12. Noah Feldman, *Divided by God* (New York: Farrar, Straus and Giroux, 2005).

13. 370 U.S. 421 (1962).

14. 374 U.S. 203 (1963).

15. 472 U.S. 38 (1985).

16. 536 U.S. 639 (2002).

17. 403 U.S. 602 (1971).

18. 505 U.S. 577 (1992).

19. 530 U.S. 290 (2000).

20. 249 U.S. 247 (1919).

21. 341 U.S. 494 (1951).

22. 304 U.S. 144 (1938).

23. 395 U.S. 444 (1969).

24. Harry Kalven, *A Worthy Tradition: Freedom of Speech in America* (New York: Harper & Row, 1988).

25. 376 U.S. 254 (1964).

26. Anthony Lewis, *Make No Law: The Sullivan Case and the First Amendment* (New York: Vintage Books, 1992).

27. 403 U.S. 713 (1971).

28. 413 U.S. 15 (1973).

29. 521 U.S. 844 (1997).

30. John W. Johnson, *The Struggle for Students' Rights:* Tinker v. Des Moines *and the 1960s* (Lawrence: University Press of Kansas, 1997).

31. *Tinker v. Des Moines* (393 U.S. 503 (1969)).

32. 391 U.S. 367 (1968).

33. 491 U.S. 397 (1989).

34. Robert Justin Goldstein, *Flag Burning and Free Speech: The Case of* Texas v. Johnson (Lawrence: University Press of Kansas, 2000).

35. Philippa Strum, *When the Nazis Came to Skokie: Freedom for Speech We Hate* (Lawrence: University Press of Kansas, 1999).

36. 528 U.S. 343 (2003).

37. Milton Heumann and Thomas W. Church, eds., *Hate Speech on Campus* (Boston: Northeastern University Press, 1997).

38. 554 U.S. 570 (2008).

39. 561 U.S. ____ (2010)

40. Lucas A. Powe Jr., *The Warren Court and American Politics* (Cambridge, MA: Belknap Press of Harvard University, 2002).

41. 389 U.S. 347 (1967).

42. 367 U.S. 643 (1961).

43. *Kyllo v. United States*, 533 U.S. 27 (2001).

44. It should be noted, however, that a majority of states have chosen to use grand juries, even without being compelled to do so by the U.S. Constitution.

45. 384 U.S. 436 (1966).

46. Gary Stuart, *Miranda: The Story of America's Right to Remain Silent* (Tucson: University of Arizona Press, 2004).

47. 372 U.S. 335 (1963).

48. 536 U.S. 304 (2002).

49. Austin Sarat, *When the State Kills* (Princeton, NJ: Princeton University Press, 2002).

50. 381 U.S. 479 (1965).

51. John W. Johnson, Griswold v. Connecticut: *Birth Control and the Constitutional Right of Privacy* (Lawrence: University Press of Kansas, 2005).

52. 410 U.S. 113 (1973).

53. N. E. H. Hull and Peter Charles Hoffer, Roe v. Wade: *The Abortion Rights Controversy in American History* (Lawrence: University Press of Kansas, 2001).

54. 505 U.S. 833 (1992).

55. 550 U.S. 124 (2007).

56. 539 U.S. 558 (2003).

CHAPTER 5

1. Louis R. Harlan, *Booker T. Washington: The Making of a Black Leader* (New York: Oxford University Press, 1975).

2. David Levering Lewis, *W. E. B. DuBois, 1868–1919: Biography of a Race* (New York: Owl Books, 1994).

3. 347 U.S. 483 (1954).

4. 60 U.S. 393 (1857).

5. Eric Foner, *Reconstruction: America's Unfinished Revolution* (New York: Harper, 2000).

6. 83 U.S. 36 (1873).

7. 109 U.S. 3 (1883).

8. 163 U.S. 537 (1896).

9. For a comprehensive account of the NAACP's strategy, see Richard Kluger, *Simple Justice* (New York: Vintage Books, 1975).

10. 358 U.S. 1 (1958).

11. Jennifer Hochschild, *The New American Dilemma: Liberal Democracy and School Desegregation* (New Haven, CT: Yale University Press, 1984).

12. See Taylor Branch, *Pillar of Fire: America in the King Years, 1963–65* (New York: Simon & Schuster, 1999).

13. Charles Whalen and Barbara Whalen, *Longest Debate: A Legislative History of the Civil Rights Act* (Santa Ana, CA: Seven Locks Press, 1984).

14. 438 U.S. 265 (1978).

15. Howard Ball, *The* Bakke *Case: Race, Education and Affirmative Action* (Lawrence: University Press of Kansas, 2000).

16. 515 U.S. 200 (1995).

17. 539 U.S. 306 (2003).

18. 539 U.S. 244 (2003).

19. U.S. Census Bureau, "Income, Poverty, and Health Insurance Coverage in the United States: 2010" (report issued September 2011).

20. "Vital Signs: Statistics That Measure the State of Racial Inequality," *Journal of Blacks in Higher Education*, no. 44 (Summer 2004).

21. Michael Jones and Eileen Poe-Yamagata, *And Justice for Some* (Washington, DC: Building Blocks for Youth Press, 2000).

22. 208 U.S. 412 (1908).

23. 335 U.S. 464 (1948).

24. 368 U.S. 57, 61 (1961).

25. 404 U.S. 71 (1971).

26. 411 U.S. 677 (1973).

27. 429 U.S. 190 (1976).

28. 517 U.S. 620 (1996).

Chapter 6

1. Woodrow Wilson, *Congressional Government* (Baltimore: Johns Hopkins University Press, 1981; originally published in 1885).

2. For a good discussion of the Constitutional Convention and issues related to Congress, see Charles Stewart III, "Congress and the Constitutional System," in *Institutions of American Democracy: The Legislative Branch,* ed. Paul J. Quirk and Sarah A. Binder (New York: Oxford University Press, 2005).

3. Alexander Hamilton, James Madison, and John Jay, *The Federalist Papers* (Chicago: The New American Library of World Literature; reprinted in 1961).

4. Thomas Mann, *Unsafe at Any Margin: Interpreting Congressional Elections* (Washington, DC: Brookings Institution Press, 1978).

5. Paul Finkelman and Peter Wallenstein, *The Encyclopedia of American Political History* (Washington, DC: CQ Press, 2001), 55–56.

6. See, for example, *Baker v. Carr,* 369 U.S. 186 (1962); *Reynolds v. Sims,* 377 U.S. 533 (1964); *Wesberry v. Sanders,* 376 U.S. 1 (1964).

7. See James Madison, Federalist No. 63.

8. For a discussion of leadership in Congress, see Burdett A. Loomis, *The Contemporary Congress,* 3rd ed. (Boston: Bedford St. Martin's, 2000), chapter 6.

9. See Eric Schickler, "Institutional Development of Congress," in *Institutions of American Democracy: The Legislative Branch,* ed. Paul J. Quirk and Sarah A. Binder (New York: Oxford University Press, 2005), chapter 2.

10. A classic work on congressional committees is Richard F. Fenno Jr., *Congressmen in Committees* (Boston: Little, Brown, 1973).

11. See Stephen S. Smith and Christopher Deering, *Committees in Congress,* 2nd ed. (Washington, DC: CQ Press, 1990).

12. See Roger Davidson and Walter Oleszek, *Congress and Its Members,* 4th ed. (Washington, DC: CQ Press, 1994).

13. A classic piece on the topic is John Manley, "Wilbur Mills: A Study of Congressional Influence," *American Political Science Review,* vol. 63 (1969): 442–464.

14. Eric Redman, *The Dance of Legislation* (Seattle: University of Washington Press, 1974).

15. For a discussion of the motivations for senators to filibuster, see Sarah A. Binder and Stephen S. Smith, *Politics or Principles? Filibustering in the United States Senate* (Washington, DC: Brookings Institution Press, 1997).

16. Morris P. Fiorina, *Congress: Keystone of the Washington Establishment,* 2nd ed. (New Haven, CT: Yale University Press, 1989).

17. For an excellent discussion of the executive appointment process, see David E. Lewis, *The Politics of Presidential Appointments: Political Control and Bureaucratic Performance* (Princeton, N.J.: Princeton University Press, 2008).

18. Richard F. Fenno Jr., *Home Style: House Members in Their Districts* (Boston: Little, Brown, 1978).

Chapter 7

1. Joseph Ellis, *His Excellency: George Washington* (New York: Knopf, 2004).

2. Dates provided after a president's name refers to year(s) of service as president of the United States.

3. H. W. Brands, *Andrew Jackson: His Life and Times* (New York: Random House, 2005).

4. John Seigenthaler, *James K. Polk, 1845–1849* (New York: Times Books, 2003).

5. See *Ex Parte Merryman,* 17 Fed. Cas. 144 (1961).

6. Edmund Morris, *Theodore Rex* (New York: Random House, 2001).

7. See Clinton Rossiter, *The American Presidency* (Baltimore: Johns Hopkins University Press, 1987).

8. See John Locke, *Two Treatises of Government and a Letter Concerning Toleration,* ed. Peter Laslett (Cambridge: Cambridge University Press, 1963).

9. Baron de Montesquieu, *The Spirit of the Laws* (Anne M. Cohler et al., eds.) (Cambridge: Cambridge University Press, 1989).

10. Michael J. Gerhardt, *The Federal Appointments Process: A Constitutional and Historical Analysis* (Durham, NC: Duke University Press, 2003).

11. Robert F. Kennedy Jr., *Thirteen Days: A Memoir of the Cuban Missile Crisis* (New York: W. W. Norton, 1999).

12. Mark Peterson, *Legislating Together: The White House and Capitol Hill from Eisenhower to Reagan* (Cambridge, MA: Harvard University Press, 1990).

13. Paul Light, *The President's Agenda: Domestic Policy Choice from Kennedy to Clinton* (Baltimore: Johns Hopkins University Press, 1999).

14. Lee Hamilton and Jordan Tama, *A Creative Tension: The Foreign Policy Roles of the President and Congress* (Washington, DC: Woodrow Wilson Press, 2003).

15. Kenneth Mayer, *With the Stroke of a Pen: Executive Orders and Presidential Power* (Princeton, NJ: Princeton University Press, 2001).

16. The updated version of this work is Richard Neustadt, *Presidential Power and the Modern Presidents: The Politics of Leadership from Roosevelt Through Reagan* (New York: Free Press, 1991).

17. Jules Witcover, *Crapshoot: Rolling the Dice on the Vice Presidency* (New York: Crown, 1991).

18. Bob Woodward, *Plan of Attack* (New York: Simon & Schuster, 2004).

19. For a comprehensive discussion of the various ways that modern presidents have organized the White House, see Stephen Hess, *Organizing the Presidency* (Washington, DC: Brookings Institution Press, 1988).

20. Bill Adler, *America's First Ladies* (New York: Taylor, 2002).

21. Samuel Kernell, *Going Public: New Strategies of Presidential Leadership* (Washington, DC: CQ Press, 1992).

22. Elizabeth Drew, *On the Edge: The Clinton Presidency* (New York: Touchstone, 1995).

23. See Kathleen Hall Jamieson and Paul Waldman, *The Press Effect: Politicians, Journalists, and the Stories That Shape the Political World* (New York: Oxford University Press, 2002).

24. John A. Maltese, *Spin Control: The White House Office of Communications and the Management of Presidential News* (Chapel Hill: University of North Carolina Press, 1992).

25. Ted Rueter, *The 267 Stupidest Things Republicans Ever Said/The 267 Stupidest Things Democrats Ever Said* (New York: Three Rivers Press, 2000).

CHAPTER 8

1. See *Washington Monthly,* a periodical that regularly reports on the excesses and waste in the federal bureaucracy.

2. For a comprehensive discussion of the virtues of contemporary bureaucracy, see Charles T. Goodsell, *The Case for Bureaucracy* (Chatham, NJ: Chatham House Publishers, 1994).

3. Max Weber, chapters 11 and 12 in *Economy and Society,* ed. Guenther Roth and Claus Wittich (New York: Bedminster Press, 1968).

4. For a good discussion of organizational issues in the federal bureaucracy, see James Q. Wilson, *Bureaucracy: What Government Agencies Do and Why They Do It* (New York: Basic Books, 1989).

5. See Joel Aberbach, *Keeping a Watchful Eye: The Politics of Congressional Oversight* (Washington, DC: Brookings Institution Press, 1990).

6. Beverly Cigler, "The Paradox of Professionalization," in *Democracy, Bureaucracy and the Study of Administration,* ed. Camilla Stivers (Boulder, CO: Westview Press, 2001).

7. For a good discussion of the growth of the federal bureaucracy during the FDR years, see Brian J. Cook, "Serving the Liberal State," chapter 5 in *Bureaucracy and Self-Government: Reconsidering the Role of Public Administration in American Politics* (Baltimore: Johns Hopkins University Press, 1996).

8. David Osborne and Ted Gaebler, *Reinventing Government: How the Entrepreneurial Spirit Is Transforming the Public Sector* (New York: Penguin Books, 1993).

9. Harold S. Stanley and Richard G. Niemi, *Vital Statistics on American Politics, 2005–2006* (Washington, DC: CQ Press, 2006), 266.

10. Robert H. Wiebe, *The Search for Order: 1877–1920* (New York: Hill and Wang, 1967).

11. Data from the U.S. Bureau of Labor Statistics Web site, http://www.bls.gov/oco/cg/cgs041.htm.

12. See Ari Hoogenboom, *Outlawing the Spoils: A History of the Civil Service Reform Movement, 1865–1883* (Champaign: University of Illinois Press, 1961).

CHAPTER 9

1. For an account of the ways in which the Supreme Court's methods contribute to its image and status as an institution, see John Brigham, *The Cult of the Court* (Philadelphia: Temple University Press, 1987).

2. John Merryman, *The Civil Law Tradition* (Palo Alto, CA: Stanford University Press, 1985).

3. G. Alan Tarr and Mary Cornelius Porter, *State Supreme Courts in State and Nation* (New Haven, CT: Yale University Press, 1988).

4. 5 U.S. 137 (1803).

5. Arthur Hellman, *Restructuring Justice: The Innovations of the Ninth Circuit and the Future of the Federal Courts* (Ithaca, NY: Cornell University Press, 1991).

6. One rare exception to the strict use of the adversarial approach in the American legal system comes in the form of "structural reform litigation," a term that describes certain types of lawsuits brought against bureaucracies such as prisons, school systems, or welfare systems. Judges in these types of cases often assume a more active "managerial approach" in the process, overseeing the implementation of remedies and occasionally taking a proactive role to ensure that the lawyers are properly representing their client's interests. For comprehensive analysis of one example of structural reform litigation in action, see Malcolm Feeley and Edward Rubin, *Judicial Policymaking and the Modern State: How the Court Reformed America's Prisons* (Cambridge: Cambridge University Press, 2000). Of course, the more traditional adversarial system still tends to predominate in most other forms of civil litigation.

7. See George Fisher, *Plea Bargaining's Triumph: A History of Plea Bargaining in America* (Palo Alto, CA: Stanford University Press, 2003); Milton Heumann, *Plea Bargaining: The Experiences of Prosecutors, Judges, and Defense Attorneys* (Chicago: University of Chicago Press, 1981).

8. James Eisenstein, Roy Flemming, and Peter Nardulli, *The Contours of Justice* (New York: Addison-Wesley Publishing, 1988).

9. R. Kent Newmyer, *The Supreme Court Under Marshall and Taney* (Arlington Heights, IL: Harlan Davison, 1968).

10. 17 U.S. 316 (1819).

11. 1 Wheat (14 U.S.) 304 (1816).

12. 358 U.S. 1 (1958).

13. 60 U.S. 393 (1857).

14. 347 U.S. 483 (1954).

15. 418 U.S. 683 (1974).

16. 506 U.S. 224 (1993).

17. 6 Pet. (31 U.S.) 515 (1832).

18. See Bob Woodward and Carl Bernstein, *The Final Days* (New York: Simon & Schuster, 1975).

19. Bradley Canon and Charles Johnson, *Judicial Policies: Implementation and Impact,* 2nd ed. (Washington, DC: CQ Press, 1999).

20. 347 U.S. 483 (1954).

21. 370 U.S. 421 (1962).

22. Robert Dahl, "Decision-making in a Democracy: The Supreme Court as a National Policy-Maker," *Journal of Public Law,* vol. 6 (1957): 279–295.

23. Philip DuBois, *From Ballot to Bench: Judicial Elections and the Quest for Accountability* (Austin: University of Texas Press, 1980).

24. Sheldon Goldman, *Picking Federal Judges* (New Haven, CT: Yale University Press, 1997).

25. Barbara Perry, *A Representative Supreme Court* (Westport, CT: Greenwood Press, 1991).

26. John Maltese, *The Selling of Supreme Court Nominees* (Baltimore: Johns Hopkins University Press, 1995).

27. Ethan Bronner, *Battle for Justice: How the Bork Nomination Shook America* (New York: W. W. Norton, 1989).

28. 410 U.S. 113 (1973).

29. Richard Pacelle, *Between Law and Politics: The Solicitor General and the Structuring of Race, Gender, and Reproductive Rights Litigation* (College Station: Texas A & M University Press, 2003).

30. 376 U.S. 254 (1964).

31. 478 U.S. 186 (1986).

32. 539 U.S. 558 (2003).

33. 384 U,S. 436 (1966).

34. Jeffrey Segal and Harold Spaeth, *The Supreme Court and The Attitudinal Model* (Cambridge: Cambridge University Press, 1993), 246.

35. See, for example, Sheldon M. Novick, *Honorable Justice: The Life of Oliver Wendell Holmes, Jr.* (Boston: Little, Brown & Co., 1989).

36. 531 U.S. 98 (2000).

37. Justice Antonin Scalia, Interview with CNBC, October 10, 2005.

CHAPTER 10

1. Vincent Price, *Public Opinion* (Newbury Park, CA: Sage Publications, 1992), 5–22.

2. E. E. Schattschneider, *The Semisovereign People: A Realist's View of Democracy in America* (New York: Holt, Rinehart and Winston, 1960).

3. V. O. Key Jr., *Public Opinion and American Democracy* (New York: Knopf, 1961).

4. Samuel P. Huntington, *American Politics: The Promise of Disharmony* (Cambridge, MA: Harvard University Press, 1981).

5. For a good discussion of the value of individualism in the American culture, see Herbert McCloskey and John Zaller, *The American Ethos* (Cambridge, MA: Harvard University Press, 1984).

6. The concept of partisanship and controversies surrounding it over the years are presented in Warren E. Miller and Merrill Shanks, *The New American Voter* (Cambridge, MA: Harvard University Press, 1996).

7. See M. Kent Jennings and Richard G. Niemi, *Generations and Politics: A Panel Study of Young Adults and Their Parents* (Princeton, NJ: Princeton University Press, 1981).

8. James Madison, Alexander Hamilton, and John Jay, Federalist No. 51, in *The Federalist Papers*, (New York: Doubleday, 1966, originally published in 1788).

9. Walter Lippman, *Public Opinion* (New York: Harcourt Brace Jovanovich, 1922).

10. Angus Campbell, Phillip E. Converse, Warren E. Miller, and Donald E. Stokes, *The American Voter* (New York: John Wiley and Sons, 1960).

11. This survey was commissioned by the Intercollegiate Studies Institute and included a national adult sample of 2,500 respondents, conducted by telephone.

12. V. O. Key Jr., *The Responsible Electorate* (Cambridge, MA: Belknap Harvard, 1966).

13. Benjamin I. Page and Robert Y. Shapiro, *The Rational Public: Fifty Years of Trends in Americans' Policy Preferences* (Chicago: University of Chicago Press, 1992).

14. Samuel Kernell, *Going Public: New Strategies of Presidential Leadership* (Washington, DC: CQ Press, 1997).

15. Jack Dennis, ed., *Socialization to Politics* (New York: John Wiley and Sons, 1973).

16. See, generally, David Easton, *A Systems Analysis of Political Life* (New York: John Wiley and Sons, 1965).

17. Michael X. Delli Carpini and Scott Keeter, *What Americans Know About Politics and Why It Matters* (New Haven, CT: Yale University Press, 1996).

18.Herb Asher, *Polling and the Public*, 6th ed. (Washington, DC: CQ Press, 2004).

19. Charles W. Roll and Albert H. Cantril, *Polls: Their Use and Misuse in Politics* (New York: Basic Books, 1972).

20. An important book spelling out the variety of problems and issues with the wording of survey questions is Howard Schuman and Stanley Press, *Questions and Answers in Attitude Surveys* (New York: John Wiley and Sons, 1981).

21. For a more detailed discussion of these concepts, see W. Lance Bennett, *Public Opinion in American Politics* (New York: Harcourt Brace Jovanovich, 1980).

CHAPTER 11

1. James Madison, Federalist No. 10, in *The Federalist Papers* (reprinted by Mentor Books, 1961), 77.

2. Alexis de Tocqueville, *Democracy in America* (New York: Mentor Books, reprint edition, 1956).

3. Robert Dahl, *A Preface to Democratic Theory* (Cambridge: Cambridge University Press, 1956).

4. David B. Truman, *The Governmental Process* (New York: Alfred Knopf, 1951).

5. C. Wright Mills, *The Power Elite* (New York: Oxford University Press, 1956).

6. John P. Heinz, Edward O. Laumann, Robert L. Nelson, and Robert H. Salisbury, *The Hollow Core* (Cambridge, MA: Harvard University Press, 1993).

7. David Lowery and Holly Brasher, *Organized Interests and American Government* (New York: McGraw-Hill, 2004), 8.

8. See http://www.opensecrets.org/lobbyists/index .asp.

9. See Theodore J. Lowi, *The End of Liberalism* (New York: W. W. Norton, 1979).

10. See William Gormley, "Regulatory Issue Networks in a Federal System," *Polity*, vol. 18 (1986): 595–620.

11. See http://www.uschamber.com.

12. Mancur Olson, *The Logic of Collective Action: Public Goods and the Theory of Groups* (Cambridge, MA: Harvard University Press, 1971), 22–35.

13. Robert Salisbury, "An Exchange Theory of Interest Groups," *Midwest Journal of Political Science*, vol. 13 (1969): 1–32.

14. Peter B. Clark and James Q. Wilson, "Incentives Systems: A Theory of Organization" *Administrative Science Quarterly*, vol. 6 (1961): 129–166.

15. For a good discussion of the influence of group member dedication to group effectiveness, see Olson, *The Logic of Collective Action: Public Goods and the Theory of Groups*, op. cit.

16. Olson, *The Logic of Collective Action: Public Goods and the Theory of Groups*, op. cit.

17. See http://www.commoncause.org.

18. David Lowery and Holly Brasher, *Organized Interests and American Government* (New York: McGraw-Hill, 2004), 247.

CHAPTER 12

1. 438 U.S. 726 (1978).

2. See Philip Meyer, *Precision Journalism: A Reporter's Introduction to Social Science Methods* (Lanham, MD: Rowman & Littlefield, 2002).

3. The word *muckrakers* is derived from the idea that this group was "raking up the mud" from scandals and corruption of government and industry.

4. For a chronicle of the Watergate story, see Bob Woodward and Carl Bernstein, *All the President's Men* (New York: Simon & Schuster, 1974).

5. For a thorough review of the history of news, see Mitchell Stephens, *A History of News: From the Drum to the Satellite* (New York: Viking, 1989).

6. Kurt Lang and Gladys Lang, *Television and Politics* (Edison, NJ: Transaction Publishers, 2001).

7. For a good review of the process and impact of presidential debates, see Alan Schroeder, *Presidential Debates* (New York: Columbia University Press, 2000).

8. Marshall McLuhan, *Understanding Media: The Extensions of Man* (New York: McGraw-Hill, 1964).

8. See Doris Graber, *Processing Politics: Learning from Television in the Internet Age* (Chicago: University of Chicago Press, 2001).

9. Mass communications researcher Joseph Klapper was a pioneer of the minimal effects (or limited effects) theory. He introduced the theory in a book titled *The Effects of Mass Communication* (New York: Free Press, 1960).

10. For a good discussion of selection retention, see D. Sears and J. Freeman, "Selective Exposure to Information: A Critical Review," in *The Process and Effects of Mass Communication,* ed. Wilbur Lang Schramm (Chicago: University of Illinois Press, 1972).

11. For a good discussion of social learning theory, see Albert Bandura, *Social Foundations of Thought and Action* (Englewood Cliffs, NJ: Prentice-Hall, 1986).

12. See L. Berkowitz, "Some Effects of Thought on Anti- and Pro- Social Influences of Media Effects," *Psychological Bulletin,* vol. 95 (1984): 410–427.

13. A pioneer in developing cultivation theory was George Gerbner. See George Gerbner et al., "Growing Up with Television: The Cultivation Perspective," in *Media Effects: Advances in Theory and Research,* ed. Jennings Bryant and Dolf Zillman (Hillsdale, NJ: Lawrence Erlbaum, 1994), 17–41.

14. A number of studies have demonstrated the agenda-setting power of the media, including Maxwell E. McCombs, "The Agenda-Setting Approach," in *Handbook of Political Communication,* ed. Dan D. Nimmo and Keith Sanders (Thousand Oaks, CA: Sage, 1981), 121–140; and Shanto Iyengar and Donald R. Kinder, *News That Matters* (Chicago: University of Chicago Press, 1987).

17. Doris A. Graber, *Mass Media and American Politics* (Washington, DC: CQ Press, 2002), 207.

18. Kenneth Dautrich and Thomas H. Hartley, *How the News Media Fail American Voters* (New York: Columbia University Press, 1999), 92–95.

CHAPTER 13

1. "Toward a More Responsible Party System: A Report of the Committee on Political Parties, American Political Science Association," *American Political Science Review*, vol. 44, no. 3 (September 1950).

2. E. E. Schattschneider, *Party Government* (New York: Farrar and Rinehart, 1942).

3. See chapter 2 in John F. Bibby, *Politics, Parties and Elections in America,* 5th ed. (Belmont, CA: Wadsworth, 2002).

4. See Paul Finkelman and John Moore, "Political Parties," in *The Encyclopedia of American Political History,* ed. Peter Wallenstein and Paul Finkelman (Washington, DC: CQ Press, 2001).

5. See chapter 2 in Bibby, *Politics, Parties and Elections in America,* op. cit.

6. V. O. Key Jr., "A Theory of Critical Elections," *Journal of Politics*, vol. 16, no. 1 (1955): 13–18.

7. See Walter Dean Burnham, *Critical Elections and the Mainsprings of American Politics* (New York: W. W. Norton, 1970).

8. For a thorough analysis of how the American party system has changed since the New Deal, see Sidney M. Milkus, *The President and the Parties: The Transformation of the American Party System Since the New Deal* (New York: Oxford University Press, 1993).

9. Paul Allen Beck, "The Dealignment Era in America," in *Electoral Change in Advanced Industrial Democracies: Realignment or Dealignment,* ed. M. N. Dalton, T. T. Flanagan, and H. Beck(Princeton, NJ: Princeton University Press, 1984).

10. Angus Campbell, Philip E. Converse, Warren E. Miller, and Donald E. Stokes, *The American Voter* (New York: Wiley, 1960).

11. For a thorough discussion of the concept of party identification, see Warren E. Miller and J. Merrill Shanks, *The New American Voter* (Cambridge, MA: Harvard University Press, 1996).

12. Philip E. Converse, "The Concept of the Normal Vote," in *Elections and the Political Order,* ed. Angus Campbell, Philip E. Converse, Warren E. Miller, and Donald E. Stokes (New York: Wiley, 1966).

13. For a discussion of governance and the parties, see John H. Aldrich, *Why Parties? The Origin and Transformation of Political Parties in America* (Chicago: University of Chicago Press, 1995), chapter 7.

14. See Richard S. Conley, *The Presidency, Congress and Divided Government* (College Station: Texas A&M University Press, 2002).

15. For a good discussion of the rationale for America's two-party system, see Frank J. Sorauf, *Party Politics in America,* 5th ed. (Boston: Little, Brown, 1984).

16. For a good discussion of nineteenth- and twentieth-century third-party candidacies, see Steven J. Rosenstone, Roy L. Behr, and Edward H. Lazarus, *Third Parties in America,* 2nd ed. (Princeton, NJ: Princeton University Press, 1996).

17. Martin Wattenberg, *The Decline of American Political Parties* (Cambridge, MA: Harvard University Press, 1998).

18. See, for example, Jeff Cohen, Richard Fleisher, and Paul Kantor, eds., *American Political Parties: Decline or Resurgence?* (Washington, DC: CQ Press, 2001).

19. For a comprehensive discussion of political participation, see M. Margaret Conway, *Political Participation in the United States,* 3rd ed. (Washington, DC: CQ Press, 2000).

20. For a discussion of the struggle for suffrage, see William H. Flanigan and Nancy H. Zingale, *Political Behavior of the American Electorate* (Washington, DC: CQ Press, 1998), chapter 2.

21. See Margaret M. Conway, *Political Participation in the United States* (Washington, DC: CQ Press, 2000), chapter 5.

22. Some southern states continued to use the poll tax in state elections after passage of the Twenty-fourth Amendment. In 1966, the U.S. Supreme Court in *Harper v. Virginia State Board of Elections* outlawed the use of the poll tax in state elections as well as federal elections.

23. See Nancy McGlen and Karen O'Connor, *Women, Politics and American Society,* 2nd ed. (Upper Saddle River, NJ: Prentice-Hall, 1998).

24. A thorough discussion of the development of states' voter registration systems can be found in Joseph P. Harris, *Registration of Voters in the United States* (Washington, DC: Brookings Institution Press, 1929).

25. A federal statute requires that the waiting period from becoming a state resident to being eligible to vote may not exceed 30 days.

26. Michael D. Martinez and David B. Hill, "Did Motor Voter Work?" *American Politics Quarterly,* vol. 27 (1999): 296–315.

27. See Lee Sigelman et al., "Voting and Non-voting: A Multi-Election Perspective," *American Journal of Political Science,* vol. 29 (November 1985): 749–765.

28. See Raymond E. Wolfinger and Steven J. Rosenstone, *Who Votes?* (New Haven, CT: Yale University Press, 1980), 44–46.

29. Norman H. Nie, Jane Junn, and Kenneth Stehlik-Barry, *Education and Democratic Citizenship in America* (Chicago: University of Chicago Press, 1996).

30. Todd G. Shields and Robert K. Goidel, "Participation Rates, Socioeconomic Class Biases and Congressional Elections: A Cross Validation," *American Journal of Political Science,* vol. 41 (1997): 683–691.

31. Anthony Downs, *An Economic Theory of Democracy* (New York: Harper and Brothers, 1957).

32. Angus Campbell, Philip E. Converse, Warren E. Miller, and Donald E. Stokes, *Elections and the Political Order* (New York: Wiley, 1966).

33. For a comprehensive examination of the trends in voter turnout, see Thomas E. Patterson, *The Vanishing American Voter: Public Involvement in an Age of Uncertainty* (New York: Alfred A. Knopf, 2002).

34. See Ivor Crewe, "As the World Turns Out," *Public Opinion* 4 (February–March 1981).

35. For a discussion of trends in political efficacy, see also M. Margaret Conway, *Political Participation in the United States,* 3rd ed. (Washington, DC: CQ Press, 2000), 51–53.

36. Robert Putnam, *Bowling Alone* (New York: Simon & Schuster, 2000).

CHAPTER 14

1. See Lawrence D. Longley and Neal R. Pierce, *The Electoral College Primer* (New Haven, CT: Yale University Press, 1996).

2. For a good discussion of the development of parties in the early republic, see Stanley Elkins and Eric McKitrick, *The Age of Federalism: The Early American Republic 1788–1800* (New York: Oxford University Press, 1993).

3. See Paul Finkelman and John Moore, "The Democratic Party," in *The Encyclopedia of American Political History,* ed. Peter Wallenstein and Paul Finkelman (Washington, DC: CQ Press, 2001).

4. See Tadahisa Kuroda, *The Origins of the Twelfth Amendment: The Electoral College in the Early Republic 1787–1804* (Westport, CT: Greenwood Press, 1994).

5. A thorough discussion of the nomination process as well as other aspects of the presidential campaign can be found in Stephen Wayne, *The Road to the White House 2008,* 8th ed. (Boston: Wadsworth Press, 2008).

6. Larry M. Bartels, *Presidential Primaries and the Dynamics of Public Choice* (Princeton, NJ: Princeton University Press, 1988).

7. See John F. Bibby, *Politics, Parties and Elections in America* (Chicago: Nelson-Hall, 1992), chapter 6.

8. Ibid.

9. For a good discussion of the relevance of the New Hampshire primary, see Dante J. Scala, *Stormy Weather: The New Hampshire Primary and Presidential Politics* (New York: Palgrave Macmillan, 2003).

10. Nevada disrupted this traditional order in 2008 when it scheduled its Republican and Democratic caucuses for January 19, three days before the New Hampshire primary. New Hampshire then moved its primary to January 8.

11. See William G. Mayer and Andrew Busch, *The Frontloading Problem in Presidential Nominations* (Washington, DC: Brookings Institution Press, 2003).

12. For an excellent discussion of the 2008 presidential contest and some of its leading candidates, see Mark Halperin and John Harris, *The Way to Win: Taking the White House in 2008* (New York: Random House, 2006); John Heilemann and Mark Halperin, *Game Change: Obama and the Clintons, McCain and Palin, and the Race of a Lifetime* (New York: Harper, 2010).

13. For a history of party conventions, see CQ Press's *National Party Conventions 1831–2004* (2005).

14. The supporters of Herbert Hoover, the Republican candidate in 1928, briefly considered putting Dawes on the ticket as vice president once again, but backed down when the move was opposed by President Coolidge.

15. See, for example, James Druckman, "The Power of Television Images: The First Kennedy-Nixon Debate Revisited," *Journal of Politics,* vol. 65, no. 2 (2003): 559–571.

16. See Alan Schroeder, *Presidential Debates: 40 Years of High Risk TV* (New York: Columbia University Press, 1997).

17. See Darrell M. West, *Television Advertising in Election Campaigns 1952–1996* (Washington, DC: CQ Press, 1997).

18. For an analysis of the effects of negative ads on voters, see Richard R. Lau and Gerald M. Pomper, *Negative Campaigning: An Analysis of U.S. Senate Elections* (Lanham, MD: Rowman and Littlefield, 2004).

19. For a discussion of why the electoral college was created and how it has changed, see Lawrence D. Longley and Neal R. Peirce, *The Electoral College Primer 2000* (New Haven, CT: Yale University Press, 1999), chapter 2.

20. See Longley and Peirce, chapter 4.

21. The psychological concept of party identification is developed in Angus Campbell, Philip E. Converse, Warren E. Miller, and Donald E. Stokes, *The American Voter* (New York: Wiley, 1960).

22. For discussion of the role of party identification in forming vote choices, see Warren E. Miller and J. Merrill Shanks, *The New American Voter* (Cambridge, MA: Harvard University Press, 1996); and William H. Flanagan and Nancy H. Zingale, *Political Behavior of the American Electorate,* 9th ed. (Washington, DC: CQ Press, 1998).

23. See Martin P. Wattenberg, *The Decline of Political Parties 1952–1996* (Cambridge, MA: Harvard University Press, 1998).

24. Warren E. Miller and J. Merrill Shanks, *The New American Voter* (Cambridge, MA: Harvard University Press, 1996), chapter 12.

25. See Norman Nie, Sidney Verba, and John Petrocik, *The Changing American Voter* (Cambridge, MA: Harvard University Press, 1979).

26. Morris P. Fiorina, *Retrospective Voting in American National Elections* (New Haven, CT: Yale University Press, 1981).

27. See David B. Magleby and Candice J. Nelson, *The Money Chase* (Washington, DC: Brookings Institution Press, 1990).

28. *Buckley v. Valeo,* 424 U.S. 1 (1976).

29. *McConnell v. F.E.C.,* 540 U.S. 93 (2003).

30. For a thorough discussion of congressional elections, see Paul S. Herrnson, *Congressional Elections: Campaigning at Home and in Washington,* 2nd ed. (Washington, DC: CQ Press, 1998).

31. For a complete discussion of the coattail effect, see Gary C. Jacobson, *Electoral Origins of Divided Government 1946–1988* (Boulder, CO: Westview Press, 1990).

32. See Gary C. Jacobson, *The Politics of Congressional Elections,* 5th ed. (New York: Longman, 2001), chapter 3.

CHAPTER 15

1. Charles Lindblom, "The Science of Muddling Through," *Public Administration Review*, vol. 19 (Spring 1959): 79–88.

2. Paul R. Cutright, *Theodore Roosevelt: The Making of a Conservationist* (Urbana: University of Illinois Press, 1985).

3. Carl E. Van Horn, Donald Baumer, and William T. Gormley Jr., *Politics and Public Policy,* 3rd ed. (Washington, DC: CQ Press, 2001).

4. Ibid., 193–230.

5. William T. Gormley Jr., "Interest Group Interventions in the Administrative Process" in *The Interest Group Connection,* ed. Paul C. Herrnson, Ronald G. Shaiko, and Clyde Wilcox (Chatham, NJ: Chatham House, 1998), 213–223.

6. See Adam Smith, *The Wealth of Nations* (reprinted by New York: Modern Library, 1994).

7. John Maynard Keynes's most famous work is *The General Theory of Employment, Interest, and Money* (New York: Harcourt Brace Jovanovich, 1936).

8. See David Stockman, *The Triumph of Politics: How the Reagan Revolution Failed* (New York: Harper & Row, 1986).

9. John Steele Gordon, *Hamilton's Blessing: The Extraordinary Life and Times of Our National Debt* (New York: Penguin, 1998).

10. For a more detailed discussion of this argument, see the work of Michael Lewis-Beck, including *Economics and Elections: The Major Western Democracies* (Ann Arbor: University of Michigan Press, 1990).

11. Shelley Lynne Tomkin, *Inside OMB: Politics and Process in the President's Budget Office* (Armonk, NY: M. E. Sharpe, 1998).

12. See Allen Schick and Felix Lostracco, *The Federal Budget: Politics, Policy, Process* (Washington, DC: Brookings Institution Press, 2000).

13. Elizabeth Drew, *Showdown: The Struggle Between the Gingrich Congress and the Clinton White House* (New York: Touchstone, 1997).

14. *Bowsher v. Synar,* 478 U.S. 714 (1986).

15. Forbes's most recent proposal for a flat tax is discussed in Steve Forbes, *Flat Tax Revolution: Using a Postcard to Abolish the IRS* (Washington, DC: Regnery, 2005).

16. William Greider, *Secrets of the Temple: How the Federal Reserve Runs the Country* (New York: Simon & Schuster, 1989).

17. This was especially true when Alan Greenspan headed the Federal Reserve. See Bob Woodward, *Greenspan's Fed and the American Boom* (New York: Simon & Schuster, 2001).

18. Herbert Packer, *The Limits of the Criminal Sanction* (Stanford, CA: Stanford University Press, 1968).

19. For a discussion of criminal justice in America more generally, see George Cole and Christopher Smith, *The American System of Criminal Justice* (Belmont, CA: Wadsworth, 2001).

20. Larry J. Siegel and Joseph J. Senna, *Introduction to Criminal Justice* (Boston: Wadsworth, 2005), 412.

21. David Baldus, George Woodworth, and Charles Pulaski, *Equal Justice and the Death Penalty: A Legal and Empirical Analysis* (Boston: Northeastern University Press, 1990).

22. Lawrence M. Friedman, *Crime and Punishment in American History* (New York: Basic Books, 1993), 264–265.

23. Jeffrey Rosen, "Dual Sovereigns," *The New Republic* (July 28, 1997), 16–19.

24. *United States v. Lopez,* 514 U.S. 549 (1995).

25. Hermann Beck, *The Origins of the Authoritarian Welfare State in Prussia* (Ann Arbor: University of Michigan Press, 1997).

26. William Leuchtenberg, *Franklin Roosevelt and the New Deal* (New York: HarperCollins, 1963).

27. Kristen Lindenmeyer, *A Right to Childhood: The U.S. Children's Bureau and Child Welfare* (Urbana: University of Illinois Press, 1997).

28. Jonathan Oberlander, *The Political Life of Medicare* (Chicago: University of Chicago Press, 2003).

29. Jeffrey Lehman and Sheldon Danziger, "Turning Our Back on the New Deal: The End of Welfare in 1996," in *Race, Poverty and Domestic Policy,* ed. C. Michael Henry (New Haven, CT: Yale University Press, 2004).

30. Robert Hudson, ed., *The New Politics of Old Age Policy* (Baltimore: Johns Hopkins University Press, 2005).

31. See Paul Light, *Still Artful Work: The Continuing Politics of Social Security Reform* (New York: McGraw Hill, 1994).

32. "Baby Boomers Envision Retirement II: Survey of Baby Boomers' Expectations for Retirement," survey conducted for AARP by RoperASW, October 9–23, 2003 (see http://www.research.aarp.org/).

33. Jan Gregoire Coombs, *The Rise and Fall of HMOs: An American Health Care Revolution* (Madison: University of Wisconsin Press, 2005).

34. William Gesler and Thomas Ricketts, eds., *Health Care in Rural North America: The Geography of Health Care Services in North America* (Newark, NJ: Rutgers University Press, 1992).

CHAPTER 16

1. Robert Dallek, *Franklin Delano Roosevelt and American Foreign Policy, 1932–1945* (New York: Oxford University Press, 1995).

2. A detailed (if uncritical) look at the events leading up to the Truman Doctrine and the Marshall Plan can be found in Joseph M. Jones, *The Fifteen Weeks* (New York: Harcourt, Brace, 1955).

3. D. F. Flemming, *The Cold War and Its Origins: 1917–1960* (New York: Doubleday, 1961).

4. David DiLeo, *George Ball, Vietnam and the Rethinking of Containment* (Chapel Hill: University of North Carolina Press, 1991).

5. Stanley Karnow, *Vietnam: A History* (New York: Penguin, 1997).

6. Frank Snepp, *Decent Interval: An Insider's Account on Saigon's Indecent End* (New York: Vintage Books, 1978).

7. Robert Litwak, *Détente and the Nixon Doctrine* (Cambridge: Cambridge University Press, 1986).

8. John Newhouse, "The Missile Defense Debate," *Foreign Affairs*, vol. 80, no. 4 (July/August 2001).

9. John Lewis Gaddis, *The Cold War: A New History* (New York: Penguin, 2005).

10. One of the key architects of this new understanding was Bush's secretary of state, James A. Baker III. See James A. Baker III, *The Politics of Diplomacy* (New York: Putnam, 1995).

11. Many of these criticisms are discussed in Samantha Power's award-winning book, *A Problem from Hell: America and the Age of Genocide* (New York: Harper Perennial, 2003).

12. Perhaps the best book written to date about the problems in the military's 2003 intervention in Iraq is Michael Gordon and Bernard Trainor's *Cobra II: The Inside Story of the Invasion and Occupation of Iraq* (New York: Pantheon, 2006).

13. Niall Ferguson, *Colossus: The Rise and Fall of the American Empire* (New York: Penguin Books, 2005).

14. Joseph Nye, *Soft Power: The Means to Success in World Politics* (New York: PublicAffairs, 2005).

15. Louis Fisher, "Without Restraint: Presidential Military Initiatives from Korea to Bosnia," in *Domestic Sources of American Foreign Policy,* 3rd ed., ed. Eugene Wittkopf and James McCormick (Lanham, MD: Rowman and Littlefield, 1999), 141–155.

16. Powell's shuttle diplomacy was described in great detail in Bob Woodward, *Plan of Attack* (New York: Simon & Schuster, 2004).

17. Geoffrey Kemp, "Presidential Management of the Executive Bureaucracy," in *United States Foreign Policy: The Search for a New Role*, ed. Robert J. Art and Seyom Brown (Upper Saddle River, NJ: Prentice Hall, 1993).

18. See Bruce Berkowitz, "Information Age Intelligence," *Foreign Policy*, vol. 103 (Summer 1996): 35–50.

19. Jeremy D. Rosner, *The New Tug-of-War: Congress, the Executive Branch and National Security* (Washington, DC: Carnegie Endowment for International Peace, 1995).

20. George Crile, *Charlie Wilson's War* (New York: Grove Press, 2004).

21. Perot's daring rescue effort is described in dramatic fashion in Ken Follett, *On Wings of Eagles* (New York: William Morrow, 1983).

22. See William B. Quandt, "The Electoral Cycle and the Conduct of American Foreign Policy," *Political Science Quarterly*, vol. 101 (1986): 825–837.

23. John Mueller, "Public Opinion and Foreign Policy: The People's Common Sense," in *Domestic Sources of American Foreign Policy*, 3rd ed., ed. Eugene Wittkopf and James McCormick (Lanham, MD: Rowman and Littlefield, 1999), 51–60.

24. Peter Boone, "The Impact of Foreign Aid on Savings and Growth," Center for Economic Performance Working Paper No. 1265, London, October 1994, 25–26.

INDEX

Note: Terms in boldface type are key terms defined in the glossary. Page numbers in italics refer to tables, figures, and boxed features.

A

AARP, 131, 294–295, 302
   grassroots lobbying by, 310
   money spent on lobbying, *306*
   poll on Social Security, 443
Abbott Laboratories, 309
ABC, 334–335
Abington School District v. Schempp (1963), 81
abolition movement, 110
abortion, 97, 98–99
Abramoff, Jack, 293
Abrams v. United States (1919), 320
Abu Ghraib prison, 333
accommodation, philosophy of, 109, 113
ACLU. *See* American Civil Liberties Union (ACLU)
ActBlue, *310*
ADA. *See* Americans for Democratic Action (ADA)
Adams, John, 175
   Constitutional Convention and, 32
   Declaration of Independence and, 29
   in election of 1796, 350
   in election of 1800, 6, 350, 392
   French Revolution and, 74
   justices and judges appointed by, 239
   precedent of peaceful transition between presidents by, 175
   reelected as vice president, 350
Adams, John Quincy, 162, 175, 390
   election of 1824, 350, 404
   Monroe Doctrine and, 177
   popular vote in 1824, *377*
Adarand v. Peña (1995), 122
administrative discretion, 206–207
administrative law, 207, 232
The Adventures of Huckleberry Finn (Twain), 329
The Adventures of Tom Sawyer (Twain), 329
adversarial system of justice, 236–238
advertising, presidential campaign, 404
AFDC (Aid to Families with Dependent Children), 440–441
affirmative action, 14, 119, 121–123, 126, 270
Afghanistan, 182, 188, *467,* 468
AFL (American Federation of Labor), 298
AFL-CIO, 298, 300, 302

African Americans
   affirmative action and, 119, 121–123
   black nationalism, 118–119
   civil rights movement, 115–119, 368
   Congressional Black Caucus, *109, 155*
   crime control policy and, 438–439
   differing approaches to civil rights among, 108–110
   equal rights for, 109
   first in cabinet, 216
   first Supreme Court Justice, 230, 247
   Ku Klux Klan and, 84
   mean/median income, 123
   political offices held by, 120–121
   race riots (1992) and, 94
   racial discrimination of, 110–111
   racial profiling of, 123–124
   racial segregation of, 112–115
   struggle for equality and civil rights, 110–124
   suffrage for, 367
   voting rights for, 107, 110, 118, 367–368
   "Year of Birmingham" and, 116–118
age, voter turnout and, 371, *371*
agencies
   independent, 218
   regulatory, 218–219
agenda setting theory, 337
agents of political socialization, 273
agitation, philosophy of, 109
Agnew, Spiro, 162
Agricultural Adjustment Act, 253
Agricultural Party, 360
Aguilera, Christina, *328*
Aid to Dependent Children, 440–441
Aid to Families with Dependent Children (AFDC), 440–441
Airline Pilots Association, *305*
Alaska, 357
Albany Congress of 1754, 142
Albany Plan of Union, 142
Albright, Madeleine, 216
Alcatraz Island, 128, *128*
Alien Act (1798), 74, *100*
Alien Enemies Act, 74
Alito, Samuel, 246, *246*
Allen, George, 339
Allison, Jim, 28
All the President's Men (Woodward/Bernstein), 331
All Things Considered (radio news show), 336

"alphabet soup" agencies, *210*

Al Qaeda, *461,* 462

Alston & Byrd, 309

Amazon, 423

amendments. *See also* individual amendments
  Balanced Budget Amendment, 431
  Civil War, 111, 367
  defined, 41
  extending voting rights, *11*

American Association for Justice, *310*

American Association of Retired Persons (AARP), 131.
  See also AARP

American Bar Association (ABA), 246, *256,*
  305–306, 311

American Civil Liberties Union (ACLU), 125, 307, 311

American democracy, in a state of decline, 15–19

American Farm Bureau Federation (AFBF), 301

American Federation of Labor (AFL), 298

American Federation of Labor-Congress of Industrial
  Organization (AFL-CIO), 298, 300, 302

American Federation of State, County and Municipal
  Employees, *310*

American Federation of Teachers, *310*

American government
  branches of, 8
  enduring democracy of, 9–10
  legitimacy of, 8–9, 10
  levels of, *9*

American Hospital Association, *306*

American Independent Party, *362*

American-Israel Public Affairs Committee (AIPAC),
  302, 466

American Medical Association (AMA), 300,
  305–306, *306*

American Minerva (Webster), 324

American political culture, 10–14

American Political Science Association (APSA), 348

American Public Media, 335

American Recovery and Reinvestment Act (ARRA),
  173, 182

Americans for Democratic Action (ADA), 307, 311

Americans for Free-Choice, 307

American Socialist Party, 84

American Society of Travel Agents (ASTA), 303

Americans with Disabilities Act (1990), 131

American Trial Lawyers Association (ATLA), 301

The American Voter (Converse), 271, 356

American Woman Suffrage Association, 106

AmeriCorps, *445*

Ames, Oakes, 292

Ames, Oliver, 292

amicus curiae briefs, 311

Amish, 78, *78,* 79

anarchy, 7

Anderson, John, *362*

Annapolis Convention, 31–32

Anthony, Casey, 257

Anthony, Susan B., 106

Anti-Federalists, 39
  beliefs, 349
  in history of political parties, 349

Anti-Federalists, 37

Anti-Masonic Party, *362*

antitrust laws, 183

appeals court, 235

appellate jurisdiction, 243

Apple (company), 424

appropriations committees, 429–430

Arizona, immigration law, 53

Ars Technica, *322*

Article I, 56, 57, 60, 90, 142, 241, 366

Article II, 174, 175, 177, 182, 189, 206, 405

Article III, 58, 234, 239, 242

Article IV, 57, 58

Articles of Confederation, 30–32
  changes to, 37
  confederation and, 54
  defined, 30
  key features of, *30*
  limitations of central government under, 30–31
  proposals to revise, 31–32
  ratification of, 30

Article V, 42

Article VI, 57, 239

Article VII, 35

Asian Americans, civil rights for, 128

assassinations, 175, *461–462*

Associated Press (AP), 331, 334

Association for Intercollegiate Athletics for Women, *133*

Association of Trial Lawyers of America (ATLA), 302

Atlanta Journal-Constitution, 85, 86

AT&T, *306, 310*

The Audacity of Hope (Obama), *400*

authoritarianism, 6, 7

authority, 7

Aviation Committee, 151

Ayers, William, 338

B

Bachmann, Michelle, 6, *153, 393,* 393–394

bail, 97

Baker, Jack, 107

Bakke, Alan, 119, 121

Balanced Budget Amendment, 431

balance-of-trade figures, 428–429

Baldus, David, 123

Balkans, 460

ballots, 371–373, *372*

banking system, central, 435–437

Barkley, Alben, 400

Barnett, Ross, 114

battleground states, 401, 402

Battle of New Orleans (1815), 177

Belgium, death penalty abolished in, *98*

Benton v. Maryland (1969), *77*

Bernanke, Ben, 436, *436,* 436–437

Bernstein, Carl, 323, *324,* 331

bias, media, 339

bicameral legislature, 143–144

Biden, Joseph, 191, *191,* 248, 398, 399, *401*

Big Brothers, *445*

Big Sisters, *445*

bill

    becoming a law, *156,* 156–160

    conference committee action, 159

    defined, 150

    to House and Senate for consideration, 158–159

    introduction of, 156–157

    presidential action, 160

    sent to standing committee for action, 157

bill of attainder, 90

Bill of Rights, 11, 73. *See also* civil liberties; specific
    amendments

    applicable to the states, *77,* 77–78

    defined, 41

    formation of, 41

    natural rights and, 12

    origin and evolution of, 76–78

    rights protected under, 41

    Supreme Court interpretation of, 76–77

bin Laden, Osama, *185, 186, 461, 462*

Bipartisan Campaign Reform Act (BCRA) (2002), 413

Birmingham, Alabama, civil rights movement in, *116,*
    116–118

birth control, right to, 97–98

Bituminous Coal Conservation Act, 253

Black, Hugo, 195

Black Codes, 111

Blackmun, Harry, 98

Black Muslims, 119

black nationalism, 118–119

Black Panther Party, 119

Blair, Sheila, *157*

block grants, 62, 66

blogs, *267*

    defined, 334

political, *339*

    public opinion expressed through, 268

    top 10 political, *322*

Blue Cross/Blue Shield, *306*

Boehner, John, *146, 431*

Boeing, *306*

books, 330–331

Boone, Peter, 470

Bordley, Stephen, 240

Bork, Robert H., 46, 248, *248*

Bosnia, 459

Boston Globe, 276

Boston Tea Party (1773), 27

Bowers v. Hardwick (1986), 252, 253

boycotts, 111, 115

Boys and Girls Club, *445*

Bradley, Bill, 18, 411

Brady, James, 90

Brady, Sarah, 90

Brady Bill (1993), 67, 90

Brady Handgun Violence Prevention Act (1993), 90

Brafman, Benjamin, 238

Brandeis, Louis, 67, *442*

Brandenburg v. Ohio (1969), 84

Brennan, William, 46, 245, 255

Breyer, Stephen, *246,* 247, 257

British Parliament, 143

Brooks, Preston, 140

Brown, Scott, 339, *414*

Brownlow, Louis, 210

Brownlow Committee, 210

***Brown v. Board of Education* (1954),** 110, *113,*
    113–114, 230, 242, 243

"Brutus" pseudonym, 39

Brzezinski, Zbigniew, 217

Buchanan, James, 177, 192, 352, 377

Buchanan, Pat, *363*

***Buckley v. Valeo* (1976),** 412

Budget and Accounting Act (1921), 429

Budget and Impoundment Act (1974), 430

budget authority, 433

budget deficit, 428

Budget Enforcement Act (1990), 431

budget surplus, 428

Buffet, Warren, 433

"Buffet plan," 433

"bull moose" keychain, *352*

Bull Moose Party, 353, 361, *362*

"bully pulpit," 454

bureaucracy, 201–224

    Bureau of Consumer Financial Protection (BCFP), 203

    cabinet departments, 212–216, 217

bureaucracy (*continued*)
    characteristics of effective, 204
    control of growing, 211–212
    defined, 204
    Department of Homeland Security, 216
    deregulation of, 211
    development of, 209–210
    devolution of, 211
    Executive Office of the President, 220
    federal workforce, 220–222
    Golden Fleece Awards, *208*
    government corporations, 219–220
    independent agencies, 218
    legislation, 206–207
    organization of, 204, *205,* 206, 212–220
    policy implementation by, 206
    regulatory agencies, 218–219
    Securities Exchange Commission and, 202
bureaucratic adjudicating, 209
bureaucratic agencies, interest groups and,
    299–300
Bureau of Consumer Financial Protection (BCFP), 203
Bureau of Forestry, 422
Bureau of Indian Affairs, 128
Bureau of Labor, 209
Bureau of Labor Statistics, 213
Burns, Ken, 335
Burr, Aaron, 350, 392
Burris, Roland, 119
bus boycott, 115
Bush, Barbara, 192–193
Bush, George H.W.
    becoming president after vice president, 174
    election of 1992, 408
    global trade and, 459
    losing reelection bid, 175
    nomination for defense secretary, 184
    pardons by, 184
    presidency of, 181
    relations with Bush, George W., 175
    selected as vice-presidential candidate, 400
    Supreme Court nomination by, 248–249
    tax policy, 433
    as two-term vice-president, 18
    vetoes issued by, *188*
    vice presidential candidate of, 401
    war-making powers, 188
Bush, George W.
    background of, 18
    book on propaganda by, 323–324
    cabinet of, 216, 217
    Clarence Thomas nominated by, 162

Department of Homeland Security, 216
    discretionary spending under, 434–435
    election of 2000, 404, 407
    election of 2004, 400, 414
    executive orders by, 190
    on Hispanic Americans, 129
    Iraq war and, 462–463, 467
    judicial appointments by, 249
    media and, 195, 196
    Middle East policy, 460
    poll predicting election outcome of, *277*
    post-9/11 antiterrorism policies/actions, 75, 189
    preemption doctrine and, 469
    presidency of, 182
    press conferences by, 328
    racial profiling and, 124
    relationship with Cheney, 191
    relations with Bush, George H.W., 175
    signing statements used by, 187
    Supreme Court nomination by, 184, 244–245, 246
    tax cuts by, 151
    USA Patriot Act and, 183–184
    vetoes issued by, 187, *188*
    vice presidential candidate of, 401
    war on terror policies, *100*
Bush v. Gore (2000), 257
businesses
    interest groups of, 303–304
    ownership of news media outlets, 334–335, *335*
    satisfaction with size and power of, *66*
Business Insider blog, *322*
Business Roundtable, *306*
busing, 115
BuzzFeed, *322*
Byrnes, James F., 240

C

cabinet, 191–192
    bureaucracy of, *205*
    conflicts within, 217
    departments of, 212–216
    diversity in, 216
cabinet departments, 212–216
Cain, Herman, 6, *393,* 393–394
Calderon, Felipe, *463*
Calhoun, John, *61*
California
    delegates in, 396
    deregulation of utilities, 67
    House of Representatives, number of seats in, 145
    state expenditures, *63*

California v. Ciraolo (1986), 93
cameras
    in the courtroom, 257–258
    surveillance, 92, 94
Cameron, David, *348*
Cammermeyer, Margarethe, 132
campaign buttons, *352*
campaign contributions, 16–17, 18–19, *310*
campaign funding, 409–413
    regulating, 412–413
    sources of, 409–412, *410, 411*
campaigns
    negative, 6–7
    persuasion, 311
    televised debates and, 325–327
    use of social media for, 4
    use of television, 4–5
Campbell, Angus, 373
Canada
    death penalty abolished in, *98*
    as a federal system, 55
    immigrants from, *130*
    legislatures in, 143
    NAFTA and, 186
candidate image voting, 409
Cannon, Joe, 147–148
Cantwell v. Connecticut (1940), *77*
capitalism, 15–16, 18, 439
Carlin, George, 321
Carswell, G. Harrold, 248, *248*
Carter, Jimmy, 400
    cabinet of, 217
    election of 1980, 408, 409
    foreign policy in Middle East, 460
    losing reelection bid, 175
    Panama Canal Treaty, 186
    presidency of, 181
    relationship with Mondale, 191
    televised debate with Ford, 326–327, 403
    town meetings by, 193
    vetoes issued by, *188*
    winning nomination for presidency, 391
Carter, Rosalyn, 192
Carville, James, 433
casework, 164, 166
Castro, Fidel, *461*
caucus, *155,* 395–396
CBS, 334–335
CBS Corporation, *335*
CBS/*New York Times* poll, 268, 282
Center for Auto Safety, 307
Central Intelligence Agency (CIA), *462,* 465–466

chairs, congressional committee, 153
Change We Can Believe In (Obama), 400
Chase, Samuel, 240
checks and balances, 36, *36*
Cheney, Dick, 191, 211, 400, 401, 464–465
Chicago Daily Tribune, 277
child labor amendment, 44
child labor laws, 61
child pornography, 87
China
    as economic superpower, 15, 17
    immigrants from, *130*
    projected gross domestic product, *15*
Chinese Exclusion Act (1882), 128
Chisholm, Shirley, *155*
Christian Coalition of America (CCA), 301, 307
Christie, Chris, 40, 394, 399
Church, Frank, *461*
Church of Jesus Christ of Latter-Day Saints, 79–80
church-state separation, 78, 80, 82
CIA (Central Intelligence Agency). *See* Central
    Intelligence Agency (CIA)
CIO (Congress of Industrial Organizations), 298
CIRCLE (Center for Information and Research on Civil
    Learning and Engagement), 19
Citadel, Charleston, South Carolina, 126
citizenship
    for African Americans, 111
    for Native Americans, 127–128
Citizens United v. FEC (2010), 16–17, 253, 255,
    298, 299
City Year, *445*
civil disobedience, 110, 379
Civilian Conservation Corps, 210
civil law, 232
civil liberties. *See also* Bill of Rights
    Americans' attitudes on, *96*
    defined, 73
    freedom of expression, 83–89
    freedom of religion, 78–80
    historical background, 74
    post-9/11 antiterrorism policies and, 75
    right to bear arms, 89–90
    right to privacy, 97–99
civil litigation, 236–237
civil rights
    for African Americans, 110–124
    for Asian Americans, 128
    defined, 108, 109
    differing approaches in achieving, 108–110
    for gays and lesbians, 131–132
    gender equality and, 124–127

civil rights (*continued*)
    for Hispanic Americans, 129–130
    for individuals with disabilities, 132
    for Muslim Americans, 129
    for Native Americans, 127–128
    for older Americans, 130–131
    same-sex marriage, 107
    women's suffrage, 106
Civil Rights Act (1875), 111
Civil Rights Act (1964), 118
    Title VII, 126, 127
Civil Rights Act (1968), 118
civil rights movement, 115–119, 318, 368
civil rights protests (1960s), 12
civil service, 221–222
Civil Service Reform Act of 1978, 222
Civil War (1861-1865), 111
    modern party system and, 352
    PBS documentary on, 335
    presidency of Lincoln and, 177
    slavery issue and, 35, 44
    state-federal government relationship and, 61
    suffrage and, 367
    Whig Party and, 351–352
Civil War Amendments, 111, 367
Clarke, John Hessin, 240
class action lawsuit, 242
Clay, Henry, 351
Clean Air Act (1963), 207
clear and present danger test, 84
Cleveland, Grover, *377*
Clinton, Bill, *194*
    antitrust laws, 183
    bureaucratic accountability under, 211
    chief of staff and, 192
    election of 1992, 400
    on gays in the military, 132
    global trade and, 459
    government shutdowns and, 66, 430
    impeachment, 163, 175
    NAFTA and, 186
    pardons issued by, 184
    popular vote in 1992, *377*
    presidency of, 181–182
    press conferences, 328
    public opinion and foreign policy of, 468
    on racial profiling, 124
    relationship with Congress, 194, 195
    as Rhodes Scholar, 18
    same-sex unions and, 107
    serving two terms, 181
    speaking at national convention, 2008, 398
    speaking at national convention, 2012, 399
    Supreme Court nominations by, 247
    town meetings by, 193
    vetoes issued by, *188*
    war-making powers, 188
    welfare and, 194, 441
    women in cabinet of, 216
Clinton, George, 350
Clinton, Hillary Rodham
    diversity of Obama's cabinet and, 216
    election of 2008, *355,* 397, 407
    health care reform and, 193
    New Hampshire Democratic primary election
        and, *277–278*
    as secretary of state, 464
    speaking at national convention, 2008, 398
closed primary, 395
closed rule, 158
closed shop, 305
cloture rule, 158
CNN website, 334
Coast Guard, 465
coattail effect, 414
Coercive Acts (1774), 27
Colbert, Stephen, *275,* 329–330, *330*
Cold War, 181, 210, 212, 458
college, attending close to home, *68*
college students
    military draft and, *473*
    Occupy Wall Street, 286, *286*
    PIRG and, 312
    political campaign involvement, *416*
    political participation by, *416*
Colombia, immigrants from, *130*
colonies
    British raising money in, 26
    political parties in, 349
    political structure in, 26
    response to British policies, 27, 29
Colossus: The Rise and Fall of the American Empire
    (Ferguson), 463
Commerce Agency, 209
committee chairs, 153
committee system in Congress, 150–154
Common Cause, 307, 377
common law, 232
Common Sense (Paine), 29
Commonwealth Fund, *59*
complaint, 236
computerized response audience polling
    (CRAPs), 280
computer punch cards, 372, *372,* 373

concurrent powers, 56

concurring opinion, 251

confederation, 54

conference committees, 152–153, 159

confirmation of presidential nominations, 162, 247–249

Congo, *461*

Congress, 137, 139–166

    111th, 141, 158

    African American participation in, 111, 119, *120*

    appointment of federal judges by, 244

    approval ratings, 2012, 141

    Article I and creation of, 142

    under Articles of Confederation, 30

    authority to regulate interstate commerce, 64

    bicameralism, 143–144

    bill becoming a law in, *156,* 156–160

    casework by, 164, 166

    changes in health care, sources for consideration on, *160*

    committee system in, 150–154

    conference committees, 152–153

    confidence in, *143*

    confirmation of presidential nominations, 162–163

    constituent service by, 163–164, 166

    divided government in, 359

    divisions in, during 1850s, 140

    federal bureaucracy and, 206–207

    first, 145

    following Lincoln's assassination, 177

    foreign policy powers, 454, 466

    founding fathers on, 142

    impeachment powers, 161, 163

    internships in, *165*

    joint committees, 153

    leadership in, 146–149

    midterm elections, 413–416

    oversight, 161–162

    partisan divisiveness in, 140, 141

    partisan voting in, *359*

    "pork-barrel" legislation, 166

    president's legislative role and, 186–187

    president's relationship with, 193–194

    select committees on, 152

    separation of powers and, 36

    staffing, 153–154

    standing committees, 151, *152*

    structure and organization of, 143–149

    treaty approval by, 163

    vetoes overridden by, 187

    war-making powers, 188

congressional agencies, 154

Congressional Black Caucus (CBC), *109, 155*

Congressional Budget Office (CBO), 154, 173, 207, 430

congressional caucuses, 147, 149, *153, 155*

congressional committees, 151–153, *152*

    interest groups and, 299–300

congressional committee staff, 154

congressional districts, 145

congressional elections, 374, 413–416, *415*

Congressional Government (Wilson), 142

Congressional Hispanic Caucus, *165*

Congressional Member Organization, *155*

congressional oversight, 207

congressional personal staff, 153–154

congressional power

    under Articles of Confederation, 30–31

    under dual federalism, 61

Congressional Research Service (CRS), 154

Congress of Industrial Organization (CIO), 298

Congress on the Armed Services Committee, 308

Congress: The Keystone of the Washington Establishment (Fiorina), 162

"Connecticut Compromise" (The Great Compromise), 33–34

Connor, Eugene "Bull," 117

conservative ideology, 270

Conservative Party, 360

Constitution. *See also* Bill of Rights; individual amendments

    amendment process, 42, *42, 43,* 44–45

    amendments extending voting rights, 11

    American political culture and, 12

    Articles of Confederation and, *30*

    capacity to evolve, 24

    checks and balances in, 36, *36*

    conflict and, 9–10

    creation of, 9

    electoral college and, 404

    federal and state powers under, *56*

    foreign policy and, 454

    full faith and credit clause, 57–58

    health care reform and, 25

    informal change processes, 45–47

    on judicial review, 239

    as a "living document," 37, *46*

    loose interpretation of, 45–47

    national supremacy period of federalism and, 60

    popular support for amendments, *44*

    preamble, 10

    on presidential powers, 182, 183

    presidential powers in, 189

    on presidential requirements, 174

    privacy rights in, 97

    privileges and immunities clause, 58

    provisions in, 35–37

Constitution (*continued*)

    on public opinion, 266

    ratification, 37–41

    separation of powers in, 36

    strict interpretation of, 45–46

    supremacy clause, 57

    on Supreme Court, 234

    voting and, 366

Constitutional Convention, *8,* 32–35

    delegates at, 32

    Great Compromise, 33–34, 143

    New Jersey Plan, 33

    slavery issue at, 34–35

    Three-Fifths Compromise, 35

    Virginia Plan, 32–33

constitutional law, 232

Constitution Party, *363*

consumer confidence index (CCI), 428, *429*

Consumer Financial Protection Bureau, 212

consumer price index (CPI), 427

Consumer Product Safety Commission (CPSC), 219

consumer protection movement, 297

containment, 458

continuing resolutions, 430

continuity (in public opinion), 284

Contract with America, 66

Converse, Philip, 271

Coolidge, Calvin, 175, *188,* 400

cooperative federalism (1937-1990), 59, 62–64

Cooper v. Aaron (1958), *113,* 114, 241

Corcoran, Tommy, 309

Cordray, Richard, *203*

Corporation for Public Broadcasting (CPB), 335

corporations. *See* businesses

Corzine, Jon, 410

cost-of-living adjustments (COLAs) in Social Security, 294–295

Coughlin, Charles, 325

county government, 9

courts. *See also* legal system; U.S. Supreme Court

    cameras in the courtroom, 257–258

    electing and appointing judges of, 244–249

    federal court system, 234–235

    limitations on, 241–243

    state, 233, *234*

Craig v. Boren (1976), 125

Crédit Mobilier, 292

crime control model, 438–439

crime policy, 438–439

criminal law, 232

criminally accused, rights of, 90–97

critical election, 352

Cronkite, Walter, *325*

Crozer Theological Seminary, 115–116

Cuba, immigrants from, 129, *130*

Cuban missile crisis (1962), *185,* 458

cultivation theory, 337

CVS, 309

cyberbullying, 88–89

D

Dahl, Robert, 243, 295

The Daily Beast, *322*

The Daily Kos blog, *267,* 268

The Daily Show, 330

"Daisy Girl" commercial, 5

Daley, Richard J., 398

The Dance of Legislation (Redman), 156

Daniels, Mitch, 394

Daschle, Tom, 184, 309, *309*

Dateline, 323

Dawes, Charles, 400

Dawes Severalty Act (1887), 127

Day O'Connor, Sandra, 64

dealignment, 354

Dean, Howard, 411

death penalty, *98,* 123

debates, presidential, 325–327, 403–404

Debs, Eugene V., *362*

debt, national, 428, *432*

Declaration of Independence

    "all men are created equal" in, 268–269

    inalienable rights in, 29

    "inalienable rights" in, 76

    natural rights and, 9

    political culture and, 12

    writing of, 29

Declaration of Rights and Grievances, 26

Declaratory Act, 27

"Deep Throat," 323

de facto discrimination, 115

defendant, 236

Defense of Marriage Act (DOMA) (1996), *57,* 58, 107

de jure discrimination, 115

DeKalb, George, 82

Delaware v. Van Arsdall (1937), *77*

DeLay, Tom, 292

delegated congressional power, 207

democracy

    defined, 7

    direct, 10, 11

    indirect, 10

    public opinion and, 267

representative, 10, 365–366
Democratic National Committee, 396
Democratic National Party Conventions, 398, *398,* 399
Democratic Party. *See also* political parties
  Adam Clayton Powell and, *120*
  congressional caucuses, *155*
  congressional leadership by, 147
  convention of 1968, 398, *398*
  convention of 2008, 398
  convention of 2012, 399
  before election of 1890, 346
  first national party convention, 351
  formation of, 351
  founding of, 390
  Hispanic Americans voting for, 129
  in history of political parties, 351–354
  interest groups and, 311
  liberal ideology and, 270
  New Deal coalition and, 353–354
  on same-sex marriage, 107
  seat gains in House of Representatives, *149*
  Supreme Court confirmations and, 249
Democratic-Republican Party
  election of 1796, 350
  election of 1800, 350
  election of 1824, 350–351
  elections of 1792, 349–350
  Federalist Party and, 349
  nominating candidates for presidency, 390
  supported in the South, 350
Democratic Select Committee, *155*
de Montesquieu, Baron, 36
Denmark, *98*
Dennis v. United States (1951), 84
Department of Commerce (DOC), *214*
Department of Commerce and Labor, *214*
Department of Defense, 213, 300, 308
Department of Defense, 212, *214,* 216, 464
Department of Education, 66, 212, *215,* 223
Department of Energy (DOE), *215,* 216
Department of Health and Human Services, *215*
Department of Homeland Security (DHS), 212, *215,* 216, 465
Department of Housing and Urban Development, *215*
Department of Justice (DOJ), 209, *214*
Department of Labor, 211, 213, *215,* 298
Department of State, 209, *214,* 454, 464
Department of the Interior (DOI), 209, *214*
Department of Transportation (DOT), *215*
Department of Treasury, 209, *214*
Department of Veterans Affairs, *215*
Department of War, 209, 454
deregulation, 211

desegregation, 110, 114, 117, 242
Detainee Treatment Act (2005), 187
de Tocqueville, Alexis, 12–13, 295
devolution, 64, 66, 211
Dewey, Thomas, *277*
Dexter Avenue Baptist Church, 115
DHS. *See* Department of Homeland Security (DHS)
digital divide, 334
digital media, *332,* 332–334
direct democracy, 10, 11
direction (of public opinion), 284
direct primary elections, 365, 391
disabilities, civil rights for individuals with, 131
discount rate, 436
discovery, 236
discretionary spending, 433–434
discrimination
  of Asian Americans, 128
  of gays and lesbians, 131–132
  gender, 125–127
  against Hispanics, 129
  of individuals with disabilities, 131
  racial, 110–111, 115, 118
Disney Corporation, 335, *335*
dissenting opinion, 251–252
distributive tax policies, 432
District of Columbia, *112,* 368, 392, 404
District of Columbia v. Heller (2008), 90
diversity
  American political culture and, 13
  federalism and, 67
  in Obama's cabinet, 216
divided government, 359
DNA testing, 92
doctrine of preemption, 57
Dodd-Frank Financial Reform Act (DATE), 203
Dole, Bob, 400
domestic policy, 421
  crime policy, 438–439
  environmental, 423
  fiscal policy theories and practice, 426–435
  health care, 423
  health care policy, 444
  monetary policy theories and practice, 435–437
  policymaking process, 424–426
  Social Security System, 441, 443
  states as laboratories for national policies, *442–443*
  think tanks, *423*
  welfare state and programs for the poor, 439–441
Dominican Republic
  immigrants from, *130*
domino theory, 458

"don't ask, don't tell" policy, 132
"Doonesbury" (Trudeau), 329
double jeopardy clause, 94
Douglas, William O., 254
Dow Jones Industrial Average, 428
Dow Jones Industrial index, 202
Downs, Anthony, 373, 408
draft, military, *473*
Dred Scott v. Sandford (1857), 110–111, 241, 367
drug use, freedom of religion and, 80
dual federalism, 61
Du Bois, W.E.B., 109, 113
due process model, 438
Dukakis, Michael, 403
Duncan v. Louisiana (1968), *77*

E

Eagleton, Thomas, 401
Easton, David, 274
Eastwood, Clint, 399
Economic and Social Council (UN), 470
economic disparities among states, 68
economic equality, 108
economic interest groups, 303–306
economic policy. *See* fiscal policy
economic recession. *See* Great Recession of 2007-2010;
    recession
economic superpower, United States as, 15, 17
economy. *See* fiscal policy
Ecuador, immigrants from, *130*
Edison Electric Institute, *306*
education. *See* schools
educational level, voter turnout and, 371, *371*
Edwards, John, 338, 405
Eighteenth Amendment, *43,* 44–45
Eighth Amendment, *43, 77,* 78, 90, 97
Eisenhower, Dwight D.
    on civil rights, 318
    on Nixon, 191
    press conferences, 327
    Supreme Court appointments by, 245
    vetoes issued by, *188*
Elazar, Daniel, *13*
election poster, *350*
elections, 387–389. *See also* presidential elections;
    voting
    1792, 349–350
    1796, 350
    1800, 6, 175, 350, 392
    1824, 350–351, 390, 404
    1856, 352
    1860, 352

1876, 162
1888, 346, 404
1890, 346
1896, 352
1900, 391
1912, 353
1932, 5, 358
1936, 276
1946, 414
1948, 277
1952, 325, 400
1960, 4–5, 325–326, 403
1964, 6, 394
1968, 175, 398
1972, 401
1976, 403
1980, 400, 409
1984, 396–397, 409, 414
1988, 401
1992, 408
1994, 414
2000, 277, 404, 405, 406, 407
2004, 401, 405, 411, 414
2006, 129, 414
2008, 4, 129, 277–278, 359, 396–397, 398, 401,
    407, 411
2010, 346, 354, 414
2012, 5–6, 257, 354, 393–394, 396, 397, 399,
    401, *402, 403,* 403–404, 408, 411
    congressional, 413–416, *415*
    contesting, by political parties, 354–355
    critical, 352
    interest groups supporting candidates in, 310–311
    recruiting and nominating candidates for, 354
    selecting presidential electors, 351
Electoral College, 360, 392–393, 404–406
electoral college map, *405*
electors, 405
electronic media, 328, 332–334
electronic voting systems, 372, 373
Eleventh Amendment, *43,* 64
Elizabeth II, Queen of Great Britain, 7
Ellis Island, 58
Ellison, Keith, *120, 121*
El Salvador, *130*
Ely, John Hart, 46
emancipation, 35
Emancipation Proclamation, 111
Emergency Management Committee, 151
Employment Act (1946), 429
Employment Division v. Smith (1990), 80
Engel v. Vitale (1962), 81, 243

enumerated powers, 37, 56, *56*, 57

environmental policy, 422, 425

Environmental Protection Agency (EPA), 207, 209, 219

EOP (Executive Office of the President), 192

Equal Employment Opportunity Commission (EEOC), 118, 162, 209, 219

equality

    African American struggle for, 110–124

    approaches and tactics for achieving, 108–110

    for Asian Americans, 128

    economic, 108

    for gays and lesbians, 131–132

    gender, 124–127, *133*

    for Hispanic Americans, 129–130

    for individuals with disabilities, 131

    for Muslim Americans, 129

    for Native Americans, 127–128

    for older Americans, 130–131

    political, 108

    social, 108

    types of, 108

equality of opportunity, 14

Equal Rights Amendment (ERA), 44–45, 125

equal time rule, 321

establishment clause, 80–83

ethnic diversity, 13

Europe, political parties in, 348

European Community, as a confederation, 54

European Court of Human Rights, 252

Everson v. Board of Education (1947), *77*

exclusionary rule, 91

executive agreements, 190

executive branch, 8, 358. *See also* cabinet; presidency

    bureaucracy of, *205,* 206

    delegation of congressional power to, 161

    Federalist Papers on, 38–39

    in New Jersey plan, 33

    separation of powers and, 36

    in Virginia Plan, 32

Executive Office of the President (EOP), 192, 220

executive orders, 190

executive power, 36

expansionism, 456

ex post facto laws, 90–91

Exxon Mobil, *306*

F

Facebook, 44

FAFSA form, 223

fairness doctrine for broadcast media, 321

family, political socialization and, 273

Farrakhan, Louis, 119

Faubus, Orval, 114

FCC v. Pacifica Foundation (1978), 321

FDIC. *See* Federal Deposit Insurance Corporation (FDIC)

Federal Aviation Administration, *215*

federal budget, 426, 429–431

federal bureaucracy. *See* bureaucracy

Federal Bureau of Investigation (FBI), 93

Federal Communications Commission (FCC), 209, 219, 320–321

federal court system, 234–235. *See also* U.S. Supreme Court

Federal Deposit Insurance Corporation (FDIC), *157,* 179

Federal Educational Amendments (1972), 126

Federal Election Campaign Act (FECA), 299, 412, 413

Federal Election Commission (FEC), 410

Federal Emergency Management Agency (FEMA), 216, 465

Federal Emergency Relief Administration, 440

federal expenditures, *63*

"Federal Farmer" pseudonym, 39

federal government

    on cooperative federalism, 62

    grants-in-aid from, 62

    involvement in state government, 65

    powers of, *56*

    satisfaction with size and power of, *66*

    transferring authority to state government, 64

Federal Highway Administration, *215*

Federal Housing Administration, 309

federal immigration law, 53

Federal Incident Computer Response Center, 216

federalism, 52–69

    advantages of, 67

    common configurations for, *55*

    compared to other systems of government, 54–56

    in the Constitution, 37

    cooperative, 59, 62–64

    defined, 53, 54

    disadvantages of, 67–69

    dual, 61

    government powers in, 56–57

    historical background, 52

    history of American, 58–66

    immigration and, 53

    issues related to, 54

    layer cake, 62

    national supremacy period, 60–61

    "new federalism" (1990-present), 59, 64, 66

    sovereignty and, 54

    state-centered, 60

Federalist Papers, 38–40, 41, 67

Federalists, 37–38
  beliefs, 349
  defined, 37
  election of 1796, 350
  election of 1800, 350
  gerrymandering and, 145
  in history of political parties, 349
  judicial review and, 239
  nominating candidates for presidency, 390
  supported in the North, 350
Federal Management Agency (FEMA), 189
Federal Railroad Administration, *215*
Federal Register, 206
Federal Reserve Act (1913), 161, 436
Federal Reserve Banks, 435–437
Federal Reserve Board, 161
Federal Reserve Board, 435–436
Federal Reserve Chair, 436
Federal Reserve System, 435–436
Federal Trade Commission (FTC), 219
federal workforce
  changes in number of, *221*
  civil service, 221–222
  presidential appointees, 220, 221
  Senior Executive Services (SES), 220
Feingold, Russell, 413
Felt, Mark, 323
FEMA (Federal Emergency Management Agency), 216, 465
Fenno, John, 324
Fenno, Richard F., 164
Ferguson, Niall, 463
Ferraro, Geraldine, 193
Fifteenth Amendment, *11, 43,* 111, 367, 368
Fifth Amendment, 41, *77*
  defendant's rights in, 238
  providing protection against federal government only, 78
  ratification of, *43*
  rights of the criminally accused in, 90, 94–96
filibuster, 140, 141, 158, 249
Fillmore, Millard, *362*
financial crisis 2007-2010, 426, *427,* 436–437
Fiorina, Morris, 162
fireside chats, 179, 180, 193, 325
First Amendment, 41, *77*
  establishment clause, 80–83
  freedom of religion, 78–80
  freedom of the press, 320
  free expression rights, 83–89
  interest groups and, 295
  public opinion and, 267
  ratification of, *43*
First Continental Congress (1774), 27, 142

first ladies, 192–193
fiscal policy, 426–435
  defined, 426
  economic theories guiding, 426
  federal budget-making process, 429–431
  Keynesian, 173
  measures used to assess economic performance, 427–429
  spending policies, 434–435, *435*
  taxation policy, 432–434
flag-burning, 87–88, *88*
flat tax, 433
Florida
  election of 2000 and, 406
  electoral votes in, 405
  primary election in, 391, 396–397
  racial profiling, 124
Forbes health care study, *59*
Ford, Gerald R., *184*
  Congress supporting nomination of, 162
  election of 1976, 400
  losing reelection bid, 175
  pardon of Nixon by, 184
  televised debate with Carter, 326–327, 403
  vetoes issued by, 187, *188*
foreclosed homes, 203
foreign aid, 470
foreign policy, 451
  after September 11th attacks, 462–463
  under Bush, H.W., 181
  Cold War and, 458–459
  Congress and, 466
  constitutional framework for, 454
  Department of State, *214*
  expansionism and manifest destiny, 456–457
  foreign aid and, 470
  under Franklin D. Roosevelt, 179
  internationalism, 457–458
  isolationism, 455–456
  under Johnson, 181
  in the Middle East, 460, 462
  Monroe Doctrine, 456
  new world order and, 459–460
  preemption doctrine and, 469
  president's power and, 454, 463–464
  president's role in, 182–183
  presidents' successes with, *185–186*
  public opinion and, 467–468
  under Reagan, 181
  roots of, 454–460, 462–463
  Russian Federation and, 469–470
  structure of, 463–468

under Theodore Roosevelt, 178–179
under Truman, 181
twenty-first century dilemmas, 468–471
United Nations (UN) and, 470–471
Fortas, Abe, *248*
Fort McClellan, 117
Founding Fathers
on Congress, 142
on elections, 390
on electoral college, 406
on executive power, 183
on inevitable conflict, 9
on political parties, 348–349
on presidential reprieves and pardons, 184
rating most important, 28
on Senate, 145–146
on term limit of presidents, 175–176
401(k) plans, 443
Fourteenth Amendment, 77, 111, 367
affirmative action and, 121
Bill of Rights incorporated by, 76–77
gender discrimination and, 126
ratification of, *43*
Fourth Amendment, 41, *77*
ratification of, *43*
rights of the criminally accused in, 90, 91–92, 93, 94
students rights in schoolhouse, 100
Fox News, 335
Fox News/Opinion Dynamics poll, 268
France
American isolationism and, 455
death penalty abolished in, *98*
in French and Indian War, 26
legislatures in, 143
system of justice in, 236
unitary system of government and, 54
value of individualism in, *14*
franchise, 367. *See also* suffrage
franking privilege, 416
Franklin, Benjamin, *10*
on the Constitution, *10*
at Constitutional Convention, 32
Declaration of Independence and, 29
lobbying by, 309
political party identification, 349
Free Application for Student Aid (FAFSA) form, 223
Freedman's Bureau, 440
freedom of expression, 83–89
freedom of religion, 78–80
freedom of the press, 85–86, 320, 334
Freedom Rides, 116

free exercise clause, 78
free expression rights, 83–89
"free marketplace of ideas," 320
free riders, 304
Free Soil Party, 352
Fremont, John, 352
French and Indian War (1754-1763), 26
French Revolution, 74
Friedman, Thomas, 322
friends, political socialization and, 271-272
Frontiero v. Richardson (1973), 125
Frontline, 336
frontloading, 396
full faith and credit clause, 57, *57,* 59

G

G-7 nations, *437*
Gallup, George, 276
Gallup Poll, 268
accuracy of, *279*
on gay marriage, 107
history of, 276, 278
partisan differences on what is "morally acceptable," 356, *357*
on state demographics of party identification, *358*
wording of poll and, 282
Gandhi, Mohandas, 110, *115,* 116
Garner, John Nance, 191
Garrison, William Lloyd, 110
gays and lesbians, civil rights for, 131–132
Gazette of the United States (Fenno), 324
gender, voter turnout and, 371, *371*
gender equality, 124–127
General Accounting Office (GAO), *165,* 431
General Assembly (UN), 470, *472*
general election campaign, 393, 399–401, 403–406
General Electric (GE), *306,* 335, *335*
General Motors (GM), 303, *306,* 307, 335–336
Gentleman's Agreement (1907), 128
George II, King of England, 12
Georgia (country), 469
Geragos, Mark, 238
Germany
as a federal system, 55
immigrants from, *130*
legislatures in, 143
value of individualism in, *14*
Gerry, Elbridge, 28, 145
gerrymandering, 145
Gibbons v. Ogden **(1824),** 60
Gideon v. Wainwright (1963), 65, *77,* 96
Gingrich, Callista, *395*

Gingrich, Newt, *296, 395*
   budget bill (1995) and, 430
   "Contract with America," 66
   election of 2012, 397
   primary election of 2012, 6
Ginsburg, Douglas H., *248*
Ginsburg, Ruth Bader, 125, *246,* 247, *311*
Gitlow v. New York (1925), *77*
"glass ceiling," 126
Goesaert v. Cleary (1948), 125
Golden Fleece Awards, *208*
Goldman Sachs, *310*
Goldwater, Barry, 6, 394
Gonzales, Alberto, 216
Gonzales v. Carhart (2007), 99
Goode, Virgil, *121*
good faith exception, 91
Google, 333
Gorbachev, Mikhail, *458,* 459
Gore, Al, 191, *277,* 405
government. *See also* American government
   colonial, 26
   concurrent powers in, 56
   defined, 7
   forms and functions of, 7–8
   regulation of the media, 320–321
   reserved powers in, 56
   unitary system of, 54
Government Accountability Office (GAO), 154, 207
government corporations, *205,* 219–220
government interest groups, 308
Government Performance and Results Act (1997), 211
Government Printing Office, 154
government shutdowns, 15, 18, 66
GPS tracking devices, *93*
Gramm-Rudman-Hollings Act (1985), 431
grand jury, 94, 237
Grant, Ulysses S., 177, *377*
grants-in-aid, 62
Grassley, Charles, 257
grassroots lobbying, 310
Gratz v. Bollinger (2003), 122
Great Britain
   colonial response to policies of, 27, 29
   in French and Indian War, 26
   parliamentary system in, 143
   regulation of colonies, 26–27, 29
   unitary system of government and, 54
   value of individualism in, *14*
Great Compromise, 33, *33*
"Great Compromise," 143
Great Depression, 24, 440

Great Recession of 2007-2010, 4, 15, 18, 173, 203, 426, *427,* 436–437
Great Society, 181, 187, 210
   interest groups and, 298
   mandatory spending and, 434
   welfare state and, 440
Green Party, 361, *362, 363*
Greenspan, Alan, 436, *436*
Gregoire, Christine, *107*
Grenada, 188
gridlock, legislative, 151
Griswold v. Connecticut (1965), 97
gross domestic product (GDP), *15,* 427
Ground Transportation Committee, 151
Ground Zero, 129, 189, 195
Grutter v. Bollinger (2003), 122
Guantanamo Bay, Cuba, 75
Guatemala, immigrants from, *130*
Guiana, 456
Gulf War conflicts, 188
gun control, Supreme Court on, 64
Gun-Free School Zones Act (1990), 439
gun ownership, 89–90
Guyana, 456

H

Haiti, 188
Haiti, immigrants from, *130*
Hall, John, 240
Halliburton, 211
Hamilton, Alexander, *349*
   on a bill of rights, 41
   at Constitutional Convention, 32
   Federalist Papers written by, 38, 39
   freedom of the press and, 320
   on the judiciary, 241
   National Bank and, 60
   on presidents serving for life, 175
   on public opinion, 271
   rating importance of, 28
   in Washington's cabinet, 217
   Washington siding with, 176
handgun possession, 89–90
Hannity, Sean, *323*
Hannity's America, 323
Hard Ball with Chris Matthews, 323
Harding, Warren G., 174, *377*
hard money, 412
Harrisburg Pennsylvanian, 274
Harrison, Benjamin, 175, 346, *377,* 404
Harrison, William Henry, 174, 175, *176*
Hatch Act of 1939, 222

hate speech, 88
Hatfield, Mark, 394
Hawaii, 456
hawks, 464–465
Hayes, Rutherford B., 162, *377*
Haynsworth, Clement, *248*
Haysbert, Dennis, *380*
Hazardous Materials Committee, 151
Head Start preschool education, 441
health care, 444
Health Care and Education Reconciliation Act
    (2010), 444
health care reform
    media and, 319
    Obama's agenda, 423
    Supreme Court ruling on, 249
    variations in state-level approaches to health
        care and, *59*
Health Care Reform Law (2010), 328
health maintenance organizations (HMOs), 444
HealthSouth, 309
Heinz, John, 296
Henry, Patrick, *27, 76*
Higher Education Act, Title IX Amendment, *133*
Hill, Anita, 162
Hispanic Americans
    civil rights for, 129–130
    first in cabinet, 216
Hitler, Adolf, 13
Hobbes, Thomas, 7, 11–12
Holder, Eric, 216
Holmes, Oliver Wendell, 83, 84, 131, *251,* 251–252,
    254, 320
Home Style: House Members in Their Districts
    (Fenno), 164
Honduras, immigrants from, *130*
Hong Kong, immigrants from, *130*
Hoover, Herbert
    as commerce secretary before president, 174
    election of 1928, 353
    popular vote in 1928, *377*
    presidency of, 179
    radio addresses for 1932 campaign, 5
    vetoes issued by, *188*
Hot Aire blog, *322*
House Appropriations Committee, 207, 430
House Armed Services Committee, 207
House of Representatives. *See also* Congress
    African Americans serving in, 119
    Appropriations Committee of, 429–430
    Armed Serviced Committee, 207
    committees in, *152*
    first female to serve in, *120*

founding fathers on, 144
    impeachment process, 163
House of Representatives. (*continued*)
    Judiciary Committee, 157
    leadership in, 147–148, 358
    member requirements, 145
    members becoming president, 174
    number of representatives per state, 144–145
    party-line voting in, 365
    as the "people's house," 144–145
    Rules Committee, 147–148, 158
    Speaker of the House, 147–148
    tax and revenue bills originating in, 156
    term of member, 144
    top 10 largest partisan gains in, *149*
    Transportation and Infrastructure Committee, 151
    Ways and Means Committee, 151
House Rules Committee, 147–148
House Science and Technology Committee, 207
House-Senate Intelligence Committee, 466
Housing and Urban Development (HUD), *157*
Houston, Charles, 113
Houston, Whitney, 338
Hoyt v. Florida (1961), 125
HUD (Department of Housing and Urban Development), *215*
Huffington, Arianna, *322*
Huffington Post, *322*
Humphrey, Hubert, 398
Huntington, Samuel, 268
Hurricane Katrina, 195
Hussein, Saddam, 7, 217, 460, 462, 469
hypercentralism, 54

I

Iceland, *98*
Idaho, 357
"I Have a Dream" speech (King), 118
illegal drug use, 80
immigrants/immigration
    countries sending most, to U.S., *130*
    from East Asia, 128
    equality of opportunity for, 14
    federalism and, 53
    restrictive, 13, *13*
impeachment, 161, 163, 175
income. *See* wages
income tax rates, *437*
incorporation, 77
incorporation, 77–78
incumbent race, 399–400
independent agencies, 218
independent campaign expenditures, 413

Independent Party, *362*

India, immigrants from, *130*

Indian Gaming Regulatory Act (1988), 292

indictment, 237

indirect democracy, 10

individualism, 13–14, *14,* 269

individualistic political subculture, *13*

individual retirement accounts (IRAs), 443

individuals with disabilities, civil rights for, 131

Industrial Party, 360

inflation, 426

inquisitorial system of justice, 236

in re Oliver (1948), *77*

in-state tuition, *68*

intensity of public opinion, 284

intercept polls, 280

interest groups

    biggest contributors to political campaigns, *310*

    defined, 294

    de Tocqueville on, 295

    economic, 303–306

    factors impacting influence of, 301

    free rider problem, 304

    government, 308

    growth of, 298–299

    iron triangles and, 299–300

    issue and ideological, 307

    labor-business tensions and, 298

    litigation by, 311

    lobbying by, 308–310

    membership in, 300–301

    noneconomic, 306–308

    passage of a bill and, 159

    PIRG and, 312

    pluralism and, 295

    political parties *vs.,* 296–297

    pros and cons of, 295–296

    public, 307

    scandalous activities of lobbyists, 292, 293

    senior citizen, 294–295

    social movements and, 297–298

    spending the most on lobbying, *306*

    supporting for candidates and parties in elections, 310–311

    top 10 most influential, 302

intergovernmental lobbies, 308

intermediate scrutiny, 126

International Brotherhood of Electrical Workers, *310*

International Court of Justice (UN), 470

internationalism, 457–458

international organizations, 464

Internet. *See also* blogs

    digital divide and, 334

    impact on American politics, 4

    news coverage from, 333–334

    obscenity/pornography and, 87

    regulating, 88–89

    as source of news, 331

Internet voting, 373

internships, in Congress, *165*

Interstate Commerce Commission (ICC), 218

Intolerable Acts (1774), 27

Investigations Committee, 151

invisible primary, 393–394

Iowa caucus, 395, 396, 397

Iran-Contra scandal, 184, 464

Iraq

    authoritarian government in, 7

    war-making powers to invade, 188

Iraq war

    active military force for, *473*

    American foreign policy and, 460, 462–463, 464–465

    Bush and, 182

    Bush-Cheney relationship and, 191

    cabinet conflicts over, 217

    Congress and, 466

    news coverage of, 332–333

    preemption doctrine and, 469

    Russia and, 470

IRAs (individual retirement accounts), 443

Iredell, James, 240

iron triangles, 299–300

isolationism, 455–456

Israel, 143, 360, 466

issue and ideological groups, 307

issue networks, 300

issue voting, 408

Italy

    death penalty abolished in, *98*

    legislatures in, 143

J

Jackson, Andrew

    campaign use of penny press, 5

    Democratic Party formed by, 351

    election of 1824, 350, 390

    election of 1832, 351

    election poster for (1828), *350*

    federal workforce under, 221–222

    on National Bank, 60

    national party organizations and, 362

    popular vote in 1828, *377*

    portrait, *177*

    presidency of, 177

on public opinion, 266
Tariff of 1828 and, 60–61
Worcester v. Georgia and, 243
Jackson, Jesse, 124, *369*
Jackson, Michael, 238, 338
Jamaica, immigrants from, *130*
Jamieson, Kathleen Hall, 195
Japan
  economy, 17
  Gentleman's Agreement, 128
  legislatures in, 143
  Pearl Harbor, 179
Japanese internment camps, 12, 128
Jay, John, 162
Jefferson, Thomas, *349*
  on a bill of rights, 41, 76
  Constitutional Convention, 32
  Declaration of Independence and, 29
  Democratic-Republican Party and, 349
  election of 1796, 350
  election of 1800, 6, 350
  George Washington and, 176
Jefferson, Thomas (*continued*)
  on individualism, 269
  on limited government, 12
  National Bank and, 60
  on natural rights, 9
  presidency of, 176
  selected as president by Congress, 162
  strict construction and, 45
  in Washington's cabinet, 217
Jehovah's Witnesses, 78
Jewell, Richard, 85–86
Jezebel, *322*
Jim Crow laws, 112–113
Johnson, Andrew, 163, 174, 175
Johnson, Lyndon B. *See also* Great Society
  becoming president after Kennedy's assassination, 175
  choosing not to run for reelection, 175
  civil rights legislation, 118, 318
  "Daisy Girl" commercial and, 5
  election of 1964, 6, 7, 394
  New Deal coalition and, 353–354
  popular vote in 1964 election, *377*
  presidency of, 181
  press conferences, 327
  religion of, 174
  Supreme Court nomination by, 230, 247
  Vietnam and, 181, 193, 467
Johnson, Thomas, 240
Joint Chiefs of Staff (JCS), 464
joint committees, 153

Jordan, Barbara, 111
Journal of Blacks in Higher Education, 123
judges. *See also* Supreme Court justices
  confirmation of, 247–249
  electing and appointing, 244–249
  electing *vs.* appointing, 255–256
  nomination of, 244–247
  selection of federal, 244
judicial activism, judicial restraint *vs.,* 255
judicial branch, 8. *See also* legal system; U.S. Supreme
  Court
  bureaucracy of, *205*
judicial power, 36, 255–258
judicial restraint, judicial activism *vs.,* 255
judicial review, 238–239, 241
Judiciary Act (1789), 239
Justice Department, 183, 244, 245

K

Kagan, Elena, *245, 246,* 247
Kansas-Nebraska Act (1854), 140
Kashlari, Neel, *157*
Katz, Charles, 93
Katz test, 91
Katz v. United States (1967), 93
Kemp, Jack, 400
Kennedy, Anthony, 64, *246,* 252, 254
Kennedy, Edward M., *442*
Kennedy, John F., *195, 369*
  Birmingham riots, 117
  campaign use of social media, 4–5
  as a Catholic, *369*
  Cuban Missile Crisis and, 458
  debate with Nixon (1960), 403
  foreign policy success of, *185*
  media and, 195
  moving from Senate to president, 174
  New Deal coalition and, 353–354
  presidency of, 181
  press conferences, 327
  religion of, 174
  televised debate with Nixon, 325–326
  vetoes issued by, *188*
Kennedy, Joseph P., 202, *202*
Kernell, Samuel, 193, 272
Kerry, John, 400, 403, 405
Kevorkian, Jack, 99
Key, V.O., Jr., 267–268, 272, 352
Keynes, John Maynard, 173, 426
Keynesian economic theory, 426
Khomeini, Ayatollah, 460, 462
Kim Jong II, 7

King, Martin Luther Jr., 110, *115*
  assassination of, 119
  Birmingham demonstrations, 117
  Gandhi and, *115*
  "I have a Dream" speech, 118
  March on Washington, 118
  nonviolent protest, 115–116
King, Rodney, 94
King, Rufus, 28
King Leopold's Soliloquy (Twain), 329
Kirk, Ron, 216
Klopfer v. North Carolina (1967), *77*
Know-Nothing Party, 352, *362*
Korea, immigrants from, *130*
Korean War, 184, 188
Krauthammer, Charles, 322
Ku Klux Klan, 111, 117
Kuwait, 460

L

Laborers Union, *310*
labor unions, interest groups of, 304–305
Lady Chatterley's Lover (film), *86*
laissez-faire economics, 426
"land-lease" policy, 179
Landon, Alfred, 276
L.A. Now blog, *322*
"large states plan" (Virginia Plan), 32–33
Lasswell, Harold, 8
law
  administrative, 207
  antitrust, 183
  how a bill becomes a, *156,* 156–160
  Jim Crow laws, 112–113
  types of, 232–233
Lawrence v. Texas (2003), 99, 132, 252, 254
law school, *256*
layer-cake federalism, 62
Lazarus, Emma, 13
League of Nations, 179, 457
League of Women Voters, 307, 377
Lee, Richard Henry, 29
Lee v. Weisman (1992), 83
Legal Aid, 441
legal protests, 378
legal system
  adversarial system, 236–238
  categories of law, 232–233
  criminal trials, 237–238
  development of federal, 234–235
  electing and appointing judges, 244–249
  elements of civil litigation, 236–237

inquisitorial system, 236
  limitations on courts, 241–243
  state, 233
  structure of U.S., 233–235
legislation, bureaucratic, 206–207
legislative branch, 8, *205. See also* Congress; House of
  Representatives; Senate
legislative power, 36
legislative role of president, 186–187
legitimacy, 8–9, 10
Lemke, William, 276
Lemon test, 82
Lemon v. Kurtzman (1971), 82
Leno, Jay, *336*
Lesbian and Gay Rights Rally (1993), *112*
Lett-Smitton, Barbara, 405
lever voting machine, 372, *372*
Lewinsky, Monica, 328
libel, 85–86
liberal ideology, 270
liberals, blogs of, 268
The Liberator, 110
Libertarian Party, *363*
liberty, American political culture and, 12
Library of Congress, 154, *165*
Lieberman, Joe, 405
Light, Paul, 187
Limbaugh, Rush, 320, 323
limited government, 12
Lincoln, Abraham
  delivering Gettysburg Address, *178*
  election of 1860, 352
  Emancipation Proclamation, 111
  popular vote in 1860, *377*
  presidency of, 177
  suffrage and, 367
Lippman, Walter, 271
literacy test, 111, 118, 368
Literary Digest, 276, 281
litigation, 109–110
  defined, 236
  elements of civil, 236–237
  by interest groups, 311
Little Rock, Arkansas, 114
Little Rock's Central High School, 114, *114*
Livingston, Robert, 29
lobbying
  defined, 308
  grassroots, 310
  high-powered lobbyists in American history, 309
  interest groups achieving goals through, 308, 310
  interest groups spending the most on, *306*

introduction of a bill and, 157
   passage of a bill and, 159
local party organizations, 363–364
Lochner v. New York (1905), 40
Locke, John, 29, 41, 267
   American political culture and, 11–12
   on executive power, 183
   on natural rights, 9, 29
Lockheed Martin, *306*
Lodge, Henry Cabot Jr., 394
Log Cabin Republicans, 132
log-in polls, 280
logrolling, 159
Long, Huey, 325
loose construction, 45–47
Lumumba, Patrice, *461*
Luxembourg, death penalty abolished in, *98*

M

MacArthur, Douglas, 184
Madison, James
   on a bill of rights, 41
   Democratic-Republicans and, 349
   on division of powers, 67
   on federalism, 55
   Federalist Papers, 38
   on the Great Compromise, 35
   on House of Representatives, 144
   on individual rights, 76
   on interest groups, 294, 295, 298
   judicial review and, 239
   National Bank and, 60
   on political parties, 348
   portrait, *38*
   presidency of, 176
   on public opinion, 267, 271
   rating importance of, 28
   related to Zachary Taylor, 175
   strict construction and, 45
magazines, 330
Maine
   caucus, 395
   voter registration in, 370
majoritarianism, 295, 365–366
majority caucus, 147, 149, 153
majority leader, 148, 358
majority opinion, 251
majority rule, 12
Makin, Michelle, 268
Malcolm X, 118–119
Malloy v. Hogan (1964), *77*
Maltese, John, 248

mandatory spending, 433
manifest destiny, 456
Mann, Thomas, 144
Mapp v. Ohio (1961), *77*, 91
marble-cake federalism, 62
Marbury, William, 239
Marbury v. Madison (1803), 47, 234, 239
March for Women's Lives (2004), *112*
March on Washington (1963), *112,* 118
March on Washington II (1983), *112*
marginal seats, 415
Marshall, John, 234, 239, 241, 243
   on interpretation of the Constitution, 45
   national supremacy doctrine of federalism, 60
Marshall, Thurgood, 113, 230, *230,* 247
Marshall Plan, 458
Martin, Trayvon, 124, *124*
***Martin v. Hunter's Lessee* (1819),** 57, 241
Mary Baldwin College, 126
Maryland, 107
Mason, George, 28, 76
Massachusetts
   health care reform in, *442–443*
   same-sex marriage in, 107
   state expenditures, *63*
   voter registration in, 370
Masters Golf Tournament (2003), 110
material benefits (of group membership), 300
McCain, Cindy, 398
McCain, John, 398, 411, 413
McCarthy, Eugene, 398
McCarthy, Joseph, 321
McConnell, Michael, 107, *150*
McConnell v. F.E.C. (2003), 413
McCorvey, Norma, 98
McCotter, Thaddeus, *393*
***McCulloch v. Maryland* (1819),** 45, 47, 60, 241
McCullough, David, 29
McDonald v. Chicago (2010), 65, *77*
McGovern, George, 398, 401
McGraw, Muffet, *133*
McKinley, William, 177, 178
McLaurin v. Okla. State Regents (1950), *113*
McNamara, Robert, 464
McSweeney, Miles B., 240
mechanical lever ballots, 372, *372*
media
   Americans' primary news sources, *331*
   in courtrooms, 257
   criticism of news, 337–339
   effects of, 336–337
   electronic, 328, 331–334

ia (*continued*)

facilitating public debate, 322–323

facts about American, 320

freedom of the press and, 85–86, 320

functions in American politics, 321–324

generational divide in use of digital, *332*

government regulation of, 320–321

government watchdog role of, 323–324

historical development of, 324–328

Obama's use of, 319

objectivity in, 321–322

ownership of, 334–336, 337–338

political satire, 329–330

political socialization and, 275

president and, 195–196

print, 328, 330–331

protests covered by, 379

public broadcasting, 335–336

public opinion expressed through, 267–268

sensationalism in, 338

today's mass, 328, 330–336

Mediaite blog, *322*

Medicaid, 181, 441

Medicare, 181, 441

Medvedev, Dmitri, 469–470

Meet the Press, 323

"melting pot" concept, 13

merit system, 222

Merit Systems Protection Board (MSPB), 222

Mexico

immigrants from, 129, *130*

legislatures in, 143

NAFTA and, 186

Woodrow Wilson and, 183

Meyer, Philip, 321

Michigan, 396–397

Microsoft Corporation, 183

Middle East, 460, 462

midterm congressional elections, 413–416, *415*

Miers, Harriet, 184, 246, *248*

military

homosexuality in, 132

presidents having served in the, 174

president's leadership role in, 188

military draft, *473*

military-industrial complex, 467

Miller v. California (1973), 87

Million Man March (1995), *112,* 119

Mills, C. Wright, 296

minimal effects theory, 336

Mink, Patsy, *133*

Minnesota, voter registration in, 370

minority caucus, 147, 148, 149

minority leader, 148

minority rights, 12

minor parties, 348, 360, 361–362, *362, 363*

Miranda, Ernesto, 94–95

Miranda v. Arizona (1966), 252

Miranda warnings, 94–95, 94–96

Missouri ex. rel. Gaines v. Canada (1938), *113*

Missouri Plan, 244

Mitchell, George, 194

monarchy, 7

Mondale, Walter, 191, 403, 414, 433

monetary policy, 435–437

Monroe, James, 176–177, 456

Monroe Doctrine, 177, 178, 456

Montesquieu, Baron de, 183

Montgomery, Brian, *157*

Moore, Roy, 243

moralistic political subculture, *13*

Mormons, 78, 79–80

Morning Edition (radio news show), 336

Morris, Gouverneur, 28

MOSAIC, 333

Motor Voter law, 370

MTV "Rock the Vote" campaign, 377–378

muckrakers, 323

Mujahidin, the, 466

Muller v. Oregon (1908), 124

multiparty system, 359–360

municipal government, 9

Murrow, Edward R., 325

Murtha, John, 466

Muslim Americans

civil rights for, 129

in Congress, *121*

racial profiling and, 124

Myers v. United States (1926), 184

N

NAACP, 109–110, 113

Nader, Ralph, 297, 307, 361, *362, 363*

NAFTA (North American Free Trade Agreement), 186, 459

Napoleon Bonaparte, 74

Napolitano, Janet, 216

NASA (National Aeronautics and Space Administration), 207, *218*

The Nation, 323

National Advancement for the Association of Colored People (NAACP), 230

National Aeronautics and Space Administration (NASA), 207, *218*

National Association for the Advancement of Colored People (NAACP), 109–110, 113

National Association of Manufacturers (NAM), 298

National Association of Real Estate Investment Trusts, 309

National Association of Realtors (NAR), 306, *306, 310*

National Bank, 60

National Bank of the United States, 60

National Collegiate Athletic Association (NCAA), *133*

national committee, 362–363

national committee chair, 363

National Community and Service Trust Act (1993), *445*

national conventions, 392

national debt, 428, *432*

National Domestic Preparedness Office, 216

National Education Association (NEA), 302, 305, *310*

National Federation of Independent Businesses (NFIB), 302

national forest preserves, 422

National Gazette, 324

National Highway Traffic Safety Administration, *215*

National Incident Protection Center, 216

National Industrial Recovery Act (NIRA), 24

National Intelligencer, 324

National Journal, 141

National Minimum Drinking Age Amendment (1984), 63–64

National Organization for Women (NOW), 125, 307

National Organization for Women March for Women's Lives (1992), *112*

national party conventions, 351

national party organization, 362

National Performance Review, 191

National Public Radio (NPR), 335–336

National Republicans, 351

National Restaurant Association, 302

The National Review, 323

National Rifle Association (NRA), 89, 297, 302

National Right to Life Committee (NRLC), 301, 302, 307

National Security Act (1947), 465

National Security Council (NSC), 192, 464

national service, *445*

national supremacy doctrine, 60, 62

national supremacy period (1819-1837), 59, 60–61

National Unity Party, *362*

National Voter Registration Act (1993), 370

National Women's Party, 125

Nation of Islam, 119

Native Americans
  Abramoff scandal and, 293
  civil rights for, 127–128
  as concern of Constitutional Convention delegates, 32
  peyote use by, 80
  voting rights, 366, 368

NATO (North Atlantic Treaty Organization), 458

natural law, 9, 12

Natural Law Party, *363*

natural rights, 9, 29

Nature Conservancy, 307

NBC, 334–335

NBC/*Wall Street Journal* poll, 268

Near v. Minnesota (1931), *77*

necessary and proper clause, 57

Nelson, Ben, 16

neo-Nazis, 88

Netanyahu, Benjamin, *348*

net exports, 428–429

Netherlands, *98*

Neustadt, Richard, 190

Nevada, 395

New Deal, 179
  borrowing from state experiences and, 67
  cooperative federalism and, 62
  dual federalism and, 61
  federal bureaucracy and, 209–210
  Great Society and, 181
  interest groups and, 298
  mandatory spending and, 434
  public support and, 193
  as unconstitutional, 241
  welfare state and, 440–441

New Deal coalition, 353–354

New England Woman Suffrage Association, 106

"new federalism" (1990-present), 59, 64, 66

New Hampshire primary, 396, 397

New Hampshire primary poll, *277–278*

New Jersey, anti-profiling law in, 124

New Jersey Plan, 33, *33*

New Jersey v. TLO (1985), 100

new media, 332–334

News Corporation, 335, *335*

News Hour with Jim Lehrer, 336

newspapers, 328
  campaign use of, 5
  decline in use, 331
  historical development of, 324–325
  wire services, 331

Newsweek, 330

new world order, 459–460

New York (state), 396

New York Herald, 276

New York Times v. Sullivan (1964), 85, 252

New York Weekly Journal, 320

NFIB v. Sebelius (2012), 255

Nineteenth Amendment, *11, 43,* 106, 125, 368

Ninth Amendment, 76
    privacy rights and, 97
    ratification of, *43*

Nixon, Richard M., *184*
    debate with Kennedy (1960), 403
    election of 1960, 5
    executive order by, 190
    popular vote in 1968, *377*
    popular vote in 1972, *377*
    presidency of, 181
    public opinion and, 193–194
    resignation of, 175
    "set speeches" by, 193
    Supreme Court nomination by, 248
    televised debate with Kennedy, 325–326
    vetoes issued by, 187, *188*
    as vice-president, 191
    Watergate and, 181, 193–194, 242, 243

Nixon v. United States (2003), 242

No Apology: The Case for American Greatness
    (Romney), 400

No Child Left Behind legislation, *65*

nominating conventions, 398–399

nomination campaign, 392, 395–399

nomination process, 244–247

nominations, confirmation of, 162–163, 184

noneconomic interest groups, 306–308

normal vote, 356–357

North American Free Trade Agreement (NAFTA),
    186, 459

North Atlantic Treaty Organization (NATO), 458

North Dakota, 370

North Korea, 7

Northrop Grumman, *306*

Northwest Airlines, 309

Norway, death penalty abolished in, *98*

"no taxation without representation," 26

NPR (National Public Radio), 335–336

"nuclear club," *471*

Nuclear Non-Proliferation Treaty (NPT), *471*

nullification crisis, 60–61

Nye, Joseph, 463

O

Obama, Barack, *132, 245, 336, 366, 399*
    Afghanistan and, 188, 467, 468
    on Arizona immigration law, 53
    Bin Laden and, *185*
    books written by, *400*
    breaking down racial barriers, *369*
    budget cuts and, 430–431
    cabinet of, *213,* 216
    campaign funding and, 411–412, *412*
    campaign use of Facebook, 4
    crisis manager role of, 189
    Defense of Marriage Act (DOMA) and, 107
    economic recession and, 173
    election of 2008, *355,* 398
    election of 2012, 5–6, *366,* 394, 400
    executive order by, 190
    federal bureaucracy and, 212
    as first African American president, 119
    health care reform by,, 423
    Keynesian economic theory used by, 426
    killing of bin Laden and, *461*
    media and, 195, 319
    Middle East foreign policy, 463
    moving from Senate to president, 174
    New Hampshire Democratic primary election
        and, *277–278*
    nomination for secretary of health and human
        services, 184
    opposition to health care reform of, 141
    overcoming racial barriers, *380*
    post-9/11 antiterrorism policies, 75
    presidency of, 182
    press conferences of, 328
    public opinion and, 193
    signing health care reform bill, *161*
    signing statements used by, 187
    social media used by, 197
    Supreme Court nomination by, 231, 247
    Supreme Court ruling on health care law, 241, 257
    taking oath of office, *117*
    tax policy, 434
    Tea Party and, 347
    universal health care and, 25
    U.S.-Russian relations and, 469–470
    vetoes issued by, 187, *188*
    on war on terror policies, *100*

Obama, Michelle, *192,* 193, 399

Obama's Wars (Woodward), 217

objective coverage, by the media, 321–322

objectivity, 321

obscenity, 86–87

Occupational Safety and Health Administration (OSHA),
    207, 213, 308

Occupy Wall Street movement, *286,* 378, *379*

O'Connor, Sandra Day, 247

Office of Congressional Relations (OCR), 194

Office of Economic Opportunity, 190

Office of Labor-Management Standards, 213
Office of Management and Budget (OMB), 154, 192, 429, 430
Office of Personnel Management (OPM), 222
Office of the U.S. Trade Representatives, 192
Ohio State University, *416*
old age pensions, *442*
older Americans, civil rights for, 130–131
oligarchy, 7
Olson, Mancur, 303
"one person, one vote" principle, 145
open election, 400
open market operations, 435
open primary, 395
open rule, 158
open shop, 305
Operation Restore Hope, 468
optical scan ballots/cards, 372, *372,* 373
O'Reilly, Bill, 329, *333*
Organization for Economic Cooperation and Development (OECD), *437*
originalism, 252
original jurisdiction, 243
Oslo accords, 460
outlays, 433
overriding (a veto), 160
oversight, congressional, 161–162
Oversight Committee, 151

P

pacifism, 456
Packer, Herbert, 438
Packwood, Robert, 309
Page, Benjamin, 272
Paine, Thomas, 29
Palestine Liberation Organization (PLO), 183
Palin, Sarah, 129, 193, 394, 398
Panama, 188
Panama Canal Treaty, 186
paper ballots, 371–372, *372*
pardon, 184
Paris Peace Conference, 179
Parker, John J., *248*
Parker v. Gladden (1966), *77*
Parks, Rosa, 115
Parliament, British, 143
parochial schools, 82
Partial Abortion Act (2003), 99
partisan newspapers, 324
partisan press era, 324
partisanship

in congressional committees, 153
political orientation and, 269–270
Senate leadership, 149
trends in, *269*
party identification, 407–408
party identification, 356, 357, *358, 407-408.*
party platform, 351
Patient Protection and Affordable Care Act of 2010 (PPACA), 241, 243, 444
Patrick, Deval, 119
patronage, 222
Paul, Rand, *155,* 347
Paul, Ron, 6, *393,* 393–394, *397*
Pawlenty, Tim, 394
PBS (Public Broadcasting Service), 335–336
Peace Corps, *445*
Pearl Harbor, 179
peer groups, political socialization and, 273–274
Pelosi, Nancy, 125
Pendleton Civil Service Reform Act (1883), 222
penny press, 5, 324
pension plans, *442,* 443
"People's Party," 346
Perot, Ross, 361, *362, 363,* 403, 410, 466
Perry, Rick, 6, 393–394
Persian Gulf War (1991), 460, 468, 469
Personal Responsibility and Work Opportunity Reconciliation Act (1996), 66, 441
persuasion campaigns, 311
Peru, immigrants from, *130*
peyote use, 80
Pharmaceutical Research and Manufacturers of America, *306*
Philippine-American Wars, 456
Philippine Islands, 456
Philippines, immigrants from, *130*
physician-assisted suicide, 99
Pierce, Franklin, 177
Pinckney, Charles, 350, 392
Pipeline Transportation Committee, 151
plaintiff, 236
Planned Parenthood v. Casey (1992), 99, 254
Plan of Attack (Woodward), 330–331
plea bargain, 237–238
Plessy, Homer, 112–113
Plessy v. Ferguson (1896), 113
PLO (Palestine Liberation Organization), 183
pluralism, 295
pocket veto, 160, 187
Pointer v. Texas (1965), *77*
Poland, *130,* 458
police searches, 91
policy implementation, 206

political action committees (PACs)
    campaign contributions from, 410, 413
    contributions from, 16–17
    defined, 299
    growth of, *411*
    supporting Gingrich in 2012 primaries, 6
political blogs, 322, 339
political culture
    of America, 10–14
    defined, 10, 11
political equality, 108
political ideology, 270
political orientations, 269–270
political participation, *367,* 378–379, *416. See also* voting
political parties, 345. *See also* individual party names
    candidates recruited and nominated by, 355, 390
    contesting elections, 354–355
    defined, 348
    development of, 348–354
    first in America, 349–351
    framework for voters provided by, 355–357
    functions of, 354–359
    future of, 364–365
    interest groups *vs.,* 296–297
    leadership in Congress and, 147
    modern party system, 352–354
    organizations, 362–364
    passage of a bill and, 159
    policy paralysis caused by partisan gridlock between, 16, 18
    providing organization for operations of government, 358–359
    third/minor, 360, 361–362, *362, 363*
    in two-party system, 359–360
political partisanship. *See* partisanship
political preferences, 270, *271*
political satire, 329–330
political socialization, 272–275
political talk radio shows, 325
politics, 8
Polk, James K., 177
polls. *See* public opinion polls
poll taxes, 111, 118, 368
polygamy laws, 79
popular sovereignty, 10, 12
popular vote, 406, *406*
Populist Party, 346, *362*
pork-barrel legislation, 166
pork-barrel spending, *208*
pornography, 86, 87
Portugal, *98*

positive rights, 76
Powell, Adam Clayton Jr., *120–121*
Powell, Colin, 216, 217, 460, 464, 465
Powell, Lewis, 253, *253,* 253–254
Powell Doctrine, 464
Powell v. Alabama (1932), *77*
Powell v. McCormack (1969), *120–121*
power, 8
The Power Elite (Mills), 296
Powerline (blog), 268
power of appointment, 184
power of incumbency, 414–415
Pratt & Whitney, 300, 308
prayer
    at graduation ceremonies and football games, 82–83
    school, 81–82
preemption, 57
preemption doctrine, 469
A Preface to Democratic Theory (Dahl), 295
"preferred freedoms" doctrine, 84–85
prenomination campaign, 393–394
presidency. *See also* presidents
    attack of imperial (1945-1980), 180–181
    birth of modern, 178–179
    cabinet, 191–192
    decline in candidates for, 16, 18
    in era of divisiveness (1981-2012), 181–182
    evolution of American, 175–182
    executive office and staff, 192
    express powers and responsibilities in, 182–188
    Federal Reserve Chair and, 436
    first lady and, 192–193
    foreign policy powers, 454, 463–464
    passage of a bill and, 159, 160
    power of, Constitution and, 47
    separation of power and, 36
    in Wilderness Years (1837-1900), 177
presidential debates, 325–327, 403–404
presidential elections
    advertising, 404
    amendments altering process of, 392
    battleground states and, 401, 402
    breaking down traditional barriers, *369*
    campaign funding, 409–413
    caucuses, 395–396
    electoral college vote, 404–406
    five stages of, 392–393
    general election phase, 391–393, 399–401, 403–406
    incumbent race *vs.* open election, 399–401
    nominating conventions, 398–399
    nomination phase, 390–391, 395–399

polls measuring outcome of, 276, 277–278
presidential debates, 325–327, 403–404
primary elections, 5–6, 391, 395–396
race for nomination, 394
televised debate, 325–327
vice president, choosing, 400–401
Presidential Power: The Politics of Leadership
(Neustadt), 190
presidential primary, 395–396
president pro tempore, 148
presidents
assassination of, 175
birthrights of, 174–175
as "chief clerk" (1789-1836), 176–177
as chief diplomat, 186
as chief executive and head of government, 183–184
as chief legislator, 186–187
as commander in chief, 188
as crisis manager, 189
dying of natural causes while in office, 175
executive orders and agreements by, 190
federal judicial appointments by, 244
as head of state, 182–183
impeachment of, 175
implied powers and responsibilities of, 189–190
important relationships of, 193–196
losing reelection bids, 175
as party leader, 189–190
previous government experience of, 174
relationship with Congress, 194–195
relationship with the media, 195–196
relationship with the public, 193–194
requirements of, 174
resources of, 190–193
signing statements by, 187, *189*
ten greatest, *180*
two-term, 175
vetoes issued by, 187-188
vice-president's relationship with, 191
President's Council of Economic Advisors, 192
press
freedom of the, 85–86, 334
partisan era of, 324
press conferences, 195, 196, *327,* 327–328
Priebus, Reince, *358*
primacy tendency, 273
primary elections, 5–6, 391, 395–396
print media, 328, 330–331
prior restraint, 86
privacy rights, 93, 97–99
private law, 233
privatization, 211

privileges and immunities clause, 58, *58*
Pro-Choice Rally (1989), *112*
Proclamation of 1763, 26
professional associations, interest groups of, 305–306
Progressive Party, *362*
progressive tax, 432–433
pro-Israel lobby, 466
proportional representation, 360
Protect Intellectual Property Act, 89
Protestantism, 78
protests, *266,* 378–379, *379*
Proxmire, William, *208*
pseudo-polls, 281
Public Allies, *445*
Public Broadcasting Act (1967), 335
Public Broadcasting Service (PBS), 335–336
Public Citizen, 297, 307
public debate, media facilitating, 322–323
public interest groups, 307
Public Interest Research Group (PIRG), 312
public law, 232
public opinion, 263–286. *See also* public opinion polls
American foreign policy and, 467–468
in American politics, 266–267
continuity of, 284, *285*
defined, 267–268
direction of, 284
expressed through the news media, 267–268
expressed through voting, 267
formation of, 272–275
ideological nature of, 360
ill-informed, 271–272, *272*
intensity of, 284
interpreting data, 284
levels of, 268–271
Occupy Wall Street movement, *286*
political orientation and, 269–270
political preferences and, 270, *271*
values and beliefs, 268–269
public opinion polls, 193, 267, 275–283
accuracy of Gallup Poll, *279*
asking questions on, 282–283
on attitudes about the environment, *285*
defined, 275
examples, 268
history of, 276, 278
items disclosed about publicly released, *283*
large role of, 275–276
on news media, 338
presidential elections and, 276, 277–278
pseudo, 281
on public perception of new coverage, 338, *338*

public opinion polls (*continued*)
    sample size for, 281–282
    scientific sampling, 278
    on TV tobacco advertising, *284*
    unscientific, 278, 280–281
public policy
    defined, 423
    public opinion and, 272
Public Radio International, 335
Publius, 38
punch cards, 372, *372*, 373
Puritans, 13
purposive benefits (of group membership), 300–301
Putin, Vladimir, 470
Pyne, Joe, 325

Q

Quayle, Dan, 401
questions, on public opinion polls, 282–283

R

Rabin, Yitzhak, 460
race
    sentencing decisions and, 438–439
racial discrimination, 110–111
    Civil Rights Act (1964), 118
    de facto, 115
    de jure, 115
racial diversity, 13
racial profiling, 53, 123–124, 439
racial segregation, 112–115
    Brown v. Board of Education, 113–114
    de jure *vs.* de facto discrimination, 115
    Little Rock, Arkansas High School, 114
    Supreme Court cases, *113*
radio
    campaign use of, 5
    equal time rule, 321
    "fireside chats" on, 325
    government regulation of, 320–321
    historical development of, 325
    public broadcasting, 335
    satellite, 320
    talk radio, 333
railroad worker strike, Pennsylvania, 2009, *304*
Rainey, Joseph, *142*
Randolph, Edmund, 28
random-digit dialing (RDD), 282
random sampling, 278, 281–282

Rangel, Charles, *155, 473*
Rankin, Jeanette, *120, 144*
ratification
    of amendments, 42, *43*, 44, 45
    Articles of Confederation, 30
    Bill of Rights, 41, 42
    of the Constitution, 37–41
    Equal Rights Amendment (ERA), 44–45
rational basis (minimum) scrutiny, 126
rational choice theory, 373
The Rational Public (Page/Shapiro), 272
Reagan, Nancy, 192
Reagan, Ronald, *194, 458*
    abortion and, 99
    antitrust laws, 183
    attempted assassination of, 90
    background of, 18
    control of bureaucracy under, 211
    devolution policies, 64
    election of 1976, 398
    election of 1980, 408, 409
    election of 1984, 409, 414
    federalist policy of, 66
    media and, 195–196
    popular vote in 1984, *377*
    presidency of, 181
    press conferences of, 327–328
    Reaganomics, 172
    "set speeches" by, 193, *194*
    Strategic Defense Initiative proposed by, 459
    supply-side economics used by, 426
    Supreme Court appointees under, 64, 245, 247
    Supreme Court nominations by, 244
    tax reform and, 432, 433
    on U.S. sponsoring assassinations, *461*
    vetoes issued by, *188*
    vice presidential selection by, 400
    war-making powers, 188
realists, 465
reapportionment, 145
recession, 426. *See also* Great Recession of 2007-2010
    defined, 426
    Great Recession of 2007-2010, 426, *427*
    1981, 172
    Reaganomics and, 172
Reconstruction era (1865-1877), 111, 112
redistributive tax policies, 432
redistricting, 145
Redman, Eric, 156
Reed v. Reed (1971), 125
Reform Party, 361, *362, 363*

Regents of the University of California v. Bakke (1978), 119, 253

regressive tax, 433

regulations, 206

regulatory agencies, 218–219

Rehnquist, William, 245

Reid, Harry, 129, *150*

Reinventing Government (Osborne), 211

religion

    drug use and freedom of, 78–80

    establishment clause and, 80–82

    peyote use and, 80

    political socialization and, 275

    school prayer, 81–82

Reno, Janet, 216

Reno v. ACLU (1997), 87

reporting legislation, 151

representative democracy, 10, 365–366

reprieve, 184

republican form of government, 10

Republican Party. *See also* political parties

    congressional caucuses, *155*

    congressional leadership by, 147

    conservative ideology and, 270

    in history of political parties, 351–354

    interest groups and, 311

    Jeanette Rankin and, *120*

    Obama and, 182

    primary election of 1964, 6–7

    primary election of 2012, 5–6

    seat gains in House of Representatives, *149*

Republic of Chechnya, 469

requisition system, 30

reserved powers, 56, *56*

reserve requirement, 436

The Responsible Electorate (Key),, 272

restrictive immigration policy, 13, *13*

retrospective voting, 408–409

Revenue Reconciliation Act (1990), 433

Reynolds, George, 79–80

Rice, Condoleezza, 216, 464–465

Rich, Marc, 184

Roberts, John, 245, 246, *246*

Roberts, Owen, 62, 253, *253*

Robinson v. California (1962), *77*

Rockefeller, Nelson, 6–7, 162

Rock the Vote campaign, 19, *328, 378*

Roe v. Wade (1973), 98,, 248, 252, 301

Romania, 458

Romer v. Evans (1996), 132

Romney, Ann, 399

Romney, George, 7

Romney, Mitt, *364, 397, 442, 465*

    book written by, *400*

    election of 2012, 394, 397, *397*, 401

    issue voting and, 408

    prenomination campaign, 393–394

    primary race of 2012, 5–6

Roosevelt, Eleanor, 192

Roosevelt, Franklin Delano (FDR), *24, 325.*
    See also New Deal

    becoming president from vice president, 175

    campaigning in 1936, *353*

    changing images of, *174*

    cooperative federalism and, 61

    death, 175

    development of bureaucracy under, 209–210

    election of 1932, 5, 353, 400

    evolution of Constitution under, 24

    executive orders by, 190

    fireside chats of, 179, 180, 193, 325

    foreign policy and, 457

    learning from states' experiences, *442*

    lobbying by Corcoran and, 309

    media and, 195

    poll measuring election outcome of, 276

    popular vote in 1936,, *377*

    presidency of, 179

    radio addresses for 1932 campaign, 5

    relationship with the public, 193

    relationship with vice president, 191

    Supreme Court size and, 234, 253

    vetoes issued by, *188*

Roosevelt, Theodore

    Bull Moose Party and, 353, 361

    on "bully pulpit," 159

    conservation projects of, 422

    election of 1912, *362*

    foreign policy success of, *185*

    popular vote in 1904, *377*

    presidency of, 178–179

    "speak strongly and carry a big stick" approach, *457*

    vetoes issued by, *188*

    at Yosemite National Park, *422*

Roosevelt Corollary, 178–179

Roper Organization, 282

Rule of Four, 249

"rule of law" value, 269

Rules Committee, 158

Rumsfeld, Donald, 217, 464–465, 469

Russia, Treaty of Portsmouth and, *185*

Russian Federation, 469–470

Rutledge, John, 28, 162

Ryan, Paul, 399, 401, *401*, 433

S

safe seats, 415, *415*

SALT I, 459

SALT II, 459

same-sex marriage, 107

    Defense of Marriage Act (1996), *57,* 58

    Federalist No. 51 and, 40

    full faith and credit clause and, 57–58

    political preferences and, 270, *271*

sample, defined, 278

sampling error, 281–282

Sanders, Bernie, *363*

Sanford, Mark, 338

Santa Fe v. Doe (2000), 83

Santorum, Rick, 6, *294, 361, 393,* 393–394, *397*

satellite radio, 320

Saudi Arabia, 460, 465

SB 1070, 53

Scalia, Antonin, 46, 64, *246, 255,* 257–258

scandals, by lobbyists, 292, 293

Schattschneider, E.E., 266, 348

Schechter Poultry Corp v. U.S. (1935), 24

Schenck, Charles, 84

Schenck v. United States (1919), 84

Schlesinger, Arthur M., Jr., *180*

school desegregation, 113–115

school prayer, 81–82

schools

    Amish and attendance in, 79

    busing and, 115

    financial aid and the Lemon test, 82

    guns in, 64

    Internet regulation and, 88–89

    political socialization and, 274–275

    racial segregation in, *113,* 113–115

Schultz, Ed, 323

scientific sample, 278, 279

Scranton, William, 394

Sebelius, Kathleen, 216

Second Amendment, *43,* 65, *77,* 89–90

Second Continental Congress (1776), 29, 30, 142

Second National Bank, 177

Secretariat (UN), 470

secretary of state, 464

Securities Act (1933), 202

Securities and Exchange Commission (SEC), 202, 210, 219, 309

Security Council (UN), 470

Sedition Act (1798), 74, 85, *100*

Segal AmeriCorps Education Award, *445*

segregation

    of Mexican students, 129

    racial, 112–115

select committees, 152

self-incrimination clause, Fifth Amendment, 94

self-selected listener opinion polls (SLOPs), 280

The Selling of Supreme Court Nominees (Maltese), 248

The Semisovereign People (Schattschneider), 267

Senate. *See also* Congress

    Appropriations Committee, 429–430

    Banking Committee, *157*

    bills becoming laws in, 156–160

    cloture rule, 158

    committees in, *152*

    Environment and Public Works Committee, 207

    founding fathers on, 145–146

    Judiciary Committee, 246

    Labor and Human Resources Committee, 157

    leadership in, 148–149, 358

    majority leader, 358

    moving to presidency from, 174

    party-line voting in, 365

    president of, 148

    qualifications of senators, 146

    selection of senators, 145–146

    Supreme Court confirmation and, 247–248

    terms of senators, 146

    total number of members, 146

Seneca Falls, New York convention (1848), 368

senior citizen interest groups, 294–295

Senior Executive Service (SES), 220

sensationalism, in elections, 338

separate but equal doctrine, 113, 126

separation of powers, 36

September 11th terrorist attacks, *459*

    Bush's visit to Ground Zero, 189

    CIA and, 465–466

    civil liberties and policies following, 75

    Congress acting after, 142

    foreign policy following, 462–463

    Muslim Americans and, 129

    national security policy, 464

    support for federal government and, 66

Service Employees International Union, *310*

Seventeenth Amendment, 11, *43*

Seventh Amendment, *43,* 78

Seventh-Day Adventists, 78–79

sexual harassment, 127

Shapiro, Robert, 272

Sharma, Ruchir, 18

Shays, Daniel, 32

Shay's Rebellion, 32

Shepard, Matthew, 132

Sherbert v. Verner (1963), 78–79

Sherman, Roger
  Declaration of Independence and, 29
  the Great Compromise and, 33
  rating importance of, 28
Sherman Anti-Trust Act, 346
Shields, Mark, 322
Shriver, Sargent, 401
Sidarth, S.R., 339
Sierra Club, 301, 307
"signing statement," 187
Simpson, O.J., 232
Sipuel v. Bd. of Regents of Univ. of Okla. (1948), *113*
sit-ins, 116
Sixteenth Amendment, *43,* 432
Sixteenth Baptist Church, 118
Sixth Amendment, *43, 77,* 90, 96, 238
60 Minutes, 323
SLAPS test, 87
The Slaughterhouse Cases (1873), 111
slavery
  abolition movement, 110
  concentration of, by county (1790), *34*
  as issue at Constitutional Convention, 34–35
  southerners' approach to, 110–111
  uniform policies of states and, 65
  as violation of minority rights, 12
SLOPs (self-selected listener opinion polls), 280
"small states plan" (New Jersey Plan), 33
Smith, Chris, 158
Smith, Margaret Chase, 394
Smits, Jimmy, *380*
Snowe, Olympia, 16
social capital, 376
social contract, 7
social equality, 108
socialism, 439
Socialist Party, 360, *362, 363*
social learning theory, 337
social media, 4
social movements, 297–298
social policy
  crime policy, 438–439
  defined, 423
  health care policy, 444
  Social Security system, 441, 443
  welfare state, 439–441
Social Security Act (1935), 206, 440
Social Security Administration, 206, 210
Social Security system, 179
  cost-of-living adjustments in, 294–295
  long-run solvency of, 441, 443
  mandatory spending and, 434, 435

  state program as model for, *442*
Social Security taxes, 433
sodomy, criminalizing, 99
soft money, 299, 412
Soft Power: The Means to Success in World Politics (Nye), 463
solicitor general, 251
Solidarity Day for Labor (1991), *112*
Solidarity Day Labor Rally (1981), *112*
solidary benefits (of group membership), 301
Solis, Hilda, 216
Somalia, 459, 460
Sons of Liberty, 298
Sotomayor, Sonia, 129, 231, *231, 246,* 247
Souter, David, 248–249
South Carolina, 397
***South Dakota v. Dole* (1987),** 64
Southern Christian Leadership Conference (SCLC), 116
Southern Co., *306*
Southern Conference on Human Welfare, 192
"Southern Manifesto," 114
sovereignty
  cooperative federalism and state, 63
  defined, 54
  federalism and, 54
Soviet Union. *See also* Cold War
  Cuban missile crisis and, *185*
  Eastern Europe and, 458
  fall of, 469
Spain, value of individualism in, *14*
Speaker of the House, 358
  defined, 147
  first woman serving as, 125
  House of Representatives, 147–148
  passage of a bill and, 156, 157
special district governments, number of, 9
special interests, 297. *See also* interest groups
Spitzer, Elliot, 338
spoils system, 222
staff, congressional, 153–154
Stamp Act (1765), 26
Standard & Poor's 500 Index, 428
standing, 242
standing committees, 151, *152,* 157
"Stand Your Ground Law," 124
Stanford University, 88
stare decisis, 252
Stassen, Harold, 394, *396*
state and local government
  attracting in-state college students, *68*
  bill of rights in, 76
  in cooperative federalism, 62

state and local government (*continued*)
  under dual federalism, 61
  federal government involvement in, 65
  grants-in-aid to, 62
  number of, 9
  policymaking authority of, 63–64
  powers of, *56,* 56–57
state-centered federalism (1789-1819), 59, 60
state courts, 233, *234*
state expenditures, *63*
state legal systems, 233
State of the Union Address, 187, 193
states
  Bill of Rights applicable to, *77,* 77–78
  incorporating Bill of Rights to apply to, *77*
  judicial review and, 241
  as laboratories for national domestic policy, *442–443*
  number of House representatives per, 144–145
  party identification in, 357, *358*
  relations between, 57–58
  serving as birthplaces of presidents, 174
States' Rights Party, *362*
Statue of Liberty, 13
statutory law, 232
Stem Cell Research Enhancement Bill, 187
Stern, Howard, 320
Stewart, Jon, 320, 330
Stewart, Potter, 86
stock market crash (1929), 18, 202
Stone, Harlan Fiske, 84
Stop On-Line Piracy Act (SOPA), 89
strategic arms limitation treaties (SALT), 459
Strategic Defense Initiative (SDI), 459, 460
straw poll, 276
strict construction, 45–46
strict scrutiny, 114
Student Tools for Online Republican Mobilization (STORM), *416*
subcultures, American political, *13*
suffrage
  African American, 107, 110, 118, 367–368
  constitutional amendments extending, *11*
  Constitution and, 366
  Voting Rights Act (1965), 118
  women's, 106, 107, 367, 368
Sugar Act (1764), 26
SUGing (selling under the guise of polling), 281
Sumner, Charles, 140
Sunrise Research Group, 309
Sunshine in the Courtroom Act, 257
super-PACs, 299
  campaign contributions from, 16–17

in primary 2012 election, 6
superpower, China *vs.* U.S. as, 15, 17
"Super Tuesday," 397
supply-side economics, 426
Support Our Law Enforcement and Safe Neighborhood Act (2010), 53
supremacy clause, 57
Supreme Court. *See* U.S. Supreme Court
Supreme Court building, Washington D.C., *233*
Supreme Court justices. *See also* individual names of justices
  confirmation process, 247–249
  current, *246, 247*
  factors playing role in decisions of, 252, 254–255
  failed nominees, *248*
  lacking formal law school degrees, 240
  nomination process, 244–247
  "swing," 253–254
surveillance cameras, 92
surveillance techniques, 92–94
Sweatt v. Painter (1950), *113*
Sweden, 434
swing states, 401
Switzerland, 55
symbolic speech, 87–88

T

Taft, William Howard, *188,* 247, 400
Taft-Harley Act (1947), 305
Taiwan, immigrants from, *130*
Tajikistan, 469
Taliban, 182
Talking Points Memo (blog), 268
talk radio, 325, 333
Taney, Roger, 100–111
TANF (Temporary Assistance to Needy Families), 441
Tariff of 1828, 60
taxation
  by British on colonies, 26–27
  Reaganomics and, 172
taxation policy, 432–434
Taylor, Zachary, 175, *377*
Teach for America, *445*
Tea Party, 347, 378
Tea Party Caucus, *155*
tea tax, 27
technology
  newspapers and, 324
  surveillance, 92–94
telegraph, 5
television, 328
  campaign advertising on, 404

civil rights movement and, 318
election politics and, 398
emergence of, 325
equal time rule, 321
facts about American use of, 320
Kennedy's campaign using, 4–5
network ownership, 334–335
news programming on, 332
presidential debates on, 325–327
presidential press conferences on, 327–328
public broadcasting, 335–336
shaping vies on what is politically possible, *380*
visual images of presidential candidates on, 409
visual nature of, 332–333
Temporary Assistance to Needy Families (TANF), 441
Ten Commandments, public displays of, 81
Ten Commandments monument, *81,* 243
Tenet, George, 465
Tennessee Valley Authority (TVA), 220, 309
Tenth Amendment, *43,* 76
theocracy, 7
thermal imaging scans, 92, *92*
Think Progress, *322*
think tanks, *425*
Third Amendment, *43,* 78
third parties, 348, 360, 361–362, *362, 363*
Thirteenth Amendment, *43,* 111, 367
Thomas, Clarence, 64, 162, *246*
Thornberry, Homer, *248*
Three-Fifths Compromise, 35
Thurmond, Strom, 158, *362*
Time, 330
Tinker v. Des Moines (1967), 100
Title IX, 126, *133*
Tonight Show, 336
Tories, 349
touch-screen computer ballot, *372*
Tower, John, 184
Townsend Acts (1767), 27
township/town government, 9
trade associations, 303
traditionalistic political subculture, *13*
Transfer Act (1905), 422
Treasury Department, 209, *214*
treaties, congressional approval of, 163
Treaty of Paris (1763), 26
Treaty of Portsmouth (1905), *185*
Treaty of Versailles (1919), 163, 457
trial courts, 233
Tribe, Lawrence, 46
Trudeau, Garry, 329
Trujilo, Rafael, *461–462*

Truman, David B., 295
Truman, Harry S., 400
    becoming president from vice president, 175
    Korean War and, 188
    New Deal coalition and, 353–354
    poll predicting election outcome of, *277*
    presidency of, 181
    Truman Doctrine, 458
    vetoes issued by, *188*
Truman Doctrine, 181, 458
Trump, Donald, 394
Tuskegee Normal and Industrial Institute, 109
Tuskegee University, 109
Twain, Mark, 329
Twelfth Amendment, *43,* 350, 392
Twentieth Amendment, *43*
Twenty-fifth Amendment, *43*
Twenty-first Amendment, 42, *43*
24 (television show), *380*
Twenty-fourth Amendment, *11, 43,* 118, 119, 368
Twenty-second Amendment, *43,* 175, 392
Twenty-seventh Amendment, 41, *43,* 45, *46*
Twenty-sixth Amendment, *11, 43,* 368
Twenty-third Amendment, *11, 43,* 45, 368, 392
Twitter, 197
two-party systems, 359–360
two presidencies theory, 454
Tyler, John, 174, 175

U

undue burden test, 99
unemployment rate, 427–428
unicameral legislatures, 143
Union, the
Union Pacific Railroad, 292
union shop, 305
unitary system of government, 54
United Kingdom, *98, 130*
United Nations (UN), 54, 457, 470–471
United States v. Carolene Products (1938), 84
United States v. Dickerson (2000), 96
United States v. Lopez (1995), 64
United States v. Morrison (2000), 64
United States v. Nixon (1974), 242, 243
United States v. O'Brien (1968), 87
United We Stand America Party, *362*
unit rule, 405
universal health care, 25, 423, 444
universal suffrage, 367
University of California-Davis Medical School, 119, 121
University of Michigan, 88, *122*

University of Texas, 123

Unsafe at Any Speed: The Designed-in Dangers of the American Automobile (Nader), 307

unscientific poll, 278, 279, 280

U.S. Air Force, 213

USA Patriot Act, 75, 129, 142, 183–184

U.S. Army, 132, 213

USA Today/Gallup Poll, 268

U.S. Census Bureau, 123

U.S. Chamber of Commerce, 300, 302, 303, *306*

U.S. Coast Guard, 465

U.S. Constitution. *See* Constitution

U.S. Courts of Appeals, 235

U.S. Department of Agriculture, 209, *214*

U.S. Department of Commerce, Bureau of Economic Analysis, 68

U.S. Forest Service, 422

U.S. National Guard, 213

U.S. Navy, 213

U.S. Postal Service (USPS), 220

U.S. Supreme Court. *See also* Supreme Court justices
    abortion, 98, 99
    affirmative action, 119, 121, 122
    Bill of Rights interpreted by, 76–77
    cameras in, 257–258
    campaign financing, 413
    "clear and present danger" test by, 84
    confirmation of nominees for, 162
    current membership in, *246, 247*
    exclusionary rule, 91
    factors playing a role in judge's decisions in, 252, 254–255
    failed nominees for, *248*
    Federalist Papers cited by, 40
    freedom of religion, 78–80, 82
    freedom of speech, 84–85
    freedom of the press, 85–86
    gender discrimination, 125–126
    George Washington consulting with, 176
    good faith exception, 91
    guns in school zones, 64
    hate speech, 88
    how a case proceeds within the, 249–252, *250*
    Japanese internment, 128
    judicial review and, 239, 241, 255–258
    limitations on, 241–243
    Miranda warnings and, 95, 96
    new federalism and, 64
    Obama's health care reform, 241
    obscenity, 86
    petitioning for review, 235
    physican-assisted suicide, 99
    politics and, 256–257
    presidential nominations of, 230, 231
    presidential power of appointment and, 184
    privacy rights, 97–98
    racial segregation, 113, *113*
    rights of the criminally accused, 91, 96
    right to bear arms, 90
    same-sex partners, 132
    school prayer, 81–82
    separation of power and, 36
    size of, 234
    state courts and, 233
    state uniformity on issues and, 65
    strict *vs.* loose construction approach to Constitution and, 45–47
    suffrage, 367
    surveillance techniques, 92, 93
    symbolic speech, 87–88
    women's labor, 124

U.S. Treasury, 177

U.S. v. Jones (2012), 93

Utah, 357

V

values and beliefs, 268–269

Van Buren, Martin, 174, 191

Vance, Cyrus, 217

Venezuela, 456

Verizon, *306*

Verizon Communications, 309

Vermont, same-sex unions in, 107

Veterans Affairs Department, 216

veto, 160, 187

Viacom, 335

vice president, 191
    becoming president, 174, 175
    choosing as a candidate, 400–401
    congressional approval of president's nomination for, 162
    powers/duties of president devolving on, 175
    as president of the Senate, 148

Vietnam, immigrants from, *130*

Vietnam Moratorium Rally (1969), *112*

Vietnam "Out Now" rally (1971), *112*

"Vietnam syndrome," 460

Vietnam War, *455*
    domino theory and, 459
    Johnson and, 181, 193, 467
    lesson learned from, 460
    news coverage of, 332
    protests against, 87–88, 379

public opinion and, 193
Vietnam War protests, 87–88
violent protests, 379
Virginia Declaration of Rights of 1776, 41
Virginia Military Institute (VMI), 126
Virginia Plan, 32–33, *33*
Virginia Resolves, 26
Virginia v. Black (2003), 88
Virginia Women's Institute for Leadership (VMIL), 126
von Bismarck, Otto, 439
Voter News Service (VNS), *277*
voter registration, *118*
voter turnout
    around the world, *375*
    for congressional elections, 374
    defined, 371
    demographic differences and, 371, *371*
    low, 377–378
    reasons for low, 375–376
    types of elections and, 373–374
    in U.S. compared with other democracies,
        374–376
    in U.S. congressional and presidential
        elections, *374*
voting, 365–378
    candidate image, 409
    defined, 366
    determinants of vote choice, 407–409
    electoral college and, 404–406
    eligibility for, 366–367
    encouraging, 377–378
    factors explaining reasons for, 370
    issue, 408
    legal structure for, 366
    methods of casting a ballot, 371–373
    normal vote and, 356–357
    party identification and, 356, 407–408
    popular vote, 406, *406*
    providing a framework for voters to make choices,
        355–357
    public opinion expressed through, 267
    representative democracy and, 365–366
    retrospective, 408–409
    top 10 and bottom 10 popular winners in presidential
        elections, *377*
    universal suffrage and, 367–368
    in U.S. compared with other democracies, 374–376
    voter registration laws, 368, 370
    voter turnout, worldwide, *375*
    by youth, 19
voting rights. *See* suffrage
Voting Rights Act (1965), 118, 368

wages
    of African Americans, 123
    gender differences in, 126–127
Waldman, Paul, 195
Wallace, George, 114, *362*
Wallace, Henry, *362*
Wallace v. Jaffree (1985), 81
war-making powers, 188
War of 1812, 176, 209
war on drugs, 439
war on terrorism, 75, 182, 212
War Powers Resolution (1973), 188, 454
warrantless searches, 91
warrants, 91, 93
Warren, Earl, 84, 245, 255
Warren, Elizabeth, 203, *414*
Warren Court, 84–85, 91
Warsaw Pact, 458
Washington, Booker T., 108–109, 113
Washington, George, *349*
    becoming president, 390
    cabinet of, 217
    Constitutional Convention of 1787, *8*, 32
    development of bureaucracy under, 209
    political parties and, 349
    portrait of, *32*
    as president, 176
    Supreme Court appointments by, 162, 240
    two-term precedent set by, 175
Washington D.C., 11 largest demonstrations held in, *112*
Washington v. Texas (1967), *77*
Wasserman-Schultz, Debbie, *358*
Watergate scandal, 181, 193–194, 323, *324*
Water Resources and Environment Committee, 151
Watson, Greg, *46*
Waxman, Henry, 158
weapons of mass destruction, 460
Weather Underground, 338
Weaver, James, *362*
weblogs, 334
Webster, Noah, 324
Weinberger, Casper, 184
welfare programs, 66, 68, 69
welfare reform, 194, 211
welfare state, 439–440
West, Allan, *164*
West, Theodore, 119
West Virginia v. Barnette (1943), 78
West Wing, The, 380
What Happened (McClellan), 323–324

Whig Party, 351–352

whip (majority and minority), 148

White, George Henry, 111

White House chief of staff, 192

White House Office of Legislative Affairs, 187

White House press secretary, 195

Wildavsky, Aaron, 454

Wilderness Years (1837-1900), weakened presidency during, 177

Will, George, 322

Williams, Brian, *325*

Wilson, Charlie, 466

Wilson, Edith, 192

Wilson, Ellen, 192

Wilson, James, 28

Wilson, Joe, 141, *141*

Wilson, Woodrow, 400

    on Congress, 142

    Mexico and, 183

    popular vote in 1912, *377*

    presidency of, 179

    Supreme Court appointment by, 240

Wilson, Woodrow (*continued*)

    Treaty of Versailles and, 163, 457

    vetoes issued by, *188*

    wives of, 192

    women's suffrage and, 106

winner-take-all system, 360

Wirt, William, *362*

Wisconsin, voter registration in, 370

Wisconsin v. Yoder (1972), 79

Wolfowitz, Paul, 469

Wolf v. Colorado (1949), *77*

women

    affirmative action and, 119

    Equal Rights Amendment (ERA), 125

    first in cabinet, 216

    legal challenges to gender discrimination, 125–127

    salary discrepancies, 126–127

    voting rights for, 106, 107, 367, 368

    women's college basketball, *133*

    women's movement, 124–127

Woods, Tiger, 338

Woodside, D.B., *380*

Woodward, Bob, 217, 323, *324,* 330–331

workforce, federal. *See* federal workforce

Works Progress Administration, 440

World Bank, 470

World War I, 106, 179, 457

World War II, 179, 457

Wright, Jeremiah, 338

writ of certiorari, 235, 249–250

writ of habeas corpus, 177

writ of mandamus, 239

Wyoming, 357

Y

Yahoo, 333

Yosemite National Park, *422*

Young, Andrew, 111

YouthVote.org, 19

youth voters, 19

Yu, Susan, 238

Z

Zenger, John Peter, 85, *100*

Zenger, Peter, 320

Zimmerman, George, 124

zone of privacy, 98

Electoral College

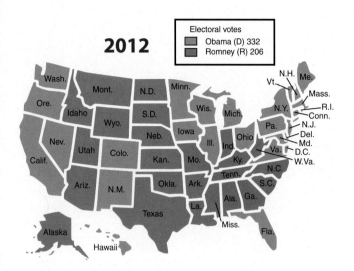

2012

Electoral votes
- Obama (D) 332
- Romney (R) 206

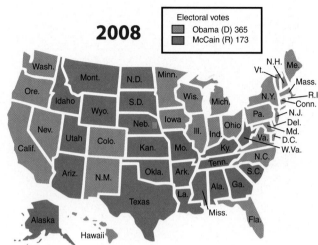

2008

Electoral votes
- Obama (D) 365
- McCain (R) 173

2004

Electoral votes*
- Kerry (D) 251
- Bush (R) 286

*A Minnesota elector pledged to Kerry cast a ballot for John Ewards [sic].

2000

Electoral votes*
- Gore (D) 266
- Bush (R) 271†

*A District of Columbia elector pledged to Gore cast no ballot as a protest against the District of Columbia's lack of representation in the U.S. Congress

†The state of Florida certified Bush the winner on November 26, a result that Gore contested in court.

Results from 1984 to 2012

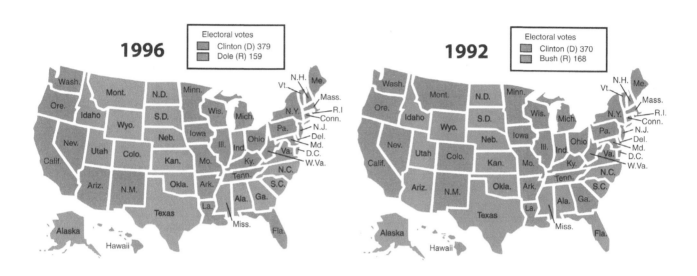

1996

Electoral votes
- Clinton (D) 379
- Dole (R) 159

1992

Electoral votes
- Clinton (D) 370
- Bush (R) 168

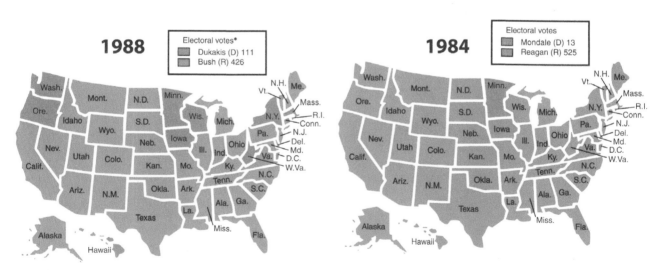

1988

Electoral votes*
- Dukakis (D) 111
- Bush (R) 426

1984

Electoral votes
- Mondale (D) 13
- Reagan (R) 525

* A West Virginia elector pledged to Dukakis cast her ballot for Democratic vice presidential candidate Lloyd Bentsen.

GEORGIA'S CONSTITUTION AND GOVERNMENT
6th edition

Arnold Fleischmann
University of Georgia

and

Carol Pierannunzi
Kennesaw State University

Introduction

Colleges and universities across the United States offer numerous courses on American government and politics. Many of them cover only the national government despite the ways that state and local governments affect the daily lives of most U.S. citizens. These activities range from basic local services such as streets, water, and fire protection to state support for public schools and universities. State and local governments spent $1.5 trillion in 2003, less than the federal government's $2.1 trillion, but still a significant amount. Moreover, while the federal government had 2.7 million civilian employees in 2002, state governments employed 5 million workers; local governments such as cities, counties, and school districts had another 13.3 million employees.[i]

Georgia is among the states requiring students to know something about state and local government. Specifically, the legislature has passed a law requiring graduates of public colleges and universities to demonstrate proficiency with both the United States and Georgia constitutions. This monograph is intended to assist students in satisfying that requirement.

1. The U.S. Constitution and Federalism

Constitutions are important because they establish the basic "rules of the game" for any political system. They specify the authority of government, distribute power among institutions and participants in the political system, and establish fundamental procedures for conducting public business and protecting rights. Just as drawing up or changing the rules can affect the outcome of a game, individuals and groups battle over constitutions, which can help determine who wins or loses politically.

When it was ratified in 1789, the United States Constitution included federalism as one of its most important elements. Federalism is a type of political system that gives certain powers to the national government, others to the states, and some to both levels of government. This differs from a unitary system such as in Great Britain or France, where all authority rests with the national government, which can distribute it to local or regional governments. Federalism also stands in contrast to a confederation, where all power is in the hands of the individual states, and the national government has only as much power as the states give to it. The United States used such a system during 1781-1788 under the Articles of Confederation, as did the Confederate States of America. More recently, confederations were tried following the break-up of the former national governments in the Soviet Union and Yugoslavia.

The American federal system is not static; in fact, it has changed significantly over the years. Below, we will discuss four key features that have had a major influence on the way federalism has developed. Three of these are found in the U.S. Constitution: the principle of national supremacy, the 10th Amendment, and the 14th Amendment. The last feature, state constitutions, is covered in Part 2.

National Supremacy

The U.S. Constitution's stability is due in large part to its broad grants of power and its reinterpretation in response to changing conditions. Article 1, section 8 grants Congress a series of "enumerated powers" such as taxing, spending, declaring war, and regulating interstate commerce. It also permits Congress to do whatever is "necessary and proper" to exercise the enumerated powers. This language is referred to as the "elastic clause" because of its flexible grant of authority. Article 6 reinforces the power of the national government by declaring that the Constitution and federal law are "the supreme law of the land." This so-called supremacy clause thus identifies the U.S. Constitution as the ultimate authority whenever there is a need to resolve a dispute between the national government and the states.

In an 1819 case, *McCulloch v. Maryland*, the U.S. Supreme Court adopted a broad view of the national government's powers when it decided that the elastic clause allowed Congress to exercise "implied powers" not mentioned explicitly in the U.S. Constitution but that could be inferred from the enumerated powers. The supremacy clause and implied powers have been cornerstones for the expansion of the national government's powers. Congress occasionally has turned programs over to states, as with changes in welfare laws during the 1990s, and has imposed new requirements and costs on them, as under the No Child Left Behind Act adopted in 2002.

The 10th Amendment

The constitutions, laws, and policies of the states cannot contradict the U.S. Constitution. Thus, federalism allows states many opportunities to develop in their own way, but it always holds out the possibility that the national government may act to promote uniformity for the country. Much of the debate over ratification of the U.S. Constitution focused on claims that the national government would be too powerful. This concern was reflected in proposals to add twelve amendments in 1789. Ten of the proposed changes were ratified by the states in 1791 and are commonly referred to as the Bill of Rights.

The 10th Amendment reads:

> The powers not delegated to the United States by the Constitution, nor prohibited by it to the States, are reserved to the States respectively, or to the people.

The amendment grants the states "reserved powers," but it does not define them. As one might expect, this has produced conflicts between the national and state governments, many of which have had to be resolved by the U.S. Supreme Court. For much of the period from the 1890s through the mid-1930s, for instance, the Court restricted efforts by Congress to enhance the power of the federal government. Since then, the power of the national government has grown, although some recent court cases have favored the states.

The 14th Amendment

The national government's power over the states was strengthened by the 1868 addition of the 14th Amendment to the U.S. Constitution. One of three amendments designed to end slavery and grant rights to blacks after the Civil War, the 14th states in part:

> No state shall make or enforce any law which shall abridge the privileges or immunities of citizens of the United States; nor shall any State deprive any person of life, liberty, or property without due process of law; nor deny to any person within its jurisdiction the equal protection of the laws.

This language essentially restates the fundamental principle of dual citizenship: Americans are citizens of both the nation and their state, and they are governed by the constitutions of both governments. The U.S. Constitution guarantees minimum rights to citizens that may not be violated by the states. The states, however, may grant broader rights to their citizens than are guaranteed by the U.S. Constitution.

The 14th Amendment has had an interesting and controversial history. The U.S. Supreme Court generally has defined the amendment's somewhat vague guarantees in terms of other provisions found in the U.S. Constitution. Since 1925, the Court has employed a process known as "selective incorporation" through which it incorporates into the meaning of the 14th Amendment the protections offered by the Bill of Rights. It does this selectively, that is, by applying these guarantees to the states on a case-by-case basis. Congress, too, has used the 14th Amendment in support of laws that restrict the power of state and local governments.

2. State Constitutions

States adopt their constitutions within the context of national supremacy; enumerated, implied, and reserved powers; dual citizenship; and the provisions of the 10th and 14th Amendments. Many state constitutions are modeled after the U.S. Constitution. Because state constitutions generally do not include implied powers, they tend to be more detailed and restrictive in defining the powers of government. State constitutions often include policies that seemingly could be decided by passing laws, as with Georgia's lottery. Putting such decisions in constitutions makes it harder for opponents to change them.

States also possess "police power," namely, the ability to promote public health, safety, morals, or general welfare. The police power is among the "reserved powers" in the 10th Amendment to the U.S. Constitution. Police powers are often delegated by states to local governments, which are covered in great detail in state constitutions, but are not mentioned at all in the U.S. Constitution.

Basic Differences in State Constitutions

Unlike the U.S. Constitution, which has been amended only 27 times, state constitutions are amended frequently, often to make narrow policy changes. Numerous amendments, provisions about local governments, and the lack of implied powers are major reasons that many state constitutions are so long, in contrast to the 8,700 words in the U.S. Constitution.

Table 1 indicates the number, length, and amendments for each state constitution. Georgia is noteworthy in two ways. First, it has had ten constitutions, second only to Louisiana. Second, Georgia's current constitution took effect in 1983, making it among the second youngest. Only Rhode Island can be considered to have a newer constitution, following the 1986 adoption of a revised version of its 1842 constitution.

Table 1
State Constitutions as of January 1, 2005

State	Number of Constitutions	Estimated Number of Words	Number of Amendments
Alabama	6	340,136	766
Alaska	1	15,988	29
Arizona	1	28,876	136
Arkansas	5	59,500	91
California	2	54,645	513
Colorado	1	74,522	145
Connecticut	4	17,256	29
Delaware	4	19,000	138[a]
Florida	6	51,456	104
Georgia	10	39,526	63
Hawaii	1	20,774	104

Idaho	1	24,232	117
Illinois	4	16,510	11
Indiana	2	10,379	46
Iowa	2	12,616	52
Kansas	1	12,296	92
Kentucky	4	23,911	41
Louisiana	11	54,112	129
Maine	1	16,276	169
Maryland	4	46,600	218
Massachusetts	1	36,700	120
Michigan	4	34,659	25
Minnesota	1	11,547	118
Mississippi	4	24,323	123
Missouri	4	42,600	105
Montana	2	13,145	30
Nebraska	2	20,048	222
Nevada	1	31,377	132
New Hampshire	2	9,200	143
New Jersey	3	22,956	36
New Mexico	1	27,200	151
New York	4	51,700	216
North Carolina	3	16,532	34
North Dakota	1	19,130	145
Ohio	2	48,521	161
Oklahoma	1	74,075	171
Oregon	1	54,083	238
Pennsylvania	5	27,711	30
Rhode Island	3	10,908	8
South Carolina	7	22,300	485
South Dakota	1	27,675	212
Tennessee	3	13,300	36
Texas	5	90,000	432
Utah	1	11,000	106
Vermont	3	10,286	53
Virginia	6	21,319	40
Washington	1	33,564	95
West Virginia	2	26,000	71
Wisconsin	1	14,392	133	Wyomin

[a]Amendments are not subject to voter approval.

Source: *The Book of the States: 2005 Edition*, pp. 10-11.

Amending State Constitutions

5

The states vary in the methods used to amend their constitutions (see Table 2). Seventeen states require only a majority in their legislatures to submit a proposed amendment to voters; others are more restrictive. Georgia is among the 20 states requiring a two-thirds vote by its legislature. Some states face the obstacle of getting an amendment approved in two legislative sessions before it can be submitted to voters. Four states, but not Georgia, also limit the number of amendments submitted to the voters at one election.

In terms of voter approval, 39 states require that a majority vote "yes" on an amendment for it to be ratified. A few states require more than a simple majority, e.g., a two-thirds vote in New Hampshire. Some require a simple majority on most amendments, but larger majorities for certain types of amendments, as with a two-thirds requirement in Florida to approve new taxes or fees. Other states require approval by a majority of those voting in an election, not just those voting on the amendment. The latter procedure can be especially difficult when people vote for highly visible offices like governor but skip proposed amendments. In such cases, not voting on the amendment is the same as voting "no."

The Georgia legislature can ask the state's voters to create a convention to amend or replace the constitution. The General Assembly also can propose amendments if they are approved by a two-thirds vote in each legislative – a procedure like that at the national level. The governor has no formal role in this process, but may be influential in recommending amendments and mobilizing public opinion before voters go to the polls. It is also worth noting that Georgia is not among the 18 states whose constitutions allow amendments through the initiative process, in which voters circulate petitions to place proposed amendments on the ballot for voters to ratify or reject in a statewide referendum.

The U.S. Constitution requires ratification of amendments by legislatures or conventions in three-fourths of the states. In contrast, the Georgia Constitution requires ratification by a majority of the voters casting ballots on the proposed amendment. Such proposals are voted upon in the next statewide general election after being submitted to the electorate by the General Assembly (November of even-numbered years).

During 2004, 33 states considered a total of 113 constitutional amendments of statewide applicability, of which 81 (72 percent) were adopted. Thirty-two of the proposed amendments dealt with government finance, taxation, and debt. Voters in 11 states considered 31 initiatives placed on the ballot by petition and approved 17 (55 percent).[ii]

Table 2
Amending State Constitutions Through Their Legislatures[a]
(Method in Georgia Marked with ✓)

Procedure	Approval Required	Number of States
Vote in Legislature	Majority	18
	2/3	19 ✓
	3/5	9
	Other	4[b]
Number of Legislative Sessions	One	38 ✓
	Two	12

6

Voter Approval Majority on Amendment	44[c] ✓
Majority in Election	3
Other	3[d]

[a]Eighteen states also allow their citizens to use the initiative process to place amendments on the ballot.
[b]Includes 3 states that require larger majorities if passed in one session, but only a majority if passed in two legislative sessions.
[c]Includes 5 states with different majorities for certain types of constitutional changes.
[d]Includes Delaware's constitution is amended by a two-thirds vote in two sessions of the legislature and does not require voter approval in a referendum.

Source: *The Book of the States: 2005 Edition*, pp. 12-14.

3. Constitutional Development in Georgia[iii]

Each of Georgia's ten constitutions can be considered a political response to some conflict, problem, or crisis. Replacing any state's constitution is a rare event, however. Amending a constitution is much more common. Both types of change, however, have produced long and often complicated documents. Such changes have also been linked to politics.

Politics and State Constitutions

Unlike the U.S. Constitution, most state constitutions include a wide range of very specific policies. Of course, legislatures normally enact policies by passing laws. Why "clutter up" state constitutions rather than limiting them to more fundamental issues? At least three reasons stand out: efforts to gain political advantage, state court decisions, and the requirements of the national government. Georgia's constitution has numerous examples of these processes.

Efforts to Gain Political Advantage. Many policies in state constitutions result from efforts by groups to gain a strategic advantage over their political opponents. If a group is able to get its position on an issue included in a state's constitution, it becomes much more difficult to change the policy. This is really a matter of taking advantage of the "rules of the game" by forcing the opposition to get its own amendment passed rather than simply getting a law enacted. Amendments that have added policies to Georgia's constitution deal with earmarking, tax breaks, morality issues, and limitations on decision making.

Like many state constitutions, Georgia's "earmarks" certain funds (identifies revenue sources that must be spent for designated purposes) that could benefit specific interests. The most significant are motor fuel taxes, which Article 3 requires to be spent "for all activities incident to providing and maintaining an adequate system of public roads and bridges" and for grants to counties. Morever, this money goes for these purposes "regardless of whether the General Assembly enacts a general appropriations Act."[iv] Thus, the Constitution provides those interested in highway construction with a guaranteed source of funds.

In other cases, the Constitution merely permits the earmarking of funds.[v] For instance, the General Assembly can use taxes on alcoholic beverages for programs related to alcohol and drug abuse. The legislature is also allowed to create a variety of trust funds for programs ranging from prevention of child abuse to promotion of certain crops. The 1992 amendment creating the state lottery requires that net proceeds (after expenses and prizes) go to "educational programs and purposes," with the governor's annual budget including recommendations for using these funds.[vi] An amendment approved by voters in November 1998 further restricted the use of lottery funds.

The Constitution provides special tax treatment to various groups and activities. An example is the taxation of timber, one of Georgia's major industries. An amendment approved by voters in 1990 requires that timber be taxed at fair market value only at the time of its harvest or sale.[vii] Previously, it was taxed annually at market value. This change produced a major drop in property taxes for some counties and school districts. The Constitution also requires that certain agricultural land be assessed at 75 percent of its value[viii] and exempts part of the value of a disabled veteran's home from property taxes.[ix] Other sections of the Constitution authorize rather than require the General Assembly to provide certain types of tax preferences, as with a 1988 amendment that applies to property on a historic register and a 1992 amendment that permits special treatment for heavy motor vehicles owned by nonresidents.[x]

Various groups often attempt to use state constitutions to establish their position on controversial social issues. This happened with the U.S. Constitution when the 18th Amendment was added in 1919 to ban the sale of alcohol. It was repealed, however, by the 21st Amendment in 1933. Similar provisions exist in the Georgia Constitution. The 1983 Constitution retained the prohibition against whipping as a punishment for a crime out of fear that the General Assembly might pass bills permitting whipping in schools or prisons.[xi] The 1983 Constitution, like all of its predecessors since 1868, prohibited lotteries. After being elected governor in 1990, Zell Miller convinced the General Assembly to submit a proposed amendment to voters to create state-run lotteries whose proceeds would be spent on education. That amendment was ratified by a narrow majority in November 1992 following a vigorous campaign. In 2004, Georgia voters were asked by the legislature to vote on amendment that would define marriage as the "union of man and woman." Even though Georgia already had a law banning the practice, the legislature voted to submit an amendment on the matter, which passed in every Georgia county and carried by 76-24% statewide.

Constitutions can also specify who gets to participate in key decisions, as well as limit the discretion of government agencies. For example, Article 4 creates six state boards and commissions, and Article 8 creates two more for education. The Constitution also establishes important political ties between the State Transportation Board and the General Assembly, thereby reducing the power of the executive branch over highways. The Georgia Constitution also empowers certain interests through residency requirements, as with membership from each congressional district on certain boards and commissions and the requirement that at least one member of the Board of Natural Resources be from one of six coastal counties.[xii] An example of constitutional limits on the discretion of government agencies is the requirement that veterans be given a preference in state civil service employment.[xiii]

State Court Decisions. A second reason for including policies in a constitution is to respond to a state court decision. For example, the Georgia Supreme Court might hold that a state law or an action by a local government violates the Georgia Constitution. Almost the only way to undo the court's action is to amend the state constitution. A 1994 amendment permits local governments to prohibit alcohol sales at clubs with nude dancing. This was a way to get around a Georgia Supreme Court ruling that nude dancing was expressive conduct protected by the Georgia and U.S. constitutions. Alcohol sales are not constitutionally protected, so regulating them is a way to try to drive nude dancing clubs out of business, which was subsequently considered allowable under the Georgia Constitution.[xiv]

Several decisions by the Georgia Supreme Court during the 1980s created confusion about sovereign immunity (the ability of citizens to sue the state or its local governments). As a result, an amendment was ratified in 1990 that attempted to clarify the matter.[xv] Similarly, the 1983 Constitution added language to clarify a somewhat confusing series of cases regarding the authority of the state, cities, and counties regarding planning and zoning.[xvi]

National Government Requirements. A third way in which politics affect state constitutions is to satisfy some requirement of the national government. For example, the Georgia Constitution was amended in 1988 and 1992 to create a trust fund to provide medical services for the poor through the federal Medicaid program. Without the trust fund, money unspent at the end of the budgetary year would have to go to the state's general fund and could be used for any purpose, as specified elsewhere in the Constitution.[xvii] With the trust fund, the unspent money can be carried over to the next year to pay for medical care. Another example can be found in Article 3, which is written in order to satisfy federal court decisions about how legislative districts must be drawn.

A Brief Comparison of the U.S. and Georgia Constitutions

It is useful at this juncture to compare the current U.S. and Georgia constitutions. Keep in mind, though, that constitutions are not static. Georgia has had ten constitutions, and the current one has been amended more than 60 times during its brief life. In addition, Georgia's constitutions have evolved because of the ways they have been interpreted by the courts.

Similarities. The most obvious similarity between Georgia and the national government is the presence of a bill of rights in each constitution. These guarantees were added as the first ten amendments to the U.S. Constitution, but the bill of rights is included prominently in Georgia's constitution as the first article. Both governments adopt separation of powers with distinct legislative, executive, and judicial branches. The president and Georgia's governor have substantial power to appoint officials and veto bills, although there are some important differences discussed below. Both the U.S. Congress and the Georgia General Assembly are bicameral, and each calls its two chambers the senate and house of representatives. Both governments allow judicial review (the power of courts to declare acts unconstitutional). Georgia courts are given this power in the state constitution,[xviii] while this authority at the federal level was laid down in 1803 by the Supreme Court itself in the case of *Marbury v. Madison*.[xix]

Differences. Perhaps the most visible difference between the two constitutions is how much longer Georgia's is, mainly because it includes many detailed policies. These range from specific taxes to sections on retirement systems, local government services, the state lottery, and even nude dancing.

The two constitutions also include differences in both procedures and the structure of government. One procedural distinction deals with constitutional amendments. Georgia voters must approve all amendments to the state's constitution. There is no comparable role for citizens in amending the U.S. Constitution, where amendments require a two-thirds vote in each house of Congress and then must be ratified by three-fourths of the states, in either their legislature or conventions. Another procedural difference is that the Georgia Constitution requires the state to have a balanced budget, but the U.S. Constitution imposes no such limitation on the federal government. The Georgia Constitution also grants the governor a line-item veto (the ability to kill a specific item in a spending bill), but the U.S. Constitution grants the president no such power over legislation passed by Congress.[xx]

There are striking structural differences among the three branches of governments. Unlike the national government, where judges are nominated by the president subject to Senate confirmation, Georgia elects almost all of its judges on a nonpartisan ballot. In addition, Georgia's attorney general issues advisory opinions, which generally have the force of law unless reversed by a court. There is no comparable process at the national level.

The legislative branches also exhibit some interesting differences. All legislators in Georgia (both the House and the Senate) serve two-year terms and are elected from districts based on population. This contrasts with the national government, where representatives serve two-year terms and senators are elected for six years. Moreover, while members of the U.S.

House are elected from districts based on population, two senators are elected from each state – the same for California and Wyoming – which builds in a bias in favor of less populous states.

The most glaring difference in the two executive branches is the lack of a cabinet system in Georgia. The president has the authority to appoint and fire heads of almost all major federal agencies. In contrast, Georgia's constitution requires that voters elect six department heads. This "plural executive" can make life difficult for a governor, who has limited authority over these independently elected officials, who may not share the same views or political party as the governor. The constitution also requires that several other department heads be chosen by boards and commissions rather than by the governor or the voters.

Perhaps the most noticeable structural difference between Georgia and the national government deals with local government. Georgia's constitution is quite specific about the organization of local governments, the services they can provide, the ways they can raise and spend money, and similar matters. It even limits the maximum number of counties at 159. The U.S. Constitution never mentions local government.

Georgia's Previous Constitutions

In addition to substantive differences, Georgia's constitutions also vary in the methods used to draft and approve them (see Table 3). Seven were written by conventions composed of elected delegates. Two were prepared by bodies whose members were either appointed or included because they held specific offices. The 1861 constitution was the first to be ratified by voters. The Constitution of 1976 resulted from a request by Governor George Busbee to have the Office of Legislative Counsel prepare an article-by-article revision of the Constitution of 1945 for the General Assembly.

Table 3
Georgia's Ten Constitutions

Year Implemented	Revision Method[a]	Major Characteristics
1777[b]	convention	Separation of powers, with most in the hands of the unicameral legislature.
1789[b]	convention	Bicameral legislature, which chose the governor; no bill of rights.
1798[b]	convention	Popular election of governor; creation of Supreme Court; greater detail than predecessors.
1861	convention	Long bill of rights; first constitution submitted to voters.
1865	convention	Governor limited to two terms; slavery abolished; Ordinance of Secession repealed; war debt repudiated; some judges made elective.
1868	convention	Authorization of free schools; increased appointment power for governor; debtors' relief.
1877	convention	More restrictions on legislative power; two-year terms for legislators and governor; no gubernatorial succession; most judicial appointments by legislature.
1945	commission	Establishment of lieutenant governorship, new constitutional officers, new boards, state merit system; home rule granted to counties and cities.
1976	Office of Legislative Counsel[c]	Reorganization of much-amended 1945 constitution.
1983	select committee[d]	Streamlining of previous document, with elimination of authorization for local amendments.

[a]Group responsible for proposing new document.
[b]Not submitted to voters for ratification.
[c]State employees, attorneys.

Source: Hill, *The Georgia State Constitution*, pp. 3-20.

Even before American independence in 1776, Georgians were exerting their independence from England. Colonial Georgia, dependent upon imports for most manufactured items, was hard hit by the various import taxes which had led to colonial protests. Public opinion in Georgia favored independence and citizens mobilized to break with England. The first self-government in Georgia was defined by the Rules and Regulations of 1776. This short and simple document was written hurriedly and adopted before the signing of the Declaration of Independence. All current laws were maintained except those in conflict with actions taken by the Continental Congress. It declared that governmental authority resided within the state, not with the British monarchy, and that power originated from the governed. While this document was not officially a state constitution, many have noted that it served as one. The Declaration of Independence prompted Georgians to establish a more permanent government, and the state adopted the first of its ten constitutions in 1777.

The Constitution of 1777. Georgia's first constitution included now familiar ideas such as separation of power among the legislative, executive, and judicial branches of government; proportional representation on the basis of population; and provisions for local self-government. This constitution, like the Rules and Regulations of 1776, included little expressed protection of individual liberties. Despite this omission, Georgia's political culture at the time was more liberal than other states, and the constitution was written to empower the "common man" (although only white males of 21 years who had paid property taxes in the previous year were permitted to vote). The Anglican Church was disestablished, and language in the document was easily understood. Local control of the judiciary was insured by the fact that no courts were established above the county courts.

The transition from the Rules and Regulations of 1776 to a new constitution in 1777 was little noted by citizens. This document governed the state until the demise of the Articles of Confederation. Georgia ratified the U.S. Constitution in January 1788 (the fourth state to do so) and redrafted the state constitution to reflect this monumental change in national government.

The Constitution of 1789. The Constitution of 1789 provided for a bicameral legislature. Although there were some accommodations made for representation on the basis of population in the House of Representatives, all legislative districts were drawn within counties, which could have from two to five representatives and one senator. Slaves were counted as three-fifths of a person, in accord with the U.S. Constitution and to meet the demands of landowners seeking to enhance representation for areas with large plantations. The state capital was moved to Louisville from Augusta,[xxi] provisions were included to mandate public education at the county level, and new counties were created to be represented in the legislature. In addition, the constitution authorized the legislature to elect the governor and most other state elected officials except the legislature itself. Restrictions on voting included race, age, residence, and the payment of taxes in the previous year.

The Constitution of 1798. The short life of the Constitution of 1789 can be attributed to a scandal over land speculation by legislators. The Constitution of 1798 was written by a convention and retained much of the language of the previous document. However, it was much longer due to increased detail about the powers of the legislature. As time passed, this constitution was amended to permit more democratic requirements for voting, establish executive offices to handle some of the duties of the legislature, outlaw foreign slave trade, and establish local governments. This constitution proved to be more enduring than its predecessors and was in effect until the formation of the Confederacy in 1861.

The Constitution of 1861. Secessionist fever at the start of the Confederacy could hardly allow the state constitution to go untouched. T.R.R. Cobb, the main author of the Confederate Constitution, was also the author of the Georgia Constitution under the Confederacy. The size of the state legislature was reduced by permitting senators to represent more than one county, and the governor's power was increased significantly. Judicial review was institutionalized in this document, and state judgeships were established as elective offices.

The Constitution of 1861 was the first to be submitted to the voters for approval in a referendum. This was also the first Georgia constitution with an extensive list of personal liberties, including freedom of thought and opinion, speech, and the press. Citizens were warned, though, that they would be responsible for "abuses of the liberties" guaranteed to them. Naturally, the Georgia Constitution under the Confederacy included ideals of states' rights.

The Constitution of 1865. The Constitution of 1865 was drafted by reluctant Georgians in order to accommodate the demands of Congress for readmission to the Union. Only men who expressed moderate political beliefs before and after the war were permitted to work on the document, which included the abolition of slavery, repudiation of Civil War debt, and repeal of the acts of secession. This repeal was not met with great enthusiasm by the North, which had insisted that the ordinance of secession be declared void. Also absent was enfranchisement of the black population of the state, although this was not as likely to stir animosity in the North since blacks could only vote in six northern states at the time. These omissions put pressure on Georgia to rewrite the constitution just three years later in order to meet the requirements for reentry into the Union. The Constitution of 1865 was viewed largely as the work of northern "carpetbaggers" trying to make quick fortunes in the postwar South, or, worse yet in the eyes of many, "scalawags" (southerners willing to cooperate with Yankees).

The Constitution of 1868. When a constitutional convention was called in 1867, it was boycotted by most of Georgia's popular leaders. The state capital, at that time in Milledgeville, refused to accommodate many of the delegates, some of whom were black. Therefore, the convention was held in Atlanta, and the new constitution, perhaps in retaliation for the inhospitable treatment by the city of Milledgeville, specified Atlanta as the capital. The Constitution of 1868 met the requirements of Congress for readmission to the Union and eliminated all debts incurred prior to 1865. Public education was also provided for, to be funded by poll and liquor taxes, although it was some time before this policy actually was implemented. Black citizens were insured equal rights, at least on paper, and property rights for women were upheld. Moreover, some attempts were made to enhance the business climate in order to build a stronger tax base.

Due to the high representation of poor and black citizens at this convention, the Constitution of 1868 was a liberal document for the times, particularly after blacks were seated in the General Assembly in 1870. Overall, the new constitution was widely unpopular due to its compliance with northern demands, which were symbolized by the presence of northern troops until 1876. It remained a symbol of southern defeat until replaced in 1877.

The Constitution of 1877. Georgia's post-Reconstruction constitution was a return to more conservative ideals. It reduced the authority of state officials and shifted power to counties, most of which were rural. Most noteworthy was its not-so-subtle disenfranchisement of blacks and poor whites through the mandate that only those who had paid all back taxes would be eligible to vote. As the Constitution of 1877 was being drafted, factionalism within the ranks of the Democratic party erupted. Many who were sympathetic to old southern culture were reluctant to compromise with those who called for economic development and progressive policies. An agreement was reached to comply with northern demands for reconstruction, as well as demands from more industrialized northern states that the South continue to supply raw materials. This compromise stirred up a faction of the Democratic party labeled Bourbons, who were dedicated to pre-Civil War agrarian economic and social norms, white supremacy, and local and state self-determination. The Republicans found that the compromise left them with little power in Georgia, and it would be quite some time before the Republican party reasserted itself in the state.

The Constitution of 1877 was not well suited to changing conditions. For example, it forbade public borrowing, thereby eliminating the possibility of large-scale improvements in transportation or education financed by the state. The constitution eventually included 301 amendments, many of which were temporary or dealt with local rather than statewide issues. Others made Supreme Court justices elected officials, established juvenile courts and a court of appeals, empowered an elected Public Service Commission to regulate utilities, and modified the boards overseeing education.

This constitution also codified the system of representation under which the six counties with the largest population were to be represented in the lower house of the legislature by three persons each, the next 26 most populous counties by two each, and the remaining counties by one member. This 3-2-1 ratio became the basis for the Democratic party's use of the county-unit system to elect statewide candidates—a custom that became state law in 1917 with passage of the Neill Primary Act.

Under the county-unit system, Democratic candidates for statewide office were chosen in primaries based on county-unit votes, which were similar to the electoral votes used to elect the U.S. president. Each county had twice as many unit votes as it had seats in the Georgia House of Representatives under the 3-2-1 formula. Beginning in 1920, the eight largest counties had six unit votes, the next 30 counties had four unit votes, and the remaining counties had two unit votes. Thus, Fulton County, which had more than 6,000 voters go the polls in 1940, had 6 unit votes; Quitman and Chattahoochee Counties, which each had fewer than 250 votes cast the same year, had 2 unit votes each. A county's unit votes were awarded on a winner-take-all basis, which meant that the candidate finishing first got all the unit votes. Under this system, candidates could concentrate their campaigns in rural areas and could win a primary without getting a majority of the popular vote. In 1940, the 121 counties with 2 unit votes had 43.5 percent of Georgia's population, but 59 percent of the unit votes. In contrast, Georgia's eight most populous counties, with 6 unit votes each, had 30 percent of the state's population but a mere 12 percent of the unit votes. In 1946, Eugene Talmadge finished second in the primary for governor by about 6,000 popular votes. He won the Democratic nomination, however, by besting his opponent 242 to 146 in unit votes.[xxii] The county-unit system remained intact until

1963, when the U.S. Supreme Court held that this underrepresentation of urban areas violated the "equal protection" clause of the 14th Amendment.

The Constitution of 1945. The Constitution of 1877 lasted until 1945, albeit in much amended form. A 23-member commission appointed by the governor to draft a new constitution was finally created because of dissatisfaction with the 1877 constitution, a careful study of the document in the 1930s, and prodding by Governor Ellis Arnall. The use of a commission rather than an elected convention reflects the governor's wish to depoliticize the constitution and bring it up to date, as well as the General Assembly's previous failure to muster the two-thirds vote to call a convention.[xxiii]

The new constitution included limited substantive changes. Its main effect was to condense its heavily amended predecessor. Perhaps the most notable changes were the creation of the office of lieutenant governor and new boards for corrections, state personnel, and veterans services. One contested issue was the ban against governors succeeding themselves, which the General Assembly retained in the draft submitted to the voters. The new constitution also authorized women to serve on juries and gave home rule to local governments, which increased their authority. The document also addressed the controversial issue of the poll tax.

With a turnout of less than 20 percent of those registered, voters approved the document by slightly more than a three-to-two margin following an active campaign on its behalf. Georgia thus became the first state to adopt a constitution proposed by commission rather than by an elected convention. The limits of this constitution emerged quickly. Within three years, the new constitution added its first amendments, with a total of 1,098 amendments proposed between 1946 and 1974. Voters ratified 826, of which 679 (82 percent) were local in nature.

The Constitution of 1976. An effort to revise the 1945 constitution occurred during the early 1960s, but a federal court ruling prevented voters from considering it during the 1964 general election. Another attempt died in 1970 when the House but not the Senate approved a document for submission to the electorate.

After assuming office in 1975, Governor George Busbee asked the Office of Legislative Counsel to draft a revision of the 1945 constitution in time for the 1976 election. The proposal included no real changes, but it did reorganize the constitution on an article-by-article basis so that it was easier to understand and interpret. After some revisions by the General Assembly, voters approved the document in November of that year. With no substantive changes in the new constitution, the General Assembly almost immediately set out to consider a more thorough revision, creating the Select Committee on Constitutional Revision during its 1977 session.

Georgia's Current Constitution

Adoption. Georgia's 1983 constitution was neither easily written nor quickly adopted. In fact, the Constitution of 1983 is a good example of how factionalism can play a role in state politics. Because the 1945 and 1976 constitutions so restricted local governments, cities and counties often were forced to amend the constitution in order to make changes in taxation or municipal codes. Amendments were proposed by the legislature and approved through popular vote, with those proposals affecting the entire state appearing on the statewide ballot and those affecting only one county or city appearing on the ballot only in that jurisdiction.[xxiv] As a result, ballots were brimming with proposed amendments that often irritated voters.

Between 1946 and 1980, Georgians were asked to vote on 1,452 proposed amendments (1,177 of them purely local in nature) and ratified over 1,105. This created an unwieldy document understood by only the most diligent of constitutional students. Voters became so annoyed with the large number of proposals that they began to vote them down. In 1978, the statewide ballot included over 120 proposed changes in the state's constitution, one-third of which failed to pass.[xxv]

By the late 1970s, many were pleased when Governor George Busbee sought the rewriting of the constitution, although Busbee may not have realized the political difficulty of such a task. The proposed constitution was debated for three years by a Select Committee on Constitutional Revision whose members included the governor, lieutenant governor, speaker of the House, attorney general, and eight other elected officials. The Select Committee began work in May 1977 and appointed committees with broader citizen membership to revise individual articles of the constitution for consideration by the General Assembly and the electorate. In November 1978, two articles were submitted to voters, who rejected them.

Subsequent efforts by the Select Committee and the 1980 session of the legislature failed to produce a new constitution. During its 1981 session, though, the General Assembly created a Legislative Overview Committee on Constitutional Revision, with 31 members from each chamber, to work with the Select Committee. These efforts produced a document that was approved in a 1981 special session and modified at the 1982 regular session of the General Assembly before being submitted to the electorate.

Like constitutional revisions generally, this one was quite political. Lobbyists and others representing specific interests were quick to get involved in the process. The 1981 special session was also an expensive one, with one estimate that it cost $30,000 per day.[xxvi] A confrontation occurred between the Speaker of the House of Representatives, Tom Murphy, and the governor over the powers to be granted to the legislature under the new constitution. This debate was fueled by the fact that governors had built up many informal powers under previous constitutions, including the naming of presiding officers of the House and Senate, as well as most legislative committee and subcommittee chairs. This practice ended with the 1966 election, when the legislature chose Lester Maddox as governor because no candidate got a majority of the popular vote. The General Assembly also organized itself without input from the governor and gained more power in subsequent years. Thus, by the early 1980s, legislators wanted to guard their political gains, but Governor Busbee favored the delegation of some powers to bureaucratic offices and state boards. The governor and the General Assembly also disagreed over taxes and gubernatorial term limits. At one point, Busbee asked legislators to forget the proposal and spend the remaining days of the session on other topics.[xxvii] Agreement was eventually reached, and voters approved the new constitution in November of 1982 by a nearly three-to-one margin. It took effect in July of 1983.

Major Provisions of the 1983 Constitution. The new constitution included eleven articles, many of them detailed and complicated. Still, the document was indeed much shorter than its predecessor and was written in simpler and gender-neutral language. Although it can be argued that the new constitution was one of evolution rather than revolution, it included many noteworthy changes:[xxviii]

✓ eliminating the requirement that local governments place changes in taxation, municipal codes, and employee compensation on the state ballot;

- ✓ establishing a unified court system, consolidating the duties of justices of the peace and small claims courts into magistrate courts, and strengthening the state Supreme Court;

- ✓ requiring nonpartisan election of state court judges;

- ✓ enhancing the power of the General Assembly to enact laws and authorize the appropriation of taxes;

- ✓ giving the Board of Pardons and Paroles power to stay death sentences;

- ✓ establishing an equal protection clause;

- ✓ reducing the total amount of debt that the state may assume;

- ✓ providing more open-to-the-public committee and legislative meetings; and,

- ✓ incorporating more formal separation of powers between the legislative and executive branches.

It is worth noting that the new constitution did not repeal the long list of local amendments in the old constitution. It simply allowed them to continue in force if approved by the General Assembly or the affected local government and "froze" them by prohibiting the addition of new local amendments.

Constitutional Amendments. The Georgia legislature can ask the state's voters to create a convention to amend or replace the constitution. The General Assembly also can submit proposed amendments to voters by a two-thirds vote in the House and the Senate – a procedure like that at the national level. The governor has no formal role in this process, but may be influential in recommending amendments and mobilizing public opinion. The U.S. Constitution requires ratification of amendments by legislatures or conventions in three-fourths of the states. In contrast, the Georgia Constitution requires ratification by a majority of the voters casting ballots on the proposed amendment. Such proposals are voted upon in the next statewide general election after being submitted to the electorate by the General Assembly (November of even-numbered years).

Despite the relatively young age of the Georgia Constitution, efforts to amend it have become somewhat common, although the number of proposals has not reached the dizzying heights of the previous constitution. There were 83 proposed general amendments on the ballot between 1984 and 2004, and voters approved 63 (76 percent). The total includes at least two proposals each year, with a high of 15 in 1988.

The November 2000 election included seven proposed amendments. The only proposal defeated by voters (52 percent opposed) would have allowed changes in the way marine vessels are taxed. Three amendments were approved to allow benefits for law enforcement officials, firefighters, public school employees, and state highway employees killed or disabled in the line of duty. One allowed members of the General Assembly to be removed from office after conviction for a felony rather than after exhausting all of their appeals. Another amendment raised from five to seven years the amount of time that state court judges must have been able to practice law before they can begin their judicial service. Finally, voters approved a measure related to property tax relief.

The 2002 election included six proposed amendments. Voters rejected two of these proposals. The first defeated proposal (54% opposed) would have established separate valuation standards and property tax rates for low-income residential developments. The other failed proposal (57% opposed) would have affected tax rates for commercial docksides used in the landing and processing of seafood. Of the four amendments approved by voters, two provided tax incentives for the redevelopment and clean-up of deteriorated or contaminated properties. Another amendment established a program of dog and cat sterilization funded by special license plates. Finally, voters approved a measure to prohibit individuals from holding state office if they have defaulted on their federal, state, or local taxes.

The November 2004 ballot included only two proposed amendments. One was a rather obscure question regarding the jurisdiction of the state supreme court. The other, however, was a contentious measure banning same-sex marriage.

Table 4
Proposed Amendments to the Georgia Constitution

Year	Number of Amendments Submitted to Voters	Number Approved	
1984	11	10	
1986	9	8	
1988	15	6	
1990	9	8	
1992	8	7	
1994	6	5	
1996	5	4	
1998	5	3	
2000	7	6	
2002	6	4	
2004	2	2	
TOTAL	83	63	(76%)

Sources: for 1984-1992: Hill, *The Georgia State Constitution*, pp. 20-23; for 1994: *Georgia Laws 1995 Session*, vol. 3, pp. CCCXVII-CCCXIX; for 1996-2004: Georgia Secretary of State Elections Division, "Georgia Election Results" (available www.sos.state.ga.us/elections/election_results/default.htm).

4. Georgia's Governmental Institutions

Like most states, Georgia's constitution mirrors the separation of powers adopted by the framers of the U.S. Constitution. Perhaps the most important aspect of the Georgia Constitution is what Melvin Hill calls its status as "a power-limiting document rather than a power-granting document."[xxix] Thus, many provisions specify things that the state of Georgia and its local governments <u>cannot</u> do.

The Georgia Constitution spells out the organization and authority of the legislative branch in Article 3 and the judicial branch in Article 6. Beyond that, the organization of government looks a bit different than at the national level. Executive responsibilities are spread among provisions in Article 4, which covers six boards and commissions, and Article 5, which encompasses the governor, lieutenant governor, and the six elected department heads. Other provisions affecting administration and local government are found in Article 8, which considers Georgia's system of education. The framework for local government is in Article 9, which comprises almost 20 percent of the Constitution.

The Georgia General Assembly

Comparisons to Congress and Other State Legislatures.[xxx] On the surface, there are few differences between the U.S. Congress and Georgia's legislature, which is officially named the Georgia General Assembly. Both are bicameral. The presiding officer of the house of representatives is called the speaker and is chosen by the members, but the leader of the senate (vice president of the United States and the lieutenant governor of Georgia) is elected independently of its members. Unlike Congress, where the entire House and one-third of the Senate are elected every two years, all 236 members of the General Assembly are up for election every two years. The General Assembly also meets for a very limited time each year and lacks the salary and staff support found in Congress.

The Georgia General Assembly has much in common with other state legislatures. Its members are charged with representing the people of their districts, reapportioning legislative seats following the census, enacting laws, adopting taxing and spending measures, overseeing enforcement of current laws, and interceding for constituents. Except for Nebraska, every state legislature is bicameral, elects its members on a partisan basis, and has an upper chamber called the senate. Forty-one states call their lower chamber the house of representatives, and Georgia and 41 other states convene regular legislative sessions annually. The fact that only eight state legislatures still meet biennially reflects the view that meeting once every two years may be too infrequent to keep up with problems in the modern world.

Differences do exist among legislatures, however. Size varies from a low of 49 in Nebraska's unicameral legislature to a high of 424 in the small state of New Hampshire. Georgia, with its 236 members, has the third-largest legislature. For the 49 bicameral legislatures, the average senate has 40 members, as compared to Georgia's 56. The average house of representatives has 109 members, much smaller than the 180 found in the Georgia House.[xxxi]

Qualifications such as minimum age, length of residence, and term limits vary. So do terms of office. Georgia is one of 11 states using only two-year terms. Members of Nebraska's unicameral legislature have terms of four years; four states have four-year terms for both chambers; the remaining 34 states elect their upper chamber to a four-year term and their lower chamber for two years. Unlike fifteen other states, neither Georgia's constitution nor its laws limit the number of terms that someone can serve in the legislature.[xxxii]

Regular legislative sessions range from off-year limits of 30 calendar days in New Mexico and Virginia and 20 legislative days in Wyoming to unlimited length for annual sessions in 13 states. Georgia is somewhere in the middle, with an annual session of 40 legislative days. Leadership, procedures, and compensation also vary widely among the states.

Representation. Georgia's earliest legislatures were based on county representation, initially with at least one representative for each county, which meant that the size of the General Assembly fluctuated over the years. During the 1960s, for example, the House had over 200 members at one point. As population changed and the number of counties grew to 159, the legislature became relatively large, but sparsely populated counties were represented equally with larger ones. Senate districts had three counties, and each seat rotated among its three counties at the end of each term. With each senator serving only one term and then giving way to someone from a neighboring county, power in the legislative branch was concentrated in the House, where members could hold unlimited tenure.[xxxiii]

The Constitution of 1983 restricted the Senate to not more than 56 members, while the House must have at least 180 members (size can be changed by law within these limits). Reapportionment occurs following the U.S. census held every ten years. The General Assembly has substantial flexibility in drawing legislative districts. This authority became more limited beginning in the 1960s, however when federal courts ruled that all representation within state legislatures must be based on population rather than county and Congress adopted the Voting Rights Act.[xxxiv] The practice of rotating Senate seats among counties in a district also ended, which allowed senators to run as incumbents and increased the power of the Senate as a whole.

After the 1990 census, the legislature abandoned multi-member House districts, which elected several representatives within the same district, with candidates required to run for a designated seat. This contrasts with a single-member district, where voters elect only one legislator. For example, District 72 might have two seats and would therefore have twice the population of a single-member district. People running for District 72, Post 1 did not compete with candidates for District 72, Post 2, although the electorate consisted of the same voters. With over 8.2 million residents in 2000, the average Senate district had about 147,000 people living in it, and there were approximately 46,000 resident per House district. During its 2001 session on redistricting, the General Assembly created more than 20 large, multi-member House districts where voters would elect two, three, or four representatives. Subsequent litigation, however, modified the boundaries for seats in both the Senate and the House, which saw the replacement of its multi-member districts with single-member districts.

Qualifications of Members. Article 3, section 2 of the Georgia Constitution requires that persons seeking office in the General Assembly be registered voters, U.S. citizens, and Georgia citizens for at least two years. It also requires that representatives live within their districts for at least one year. Those elected to the Senate must be at least 25 years old, while members of the House must be 21 or older. Persons may not simultaneously run for more than one office or in the primaries of two political parties. Also ineligible are persons on active military duty, those who hold other elected or civil offices within the state (unless they resign), and convicted felons.

Legislative Sessions. The Georgia General Assembly meets annually in a regular session that begins on the second Monday of January and lasts up to 40 legislative days. These are not calendar days, but days that the General Assembly is in session (not in recess or adjourned). The General Assembly may be called into special session by the governor, who sets the agenda, or by agreement of three-fifths of the membership of each chamber. Special sessions may be called to deal with unexpected crises, such as natural disasters, budgetary shortfalls, or other state emergencies. Special sessions may not last longer than 40 days and generally cannot be used for matters unrelated to the official agenda.[xxxv]

Legislative Leadership. When members of the General Assembly arrive in Atlanta for the beginning of a new legislative session, their first priorities include selecting leaders and organizing committees. The Georgia Constitution provides for the selection of presiding officers in each chamber. In the Senate, the lieutenant governor serves as president, just as the vice president of the United States is formally the presiding officer of the U.S. Senate. Thus, the presiding officer of the Senate is chosen by Georgia's voters in a statewide election, although the winner is chosen independently from the governor. It is worth noting that 25 other states (including Nebraska's unicameral legislature) also make the popularly elected lieutenant governor presiding officer of the senate. In the remaining 24 states, the senate chooses its own presiding officer. The Georgia Senate also elects one of its members as president pro tempore should the need arise to replace the presiding officer.

In the House, the representatives elect a speaker from among their members, as do the lower houses in the other 48 bicameral legislatures and the U.S. House of Representatives. In Georgia, House members also elect a speaker pro tempore, as do 25 other states; the other 23 legislatures either have no such position or have their speaker appoint someone.[xxxvi] In the speaker's absence, the speaker pro tempore presides.

Types of Legislation. Article 3 of the Georgia Constitution includes several sections detailing the General Assembly's procedures and powers for enacting laws, conducting impeachments, and spending public money. Bills before the General Assembly can be classified as resolutions, general legislation, and local legislation. All currently enforceable statutes are published in the *Official Code of Georgia Annotated*, which is updated periodically to include both new laws and legal opinions on implementation of current law.

Much of what passes through the General Assembly is not intended to be implemented as statute. Some of the items brought up for consideration are intended as statements of legislative opinion and may be enforceable only on the membership of the legislature itself. For example, the legislature may wish to recognize individuals or a sports team, in which case the General Assembly might pass a "resolution" describing the honoree's achievements. Resolutions also might be used to create special committees, to determine compensation for citizens who have been injured or suffered damages by state actions, or to set requirements for legislative staff. The resolution would therefore have little impact on other citizens of the state. It does, however, express the approval of the state government.

Resolutions might be passed to require the General Assembly itself to behave in a specific manner, as with rules of conduct, scheduling, or agreements on budgetary matters. In some cases, resolutions are passed by one chamber to establish rules only for the membership of that body, but joint resolutions require passage through both chambers. Resolutions generally do not require the signature of the governor because they do not require implementation outside the legislature itself. However, joint resolutions which are enforceable as law do require the governor's signature and may be vetoed.

General legislation has application statewide. Laws regarding election procedures or speed limits on state highways are examples. Local governments may not pass ordinances which contradict general law. Most general legislation intended to change existing law will specify exactly which statutes will be changed, but any new legislation supersedes past legislation.

Local legislation refers to those laws passed by the Georgia General Assembly which apply only to specific cities, counties, or special districts within the state. The General Assembly retains the power to govern localities through the passage of local legislation.[xxxvii] Local legislation may not contradict general legislation and may not be used to change the tenure of particular local officials. It can, however, be used to create or change political boundaries. The passage of local legislation differs in some ways from the passage of general law. Local bills must be preceded by a period of advertisement in which citizens of the jurisdiction concerned are notified of the potential law. This most often occurs in local newspapers.

Consideration of Bills. Only members of the General Assembly may introduce legislation, although by custom governors have had members introduce bills on their behalf. Bills generally are written by several persons and may be sponsored by multiple legislators. Bills may be introduced in either chamber of the General Assembly or at the same time in both chambers. One exception is legislation dealing with public revenues or appropriation of public money, which the Constitution requires to begin in the House of Representatives.[xxxviii]

Bills must adhere to a specific format dictated by the Constitution and the rules of each chamber. The title of the bill must relate directly to its content, and bills are constitutionally restricted to no more than one purpose. The Constitution mandates that all general legislation be read three times from the floor on three separate days. Because the title is required to be a summary of intent, reading the title only is substituted for the first reading of the entire bill. A second reading of the bill, which occurs on the second day after introduction, will also be of the title only. The Constitution forbids the introduction of bills which deal with specific individuals or which might limit the constitutional authority of the General Assembly. Population bills (those which apply to jurisdictions of a certain population) are also forbidden, as are bills that would have the effect of limiting business competition or creating monopolies within the state. Local legislation may be voted on after only one reading. The media may follow the passage of a bill, and the Constitution requires that floor action and committee meetings must be "open to the public," but this guarantee is not absolute.[xxxix]

Bills are passed by a simple majority of the entire membership of each chamber, although there are several exceptions to this rule. Tax legislation, proposed amendments to the constitution, veto overrides, punitive action taken against a member of the General Assembly, or motions to change the order of business require two-thirds majorities. Bills which have been rejected once in a legislative session also require a two-thirds majority to be reconsidered. Procedural changes may only require a majority of those members present. Once a bill has achieved a majority vote in one chamber, it must be passed in identical form by a majority vote in the other chamber in order to continue on the path to becoming a law.

The State Budget.[xl] The budget is a special type of lawmaking. The Georgia Constitution directs the governor to prepare the state's annual budget and submit it to the General Assembly during the first five days of the regular legislative session. This leaves the governor with substantial authority in the early stages of budget formation. This is countered, however, by the legislature's virtually unlimited power to change the budget submitted by the governor. The Constitution also requires that the state adopt a balanced budget, something the federal government is not obligated to do. Georgia's governor can exercise a line-item veto in an attempt to remove specific spending without vetoing the entire budget. Like a regular veto, the line-item veto can be overridden by a two-thirds vote of the membership in each chamber of the General Assembly.[xli]

The Executive Branch

One of the most striking differences between the U.S. and Georgia constitutions is the number of elected officials in the executive branch. The most visible in Georgia are the governor and the lieutenant governor. While they may be compared to the U.S. president and vice president, they are not elected together as a team and may represent different views and political parties.

Like the majority of states, Georgia has a plural executive, meaning that voters elect various department heads rather than having them picked by the governor like presidents choose the members of their cabinet. All but six states elect executive branch officials in addition to a governor (see Table 5).[xlii] In fact, voters around the country choose over 500 officials in statewide elections (a number virtually unchanged since the mid-1950s). Some of these officials are required to be elected by state constitutions; others are provided for by law. Their tasks vary significantly. Financial monitoring, for instance, is assigned to elected auditors, comptrollers, and treasurers, as well as appointed officials. Education is also diverse: seven states elect boards to govern public education, while Colorado, Michigan, and Nebraska voters elect the board of regents for their state universities.[xliii]

The Governor. Governors are generally the most powerful political figures in their states. Their political clout is based on the formal authority granted in a state's constitution, as well as several other sources of power, including laws, the media, public opinion, ties to political parties and interest groups, and personal characteristics. Professor Thad Beyle has compared the formal power of nation's governors, including their tenure potential, appointment powers, budgetary control, veto power, and the number of separately elected executive officials.[xliv]

The tenure potential (number of consecutive terms permitted for a governor) has been a contentious issue in Georgia's political history. The 1877 constitution limited the governor to two consecutive, two-year terms. A 1941 constitutional amendment provided for a four-year term, but prohibited governors from succeeding themselves in office. That was changed in 1976 to permit successive terms, but the lifetime limit for any governor was also two terms. The Constitution of 1983 permits two consecutive, four-year terms with no lifetime restriction on the time of a governor's service. That earned Georgia's governor a score of 4 on Beyle's 5-point scale for tenure potential. The most powerful tenure potential, which received a score of 5, exists in the nine states where governors face no limit on the number of four-year terms. At the opposite pole is Virginia, which does not allow governors to succeed themselves.[xlv] Unlike the governor, Georgia's other statewide elected officials face no constitutional limit on the number of consecutive terms they can serve, and some have served for decades.

24

Table 5
Executive Branch Officials Elected by the Public

Office	Number of States Electing	Georgia
Governor	50	elected statewide
Lieutenant Governor	42	elected statewide
Attorney General	43	elected statewide
Secretary of State	36	elected statewide
Education Superintendent		14[a] elected statewide
Agriculture Commissioner		13 elected statewide
Insurance Commissioner	11	elected statewide
Labor Commissioner	5	elected statewide
Utilities Commissioners	7[b]	5 elected statewide
Treasurer	36	appointed by governor[c]
Auditor	23	chosen by the legislature

[a]Another 8 states elect their boards of education.
[b]As in Georgia, these are multi-member boards regulating matters such as quality and prices for services such as natural gas, telephone, and electricity.
[c]Tasks are performed by the director of finance.

Source: *The Book of the States: 2005 Edition*, pp. 233-238, 350-351.

In terms of appointment power, Beyle classifies Georgia's governor in the weakest category because of limited power in six key areas: health, education, transportation, corrections, public utilities regulation, and welfare. In each of these cases, top administrators are chosen by voters (school superintendent and members of the Public Service Commission) or by boards. Gubernatorial control over boards and commissions is weakened because terms are long and staggered, which means that it can take some time before a governor's appointees are in control. In the case of one board (Transportation), the governor does not even appoint the members – the General Assembly chooses them.

Perhaps the most important appointment power of Georgia governors is their constitutional authority to fill vacancies in the executive and judicial branches without Senate confirmation.[xlvi] In the case of elected positions, the governor picks someone who finishes an unexpired term, thus becoming the incumbent in the next campaign. By law, the governor also can fill vacancies at the local level when an official has been removed temporarily following an indictment.[xlvii]

Beyle's 1-5 scale of budgetary power assigned a value of 1 to a governor who prepared the budget with other officials and faced unlimited legislative ability to amend, while 5 was for a budget prepared by a governor whose legislature was prohibited from increasing it. Like 42 other states, the Georgia governor rated a 3 on budgetary powers: the governor has full responsibility for preparing the budget, but the legislature has unlimited ability to change it.

Using a similar 1-5 scale for veto power, Beyle rated Georgia's governorship a 5, meaning that the governor has both simple and line-item vetoes along with a requirement for a large majority of the legislature to override (two-thirds of the total membership of each chamber). Twenty-three states make it easier to override a gubernatorial veto: six require only a majority of legislators elected, five mandate three-fifths of those elected, and twelve specify three-fifths or two-thirds of those present for the override vote.[xlviii]

The governor's veto power is included in the legislative, not the executive, article of the Georgia Constitution.[xlix] The governor has authority to act on legislation passed by the General Assembly that would have the effect of law, except for changes in the Constitution. If the governor signs a bill, it becomes law on a specified date, usually with the start of the fiscal year on July 1. The governor has six days to act on a bill while the General Assembly is in session. If the General Assembly has adjourned for the session or for more than forty days (like a recess), the governor has forty days after adjournment to act. When vetoing a bill, the governor is required to return it to the chamber where it originated within three days during the session or sixty days after adjournment. Once the General Assembly has received a veto message, the originating chamber may consider the vetoed bill immediately. Those bills vetoed during adjournment can be overridden during the next legislative session, as long as an election has not intervened.

A bill also becomes law if the governor does nothing (neither signs nor vetoes it). If the governor fails to act on a bill, it will become law following a six-day waiting period for bills passed during the first thirty-four days of the legislative session, or following a forty-day waiting period for bills passed during the final six days of the session. Thus, bills may sit on the governor's desk after adjournment of the legislature and become law even if the governor does not sign them.

Georgia is among the 43 states that provide for two types of vetoes, full and line-item. A full veto is a rejection of an entire bill. Line-item vetoes are rejections of specific passages in appropriations bills, which give the governor the power to kill spending for specific projects without having to veto an entire state budget. Reconsideration of bills in which specific funding has been line-item vetoed is not necessary, and the governor's actions officially reduce the appropriation if not overridden. A successful override allows a bill to become law in spite of the governor's veto. If an override fails in either chamber of the Georgia General Assembly, a bill is dead.

The Plural Executive. The Georgia Constitution requires voters to elect six department heads in addition to the governor and lieutenant governor. Together, these eight officials are referred to as the state's "elected constitutional officers."[l] Like a majority of states, Georgia elects an attorney general and secretary of state. Georgia is among the few states, however, letting voters pick a state school superintendent and individuals to head departments of agriculture, insurance, and labor.[li]

The six elected department heads possess power independent of the governor. They do so in part because of the prerogatives of their offices. The attorney general, for instance, exercises great discretion regarding the handling of litigation in which the state is a party and issues opinions on the legality or constitutionality of actions taken by the state.[lii] The insurance and agriculture commissioners have substantial power to regulate certain types of businesses. In addition to the power they derive from being elected separately from the governor, the narrow focus of their offices means that constitutional officers' natural constituencies (for votes and campaign money) are the interests affected most directly by their decisions. In fact, they are often seen as advocates of the industries they oversee.[liii] Elected department heads may even be in conflict with one another. Thus, despite the image of the governor's power in Georgia, executive power in the state is dispersed.

Georgia's elected department heads must have reached the age of 25, been a U.S. citizen for at least ten years, and been a Georgia resident at least four years when they assume office. The attorney general also is required to have had seven years as an active-status member of the State Bar of Georgia, which supervises the legal profession in the state. The Constitution leaves it to the General Assembly to spell out the power and duties of these officers, to determine their salaries, and to fund their agencies.[liv] There is also a procedure under which four of the eight constitutional officers can petition the Georgia Supreme Court to hold a hearing to determine if a constitutional officer is permanently disabled and should be replaced.[lv]

Constitutional Boards and Commissions. States commonly assign decision making in certain policy areas to multi-member boards rather than departments headed by a single individual. Georgia is no exception. Eight boards have their authority spelled out in the Georgia Constitution (see Table 6) Others have been created by law or executive order.

The eight boards and commissions required by the Constitution are among the most powerful agencies in Georgia, in part because any changes in their basic authority and membership require a constitutional amendment rather than passage of a law by the General Assembly. Their power is also reflected in the resources they control. In fiscal year 2005, for instance, the University System Board of Regents had a budget of roughly $3.5 billion, slightly less half of which was state funds. Some funds are earmarked in the Constitution: Article 3 requires that state motor fuel taxes, which were expected to total more than $634 million in fiscal 2005, must be spent for "an adequate system of public roads and bridges." That provides substantial power to the Department of Transportation, which had a total budget of more than $1.6 billion in fiscal 2005.[lvi]

Table 6
Constitutional Boards and Commissions in Georgia

Board/Commission	Members	Membership Selection
Public Service	5	Elected statewide on a partisan ballot for six-year terms.
Pardons and Paroles	5	Appointed by the governor to seven-year terms subject to Senate confirmation.
Personnel	5	Appointed by the governor to five-year terms subject to Senate confirmation.
Transportation	13[a]	One member per congressional district elected by majority vote of General Assembly members whose districts overlap any of the congressional district.

Veterans Services	7	Appointed by the governor to seven-year terms subject to Senate confirmation.
Natural Resources	18[a]	One member per congressional district and five at large (at least one of whom is from a coastal county) appointed by the governor to seven-year terms subject to Senate confirmation.
Education	13[a]	One member per congressional district appointed by the governor to seven-year terms subject to Senate confirmation.
Regents	18[a]	One member per congressional district and five at large appointed by the governor to seven-year terms subject to Senate confirmation.

[a]Membership can vary because it depends on the number of seats that Georgia has in the U.S. House of Representatives, which increased to 13 following the 2000 census and reapportionment.

Source: *Constitution of the State of Georgia*, art. 4 (for the first six boards); art. 8, sect. 2 (State Board of Education); art. 4, sect. 4 (Board of Regents).

The Constitution insulates these boards from political pressure to some degree by providing relatively long terms that are staggered. In the case of the State Board of Education and the University System Board of Regents, the governor is specifically prohibited from being a board member. Most constitutional boards and commissions use some geographical representation. Assigning one seat per congressional district has the effect of assuring South Georgia seats on boards that otherwise might be dominated by people from the Atlanta area. It also means that the size of a board can change as Georgia gets additional seats in the U.S. House of Representatives.

The Public Service Commission was originally created by statute in 1879 to regulate railroads. Today it is composed of five members who are elected statewide for staggered, six-year terms and regulates telephone services, utilities such as gas and electricity, communication networks, and transportation such as trucking and rail systems. The State Transportation Board may seem like the essence of pork-barrel politics, with one member chosen from each congressional district by the state legislators whose districts overlap it (and benefit from highway construction). Members of the remaining six boards are appointed by the governor, subject to confirmation by the Senate.

The Judicial Branch

There are essentially 51 legal systems in the United States, one at the federal level and a distinct system in each of the 50 states. Like the federal government and other states, Georgia has an elaborate system of trial and appellate courts (see Figure 1). Trial courts apply laws to the facts in specific cases, as when they render a verdict in a criminal or civil case. Appellate courts review the actions of trial courts to determine questions of law (whether statutes or constitutional questions were interpreted or applied correctly). Decisions in appellate courts are made by groups of judges with no witnesses or juries. The appellate courts rely on written and oral arguments by the parties in the case being appealed, although they can permit other parties to submit written briefs in support of either side in a case. Unlike the U.S. Constitution, which grants Congress broad authority regarding the legal system, Article 6 of the Georgia Constitution includes substantial detail about the operation of trial and appellate courts, the selection and conduct of judges, the election and performance of district attorneys, and a range of procedures.

The Georgia Constitution requires that state judges be elected, primarily on a nonpartisan ballot. Georgia's district attorneys, who are local officials responsible for criminal prosecutions, also are elected. This is quite different from the national level, where, subject to Senate confirmation, local prosecutors are presidential appointees under the authority of the U.S. Department of Justice, and judges are nominated by the president and can serve for life.

There is some link between Georgia's executive and judicial branches because the governor is permitted to appoint people to vacant or newly created judgeships.[lvii] One study calculated that 66 percent of superior court judgeships between 1968 and mid-1994 were filled by appointment. Because judges are routinely reelected in Georgia and so many vacancies are filled by appointment, judicial selection in Georgia is often seen as a system of gubernatorial selection, as when Governor Sonny Perdue appointed his top legal advisor to the Georgia Supreme Court in 2005.[lviii] Another practice not found at the national level is the ability of the attorney general to issue advisory opinions, which can have the force of law in Georgia unless overturned in court.

Trial Courts. Georgia is often characterized as one of the more complicated court systems, in large part because of the many trial courts of limited jurisdiction, some of which operate in only a few cities or counties rather than being uniform throughout the state. The Georgia Constitution grants the General Assembly discretion over the creation, jurisdiction, and operation of the state's courts, but it also requires that each county have at least one superior court, magistrate court, and probate court.[lix]

Superior court is the court of general jurisdiction, hearing a broad range of serious cases. The state is divided for administrative purposes into circuits that vary in population and size. Each county has its own superior court, but judges may handle cases in more than one county within a circuit. Superior courts hear divorces, felonies, most civil disputes, and similar matters. As workloads have increased, the General Assembly has added more judges and circuits.

There are also trial courts of limited jurisdiction, which hear specialized cases that are usually less serious than those in courts of general jurisdiction. These are primarily municipal courts dealing with traffic laws, local ordinances, and other misdemeanors. They also process warrants and may conduct preliminary hearings to determine if "probable cause" exists in a criminal case. Local acts passed by the General Assembly set courts' jurisdiction and the requirements for selecting municipal court judges.

The probate court in each county deals with wills, estates, marriage licenses, appointment of guardians, and involuntary hospitalizations of individuals. Probate courts may also issue warrants in some cases. Magistrate courts deal with bail, misdemeanors, small civil complaints, and search and arrest warrants. They also may conduct preliminary hearings.

Some counties have state and juvenile courts. The General Assembly passes local legislation to create state courts, which hear civil cases, traffic violations, or other misdemeanors. They may also hold preliminary hearings and act on applications to issue warrants. State courts operate in less than half of Georgia's counties and often have part-time judgeships. There may not be a separate juvenile court judge in small counties, where superior court judges often serve in juvenile court.

Appellate Courts. Like most states, Georgia has two levels of appellate courts. Cases decided by trial courts may be appealed to the Court of Appeals, except in cases reserved for other courts, such as the Georgia Supreme Court's exclusive jurisdiction over election contests. The Court of Appeals, which was created in 1907 to relieve some of the burden on the Supreme Court, is elected statewide on a nonpartisan basis for staggered, six-year terms. The Court of Appeals can be affected by state law, as when the General Assembly added a tenth

SUPREME COURT

COURT OF APPEALS

Certain counties

Capital felonies.
Constitutional issues.
Title to land.
Wills, equity, and divorce.

SUPERIOR COURT

| STATE COURT | JUVENILE COURT | PROBATE COURT | MAGISTRATE COURT |

| MUNICIPAL COURTS | COUNTY RECORDER'S COURT | CIVIL COURT | MUNICIPAL COURT |

judge in 1996 to help with the increased work load. Another two positions were added in 1999, leaving a court with twelve judges. The court often hears appeals on child custody, worker's compensation, and criminal cases that do not involve the death penalty. Cases appealed to the Court of Appeals are usually heard by a panel of three judges. If one of the judges on a panel dissents, however, a case may be heard by the full Court of Appeals.[ix]

The Supreme Court is comprised of seven justices elected statewide on a nonpartisan basis to six-year terms. They choose whether to hear appeals from lower courts through the process of certiorari (request for information from lower courts). The Court has exclusive appellate jurisdiction over all cases regarding the Georgia Constitution, the U.S. Constitution (as it applies within the state), elections, and the constitutionality of laws. It also may hear cases on appeal from the Court of Appeals or may be called upon to decide questions of law from other state or local courts. It has authority to hear appeals for all cases in which a sentence of death may be given. The Supreme Court is also involved in administering the state court system and regulating the legal profession.[lxi]

Selection of Judges.[lxii] The 50 states employ five methods for choosing judges. Some states elect judges in partisan elections; others hold nonpartisan elections; others require that judges be appointed by the governor; three states have at least some judges elected by the legislature; still others allow for the selection of judges under a merit system of screening by nominating commissions that submit candidates to a state's governor for selection. Once in office, such judges stand periodically for election.

Georgia has a long-standing commitment to electing judges, although there are some qualifications about age, living in certain counties or circuits, and membership in the state bar. The Constitution requires that members of the Supreme Court and Court of Appeals be elected in statewide nonpartisan elections for six-year terms. The justices of the Supreme Court choose a chief justice from among themselves. Superior court judges are also elected in nonpartisan elections, but serve four-year terms and are elected by voters who live within their circuits. State court judges are elected in nonpartisan, countywide elections for four years. Juvenile court judges are appointed, not elected, by the superior court judges of the counties they serve. The Georgia Constitution requires that all appellate and superior court judges shall have been admitted to practice law for seven years prior to assuming their judicial positions. Voters approved an amendment to the Constitution in 2000 imposing a similar seven-year requirement for state court judges (it had been five years).

The methods for choosing probate judges, magistrates, and municipal court judges are determined by law and can vary widely. In Athens-Clarke County, for instance, the probate judge and magistrate are elected on a partisan ballot, but municipal court judges are appointed. Unlike the rest of the judiciary, the Georgia Constitution does not require that probate judges, magistrates, or municipal court judges have been admitted to practice law for a minimum number of years. It leaves such matters for the General Assembly to specify by law, which means that non-lawyers could serve in such positions. This has often been a controversial issue, and state law does require certain training for those assuming such positions.

The Constitution allows the Judicial Qualifications Commission to suspend, remove, or discipline judges who have been indicted or convicted of a crime, cannot perform the duties of their office, or "for conduct prejudicial to the administration of justice which brings the judicial office into disrepute." The Georgia Supreme Court must review the case before a judge is removed from office.[lxiii] Except in magistrate, probate, and juvenile courts, the Georgia Constitution authorizes the governor to appoint a replacement to serve the remainder of a judge's term when a position becomes vacant for any reason. The Judicial Nominating Commission assists the governor in making such appointments, although the selection process includes input from political leaders and members of the legal profession.

District Attorneys.[lxiv] District attorneys are elected for four-year terms in each judicial circuit in Georgia. Qualifications for office include active membership in the State Bar of Georgia for three years. District attorneys represent the state as prosecutors in all criminal cases and in all cases heard by the Supreme Court and Courts of Appeals.

Juries.[lxv] The Georgia Constitution provides limited detail on juries, although it is significant that the matter is in Article 1 with the bill of rights rather than in the article on the judiciary, as it was in the Constitution of 1976. Citizens may be chosen to serve on grand juries or trial juries. While trial juries are the better known to the public because of media coverage of criminal cases, grand juries are important in determining how and if a case will proceed against a defendant.

Juries are not required for all trials in Georgia, but the size of the jury is determined by the level of the court. The Constitution specifies trial juries of 12 members, but allows the General Assembly to permit smaller juries and nonunanimous decisions in misdemeanor cases and in courts of limited jurisdiction. Magistrate courts and juvenile courts never hold jury trials, and other lower courts are not likely to use juries. Superior courts have juries of 12 members. State courts have six-member juries. Juries in civil cases consist of six or 12 members, depending on the dollar amount of damages sought and whether either party requests a jury of 12 rather than six members in state court. Unanimous decisions are required in criminal cases, where the decision to use a jury rather than a judge for the verdict rests with the defendant. The General Assembly has other authority over the composition of juries. In 2005, for instance, legislators passed a law that gave the defendant and the prosecutor in a criminal case an equal number of "strikes" to remove potential jurors from a jury pool. Previously, the prosecutor was allowed only half as many strikes as the defendant.[lxvi]

Grand juries are used by over half the states to issue an indictment (a formal charge accusing someone of a crime). Four states require grand juries for all indictments. Georgia is one of fifteen states that requires a grand jury for felony indictments. Six states require grand jury indictments for capital crimes, and the state of Pennsylvania does not empower the grand jury to indict. All other states make grand jury indictments optional, with the prosecutor filing an "information" in order to enter a formal charge against someone.

In deciding whether to issue an indictment, a grand jury must conclude that there is "probable cause" that the person committed the crime as charged. This a far less rigorous standard, however, than the "proof beyond a reasonable doubt" needed to convict the accused in a trial. Because the grand jury decides merely if sufficient evidence exists for an indictment, only the prosecution is heard, business is conducted in secret, and the defense has no right to cross-examine witnesses. Many have argued that this makes grand juries unnecessary and merely a "rubber stamp" for the prosecutor.

Grand juries in Georgia consist of 16-23 members. In addition to issuing indictments, grand juries have broad powers to study the records and activities of county governments, issue reports, and make certain decisions. For instance, grand juries in both counties had to review a request by some citizens to transfer the territory where they lived from Fulton County to Coweta County. Also, grand juries selected school boards in some counties until the Georgia Constitution was amended in 1992.

Local Government in Georgia[lxvii]

In addition to allocating authority among the three branches of state government, the Georgia Constitution also establishes a framework for the operation of local government.[lxviii] This is especially important since the U.S. Constitution says nothing about the matter. Local government in Georgia includes a range of counties, cities, and special districts (see Table 7).

Counties and Cities. The Georgia Constitution is very detailed regarding local government, although it is somewhat more specific regarding counties than cities and special districts. Article 9 even restricts the number of counties to no more than 159, although no such limit applies to other local governments. The Constitution also requires all counties to have certain elected officials. These local "constitutional officers" include a clerk of the superior court, judge of the probate court, sheriff, and tax commissioner (or tax collector and tax receiver), each of whom is elected to a four-year term. The Constitution leaves it to state law to spell out the characteristics of local legislative bodies such as county commissions and city councils.

The Constitution goes to some length to prohibit counties from taking several types of actions, such as those affecting local school systems or any court. It also lists functions that cities and counties may perform, including public transportation, health services and facilities, libraries, and enforcement of building codes. This is especially important to counties, which were first authorized to provide urban services by a constitutional amendment ratified in 1972. Article 9 also allows counties and cities to use planning and zoning, take private property, make agreements with one another, and consolidate.

Table 7
Number and Type of Local Governments in Georgia, 1952-2002

Year	Counties[a]	Municipalities[a]	School Districts	Special Districts
1952	159	475	187	154
1957	159	508	198	255
1962	159	561	197	301
1967	159	512	194	338
1972	159	529	189	366
1977	159	529	188	387
1982	159	532	187	390
1987	159	531	186	410
1992	159	534	183	421
1997	159	534	180	473
2002	159	528	180	581

[a]Following the mergers between Columbus and Muscogee County in 1970, Athens and Clarke County in 1991, and Augusta and Richmond County in 1995, the U.S. Census Bureau counted

33

the new governments as a municipality, not a county. This table treats each merged government as a county because of its organization and functions.

Sources: U.S. Bureau of the Census, *Census of Governments*, selected years.

Special Districts. A wide range of special districts is permitted by the Georgia Constitution, but their characteristics are covered by general laws. Probably the most visible special districts are local school systems. Policy making for education at the local level is the responsibility of elected school boards, who hire a superintendent as chief administrator. Prior to ratification of a constitutional amendment in November 1992, two-thirds of the county superintendents and 85 percent of the boards were elected.[lxix]

Perhaps the most important characteristic of special districts is their relative independence from county and municipal governments. For instance, areas can set up "community improvement districts" under state law to tax themselves extra for services beyond what their city or county provides. There are districts for major malls in suburban Atlanta, plus one that collects $1.7 million annually for services in downtown Atlanta.[lxx]

In addition to districts that cover only part of a local government's area, larger ones have been established to deal with regional issues. For example, MARTA (Metropolitan Atlanta Regional Transportation Authority) provides bus and subway service in Fulton and DeKalb Counties. The Georgia Regional Transportation Authority (GRTA) was created by the General Assembly in 1999 to oversee transportation and major development decisions in areas not meeting federal clean air standards.[lxxi] The General Assembly also created the North Georgia Metropolitan Water Planning District in 2001 to address water problems in 18 counties in the Atlanta area.[lxxii] As public needs and demands continue to arise, the General Assembly will undoubtedly use its constitutional power to establish local governments to create more special districts on top of the state's counties and cities.

Home Rule. The Georgia Constitution provides "home rule" for cities and counties. In most states, this means that a local government is granted broad powers to write and amend its charter (the equivalent of a local government's constitution) and to take any action not prohibited by the state. Home rule has proven more limited in Georgia, however. One study found that Georgia was one of 25 states in 1990 without a general law providing optional forms of government for counties, and one of 26 that did not grant them some autonomy in choosing their form of government. The same was true regarding municipalities, where Georgia was one of 13 states that did not have a general law regarding optional forms, and one of only ten that did not give cities any choice in their organizational structure. Unlike 30 states, Georgia did not divide its cities into "classes" (usually based on population), with different levels of authority granted to each class. Georgia does grant flexibility to cities and counties in carrying out local government functions.[lxxiii] Thus, Georgia grants its local governments some autonomy in day-to-day operations, but little authority to determine their own organizational structure.

A major reason for this limited local power is the Constitution itself, which places some restrictions directly on counties and cities. It also permits the legislature to adopt local acts, which are applied to specific cities, counties, and special districts. Local acts were 51 percent of the bills passed between 1970 and 1996 and can cover a wide range of topics. For example, it took action by the General Assembly to establish procedures for citizens to vote on merging governments such as Athens-Clarke County and Augusta-Richmond County.[lxxiv] Many other state constitutions prohibit the adoption of local laws.

Local Government Finances.[lxxv] The Constitution generally leaves the question of how local governments can raise and spend money to the General Assembly. In contrast, debt is covered in substantial detail. Georgia employs several restrictions common among the states. One is that debt cannot exceed ten percent of the assessed value of taxable property within the jurisdiction. Second, the Constitution places an annual limit on the amount that can be borrowed on a short-term basis.

A third requirement is that voters must approve the issuance of new debt by a simple majority in an election. However, this applies only to general obligation debt (borrowing in which the local government pledges tax revenues to pay off bonds sold to raise money, usually for major construction projects). The required voter approval and debt limitation do not apply to revenue bonds, which are not backed by taxes, but by revenues from projects being financed by the bonds. Airport revenue bonds, for example, are generally paid off with parking fees, aircraft landing charges, rents from airlines and concessionaires, and the like. With all types of local government borrowing, though, the real limit is the willingness of investors to buy bonds issued by a local government. In addition, local governments are required by state law to adopt a balanced budget each year.[lxxvi]

Georgia, like most states, limits local tax rates, mainly through laws passed by the General Assembly. State law allows counties and municipalities to levy a one percent general sales tax in addition to the four percent state tax. They cannot levy the tax without the approval of their voters. Since 1985, counties have been permitted by law to use a one-percent special purpose local option sales tax (SPLOST). The SPLOST is temporary, must be approved in a referendum, and must finance specific projects such as streets and roads, bridges, landfills, and solid waste.

In November of 1996, Georgia voters ratified a constitutional amendment to allow school districts to use a one-percent sales tax for construction. This tax is similar to the SPLOST used by counties and must be approved by a school district's voters in a referendum. This new revenue source can generate millions of dollars of funds, especially in rapidly growing school systems, and help school boards reduce their debt and dependence on property taxes. Despite the narrow statewide majority ratifying the amendment, the tax quickly proved popular at the local level.[lxxvii]

5. Elections

Just as constitutions specify the ways in which political institutions are organized, they also establish processes considered essential for a democracy. These include procedures for conducting elections, which are found in Article 2 of the Georgia Constitution.

Types of Elections

The Georgia Constitution provides basic ground rules for elections, such as the use of secret ballots and establishment of 18 as the minimum voting age (Georgia adopted this minimum age in the 1940s and was the first state to do so). Runoff elections and recalls are constitutionally established, as are procedures for removing and/or suspending public officials. However, the Constitution leaves most of the specifics regarding voter registration and election procedures to be decided by the General Assembly.

Primary and General Elections. All states have general elections in which voters choose from a number of candidates to fill an office. In most states, including Georgia, voters select party nominees from a group of potential candidates in a primary election. Some states also use party conventions to nominate candidates for certain offices. Primaries are not specified in the Georgia Constitution, but procedures are provided for by state law or political party rules.

Runoffs. In most states, the individual who receives the most votes in an election is declared the winner, but others require that the winner of a primary or general election receive over a certain percentage of the votes cast. Seven states, including Georgia, hold runoffs if no single candidate is able to capture 50 percent of the vote. North Carolina also employs runoffs, but reduced the threshold from 50 percent to 40 percent in 1989. Georgia's runoff was originally adopted in 1917, but has changed somewhat since then.

The logic behind the runoff system is based, in part, on the assumption that elections should reflect the will of the majority of the electorate. In places where there is a tradition of one-party politics with little or no opposition in the general election, candidates have faced their strongest opposition in primaries. If only a plurality were required, it would be possible to achieve elected office by finishing first in a primary with many candidates but still receiving well under 50 percent of the vote. To prevent that from occurring, the top two finishers face each other in a subsequent runoff, where the winner would be the candidate getting a majority in this two-person race.[lxxviii]

Traditionally, runoffs occurred after primaries, but in 1992 a runoff was held after a general election in Georgia between candidates for the U.S. Senate. In that instance, a third candidate prevented front-runner Wyche Fowler, the Democratic incumbent, from earning over 50 percent of the vote. His Republican opponent, Paul Coverdell, won the runoff. The General Assembly prevented this from occurring again when it adopted laws in 1994, 1996, 1997, and 1998 governing the use of such elections. A plurality (not a majority) is all that is needed to win a general election for a state office, except for the statewide constitutional officers, who still must achieve 50 percent. A majority remains required for party primaries and special elections, so runoffs could be common in such cases.[lxxix] Runoff requirements also remain a requirement in many local elections.

Runoffs have been criticized as being biased against minority candidates, who might finish first in an election but not get a majority. A minority candidate could then be defeated in a runoff as whites voted in a bloc for the remaining white candidate. Runoffs have been the subject of litigation in Georgia. The U.S. Supreme Court permitted their continued use in 1999, however, when it refused to hear an appeal from a lower court, which had held that the law requiring primary runoffs was not racially discriminatory.[lxxx]

Referendum Elections. States also conduct elections in which candidates are not running for office. The most common is a referendum, in which legislative bodies place issues on the ballot for public approval. Critics often complain, though, that asking people to vote "yes" or "no" on a question is not a good way to decide complex issues. Georgia voters are accustomed to referenda on whether to amend the state constitution. In their communities, they can be asked to decide whether local governments should levy sales taxes or be permitted to go into debt to by selling bonds to pay for public improvements such as roads and buildings.

Removal of Elected Officials. Recalls are elections to remove public officials from office before their terms have expired. Recall of state officials is allowed in Georgia and 15 other states; recall of local officeholders is more widely permitted. Some states exempt certain officeholders, usually judges, from the recall process. In Georgia, all persons who occupy elected state or local offices, even if they were appointed to fill unfinished terms, are subject to removal. Recalls are placed on the ballot through a petition process established by law. If an office becomes vacant through recall, a special election is held to fill the position.[lxxxi]

The Constitution allows other means for removing public officials. The House of Representatives may impeach any executive or judicial officer of the state, as well as members of the General Assembly. If the House votes in favor of impeachment charges, a two-thirds vote in the Senate is required to convict and remove the official from office.[lxxxii] The Constitution also includes procedures for the temporary suspension of the governor, the lieutenant governor, any of the other six constitutional officers, or a member of the General Assembly indicted for a felony by a grand jury.[lxxxiii]

Timing of Elections[lxxxiv]

The 1983 Constitution set the dates for the first general elections after its implementation; it also gave the General Assembly power to change the dates. This has not occurred, so elections for state offices are held the first Tuesday after the first Monday in November of even-numbered years. The members of the General Assembly are elected for two-year terms, which means that elections for these offices are at the same time as the U.S. House of Representatives. The governor and other statewide officeholders have four-year terms and are elected in years when the presidency is not on the ballot, which can protect Georgia candidates if their political party has an unpopular presidential candidate.

The Constitution sets length of terms for other elected officials, but leaves it to the General Assembly to determine by law when judges and most local officials will be elected.[lxxxv] County elections in Georgia are generally at the same time as major state and national races, but most city elections are held at different times, usually in odd-numbered years.

Redistricting

Like other states, Georgia redraws district boundaries for its legislature and the U.S. House of Representatives every ten years following the U.S. census. A similar process occurs for city councils and county commissions whose members are elected from districts rather than at large. Gerrymandering (the practice of drawing districts in order to achieve political outcomes) is one method by which incumbents may protect their political careers, minority political parties may be prevented from gaining legislative seats, rural or urban districts may dominate, or the voting strength of minority groups may be diluted.

Although it did not originate in Georgia, the U.S. Supreme Court's 1962 decision in *Baker v. Carr*[lxxxvi] affected Georgia profoundly. This landmark ruling and subsequent decisions forced states to draw legislative districts on the basis of population rather than political boundaries such as county lines. The "one person, one vote" standard required districts of equal population, although slight variation is tolerated. Based in part on crucial litigation in Georgia, the U.S. Supreme Court has also limited the use of race in drawing legislative districts (see below).

6. Rights and Liberties[lxxxvii]

Just as constitutions establish governmental institutions and basic processes such as elections, they also guarantee rights to individuals and regulate government's ability to interfere with people's liberties. Amending a constitution is normally a very difficult process. Therefore, including rights and liberties in a constitution is designed to protect them better than if such guarantees could be reduced or eliminated simply by passing a law. State constitutions may not infringe upon liberties and rights protected by the U.S. Constitution. Because of dual citizenship and the 14th Amendment to the U.S. Constitution, these federal guarantees are minimum standards, however, and states may grant their citizens broader rights.

Article 1 of the Georgia Constitution allows state courts to determine whether laws or actions comply with the state or U.S. constitutions.[lxxxviii] This process of judicial review is similar to that at the national level. Any law or administrative rule in Georgia, whether adopted by the state or by local governments, may be challenged in court. In addition, some private practices may be challenged, such as activities of businesses or individuals. Unlike the U.S. Constitution, which specifies most rights in amendments, Georgia's constitutions since 1861 have included a bill of rights as an integral part of the document. Article 1 in the 1983 Constitution included 28 paragraphs covering "Rights of Persons."

The discussion below covers some of the major provisions in Georgia's bill of rights. Under each heading, the first section describes how Georgia courts have applied these guarantees in specific cases. This is followed by a discussion of related federal court cases originating in Georgia. These cases are based on the U.S. Constitution and often brought about substantial changes not only in Georgia, but in the nation as a whole.

The first section covers civil rights, which are often thought of as the freedom to participate in the political system. It is generally linked to the guarantee of "equal protection" in the eyes of the law, which is the basis for much of the litigation on discrimination. The next three sections deal with civil liberties—the basic protection against unwarranted government intrusion into one's life. The fifth section deals with the right to privacy – a protection not written explicitly into either the U.S. or Georgia constitutions. Each section summarizes major federal court cases in a tables with full legal citations. Citations for decisions by Georgia courts are found in the endnotes.

Equal Protection[lxxxix]

Georgia Courts. The second paragraph in Georgia's bill of rights guarantees that, "No person shall be denied the equal protection of the laws." This language mirrors the 14th Amendment to the U.S. Constitution. While the Georgia Supreme Court has held that the federal and state equal protection guarantees "coexist," the justices have acknowledged that the state may interpret the Georgia Constitution to offer broader rights than are available under the U.S. Constitution.

A great deal of the controversy over equal protection involves government's classification of groups, with the courts being most vigilant regarding sex and race. In 1984, the Georgia Supreme Court found unconstitutional a law that provided benefits to children whose mothers were wrongfully killed but did not afford the same protection to children whose fathers were wrongfully killed. The Court also struck down Atlanta's program to set aside a share of contracts for minority- and female-owned businesses because the city failed to demonstrate the need for a race-conscious program.[xc] Local governments have continued to adopt set-aside programs, however, after studies to determine the effects of prior discrimination. Such policies remain highly contentious and must operate within guidelines laid out by the U.S. Supreme Court, which has become increasingly skeptical of such initiatives. Similar controversies have surrounded the use of affirmative action in admissions decisions at Georgia's public colleges and universities.[xci]

Perhaps more controversial have been several Atlanta ordinances dealing with gay rights. In 1995, the Georgia Supreme Court held that Atlanta could create a registry of unmarried couples (both heterosexual and homosexual) and forbid discrimination based on sexual orientation. However, the Court concluded that the city exceeded its authority by extending insurance benefits to the domestic partners of city employees.[xcii]

Federal Courts and Discrimination. On the surface, the 14th Amendment would seem to prohibit discrimination based on race. Yet Georgia, like other southern states, used a number of strategies to disenfranchise black citizens from the 1870s to the 1960s. These included the poll tax, the white primary, and other restrictions eventually eliminated by federal legislation and court decisions.[xciii]

The poll tax required citizens to pay an annual levy to be eligible to vote, thereby making it harder for the poor to vote. Georgia had used a poll tax earlier in its history, but it became particularly restrictive when the 1877 constitution made it cumulative, which meant that anyone falling behind in the annual tax had to make back payments. The poll tax was not repealed until 1945, when Governor Ellis Arnall made it a major issue during the legislative session. In other southern states, the poll tax lasted until the 24th Amendment to the U.S. Constitution banned it in 1964.

Perhaps the most blatant attempt to disenfranchise blacks was the white primary, which restricted voting in party primaries to whites only. Blacks could participate in the general election, but their votes were inconsequential because there was seldom Republican opposition on the ballot.

White primaries in Georgia were adopted in some counties by the 1890s. Beginning in 1900, only whites could vote in the Democratic party's primary elections. In a 1927 Texas case, the U.S. Supreme Court held that it was unconstitutional for state law to restrict primary voting on the basis of race. Virtually the entire South was controlled by the Democratic party then, and party leaders thereafter used party rules to enforce the white primary. Unlike general elections, which are processes of government, primaries could be regarded as activities of political parties, which are "private" organizations.

It was not until 1944 that the U.S. Supreme Court held that party rules enforcing a white primary also abridged the right to vote based on race. Georgia's white primary was overturned the following year by a federal appeals court in *King v. Chapman*. Perhaps the most immediate effect of this decision was in Atlanta, where business and political leaders began developing a coalition with the city's large black middle class.[xciv]

Three other restrictions were included in the Disenfranchisement Act of 1908, which voters approved as an amendment to the Georgia Constitution by a two-to-one margin:

The literacy test required that voters be able to read and explain any paragraph of the federal or state constitution; while the property qualification required ownership of 40 acres of land or property assessed at $500. The grandfather clause enfranchised men who had served in the United States or Confederate military forces and their descendants; no one could register under that provision after 1914.[xcv]

Implementation of the literacy test was in the hands of local election officials, who exercised great discretion, especially their power to purge voter registration rolls of those judged to be unqualified.

As the momentum grew to desegregate during the 1950s and 1960s, the Georgia General Assembly produced an array of legislation to forestall the process.[xcvi] At one point, all state aid was removed from any public school that was integrated, and payments were authorized to parents of children who attended segregated private schools. In order to prevent blacks from attending college in the state, requirements for admission were set to include letters of recommendation from two former graduates of the institution to which a student was applying. Since no blacks had attended most of these institutions, such letters would be difficult to obtain. Although most actions by the Georgia General Assembly were struck down as unconstitutional, white parents were able to move to different school districts or to send their children to private academies which did not admit blacks. Segregation was largely maintained until Congress passed the 1964 Civil Rights Act, but it continued in many respects long after that date. Local school districts also tried to prevent or minimize desegregation, including the Chatham County school board's unsuccessful effort to claim that integration would heighten black children's feelings of inferiority.[xcvii]

The Civil Rights Act of 1964 was designed to end discrimination in public accommodations (hotels, restaurants, transportation, etc.). In *Heart of Atlanta Motel v. United States*, the U.S. Supreme Court took a broad view of the U.S. Constitution's commerce clause and upheld the Civil Rights Act as a valid exercise of Congress's authority. The Court rejected the motel's claim that it was a local business. Because the motel served interstate travelers, its practice of refusing lodging to blacks was held to obstruct commerce, and the motel would therefore have to serve blacks.

Not all discrimination falls under the 14th Amendment. Congress has also passed laws dealing with characteristics such as religion, age, and disability. One of the leading cases regarding the disabled was based on the ways in which the Georgia Department of Human Resources had institutionalized people involuntarily after it was determined that such people could be placed in a community setting. In *Olmstead v. L.C.*, the U.S. Supreme Court held that such action violated the protection of the Americans with Disabilities Act of 1990.

Table 8
Major Federal Cases on Discrimination

King v. Chapman 154 F.2d 450 (1946)	Building on a 1944 U.S. Supreme Court case covering Texas, the circuit court of appeals found that the rules of Georgia's Democratic party, which restricted voting in primary elections to whites only, violated the equal protection guarantee of the 14th Amendment.
Heart of Atlanta Motel v. United States 379 U.S. 241 (1964)	Upheld constitutionality of Title 2 of the Civil Rights Act of 1964, which prohibited racial discrimination in public accommodations.
Olmstead v. L.C.	The state's practice of involuntarily institutionalizing

| no. 98-536 (1999) | disabled individuals judged suitable to live in less restrictive settings violates the Americans with Disabilities Act of 1990. |

Federal Courts and Equal Representation. Since the early 1960s, federal courts have become increasingly active in the process of drawing districts for legislative bodies. The courts have interpreted the equal protection guarantee of the 14th Amendment to mean that one person's vote should have the same weight in an election as another person's; to do this requires districts of roughly equal population. In *Toombs v. Fortson*, the Court ruled that reapportionment for the General Assembly must be made on the basis of the population of the state rather than by county or other political boundaries. Each district must have roughly the same number of inhabitants. After four earlier challenges had failed, in *Gray v. Sanders*, the U.S. Supreme Court struck down the county-unit system as a violation of the 14th Amendment's equal protection guarantee because the system malapportioned votes by underrepresenting urban residents. Other litigation also forced the General Assembly to redraw congressional districts in the state.[xcviii]

Questions of representation have become increasingly linked to race since Congress passed the Voting Rights Act (VRA) in 1965. The VRA suspended use of literacy tests, allowed for federal election examiners and observers, and required affected state and local governments to receive approval from the national government before making changes in their electoral systems. This "preclearance" by the U.S. Department of Justice is especially wary of changes which might dilute the voting strength of minorities.

The U.S. Department of Justice objected to congressional redistricting by the Georgia General Assembly following the 1990 census. After two unsuccessful attempts to redraw districts, state lawmakers finally satisfied federal guidelines to protect minority voting strength in the 1992 elections.[xcix] Ironically, in 1995 those districts were ruled unconstitutional in *Miller v. Johnson* because race was a "predominant factor" used in drawing the district lines.[c] Similar litigation occurred following redistricting based on the 2000 census: in *Georgia v. Ashcroft*, the U.S. Supreme Court again required Georgia to consider factors other than race in drawing legislative districts.

Table 9
Major Federal Cases on Representation

Gray v. Sanders 372 U.S. 368 (1963)	Held that Georgia's county-unit system violated the 14th Amendment's equal protection guarantee because it malapportioned votes among the state's counties.
Fortson v. Toombs 379 U.S. 621 (1965)	Upheld a lower court's 1962 decision that the 14th Amendment required seats in the General Assembly to be apportioned with districts of roughly equal population rather than being based on county or other political boundaries.
Miller v. Johnson 515 U.S. 900 (1995)	Invalidated Georgia's congressional redistricting following the 1990 census as a violation of the 14th Amendment's equal protection clause because race was the predominant factor in drawing district

	boundaries. The General Assembly had created three black-majority districts, with the eleventh district having a very irregular shape.
Georgia v. Ashcroft no. 02-182 (2003)	Held that courts reviewing redistricting under the Voting Rights Act have to consider all relevant factors affecting minority voters, not just the chance of electing minority candidates.

Right to Life, Liberty, and Property[ci]

Georgia Courts. Life, liberty, and property are the first rights listed in the Georgia Constitution. Like guarantees in the U.S. Constitution, they cannot be abridged "except by due process of law." State courts have found this guarantee to be broader than under the U.S. Constitution.[cii] Georgia courts traditionally have found that the state has the power to regulate businesses so long as the regulation is applied equally to all who engage in the same types of businesses and has some "rational relationship" to a valid purpose. Only when litigants are able to show that their due process has been violated are they able to convince the courts that government regulation is "arbitrary" or "unreasonable." Thus, laws regulating the licensing and training of professionals have largely been upheld. The Georgia Supreme Court has held that a mandatory life sentence for a second drug conviction does not violate due process or equal protection despite statistical evidence that a larger percentage of blacks end up serving life sentences under the law.[ciii]

The Georgia Supreme Court has taken a broad view of government compensation owed to the owners of private property taken for public use. All states and the federal government have some power of eminent domain (the taking of private property for public use such as expanding a highway, constructing facilities, and laying water or sewer lines). While most Georgia court decisions have permitted government to determine the size and use of land taken, restrictions have been imposed on compensation for property. The courts also have applied the notion of "taking" to regulation of private property, i.e., government regulation may be so restrictive that it has the same effect as seizing someone's land. In this regard, the Georgia Supreme Court has reviewed a great many cases dealing with land-use regulation and has tended to favor property owners over cities and counties. There are no landmark federal cases from Georgia dealing directly with this issue, although the state has produced major cases dealing with the related question of privacy (see below).

Rights Related to Expression and Association

Georgia's bill of rights includes a number of provisions designed to allow people to hold and express opinions, to associate with others, and to participate in the political process. These include two paragraphs on religion, as well as one on and the press, another on the right to assemble and petition, and one on libel, which is not mentioned in the U.S. Constitution.

Georgia Courts and Freedom of Conscience and Religion.[civ] Religious freedom was the earliest liberty to be addressed by Georgia's constitution drafters. Even the Rules and Regulations of 1776 included a provision for freedom of religion. The Georgia Constitution includes somewhat different language from the 1st Amendment to the U.S. Constitution. Perhaps the most striking difference is Georgia's limitation on religious practices: "but the right of freedom of religion shall not be so construed as to excuse acts of licentiousness or justify practices inconsistent with the peace and safety of the state."[cv] Thus, Courts in Georgia have at times limited freedom of religion, as when the Georgia Supreme Court found that freedom of religion did not include the distribution of literature in public. Nor has the Court extended freedom of religion to the use of controlled substances.

Georgia Courts and Freedom of Speech and the Press.[cvi] Georgia courts have adopted a broad interpretation of freedom of speech. For example, while the U.S. Constitution held that screening of movies was not in and of itself a violation of free speech, the Georgia Supreme Court found that an ordinance requiring approval of a censor before screening movies was unconstitutional in Georgia. The Court also held that it violated free speech to ban those between the ages of 18 and 21 from premises with sexually explicit performances.[cvii]

Free speech, as interpreted by the Georgia courts, includes limits. Indeed, the Georgia Constitution says that people "shall be responsible for the abuse of that liberty," as in cases involving incorrect publication of delinquent debt, inaccurate information regarding criminal activity, or use of photographs for advertising without the subjects' permission. The Georgia Supreme Court has upheld an injunction against anti-abortion protesters on the ground that the protest was limited by reasonable restrictions regarding time, place, and manner. The Court has held, however, that picketing was not protected free speech when the protest included an illegal strike. The Court also upheld the state's "Anti-Mask Act," which targets groups such as the Ku Klux Klan by prohibiting intimidating or threatening mask-wearing behavior, despite a claim that the law violates a person's freedom of speech.[cviii]

The press does not have a constitutional right to withhold a confidential news source.[cix] However, the media have been granted limited protection by a state law that allows reporters to be forced to turn over information from confidential sources when the evidence is material and relevant, is necessary for one of the parties to prepare a case, and cannot reasonably be gathered by other means.[cx] In terms of other publications, the Georgia Supreme Court has held that it violates free speech for a city to prohibit the distribution of printed materials to homes.[cxi]

Controversies have swirled around language or behavior judged offensive by many people. For instance, the Georgia Supreme Court struck down a state law attempting to outlaw bumper stickers considered profane as being too vague and a violation of free speech. Even greater debates have involved sexually-oriented communication, particularly after the Georgia Supreme Court ruled that nude dancing was protected expression and overturned local regulations banning such entertainment as too broad or outside the authority granted to local governments. To reverse this action, Georgia voters approved a constitutional amendment in 1994 to increase local governments' control over nude dancing through their power to regulate alcoholic beverages. A number of local governments subsequently adopted ordinances to prevent clubs with nude dancing from serving alcohol. The Georgia Supreme Court has held that such alcohol regulations do not violate the free speech rights associated with such entertainment.[cxii]

Federal Courts and Freedom of Speech and the Press. The U.S. Supreme Court has considered many cases during the past 40 years dealing with the 1st Amendment's guarantees regarding religion, speech, the press, and association. Two major cases on obscenity originated in Georgia. In a 1969 decision, *Stanley v. Georgia*, the Court found that "the mere private possession of obscene matter cannot constitutionally be made a crime," which Georgia law had done. Police had a warrant to search Stanley's home for materials related to illegal gambling, but they found allegedly obscene material. The state claimed that certain types of materials should not be possessed or read, and that obscene materials may lead to sexual violence or other acts. The Court rejected these claims, holding that the state asserted the "right to control the moral content of a person's thoughts . . . but it is wholly inconsistent with the philosophy of the First Amendment."

In a 1973 case, *Paris Adult Theatre I v. Slaton*, the Supreme Court was asked to determine whether the state could ban a commercial theater from showing films considered obscene. Here the Court reached an opposite result from *Stanley*, holding that the state had an interest in "stemming the tide of commercialized obscenity." The Court held that it did not make a difference that the films in question were shown only to consenting adults and the business posted warnings of films' content and prohibited minors from entering. Instead, the Court held that the state had a valid interest in "the quality of life and the total community environment, the tone of commerce in the great city centers, and, possibly, the public safety itself."

Cox Broadcasting Corp. v. Colin dealt with Georgia's law prohibiting publication of a rape victim's name. Pitted against each other were the desire to protect the victim's privacy and the freedom of the press. The Court held that it would violate press freedom to prohibit the publication of crime victims' names obtained from public records.

Table 10
Major Federal Cases on Freedom of Speech and the Press

Stanley v. Georgia 394 U.S. 557 (1969)	Overturned state law making private possession of obscene material a crime. The Georgia law was held to violate the 1st and 14th Amendments to the U.S. Constitution.
Paris Adult Theatre I v. Slaton 413 U.S. 49 (1973)	Banning the showing of allegedly obscene films to consenting adults in a commercial theater was held not to violate the 1st Amendment or the right to privacy.
Cox Broadcasting Corp v. Colin 420 U.S. 469 (1975)	Overturned the Georgia law prohibiting publication of the name of a rape victim obtained from public records.
Forsyth County, Georgia v. Nationalist Movement 505 U.S. 123 (1992)	Invalidated a local ordinance requiring participants to pay law enforcement costs for demonstrations and empowering the county administrator to determine how much to charge a group seeking a permit for a demonstration. The court found

Forsyth County was the scene of several marches by civil rights supporters and countermarches by the Ku Klux Klan during the 1980s. To manage these events, the county commission adopted an ordinance requiring those seeking a demonstration permit to pay a fee for law enforcement protection. The county administrator had discretion about the size of the fee, which could not exceed $1,000. One group refused to pay a $100 fee and sued the county. In *Forsyth County, Georgia v. Nationalist Movement*, the U.S. Supreme Court found that the county ordinance contained no standards for the administrator to follow and was thus unconstitutional because it "contains more than the possibility of censorship through

45

uncontrolled discretion [and] the ordinance often requires that the fee be based on the content of the speech" of the group seeking the permit.

Rights of Those Accused and Convicted of Crimes[cxiii]

The Georgia Constitution includes several provisions to protect people in dealing with the state's legal system. These include conditions regarding searches, seizures, and warrants by law enforcement officials; access to the courts and the use of juries; the right to an attorney and to cross-examine witnesses in criminal cases; the right against self-incrimination; protection against excessive bail and "cruel and unusual" punishment; and a prohibition against double jeopardy. Most of these guarantees parallel those in the U.S. Constitution's bill of rights, although Georgia has added other guarantees. For instance, the state bill of rights explicitly prohibits whipping and banishment from the state as punishment for crimes,[cxiv] imprisonment for debt,[cxv] and being "abused in being arrested, while under arrest, or in prison."[cxvi]

Georgia Courts. One of the most notable distinctions between the Georgia and U.S. constitutions is that the state offers more protection to defendants against unreasonable searches and seizures by law enforcement authorities. In addition, Georgia has long recognized the right of indigents to have a lawyer appointed, although this right does not extend to civil cases.[cxvii] A major problem with providing attorneys to poor criminal defendants has been in appropriating sufficient funds to make the guarantee work well.

Arguments often are made that certain punishments are "cruel and unusual." Georgia courts have held that punishment exceeding the crime is, in some cases, constitutional. For example, fines larger than amounts taken by theft have been permitted. In some instances, defendants have been banished from certain counties, but the Georgia Supreme Court has not upheld banishment from the state as a whole. Georgia's use of the death penalty was found to be unconstitutional in 1972 by the U.S. Supreme Court because the state did not have standards to protect against unequal application of capital punishment. Currently, Georgia law lists the conditions under which the death penalty may be sought and is in line with later U.S. Supreme Court rulings permitting executions. The Georgia Supreme Court, however, has considered it cruel and unusual punishment to execute someone who is mentally retarded,[cxviii] but reached the opposite conclusion when considering life in prison for a second conviction for selling cocaine.[cxix]

Federal Courts and Search and Seizure. Georgia has produced few major federal cases related to the search and seizure rights of criminal defendants in the U.S. Constitution's 4th Amendment. In 1997, however, the U.S. Supreme Court overturned a Georgia law requiring candidates for state office to pass a drug test, which the General Assembly had passed as part of its anti-drug efforts during the 1980s. Walker Chandler filed to run as Libertarian party candidate for lieutenant governor in 1994 but refused to take the test. In *Chandler v. Miller*, the Court held that the drug tests did not fall within the category of constitutionally permissible suspicionless searches. Indeed, the Court found that the test was essentially "symbolic" rather than being directed at some identifiable problem that might demand such a search.

Federal Courts and the Rights of Criminal Defendants. The U.S. Constitution's 6th Amendment includes the right to a fair trial, which is not spelled out in detail. Therefore, the courts have had to define what that right means in practice. Some of these cases have dealt with the size of trial juries and whether they must reach a unanimous decision. In a 1973 Florida case, the U.S. Supreme Court had permitted six-member juries in civil cases. In *Ballew v. Georgia*, however, the Court ruled in 1978 that Georgia's use of five-person juries in misdemeanor cases violated the right to a fair trial, in part because of the reduced deliberation and bias in favor of the prosecution regarding hung juries. Georgia's current constitution allows the General Assembly to permit six-member juries in misdemeanor cases or in courts of limited jurisdiction.[cxx]

Federal Courts and the Death Penalty. Two appeals to the U.S. Supreme Court from Georgia during the 1970s became the landmark cases regarding the use of capital punishment in the United States. The first, *Furman v. Georgia* in 1972, effectively ended executions throughout the country. Four years later, *Gregg v. Georgia* allowed the state's rewritten capital punishment law to stand, thereby opening the door for states to resume executions.

What was different about these two cases? The members of the U.S. Supreme Court had a range of views regarding capital punishment, but the major concern was how the death penalty was applied. In *Furman*, the Court was concerned with both the lack of guidelines to use in deciding when to impose a death sentence and the wide variation in its use for similar crimes. The states then began revising their laws, and the Court decided several cases in 1976 based on the new statutes. In *Gregg*, the Court upheld Georgia's new capital punishment law, in part because it required specific findings by the jury regarding the facts of the crime and the character of the defendant; it also had a process for appellate courts to review death penalty cases.

Table 11
Major Federal Cases Affecting Those Accused or Convicted of Crimes

Chandler v. Miller 520 U.S. 305 (1997)	Held that Georgia's requirement that candidates for state office pass a drug test violates the 4th and 14th Amendment protections against suspicionless searches.
Ballew v. Georgia 435 U.S. 223 (1978)	Held that a criminal trial using a jury of less than six members violated the 6th and 14th Amendment guarantees to a fair trial.
Furman v. Georgia 408 U.S. 238 (1972)	Held that Georgia's methods of administering the death penalty violated the 8th Amendment's guarantee against cruel and unusual punishment. The decision effectively ended executions in the United States for more than a decade.
Gregg v. Georgia 428 U.S. 153 (1976)	Upheld Georgia's revised law on capital punishment, which limited the crimes for which the death penalty could be imposed and specified the factors to be considered and procedures to be used in deciding when to impose capital punishment.
Coker v. Georgia 433 U.S. 584 (1977)	Found that Georgia's imposition of the death penalty for the crime of rape was grossly disproportionate and thus a violation of the 8th Amendment's ban on cruel and unusual punishment.

McCleskey v. Kemp 481 U.S. 279 (1987)	Rejected the claim that racial differences in the imposition of the death penalty violated the equal protection guarantee of the 14th Amendment and amounted to cruel and unusual punishment in violation of the 8th Amendment.

Two other cases tested the constitutionality of the conditions under which Georgia imposed the death penalty. In *Coker v. Georgia*, the U.S. Supreme Court held that the death sentence for the crime of rape was grossly disproportionate to the offense and thus violated the 8th Amendment ban on cruel and unusual punishment. In *McCleskey v. Kemp*, the Court confronted the issue of bias in imposing the death penalty. McCleskey presented a study showing that the use of the death sentence in Georgia was statistically related to the race of the murder victim and, to a lesser extent, the race of the defendant. This pattern, he argued, violated the 8th and 14th Amendments. The Supreme Court rejected these claims, citing appellate courts' review of cases with facts similar to McCleskey's case.

The Right to Privacy

Georgia Courts. Like the U.S. Constitution, Georgia's does not mention a right to privacy. In 1904, though, Georgia became the first state to recognize a privacy right when the Georgia Supreme Court found this right in natural law and the guarantees of liberty found in the U.S. and state constitutions.[cxxi] Privacy has been extended to the right of a prisoner to refuse to eat, even to the point of starvation, and a person's right to refuse medical treatment even if it was certain to lead to death.

Table 12
Major Federal Cases on the Right to Privacy

Doe v. Bolton 410 U.S. 179 (1973)	This is the less famous Georgia case decided along with *Roe v. Wade*. It overturned Georgia's ban on abortions as a violation of a woman's right to privacy.
Bowers v. Hardwick 478 U.S. 186 (1986)	Held that the right to privacy did not protect consensual homosexual sex from prosecution under Georgia's sodomy law.

Federal Courts. The U.S. Supreme Court first recognized a right to privacy in a 1965 Connecticut case dealing with government regulation of contraception. Since then, the courts have been forced to define the limits of privacy rights. These debates include two Georgia cases. *Doe v. Bolton* remains almost unnoticed today, but it was the challenge to Georgia's abortion law decided along with *Roe v. Wade*, the more widely known Texas case in which the Supreme Court held that the right to privacy included a woman's right to abortion.

The second Georgia case was *Bowers v. Hardwick*. In this case, Michael Hardwick challenged Georgia's sodomy law as a violation of the right to privacy in so far as it applied to consensual conduct. He also argued that as a homosexual he faced constant threat of arrest and prosecution. The Supreme Court rejected Hardwick's claim and upheld Georgia's sodomy law, which prohibited certain acts but did not specify the gender or sexual orientation of the participants.

Dual Citizenship and the Right to Privacy. Georgia's sodomy law provides a good example of the way in which dual citizenship can produce different rights under state and U.S. constitutions. The Georgia Supreme Court reinforced the *Hardwick* decision in 1996, when it ruled, in *Christensen v. State*,[cxxii] that the state's sodomy law did not violate Georgia's right to privacy. That all changed in 1998, however. Based on facts involving a heterosexual couple, the Georgia Supreme Court, in *Powell v. State*, held, "insofar as it criminalizes the performance of private, non-commercial acts of sexual intimacy between persons legally able to consent, [the sodomy law] 'manifestly infringes upon a constitutional provision' . . . which guarantees to the citizens of Georgia the right to privacy."[cxxiii] Shortly thereafter, however, the Court rejected the claim that Georgia's right to privacy also protected commercial sexual activity.[cxxiv]

Thus, while any given state's law criminalizing sodomy would not violate the federal right to privacy as applied in *Bowers v. Hardwick*, state courts around the country could consider such a law in violation of broader rights guaranteed in their state constitutions. That possibility changed rather dramatically in 2003, however, when the U.S. Supreme Court's *Lawrence v. Texas* decision overturned sodomy laws in those states that still had them.[cxxv]

The most recent frontier in battles over privacy rights deals with medical treatment. For instance, a 1997 U.S. Supreme Court decision left the door open for states to either ban or allow doctor-assisted suicide. This produced a conflict when former U.S. Attorney General John Ashcroft attempted to keep Oregon from implementing its law allowing the practice.[cxxvi] Such disputes will undoubtedly continue to pit the states against the national government in the face of breakthroughs in medical treatment and research.

7. The Continuing Significance of Georgia's Constitution

A constitution is not some kind of sacred or unchanging blueprint for government. Constitutions are essentially political documents. That is why individuals, businesses, political parties, and interest groups often fight vigorously about interpreting and amending constitutions. For instance, lawsuits have attacked as racially biased the methods of selecting Georgia's judges and juries.[cxxvii] By approving an amendment to create a state-sponsored lottery in 1992, voters gave the governor, legislature, and bureaucracy millions of dollars to distribute to programs and individuals. They also paved the way for firms to profit from the production, sale, and marketing of lottery tickets. Another amendment granted a property tax break for growing timber,[cxxviii] although voters rejected a similar proposal for blueberries in 1994. The 1992 amendment requiring that local school board members be elected and superintendents be hired allows boards to recruit superintendents from anywhere. Under the old system of electing school superintendents in some counties, only local residents could run for the office.[cxxix]

As the preceding examples demonstrate, constitutions help distribute political and economic power. Constitutions also adopt policies that under other circumstances might be made simply by passing a law. Given the extensive detail in the Georgia Constitution, voters undoubtedly will face proposed amendments every even-numbered year as various interests try to modify the document to achieve their ends. If a large number of changes are ratified by voters, the Constitution might become so littered with amendments that it is unwieldy and difficult to interpret. A second possibility is that Georgians will become so annoyed with proposals on the ballot that they rebel by voting "no" on amendments. Finally, both groups and members of the General Assembly might regularly use constitutional change as just another way to achieve their political ends. If so, Georgians might treat amendment battles as just an ordinary part of the election process even though it would not be on the scale of western states using the initiative. None of these scenarios bodes well, however, for the durability of the 1983 Georgia Constitution.

NOTES

[i] U. S. Bureau of the Census, *Statistical Abstract of the United States: 2004-2005* (Washington: Government Printing Office, 2005), Tables 426, 453, 461.

[ii] On procedures for amending state constitutions, see Janice C. May, "State Constitutional Developments in 2004," pp. 3-9 in Council of State Governments, *The Book of the States: 2005 Edition* [hereafter cited as *The Book of the States*] (Lexington, KY: Council of State Governments, 2005) [also see Table 1.6 on p. 18].

[iii] This section draws heavily from Melvin B. Hill, Jr., *The Georgia State Constitution: A Reference Guide* (Westport, CT: Greenwood Press, 1994). Rather than weigh down this section with extensive endnotes, specific references are used only when necessary. Readers are urged to consult Hill's exhaustive work for more detail.

[iv] *Constitution of the State of Georgia*, art. 3, sect. 9, para. 6b.

[v] *Constitution of the State of Georgia*, art. 3, sect. 9, para. 6c-j.

[vi] *Constitution of the State of Georgia*, art. 1, sect. 2, para. 8c.

[vii] *Constitution of the State of Georgia*, art. 7, sect. 2, para. 3e.

[viii] *Constitution of the State of Georgia*, art. 7, sect. 1, para. 3c.

[ix] *Constitution of the State of Georgia*, art. 7, sect. 2, para. 5.

[x] *Constitution of the State of Georgia*, art. 7, sect. 1, para. 3d. Also see Hill, *The Georgia State Constitution*, pp. 152-155.

[xi] Hill, *The Georgia State Constitution*, p. 49.

[xii] *Constitution of the State of Georgia*, art. 4; art. 8, sects. 2 and 4.

[xiii] *Constitution of the State of Georgia*, art. 4, sect. 3, para. 2.

[xiv] *Constitution of the State of Georgia*, art. 3, sect. 6, para. 7.

[xv] Hill, *The Georgia State Constitution*, pp. 56-59.

[xvi] Hill, *The Georgia State Constitution*, pp. 194-195; *Constitution of the State of Georgia*, art. 9, sect. 2, para. 4.

[xvii] Hill, *The Georgia State Constitution*, p. 99.

[xviii]*Constitution of the State of Georgia*, art. 1, sect. 2, para. 5.

[xix]5 U.S. 137.

[xx]Congress passed a law in 1996 giving the president limited line-item veto authority. The U.S. Supreme Court ruled that this action was unconstitutional, however, after President Clinton used it with 11 laws. See *Clinton v. City of New York*, 524 U.S. 417 (1998).

[xxi]On the changing location of the state capital, see Kenneth Coleman, editor, *A History of Georgia* 2nd edition (Athens: University of Georgia Press, 1991), pp. 91, 96, 107, 208-209.

[xxii][xxii][xxii]V.O. Key, Jr., *Southern Politics* (New York: Vintage, 1949), pp. 119-122; Hill, *The Georgia State Constitution*, pp. 224-225.

[xxiii]For a thorough account, see Harold P. Henderson, *The Politics of Change in Georgia: A Political Biography of Ellis Arnall* (Athens: University of Georgia Press, 1991), pp. 77-96.

[xxiv]For an example of the politics surrounding the use of local amendments, see the account of the 1970 consolidation of Columbus and Muscogee County in Arnold Fleischmann and Jennifer Custer. "Goodbye, Columbus," pp. 46-59 in *Case Studies of City-County Consolidation: Reshaping the Local Government Landscape*, edited by Suzanne M. Leland and Kurt Thurmaier (New York: M.E. Sharpe, 2004).

[xxv][xxv][xxv]Bill Montgomery, "New Constitution in Hands of Voters," *Atlanta Constitution*, November 2, 1982, p. 9A; Hill, *The Georgia State Constitution*, pp. 15-23.

[xxvi][xxvi][xxvi][xxvi]"A Constitutional Mess," *Atlanta Constitution*, August 28, 1981, p. 4A.

[xxvii][xxvii][xxvii][xxvii]Bill Shipp, "Do the State a Favor: Forget the New Constitution," *Atlanta Constitution*, August 15, 1981, p. 2B. On the shifting power of governors and the General Assembly, see Harold P. Henderson and Gary L. Roberts, editors, *Georgia Governors in an Age of Change* (Athens: University of Georgia Press, 1988), pp. 199-207, 234-237, 267-269.

[xxviii]"Streamlined State Constitution," *Atlanta Constitution*, June 30, 1983, p. 22A; "New State Constitution Deserves Ratification" (editorial), *Atlanta Constitution*, October 24, 1982, p. 2C.

[xxix]. [xxix][xxix]Hill, *The Georgia State Constitution*, p. 70.

[xxx]. [xxx][xxx]*Constitution of the State of Georgia*, art. 3. For comparisons to other states, see *The Book of the States*, chap. 3.

[xxxi]*The Book of the States*, pp. 130-131.

[xxxii]Jennifer Drage Bowser, "The Effects of Legislative Term Limits," pp. 111-115 in *The Book of the States*.

xxxiiiSee Edwin L. Jackson and Mary E. Stakes, *Handbook for Georgia Legislators* 10th ed. (Athens: Carl Vinson Institute of Government, University of Georgia, 1988), pp. 1-10.

xxxiv*Constitution of the State of Georgia*, art. 3, sect. 2, paras. 1 and 2.

xxxv*Constitution of the State of Georgia*, art. 5, sect. 2, para. 7.

xxxvi*Constitution of the State of Georgia*, art. 3, sect. 3. Although the president pro tempore can become president of the Senate, the lieutenant governorship is left unfilled until the next general election should the position become vacant (see art. 5, sect. 1, para. 5). On other states, see *The Book of the States*, pp. 136-141.

xxxvii*Constitution of the State of Georgia*, art. 3, sect. 5, para. 8.

xxxviii*Constitution of the State of Georgia*, art. 3, sect. 5, para. 2.

xxxix*Constitution of the State of Georgia*, art. 3, sect. 4, para. 11.

xl*Constitution of the State of Georgia*, art. 3, sect. 9.

xliThe line-item veto is not covered in the section dealing with appropriations in the *Constitution of the State of Georgia*, but in art. 3, sect. 5, para. 13, which covers use of the veto in the enactment of laws.

xliiTable 5 excludes all judicial positions and some executive branch officials. Lieutenant governors are included despite their status as presiding officers in 27 legislatures because of their right to succeed governors and their executive responsibilities in several states.

xliii*The Book of the States*, pp. 233-238.

xlivThad Beyle, "The Governors," pp. 194-231 in *Politics in the American States: A Comparative Analysis* 8th ed., edited by Virginia Gray and Russell L. Hanson (Washington: CQ Press, 2004).

xlvSee *Constitution of the State of Georgia*, art. 5, sect. 1; *The Book of the States*, pp. 215-216. For a brief history of the Georgia governor's office, see Edwin L. Jackson and Mary E. Stakes, *Handbook of Georgia State Agencies* 2nd edition (Athens: Carl Vinson Institute of Government, University of Georgia, 1988), pp. 38-39.

xlvi*Constitution of the State of Georgia*, art. 5, sect. 2, paras. 8 and 9; art. 6, sect. 7.

xlvii*Official Code of Georgia Annotated* [hereafter cited as OCGA], title 45, chap. 5.

xlviii*The Book of the States*, pp. 161-165. Four states require larger majorities to override taxing, spending, or emergency measures.

xlix*Constitution of the State of Georgia*, art. 3, sect. 5.

[li] *Constitution of the State of Georgia*, art. 5, sect. 4, para. 1.

[lii] *Constitution of the State of Georgia*, art. 5, sect. 3.

[liii] OCGA, title 45, chapter 15; Jackson and Stakes, *Handbook of Georgia State Agencies*, pp. 63-69.

[liii] Rhonda Cook, "Oink If You Know the Secret Menu for Legislature's Wild Hog Supper," *Atlanta Journal and Constitution*, January 10, 1993, pp. A1, A12; and "Legislators Being Feted in Daytona," *Atlanta Journal and Constitution*, February 13, 1993, pp. A1, A6.

[liv] *Constitution of the State of Georgia*, art. 5, sect. 3.

[lv] *Constitution of the State of Georgia*, art. 5, sect. 4.

[lvi] Governor's Office of Planning and Budget, "Fiscal 2005 Budget-as-passed" (available http://www.legis.state.ga.us/legis/budget/GEN05.htm).

[lvii] *Constitution of the State of Georgia*, art. 6, sect. 7.

[lviii] Georgia Supreme Court Commission on Racial and Ethnic Bias in the Court System, *Let Justice Be Done: Equally, Fairly, and Impartially* (final report, August 1995), p. 56; Bill Rankin, "Perdue's Court Pick Historic," *Atlanta Journal-Constitution*, June 9, 2005, p. A1.

[lix] *Constitution of the State of Georgia*, art. 6, sects. 1-4. For detail on Georgia's courts, see the web site for the Administrative Office of the Courts: http://www.georgiacourts.org/.

[lx] *Constitution of the State of Georgia*, art. 6, sects. 5 and 7; Court of Appeals of Georgia, "History of the Court of Appeals" (available http://www.gaappeals.us/history/).

[lxi] *Constitution of the State of Georgia*, art. 6, sects. 6 and 7.

[lxii] On differences in states' methods of selecting judges, see Henry R. Glick, "Courts: Politics and the Judicial Process," pp. 232-260 in *Politics in the American States*. On judicial selection in Georgia, see *Constitution of the State of Georgia*, art. 6, sect. 7.

[lxiii] On the Judicial Qualifications Commission, see http://www.georgiacourts.org/agencies/jqc/index.html.

[lxiv] *Constitution of the State of Georgia*, art. 6, sect. 8.

[lxv] On jury selection in Georgia, see OCGA, title 15, chap. 12, art. 5; on juries generally, see Henry R. Glick, *Courts, Politics, and Justice* 3rd edition (New York: McGraw-Hill, 1993), pp. 222-223.

[lxvi] Georgia General Assembly, "2005 Summary of General Statutes" (available

http://www.legis.state.ga.us/legis/2005_06/05sumdocnet.htm) and the text of HB 170 (available http://www.legis.state.ga.us/legis/2005_06/pdf/hb170.pdf). Also see Jim Tharpe, "Parents' Grief Leads to a Victory," *Atlanta Journal-Constitution*, April 6, 2005, p. B1.

lxvii See Arnold Fleischmann and Carol Pierannunzi, *Politics in Georgia* (Athens: University of Georgia Press, 1997), chap. 9.

lxviii *Constitution of the State of Georgia*, art. 9, sects. 1 and 2; Hill, *The Georgia State Constitution*, pp. 184-200.

lxix *Constitution of the State of Georgia*, art. 3, sect. 5, paras. 1 and 2.

lxx Steve Visser, "A Taxing Decision," *Atlanta Constitution*, June 14, 1999, p. E7.

lxxi David Goldberg and Kathey Pruitt, "GRTA Occupies Hot Seat," *Atlanta Constitution*, June 4, 1999, pp. A1, A8; Lucy Soto, "Public Still Skeptical About Transportation Board," *Atlanta Constitution*, June 7, 1999, pp. E1, E4.

lxxii Charles Seabrook, "Water Planning District" *Atlanta Constitution*, March 26, 2001, pp. E1, E6.

lxxiii U.S. Advisory Commission on Intergovernmental Relations, *State Laws Governing Local Government Structure and Administration*, report M-186 (Washington: Government Printing Office, 1993), pp. 7-9, 17-22.

lxxiv On local acts, see Fleischmann and Pierannunzi, *Politics in Georgia*, pp. 157-159, 233-238; on consolidation in Georgia, see Leland and Thurmaier, editors, *Case Studies of City-County Consolidation: Reshaping the Local Government Landscape*, chaps. 3, 6, and 10.

lxxv Taxation, debt limits, and revenue bonds are covered in *Constitution of the State of Georgia*, art. 9, sects. 4-6. Also see OCGA, title 36: chap. 5 on the property tax, chap. 7 on the income tax, and chap. 8 on the sales tax.

lxxvi OCGA, title 36, chap. 81, sect. 3b.

lxxvii *Constitution of the State of Georgia*, art. 8, para. 4; also see James Salzer, "Georgia Voters Throw Weight Behind Desire for Better Schools with Sales Tax Approvals," *Athens Daily News and Banner-Herald*, October 19, 1997, p. 6A.

lxxviii In addition to Georgia, runoffs are held in Alabama, Florida, Mississippi, North Carolina, Oklahoma, South Carolina, and Texas. Virginia repealed the runoff requirement in 1969, and Louisiana abandoned the runoff in favor of a nonpartisan primary in 1975. Arkansas, Kentucky, Maryland, and Utah have also used the runoff in the past. Arizona adopted a runoff for statewide general elections in 1988. See Key, *Southern Politics*, pp. 416-23; Charles S. Bullock III and Loch K. Johnson, *Runoff Elections in the United States* (Chapel

Hill: University of North Carolina Press, 1992).

lxxix On the rules for runoffs in Georgia, see OCGA, title 21, chap. 2, sect. 501.

lxxx *Brooks et al. v. Miller et al.*, 158 F.3d 1230 (1998); *Brooks et. al. v. Barnes et al.*, no. 98-1521, cert. denied May 24, 1999; Kathey Pruitt, "Majority Vote Still Needed in Primaries," *Atlanta Constitution*, May 25, 1999, p. B3.

lxxxi OCGA, title 21, chap. 4.

lxxxii *Constitution of the State of Georgia*, art. 3, sect. 7.

lxxxiii *Constitution of the State of Georgia*, art. 2, sect. 3.

lxxxiv *Constitution of the State of Georgia*, art. 3, sect. 2, para. 5; art. 5, sect. 1, paras. 2 and 3; art. 5, sect. 3, para. 1.

lxxxv *Constitution of the State of Georgia*, art. 6, sect. 7, para. 1; art. 8, sect. 5, para. 2; art. 9, sect. 1, para. 3.

lxxxvi 296 U.S. 186 (1962).

lxxxvii It does not seem necessary to include detailed citations to Georgia court cases in a general work such as this. Therefore, each section will include a citation to the appropriate location in Hill's definitive work on the Georgia Constitution, plus updates from the *Official Code of Georgia Annotated*. Many of these cases are discussed in more detail, with full citations in the endnotes, in Fleischmann and Pierannunzi, *Politics in Georgia*, pp. 62-67.

lxxxviii *Constitution of the State of Georgia*, art. 1, sect. 2, para. 5.

lxxxix *Constitution of the State of Georgia*, art. 1, sect. 1, para. 2; Hill, *The Georgia State Constitution*, pp. 33-36.

xc *American Subcontractors Association v. City of Atlanta*, 259 Ga. 14, 376 S.E.2d 662 (1989).

xci Doug Cumming, "Applicants Nervously Await Decisions," *Atlanta Constitution*, March 25, 1998, p. C5. Following years of litigation over policies at the University of Georgia, the U.S. Supreme Court gave support to the limited use of affirmative action in college admissions in two cases involving the University of Michigan: *Gratz v. Bollinger*, no. 02-516 (2003), and *Grutter v. Bollinger*, no. 02-241 (2003).

xcii Douglas A. Blackmon and Holly Morris, "Court Gives Split Ruling on Gay Rights," *Atlanta Constitution*, March 15, 1995, p. E1.

xciii On the right to vote, see Laughlin McDonald, Michael B. Binford, and Ken Johnson, "Georgia," pp. 67-102 in *Quiet Revolution in the South: The Impact of the Voting Rights*

Act, 1965-1990, edited by Chandler Davidson and Bernard Grofman (Princeton: Princeton University Press, 1994).

[xciv]For a thorough discussion, see Clarence N. Stone, *Regime Politics: Governing Atlanta, 1946-1988* (Lawrence: University Press of Kansas, 1989).

[xcv]William F. Holmes, "Part Five: 1890-1940," in *A History of Georgia* 2nd edition, edited by Kenneth Coleman (Athens: University of Georgia Press, 1991), p. 280.

[xcvi]For a good synopsis of postwar racial change, see Numan V. Bartley, "Part Six: 1940 to the Present," in *A History of Georgia* 2nd edition, edited by Kenneth Coleman (Athens: University of Georgia Press, 1991), pp. 361-74.

[xcvii]*Stell v. Savannah-Chatham County Board of Education*, 333 F.2d 55 (1964).

[xcviii]*Wesberry v. Sanders*, 376 U.S. 1 (1964).

[xcix]See Hill, *The Georgia State Constitution*, p. 225.

[c]Linda Greenhouse, "Justices, in 5-4 Vote, Reject Districts Drawn with Race the 'Predominant Factor'," *New York Times*, June 30, 1995, pp. A1, A13.

[cici]*Constitution of the State of Georgia*, art. 1, sect. 1, para. 1; Hill, *The Georgia State Constitution*, pp. 30-33.

[cii]*Suber v. Bulloch County Board of Education*, 722 F.Supp. 736 (S.D. Ga., 1989).

[ciii]*Stephens v. State*, 265 Ga. 356, 456 S.E.2d 560, cert. denied 516 U.S. 849 (1995).

[civ]*Constitution of the State of Georgia*, art. 1, sect. 1, paras. 3 and 4; Hill, *The Georgia State Constitution*, pp. 36-38.

[cv]*Constitution of the State of Georgia*, art. 1, sect. 1, para. 4.

[cvi]*Constitution of the State of Georgia*, art. 1, sect. 1, para. 5; Hill, *The Georgia State Constitution*, pp. 38-40.

[cvii]*State v. Café Erotica*, 269 Ga. 486, 500 S.E.2d 547 (1998).

[cviii]*State v. Miller*, 260 Ga. 669, 398 S.E.2d 547 (1990).

[cix]*Vaughn v. State*, 259 Ga. 325 , 381 S.E.2d 30 (1989).

[cx]See OCGA, title 24, chap. 9, sect. 30.

[cxi]*Statesboro Publishing Co. v. City of Sylvania*, 271 Ga. 92, 516 S.E.2d 926 (1999).

[cxii]*Goldrush II v. City of Marietta*, 267 Ga. 683, 482 S.E.2d 347 (1997)

[cxiii]*Constitution of the State of Georgia*, art. 1 sect. 1, paras. 11-24; Hill, *The Georgia State Constitution*, pp. 42-51.

[cxiv]*Constitution of the State of Georgia*, art. 1, sect. 1, para. 21.

[cxv]*Constitution of the State of Georgia*, art. 1, sect. 1, para. 23.

[cxvi]*Constitution of the State of Georgia*, art. 1, sect. 1, para. 17.

[cxvii]*Bergman v. McCullough*, 218 Ga. App. 353, 461 S.E.2d 544 (1995), cert. denied 517 U.S. 1141 (1996).

[cxviii]*Fleming v. Zant*, 259 Ga. 687, 386 S.E.2d 339 (1989).

[cxix]*Crutchfield v. State*, 218 Ga. App. 360, 461 S.E.2d 555 (1995).

[cxx]*Constitution of the State of Georgia*, art. 1, sect.1, para. 1b.

[cxxi]*Pavesich v. New England Life Insurance Co.*, 122 Ga. 190, 50 S.E. 68 (1904).

[cxxii]*Christensen v. State*, 266 Ga. 474, 464 S.E.2d 188 (1996).

[cxxiii]*Powell v. State*, 270 Ga. 327, 510 S.E.2d 18 (1998).

[cxxiv]*Morrisaon v. State*, 272 Ga. 129, 526 S.E.2d 336 (2000).

[cxxv]*Lawrence v. Texas*, no. 02-102 (2003).

[cxxvi]For the U.S. Supreme Court's view of assisted suicide and the right to privacy, see *Washington v. Glucksberg*, 521 U.S. 702 (1997) and *Vacco v. Quill*, 521 U.S. 793 (1997). On the Oregon conflict, see *Oregon v. Ashcroft*, 368 F.3d 1118 (2004), the case was appealed to the U.S. Supreme Court, which heard oral arguments on the appeal in October 2005.

[cxxvii]See Mark Curriden, "Is Naming Judges Serving Justice?" *Atlanta Journal and Constitution*, November 29, 1992, pp. G1, G3; Andrew Kull, "The Slow Death of Colorblind Justice," *Atlanta Journal and Constitution*, November 29, 1992, pp. H1, H5; Mark Curriden, "Road to a Judicial Appointment Not Clear—Even to State's Judges," *Atlanta Constitution*, December 21, 1992, p. C3.

[cxxviii]*Constitution of the State of Georgia*, art. 7, sect. 1, para. 3e.

[cxxix]*Constitution of the State of Georgia*, art. 8, sect. 5, paras. 2 and 3.

Filename: Fleischmann 6th Edition.wpd
Directory: T:\Joel Brennecke
Template: C:\Documents and Settings\jbrennecke\Application
     Data\Microsoft\Templates\Normal.dot
Title:
Subject:
Author: TL User
Keywords:
Comments:
Creation Date: 3/12/2006 7:08:00 AM
Change Number: 1
Last Saved On:
Last Saved By:
Total Editing Time: 3 Minutes
Last Printed On: 3/12/2006 7:11:00 AM
As of Last Complete Printing
                    Number of Pages: 59
                    Number of Words: 22,680 (approx.)
                    Number of Characters: 129,277 (approx.)